Some Georgia County Records

Vol. 6

Being Some of the Legal Records

of

Cobb, Cherokee, Dawson,
Forsyth, Gilmer,Gordon,
Gwinnett, Hall, Lumpkin,
Murray, Pickens, Paulding,
Rabun, Walton & Whitfield Counties

Compiled by:
The Rev. Silas Emmett Lucas

SOUTHERN HISTORICAL PRESS
INC

Please direct all correspondence and book orders to:

Southern Historical Press, Inc.
P.O. Box 1267
Greenville, S.C. 29602-1267

ISBN # 0-89308-686-X

Printed in the United States of America

Table of Contents

THE 1834 STATE CENSUS OF COBB COUNTY

From the county files, Telamon Cuyler Collection, Special
Collections, University of Georgia Libraries. Reproduced by
permission.

Cobb County. Return of the Census taken under the act of 1833 &
received at the Executive Dept. 22nd March 1834. 1576 white
inhabitants.

HEADS OF FAMILIES AND NUMBER OF WHITE PERSONS

William Carlile-7
Josiah Luther-3
Martin Adams-4
Josiah Massey-8
John Thompson-8
Gallant Runnels-8
Enoch R. Mills-4
James Henderson-9
G. W. Gober-10
Charles Harris-9
John D. Mullins-2
Riley Harvel (Harrel?)-8
Henry Cupp Sr.-4
Samuel N. Maloney-4
Jesse Harris-3
Wm. P. Maloney-4
Silas McLain-6
John W. Lowrey-8
Henry Cupp Jr.-3
Michael Cupp-4
James W. Pollard-4
William Brumbalow-5
William M. Davis-6
Daniel Bruice-5
John Moore-13
John Pace-11
R. B. Hornbuckle-4
Benjamin Hearndon-6
Robert Malom (Malone?)-9
Samuel Conn-9
George Henry-1
Warner A. Belk-1
Robert Carter-9
Joseph Chastain-8
William B. Malone-8
Gideon Trout-11
Caleb Clark-6
Charles Long-5
William Harris-7
Elijah Croxton-2
Abner Camp-7
Elizabeth Whitfield-2
John Hubbard-4
Martin Ingram-8
Silas Ellis-3
Lewis R. Powel-9
Thomas Whitehead Sr.-3
Thomas Whitehead Jr.-5
William Rice-3
David Brogdin-1
Dicey Simpson-6
Daniel Reid-12

William Barber-12
William Pearce-3
Peter Wallice-7
Stephen Dale-5
Joseph A. Murdock-6
William Price-9
John C. Murriner-8
Ephram Haynes-5
Haley Shaw-8
Reddin Blocker-8
Archibald Harris-5
Ester Harris-4
Elizabeth H. Arnold-5
John Bolton-5
Robert McDowell-4
Nathaniel Crenshaw-8
Willis Cox-3
Richard Barber-2
John C. Low-6
Absalom Smith-4
Joel Moore-9
James B. Waller-1
Mary Wolf-2
William Morris-9
Oliver Hacket-7
John R. Tucker-8
William Baker-12
Absalom Baker-3
Nelson Tucker-1
Gideon Whitihead-2
James Rush-3
Silas N. Clay-2
John Clay-10
William Bullard-8
John A. Wells-5
Berry Mulligan-6
Francis Stinson-1
William Sansom-10
George Harper-5
John Martin-6
Notley Gour-6
Martha Barnes-7
James Harris-3
John James-4
Josiah Johnson-7
Thomas Brown-6
William Harris-5
James Clay-7
John Kimbarl-6
Isaac Henson-5
William W. Duncan-8
Thomas Copelan(Capelan?)-10

1

THE 1834 STATE CENSUS OF COBB COUNTY

Johnston Williams-5
Samuel Harmon-12
Joseph D. Shumate-8
Thomas Davenport-5
Ira Kemp-3
William W. Maloney-7
John Glen-8
John Jefries-12
Thomas C. West-3
Daniel May-7
John Stroud-7
John Hi-1-5
Wilson F. Blackstock-2
William Dobbins-8
Jesse Thrasher-8
A.G.W. Stroud-2
John Rowe-6
Archibald Johnston-1
Jacob Meadows-4
Robert Stewart-7
James Hunter-3
Jeremiah Nesbit-2
Linsey Elsberry-11
Joshua Hill-9
Burgis Mullins-8
Buda Mullins-3
Jonathan R. Davis-8
Ausburn Mullins-9
James Rowel-7
Briant Williams-6
William Pruit-3
George H. Maway-3
William Williams-4
James Stewart-5
William B. Binson-4
Robert M. Minor-3
Levi Hollaway-4
Elijah Williams-2
George Stewart-4
Jesse Winfra-10
Nelson Porterfield-3
Samuel Hollaway-4
Narcissa Austin-8
Elizabeth Gurley-3
John Austin-5
David G. Austin-6
Isaac Gray-3
Samuel Mullins-4
Martin Dobbs-4
Abraham Leathus-6
William Wilson-6
Henry Dunn-3
Huzial Baggett-10
John Collins-8
Benjamin Hollins-3
Robert Caruth-9
John T. Camp-6
William Canada-4
Nathaniel Guess-13
Samuel Hulbut-9
John Linsey-9

Moses Morris-6
William Morris-3
James Carnes-3
Lydia Carnes-9
Green Carnes-6
Joseph Roper (Raper?)-6
George Bell-8
Gideon Smith-3
Joseph Carnes-2
David Canada-7
Josiah Morris-9
John McKenzie-9
John Goodard-5
John Pritchard-4
Thompson Hawk-8
John Dozier-2
B.B.S. Sandres-1
John S. Davis-6
Charles Collins-4
Daniel Dudley-4
Garry Davis-9
James L. Davis-7
William Guess-9
Joseph Quinton-7
James Grizzel-5
William Tait-3
Ferdinand Jett-10
Henry Bredwell-5
Wiley Kemp-4
Abraham Pace-9
Stephen Smith-2
John Pace-5
Stephen Smith-2
Hiram Burnet-2
Jacob Crow-11
David Wadkins-2
Jesse Wadkins-4
David Delk-2
David B. Ellington-4
Moses Dukes-2
Charles Anderson-2
William Dunn-9
Austin Martin-5
Clinton Web-4
James Hestalir-8
Richard Glover-5
Margaret Booth-2
Tandy K. Martin-5
Hezekiah Treadaway-4
Robert Martin-3
D. D. Baker-5
Alexander Pucket-5
Richard Coleman-4
Renne Coleman-3
Robert Cox-3
James T. McAfee-4
Jackson Gregory-6
Gabriel Jowet-9
William Hill-7
Elihu Goggins-4
Robert Watson-5

THE 1834 STATE CENSUS OF COBB COUNTY

Joseph McDonald-5
John Sims-8
Mastin Pearce-7
Amos Brown-10
George W. Brown-3
Jacob R. Brooks-9
Thomas Akins-8
John B. Brockman-7
Thomas Womack-5
James Berry-9
Renne Coleman-7
Solomon Griffin-6
B. A. Baber-5
James Baber-2
John M. Williford-13
Bird Womack-5
John Cudd-11
Riley Goss-6
James Dougherty-7
William Worthy-4
Mahaffey Henderson-3
Nathan Martin-5
Larkin Martin-6
Samuel A. Power-3
Micajah Pope-6
Martin R. Paxton-4

George Butler-8
Jesse Davis-5
Elizabeth Wallace-2
William York-8
Henry L. Hicks-8
Elijah Stancel-4
Thomas Cupp-4
John Akins-9
Alfred Edwards-4
John Richards-8
Benjamin Hearndon-6
James Collins-7
George Fielder-7
John Coleman-4
James Power-2
Bradley Smith-3
William Brumbalow Sr.-1
Edward Mays-6
James Anderson-6
Mary Beavers-5
Lemma Kirttey-6
George Baber-6
George W. Winter-9
Elizabeth Pearce-4
Leonard Simpson-4

TOTAL - 1576

I Ferdinand Jett, do hereby certify that I have taken the number and census of the whole population, who are citizens of Cobb County, to the best of my skill and information, which number is one thousand five hundred and seventy six this 4th March 1834.
    /s/ Ferdinand Jett; appointed for the above purpose

Georgia   ) I hereby certify that the above is a correct
Cobb County) copy of the enumeration or census of the free
               white persons who reside in this county, as taken
and returned to my office by Ferdinand Jett. Given under my hand at Office this 11th March 1834.
                        /s/ Enoch R. Mills
                        Clk. Inferior Court

Groom - Bride - Date of license - Ordinary - Marriage Date - Officer

Page 7:
Francis M. Watson - Mary A. Glasco - 1 Feb. 1865 - Jno. G. Campbell -
2 Feb. 1865 - Wm. S. Brown, J.P.

Mr. Michael Burtz - Miss A. S. Bellah - 17 Dec. 1864 - Jno. G. Campbell
18 Dec. 1864 - Walter Manning, O.M.G.

Page 8:
John C. Miller - Mary L. Veal - 4 June 1864 - Jno G. Campbell - 9 June 1864 -
David N. McEachern, J.P.

John Mahaffy - Sarah A. Landmond - 22 June 1865 - Jno G. Campbell -
25 June 1865 - William S. Brown, J.P.

Page 9:
Perrin Turner - Margaret R. Robb - 29 June 1865 - Jno G. Campbell -
2 July 1865 - E. H. Lindley, J.I.C.

Edwin W. Compton - Fannie P. Gann - 8 June 1865 - Jno G. Campbell -
9 June 1865 - J. T? Robertson, J.P.

Page 10:
Gurley (written over Genley) B. Chase - Martha E. Drennan - 1 Jan. 1861 -
A. A. Brown 1st Lieut & Pro Mar - 26 July 1865 - Gurley B. Chase &
MEO m E. P. Palmer O.M.G.

Lafayette Conat - Julia Dabbs - 17 July 1865 - Jno G. Campbell -
18 July 1865 - Thos. P. Whitfield, J.P.

Page 10:
Hiram Owens - Permelia Reeves - 30 June 1865 - Jno G. Campbell - 2 July 1865 -
W. Manning, O.M.G.

John O. Allen - Eliza Dodgen - 7 Aug. 1865 - Jno. G. Campbell - 27 Aug.
1865 - Benjamin Bullard, J.P.

Page 12:
Richard P. Hadaway - Susan Haynes - 23 Aug. 1865 - 27 Aug. 1865 James Green
O.M.G.

John W. Hodge - E. A. MAULDING - 29 Aug. 1865 - Jno G. Campbell -
29 Aug. 1865 - W. W. Carroll O.M.G.

Page 13:
Wilson B. Morris - Eliza Davis - 5 Aug. 1865 - 16 Aug. 1865 - William C.
Dorris, J.P.

George Weight - Nany J. Willis - 12 Aug. 1865 - O. B. Rockwell, Capt. &
Prov. Mar - 7 Aug. 1865 - W. W. Carroll, O.M.G.
Page 14:
Andrew J. Reynolds - Mary M. Dobbs - 22 Aug. 1865 - Jno G. Campbell -
22 Aug. 1865 - W. W. Carroll, O.M.G.

Henry A. Barber - Nancy Scoggins - 7 Aug. 1865 - O. B. Rockwell, Capt. &
Prov. Mar - 7 Aug. 1865 - W. W. Carroll, O.M.G.

Page 15:
Milton W. Steele - Martha A. W. Everett - 6 Sept. 1865 - Jno. G. Campbell -
28 Sept. 1865 - Manning Cain J.P.

Louis Smith - Mary A. Cram - 21 Sept. 1865 - Jno. G. Campbell - 21 Sept. 1865
John F. Lanneau, O.M.G.

Page 16:
Bennett H. McClain - Martha Jordan - 30 Sept. 1865 - Jno G. Campbell -
1 Oct. 1865 - Walter Manning, O.M.G.

David D. Barfield - Martha Pickens - 2 Sept. 1865 - Jno G. Campbell -
5 Sept. 1865 - W. W. Carroll, O.M.G.

Page 17:
Juliah D. Delk - Mary Walker - 14 Sept. 1865 - Jno. G. Campbell -
14 Sept. 1865 - W. W. Carroll, O.M.G.

Orville T. Andrews - Nancy P. Smith - ___ Sept. 1865 - Jno G. Campbell -
24 Sept. 1865 - Thomas P. Whitfield

Page 18:
James L. Wylie - Nancy E. Wise - 25 Sept. 1865 - Jno G. Campbell -
26 Sept. 1865 - Jeremiah (his X mark) Daniel

Mason J. Florence - Sallie E. Clonts - 18 Sept. 1865 - Jno G. Campbell -
20 Sept. 1865 - J. B. C. Quillian, M.G.

Page 19:
John B. Chapman - Elizabeth Kuykendall - 28 Sept. 1865 - Jno G. Campbell -
1 Oct. 1865 - J. C. Hedgecock, J.P.

John C. Butner - Elizabeth E. Lindley - 13 Sept. 1866 - Jno G. Campbell -
14 Sept. 1865 - E. H. Lindley, J.I.C.

Page 20:
William F. Brooks - Nancy Tate - 14 Sept. 1865 - Jno G. Campbell -
14 Sept. 1865 - E. T. Palmer, O. M.G.

James W. Reed - T. Charlotte Power - 3 Oct. 1865 - Jno G. Campbell -
17 Oct. 1865 - W. W. Jolly, J.P.

Page 21:
William Gassett - Angeline Coleman - 15 Oct. 1865 - Jno G. Campbell, Ordy -
15 Oct. 1865 - Thomas P. Whitfield, J.P.

E. R. Davis - Tempy S. Roberts - 4 Oct. 1865 - Jno G. Campbell - 8 Oct.
1865 - David N. McEachern, J.P.

Page 22:
William C. Green - Julia Colder - 12 Oct. 1865 - Jno G. Campbell -
12 Oct. 1865 - E. P. Palmer, O.M.G.

John P. Bartlett - Mary Miller - 10 Oct. 1865 - Jno G. Campbell - 12 Oct.
1865 - David V. McEachern

Page 23:
Jasper Oneil - Adeline Cook - 30 Oct. 1865 - Jno G. Campbell -
31 Oct. 1865 - E. P. Palmer O.M.G.

Harbin H. McIntire - Harriet H. Scroggins - 7 Oct. 1865 - Jno G. Campbell
8 Oct. 1865 - W. W. Carroll, O.M.G.

Page 24:
Evan J. Loveless - Louisa S. Runyan - 14 Oct. 1865 - Jno G. Campbell -
19 Oct. 1865 - J. Daniel

Thomas Paine - Mary Neighbors - 6 Oct. 1865 - Jno G. Campbell - 6 Oct. 1865 -
E. P. Palmer, O.M.G.

Page 25:
W. Patt Berry - Fannie E. Boyd - 3 Oct. 1865 - Jno G. Campbell -
12 Nov. 1865 - E. P. Palmer O.M.G.

A. J. Foster - Mary Jane Sprouce - 26 Oct. 1865 - 19 Oct. 1865 -
S. R. McClesky, J.P.

Page 26:
Isaac A. Reed - Martha E. Gaines - 27 Oct. 1865 - Jno G. Campbell -
5 Nov. 1865 - S. J. Bellah, M.G.

Charles W. Nichols - Mahala E. Ellison - 11 Nov. 1865 - Jno G. Campbell -
14 Nov. 1865 - G. T. Carrie, J.P.

Page 27:
Israel P. Runyan - Miss A. V. Kirk - 14 Nov. 1865 - Jno G. Campbell -
16 Nov. 1865 - Thomas P. Whitfield, J.P.

George Foltz - Mary E. Gray - 3 Nov. 1865 - Jno G. Campbell - 3 Nov. 1865 - J. S. Heaton Minister of the Gospel.

Page 28:
John W. Dodgen - Miss Jane Pope - 20 Nov. 1865 - Jno. G. Campbell - 28 Nov. 1865 - Benjamin Bullard, J.P.

Mr. T. J. Ousley - Miss Harry O. Wallis - 11 Dec. 1865 - Campbell - 11 Dec. 1865 - G. W. Given, O.M.G.

Page 29:
Geo. W. Conant - Jane L. Hadaway - 11 Nov. 1865 - Campbell - 30 Nov. 1865 - Cocero A. Pool, J.P.

Elias S. Welch - Amanda Smith - 28 Nov. 1865 - Campbell - 29 Nov. 1865 - E. P. Palmer, O.M.G.

Page 30:
Albert T. Lea, Major - Virginia A. Donnall - 13 Dec. 1865 - Campbell - 14 Dec. 1865 - G. W. Givens, O.M.G.

Mr. J. F. Hadard - Miss Louisa Gittery - 18 Dec. 1865 - Campbell - 21 Dec. 1865 - J. O. Reed, M.G.

Page 31:
W. H. H. Orr - Sarah M. Scott - 20 Dec. 1865 - Campbell - 24 Dec. 1865 - James D. Reed, M.G.

John Hayden - Mary L. Simmon - 15 Sept. 1865 - Campbell - 16 Sept. 1865 - Thomas P. Whitfield, J. P.

Page 32:
William O. Waters - Hannah M. Mason - 18 Jan. 1866 - Campbell - 18 Jan. 1866 - Wm. L. Mansfield, M.G.

Mr. Jasper L. Clay - Miss Martha A. Pace - 25 July 1866 - Campbell - 29 July 1866 - John C. Clay, J.P.

Page 33:
David S. Pool - Susan L. Moon - 8 June 1866 - 14 June 1866 - Campbell, ordy - Cicero A. Pool, J.P.

Marion P. Morris - Miss Cautie Mayes - 6 June 1866 - Jno G. Campbell - 17 June 1866 - S. R. McClesky, J.P.

Page 34:
Burrell T. Vann - Lucinda Attaway - 30 June 1866 - Jno G. Campbell - 2 July 1866 - G. W. Johnson, J.P.

William S. Green - Malinka Kirk - 16 July 1866 - Jno G. Campbell - 19 July 1866 - D. N. McEachen, J.P.

Page 35:
Hezekiah Hany - Lavinia Gant - 23 July 1866 - Jno G. Campbell - 25 July 1866 - Wm. H. Campbell, O.M.G.

James M. Stewart - Fannie Pattillo - 28 Nov. 1865 - Jno. G. Campbell - 3 Dec. 1865 - G. W. Gwinn, O.M.G.

Page 36:
H. W. Coleman - Frances Tatu - 11 Nov. 1866 - Jno G. Campbell - 16 Nov. 1865 - Daniel Wright, J.P.

James H. Kellar - Elizabeth Knight - 12 Dec. 1865 - Jno. G. Campbell - 13 Dec. 1865 - James Pool, O.M.G.

Page 37:
R. E. Keker - Miss F. S. Clonts - 2 Dec. 1865 - Jno G. Campbell - 7 Dec. 1865 - J.B.C. Quilliam, M.G.

James R. Harbin - Miss Earralie C. Eason - 16 Dec. 1865 - Jno. G. Campbell - 24 Dec. 1865 - Cocero A. Pool, J.P.

Page 38:
Mr. John F. Davis - Miss Martha Tully - 16 Dec. 1865 - Jno G. Campbell -
17 Dec. 1865 - S. R. McClesky, J.P.

Mr. Garrett S. Oglesby - Mrs. C. D. Lemon - 19 Dec. 1865 - Jno G. Campbell -
19 Dec. 1865 - Geo. W. Gwin, M.G.

Page 39:
Wiley G. Armor - Miss Rebecca Searight - 30 Jan. 1866 - Jno G. Campbell -
1 Feb. 1866 - J. G. Denton, M.G.

Mr. William W. Hawkins - Miss Caroline Caldwell - 19 Dec. 1865 - Jno G.
Campbell - 24 Dec. 1865 - G? W? Gwin, O.M.G.

Page 40:
Joshua P. Stevens - Mary C. Barnister - 15 Nov. 18656 (marked over) -
Jno G. Campbell - 18 Nov. 1866 - Peter Groover, M.G.

Mr. D. F. McClatchy - Miss (written over) Mrs. E. H. Lyon - 26 Dec. 1865 -
Jno. G. Campbell - 26 Dec. 1865 - J. M. Loury, M.G.

Page 41:
Mr. James Ham - Elizabeth M. Rutherford - __ Dec. 1865 - Jno G. Campbell -
31 Dec. 1865 - R. H. Marchman, J.P.

Mr. J. J. Tatum - Miss Flanada Wood - 13 Dec. 1865 - Jno G. Campbell -
26 Dec. 1865 - A. J. Deavors, O.M.G.

Page 42:
Mr. W. B. Knox - Miss Martha A. Seale - 19 Dec. 1865 - Jno G. Campbell -
21 Dec. 1865 - J. G. Denton, M.G.

Joseph Green - Sarah Poor - 28 Jan. 1865/6 Jan. 1865 - B. F. Strain, M.G.
Campbell, ordy.

Page 43:
Gazaway Hames - Marietta Hames - 18 Dec. 1865 - Jno G. Campbell - 21 Dec.
1865 - Peter Groover, M.G.

Walton R. Lowry - Martha M. Hardman - 15 Dec. 1865 - Jno G. Campbell -
21 Dec. 1865 - Peter Groover, M.G.

Page 44:
Mr. George Hendricks - Miss Amanda Gramling - 19 Dec. 1865 - Jno G.
Campbell - 24 Dec. 1865 - Geo (last name written over...may be Gramling or
Hamsley)

Alfred B. Lowry - Elizabeth Fain - 25 Jan. 1866 - Jno G. Campbell - 25
Jan. 1866 - J. T. Robertson, J.P.

Page 45:
David Johns - Miss Augusta Elis - 9 Jan. 1866 - Jno G. Campbell - 14 Jan.
1866 - C. D. Moon, J.P.

Robert M. Brumbalow - Susan J. Bullard - 27 Jan. 1866 - Jno G. Campbell -
4 Feb. 1866 - C. D. Moon, J.P.

Page 46:
James M. Abner - Elizabeth Yarber - 25 Sept. 1866 - Jno G. Campbell -
27 Sept. 1866 - James D. Reed, M.G.

James P. T. Roper - Martha A. Oglesby - 28 Sept. 1866 - Jno G. Campbell -
4 Oct. 1866 - C. D. Moon, J.P.

Page 47:
William J. Strong - Eliza E. Strong - 8 Sept. 1866 - Jno G. Campbell -
9 Sept. 1866 - G. W. Johnson, J.P.

James R. Brumby Laura M. Smith - 28 Aug. 1866 - Jno G. Campbell -
28 Aug. 1866 - Samuel Benedict, Rector of St. James Church, Marietta, Ga.

Page 48:
Asa Darby - S. C. Mayes - 18 Aug. 1866 - Jno. G. Campbell - 19 Aug. 1866 -
D. N. McEachern, J.P.

7

George W. Daniel - Miss Martha C. Johnson - 10 Aug. 1866 - Jno G. Campbell -
12 Aug. 1866 - J. M. Daniel, M.G.

Page 49:
Mr. Joseph T. Foury - Miss Charlotte A. Northup - 11 April 1866 - Jno G.
Campbell - 12 April 1866 - Atticus G. Haggood, M.G.

Benjamin W. Van Dyke - Elizabeth C. Lowry - 16 Nov. 1866 - Jno. G. Campbell -
21 Nov. 1866 - Atticus G. Haggood, M.G.

Page 50:
John S. Goodwin - Miss Margaret L. Williams - 13 Aug. 1866 - Jno G. Campbell -
16 Aug. 1866 - D. N. McEachern, J.P.

Mr. James B. Young - Miss Mattie Wallis - 20 Sept. 1866 - Jno G. Campbell -
20 Sept. 1866 - Edw. Porter Palmer, O.M.G.

Page 51:
William A. McElreath - Matilda J. McEachin - 8 Sept. 1866 - Jno G.
Campbell - 13 Sept. 1866 - R. Baber, M.G.

Elisha H. Stiles - Mary Ann Hall - 27 Sept. 1866 - Jno. G. Campbell - 28
Sept. 1866 - George W. Johnson, J.P.

Page 52:
James L. Davis - Emma Willmoth - 14 Aug. 1866 - Jno. G. Campbell - 15 Aug.
1866 - E. Porter Palmer, O.M.G.

Joseph Lacy - Sarah M. Smith - 8 Aug. 1866 - Jno. G. Campbell - 12 Aug.
1866 - John C. Clay, J.P.

Page 53:
John Rice - Nancy J. West - 2 Aug. 1866 - Jno G. Campbell - 9 Aug. 1866 -
Robt Baber, M.G.

George M. Smith - Harriet C. Mitchell - 8 Aug. 1866 - Jno G. Campbell -
9 Aug. 1866 - S. R. McClesky, J.P.

Page 54:
Willis F. Murdock - Margaret J. Reid - 18 July 1866 - Jno G. Campbell -
19 July 1866 - J. P. McPherson, J.P.

Iverson or Averson Y. David - Nancy Ann L. Sewel - 23 July 1866 -
Jno G. Campbell - 26 July 1866 - D. N. McEachen, J.P.

Page 55:
Charles M. Barrett - Mary L. Scott - 2 Oct. 1866 - Jno G. Campbell -
4 Oct. 1866 - E. H. Lindly, J.I.C.

Andrew H. Pickens - Mary J. Dial - 10 Oct. 1866 - Jno G. Campbell - 10 Oct.
1866 - D. N. Eachen, J.P.

Page 56:
Peter D. Wheeland - Amanda Chastain - 30 Oct. 1866 - Jno. G. Campbell -
1 Oct. 1866 - Wm. S. Foster, M.G.

George W. Pharr - Mary E. Sasseman - 30 Oct. 1866 - Jno. G. Campbell - 1 Nov.
1866 - R. Baber, M.G.

Page 57:
A. S. Hamby - Miss Ely Mayes - 14 Nov. 1865 - Jno. G. Campbell -
14 Nov. 1865 - W. H. Campbell, M.G.

G. T. Hulland - Miss Mary Ann Johnson - 8 Dec. 1865 - Jno G. Campbell -
14 Nov. 1865 - Beaton Daniel, M.G.

Page 58:
Pinckney Clanton - Julia Culp - 29 Sept. 1866 - Jno G. Campbell - 30 Sept.
1866 - William H. Campbell, M.G.

William P. Dawson - Miss Jane McClesky - Jno G. Campbell - 4 Sept. 1866 -
S. R. McClesky, J.P.

Page 59:
Mr. J. B. Blackwell - Mrs. E. L. Bellinger - 18 Dec. 1865 - Jno G. Campbell -
19 Dec. 1865 - John F. Lanneau, O.M.G.

Robert T. Foster - Louisa Oliver - 3 Jan. 1866 - Jno G. Campbell - 9 Jan.
1866 - James B. Dunwoody, Preacher of Gospel.

Page 60:
Carson Thirley (Shirley?) - Mary J. Braswell - 20 Jan. 1866 - Jno. G.
Campbell - 21 Jan. 1866 - W. W. Jolley, J.P.

E. J. Simpson - Eliza Jane Robertson - 21 Dec. 1865 - Jno G. Campbell -
21 Dec. 1865 - John L. or T. Robertson, J.P.

Page 61:
Sanders B. Ragsdale - Rebecca M. Eason - 13 March 1866 - Jno G. Campbell -
15 March 1866 - Cocero L. Pool, J.P.

Mr. J. C. Freltz - Mrs. Mary A. Lane - 5 March 1866 - Jno G. Campbell -
8 March 1866 - Robert Baber, M.G.

Page 62:
James A. Aikins, Miss Nancy C. Caper - 17 March 1866 - Jno G. Campbell -
18 March 1866 - Benjamin Bullard, J.P.

Thos. Potts - Pheobe Booker - 16 March 1866 - Jno G. Campbell - 16 March
1866 - T. J. Atkinson, J.I.C.C.

Page 63:
Mr. Reuben Kendrick - Amanda Wellmoth - 18 March 1866 - Jno G. Campbell -
W. W. Carroll, O.M.G.

Andrew B. Ivey - Delitha A. Edwards - 10 May 1866 - Jno G. Campbell -
10 May 1866 - T. J. Atkinson, J.I.C.C.

Page 64:
Martin Boyle - Margaret Mitchell - 13 May 1866 - Jno G. Campbell - 13 May
1866 - T. J. Atkinson, J.I.C.C.

Marcus L. Green - Eliza M. Stanley - 2 March 1866 - Jno G. Campbell - 4 March
1866 - Thomas P. Whitfield, J.P.

Page 65:
Mr. John Fitts - Miss Susan Bradly - 28 March 1866 - Jno G. Campbell -
13 May 1866 - Daniel Wright, J.P.

John W. McClesky - Sarah E. Payne - 5 March 1866 - Jno G. Campbell -
6 March 1866 - C. M. McClure, M.G.

Page 66:
Thomas M. WestBrooks - Hester Ann Ellis - 11 Oct. 1866 - Jno G. Campbell -
17 Oct. 1866 - Golson M. Hook, J.P.

Augustus Hill - Delilah W. Ragsdale - 29 Oct. 1866 - Jno G. Campbell -
21 Nov. 1866 - T. J. Atkinson, J.I.C.

Page 67:
Henny Call - Doxay Simpson - 22 March 1866 - Jno G. Campbell - 25 March
1866 - Hartwell A. Baldwin, J.P.

John W. Hicks - Emma E. Wright - 2 March 1866 - Jno G. Campbell -
6 March 1866 - F. A. Bell, M.G.

Page 68:
Lemuel A. Ragland - Martha A. Bennett - 17 Oct. 1866 - Jno. G. Campbell -
25 Oct. 1866 - J. B. C. Quillian, M.G.

William C. Burton - Nancy E. Eddleman - 22 Feb. 1866 - Jno G. Campbell -
22 Feb. 1866 - T. J. Atkinson, J.I.C.

Page 69:
William F. Bohannon - Demary F. Harris - 27 Feb. 1866 - Jno G. Campbell -
1 March 1866 - Robert Daniel, M.G.

John A. G. Anderson - Luella McAfee - 1 Feb. 1866 - Jno. G. Campbell -
1 Feb. 1866 - E. Porter Palmer, O.M.G.

Page 70:
Robert Lacy - Lavonia Hight - 22 May 1866 - Jno G. Campbell - __ May 1866 -
John C. Clay, J.P.

Cary C. Murdock - Martha Cornett - 23 June 1866 - Jno. G. Campbell -
26 June 1866 - P. O. McPherson, M.G.

Page 71:
David W. Henderson - Jane R. Brown - 5 June 1866 - Jno G. Campbell -
7 June 1866 - T. J. Atkinson, J.I.C.C.

Thomas W. B. Garrett - Mary C. Lacy - 22 May 1866 - Jno G. Campbell -
22 May 1866 - H. C. Hornady, M.G.

Page 72:
Henry C. White - Sophia L. Ruede - 23 May 1866 - Jno G. Campbell - 24 May
1866 - E. Porter Palmer, O.M.G.

Joel S. Reid - Nacy E.O.J. Haye - 17 May 1866 - Jno. G. Campbell - 20 May
1866 - W. W. Jolly, J.P.

Page 73:
William R. Montgomery - Emma J. Northcutt - 17 May 1866 - Jno G. Campbell -
17 May 1866 - E. Porter Palmer, O.M.G.

James Rice - Sarah Jones - 17 May 1866 - Jno G. Campbell - 20 May 1866 -
Robert Baber, M.G.

Page 74:
John Robinson - Caroline Simpson - 26 May 1866 - Jno G. Campbell - 27 May __
T. J. Atkinson, J.I.C.

Charles M. Vann - Dyalphia Baker - 9 June 1866 - Jno G. Campbell -
12 or 14 June 1866 - G. W. Johnson, J.P.

Page 75:
Pascal F. Ferguson - Charity W. Williams - 17 June 1866 - Jno G. Campbell -
17 June 1866 - Thomas P. Whitfield, J.P.

Mr. Jesse M. Penley - Miss Louisa Casey - 18 May 1866 - Jno. G. Campbell -
20 May 1866 - D. W. McEachen, J.P.

Page 76:
James Ray - Miss Leonna Foster - 17 May 1866 - Jno G. Campbell - 20 May 1866 -
F. A. Bell, M.G.

Charles A. Hawkins - Miss Harriet B. Tucker - 5 April 1866 - Jno G. Campbell -
8 April 1866 - E. Porter Palmer, O.M.G.

Page 77:
Jonathan J. Vinson - Amanda Lea - 27 Feb. 1866 - Jno. G. Campbell -
1 March 1866 - William S. Brown, J.P.

Thomas Parr - Joicy Wade - 23 Feb. 1866 - Jno G. Campbell - 25 Feb. 1866 -
William S. Brown, J.P.

Page 78:
James W. Cochran - Easter Robertson - 1 Feb. 1866 - Jno. G. Campbell -
1 Feb. 1866 - Hartwell A. Baldwin, J.P.

Larkin James - Amanda James - 5 Feb. 1866 - Jno. G. Campbell - 5 Feb. 1866 -
R. W. Milner, M.G.

Page 79:
Mr. Laurence E. Emmons - Miss Eliza H. Fletcher - 16 May 1866 -
Jno. G. Campbell - 17 May 1866 - Samuel Benedict, Rector of St. James Church,
Marietta.

John T. Fannin - H. A. Robinson - 21 March 1866 - Jno. G. Campbell -
22 March 1866 - G. T. Carrie, J.P.

Page 80:
Mr. F. J. Ansley - Miss H. J. Lawthorn - 22 Feb. 1866 - Jno. G. Campbell -
25 Feb. 1866 - R. M. Milner, M.G.

Enoch A. Spinks - Miss Nancy Boswell - 10 May 1866 - Jno. G. Campbell -
13 March 1866 - Francis A. Bell, M.G.

Page 81:
Mr. Samuel F. Mayes - Miss Nancy C. Williams - 7 Feb. 1866 - Jno. G.
Campbell - 8 Feb. 1866 - D. N. McEachern, J.P.

Mr. Nathan T. Gann - Miss Susan Gann - 10 Feb. 1866 - Jno G. Campbell -
11 Feb. 1866 - Benjamin Bullard, J.P.

Page 82:
James M. Mitchell - Miss Julia A. Kirk - 12 Feb. 1866 - Jno G. Campbell -
13 Feb. 1866 - Thomas P. Whitfield, J.P.

Chas. D. Philips - Miss Ella M. Combs - 20 Feb. 1866 - Jno. G. Campbell
21 Feb. 1866 - Jas. W. Hames, M.G.

Page 83:
Robert A. Johnson - Rhoda M. Ferguson - 17 June 1866 - Jno. G. Campbell -
17 June 1866 - Thomas P. Whitfield, J.P.

William S. Varner - Cornelia Moore - 31 Oct. 1866 - Jno. G. Campbell -
1 Nov. 1866 - G. W. Johnson, J.P.

Page 84:
Joseph C. A. Shinn - Frances A. Hawkins - 12 Oct. 1866 - Jno. G. Campbell -
16 Oct. 1866 - Geo. W. Johnson, J.P.

James A. Hardman - Sylvania A. Jackson - 2 Nov. 1866 - Jno. G. Campbell
8 Nov. 1866 - Walter Manning, M.G.

Page 85:
James M. Hartsfield - Martha H. Jackson - 18 Oct. 1866 - Jno. G. Campbell -
25 Oct. 1866 - William H. Campbell, M.G.

John W. Beaty - Tabitha T. Mitchell - 2 Oct. 1866 - Jno. G. Campbell -
2 Oct. 1866 - Wm. L. Mansfield, M.G.

Page 86:
John V. Williams - Narcissa Johnson - 3 Oct. 1866 - Jno. G. Campbell -
4 Oct. 1866 - Geo. W. Johnson, J.P.

Mrs. Thomas W. Nichols - Miss Ibbie Smith - 3 Oct. 1866 - Jno. G. Campbell -
3 Oct. 1866 - G. W. Gwin or Given, M.G.

Page 87:
Martin M. Johnson - Nancy Smith - 19 Oct. 1866 - Jno. G. Campbell -
21 Oct. 1866 - A. J. Norton, J.P.

David B. Whitfield - Sarah M. Power - 18 Oct. 1866 - Jno. G. Campbell -
18 Oct. 1866 - A. G. Dempsey, M.G.

Page 88:
James N. Clay - Caroline Edwards - 19 Oct. 1866 - Jno. G. Campbell -
20 Oct. 1866 - John C. Clay, J.P.

Asberry J. Vann - Frances Dobbs - 3 Nov. 1866 - Jno. G. Campbell - 4 Nov.
1866 - G. W. Johnson, J.P.

Page 89:
Samuel L. Anderson - Julia P. Talley - 1 Nov. 1866 - Jno. G. Campbell -
4 Nov. 1866 - James Peek, M.G.

Jeremiah Freeland - Frances E. Kilgore - 24 March 1866 - Jno. G. Campbell -
22 ___ 1866 - not signed by any minister or J.P.

Page 90:
Thomas E. Bolden - E. V. Danforth - 1 Nov. 1866 - Jno. G. Campbell -
4 Nov. 1866 - Hartwell A. Baldwin, J.P.

Captain Gauslin - Martha Johnson - 26 Nov. 1866 - Jno. G. Campbell - 26 Nov. 1866 - T. J. Atkinson, J.I.C.C.

Page 91:
Edmund Gann - Clementine Wade - 23 Nov. 1866 - Jno. G. Campbell - 25 Nov. 1866 - W. H. Campbell, O.M.G.

John A. Richardson - Martha A. Dukes - 14 Nov. 1866 - Jno. G. Campbell - 15 Nov. 1866 - W. H. Campbell, O.M.G.

Page 92:
Andrew W. Skelton - Lucy A. Bell - 10 Nov. 1866 - Jno. G. Campbell - 11 Nov. 1866 - John R. Sanger, O.M.G.

James E. McGinty - Mary C. Gault - 17 Nov. 1866 - Jno. G. Campbell - 18 Nov. 1866 - John R. Sanger, O.M.G.

Page 93:
William W. White - Pauline Kirkpatrick - 12 Dec. 1866 - Jno. G. Campbell - 13 Dec. 1866 - E. P. Palmer, O.M.G.

William J. Goodwin - Louisa Bennett - 21 Nov. 1866 - Jno. G. Campbell - 22 Nov. 1866 - R. Baber, M.G.

Page 94:
Robert A. Montgomery - India G. Cowan - 10 Nov. 1866 - Jno. G. Campbell - 11 Nov. 1866 - H. J. Scruggs, M.G.

Matthew A. Youngblood - Narcissa White - 13 Dec. 1866 - Jno. G. Campbell - 13 Dec. 1866 - G. T. Carrie, J.P.

Page 95:
William P. Johnson - Mattie R. Perkerson - 2 Jan. 1867 - Jno. G. Campbell - 3 Jan. 1867 - R. P. Roger, M.G.

Joel P. Queen - Sophronia Hooker - 21 Oct. 1866 - Jno. G. Campbell - 23 Oct. 1866 - A. Melton, M.G.

Page 96:
Kinson M. Green - Easter E. Kelly - 15 Jan. 1867 - Jno. G. Campbell - 15 Jan. 1867 - T. J. Atkinson, J.I.C.

James Melton - Eliza Allen - 21 Oct. 1866 - Jno. G. Campbell - 28 Oct. 1866 - A. Melton, M.G.

Page 97:
Thomas J. Hindsman - Harriet E. Elmore - 14 Dec. 1866 - Jno. G. Campbell - 26 Dec. 1866 - John A. Casey, J.P.

Sidney P. Parr - Lucinda J. Shaw - 3 Nov. 1866 - Jno. G. Campbell - 4 Nov. 1866 - William S. Brown, J.P.

Page 98:
William A. Seals - Indiana C. Pruett - 14 Dec. 1866 - Jno. G. Campbell - 16 Dec. 1866 - William S. Brown, J.P.

Louis B. Cape - Haseltine Wilson - 26 Dec. 1866 - Jno. G. Campbell - 27 Dec. 1866 - A. Melton, M.G.

Page 99:
William Edwards - Frances C. Cape - 27 Nov. 1866 - Jno. G. Campbell - 29 Nov. 1866 - A. Melton, M.G.

William R. Haney - Frances Brand - 22 Jan. 1867 - Jno. G. Campbell - 23 Jan. 1867 - W. H. Campbell, M.G.

Page 100:
William P. Stanley - Fannie J. Wade - 24 Dec. 1866 - Jno. G. Campbell - 27 Dec. 1866 - G. T. Carrie, J.P.

John B. Seawell - Miss Sallie R. Lacy - 2 Feb. 1867 - Jno. G. Campbell - 3 Feb. 1867 - G. W. Gwin or Given, M.G.

Page 101:
James L. Pace - Martha S. Fults - t Sept. 1866 - Jno. G. Campbell -
6 Sept. 1866 - Robert Daniell, M.G.

Pinckney Goggins - Julia Pace - 1 March 1867 - Jno. G. Campbell - 3 March 1867
D. N. McEachern, J.P.

Page 102:
Daniel R. Thomas - Jennie H. E. Manget - 13 Feb. 1867 - Jno. G. Campbell -
13 Feb. 1867 - E. P. Palmer, O.M.G.

John C. Welch - Georgia Henderson - 20 Dec. 1866 - Jno. G. Campbell -
20 Dec. 1866 - W. W. Carrell, Ord. M. G.

Page 103:
George H. Gramling - Lois J. Green - 7 Feb. 1867 - Jno. G. Campbell -
7 Feb. 1867 - E. Porter Palmer, O.M.G.

Neal E. Williams - Margaret R. Mayes - 7 Feb. 1867 - Jno. G. Campbell -
7 Feb. 1867 - D. N. McEachern, J.P.

Page 104:
Franklin M. Mullins - Sallie M. Sanges - 5 Dec. 1866 - Jno. G. Campbell -
6 Dec. 1866 - J. R. Mayson, L. D.

William P. Duncan - Ann N. Grisham - 24 Dec. 1866 - Jno. G. Campbell -
26 Dec. 1866 - R. Baber, M. G.

Page 105:
James E. Johnson - Margaret L. Davis - 17 Dec. 1867 - Jno. G. Campbell -
27 Dec. 1866 - Daniel Wright, J.P.

Edward Pharr - Mary Smith - 30 Jan. 1867 - Jno. G. Campbell - 13 Feb. 1867 -
R. Baber, M.G.

Page 106:
Thomas F. Maddux - Elizabeth J. Scott - 14 Jan. 1867 - Jno. G. Campbell -
17 Jan. 1867 - John Anderson, M.G.

Thomas Henderson - Julia Ann Stephens - 11 Jan. 1867 - Jno. G. Campbell -
13 Jan. 1867 - J. M. Daniell, M.G.

Page 107:
Perry F. York - Lizzie E. Shockley - 18 Dec. 1866 - Jno. G. Campbell -
20 Dec. 1866 - G. W. Given or Gwin, M.G.

Reuben F. Hill - Elizabeth Biles - 10 Jan. 1867 - Jno. G. Campbell -
10 Jan. 1867 - Hartwell A. Baldwin, J.P.

Page 108:
James F. McLarty - Eliza R. Barnes - 28 July 1866 - Jno. G. Campbell -
29 July 1866 - Benjamin Bullard, J.P.

Glenn O. Moseley - Sarah E. Maroney - 20 Dec. 1866 - Jno. G. Campbell -
21 Dec. 1866 - John C. Bowden, J.I.C.

Page 109:
Jasper L. Gant - Margaret E. Shirley - 4 Sept. 1866 - Jno. G. Campbell -
4 Sept. 1866 - H. B. Johnson, M.G.

James T. Johnson - Mary Francis Delk - 10 Nov. 1866 - Jno. G. Campbell -
15 Nov. 1866 - H. B. Johnson, M.G.

Page 110:
James L. Root - Caledonia Leverton - 16 Jan. 1867 - Jno. G. Campbell -
17 Jan. 1867 - E. Porter Palmer, O.M.G.

Joseph M. Tanner - Eliza Ragsdale - 3 Dec. 1866 - Jno. G. Campbell -
5 Dec. 1866 - A. G. Dempsey, M G.

Page 111:
John M. Martin - Frances Brown - 2 Jan. 1867 - Jno. G. Campbell -
2 Jan. 1867 - George W. Given, M.G.

John C. Powell - Rebecca A. Post - 24 Dec. 1866 - Jno. G. Campbell -
25 Dec. 1866 - W. W. Carroll, M.G.

Page 112:
Benjamin F. Mackey - Emeline Rutherford - 8 Jan. 1867 - Jno. G. Campbell -
8 Jan. 1867 - R. H. Marchman, J.P.

Bryant Wadkins - Mary Grace - 13 Nov. 1866 - Jno. G. Campbell -
17 Nov. 1866 - Benjamin Bullard, J.P.

Page 113:
Robert A. Watson - Mary H. Stanley - 12 Nov. 1866 - Jno. G. Campbell -
15 Nov. 1866 - R. W. Milner, M.G.

John Mitchel - Einefore Bass - 24 Sept. 1866 - Jno. G. Campbell -
27 Sept. 1766 - Daniel Wright, J.P.

Page 114:
Lemuel W. Wright - Matilda J. Hardman - 8 Jan. 1867 - Jno. G. Campbell -
10 Jan. 1867 - A. H. McGay, O.M.G.

Enoch Walraven - Louisa E. Philips - 19 Jan. 1867 - Jno. G. Campbell -
27 Jan. 1867 - W. H. Campbell, O.M.G.

Page 115:
William A. Steel - Elvira A. E. Evans - 20 Dec. 1866 - Jno. G. Campbell -
23 Dec. 1866 - W. W. Carroll, M.G.

John T. Ashley - Mary A. Leeroy - 24 July 1867 - Jno. G. Campbell -
28 July 1867 - W. G. Wigley, J.P.

Page 116:
John B. Putnam - Mary Grisham - 20 Dec. 1866 - Jno G. Campbell -
21 Dec. 1866 - W. H. Dean, M.G.

Mr. John Tate - Miss Jane A. Benson - 10 Feb. 1866 - Jno. G. Campbell -
13 Feb. 1866 - William H. Dean, M.G.

Page 117:
Isaac L. Magill - Sarah E. Orr - 16 July 1867 - Jno. G. Campbell - 1 Aug. 1867
R. W. Milner, M.G.

Charles T. Shephard - Miss Martha A. Lowry - 22 Aug. 1867 - Jno. G. Campbell -
22 Aug. 1867 - J. W. Yarborough, M.G.

Page 118:
William M. Knox - Miss Harriet L. Campbell - 1 March 1867 - Jno. G. Campbell
5 March 1867 - E. H. Lindley, J.I.C.

L. H. Willmoth - Elizabeth N. Beavers - 18 Feb. 1867 - Jno. G. Campbell -
7 March 1867 - W. W. Carroll, M.G.

Page 119:
Mr. Henry L. Tant - Miss Ellen F. Summerhill - 10 March 1867 - Jno. G.
Campbell - 10 March 1867 - John R. Sanger, O.M.G.

James M. Kirk - N. Eveline Martin - 15 May 1867 - Jno. G. Campbell -
16 May 1867 - John C. Clay, J.P.

Page 120:
John M. Kirk - M. Jane Martin - 15 May 1867 - Jno. G. Campbell -
16 May 1867 - John C. Clay, J.P.

Samuel P. Rose - Miss Celestia M. Coombs - 29 April 1867 - Jno. G. Campbell
3 April 1867 - Samuel Benedict, Rector St. James Ch.

Page 121:
Hiram R. Delay - Matilda S. Jones - 18 Feb. 1866 - Jno. G. Campbell -
20 Feb. 1866 - W. H. Dean, M.G.

Sidney M. Burden - Miss Emma F. White - 12 March 1867 - Jno. G. Campbell -
14 March 1867 - A.G. Dempsey, M.G.

Page 122:
James Thompson - Miss Julia Holbrook - 20 Feb. 1867 - Jno. G. Campbell -
21 Feb. 1867 - A. Melton, M.G.

Edwin R. Coker - Mary Matilda Pursley - 19 Aug. 1867 - Jno. G. Campbell -
22 Aug. 1867 - W. Manning, O.M. G.

Page 123:
Jacob L. Cook - Henrietta H. Meigs - 4 Sept. 1867 - Jno. G. Campbell -
4 Sept. 1867 - Samuel Benedict Rector St. James Ch.

James H. Fraser - Eliza J. Dickerson - 3 Aug. 1867 - Jno. G. Campbell -
13 Aug. 1867 - W. W. Jolly, J.P.

Page 124:
Joseph Norris - Mrs. Charlotte Ivey - 10 Aug. 1867 - Jno. G. Campbell -
11 Aug. 1867 - W. W. Jolley, J.P.

Thomas M. Chandler - Martha E. Hannon - 4 May 1867 - Jno. G. Campbell -
5 May 1867 - William S. Brown, J.P.

Page 125:
David H. Reeves - Sophronia A. R. Augburn - 27 Aug. 1867 - Jno. G. Campbell -
28 Aug. 1867 - R. Baber, M.G.

Joseph Mitchell - Elizabeth Henderson - 18 June 1867 - Jno. G. Campbell -
24 June 1867 - R. Daniel, M.G.

Page 126:
C. J. Ireland - Nancy C. Gann - 7 Sept. 1867 - Jno. G. Campbell -
8 Sept. 1867 - Wm. S. Brown, J.P.

George H. Power - Martha C. Bishop - 6 Feb. 1867 - Jno. G. Campbell -
7 Feb. 1867 - W. H. Campbell, M.G.

Page 127:
Thomas D. Spragins - Elimira Chastain - 18 March 1867 - Jno. G. Campbell -
28 March 1867 - G. W. Johnson, J.P.

John L. Teat - Eliza L. Tippins - 1 Feb. 1867 - Jno. G. Campbell -
3 Feb. 1867 - E. Northcutt, M.G.

Page 128:
John W. Garrison - Catherine Nickles - 27 July 1866 - Jno. G. Campbell -
31 July 1866 - E. Northcutt, M.G.

John Brown - Caroline R. Tanner - 3 Dec. 1866 - Jno. G. Campbell -
6 Dec. 1866 - E. Northcutt, M.G.

Page 129:
Hugh L. Winn - Miss Fannie E. Latimer - 30 July 1867 - Jno. G. Campbell -
1 Aug. 1867 - John R. Gaines, M.G.

Joseph E. Anderson - Farency Queen - 16 Nov. 1866 - Jno. G. Campbell -
17 Nov. 1866 - James Peek, O.M.G.

Page 130:
John H. Ketner - Miss Julia S. Hansell - 11 Sept. 1867 - Jno. G. Campbell -
11 Sept. 1867 - E. P. Palmer, M.G.

David A. Barrett - Louisa Barrett - 25 Jan. 1867 - Jno. G. Campbell -
29 Jan. 1867 - R. Baber, M.G.

Page 131:
James M. Allen - Cerena E. Tanner - 10 Dec. 1866 - Jno. G. Campbell -
16 Dec. 1866 - E. Northcutt, M.G.

Aron Thompson - Catherine Baine - 26 May 1866 - Jno. G. Campbell -
27 May 1866 - Benjamin Bullar, J.P.

Page 132:
Daniel Moss - Miss Frances Ray - 25 Oct. 1862 - Jno. G. Campbell -
26 Oct. 1862 - Benjamin Bullard, J.P.

J. M. Coker (Koker) - Mary A. Pullin - 17 May 1867 - Jno. G. Campbell -
19 May 1867 - E. J. Fowler, J.P.

Page 133:
Joseph B. Richardson - Martha Simpson - 16 July 1867 - Jno. G. Campbell -
16 July 1867 - W. W. Carrell, Ord. M.G.

Atlas A. Daniel, Jr. - Emeline Simpson - 7 Feb. 1867 - Jno. G. Campbell -
7 July 1867 - T. J. Atkinson, J.I.C.

Page 134:
William W. Briner - Mary Blythe - 8 Jan. 1867 - Jno. G. Campbell -
8 Jan. 1867 - R. A. Marchman, J.P.

Robert A. Hamilton - Miss Martha A. Wright - 11 July 1867 - Jno. G. Campbell
14 July 1867 - John Grest O.M.G.

Page 135:
Hugh B. Greenwood - Marietta Tapp - 16 Jan. 1867 - Jno. G. Campbell -
17 Jan. 1867 - Janus G. Ryals, M.G.

Fletcher L. Delk - Mary E. Parnell - 24 Oct. 1867 - Jno. G. Campbell -
25 Oct. 1867 - H. B. Johnson, M.G.

Page 136:
James D. Carruth - Susan F. Kemp - 6 Feb. 1866 - Jno. G. Campbell -
8 Feb. 1867 - E. Northcutt, minister gospel.

J. M. Welchel - Elizabeth Welchel - 17 June 1867 - Jno. G. Campbell -
20 June 1867 - W. G. Wigley, J.P.

Page 137:
Leroy H. Turner - Anna V. McConnell - 14 Sept. 1867 - Jno. G. Campbell -
15 Sept. 1867 - J. C. Hedge Cock, J.P.

Adolphus C. Hawkins - Martha C. S. Hans - 31 Aug. 1865 - Jno. G. Campbell -
3 Sept. 1865 - W. H. Deen, M.G.

Page 138:
Henry Myers - Jane Eliza Green - 2 May 1867 - Jno. G. Campbell -
2 May 1867 - Samuel Benedict, Rector of St. James Church

William Copland - Sarah Teal - 25 May 1867 - Jno. G. Campbell -
26 May 1867 - John T. Robertson, J.P.

Page 139:
William Thompson - Elizabeth Dodle - 6 April 1867 - Jno. G. Campbell -
7 April 1867 - A (X his mark) Melton, M.G.

James Wallace - Nancy Queen - 10 March 1867 - Jno. G. Campbell -
10 March 1867 - A. (X his mark) Melton, M.G.

Page 140:
Jesse F. Murner - Sarah J. F. Stone - 2 May 1867 - Jno. G. Campbell -
2 May 1867 - W. Manning, O.M.G.

William N. Reese - Isabella D. Hill - 24 April 1867 - Jno. G. Campbell -
25 April 1867 - Wm. L. Mansfield, M.G.

Page 141:
James B. Baggett - Miss Martha Sorrells - 15 Aug. 1867 - Jno. G. Campbell
18 Aug. 1867 - John Murphy Minister Gospel

Malachi L. Reed - Martha Gann - 12 Sept. 1867 - Jno. G. Campbell -
15 Sept. 1867 - William S. Brown, J.P.

Page 142:
Charles M. Fitzgerald - L. Camilla Calder - 25 Sept. 1867 - Jno. G. Campbell -
25 Sept. 1867

William M. Alexander - Mary White - 28 March 1867 - Jno. G. Campbell -
28 March 1867 - A. G. Dempsey, M.G.

16

Page 143:
Henry B. Johnson - Eliza Jane Knight - 1 May 1867 - Jno. G. Campbell -
7 May 1867 - Beaton Daniell, M.G.

George L. Mitchell - Georgia E. Hunt - 14 Feb. 1867 - Jno. G. Campbell -
18 Feb. 1867 - E. Porter Palmer, O.M.G.

Page 144:
John S. Eason - Martha Jane Lee - 27 Feb. 1867 - Jno. G. Campbell -
3 March 1867 - Cocero A. Pool, J.P.

James F. Hooper - Sarah Alsabrooks - 5 Aug. 1868(?) - Jno. G. Campbell -
1 Sept. 1867 - Hartwell A. Baldwin, J.P.

Page 145:
Andrew R. Groover - Nancy J. Richardson - 20 July 1867 - Jno. G. Campbell -
21 July 1867 - Peter Groover, M.G.

Robert A. Bellinger - Georgia A. Wallace - 29 April 1867 - Jno. G. Campbell -
5 May 1867 - Wm. L. Maysfield, M.G.

Page 146:
Isaac D. Williams - Cornelia Malone - 4 Oct. 1867 - Jno. G. Campbell -
4 Oct. 1867 - A. G. Dempsey, M.G.

Adam J. Lester - Miss Elizabeth West - 8 Oct. 1867 - Jno. G. Campbell -
8 Oct. 1867 - R. Baber, M.G.

Page 147:
Alexander A. Gullat - Mary J. Heren - 8 Oct. 1867 - Jno. G. Campbell -
8 Oct. 1867 - R. Baber, M.G.

Page 148:
John D. Sherman - H. E. Crochran - 26 Sept. 1867 - Jno. G. Campbell -
13 Oct. 1867 - Thomas Burge, M.G.

William G. Robertson - Lucia D. Childers - 23 July 1867 - Jno. G. Campbell
24 July 1867 - E. Porter Palmer, M.G.

Page 149:
Randall Hughey - Sarah Shellgore - 23 Sept. 1867 - Jno. G. Campbell -
24 Sept. 1867 - Isaac Rutherford, M.G.

John B. Seago - Frances E. Adams - 27 Oct. 1867 - Jno. G. Campbell -
John R. Gaines, M.G.

Page 150:
William Casey - Miss Rebecca McKey - 9 Nov. 1867 - Jno. G. Campbell -
10 Nov. 1867 - G. T. Carrie, J.P.

Little B. Hairston - Miss Julia Ann Watson - 21 Oct. 1867 - Jno. G. Campbell -
27 Oct. 1867 - Joseph M. Gable, M.G.

Page 151:
Andrew J. Barker - Miss Harriet Cooper - 2 Nov. 1867 - Jno. G. Campbell -
3 Nov. 1867 - C. D. Philips, J.C.C.C.C.

George Ridings - Maria Gadden - 7 Nov. 1867 - Jno. G. Campbell -
13 Nov. 1867 - C. T. Carrie, J.P.

Page 152:
George W. Tatum - Sarah Ann Todd - 1 Oct. 1867 - Jno. G. Campbell -
3 Oct. 1867 - John G. Grane, M.G.

Francis M. Hembree - Miss Lou E. Ash - 16 Oct. 1867 - Jno. G. Campbell -
16 Oct. 1867 - Joseph M. Gable, M.G.

Page 153:
Alexander N. Boring - Cassie A. E. Johnson   3 Dec. 1866 - Jno. G. Campbell -
11 Dec. 1866 - C. M. McClure, M.G.

Henry Driscoll - Catherine Turner - 19 Oct. 1867 - Jno. G. Campbell -
20 Oct. 1867 - Cocero A. Pool, J.P.

Page 154:
John M. Green - Miss Clara J. Kirk - 13 Sept. 1867 - Jno. G. Campbell -
15 Sept. 1867 - J. G. Eubanks, M.G.

Walter B. Dismuke - Miss Nancy E. Way - 5 Dec. 1867 - Jno. G. Campbell -
5 Dec. 1867 - Wm. L. Mansfield, M.G.

Page 155:
Elijah Walraven - Mary C. Channell - 9 Oct. 1867 - Jno. G. Campbell -
10 Oct. 1867 - John G. Eubanks, M.G.

Lemuel Johnson - Elizabeth Groover - 26 Oct. 1866 - Jno. G. Campbell -
7 Nov. 1866 - C. M. McClure, M.G.

Page 156:
David Herndon - Martha Fowler - 16 Oct. 1867 - Jno. G. Campbell -
24 Oct. 1867 - Wm. L. Foster, M.G.

James Burton - Mary Ann Simpson - 8 Dec. 1866 - Jno. G. Campbell -
3 June 1867 - John G. Evans, M.G.

Page 157:
Andrew J. Ball - Mary E. Power - 9 Jan. 1867 - Jno. G. Campbell -
10 Jan. 1867 - Wm. Power, J.P.

Charles T. Henderson - Eugenia Rice - 29 Sept. 1865 - Jno. G. Campbell -
5 Oct. 1865 - James Lindley, J.P.

Page 158:
Jeremiah J. Pruett - Nancy Harbin - 20 Nov. 1866 - Jno. G. Campbell -
30 Nov. 1866 - James Lindley, J.P.

Willis Scoggins - Mary E. McCannon - 2 Dec. 1867 - Jno. G. Campbell -
2 Dec. 1867 - J. R. Saye O.M.G.

Page 159:
Monroe F. Campbell - Mrs. Amelia M. Kemp - 11 Nov. 1867 - Jno. G. Campbell -
12 Nov. 1867 - R. W. Milner, M.G.

Wm. T. Edwards - Martha E. McGinty - 28 Nov. 1867 - Jno. G. Campbell -
28 Nov. 1867 - J. R. Sanges, M.G.

Page 160:
Frances N. Cowan - Miss Mary M. Gresham - 13 Nov. 1867 - Jno. G. Campbell -
21 Nov. 1867 - R. W. Milner, M.G.

John W. Newel - Miss Sarah A. Abbott - 2 Oct. 1867 - Jno. G. Campbell -
30 Oct. 1867 - Robt. Baber, M.G.

Page 161:
Gustavus A. Hardage - Miss Martha Guess - 25 Oct. 1867 - Jno. G. Campbell -
27 Oct. 1867 - John G. Eubanks, M.G.

Levi Watts - Clara Mitchem - 23 Nov. 1867 - Jno. G. Campbell -
28 Nov. 1867 - F. A. Bell, M.G.

Page 162:
William N. Pace - Elizabeth C. Ruff - 19 Nov. 1867 - Jno. G. Campbell -
20 Nov. 1867 - J. R. Sanger, O.M.G.

Robert C. Irwin - Miss Mary W. Lane - 13 Nov. 1867 - Jno. G. Campbell -
14 Nov. 1867 - Rob't Baber, M.G.

Page 163:
George W. Powell - Nanie C. Glore - 26 Nov. 1867 - Jno. G. Campbell -
28 Nov. 1867 - William L. Brown, J.P.

Alfred G. Duke - Miss Martha E. Hill - 15 Nov. 1867 - Jno. G. Campbell -
28 Nov. 1867 - C. D. Moore, J.P.

Page 164:
William Rakestraw - Jane Rakestraw - 26 Sept. 1867 - Jno. G. Campbell -
6 Oct. 1867 - C. D. Moon, J.P.

James N. Hardman - Miss C. A. Megarity - 19 Oct. 1867 - Jno. G. Campbell -
27 Oct. 1867 - Walter Manning, O.M.G.

Page 165:
Robert P. Bush - Mary E. Murdock - 3 Oct. 1867 - Jno. G. Campbell -
5 Sept. 1867 - W. H. Campbell O.M.G.

William B. Stroud - Miss Jane Davis - 3 Aug. 1867 - Jno. G. Campbell -
4 Aug. 1867 - Benjamin Bullard, J.P.

Page 166:
John A. Hill - Nancy A. Brooks - 7 Sept. 1867 - Jno. G. Campbell -
8 Sept. 1867 - Benjamin Bullard, J.P.

Jasper N. Brown - Miss Amanda J. Bell - 15 Aug. 1867 - Jno. G. Campbell -
17 Aug. 1867 - W. H. Campbell, M.G.

Page 167:
John B. Mathis - Miss Marietta A. A. Mays - 5 Dec. 1867 - Jno. G. Campbell -
5 Dec. 1867 - John R. Gaines, M.G.

Isaac B. Stroud - Mary E. Scroggins - 17 Dec. 1867 - Jno. G. Campbell -
26 Dec. 1867 - Benjamin Bullard, J.P.

Page 168:
Samuel M. Queen - Miss Cynthia C. Pope - 30 Oct. 1867 - Jno. G. Campbell -
31 Oct. 1867 - Benjamin Bullard, J.P.

Billington S. Florence - Lizzie O. Kiser - 4 Dec. 1867 - Jno. G. Campbell -
5 Dec. 1867 - R. Baber M.G.

Page 169:
William B. Paucl(?) - Elizabeth Gazaway - 24 Aug. 1867 - Jno. G. Campbell -
24 Aug. 1867 - E. J. Fowler, J.P.

J. Byron Montgomery - Miss Eugenia F. Holt - 12 June 1867 - Jno. G. Campbell -
13 Aug. 1867 - E. P. Palmer, O.M.G.

Page 170:
James M. Jordan - Mary A. Bolden - 28 Dec. 1867 - Jno. G. Campbell -
29 Dec. 1867 - Hartwell A. Baldwin, J.P.

James C. Hill - Miss Josephine Hill - 10 July 1867 - Jno. G. Campbell -
10 July 1867 - T. J. Atkinson, J.I.C.

Page 171:
John D. Perkerson - Martha J. McClarty - 4 Jan. 1868 - Jno. G. Campbell -
9 Jan. 1868 - E. H. Lindley, J. Inf. Ct.

Levi G. Haygood - Victoria C. Garrison - 4 Jan. 1868 - Jno. G. Campbell -
9 Jan. 1868 - A. H. Teasley, J.I.C.

Page 172:
James W. Hatcher - Miss Mary M. Pate - 5 Nov. 1867 - Jno. G. Campbell -
6 Nov. 1867 - E. H. Lindley, J.I.C.

Edward D. Stephens - Mary E. Duncan - 27 Aug. 1867 - Jno. G. Campbell -
29 Aug. 1867 - H. B. Johnson M.G.

Page 173:
Joseph G. Brooks - Martha Williams - 27 Aug. 1867 - Jno. G. Campbell -
29 Aug. 1867 - John W. Hill, J.P.

Joel C. Stansell - Eva Kimberly - 24 Dec. 1867 - Jno. G. Campbell -
24 Dec. 1867 - H. B. Johnson, M.G.

Page 174:
B. F. Richardson - Sarah A. Kirk - 24 Dec. 1867 - Jno. G. Campbell -
24 Dec. 18678 (written over)

Silas M. Simpson - Mary M. Campbell - 3 Jan. 1868 - Jno. G. Campbell -
9 Jan. 1868 - Robert Baber, M.G.

Page 175:
Kelly McHaffy - Sarah F. Greier - 1 Feb. 1868 - Jno. G. Campbell -
9 Feb. 1868 - W. F. Cook, M.G.

Warren C. Kehely - Elizabeth L. Kemp - 2 Jan. 1868 - Jno. G. Campbell -
2 Jan. 1868 - D. N. McEachen J.P.

Page 176:
James M. Lindley - Margaret Johnson - 16 Jan. 1868 - Jno. G. Campbell -
19 Jan. 1868 - C. D. Moon, J.P.

James A. Smith - Elizabeth Barrett - 18 Jan. 1868 - Jno. G. Campbell -
19 Jan. 1868 - John C. Clay, J.P.

Page 177:
David Beaty - Ann Mitchell - 31 Dec. 1867 - Jno. G. Campbell -
2 Jan. 1867 - E. J. Fowler, J.P.

Thomas J. Winn - Priscilla Burns - 6 Feb. 1868 - Jno. G. Campbell -
6 Feb. 1868 - T. J. Atkinson, J.I.C.

Page 178:
John H. Cantrell - Roancy L. Eaton - 22 Feb. 1868 - Jno. G. Campbell -
22 Feb. 1868 - Hartwell A. Baldwin, J.P.

John P. Farrar - Mary F. Dodgen - 15 Jan. 1868 - Jno. G. Campbell -
23 Jan. 1868 - Hartwell A. Baldwin, J.P.

Page 179:
James C. Greer - S. Isabella Ray - 22 Feb. 1868 - Jno. G. Campbell -
25 Feb. 1868 - Robt. Baber, M.G.

Joseph S. Shaw - Eliza E. Wade - 11 Dec. 1867 - Jno. G. Campbell -
12 Dec. 1867 - William S. Brown, J.P.

Page 180:
John L. Reed - Nancy A. Ruff - 21 Jan. 1868 - Jno. G. Campbell -
23 Jan. 1868 - Robert Daniell, M.G.

John K. or R. McKenny - Josephine Florence - 23 Dec. 1867 - Jno. G. Campbell -
25 Dec. 1867 - R. Baber, M.G.

Page 181:
Michael S. Wheelan - Medora M. Pilgrim - 15 Jan. 1868 - Jno. G. Campbell -
15 Jan. 1868 - W. F. Cook M.G.

James J. Bolden - Amanda Manor - 7 Feb. 1868 - Jno. G. Campbell -
9 Feb. 1868 - Hartwell A. Baldwin J.P.

Page 182:
Newton M. Morris - Margaret A. Mayes - 3 Jan. 1868 - Jno. G. Campbell -
5 Jan. 1868 - W. Manning O.M.G.

Ranson W. Keheley - Ruhama Meek - 17 Dec. 1867 - Jno. G. Campbell -
19 Dec. 1867 - A. G. Dempsey M.G.

Page 183:
Wm. J. Cannon - Sarah J. Brown - 27 Feb. 1868 - Jno. G. Campbell -
27 Feb. 1868 - A. G. Dempsey M.G.

Francis A. Anderson - Jane E. Fleming - 21 Jan. 1868 - Jno. G. Campbell -
23 Jan. 1868 - John F. Rowns L.M.

Page 184:
John A. Massey - Miss Georgia A. Keefe - 22 April 1868 - Jno. G. Campbell -
22 April 1868 - Samuel Benedict Rector of St. Johns Church, Savannah, Ga.

Michael Klahar - Mary J. Echols - 16 April 1868 - Jno. G. Campbell -
16 April 1861 - John C. Clay, J.P.

Page 185:
Thomas P. Moore - E. J. Hunton - 24 Oct. 1867 - Jno. G. Campbell -
29 Oct. 1867 - L. H. West, J.P.

Henry C. Ruff - Minerva A. Dowda - 20 April 1868 - Jno. G. Campbell -
23 April 1868 - Robert Daniell, M.G.

Page 186:
Ittai Prewett - Miss Eliza Wright - 1 April 1868 - Jno. G. Campbell -
2 April 1868 - Robert Daniell, M.G.

James W. Melton - Martha E. Cape - 7 Feb. 1868 - Jno. G. Campbell -
11 Feb. 1868 - Benjamin Bullard, J.P.

Page 187:
William R. Wilson - Mary R. Conger - 19 Feb. 1868 - Jno. G. Campbell -
20 Feb. 1868 - Benjamin Bullard, J.P.

Thos. Alexander - Mattie Loveless - 4 Feb. 1868 - Jno. G. Campbell -
6 Feb. 1868 - Benjamin Bullard, J.P.

Page 188:
Thomas B. Cates - Julia Waits - 13 March 1868 - Jno. G. Campbell -
15 March 1868 - Berton Daniell M.G.

Henry L. Echols - Rhoda Walraven - 31 March 1868 - Jno. G. Campbell -
31 March 1868 - John C. Clay, J.P.

Page 189:
Thomas W. Whitfield - Eliza L. Bowie - 10 March 1868 - Jno. G. Campbell -
12 March 1868 - A. G. Dempsey, M.G.

John C. Waters - Miss Mary J. Wallis - 25 March 1868 - Jno. G. Campbell -
25 March 1868 - W. F. Cook, M.G.

Page 190:
Wm. J. Eubanks - Mary C. Bates - 8 Jan. 1868 - Jno. G. Campbell -
9 Jan. 1868 - John G. Eubanks, M.G.

James F. Kirk - Amanda M. Fowler - 7 Feb. 1868 - Jno. G. Campbell -
9 Feb. 1868 - W. G. Wigley, J.P.

Page 191:
John T. Basel - Sarah A. Spinks - 4 Jan. 1868 - Jno. G. Campbell -
9 Jan. 1868 - W. H. Campbell, O.M.G.

John Brooks - Martha Kirk - 28 Dec. 1867 - Jno. G. Campbell -
29 Dec. 1867 - John G. Eubanks M.G.

Page 192:
Pleadious M. T. Medlin - Miss Martha E. Whitfield - 18 Feb. 1868 -
Jno. G. Campbell - 19 Feb. 1868 - V. E. Manget M.G.

Robert Holland - Marinda Barker - 27 Feb. 1868 - Jno. G. Campbell -
1 March 1868 - Jno. G. Campbell M.G.

Page 193:
William A. Howell - Miss Clara P. Scroggins - 12 Nov. 1867 - Jno. G. Campbell-
14 Nov. 1867 - Jas. P. Prickett M.G.

Adolphus B. Hairston - Sarah L. Bell - 18 Dec. 1867 - Jno. G. Campbell -
19 Dec. 1867 - John G. Eubanks, M.G.

Page 194:
George M. Manning - Kate L. Sanges - 20 Feb. 1868 - Jno. G. Campbell -
20 Feb. 1868 - W. F. Cook M.G.

Joshua H. Segars - Ara Anna Gable - 14 April 1868 - Jno. G. Campbell -
14 April 1868 - W. F. Cook M.G.

Page 195:
Cicero M. Adams - Miss Sarah A. Voss - 12 Jan. 1868 - Jno. C. Campbell
16 Jan. 1868 - Wm. C. Doeris J.P.

Elijah Congo - Miss Lizzie Vinson - 16 Jan. 1868 - Jno. G. Campbell -
17 Jan. 1868 - E. H. Lindley J.I.C.

Page 196:
Warren H. Medlin - Louisa C. Whitfield - 22 April 1868 - Jno. G. Campbell -
22 April 1868 - V. E. Manget M.G.

John T. Hairston - Nancy E. Ireland - 25 March 1868 - Jno. G. Campbell -
25 March 1868 - H. B. Johnson.

Page 197:
Thomas M. Graham - Louisa S. Bell - 29 April 1868 - Jno. G. Campbell -
20 May 1868 - H. B. Johnson

J. H. Whitehead - Mrs. Martha Polston - 11 May 1868 - Jno. G. Campbell -
14 May 1868 - D. N. McEachen J.P.

Page 198:
Richard T. Verhine - Miss Joisey L. Collins - 1 May 1868 - Jno. G. Campbell -
3 May 1868 - J. C. Hedgecock J.P.

W. N. Willson - M. E. Scroggins - 6 June 1868 - Jno. G. Campbell -
7 June 1868 - J. R. Sanges, M.G.

Page 199:
Early A. Griffin - Miss Mary Emanuel - 13 June 1868 - Jno. G. Campbell -
14 June 1868 - James G. Ryals O.M.G.

Wm. B. Patton - Elizabeth Q. Summy - 15 July 1868 - Jno. G. Campbell -
16 July 1868 - C. A. Evans M.G.

Page 200:
John R. Newton - Nancy A. McWilliams - 19 May 1868 - Jno. G. Campbell -
21 May 1868 - Hartwell A. Baldwin J.P.

John Morris - Miss Emily Goodson - 30 Oct. 1867 - Jno. G. Campbell -
3 Nov. 1867 - Cicero A. Poole, J.P.

Page 201:
Andrew J. Williams - Miss Caroline Clanton - 6 Aug. 1868 - Jno. G. Campbell -
6 Aug. 1868 - W. W. Jolley, J.P.

Oscar A. Alden - Mrs. C. V. Howel - 20 April 1868 - Jno. G. Campbell -
22 April 1868 - Jas. P. Prickett M.G.

Page 202:
Newton Cook - Nancy Wallace - 24 April 1868 - Jno. G. Campbell -
25 April 1868 - A. Melton O.M.G.

Robert C. Pressley - Nancy J. Sherman - 2 Jan. 1868 - Jno. G. Campbell -
2 Jan. 1868 - W. W. Jolly, J.P.

Page 203:
John W. Barnett - Amanda J. Rowland - 1 July 1868 - Jno. G. Campbell -
2 July 1868 - W. Manning O.M.G.

James J. Price - Mary E. Kirk - 24 June 1868 - Jno. G. Campbell -
25 June 1868 - J. G. Eubanks M.G.

Page 204:
James H. Albutton (also written Albotton) - Mary E. Huskins - Jno. G.
Campbell - 14 April 1868 - D. R. Hembree J.P.

Albert J. McGullin - Martha J. Hicks - 11 July 1868 - Jno. G. Campbell -
19 July 1868 - W. W. Jolley, J.P.

Page 205:
Thomas J. Minhinnett - Martha Eldridge - 5 June 1868 - Jno. G. Campbell -
9 June 1868 - N. A. Pratt O.M.G.

Dillard M. Young - Harriet Burt - 11 July 1868 - Jno. G. Campbell -
12 July 1868 - W. F. Cook M.G.

Page 206:
Philip E. Norton - Mildred W. Oglesby - 10 March 1867 - Jno. G. Campbell -
21 March 1867 - M. D. Norton M.G.

Uriah Owen - Fannie Moore - 27 July 1868 - Jno. G. Campbell - 29 July 1868 -
J. G. Eubanks, M.G.

Page 207:
Cicero N. Marchman - Miss Fannie Hill - 7 Aug. 1868 - Jno. G. Campbell -
9 Aug. 1868 - D. B. Hamilton M.G.

Henry Baldwin - Miss Sarah Johnson - 7 Aug. 1868 - Jno. G. Campbell -
15 Aug. 1868 - A. G. Dempsey M.G.

Page 208:
J. T. Shirtley - Mary T. Cobb - 27 Aug. 1868 - Jno. G. Campbell -
27 Aug. 1868 - G. F. Carrie, J.P.

W. E. Gramling - Sarah W. Reid - 1 Sept. 1868 - E. A. Dobbs, ordy -
2 Sept. 1868 - W. F. Cook M.G.

Page 209:
Thomas W. Nox - Hannah Green - 17 Sept. 1868 - E. A. Dobbs, ordy -
17 wept. 1868 - G. F. Carrie J.P.

George W. Guthrey - Elizabeth C. Abney - 23 Aug. 1868 - Jno. G. Campbell -
3 Sept. 1861 - A. B. Mitchell.

Page 210:
J. Monroe Steel - Miss T. A. Adams - 21 Aug. 1868 - Jno. G. Campbell -
27 Aug. 1868 - J. G. Eubanks, M.G.

G. B. Cheatham - Miss Nanny Adams - 10 Sept. 1868 - E. A. Dobbs -
10 Sept. 1868 - J. G. Eubanks M.G.

Page 211:
George J. Yoler - Milly A. Walraven - 29 Sept. 1868 - E. A. Dobbs -
1 Oct. 1868 - J. G. Eubanks M.G.

James P. McClain - Mary Everett - 17 Sept. 1868 - E. A. Dobbs -
24 Sept. 1868 - J. G. Eubanks M.G.

Page 212:
William P. Embry - Miss Benneth J. Simms - 14 Sept. 1868 - Jno. G. Campbell -
16 Aug. 1868 - J. G. Ryals O.M.G.

William Griggs - Mary Ann Carroll - 7 Aug. 1868 - Jno. G. Campbell -
9 Aug. 1868 - C. D. Moon J.P.

Page 213:
Thomas Campton - Mrs Temperance S. Davis - 7 Sept. 1868 - E. A. Dobbs -
13 Sept. 1868 - C. D. Moon J.P.

P. F. Tapp - Miss Susan Jackson - 24 Sept. 1868 - E. A. Dobbs -
1 Oct. 1868 - H. B. Johnson M.G.

Page 214:
David Black - Miss E. M. Marlow - 29 Sept. 1868 - E. A. Dobbs -
4 Oct. 1868 - Williams S. Brown, J.P.

John King - Frances Duncan - 10 Oct. 1868 - E. A. Dobbs - 11 Oct. 1868 -
H. B. Johnson, M.G.

Page 215:
James Blankenship - Miss Nancy Burton - 24 Oct. 1868 - E. A. Dobbs -
25 Oct. 1868 - Thomas P. Whitfield, J.P.

William M. Donehoo - Miss Mary J. Shirley - 17 Nov. 1868 - E. A. Dobbs -
18 Nov. 1868 - J. M. Gable

Page 216:
J. C. Wilson - Samantha Randall - 23 Nov. 1868 E. A. Dobbs -
23 Nov. 1868 - W. W. Carroll Ord. M. G.

Charles Smith - Miss Mary Folds - 31 Oct. 1868 - E. A. Dobbs - 29 Nov. 1868 -
John C. Clay, J.P.

Page 217:
B. M. Stanley - Miss Jane Williams - 23 Sept. 1868 - E. A. Dobbs -
24 Sept. 1868 - W. H. Campbell O.M.G.

James N. Clay - Miss Georgia Ann Rice -23 Oct. 1868 - E. A. Dobbs -
25 Oct. 1868 - John Anderson M.G.

Page 218:
Haston Dunn - Miss Rebecca Tucker - 3 Nov. 1868 - E. A. Dobbs -
30 Nov. 1868 - W. H. Campbell O.M.G.

Sanford N. Green - Miss N. Lou Manning - 1 Dec. 1868 - E. A. Dobbs -
3 Dec. 1868 - J. M. Gable Ord. minister.

Page 219:
James E. Beasley - Miss M. A. Cook - 4 Nov. 1868 - E. A. Dobbs - 4 Nov.
1861 - Samuel Benedict Recotr of St. Johns Church, Savannah

W. M. Roberts - Mary M. Gray - 26 Sept. 1868 - E. A. Dobbs - 4 Oct. 1868 -
W. H. Campbell O.M.G.

Page 220:
James M. Latimer - Miss Henerietta Dunn - 6 Nov. 1868 - E. A. Dobbs -
12 Nov. 1868 - Wm. L. Mansfield M.G.

Joseph Barton - Miss Catherine Reynolds - 2 Nov. 1868 - E. A. Dobbs -
5 Nov. 1868 - G. T. Carrie J.P.

Page 221:
E. M. Hudsputh - Charlotte Hays - 17 Oct. 1868 - E. A. Dobbs - 22 Oct. 1868 -
J. M. Gable M.G.

P. B. Cornett - Miss Eleanor J. Murdock - 26 Oct. 1868 - E. A. Dobbs -
29 Oct. 1868 - J. M. Gable M.G.

Page 222:
J. W. Taylor - Miss T. C. McEachern - 26 Oct. 1868 - E. A. Dobbs -
29 Oct. 1868 - Rev. James N. Myears

Green B. Goswick - Miss Martha Martin - 31 Oct. 1868 - E. A. Dobbs -
3 Nov. 1868 - W. P. Harrison, minister

Page 223:
Hiram M. Adams - Miss Allice Hunt - 15 Oct. 1868 - E. A. Dobbs -
18 Oct. 1868 - O. M. Dodgen, J.P.

Newton A. Dempsey - Miss Sarah J. Meek - 9 Dec. 1868 - E. A. Dobbs -
10 Dec. 1868 - Bazzel Lowery, M.G.

Page 224:
W. A. Weaver - Miss Lois F. White - 12 Dec. 1868 - E. A. Dobbs - 13 Dec. 1861 -
James G. Ryals, O.M.G.

George Mahon - Rachel A. James - 30 July 1869 - C. J. Shepherd, ordy -
30 July 1869 - A. N. Simpson N.P.

Page 225:
John Wade - Georgia Davis - 22 July 1869 - H. M. Hammett ex offico Clerk Ct.
Ordy - 24 July 1869 - Benjamin Bullard, J.P.

Geo. W. Johnson - Fannie Smith - 22 July 1869 - H. M. Hammett, ex offico
Clk Ct. Ordy - 25 July 1869 - Robert Baber, M.G.

Page 226:
Chas. T. Carnes - Nancy A. Batson - 21 Aug. 1869 - C. J. Shepherd, ordy
22 Aug. 1869 - Wm. L. Mansfield M.G.

James C. Chalker - Harriet M. Summers - 18 Aug. 1869 - C. J. Shepherd -
19 Aug. 1869 - G. T. Carrie J.P.

Page 227:
B. K. Allread - Miss Ellen Malona - 12 Aug. 1869 - C. J. Shepherd per W.
Shepherd, Clerk - 12 Aug. 1869 - D. N. McEachern J.P.

J. P. Carson - Mary A. Baty - 5 Aug. 1869 - C. J. Shepherd - 7 Aug. 1869 - Robert Daniel M.G.

Page 228:
Asa Darby - Elizabeth Keith - 28 Aug. 1869 - C. J. Shepherd - 31 Aug. 1869 - John B. Bates M.G.

H. H. Turley - Nancy E. Burgess - 31 Aug. 1869 - C. J. Shepherd - 5 Sept. 1869 - J. H. King, J.P.

Page 229:
J. M. Green - Miss Ennice Clifton - 31 Aug. 1869 - C. J. Shepherd, ordy per W. Shepherd, clk - 1 Sept. 1869 - C. M. Irwin M.G.

Pinkney C. Fields - Sarah F. Drenon - 15 Sept. 1869 - C. J. Shepherd - 16 Sept. 1869 - G. M. Hooker J.P.

Page 230:
Joseph M. Bishop - Nancy A. Spruell - 25 March 1868 - Jno. G. Campbell - 16 July 1868 - Wm. Power, J.P.

Timothy Stephens - Miss Nancy Colley - 17 Sept. 1869 - C. J. Shepherd - 14 Sept. 1869 - Wm. L. Mansfield M.G.

Page 231:
Samuel P. Conner - Miss Sarah J. Clanton - 24 Sept. 1869 - C. J. Shepherd - 26 Sept. 1869 - J. T. Alexander, J.P.

E. C. Hulbert - Miss Susie Carrie - 15 Oct. 1869 - C. J. Shepherd - 17 Oct. 1869 - W. L. Mansfield, M.G.

Page 232:
W. O. Kirkley - E. G. Edgeworth - 30 Oct. 1869 - C. J. Shepherd - 1 Nov. 1869 - W. F. Cook M.G.

John H. Sprouse - Nancy E. Kemp - 23 Aug. 1869 - C. J. Shepherd - 26 Aug. 1869 - A. W. McVay M.G.

Page 233:
J. Calvin Hardy - Miss Julia Rakestraw - 8 Nov. 1869 - C. J. Shepherd - 14 Nov. 1869 - Robt Baber M.G.

Robert Griffin - Miss J. Sparks - 27 Oct. 1869 - C. J. Shepherd - 27 Oct. 1869 - Wm. C. Dorris, Ex. Off, J.P.

Page 234:
James Hardy - Miss Susan Lee - 8 Nov. 1869 - C. J. Shepherd - 11 Nov. 1869 - W. B. Smith M.G.

L. D. Jackson - Miss Jane Stanley - 2 Nov. 1869 - C. J. Shepherd - 4 Nov. 1869 - J. G. Eubanks M.G.

Page 235:
Joseph H. Goodwin - Martha C. Osburn - 8 Nov. 1869 - C. J. Shepherd - 12 Nov. 1869 - J. G. Eubanks, M.G.

T. W. Ogle - Martha E. Haney - 6 Nov. 1869 - C. J. Shepherd - 7 Nov. 1869 - J. G. Eubanks, M.G.

Page 236:
Wm. C. Kemp - Angelina Mitchel - 13 Nov. 1869 - C. J. Shepherd - 18 Nov. 1869 - J. G. Eubanks, M.G.

E. W. Gilham - S. M. E. McKey - 24 Nov. 1869 - C. J. Shepherd - 25 Nov. 1869 - J. M. Gable, M.G.

Page 237:
E. W. Gillham - S. M. F. McKey - 24 Nov. 1869 - C. J. Shepherd - 25 Nov. 1869 - J. M. Gable, M.G. (repetition of previous page)

E. P. Gaines - Mrs. Mary A. Sharp - 18 Nov. 1869 - C. J. Shepherd - 23 Nov. 1869 - J. M. Gable, M.G.

Page 238:
James M. Chastain - Lousanne E. Dodgen - 8 Nov. 1869 - C. J. Shepherd -
17 Nov. 1869 - A. H. McVay, M.G.

Robert C. McCall - Sarah J. Tatum - 12 Nov. 1869 - C. J. Shepherd -
18 Nov. 1869 - A. H. McCall, M.G.

Page 239:
W. M. Shaw - S. E. Gady - 13 Nov. 1869 - C. J. Shepherd - 14 Nov. 1869 -
A. H. McVay, M.G.

P. M. Hairston - Julia C. Wallace - 6 Oct. 1869 - C. J. Shepherd -
14 Oct. 1869 - W. H. Campbell, O.M.G.

Page 240:
J. A. Garrison - Miss Nancy Kelphin - 8 Nov. 1869 - C. J. Shepherd -
9 Nov. 1869 - J. Chambers, M.G.

Geo. L. Jones - Isabel J. Drysdale - 2 Dec. 1869 - C. J. Shepherd -
2 Dec. 1869 - W. Eston Eppes Rector St. James Marietta

Page 241:
Jasper Bullard - Nancy McCain - 26 Oct. 1869 - C. J. Shepherd -
4 Nov. 1869 - A. B. Mitchell M.G.

J. W. Scoggins - Miss E. Sorrels - 2 Dec. 1869 - C. J. Shepherd -
4 Dec. 1869 - J. G. Alexander J.P.

Page 242:
James H. Smith - Nancy Gann - 16 Sept. 1869 - C. J. Shepherd -
16 Sept. 1869 - W. H. Campbell, O.M.G.

John H. Hicks - Mary F. Gann - 20 Sept. 1869 - C. J. Shepherd -
23 Sept. 1869 - W. H. Campbell, O.M.G..

Page 243:
Jesse Mackey - Miss Frances Kirk - 17 Dec. 1869 - C. J. Shepherd -
19 Dec. 1869 - Rob't Daniell, M.G.

J. M. Daniell, Jr. - Miss Emma Wallace - 6 Dec. 1869 - C. J. Shepherd -
7 Dec. 1869 - Rob't Daniell, M.G.

Page 244:
Albert J. Fambrough - Sallie E. McDonald - 22 Dec. 1869 - C. J. Shepherd -
23 Dec. 1869 - J. M. Stewart, M.G.

James Hogan - Margaret M. Smith - 24 Dec. 1869 - C. J. Shepherd -
26 Dec. 1869 - Rob't Daniell, M.G.

Page 245:
C. W. Pyrom - E. P. Spragin - 17 Oct. 1869 - C. J. Shepherd - 17 Oct. 1869 -
J. M. Brittain, J.P.

J. T. Moseley - Nancy T. Cox - 1 Nov. 1869 - C. J. Shepherd -
11 Nov. 1869 - Benj. Bullard, J.P.

Page 246:
Sam'l Gordon - Miss Julia A. Davis - 18 Nov. 1869 - C. J. Shepherd -
25 Nov. 1869 - Benj. Bullard, J.P.

John E. Pritchet - Eliza C. Rice - 1 Jan. 1870 - C. J. Shepherd -
2 Jan. 1870 - Robt. Baber, M.G.

Page 247:
S. L. Roper - Elizabeth Elliott - 21 Dec. 1869 - C. J. Shepherd -
26 Dec. 1869 - Robt Baber, M.G.

S. J. Scott - V. E. Kemp - 20 Dec. 1869 - C. J. Shepherd - 23 Dec. 1869 -
Robt Baber, M.G.

Page 248:
Thomas McGarity - Miss Molly Whorton - 20 Dec. 1869 - C. J. Shepherd -
22 Dec. 1869 - A. H. McVay, M.G.

B. F. Scott - Louisa P. West - 13 Dec. 1869 - C. J. Shepherd - 16 Dec. 1869 - C. Rakestraw, J.P.

Page 249:
W. H. Covington - Ursullar (also written Urcillar) Wallace - 6 Jan. 1870 - C. J. Shepherd - 6 Jan. 1870 - W. W. Carrell, ord. M. G.

A. A. Fletcher - Miss Maggie Boyd - 8 Jan. 1870 - C. J. Shepherd - 10 Jan. 1870 - D. L. Buttolph

Page 250:
Thomas McCutcheson - Mattie Bedford - 14 July 1869 - E. A. Dobbs - 15 July 1869 - W. W. Carrell, ord. M.G.

G. C. Hames - Fannie Graham - 8 Jan. 1870 - C. J. Shepherd - 8 Jan. 1870 - Wm. L. Mansfield, M.G.

Page 251:
W. T. Cramer - Miss S. L. Coleman - 22 Jan. 1870 - C. J. Shepherd - 23 Jan. 1870 - J. T. Alexander, J.P.

James A. Merritt - F. A. Morris - 12 Feb. 1870 - C. J. Shepherd - 17 Feb. 1870 - A. H. McVay, M.G.

Page 252:
Samuel Davis - Georgianna Strop - 12 Jan. 1870 - C. J. Shepherd - 23 Jan. 1870 - A. H. McVay, M.G.

Jno. R. Ward - Miss Catherine Greer - 1 March 1870 - C. J. Shepherd - 1 March 1870 - D. N. McEachern, J.P.

Page 253:
John M. Hewitt - Sarah Ann N. Smith - 26 Feb. 1870 - C. J. Shepherd - 1 March 1870 - Nathan W. Smith, M.G.

James L(?) Gault - Mira Hardiman - 1 March 1870 - C. J. Shepherd - 3 March 1870 - M. Puckett, M.G.

Page 254:
H. H. Wooten - Alyann Sorrow - n.d. - C. J. Shepherd - 6 March 1870 - D. A. King, N.P. ex off J.P.

Isaac Williams - Francis Bond - 12 March 1870 - C. J. Shepherd - 13 March 1870 H. J. Hopkins, N.P.

Page 255:
R. P. McElwreath - M. A. McEachern - 18 Feb. 1870 - C. J. Shepherd - 24 Feb. 1870 - R. J. Harwell, M.G.

J. T. Harris - Miss Hattie Carpenter - 10 Dec. 1869 - C. J. Shepherd - 16 Dec. 1869 - W. J. Scott, M.G.

Page 256:
Henry Braswell - Nancy A. Clanton - 19 March 1870 - C. J. Shepherd - 20 March 1870 - J. T. Alexander, J.P.

G. D. Collins - Miss Laura Gragg - 1 March 1870 - C. J. Shepherd - 3 March 1870 - W. J. Scott, M.G.

Page 257:
James A. Folze - Jane Merritt - 30 Sept. 1869 - C. J. Shepherd - 30 Sept. 1869 - Jno. Anderson, M.G.

J. W. Bennett - Mattie Chalker - 22 Dec. 1869 - C. J. Shepherd - 28 Dec. 1869 - G. T. Carrie, J.P.

Page 258:
Alfred B. Rutledge - Eliza A. Kennon - 5 May 1870 - C. J. Shepherd - 5 May 1870 - A. N. Simpson, N.P.

James Norris - Sarah L. R. Kelly - 3 May 1870 - C. J. Shepherd - 5 May 1870 - G. T. Carrie, J.P.

Page 259:
Alexander Fields - Dora Stanley - 9 April 1870 - C. J. Shepherd -
12 April 1870 - H. J. Hopkins, N.P.

Wm. Nix - Mary M. Norris - 22 April 1870 - C. J. Shepherd - 23 April 1870 -
J. T. Alexander J.P.

Page 260:
J. J. Caloway - Julia A. Lindley - 10 May 1870 - C. J. Shepherd -
12 May 1870 - Robert Baber, M.G.

James T. Baker - Mary L. Akins - 14 May 1870 - C. J. Shepherd -
13 May 1870 - G. T. Carrie, J.P.

Page 261:
Ephraim R. Brumby - Miss Mary McPherson - 21 May 1870 - C. J. Shepherd -
31 May 1870 - D. L. Buttolph, M.G.

Jacob Caldwell - Sarah Hastings - 8 June 1870 - C. J. Shepherd - 9 June 1870 -
W. Eston Eppes, Presbiter & Rector St. James Church, Marietta.

Page 262:
A. H. Timms - Elizabeth Emaniel - 8 June 1870 - C. J. Shepherd - James G.
Ryals, O.M.G.

Wm. H. Wilcox - Emily Shaw - 21 April 1870 - C. J. Shepherd - 21 April 1870 -
Wm. S. Foster, M.G.

Page 263:
L. W. Morris - Elizabeth Hicks - 24 Dec. 1869 - C. J. Shepherd -
26 Dec. 1869 - W. H. Campbell O.M.G.

J. E. Johns - Mary M. Ward - 11 Jan. 1870 - C. J. Shepherd - 13 Jan. 1870 -
W. H. Campbell, O.M.G.

Page 264:
Alfred Tucker - Miss Mary Brown - 8 Feb. 1870 - C. J. Shepherd -
10 Feb. 1870 - J. B. C. Quillian, M.G.

Henry H. Gentry - Nancy King - 2 July 1870 - C. J. Shepherd - 3 July 1870 -
C. T. Carrie, J.P.

Page 265:
Robert Brown - Martha R. C. Brown - 27 April 1870 - C. J. Shepherd -
27 April 1870 - Nathaniel A. Pratt - Minister of the gospel

John H. Huff - Frances Rakestraw - 17 July 1870 - C. J. Shepherd -
14 July 1870 - R. Baber, M.G.

Page 266:
Jesse Lancaster - Martha A. Quinn - 2 Aug. 1870 - C. J. Shepherd -
2 Aug. 1870 - W. L. Mansfield, M.G.

Mitchel Dalton - Leander Edwards - 1 Aug. 1870 - C. J. Shepherd -
1 Aug. 1870 - Wm. M. Rsses?, M.G.

Page 267:
M. H. McCombs - Miss Minnie Glover - 12 July 1870 - C. J. Shepherd -
12 July 1870 - W. Eston Eppes, Presbiter & Rector St. James, Marietta

Almon R. Moon - Frances L. Hargroves - 18 Aug. 1870 - C. J. Shepherd -
18 Aug. 1870 - A. J. Jarrell, M.G.

Page 268:
Geo. L. Kendrick - Lizzie Mabry - 4 Aug. 1870 - C. J. Shepherd -
14 Aug. 1870 - W. L. Mansfield, M.G.

James E. Graham - Angelina Hood - 21 March 1870 - C. J. Shepherd - 21 March
1870 - Wm. L. Mansfield, M.G.

Page 269:
W. W. Holcom - Mary Ginn - 26 Aug. 1870 - C. J. Shepherd - 28 Aug. 1870 -
S. H. Smith, M.G.

28

W. K. Smith - Miss R. C. Nichols - 27 Aug. 1870 - C. J. Shepherd -
30 Aug. 1870 - Wm. L. Mansfield, M.G.

Page 270:
Nathan Noble - Violet Ridings - 6 Sept. 1870 - C. J. Shepherd -
11 Sept. 1870 - G. T. Carrie, J.P.

Mr. James Fain - Miss Martha Hildebrand - n.d. - C. J. Shepherd -
11 Sept. 1870 - G. T. Carrie, J.P.

Page 271:
Wm. A. Reed - Miss Laura V. Wallis - 14 Sept. 1870 - C. J. Shepherd -
15 Sept. 1870 - A. J. Jarrell M.G.

William Oliver - Nancy Leverett - 20 July 1870 - C. J. Shepherd -
21 July 1870 - A. H. McVay, M.G.

Page 272:
George N. Johnson - Miss Ophelia W. Sewell (may be Lewell) - 19 Sept. 1870 -
C. J. Shepherd - 20 Sept. 1870 - A. J. Jarrell, M.G.

Henry W. Dews - Miss Lila Trenhohm - 28 Sept. 1870 - C. J. Shepherd -
28 Sept. 1870 - W. L. Mansfield, M.G.

Page 273:
J. M. Dorsey - Miss Ellen Robertson - 24 Nov. 1870 - C. J. Shepherd -
2 Oct. 1870 - A. J. Jarrell, M.G.

John C. Mohon - Mrs. Margaret R. Leavell - 27 June 1870 - C. J. Shepherd -
28 June 1870 - Burrell Kemp, J.P.

Page 274:
William R. Mullins - Sarah S. Scroggins - 1 Sept. 1870 - C. J. Shepherd -
8 Sept. 1870 - A. N. Simpson N.P. ex off. J.P.

John R. Brown - Mary J. Baker - 20 Aug. 1870 - C. J. Shepherd -
21 Aug. 1870 - W. L. Davenport, M.G.

Page 275:
J. A. Garmon - Nancy E. Sherman - 20 Oct. 1870 - C. J. Shepherd -
20 Oct. 1870 - W. L. Mansfield, M.G.

Joseph G. Holden - Eliza J. Garmon - 20 Oct. 1870 - C. J. Shepherd -
20 Oct. 1870 - W. L. Mansfield, M.G.

Page 276:
L. M. Brockman - E. F. Johnson - 26 Oct. 1870 - C. J. Shepherd -
27 Oct. 1870 - Robt. Baber, M.G.

E. C. Wright - Martha F. Newton - 27 Sept. 1870 - C. J. Shepherd -
29 Sept. 1870 - A. F. McVay, M.G.

Page 277:
Wm. P. Forrester - Margaret J. Lassaman - 5 Nov. 1870 - C. J. Shepherd -
10 Nov. 1870 - F. A. Bell, M.G.

John Gwin - Mary E.(?) Aycock - 17 Nov. 1870 - C. J. Shepherd -
17 Nov. 1870 - J. B. C. Quillian, M.G.

Page 278:
Y. T. Anderson - L. J. Butner - 9 Nov. 1870 - C. J. Shepherd -
9 Nov. 1870 - Rob't Daniell, M.G.

G. L. Daniell - E. T. Hamby - 14 Nov. 1870 - C. J. Shepherd -
17 Nov. 1870 - Beaton Daniell, M.G.

Page 279:
James C. Bell - Lucy McAfee - 15 Nov. 1870 - C. J. Shepherd -
17 Nov. 1870 - W. M. Crumley, M.G.

Welcome W. Almond - Sarah Frith - 16 Nov. 1870 - C. J. Shepherd -
see next page

Page 280:
Welcome V. Almond - Sarah Frith - 16 Nov. 1870 - C. J. Shepherd -
20 Nov. 1870 - Robert Baber, M.G.

James B. Turner - Mary A. Griggs - 23 Aug. 1870 - C. J. Shepherd -
28 Aug. 1870 - J. G. Eubanks, M.G.

Page 281:
B. A. Pilgrim - Miss H. Turner - 24 Sept. 1870 - C. J. Shepherd -
25 Sept. 1870 - J. G. Eubanks, M.G.

Daniell Wright - Mary A. M. Dodgens - 23 Nov. 1870 - C. J. Shepherd -
23 Nov. 1870 - J. A. H. McVay, M.G.

Page 282:
R. H. Bryan - Georgia Hunt Dodgins - 8 Nov. 1870 - C. J. Shepherd -
10 Nov. 1870 - A. H. McVay (M.G.)

Wm. Crenshaw - Alberta Hansell - 23 Nov. 1870 - C. J. Shepherd -
23 Nov. 1870 - J. W. Baker minister of the gospel.

Page 283:
Thos. J. Channell - Penelope L. Adams - 15 Dec. 1870 - C. J. Shepherd -
18 Dec. 1870 - John C. Clay, M.G.

William H. Wylie - Angelina P. Thomas - 20 Dec. 1870 - C. J. Shepherd -
20 Dec. 1870 - John McElroy, M.G.

Page 284:
George Durham - Laura Whitfield - 17 Dec. 1870 - C. J. Shepherd -
18 Dec. 1870 - G. T. Carrie, J.P.

Thomas J. Buchanan - Josie H. Bowie - 24 Dec. 1870 - C. J. Shepherd -
25 Dec. 1870 - A. G. Dempsey, M.G.

Page 285:
Doctor F. Moore - Isabella C. Hill - 1 Sept. 1870 - C. J. Shepherd -
1 Sept. 1870 - Wiley Steed, Elder.

Nelson McAffee - Fanny Durham - 3 Jan. 1871 - C. J. Shepherd -
7 Jan. 1871 - J. B. Kindrick, N.P.

Page 286:
William Spencer - Rhoda Northcutt - 24 Dec. 1870 - C. J. Shepherd -
25 Dec. 1870 - Wm. L. Mansfield, M.G.

Mr. J. Theodore(?) Carrie - Miss Yenobia Harris - 6 Dec. 1870 -
C. J. Shepherd - 8 Dec. 1870 - Wm. L. Mansfield, M.G.

Page 287:
Wm. R. Haney - Mary E. Camp - 23 Dec. 1870 - C. J. Shepherd - 25 Dec. 1870 -
James M. Stewart M.G.

W. H. H. Orr - N. A. Leavell - 18 Nov. 1870 - C. J. Shepherd -
27 Nov. 1870 - R. W. Millner - M.G.

Page 288:
Richard W or V Bellah - Emily T. Power - 20 Dec. 1870 - C. J. Shepherd -
3 Jan. 1871 - W. Manning, O.M.G.

T. B. Cook - L. A. Barmon - 31 Dec. 1870 - C. J. Shepherd - 1 Jan. 1871 -
Joseph Gantt, J.P.

Page 289:
D. P. Mitchel - Maggie J. Beatz - 30 April 1870 - C. J. Shepherd -
1 May 1870 - W. S. Dodgen, N.P. ex off. J.P.

Lawson Baldwin - Marietta Gann - 31 Dec. 1870 - C. J. Shepherd -
1 Jan. 1871 - W. B. Smith, M.G.

Page 290:
Geo. Watson - Martha Allen - 21 Jan. 1871 - C. J. Shepherd -
22 Jan. 1871 - A. G. Dempsey, M.G.

James A. Fraser - Mary E. Warren - 27 Dec. 1870 - C. J. Shepherd -
29 Dec. 1870 - A. H. McVay, M.G.

[Correct spelling of the name Shephard is Shepard]
Page 291:
J. R. Hill - Bessie W. Williams 4 Jan. 1871, C. J. Shephard, ordy
5 Jan. 1871, W. Eston Eppes, Rector St. James Church, Marietta.

James W. Cochron - Maria Linsey 14 Jan. 1871, C. J. Shephard, ordy
15 Jan. 1871, W. B. Smith, M.G.

Page 292:
W. H. Davis - Sally Mitchell 20 Dec. 1870, C. J. Shephard, ordy
27 Dec. 1870, A. H. McVay, M. G.

John T. Conn - Sarah M. Furgeson 30 July 1870, C. J. Shephard, ordy
4 Aug. 1870, J. T. Alexander, J.P.

Page 293:
Frank A. Black - Ann M. White 26 Nov. 1870, C. J. Shephard, ordy
27 Nov. 1870, J. T. Alexander, J.P.

J. M. Barefield - Sarah A. Smith 5 Jan. 1871, C. J. Shephard, ordy
5 Jan. 1871, J. T. Alexander, J.P.

Page 294:
Stephen B. Moon - Miss Martha Jane Hilton 7 Jan. 1871, C. J. Shephard, ordy
8 Jan. 1871, A. Melton, ord. M.G.

Thomas Peters - Angelina Slocum 18 Aug. 1870, C. J. Shephard, ordy
21 Aug. 1870, D. A. King, N.P. Ex O.J.P.

Page 295:
Newton Cochran - Miss Fannie Darnell 2 Feb. 1871, C. J. Shephard, ordy
2 Feb. 1871, Alfred Maner, N.P. EX O.J.P.

James H. Covington - Molly Spoor 18 Jan. 1871, C. J. Shephard, ordy
19 Jan. 1871, Geo. R. Kramer, M.G.

Page 296:
John J. Robertson - Mrs. Elizabeth Elrod 9 Feb. 1871, C. J. Shephard
9 Feb. 1871, F. A. Bell.

John D. Brown - Miss M. J. Bennett 4 Feb. 1871, Shephard, ordy
9 Feb. 1871, R. Baber, M.G.

Page 297:
W. D. Atkinson - Mrs. L. N. Gignilliat 5 Jan. 1871, C. J. Shephard, ordy
5 Jan. 1871, W. Lillomfield, M.G.

Richard Holmes - Matilda Cunningan 14 March 1871, Shephard, ordy
16 Feb. 1871, Natha Prutt, minister of the gospel

Page 298:
Wm. Ashby - Mattie Brown. 24 Dec. 1870, C. J. Shephard, ordy pr Wm. O.
Shephard, clerk. 28 Dec. 1870, H. J. Hopkins, N.P.

L. or S. A. Darnell - Susie Hotchkiss 22 Feb. 1871, Shephard, ordy
22 Feb. 1871, W. L. Mansfield, M.G.

Page 299:
Mr. C. C. Kiser - Ellen Roberts 8 Feb. 1871, Shephard, ordy
8 Feb. 1871, W. L. Mansfield, M.G.

Wm. H. Crawford - E. J. Wright 22 Feb. 1871, Shephard, ordy
23 Feb. 1871, Robert Daniel, M.G.

Page 300:
Wade H. Wallace - Molly Covington 18 Jan. 1871, C. J. Shephard, ordy
19 Jan. 1871, John R. Sanges, ordained minister

W. H. Joiner - Miss Sue Goodman 13 Feb. 1871, C. J. Shephard, ordy
15 Feb. 1871, D. L. Butteth, M.G.

Page 301:
William W. Jolly - Catherine Castlebary 18 March 1871, Shephard
18 March 1871, J. Z. or Y Alexander, J.P.

Harrison Hollafield - Nannie Dobbins 1 March 1871, Shephard
2 March 1871, J. Y. Alexander, J.P.

Page 302:
Albert A. Sharp - Anna Holtzclaw (ink blot covering name) 8 June 1870
C. J. Shephard, ordy, 14 June 1870, R. W. Milner, M.G.

William A. Wallis - Jane T. Wallace 20 Feb. 1871, Shephard ordy
23 Feb. 1871, A. B. Mitchell, M.G.

Page 303:
James Winter - Lalisia Griggs 7 March 1871, Shephard, ordy
7 March 1871, J. D. Vaughn, J.P.

Only one license on this page.

Page 304:
John Barnes - Miss Mary Canon 13 Feb. 1871, Shephard, ordy
16 March 1871, Thos. Hooper, J.P.

Thomas F. Bryant - S. Tabitha Chapel 21 Feb. 1871, Shephard, ordy
23 Feb. 1871, W. L. Dodgen N.P. & Ex O.J.P.

Page 305:
("Colored license recorded here by mistake")
A. J. Rogers - Emma Taylor 6 Feb. 1871, Shephard, ordy
6 Feb. 1871, Thomas N. Allen, M.G.

Adam Haygood - Milly Irwin 8 Dec. 1870, Shephard, ordy
8 Dec. 1870, Wm. Barnes, M.G.

Page 306:
Henry Nichols - Susan Johnson 18 Nov. 1870, Shephard, ordy
20 Nov. 1870, A. B. Davis, M.G.

James R. Loyd - Mrs. P. Fincher 26 Feb. 1871, Shephard, ordy
26 Feb. 1871, George R. Kramer, minister of gospel

Page 307:
James M. Pickens - Caladonia Mays 11 Jan. 1871, Shephard, ordy
12 Jan. 1871, W. H. Campbell, O.M.G.

D. L. Braswell - Elizabeth Guess 21 Dec. 1870, Shephard, ordy
22 Dec. 1870, W. H. Campbell O.M.G.

Page 308:
Rolly J. Shipp - Eliza Dobbs 22 Dec. 1870, Shephard, ordy
28 Dec. 1870, John A. Gemer, M.G.

Daniel W. Barker - Miss Mary E. Green 23 Dec. 1870, Shephard, ordy
25 Dec. 1870, W. H. Campbell O.M.G.

Page 309:
Warren L. Watson - Mary J. Taylor 17 Oct. 1870, Shephard, ordy
27 Oct. 1870, W. H. Campbell O.M.G.

Henry M. Davis - Sarah C. West 6 Dec. 1870, Shephard, ordy
11 Dec. 1870, W. H. Campbell O.M.G.

Page 310:
William L. Johns - Miss Arminitha Fannin - 7 March 1871, Shephard
9 March 1871, W. H. Campbell O.M.G.

Thomas J. Turner - Urina Jane Bloodworth 11 March 1871, Shephard
16 March 1871, W. H. Campbell O.M.G.

Page 311:
W. H. Pratt - Elvira Maloney 3 Jan. 1871, Shephard, ordy
5 Jan. 1871, W. H. Campbell O.M.G.

Hiram W. Baggett - Miss Julia Ward   20 Feb. 1871, Shephard, ordy
23 Feb. 1871, W. H. Campbell O.M.G.

Page 312:
Wells B. Whitmore - Nannie A. Emons   4 April 1871, Shephard, ordy
5 April 1871, W. Eston Eppes, Rector of St. James Church, Marietta

Sylvanua Scoggins - Susan Ann Burnett   2 April 1871, Shephard, ordy
11 April 1871, Walter Manning O.D.M.G.

Page 313:
David Smith - Mahala Shields   13 Jan. 1871, Shephard, ordy
17 Jan. 1871, J. Y. Alexander N.P. Ex O.J.P.

Irwin C. Cockram - Matilda E. Dickerson   31 March 1871, Shephard
9 April 1871, J. T. Alexander, J.P.

Page 314:
Riley Owens - Mary Ann E. Fuller   3 Feb. 1871, Shephard, ordy
12 Feb. 1871, James M. Stewart, M.G.

Robert H. Runyan - Emma C. Garmon   13 April 1871, Shephard, ordy
27 April 1871, W. W. Carrell, Ord. M.G.

Page 315:
James H. Evans - Adaline Boswell   5 May 1871, Shephard, ordy
7 May 1871, Jno. Anderson, M.G.

John Branon - Eliz. Ann Chapman   8 April 1871, Shephard, ordy
9 April 1871, John Anderson O.M.G.

Page 316:
Gabriel W. Quarles - Sarah E. Stephens   5 May 1871, Shephard, ordy
16 June 1871, N. H. McVay, M.G.

Page 316: Continued
Elisha H. Simpson - Emma C. Blankenship   7 June 1871, Shephard
18 June 1871, J. R. Sanges, ord. minister

Page 317:
Aaron Nichols - Betsy Strickland   1 July 1871, Shephard
2 July 1871, John W. Hill, N.P. Ex O.J.P.

William R. Maynor - Miss Lucy Ann Goodson   12 May 1871, Shephard
14 May 1871, Alfred Maner, N.P.

Page 318:
Robt E. Hipp - Guvicy? J. Hicks   20 June 1871, Shephard
22 June 1871, W. H. Campbell O.M.G.

Meridith W. Griffin - Louisa E. Price   27 April 1871, Shephard
28 April 1871, John W. Hill N.P. EX O.J.P.

Page 319:
Jasper N. Barber - Eliza Alexander   18 May 1871, Shepard
19 May 1871, W. W. Carrell ord. M.G.

M. W. Barber - Miss Nancy M. Casey   29 June 1871, Shephard, ordy.
29 June 1871, W. W. Carrell Ord. M.G.

Page 320:
Samuel Gaddy - Martha L. Young   8 July 1871, Shephard
6 July 1871, J. M. Stewart Min. G.

Dr. J. M. Moore - Martha J. Alexander   5 June 1871, Shephard
8 June 1871, W. H. Campbell, O.M.G.

Page 321:
Daniel W. Johns - Marky E. Skinner   24 March 1871, Shephard
28 March 1871, W. H. Campbell O.M.G.

John N. Calet(?) - Eliza Spinks   13 April 1871, Shephard
14 April 1871, J. Y. Alexander, J.P.

Page 322: William N. Landmon - Mary Brown 26 May 1871, Shephard, ordy
28 May 1871, W. L. Davenport, M.G.

J. T. Buffington - A. V. Teach or Teal 3 Jan. 1871, Shephard
26 Jan. 1871, W. L. Davenport, M.G.

Page 323:
John Greenwood - Miss Fannie Dempsey 1 Sept. 1871, Shephard
10 Sept. 1871, James G. Ryals, M.G.

Frany Lawrence - Hester Ann Boyd 15 Aug. 1871, Shephard
15 Aug. 1871, A. N. Simpson, N.P.

Page 324:
Crawford K. Lewis - May E. Arnold 1 July 1871, Shephard
6 July 1871, Thos. Boling, M.G.

H. H. King - Martha A. Hampton 4 July 1871, Shephard
9 July 1871, G. T. Carrie, J.P.

Page 325:
James B. Buchanon - Frances J. Gann 3 Aug. 1871, Shephard
3 Aug. 1871, Robert Daniel, M.G.

Calvin Newton Price - Frances E. Brooks 9 Aug. 1871, Shephard
10 Aug. 1871, John W. Hill, N.P.

Page 326:
Elija N. Brooks - Nancy J. Price 10 Aug. 1871, Shephard
11 Aug. 1871, John W. Hill, N.P.

Drury Hollafield - Miss Elizabeth Castleberry n.d., Shephard
24 Aug. 1871, J. Y. Alexander, J.P.

Page 327:
D. P. Myers - Jennie Brown 24 Aug. 1871, Shephard
27 Aug. 1871, James G. Ryals, M.G.

Chas. C. Clayton - Maria Myers 7 Sept. 1871, Shephard
10 Sept. 1871, James G. Ryals, M.G.

Page 328:
Willis C. McGarity - Miss Lizzia Henry 19 Aug. 1871, Shephard
23 Aug. 1871, J. M. Gable, M.G.

James Jones - Fannie Montgomery 23 Nov. 1870, Shephard, ordy
7 Jan. 1871, Rev. John F. Rowan, M.G.

Page 329:
G. W. Anderson - Frances Chandler 20 Jan. 1871, Chephard
22 Jan. 1871, Rev. John F. Rowan, M.G.

Benj. F. McDuffe - Edna A. Buchanan 4 July 1871, Shephard
7 July 1871, W. H. Campbell, O.M.G.

Page 330:
Veston L. Goodwin - Julia A. M. Leavell 23 March 1871, Shephard
25 March 1871, W. H. Campbell, O.M.G.

J. W. Robertson - M. A. Winn 18 Sept. 1871, Shephard
21 Sept. 1871, J. R. Mayson, M.G.

Page 331:
Joseph P. Wallace - Elizabeth A. Barrett 20 Sept. 1871, Shephard
21 Sept. 1871, P. M. Ryburn, M.G.

J. P. Brockman - Miss S. E. Gober 29 Nov. 1870, Shephard
29 Nov. 1871, J. W. Baker minister of the gospel

Page 332:
John Y. Alexander - Sarah A. Reed 18 Sept. 1871, Shephard
21 Sept. 1871, J. W. Baker, minister of the gospel

Thos. B. Dodgeon - L. N. Gann 6 Sept. 1871, Shephard
10 Sept. 1871, W. H. Campbell, O.M.G.

Page 333:
James Denson - Emeline Congo 20 Sept. 1871, Shephard, ordy
21 Sept. 1871, W. H. Campbell, O.M.G.

Hutson Lindley - Maretta Scott 5 Oct. 1871, Shephard, ordy
5 Oct. 1871, John M. Henderson

Page 334:
Frederick J. Inzer - Mary Ann Weems 17 Oct. 1871, Shephard, ordy
19 Oct. 1871, Walter Manning, O. M. G.

Joseph Smith - Martha Davis 15 Oct. 1871, Shephard, ordy
16 Oct. 1871, Walter Manning, O.M.G.

Page 335:
Mary Pritchard - James R. Williams 3 Oct. 1871, Shephard, ordy
8 Oct. 1871, John W. Hill, N.P. Ex O.J.P.

Jonathan Potts - Louisa P. Bell n.d., Shephard
19 Sept. 1871, Geo. R. Kramer, M.G.

Page 336:
William Robison - Mrs. Huldah Stansell 24 Sept. 1871, Shephard
24 Sept. 1871, Geo. R. Kramer, M.G.

Joseph C. Wilson - Sarah Fridell 21 Oct. 1871, Shephard, ordy by Wm. H.
Shephard D.C.C.O. 22 Oct. 1871, Walter Manning O.M.G.

Page 337:
Isaac B. Seay - Amanda G. Barnes 1 April 1871, Shephard
3 April 1870, Benj. Bullard, J.P.

Elias Potts - Sarah A. Bell 18 Sept. 1871, Shephard by Wm. H. Shephard,
D.C.C.O. 19 Sept. 1871, Geo. R. Kramer, M.G.

Page 338:
William S. Thompson - Miss Nena Danner 1 Nov. 1871, Shephard
2 Nov. 1871, W. F. Cook m of G

Adolphus Durham - M. P. Hargroves 14 Nov. 1871, Shephard
14 Nov. 1871, P. M. Ryburn, M.G.

Page 339:
Birdine Kirk - Frances M. Martin 24 Oct. 1871, Shephard
26 Oct. 1871, John C. Clay, N.P.

Allen Estes - Frances E. Stuard 3 Nov. 1871, Shephard
5 Nov. 1871, Joseph Gault, J.P.

Page 340:
David M. Elliott - Miss Sally Dobbs 28 Nov. 1871, Shephard
29 Nov. 1871, W. L. Mansfield, M.G.

John J. Brown - Henrietta Arnold 26 Oct. 1871, Shephard, ordy
26 Oct. 1871, W. L. Mansfield, M.G.

Page 341:
John A. Griggs - Elizabeth Alexander 13 April 1871, Shephard
14 April 1871, W. L. Mansfield, M.G.

J. F. Farbrough - Miss Martha M. Daniel 27 Nov. 1871, Shephard
28 Nov. 1871, Robert Daniel, M.G.

Page 342:
Andrew Reeves - Mattie Mitchell 31 Oct. 1871, Shephard
2 Nov. 1871, James M. Stewart, M.G.

Page 343:
Norval C. Jordan - Sarah E. Cape 10 Nov. 1871, Shephard
16 Nov. 1871, W. B. Smith, M.G.

Page 344:
William K. Coleman - Nancy E. Swan 13 Sept. 1871, Shephard
14 Sept. 1871, J. Y. Alexander, J.P.

Page 345:
William P. Foster - Mary J. Malony 7 Oct. 1871, Shephard
15 Oct. 1871, J. Y. Alexander, J.P.

Page 346:
John E. Ray - Elizabeth Barber 18 Oct. 1871, Shephard
22 Oct. 1871, J. Y. Alexander, J.P.

Page 347:
Thomas J. Baker - Cynthia A. C. Howell 30 Nov. 1871, Shephard
30 Nov. 1871, Rev. J. F. Rowan

Page 348:
W. W. Saunders - A. L. Gann 30 Nov. 1871, Shephard
30 Nov. 1871, Robert Daniel, M. G.

Page 349:
Newton J. Steen - Nancy A. Everett 16 Dec. 1871, Shephard
17 Dec. 1871, G. T. Carrie, J.P.

Page 350:
L. M. Wilson - Mary Scroggins - 21 Dec. 1871, Shephard
21 Dec. 1871, Samuel J. Pinkerton, M.G.

Page 351:
Aaron A. Hilberbrand - Harriet A. Baldwin 21 Dec. 1871, Shephard
24 Dec. 1871, J. B. Kendrick, N.P.

Page 352:
Henry Pate - Jane Hannon 4 Nov. 1871, Shephard
12 Nov. 1871, Rev. J. F. Rowan

Page 353:
S. W. E. Adair - Mary P. Oglesby 28 Nov. 1871, Shephard
7 Nov. 1871, Rev. J. F. Bowen

Page 354:
Perry Strickland - Mary Pickens n.d., Shephard, 21 Dec. 1871,
A. B. Davis, M.G.

Page 355:
William R. Lee - Rebecca A. Argroves 8 Nov. 1871, Shephard
10 Nov. 1871, C. C. Davis

Page 356:
Clias E. Johns - Mattie Chatman 18 Nov. 1871, Shephard
19 Nov. 1871, Jno. Anderson, M.G.

Page 357:
Reubin G. D. Mullins - Nancy A. Garrison 5 Dec. 1871, Shephard
6 Dec. 1871, John Mehaffee, N.P.

Page 358:
Robert M. Echols - Mary V. Gilbert 4 Dec. 1871, Shephard
10 Dec. 1871, John Clay, N.P.

Page 359:
William R. Blackman - Miss Jane Dunn 25 Dec. 1871, Shephard
25 Dec. 1871, W. Manning, O.M.G.

Page 360:
W. A. Kehely - Jennette N. Lovell 4 Jan. 1872, Shephard
4 Jan. 1872, A. G. Dempsey, M.G.

Page 361:
Andrew J. Steadham - Elizabeth A. Blankenship 27 Dec. 1871, Shephard
27 Dec. 1871, W. L. Mansfield, M.G.

Page 362:
Berrien Attaway - Martha Chadwic 25 Dec. 1871, Shephard
27 Dec. 1871, W. L. Mansfield, M.G.

Page 363:
Thos. B. Price - Nancy A. M. Waters 27 July 1871, Shephard
28 July 1871, John W. Hill, N.P. & Ex. O.J.P.

Page 364:
Wm. T. Holley - Mrs. S. C. Drake 6 Dec. 1871, Shephard
7 Dec. 1871, John W. Hill, N.P.

Page 365:
Wm. R. Hall - Mary E. Davis 22 Dec. 1871, Shephard
31 Dec. 1871, G. T. Carrie, J.P.

Page 366:
A. J. Stewart - Miss Mary Butler 19 Dec. 1871, Shephard
21 Dec. 1871, J. H. King, J.P.

Page 367:
James R. Glore - Mary F. Gann 11 Dec. 1871, Shephard
21 Dec. 1871, W. B. Smith, M.G.

Page 368:
Garmon A. Jordan - Clara C. Daniell 27 Dec. 1871, Shephard
11 Jan. 1872, W. B. Smith, M.G.

Page 369
Simeon B. Brirner - Analine Rutherford 28 Dec. 1871, Shephard
31 Dec. 1871, J. B. Kendrick, J.P.

Page 370:
William Adair - Ada Moore 18 Jan. 1872, Shephard
31 Jan. 1872, G. T. Carrie, J.P.

Page 371:
William R. Boyle - Miss Carrie Leroy 11 Jan. 1872, Shephard
14 Jan. 1872, J. H. King, J.P.

Page 372:
James A. Pierson - Miss Nancy Sainders 13 Jan. 1872, Shepard
15 Jan. 1872, C. J. Shepard, ordy.

Page 373:
Larkin V. Haney - Georgia A. Red 7 June 1871, Shepard
11 June 1871, H. B. Johnson, M.G.

Page 374:
Mathew W. Christopher - Samantha A. Haney 24 Nov. 1871, Shepard
23 Nov. 1871, H. B. Johnson, M.G.

Page 375:
Andy Webb - Miss Caroline Dickerson 20 Jan. 1872, Shepard
21 Jan. 1872, J. Y. Alexander, J.P.

Page 376:
Robert Vasser - Miss Lucy Taylor 3 Feb. 1872, Shepard
6 Feb. 1872, W. B. Smith, M.G.

Page 377:
Clias J. Martin - Lula M. Wallace 31 Jan. 1872, Shepard
31 Jan. 1872, D. L. Buttolph, M.G.

Page 378:
James H. Ross - Susie Smith 20 Dec. 1871, Shepard
29 Dec. 1871, J. R. Mayson, M.G.

Page 379:
Benson O. Boulton - Lula Winn 20 Dec. 1871, Shepard
11 Jan. 1872, J. R. Mayson, M.G.

Page 380:
Joseph N. Guess - Lou P. Moore 21 Feb. 1872, Shepard
21 Feb. 1872, John C. Clay, N.P.

Page 381:
J. D. Frazier - Emma J. Kiser 26 Aug. 1871, Shepard
27 Aug. 1871, J. A. Gandy, M.G.

Page 382:
R. DeLong - Ellen Barber 24 Jan. 1872, Shepard
25 Jan. 1872, Wm. G. Akins, M.G.

Page 383:
W. J. Brown - Mattie J. Eaton 13 Feb. 1872, Shepard
13 Feb. 1872, Robert Daniell, M.G.

Page 384:
Benson R. Whitfield - Mrs. Nancy C. Williams 24 Feb. 1872, Shepard
29 Feb. 1872, Robt Daniell, M.G.

Page 385:
Elias N. Dobbs - Nancy E. Hardman 4 March 1872, Shephard
7 March 1872, M. Puckett, M.G.

Page 386:
N. J. Huffaker - Miss E. R. Slaton 21 March 1872, Shepard
21 March 1872, D. L. Buttolph, M.G.

Page 387:
Emory S. D. Byrd - Mary E. Roberson 25 Jan. 1872, Shepard
25 Jan. 1872, Alfred Manor, J.P.

Page 388:
J. J. Stewart - Mary Stean 9 March 1872, Shepard
10 March 1872, N. A. Pratt, M.G.

Page 389:
Orren M. Jordan - Lucinda D. Duffy 10 March 1872, Shepard
17 March 1872, J. B. O'Neill, J.P.

Page 390:
Lemuel Burgess - Miss Mary Barton 25 Sept. 1871, Shepard
5 Oct. 1871, S. R. McClesky

Page 391:
Henry A. Butler - Fannie L. Northcutt 29 Feb. 1872, Shepard
29 Feb. 1872, W. L. Mansfield, M.G.

Page 392:
Thomas J. Helton - Sarah E. Morris 19 March 1872, Shepard
7 April 1872, Joseph Kincaid, min of gos

Page 393:
David Swann - Rachel Johnson 20 March 1872, Shepard
28 April 1872, J. Y. Alexander, J.P.

Page 394:
Thomas Clanton - Nancy Tummis 8 April 1872, Shepard
14 April 1872, A. H. McVay, M.G.

Page 395:
Charles A. Waters - J. Mattie Anderson 1 May 1872 Shepard
1 May 1872, W. L. Mansfield, M.G.

Page 396:
Nathanill Gibson - Fannie Sinson 11 May 1872, Shepard
12 May 1872, D. L. Buttolph, M.G.

Page 397:
Marcus L. Boatner - Rosina E. Fitts 16 April 1872, Shepard
18 April 1872, Walter Manning, O.M.G.

Page 398:
Samuell N. House - Willis J. Gresham 5 March 1872, Shepard
14 March 1872, J. R. Mayson, M.G.

Page 399:
James R. Carrell - Mary Wilson 22 March 1872, Shepard
23 March 1872, J. R. Mayson, M.G.

Page 400:
John T. H. Smith - Sophia J. Brumbelow   22 May 1872, Shepard
23 May 1872, J. A. Gandy, M.G.

Page 401:
Thos. B. Irwin - Lilla C. Atkinson   3 Jan. 1872, Shepard
3 Jan. 1872, J. W. Baker minister of the gospel

Page 402:
James D. Carnes - Miss Lou E. Smith   16 May 1872, Shepard
16 May 1872, G. T. Carrie, J.P.

Page 403:
Thomas J. Garrison - Mary E. Dawes   30 May 1872, Shepard
30 May 1872, James Lindley, J.P.

Page 404:
Wm. L. McRea - Elizabeth F. Harris   2 July 1872, Shepard
4 July 1872, G. T. Carrie, J.P.

Page 405:
William W. Reed - Mrs Mary Crow   13 July 1872, Shepard
14 July 1872, J. B. Harry, M.G.

Page 406:
Frank J. E. Medley - Malvinia Fridell   4 May 1872, Shepard
5 May 1872, J. M. Gable, M.G.

Page 407:
Anderson Brimer - Miss Mary Newton   13 July 1872, Shepard
13 June 1872, J. M. Gable, M.G.

Page 408:
John T. M. Spinks - Samantha E. Thomas   18 July 1872, Shepard
18 July 1872, Joseph M. Gable, M.G.

Page 409:
Washington T. Weems - Harriet Manning   1 Aug. 1872, Shepard
4 Aug. 1872, W. Manning, O.M.G.

Page 410:
Parker E. Scott - Mattie McCown   16 July 1872, Shepard
22 July 1872, R. Baber, M.G.

Page 411:
Mary Reeves - Miss Nancy E. Haygood   28 Aug. 1872, Shepard
28 Aug. 1872, J. M. Gable, M.G.

Page 412:
James Johnson - Nancy Reeves   13 Jan. 1872, Shepard
18 Jan. 1872, M. Puckett, M.G.

Page 413:
Raymond B. Simpson - Tabitha Robertson   1 June 1872, Shepard
13 June 1872, Thomas Hooper, J.P.

Page 414:
Walter T. Ogle - Frances A. Bryant   24 June 1872, Shepard
25 June 1872, A. H. McVay, M.G.

Page 415:
Moses J. McLendon - Sallie J. Wingo   20 Aug. 1872, Shepard
8 Sept. 1872, J. B. Kendrick, N.P.

Page 416:
John G. Brumby - Miss Carie L. Cason   17 Sept. 1872, Shepard
17 Sept 1872, William A. Rogers, M.G.

Page 417:
J. F. C. Williams - Miss Mattie A. George   18 Sept. 1872, Shepard
18 Sept. 1872, W. E. Eppes, Pastor St. James Church

Page 418:
D. A. Armistead - M. C. Pain 28 Sept. 1872, Shepard
29 Sept. 1872, Walter Manning, O.M.G.

Page 419:
Burton B. Baggett - Mary F. Bingham 22 Dec. 1871, Shepard
24 Dec. 1871, J. A. Gandy, M.G.

Page 420:
James D. Chadwick - Elizabeth Smith 26 Aug. 1872, Shepard
1 Sept. 1872, J. R. Sanges, minister

Page 421:
James O. Carpenter - Elizabeth D. Burney 2 Sept. 1872, Shepard
5 Sept. 1872, J. H. King, J.P.

Page 422:
Daniel B. Wooten - Sally Harris 13 Sept. 1872, Shepard
22 Sept. 1872, A. H. McVay, M.G.

Page 423:
Henry C. Shaw - Mary D. Anderson 28 Sept. 1872, Shepard
26 Sept. 1872, John C. Clay, N.P.

Page 424:
Elisha E. B. Clanton - Sarah J. Smith 9 Oct. 1872, Shepard
10 Oct. 1872, J. Y. Alexander, J.P.

Page 425:
John F. Byrd - Rachel McKehely 17 Oct. 1872, Shepard
17 Oct. 1872, A. H. McVay, M.G.

Page 426:
William H. Baldwin - Rosetta Gann 11 Dec. 1872, Shepard
12 Dec. 1872, A. B. Mitchell, M.G.

A. J. Johnson - Martha L. Calder n.d., Shepard 30 May 1871
W. L. Mansfield, M.G.

Page 427:
J. M. Chalker - Miss Emily Hill 22 Nov. 1872, Shepard
24 Nov. 1872, W. L. Mansfield, M.G.

Lewis M. Ataway - Miss Elizabeth Taylor 3 Dec. 1872, Shepard
5 Dec. 1872, Wm. A. Parks, M.G.

Page 428:
John B. Alexander - Miss Catharine Esters 28 Dec. 1872, Shepard
29 Dec. 1872, Bazzel Mowry, M.G.

P. T. Hambry - Miss Theresa E. Gober 10 Dec. 1872, Shepard
10 Dec. 1872, Jos. M. Gable, M.G.

Page 429:
George M. Bradley - Elizabeth S. Donehoo 29 July 1872, Shepard
30 July 1872, Jos. M. Gable, M.G.

Page 429:
T. B. Cantrell - C. F. Eaton 5 Dec. 1873, Shepard
8 Dec. 1872, Albert B. Vaughn, M.G.

Page 430:
John M. Haus - Martha A. Runyan 25 Oct. 1872, Shepard
27 Oct. 1872, W. L. Davenport, M.G.

Ephraim G. Deel - Viny E. Bingham 30 Oct. 1872, Shepard
31 Oct. 1872, H. J. Hopkins, N.P.

Page 431:
Pack South - Mary Gober 17 Oct. 1872, Shepard
20 Oct. 1872, J. H. King, J.P.

Elijah N. Davenport - Miss S. A. Prichard 27 Nov. 1872, Shepard
29 Nov. 1872, J. L. Rogers, M.G.

Page 432:
Robert A. Sorrels - Julia E. Phillips   25 Oct. 1872, Shepard
31 Oct. 1872, Robert Baber, M.G.

J. B. Barefield - Minerva J. Honea   9 Nov. 1872, Shepard
10 Nov. 1872, J. Y. Alexander, J.P.

Page 433:   Robert G. McWilliams - Mary E. Dewberry   9 Nov. 1872, Shepard
17 Nov. 1872, J. Y. Alexander, J.P.

James A. Thomas - Frances Congo   23 Nov. 1872, Shepard
24 Nov. 1872, Hartwell A. Baldwin, N.P.

Page 434:
Columbus Allen - Sarah Bone   19 Sept. 1872, Shepard
19 Sept. 1872, A. Melton, M.G.

Thomas Gresham - Lavilia Hill   24 Dec. 1872, Shepard
26 Dec. 1872, Robt. Baber, M.G.

Page 435:
James P. Stark - Joanna Wood   16 Dec. 1872 Shepard
19 Dec. 1872, Robt. Baber, M.G.

William P. Moseley - Elvira F. Neill   9 Dec. 1872, Shepard
19 May 1872, Robt Baber, M.G.

Page 436:
Eliza Pierson - Jane McLillen   11 May 1872, Shepard
12 May 1872, W. L. Mansfield, M.G.

Chas. W. Northcutt - Miss Vick Mayes   9 Dec. 1872, Shepard
22 Dec. 1872, A. H. McVay, M.G.

Page 437:
Calvin W. Wallace - Miss Athie Bishop   5 Dec. 1872, Shepard
5 Dec. 1872, A. M. McVay, M.G.

Zavhariah Norris - Amazonia Thaxton   23 Nov. 1872, Shepard
24 Nov. 1872, J. Y. Alexander, J.P.

Page 438:
Benjamin P. Baswell - Miss Ellen Frazier   26 Nov. 1872, Shepard
26 Nov. 1872, J. Y. Alexander, J.P.

Chas. W. Barfield - Mary E. Porter   5 Dec. 1872, Shepard

Page 439
8 Dec. 1872, J. Y. Alexander, J.P.

F. E. Legg - Amanda Gresham   9 Dec. 1872, Shepard
19 Dec. 1872, John Durham, N.P.

James S. Durham - Miss Louisa Dabbs

Page 440:
13 Jan. 1873, H. M. Hammett, ordy   16 Jan. 1873, J. L. Rogers, M.G.

James R. Bagwell - Sarah A. Neese   15 Jan. 1873, H. M. Hammett
20 Jan. 1873, Jno. Y. Alexander, J.P.

Page 441:
J. T. Smith - Miss M. J. Pickens   20 Jan. 1873, H. M. Hammett
21 Jan. 1873, Jno. Y. Alexander, J.P.

James Attaway - Mary A. Winn

Page 442:
31 Jan. 1873, J. H. Hammett   4 Feb. 1873, J. B. Kendricks, J.P.

Daniel Bullard - Martha F. Lee   28 Jan. 1873, H. M. Hammett
30 Jan. 1873, Rec. C. C. Davis.

41

Page 443:
Westley Rakestraw - Harriett Forester   1 Jan. 1873, Shepard
19 Jan. 1873, C. R. Rakestraw, J.P.

A. P. Taylor - Miss A. C. Hales 16 Jan. 1873, H. M. Hammett

Page 444:
16 Jan. 1873, Albert B. Vaughn, M.G.

John A. Parr - Nancy Congo 12 Jan. 1873, H. M. Hammett
12 Jan. 1873, R. Beber, M.G.

John T. Hoard - Henrietta E. J. Wright

Page 445:
9 Jan. 1873, Shepard 12 Jan. 1873, R. Baber, M.G.

Josiah Coombs - Sarah A. Hammett 22 Feb. 1872, Shepard
22 Feb. 1872, W. W. Carroll, O.M.G.

Page 446:
K. L. Foster - Miss Lila Alexander 28 Dec. 1872, Shepard
2 Jan. 1873, W. W. Carroll, O.M.G.

N. A. Alexander - Geneva Sanges 2 Jan. 1873, Shepard

Page 447:
2 Jan. 1873, W. W. Carroll, O.M.G.

Page 447: Cont.
Henry P. Sauls - Nancy P. Shirley 23 Jan. 1873, H. M. Hammett
23 Jan. 1873, Joseph M. Gable.

Page 448:
James M. McCurley - Laura Wardlaw 14 Jan. 1873, H. M. Hammett
16 Jan. 1873, E. K. Aiken, M.G.

William P. Clay - E. P. Bullard 13 Feb. 1873, H. M. Hammett
13 Feb. 1873, E. K. Aiken, M.G.

Page 449:
Thomas M. Smith - Miss Rebecca Mitchell 4 March 1865, Jno. G. Campbell, ordy
17 March 1865, J. T. Robertston, J.P. (recorded 1 Feb. 1873)

Mr. Ezekiel C. Harris - Mrs. Margaret L. Tucker

Page 450:
17 April 1865, Jno. G. Campbell, ordy 18 April 1865 R. A. Holland, M.G.

Cornelius J. Murphy - Rachel E. Elyard 29 June 1865, Jno. G. Campbell, ordy
29 ___ 1865, W. W. Carroll, O.M.G. (recorded 1 March 1873)

Page 451:
Zacariah Conger - Parmelia Parks 4 July 1865, Jno. G. Campbell
4 July 1865, W. W. Carroll, O.M.G.

Mr. Harris Wade - Amanda Cox 25 Jan. 1865, Jno. G. Campbell

Page 452:
26 Jan. 1865, Benjamin Bullard, J.P. (recorded March 1873)

B. A. Mullins - Julia Dunn 14 Feb. 1873, H. M. Hammett

Page 453:
16 Feb. 1873, J. R. Sanger, O.M.G.

Jno. D. Baker - Lucy A. Hilderbrand 13 Feb. 1873 - H. M. Hammett
23 Feb. 1873, J. R. Kendrick, J.P.

John W. Simmons (heading of page is Summers), E. R. Baker

Page 454:
13 Feb. 1873, H. M. Hammett 23 Feb. 1873, W. A.? Simmons, M.G.

George S. Owen - Lucy A. Rayburn 6 Feb. 1873, H. M. Hammett
9 Feb. 1873, Wm. A. Simmons, M.G.

Page 455:
T. G. Greer - E. L. Chambers 24 Feb. 1873, H. M. Hammett
27 Feb. 1873, N. A. Pratt, M.G.

J. C. Pickets - Sarah A. Johnson 8 Feb. 1873, H. M. Hammett
19 Feb. 1873, H. B. Johnson, M.G.

Page 456:
Thomas Whitfield - Sophia Buchanan - 1 March 1873, H. M. Hammett
2 March 1873, M. T. McCluskey, J.P.

Laurence Kelly - Sallie C. Hunt 22 March 1873, H. M. Hammett
23 March 1873, J. B. Kendrick, J.P.

Page 457:
James Bryant - Francis Pendley 10 March 1873, H. M. Hammett
11 March 1873, V. or N. B. Smith, M.G.

Daniel Ogle - Harriett F. T. Bryant 11 Jan. 1873, Shepard
12 Jan. 1873, A. H. McVay, M.G.

Page 458:
J. M. Daniell - Alice Sheffield 20 March 1873, H. M. Hammett
20 March 1873, W. W. Carroll, O. M. G.

Thomas B. Moon - Julia A. Hardy 11 Feb. 1873, H. M. Hammett
27 Feb. 1873, J. G. Eubanks, M.G.

Page 459:
Jasper N. Dorsey - Mrs Junius Cornelia Brown 29 April 1873, H. M. Hammett
2 May 1873, D. L. Buttolph, M.G.

J. T. Kennan - Fannie Lee 19 March 1873, H. M. Hammett
12 March 1873, Rev. C. C. Dabis

Page 460:
John C. Fowler - Emma L. Paden 3 May 1873, H. M. Hammett
6 May 1873, N. A. Pratt, M.G.

J. F. Nutting - Miss C. M. Morris 1 May 1873, H. M. Hammett
6 May 1873, Geo. W. Yarbrough, M.G.

Page 461:
Lee C. Smith - Sarah E. Melton 11 Dec. 1872, Shepard
11 Dec. 1872, A. Melton, M.G.

William Fincher - Mary A. Smith 10 May 1873, H. M. Hammett
11 May 1873, A. N. Simpson, Not. Pub. Cobb Co.

Page 462:
Bird Pierce - Mary J. Waits 10 May 1873, H. M. Hammett
12 May 1873, J. T. Talley, J.P.

Frederick A. Shephard - Mary Clifford/Hansell 14 May 1873, H. M. Hammett
14 May 1873, J. W. Baker, M.G.

Page 463:
Benjamin N. Brown - Sarah L. Hammett 31 May 1873, H. M. Hammett
1 June 1873, John Sanges, M.G.

Mitchell Smith - Martha J. Black 17 May 1873, H. M. Hammett
26 May 1873, J. Y. Alexander, J.P.

Page 464:
Dillard Ferguson - Laura Ann Woodruff 7 April 1873, H. M. Hammett
8 April 1873, J. Y. Alexander, J.P.

Campbell Barber 0 Sophrona Hogan 12 Oct. 1872, Shepard
13 Oct. 1872, John W. Hill, N.P.

Page 465:
John W. Rogers - Mrs. Jane Henderson   28 June 1873, H. M. Hammett
29 June 1873, J. R. Sanges, O.M.G

M. E. Clanton - Lucinda Dickerson   7 June 1873, H. M. Hammett
8 June 1873, J. Y. Alexander, J.P.

Page 466:
John L. Lowe - Miss Pheriby L. Moble   1 July 1873, H. M. Hammett
3 July 1873, J. W. Baker, M.G.

Leroy Smith - Martha A. Caylor   28 May 1873, H. M. Hammett
29 May 1873, Albert B. Vaughn, M.G.

Page 467:
W. J. McGinn - Fannie Pierce   1 July 1873, H. M. Hammett
2 July 1873, J. Y. Alexander, J.P.

Wm. Haygood - R. M. Garrison   4 June 1873, H. M. Hammett
8 June 1873, A. H. Tally, J.P.

Page 468:
J. C. Ireland - Miss Mattie L. Davis   1 July 1873, H. M. Hammett
3 July 1873, Rev. J. F. Rowan

William T. Harris - Miss Mary W. Queen   7 May 1872, Shepard

Page 469:
9 May 1872, Rev. J. F. Rowan

S. J. Wooten - Miss Mary Thompson   26 June 1873, H. M. Hammett
26 June 1873, Rev. W. L. Davenport

Page 470:
James E. Holmes - Madge Gigrilliant   24 June 1873, H. M. Hammett
24 June 1873, W. Eston Eppes, Rector St. James Church, Marietta

Page 471:
John T. Myers - Sarah E. Watson   7 Dec. 1871, Shepard
10 Dec. 1871, W. H. Campbell, O.M.G.

Page 472:
Benjamin Phillips - Emaline Hardage   11 Oct. 1872, Shepard
13 Oct. 1872, W. H. Campbell O.M.G.

Page 473:
Willis L. Guess - Miss Louisa McCurdy   9 Jan. 1872, Shepard
13 Jan. 1872, W. H. Campbell, O.M.G.

Page 474:
W. H. Jackson - Tallulah Durham   10 Jan. 1872, Shepard
12 Jan. 1872, W. H. Campbell

Page 475:
Warren A. Dodgen - Miss Georgia A. Clay   20 Aug. 1872, Shepard
12 Sept. 1872, W. H. Campbell, O.M.G.

Page 476:
William G. Williams - Miss A. V. Kemp   15 Jan. 1872, Shepard
15 Jan. 1872, W. H. Campbell, O.M.G.

Page 477:
Z. L. Wyatt - C. E. Clay   11 Jan 1873 Shepard
14 Jan. 1873 W. H. Campbell, O.M.G.

Page 478:
James G. McCurdy - Nancy J. Barron   2 Dec. 1872, Shepard
5 Dec. 1872 _____

Page 479:
J. C. Hull - Fannie Bradford   18 March 1873, H. M. Hammett
23 March 1873, W. H. Campbell, O.M.G.

Page 480:
Thomas J. Scott - Barbara McCurdy 1 Nov. 1872, Shepard
3 Nov. 1872, W. H. Campbell, O.M.G.

Page 481:
C. J. Ward - C. A. Mayes 15 Dec. 1871, Shepard
19 Dec. 1872, W. H. Campbell, O.M.G.

Page 482:
P. H. Green - Georgia F. York 18 April 1873, H. M. Hammett
19 April 1873, W. H. Campbell, O.M.G.

Page 483:
William F. Robinson - Louisa J. Rankford 18 Dec. 1872, Shepard
19 Dec. 1872, W. H. Campbell, O.M.G.

Page 484:
George McGee - M. A. Baggett 6 Feb. 1873, H. M. Hammett
13 Feb. 1873, R. Baber, M.G.

Page 485:
John M. Johnson - Henrietta Northcutt 3 Dec. 1872, Shepard
5 Dec. 1872, James G. Ryals, M.G.

Page 486:
John D. Benson - Mary A. Brantley 8 Sept. 1871, Shepard
10 Sept. 1871, W. H. Dean, M.G.

Page 487:
John Wesley - Francis McAfee 16 Dec. 1870, Shepard
22 Dec. 1870, W. H. Dean O.M.G. (recorded 24 Sept. 1873)

Page 488:
George W. Gresham - Miss Mollie A. Hoy (Hay?) 13 Jan. 1869, E. A. Dobbs, ordy
17 Jan. 1869, W. H. Dean, minister (recorded 27 Sept. 1873)

Page 489:
John L. Reed - Sue M. Fowler 5 Nov. 1870, Shepard
10 Nov. 1870, W. H. Dean, M.G. (recorded 24 Sept. 1873)

Page 490:
L. M. Dawson - Mrs. E. A. Walraven 31 Dec. 1868, E. A. Dobbs, ordy
31 Dec. 1868, W. H. Dean, minister (recorded 24 Sept. 1873)

Page 491:
Joseph C. Kelphin - Susan E. Drake 17 Dec. 1872, Shepard
25 Dec. 1872, N. A. Pratt, minister gospel (recorded 1 Oct. 1873)

Page 492:
Thomas R. Rutherford - Caroline Wilson 11 April 1872, Shepard
11 April 1872, M. Groover, M.G.

Page 493:
Giffen Gentry - Albletine Rutherford 27 Nov. 1872, Shepard
28 Nov. 1872, M. Groover, M.G.

Page 494:
J. L. Baker - Miss Elizabeth Mackey 27 Dec. 1871, Shepard
29 Dec. 1871, John T. Paden, M.G.

Page 495:
Joseph Brown - Ann E. Cromer 3 April 1872, Shepard
4 April 1872, M. Groover, M.G.

Page 496:
Henry Moore - Florida Rogers 13 March 1874, H. M. Hammett
13 March 1874, John R. Sanges, M.G.

Page 497:
Mr. Isaac Petty - Miss Jane Davis 18 Jan. 1873, H. M. Hammett
19 Jan. 1873, James Peck, M.G.

Page 498:
Marshall Davis - Elizabeth Petty 1 Jan. 1872, Shepard
2 Jan. 1872, J. Peck, M.G. (recorded 30 March 1874)

Page 499:
Augustus Garrison - Miss Mary E. Bentley 13 Oct. 1869, Shepard
14 Oct. 1869, C. M. McClure, M.G. (D. O. Green, clerk)

Page 500:
Mitchell T. Burtz - Sarah A. Haney 2 Sept. 1870, Shepard
13 Sept. 1870, C. M. McClure, M.G. Recorded 11 April 1874, D. O. Green, clerk

Page 501:
George B. Burtz - Cara L. Garrison 4 Oct. 1870, Shepard
5 Oct. 1870, C. M. McClure, M. G. (recorded 11 April 1874, Green)

Page 502:
B. F. Callahan - E. A. Teary 2 May 1874, H. M. Hammett
6 May 1874, A. H. McVay, M.G.

Page 503:
"Colored license recorded by error in this book"
Thomas Mosley - Killie Lawson 30 July 1874, H. M. Hammett
11 Aug. 1874, Charles Hines, M.G.

Page 504:
T. W. Smith - Mrs. Jane Hammett 24 Sept. 1874, H. M. Hammett
24 Sept. 1874, J. R. Sanges, M.G.

Page 505:
James H. Elliott - Rachael R. Moon 1 Sept. 1874, H. M. Hammett
26 Sept. 1874, E. M. Compton, N.P.

Page 506:
Mr. Thomas A. P. Lindley - Miss Georgia A. Turner 5 Aug. 1868 , John G.
Campbell, ordy 6 Aug. 1868, Luke T. Mizell, M.G.

Page 507:
David L. McEarcherson - Mary L. Baggett 17 Oct. 1870, Shepard
20 Oct. 1870, L. T. Mizell, M.G.

Page 507:
F. Lowery - Mary Jane Mote 14 Nov. 1874, H. M. Hammett
17 Nov. 1874, G. T. Carrie, N.P. Ex Off J.P.

Page 508:
Joseph H. Murray - Miss Eugenia P. Reynolds 2 May 1871, Shepard
4 May 1871, L. T. Mizell, M.G.

Page 509:
A. L. Smith - Miss A. P. McElwnath 14 Dec. 1869, Shepard
2 Dec. 1869, L. T. Mizell, M.G.

Page 510:
R. P. Doss - E. J. Congo 1 Oct. 1874, H. M. Hammett
4 Oct. 1874, M. T. McClesky, J.P.

Page 511
McAbraton (only one name given) - Harriet Ragins 24 Dec. 1873, H. M. Hammett
25 Dec. 1873, M. T. Mizell, M.G.

Page 512:
Wm. L. Meadows - Sarah R. Eliot 21 Dec. 1872, Shepard
22 Feb. 1872, L. T. Mizell, M.G.

Page 513:
Auston A. Wills - Miss Kinns L. Wilson 3 Aug. 1872, Shepard
4 Aug. 1872, L. T. Mizell, M.G.

Page 514:
B. H. Almond - M. J. Hims 12 Nov. 1874, H. M. Hammett
13 Nov. 1874, J. Y. Alexander, J.P.

Page 515:
J. L. Landrum - A. J. Hopkins 1 Dec. 1874, H. M. Hammett
10 Dec. 1874, E. S. Hewk, M.G.

Page 516:
William A. Petty - Jennie Wilson 13 Jan. 1875, H. M. Hammett
14 Jan. 1875, Rev. L. L. Bailey, M.G.

Page 517:
J. D. Frazier - Emma H. Kiser 26 Aug. 1871, Shepard
27 Aug. 1871, B. S. Florence

Page 518:
C. A. Fridell - Miss N. E. Smith 1 March 1873, H. M. Hammett
2 March 1875, Joseph M. Gable, M.G.

Page 519:
George S. Owens - Miss Sallie Knight 13 Feb. 1869, E. A. Dobbs, ordy
14 Feb. 1869, W. W. Carrell, Ord. M.G. (recorded 28 Oct. 1875)

Page 520:
Joseph N. Wallis - Miss M. E. Jemion 30 Jan. 1869 E. A. Dobbs, ordy
31 Jan. 1869, Benjamin Bullard, J.P.

John Evagin - Hariett Jones 22 May 1869 E. A. Dobbs, Ordy
23 May 1869, Isaac (X) Gresham

Page 521:
Asa McKnight - Mrs. Martha Ables 21 Jan. 1869, E. A. Dobbs, ordy
21 Jan. 1869, Benjamin Bullard, J.P.

H. P. Stephens - Miss Emma Sanders 29 Dec. 1868, E. A. Dobbs, ordy
28 Jan. 1869, A. B. Mitchell, M.G.

Page 522:
Wm. C. Turner - Miss Sallie Smith 13 Jan. 1869, E. A. Dobbs, ordy
13 Jan. 1869, A. N. Simpson, N.P. & J.P.

Perry Jones - Hester A. Welchin 14 June 1869, E. A. Dobbs, ordy
14 June 1869, A. N. Simson, N.P.

Page 523:
J. Sidney Dobbins - Miss Mary Pace 15 April 1869, E. A. Dobbs, ordy
18 April 1869, Burrell Kemp, J.P.

C. E. Bapford (Basford?) - Miss Laura King 16 Jan. 1869, E. A. Dobbs, ordy
17 Jan. 1869, A. G. Dempsey, M.G.

Page 524:
J. B. Legg - Miss Lou Smith 22 Feb. 1869, E. A. Dobbs, ordy
23 Feb. 1869, W. F. Cook, M.G.

T. J. Green - Miss Ardisha Roney 17 Feb. 1869, E. A. Dobbs, ordy
18 Feb. 1869, J. G. Eubanks, M.G.

Page 525:
Charles B. C. Holeman - Miss Mary H. Root 13 Jan. 1869, E. A. Dobbs, ordy
13 Jan. 1869, D. L. Buttolph, M.G.

John D. Somers - Miss Martha J. Moon 16 March 1869, E. A. Dobbs, ordy
17 March 1869, James Lindley, J.P.

Page 526:
George W. Pitman - Miss Emma J. Howell 17 Nov. 1868, E. A. Dobbs, ordy
19 Nov. 1868, J. F. Rowan, M.G.

Richard Johnson - Malissa Goswick 28 Nov. 1869, E. A. Dobbs, ordy
29 Nov. 1868, J. R. Sanges, M.G.

Page 527:
W. J. Palmer - Miss Ellen L. Lane 19 Sept. 1868, E. A. Dobbs, ordy
29 Sept. 1868, R. W. Melner, M.G.

W. J. Brannen - Miss Cinthia L. Green 24 Dec. 1868, E. A. Dobbs
27 Dec. 1868, John R. Bates, M.G.

Page 528:
R. S. Eidson - Miss C. E. Steele 21 Dec. 1868, E. A. Dobbs, ordy
22 Dec. 1868, W. H. Campbell, O.M.G.

Page 529:
Robert M. C. Moon - Miss Catharine M. Daniell 21 Dec. 1868, E. A. Dobbs, ordy
24 Dec. 1868, Thos. P. Whitfield, J.P.

Berry Marlow - Martha Smith 14 Nov. 1868, E. A. Dobbs, ordy
14 Nov. 1868, no signature of minister

Page 530:
Nathan P. Medlin - Miss Nancy Moon 14 Jan. 1869, E. A. Dobbs, ordy
14 Jan. 1869, W. W. Jolly, J.P.

Hartwell A. Baldwin - Miss Sarah A. Dorsett 27 Jan. 1869, E. A. Dobbs, ordy
28 Jan. 1869, Robert Kemon, J.P.

Page 531:
James Stanley - Miss Georgia Williams 16 Jan. 1869, E. A. Dobbs, ordy
17 Jan. 1869, J. G. Eubanks, M.G.

James L. Johnson - Miss Lucy G. Harris 11 March 1869, E. A. Dobbs, ordy
11 March 1869, V. A. Gaskill, M.G.

Page 532:
E. A. Rays - Miss L. K. Humphries 15 Feb. 1869, E. A. Dobbs, ordy
16 Feb. 1869, H. F. Buckannon, M.G.

James M. Smith - Miss Edna Sanders 28 Jan. 1869, E. A. Dobbs, ordy
28 Jan. 1869, A. B. Mitchell, M.G.

Page 533:
Henry A. Dunwoody - Miss Hattie W. Morris 6 April 1869, Ellison A. Dobbs,
ordy 7 April 1869, G. W. Yarbrough, M.G.

Lott Reeves - Mary Miles 20 Jan. 1869, E. A. Dobbs, ordy
21 Jan. 1869, Robt. Baber, M.G.

Page 534:
William R. Copeland - Miss Carrie Whitfield 17 April 1869, E. A. Dobbs, ordy
18 April 1869, A. G. Dempsey, M.G.

W. W. Brown - Miss Elizabeth Wingo 2 April 1869, E. A. Dobbs, ordy
4 April 1869, G. T. Carrie, J.P.

Page 535:
Thomas S. Causey - Miss Milly M. Pruett 17 Feb. 1869, E. A. Dobbs
17 Feb. 1869, J. T. Robertson, J.P.

M. W. Murdock - Miss Jamima Steel 19 Dec. 1868, E. A. Dobbs, ordy
24 Dec. 1868, W. Manning, O. M. G.

Page 536:
John J. C. McMahan - Georgia Lyers 10 July 1869, E. A. Dobbs, ordy
11 July 1869, James G. Ryals, O.M.

Francis M. Simpson - Gracie M. McEntyre 8 July 1869, E. A. Dobbs
8 July 1869, J. M. Britton, M.G.

Page 537:
Samuel Thomas - Mary L. Evis 7 July 1869, E. A. Dobbs, ordy
8 July 1869, J. M. Brittain, M.G.

R. M. Gramling - Miss Sabrina Skelton 20 April 1869, E. A. Dobbs
22 April 1869, A. G. Dempsey, M. G.

Page 538:
Daniel Reed - Miss Mary A. Ruff 1 April 1869, E. A. Dobbs
4 April 1869, Robert Daniell, M.G.

48

Page 538:
J. F. Lindley - Miss Keren H. Kirkpatrick 15 April 1869, E. A. Dobbs
15 April 1869, D. L. Buttolph, M.G.

Page 539:
John D. Hall - Lucinda Smith 9 July 1869, E. A. Dobbs
11 July 1869, J. M. Brittain, M.G.

Samuel A. Blamer - Miss Susan Green 17 April 1869, E. A. Dobbs
18 April 1869, G. T. Carrie, J.P.

Page 540:
W. W. Cassel - Miss Mary A. M. Mullins 23 Jan. 1869, E. A. Dobbs
28 Jan. 1869, A. N. Simpson, N.P. Ex Off J.P.

Sylvanus Scroggins, Jr. - Miss Francis Dunn 17 Feb. 1869, E. A. Dobbs
17 Feb. 1869, N. B. Johnson, M.G.

Page 541:
Hiram Moss - Margarett Marlow 19 Nov. 1868, E. A. Dobbs
19 Nov. 1868, William S. Brown, J.P.

W. H. Richardson - Miss Mary Steele 22 Dec. 1868, E. A. Dobbs
27 Dec. 1868, W. Manning, O.M.G.

Page 542:
William J. Davis - Eleanor P. Strickland 18 Nov. 1868, E. A. Dobbs
19 Nov. 1868, J. G. Eubanks, M.G.

E. M. Crow - Miss Eleanor D. Leadford 12 Jan. 1869, E. A. Dobbs
13 Jan. 1869, W. W. Jolly, J.P.

Page 543:
Robert A. Patterson - Miss Mary P. Stansell 3 Feb. 1869, E. A. Dobbs
11 Feb. 1869, G. T. Carrie, J.P.

William J. Stephens - Miss Sarah A. Moore 16 Dec. 1868, E. A. Dobbs
17 Dec. 1868, Benjamin Bullard, J.P.

Page 544:
Mr. John T. Knight - Miss Sylvia M. Daniell 4 Nov. 1868, E. A. Dobbs
8 Nov. 1868, Benjamin Bullard, J.P.

John M. Harvill - Polly Stephens 27 Aug. 1868 Jno. G. Campbell
31 Aug. 1868, Benjamin Bullard, J.P.

Page 545:
James Summers - Miss Elizabeth Moon 3 April 1869, E. A. Dobbs
4 April 1869, D. N. McEachern, J.P.

James Skelton - Miss M. V. Chalker 5 April 1869, E. A. Dobbs
15 April 1869, G. T. Carrie, J.P.

Page 546:
John P. Bryan - Miss Salema Mitchell 17 Feb. 1869, E. A. Dobbs
18 Feb. 1869, E. J. Fowler, J.P.

Williamson Kirkland - Salitia M. Blackman 17 Jan. 1866, Jno. G. Campbell,
18 Jan. 1866, C. N. Woodall, J.P.

Page 547:
P. J. Wilson - Miss Mary Magarity 8 March 1869, E. A. Dobbs
10 March 1869, W. Manning, O. M. G.

Mr. Samuel J. Molock - Miss Sarah J. Martin 8 Feb. 1869, E. A. Dobbs
9 Feb. 1869, W. W. Carrell, Ord. M.G.

Page 548:
W. S. Stansell - Miss Gertrude J. Bryson 23 Dec. 1868 Ellison A. Dobbs, ordy
23 Dec. 1868, L. F. Mizell, M.G.

F. M. Rice - Mrs. Rachell Lindsay 20 Nov. 1868, E. A. Dobbs
22 Nov. 1868, Luke T. Mizell, M.G.

Page 549:
C. F. Pope - Miss N. E. Scroggins   12 Dec. 1868, E. A. Dobbs
13 Dec. 1868, John F. Rowan, M.G.

T. P. Anderson - Elizabeth A. Hooker   23 Dec. 1868, E. A. Dobbs
31 Dec. 1868, John C. Clay, J.P.

Page 550:
C. C. Watford - Mrs. Annie Tate   8 April 1869, E. A. Dobbs
8 April 1869, A. N. Simson, N.P.

Johnathan H. Ragsdale - Mary L. McEver - 18 Aug. 1868, Jno. G. Campbell
18 Aug. 1868, R. W. Milner, M.G.

Page 551:
Joseph Bell - Miss Susan Barber   24 Oct. 1868, E. A. Dobbs (no signature
of minister)

J. A. Williams - Miss Ellin Cheatham   29 Dec. 1868, E. A. Dobbs
29 Dec. 1868, W. H. Campbell, O.M.G.

Page 552:
Emanuel Patton - Miss Sarah Matilda Gresham   17 Dec. 1868, E. A. Dobbs
20 Dec. 1868, J. G. Eubanks, M.G.

Dewitt C. Winn - Miss Mary C. Johnson   21 Dec. 1861, E. A. Dobbs
24 Dec. 1868, G. T. Carrie, J.P.

Page 553:
William E. Buckner - Miss Josephine Pope   10 Nov. 1868, E. A. Dobbs
13 Nov. 1861, Robert Lemon, J.P.

William P. Cash - Miss Sarah J. Ragsdale   13 March 1868, Jno. G. Campbell
15 March 1868, Robert Lemon, J.P.

Page 554:
Benjamin Asbury - Margaret Queen   26 Aug. 1868, Jno. G. Campbell
26 Aug. 1868, Robert Lemon, J.P.

Newton N. Gober - Miss Sarah T. Farrington   19 Nov. 1868, E. A. Dobbs
19 Nov. 1868, Luke T. Mizell, M.G.

Page 555:
Joseph P. Jolley - Rachael Edward   20 April 1876, H. M. Hammett
20 April 1876, J. Y. Alexander, J.P.

William P. Cash - Miss Sarah J. Ragsdale   13 March 1868, Jno. G. Campbell
15 March 1868, Robert Lemon, J.P.

Page 554:
Benjamin Asbury - Margaret Queen   26 Aug. 1868, Jno. G. Campbell
26 Aug. 1868, Robert Lemon, J.P.

Newton N. Gober - Miss Sarah T. Farrington   19 Nov. 1868, E. A. Dobbs
19 Nov. 1868, Luke T. Mizell, M.G.

Page 555:
Joseph P. Jolley - Rachael Edward   20 April 1876, H. M. Hammett
20 April 1876, J. Y. Alexander, J.P.

Cobb County, Georgia was formed December 8,1832 from Cherokee County, and its county seat is Marietta. All of the Cobb County records have been microfilmed, and security copies of these microfilmed records have been placed in the Georgia State Department of Archives and History. Cobb County officials will not allow these microfilmed copies in the Archives to be used by the public, and therefore, anyone desiting information about Cobb County must co to the Courthouse in Marietta to do research.

The index in the office covers to 1967 but for these purposes only to 1900 were copied. Although the various items for each estate have been copied into the various books the loose papers are filed in manila folders by case numbers and may be xeroxed easily. The system is a very good one but only those papers which were FOUND have been filed.

ESTATE #	PRINCIPAL	ADMINISTRATOR - EXECUTOR, ETC.	DATE	ITEMS
3	Levi Abbott	Wm. Henderson, Admr.	1888	6
4	Docie Abbott	Wm. Henderson, Admr.	1889	8
12	H.S. Adams, Minor		1872	6
13	May E. Adams, Minor	R.E. Cason, Gdn.	1875	3
14	F.W. Adams	H.J. Adams, trustee	1878	1
15	Melissa Adams, Inc.	W.P. Clay/J.T. Adams, Admr	1900	8
5001	H.M. Adams	Alice & John Q. Adams, Exor.	1897	23
25	Aldridge, Ellenor, et al	Nancy Aldridge, Gdn.	1880	3
26	Allen, R.A.	Susan A. Allen, Exor	1878	4
27	Allen, Charles C.	W.P. McClatchey, Admr.	1894	3
28	Allen, R.A.	J.O. Allen, Admr.	1900	7
37	Aleywine, Lena & Sallay	John Dunn, Gdn.	1889	3
38	Aleywine, Zacharia	Irene Aleywine, Wid.	1889	1
39	Alexander, R.G.	J.Y. Alexander, Exor.	1870	10
40	Alexander, Nathan	J.R. Alexander, Admr.	1881	12
41	Alexander, John	W.R. Montgomery, Admr.	1881	9
42	Alexander, Mary	Milley S. Alexander, Gdn.	1882	2
43	Alexander, P.W.	Theresa Alexander, Exor.	1886	3
44	Alexander, J.B.	J.Y. Alexander, Admr.	1890	5
45	Alexander, W.C.	Josie Alexander, Gdn.	1893	1
51	Allgood, John W.	John E. & Francis Allgood, Exor.	1897	6
57	Anderson, W.P.	Catherine Anderson	1885	4
(Notation: same as Estate #62)				
58	Anderson, H.S.	D.N. Anderson	1891	6
59	Anderson, Henry	Ella Anderson, Gdn.	1891	1
60	Anderson, Henry N.	D.N. Anderson, Gdn.	1893	7
61	Anderson, Leila, et al	Leila H. Anderson, Gdn.	1894	3
62	Anderson, Wm. P.	Saxon Anderson, Admr.	1896	7
(Notation: same as Estate #57)				
79	Andrews, C.C.	Julia Andrews, Wid.	1878	1
80	Andrews, Emma, et al	Julia E. Andrews & M.P. Appling Guardians	1878	5
83	Appling, Walter, Sr.	Walter Appling, Admr.	1868	5
93	Armstrong, Wm.	J.O. Allen, Admr.	1881	12
103	Arwood, Barbay A.	A.C. Edwards, Gdn.	1870	6
107	Atkins, Enerest B.	J.H. Atkins, Exor.	1897	13
108	Atkins, James H., et al	James M. Atkins, Gdn.	1889	3

109	Atkinson, Tillman J.	Saphonia Atkinson, Admr.	1882	12
112	Austin, Wm. A.	Lucinda Austin, Exor.	1882	4
116	Awtrey, Merrill C.	Orlando Awtrey, Exor.	1890	5
117	Awtrey, Sarah	S.H. Alexander, Exor.	1891	6
119	Avery, Lucinda	Benjamin Bullard	1866	9
120	Avery, Sara E.	M.M. Sessions, Admr.	1883	7
121	Avery, Holmes, M.	Mary B. Avery, Wid.	1893	1
128	Baggett, Burton	A. Reynolds, Exor.	1870	10
130	Bagwell, Parthena, et al	Sara Bagwell, Gdn.	1874	3
131	Bagwell, Bryant	G.L. Chatham, Admr.	1893	8
134	Bain, John	Mary Bain, Exor.	1881	1
135	Baker, John V.	Margaret M. Baker, Wid.	1886	2
136	Baker, Mrs. Charlotte & children	John W. Baker, trustee	1866	7
137	Baker, William	A. Baker, Admr.	1871	11
138	Baker, A.	W.A. Wilson, Admr.	1876	17
139	Baker, Francis	R.B. Baker, Exor.	1880	3
148	Baldwin, Sylvanus	J.F. Baldwin, Admr.	1877	7
149	Baldwin, John F.	Vina Baldwin, Admr.	1884	11
150	Baldwin, T.D., et al	Martha Gulliver, Gdn.	1887	3
151	Baldwin, Henry H.	Sarah Baldwin, Wid.	1894	1
159	Ballinger, Mary F.	E.E. Ballenger, Gdn.	1863	1
162	Banks, W.R.	Mrs. G.W. Banks, Admr.	1870	3
163	Banks, W.P.	J.Z. Foster, Admr.	1888	8
168	Barber, Rachel	Sarah & Wm. Barber, Gdn.	1876	9
169	Barber, William	Sarah J. Barber, Admr.	1876	6
170	Barber, R.V.	Sarah J. Barber, Gdn.	1888	2
171	Barber, J.N.	Mrs. E.A. Barber, Admr.	1896	5
120-A	Barrett, James S.	Dora Barrett, Wid.	1896	1
175	Barfield, Alex, et al	D.D. Barfield, Admr.	1885	1
176	Barfield, D.D.	Martha Barfield & S.C. Barfield Administrators	1894	14
180	Barmore, Wiley	Sarah A. Barmore, Wid.	1867	2
182	Barnes, John J.	W.L. Barnes, Gdn.	N.D.	3
183	Barnes, John J. & Barnes, Nancy A.	William L. Barnes, Gdn.	N.D.	1
184	Barnes, Elizabeth & Barnes, Amanda	W.S. Brown, Gdn.	N.D.	4
185	Barnes, James J.	J.W. Barnes & J.J. Barnes Admr.	1884	9
186	Barnes, Mattie	John W. Barnes, Gdn.	1885	4
187	Barnes, Linwood	John E. Moseley, Gdn.	1895	3
188	Barnes, Blanch, et al	H.A. Barnes, Gdn.	1897	3
193	Barnwell, Robert	W.R. Montgomery, Admr.	1881	8
197	Barrett, Charles	D.A. Barrett, Exor.	1870	11
198	Barrett, John	Annie Barrett, Exor.	1890	3
199	Barrett, George	Juda Barrett, Wid.	1892	1
200	Barrett, J.D.	Dora Barrett, Wid.	1896	1
205	Bartles, Sarah H., et al	J.N. Bartles, Gdn.	1885	5
208	Basford, Estell, et al	Laura Bassford	N.D.	1
209	Baswell, John C.		1887	2
210	Baswell, W.P.	Cordelia Baswell, Exor.	1898	4
216	Bates, Mathais	Russell J. Bates & Charles Nix, Exors	1883	22

223	Baxter, William B.	Mrs. S.C. Baxter, Wid.	1871	2
224	Beasley, J.F.	B.H. Curmerson, Admr.	1893	6
232	Bell, W.R.	Margaret Bell, Admr.	1876	26
233	Bell, G.C. & W.A.	Allen J. Bell, Gdn.	1877	11
234	Bell, Narcissa	J.C. Bell, Gdn.	1878	7
235	Bell, Julia H.	D.A. Bell, Gdn.	1878	7
236	Bell, Abby, et al	B.F. Bishop & John H. Marlon Guardians	1878	4
237	Bell, J.C.	Lucy M. Bell, Wid.	1881	1
238	Bell, Margaret J.	Margaret Bell, Gdn.	1888	7
239	Bell, Mamie A.	B.A. Bell, Gdn.	1892	2
240	Bell, Margaret	Fannie L. Bell, Admr.	1892	11
244	Bellenger, John	Albert C. & John F. Ballenger Executors	1866	5
245	Ballenger, Mary F.	J.B. & E.E. Ballenger, Gdn.	1866	3
246	Bice, M.	Lavonia Swetman, Wid.	1893	1
251	Bennett, D.A.	I.N. Scott, Admr.	1895	16
252	Bennett, J.B.	Ida Bennett, Exor.	1895	3
253	Bennett, Francis, et al	I.N. Scott, Gdn.	1896	12
264	Benson, Andrew M.	R.M. Benson & L.W. Fowler, Admr.	1878	10
267	Bentley, Sam	W.J. Hudson, Admr.	1869	6
274	Betterton, J.B.	E. Faw, Exor.	1870	4
277	Bingham, S.A.	W.F. Bingham, Exor.	1888	11
278	Bingham, S.A., et al	Mrs. E.C. Bingham, Gdn.	1889	2
281	Bishop, S.E.	L.A. Bishop, Gdn.	1892	3
287	Byrd, James, et al	James Pitner, Gdn.	1866	2
288	Byrd, W.J.	T.D. Power, Admr.	1889	16
289	Byrd, Willie	J.F. Byrd, Gdn.	1890	1
290	Byrd, Mrs. S.N.	E.S.D. & J.F. Byrd, Exors.	1895	7
291	Byrd, Willie, et al	E.W. Frey & Edgar R. Anderson Guardians	1892	23
297	Blackwell, J.B.	G.B. Waddell, Admr.	1894	20
298	Blackwell, Elizabeth	J.Y. Alexander, Admr.	1895	4
303	Blankenship, Lillian	G.F. Blankenship	1882	4
305	Blyth, Wm. C.	W.W. Brimer, Gdn.	1871	5
306	Blyth, Sarah (Nee Hirsh)	Raphael Hirsh, Gdn.	1874	1
307	Bobo, Callabat E., et al	Matilda Bobo, Gdn.	1872	5
311	Bolden, William	John V. Steele, Gdn.	1881	2
314	Bond, Thomas, et al	T.B. Bond, Gdn.	1896	3
317	Bonner, Claborn	John Alexander, Exor.	1876	6
320	Boring, Mary M., et al	John P. Boring, Gdn.	1890	4
325	Bostwick, C.C.	Andrew J. Hansel, Admr.	1873	5
337	Boyd, Robert M.	Mary A. Boyd, Exor.	1865	5
338	Boyd, Iseral	H.M. Hammett, Admr.	1867	13
339	Boyd, David	Levina Boyd, Exor.	1877	2
348	Bradford, Ella T.	W.R. Montgomery, Gdn.	1887	3
353	Branan, Sarah	Sarah E. Campbell	1874	2
354	Brand, Elisha	W.R. Power, Admr.	1896	2
357	Branham, Eva	E.W. Frey, Admr.	1900	2
358	Brantley, Wm. R.	E.W. Faw, Admr.	1864	1
359	Brantley, John Q., et al	E.W. Frey, Gdn.	1898	15

360	Brantley, Q.L.	E.W. Frey, Admr. Sarah Brantley Widow	1900	5
362	Braswell, Mattie L. & J.W.-Alfred I. James, Gdn.		1883	4
363	Braswell, Ulea, et al	Alfred I. James, Gdn.	1883	5
364	Braswell, Clifford, et al	A.I. James, Gdn.	1888	3
370	Brinkley, Mrs. E.F.	J.F. Brinkley, Exor.	1896	8
372	Bryant, R.R.	Susan Bryant, Admr.	1874	7
373	Bryant, T.J.	P.P. Allgood, Admr.	1877	27
379	Brockman, John B.	J.A. Johnson, Exor.	1880	9
381	Brooks, Josephine	B. Holleman, Gdn.	1886	2
382	Brooks, M.J.	Charles A. Brooks & Mrs. M.L. Brooks, Admr.	1892	13
383	Brooks, George F., et al	Mary L. Brooks, Gdn.	1894	3
980	Brown, A.C.	Wm. S. Brown, Admr.	1866	1
981	Brown, Robert	Susan Brown, Wid.	1867	2
982	Brown, Hiram	Wm. S. Brown, Admr.	1867	12
983	Brown, Eula, et al	Louise N. Brown, Gdn.	1867	2
984	Brown, Silas	Robart A. Brown, Exor.	1869	17
985	Brown, Clayborn	J.Y. Alexander, Exor.	1875	1
986	Brown, W.S.	W.R. Montgomery, Admr.	1879	19
987	Brown, James		1879	11
988	Brown, Matilda, et al	James & Ludie Brown, Gdn.	1880	6
989	Brown, M.L. & P.A. Brown	M.L. Brown, Gdn.	1882	5
990	Brown, John C.	W.L. Brown, Gdn.	1882	4
991	Brown, James H.	M.A.E. Brown, Gdn.	1883	1
992	Brown, W.S. & E.W. Brown	Luddie Brown, Gdn.	1887	3
993	Brown, James W.	W.H. Nutting & R.E. Brown, Exors.	N.D.	7
994	Brown, William G.	J.J. Eubanks, Admr.	1890	11
995	Brown, Hiram	John D. Perkinson, Admr.	1890	7
997	Brown, S.M.	E.J. Brown, Admr.	1890	7
998	Brown, Robert, et al	E.J. Brown, Gdn.	1890	2
999	Brown, Winnie	Wm. F. Brown, Gdn.	1891	10
1000	Brown, James R.	James W. McFall, Gdn.	1891	5
1001	Brown, P.E.	A.E. Brown, Admr.	1893	6
1002	Brown, W.M.	Hiram Brown, Gdn.	1895	6
399	Brumbalow, Jackson	H.M. Hammett, Admr.	1868	5
401	Brumby, T.M.	Mary D. Heyward, Admr.	1900	5
404	Buice, James D.	Minnie L. Buice, Admr.	1889	3
405	Buice, Louie	S.G. Mozley, Admr.	1899	3
407	Bullard, Robert	Margaret Bullard, Exor.	1845	1
408	Bullard, Micajah	A.D. McEwen, Admr.	1866	13
409	Bullard, William	Benjamin Bullard, Adrm.	1874	13
410	Bullard, Ruby	James Powell, Gdn.	1897	1
418	Bunn, M.H.	Catherine Bun, Exor.	1884	4
420	Burge, J.B.	H.A. Burge, Gdn.	1900	3
425	Burnap, George S.	G.C. Burnap, Admr.	1891	5
426	Burnap, G.C.	Annie S. Burnap, Exor.	1896	4
429	Burney, I.H.	J.O. Carpenter, Admr.	1889	1
440	Burtz, J.M.	Fannie L. Purtz, Admr.	N.D.	1
443	Buse, E.W., et al	Mrs. M.A. Buse, Gdn.	1888	3

444	Buse, W.F.	E.W. Buse, Admr.	1890	2
445	Buse, Asa	H.E. Bush, Admr. D.B.N.	1881	17
446	Bush, Henry, et al	Emily V. Bush, Gdn.	1882	16
447	Bush, Frankie	Henry E. Bush, Admr.	1890	10
450	Bussey, W.P.	Mrs. F.G. Bussey, Admr.	1892	1
451	Bussey, Harry, et al	Mrs. G. Bussey, Gdn.	1892	9
452	Bussey, Thomas L.	M. Sessions, Admr.	1895	7
453	Bussey, M.L., et al	Mrs. M.L. Bussey, Gdn.	1895	4
466	Buttolph, et al	Sallie P. Buttolph, Gdn.	1899	3
467	Buttolph, W.S.	C.S. McCandlish, Admr.	1899	13
474	Caldwell, Francis	John H. Boston, Admr.	1882	2
478	Calloway, John	J.J. Calloway, Admr.	1888	3
480	Camp, Benjamin T.	Samuel N. Scott, Admr.	1866	2
481	Camp, Thomas, et al	Sarah Camp, Gdn.	1867	3
482	Camp, Lutitia L.	Sarah J. Camp, Gdn.	1869	5
483	Camp, Maud	D.C. Camp, Admr.	1886	7
484	Camp, Ed. & Freddie	D.C. Camp, Gdn.	1887	12
485	Camp, Thomas L.	Mary C. Camp, Admr.	1889	6
486	Camp, Paul, et al	Mary C. Camp, Gdn.	1892	2
487	Camp, T.A.	J.T. Camp, Admr.	1900	4
494	Campbell, Alice, et al	Sarah E. Campbell & S.A. Campbell, Guardians	1867	8
495	Campbell, John	Mary A. Campbell, Wid.	1873	1
496	Campbell, Alice & Porter Campbell	S.A. Anderson, Gdn.	1880	2
497	Campbell, G.B.	Nancy E. Campbell, Wid.	1895	1
501	Cantrell, et al	J.F. Lee, Gdn.	1900	5
505-A	Cape, J.R.	Mrs. M.L. Cape, Wid.	1882	1
506	Carlile, James	James H. Carlile & A. Reynolds, Admr.	1877	11
510	Carmichael, J.T.	C.C. Davis, Admr.	1873	6
511	Carmichael, Mrs. M.J.	J.W. Carmichael, Admr.	1893	5
515	Carnes, W.B.	C.T. Carnes, Admr.	1899	8
523	Carr. Tolbert	Mary A. Carr, Wid.	1887	1
530	Cary, Georgia E.	Thomas H. Shockley, Admr.	1885	5
534	Cason, Walter, et al Minors	R.E. Cason, Gdn.	1880	3
535	Cason, Myrtis, et al Minors	Carrie C. Brumby	1895-1906	12
538	Castleberry, H.C.	W.M. Jolly, admr.	n.d.	16
541	Cattell, J.C.	Jane C. Cattell, admr.	1889	8
542	Causey, Israel	Wm. M. Causey/Wm. Mitchel Margaret Causey, widow	1880	19
543	Causey, Margaret	R.W. Perkerson, admr.	1885	4
546	Chadzy, H.A.	S.R. Collins, admr.	n.d.	1
547	Chalker, Phillip	J.T. & J.C. Chalker, admr.	April 1881	20
548	Chalker, Emma	S.L. Brinkley, gdn.	1883	7
559	Chambers, Rebecca(minor)	Givens, W. Arnold, gdn.	1873	1
560	Chamberlin, Augustus	C.R. Chamberlin, gdn.	1894	4
561	marked out			
563	Chandler, Robert	W.J. Hudson & H.M. Hammett, admr. June 1874	1869-	12

571	Chappell, John	Arena Chappell, widow	1866	7
		Wilson Chappell, exor.		
572	Chappel, Nancy (minor)	Mathew J. Bell, gdn.	1871	1
573	Chase, Mary O-Ida Mae (minor)	Mary C. Nichols, gdn.	1881	3
574	Chastain, J.H. (minor)	Charles W. Pyron, gdn.	1870- Jan. 1885	7
575	Chastain, Joseph	E.C. Stansell, admr.	1880- Aug. 1883	12
576	Chastain, Nancy	E.W. Frey, admr.	1895- Apr. 1897	7
580	Chatham, Naomi		1893	3
585	Chester, N.L.	Elizabeth L. Chester, admr.	1877	4
586	Cheney, A.J.	W.S. Cheney & James N. Cheney, exors. Jan.	1886 1906	79
587	Cheney, Cora (minor)	W.S. Cheney, gdn.	1891	14
588	Cheney, W.S.	John P. *J.N. Cheney, Exors.	1899	13
592	Christain, Homer, et al (minors)	L.C. Upshaw, gdn.	1897	3
597	Clackum, Elizabeth	A.C. Dpnehoo, admr. Apr.	1889- 1890	90
599	Clark, Jane	Stephen Cowan, exor.	1885	2
600	Clark, Susan S.	James F. & Eva Clark, exors.	1895	2
603	Clay, Thomas C.	Jasper L. Clay, exor. Dec.	1899- 1900	8
628	Cochran, R. Lee (minor)	William D. Anderson gdn. (ex officio admr.) June Jan.	1874 1879 1880	7
629	Cochran, W.B. (minor)	E.B. Cochran, gdn.	1880	3
630	Cochran, J.B.	Ella Cochran, widow	1886	1
631	Cochran, S.R.	Mrs. M.G. Cochran, exor.	1894	3
642	Coker (minors)	W.C. Coker, gdn.	1883	2
5424	Cole, Henry G.	A.A. Fletcher, exor. Mary Cole, admr.(de bonis non) D.C. Cole, admr. de bonis non)	1875- 1939	33
649	Collier, Eugene et al (minors)	Lawson F. Collier, gdn.	1891	2
658	Collins, James A. Transferred to Fulton Co.	W.R. Venable, admr.	1866	6
659	Collins, Albert R. (minor)	Cyntha Collins, gdn.	1873	1
660	Collins, Charles H. & Richard A., (minors)	Cytha Collins, gdn.	1867	3
661	Collins, Jessie E.(minor)	Daniel Collins, gdn.	1889	4
662	Collins, Ernest, et al (minors)	George B. Collins, gdn. Aug.	1890- 1913	9
671	Combs, Sarah, D.B. Hammett, Eliza A. McLean, (minors)	John B. Campbell, gdn.	1878	5
674	Conaway, Thomas	R.L. Jackson, gdn.	1897	3
675	Conger, Zacariah	Bird Conger, admr.	n.d.	1
678	Converse, Charles A.	George Newell, admr.	1888	5
679	Cook, Francis	W.F. Cook, exor.	1872	11
680	Cook, Mrs. Elizabeth	John B. Barfield, admr. May	1898- 1907	15
681	Cook, Nathan M.	S.E. Merwin, exor	1889	3
684	Cooper, Annie & Flonnie, (minors)	J.H. Cooper, gdn.	1891	4

685	Cooper, B.F.	B.F. Simpson, admr.	1893	1
693	Cotton, Alonzo	Mrs. L.J. Cotton, admr.	1886	6
696	Couper, Hannah P.	B.K. Couper, exor.	1897	3
697	Coursen, Mrs. Harriet	Van Wich B.	n.d.	1
698	Covington, W.H.	Ursilla Covington, exor. John Cheney, admr.(will annexed)	1896	10
701	Cowan, Francis M.	W.D. Anderson July	1866- 1871	26
702	Cowan, F.J.	F.N. Cowan, Temp. admr. J.J. Northcutt, Perm. admr.	1900- 1903	11
708	Cox, Andrew (Anderson?) (minor)	W.P. Johnson, gdn.	1881- 1882	6
709	Cox, A.J.	Mrs. A.J. Cox, gdn.	n.d.	1
710	Cox, Anderson	Wm. Hill, gdn.	1883	1
711	Cox, Margaret	Stephen Cox, admr.	1887-	7
712	Cox, George W.	Mrs. Queen H. Cox, admr. May	1896- 1898	10
717	Cox, Miranda	J.W. Cox & Henry Brown, admr. Stephen Cox, admr.(de bonis non)1888	1883-1884	25
718	Cox, S.A. (inc)	Cox, Adela (Mrs. A.J.) gdn.	1883	18
740	Cumming, W.H.	Montgomery Cumming, exor	1893	3
741	Cumming, Mrs. E.R.	W.S. Buttolph, admr.	1895 1898	9
743	Cunningham, Leola, et al. (minors)	F. Cunningham, gdn.	1889	2
747	Curry, Rebecca	C.E. Youngblood, exor.	1889	3
750	Daniel, Jeremiah	J.B. Daniel; G.M. Daniel; M.M. Sessions, trustees	1873	9
751	Daniell, Mrs. Henrietta	J.N. Daniell, trustee	1873	9
752	Daniell, H.V.	Inez N. Daniell, trustee	1876	1
753	Daniel, W.R.	George M. Daniell, admr.	1878- 1879	18
754	Daniel, A.A.	John M. Fleming, admr.	1878- 1884	12
755	Daniel, S.N. & G.B. Minors/H.J. Daniel, gdn.		1878	4
756	Daniell, et al, Minors	H.J. Daniell, gdn.	n.d.	1
757	Daniell, Robert	R.P. Daniell & J.S. Daniel, exors	1881- 1915	23
758	Daniell, S.N.	Josephine Daniell, widow	1890	1
774	Darby, John	Asa Darby, exor.	1880- 1907	22
775	Darby, Mary F.	John B. Kemp, exor.	1886- 1889	8
782	Davenport, Marcus L.	Thomas Davenport, admr.	1867- 1871	14
783	Davenport, Sanford H. et al., minors	Mrs. S.L. Davenport, gdn.	1870	9
784	Davenport, T.J.	E.N. Davenport, admr.	1899	6
786	Davis, E.R.	Tenperance S. Davis, widow	1868	4
787	Davis, Gray	P.L. Davis, exor; G.F.D. Davis, admr. de bonis non	1875	16
788	Davis, Orelia, minor	James B. Davis, gdn.	1885	2
789	Davis, Ida, et al, minors	George H. Crow, gdn.	1893	3
812	Dawson, William	William P. Dawson, admr.	1876- 1880	13

816	Deal, Jacob	Mary Deal, widow	1883	1
820	Delk, William J.	Elizabeth Delk, admr. Will annexed J.D. Delk, admr. de bonis non	1870	12
821	Delk, Jackson	W.P. & R.D. Delk, exor.	1897-1890	10
829	Dempsey, L.	Pliny R. Fleming, exor.	1883	3
830	Dempsey, A.F.	N.A. Dempsey, admr.	1899-1900	9
842	Dickson, D.W.	William C. Dickson, exor.	1864-1870	11
843	Dickson, Mary E. Davis; minors	William C. Dickson, gdn.	1866	3
844	Dickson, E.A., minor	J.A.L. Born, gdn.	1869	4
845	Dickson, D.W., minor	W.C. Dickson	n.d.	2
846	Dickson, W.D.	J.D. Perryman, admr.	1893	6
849	Dockerson, John	J.Y. Alexander, exor. R.J. Dickerson, admr. de bonis non, will annexed	1874-1909	12
850	Dickerson, Allen	Ellen Dickerson, widow	1878	1
853	Denmead, Tolbott	A.N. Simpson, atty. for exors.	1877	1
854	De Trevilie, Mrs. Eliza	John H. Glover, trustee	1862	1
855	De Trevelle, Robert & Ruth, minors	J.B. Glover, gdn.	1872	4
862	Dobbs, Rosalinda	H.M. Hammett, admr.	1867-1873	16
863	Dobbs, David	David J. Dobbs, exor.	1871	8
864	Dobbs, William	H.M. Hammett, admr.	1872	10
865	Dobbs, David J. (Transferred to Cobb Superior Court)	Mattie J. Dobbs, exor.	1877	9
866	Dobbs, Addie M. & Mamie, minors	Amanda C. Dobbs, gdn.	1884	2
867	Dobbs, George H.	Jane E. Dobbs, admr.	1884	3
868	Dobbs, James P.	Albert & James E. Dobbs, exors	1884	4
869	Dobbs, W.B.	W.J. Dobbs, admr.	1887	10
870	Dobbs, William M.	H.I. Seals; W.O. Dobbs, exor.	1892	5
871	Dobbs, W.P.	J.L. Dobbs, Temp. admr. Mrs. Alice Dobbs, Perm. admr.	1894-1897	21
872	Dobbs, O.S.	Mrs. M.C. Dobbs, widow	1894	1
873	Dobbs, David et al, minors/	D.W. Dobbs, gdn.	1895	5
874	Dobbs, Willie C.	Alice C. Dobbs, gdn.	1897	1
890	Dobbins, Drurie	Sarah F. Dobbins, widow	1890	1
896	Dodd, Julia & George, minors	Ann Dodd, gdn.	1884	2
897	Dodd, Henry C.	Marion S. Dodd, Temp. admr. T.M. Hooper, Perm. admr.	1884-1890	22
898	Dodd, Peter S.	Ann Dodd; G.S. Dodd, exors.	1885-1904	5
901	Dodgen, John L.	Thomas & Warren Dodgen, exors.	1885	3
902	Dodgen, O.M.	George N. Dodgen, exor.	1887	5
911	Donehoo, Laura L. et al, minors	William Donehoo, gdn.	1889	3
912	Donehoo, Cornelius	Barnett Donehoo, exor.	n.d.	2
914	Dorsett, M.J.	Mrs. Martha Dorsett, widow	1899	1
918	Drake, Cargill	Martha Drake, exor.	1881	2
922	Duncan, Bobbie, minor	Lena Duncan, gdn.	1885	1
923	Duncan, Martha B.	R.T. Nesbit, exor.	1896-1899	8
927	Dunn, D.D., minor	Nancy Dunn, gdn.	1868	4

928	Dunn, William	Sam R. McCleskey, admr.	1873-1874	15
929	Dunn, W.S.	I.J. Dunn & E.W. Frey, admr.	1890-1901	9
930	Dunn, I.J.	Mrs. M.E. Dunn; J.H. Dunn; E.W. Frey, admrs.	1895-1901	19
931	Dunn, William N.	W.G. Dunn, admr.	1895-1897	10
932	Dunn, J.M.	J.C. Grover, appraiser for 3 minor children	1897	1
933	Dunn, Mary, minor	J.H. Dunn, gdn.	1897	3
944	Dunton, Frances P.	Mary Dunton, Perm. admr.	1874	4
945	Dunton, John C. et al, minor	Nancy Dunton, gdn.	1885	5
946 ;	Dunwoody, Ellen C.	Chas. A. Dunwoody, exor.	1895	3
949	Dupree, E.M.	E.L. Litchfield, admr.	1864	1
950	Dupree, A.N.	Samuel A. Dupree, exor.	1866	11
951	Dupree, (B) D.D.	Samuel A. Dupree, exor.	1867	4
952	Dupree, minors	E. Faw, trustee	1872	3
953	Dupree, E.F.	M.M. Sessions	1883	2
954	Dupre, C.W.	Mrs. J.A. & W.A. Dupree, admr.	1895	5
960	Durham, Lacy W. minors (same as estate #962)	Robert Daniell, admr.	1866-1880	7
961	Durham, Charlot, minor	J.M. Tanner, gdn.	1875	4
962	Durham, A.N. et al	Robert Daniell, trustee June	1880	2
963	Durham, Mamie, et al, minors	Mattie J. Durham, gdn.	1896	3
964	Durham, J.O.	Laura J. Wigley, admr.	1898	5
972	Dutton, D.S.	A.N. Simpson, admr.	1865	4
973	Dutton, R.	A.N. Simpson, gdn.	1866	1
976	Dyson, James T.	W.P. McClatchey, admr.	1876-1883	25
977	Dyson, J.C. et al	J.F. Lindley, gdn.	1878	20
978	Dyson, Marion M., minors	Thomas H. Shockley, gdn.	1889	3
1028	Earle, Samuel	Mrs. E.W. Earle, exor. Mrs. A.L. Earle, admr(will ann)	1910	16
1031	Easley, Julia	T.D. Power, gdn.	1892	6
1032	Eason, Rasberry	O.R. Eason, admr.	1866	16
1033	Eason, Rebecca M., minor	Obed R. Eason, gdn.	1866	3
1034	Eason, Manister M., minor	John L. Eason, gdn.	1866	4
1035	Eason, Nathan, et al, minors	Emily Eason, gdn.	1886	5
1036	Eason, Emily	J.S. Eason, temp admr./perm. admr.	1869	12
1041	Echols, Wm. et al, minors	J.R. Echols, gdn.	1880	2
1047	Edwards, Simeon	W.N. Edwards, exor.	1893	4
1048	Edwards, A.C.	A.N. & A.M. Edwards, exors	1898-1900	7
1050	Edwards, Gussie, et al, minors	A.M. Edwards	n.d.	3
1051	Edwards, Annie W., minor	J.C. Fultz, gdn.	n.d.	1
1061	Eldridge, J.W.	Mrs. M.J. Eldridge, admr.	1895	4
1063	Eldridge, Willie, et al, minor	W.R. Power, gdn.	1895	1
1065	Ellington, C.	E.W. Frey, admr.	1895-1897	7
1069	Elliott, Elmira A.	William M. Dobbs, admr.	1881	9
1070	Elliott, G.L.	L.V. Elliott, gdn.	1882	4

1071	Elliott, M.M.	J.Z. Foster, Tem/Perm. admr.	1889	18
1072	Elliott, W.H.	F.A. Elliott, exor.	1896	4
1076	Ellison, Ezra T., minor	W.S. Williams, gdn.	1891	5
1077	Ellison, Lumpkin J.	Thomas Hairston, admr.	n.d.	2
1078	Elmer, J.B.	Edward Dunmead, admr.	1871	4
1079	Elmore, F.T., minor	Eliza Elmore, gdn.	1888	3
1080	Emanuel, David	Elizabeth Emanuel, exor.	1866	6
1081	Esler, Sara	?	1881	2
1082	Este, William M.	Mrs. Rosine M. Este, widow	1900	3
1084	Eubanks, Joseph	G.T. & I.B. Eubanks, exors.	1898	5
1086	Evans, Bertha & Edward P,/Jennie Evans, gdn.		1888	4
	minors			
	(Case number is erased & case repeated as:)			
1090	Evans, Bertha & Edward P/	J.E. Stephens, gdn.;	1900-1903	9
	minors	Dorothy Stephens, gdn.		
1087	Evins, George G.	Thom. Davenport	1889	4
1088	Evans, T.A.	E.H. Lindley, Temp/Perm adm.	1891	13
1089	Evans, Geo. C. et al,	Henrietta C. Evans, gdn.	1895	4
	minors			
1099	Fair, Sanford	Tena C. Fair, widow	1899	1
1110	Fannin, Benj.	C.C. Fannin, exor.	1890-1895	16
1112	Faw, Thom. A.	Walter P. Faw	1890	1
1115	Fenn, S.E.	Russell R. Petree, exor.	1890	5
1121	Flemming, Pliny	Mary L. Flemming, widow	1889	1
1128	Florence, William	M.J. & I.B. Florence, exors.	1884	21
		T.F. Hardage, adm de bonis non		
1129	Florence, Julia A.	I.B. Florence, trustee	1885	1
1135	Flournoy, George (inc)	John Griffis, gdn.	1881	1
1136	Floyd, A.T.	S.E. Floyd, widow	1876	1
1140	Foster, John L. et al,	J.G. Foster, gdn.	1882	2
	minors			
1141	Foster, Jensie M.	Mrs. M.J. Spragins, admr.	1895-1897	12
1148	Fowler, Frances	Balis Simpson, admr.	1883	7
1149	Fowler, Geo. T.	W.P. Fowler, exor.	1888	4
1152	Fraser, Anna	James L. Nichols, admr.	1874	9
		Rebecca L. Frazier, admr de bonis non		
790	Frasier, Elsie	Edward & William, minors	1895	1
1156	Frey, Martin W. (see 1161)	B.T. Frey, admr.	1895	4
1157	Frey, Martin et al, minors	/B.T. Frey, admr.	1895	3
		(carried to 1916)		
1171	Fridell, John L.	Lucinda Fridell, exor.	1876	4
1172	Fridell, J.L.	C.A. Fridell, Temp. admr.	1900	7
1175	Fuller, W.G.	William Fuller, exor.	1871-1874	15
		John B. Watson, exor.		
1176	Fuller, Laura, et al,	R.L. Waters, gdn.	1872	5
	minors (Transferred to Milcon Co.)			
1171	James A. Fuller	Mary Fuller, gdn.	1874	2
1178	Fuller, Helen, et al,	J.D. Fuller, gdn.	1891	5
	minors			
1181	Gable, Elizabeth, et al,	Joshua Segars, gdn.	1869	4
	minors			
1184	Gaines, James M.	Mrs. Mary Gaines, widow	1869	3
1185	Gaines, Edmond	Mary A. Gaines, admx.	1881	1

1189	Gann, Edward	Frances Gann, widow	1867	2
1190	Gann, John	Nancy E. Gann, widow	1881	1
1191	Gann, E.C., minor	G.B. Gann, gdn.	1882	2
1200	Gantt, Rosa L., et al, minors	J.L. Gantt, gdn.	1890	2
1202	Gappins, Jordan (col.)	Sam Earle, exor.	1888	4
1203	Gantt, Joseph	Elizabeth A. Gantt, exrx.	1884	2
1206	Garmon, James A.	Nancy Garmon, admr.	1878	4
1212	Garrison, T.W.	T.W. Garrison, Jr., Temp. adm.	1899	3
1213	Garrison, Dora, et al, minors	T.W. Garrison, Jr., gdn.	1898	3
1214	Garrison, Wm. L., et al, minors	J.A. Garrison, gdn.	1900-1909	5
1219	Garwood, F.P., et al, minors	Robt. B. Garwood, gdn.	1883	4
1224	Gault, William L.	Mary E. Gault, admr.	1866	6
1225	Gault, Edward N. (Transf. to Whitfield Co)	Elizabeth Gault, widow J.A.R. Hanks, admr.	1866	7
1226	Gault, William	Wm. R. Powers, admr.	1880-1885	7
1227	Gault, Emma et al, minors	W.P. Powers, gdn.	1880	6
1228	Gault, Edward et al, minors	T.G. Lawhorn, gen.	1880	8
1229	Gay, Eliza, minor	John Gay, gdn.	1889	1
1232	Geiger, Ann M.	Charles A. Geiger, admr.	1884	7
1233	Giger, Caroline, et al, minors	C.A. Giger, gdn. C.A. Giger, Jr., gdn.	1887-1895	16
1235	Gibson, Annie	John H. Glover, trustee	1864	1
1236	Gibson, John S.	J.F. Gibson Temp/Perm admr.	1883-1888	17
1237	Gibson, A.T., minor	Nancy A. Gibson, gdn.	1884	4
1238	Gibson, Frank T., minor	Nancy Gibson, gdn.	1884	5
1239	Gibson, I.R.	B.H. Carrie, exor.	1898-1902	6
1244	Gignillant, N.P.	Charlotte T. Gignillant, exor	1871	3
1245	Gigniliatt, Wm. R.	Janette Gigniliatt, exrx.	1882	3
1246	Gigniliatt, Joseph, et al, minors	Mrs. C.T. Gigniliatt, gdn.	1896	8
1250	Gilbert, W.E.	E.G. Gilbert, Temp/Perm admr.	1900-1903	23
1255	Gladen, Birtee	Amanda M. House, gdn.	1891	16
1256	Glasgo, Miles	H.M. Hammett, admr.	1867	4
1258	Glore, Geo. W.	Rhoda E. Glore, admr.	1865	20
1259	Glore, Abram	John T. Glore, admr.	1885-1888	12
1260	Glore, Tobitha (inc)	Alex Mable, gdn.	1886-1888	9
1261	Glore, A.E., et al, minors	Mary F. Glore, gdn.	1886-1899	11
1262	Glore, J.R.	Geo. W. & Mary F. Glore, Temp admr.; Geo. W. Glore, Perm.	1886-1889	17
1266	Glover, Miss Maria	John H. Glover, gdn.	1862	1
1267	Glover, Thos. W., minor	J.H. Glover, gdn.	1862	1
1268	Glover, Edward, minor	John H. Glover, gdn.	1862	1
1269	Glover, Jane S.	John H. Glover, gdn.	1862	1
1270	Glover, Joseph, minor	John H. Glover, gdn.	1862	1
1271	Glover, Annie	John H. Glover, gdn.	1862	1
1272	Glover, Edward, et al, minors	J.B. Glover, gdn.	1872	4

1273	Glover, J.B., Jr.	J.B. Glover, Sr., exor.	1897	3
1279	Gover, John E.	James E. Moss, admr.	1865	10
1280	Gover, Elza V., minor	Walter Manning, gdn.	1865	3
1286	Goodman, Mary et al, minors	Robert B. Goodman, gdn.	1885	3
1287	Goodman, Miriam P.	Wm. P. Alston, admr.	1892	5
1294	Goss, Dr. I.J.M.	Frances A. Goss, Temp/Perm adm.	1897	5
1295	Goulding, Matilda	Henry C. Reece; O.H. King, exors.	1895-1911	8
1296	Gragg, John	Geo. S. Avery, exor.	1891	6
1307	Gray, Daniel S.	Eliza Gray, Temp/Perm admr.	1873	11
1308	Gray, Eliza A.	William I. Goodwin, exor.	1878-1883	13
1309	Gray, Lou Ella	W.S. Williams, gdn.	1882-1888	12
1310	Gray, Virgil, et al, minors	Jennie (Burt) Gray, gdn.	1891-1910	9
1315	Graves, Eleanor	W.H. Welch, admr.	1883	1
1316	Gregg, E.A. (Trans. to Bartow Co.)	Thos. E. Smith, Temp/Perm adm. H.J. Gregg, Temp. admr.	1874	12
1319	Green, W.C.	N.M. Mayes, exor.	1870	5
1320	Green, Joseph P.	Joel A. Green, exor.	1870	7
1321	Green, Abraham	Edward Dunmead, Temp. admr. A.N. Simpson, Perm. admr.	1872	14
1322	Green, Napoleon B.	Mrs. Clotilda Green, admr.	1874-1877	12
1323	Green, Joel A.	Fannie Green, exrx	1886-1889	11
1324	Green, Clotilda	Geo. F. Gober, exor.	1892-1893	7
1325	Green, Clara J.	W.N. Green; I.P. Runyan, exor.	1894	4
1338	Greer, J.	Catherine Greer, admr.	1869-1872	7
1341	Grier, C.A., Jr., et al, minors	Dr. C.A. Grier, gdn.	1894	1
1345	Gresham, Watson	William Florence, admr. Will annexed de bonis non	1867	13
1346	Gresham, William	Green B. Bentley; Jane Gresham, admr.	1867-1871	17
1347	Gresham, Geo. W.	Mary A. Gresham; G.B. Bentley, N.A. Fowler, exors.	1868-1906	10
1348	Gresham, T.R., et al, minors (Trans. to Douglas Co.)	William P. Duncan, gdn.	1868	11
1349	Gresham, Amanda, minor	John B. Putnam, gdn.	1871-1874	6
1372	Grogan, Thomas W.	J.R. Humphries, admr.	1877-1882	9
1380	Groves, Joseph L., minor	M.A. Mayes, gdn.	1874	3
1381	Groves, Grave M.	T.L. Hunt, admr.	1889	8
1382	Groves, W.E.	Mrs. Grace M. Groves, widow	1886	1
1383	Groves, William F.	Camille Groves, exor.	1893	3
1385	Groover, J.N.	Wm. F. & Laura Groover, exors	1876-1878	8
1386	Groover, P.L.	J.M. Gable, Temp/Perm. admr.	1888-1890	18
1387	Groover, L.H., et al, minors	Mrs. L.P. Groover, gdn.	1888	2
1388	Groover, L.C.	J.P. Groover, admr.	1893-1894	12
1389	Groover, Fannie Mae	J.C. Groover, gdn.	1893	2
1390	Groover, M.C.	J.P. Groover, gdn.	1893	4
1405	Gunnell, W.B.	C.A. & G.A. Gunnell, exors.	1885-1902	6
1407	Gunter, David	D.P. Morris, exor.	1889	3
1409	Guess, Henry	Jerusha Guess, admr.	1867	19

1410	Guess, Willie L.	R.L. Guess, widow	1885	1
1411	Guess, Jerusha	J.N. & H.N. Guess, admr.	1892	13
1415	Hairston. Thomas J.	Thomas Hairston, admr.	1866	3
1416	Hairston, Julia, minor	Little P. Hairston, gdn.	1880	3
1418	Hall, Mrs. M.O.	J.B. Campbell, admr.	1874	7
1421	Hales, Elizabeth	T.J. Hales, admr.	1896-1897	7
1422	Hales, John	Amanda P. Hales, widow	1896	1
1423	Hamby, D.C.	J.M. Daniel, admr.	1864-1886	3
1424	Hamby, P.T., et al, minors	B.J. Hamby, gdn.	1866	6
1425	Hamby, T.K.	Mary Ann Hamby, exor.	1896	5
1430	Hamilton, Josephine, et al, minors	Robert Barber, gdn.	1862-1870	5
1437	Haney, William	Elizabeth J. Haney, widow	1866	7
1438	Haney, A.J.	J.A. Groover, admr.	1869	1
1439	Haney, Martha, et al, minors	Hezekiah Haney, admr.	1874	3
1440	Haney, William	Hezekiah Haney, admr.	1875-1886	9
1441	Haney, Daniel J.	Sarah A. Haney, admr.	1877	11
1442	Haney, G.W., et al, minors	Sarah A. Haney, gdn.	1880	2
1445	Hannan, Sam B.	Thomas M. Chandler, admr.	1877	5
1446	Hansell, Mrs. Caroline	A.J. Hansell, trustee	1866	1
1447	Hansell, Andrew J.	William Hansell, admr.	1881	10
1448	Hansell, Mrs. C.C.	W.A. Hansell, admr.	1890	6
1450	Harbin, Richard G.	James R. Harbin, Temp. admr.	1866-1887	22
1451	Harbin, Richard, et al, minors	Wm. (F.M.) Mitchell, gdn.	1866	11
1452	Same as #1451 but with M. Harbin (Ward)		1881	7
1453	Harbin, Joel	F.M. Mitchell, gdn.	1882	8
1454	Harbin, B.T., minor	James R. Harbin, gdn.	1866	4
1461	Hardman, James, et al, minors	Parks Hardman, gdn.	1863	1
1462	Hardman, Harriet M., minor	Matilda S. Hardman, gdn.	1864	1
1463	Hardman, John J.	Parks Hardman, gdn.	1864	4
1464	Hardeman, Parks	Thos. N. Hardman, admr.	1898-1902	16
1465	Hardeman, Naaman	H.M. Hammett, admr.	1870	10
1466	Hardeman, Ada, minor	T.G. McHarrity, gdn.	1885	2
1467	Hardeman, Ida Lee, minor	T.G. McCarrity, gdn.	1885-1902	3
1469	Harden, R.R.	Martha Harden, exrx.	1879	3
1475	Hqrdy, H.	T.M. Hardy, admr.	1891-1892	12
1476	Hardy, Jane	Ed. W. Frey Co., admr.	1899-1901	9
1477	Hardy, K. Luxicanah minor	J.H. Kincaid	1900	3
1484	Hatgrove, Ashbury	F.A. Hargrove, exor.	1879-1892	11
1488	Harlow, T.B.	Enoch Faw, admr.	1874	3
1489	Harlow, Cinthia	C.D. Phillips, exor.	1897	5
1490	Harper, Carrie P., et al, minors	Mrs C. Harper, gdn.	1895	3
1493	Harrington, Jackson	John B. Campbell, exor.	1879	5
1496	Harris, S.Y.	Mary C.A. Harris, admr.	1869	3
1497	Harris, Margaret L.	Ezikial Harris, admr.	1877-1881	8

1498	Harris, Thomas	Mattie Harris, widow	1882	1
1499	Harris, Mollie	Lemuel C. Harris, admr.	1883	8
1500	Harris, Bessie S. (nee Cason)	Lemuel C. Harris, gdn.; William L. McCreary, gdn.; Martha Gulliver, gdn.	1901	21
1516	Harrison, A.H.	Orlanda Awtey, Temp/Perm adm.	1883-1885	16
1517	Harrison, D.A., minor	Birding Rainey, gdn.	1883	1
1518	Harrison, J.P.	Samuel Earl, Temp/Perm. adm. J.M. & J.E. Fields, Perm. adm.	1887	7
1521	Hartsfield, Moses A.	Daniel Wright, admr.	1864	1
1522	Hartsfield, James M., minor	John L. Dodgen, gdn.	Dec.1863	3
1523	Hartsfield, James M.	Louise M.A. Hartsfield, Temp/Perm. admr.	1891-1901	23
1540	Hayes, J.O.	Louisa A. Hayes, exrx.	1878	4
1541	Hayes, Geo. N.	I.N. Hayes, Gdn.	1891	2
1560	Heggie, Mrs Carrie	A.C. Haggie, exor.	1894	7
1562	Helderbrand, J.E.	Celia Hilderbrand, admr.	1873	6
1563	Helderbrand, John E.	J.D. Baker, adm. de bonis non	1899-1900	7
1566	Hice, Florence, et al minors	Chas. E. Hill, gdn.	1885	7
1567	Hicks, S.A.	Polly Hicks, widow	1877	1
1568	Hicks, Henry L.	Robert B. Hicks, admr. Geo. Johnson	1880-1883	11
1570	Hicks, Robert S. et al. minors	A.S. Clay, gdn.	1892-1900	7
1575	Higgins, R.T.	Catherine Higgins, widow	1880	1
1578	Hilburn, L.J.	Elizabeth J. Hilburn, widow	1886	1
1581	Hill, John	Sylvester Hill, widow	1873	2
1582	Hill, R.C.	Robecca Hill, admrx.	1880	7
1583	Hill, J.C. et al, minors	John W. Hill, gdn.	n.d.	1
5004	Hill, John W.	Elvira S. & E.J. Hill, exors. E.G. Hill, admr.	1884	16
1584	Hill, Florence et al, minors	Charles E. Hill, gdn.	1887	2
1585	Hill, L.B.	Mrs. L.A. Hill, admr.	1891	1
1586	Hill, Curtis J.	Mary E. Hill, widow	1893	1
1587	Hill, N.A. (inc)	A.Y. Moss, gdn.	1893	3
1588	Hill, T.A.	J.J. Hill et al, heirs	1899	2
1602	Hyde, J.W.	Aveline Hyde, widow	1892	1
1603	Hyde, Mary A.	E.W. Hyde, admr.	1897	4
1606	Hembre, S.G.	Sarah Ann Hembree, admr. with will annexed	1865-1868	17
1607	Hembree, Warren W.	E.J. Hembree, admr.	1866	7
1608	Hembree, Elizabeth J.	Newton J. Fenn, admr.	1867-1870	10
1609	Hembree, Cicero, minor	F.M. Hembree, gdn.	1869-1877	5
1613	Henderson, G.W. (see estate below)	Hugh Harris; William Henderson; Temp/Perm. admr.		
1614	Henderson, G.W. (see estate above)	High Harris, admr.	1905	4
1615	Henderson, S.S.	N.W. Smith, admr.	1872	6
1616	Henderson, D.B., minor	David S. Wiley, gdn.	1873	4
1617	Henderson, John W., minor	T.J. Hightower, gdn.	1877	5
1618	Henderson, Will	Adaline Henderson, widow	1882	1

1627	Henry, Andrew J.	John C. Groover, admr.	1866-1872	16
1633	Herrington, Ilsa	James T. Echols, admr.	1894-1898	11
1635	Hirsch, Sarah, minor	Raphail Hirsch, gdn.	1874	2
1636	Hirsch, Raphral	Morris Hirsch, exor. Mrs. Mena Hirsch, exrx.	1896	19
1641	Hogan, Mary	L.L. Vernon, exor.	1896	3
1642	Holcombe, Jabez J.	Mary Holcomb, exrx.; E.C. Stancil adm de bonis non with will annexed	1870-1883	13
1643	Holcombe, Willie, minor	Mary A. Holcombe, gdn.	1882	5
1648	Holford, John	John B. Campbell, admr.	1879	5
1649	Holland, Robert	Randa Holland, widow	1868	1
1650	Holland, R.E.N., minor	William D. Anderson, gdn.	1871-1880	8
1658	Holmes, Trezevant, et al, minors	Margaret Holmes, gdn.	1893	1
1660	Hooper, Thomas	Thomas M. Hooper, admr.	1879	4
1662	Hopkins, Henry J.	Charity Hopkins, exrx.	1873	3
1663	Hopkins, Charity	E.H. Lindley, Temp admr.; I.C. Butner, Temp/Perm admr.	1878	22
1664	House, John	Eliza A. House, widow	1866	2
1664?	House, William T. minor	Eliza House, gdn. Daniel S. Gray, gdn.	1867	11
1666	House, John G.	Wiley Kemp, admr.	1868	4
1667	House, Wm. T. minor	J.G. House, gdn.	1873	9
1668	House, William	Henry House & Minoca Grogan, exor.	1876	5
1669	House, Jacob	Wm. R. House, exor.	1882-1883	11
1670	House, F.C.	Pamelia House, exor.	1883	2
1671	House, Sarah	S.N. House, gdn.	1883-1887	9
1672	House, Henry	L.A. Rainey & H.F.(G) House, exor.	1890	8
1679	Howe, Millard A.(F)	T.G. Echols, Temp/Perm admr.	1895	9
1680	Howe, Lucinda R.	Mattie F. Riley, admr.	1896	3
1681	Howell, Isaac	H.P. Howell, admr.		3
1682	Howell, Clement C.	A. Baker, Temp. admr. Mrs. C.V. Howell, admr.; David Love, admr.	1867-1877	39
1683	Howell, Auguste, et al, minors	Mrs. C.V. Howell, gdn.	1878-1889	4
1689	Hoy, Andrew C.	George W. Gresham, exor.	1890	4
1697	Huff, J.F.	W.T. Hiff, admr.	1891-1893	10
1701	Hughes, James G.	Laura H. Hughes, exrx.	1894	2
1702	Hughes, Katie, et al, minors	Saxon A. Anderson, gdn.; Mrs. Laura H. Hughes, gdn.	1894	14
1709	Hughson, Mrs. K.M.	E.W. Frey, Temp/Perm. admr.	1900	8
1710	Hull, Ruby et al, minors	M.J. Abbott, gdn.	1892	3
1711	Humphrey, Rachel	I.N. Gray, exor.	1875-1882	15
1712	Humphries, J.R.	Mrs. O.H. Humphries, exrx.	1900	7
1715	Hunt, Cicaro A., minor	Rebecca A. Hunt, gdn.	1874	3
1716	Hunt, Elisha	Hiram Adams, exor.	1872-1875	13
1717	Hunt, M.E. et al, minors	Thos. W. Hunt, gdn.	1886	3
1718	Hunt, John J. Sr.	T.L. Hunt, admr.	1899	5
1719	Hunt, Mrs. I.D.	T.L. Hunt, admr.	1900	5

1732	Husk, Martha	Margaret F. Kirkham, exrx.	1891	4
1733	Huson, Thos. P. (Transferred to Bartow County)	John G. Stockes, Temp admr.	1868	
1735	Hutchins, Harris	Richard Earle, admr.	1885-1899	13
1740	Inzer, Mark P.	Rebecca Inzer, exrx.	1877	1
1741	Irby, Amanda	John R. Parnell, Temp/Perm adm	1873	11
1742	Irving, A.F.	A.H. Irvine, admr.	1880	3
1743	Irvine, Mrs. S.E.	A.H. Irvine, exor.	1900-1901	5
1747	Ivins, George	Thos. Davenport, admr.	1883	5
1749	Jackson, Martha	Joseph Chastine, trustee	1870	1
1750	Jackson, H.C.	D.W. Orr, exor.	1873-1875	10
1751	Jackson, Shadrach	A.J. Cheney, exor.	1873-1879	15
1752	Jackson, Gola, et al, minors	W.P. Jackson, gdn.	1888	2
1753	Jackson, J.C.	Martha J. Jackson, widow	1889	1
1757	See estate #1764 Jackson, Wm.	Ann Jackson, widow	1888	2
1774	James, S.T.	R.H. White, admr.	1876	1
1775	James, John	Sarah James, widow	1883	1
1780	Jenkins, Albert F., minor/V.E. Jenkins, gdn.		1891	
1784	Jervey, Mrs. Myra McCrea, minor	Mrs. Myra McCrea, gdn.	1900	4
1785	Jiles, D.G.	Ella Jiles, widow	1891	1
1788	Johns, Richmond C.	Johns, John D., Temp/Perm adm	1881-1883	16
1789	John, Dock	J.C. Johns, gdn.	1883	4
1791	Johnson, Joel	Daniel Wright, admr.	1864	1
1792	Johnson, James M.	H.M. Hammett, Temp/Perm. adm.	1867	13
1793	Johnson, Elander	C.T. Johnson, heirs; Mrs. N.E. Inzer	1873	1
1794	Johnson, Ben	Harriett Johnson, widow	1881	1
1795	Johnson, Thomas	Marie Groover, Temp admr.	1886	3
1796	Johnson, Durham	G.P. Johnson, admr.	1892-1893	10
1797	Johnson, Sallie, minor	Frances Chriswill, gdn.	1897	1
1824	Johnston, E.F. et al, minors	John B. McCollum, gdn.; Charles Johnston, gdn.	1880	7
1825	Johnston, W.M.	James T. & Chas. Johnston, exor	1880-1883	18
1826	Johnston, Ella, minor	C.E. Johnston, gdn.; J.N. Jolley, gdn.	1884	6
1828	Jones, Sam	Alexander Miller, exor.	1876	4
1829	Jones, Russell	Sarah A. Jones, widow	1887	1
1830	Jones, Sarah A.	J.B. Alexander, Temp/Perm adm.	1887	12
1831	Jones, Lula (Telula) B., minor	B.A. Bell, gdn.	1889	4
1832	Jones, S.A.	T.D. Power, admr.	1890-1891	6
1833	Jones, Jane	J.Z. Foster, admr.	1888-1889	10
1834	Jones, R.A.	C.J. Shelverton, Temp/Perm adm	1898	5
1835	Jones, J.H.	Ida Jones, admrx.	1899-1900	10
1856	Jourdan, N.C. et al, minors	Frances A. Jourdan, gdn.	1870	6
1857	Jourdan, Elbert P.	John T. Glore, admr.; Frances Jourden, widow	1871	11
1858	Jourden, James	A.P. Dodgen, admr.	1881	9

1859	Jordan, Wm. M.	E.A. Jourdon, exor.	1895	6
1860	Jourdan, Frances A.	N.C. Jordon, admr.	1896-1901	10
1861	Jordan, Mrs. E.A.(inc)	J.R. Jordan, gdn/admr.	1899-1900	8
1864	Julian, Samuel	H.M. Hammett	1870	2
1871	Kelpin, W.M.	Joseph C. Kelpin, exor.	1897	5
1872	Kelly, Julia (Col.)	Joe P. Legg, admr.	1898-1901	6
1873	Kemp, Solomon	Hiram Bennett, admr.	1865-1870	9
1874	Kemp, Mary, minor (transferred to Alabama)	Handy Harris, gdn.	1870	6
1875	Kemp, Moses	Marinda Kemp, exor.	1871	3
1876	Kemp, Ira F.	John McClain, admr.	1874-1875	13
1877	Kemp, Jennett, et al, minor	Mary J. Kemp, gdn.	1876	15
1878	Kemp, Wiley	John B. Kemp, admr.	1878-1881	12
1879	Kemp, Claudia	O.A. Kemp, gdn.	1883	3
1880	Kemp, Burrell	James C. Giles; James Kemp, Temp; J.C. Giles, Perm. admr.	1885	10
1881	Kemp, Alsey Frances (inc)	Alsey Kemp, gdn.	1888	3
1882	Kemp, Alsey	G.N. Gignilliat, exor.; Mrs. C.M. Trippe admr., with will annexed	1895	15
1883	Kemp, J.S.	A.W. Kemp & E.L. Mayes, exrs.	1896	4
1884	Kemp, M.J. (inc)	Mrs. L.A. Kemp, gdn.	1900	1
1901	Kimberly, J.E.	C.E. Kimberly, exor.	1893	4
1905	Kendricks, Dick	Rosa Kendricks, widow	1883	1
1919	King, Barrington	Chas. B. King, admr.; James Robertson, adm de bonis non	1866-1873	34
1920	King, Thomas E.	H.M. Hammett, admr.; W.J. Hudson, admr.	1867	15
1921	King, John Reed et al, minors	Mary R. Townsend, gdn. (Madison Co., Ala)	1869	2
9122	King, Harris M. et al, minors	Sarah E. King, gdn.; Sarah T. Ledford, nee King	1871	6
1923	King, Mrs. F.P.	J.R. King, trustee	1874	1
1924	King, B.	E.B. King, admr.	1875	2
1925	King, Mrs. Frances P.	Enoch Faw, exor.	1882-1894	11
1926	King, T.E.	J.R. King, admr.	1882	4
1927	King, Catherine M.	Wm. P. Baker, admr.	1887	8
1928	King, B.	W.E. Baker, admr.	1888-1893	21
1939	Kirk, John	H.M. Hammett, admr.; will ann.	1866-1888	11
1940	Kirk, George	H.M. Hammett, admr. will ann.	1866	1
1941	Kirk, Martha et al, min.	Wm. J. Eubanks, gdn. (E.L. Braswell shown on letter & bond books)	1866-1889	14
1942	Kirk, James F.	Mrs. Ann Kirk, widow	1897	1
1943	Kirk, John	F.M. Kirk, admr.	1899	8
1947	Kirkham, James M. et al, minors	James T. Kirkham	1867	3
1949	Kirkpatrick, T.M.	Parthena & John W. Kirkpatrick, Temp/Perm adm; Mrs. K.K. Lindley, admr. de bonis non	1882	22
1950	Kirkpatrick, J.W.	Mrs. S.A. Kirkpatrick, Temp/ Perm. admr.	1891-1895	17
1951	Kirkpatrick, W.L., minor	Mrs. K.K. Lindley, gdn.	1892	3
1952	Kirkpatrick, Parthen	Enoch Faw, admr. de bonis non	1894-1903	11

67

1953	Kirkpatrick, Hugh et al, minors	S.A. Kirkpatrick, gdn.	1895	3
1956	Kirksey, Mrs. M.E.	T.D. Power, admr.	1891-1895	8
1957	Kiser, John	Marion C. Kiser, exor.	1868-1871	11
1959	Kiser, Wiley J.	Winifield T. Worley, Temp/ Perm. admr.	1881	23
1959	Kiser, Nancy	W.T. Worley, Temp. admr.	1884	7
1963	Knight, E.M.E.	E.N. Knight, Temp/Perm admr.	1876	15
1964	Knight, Noel B.	Mrs. Hattie H. Knight, admr.; Mrs. N.B. Knight, widow	1887-1888	8
1965	Knight, H.H.	A.J. Harrison, exor.	1889	3
1966	Knight, N.E.	Mrs. N.J. Knight, widow	1895	1
1973	Kolb, Valentine	Mrs. Eliza Kolb, exorx.	1866	2
1974	Kolb, Clara, et al, minors	Mrs. Eliza Kolb, gdn.	1869	3
1975	Kolb, Sarah W., et al, minors	Perin Turner, gdn.	1870	6
1980	Mrs. Edna Lackey	W.R. Montgomery, exor.	1896	2
1981	Lackey, W.T.	Sarah E. Lackey, widow; (no admr.)	1883	1
1982	Lamar, A.H.	S.B. Lamar, Temp. admr.	1882	2
1996	Lane, Charles, et al, minors	J.C. Fultz, gdn.	1866	14
1997	Lane, Caroline T.	James G. Lane, exor.	1867-1872	6
1998	Lane, Mark A.	Thomas Manning, admr.	1868	5
1999	Lane, C.W.	John C. Fultz, admr.	1873	2
2000	Lane, R.A.	Matilda Lane, admr.	1874	3
2001	Lane, Matilda (Transferred to Whitfield Co., Geo.)	T.H. Harlan, exor.	1887	6
2005	Lannea, Eliza G., et al, minors	John F. Lanneau, gdn.	1867	2
2006	John F. Lanneau	A.N. Simpson, exor.	1867	5
2007	Lasiter, Henry	Eliza Neese, admr.	1878-1882	15
2008	Lasiter, Henrietta	J.E. Lasiter, gdn.	1880	3
2009	Latimer, Hezekiah R.	W.D. Anderson, admr.	1866-1869	12
2010	Latimer, Ruben	R.M. Benson & J.T. Latimer, admr.	1879-1887	13
2011	Lawhorn, Sam R.	R.E. Lawhorn, admr.	1883-1889	7
2012	Lawrence, Amanda M.	Samuel Lawrence, admr.	1866	3
2-12A	Laurence, Robert Jr.	Alex. A. Laurence, admr.	1895	9
2017	Leake, James P., minor	M.G. Whitlock, gdn.	1869	4
2019	Lee, Nichols	Asa Darby, admr.	1890-1891	11
2030	Lemon, William	Garrett S. Oglesby, admr.; will annexed	1867	18
2031	Lemon, Sara A., minor	H.M. Hammett, gdn. Sara N. Boyd, gdn.	1868	11
2032	Lemon, Robert	Lucinda Lemon & W.R. Montgomery, admr.	1881	9
2033	Lemon, Robert	J.D. Anderosn, admr.; will ann.	1895-1897	11
2034	Lemon, Robert, Sr.	E.W. Frey, admr.	1896-1900	12
2048	Lindley, Jonathan	Dr. A. Reynolds, exor.	1868	2
2049	Lindley, John B.	E.A. Lindley, exor.	1872	3

2050	Lindley, E.H.		1877-1883	12
2051	Lindley, Thomas	John C. Butner, exor.	1882-1895	7
2052	Lindley, E.H.	Jas. F.P. Lindley, admr., de bonis non	1885	3
2053	Lindley, John T.	Maggie Lindley, exor.	1893	3
2062	Lester, Margaret J.	T.D. Power, admr.	1893	4
2063	Lester, Susan	Louisa Porter, admr.	1896	4
2064	Levell, Edward F.	Johnson Williams, admr.	1866-1870	15
2066	Leavel, Charles F.	N.A. Leavel, gdn.	1869	3
2067	Leavel, A.J., minor	V.L. Goodwin, gdn.	1878	2
2069	Lewis, John	J.H. Lewis, exor.	1881	7
2070	Lewis, Agnes, et al, minors	Emma Lewis, gdn.	1883	1
2076	Litchfield, Luther, min.	Lemuel Litchfield, gdn.	1877	14
2077	Litchfield, E.L.	L.A. Litchfield, Temp/Perm adm	1883	15
2078	Litchfield, L.A.	Mary K. Litchfield, exor.	1891	12
2079	Litchfield, L.O., minor	Mary P. Smith, gdn.	1891-1897	14
2088	Love, S.E. et al, minors	D.K. Love, gdn.	1886	9
2089	Love, Mrs. M.S.H.	A.J. Harrison, Temp admr.	1899	3
2096	Loveless, James	H.H. Loveless, admr.; Sara Loveless, widow	1867	8
2097	Loveless, S.J.	L.D. Maybee, admr.	1889	4
2110	Lowery, James	George P. Lowery, admr.	1880	6
2111	Loyd, Mary	D.A. King, Trustee	1866	5
2118	Lyle Hugh G.	Amos S. Waye & James P. Lyle, exors; T. Stephens, admr. w/will annexed	1871-1878	12
2119	Lyle, Nancy L.	Timothy Stephens & John G. Camobell, exors.	1879	7
2214	McAfee, Noah	E.H. Myers, gdn.	1891	5
2215	McAfee, Harriet	Newton A. Morris, admr.	1895	5
2223	McCampbell, J.C.	A.N. Simpson, admr.	1874	7
2224	McCandlish, Elizabeth, et al, minors		1898	3
2228	McClain, James P., et al minors	Larmelia E. McClain, gdn.	1866	4
2231	McClarity, Sarah T. (See estate #2326)	Thomas J. Perkerson, gdn.	1867	6
2232	McClarity, Nancy A.(inc)	Sarah McClarity, basis for gdnship; W.S. Brown, admr.	1868	21
2235	McClellan, William C. (See estate #2333)	Thomas McClellan T. admr.	1882	6
2237	McClesky, John M., & Benjamin, minors (See estate #2239)	Samuel R. McClesky, gdn.	1888	4
2238	McClesky, Ida, minor	J.F. Kennett, gdn.	1888	4
2239	McClesky, I.F. & F.B.	S.R. McClesky, gdn.	1891	2
2249	McConnell, Mary A.	W.J. McClatchey, gdn.	1865	3
2250	McConnell, Wiley	Thomas H. Moore, admr.	1866	1
2251	McConnell, James	J.P. McConnell, exor.	1887	6
2256	McCurdy, Daniel	Amanda J. McCurdy, widow	1874	1
2257	McCurdy, James	Wm. McCurdy & Archy J. McCurdy, admrs.	1888	3
2268	McDonald, Chas. J.	A.S. Atkinson, trustee; T. Kirkpatrick & D.M. Dunwoody, exors.	1870	10

2269	McDonald, C.J.C.	A.C. Edwards, Trustee	1887	3
2272	McEachern, D.N.	John N. McEachern, exor.	1896-1899	13
2274	McElrath, John M.	W.A. McElreath, exor.	1894-1896	7
2275	McElreath, Alda & Eliza	W.A. McElreath, gdn.	1899	3
2280	McEver, John L.	Mrs. E.A. McEver, admr.; will annexed	1893	9
2285	McGarity, Archibald (See #2395 Megarity, Archibald)	Thomas C. McGarity, admr.	1883-1893	12
2286	McGee, G.M.	Henry P. Sauls, exor.	1883	1
2287	McGee, F.M.	Chalotte McGee, exor.	1887	3
2290	McGinty, Henry C., et al, minors	James E. McGinty, gdn.	1866	3
2291	McGinty, H.E.	James E. McGinty, gdn.	1867	1
2292	McGinty, Thomas	W.W. Carroll, admr.	1869	9
2293	McGriff, E.O. nee Durham	H.C. McGriff, gdn.	1880	3
2295	McHan, Barney	James & Allison McHan co-exors	1881	3
2300	McIntosh, A.C.	Amela McIntosh, admr.; S. Emma Massey, admr (de bonis non) W.W. Scott t. admr.	1885	29
2301	McIntosh, Lillie M. & Dora F., minors	W.G. Stovall, gdn.	1886	3
2304	McKee, Isaac M.	Henry Sauls, exor.	1883	2
2305	McKinney, Thomas	May McKinney, widow; W.W. Carroll, admr.	1871	3
2318	McLain, Charles P.	W.S. McLain, exor.	1897-1898	9
2326	McLarty (McClarty), Sara T.; (See #2231)	Thomas J. Perkerson, gdn.	1867	6
2327	McLarty, Nancy (inc)	Alexander Mclarty, gdn.	1870	4
2328	McLarty, Nancy (See #2232)	W.L. Brown, gdn.	1885	1
2329	McLarity, James	John D. Perkerson, admr.	1890	5
2333	McLellan, W.C. (See #2235)	Thomas C. McLellan, admr.	1883	1
2335	McLeod, Anna C.	Sara F. King, admr.	1873	10
2336	McLeod, Mary A.	William H. Burrough & Ann C. Miller, exor.	1875	13
2347	McMillan, Willis (See #2349)	B.H. Carrie, exor.	1895-1900	7
2348	McMullin, W.A.	P.A. McMullin, widow	1884	1
2349	McMullan, Willis (See #2347)	B.H. Carrie	1900	4
2361	McWilliams, Mary, et al, minors	Nancy McWilliams, gdn.	1874	3
2122	Mable, Robert	Alexander & Joseph Mable exors	1885-1919	33
2126	Maddox, J.M., et al, minors	N.E. Gunnin, gdn.	1897-1902	5
2128	Magbee, Labon	M.J. Magbee, admr.	1863	4
2132	Malone, Dr. L.	Lizzie B. Malone, widow	1873	1
2139	Maner, Hosea	J.Z. Foster, admr.	1887-1899	13
2140	Maner, Alfred	Wm. E. Manor & A.T. Hill exors	1887-1888	10
2141	Maner, Wm. A.	J.W. Boling, gdn.	1891	5
2142	Maner, Wm. G.	George A. Maner, T. admr.	1891-1892	13
2146	Manning, Simpson	Thomas Manning et al, admr.	1866-1871	10
2147	Manning, Ambrose	Mary Manning, widow	1867	2

2148	Manning, Mary A.	H.M. Hammett, T & P admr.	1867-1871	12
2149	Manning, Regenia, minor	John C. Fultz, gdn.	1868	13
2150	Manning, C.J.	Mary E. Manning, admr.	1897-1900	15
2157	Mansfield, Wm. L.	Wm. T. Winn, admr.	1873-1882	18
2158	Mansfield, Mrs. Louisa	John A. Manget, admr.	1899	7
2159	Map, J.C.	Harriet M. Durham, admr.	n.d.	2
2160	Maples, Sara F. (See #2831)	R.N. Holland, gdn.	1886	3
2161	Marchman, R.H., Sr.	R.H. Marchman, Jr.	1892	5
2165	Marks, Dennis	Amira Marks, admr.	1884	6
2168	Martin, Nathan (Transferred from Carroll County)	John P. Martin, exor.	1876-1887	14
2169	Martin, L.E., minor	G.J. Martin, gdn.	1899	3
2178	Mason, Churchill	Joshua Jackson, T. admr.	1880	5
2179	Mason, Lizzie, minor	Henry Mason, gdn.	1898	2
2183	Mathews, Alice & Ida, minors	W.T. Akers, gdn.	1877-1883	10
2184	Mathews, John, Dr.	W.T. Akers, admr.	1877-1883	10
2185	Mathews, James H.	Uriah Mathews, admr.	1895	4
2195	Maxwell, Sara L.	J.C. Maxwell & W.E. Gilbert, admr., will annexed	1895-1899	20
2199	Mayfield, G.W., minor	John G. Wigley, gdn.	1880-1883	8
2200	Mayfield, Daisy L.	C.J. Perry, gdn.	1896	9
2201	Mays, Wm.	E.L. Litchfield, admr.	1866	1
2202	Mays, Wm.	Thomas A. Gober, exor.	1871	13
2203	Mayes, Edward	John P. Mayes, admr.	1884	8
2204	Mayes, H.M.	John N. & Samuel F. Mayes, exors.	1884-1886	10
2205	Mayes, Elizabeth	James P. Brockman, exor.	1891-1893	7
2206	Mayes, Mrs. A.P., minor	A.C. Mayes, gdn.	1900	3
2210	Mayson, George W.	Henry H. Mayson, exor.	1895	4
2211	Mayson (Mason), Terannah et al, minors	Henry Mason, gdn.	1896	6
2375	Megarity, Archibald (See #2285)	Thomas C. Megarity, admr.	1883-1893	12
2376	Meinert, Annie, Henry, Grover, & John, minors	Henry Meinert, gdn.	1898-1910	8
2377	Mell, J.E.	S. Mell, admr.	1891	5
2378	Melton, James W.	Emeline Melton, widow	1885	1
2385	Miles, John	J.B. Miles, admr.	1876-1878	13
2388	Miller, George A.	John Miller, exor.	1865-1869	9
2389	Miller, Charles	Mattie Miller, widow	1876	1
2390	Millen, Ann C.	Sara E. & Wm. King, admr.	1881-1883	12
2391	Miller, John H.	David T. Miller & Charles B. Holleman, admrs.	1885-1892	24
2400	Minkinette, Francis R.	Francis Minhinette, exr.	1886	3
2401	Minton, M.W.	John Minton, exor.	1874	3
2402	Minton, Rosanna	Dan S. Arnold, exor.	1874-1878	6
2405	Merritt, Mrs. F.E.	F.P. Reynolds, admr.	1891-1893	7
2408	Mitchel, Hardy	John & Henry Mitchell, exors W.C. Kemp, admr (de bonis non)	1868-1888 will annexed	15
2409	Mitchell, Martha, et al, minors	John Mitchell, gdn.	1871	3

2410	Mitchel, Zula G. (nee Ray)	Penn Mitchel, gdn.	1890	5
2411	Mitchel, John	A.J. Reeves, admr.	1892-1893	11
2412	Mitchel, Thomas L., min.	J.G. Lazenby	1893	6
2419	Myers, Mrs. Mary A.F.	H.V. Reynolds, admr.	1893-1897	9
2421	Mohorn, John A., minor	Geo. W. Mohorn, gdn.	1881	2
2422	Monk, James G.	James M. Monk, exor.	1887	3
2423	Montgomery, H. T., minor	W.R. Montgomery, gdn.	1866	4
2424	Montgomery, Wm. R., et al, minors	E.C. Harris, gdn.	1867	2
2428	Moon, John W.	C.D. & I.N. Moon, admr.	1876-1879	19
2429	Moon, C.C. et al, minors	Mary J. Moon, gdn.	1876	3
2430	Moon, M.W.	C.D. Moon, gdn.	1876	3
2431	Moon, Elizabeth	John J. Grey, admr.	1881	6
2432	Moon, Thomas J.	Elizabeth Moon, exor.	1889	3
2433	Moon, Jessie M.	J.O. Allen, admr.	1891-1899	15
2434	Moon, C.D.	H.B. & D.C. Moon, admr.	1899-1900	22
2439	Moon, J.L. et al, minors	Melissa Moon, gdn.	1876	3
2456	Moore, Jeremiah A.	Susannah Moore, admr.	1866-1871	15
2457	Moore, Elizabeth B.	A.M Northcutt T.& P. admr.	1870	12
2458	Moore, John	Elliott Moore, admr.	1871	7
2459	Moore, John C.	Rebecca Moore, exor.	1897	3
2460	Moore, Mrs. R.A.	Mrs. Hattie L. Harden, T. admr	1899	3
2478	Morgan, David	W.A. Austin, exor. Sarah C. Morgan, widow	1868	17
2482	Morris, Newton	Margaret Morris, admr.	1885	10
2483	Morris, Newton M., et al, minors	Mrs. M.A. Morris, gdn.	1891	11
2484	Morris, Joel E.	T.D. Power T. admr. R.N. Holland T & P admr.	1891-1903	31
2485	Morris, Thompson	Oliver J. Morris, exor.	1895	7
2499	Morse, N.A.	E.W. Frey, admr.	1894	19
2500	Mosley, Elizabeth	G.O. Moseley, admr.	1866-1870	12
2501	Mosley, H.H.	S.G. Mosely, P., admr.	1882-1888	9
2509	Moss, Alfred	W.W. Moss, admr.	1863	2
2510	Moss, James C.	Harriet Moss (nee Durham)adm.	1881	24
2516	Motes, Silas	Lafaette Hauck, admr.	1880	1
2521	Murdock, William	Sara Murdock, widow	1866	2
2522	Murdock, J.R.	Mrs. Annie Murdock, widow	1899	1
2526	Murphy, Arthur F.	Jennie F. Murphy, admr.	1898-1899	11
2527	Murphy, Arthur F., minor	Jennie F. Murphy, gdn. R.W. Boone, gdn.	1899-1905	10
2534	Nash, John J., minor	M.H. Nash, gdn.	1873	5
2535	Neal, Ernest, minor	T.A. Sewell, gdn.	1875	3
2539	Neil, S.W.	W.P. Mosley, admr.	1887	11
2541	Neese, A.M.	Sara M. Neese, exor.	1893	3
2547	Nesbitt, Mary Ann	James W. Davis, exor.	1865-1870	8
2549	Nettles (Netts) Mary, et al, minors	Martaret Nettles, gdn.	1875	6
2550	Neufville, Ed L., et al, minors	John Cunningham, gdn.	1886	4
2552	Newell, D.J.	John W. Newell, exor.	1869	2

2559	Nichols, W.T.	Patrinia Nichols, exor.	1874	2
2560	Nichols, James	Mary C. Nichols, admr.	1881	5
2561	Nichols, Fannie	W.K. Smith, admr, will ann.	1890-1892	9
2572	Noe (Noah) Bennett	Sidney Noe, exor; John Dorsey P. admr., will annexed	1869-1878	14
2574	Northcutt, J.J.	R.H. Northcutt, exor.	1888	11
2575	Northcutt, Alfred M.	J.J. Northcutt, exor.	1897	6
2605	Osburn, William	Bluford Osburn, P. admr.	1871	10
2606	Osborn, Martha, et al, minors	B.A. Osborn, gdn.	1875	3
2614	Owen, Jennie, minor	George S. Owen, T. gdn.	1868	3
2615	Owen, Hiram	George Owen, exor.	1889-1891	14
2616	Owens, E.H. et al, minor	George S. Owen, gdn.	1891	1
2626	Pace, Hardy	Solomon R. Pace, admr.	1865-1884	27
2627	Pace, Stephen	Mary L. Pace, widow	1872	3
2628	Pace, James L.	Henry T. Pace, Temp admr.; W.N. Pace, Perm. admr.	1880	12
2629	Pace, L. Steva, et al, minors	Mary L. Davis, gdn.	1881	2
2630	Pace, Russell	Mary A. Pace, T. admr. & exor	1892	8
2639	Paden, R.S.	Mrs. Elizabeth S. Paden, exor.	1876	4
2642	Page, Ebenezer	Eliza A. Page, widow	1889	1
2643	Paige, Sarah C.	Joseph Paige, exor.	1897	3
2647	Pair, James L.	Sarah Pair	1877	1
2648	Pair, James M., et al, minors	S.P. Pair, gdn.	1879	2
2649	Pair, John A.	T.J. Pair, admr.	1890-1892	13
2650	Pair, J.A.	W.E. Pair, admr.	1890	6
2651	Pair, J.W.	Mrs. Frances Pair, widow	1898	1
2662	Palmer, Epenola, et al, minors	Wm. J. Palmer, gdn.	1867	6
2663	Palmer, W.J.	M.B. Hollinshed, admr.	1886-1888	12
2668	Parks, James	E.E. Parks, admr.	1864	1
2669	Parks, James	E.M. Parks, admr.	1871	9
2670	Parks, Elan N.	Mary J. Parks, admr.	1885	4
2676	Payne, Julia F.	W.R. Power, T. admr.	1896	1
2680	Peacock, Louis, et al, minors	Nathan F. Phillips, gdn.	1864	1
2681	Peacock, Payton A.	Mrs. E.C. Peacock; John W. Sewell T & P admr.	1883-1883	15
2683	Peek, James M.	N.M. Madden, admr.	1889	3
2684	Peaster, Bony P.	A.H. Irvine T & P admr.	1893-1895	13
2688	Pickens, John B., et al, minors	D.D. Barfield, gdn.	1866	11
2689	Pickens, R.H.	H.M. Hammett, admr.	1866-1888	11
2690	Pickens, M.C., minor	S.F. Mayes, gdn.	1877	4
2691	Pickens, M.J., minor	Mary P. Pickens, gdn.	1877	4
2692	Pickens, John D.	Matilda Pickens; John D. Gantt, admr.	1893-1898	12
2693	Pickens, Martha J., incomp.	Mrs. L.A. Kemp, gdn.	1900	3
2697	Pierce, Thomas M., et al, minors	Susan H. Pierce, gdn.	1890	2

73

2699	Pilgram, Burrill	I.A. Rice, exor.	1899-1900	8
2702	Penn, Benjamin J.	M.M. Phillips, exor.	1890	4
2708	Perkinson, John	W.J. Hudson, admr.; A. Reynolds, P. admr.	1874-1877	11
2709	Perkinson, Nancy S., et al, minors	C.V. Hollamon, gdn.	1876	12
2710	Perkerson, T.D.	Wm. H. Perkerson, Mary Perkerson, admr.	1876-1883	20
2711	Perkerson, James H., et al, minors	Mary Perkerson, gdn.	1879	13
2712	Perkerson, O.A.	Mary Perkerson, ex admr/gdn	1880	3
2713	Perkerson, Mariah	H.M. Putnam, admr.	1893-1894	8
2714	Perkerson, J.N.	Eliza J. Perkerson, admr.	1898-1908	7
2721	Perry, A.R.	Parthena A. Perry, admr.	1872	4
2730	Pittman, R.M.	Mary A. Pittman, widow	1873	1
2731	Pittman, M.A.	I.M. & J.A. Pittman, admrs.	1891	13
2734	Pitts, Wm.	S.R. McCleskey, admr.	1868	5
2735	Pitts, Polly Ann	H.M. Hammett, T. admr.	1872	13
2736	Pitts, M.W.	M.J. Pitts, admr.	1895	4
2750	Phillips, James D., et al, minors	Benjamin Phillips, gdn.	1874	3
2741	Phillips, M.T.	M.M. Phillips, admr.	1878	14
2742	M.M. Phillips	Mrs. Nannie E & C. C. Phillips exor.	1900	3
2747	Pledger, Mrs. Jennie, minor	G.B. Pledger & J.R. Humphreys, gdns.	1889	5
2748	Polk, John, minor	N.A. Barber, gdn.	1885	1
2749	Pomeroy, Edgar J.	Emma L. Pomeroy, exor.	1891-1901	7
2751	Pool, Elzy W.	Mrs. Amanda Pool, exor.	1898	6
2752	Pope, W.A., minor	F.M. Pope, gdn.	1875	1
2753	Pope, Mary F. (nee Palmer)	Charles Smith, T. admr.; Jowell Branham, P. admr.	1875-1881	11
2754	Pope, David	John Pope, admr.	1881-1886	15
2759	Porter, minors	Wm. Delk, gdn.	1869	5
2765	Potter, Rev. W.H.	Mrs. Georgia Potter, widow	1891	1
2787	Prather, P.H.	George H. Camp, exor. will annex; James Y. Prather, admr.	1868	7
2790	Pratt, N.A.	W.N. Pratt, exor.	1879	3
2801	Pritchard, Joshua	George N. Pritchard, admr.	1870-1880	12
2802	Pritchard, Nancy	J.B. Campbell, admr.	1877	3
2803	Pritchard, Mrs. Mamie	J.B. Campbell, admr.	1877	3
2804	Pritchard, George	James Pritchard, admr.	1881-83-98	21
2805	Pritchard, Hettie, et al, minors	James Pritchard, gdn.	1882	7
2806	Pritchard, Ruth	John R. Pritchard, gdn.	1890	5
2811	Pruett, Itai	P.B. Rolins, exor.	1890	5
2812	Pyron, James	Sadie J. Puron, admr.	1896	8
2825	Queen, Francis	N.C. Jordan, admr.	1898-1899	12
2831	See estate #2160 Rabun, Sara F., minor	(Sara Maple) R.N. Holland & Geo. F. Owen, gdn.	1881-1889	20
2836	Ragsdale, Francis	Wm. R. Montgomery, admr.	1886-1888	
2838	Rainey, O.H.	D. Rainey, admr.	1862	1

2849	Rakestraw, William	E.H. Rakestraw, admr.	1866-1872	13
2857	Randolph, John	H.M. Hammett, admr.	1867	7
2858	Ravel, A.P.	B.E. Rood, admr.	n.d.	1
2860	Ray, William	Benj. Bullard, admr.	1863	5
2861	Ray, John	H.M. Hammett, admr.	1866-1888	10
2862	Ray, Florena, et al, minors	H.M. Hammett, gdn.	1868	6
2863	Ray, George	Martha Ann Ray, widow	1870	1
2864	Ray, Emanuel	Robert Lemon, exor.	1874	5
2865	Ray, Wm. et al, minors	Martha Lee, gdn.	1879	3
2866	Ray, Jennie, et al, minors (See Estate #2747)	J.R. Humphries, gdn.	1885	8
2867	Ray, Eugene W., minor	Penn Mitchell, gdn.	1891	13
2875	Reagen, Jessie P.	George A. Fox, gdn.	1882	3
2876	Reagin, Willie B.	Green B. Chastain, gdn. Wilfield Worley, gdn.	1882	13
2877	Reagin, R.L.	Henry B. Reagin & James R Seawright, exors.	1894	3
2884	Reed, Joel B.	John L. Reed, Temp admr.; John L. Reed & Joel P. Reed, Perm admr.; will annexed	1880-1882	13
2885	Reed, Lottie L., et al, minors	Laura V. Bedford, gdn.	1888	2
2886	Reed, James T.	T.D. Power, admr.	1892-1894	8
2887	Reed, William B.	Jemina A. Reed, admr.; w/will annexed	1894	3
2888	Reed, George	Taluda Reed, widow	1897	1
2889	Reed, J.L., Sr.	Daniel Reed, admr.	1897-1902	9
2902	Reid, Andrew J.	Nathaniel Reed, exor.	1865	7
2903	Reid, Daniel	W.B. Reid & J.H. Reid, admr.	1865-1869	14
2904	Reid, T.W.	J.M. Gable, temp admr.	1886-1888	10
1905	Reid, Eliza M.	Humphrey Reid, admr.	1900-1901	8
2907	Reeves, Malachi	Parks Hardeman, exor.	1864	1
2912	Rice, Jane (Same as #2913)	S.T. & F.M. Rice, exors.	1889	6
2913	Rice, James	John P. Cheney & R.A. Hill, admr.	1911-1912	11
2919	Richardson, G.C. (Same as #2922)	J.C. Groover, admr.	1881-1883	14
2920	Richardson, T.B., minor	Paryhena Kirkpatrick, gdn.	1883	5
2921	Richardson, Nancy	W.H. Richardson, Temp admr.	1887	5
2922	Richardson, G.C.	W.H. Richardson, admr.	1887-1888	8
2924	Richardson, Ed Minor	W.L. Richardson, gdn.	1893	3
2927	Reynolds, A.	H.V. Reynolds & A. Reynolds, Jr., exors.	1892	7
2928	Reynolds, F.P.	Isie H. Reynolds, admrx.	1893	3
2930	Reynolds, Elmer, et al, minors (See #2940)	Isie H. Reynolds, gdn.	1893	10
2931	Reynolds, Nancy	Edward Heard, admr.	1895-1900	11
2942	Robenson, Richard	J.P. Porter, admr.	1896-6 (?)	12
2943	Roberts, Eliza G.	Mary E. Roberts, exrx.	1869	6
2944	Roberts, S.H.	John Roberts, admr.	1877	11
2945	Roberts, John	Geo. C. Roberts, exor.	1890-1892	9

2946	Roberts, B.G.	P.D. McCleskey, admr.	1898-1909	7
2947	Roberts, Mrs. E.J.	Mrs. W.P. Stephens, Temp admx.	1899	3
2962	Roberson, Elvina	W.T. Roberson, exor.	1890	7
2963	Robertson, Sam	Wm. C. Robertson, exor.	1885-1887	14
2964	Robertson, Robert	W.T. Robertson, admr.	1890-1891	11
2977	Robinson, John	W.M. Hammett, admr.	1866	8
2978	Robinson, William	Anna Robinson, exrx.	1868	5
2979	Robinson, John	W.H. Kemp, admr.	1873-1874	4
2980	Robinson, Joanna, et al, minors	Theresa Robinson, gdn.	1880	5
2981	Robinson, William	Geo. M. Robinson, admr.	1882-1884	11
2987	Roddy, James	S.E. Roddy, widow	1886	1
2990	Rogers, Emma	Andrew Rogers, Temp admr.; A.J. Rogers & R.A. Hill, admr.	1886	15
2991	Rogers, Minerva, et al, minors	Andrew J. Rogers, gdn.	1887	2
2992	Rogers, Charles	Chas. P. Rogers, exor.	1890	4
2993	Rogers, Annie E.	F.P. Rogers, Temp. admr.	1899	4
2994	Rogers, James R.	Mrs. Anna W. Rogers, Temp adm.	1899	3
3006	Rood, Blanche L.	Asel P. Rood, exors.	1874	5
3007	Rooney, T.A.	Mrs. S.A. Rooney, admrx.	1898	3
3008	Root, Emma	William Root, gdn.	n.d.	7
3009	Root, James L.	James B. Glover, admr.	1882-1883	11
3010	Root, Mary E., et al, minors	William Root, gdn.; Aloda C. Root, gdn.	1882	12
3014	Rovie, William	James M. Gatty, admr.	1875	7
3018	Ruff, M.L.	Martin L. Ruff, Jr. T.D. Power, admr., will annexed	1876	10
3021	Rumsey, Fields	John Maffahay, Temp. admr.	1871	11
3022	Rumsey, Rubin	W.W. Carrell, admr.	1871	4
3023	Runyan, Mrs. E.C.	R.H. Runyan, admr.	1893	7
3028	Ruskin, John W., et al, minors	Mrs Saphronia Ruskin, gdn.	1870	6
3029	Russell, Mattie V.	F.P. Reynolds, exor.	1888	6
3035	Rutherford, Wm.	Mrs. Elizabeth Rutherford, wid.	1867	3
3036	Rutherford, L., minor	Melissa Rutherford, gdn.	1873	3
3041	Sams, D.F., et al, minors	Mrs. H.S. Sams, gdn.	1896	3
3042	Sanders, Julia	T.D. Power, gdn.	1892	1
3043	Sanders, W.J.	Almendy Sanders, widow	1893	2
3044	Sanders, Nancy	E.W. Frey, admr.	1894	4
3049	Sanges, John R.	Mrs. M.T. Sanges, exrx.	1895	3
3055	Sauls, Mrs. Corrie	H.B. Sauls, admr.	1900	4
3058	Scarbrough, Susan H.	I.N. Scarbrough, admr.	1891	7
3059	Scoggins, James F.	Geo. & Nancy Scoggins, exors.	1869-1871	8
3052A	Scott, John	Edmond Scott, Temp admr.	1893	3
3053A	Scott, Netti, minor	Edmond Scott, gdn.	1893	5
3054A	Scott, Mary A. (See also #6678)	H.L. Scott, exor.	1896	4
3066	Scribner, Sara T.	John M. Green, exor.	1883-1885	6
3067	Scroggins, Geo. C.	J.L. Pace, admr.	1878-1881	11
3070	Shadenger, William	S.R. McCleskey, admr.	n.d.	5

3071	Shadengar, Sarah J., et al, minors	Elizabeth Shadenger, gdn.	1868	7
3072	Shaw, Wm.	W.S. Barnes, admr.	1875-1879	13
3073	Shaw, Joseph L.	Eliza Shaw, widow	1879	1
3073	Shaw, William	Geo. H. Shaw, admr.	1884	3
3075	Shaw. Sarah E.	Mary S. Copeland, exrx	1885	2
3076	Shaw, M.T.	Nancy O. Shaw, widow	1887	1
3081	Sharer, George	V.C. Shearer, exor.	1873	4
3083	Shelton, W.T.	E.L. Litchfield, admr.	1866	1
3084	Shelton, J.W.	S.A. Shelton, Temp/Perm admr.	1900	15
3087	Sherard, Elizabeth	E.W. Frey, admr.	1897-1898	8
3089	Sherman, Susan	Wm. Sherman, Temp. admr.; W.R. Montgomery, Perm. admr.	1881	6
3090	Sherman, Maud, et al, minors	W.R. Montgomery, gdn.	1882	3
3091	Sherman, N.L.	F.L. Crawley, admr.; H.D. McDermont; O.P. McDermont, adm. de bonis non	1893	21
3092	Sherman, Eva, minor	Mrs. Mamie Crawley, gdn.	1900	2
3098	Shinn, Wm., minor	Mary Holcomb, gdn.	1875	3
3099	Shinn, Mary, minor	Calvin C. Holcomb, gdn.	1882	5
3100	Shipp, John C.	Ralph Shipp	1887	2
3103	Shirley, James G.	H.P. Sauls, admr.	1889-1890	8
3109	Shuford, E.L. (Same as #3110)	Mrs. Kate Shuford, admr.	1886-1889	3
3110	Shuford, E.L.	R.H. Earle, admr.; J.Z. Foster Co., admr de bonis non	1886-1889	19
3112	Shuford, F.B.	A.A. Irwin, admr.	n.d.	2
3113	Shugart, John	Wm. R. Montgomery, admr.	1882	3
3115	Seals, Annie, et al, minors	John R. Seals, gdn.	1893	1
3117	Seay, Barnett	A.B. Seay & W.J. Seay, admr.	1875	13
3118	Seay, James J.	A.B. Seay, admr.	1875	9
3122	Sessions, Alice P.	M.M. Sessions, Temp. admr.	1898	3
3128	Sewell, Joseph W.	Robert Dempsey, exor.	1885-1891	14
3129	Sewell, Ellie et al, minors	Isaac Smith, gdn.	1891	2
3130	Sewell, T.R.	O.T. Sewell, exor.	1895-1903	15
3135	Seymour, B.W.	Emma P. Seymour, exrx.	1899	3
3136	Sibley, Mrs. Emma E.	A.S.J. Gardner, exor.	1898=1901	10
3140	Simmonton, James, et al, minors	Mary F. Simmonton, gdn.	1866	2
3141	Simpson, Leonard A.	Rebecca Simpson, widow	1866	2
3142	Simpson, A.N.	John H. Simpson, admr.	1884	1
3151	Sims, Archie, et al, minors	F.A. Sims, gdn.	1899	4
3153	Skelton, W.T.	J.T. Burkholter, admr.	1873	5
3157	Slaughter, Sarah	J.W. Slaughter, exor.	1890	7
3161	Slotterbeck, A.J.	H.M. Hammett, T & P admr.	1886	16
3162	Smith, Mary, et al, minors	John H. Miller, gdn.	1862	4
3163	Smith, Mongin	Laura M. Smith, exor. See #3166, James Brumby, admr.; will annexed; R.R. Cutler, admr.	1866	15

3164	Smith, Sarah	Hannah M. Smith	1866	1
3165	Smith, Benjamin F.	John H. Miller, admr.	1866	3
3166	Smith, James M. (See #3163)	Mrs. Laura M. Smith, exor.	1871	2
3167	Smith, Hannah M.	Sarah Smith, exor.	1873	1
3168	Smith, Z.A.	Mrs. Jane Smith, exor.	1875	3
3169	Smith, Elvira	A.A. Fletcher, exor.	1875	1
3170	Smith, Sarah E., minor	Judson C. Smith, gdn.	1879	1
3171	Smith, James O.	Nancy Smith, exrx.	1883	7
3172	Smith, Anna Maria	???	1880	1
3173	Smith, Joseph	Moultry Sessions, admr.	1884	2
3174	Smith, Celia A.	Mary B. Rasberry, exrx	1884	1
3175	Smith, Mamie, et al, minors	Sallie Barfield, gdn.	1885	1
3176	Smith, John T.	Wm. G. Blankership, admr.	1885-1888	10
3177	Smith, W.D.	R.B. Smith, T & P admr.	1886-1891	15
3178	Smith, Joseph	Richard Earle, admr. J.Z. Foxter co-admr.	1886-1899	8
3179	Smith, Ann M.	Arch Smith, Jr., exor.	1887	3
3180	Smith, Joseph	L.E. Litchfield, T. admr.	1889	4
3181	Smith, Archiball, Sr.	Archiball Smith, Jr.	1892	3
3182	Smith, Tillman	W.S. Smith, exor.	1892-1900	8
3183	Smith, A.S.	Rebecca J. Smith, exrx	1895	3
3184	Smith, Dr. O.	Mrs. N.E. Smith, exrx Jennie Smith, will annexed	1895-1925	12
3185	Smith, Helen Z.	Archibald Smith, admr.	1899	6
3186	Smith, Minerva	W.S. Smith, exor.	1899	3
3222	Sneed, Elijah	James Sneed, admr.	1866	1
3233	Spaulding, Harry, minor	Lewis Spaulding, gdn.; Mrs. Sadie Spaulding, gdn.	1896	5
3236	Spier, Joseph	P.H. Lyon, admr.	1868	5
3238	Spraggins, Frances, et al, minors	H.M. Hammett, gdn.	1866	1
3239	Spraggins, Thos. E.	Mrs. S. Spraggins, widow H.M. Hammett, admr.	1869	2
3241	Springer, Tobitha	H.M. Hammett, admr.	1866	9
3242	Springer, Mary, et al, minors	Mrs. Ollie Springer	1885	1
3244	Sprouse, Louella, et al, minors	Julia Sprouse, gdn.	1881	1
3253	Stansill, David	Joseph Chastain, admr.	1866-1871	14
3254	Stansell, James N., et al, minors	E.C. Stansell, gdn.	1869-1876	12
3255	Stansell, E.C.	J.R. Humphries, T & P admr.	1887	14
3265	Steel, Wm. et al, minors	Isaac Steel, gdn.	1884	3
3267	Stewart, James	Mary A. Stewart, widow	1873	2
3268	Stewart, Charles D.	Theophilus Stewart, Trustee	1873	1
3269	Stewart, Mollie, minor	Robert Benson, gdn.	1880	3
3270	Stewart, E.P.	Archibald Howell, exor.	1882	3
3271	Stewart, Susan (See also estate #3272)	B.R. Legg & E. Faw, exors.	1894	3
3272	Stewart, Theoplas & Susan	Enoch Faw, exor.	1901-1928	31

3276	Stephens, Zacharia (incomp.)	Elizabeth Stephens, gdn.	1876		3
3277	Stephens, Timothy	W.P. Stephens, exor.	1889		9
3278	Stephens, W.P.	Mrs. Dorothy Stephens, exrx	1892		3
3279	Stephens, Lena E.	Willis P. Stephens, T. admr.	1899		3
3280	Stephens, Elizabeth	E.W. Frey, admr.	1900		8
3287	Stocks, Mary L.	Parker M. Rice, exor.	1896		4
3294	Strange, M.H.	A.M. Bagley, et al	1882		1
3295	Strange, James W.	W.R. Power, exor.	1882		6
3299	Strickling, James A.	A.M. Parker, admr.	1866		2
3300	Strickling, Charity J.	Isaac McConnell, gdn.	1873		1
3301	Strickland, Hary	J.D. Strickland & Junior Humphrey, T & P admr.	1884		15
3307	Strand, Leola, minor	W.F. Groover, gdn.	1869		6
3315	Summerhill, D.	A.A. Griggs, admr.	1884	1888	11
3316	Summerlin, W.L.	Milton J. Magbee, admr.	1866		2
3317	Summers, T.F.	A.H. Summer, T & P admr.	1883-1886		16
3318	Summers, Bell, minor	Martha Summers, gdn.	1884		3
3319	Sumner, Margarete, minor	M.J. Sumners, gdn.	1885		9
3325	Sweeney, Addison	Carrie Sweeney, widow	1888		1
3331	Svedlind, Peter	Ellen Svedlund, admr.	1892-1893		9
3331	Svedlund, M.M., et al, minors	Ellen Svedlund, gdn.	1893		3

MINUTES OF COBB INFERIOR COURT FOR CIVIL PROCEEDINGS
COBB COUNTY, GEORGIA

Wed. Dec. The 20, 1865.   Cobb Inferior Court met persuant to adjournement present their honors H. M. Hammett, J.J. Northcutt and T. J. Atkinson, W. W. Carroll, Clerk I.C.

No cases to enter the court then adjourned to court in course. H. M. Hammett, J.I.C., T. J. Atkinson, J.I.C., J. J. Northcutt, J.I.C.

Page 1.   Civil Proceedings; 1866.   Official oath of Clerk of Inferior Court, Joseph Speir...in which he states he holds no other government office (except postmaster) and swears to support Constitution of state and the "United States." 29 Jan. 1866. Test: T. H. Moore, J.I.C., J. J. Northcutt, J.I.C.

Page 2.   Official oath of county surveyor, Benjamin Gregory swears to support Constitution of "United States." 5 Feb. 1866. Wit: T. J. Atkinson, J.I.C.; J. J. Northcutt, J.I.C.; H. M. Hammett, J.I.C.; Joseph Speir, Clerk.

Page 3.   Official oath of coroner, John White, same declaration as above, 31 Jany 1866. Wit: H. M. Hammett, J.I.C.; T. H. Moore, J.I.C.; Joseph Speir, Clerk.

Page 4.   State of Georgia, County of Cobb to H. M. Hammett one of the Justices of Inferior Court of sd. county, complaint and petition: William Burris of said county..."he is now and for many days" has been confined and holden in imprisonment without law or right in common jail of sd. county of John T. Robertson, jailer of sd. county...under some charge alleged against him by military authorities of United States..."he prays honor to issue the States Writ of Habeus Corporus to bring your petitioner before your honor to the end, that what appertains to justice may be done and as in duty bound your petitioner will ever pray...The facts set forth in the above petition are true to the best of petitioners knowledge and belief." Sworn to and subscribed before me this Jan. 9, 1866. John G. Campbell, ordinary. Elijah M.D. Burris.

To John T. Robertson
    You are hereby commanded to produce the body of William Burris alleged to be illegally detained by you together with the course of such detention before me on today at 3 o'clock p.m. then and there to be disposed of as the law directs. Given under my hand and official signature the Jan. 9, 1866. H.M. Hammett, J.I.C.

In obedience to the within I make this my answer the within named petitioner was turned over to me by Maj. Warner military commandant of this post. I have held him and now hold him in imprisonment in obedience....

Page 5.   To his commandants order. I have no warrant of commitment or any other papers in my hands in said case. This Jan. 9, 1866. John T. Robertson, Jailer.

Jan. 9, 1866.   Cobb Inferior Court in Chambers: Present their Honors J. J. Northcutt, T. J. Atkins, H. M. Hammett. E.M.D. Burris having been brotbefore the court from the military guard house for charge of robing on petition of Habeus Corpus the court having heard the petitioner.
    It is ordered by the court that the said Burris be and he is hereby discharged.   H. M. Hammett, J.I.C.; J. J. Northcutt, J.I.C.

T. J. Atkins, J.I.C.

(Note at bottom of the page)
This should have been recorded by former clerk Mr. W. W. Carroll
but was neglected. Recorded this 8th day Feb. 1866. Joseph
Speir, Clerk.

Page 6.   Oath of M. G. Whitlock as Justice of Inferior Court;
          sworn 12 day of Feb. 1866; witnessed by H. M. Hammett,
E. H. Lindley and T. J. Atkinson, Justices of Inferior Court,
Joseph Speir, Clerk.

Page 7.   Oath of W. W. Carroll as County Treasurer, 18 Feb. 1866;
          wit: T. J. Atkinson, M. G. Whitlock and J. J. Northcutt,
Justices of Inferior Court; Joseph Speir, Clerk.

State of Georgia) To Justices of Inferior Court: Petition of Mrs.
Cobb County   ) Chira Hendrix showeth that David Hendrix of
                    said Co. is lunatic; going at large, with a
gdn...petitions he be committed to the asylum.
Feb. 23, 1866   Chira Hendrix

Page 8.
State of Georgia) To Sheriff of sd. Co. and his deputies: you
Cobb County   ) are hereby commanded to summon the following
                    named persons to be and appear at Marietta
in sd. Co. at 2 o'clock in afternoon of 23 Feb. inst. for purposes
of trying as jurors the issue of lunancy of David Hendrix then
and theirs to be submitted...Herein fail not. Witness our hands
and official signature this 23 Feb. 1866.
1. W. R. Montgomery   5. G. R. Gilbert
2. W. W. Carroll   6. W. E. Dunwoody, M.D.
3. L. Bennett   7. Wm. Groves
4. W. W. Simpson

T. H. Moore, J.I.C.; J. J. Northcutt, J.I.C.; M. G. Whitlock,
J.I.C.; T. J. Atkinson, J.I.C.

Verdict:
We the Jury find the issue in favor of the plaintiff...David
Hendrix is an insane man and is not possess of any property by
inheritance. Signed: W. W. Carroll, Foreman; W. E. Dunwoody, M.G.;
W. R. Montgomery; G. R. Gilbert; W. W. Simpson; L. Bennett; W. F.
Groves.

Page 9-10.   ....Judgement....David Hendrix...be committed to the
             lunatic asylum of this state by sheriff or his deputy
....sd David Hendrix is a pauper and unable to pay any portion of
expenses of his keeping in sd asylum...ordered W. W. Carroll,
county Treasurer pay to Clerk and sheriff sum of ----- for their
costs for attending this case: T. H. Moore, T. J. Atkinson,
J. J. Northcutt, M. G. Whitlock, Justices of Inferior Court.
Joseph Speirs, Clerk.

Official Oath of Tax Collector: John W. McCleskey...March 30, 1866.
Wit: T. J Atkinson; T. H. Moore; J. J. Northcutt, J.I.C.; Joseph
Speirs, Clerk.

Page 10-11. Official Oath of Receiver of Tax Returns: Joshua
             Jackson, March 26, 1866: Wit: T. J. Atkinson, J. J.
Northcutt, T. H. Moore, J.I.C.; Joseph Speirs, Clerk.

MINUTES OF COBB INFERIOR COURT FOR CIVIL PROCEEDINGS

June Term 1867:   Petition of William B. Gunnett praying an order
                   of court requiring county surveyor of sd. co.
to find and run true line between lands of sd. Gunnells and
estate James Park, decd; Ordered Benjamin Gregory (having sworn
such persons to act as processioners)...

Page 12.   as he may deem proper proceed to find and run sd line
            and make a return of survey to this court.   T. J.
Atkinson, E. H. Lindley, J. J. Notrhcutt, J.I.C.   Recorded 27
Dec. 1867.

Page 13 blank   (Instead of page 14 the pages began renumbering
                as page 1 of Trial Docket)

1869:
Aug. 30   Joshua Segars applies to be appt gdn Elizabeth Emma and
           Louisia Gable Cilotein(?) Answerable Oct. term.

Oct. 4.   At a regular term of sd. ct no objection being made it
           was ordered that sd. Segars be appt gdn as aforesd upon
his complying with requisitions of law in such cases made and
provided.   C. J. Shepard, Ordy.

Aug. 28.   Mrs. Susanna Moore admr Jeremiah A. Moore applies for
           leave to sell land in Bartow Co., citation granted to
be answered Oct. term 1869.

Oct. 4.   At a regular term of sd ct: no objections being made sd
           application was granted to sd Susanna Moore to sell land
lying in Bartow Co. at public or private sale as she may think
most to the interest of sd. estate.   C. J. Shepherd, Ordy.

Aug. 2.   H. M. Mayes and W. C. Free(?) applied for letters of
           dismissal to be answered Nov. term 1869.

Dec. 7.   continued to 13 Dec. 1869

Dec. 13.   continued to 22 Dec. 1869 Suppoena issued J. G. Camp-
           bell. (transferred to p. 10)

Page 2.   Aug. 4.   App. letters of dismissal to be heard Dec. term
           1869. (The above was marked through)

Frances Bentley and minor child
Aug. 21 applies for yr's support

Sept. 6.   John G. Glore adm. Elbert P. Jordan applies for leave
           to sell. Oct. term 1869. ($800.00) Ordered sd.
application be granted...C. J. Shepherd, Ordy.

Page 3.   1869. Aug. 27. Citation for adm estate Sam'l Bentley
           dec'd to be heard Oct. term.
Oct. 7.   Order appointing clerk Superior Court, C.J. Shepherd, Ordy.

Citation for letters estate of Robert Chandler to be heard Oct.
term /69. (The above was marked through)

Aug. 24.   H. M. Hammett adm Jackson Brumbolo for leave to sell
           land to be heard Nov. term /69 (Widow and minor heirs
taking advantage of the homestead adm. discharged by order.   C. J.
Shepherd, Ordy.

MINUTES OF COBB INFERIOR COURT FOR CIVIL PROCEEDINGS

Page 4. 1869. Sept. 10. H. M. Hammett applies for leave to sell
        lands belonging to estate of Israel P. Boyd to be heard
Nov. term 1869. Nov. term: order granted C. J. Shepherd, Ordy.

Aug. 20. Citation for adm. estate of Robt Chandler dec'd to be
         heard Oct. term/69 ordered that H. M. Hammett Clerk
Superior Court be and he is hereby appointed. C. S. Shepherd,
Ordy.

Sept. 28. Petition of E. A. Dickson minor of D. W. Dickson to
          have a gdn appt. for her and selects J.A.L. Born as
gdn...to be heard Oct. term.

Oct. 4. No objections being made sd. J.A.L. Born was appt. and
        ordered papers ordering letters to be issue agreeable to
law. C. S. Shepherd, Ordy.

Page 5. Sept. 6. Petition of W. R. Vanable for change of Juris-
        diction of adm. filed.

Sept. 22. Reply of records given.

Sept. 30. Certificate of Ordy Fulton Co. filed; ordered Trans-
          ferred.

Sept. 9. W. A. Appling admr. of W. A. Appling Senr. citation to
         appear at Oct. term of ct. appeared and case conti. to
the 16 Oct. /69 Def't appeared and made oath. Inventory of
appraisement agreeable to law.

Sept. 30. Petition of W. J. Eubanks to be released from the
          gdnship of Samantha and Laura Kirk filed in office and
citation to next of kin.

1869. Nov. 1. No objection being filed it is hereby directed
       that and order be made appointing Ephrim L. Breswell gdn
of Samantha H. and Laura Kirk in place of W. J. Eubanks resigned
and that upon sd Braswell's complying with the requirement of law
letters issued to him and that upon a full and final settlement
of his trust sd. Eubanks received letters of dismissal.

Page 6. E. H. Rakestraw adm. of Wm. Rakestraw dec'd. applies for
        permission to sell the real estate belonging to sd.
estate. It appearing to the ct. that citation has been legally
granted and published sd application is hereby granted. Oct. term
1869, C. S. Shepherd.

Oct. 5. E. C. Stansell (written Stancell) applies for letters of
        gdn (written over James) citation granted. Of James N.
Calvin L Baron D and Nancy J. Stansell to be mearel(?) on 1st Mon.
in Dec. next.

Dec. 7. application granted and letters issued. C.J. Shepherd,
        ordy.

Oct. 6. J. L. Camp and others application for change of road
        commissioners ordered to report.

Nov. 2. Report of commissioners filed notice published for
        objectives to be heard 1st Tues. of Dec./69.

MINUTES OF COBB INFERIOR COURT FOR CIVIL PROCEEDINGS

Dec. 7. Continued to be heard Mon. 13 Dec. 1869.

Dec. 7. Case continued to 22 Dec. 1869.

Dec. 22. No objection being made said postponed change of road
          was by order established and entered or record. C. S.
Shepherd, Ordy.

Page 7. Aug. 27. Citation ordered requiring all persons interes-
          ted to show cause if any they could why the adm. of es-
tate of Sam'l Bentley should not be vested in the Clerk of the
Inferior Court.

Oct. 7. Letters granted.

Sept. 18. N. J. Fenn applied for letters of dismissal to be
           heard 1st Mon. in Jan.

Jan. term: letters granted.

Oct. 19. Catherine Grier applies for letters of adm. on estate of
          Josiah Grier; application citation ordered.

Dec. term: no objection being made application granted.

Page 8. 1869. Nov. 1. J. R. Harbin for release as security of
          Emily Eason gdn. minor children of Rasberry Eason dec'd
to be heard Dec. term /69 no answer the death of Emily Eason
suggested J. L. Eason be appointed admr. and time granted to sell
the gdnship of the dec'd. O. R. Eason adm. of R. Eason representative J. R. Harbin mismanagement to be heard Dec. term (conti.)

Page 9. 1869. Nov. 1. Francis Jordan widow of Elbert P. Jordan
          for years suppot for herself and eight (written over
seven) (8) minor children, appraisers appointed.

Nov. 1. Mary C. A. Harris application for letters of adm. estate
         of S. J. Harris to be heard Dec. term.

Dec. term: application granted.

Dec. 6. Geo. W. Prichard applied for letters of adm estate of
         Joshua Prichard to be heard Feb. term 7 (regular term)

Feb. 7. letters granted.

Page 10. 1869. Aug. 2. H. M. Mayes exor W. C. Green dec'd.
          applies for letters of dismissal to be heard Nov. term
1869.

Nov. term 1869. continued to Dec. term.

Dec. term 1869. continued to term Dec. 13th.

Dec. 13th. objections having been filed by consent of parties
            case continued to Dec. 22 and ct adjournes to 22 Dec.
1869.

Dec. 14. Suppos issued summoning J. G. Campbell.

Dec. 22. Came the parties by their attys Davis Irwin Esq. for

John Anderson gdn for the minor heirs of sd. W. C. Green dec'd and P. M. Green widow of sd. W. C. Green dec'd. and A. N. Simpson and M. P. Gartrell and Winn for defendent. After hearing the evidence in the case and the argument of counsel it is ordered that in lieu of $204.00 commission charged in annual return for 1866 for turning over negro property to John Anderson (in annual return of 1866-marked through) gdn sd H. M. Mays exor be allowed the sum of $50 also in lieu of the $161.00 commission for turning over property to Mrs. P. M. Green widow of W. C. Green dec'd. he be allowed the sum of $61 and that sd.H. M. Mays exor on payment of the balance to the parties thereto entitled $254 and $12.50 commission improperly charged for paying $500 to M̸/P̸/G̸a̸r̸t̸r̸e̸l̸l̸/̸&̸ W̸i̸n̸n̸ (marked through) attorneys being shall be discharged and that letters be granted to him accordingly. C. S. Shepherd, Ordy.

Dec. 23.   Parties agree to allow H. M. Mays exor till the 2nd day of Jan. 1870 to take an appeal time for appeal extended to Jany 4, 1870 case compromised.

(Pages no longer numbered)

1869
Dec. 30.   John T. Robertson cited to give new security or be removed from duty as constable. J. T. Robertson removed.

Jan. .   Petition of Perin Turner for the gdnship of orphans of Wilds Robb dec'd. to be heard Feb. term.
Feb. Term: letters granted

Jan. 4.   Petition of J. S. Eason adm Emily Eason for leave to sell real estate, to be heard Feb. 7, 1870. continued for consideration.

March term 1870. leave granted and ordered accordingly.

Feby. term 1870
Jan. 19.   Catharin Grier admr. Jonah Greer applies for leave to sell land.

Feb. 7.   Leave granted

continued from Dec. term.   Geo. W. Prichard application for adm. Jordan Prichard.

Feb. 7.   Letters granted.

Dec.   Haney Harris applied letters of gdn May C. Kemp.

Feb. 7.   Letters granted.

1870
March 3.   A. F. Northcutt applies for letters of adm. on the estate of Elizabeth M. More, citation issued.

April 6.   Letters granted and entered of record.

_____ 3.   H. M. Hammett applies for letters of gdnship of property of Mary H. Maggie E Laura A James R and Maria L Wood minors and children of Mrs. Mary J. Wood (orphans of M. J. Wood) dec'd resident of sd. county. Citation issued.

Ap 6. order passed, granted letters.

March 1. F. L. Devenport applies for letters of gdnship of her
          own children.

April term. Apr. 4. letters granted and entered of record

May term
1870
Ap 4. W. A. Appling Jr. adm rule nisi

May 2. continued at instance end of the cost of W. A. Appling
        the next regular term

June term   Je 6 1870
   came the parties and by consent case conti to July term 1870
July term conti

June term 1870
Feb. 21. W. L. Brown adm. Hiram Brown applies for dismissal,
          filed publication made conti. to Jly term

1871
June 21. R. R. Cyler, exor James M. Smith dec'd applies for
          dismission to be heard Oct. term: conti. to Nov. term

Ella Fambro   et al)
        vs   ) caveat to will of David Dobbs
David J. Dobbs   ) conti. from Aug. term

Aug. 16. commission issued to take testimony of Furman and Mary
          Roberts. commission issued to take testimony of Ella
Fambro.

Supeona, to Caroline Lyman - Jerry Dobbs - Mrs. Jane Dobbs - A. W.
          York - Mrs. E. F. Anderson - Miss Mary Mason - Wm. Dobbs
- James P. Dobbs - W. M. Dobbs - J. T. Haley

David J. Dobbs exor. etc, petition for Probate of will. Witness-
     es subpeoned: E. J. Setze, A. N. Simpson, D. N. Elliott, Mrs.
E. A. Wing.

EX 3S. Joshua H. Reed et al vs William P. Anderson   Nuisiance

Witnesses subpoened for plaintiff: R. C. Cox, John Pair, John
Pace, J. L. Reed, James L. Pair, Jas. Mehaffy, Jno. Perkerson,
Robt Clay, Barney Lee, W. C. Strickland, M. Lindley, J. C. Bartrim,
Thos. Lindley, Jas Barnes, Wm. Barnes, R. N. Anderson, Dr. A.
Reynolds, Dr. H. Reynolds, Jas. Bullock, Hardy Barnes, Dr. Baley,
E. H. Lindley, Thos. Perkerson, Bird Conger, Henry Shaw, Wm.
Anderson, Riley Wilson, R. Chandler, F. Watson, Dr. N. N. John.

Wit. for Dft:
James Wilson, B. W. Florence, B. W. Florence, C. H. Anderson,
J. H. Brown, Dr. Hardin, Dr. Tennant, Dr. Williams, Dr. Cleland,
Dr. Colton, M. C. Hatchn., Henry Pate, J. B. Cuncan, A. J. Chaney,
J. R. Ward, W. P. Anderson, Dr. J. R. Humphries, Dr. J. J. M.
Gors, Dr. Reynolds, S. A. Anderson, N. G. Gignillial

to be heard 9 Feb. 1874

verdict finding claimant a nuisiance

Archibald Megarity	Rule nisi to show cause	Sept. term
vs	for road	1873 referred
Jams T. Dobbs		to arbitrators

James S. Morris	Rule nisi to show cause	referred to
vs	for road	arbitrators
Maer A. Mayes		

Miss Mary Moore exerx of	Feby term 1873
Susannah Moore dec'd adm't	March term 1873 conti.
of estate of Jeremiah Moore	
dec'd. app letters of dismissal	

C. H. Smith applies for letters	Citation pefected
of adm. of Mary F. Pope dec'd	Letters granted Feby 3.
	1873

Application of Gerusha Guess admr &	Feb. term 1873 Petition
distributee for distribution of the	filed; March term 1873
estate of Henry Guess, dec'd.	conti. Letters granted
	Sept. term 1873

Loose in book: page partially destroyed:
Application for homestead
Peter Farmer   10 Nov. 1877
Jno. R. Ward, County Surveyor

END

On fly leaf: I owe county for nine two horse loads of Rock @50¢
                per load about 4 perches $.50   1853   Copy Nancy
E. Mitchell ¢ E. C. Mitchell Bond

Page 1 - 1833: John James, Prin. with Joashly James & John
                Jeffers as securities bonded for $500...14 Dec.
1833...John James as bailiff of #846 G.M. district before Daniel
May, JP. Reg. 7 April 1835, E. R. Mills, Clk.

Page 1:   Alexander Mohan, principal with Jesse Mohan and Josiah
           (Jackson or Johnson..blot) as securities for $500...

Page 2:   16 July 1833...Mohan as bailiff for #846 G.M. district
           before Daniel May, J.P....Reg. 7 April 1855. E. R. Mills,
Clk.

Page 2:   James Mohan, principal with William Morris and John A.
           Wells as securities for $500 on 11 July 1833..

Page 3:   ..bailiff in "said district"...before John Clay, J.P.
           Reg. April 7, 1835, E. R. Mills, Clk.

Page 3:   Cherokee Co.....Martin Ingram, principal with Gideon
           Trout and Abner Camp as securities of county aforesaid...
bonded for $500 as constable of #792 G. M. district...before
W. B. McLain, J.P.

Page 4:   Jesse Davis, principal with David McCelow and Jesse
           Griffin as securities for $500 as constable for #845
G. M. district on 15 Oct. 1833 before John M. Williford, J.P.

Page 5:   Oath of Jesse Davis before John M. Williford, J.P., Reg.
           7 April 1835, E. R. Mills, Clk.

Page 5:   Richard Coleman, principal with Tandy K. Martin and E. R.
           Mills and John M. Williford for $500 as bailiff...2 Nov.
1833...

Page 6:   ...845 G. M. district..Reg. 8 May 1835, E. R. Mills, Clk.

Page 6:   June 3, 1833...William Pierce, principal with William
           Morris and Thomas White (Head or Hurst) as securities
before Lewis Powell, J.P. bonded for $500...as bailiff for G. M.
district #792...

Page 7:   ...Reg. 7 May 1835, E. R. Mills, Clk.

Page 7:   James Waller and Willis Call bonded for $5,000..."Polly
           Wolf is mother of a bastard child and above James B.
Waller...does agree and will see that above child above mentioned
shall not be any expense to said county in terms of 12 years."

Page 8:   ...in force..9 Oct. 1833 before Thomas Whitehead, Jr.
           and Lewis R. Powell. J.P. Signed Mary Wolf, J. B. Waller
and Willis Cade. Reg. 7 May 1835, E. R. Mills, Clk.

Page 8:   William Morris, principal with William Pearce and Thomas
           Whitaker as securities bonded for $500 on 25 Feb. 1834
as constable for #852 G. M. district..L. R. Powell. J.P.   Reg.
11 May 1835.

Page 9:   John Hill, principal with Thomas C. West and Jacob
          Mathews as securities bonded for $500 on 21 Oct. 1834 as
constable for #846 G. M. district to 1 Sat. Jan. next...before J.
Rowe, J.P. and William Sansom, J.P.   Reg. 11 May 1835.

Page 9:   Martin Ingram, principal with Elijah Croxton and Abner
          Camp as securities bonded for $1,000 as...

Page 10: Constable for #852 G. M. district on 29 Jan. 1834 before
          Lewis R. Powell, J.P.   Reg. 11 May 1835..

Page 10: George Harper, principal with William Harris and John
          Rowe as securities bonded for $500 on 11 Jan. 1834...

Page 11: ...constable for #846 G. M. district before Daniel May,
          J.P.   Reg. 11 May 1834, E. R. Mills, Clk.

Page 11: John Cud, principal with Tandy K. Martin and John M.
          Williford and Amos Brown and E. R. Mills as securities
bonded for $500...as bailiff for #834 G. M. district...

Page 12: On 4 Jan. 1834 before Gabriel Powell, J.P.   Reg. 11
          May 1835, E. R. Mills, Clk.

Page 12: Oath of John Cubb on 4 Jan. 1834 before John M. Willi-
          ford, J.P.

Page 12: Joashly James as principal with George Baber and Joseph
          Chastain as securities bonded for $10,000 on 17 Feb.
1834...

Page 13: ...as county ordinary before E. R. Mills.   Reg. 25 May
          1835, E. R. Mills.   Repeats bond of above.

Page 14: Repeats oath of Joashly James as ordinary.

Page 14: William Brumbelo bonded for $1,000 (no other names) on
          20 Jan. 1835 for constable (district not given).

Page 15: ...30 Jan. 1835..signed by J. B. Waller, Martin Adams,
          William (X) Harris..   Reg. 26 May 1835, E. R. Mills.

Page 15: John Hill as principal with Daniel May and Jacob Meadows
          as securities bonded for $500 on 10 Jan. 1835 as
constable for #846 G. M. district.

Page 16: ...Reg. 26 May 1835, E. R. Mills...

Page 16: James H. Smith as principal with Daniel Grover and John
          Cud as securities bonded for $500...3 May 1835 as
constable for #897 G.M.....

Page 17: ...before Alfred B. Edwards, J.P.   Reg. 26 May 1835,
          E. R. Mills.

Page 17: John D. Mullins, principal with John Moore and Martin
          Ingram as securities bonded for $1,000 as constable for
#985 G. M. district...

Page 18: ...6 Jan. 1835...before Thomas Whitehead, J.P.   Reg. 4
          June 1835 by E. R. Mills, Clk.

Page 18:   Elijah Crasetain (Chastain?) principal with Abner Camp
           and Martin Ingram as securities for $500...

Page 19:   ...10 Jan. 1835...E. Craxton as constable for #985 G. M.
           district before Lewis R. Powell, J.P.   Reg. 5 June
1835, E. R. Mills, Clk.   Oath of Elijah Craxton before Lewis R.
Powell, J.P.

Page 20:   John M. Skelton, principal with Moses H. Guess and
           Julis Collins as securities bonded for $500...4 Feb.
1835 as constable for #851 G. M. district before Thompson Halk,
J.P. and David Kenedy, J.P.   Reg. 6 June 1835, E. R. Mills.

Page 21:   Elijah W. Mathews, principal with John Stroud as securi-
           ty for $500 on 10 Jan. 1835 bonded as constable for
#846 G. M. district. Reg. 6 June 1835, E. R. Mills, Clk.

Page 21:   John Cudd principal with Harrison T. Martin and Amos
           Brown as securities bonded for $500...

Page 22:   ...constable for #845 G. M. district on 4 Feb. 1835
           before John M. Williford, J.P.

Page 22:   Oath of John Cubb before John M. Williford, J.P. 4 Feb.
           1835.

Page 23:   Archibald Holland as principal with Thomas K. Johnson
           and John Pace as securities bonded for $1,000 on 6 Jan.
1835 as constable for #898 G. M. district by E. R. Mills and
William P. Malony, J.P.

Page 23:   Oath of Archibald Holland before Wm. P. Malony, J.P.
           Reg. 6 June 1835, E. R. Mills, Clk.

Page 24:   Alexander McClarty as principal with Wm. Guess and
           Daniel May as securities bonded for $10,000 on 3 May
1835 as county treasurer before Christopher M Crary, Dpt. Clk.
Reg. 6 June 1835, E. R. Mills.

Page 25:   James Anderson as principal with Alexander McClarty as
           security bonded for $1,000 as Clerk of Court of Ordinary
before E. R. Mills on 9 Jan. 1835. Reg. 6 June 1835, Jan. 11,
1836, E. R. Mills, Clk.

Page 26:   Notley D. Gare, principal with Robert Harper and M.H.
           Gare as securities bonded for $500 on 2 Jan. 1836 as
"bayliff" of #846 G. M. district before John Roled, J.P.   Reg.
10 Jan. 1836, E. R. Mills, Clk.

Page 27:   James Mohan, principal with Thomas Gare and George
           Harper as securities bonded for $500 on 2 Jan. 1836 as
"bayliff" of #846 G. M. district before John Rowe, J.P.   Reg. 10
Jan. 1836, E. R. Mills, Clk.

Page 27:   Joseph Mapy, principal with Martin Adams and Alexander
           McLarty as securities for $500...

Page 28:   ...4 Jan. 1836 as constable for #898 G. M. district
           before J. N. Malony, J.P.   Reg. 11 Jan. 1836, E. R.
Mills, Clk.

Page 28:   Martin Ingram as principal with Abner Kamp and John
           Wallraven as securities bonded for $500 on 5 Jan. 1836
as constable for #895 G. M. district...

Page 29:   ....before Thomas Whithill (Whithead?), J.P.   Reg. 12
           Jan. 1836, E. R. Mills, Clk.

Page 29:   James Mahon, principal with George W. Harper and Manning
           H. Gare as securities bonded for $500 on 12 Jan. 1835
as "Bayliff" of #546 G. M. district. Reg. 12 Jan. 1836, E. R.
Mills, Clk.

Page 30:   Parks Hardman as principal with Joel Reid and Wm. R.
           Turner as securities bonded for $500 on 20 July 1836 5
(written over) constable in "Capt. Brockman's district" (no
number given) before Jesse Wadkins, J.P.   Reg. 12 Jan. 1836, E.
R. Mills, Clk.

Page 31:   Willia m/Brumbelo (marked out) Larenzo Trout as princi-
           pal with A. McLarty and Jackson H. Randall as securities
bonded for $1,000 on 7 July 1835 as "Bayliff" of #898 G. M.
district. Reg. 15 Jan. 1836, E. R. Mills, Clk.

Page 31:   B. B. Hornbuckle as principal with Martin Adams and
           Charles Harris bonded for $1,000 on 25 Aug. 1836 as
constable for #898 G. M. district. Reg. 15 Jan. 1836, E. R.
Mills, Clk.

Page 32:   John Lemon, principal and William Culp and Joseph Culp
           as securities bonded for $1,000 on 25 June 1835 as
county Treasurer before Christopher McCrary. Reg. 15 Jany ____
E. R. Mills, Clk.

This book 37 bonds the recording of which amounts $23.12 at 62½
each.

Page 33:   Recd of the Justices of Inferior Court full compensation
           for recording the former bonds as contained in the book
this 8 March 1836, E. R. Mills, Clk.

Page 33:   Benjamin Sanders, principal with Malachi Reaves as
           securities bonded for $500 on 20 Feb. ____ as constable
of county (no district given)..before Jessa Wadkins, J.P.

Page 34:   Ezekiel Brumbeloe, principal with Claborn Bishop as
           security bonded for $500 on 27 Feb. 1836 as constable
for #897 G. M. district before A. B. Edwards. Reg. 18 May 1836,
Martin Adams, Clk.

Page 35:   Notly D. Gore as principal with George W. Harper and
           James B. Waller as securities bonded for $500 on 14
May 1836 as constable for #846 G. M. district...before Jos Rowe,
J.P.   Entered 13 Sept. 1836, Martin Adams, Clk.

Page 36:   James Mohorne, principle with George W. Harper and Wm.
           Norris as securities bonded for $500 on 14 May 1836 as
constable for #846 G. M. district before Jos Rowe, J.P.   Entered
13 Sept. 1836, Martin Adams, Clk.

Page 37:   Parks Hardman, principal with Joel B. Reede and Joel
           H. Babb bonded for $500 on 18 Jan. 1839 as constable

of county of Cobb...before L. J. Chamley, J.P.   Entered 19 Jan.
1839, Nathaniel F. Legg, Dpty. Clk.

Page 38:   Josiah Massey, principal with John G. Holland and James
           L. Morris as securities bonded for $1,000 on 18 Jan.
1839 as bailiff for #898 G. M. district before Jessee Dobbs, J.P.
Reg. 20 Jan. 1839, Nathaniel F. Legg, Clk.

Page 39:   Napoleon B. Green, principal with William Green and John
           Sanderson as securities bonded for $2,000 on 4 June
1839... "will pay to county treasurer all moneys which belong to
County...by 1 Jan. 1843"...before Ezekiell Brumbelo and John W.
Grovis, J.P.   (No office given)   Entered 6 June 1839, N. F. Legg,
Dept. Clk.

Page 40:   Blank

Page 41:   Elias E. Murphee, principal with Benson Roberts and
           Joshua Welch as securities bonded for $1,200 on 30 Jan.
1840 as Tax Collector before E. W. Mobly, J.I.C. and B. H. Mapy,
J.I.C.   Reg. 5 Feby 1840, D. Collins, C.I.C.

Page 42:   Elias E. Murphee, principal with John Merrett, Joshua
           Welch, to Justices of Inferior Court, to wit: E. W.
Mobley, J.P. Green, Robert Groves, B. H. May, and William Dobbs..
bonded for $2,000 on 30 Jan. 1840 as Tax Collector and recorder of
Cobb County..before E. W. Mobley, J.I.C., J. P. Green, J.I.C.
Reg. 5 Feb. 1840, D. Collins, Clk.

Page 43:   Henry Murray, principal with Thomas West and Nathan
           Parris as securities bonded for $500 on 12 Jan. 1842 as
bailiff of #942 G. M. district before J. W. Moon, J.P.   Reg.
30 Aug. 1841. D. Collins, Clk.

Page 43:   Thos. R. Brantly, principal with William J. Kisin and
           Moses Mick as securities bonded for $500 on 19 Jan.
1841 as constable for #846 G. M....

Page 44:   .... Reg. 30 Aug. 1841.

Page 44: Joel H. Babb, principal with Malithiah (?) Reeves and
         Fleming Maulding as securities bonded for $500 on 6 Jan.
1840 as constable for county. Reg. 30 Aug. 1840, Daniel Collins,
Clk.

Page 45:   Rily Goss, as principal with Hardy Pace and Samuel Den-
           ton, Martin Hasky, Joseph W. Smith as securities bonded
for $500 on 3 March 1840 as constable for #992 G. M. district
before P. H. Randall, J.P.   Reg. 30 Aug. 1841, D. Collins, C.I.C.

Page 45:   Garret Gray, principal with John C. Carson and N. B.
           Green as securities bonded for $1,000 on 11 Jan. 1840...

Page 46:   ....constable for #898 G. M. district. Reg. 30 Aug.
           1841, Daniel Collins, Clk.

Page 46:   Burton Baggitt, principal with Peleg Colly and Joseph
           Wigley as securities bonded for $500 on 6 Jan. 1840 as
constable for #942 G. M. district. Reg. 30 Aug. 1841, D. Collins,
Clk.

COBB COUNTY, GEORGIA - BOND BOOK 1833-1855

Page 47:   Jackson Delk, principal with Robert Groves as security
           bonded for $500 on 6 Jan. 1841 as constable for #897
G. M. district.   Reg. 30 Aug. 1841, D. Collins, Clk.

Page 47:   Milakiah Reeves, principal with Fleming Maulding and
           L. P. Hariston as securities bonded for $500 on 8 May
1841 as constable of county...

Page 48:   Before P. H. Rrudall, J.P.   Reg. 30 Aug. 1841, D.
           Collins.

Page 48:   Stephen Cole, principal with William S. Cole and Angus
           Johns as securities bonded for $500 on 4 Aug. 1841 as
constable for #846 G. M. dist.   Test: J.A.M. Lulus (Siles??) and
George W. Harper, J.P.   Reg. 30 Aug. 1841, D. Collins, Clk.

Page 49:   Burton Baggitt, principal with Dickson Parris and Wiley
           Glover bonded for $500 on 4 Jan. 1841 as constable for
#842, G. M. district before W. S. Cole and Burton Baggitt, J.P.
Reg. 31 Aug. 1841, D. Collins, Clk.

Page 49:   Riley Goss, principal with James A. Collins and Samuel
           G. Gane as securities bonded for $500 on 16 Feb. 1841
as bailiff for #992 G. M. district....

Page 50:   ...before P. H. Brudall, J.P.   Reg. 30 Aug. 1841, D.
           Collins, Clk.

Page 51:   Fleming Maulding, principal with Joel H. Babb and
           Malakiah Reeves as securities bonded for $500 on 9 Jany
1841 as constable for county of Cobb.   Reg. 30 Aug. 1841....

Page 51:   Joel E. Morris, principal with Joel T. Wood and John
           Babb as securities bonded for $500 on 19 May 1841 as
constable for #911 G. M. district..."fill vacancy of district by
F. P. Maulding resigning.." before Thos. H. McClusky, J.P.
Reg. 15 Nov. 1841, D. Collins, Clk.

Page 51: (Duplicate Number) Joshua B. Smith, principal with
           William C. Green and Joseph P. Green as securities bonded
for $500 on 2 June 1841 as constable in "new district formed out
of the 16, 19 and 20 district of Cobb".   Reg. 20 Jan. 1842, D.
Collins, Clk.

Page 52:   David W. McGuire, principal with William McGuire and
           F. S. McGuire as securities bonded for $500 on 1 Jan.
1842 as constable for #991 G. M. district before Thomas M. McGuire
J.P.   Reg. 20 Jan. 1842, D. Collins, Clk.

Pages 53 and 54: Blank

Page 55:   Thomas H. Highsmith, principal with David Dobbs and
           William Harris as securities bonded for $3500 on 7 Feb.
1842 as Tax Collector before Crawford Tucker, J.I.C., Benson
Roberts, J.I.C.   Reg. 16 Feb. 1842, D. Collins, Clk.

Page 56: Blank

Pages 57 & 58: Archibald Howell, principal with Clark Howell as
           security bonded for #319 on 18 Jan. 1842...
bridge contract..before John Auston.   Reg. 10 March 1840,

93

D. Collins, Clk. Bridge let at public outcry across creek at Howell Mill called Victory Crk. (great detail on the exact specifications of this bridge). Reg. 10 March 1842, Daniel Collins, Clk. Bid off to A. Howell for $319. Jos. S. Bulloch, commissioner. I acknowledge as the contract. A. Howell.

Page 59: William J. Delk, principal with Joshua Webb and Claborn Bishop as securities bonded for $1,000 on 10 Jan. 1842 as constable for #898 G. M. district. Reg. 15 May 1842, D. Collins, Clk.

Page 59: J. D. S. Foote, principal with James Foote and Asa C. Hardin as securities bonded for $500 on 12 Oct. 1841 as constable for #942 G. M. district...

Page 60: ....Reg. 15 May 1843, D. Collins, Clk.

Page 60: Thomas R. Brantly, principal with George W. Harper and Zachariah Conger as securities bonded for $500 on 8 Jan. 1842 as constable for #942 G. M. district before J. W. Moon. Reg. 15 May 1842, Collins.

Page 61: Henry Murray, principal with Thomas C. West and Peleg Cooley as securities bonded for $500 on 14 Jany 1842 as bailiff for #742 G. M. district. Reg. 15 May 1842. D. Collins, Clk.

Page 61: Henry D. Teate, principal with Henry Strickland and Wm. T. Pritchard as securities bonded for $500 on 28 Sept. 1841 as constable for #991 G. M. district...

Page 62: Thomas M. McGuire, J.P. Reg. 22 June 1842, D. Collins, Clk.

Page 62: M. W. Green, principal with William Green and N. B. Green as securities bonded for $1,000 on 10 Jan. 1842 as constable for #898 G. M. district. Reg. 22 June 1842, D. Collins, Clk.

Page 63: Nathan Parris, principal with Dickson Parris and H. A. Coleman as securities bonded for $500 on 7 Aug. 1841 as constable for #942 G. M. district before J. Wilson, J.P. Reg. 22 June 1842. D. Collins, Clk.

Page 64: John G. Clonts, principal with Jacob Clonts and William Brooks as securities bonded for $500 on 11 Oct. 1842 before J. W. Moon. Reg. 22 June 1842, D. Collins, Clk.

Page 65: William T. Popham, principal with William R. Turner as security bonded for $500 on 1 Jan. 1843 as constable for #911 G. M. district. Reg. 10 Feb. 1843, D. Collins, Clk.

Page 66: A. B. Reeves, principal with Jason Harrison and John Kirkland as securities bonded for $500 on 14 Jan. 1843 as constable for #911 G. M. district. Reg. 10 Feb. 1843, D. Collins, Clk.

Page 67: Thos. H. Highsmith, principal with Davis Dobbs and William Harris as securities bonded for $4,000 on 25 March 1843 as Tax Receiver before John Lemon, Benson Roberts, J.I.C., Compra Tucker. Reg. 18 April 1843, D. Collins, Clk.

Page 68: Thomas H. Highsmith, principal with David Dobbs and
          William Harris as securieties on 25 March 1843 as Tax
Collector..before John Lemon, Benson Roberts, J.I.C., Crawford
Tucker, J.I.C...

Page 69: Lemuel Maulden, principal with Jesse McCollum and Abram
          Smith as securities bonded for $500 on 9 Jan. 1844 as
constable for county before Hiram M. Whitworth, J.P.   Reg. 26
Jan. 1844, N. Hawthorn, Clerk.

Page 70: 1844. Isaac Osborn, principal with William Brooks as
          security bonded for $500 on 17 Jan. 1844 as
constable for #851 G. M. district. Reg. 26 Jan. 1844, N. Hawthorn
Clk.

Page 71: 1844: William Ragsdale, principal with Saunders Ragsdale
          and Elijah Ragsdale as securities bonded for $500 as
constable for #942 G. M. district on 11 Jan. 1844 before Ccorgc W.
Ragsdale. Reg. 29 Jan. 1844, N. Hawthorn, Clk. I.C.

Page 72: Henry Murray, principal with George W. Cash and Nathan
          Parris as securities bonded for $500 on 6 April 1843 as
bailiff for #942 G. M. district before John George.   Reg. 29 Jan.
1844, N. Hawthorn, Clk.

Page 73: J. H. Hardin, principal with Michael Austin and Asa C.
          Hardin as securities bonded for $500 on 25 Jan. 1844 as
constable for 942 G. M. district. Reg. 6 March 1844 by N. Hawthorn, Clerk Inferior Court, witnessed before James T. Norton and
M. V. Norton, J.P.

Page 74: Jackson Delk, principal with Israel R. Poter, security
          bonded for $500 on 27 Jan. 1844 as constable for 897 G.
M. district before John W. Groves, J.P. Reg. 23 March 1844,
Nathaniel Hawthorn, Clerk.

Page 75: William J. Delk, principal with Claborn Buishop and
          Robert Lemon, securities bonded for $1,000 on 25 March
1844 as constable for 898 G. M. district before Robert Lemon, J.P.
Reg. 25 March 1844, N. Hawthorn, Clerk I. C.

Page 76: John A. Buffington, principal with Wilson Chappell and
          David Aderholt securities bonded for $500 on 23 March
1844 as constable for 911 G. M. district before J. B. Blackwell,
J.P. Reg. 26 March 1844, A. Hawthorn, Clerk.

Page 77: Isabel C. York, principal with Jackson Delk as security
          bonded for $642.85 3/4 on 20 April 1844..."Isabel York
now pregnant with a bastard child" to protect citizens from all
costs for bringing up said child"...before John W. Groves, J.P.
Isabel (X) York. Reg. 1 May 1844, N. Hawthorn, Clk.

Page 78: Richard Carnes, principal with Henry Palmer and William
          Hoope as securities bonded for $500 on 27 April 1844 as
constable (no district given) before Hiram M. Whitworth, J.P. and
Mark (X) Sheffield. Reg. 8 July 1844, N. Hawthorn, Clk.

Page 79: Henry Murray, principal with Joel Compton & John Roe,
          securities bonded for $500 on 30 April 1844 as constable
for 942 G. M. district before John (X) Pendley. Reg. 6 Aug.
1855, Nathaniel Hawthorn, Clk.

Page 80: A. Edwards, principal with William Guiss and Joseph
Guiss as securities, bonded for $500 on 10 Jan. 1844 as
constable for #991 G. M. district before Thomas McGuire, J.P.
Reg. 10 Sept. 1844 by Nathaniel Hawthorn, Clk.

Page 81: John L. Simpson, principal with Harvey M. Mays and
Milton Turk as securities, bonded for $1,000 on 7 Jan.
1845 as constable for #898 G. M. district before Robert Lemon,
J.P. Reg. 10 Jan. 1845 by Nathaniel Hawthorn, Clerk.

Page 82: George Malone, principal with William P. Maloney as
security bonded for $1,000 on 10 Jan. 1845 as constable
for #898 G. M. district before Robert Lemon, J.P. Reg. 10 Jan.
1845, Nathaniel Hawthorn, Clerk.

Page 83: Ambrose J. Morris, principle with Isham Sheffield and
Allen Moore as securities, bonded for $500 on 11 Jan.
1845 as constable for #851 G. M. district before H. M. Whitworth,
J.P. Reg. 8 Feb. 1845. Nathaniel Hawthorn, Clerk.

Page 84: John Maloney, principle with Davis Stansell and John
Hull as securities bonded for $500 on 6 Jan. 1845 as
constable for #851 G. M. district before H. M. Whitworth, J.P.
Reg. 8 Feb. 1845 by Nathaniel Hawthorn, Clerk.

Page 85: Farrer Hall, principal with Joseph C. Picking and David
Adderhold as securities bonded for $500 (no date given)
as constable for #911 G. M. district before (no J.P. given).
Reg. 21 Feb. 1845. Nathaniel Hawthorn, Clerk.

Page 86: Garret Gray, principal with John Deveton and Moses H.
Dunnan as securities bonded for $500 on 21 Jan. 1845 as
Balliff for #942 G. M. district. Reg. 4 March 1845 by Nathaniel
Hawthorn, Clerk.

Page 87: Seborn Gann, principal with Nathan Gann and Alexander G.
Cooper as securities bonded for $500 on 11 Feb. 1845 as
constable for #992 G. M. district. Reg. 27 March 1845, Nathaniel
Hawthorn, Clk.

Page 88: John Brown, principal with Robert Harper and Thomas
Lindley as securities bonded for $500 on 11 March 1845
as constable for #846 G. M. district. Oath of John Brown before
William W. Carrie, J.P. Reg. 12 May 1845 by N. Hawthorn, Clerk.

Page 89: John Foote, principal with James Foote, Senr. and James
C. N. Foote as securities bonded for $500 on 5 April
1845 as constable (no district given). 22 March 1845. William
B. Hammellen, J.P. Reg. 12 May 1845, Nathaniel Hawthorn, Clerk.

Page 90: Mary Smith, principal with George W. Foote as security
bonded for $642.85 3/4/ "...stands charged with being
delivered of a bastard child"...protect inhabitants of county
from all costs... before W. W. Carrell, J.P. Signed: Mary (X)
Smith and G. W. Foote. Reg. 12 May 1845, Nathaniel Hawthorn, Clk.

Page 91: "Whereas W. W. Carrell and Wm. B. Hamilton, 2 of
Justices of the Inferior Court...known "Sussenah Boon"..
married woman...has been delivered of a boy child...bastard...and
is likely to become charge of the county...being before and J.P.
said Susanah to answer to the matter..." 21 July 1845. Served

the within upon the body of Susannah Boren 23 July 1845, John Brown and J. D. S. Foote. Examination before W. W. Carrell and W. B. Hamilton, P.P. 23 July 1845...that 15 April past...delivered of a bastard boy child...William Burnwell is the father...oath taken and signed Susannah Boren.

Page 92: Bond of William Burnwell, principal with Robert Burnwell as security for $642.85 3/4...26 July 1845..."protect inhabitants of county from all costs of maintenance and bring up of said child..." before William B. Hammelton, J.P. Reg. 5 Aug. 1845, Nathaniel Hawthorn, Clerk.

Page 93: Vinson Jourdan, principal with James Sweatt and James J. McWilliams as securities bonded for $500 on 31 May 1845 as constable for #992 G. M. district before David Edleman, J.P. and Silas Brown, J.P. Reg. 25 May 1845, Nathaniel Hawthorn, Clk.

Page 94: H. P. Howell, principal with M. S. Howell and Israel Causey as securities bonded for $150 on 11 Aug. 1845... "above and Isaac Howell make by 1 Oct. next good and sufficient repairs to a certain bridge known as Isaac Howell's toll bridge across Sweetwater Creek at Sweetwater Old Town and continue to keep same in good repair...five years..." road commissioners appointed by Cobb and Campbell Inferior Courts for that purpose Joseph Summetine, Comm. Robert R. Cox, Comm. Reg. 20 Aug. 1845, Nathaniel Hawthorn, Clerk.

Page 95: William F. McTyre, principal with Edward Meys, security bonded for $1,000 on 16 March 1844 as constable for #898 G. M. district. Reg. 26 May 1845, Nathaniel Hawthorn, Clk.

Page 96: James L. C. Smith, principal with William J. Kiser and Garrett Gray as securities bonded for $500 on 5 Jan. 1846 as constable for #846 G. M. district. Oath of James L. C. Smith on 5 Jan. 1846 before Wm. W. Carrell, J.P. Reg. 7 Jan. 1846, Nathaniel Hawthorn, Clerk.

Page 97: Josephua A. Baggett, principal with Wilby Abney and Burton Buggettas securities bonded for $500 on 5 Jan. 1846 as constable (no district given). Oath 5 Jan. 1846 of Josephua Baggett. Reg. 7 Jan. 1846. Nathaniel Hawthorn, Clerk.

Page 98: George Mulins, principal with William P. (Mulveny) as security bonded for $1,000 on 8 Jan. 1846 as constable for #898 G. M. district. Signed: William P. Maning. Reg. 7 Jan. 1846, Nathaniel Hawthorn, Clerk.

Page 99: Green Hill, principal with Edward Hill and John Pace as securities bonded for $1,000 on 8 Jan. 1846 as constable for #998 G. M. district before Robert Lemon, J.P. Reg. 9 Jan. 1846, Nathaniel Hawthorn, Clerk.

The end of N. Hawthorn Adm. as Clerk of Inferior Court.

Page 100: Recording commenced by J. H. McHaffey. Farrier Hall, principal with James M. Bell and Daniel Aderhold as securities bonded for $500 on 9 Jan. 1846 as constable for #911 G. M. district before James B. Blackwell, J.P. Reg. 26 Jan. 1846, James H. Mehaffey, Clerk.

Page 101: Book for the Record of Bailiff's Bonds (Written across

2 pages).   Solomon L. Strickland, principal with Michael
Austin and Jacob Meadows as securities bonded to Justices of
Inferior Court to wit, L. P. Hainston, David Moore, Napoleon B.
Green for $500 on 17 Jan. 1846 as constable for #942 G. M. district
before Jno. Rowe, J.P.   Oath of Solomon L. Strickland before
J. H. Harden, J.P.   Reg. 6 Jan. 1846, J. H. McHaffey, Clerk.

Page 102:   Israel R. Porter, principal with Jackson Delk and
            William F. Groces, as securities bonded for $500 on
29 Jan. 1846 as constable for #987 G. M. district before J. W.
Groves, J.P.   Reg. 25 March 1846, J. H. McHaffey, Clerk.

Page 103:   John Brooks, principal with John and Blare Benjamin
            Smith and Thomas Hammilton as securities bonded for
$177.50..."to build bridge across Nogans Creek at Sweetwater
formerly known as Hill's Old Bridge now known as Wood Bride..."
completed same and court having passed order to county treasurer
for $88.50 in payment...keep in order condition for 5 years.

Page 104.   Reg. 16 Sept. 1846. Nathaniel Hawthorn, Cler.   Lewis
            Hapgood, principal with Henry Mitchell and William R.
Bruntly as securities bonded for $500 on 17 Jan. 1846 as constable
for #942 G. M. district.

Page 105:   Nathaniel Hawthorn principal with William J. Delk and
            John S. Anderson as securities bonded for $3,000 on
16 Sept. 1846 Appointed Clerk of Inferior Court.

Page 106:   Before W. B. Green, Justice Inf. Ct., L. P. Hairston,
            J.I.C., M. S. Bullanger, J.I.C...Reg. 16 Sept. 1846,
Nathaniel Hawthorn, Clerk.   Oath of Nathaniel Hawthorn, 16 Sept.
1846 before N. B. Green, L. B. Hairston and M. S. Ballenger, J.I.C.

Page 107:   Milelah (Mahalah?) Mullens, principal with Thomas
            Mullens as security bonded for $642.85 3/4 on 21 Nov.
1846...protect county from all cost of lying in...of sd. child...
Reg. 7 Dec. 1846.

Page 108:   Mariah C. (X) Norten and John L. Prewett bonded for
            150 £ or $642.84 3/4 on 21 Nov. 1846..."lately been
delivered of bastard...indemify said Justices of Inferior Court
against all costs of lying in, maintenance and bringing up of
said child." before J. H. Hardin, J.P.   Reg. 7 Dec. 1846,
Nathaniel Hawthorn, Clerk.

Page 109:   Benjamin Burnett, principal with Elisha Cocron, Jackson
            Delk and F. M. Toler as securities bonded for $500 on
8 Sept. 1846 as constable for #987 G. M. district before John W.
Groves, J.P.   Reg. 5 Jan. 1847, Nathaniel Hawthorn, Clerk.

Page 110:   James S. C. Smith. principal with Jonathan Lindley and
            Elisha Lindley as securities bonded for $500 on 4 Jan.
1847 as constable for #846 G. M. district.   Reg. 16 Jan. 1847.
Nathaniel Hawthorn, Clerk.

Page 111:   T. H. Morris, principal with William Morris as security
            bonded for $500 on 2 Jan. 1847 as constable for #992
G. M. district before Silas Brown, J.P.   Reg. 16 Jan. 1847,
Nathaniel Hawthorn, Clk.

Page 112:   Farrer Hull, principal with James M. Bell and B. H.

Smith as securities bonded for $500 on 9 Jan. 1847 as constable for #911 G. M. district before J. B. Blackwell, J.P.   Reg. 16 Jan. 1847, Nathaniel Hawthorn, Clerk.

Page 113:   Joshua Welch Oath as county treasurer on 12 Jan. 1847 before N. B. Green, J.I.C., L. P. Hairston, J.I.C. and M. S. Ballinger, J.I.C.   Reg. 16 Jan. 1847, Nathaniel Hawthorn, Clerk.

Page 114:   John Palmer, principal with Thomas B. Clak and William Lindley as securities bonded for $500 on 19 Feb. 1845 as constable for #1017 G. M. district. Reg. 16 Jan. 1847, Nathaniel Hawthorn, Clerk.

Page 115:   James Morehorn, principal with John A. Dobbins and Alexander Mohan, security bonded for $500 on 9 Jan. 1847 as constable for #1017 G. M. before J. A. Green, J.P.   Reg. 30 Jan. 1847, Nathaniel Hawthorn, Clerk.

Page 116:   Muriace (?) Fleming, principal with Jesse C. Farrow, James A. Johnson and James M. Skinner as securities bonded for #00 on 11 Jan. 1847..."whereas Jacob Laseter, a minor and freeperson of collar brought before me Robert Lemon...having summoned 3 freeholders of district in terms of law at the wish of said Jacob Laister to bind him to said Maria Flemming during his monority or until he attains age of 21 years...Maria shall perform all duties..." Robert Lemon, J.P., John L. Simpson, Free H., Joaias W. Shous, Free H.   Signed: Misuce Flemming. Reg. 30 Jan. 1847, Nathaniel Hawthorn, Clerk.

Page 117:   James Morehorn (signed Mohorn) principal with John A. Dobbins, Alexander Mohorn as securities bonded for $500 on 9 Jan. 1847 as constable for #1017 G. M. district before J. A. Green, J.P. Reg. Nathaniel Hawthorn, Clerk.

Page 118:   Repetition of Page 116.

Page 119:   William W. Gibbs, principal with James W. Carlton and James Skinner as securities bonded for $1,000 on 4 Jan. 1847 as constable for #898 G. M. district before M. L. Russ, J.P. Reg. 22 Feb. 1847, Nathaniel Hawthorn, Clerk.

Page 120:   Claborn Bishop, principal with John L. Simpson, William P. Mulony, S. N. Muleny and Joseph Chastain as securities bond to David Moore, Arthur T. Camp, Littleton P. Hairson and Napoleon B. Green all justices of Inferior Court for $4,000 on 2 March 1846 as Tax Collector of Cobb County...before L. P. Harris, J.I.C. and N. B. Green, J.I.C.   Reg. 22 Feb. 1847 by Nathaniel Hawthorn, Clerk.

Page 121:   Repeats the same as above before David Moore, J.I.C. and N. B. Green, J.I.C.

Page 122:   Jackson Delk, principal with Ireael R. Poter and Josiah Land as securities bonded for $500 on 8 Jan. 1847 as constable for #897 C. M. district before John W. Groves, J.P.   Reg. 10 Feb. 1847, Nathaniel Hawthorn, Clerk.

Page 123:   William Eason, principal with Etheldred Austin and Michael Austin as securities bonded for $500 on 26 March 1847 as constable for #947 G. M. district, before Jeremiah

Wesner, J.P.   Reg. 2 May 1847, Nathaniel Hawthorn, Clerk.

Page 124:   David C. Morgan, principal with Hardy Morgan and Jesse
            Morgan as securities bonded for $500 on 10 Feb. 1847
as constable for #1017 G. M. district before John Hill, J.P. and
J. A. Green, J.P.   Reg. 10 May 1847. Nathaniel Hawthorn, Clerk.

Page 125:   William Dobbs, principal with Samuel N. Maloney and
            William Y. H. Stevens as securities bonded for $1,000
on 15 May 1847 as constable for #898 G. M. district..."to fill
vacancy of W. W. Gibbs removal".   Reg. 17 May 1847. Nathaniel
Hawthorn, Clk.

Page 126:   Starling A. Hicks, principal with Henry L. Hix & James
            H. Hill as securities bonded for $500 on 1 Jan. 1848
as constable for #897 G. M. district.   Reg. 15 Feb. 1848, Birdsong
Tolleson, Clerk.

Page 127:   Avery Jarmon, principal with Richard Grogan and Esquire
            (X) Thomason as securities bonded for $500 on 1 Jan.
1848 as constable for #851 G. M. district before H. M. Whitworth,
J.P.   Reg. 15 Feb. 1848, B. Tolleson, Clerk.

Page 128:   Farrar Hall as principal with James M. Bell and B. H.
            Smith as securities bonded for $500 on 9 Jan. 1848 as
constable for #911 G. M. district before J. B. Blackwell, J.P.
Reg. __ Feb. 1848, B. Tolleson, Clerk.

Page 129:   William Eason, principal with Thomas (X) Mullins and
            Jacob S. Clonk as securities, bonded for $500 on 29
Jan. 1848 as constable for #942 G. M. district before Solomon L.
Strickland, J.P. and Jeremiah Wiseman, J.P.   Reg. 15 Feb. 1848,
B. Tolleson, Clk.

Page 130:   James Mohorn, principal with John A. Dobbins and
            Alexander Mohon (also written as Mohorn) bonded for
$500 on 1 Feb. 1848 as constable for #1017 G. M. district before
J. A. Green, J.P.   Reg. 14 Aug. 1848, B. Tolleson, C.I.C.

Page 130:   James L. C. Smith, principal with G. W. Foots and
            James K. Cotten as securities bonded for $500 as con-
stable for #646 G. M. district on 3 Jan. 1848, before W. W.
Carrell, J.P....Reg. 14 Aug. 1848, B. Tolleson, Clerk.

Page 131:   John Brown, principal with Robert Ragin and B. Smith
            as securities bonded for $500 on 3 Jan. 1848 as con-
stable for #846 G. M. district before W. W. Carroll. J.P.   Reg.
12 Aug. 1848, B. Tolleson, Clk.

Page 131: (number repeats) A. H. Green, principal with William
            C. Green and James Mohan as securities bonded for $500
on 9 Feb. 1848 as constable for #1017 G. M. district before J. A.
Green, J.P.   Reg. 14 Aug. 1848.

Page 132:   Ephraim Knight, principal with Samuel N. Malony, John
            L. Simpson, John Walraven and William Morris, Senr.
bonded to David Moore, J.I.C., Littleton P. Hairston, J.I.C.,
Mason Ragsdale, J.I.C. and Napoleon B. Green, J.I.C. bonded for
$5,000 on 1 Feb. 1848..."elected Tax Collector on 3 Jan. 1848",
before Mason M. Ragsdale, N. B. Green.   Reg. B. Tolleson, Clerk.

COBB COUNTY, GEORGIA - BOND BOOK 1833-1855

Page 133: James Fox, principal with Noah B. Sisson and William W. Wright as securities bonded for $500 on 29 Nov. 1847 as constable for #897 G. M. district. Reg. 19 March 1849, B. Tolleson, Clerk.

Page 134: Elisha Mayfield, principal with David Blackwell & Isaiah Williams as securities bonded for $300 on 11 Dec. 1848..."repair bridge and erect handrails of good and substancial materials over Vicony's Creek at Lebanon Mills on the Alabama Road...by 11 Dec. and keep in good repair for 5 years." T. H. Roberts, J.P. and T. B. Hamrick.

Page 135: James P. Brockman, principal with John B. Brockman and Carter (X) Cudd as securities bonded for $500 on 10 Feb. 1847 as constable for #911 G. M. district before Parks Hardman, J.P. and J. B. Blackwell, J.P. Reg. 20 March 1849, B. Tolleson, Clerk

Page 136: Joseph Wofford, principal with Hiram Wofford and David Morgan as securities bonded for $500 on 10 Feb. 1849 as constable for #911 G. M. district before Parks Hardman and J. B. Blackwell, J.P. Reg. 20 March 1849, B. Tolleson, Clerk.

Page 137: Ephraim Knight, principal with John L. Simpson, S. N. Maloney, T. H. McClosky and H. H. Boroughs bonded to N. M. Calder, Washington C. Green, Elisha Lindely, Sidney Carruth and S. Lawrence (no amount given) _____ Ephraim Knight elected on 1 Jan. 1849 Tax Collector for 1849 before S. Lawrence, J.I.C. and W. C. Green, J.I.C. Reg. 20 March 1849, B. Tolleson, Clerk.

Page 138: Ephraim Knight, principal with L. Simpson, S. N. Malony, T. H. McClesky, H. W. Burroughs bonded to George W. Towns, governor for $10,000 _____ (no date) as Tax Collector before S. Lawrence, J.I.C., W. C. Green, J.I.C., Sidney M. Carruth, J.I.C. Reg. 26 March 1849, B. Tolleson, Clerk.

Page 139: Oath of A. P. Dodge before John H. Barr, J.P. as constable. Alford P. Dodgen, principal with Samuel Burdin as security bonded for $500 as constable for #895 G. M. district, no date given. Reg. 30 Nov. 1849, B. Tolleson, Clerk.

Page 140: James Mohorn, principal with John A. Dobbens as security bonded for $500 on 10 Jan. 1849 as bailiff for #1017 G. M. district before James Lindley, J.P. Reg. 30 Nov. 1849, B. Tolleson, Clerk.

Page 141: William Parris, principal with John (X) Wigley and Nathan Paris as securities bonded for $500 on 16 Jan. 1849 as constable for #941 G. M. district before Solomon L. Strickland, J.P.

Page 142: John Malony, principal with S. W. Robertson and J. A. Gober as securities bonded for $500 on 16 Jan. 1849 as constable for #851 G. M. district before H. M. Whitworth, J.P. Reg. 30 Nov. 1849, B. Tolleson, Clerk.

Page 143: James L. C. Smith, principal with Thomas (X) Lindley and A. Reynolds as securities bonded for $500 on 18 Jan. 1849 as constable for #836 G. M. district before Wm. B. Hamilton, J.P. Reg. 30 Nov. 1849, B. Tolleson, Clerk.

101

Page 144: Hugh Baker, principal with Jackson (X) Baggett and Littleton (X) M. Sewell as securities bonded for $500 on 27 Jan. 1849 as constable for #942 G. M. district before Solomon L. Strickland, J.P. Reg. 1 Dec. 1849, B. Tolleson, Clerk.

Page 145: A. H. Green, principal with Wm. G. Green and Harvey M. Mayse as securities bonded for $500 on 29 Jan. 1849 as constable for #1017 G. M. district before James M. Groves, J.P. Reg. 1 Dec. 1849, B. Tolleson, Clerk.

Page 146: Starling A. Hicks, principal with Henry L. (X) Hicks and James H. Hill securities bonded for $500 on 3 Feb. 1849 as constable for #897 G. M. district before Ellis Wright, J.P. Reg. 1 Dec. 1849, B. Tolleson, Clerk.

Page 147: Jesse Landers, principal with Thomas (X) Ballard as security bonded for $500 on 6 Feb. 1849 as constable for #895 G. M. district before T. J. Gray, J.P. Reg. 1 Dec. 1849, B. Tolleson, Clk. "The following affadavit should have been registered before the above ____ of Registered." 7 Feb. 1849, Oath of Jesse Landers.

Page 148: H. F. Bramlett, principal with Wm. P. Malony, Nathaniel Hawthorn as securities bonded for $1,000 on 24 March 1849 as constable for #898 G. M. district before Wm. J. Delk, J.P. Reg. 1 Dec. 1849, B. Tolleson, Clerk.

Page 149: John McDonald, principal with Wm. Morris and James A. McDonald as securities bonded for $500 on 5 May 1849 as constable for #992 G. M. district before P. G. Denham, J.P. and Alfred Maner, J.P. Reg. 1 Dec. 1849, B. Tolleson, Clerk.

Page 150: Jacob S. Clonts, principal with William G. (X) Black, Miles Edwards as securities bonded for $500 on 19 May 1849 as constable for #942 G. M. district before Wm. Eason, J.P. Reg. 3 Dec. 1849, B. Tolleson, Clerk.

Page 151: Archibald Carter, principal with John W. Moore and David G. Austin as securities bonded for $500 on 23 June 1849 as constable for #1043 G. M. district. Reg. 3 Dec. 1849, B. Tolleson, Clerk.

Page 152: Henry F. Bramlett, principal with John S. Anderson as security bonded for $1,000 on 7 Jan. 1850 as constable for #898 G. M. district before Nathaniel Hawthorn, J.P. Reg. 23 Jan. 1850, W. S. Johnson, Clerk.

Page 153: Felix James, principal with Henry White and Joseph J. Spiers as securities bonded for $1,000 on 10 Jan. 1850 as constable for #898 G. M. district before Jas. M. Skinner. Reg. 31 Jan. 1850, W. S. Johnson, Clerk.

Page 154: Jeremiah Matthews, principal with Wm. Weddington and Jacob S. Clonts as securities bonded for $500 on 19 Jan. 1850 as constable for #942 G. M. district before Wm. Eason, J.P. and Edward Y. Johnson, J.P. Reg. 16 Feb. 1850, T. H. Moore, deputy Clerk.

Page 155: William G. Black, principal with William Weddington and Robert H. Weddington as securities bonded for $500 on 19 Nov. 1849 as constable for #942 G. M. district before

Edward Y. Johnson, J.P.   Reg. 16 Feb. 1850, T. H. Moore, d. Clk.
I. C.

Page 156:   Starling A. Hicks, principal with Henry L. (X) Hicks
             and Alexander D. Paden as securities bonded for $500
on 26 Jan. 1850 as constable for #897 G. M. district.   Reg. 16
Feb. 1850, T. H. Moore, D. Clk.

Page 157:   James Mahorn, principal with John A. Dobbins and Laston
             H. Green as securities bonded for $500 on 9 Feb. 1850
as constable for #1017 G. M. district before James Lindley, J.P.
Reg. 23 Feb. 1850, T. H. Moore, D. Clk.

Page 158:   B. W. Donehoo, principal with William J. Delk as
             security bonded for $1,000 on 6 Jan. 1851 as constable
for #898 G. M. district before N. B. Green, J.I.C.   Reg. 10 Jan.
1851, T. H. Moore, D. Clk.

Page 159:   Miles Mullens, principal with Toliver Hicks and Allen
             W. Moore as securities bonded for $500 on 4 Jan. 1851
as constable for #851 G. M. district before H. M. Whitworth, J.P.
Reg. 10 Jan. 1851, T. H. Moore, D. Clk.

Page 160:   Thos. W. Grogan, principal with John T. Camp and Oliver
             Bussom as securites bonded for $500 on 6 Jan. 1851 as
constable for #851 G. M. district before H. M. Whitworth, J.P.
Reg. 10 Jan. 1851, T. H. Moore, D. Clk.

Page 161:   William Jones, principal with James M. Bell and B. H.
             Smith as securities bonded for $500 on 11 Jan. 1851 as
constable for #911 G. M. district before Parks Hardmon, J.P.
Reg. 13 Jan. 1851, T. H. Moore, D. Clk.

Page 162:   John D. Norton, principal with Tally Norton and Daniel
             W. Norton as securities bonded for $500 on 11 Jan. 1851
as constable before Edward Y. Johnson, J.P.   Reg. 13 Jan. 1851,
T. H. Moore, D. Clk.

Page 163:   Joshua Welch, principal with Thadeus McClesky and H.W.
             Burroughs securities bonded to Crawford Tucker, S. M.
Carruth, W. C. Green and N. M. Calder as Justices of Inferior
Court for $5,000 on 14 Jan. 1850.   Appointed County Treasurer,
William S. Johnson, Clerk Inferior Court by T. H. Moore, D. Clk.
Reg. 14 Jan. 1851.

Page 164:   Ephraim Knight, principal with Thomas H. Moore, Henry
             W. Burroughs bonded to H. Lindley, Washington C. Green,
Sidney M. Carruth, N. M. Calder and Sam'l Lawrence as Justices of
Inferior Court bonded for $5,000 on 8 Feb. 1850 as Tax Collector.
S. Lawrence, J.I.C. and E. H. Lindley, J.I.C.   Reg. 27 (?),
1851.   T. H. Moore, D. Clk.

Page 165:   James P. Brockman, principal with John B. Brockman and
             C. M. Brockman as securities bonded for $500 on 11 Jan.
1851 as constable for #911 G. M. district before Parks Hardman,
J.P.   Reg. 29 Jan. 1851, T. H. Moore, Dpt. Clk.

Page 166:   Birdsong Tolleson, principal with Joshua Welch and
             Henry W. Burroughs as securities bonded for $2,000 on
3 Feb. 1851 "elected" clerk: C. Tucker, J.I.C.; W. C. Green,
J.I.C.; S. M. Barrith, J.I.C.   Reg. 15 Feb. 1851, W.S. Johnson,
Clk. Inf. Ct.

Page 166: Birdsong Tolleson, principal with Joshua Welch and Henry W. Burroughs as securities bonded for $2,000 on 3 Feb. 1851 "elected" clerk: C. Tucker, J.I.C.; W. C. Green, J.I.C.; S. M. Barrith, J.I.C. Reg. 15 Feb. 1851, W. S. Johnson, Clk. Inf. Ct.

Page 167: Thaddeus H. McCluskey, principal with John G. (S?) Anderson and James B. Blackwell as securities bonded for $5,000 on 3 Feb. 1851.."elected Receiver of Tax Returns": C. Tucker, J.I.C.; W. C. Green, J.I.C. Reg. 15 Feb. 1851, W. S. Johnson, Clerk. Sidney W. Caruth, J.I.C.

Page 168: Elijah Maner, principal with Elijah (X) Roberts and Sandford V. Maner, securities bonded for $500 on 9 Feb. 1851 as constable for #992 G. M. district. Reg. 15 Feb. 1851, W. S. Johnson, Clk.

Page 169: Birdsong Tolleson, principal with Joseph Harkey and Wm. Chestnut as securities bonded for $1500 on 4 Feb. 1851 "appointed agent of poor school funds of said county" by C. Tucker, J.I.C.; S. M. Caruth, J.I.C.; N. M. Caulden, J.I.C. Reg. 17 Feb. 1851, T. H. Moore, Dpty Clk.

Page 170: John J. Summers, principal with Richard Robinson, Riley (X) Harwell as securities bonded for $500 on 8 March 1851 as constable for #992 G. M. district before P. G. Denham, J.P. and Alfred Maner, J.P. Oath of John Summers before Patrick G. Denham. 8 March 1851. Reg. 24 April 1851.

Page 171: Sterlin A. Hicks, principal with Henry L. Hicks and Nathaniel Reed as securities bonded for $500 on 21 Jan. 1851 as constable for #897 G. M. district. Reg. 24 April 1851, William S. Johnson, Clk.

Page 172: Thomas Whitehead, principal with John L. Anderson and John A. Dobbins, John McElereth and James Mohorne, Allston H. Green as securities bonded for $10,000...elected Tax Collector on 6 Jan. 1851 before William C. Green, J.I.C.; C. Tucker, J.I.C.; N. M. Calder, J.I.C.

Page 173: Thomas Whitehead, principal with John L. Anderson, John A. Dobbins, John McElereth, James Mohorn and Alston H. Green bonded to Justices of Inferior Court: N. M. Calder; W. C. Green; S. M. Carruth and Crawford Tucker for $6,000 on 7 Jan. 1851 as Tax Collector for 1851. Reg. 24 April 1851, William S. Johnson, Clk.

Page 174: John Hughs, principal with Robert Lemon and Richard Robinson as securities bonded for $500 on 14 June 1851 as constable for #992 G. M. district before Alfred Maner, J.P. Reg. 28 July 1851, William S. Johnson, Clerk.

Page 175: William Mote, principal with Thomas C. West and Joshua A. Baggett, Urban Pattillo as securities bonded for $500 on 20 Jan. 1852 as bailiff for #1017 G. M. district before James Lindley, J.P. Reg. 22 Jan. 1852 by John F. Arnold, Clerk. Pr R. M. C. Moore.

Page 176: Ambrose L. Morris, principal with Martin Skelton and Squire (X) Thomason as securities bonded for $500 on 9 Aug. 1851 as constable for #851 G. M. district before H. M.

Whitworth, J.P.   Reg. 22 Jan. 1852, J. F. Arnold, C.I.C. pr
R. M. C. Moore.

Page 177: Urban Pattillo, principal with John O. Smith and J. M.
           Blackwell as securities bonded for $500 on 3 Jan. 1852
as constable for #846 G. M. district before B. H. Smith, J.P.
Reg. 22 Jan. 1852, J. F. Arnold, C.I.C. pr. R. M. C. Moore.

Page 178: Job Smith, principal with Thomas C. West and Wiley (X)
           Davis as securities bonded for $500 on 3 Jan. 1852 as
constable for #846 G. M. district before B. H. Smith. J.P.   Reg.
22 Jan. 1852, John F. Arnold, C.I.C. pr. R. M. C. Moore.

Page 179: John C. Griffin, principal with William A. Austin and
           Hiram Wofford as securities bonded for $500 on 5 Jan.
1852 as constable for #911 G. M. district before Parks Hardman and
T. Hale, J.P. Reg. 22 Jan. 1852, John F. Arnold pr. R. M. C.
Moore.

Page 180: A. K. Campbell, principal with Robert Lemon and William
           H. Powell as securities bonded for $500 on 5 Jan. 1852
as constable for #911 G. M. district before Nathaniel F. Legg,
J.P. and Alfred Manor, J.P.   Reg. 22 Jan. 1852. John F. Arnold
pr. R. M. C. Moore.

Page 181: Benjamin Bullard, principal with William Bullard and
           John B. Brangford (?) as securities bonded for $500 on
3 Jan. 1852 as constable for #875 G. M. district. Reg. 22 Jan.
1852, John F. Arnold pr. R. M. C. Moore. Thos. J. Gray, J.P.

Page 182: Elisha W. Cochran, principal with B(orP.) (?) W.
           Cochran as security bonded for $500 on 6 Jan. 1852 as
constable for #897 G. M. District. Reg. 22 Jan. 1852. John F.
Arnold pr R. M. C. Moore.

Page 183: Samuel Denton, principal with Sanders W. Ragsdale and
           William Ragsdale as securities bonded for $500 on 9 Jan.
1852 as constable for #1043 G. M. district before J. Ragsdale, J.P.
Reg. 28 Jan. 1852, R. M. C. Moore, Dpt. Clk.

Page 184: William G. Black, principal with Jeremiah Matthews and
           Miles Edwards as securities bonded for $500 on 17 Jan.
1852 as constable for #942 G. M. district before Edward Y. Johnson,
J.P. and Wm. Eason, J.P.   Reg. 18 March 1852 by William F. Groves,
Dpt. C.I.C.

Page 185: James Mohan, principal with John A. Dobbin and Alexan-
           der Mohan as securities bonded for $500 on __ Jan.
1852 as constable for #1017 G. M. district before James Lindley,
J.P. and James W. Groves, J.P.   Reg. 18 March 1852, William F.
Groves, D.C.I.C.

Page 186: Thomas Whitehead, principal with Samuel M. Malone, John
           A. Dobbins, Washington C. Green, John McElereath, John
O. Gartrell bonded for $1200 on 6 April 1852.."elected 6 Jan.
1852 as Tax Collector: before W. C. Green, J.P.; Wm. B. Hamilton,
J.I.C. and Wm. R. Chesnut, J.I.C.

Page 187: Reg. 8 April 1853, William F. Groves. Urban Pattillo,
           principal with Wesley H. Pattillo and J. L. W. (X)
Cooper as securities bonded for $500 on 8 May 1852 as constable

for #849 G. M. district before J. M. Barbwell, J.P.   Reg. 14 May 1852, Wm. F. Groves, Dpt. Clk.

Page 188: Thadeus M. McClesky, principal with William Dunn, James B. Blackwell and Will A. Austin as securities bonded for $5,000 on 5 Jan. 1852 as Receiver of Tax Returns for 1852 before W. C. Green, J.I.C. and S. M. Carruth, J.I.C.   Reg. 26 May 1852, John F. Arnold pr William F. Groves.

Page 189: John F. Arnold, principal with William Phillips and A. R. White as securities bonded for $3,000 on 13 Jan. 1852.."elected Clerk of Inferior Court before W. C. Green, J.I.C.; S. M. Carruth, J.I.C.; Wm. R. Chestnut, J.I.C."   Reg. 26 May 1852, John F. Arnold pr Groves.

Page 190: Birdsong Tolleson, principal with Henry W. Burroughs and J. N. Higgie as securities bonded for $2,000 on 3 Feb. 1852.."elected Ordinary...capacity as School Commissioner".. before W. C. Green, J.I.C.; S. M. Carruth, J.I.C. and Wm. R. Chesnut, J.I.C.   Reg. Moore, agt.

Page 191: Thomas H. Moore, principal with Isaac McConnell, Jesse J. Northcutt, Aaron S. Smith as securities bonded for $3,000 on 13 Jan. 1852 as clerk for Inferior Court before S. M. Carruth, J.I.C.; Wm. R. Chesnut, J.I.C.   Reg. 27 May 1852, J. F. Arnold, Clk. pr W. F. Groves, D.C.

Page 192: Burrell Kemp, principal with William Kemp as security bonded for $500 on 20 Jan. 1852.."elected Coroner of 5 Jan. 1852"..before W. C. Green, J.I.C.   Reg. 27 May 1852. John F. Arnold pr Groves.

Page 193: William H. Young, principal with John M. Edge, T. H. McClusky and James M. Young as securities bonded for $3,000 on 30 Jan. 1852...."elected 5 Jan. 1852 as County Surveyor" before S. M. Carruth, J.I.C. and W. C. Green, J.I.C.   Reg. 27 May 1852. John F. Arnold pr Groves.

Page 194: A. R. Hicks, principal with Henry L. (X) Hicks and James Hill as securities bonded for $500 on 5 June 1852 as constable for #897 G. M. district before James Power, J.P. Reg. 8 June 1852. Wm. F. Groves, D.C.

Page 195: Ashton H. Green, principal with John C. Wright, Martin Cooley, B. W. Donehoo, J. N. Higgies, James Pattillo as securities bonded for $1,000 on __ April 1852 as constable for #898 G. M. district before N. B. Green, J.P.   Reg. 18 June 1852, Wm. F. Groves, D. C.

Page 196: Mary A. Pruitt and John J. Carnes bonded for 150 Ł being $642.85 3/4 on 23 May 1852..."Carnes charged with being reputed father of bastard child of which Mary A. Pruitt has been lately delivered of...educate, maintain said child ...to age of 14 years...expenses of lying in...indemnify Justices of Inferior Court from all costs.." before B. H. Smith, J.P.

Page 197: M. T. Castleberry, principal with Harrison (X) Baswell and J. E. Gravitt as securities bonded for $500 on __ Nov. 1852 as constable for #897 G. M. district before John Richard, J.P.   Reg. 8 Dec. 1852, William F. Groves, D. Clk.

Page 198: Thomas Whitehead, principal with Thadeus H. McCluskey,
           Lorenzo D. Trout, John L. Clerk, H. W. Burroughs, Bird
Conger, J. Welch as securities bonded to N. M. Calder, Washington
C. Green, S. M. Carruth, Wm. R. Chesnut and William B. Hamilton,
Justices of Inferior Court for $12.000 on 7 Sept. 1852 "elected
Tax Collector on 5 Jan. last for 1852" before Wm. R. Chesnut,
J.I.C.; Wm. B. Hamilton, J.I.C.; and N. M. Calder, J.I.C.   Reg.
13 Dec. 1852, William F. Groves, D.C.

Page 199: Hartwell A. Baldwin, principal with Robert Lemon and
           Jesse Landers as securities bonded for $500 on 1 Jan.
1853 as constable for #992 G. M. district before Alvred Manor,
J.P. and Nathaniel F. Legg, J.P.   Reg. 5 Jan. 1853, Groves, D.C.

Page 200: Job Smith, principal with James O. Smith and John O.
           Smith as securities bonded for $500 on 1 Jan. 1853 as
constable for #846 G. M. district before B. H. Smith, J.P. and
J. M. Blackwell, J.P.   Reg. 5 Jan. 1853, Groves, D.C.

Page 201: Joshua Welch, principal with J. B. Blackwell, Cyrus B.
           York as securities bonded to W. C. Green, S. M. Carruth,
N. M. Calder, Wm. R. Chesnut and William B. Hamilton, Justices of
Inferior Court for $5,000 on 4 Jan. 1853..."appointed County
Treasurer for 2 years"..before Wm. B. Hamilton, J.I.C.; Wm. R.
Chesnut, J.I.C.; W. C. Green, J.I.C.   Reg. 5 Jan. 1853, Groves,
D. C.

Page 202: Churchill Mason, principal with Thomas H. Harris and
          E. C. Stancil as securities bonded for $140 on 24 Dec.
1852.."built bridge across Allatoona Creek in 20th district of
county for $70..will keep in good repair for 5 years" before Wm.
B. Hamilton, J.I.C.; Wm. R. Chesnut, J.I.C.; W. C. Green, J.I.C.
Reg. 5 Jan. 1853, Groves, D.C.

Page 203: S. A. Hicks, principal with Henry L. (X) Hicks and A.R.
           Hicks as securities bonded for $500 on 10 Jan. 1853 as
constable for #897 G. M. district before John Richards, J.P.
Reg. 11 Jan. 1853, Groves, D. C.

Page 204: James M. McGuire, principal with Asa Dobbs and Seaborn
           McGuire as securities bonded for $500 on 3 Jan. 1853
as constable for #991 G. M. district before Thomas M. McGuire, J.P.
Reg. 13 Jan. 1853, Groves, D. C.

Page 205: David M. C. Black, principal with W. H. Clay, Moses
           Clay, Jesse Glasgow, Miles Glasgow as securities
bonded for $500 on 1 Jan. 1853 as constable for #895 G. M. district
before Thomas J. Gray, J.P. and John Stewart, J.P.   Reg. 23 Jan.
1853, Groves, D. C.

Page 206: Urban Pattillo, principal with John Hill, Sr. and N. M.
           Calder as securities bonded for $500 on 12 Jan. 1853
as constable for #846 G. M. district before J. M. Barnwell, J.P.
Reg. 2 Feb. 1853, Groves, Dpt. Clk.

Page 207: Nathaniel Reed, principal with Jesse (X) Daniel and
           S. N. Malony as securities bonded for $500 on 1 Feb.
1853 as constable for #897 G. M. district before R. D. Tucker, J.P.
Reg. 2 Feb. 1853, Groves, D. Clk.

Page 208: William L. (X) Robertson, principal with George Roberts and Thomas Roberts as securities bonded for $500 on 22 Jan. 1853 as constable for #991 G. M. district before Willi Roberts, J.P.   Reg. 3 Feb. 1853, Groves, D. Clk.

Page 209:   John Barrett bonded for $100 (no security) on 2 Feb. 1853.."has agreed to take an orphan child by name of John Clark Sanders and keep same for 12 mos. from 1 day Feb. 1853 for sum of $40 to be paid at end of 12 mos..." before T. M. Kirkpatrick, J.I.C., N. L. Chester, J.I.C.   Reg. 4 Feb. 1853, Groves, D. C.

Page 210:   Benjamin Bullard, principal with William Bullard and John B. Rumph as securities bonded for $500 on 5 Feb. 1853 as constable for #895 G. M. district before Thomas Brown, J.P. and John Stewart, J.P.   Reg. 15 Feb. 1853, B. Tolleson, Dpt. Clk.

Page 211:   John Turk, principal with Harvey M(?) Mayes and Angus Johnson as securities bonded for $500 on 5 April 1853 as constable for #1017 G. M. district before Joel A. Green, J.P. Reg. 14 April 1853, B. Tolleson, D.C.

Page 212:   Henry F. Bramblett, principal with Samuel N. Malony as security bonded for $1,000 on 14 Jan. 1853 as constable for #898 G. M. district before N. B. Green, J.P.   Reg. 18 April 1853, B. Tolleson, D.C.

Page 213:   Alston H. Green, principal with John C. Wright, J. N. Higgie, Martin Cooley as securities bonded for $1,000 on 14 Jan. 1853 as constable for #898 G. M. district before N. B. Green, J.P.   Reg. 18 April 1853, B. Tolleson, D. Clk.

Page 214:   Israel R. Porter, principal with Jackson Delk and Tilman (X) Smith bonded for $500 on 7 Jan. 1854 as constable for #897 G. M. district.   Reg. 18 Jan. 1854, Jas. E. Skelton, Clerk I.C.

Page 215:   James P. Brockman, principal with John B. Brockman, Isaac G. Albriton as securities bonded for $500 on 7 Jan. 1854 as constable for #911 G. M. district before Samuel R. McCluskey, J.P. and James M. Bell, J.P.   Reg. 20 Jan. 1854, Jas. E. Skelton.

Page 216:   Henry J. Hopkins, principal with Amslade Reynolds, Charles H. Andersen as securities bonded for $500 on 7 Jan. 1854 as constable for #846 G. M. district before J. M. Barnwell, J.P.   Reg. 30 Jan. 1854, Jas. E. Skelton, Clk.

Page 217:   Urban Pattillo, principal with James K. Coltan, John V. Smith as securities bonded for $500 on 7 Jan. 1854 as constable for #846 G. M. district before James M. Barnwell, J.P. Reg. 30 Jan. 1854, Jas. E. Skelton, Clk.

Page 218:   Alston H. Green, principal with J. N. Higgie, S. N Malony as securities bonded for $1,000 on 7 Feb. 1854 as constable for #898 G. M. district before N. B. Green, J.P. and Jas. W. Mumphrey, J.P.   Reg. 15 Feb. 1854, Jas. E. Skelton, Clk.

Page 219:   Henry F. Bramlett, principal with J. N. Higgie and S.N. Malony as securities bonded for $1,000 on 7 Feb. 1854 as constable for #898 G. M. district before N. B. Green, J.P. and

Jas. W. Murphy, J.P.   Reg. 15 Feb. 1854, Jas. E. Skelton, Clerk.

Page 220:   George W. Prichard, principal with James Pritchard as
            security bonded for $500 on 4 Jan. 1854 as constable
for #851 G. M. district before James S. Cheek. H. C. Jackson, J.P.
and Jas. C. Peters, J.P.   Reg. 9 March 1854, Jas. E. Skelton,
Clerk.

Page 221:   William (X) Stansell, principal with John Malony and E.
            Chastain Stansell as securities bonded for $500 on 11
Feb. 1854 as constable for #851 G. M. district before Jas. C.
Jackson, J.P. and H. C. Peters, J.P.   Reg. 9 March 1854, Skelton,
Clerk.

Page 222:   J. B. Duvall, principal with Silvanus Ballding(?) and
            W. T. Croft as securities bonded for $500 on 4 Feb.
1854 as constable for #991 G. M. district before A. J. Rigsby,
J.P.   Reg. 14 June 1854, Jas. E. Skelton, Clerk.

Page 223:   Felix James, principal with H. W. Buroughs, L. A.
            Simpson and B. S. Johnson as securities bonded for
$1,000 on 15 May 1854 as constable for #898 G. M. district before
N. B. Green, J.I.C. and J. W. Murphy, J.I.C.

Page 124 (misnumbered)   Felix James, principal with Thomas (X)
            James, Ezink (?) D. Hall bonded for $1,000 on 2 May
1854 as constable for #898 G. M. district before N. B. Green, J.P.
and J. W. Murphy, J.P.   Reg. 14 June 1854, Jas. E. Skelton, Clerk.

Page 225:   Robert Denham, principal with P. G. Denham as security
            bonded for $500 on 10 Jan. 1854 as constable for #992
G. M. District before Robert Lemon. Reg. 14 June 1854, Skelton,
Clerk.

Page 226:   John N. Underwood, principal with Jesse Landers as
            security bonded for $500 on 10 Jan. 1854 as constable
for #992 G. M. district before Robert Lemon, J.P.   Reg. 14 June
1854, Jas. Skelton, Clerk.

Page 227:   John Turk, principal with Angus Johnson as security
            bonded for $500 on 11 Feb. 1852 as constable for #1017
G. M. district. Reg. 14 June 1854, Jas. Skelton, Clerk.

Page 228:   Alexander McClarty and Hiram Brown bonded for 150 Ł or
            $642.85 3/4 on 14 March 1854..."Alexander McClarty
charged with being reputed father of bastard child..Mary Hill has
lately been delivered of...educate..maintain..pay expenses.."
before J. M. Barnwell, J.P.

Page 229:   James E. Skelton, principal with Joshua Welch and
            William Phillips as securities bonded for $3,000 on 13
Jan. 1854 as Clerk of Inferior Court before T. M. Kirkpatrick,
J.I.C.; George Roberts, J.I.C. and Norman L. Chester, J.I.C.
Reg. 24 July 1854, Skelton, Clerk.

Page 230:   John Anderson, principal with Wm. P. Anderson, Joshua
            Welch, William Phillips bonded for $20,000 on 13 Jan.
1854 as Sheriff before T. M. Kirkpatrick, J.I.C.; Norman L. Chester,
J.I.C.p George Roberts, J.I.C.   Reg. 24 July 1854, Skelton, Clk.

Page 231:   William B. Taylor, principal with Mordicai Myers,

109

Thomas R. Huson, Thomas H. Moore as securities bonded for $3,000 on 13 Jan. 1854..."elected Clerk of Inferior Court" before T. M. Kirkpatrick, J.I.C.; Norman L. Chester, J.I.C.; George Roberts, J.I.C.   Reg. 24 July 1854, Skelton, Clerk.

Page 232: Patrick G. Denham, principal with Richard Robsan, M. D. Morris, Robert Lemon and G. W. Powell as securities bonded for $6,000 on 4 April 1854 "elected Receiver of Tax Returns." Reg. 25 July 1854, Jas. E. Skelton, Clerk.

Page 233: John White, principal with James B. Blackwell and Thomas H. Moore as securities bonded for $500 on 13 Jan. 1854 as coroner of Cobb County before Norman L. Chester, J.I.C.; T. M. Kirkpatrick, J.I.C.; George Roberts, J.I.C.   Reg. 25 July 1854, Skelton, Clk.

Page 234: John W. Dewer, principal with George T. Northrop and N. B. Green as securities bonded for $200 on 1 Aug. 1854...Dewer and Northrop erected a bridge across Nickajack Creek near Mill Grove Post Office..."keep up for 5 years from 26 Feb. last."   Reg. 26 Aug. 1854, Jas. F. Skelton, Clerk.

The preceding data completes the main portion of the book. However, an index appears in the back of the book and after that upside down is the following data for 1855:

James Mohan, principal with Wm. Morris and John A. Wells as securities bonded for $500 on 11 July 1853 as bailiff (no district given) before John Clay, J.P. Reg. 7 April 1855. Christopher McCrary, Dpt. Clk.

Alexander Mohan, principal with Jesse Mohan and Josiah Johnson as securities bonded for $500 on 16 July 1855.

2nd
Alexander Mohan as bailiff for #846 G. M. district before Daniel May, J.P. Reg. 7 April 1855, E. R. Mills, Clerk.

John James, principal with Joashly James and John Jeffers as securities bonded for $500 on 14 Dec. 1855 as bailiff for #846 G.M. district before Daniel May, J.P. Reg. 7 April 1855, E. R. Mills, Clerk.

3rd
Martin (X) Ingram, principal with Gideon (X) Trout and Abner (X) Camp as securities bonded for $500 on 7 Jan. 1853 as constable for #792 G.M. district before Wm. B. Mahon, J.P. Reg. 7 April 1855, Christopher McCrary, Dpt. Clk.

Jesse Davis, principal with David McClara? and Jesse Griffin as securities bonded for $500.

4th
As constable for #845 G.M. district on 15 Oct. 1853, before John M. Williford, J.P. Reg. 7 April 1835, Enoch R. Mills, Clk.

Jesse Davis, constable oath before John M. Williford, J.P. as constable for #845 G.M. District.

June 15, 1835: Recd full compensation for recording bond to this page, E. Mills.
End

COBB COUNTY, GEORGIA - BOND BOOK A, PART I
1855-1877

This book has been placed in a binder to protect it and the center
entries are very difficult to read. The first part of the book is
in ledger form and contains what appears to be the receipts of a
county official...the names only will be copies as the payments
are for advertising, etc. as well as for bonds, etc. Pages
numbered beginning with one.

(The second part of the book gives the bonds, purposes, oaths for
various elected officials of the county. Pages renumbered there
beginning with one.)

Page 1. 1855. William H. Hunt; T. H. Moore and Lacky; J. H.
         Barr; W. Delk; G. W. Johnson; Jep. Robinson; Wm. Delk;
Elisha Buise and J. Buise; J. A. G. Anderson; S. H. Watson gdn
Bates; Geo. Roberts, adm. Burt; Wilson Harrell, adm R. Harwell;
N. A. Fletcher, guard; Wm. Easterling, adm.; Jacob Hubbard, gd.;
N. W. Smith, Adm. Wl Tinsley dec'd, J. A. G. Anderson, adm.;
W. P. Strickland; John G. Felton; Jesse Webb, adm.; J. & N. Dur-
han; Dan'l Collins, exor.; N. W. Smith...Tindley dec'd.; T. Moore;
T. Walker dec'd; J. A. Tilleson and J. Hinton; M. G. Mosepey and
S. G. Monlyde ...conti. to page 14

Page 2. 1855...John G. Campbell

Page 3. 1855...Jacob Meadows gdn Wm. C. Pruett

Page 4. 1855...Jacob Meadows

Page 6. 1855...Jacob Meadows gdn S. D. Pruett; J. A. Tolleston,
         adm.

         1854...T. B. Hamrick gdn.

Page 7.   John F. Perry

Page 8. 1855...Drs. G. Tannent and Hardy exors.

Page 9. 1855...Mrs. E. C. Ballenger, gdn.

Page 10. 1855...Keller and M. Kenny lists land warrant #4872
          Seminole War drawn by Wm. D. McGuire, private in Ashley's
Co., Ga. Militia 18th June 1855 of 120 a.

          John Renfroe adm of L. J. A. Freeny trans. to p. 90

Page 11. 1855...Isaac adm of J. Rutherford

Page 12. 1855...John W. Henley gdn Lott Henley

Page 13. 1855...J. A. G. Anderson gdn. John Anderson

Page 14 & 15. 1855...William H. Hunt mentions D. M. & S. E.
               Young admrs...W. C. Sargent gdn...W. W. Smoke, adm;
T. H. Moore; T. Walker dec'd.; John G. Campbell adm.; Frances
McElreath; R. & W. Hammock; H. B. Kemp adm; G. W. Ragsdale;
Sarah Mehaffey; G. W. Johnson, 1852; Lavinia Esterling 1852; T. H.
Moore; Elpina Fowler 1852 & 1853; Jep Robertson; H. C. Jackson
1853; John L. Simpson; Eliz. Walraven; G. W. Johnson 1854; Cuups
estate; Lackey estate; L. K. Robert; R. & W. Hammock admrs.;
Sarah R. Cash; D. W. Cooper; Jeptha Robinson; H. C. Jackson;

111

Agricola; Delk; Campbell

Page 16. 1855...William H. Hunt...C. D. Phillips (Green's es.);
          Elisha Buise (Wm. Harvell); David Morgan; A. Green;
Hardy & Tennant; D. M. Young; John Malony; Wm. & R. Hammock; J. W.
Henly; Ellis Wright ex; N. C. Daniell; A. B. Farris; Tulser Dobbs;
C. Burt; C. Burt; G. Roberts; S. A. F. Rutherford; Geo. Roberts;
M. L. Lenoir; Churchill Mason; Reuben Freeman; Wm. Stancell;
Ganaway Johnson; J. C. Brown; Clinton Webb; John H. Miller; C.
Vaughan; Jesse Oslin; Jeremiah Moore; A. N. Simpson; E. B. Foots;
J. G. Campbell

Page 17. 1855...Ruggles & Howard...(ledger type entries) amounts
          not copies as binding is to tight)

Je 29 Citation for let dism. R. E. Eason exor
July 12 Citation 2 months notice John Malong land
  "   " citation 2 months notice (W.S. Marked through) M.T.
          Phillips negro
July 18 Citation let. of adm Joseph Greer admr
  "   "   "   "   "   "   Joel Renfroe Admr
  "   "   "   "   "   guard. Joel Renfroe guard
  "   28   "   "   "   "   James Fain admr
  "   "   "   "   "   "   John Y. Alexander ad.
  "   31   "   "   "   (Whitfreeter?0 Julia H. Hollister
Aug. 4   "   "   "   gd. D. W. & Alex F. Orr
Sept. 7   "   "   ad de bonis non Geo. T. Northrup
Oct. 4   "   "   adm. Frasier & Sampler
  "   "   "   "   "   Allen Williamson
  "   "   "   "   "   John M. Kemp
  "   17   "   "   "   T. J. Ramsey
  "   "   "   "   "   Bennett (L/T?) Johnson
  "   25   "   "   "   Willis Roberts
  "   "   "   "   "   B. & Burnes
  "   "   "   adv. sale land John Malony
          "   notice Dr. & Cr N. C. Daniel
          "   "   sale land Jush Buise
          "   "   2 mos notice Wilson Harwell
          "   "   sale land Wm. Sargeant
          "   "   Geo. Roberts (sale negroes)
          "   2 mos notice Geo Roberts
          "   "   "   "   J. A. G. Anderson
          "   "   "   "   M. L. Lanoir
          "   " sale negro Clayton Vaughan
          "   " sale land C. D. Phillips
          "   "   "   "   Ellis Wright
          "   " mos notice N. W. Smith
          "   " sale land S. Dobbs
          "   "   "   "   M. L. Lanoir
          "   "   "   "   N. W. Smith
          "   "   "   "   Geo. Roberts

Page 18.   Howard & Ruggles
            Amt. brot forward $139.50
            By comm 25%   Cr   34.87
                                                    ‾‾‾‾‾‾
                                                    104.63
            By cash to Ruggles   75.00
            Amt due   ‾29.63

            By cash to Ruggles   10.00
                                                    ‾‾‾‾‾‾
                                                    $19.63

112

Pages 19-22. Blank

Page 23. Gen'l A. J. Hansell decd ad T. R. Huson
1855
1854, Dec. 9 To citation by Atkinson
            To adv. notice Dr. & crs
            To adv. sale of personal property
            To adv. 2 mos. notice
            To adv. in Georgian
            To taking record & recording bond
            To warrant of appraisement
            To recording
            To letters of adm.
            To recording order

Page 24. Gen'l. A. J. Hansell admr C. C. Bostick
1855   To citation by Adkinson
          To temp. letters
          To citation in Georgian
          To taking and recording bond
          To warrant of appraisement
          To recording of appraisement
          To prem. letters
          To recording orders

Page 25. Gen'l A. J. Hansell ad Taylor, decd
1855   To citation by Adkinson
          To cit. by ordy
          To taking & recording bond
          To letters of adm de bonis will annexed
          To recording orders

Page 26. Gen'l A. J. Hansell ad Robt B. Bostick
1855   To citation by Adkinson
          To citation in Georgian
          To taking & recording bond
          To warrant of appraisement
          To recording of appraisement
          To let. of adm
          To proving will
          To recording will
          To recording order

Page 27   Robert M. Woodman ad Bishop
1855   To citation by Adkinson
Oct. 9   By adm settled by Adkinson & receipted
          To citation in Georgian
          To taking & recording bond
          To warrant of appraisement
          To record of warrant of appraisement
          To taking & recording bond
          To letters of Administration
          To recording orders

Page 28. J. Y. Alexander ad Alexander
1855   To 2 mos notice by Adkinson
          To notice to Drs & Crs
          To citation in "Intelligender"
          To citation in "Intelligencer"
          To taking and recording bond
          To letters of administration

To warrant of appraisement
To recording warrant of appraisement
To recording orders
To taking and recording Rule absolute
To recording

By cash (not receipted)
Recording sale bill
"By cash" (not receipted but brot down)
Amt due ordy 15.75
showing that J. M. Alexander adm Martha Alexander decd.
has a credit as above of $3.00, J. A. Tolleson, Ordy.
Recd. of J. Y. Alexander $15.75 in full of above acct.

Page 29.   D. W. & A. L. Orr decd
1855   Adkinson : To notice to Drs and Crs by Adkinson
            To 2 mos notice
            To citation in "Intelligencer"
            To citation in "Intelligencer"
            To taking and recording bond
            To warrant of appraisement
            To recording warrant of appraisement
            To recording orders
            To drawing and recording Rule nisi
            To letters of administration
            To sale of land

Adkinson 1857
Jan. 29   Recd. of D. W. & A. L. Orr adm. of J. Orr dec'd 22.50
            in full of above account J. A. Tolleson
            Landing not published in both papers

Page 30.   Ganaway Johnson exor J. Fletcher
            To making title and c, by Adkinson
            To letters Dessecussory

Page 31.   N. B. Knight ad Dickson decd
            To advertising sale of land by Adkinson
            To recording exemplication
            To 2 mos notice
            To taking and recording bond

Page 32.   Blank

Page 33.   Barna 1855...(rest of page blank)

Page 34.   Blank

Page 35.   J. B. Blackwell and myself are to...buy land warrants
1855   copartnership and divide the profits equally
Nov. 1   J. B. Blackwell left in my hand $200.00
Nov. 2   I engaged a land warrant from John P. Smith to pay for
            $83.00 and paid him $5...$3 due me for getting it.
Nov. 17   To Albritains land warrant for getting
            To 4 seals to certificates
            Buy amt due on land warrants (Stancell's adm)
Nov. 22   To seals on Mathis & Albritains LW
Dec. 22   To cash by John Anderson

Page 36.   Blank

Page 37.   1855...Tho. H. Moore and myself are to buy all the land
            warrants that come to him from Washington City (if we
            can) and divide the profits equally. T. H. Moore left
            in my hands to purchase warrants with (money belonging
            to the estate of T. Walker decd) $300
Nov. 1   (I paid for a land warrant with my own money purchased
            from George Brooks)
            To cash handed you when you started to Milledgeville
            To cash a few days previous
            By amt due on Brooks warrant
            By amt due on Reuben Allen's warrant
            To seals on Brooks and Allens
            To 1 seal on Jesse Daniels
            By amt due on J. Daniels war't
Nov. 6   By amt due on Jas McCurdy's
            To 1 seal on Jas McCurdy's
Nov. 10   To 1 seal on Wm. Malony's
            Wm. Malony pd T. H. Moore $5 to obtaining his warrant
            evening before he left for M (so says W. Malony)

Nov. 13   To cash handed your father
            To cash handed J. B. Blackwell
Nov. 23   To cash handed Wm. Groves
Nov. 30   To cash handed your father
Dec.   To cash handed your father
            By cash from Pierce
Dec. 12   To cash to your father
            By cash rec'd from Coker and McDowell
            To cert. & seal Devenports and Jas. Anderson
            To cert. & seal Jas Hales
1856:
Dec. 2   To cash pd Dr. Slaughter

Page 38.   Keller & McKenney

Nov. 3   160 acres George Brooks #6382 Private, Rev. War
            20 Sept. 1855   cost $165.00
                             sold for   176.80
                             profit $ 11.80

Nov. 3   80 acres Jesse Daniels, #8162 Private Capt. Bowen's
            Co., So. Car. War 1812, Oct. 3, 1855
                        Cost.........85.60
                        Sold for.....88.40
                        Profit....... 2.80

Nov. 3   120 acres Reuben Allen #25624 Private Capt. Thomas Co.,
            Ga. militia, Oct. 16, 1855
                        Cost....................126.00
                        postage 6¢5¢ registering .11
                        Cost............126.11
                        Sold for........130.80
                        Profit.......... 4.69

Nov. 7   120 acres James McCurdy #24520, Private Capt. Benson's
            Co., S. Car. Militia War of 1812
                        Cost............128.00
                        Postage & reg...   .08
                        Cost...........128.08

115

Nov. 15   recd check for sold for 130.80
          profit $2.72

Nov. 10   80 acres Wm. Malony #7821 Private   Capt. Kelly's
          Co. S. C. War 1812
          Postage 6¢ reg. 5¢....cost86.11
                    sold for..........88.40
                    profit............ 2.29

          80 acres Joseph Devenport #10900 Priv F̶l̶o̶r̶i̶d̶a̶/̶W̶a̶r̶
          (marked through) War 1812 Capt. Garrison's Co. So.
          Car militia   6 Nov. 1855   Cost $85.00

          Joseph Anderson #30565 orderly sergeant Capt. Calhoun
          Co. Creek War 7 Nov. 1855
                    cost......$125.00

          James Hales #7454 Private Capt. Morris Co. Ga. militia
          War 1812   6 Sept. 1855......cost $84.00

Page 39. Blank

Page 40. Acct transferred from Red back book
          Elizabeth Walraven admx. Jno Walraven dec.
          To taking and recording bond
          To r̶e̶c̶o̶r̶d̶i̶n̶g̶ ̶a̶p̶p̶r̶a̶i̶s̶e̶m̶e̶n̶t̶ (marked through)
          To rule absolute
          To warrant of appraisement
          To letters of administration
          To citation in Advocate by Hunt
          To taking and recording new bond under Rule nisi 1855,
          Jany 8
          To taking Rule absolute
          By cash (n̶o̶t̶ ̶r̶e̶c̶e̶i̶p̶t̶e̶d̶ to (marked out) see Returns
          To ex. & recording return No. 1 for 1853
          To ex. & recording return No. 1 for 1854
          To roder to sell land
          By credit brot down
          To record objection to title
Dec. 31, 1856
          Recd of Eli Dodgen adm de bonis non $3.00 in full of
          above acct.

Pages 41 & 42 are blank

Page 43. 1855...John A. G. Anderson ad J. Anderson
Hunt   T̶o̶ ̶c̶i̶t̶a̶t̶i̶o̶n̶ ̶i̶n̶ ̶A̶d̶v̶o̶c̶a̶t̶e̶ (2 lines marked through)
          T̶o̶ ̶n̶o̶t̶i̶c̶e̶ ̶t̶o̶ ̶D̶t̶/̶&̶ ̶c̶t̶s̶   (error see page 13

          1855...Wilson Harvell ad Riley Harvell
Hunt   To citation in Advocate
" & Ruggles To 2 mos notice...sale land
& Campbell To citation in Advocate
          To taking bond
          To recording bond
          To warrant of appraisement
          To recording appraisement
          To recording sale bill
          To recording orders
          To notice by securities
          To Rule nisi

To recording and acct & order
To citation by _____

1856
Dec. 26   Recd pay of Geo. T. Northrup balance (marked through)
            T. H. Moore one of the adm of B. Tolleson decd

Page 44.   Abram Green exor W. Mooyer decd
1855   Hunt   notice to Drs. and Crs
            To proving will
            To recording will
            To warrant of appraisement
            To recording of appraisement
            To letters testamentary

1856
June 29   Recd of A. Green the above amt. in full J. A. Tolleson,
            adm.

Page 45.   W. P. Strickland guard.
1855 Hunt   To citation in Advocate
            To citation in Advocate
            To taking and recording bond
            To letters of gdnship
            To recording orders
            To drawing up orders

1855
May 8   by cash (receipted)
The above credit found in yellow backed book page 117   J. A.
Tolleson admr.
June 26   Recd above amount by note left by W. P. Strickland taken
            in the acct above and handed to T. H. Moore...J. A.
            Tolleson

Page 46.   John G. Felton admr Richd Felton
Hunt   To citation in Advocate
            To citation in Advocate by ordy
            To taking abd recording bond
            To recording bond (marked through)
            To drawing orders (marked through)
            To letters of appraisement
            To warrant of appraisement
            To recording of appraisement
            To order (absolute) (marked through) nisi
            To order absolute and appoint of appraisers

Page 47.   N. C. Daniell admr Campbell
Hunt   To citation in Advocate
            To citation in Advocate ordy
            To taking and recording bond
            To drawing up orders
            To letters of appraisement
            To warrant of Appraisement
            To recording Warrant of appraisement
            To recording sales bill
Ruggles   To Drs and Crs (notice)
            To order appraise per. prop

Feb 25/27 To acct recd and left with G. T. Northruff for collector
Feb 25,1857 Recd of N. C. Daniell admr of N. Campbell, decd in full
            of above acct....J. A. Tolleson, ordy

Page 48.   M. L. Lenoir ad be bonis non Ballenger decd.
1855
Hunt   To citation in Advocate
            To citation in Advocate by ordy
            To taking and recording bond
            To recording orders
            To drawing up orders
            To letters of adm de bonis non
            To ad. 2 mos. notice
            To adv. sale of land
Cr. by deducting rec. & recording up orders to orders absolute
nisi

Page 49   Churchill Mason admor Atkin
Hunt   To citation in Advocate
ordy   To citation in Advocate
            To taking and recording bond
            To drawing orders
            To recording orders absolute to sell
            To warrant of appraisement
            To recording warrant of appraisement
            To letters of administration
            To recording sale bill (wrong)
            To order appointing appraisers
            A̶t̶k̶i̶n̶s̶o̶n̶ To 2 mos. notice (Atkinson marked through)
1857
July 7   Recd of Churchill Mason adm of Jno N. Campbell decd.
            14.00 in cash in full of above acct...J.A. Toleson, adm

Page 50.   Reuben Freeman adm
Hunt   To citation in Advocate
ordy   To citation in Advocate
            To warrant of appraisement
            To recording warrant of appraisement
            To recording sale bill
            To letters of administration
            To recording orders (advs. to sell per. prop.)
            To drawing up orders
            To taking and recording bond
            Amt. due ordery $10.12½

Page 51.   John H. Miller guard.
1855   To citation in Advocate
Hunt   To citation in Advocate
ordy   To taking and recording bond
            To letters of guardianship
            To drawing orders
            To t̶a̶k̶i̶n̶g̶ (marked through) recording orders

Page 52.   Jesse Oslin ad. Oslin
            To citation in Advocate
            To citation in Advocate
            To taking and recording bond
            To drawing orders
            To recording orders
            To letters of administration
            To warrant of appraisement
            To recording warrant of appraisement
            To recording sale bills

by one book.....

1856   Cr by acct sworn to and presented as
May 6   having been previously pd Cr by recd cash

Page 53. Jeremiah Moore ad. A. Moore, decd
1855   To citation in Advocate
Hunt   To citation in Advocate
ordy   To *T̶e̶m̶p̶ l̶e̶t̶ters/of a̶d̶m (marked through)
          To taking & recording bond
          To Drawing orders
          To recording orders abs & to sell per. prop.
          To letters of administration
          To Warrant of Appraisement
          To recording of Appraisement
          To recording sales bill
          To taking & recording temp. bond
          To temporary letters
          To orders appt. temp. letters
1856
Dec. 31   Recd of Jeremiah Moore adm A. Moore, dec'd $14.25
          in full of above acct...J. A. Tolleson, adm.

Page 54. A. N. Simpson ad Holliday dec'd
1855   To citation in Advocate
          To citation in Advocate
          To temp. letters by B. S. Johnson
          To taking & recording bond
          To warrant of appraisement
          To recording of appraisement
          To recording orders
          To letters of administration

Page 55. E. B. Foote
          to ad. letters to be made and c.

Page 56. Elisha Buise, guardian

Page 57. E. E. Ballenger
1855   To recording petition and orders
          To drawing petition and orders
          To taking and recording bond
          To letters of g̶a̶n̶s̶h̶i̶p̶ a̶d̶m̶i̶n̶i̶s̶t̶r̶a̶t̶i̶o̶n̶s̶h̶i̶p̶ (MISTAKE)

Page 58. B. W. Donehoo guard. C. Donehoo
1855   unsound mind
          To r̶e̶c̶o̶r̶d̶i̶n̶g̶ petition of g̶a̶n̶s̶hip (marked through)
          To recording proceedings
          To taking and recording bond
          To l̶e̶t̶t̶e̶r̶s̶ o̶f̶ g̶a̶n̶s̶h̶i̶p̶ (marked through)
          To exe̶m̶plication a̶n̶d̶ s̶eal (marked through)
          To rule absolute
          To warrant of appraisement
          To order appt. appraisers

1856
Dec. 31   Recd of B. W. Donehoo guard of C. D. Donehoo of unsound
          mind $5.75 above acct J. A. Tolleson, adm.

Page 59. J. G. Felton exor Perkins decd
          To proving will
          To letters testamentary
          To warrant of appraisement

To recording warrant of appraisement
To recording will
To sales bill
To orders absolute and app.
1857 1st   Rec. the above acct. J. A. Tolleson, adm.

Page 60.   Ja's Fain ad. Eppy Fain decd
1855   To citation in Intelligencer
Ruggle   To citation in Intelligencer
ordy   To taking and recording bond
           To drawing orders
           To recording orders
           To letters of administration
           To warrant of appraisement
           To recording warrant of appraisement

Page 61.   Josiah Greer adm. Wm. Greer decd.
1855   To citation in Intelligencer
Ruggles   To citation in Intelligencer
ordy   To taking and recording bond
           To drawing orders
           To recording orders abs and Nisi
           To letters of administration
           To warrant of appraisement
           To recording warrant of appraisement
           To recording sales bill
           To recording and petition taking orders to sell per.
           prop.
           To n̶o̶t̶i̶c̶e̶ t̶o̶ C̶t̶s̶ a̶n̶d̶ D̶t̶s̶/(written through)

1856   Cr. by contra account & settlement for cost pd heretofore
June 16   to B. Tolleson decd not heretofore credited

Oct. 15,1856
           Recd cash of Jonah Green $2.00 settled $10.00 by contra
           acct. sworn to Benj. T. Greer...J. A. Tolleson, adm.

Page 62.   John W. Henley (guard L. Henley)
1855   To citation in Advocate
Hunt   To citation in Advocate
ordy   To taking and recording bond
           To letters of gdnship
           To drawing orders
           To recording orders

mistake
1856   Cr. by sworn acct against the estate B. Tolleson dec'd
           as sett. off said money pd as guardian Cr. by $1.12½
           balance
May 24   paid J. A. Tolleson, adm. B. Tolleson dec'd.

Page 63.   J. L. & E. M. Hembree exors A. Hembree decd
1855   To proving will
           To letters test.
           To warrant of appraisement
           To recording warrant of appraisement
           To recording will
1857, Jan. 6 By endorsing on our a/c proven and in T. H. Moore's
           hands

Page 64.   R. W. Inzer guard Loveless

1855 To taking and recording bond
    To l̶e̶t̶t̶e̶r̶s̶ o̶f̶ g̶d̶n̶s̶h̶i̶p̶ (marked through)
    To drawing orders
    To recording orders
    To recording petition

Page 65. John Clow guard J. G. S. Rumph
1855 To recording petition
    To taking and recording bond
    To letters of gdnship
    To recording orders

Page 66. Geo. T. Northrup ad. de bonis Harvill
1855 To citation in Intelligencer
Ruggles To citation in Intelligencer
    To taking and recording bond
    To recording orders
1857
June 26 by cash rec'd of Geo. T. Northrup

Page 67. Sarah E. Shaw guard _____ Shaw
1855 To drawing petition
    To recording petition
    To taking and recording bond
    To letters of gdnship

Page 68. Francis W. Robert guard B. F. Robert
1855 To recording petition and orders
    To taking and recording bond
    To letters of administration

Page 69. Wm. P. Strickland guard Strickland (Error?)
1855 Wm. Stancell adm. J. Wood decd.

Page 70. D. H. Whitfield ad. J. G. Holister
1855 To citation in Intelligencer
    To citation in Intelligencer
    To taking and recording bond
    To drawing orders
    To letters of administration
    To warrant of appraisement
    To recording warrant of appraisement
    To recording sales bill
    To granting & recording order to sell
1856
Jany 3 By cash (not receipted)
1856
Oct. 11 Showing made to D. H. Whitfield adm that there is a
    credit of $10.00. Recd cash and give recpt to D. H.
    Whitfield adm for $1.50

Page 71. Sulser Dobbs
1855
Ruggles To adv. sale of land

Page 72. Humphrey Reid
1856 By Smith work done in 1855
Jany 5 To cash...

Page 73. S. A. Adkinson
1855

Nov. To cash loaned
B̸y̸ 2̸ m̸o̸s̸ no̸t̸ic̸e̸ M̸a̸rt̸h̸a̸ A̸l̸e̸x̸a̸n̸d̸e̸r (marked through)
To 2 mos. notice John Dickson decd
To 2 mos. notice Wm. P. Young
To adv. sale land John Orr, decd
To 2 mos. not. Eppy Fain decd
Nov. 30 To 2 mos notice Hollister, decd
To 2 mos notice Drs. & Crs
To 2 mos. notice J. V. Campbell
To 2 mos. notice Drs. & Crs. S. Thompson decd
To 2 mos. notice Drs. and Crs. D. Nesbitt, decd
To 2 qiures letters of adm.
To 1 quires Temp letters 1 warrant app.
To 3 quires blanks (letters gd & bond) not heretofore cr.
Dec. 31 To cash

Page 74. Saml. T. Pharr adm Hezekiah W. Pharr
1855
Dec. 1 To citation in Intelligencer & ad.
1856 To citation by ordinary
Dec. 31 Recd of Samuel T. Pharr adm. H. W. Pharr decd in full of
above acct. J. A. Tolleson

Page 75. Fraser & Sampler adm. W. Sampler decd
1855 To citation in INtelligencer
Ruggles To citation in Intelligencer
ordy To taking and recording bond
To drawing orders
To recording orders
To letters of administration
To warrant of appraisement
To recording warrant of appraisement
To recording sales bill
1857
May 28 Recd of Simon Fraser adm Wm. Fraser decd in full of
above acct. J. A. Tolleson, adm.

Page 76. A̸l̸l̸e̸n̸ W̸i̸l̸l̸i̸a̸m̸s̸o̸n̸
1855 T̸o̸/t̸e̸m̸p̸o̸r̸a̸r̸y̸/l̸e̸t̸t̸e̸r̸s̸
Ruggles T̸o̸/c̸i̸tation in Intelligencer
T̸o̸/d̸r̸awing bond
T̸o̸/r̸e̸cording bond (marked through)
T̸o̸/t̸a̸king and recording bond
T̸o̸/l̸e̸tters of adm.
T̸o̸/w̸a̸rrant of app.
T̸o̸/r̸e̸c̸o̸rding warrant of app.
T̸o̸/r̸e̸c̸o̸rding sales bill

1855 Allen Williamson adm. of James G. Williamson decd
To temp. letters of adm.
To orders absolute
To taking and recording bond
To warrant of appraisement
To recording warrant of appraisement
To orders to sell personal property
T̸o̸ r̸e̸c̸o̸r̸d̸i̸n̸g̸ (marked through)
Ruggles To citation in Intelligencer
ordy To citation in Intelligencer
To letters of administration
To recording bond
To Rule Absolute Nisi and Ab.

1857
Feb. 28   Rec $13.62½ from Allen Williamson adm J. G. Williamson
           decd by presentation of Promisory note held by sd adm.
           against B. Tolleson dec'd for 31...this amt credited on
           sd note...J. A. Tolleson, adm

Page 77.
1855   J̶o̶h̶n̶ (marked through) Jalm M. Kemp adm. H. B. Kemp
Ruggles   To citation in Intelligencer
ordy   To Citation in Intelligencer ordy
           To taking and recording bond
           To drawing orders
           To recording orders Nisi and Absolute
           To letters of administration
           To warrant of appraisement
           To recording warrant of appraisement
           To recording sales bill

1855
Dec. 1   by cash not receipted $10.00
1856
Aug. 18   A showing made to Jehu M. Kemp that he has a credit of
           $10.00 as marked above...J. A. Tolleson, adm. B.
           Tolleson dec'd.

1857
May 29   Recd of J. M. Kemp adm the above 25¢

Page 78.   S. J. Ramsey admr Sam'l Thompson
1855   To citation in Intelligencer
Ruggles   To citation in Intelligencer
ordy   To taking and recording bond
           To drawing orders
           To recording orders
           To letters of administration
           To warrant of appraisement
           To recording warrant of app.
           To recording sales bill
Dec. 3   By cash (not receipted) $10.00
1857   June 1st showing that $8 of the above is credited as
           shown by the above entry...J. A. Tolleson, adm.

1857
June 16   Duplicate certificate given showing that above acct is
           credited with $8.00...J. A. Tolleson, adm.

Page 79.   Bennett S. Johnson
1855   To temporary letters est. F. James decd
Ruggles   To citation in Advocate
ordy   To citation in Advocate
           To drawing orders
           To recording orders
           To taking and recording bond
           To granting letters of adm.
           To granting warrant app.
           To recording warrant of app.
           To recording sale bill
Private acct Rec. orders
July 6, 1857: Give B. S. Johnson rect for $14.50 be credited on
note held by Johnson vs B. Tolleson decd now in hand of T. H.
Moore adm. also credit on sd. note private acct...Credit letters

123

adm never granted.

Page 80.   Willis Roberts adm Sy Balwin
1855
Ruggles   (first portion marked through)
ordy
            Willis Roberts adm Sylvanus Balwin
            To temporary bond
            To temporary letters
            To orders absolute
            To warrant of appraisement
            To recording warrant of appraisement
            To citation in Intelligencer
            To citation in Intelligencer ordy
            To letters of administration
            To orders to sell personal property
1857   Recd ow W. Roberts adm S. Balwin decd $12.75 in full
            of above acct...J. A. Tolleson, adm.

Page 81.   Brown & Barnes ad. Barnes
1855   To citation in Intelligencer
Ruggles   To citation in Intelligencer
ordy   To recording orders(2)
            To drawing orders
            To taking and recording bond
            To letters of administration
            To recording warrant of appraisement
            To granting warrant of appraisement
            To recording sales bill
1857
June 15   Recd of Wm. Brown and Wm. L. Barnes adm John H. Barnes
            for above fee by note due 1 day after date...J. A.
            Tolleson, adm...Handed T. H. Moore

Page 82.   Geo. Roberts adm. T. Burt decd
1855   To adv. sale of negroes
Ruggles   To adv. 2 mos notice
(& Campbell)

Page 83.   Mrs. Jane Wrigt
1855   To 2 most notice to sell negroes
Ruggles

Page 84.   1855   Clinton Webb adm.
Campbell   To letters dismissing

Page 85.   Hugh O. K. Nesbit decd exors & ex
1855   To commission to prove will
            To probate of will
            To letters of testamentary
            To 2 warrants of appraisement
            To recording appraisement (marked through)
            To recording comm. & interrogation
            To recording will
            To notice to Drs. & crs (Hunt)

1856
Apr. 29   By cash (B&A)

Page 86.   Genl. Flournoy
1854   To gold pen and handle

To 4½ # butter at 20
To paid Muschwhit (per order)

1855   O. Chastain
Mar. 30   To 2 certificates & seal

1855   John P. Winn
Nov. 1   To loaned money

1855   Ezekiel Hall
Jany 2   To loaned money

Page 87.   Wm. W. Smithwick ex E. Smithwick
1856   To signing probate of will
July 12   Recd cash...J. A. Tolleson, adm.

Page 88.   Acct brot from yellow book...transferred this book
            from page 95

Page 89.   Wm. L. Barnes guard of John J. & Nancy C. Barnes
1855   To citation in Intelligencer
            To citation in Intelligencer by ordy

1857
June 15   Recd of W. L. Barnes guard. for above fee by note due
            day after date...T. H. Moore, adm.

Page 90.   Taken from page 10
1855   Joel Rendroe adm L. A. E. (J. marked out) Freeny decd
Sept. 13   To citation by ordinary
            To citation by ordinary Intelligencer
            To taking and recording bond
            To Rule Absolute
            To letters of administration
            To warrant of appraisement
            To recording of appraisement
            To Rule Nisi & order to sell per. prop.
            To Sales Bill by cash pd B. Tolleson

1855   Joel Renfroe guard W. J. & J. Frrney
            To citation in Intelligencer by ordy
            To citation in Intelligencer by printer
            To letters of gdnship
            To taking and recording bond
            To roder (nisi marked through) absolute

1857
Dec. 31   Recd of Joel Rendroe guard in cash $4.50 & his note for
            $1.87
            J. A. Tolleson ordy handed T. H. Moore

Page 91.   Bennett S. Johnson adm Jane Holliday decd
1855   To temp letters of administration
Jan. 1   To temp bond
            To Rule Absolute
            To recording inventory
            To recording sales bill
            To warrant of appraisement
            To order for sale of per. prop.

Page 92   (not numbered)

125

Solomon Kemp adm Chas. B. Goodwin decd
Transferred from "Yellow Book" page 75

1853   To recording returns for 1851 & 1852 & 1853
To granting & recording orders leave to sell real estate

Jan. 29   By cash

1859   Recd of Solomon Kemp adm C. B. Goodwin decd 1.87½ in full above acct...J. A. Tolleson, ordy.

Transferred from "Yellow Book" page 75...Solomon Kemp guard
Narcissa John Ivey Hey and Vester Goodwin minors
Rec. & Ex Returns 1852 and 1853

1859
May 12   Recd of Solomon Kemp guard $2.25 in full payment of above acct...

End

Page 1.   State of Georgia - County of Cobb. Waide White, princi-
         pal and George R. Gable and William A. M. Lanier, securi-
ties; Jan. 9, 1865 for $500...Waide White was on 7 day this instant
elected constable for 898 district G.M....all three signed.
Witnessed: T. J. Atkinson, T. H. Moore and H. M. Hammett, JIC...
"Confederate States"

Page 2.   Oath signed. Bond for Charles B. Gable, principal and
         George R. Gilbert and W. A. M. Lanier as securites for
$500...11 Jan. 1865 said Gable elected 7 day this mos. elected
constable for 898 G.M. district...same three above witnesses.

Page 3.   Oath of Charles B. Gable to "Confederate States" sworn
         to before W. W. Carroll, Clerk.

Page 4.   Wyley S. Dodgen, principal with Nathaniel Reed and F. A.
         Dodgen as securities for $500...elected as constable for
897 G.M. district...before Atkinson and Hammett, JIC...Sworn to
"Confederate States."

Page 5.   George A. Powers principal, Hisakiah (X) Hany (written
         as Heany) and P. A. Powers as securities for $500,
elected as constable for #897 G.M. district...Jan. 16, 1865 sworn
to before W. W. Carroll, C.I.C.

Page 6.   Alfred Webb principal with S. J. Ramsey and Jonathan
         Farr and Wm. Kilphin as securities for $500, Jan. 7,
1865...elected as constable of #840 G.M. District before J. H.
Roberts J.P. and S. J. Ramsey, J.P.

Page 7.   Oath of Alfred Webb to "Confederate States" on Jan. 23,
         1856.

         Bond of William B. Turner as principal with Fletcher
McGee and John Brown as securities for $500 on 26 Jan. 1865,
elected as constable of #846 G.M. district.

Page 8.   Oath of William B. Turner sworn before W. W. Carroll.
         Jan. 27, 1865.

Page 9.   James T. Pitts principal with G. M. Crane and P. Garrison
         as securities bonded for $1000...on 8 Jan. 1865 as
constable for #911 G.M. district before H. M. Hammett and T. H.
Moon, J.I.C.

Page 10.   Oath of James T. Pitts on March 11, 1865.

Page 11.   James R. Latimer as principal with Jos. S. Morris as
          security bonded for $500 on 8 Jan. 1865 as constable
for #911 G.M. district before H. M. Hammett and T. J. Atkinson,
J.I.C....Recorded March 29, 1865, W. W. Carroll, Clk.

Page 12.   O. G. Edwards principal with Thomas Hooper and Peter S.
          Dodd as securities bonded for $500 on 11 Jan. 1865 as
constable for #992 G.M. district, before A. Maner, J.P. and H. A.
Baldwin, J.P....all three signed.

Page 13.   Haroy Waldrop as principal with Johnahan Farr and S. J.
          Ramsey as securities bonded for $500 on Jan. 7. 1865 as
constable for 845 G.M. district...Test: J. H. Roberts, J.P. Oath
of Harvey (X) Waldrop before W. W. Carroll, Jan. 25, 1865.

Page 14.   Stephen Pace and James L. Pace, security bonded for
            $500 on Jan. 7, 1865.

Page 15.   Stephen Pace, constable for $800 for #895 G.M. district.
            Test: H. M. Hammett, J.I.C.; Thos. H. Moore...signed
as Stephen L. Pace and James L. Pace.

            Oath of Stephen Pace, 7 Jan. 1865 before W. W. Carroll,
C.I.C.

Page 16.   James F. Pitts, principal with G. M. Crane and P.
            Garrison as securities bonded for $1,000, 7 Jan. 1865
as constable for #911 G.M. district...before W. M. Hammett, J.I.C.
and T. H. Moore, J.I.C....all signed.

Page 17.   Oath of Jame F. Pitts to Constitution of Confederate
            States of America...17 March 1865 before W. W. Carroll,
C.I.C.

            Appointment by Nathaniel M. Calder, Tax Receiver of
Hamilton M. Hammett as lawful deputy to receive returns of 1864
and 1865 on 14 April 1865...signed N. M. Calder, T.R.

Page 18.   Ordered: Hamilton M. Hammett hereby appointed Tax
            Receiver Protem 1864-65 according to the above appoint-
ment...April 15, 1865: signed T. H. Moon, J.I.C.; J. J. Northcutt,
J.I.C. and T. J. Atkinson, J.I.C.

            John A. Dodgins, principal with Thomas Whitehead and
A. J. McCurry as securities for $500 as constable for #1017 G.M.
district (all three signed) witnessed before Atkinson, Moon and
Hammett, J.I.C.

Page 19.   Oath of John A. Dobbins, 11 April 1865 before W. W.
            Carroll.

Page 20.   Blank

Page 21.   H. J. Hopkins retail bond: Henry J. Hopkins and W. D.
            Smith bonded for $500, Jan. 15, 1866...retail license
to retail spiritous liquors at Powder Oath of above, 15 Jan. 1866.

Page 22.   James J. Seay principal with W. L. Barns and A. B. Seay
            as securities for $500 bonded as constable for #895 G.M.
district, 22 Jan. 1866 before J. Northcutt and Hammett, J.I.C.
Recorded 31 Jan. 1866 by W. W. Carroll, J.I.C.

Page 23.   H. M. Hammett bonded, principal with G. R. Gilbert and
            William F. Groves and Lemuel Bennett as securities
bonded to Gov. Charles J. Jenkins, Governor of Georgia for $3000,
26 Jan. 1866 as Clerk of Superior Court of Cobb County...T. J.
Adkinson, T. H. Moore and J. J. Northcutt, J.I.C.

Page 24.   Official bond clerk Inferior Court: Joseph Spier as
            principal with G. R. Gilbert and J. Wils and H. J. Husk
as securities for $3,000 on Jan. 29, 1866.

Page 25.   A. F. Johnson's bond as sheriff: American F. Johnson
            as principal with T. J. Atkinson and H. B. Wallis and
Jas. S. Morris as securities $20,000 on 29 Jan. 1866, before
Joseph Spier, Clerk Inferior Ct.

Page 26.   John White's bond as coroner and principal with Dillard
           M. Young and T. Runyan as securities for $500 on 31 Jan.
1866 signed and approved by H. M. Hammett, J. Atkinson and T. H.
Wood, J.I.C.

Page 27.   Oath of T. J. White special constable before G. T.
           Carrio, J. P. 3 Feb. 1866 before Joseph Spier, Clerk
Inferior Court.

           Benjamin Gregory's bond as county surveyor and principal
with George R. Gilbert and Ebenezer Page as securities for $1000
...3 Jan. 1866.

Page 28.   Conclusion of witnesses of previous page...Atkinson,
           Northcutt and Hammett as J.I.C.

           George M. Manning bonded deputy sheriff and principal
with William F. Groves, Geo. R. Gilbert and Walter Manning as
securities for $10,000...A. F. Johnson is sheriff and he has
appointed Manning as deputy.

Page 29.   Oath of George M. Manning, Feb. 3, 1866 before Thomas P.
           Whitfield, J.P. Recd...bond returned to A. F. Johnson,
sheriff.

Page 30.   W. W. Carroll bonded as county treasurer and principal
           with George M. Daniel, Lemuel Bennett, Hilliard M.
Young, G. R. Gilbert and James S. Morris as securities for $10,000
on Feb. 19, 1866. Test and appeared: Atkinson, Whitlock and
Northcutt, J.I.C.

Page 31.   Petition and bond of L. D. Queen for ferry: To consta-
           ble: "Lorenza D. Queen desires to establish ferry in
said county...across Chattahoochee River about 1 mile below railroad bridge on land of Thomas Hooper whose consent has been ob-
tained and will appear by reference to a petition of citizens hereto annex and..." Gartrell and Winn, attys for Petn.

Page 32.   We Lorenze D. Queen, principal and Thomas Hooper and
           E. L. McGriff as securities...to Justices of Inferior
Court...bonded for $1,000..."charge for ferry amount stipulated
in order: before Atkinson, Wood and Northcutt, J.I.C."

           John Tate principal with Pickens Tate and George T.
Fowler as securities bonded for $500 as constable of #991 G.M.
district.

Page 33.   27 March 1866...(preceeding page bond) before Z. T.
           Carrio, J.P.

           Oath of J. E. Tate as constable...to "Constitution of
United States...." 27 March 1866 before Joseph Spier, Clerk.

Page 34.   Official Bond of Tax Collector: John W. McClesky as
           principal with Samuel R. McClesky, R. Latimer, Hezekiah
Gresham and W. M. Dobbs as securities for $12,000...30 March 1866.

Page 35.   (preceeding bond) sworn before Atkinson, Moore, North-
           cutt, J.I.C. recorded 5 April 1866 by Joseph Spier,
Clerk.

Official Bond of Receiver of Tax Returns...Joshuah Jackson principal with W. W. Carroll. Robert Baker and Humphrey Reed as securities for $12,000 on 26 March 1866...

Page 36. (preceeding bond) sworn before Atkinson, Northcutt and Moore, J.I.C...recorded Joseph Spier, Clerk.

John S. Johnson constable for #846 G.M. district "elected without opposition" before James Lindley, J.P.; C. H. Moore, J.P. and James O. Smith.

Page 37. Order of Court: ...so ordered...Johnson as constable, June 7, 1866 by T. H. Moore, T. J. Atkinson, M. G. Whitlock, J.I.C.

Bond of John S. Johnson as constable and principal with John B. Lindley and Uriah Matthews as securities...$500.

Page 38. 26 May 1866...bond approved and filed and returned.

Henry Call, constable for 992 G.M. district...superintendent of elections for county certifies Henry Call duly elected...H. A. Baldwin, J.P., Robert Lemon, F. H., Richard Robson, F. H. Returns approved...June 21, 1866...Atkinson, Moore, Northcutt, J.I.C. Henry Call as principal with Robert Lemon and Jasper Simpson as securities for $500.

Page 40. Sworn June 20, 1866...of Call. Lemon and Simpson before Hartwell A. Baldwin, J.P., Alfred Maner, J.P....Recorded June 23, 1866 by Joseph Spiers, Clerk.

Oath of Alfred Tarry as constable of #851 G.M. district before Burrell T. Kemp, J.P.

Page 41. William T. Wallace as principal with B. C. Irwin and W. W. Barmore as securities for $500...Sept. 8, 1866...Wallace constable of #898 G.M. district...before: Northcutt, Atkinson and Whitfield.

Page 42. Oath of William T. Wallace before Joseph Spier, Clerk, 17 Sept. 1866.

Page 43. Official bond of Tax Collector: John W. McClesky, principal with Samuel R. McClesky, A. F. Johnson, H. M. Hammett, H. A. Baldwin and J. T. Alexander as securities for $12,000...1 Oct. 1866.

Page 44. before Moore, Lindley, Northcutt, J.I.C....31 Oct. 1866, recd by Joseph Spier, Clerk.

John H. Turner's Bridge: John H. Turner, principal with T. R. Sewell and Stephen Turner as securities for $500... "letting out of builder of bridge across Nickajack Creek...said John H. Turner lowest bidder for $198"...

Page 45. "he shall keep in good order and repair for 5 years"... Nov. 6, 1866...before Atkinson, Moore and Northcutt, J.I.C., Spier, Clerk.

Bond of James A. Stewart principal with James B. Chambers as sec. for $500 "special contract with Justices of

Inferior Court for building of bridge across Sassafas...

Page 46.   Creek on lower Roswell Road...has completed said bridge
           ...let out to him at rate of $2.00 per foot same being
$200...for 5 years...Feb. 5, 1867...before: E. H. Lindley, T. H.
Moore, J. J. Northcutt, J.I.C....Recorded Feb. 15, 1867.

           W. S. Hodgen principal with William Gillham and F. A.
Hodges as securities for $500...

Page 47.   Jan. 11, 1867 bonded as constable for #897 G.M. district.
           Before: W. Manning, J.P....recorded 15 Feb. 1867,
Spier, Clerk.

           James T. Rehely, principal with William Childres and
Jasper Simpson as securities for $500, bonded as Constable for
#999 G.M. district.

Page 48.   Jan. 5, 1867...before: Hartwell A. Baldwin, J.P. Record-
           ed Feb. 15, 1867 by Jos. Spier, Clerk.

           Geo. S. Owens as principal with W. P. Stephens and W. R.
Montgomery as securities bonded for $500 as constable for #989 G.
M. district on Jan. 5, 1867.

Page 49.   Approved: Atkinson, Moore, Northcutt, J.I.C.   Record-
           ed Feb. 15, 1867 by J. Spiers, Clerk.

           John F. Perry, principal and John M. Walker and J. S.
Morris as securities bonded for $1000 as constable for 898 G.M.
district...before 11 Jan. 1868...Atkinson and Moore, J.I.C.   Recd
15 Feb. 1867 by J. Spiers, clerk.

Page 50.   Robt R. Bryan principal with S. R. McClesky and M. F.
           McClesky as securities bonded for $500 as constable for
#911 G.M. district before: Northcutt, Atkinson and Moore, J.I.C.
Recorded 25 March 186_, by J. Spiers, Clerk.

Page 51.   Bond of Howell and others: H. P. Howell administrator
           and R. M. Pitman, A. Baker, admr of estate of C. C.
Howell, deceased and A. H. G. Howell, James H. Howell, admr. of
M. S. Howell deceased, James M. Fooler and D. H. Howell, Tom B.
Howell principal and James F. Scoggins as securities bonded
Clement C. Green for $50,   August 26, 1867.   Conditions: Clement
C. Green petitions for opening and establishing a new public road
leading to said Green's ferry on Chattahoochee River...court
passed an order establishing...1st Tues August instance...whereas
said H. P. Howell, admr for R. M. Pitman: A. Baker, admr for
A. H. G. Howell; James H. Howell, admr for James M. Foster,
William B. Howell are about applying for writ of centionari in
said case now showed above pay eventual condemnation money and
court cost...before J.I.C.   Recd Oct. 2, 1867.   Stamped U.S.
Revenue state of $1.00...Joseph Spier, Clerk.

Page 52.   Charles J. Shephard principal and William Root and
           Lemuel Burnett as securities bonded for $10,000,

Page 53.   4 Nov. 1867...Shephard appointed County Treasurer...
           Approved Dix Fletcher, T. J. Atkinson, J. J. Northcutt,
J.I.C.   U.S. Revenue stamp attached $1.00.   Recorded Nov. 9,
1867, Joseph Spiers, Clerk.

Page 54.   Henry J. Hopkins principal with Jesse Black as security
        bonded for $500...applied for license to retail spiri-
tous liquors...about to be issued...he keep, maintain an orderly
and decent house...Jan. 29, 1867...before: Joseph Spiers, Clerk.

        Jno. S. Johnson, principal with John B. Lindley, Uriah
Matthias as securities bonded for $500 as constable for #846 G.M.
district.

Page 55.   Feby 1, 1868...Test and app: C. D. Moon, J.P.   Recorded
        July 13, 1868.

        Oath of J. S. Johnson, see minutes Book A page 37.

Page 56.   Blank

Page 57.   Official Bond of County Officers A.D. 1868...J. Jackson
        principal with E. H. Lindley, L. Bennett, Robert Baber,
A. Reynolds as securities bonded to Rufus B. Bullock, Governor of
Georgia for $4150...24 April 1868... Tax Receiver...Attested and
Appeared: 9 Sept. 1868 by E. A. Dobbs, Ordinary.

Page 58.   Geo. M. Manning 1868: Tax Collector...principal with
        William Phillips, Walter Manning, Lemuel Bennett and
Henry G. Cole as securities bonded for $11,100...10 Sept. 1868 as
Tax Collector of Cobb County...Appeared: E. A. Dobbs, ordinary.

Page 59.   E. A. Dobbs, principal with James P. Dobbs, David J.
        Dobbs and David Dobbs bonded as ordinary for $1,000 on
28 Aug. 1868, appearing before J. T. Robertson, J.P.

Page 60.   Henry C. White, principal with W. White, J. T. Haley,
        E. Page, William Phillips, T. J. Atkinson, H. G. Cole
as securities bonded as county treasurer for $16,000 on 9 Sept.
1868, having been elected 24 April 1868, before E. A. Dobbs,
ordinary.

Page 61.   H. M. Hammett, principal with John G. Campbell, E. Page
        & Co., H. B. Wallis as securities bonded for $3.00 as
Clerk Superior Court having been elected 24 April 1868, appearing
before E. A. Dobbs, ordinary.

Page 62.   J. R. Ward principal with William Alston and William F.
        Groves, securities bonded for $1,000 as county surveyor
on 23 Sept. 1868, having been elected 24 April 1868, appearing
before E. A. Dobbs, ordinary.

Page 63.   H. A. Baldwin, principal with Robert Lemon, E. Cochran,
        N. B. Green, Solomon K. Pace, William A. Childress,
Harvey Harris, J. M. Moon, Alexander Eaton, Richard Robertson and
Harry Love as securities, bonded for $10,000 as sheriff on 24
Sept. 1868, appearing before E. A. Dobbs, ordinary.

Page 64.   James A. Stewart Bridge Bond: Above with Samuel Stein
        as security bonded for $400 on 22 May 1868...Stewart by
contract with Inferior Court Justices for $200 built bridge across
Chinas Creek on River Road between Roswell and Marietta near
William Kelphins...to maintain for 5 years...attested before J. A.
Tolleson, Clerk, Inferior Court.

Page 65.   John B. Aycock, C. H. Anderson and others as securities bonded for $300...Nov. 1, 1867...built bridge over Sweetwater Creek on road from Marietta to Campbellton near Thomas Butners...for $165..."Will keep in good order"...for 5 years... appeared before E. H. Lindley, J.I.C.

Page 66.   𝐸𝑙𝑖𝑠ℎ𝑎 𝑁/ 𝐾𝑛𝑖𝑔ℎ𝑡 𝑀𝑎𝑟𝑡𝑖𝑛𝑠 𝐵𝑜𝑛𝑑 (marked through)

John B. Acock principal with J. L. W. Cooper, C. H. Anderson as securities bonded for $300 on 27 March 1869...contracted for $174 and built bridge across Noses Creek, said bridge known as Perkerson Bridge, leading from Powder Springs in said county to Atlanta in county of Fulton..."keep in good repair for 7 years from this date"...attested before J. J. Callaway and James Lindley, J.P.

Page 67.   George B. Manning principal with John M. Manning, Walter
           Manning, and L. S. Northcutt as securities bonded for
$16,000 as Tax Collector on 22 Jan. 1869, appearing before E. A. Dobbs, ordinary.

Page 68.   B. W. Florence Bridge Bond: B. W. Florence as principal
           with J. C. Butner as security bonded for $290 on 20
Feby 1869...contract...through C. D. Moon, Thomas Findley and J. C. Butner, committee, for $145 built bridge across Noses Creek near to residence of J. S. Hunter on road leading from Marietta to Powder Springs..."keep up for 7 years"...attested before E. A. Dobbs, ordinary.

Page 69.   Thomas J. Owsley's bond as constable and principal with
           Geo. W. Cleland, A. D. Ruedie and Wm. P. Stephens as
securities for $500 to Ellerson A. Dobbs, ordinary...for #898 G.M. district...tested and approved by E. A. Dobbs, ordy.

Page 70.   Green B. Chastain's constable bond 1869...as principal
           with David A. King, F. Chastain as securities for $500
...constable #991 G.M. district...3 April 1869...approved T. Carrio, J.P.; D. A. King, J.P. and E. A. Dobbs, ordy.

Page 71.   John T. Robertson, bonded as principal and constable
           with H. M. Hammett and A. J. Johnson as securities...
$500...constable of the #898 G.M. district...1869...tested and approved by E. A. Dobbs.

Page 71.   (page number duplicated)...Levi E. Reece principal
           bonded as constable 1869 with Samuel Buidine and F. F.
Gann as securities for $500...April 6, 1869 for #985 G.M. district ...approved by E. A. Dobbs, ordy.

Page 72.   B. W. Donehae, bonded as coroner and principal with
           Samuel Dutree and A. B. Green as securities for $500,
8 March 1869...elected on 24 April 1868...approved 8 March 1869 by E. A. Dobbs, ordy.

Page 73.   W. W. Carroll bonded as deputy sheriff principal with
           ----- as security to H. A. Baldwin, Sheriff for $5,000
on 29 Dec. 1868...approved E. A. Dobbs, ordy.

Page 74.   John B. Acock and J. L. W. Coop Bridge Bond...John B.
           Acock, James L. W. Cooper principal with James J. Barns
and C. B. Holliman as securities for $220...April 21, 1869...built bridge across Powder Springs Creek near Powder Springs on road

leading from Powder Springs to Carrollton...attest...J. W. Bingham and James Lenalie, J.P.

Page 75.   James H. Stewart, principal with Joel Gunter as security...bonded to Chas. J. Shepherd, ordy...$500 on 2 Aug. 1869..."Stewart contract has built for said county a bridge across Willis Creek at Barrington Mills on road between Roswell and Marietta...shall keep in good repair for 5 years."   Approved and attested: C. J. Shepherd, ordy.

G. B. Bently principal and John P. Berry and Andrew Benson as securities for $200, May 28, 1869...Bently by contract with said county through R. W. Benson and H. Gresham and G. T. Carie as commissioners for this purpose has for $105 built a bridge across (bond ends here and it not continued on following page)

Page 76.   Don Blake principal with Allan Grogan and Mike Blake securities for 150 Ł being $642.85 3/4...Don Blake stands charged with being the reputed father of a bastard child of which Gracy Benson is now pregnant...if Blake "do and shall from time and at all times hereafter, will and truly educate and maintain said child until it shall attain age of 15 and also pay the expenses of lying in with said child, boarding, nursing and maintenance of said Gracy until she is confined by reason of bearing said child...then the obligation be void...14 Sept. 1869 (all above signed with X mark).   Attest and approved...J. T. Alexander, J.P....Recd Sept. 14, 1869.

Page 77.   T. J. Hardage, principal with J. B. Florence and William Florence as securities for $238...20 Sept. 1869...said T. J. Hardage built bridge across Sweetwater on line of Paulding & Cobb county known as Miller's Bridge leading from Marietta to Villa Rica...keep up 7 years.   Recd Oct. 15, 1869.

Page 78.   J. G. Bently, principal with John P. Boring and Andrew Benson as securities for $200...May 28, 1869...Bently appointed by commissioners B. W. Benson, H. Gresham and G. T. Carrie "for $105 built bridge across Noonday Creek known as Shallow Ford Road...keep up 7 years."...Attested John Durham, J.P....Recd Oct. 15, 1869.

Page 79.   Jesse Pope, principal and John Bullard and S. R. Cochran as securities for $500...Oct. 16, 1869...Pope appointed constable of #895 G.M. district...Benjamin Bullard, J.P.; John Mahaffy, N.P. & ex off of J.P.   Recd Oct. 20, 1869.

Page 80.   George T. Fowler, principal with Thomas F. Summers and William Phillips as securities for $180...under contract with G. T. Carrie, R. M. Benson and H. Gresham, commissioners for that purpose...for $91.75 built bridge across Noonday Creek on what is known as Bell's Ferry Road...keep up 7 years...Nov. 2. 1869.   Approved C. J. Shepherd, ordy.

Page 81.   Sanford Gorham, principal with J. M. Wilson and John M. Walker as securities for $500...approinted constable for #898 G.M. district...approved C. J. Shepherd, ordy...Nov. 24, 1869. Recd. Nov. 24, 1869.

Page 82.   Ansley Hayes, principal and ------ as securities bonded for $400 on 5 Dec. 1869...built bridge across Sweetwater

Creek in Cobb County known as Hayes Bridge...bid off for $235...
keep in good repair for 7 years." "Signed and approved and further
I certify that this is the best bond I ever witnessed this 4 Dec.
1869...James Lindley, J.P."...No securities given in body of
document but the following signed: Ansley Hayes, Alfred McAtaney,
W. Neil, Almon Hays, Jas. O. Smith, James L. W. Cooper and John
Duncan. Recd. Dec. 21, 1869.

Page 83. S. M. Owen, principal with J. G. Havroe as security for
$500 on 4 Dec. 1869...building of bridge across road
from Acworth to Dallas and on road also from Marietta to Rome and
other places...ordinary appointed J. W. Hill, S. Lemon and S.
Collins to let bridge..."he shall keep in good repair for 7 years."
Test: S. Lemon, J. W. Hill and S. Collins...Recd Dec. 21, 1869.

Page 84. Joseph Lary principal with Zacharia Smith and W. C.
Green as securities for $500...appointed constable G.M.
not given...Test and approved: J. W. Hill, J.P.....Recd Dec. 27,
1869.

Page 85. John Mohan principal with Wm. Hedgpeth of Paulding
County and D. W. Johns of Cobb County as securities for
$500...elected as constable of #851 G.M. district...April 8, 1869.
John W. Hill, N.P....recd Jan. 11, 1870...The above bond was
found amongst old papers and recorded.

Page 86. Wm. A. Barefield principal and R. G. Alexander and
Gilman Smith as securities for $500 on Dec. 27, 1869...
appointed constable for #897 G.M. district...approved C. J.
Shepherd, Ordy...Recd Jan. 15, 1870.

Page 87. S. T. Batson, principal with W. B. Carnes and Jno. T.
Robertson as securities for $500 applied for license to
sell spirituous liquors at his store on Canton Road known as
"Mitchell's Old Stand"...maintain good and orderly house...Test
T. S. Gann, Recd. March 11, 1870.

Page 89. Tanner and Patterson as principal with W. D. Smith as
security, bonded for $500...applied for license to
retail spirituous liquors...maintain orderly house...Test and
approved C. J. Shepherd, ordy...Recd March 30, 1870.

Page 90. Geo. T. Fowler as principal with H. Gresham and A. A.
Winn as securities for $206...contract with court of
Ordinary through R. M. Benson and H. Gresham as commissioners for
$103...built bridge across Noonday Creek on road leading from Big
Shanty to Roswell near residence of A. A. Winn...keep in good
repair for 7 years...18 May 1870...approved C. J. Shepherd, ordy
...recd May 18, 1870.

Page 91. Lawrence M. Dawson, principal with W. Asbury Batson and
Turner Batson as securities for $500...as constable
(no G.M. district) 12 April 1870...approved Jno. Durham, N.P.

J. N. Limlick principal with Henry White and R. H.
McCutcheson as securities for $500...license to retail spirituous
liquors at his store in Big Shanty...keep and maintain an orderly
house (no date) in presence of T. Laurence Hunt...recd July 18,
1870.

Page 92. Thos. Anderson prin R. C. Irwin, W. P. Stephens and

Archibald Howell as securities for $200 on 7 July 1870 bonded...appointed constable by Joseph Gault, J.P. for #898 G.M. district to fill vacancy of John T. Robertson (resigned)...personally appeared before me...C.J. Shepherd, ordy...T. J. Anderson appointed...sworn oath of T. J. Anderson, 12 Aug. 1870.

Page 93.   Joel Britt, principal with A. H. Simms and Geo. L. Avery as securities for $500...constable #851 G.M. district on Oct. 31, 1870. Oath of Joel Britt on 1 Nov. 1870 before C. J. Shepherd, ordy.

Page 94.   Camp and Brown principal with W. B. Rakestraw as security for $500...leave to sell spirituous liquors at their store in Powder Springs for 3 months...maintain orderly house. Test and approved: C. J. Shepherd, ordy...recd Nov. 9, 1870.

Page 95.   A. A. Griggs as principal with A. D. Griggs and Elija West as securities for $500 as constable for #1017 G.M. district on Jan. 9, 1871...approved C. J. Shepherd, ordy... official oath of A. A. Griggs on 9 Jan. 1870...rec. Jan. 12, 1871.

Page 96.   John Nix principal with W. White and A. Keeter and L. Bennett as securities for $500 bonded as constable for #898 district before C. J. Shepherd, ordy...Oath of John Nix on 10 Jan. 1871...recd Jan. 12, 1871.

Page 97.   Amaziah South as principal with R. B. Anderson and Joel A. Gunter as securities for $500...bonded as constable for #845 G.M. district approved J. H. King, J.P.   Oath of Amaziah South 14 Jan. 1871 before C. J. Shepherd, ordy...recd.19 Jan. 1871.

Page 98.   Jesse H. Nelms, principal with Robert Lemon and W. J. Lee as securities bonded for $500 as constable for #992 G.M. district Jan. 14, 1871...approved Thos. Hooper, J.P.; Alfred Maner, NP & JP...Oath as constable #992 G.M. district 18 Jan. 1871 before C. J. Shepherd, ordy...recd Jan. 19. 1871.

Page 99.   Wm. P. Stephens as principal with Timothy Stephens and A. L. Edmondson and L. Burnett, E. Page and Wm. R. Montgomery and William D. Anderson as securities bonded for $10,000 on 14 Jan. 1871 as sheriff...tested and approved C. J. Shepherd, ordy...recd Jan. 19, 1871.

Page 100.   H. M. Hammett as principal with Chas D. Phillips, Henry G. Cole and A. N. Simpson as securities bonded for $3,000 on 20 Jan. 1871 as Clerk of Superior Court of Cobb County. Attested and approved C. J. Shepherd, ordy...recd Jan. 23, 1871.

Page 101.   J. R. Ward, principal with D. H. Whitfield, J. B. Blackwell, H. G. Cole, Wm. Phillips as securities bonded for $1,000...elected 22 Dec. 1870 as county surveyor of Cobb... before C. J. Shepherd, ordinary on 20 Jan. 1871...recd 23 Jan. 1871.

Page 102.   John Thomason principal with G. W. Perkerson and James M. Brown as securities bonded for $500...elected constable of #895 G.M. district before John Mahaffy, J.P....recd 25 Jan. 1871 by C. J. Shepherd, ordinary.

Page 103.   J. C. Oglesby principal with J. L. Camp and _____ (blank but signed by E. H. Linaly) as securities bonded for $500 on 6 Feb. 1871 as Receiver of Tax Returns before C. J. Shepherd, ordinary...recd 6 Feb. 1871, Shepherd.

Page 104. Henry C. White, principal with B. Stripling, W. White, T. J. Atkinson, H. G. Cole and Wm. Phillips bonded for $22,000 on 4 Feb. 1871 as county Treasurer...recorded 6 Feb. 1871, Shepherd.

Page 105. William H. Barfield, principal with Tillman (X) Smith, E. J. Smith as securities bonded for $500 on 9 Jan. 1871 as constable for #897 G.M. district before J. Z. Alexander, J.P....recorded 14 Feb. 1871, C. J. Shepherd, Ordinary.

Page 106. James W. Kehely, principal with Alvin G. Dempsey, T. G. McAffee as securities bonded for $500 on 15 Jan. 1871 as constable for #992 G.M. district before Alfred Maner, N.P. & Ex O J.P...recd 14 Feb. 1871, Shepherd.

Page 107. J. H. Simpson, principal with Raphael Hirsch and W. W. Simpson as securities bonded for $500 on 26 Jan. 1871 as county coroner before C. J. Shepherd, ordinary...recd 15 Feb. 1871, ordy.

Page 108. Robert Lemon, principal with Richard Robison and E. J. Simpson as securities bonded for $500 on 10 Jan. 1871... "license to retail spiritous liquors"...approved C. J. Shepherd, ordinary...recd 2 March 1871, C. J. Shepherd, ordy.

Page 109. J. S. T. Batson, principal with C. T. Carnes as securities bonded for $500 on 1 March 1871..."license to retail spiritous liquors for 6 months from 12 Jan. 1871...keep and maintain an orderly house." Recorded 2 March 1871, C. J. Shepherd, ordinary.

Page 110. Camp & Brown, principal (signed by M. P. Camp) with J. C. Grier as security bonded for $500 on 3 March 1871..."license to retail spiritous liquors for 12 months from 1 Jan. 1871." Approved C. J. Shepherd, ordinary. Recorded C. J. Shepherd, ordy.

Page 111. H. J. Hopkins and A. B. Rutledge, trading under name and style of Hopkins and Rutledge as principal with J. M. Lindley as security bonded for $500 on 27 Feb. 1871... "license to retail spiritous liquors in said county." Recorded 3 March 1871, C. J. Shepherd, ordinary.

Page 112. John Mahaffy, principal with --------- security bonded for $500 on 16 Feb. 1871..."retail spiritous liquors." (No security signed) Recorded 23 March 1871, C. J. Shepherd, ordinary.

Page 113. G. A. Baldwin and H. A. Baldwin, principal & security bonded for $500 on 20 March 1871..."license to retail spiritous liquors at the Baldwin place about 2 miles north of Chattahoochee River." Recorded 28 March 1871, C. J. Shepherd, ordinary.

Page 114. J. F. Chastain, principal with R. H. McCutchens and H. C. White as securities bonded for $500 on 28 April 1871..."license to retail spiritous liquors at Kenesaw from 28

April 1871 for 1 year."

Page 115.   W. A. M. Lanier, principal with Timothy Stevens and
            H. M. Hammett as securities bonded for $500 on 10 Jan.
1871 as constable of #898 G.M. district...approved 11 Jan. 1871,
C. J. Shepherd, Ordy...Oath of W. A. M. Lanier as constable before
Shepherd.

Page 116.   William J. Manning, principal with William H. Kemp as
            security bonded for $600..."letting of bridge across
Nose Creek near Fultz Mill...W. J. Manning, lowest bidder for
$345...keep up for 7 years."...on 13 May 1871...C. J. Shepherd,
ordinary.

Page 117.   Geo. M. Manning, principal with Wm. Phillips, Lemuel
            Bennett, Henry G. Cole, Benj. Stripling as securities
bonded for $16,500 on 25 May 1871 as Tax Collector for 1871 before
C. J. Shepherd, ordinary...recd 26 May 1871, C. J. Shepherd.

Page 118.   G. M. Manning, principal with Thos. M. Kirkpatrick,
            Timothy Stephens and A. S. Edmondson as securities
bonded for $12,000 on 25 May 1871 as Tax Collector...C. J.
Shepherd, ordinary.

Page 119.   W. H. Dooly, principal with P. H. Lyon as security
            bonded for $500..."retail spiritous liquors at his
store in Cobb County." before A. J. Julian...recd 14 Sept. 1871.

Page 120.   Jackson Delk, principal with W. L. (X) Bishop, security
            bonded for $500 on __ Aug. 1871..."build a bridge ac-
ross Soaps Crk near residence of said Jackson Delk for $275...60
feet long and 12 feet wide with good railings and built a rock
wall to extend from ending of said bridge to foot of hill"...to
be completed by 15 Nov. 1871 and kept in good order for 7 years."
C. J. Shepherd, ordy...recd 15 Sept. 1871.

Page 121.   James Burton, principal with Harvey McVey and N. M.
            Morris as security bonded for $500 as constable of
#911 G.M. district...recd 15 Sept. 1871.

Page 122.   Nelson Timlick, principal with W. S. Allen security
            bonded for $500..."retail spiritous liquors." 17 June
1871...approved C. J. Shepherd, ordinary...recd 23 Oct. 1871.

Page 123.   John Mahaffey, principal with John Thomason as security
            bonded for $500 on 23 Nov. 1871..."sell spiritous
liquors at store at Coxes Courtground." Recorded 12 Dec. 1871.

Page 124.   J. F. & L. J. Baldwin...dealing as Baldwin & Bros.,
            principal with R. Hirsch as security bonded for $500
on 14 Dec. 1871..."retail spiritous liquors at their store in
Big Shanty." Recorded 14 Dec. 1871.

Page 125.   J. H. Elliott, principal with T. L. Roper, security
            bonded for $500 on 4 Jan. 1872..."retail spiritous
liquors." Recorded 5 Jan. 1872.

Page 126.   G. W. Cox and R. T. Cox security bonded for $500 on
            22 Nov. 1871 to "retail spiritous liquors." Recorded
5 Jan. 1872.

Page 127.   J. R.(?) Alexander, principal with Nathan Alexander
             as security bonded for $350 on 1 Dec. 1871..."Bridge
across Allatoona Creek on Dallas-Acworth Road near F. N. Cowan"
...lowest bidder at $175...keep in good repair for 7 years...
before J. W. Hill, N.P....signed by J. W. Hill, H. B. McConnell
and J. G. Homer, securities.

Page 128.   H. J. Hopkins, A. B. Rutledge and M. P. Camp, merchants
             and traders principal with Joseph L. Camp as security
bonded for $500 on 11 Jan. 1872...to retail spiritous liquors.
Recorded 15 Jan. 1872.

Page 129.   Jasper N. Barber, principal and Edmund B. Barber and
             ------- bonded for $500 on 24 Jan. 1872 as constable
of #898 G.M. district...recd 24 Jan. 1872.

Page 130.   Joseph W. Walker, principal with W. B. Howell as
             security bonded for $500 on 10 Feb. 1872..."to retail
spiritous liquors"...recd 15 Feby 1872.

Page 131.   John James, principal with Albert B. Rutledge and M.P.
             Camp as securities bonded for $500 on 20 Feb. 1872,
#848 G.M. district constable before James Lindley, J.P. and Henry
J. Hopkins, N.P.   Recorded 23 Feb. 1872.

Page 132.   Robert Lemon, principal with W. J. Lee as security
             bonded for $200 on 5 March 1872..."to retail spiritous
liquors"...recd 6 March 1872.

Page 133.   B. W. Donohue, principle with B. G. Roberts and Henry
             C. White as securities bonded for $500 on 5 March 1872
as constable for #898 G.M. district...recd 7 March 1872.

Page 134.   D. W. Johns, principal with A. R. Hicks as security
             bonded for $500 on 7 March 1872..."to retail spiritous
liquors"...before C. J. Shepherd, ordy...recd 7 March 1872.

Page 135.   J. M. (X) Gray, principal with P. H. Lyon as security
             bonded for $500 on 27 Jan. 1872..."to retail spiritous
liquors"...before Frank Shepherd...recd 1 March 1872.

Page 136.   G. B. Chastain, principal with J. B. Kendricks as
             surety bonded for $500 on 23 March 1872 as constable.
D. A. King was surety on the original bond and in consequence of
his reported insolvency said Chastain ordered to strengthen bond.
Recorded 15 March 1872.

Page 137.   John T. Harris, principal with Thos F. Summers as
             surety bonded for $500 on 7 May 1872..."to retail
spiritous liquors"...recd 7 May 1872.

Page 138.   W. L. McRae, principal with Jas. L. Wyhes, security
             bonded for $500 on 15 June 1872..."to retail spiritous
liquors at his house at Big Shanty"...recorded 20 June 1872...
Frank C. Shepherd, D.C.C.O.

Page 139.   Jam (X) Gray, principal with Dillard M. Young as secur-
             ity bonded for $500 on 29 June 1872..."license to re-
tail spiritous liquors at Abe White's house at Smyrna, Ga."
before C. J. Shepherd, ordy...recd 29 June 1872, Frank C. Shepherd, D.C.C.O.

Page 140. J. L. Dodgson & Sons, principal with W. S. Dodgson
as security bonded for $500 on 24 Aug. 1872..."retail
spiritous liquors in said county."

Page 141. (unnumbered page)   J. H. Elliott, principal with T. L.
Roper as security bonded for $500 on 10 Sept. 1872...
"retail spiritous liquors."

Page 142. D. W. John, principal with A. R. Hicks as security
bonded for $500 on 10 Sept. 1872..."maintain quiet
orderly house."

Page 143. W. H. Dewels and principal with H. C. White as security
bonded for $500 on 10 Sept. 1872..."license to retail
spiritous liquors at the Mitchell place."

Page 144. Robert Lemon, principal with W. J. (X) Lee as security
bonded for $500 on 13 Sept. 1872..."retail spiritous
liquors at Lemon's Courtground." Attested C. J. Shepherd, ordy...
recd 16 Sept. 1872...Frank C. Shepherd, D.C.C.O.

Page 145. B. G. (X) Roberts principal with S. H. Hicks and
Walter Manning as securities bonded for $500 on 2 Oct.
1872 as constable of #897 G.M. district...recd 22 Oct. 1872...
Frank C. Shepherd, D.C.C.O.

Page 146. J. B. Gordon, principal with W. A. Childress as
security bonded for $500 on 22 Oct. 1872..."retail
spiritous liquors." Recorded 22 Oct. 1872...Frank C. Shepherd,
D.C.C.O.

Page 147. J. T. Harris, principal with H. B. Williams as security
bonded for $500 on 5 Nov. 1872..."retail spiritous
liquors for 6 months at his store in Big Shanty." C. J. Shepherd.
Recorded 7 Nov. 1872.

Page 148. G. W. Cox, principal with R. T. Cox as security bonded
for $500 on 26 Sept. 1872..."retail spiritous liquors."
Recorded 6 Nov. 1872.

Page 149. W. H. Dewes, principal with Thos. M. Smith as security
bonded for $500 on 12 Dec. 1872..."retail spiritous
liquors." C. J. Shepherd...recd 19 Dec. 1872.

Page 150. John F. Baldwin, principal with L. J. Baldwin as security bonded for $500 on 23 Dec. 1872..."retail spiri-
tous liquors at Big Shanty."

Page 151. John D. (X) Sanders, principal with H. J. Hill and
M. T. Dorsett as securities bonded for $500 as constable
for #895 G.M. district before C. J. Shepherd.

George N. Shaw, principal with H. J. Hill and N. D.
Stephens as securities bonded for $500 as constable of #895 G.M.
district 7 Jan. 1872 before C. J. Shepherd, ordy.

Page 152. F. M. Mullins, principal with A. W. York and Gei. M.
Manning as securities bonded for $500 on 6 Jan. 1873 as
constable for #898 district before A. N. Simpson, N.P.

Page 153. Wm. J. Hudson, principal with J. F. Lindley, J. T.

Haley, B. Stripling and A. S. Edmondson as securities bonded for $3,000 on 11 Jan. 1873..."elected as Clerk of Superior Court for 1873 and 1874 before C. J. Shepherd, 11 Jan. 1873." Recorded 16 Jan. 1873, H. M. Hammett, ordy.

Page 154.   Hamilton M. Hammett, principal with Humphrey Reid, Joseph Elsas, Timothy Stephens, J. B. Blackwell as securities bonded for $1,000 on 11 Jan. 1873..."elected ordinary" 11 Jan. 1873 before A. N. Simpson, N.P. & Ex Offico J.P.and N.B. Knight, J.S.C....recorded 18 Jan. 1873.

Page 155.   Archibald P. Griggs, principal with James M. Griggs and A. A. Griggs as securities bonded for $500 as bailiff of #1017 G.M. district on 13 Jan. 1873 by H. M. Hammett, ordy.

Hasten Dunn, principal with W. J. Richards and J. M. Green as securities bonded for $500 on 4 Jan. 1873..."elected constable."

Page 156.   (continued)   for #897 G.M. district before J. Z. Alexander, J.P.   Recorded 18 Jan. 1873, F. M. Hammett, ordy.

John R. Ward, principal with Wm. F. Groves, C. J. Shepherd, W. L. Cooper and N. B. Green as securities bonded for $1,000 on 22 Jan. 1873..."elected county surveyor."

Page 157.   (continued)   approved 22 Jan. 1873, H. M. Hammett, ordy.

G. W. Pharr, principal with Wm. H. Campbell as security bonded for $500 7 Jan. 1873 as constable for #1017 G.M. district ...approved by Jno. C. Clay, J.P.

Page 158.   R. L. Eidson, principal with M. M. Phillips, R. C. Hill and W. J. Kiser as securities bonded for $16,900 on 28 Jan. 1873..."elected Tax Collector."   Recorded 29 Jan. 1873 H. M. Hammett, ordy.

Page 159.   J. E. Verhine, principal with J. B. Kendrick and A. M. Puckett as securities bonded for $500 as constable of #991 G.M. district on 29 Jan. 1873 before G. F. Caine, J.P.

William P. Stephens, principal with W. B. Walles, L. Black, A. S. Edmondson, L. Bennett, B. Stripling, B. H. Marchman and J. W. Henderson as securities bonded for $10,000.

Page 160.   (continued) on 20 Jan. 1873..."elected sheriff" before H. M. Hammett, ordy...recd 30 Jan. 1873.

M. T. Grist, principal with P. H. Lyon and G. M. Manning as securities bonded for $1,000 on 22 Jan. 1873...

Page 161.   (continued)   as coroner on 22 Jan. 1873 before H. M. Hammett, ordy...rec 6 Feb. 1873.

Hopkins and Moon, principal with A. J. Kiser as security bonded for $500 on 6 Feb. 1873..."retail spiritous liquors" before H. M. Hammett.

Page 162.   Robert Lemon, principal with Edward Lemon as security

141

bonded for $500 on 7 Feb. 1873..."retail spiritous liquors at his house"...before H. M. Hammett...recd 12 Feb. 1873, H. M. Hammett, ordy.

Page 163.   J. H. Elliott, principal with T. L. Ryer, security bonded for $500 on 14 July 1873..."retail spiritous liquors"...H. M. Hammett, ordy.

Page 164.   N. J. Garrison, principal with H. M. Putnam, James L. Lemon, L. H. Tanner, E. L. Litchfield as securities bonded for $6350 on 31 Jan. 1873..."Receiver of Tax Returns"... before H. M. Hammett, 21 Feb. 1873.

Page 165.   Henry C. White, principal with Benjamin Stripling, T.J. Atkinson, H. B. Wallis as securities bonded for $16,000 on 22 Feb. 1873 "elected county Treasurer"...before H. M. Hammett.

Page 166.   D. W. Johns, principal with J. M. Skinner, as security bonded for $500 on 12 March 1873..."retail spiritous liquors"... before H. M. Hammett, ordy...oath of D. W. John before H. M. Hammett 12 March 1873.

Page 167.   James W. Keley, principal with N. N. Gober and Wm. A. Childress as securities bonded 12 March 1873 as constable for #992 G.M. district $500 before Alfred Maner, N.P.... recd 27 March 1873, H. M. Hammett.

Page 168.   A. South, principal with G. W. Arnold and R. B. Anderson as securities bonded for $500 as constable for #845 G.M. district before J. T. Talley, NP...filed 11 April 1873, recorded 14 April 1873, H. M. Hammett, ordy.

Page 169.   William B. Pilgrim, principal with P. H. Lyon and W. B. Wallis as securities bonded for $500 appointed constable for #898 G.M. district on 19 April 1873 before M.A.M. Lanier, J.P. Filed 19 April 1873...recorded 19 April 1873, H. M. Hammett (commission issued).

Page 170.   James Burton, principal with J. H. Wells and Wm. Davis securities bonded for $500 as constable for #911 G.M. district on 22 April 1873 before H. M. Hammett...filed 29 April 1873...recd 1 May 1873 (commission issued).

Page 171.   Daniel Reid, principal with J. H. Reid security bonded for $500 on 5 May 1873..."build bridge across Stopes Creek on road leading from Powder Springs to Sweetwater old town... keep in good repair for 7 years"...before H. M. Hammett.

Page 172.   J. F. Baldwin and Bros., principal with A. D. Edwards security bonded for $500..."license to retail spiritous liquors"...2 July 1873, H. M. Hammett, ordy....Oath of J. T. Baldwin...9 months...before H. M. Hammett.

Page 173.   Oath of G. W. McClarty...retail spiritous liquors for 8 months on 6 May 1873 before H. M. Hammett, ordy.

Oath of R. A. Ballenger...6 months retail spiritous liquors on 30 June 1873 before H. M. Hammett.

Page 174.   John McTyre, principal with Robert N. Anderson, James H. Brown, Z. T. Anderson as securities bonded for $500..

"keep in good repair bridge over Olly's Creek leading from Powder Springs to Atlanta." 11 Aug. 1873...H. M. Hammett, ordy.

Page 175. Robert Lemon, principal with John Burns, security bonded for $500..."retail spiritous liquors"...22 July 1873, H. M. Hammett, ordy...Oath of Robert Lemon...1 mo...22 July 1873, H. M. Hammett, ordy.

Page 176. Sidney F. Powell, principal with L. M. Simpson security bonded for $500..."retail spiritous liquors on 10 Oct. 1873"...brfore H. M. Hammett, ordy...Oath of S. F. Powell...6 mos. ..10 Oct. 1873.

Page 177. W. H. Lacell, principal with J. S. Hames, security bonded for $500 on 12 Sept. 1873..."to retail spiritous liquors"...before H. M. Hammett, ordy...Oath of Lacell and Hames ...3½ months...12 Sept. 1873, H. M. Hammett.

Page 178. D. W. Johns, principal with J. M. Skinner security bonded for $500 on 7 Sept. 1873 before H. M. Hammett... Oath of D. W. Johns...6 months.

Page 179. J. N. Dodgen, principal with J. L. Dodgen security bonded for $500..."retail spiritous liquors"...22 Oct. 1873 before H. M. Hammett, ordy...Oath of J. N. Dodgen...3 months.

Page 180. J. M. Lee, principal with W. J. Lee, security bonded for $500..."retail spiritous liquors"...10 Nov. 1873 before H. M. Hammett, ordy....Oath of J. M. Lee.

Page 181. R. S. Eidson, principal with J. R. Humphries, Thos. F. Simmons and Geo. Kendrick, security bonded for $28,000 as Tax Collector...-- Sept. 1873 before H. M. Hammett.

Page 182. Elliott and Oglesby, principal with A. B. Moon security bonded for $500..."retail spiritous liquors at Powder Springs"...25 Dec. 1873 before H. M. Hammett, ordy...Oath of J. H. Elliott and J. E. Oglesby...12 months.

Page 183. Lasell Hames, principal with H. C. Hames, security bonded for $500...2 Jan. 1874..."retail spiritous liquors"...before H. M. Hammett...Oath of W. J. M. Hames...3 months.

Page 184. Joel B. Tribble, principal with S. T.(?) Moon as security bonded for $800..."letting of bridge across Big Allatoona Creek near town of Acworth...lowest bidder @ $399... keep in good repair for 7 years..." 26 Feb. 1874.

John James, principal with A. B. Rutledge, security bonded for $500 on 3 Jan. 1874...

Page 185. John James elected constable for #846 G.M. district, before W. H. Goodwin, N.P. & Ex. O J.P.

Z. B. Moon, principal with J. J. Barnes security bonded for $500 on 3 Jan. 1874 as constable for #846 G.M. district.

Page 186. (continued)...before James Lindley, J.P. 7 W. H. Goodwin, N.P. Ex. O J.P.

Thomas Hooper, principal with William Buckner security bonded for $300..."built bridge across Nicksjack Creek leading from Masons and Turner's Ferry to Powder Springs...maintain good repair for 7 years."...3 Feb. 1874. Signed by T. M. Hooper, Wm. Buckner and Thomas Hooper.

J. M. Moore, principal with T. H. Moore, security bonded for $1,000.

Page 187. ..."Letting out of bridge across Soaps Creek near Oakley Mills...lowest bidder @ $494...keep in good repair for 7 years." 3 Feb. 1874. J. M. Moore, M.D. and T. H. Moore signed.

20 Jan. 1874 #851 G.M. district. George McMillan, principal with J. R. Humphries as security bonded for $1,000... George McMillan bid bridge on Santown road between George McMillan and Thos. Moore's...keep in good repair for 7 years...bid @ $179.00...signed J. W. Hill and W. J. Palmer, commissioners.

Page 188. Calvin Fults, principal with D. W. Johns security bonded for $68.00...lowest bidder for bridge across Mud Creek near Irwin old place on Powder Springs road...bid @ $34.00...good repair for 5 years...4 Feb. 1874...approved T. R. Echold, J.P.

James L. Hughs, principal with J. A. Buffington and ---- ----(?) as securities bonded for $500.

Page 189. 16 March 1874...James L. Hughes appointed constable for #991 G.M. district before John A. Booth, N.P.

R. A. Ragland, principal with Almond Hays bonded for $150..."built bridge across Powder Springs Creek on road leading from Powder Springs to Dallas...maintain 7 years"...before H. M. Hammett, ordy.

Page 190. Ezekill Stabley, principal with L. L. Northcutt, security bonded for $150..."build bridge across Noses Creek on road leading from Paulding Road to Cassvill Road by New Salem Church...for $75.50...good repair for 7 years"...before H. M. Hammett, ordy.

Page 191. William B. Pilgrim, principal with Benjamin Stripling security bonded for $500 as constable for #898 G.M. district...before H. M. Hammett, ordy on 5 Jan. 1875...also signing was N. B. Wallis...Oath of William B. Pilgrim.

Page 192. T. W. Wallis, principal with H. B. Wallis as security bonded for $500 as constable for #898 G.M. district on 5 Jan. 1875, before H. M. Hammett, ordy...Oath of T. W. Wallis.

Page 193. Jessie H. Nelms, principal with W. J. Lee and John T. Thompson as securities bonded for $500 as constable for #992 G.M. district..."elected"...on 5 Jan. 1875 before H. M. Hammett, ordy...oath of Jessie H. Nelms.

Page 194. J. B. Gordon, principal with J. W. Kirkpatrick and L. M. Simpson as securites bonded for $500 as "constable for #992 G.M. district for 2 years"...on 4 Jan. 1875 before H. M. Hammett, ordy...Oath of J. B. Gordon.

Page 195. Hasten Dunn, principal with J. L. Gantt (signed J. D.
          Gantt) and W. J. Richards as securities bonded for
$500..."elected constable for #897 G.M. district"...9 Jan. 1875
before H. M. Hammett, ordy...Oath of Hasten Dunn.

Page 196. E. A. Spinks, principal with W. W. Carroll and J. J.
          Jolly as securities bonded for $500..."elected consta-
ble for #897 G.M. district"...5 Jan. 1875 before H. M. Hammett,
ordy...Oath of E. A. Spinks.

Page 197. I. J. Morris, principal with R. T. Seay and William
          Henderson as securities bonded for $500..."elected
constable for #895 G.M. district"...on 6 Jan. 1875 before H. M.
Hammett, ordy...oath of I. J. Moon.

Page 198. P. C. Priest, principal with R. M. Benson, J. T.
          Chalker, T. E. Kendrick, as securities bonded for $500
as constable for #991 G.M. district before J. B. Kendrick, J.P.
and G. T. Carrie, J.P....Oath of P. C. Priest.

Page 199. Samuel J. Scott, principal with J. F. Johnson as
          security bonded for $500..."elected constable for
#1017 G.M. district"...5 Jan. 1875 before H. M. Hammett, ordy...
oath of Samuel J. Scott.

Page 200. J. J. Callaway, principal with T. P. Lindley and J. C.
          Butner, securites bonded for $500 on 2 Jan. 1875...
"elected constable for #846 G.M. district before W. H. Goodwin,
N.P. & Ex O., J.P. and James Lindley, J.P....certification of
elected of J. J. Callaway by W. H. Doowin and James Lindley...
oath of J. J. Callaway before H. M. Hammett, ordy.

Page 201. J. C. Mohon, principal with D. W. Johns, and J. H.
          Cooper as securities bonded for $500 on 14 Jan. 1875
as constable for #1017 G.M. district before H. M. Hammett, ordy...
oath of J. C. Mohon (probably Mahan).

Page 202. J. J. Hunter, principal with T. G. Green and J. H.
          Burney as securities bonded for $500..."elected con-
stable for #845 G.M. district"...18 Jan. 1875 before H. M. Hammett, ordy...oath of J. J. Hunter.

Page 203. James Burton, principal with A. H. McVay and J. G.
          Morris as securities bonded for $500 as constable for
#911 G.M. district before H. M. Hammett, ordy. n.d...oath of
James Burton.

Page 204. William P. Stephens, principal with Benjamin Stripling
          and T. A. Gober, H. D. McCutchson and R. H.Marchman as
securities bonded for $10,000 on 23 Jan. 1875...elected Sheriff
before Hammett, ordy.

Page 205. John Bela Campbell, principal with John G. Campbell,
William J. Hudson, J. S. Clifton and W. E. Gilbert as securities
...bonded for $3,000 on 23 Jan. 1875 as Clerk of Superior Court
before H. M. Hammett, ordy.

Page 206. James B. Glover, principal with H. G. Cole, J. B.
          Blackwell and L. L. Northcutt, securites bonded for
$31,000 on 23 Jan. 1875 as Tax Collector before H. M. Hammett,
ordy.

Page 207. Repeats page 206.

Page 208. Wesley H. Jackson, principal with J. Jackson, J. F.
Lindley, N. M. Gober, J. P. Dobbs as securities bonded
for $12,000 on 29 Jan. 1875 as Tax Receiver.

Page 209. Henry C. White, principal with H. B. Wallis, B. Stripling, and L. L. Northcutt as securities bonded for
$10,000 on 6 Jan. 1875 as County Treasurer before H. M. Hammett,
ordy.

Page 210. John R. Ward, principal with R. H. Marchman, B. Stripling, Wm. B. Clinkscales, W. L. Cooper as securities
bonded for $10,000 on 8 Feb. 1875 as County Surveyor before H. M.
Hammett, ordy.

Page 211. M. T. Grist, principal with A. L. Edmondson, J. T.
Maley as securities bonded for $1,000 on 27 Jan. 1875
as Coroner before Hammett, ordy.

Page 212. John James, principal with F. C. House, Ezrah James as
securities bonded for $500 on 2 Jan. 1875 as constable
for #846 G.M. district before W. H. Goodwin, N.P. & EX O. J.P.
...Certification of election of John James by William Goodwin,
heading Powder Springs.

Page 213. Toliver W. Wallace, principal with R. H. McCutcheson
and P. H. Lyon as securities bonded for $500 on 22 May
1875..."elected constable for #898 G.M. district"...before H. M.
Hammett, ordy...oath of T. W. Wallace.

Page 214. Almond Hays, principal with L. A. Ragland, security
bonded for $500..."letting out of bid for bridge
across Sweetwater near Mrs. Barnes on road leading from Atlanta
and Powder Springs road across to old Tallapoosa road...low bid
@ $200...good repair for 4 years"...1 Nov. 1874, H. M. Hammett,
ordy.

Page 215. John Read, principal with M. L. Ruff, H. C. Ruff by
J. L. Reed as securities bonded for $125.00..."letting
out of bridge...across Powder Springs Creek on road from Marietta
to Dallas near John Moon's...lowest bidder at $60.00"...on 14
Aug. 1875...before H. M. Hammett, ordy.

Page 216. L. F. Mayes, principal with J. B. Blackwell security
bonded for $500..."elected constable for #1017 G.M.
district"...11 Jan. 1876 before H. M. Hammett, ordy...oath of
S. F. Mayes.

Page 217. J. C. Hunter, principal with G. W. Arnold and C. A.
Dunwoody as securities bonded for $500 as constable
for #845 G.M. district before J. T. Talley, J.P....n.d.

Page 218. William T. Harris, principal with Hugh Queen and Francis
Queen as securities bonded for $500 as constable for
#895 G.M. district before W. B. Howell, J.P....n.d.

Page 219. William S. Echols, principal with J. G. Wright security
bonded for $38.00..."bridge across Smith Creek near
Esq. Echols on Villa Rica Road...low bid of $19...5 years good
repair"...before T. R. Echols, J.P.

Page 220.   T. W. Wallace, principal with J. P. Wallace and H. B.
            Wallace as securities bonded for $500 on 13 Jan. 1876
..."appointed constable of #898 G.M. district"...before H. M.
Hammett, ordy...oath of Toliver Wallace.

Page 221.   James O. Fraser, principal with C. K. Lewis and Simon
            Fraser as securities bonded for $500 on 29 Nov. 1875
as constable of #895 G.M. district before H. M. Hammett, ordy...
oath of James O. Fraser.

Page 222.   Certiorarie Bond...James H. Howell and J. C. Mohon for
            $25.00 on 30 July 1875...J. H. Howell has presented
his petition of certiorari to Hon. N. B. Knight, J.S.C. to be
directed to H. M. Hammett, ordinary requiring ordinary to certify
and sent to said Superior Court his actings and doings in a certain
cause in which John Pope was petitioner and J. B. Howell up which
judgment has been rendered against said J. B. Howell in order
that the errors alledged to have been committed may be corrected..
.." 30 July 1875.

Page 223.   A. C. Sorrells, principal with C. C. Sorrell as secur-
            ity bonded for $590 on 20 Jan. 1876..."B. Rainey, John
M. McLain and W. D. Stansell Road Commissioners let out building
of new bridge across Proctor Creek on road leading from Acworth
to Dallas near Acworth...keep in good repair for 7 years"...be-
fore H. M. Hammett, ordy...C. C. Sorrells security of above bond...

Page 224.   ...on oath says he is worth the amount of said bond
            over and above his debts, exemptions homestead and
otherwise...sworn 20 Jan. 1876 before R. M. Mitchells, resident
of town of Acworth.

            Allen C. Sorrells, principal with Clark C. Sorrells,
security bonded for $786 on 24 April 1876..."build of public
road bridge on ----- Creek for $374 by James W. Robertson and
William Kelph, Road Commissioners of Roswell district...near
Roswell and 130 feet long...7 years in good repair"...before J. P.
Lauthon, N.P. & Ex O. J.P....to be completed on or before 1 July
next...before H. M. Hammett, ordy.

Page 225.   H. T. Holtsclaw, principal with Almond Hayes, security
            bonded for $19..."keeping in good repair of bridge
lately built near said H. T. Holtsclaw across Gothards Creek near
Millers Weavers on said creek...on road leading from J. H. Millers
to Tallapoosa road...good repair for 7 years"...19 Sept. 1876...
before H. M. Hammett, ordy.

Page 226.   NOTARY'S COURT...#851 district, 15 Jan. 1875...There
            being no constable elected in and for said district...
ordered that James M. Griggs be appointed until an election be
held...J. P. Lawthorn, N. P. & Ex O. J.P.

            Oath of J. M. (X) Griggs, 15 Jan. 1875...Bond of James
M. Griggs, principal with J. T. (X) Hix and Hugh Griggs as securities for $500 as constable on 22 Jan. 1875 before H. M. Hammett,
ordy.

Page 227.   John T. Thompson, principal with J. W.(?) Kirkpatrick
            and Robert Lemon as securities bonded for $500 on 16
June 1876...appointed constable for #992 G.M. district...caused
by resignation of J. B. Gordon and Jessie H. Nelms, before

Alfred Maner, N.P. and J. V. Stanback, J.P.

Page 228.   James L. Hughs, principal with John A. Gibson and W. H.
            Bates securities bonded for $500 on 30 Oct. 1876 as
constable of #991 G.M. district before H. M. Hammett, ordy...oath
of James L. Hughs.

Page 229.   James E. Verhine, principal with S. J. Burnett and H.
            B. Williams as securities bonded for $500...appointed
constable for #991 G.M. District by G. T. Carrie and D. B. Kendricks, J.P. for #991 G.M. district to fill unexpired term of P. C.
Priest, 27 Nov. 1876 before G. T. Carrie and D. B. Kendricks.

Page 230.   John R. Alexander, principal with L. N. Alexander and
            Nathan (X) Alexander as securities bonded for $120...
7 Nov. 1876..."bridge across Little Allatoona Creek on Stiled-
borough road near T. N. Cowan's was let out to low bid of J. R.
Alexander...good repair for 7 years...approved and ordered an
order be issued to J. R. Alexander for $60 the amount for building
said bridge...H. M. Hammett, ordy.

Page 231.   Acworth, Ga., 20 Nov. 1876...H. M. Hammett, ordinary:
            Sir: This is to certify that J. A. Alexander has com-
pleted said bridge named in above bond and it is hereby recorded.
B. Rainey and John McLain and W. D. Stansell.

Page 232.   W. M. McMillan, principal with J. A. Johnson and J. B.
            Brockman securities bonded for $595..."keeping in good
repair of bridge about to be built by W. M. McMillen across
Willis Creek at Starch Mills on road known as Roswell River Road
...for 7 years from 21 Oct. 1876"...before Dewitt O. Green.

END

148

VOTERS LIST, CHEROKEE COUNTY, 1832

At an election held at the house of Ambrose Harnage, in the county and state aforesaid, on Monday, the sixth day of February, in the year 1832, it being the first Monday in that month, for Clerk of the Superior Court, Clerk of the Inferior Court, Sheriff, Receiver of Tax Returns, Tax Collector, Coroner, County Surveyor, and five Justices of the Inferior Court, county officers of said county, the following named persons cast their ballots:

William Bradford	Joshua Davis	Joseph S. Dyer
Joseph Bradford	H.J. McGallion	John McBryer
Leroy Hammons	Robert Gatling	John Middleton
Thomas Atkins	Edward Gilbert	Elijah Bersawn
Reuben Holloway	Wm. A. Coleman	John Thompson
John McConnell	Uriah Holden	Joseph Eaton
George Barber	Daniel Ledbetter	Jesse Smith
Wilson Young	Evans Thomas	Jesse Thompson
John Williams	Charles Smith	David Wilkey
William Stansill	Robert T. Fowler	John Holcomb
Lacy Witcher	Joseph McSherry	Philo Smith
J.L. Parker	Elisha Robertson	Daniel R. Mitchell
J.H. Raundsevill	Thos. W. Bolton	John C. Johns
Henry Witcher	William Gunter	Geo. W. Gaddis
Ephraim Mabry	Wm. Williamson	Joseph Keyton
Hinson Dorsey	Jeremiah S. Chastain	John Doss
William Nolen	Wm. McKinsey	John Sharp
Dennis Knight	James Batey	John T. Mattox
Archibald Bradford	John Kimball	Lewis Polston
Daniel Hammons	Jesse Wisdom	B.S. Hardman
David B. Ellington	Robert Henderson	David Allison
Edward Pilburn	Thos. Rogers	Sherwo'd Bowman
Andrew Johnson	Robert McClure	Wm. Grant
William McClure	Jonathan Cox	Elisha Dooly
Thomas Wilson	John Say	Nathaniel Wofford
George Post	Cornelius Cooper	L.L. Langston
David Raundsville	Lewis Arter	Vincent Bowman
Lewis Tumlin	Nimrod H. Pendley	Lowry Williamson
John Cockrell	David Utry	John Corner
Jeremiah Cloud	Pleasant Henderson	Barnaby Thomvill
Levi McGinis	Philip Burns	Benjamin Jones
John Jack	Reuben Sams	Obadiah Hooper
Wm. McDaniel	James Daniel	John Witcher
Samuels Mans	James Cantrell	Gennubuth Winn
John Holland	John B. Garrison	Elisha Wilburn
Jas. Holesonback	Wm. B. Malone	Moses Anderson
James Wilson	John Jolly	James McBrayer
James Cochrane	John P. Brooks	John D. Chastain
Asa Keith	James Jones	Redden Pinson
Riley Wilson	Henry Holcomb	Jabez Holcomb
Bythel Bradbury	Mason Ezzard	Joab Ashworth
Lawson Bowman	David Densmore	Jeremiah Cruse
Henry Bright	Wm. Hammons	Allen H. Murdock
Wm. T. Williamson	Andrew Wood	Chester Hawks
John Greenwood	John Armstrong	Edward Edwards
John Pittman	Barrow Mullins	Benj. Bracketts
David Gutury	William Loveless	Green B. Durham
Thomas Higgs	Jesse Townsend	Nathaniel G. _____
Noah Langley	Berry Hill	Hiram Hall
Wm. H. Ray	Eli Dogins	Elias Henderson
George R. Glenn	Archibald Lindsey	Isaac Green
John P. Winn	Elias Goddard	James Mayes
John Langley	Grenn Doss (Dees?)	Isaac Horton
Washington Willis	Wm. Willis	John Hendricks
James Sample	Moses Perkins	James Middleton

VOTERS LIST, CHEROKEE COUNTY, 1832

Reuben Daniel
Daniel Davis
Daniel May
R.L. Goodman
Wm. Hendrick
Elijah Roberts
John Wood
Benj. Bradley
John Roach
James Simmons
Martin Culbertson
Reuben Thomton
Jacob M. Scudder
Wm. Wood
Wm. Baker
Wm. Lay
Oliver Strickland
Jas. Hemphill

James Bell
Reuben F. Daniel
Benj. Cooper
John Dawson
Eli McConnell
Charles Harris
Wm. May
Allen Stephens
Noble Simmons
Moses Cantrell
Michael C. Wood
Joel M. Bryant
Reuben Eaton
Wm. Parley
Holmon Simmons
William S. Simmons
John Smith

Robert O'Bar
Jesse Day
Benj. Forester
Daniel Love
Lackley Langley
John Daniel
Wm. K. Love
Willis Hendricks
M. Brabett
Abraham Wood
James Hendricks
Hubbarn Barker
James White
William _____
Robert Berry
Wm. Smith
Lewis Dobbs

The men elected to the various county officers were:

Oliver Strickland, Clerk Superior Court; William T. Williamson, Clerk Inferior Court; John Jolly, Sheriff; Hubbard Barker, Receiver of Tax Returns; Lewis Tumlin, Tax Collector; Asa Keith, Coroner; Jesse Watkins, County Surveyor; John McConnell, John Witcher, Robert O'Barr, Gennubeth Winn, Henry Holcombe, Justices of the Inferior Court.

150

THE 1834 CENSUS OF CHEROKEE COUNTY

Reproduced from the original in the county files, Telamon Cuyler Collection, Special Collections, University of Georgia Libraries, with the permission of University of Georgia Libraries.

Georgia   )   I Abraham C. Avery having been Duly appointed
Cherokee County)   and Sworn to take the Census of the white
                    population of Cherokee County and by Law to
make my return on or before the first of April 1834, do hereby
certify that the foregoing four pages hereto annexed doth contain
a true statement of the Census of the white population in Said
County at this time from the best & most authentic information in
my power to obtain.   Given under my hand this 29th day of March
1834.   There being thirteen hundred and forty two white free
inhabitant Citizens in Said County.   /s/ Absalem C. Avary
Philip Kroft C.I.C.
Numeration of Cherokee County (Names of Heads of Families and
numer of white persons).

John P. Wiley-6
William Grisham-5
John Priest-5
Howell Colb-7
Stephen Whitmire-6
Jeremiah Dean-1
Benjamin F. Johnston-6
Joseph Donaldson-5
Philip Kroft-6
Beverly Daniel-6
John Edwards-7
Robert Guthrie-9
John McCanless-5
William McCanless-2
Rewben F. Daniel-3
William W.B. Key-2
Georg Brock-12
Andrew Cathey-6
Jane Parker, wid-4
Roger Green (Grum?)-9
Nancy Nelson-4
Solomon Floyd-6
James Burnes-5
John S. Holcombe-7
John Nix-7
John Rogers-4
George McCaskey-5
Eli McConnell-8
James Tippen-4
William Tippen-4
Thompson Tippen-3
Pleasant Logan-2
John B. Garrison-6
Eli Grimes-2
Danel Butler-6
Martin Evans-8
James Chambers &
John M. Chambers-2
Jacob Cagle-3
Elias Putnam (Butram?)-7
Joseph Cagle-4
Elisha Dyer-5
Peter C. Boger-6

James S. Elliett-10
Stephan Kemp-7
Alsey Kemp-3
Jacob Avery-4
Squire Herring-6
Robert T. Fowler-2
George A. Bolch-4
William Lawless-2
William Ward-8
John Black-5
John H. King-6
Garvin Black-5
John Wilson-6
Solomon Peck-7
Bryant Ingram-2
Linsey Peck-5
John Mileer-10
Enoch Rogers-11
Jeptha Maddox-4
John B. Bird-2
Dennis Miller-2
William M. Bird-5
Edward Maddox-6
John McConnell (McCornrell?)-10
John Landram-4
Lucy Bradford, wid-8
Charles Blythe-4
Archabald Bradford-11
John P. Brook-13
James Wilbon-3
James Young-8
Daniel R. Mitchell-4
Ferdinand Bailey-9
Wyatt Walbrit-3
Moses Perkins-4
Jonathan Crow-6
William Crow-4
Abraham Crow-4
William Poque-6
Henry Wheeler-3
William White-6
Joiner C. Bailey-5

Caless Sanders-5
Noble Timmons-12
John Pugh-6
Andrew Scott-2
John M. Mullins-10
Burton Mullins-2
Nancy Ann Mullins, wid-4
William T. Bates-6
Stephen Bates-6
Enoch Vandervier-6
Thomas T. Bates-2
Joseph Fincher-8
James Cooper-1
Joel Leathers-10
James Whorton-2
Samuel C. Candler-2
Noble P. Bell-10
Jonathan J. Johnson-3
James H. Beal-2
Sympson C. Dyer-2
William O. Beal-5
John Brewster-9
James Minton-4
John Cannon-7
Charles McGrady-5
George Heard-0
Martin Smith-1
William Crain-4
Danel Methvin-4
Bennett Morgan &
William Milnor (?) &
William Eids (?)-8
Richard Ragsdale-7
Kertus Sadderfee-7
Andrew Hicks-7
William Chamblee-9
William Wayne-2
Tarrett Chamblee-3
James Barnett-13
Gamuel Jackson-4
Martin Chamblee-5
Gideon H. Trout-3
Robert T. Griffin-0
John Waggoner-11
Joseph Nailer-4
Henry G. Ellison-5
Henry Wright-4
Jesse Bates-11
Thomas Johnson-7
Anny Bostwick, wid-4
John Epperson-8
James Jourdon-5
George Post-3
Guilford W. Jones-6
Jeremiah Wafford-3
William Lay-3
Thomas Heggs-3
George Hinkle-4
John P. Winn-7
David Qualls-8
Randol McDaniel-8

Henry Holcombe-5
James T. Sitten-4
Elisha Dooley-5
James W. Dooley-6
Robert Sweat(Tweat?)-14
Lodderick Nix-9
William Nix-4
Wiley Petty-2
Emariah Popham-8
William P. Nix-5
Flemming Bates-9
Elisha Wright-6
Charles Christian-9
Abram Harbon-2
Nathaniel Harbon-6
Felix Moss-9
James Copelin-6
Charles F. Lay-3
George Kitchens-6
Simeon B. Rucker-8
John Nailer-7
James Thward(Shward?)-4
Joseph S. Dial (Diel?)-6
Elijah Greyham-4
David Rusk-8
Edward Townsend-12
Thomas Townsend-11
John Tate-9
William Tate, Jr.-2
William Priest-3
Thomas Priest-5
Simond Tate-6
Solomon Sawbury-4
James Kurkendoll-4
John Blythe-10
Busy Barnett-3
Holman F. Simmons-11
Ausburn Reeves-4
Jesse Grum (Green?)-5
Moses Whitsitt-6
David Stancel-9
William Townsend-3
William Priest-3
John Waitrs-10
Rewben Harrison-9
Alexander Miller-7
Thomas B. Wells-3
Musten Wells-4
Thomas Smith-6
William Dean-4
John Maddox-8
Abner Philips-10
Joseph Walker-5
John Williamson-4
William Holland-3
Joseph Watt-4
Levi Merrett-7
Andrew Boyd-10
William Tate Sr.-3
John Black-8
Wiley Barber-3

Elias Chafin-4
Amos Chaffin-2
Elijah Chaffin-6
Joseph Chaffin-6
Robert Blythe-4
Elizabeth Blake, wid-8
Robert Chandler-6
Christopher Rinehart-3
John Semore-3
Lawson Fields-3
Archabald Cogburn-6
David Densemore-6
David Dudley-12
Jesse Wallis-4
Charles Sawyer-8
Harla Attaway Sawyer-3
Thomas Hendrix-10
Zachariah Davis-10

John Hendrix-6
Wiley A. Roberds-5
Hiram Dimsdale-6
William Trible-6
William May-12
James Ellerd-6
Alford Dockirss-6
Mary Rustin-1
Isaac George-6
William Lay-3
James Conn-5
Henry Wilson-8
John Stancel-3
Richard Lethral-4
William M. McAfee-2
James Barmore-6
John Searjeant-8
Absalem C. Avery-4

End

County organized 1832, County site, Canton, Ga. Present court
house, built in 1873, dilapidated and inadequate. In Bartow
county, when the Federal army reached Cassville the then **Ordinary**
had loaded most of the public records in wagons, carried them
four miles in the woods and buried them, so that they escaped
the holocaust of the town. Here practically the same thing oc-
curred; the clerk of the Court removing all the records of his
office, and apparently most of those from the Ordinary's office
and hiding them several miles in the country, so that when
Sherman's torch bearers arrived here to do their work the records,
or most of them, were saved. Judge Burtz, the Ordinary, says
that this faithful officer now rests in an unmarked grave in the
county, and he hopes that the County may yet recognize his valu-
able services by placing a marker over it.

CLERK'S OFFICE. Records begin with the organization of the county and seem to be complete, though the separate indexes to some
of the early deed books are missing. The earliest book of deeds,
1832-1833, which is not very legible, has been re-written, both
the original and the copy being found in the vault. The following two or three volumes are the most beautifully written that I
have ever seen. Covers are getting loose, but otherwise in good
condition.
   Samuel C. Candler was the second Sheriff of the County, beginning in 1834 and serving for several years.

ORDINARY'S OFFICE. Marriage Licenses complete from 1841, with a
few in 1840 recorded in that volume. Minutes of the Court of
Ordinary, Book A, begins 1856. Bonds and Wills, Book B, 1848-
1866. Judge Burtz says that the former Ordinary told him there
is an earlier volume somewhere in the office, but he has not been
able to find it. Beginning with 1866 wills are recorded separa-
tely, and are continuous. Tax digests back to 1870. County
gazettes for probably 30 or 40 years, unbound, in pigeon holes,
part in the office and part in vault: Large cabinet of original
papers in the office, unclassified.
   Book A, County Officer's bonds, starts 1848. Found no early
Appraisals, Administrations or Sales.
   On top of steel shelving in the vault are some high piles of
account books and the bottom three in one of these piles appeared
to be very old, and I took them to be among the earliest records
of the county, but as the Ordinary seemed unwilling for me to dis-
turb the pile, I did not find out what they were.

This county, like Bartow, Floyd, Polk and probably all of the
counties in the Cherokee section, carries a numberical lot index
to deeds, in additional to the regular index.

GROOM	BRIDE	MARRIED	PAGE
Hezekiah Miller	Minerva Emmerson	11/10/1840	1
John S. Russell	Martha Baker	2/11/1841	1
John Gibbs	Eliza Ann Smithwick	2/16/1841	2
John O'Neal	Nancy Blythe	1/14/1841	2
Charles Clayton	Charlotty Corbin	3/ 3/1841	3
William Presley	Abbaline Langly	1/ 7/1841	3
Humphrey P. Rice	Leviny Kerkendall	2/11/1841	3
Robert C. Smith	Eliza Brown	1/21/1841	4
Hezekiah Miller	Manervia Emmerson	11/10/1840	4
George Wilkie	Anna Crofford	3/ 2/1841	5
William Anderson	Jane Wilson	3/ 4/1841	5
Jesse Keykendall	Nancy Blythe	3/15/1841	6
Austin R. Pearce	Ann Dobson	3/14/1841	6
Blewford Holcomb	Caroline McDaniel ✓	4/ 8/1841	7
Thomas N. White	Louisa C. Gilmore	5/13/1841	7
Joseph Rodgers	Demarsa Mills	11/30/1840	8
John Corbin	Laura P. Clayton	4/ 4/1841	8
James M. Bates	Sary Ann Williamson	2/ 4/1841	9
William P. Hammond	Mary Ann Sargent	7/ 4/1841	9
Robert C. Thomas	Frances D. Baker	7/15/1841	10
William Wilson	Harriet L. Fowler	3/11/1841	10
George W. Jefferson	Jane M. Dent	12/29/1840	11
William H. Brown	Nancy Brown	8/ 3/1841	11
Hugh A. Thompson	Rachel Hogan	12/27/1840	12
Martin Phillips	Rebecca Walraven	5/30/1841	12
George S. Hoyt	Margaret Amanda Erwin	10/24/1841	13
Berryman H. Corley	Sindy Bennet	8/29/1841	13
Elijah Jackson	Elizabeth Wright	7/23/1841	14
Jesse Ellis	Nancy Lay	9/23/1841	14
Hugh A. Longino	Margaret S. Brewster	10/24/1841	15
William Chamlee	Elizabeth Ann Pew	9/29/1841	15
Sion Honey	Rebecca White	10/10/1841	16
Augustin I. Martin	Mary Thompson	4/ 6/1841	16
Abner Phillips	Nancy Broadwell	9/ 9/1841	17
Cornelius Kuykendall	Jane Simpson	10/14/1841	17
Allen Walston	Elizabeth M. Daniel	11/12/1841	18
Sampson Boatner	Rebecca Burch	10/24/1841	18
Thomas Harris	Lucinda Deadman	11/22/1841	19
John F. Brooks	Elizabeth G. Moss	1/20/1842	19
THERE IS NO PAGE 20			
David Walraven	Elizabeth White	9/30/1841	21
Arthur T. Camp	Nancy Maxwell	12/12/1841	21
John Weatherford	Elizabeth Coller	12/12/1841	22
Asa M. Griffin	(not given)	2/20/1842	22
Noel G. Jones	Lucinda Hollans	12/ 7/1841	23
G. W. Bush	Sarah Ann D. Griffin	12/23/1841	23
William B. Colb	Jane Hillhouse	12/ 2/1841	24
Walter Maddox	Charlotte Rhodes	2/25/1842	24
James M. Brooks	Elizabeth Stegall	8/19/1841	24
Tyre H. Smithwick	Martha Latham	12/10/1840	24
David Welch	Elizabeth Smithwick	12/10/1840	25
John Kuykendall	Martha Tate	11/11/1841	25
William W. Williamson	Caroline McWhorter	7/11/1841	26
J.T.D. Harvin	Elvira E. Strain	2/27/1842	26
John Daniel Harbin	Mary Boon	7/ /1841	27
John Howell	Nancyville Brown	8/ 2/1842	27
Benjamin Hill	Nancy Brock	8/ 3/1842	28
Joseph B. Sims	Eliza Ann Wilson	8/ 3/1842	28
Elijah R. Bennett	Kesiah Tate	8/ 3/1842	29

155

GROOM	BRIDE	MARRIED	DATE
Louis M. Hook	Elizabeth W. McMeekin	8/ 7/1842	29
John W. Armstrong	Clara Hagen	1/ 9/1842	30
Samuel Masell	Louisa Avery	8/ 8/1842	30
Jefferson Jones	Sophia Boatner	8/10/1842	31
John Simpson	Elizabeth McKinney	8/11/1842	31
Joshua Roberts	Mary Ann McConnell	8/12/1842	32
Benjamin Denton	Jane Pittman	8/17/1842	32
William P. Head	Dinnia Dobbs	8/17/1842	33
George W. Simms	Emeline Coward	8/17/1842	33
Harbin Grimes	Ann Barrett	5/12/1842	34
James Welchel	Vina Pool	3/ 8/1842	34
John Taylor	Matilda Satterfield	2/ 7/1842	35
William White	Mary Armstrong	8/31/1842	35
Larkin A. Ragsdale	Judy Gipson	11/15/1842	36
William Welchel	Susan Copland	8/25/1842	36
Benjamin Dowdy	Margaret Wilson	12/ 8/1841	37
William Pharr	Rutha Ingram	11/ 3/1842	37
John K. Moore	Frances I. Garrison	9/ 8/1842	38
Jeffrey Saunders	Sarah Petty	9/ 8/1842	38
Joseph Dobbs	Melissa Tippin	7/14/1842	39
James A. Fowler	Clarissa Castleberry	5/ 8/1842	39
Joseph Paterson	Mary Denton	9/ 4/1842	40
Charles Dean	Lucinda Wilson	9/25/1842	40
John Q. Gipson	Sary Ann Broadwell	10/27/1842	41
John A. J. Wayne	Lydia Chandler	2/10/1842	41
Henry G. Boasman	Jane C. McCutchen	8/20/1842	42
Jesse Cloud	Elizabeth Conner	9/13/1842	42
Chiles P. Ingram	Sara Ann Holland	9/ 4/1842	43
John H. Wood	Sarah S. Brewster	8/10/1842	43
William W. Worley	Lucena Holland	11/19/1840	44
Ambrose Worley	Sarah E. Doss	7/16/1840	44
Eli Odum	Nelly Ann Taylor	10/22/1840	45
William Wood	Elizabeth M-rewood(sic)	5/ 5/1841	45
Jackson Bennet	Eliza Cloud	11/14/1841	46
Isaac Pagett	Artilla Coward	10/16/1840	46
Elijah Dene	Eliza Fowler	9/15/1842	47
Winston Worley	Eliza Willbank	2/18/1841	47
Joseph Wood	Malissa Care	5/20/1841	48
James R.G. Martin	Casinda Ward	11/10/1842	48
Martin Ingram	Beedy Boseman	11/24/1842	49
Ciceron White	Margaret Tarkendell	11/27/1842	49
Lewis McKinney	Lucindy Webb	10/10/1842	50
William Pitman	Polly Cook	11/ 6/1842	50
George V. Bates	Antuza M. Walker	9/29/1842	51
William I. Lynch	Jane Bagley	1/17/1843	51
James Holt	Liner Williams	12/29/1842	52
Jacob Norton	Ervisena Sparks	1/21/1843	52
John Kerkendall	Malinda Ervin (?)	2/16/1843	53
Elias Caine	Martha Broadwell	11/24/1842	53
Sanford V. Harbin	Martha Colley	2/ 2/1843	54
Green B. Hunt	Polly Ann Kuykendall	1/10/1843	54
William Butler	Sarah Rogan	12/27/1842	55
Thomas Nix	Brunetta Boon	1/12/1843	55
John Sitton	Elizabeth C. Roberts	12/29/1842	56
Moses W. Paden	Rosannah M. Delany	12/ 6/1842	56
John Fowler	Nancy Moody	1/12/1843	57
John Henderson	Maryan Grice	12/29/1842	57
William F. Davidson	Elizabeth M. Roberts	2/ 3/1842	58
Robert Nancel	Hannah McCollum	2/ 2/1843	58

GROOM	BRIDE	MARRIED	DATE
Charles Treadaway	Elizabeth Bailey	10/30/1842	59
John A. Yancy	Ann Christian	4/12/1842	59
James Baker	Mary A. McConnell	12/26/1842	60
Alexander Williams	Nancy Peak	8/11/1843	60
Samuel Cooker	Mary Ann Mayfield	12/15/1842	61
Isham McMakin	Mary Ford	3/ 9/1843	61
Rufus M. Hardbarger	Martha M. Tippins	3/18/1843	62
Thomas Smith	Louisa Strain	5/14/1843	62
Austin Field	Gaban (?) Lee	1/22/1843	63
Charles Patton	------ Buchanan	12/ 1/1842	63
Jetham (?) K. McMakin	Mary Ford	3/ 9/1843	64
Samuel Cooker	Maryann Mayfield	12/13/1842	64
Reuben Denton	Susan Pitman	5/ 3/1843	65
Nathaniel D. Pain	Elizabeth Bates	3/15/1843	65
A. B. Roberts	Elizabeth Beck	5/21/1843	66
Henry Miller	Martha S. Bell	8/17/1843	66
Elijah Springs (?)	Elizabeth Rice (?)	9/28/1843	67
Anderson McKay	Caroline Speir	9/28/1843	67
Samuel W. Major	(not given)	11/30/1843	68
James McCay	Sary Cook	12/17/1843	68
Andrew Chalmore	Peggy Landrum	10/ 8/1843	69
James J. Reaves	Elizabeth Williams	6/15/1844	69
James Brannon	Mary Mann	5/ 4/1844	70
John A. Brannon	Jane Mann	5/ 4/1844	70
(The two above: License date; double wedding)			
Solomon W. Peek	Mary Ann Tinker	7/27/1843	71
Pinkney Blackburn	Sarah Mason	9/14/1843	71
Elisha Brown	Charlotte Chaffin	5/ 5/1844	72
George W. Tippin	Sary J. Kemp	11/ 7/1843	72
A. B. Roberts	Elizabeth Beck	5/ 2/1843	73
Thomas H. Moore	Amanda N. Fleming	1/25/1844	73
James Pindey (?)	Matilda Teasley	3/26/1843	74
William Martin	Viney Dover	11/10/1844	74
Benjamin F. Strain	Martha E. Jaison	10/27/1844	75
Pleasant C. Dobbs	Caroline Wilks	6/30/1844	75
John Honey	Elizabeth M. Honey	6/ 6/1843	76
Henry M. Newton	Amystana Finn	11/ 2/1843	76
Wesley O'Brven	Lydia Tyler	4/ 2/1844	77
John Fielden	Mary Simpson	12/14/1843	77
Jacob J. Robbins	Rebecca Allred	12/24/1843	78
Hiram Bennet	Leah Eddington	1/ 2/1844	78
James Peyton	Elizabeth Robberts	9/21/1843	79
James M. Stephens(?)	Lucinda Smith	5/23/1843	79
William Gunn	Martha White	12/ 4/1844	80
Charles Pruett	Elizabeth Bennet	3/27/1844	80
John M. Childress	Martha Crandall	8/27/1843	81
Thomas Black	Rachel Odell	7/12/1843	81
Cicero Mouson	Mary Gilleland	2/18/1844	82
William Smithwick	Louranzy Boatman	7/31/1842	82
Daniel Bridgman	Catherine L. Taylor	10/17/1843	83
Salathial Martin	Narissa Roach	7/10/1843	83
James Ramsey	Sally Martin	8/10/1843	84
John L. White	Caroline Rodgers	7/11/1843	84
William Hill	Rosanna Mayfield	12/ 4/1843	85
Samuel M. Lambert	Mary Jenkins	12/23/1843	85
John B. Summerlin	Emily Howell	12/26/1843	86
Sanford Vandiver	Julyan Dobbs	10/12/1843	86
Maulden B. Nally	Mary Smith	11/ 6/1842	87
George Roberts	Nancy Dean	11/16/1843	87

GROOM	BRIDE	MARRIED	PAGE
William Simmons	Vashti Manning	10/26/1843	88
James Summerlin	Tabitha Swinford	12/28/1843	88
Robert Wood	Margaret Summer (?)	12/20/1843	89
Joel M. Bennet	Lourany -----	7/ 4/1843	89
Noah Williams	Martha Hendrix	10/20/1844	90
Isham Fielding	Malinda Simpson	10/17/1844	90
Benjamin F. Matthews	Catherine Malroy (?)	10/22/1844	91
Andrew Lovalady	Sarah Monroe	1/30/1844	91
Bennett M. Hardman (License date)	Lucinda McAsky	8/ 5/1844	92
Perry Dobbs	Vesty M. Dobbs	2/11/1844	92
John S. Oliver	Cynthia E.N. Blackburn	8/10/1843	93
Oliver Farr	Matilda Corbin	8/10/1844	93
John Christopher	Nancy Christopher	5/ 6/1844	94
Archibald Payne	Esther Simms	4/14/1844	94
Willson Sharp	Harriet Johnson	1/25/1844	95
Fletcher Lowry	Ann Bradford	5/ 7/1844	95
Thomas Dooly	Patsyann Townsend	5/19/1844	96
Samuel Hudgins	Eliza Townsend	5/19/1844	96
William Thompson	Frances Paine	7/ 4/1844	97
Absalom Pressly	Demaris Langly	2/15/1844	97
Robert Hogen	Martha M.L. Noris	2/ 4/1844	98
Benjamin F. Cockrum	Hannah Eaton	12/21/1843	98
John Darly	Julian Widanell	4/25/1844	99
Joshua F. Harris	Mariah Robertson	8/14/1844	99
Hezekiah Ingram	Delitha Sary Ann Tarbuton	10/13/1844	100
Solomon Wood	Jenny Catherine Tarbuton	10/13/1844	101
Anderson Ward	Winny Catherine Durham	10/ 3/1844	101
James Brannon	Marian S.T. Man	7/ 4/1844	102
Solomon W. Peek	Maryan Tucker	7/27/1844	102
Samuel B. Martin	Mary King	1/22/1844	103
Solomon R. Summer	Martha George	10/19/1843	103
Samuel Huggins	Eliza Townsend	5/ 9/1844	100
Richard White	Jane Kuykendall	9/ 1/1844	104
Edward Manning	Rutha Edwards	9/29/1844	104
Mathew Christopher	Caroline McKinney	8/14/1844	105
William Henson	Eliza Ann Hardyman	7/30/1844	105
Robert Reece	Emily Gregory	12/19/1844	106
David Moody	Hanner M. Dover	12/19/1844	106
Henry B. Herold (?)	Jane Ponder	5/12/1844	107
David Kiker	Mary Cray	12/17/1843	107
Thomas S.M. Spurlin	Lucy King	7/23/1844	108
Martin Corbin	Sary Paul	8/15/1844	108
Hemsberry Brown	Martha Ann Merritt	10/ 1/1844	109
Loarer Carr	Sary Bates	11/ 4/1844	109
Joel S. Galt	Malinda C. Gresham	10/ 6/1844	110
Thomas B. Cook	Ann McDonnell	11/24/1844	110
Willis Ward	Martha Obriant	9/ 4/1844	111
Thomas Kelly	Frances E. Harp	9/19/1844	111
Thaddous C. Daniel	Maryan Pugh	9/23/1844	112
Perry C. Pagett	Melinda Bent	5/16/1844	112
David P. Roberts	Nancy Black	6/23/1844	113
Thomas Baker	Sarah Pruit	11/26/1844	113
Robert J. Sample	Frances Meritt	10/30/1844	114
William D. Newton	Jane A. Atkins	12/19/1844	114
John Bennet	Nancy Ann Jourden	8/24/1844	115
Abner Wiggins	Jane Hansford	12/23/1844	115

GROOM	BRIDE	MARRIED	PAGE
Joseph M. Curbow	Martha Beck	10/24/1844	116
Joseph Edwards	Jane Owens	1/30/1845	116
James M. Adnderson	Clarissa Johnson	9/24/1844	117
Ezekiah Wiggin	Angeline Fowler	1/30/1845	117
Noniman C. Shelton	Sarah K. Ingram	1/12/1845	118
George T. Fowler	Fanna Cockburn	1/14/1845	118
Marida Fisher	Sarah Heath	7/ 7/1844	119
Allen Dover	Mary M. Cloud	2/16/1845	119
Hamilton Gragg	Frances Cobb	12/15/1844	120
William B. Chambers	Barbary Sawyers	1/ 2/1845	120
James Barrett	Rebecca Head	6/ 8/1845	121
Nathaniel I. Cook	Mary Cook	4/ 6/1845	121
James Falkner	Lydda A. Gilmer	7/ 4/1845	122
Ansell Duncan	Catherine Cook	6/22/1845	122
Wilds Brown	Elizabeth Pharr	7/ 7/1845	123
Andrew J. Nally	Catherine Everett	7/25/1845	123
John P. Minton	Anna Cook	7/24/1845	124
Levi Yancy	Christian Spears	2/27/1845	124
John Gossit	Rebecca Hickman	5/23/1845	125
Elijah Owens	Isabella I. Heard	8/17/1845	125
William C. Howell	Margaret Beck	8/24/1845	126
Jonathan Potts	Ebby Gordon	8/17/1845	126
John H. Gregory	Christiana Payne	11/11/1844	127
Erwin C. Disheroon	(not given)	9/30/1845	127
John L. Monday	Almira Fitzsimmons	6/ 8/1845	128
James A. McCamie	Martha Roberts	9/30/1845	128
William C. Seargent	Polly Tate	3/13/1845	129
Daniel McDonald	Elizabeth Hyle	6/ 5/1845	129
Thomas Tippins	Jincy Fielding	12/29/1844	130
Henry H.W. Osborn	Sarah M. Roberts	12/ 5/1844	130
E. B. Sergeant	Elizabeth J. Hunt	1/ 9/1845	131
Hartwell Richards	Elizabeth Tallow	3/29/1845	131
Choice Duncan	Elizabeth Tate	12/19/1844	132
William W. Wilson	Malinda E. Williamson	6/15/1845	132
Thomas Sawyers	Micky Loveless	12/27/1844	133
Burton Bruce	Elizabeth Mayfield	10/30/1845	133
John J. Epperson	Jane A. Coulter	11/ 7/1845	134
Henry Swinford	Mary Priest	10/21/1845	134
Robert Evans	Martha E. Dobson	2/ 6/1845	135
Albert Gay	Nancy Ward	11/30/1845	135
Andrew J. Copeland	Elizabeth Jordan	12/21/1845	136
Jesse King	Manda Stover	12/22/1845	136
Calvin Holcombe	Lanceler Hart	9/21/1845	137
Stephen Johnson	Elizabeth Moody	5/21/1843	137
Josiah Thompson	Melinda Ashworth	12/28/1843	138
Michael Shelings	Mary Ann Paynolds	11/18/1843	138
Nicholas Spearings	Elizabeth Gilbert	11/18/1843	139
Albert E. Holcombe	Harriet E. Gibbs	2/15/1844	139
John Connor	Margaret Welch	8/21/1844	140
Isaac Nix	Elizabeth Nix	11/12/1843	140
Hubbard P. Carnes	Sidney Welch	10/ 3/1844	141
William Hogan	Susanna M. Wooten	10/29/1844	141
Joseph L. Simmons	Eliza Tuglar	11/ 7/1844	142
Robert C. Tyson	Sarah Moody	9/ 3/1843	142
William Dowdy	Julia Ann Williams	1/25/1846	143
Aaron Reece	Nancy O'Bryant	1/29/1846	143
William Castleberry	Elizabeth A. Doss	1/29/1846	144
G. W. Sams	Candis E. Anderson	3/ 5/1846	144
Greenberry Jackson	Caroline Hutcheson	2/ 5/1846	145

GROOM	BRIDE	MARRIED	PAGE
Thomas T. Johnson	California Christian	10/13/1846	145
James E. Rainwaters	Susan Henson	1/25/1846	146
William P. Nichols	Catherine M. Blackburn	10/ 7/1845	146
Martin Helton	Sarah M. Chaffin	2/15/1846	147
William M. League	Martha Farr	11/23/1845	147
Lewis A. Carpenter	Artaminsa Mathis	3/ 1/1846	148
Allen Phillips	Elizabeth Nix	3/13/1845	148
Matthew Samples	Malinda Hanshard	2/20/1845	149
Bennett Hosia	Lydia Priest	1/ 6/1846	149
William Coward	Susannah Bailey	2/27/1845	150
Jacob C. Hook	Frances M. Edwards	7/13/1845	150
Josiah P. Blythe	Esebell House	10/21/1845	151
William W.W. Flemming	Elisiah H. Braselton	12/23/1845	151
John Boren	Rosanna Young	2/18/1845	152
William D. McClesky	Frances Morris	11/ 6/1845	152
Elcaney B. Newton	Elizabeth Ann Ezzard	11/ 6/1846	153
Daniel Knight	Rosella Barnette	12/22/1845	153
Isaac Petty	Partheny Mullinax	12/ 3/1845	154
Vardry McGinness	Louisa Shotwell	11/29/1846	154
J. E. Whithead	Sarah Ann Matilda Baker	11/ 5/1846	155
Alby Griffin	Eliza Adaline Hinkle	6/ 7/1846	155
William S. Epperson	Sarah E. Yancy	12/13/1845	156
Isaac Beck	Emeline Brewer	11/23/1845	156
James Carr	Lauressa Carr	2/25/1845	157
Simon Cameron	Mary Bates	6/11/1845	157
John M. Nuckells (License date)	Nancy E. Bates	8/28/1845	158
James L. Wiley	Rebecca Johnson	8/ 3/1845	158
Samuel J. Messer	Louisa E. Gaines	2/ 4/1845	159
John M. Watson	Nancy C. Pugh	12/29/1844	159
Matthew R. Adams	Elizabeth J.Bradford	5/17/1846	160
John Butler	Mary Butler	7/24/1846	160
William Davis	Martha Davis	3/22/1846	161
Robert M. White	Elizabeth A. Adkins	9/ 4/1846	161
George W. Gray	Lucinda Castleberry	8/16/1846	162
Jeptha Moss	Hepsey Legrand	10/ 7/1846	162
Harrison D. Hill	Martha Moss	10/ 1/1846	163
John Brock	Leacy Tedder	10/ 1/1846	163
Henry McIntyre	Eliza Gregory	7/16/1846	164
Horace Osborn	Susan Grimes	4/16/1846	164
Warren R. Haynes	Caroline Reece	2/24/1846	165
Archibald Robinett	Rebecca Dean	9/11/1845	165
John Priest	Rachel Numen	4/23/1846	166
Rice Arrendale	Sarah McElroy	2/29/1844	166
Ransom Roe	Malinda McDonald	7/ 2/1846	167
Elisha McCoy	Mariah Elrod	9/ 6/1846	167
James L. Craig	Susan Hopgood	9/11/1845	168
Linden Gaddiss	Emily Dickerson	3/ 6/1845	168
Joathan G. Ellison	Serena Whitlock	4/12/1846	169
John McCracken	Rachel H. Neal	12/ 7/1845	169
M.D.P. Dempsey	Susan Baker	11/12/1846	170
Jesse W. Delay	Mary Paton	3/14/1846	170
William R. Craig	Caroline Rice	11/ 5/1846	171
Warren Moss	Nancy Hill	1/ 7/1847	171
William Kelton	Ruthy Starnes	6/ 1/1847	172
Elias E. Field	Susan S. McKinney	6/20/1847	172
Thomas Swearingen	Margaret M. Sleedel	6/20/1847	173
Umphrey Tarbutton	Nancy Young	12/10/1847	173

GROOM	BRIDE	MARRIED	PAGE
Jonathan Williams	Tabitha Starrell	9/17/1846	174
John W. Lowry	Sarah M. Fisher	7/22/1847	174
James P.J. Ward	Nancy Riggins	11/ 5/1846	175
John Taylor	Ary Howell	9/ 6/1846	175
David J. Dimsdale	Martha Malinda Hendricks	1/ 7/1846	176
Malcijah Morris	E. Ford (?)	3/25/1847	176
H. R. Carmichael	Eveline Fincher	7/ 4/1847	177
Leonard Hitt	Elizabeth Swinford	7/25/1847	177
Silas Dobbs	Nancy S. Fountain	7/ 5/1846	178
David H. Collins	Sarah Ann Jefferson	7/22/1847	178
James M. Fountain	Malissa Odle	11/28/1844	179
Benjamin C. Pugh	Elizer Emeline Pugh	10/12/1846	179
Thomas Long	Martha Johnson	2/ 9/1847	180
John McRea	Patsey Lackey	12/ 2/1847	180
Washington Gossett	Rebecca Mitchell	7/ 5/1846	181
Clvin H. Carson	Nancy Sudeath	11/13/1846	181
William P. Fenn	Susan Emaline Petree	10/ 7/1847	182
Carson Cox	Rachel McCarter	7/ 4/1847	182
Pinkney Putnam	Mary Ann Brooke	9/28/1847	183
John L. Wood	Mary Quinton	7/13/1847	183
Stephen McPherson	Lucy J. Wynn	11/ 2/1847	184
Abraham Walker	Mariah Kirk	9/ 5/1846	184
Philip Willson	Nancy Willson	9/ 4/1847	185
David L. Smith	Adaline Brock	12/20/1846	185
Robert F. Jenkins	Elizabeth Black	7/30/1844	186
Matthew Holcombe	Lydia Jarrett	4/15/1846	186
David Elmore	Lucy McCormack	2/21/1844	187
Marmer D. George	Jane Thacker	4/ 9/1846	187
Joshua McConnell	Nancy Steadman	10/28/1847	188
Felix McMinn	Elizabeth Johnson	9/ 8/1846	188
Jesse P. Fountain	Artaminsa Williamson	3/ 5/1844	189
Albert Honea	Mary Ann Hughs	2/25/1847	189
Samuel C. Marbin	Sarah Harper	12/31/1846	190
Oliver Payne	Martha Johns	7/20/1847	190
Asa Holcombe	Polly Ann Townsend	8/13/1846	191
J.P. Sayers	Sarah Ann Braselton	3/28/1847	191
George W. Kirk	Sarah Ann E. Jackson	12/ 5/1847	192
Francis A. Wales	Mary Ann Epperson	2/18/1848	192
John Q.A. Christopher	Susan Batson	12/23/1847	193
R. W. Trout	Elizabeth Paden	11/ 4/1847	193
William Halcomb	Mahulda McCraw	6/20/1847	194
William Pitts	Drucilla Brooks	2/14/1848	194
Levi Land	Mary H. Wood	2/17/1848	195
Thomas Bell	Nancy Oliver	1/23/1848	195
Nehemiah S. Dickerson	Nancy J. Wheeler	2/23/1847	196
Daniel C. Boger	Terrissa Moss	11/12/1846	196
Benjamin F. Freeman	Lotty Fry	2/14/1847	197
Nelson Gilreath	Martha E. Hardin	7/ 1/1847	197
David Dobbs	Martha C. Griffin	1/ 9/1848	198
Perry M. Hall	Eliza Newman	1/30/1848	198
Robert Christopher	Margaret A.Christopher	11/14/1847	199
Jesse Burtz	Eliza L. Mothershead	12/20/1847	199
Edley Williams	Jane A. Jarrett	11/16/1847	200
Elisha Gentry	Elizabeth Conn	9/ 9/1847	200
Edward Bagby	Sarah Green	1/ 5/1848	201
Levi Yancy	Anna Rice	12/19/1847	201
Robert Chamble	Mary E. Haley	2/10/1848	202
William Ashley	Mary Ann Whitmire	1/20/1848	202

GROOM	BRIDE	MARRIED	PAGE
Wilson P. Coward (by J. H. Bibb, JP)	Polly Bailey	1/ 2/1844	203
James W. McCollum	Mary Martin	12/ 2/1847	203
James Brown	Mary Ann Johnson	12/ 7/1847	204
William Gregory	Emily Waddell	1/ 2/1848	204
N. H. Wiley	Sarah Rudisill	1/21/1848	205
Monroe Lawrence	Adaline Thacker	1/30/1848	205
Stephen Justice	Ann C. Crandal	2/ 8/1848	206
Francis Kirkendall	Elizabeth Thompson	11/21/1847	206
Joseph Kidd (Licnese date)	Malissa Ann Hopper	3/ 5/1847	207
Leonard Mann	Malissa Blackwell	7/19/1846	207
L. D. Watson	Elizabeth R.J. Tyson	12/20/1847	208
Joseph Lawrence	Elizabeth Jane Jackson	1/17/1847	208
William Presley	Mahaly Ray	12/25/1847	209
George Lathen	Eliza Burdine	1/26/1848	209
William H. Riley	Catherine Thomas	9/ 2/1847	210
Francis C. Tate	Hannah J. Cambron	2/--/1847	210
William Lile	Elvina Mullins	9/ 7/1846	211
Levi F. Lambers	Sarah McClesky	8/26/1847	211
Abner Smith	Amanda Harris	9/16/1848	212
Daniel Curbow Jr.	Melissa Bradley	10/18/1846	212
William Hendricks	Elizabeth Freeman	1/18/1848	213
Mitchell Griffin	Mary Rudasill	1/20/1848	213
Sylvester Dinsmore	Caroline Reavis	9/ 9/1847	214
Isaac Bichop	Margaret M. Petitt	7/16/1846	214
Alston Phillips	Polly Nix	11/26/1846	215
James Wood	Mary Freeman	1/16/1848	215
William Griffin	Mary Ann Palmore	12/26/1847	216
Allen Justice	Mary Haygood	12/16/1847	216
Hartwell D. Freeman	Eliza E. Freeman	12/26/1846	216
William F. McTere	Kiza Tate	5/ 6/1847	216
D. C. Newman	Sarah Wallace	2/17/1848	217
Daniel Pettit	Lavina H. Tillison	1/16/1848	217
Levi Yancy Jr.	Emily Bennyfield	3/21/1847	218
John Welchel	Amanda Elvina Bates	11/18/1847	218
Henry Newton	Jane Farmer	2/ 2/1848	219
Isaac Cox	Amanda Adams	5/14/1848	219
Joseph B. Cook	Altha Pool	7/11/1848	220
George W. Paine	Tempey Gregory	7/ 4/1848	220
Samuel M. McConnell	Mary J. Brewster	4/12/1848	221
John P. Rhodes	Elizabeth Pullen	4/ 6/1847	221
Daniel L. Bailey	Margaret Rhodes	5/25/1848	222
Benjamin F. Freeman	Elizabeth M. Evans	5/30/1848	222
William Lile	Elvina Mullins	9/ 4/1846	223
Elias W. Allred	Martha Arthur	1/11/1848	223
George Hitt	Rachel Hopkins	8/24/1848	224
Andy C. Kuykendall	Sarah Darnal	8/13/1848	224
Adam H. Rinehardt	Mary Hardie	11/26/1848	225
Moses Pinson	Mary Adeline Coley	11/15/1848	225
James Paddis	Synthia Findley	12/26/1848	226
William Coley	Salenia A. Coley	1/12/1845	226
J. M. Davis	Jane S. Tate	12/ 2/1847	227
Alexander Simmonds	Julia P. White	7/15/1846	227
John Franklin Amos	Emerline Satterfield	9/21/1848	228
Charles Huggins	Elizabeth Quarles	6/29/1848	228
James Cooley	Rutha Eaton	3/14/1848	229
Abraham Mayfield	Martha Williams	8/ 1/1847	229
Newton N. Edge	Virginia A.S. Holland	8/29/1848	230

CHEROKEE COUNTY, GA. - MARRIAGES

GROOM	BRIDE	MARRIED	PAGE
William Worley	Elizabeth Martin	8/ 3/1848	230
Benjamin F. Loveless	Sarah Adams	7/31/1848	231
George Gunnely	Catherine L. Coulter	5/12/1848	231
William G. Elrod	Louisa Jane Cogswell	11/ 5/1848	232
Levi T. Hughes	Dotia Fowler	5/ 1/1848	232
John Voss	Susan Fletcher	4/27/1848	233
Noble Simmonds	Nancy Adeline Evans	9/28/1848	233
Thomas E. Dickerson	Selenia Knox	10/19/1848	234
Oliver Fincher	Hessa Ann Reece	8/25/1848	234
Isham S. Seals	Amanda E. Jackson	8/ 4/1848	235
Jesse W. Harbin	Catherine M. Strain	8/31/1848	235
Jeptha P. Carr	Narcissa M. Doss	9/ 7/1848	236
Edley Corbin	Mary H. Clayton	10/ 1/1848	236
William J. Honea	Almyra Ellis	9/21/1848	237
William J. Bennett	Nancy C. Wilson	9/21/1848	237
Nathaniel Brooks	Elizabeth T. Tripp	9/28/1848	238
Spencer Ragsdale	Sarah Ann Gibson	12/ 5/1848	238
William T. Hall	Katherine Martin	12/28/1848	239
James S. White	Sarah J. Field	8/13/1848	239
George H. Willcox	Rebecca Priest	11/ 5/1848	240
Isaac S. Gilbert	Minerva L. Wiley	1/16/1848	240
Nicholas Waddell	Sarah Stapp	10/ 5/1848	241
Enoch Hammons	Canzala Jeffers	2/24/1848	241
Lemuel J. Padget	Mary M. Scruggs	7/12/1848	242
Thomas Hill	Martha Dyers	10/ 8/1848	242
John Mullenacks	Eliza Adeline Forrester	11/30/1848	243
James McMahon	Sarah Little	1/ 7/1849	243
Oliver H.P. Norwood	Margaret C. Hammond	12/10/1848	244
John Fowler	Elizabeth Carmichael	12/19/1848	244
John E. Johnson	Artamissa Kemp	1/11/1849	245
Car Cox	Mary Jane Finch	1/14/1849	245
Anderson D. Lowery	Mary Chapman	1/25/1849	246
Leroy McRady	Catherine Fitzsimmons	12/24/1848	246
William I. Cook	Nancy Underwood	2/ 4/1849	247

CORRECTION TO A MARRIAGE IN CHEROKEE CO, GA.

The correct name is JAMES J. P. WOOD - Nancy Riggins 11/5/1846
The 1850 Federal Census, Cherokee County, Ga. enumerates:
15 District: household 355-346
   James J. P. Wood age 33, born S.C.; Nancy, age 31, born Ga.;
William A., 12, Ga.; Virgil L., 11, Ga.; James E., 10, Ga.;
Sarah A., 8; Jasper L. 6 (my grandfather); Lydia C., age 5;
Laura D., 2.

James J. P. Wood enlisted in The War between The States in the
28th Regt., Ga. Volunteer Infantry March 4, 1862 at Orange, Ga.
He was reported wounded May 9, 1863 and was transferred to General Hospital, Atlanta, Ga., June 16, 1863.

The family Bible is in possession of a relative in Cedartown,
Ga. and these records come from the Bible:
James J. P. Wood was born Jan. 10, 1827, S.C. Died May 5, 1895.
Nancy Riggins was born January 23, 1828. Died April 10, 1864.
Married November 5, 1846. Cherokee County, Ga.
                Children:
            William Andrew Wood born Sept. 3, 1847
            Virgil L. Wood born Feb. 20, 1849
            James Edward Wood born Nov. 27, 1850

(Tripletts) Sara Ann, Mary Ann & Catherine Jane wood born Apr.
9, 1852
        Jasper Lewis Wood born Nov. 19, 1854
        Lydia Caroline Wood born Mar. 28, 1854
        Mary Abigail Wood Born Jan. 25, 1858
        Laura Victoria Wood born Nov. 28, 1859
        George Newton Wood born Mar. 10, 1861
        David Beauregard Wood born June 30, 1862
James J. P. Wood married as second wife Amanda origin Mullins.
Their Children:
        Margaret Lula Wood born Feb. 23, 1866
        Reverdie Eugene Wood born Nov. 3, 1868
James J. P. Wood married as third wife Ellender Frances Cox.
No children.

In the 1880 Federal Census Floyd County, Ga.
Chulio District: Household 167   James P. Wood is living with
           third wife and children:
        George N., Laura V., Margaret L., and Eugene R.

James J. P. Wood is buried in Silver Creek Primitive Baptist
Church Cemetery, Wax Community, Floyd County, Ga.

Evidently, Nancy Riggins Wood died in Cherokee County, Ga. Either her grave is unmarked, or else the cemetery is unlocated
even though I have searched through cemetery after cemetery in
the county.

On page 159, Cherokee County, Ga. Marriages:
Solomon W. Peek is named for his father Solomon W. Peek Sr. His
mother's name was Rachel -----. The family removed from Hall
County, Ga. around 1832 to Cherokee County, Ga.

Mary Ann Tucker was daughter of Willis Tucker and Chloe Ann
Bryan (or Bryant). The family removed from South Carolina to
Cherokee County, Ga. between 1838 and 1840.

There also are relatives. My great grandfather, Samuel Lewis
Tucker, was sister to Mary Ann Tucker and his wife, Rachel Peek,
was niece of Solomon W. Peek. The parents of Rachel Peek were
Lindsay and Esther Maddox Peek. Some of the Tuckers and most of
the Peeks removed to Alabama and mostly settled in Blount and
Cherokee Counties, Alabama.

End

CHEROKEE COUNTY SUPERIOR COURT MINUTES

Created by Act of the Legislature in House Bill #7 and was signed into law by Wilson Lumpkin, Governor on 26 Dec. 1831. The first grand jury met March 1832 and represented the original Cherokee County which included ALL the lands formerly occupied by the Cherokee Indians. Senate Bill #23 in December 1832 changed this large county into smaller ones and created other then Cherokee County: Cass, Cobb, Forsyth, Floyd, Murray, Gilmer, Lumpkin, Pauling, Cherokee and Union.

On December 4, 1980 the Cherokee County Historical Society will hold a "Kick-off" Birthday Dinner to begin a year long celebration of the 150th Anniversay of the founding of the county.

Pasted on inside of cover:
Oct. 1837

Canton	139	76	127	66	150	12
Fords	112	38	113	35	139	2
McDonalds	57	13	54	12	41	23
Elliotts	58	6	52	7	61	0
Townsend	10	9	18	0	11	7
Gobers	9	17	3	22	14	4
	385	159	367	142	416	48

(On one of end pages not in original hand: Cherokee County authorised Dec. 26, 1831 by Ga. Legislature)

Page 1.   Monday March 26, 1832

At Superior Court began and holden at the house of Ambrose Harnage now Harnageville in and for the county of Cherokee, State of Ga. On 26 day it being the 4th Monday of March 1832, the following business was done:

Present Hon. Charles Dougherty Judge of said Court Following persons <u>Haveing</u> been selected frawn and summoned to attend this term of said court as grand jurors were empaneled and sworn, to wit:

1. James Hemphill, Foreman
2. John Dawson
3. James Cantril
4. Franklin Daniel
5. Green B. Durham
6. Robert Fowler
7. John Jack
8. Reuben Sams
9. John P. Brook
10. Charmes Haynes
11. George Baber
12. Noble Timmons
13. John S. Holcomb
14. Leory Hammond
15. Samuel Means
16. William H. Ray
17. Hubbard Barker
18. William Smith
19. William Lay

Following persons...empaneled as petit jurors:

1. Burton Mullens
2. Edward Gilbert
3. William Milhene?
4. John Armstrong
5. Thomas Higgs
6. Richard Coleman
7. Elias Goddard
8. Benny Hill
9. James Simmons
10. Wm. S. Simmons
11. Thomas Rogers
12. Joel Ashworth

Following persons Petit Jury #2   (12 places marked off but are blank)

Page 2.   Monday March 26, 1832

State	)	Illegal Residence
vs.	)	It is ordered by the court that John Agnew be
John Agnew	)	discharged from further attendance on the above
		stated case.

State	)	Residing in the Cherokee Nation without a
vs.	)	licens
Jeremiah Towns	)	True Bill, James Hamphill, Foreman

State	)	Hog Stealing
vs.	)	
Thomas Cantril	)	True Bill, James Hemphill, Foreman
Enoch Earley	)	
& George Downs	)	

State	)	Residing in the Cherokee Nation without licens
vs.	)	
Eluas Goddard	)	True Bill, James Hemphill, Foreman

State	)	Hog Stealing
vs.	)	Thomas Cantril arraigned and pled not gilty
Thomas Cantril	)	and continued by Travern
Enoch Earley	)	T. H. Tripp, Sol. Gen'l.
& George Downs	)	

Page 3.

State	)	Residing in the Cherokee Nation without licens
vs.	)	Arraigned and plead not guilty, copy bill and
Jeremiah Towns	)	list of witnesses wanted. T.H. Tripp, Sol.Gen'l.

State	)	Digging gold
vs.	)	True Bill, James Hemphill, Foreman
Charles Duncan	)	

State	)	Assault and Battery
vs.	)	Grue Bill, James Hemphill, Foreman
Harrison Riley	)	

Following persons drawn as grand jurors to serve next term of the court:

1. John Lay
2. Soward Clayton
3. Robert Guthery
4. John P. Winn
5. Reuben Thornton
6. Archibald Bradford
7. Elias Putnam
8. James Daniel
9. Henry Witcher
10. Tho. W. Bolton
11. Jas. McShinny
12. No #
13. Jas. Willson
14. J. B. Chastian
15. John Gray
16. James Bell
17. Hoalman F. Simmons
18. John Kimbol

19. Jas. Parker
20. Moses Cantril
21. Eli McConnel

Page 4.

22. Geo. R. Glenn
23. Edward Harrel
24. Jacob McScudder
25. Chester Hawks
26. John Smith
27. Robert Obarr
28. Robert Henderson
29. John Witcher
30. John S. Chastian
31. John McConnel
32. Genwleth (?) Winn
33. John B. Garrison

34. Rabdle McDannel   36. Wm. Baker
35. James Tippens

The following drawn to serve as petit jours next term:

1. Felix Arther   27. Stephen Dale
2. Elijah Stansel   28. Willis Cox
3. Berry or Benj. Jones   29. John Mullens
4. Lewis Kenam   30. Haley Shaw
5. Sterling Goodwin   31. Danniel Hammond
6. Hiram Proctor   32. Eaphus Mabrey
7. James B. White   33. John Williams
8. Benj. or Berry Brackett 34. Bradley Smith
9. Jeffrey Smith   35. Ferdinand Bailey
10. Joseph Eaton   36. James Murphey
11. Reling Willson   37. James Cochran
12. Tilman Shamley   38. Willis McDaniel
13. John T. Cox   39. Reuben Holloway
14. Squire Herren   40. Richard Hays
15. Reddin Pinson   41. James Landrum
16. Dennis Knight   42. Alfred Hudson
17. Abner Kemp   43. William Mathis
18. Gideon Trout, Sr.   44. Robert Nailor
19. Rich'd. B. White   45. Elisha Dooley
20. Henry Johnson   46. David Allison
21. John Albright   47. Wm. Mathis
22. Ridden Blocker   48. West Walker
23. John Ragsdale   49. L. S. Langston
24. Daniel Ried   50. Bethel Bradley
25. Washington W. Winters 51. John Greenwood
26. Arch'd. Harris

Page 5. Monday March 26, 1832

We, the Grand Jury chosen and sworn for the county of Cherokee
refrain the expression of our grattification of the organization
of the country into a county, we know that new as our county is
the extent of its territory and the few person yet cittizens of
it that much cannot be done toward the improvement & repair of
our roads we would however recommend the inferior court to use
all the means within their countrol to has this object attended
to...the roads in the county have been so long neglected that they
are in some places...almost impassable and knowing as we do that
during the ensuing summer an unusual number of persons will visit
the country we would respectfully urge the inferior court to the
accomplishment of a purpose so interesting to the whole community.
The opion of his honor Judge Doughtery upon the right for it and
over it merits our approbation as well as his administration during
the present term. To which we tender respects to the solicitor
Mr. Tripp we also tender our acknowledgements for the manner in
which he has discharged his duty. We request that our presentments may be published in the Federal Union and the Georgia
Journal.

James Hemphill, Foreman   George Baber
John Dawson   Noble Timmons
R. T. Fowler   John S. Holcomb
James Cantril   Leroy Hammond
R. F. Daniel   Wm. H. Ray
G. B. Durham   Hubbard Barker
John Jack   Wm. Smith

Reuben Sams   Wm. Lay
John P. Brook   Charles Haynes

Motion of <u>Turner</u> H. Tripp, Sol. Gen'l. ordered, be published.
Court adjourns...Oliver Strickland, Clk. Signed: C. Doughtery.

Page 6. Monday Sept. 24, 1832

At Superior Court, holden at Cherokee Courthouse in and for the
county of Cherokee, 24 day of Sept. being the 4th Monday. Present
His Honor Charles Doughtery, Judge. Following persons grand jury-
<u>Tanner</u> H. Tripp, Sol. Gen'l. of Western Circuit being absent on
account of the indisposition of his family - It is ordered that
Daniel R. Mitchell be appointed Sol. Gen'l. protem for this court.

Grand Jurors:
1. Eli McConnell, Foreman   10. Micajah Goodin
2. John P. Winn   11. Roberte Guthry
3. Randle McDaniel   12. John Lay
4. John Withcer   13. George R. Glenn
5. Henry McConnel   14. Robert Obarr
6. Thos. M. Botton   15. John B. Garrison
7. Isaac W. Parker   16. James Tippens
8. Joseph McElhenny   17. William Baker
9. R̶o̶b̶e̶r̶t̶/̶H̶e̶n̶d̶e̶r̶s̶o̶n̶ (marked through) 18. John McConnel
9. John Smith   19. Elias Putnam

Page 7. Petit Jurors Sept. 24, 1832

1. Benjamin Jones   8. John Ragsdale
2. James B. White   9. John Landrum
3. John T. Cox   10. Riley Wilson
4. Squire Herring   11. Alfred Hudson
5. Abner Camp   12. David Elington (Allison?)
6. Bethel Bradley

William N. Bishop   ) Debt
     vs.   ) I confess Judgement to the plantiff &c for
Johnson Rogers   ) thirty two dollars with interest and cost
                       with Liberty of appeal. Johnson Rogers.

William N. Bishop   ) Debt
     vs.   ) I confess judgement to the plaintiff &c for
Matrin Evans   ) $36.96 with interest & cost of suit with
                       liberty of appeal. McDaniel, Dft. attorney

Calvin Gings for the) Debt
use of P.P. Murray   ) I confess judgement to the plaintiff &c for
     vs.   ) $50 with interest & cost. Chas. Haynes
Charles Haynes   )

Wood & Hobson   ) Debt
     vs.   ) I confess judgement to plaintiff for $53.42½
William H. Love   ) with interest & cost. Witton H. Gathright,
                       deft. atty.

Page 8. Monday Sept. 24, 1832

John Totty & Co.   ) Debt
     vs.   ) I confess judgement to plaintiff for $78.50
Reuben Thornton   ) principal with interest & cost. Z.B.Hargrove,
                       dft. atty.

State) Digging for gold
vs.) True Bill: Eli McConnel, Foreman
Walnut)

State) Horse Stealing
vs.) True Bill: Eli McConnel, Foreman
John Kimble)
Butler Kimble)

State) Digging for gold
vs.) True Bill: 24 Sept. 1832, Eli McConnel, Foreman
Thomas Howell)

State) Digging for gold
vs.) True Bill: Eli McConnel, Foreman
Nathan Howard)

Page 9.

Ambrose Harnage) Trover & conversion
vs.) This case came before petit jury #1
John Bell & Joseph Linch) who returned following verdict. in
favor of plaintiff for the negro to
be delivered in 15 days as good as he was when taken or $600 for
said negro together with $150 for hire of said negro the 2 years
with all costs.

Sept. 24, 1832   John T. Cox

State) Hog Stealing
vs.) Sept. 24, 1832   NOT GUILTY
Thomas Cantril) John T. Cox, foreman

Petit Jury #2
1. Mercer Acles   7. Kirk Langley
2. J. C. Bailey   8. John Ragsdale
3. John Langley   9. J. S. Langston
4. John McClien   10. T. Shamley Chambers (marked
                                      through)
5. Washington Lumpkin   11. Stephen Dale
6. Winchester Dumas   v Robert McClure (written above)
                                  12. Elisha Dooley

Page 10.

Ambrose Harnage) Trover
vs.) Verdict for plaintiff requiring defendant to
John Bell &) deliver negro within 15 days or defendant to
Joseph Lynch) pay $600 together with $150 for hire of negro
together with all costs: The defendant being
dissatisfied with verdict of jury rendered in foregoing case come
into court by the attorney Z. B. Hargrove pays all cost on above
case and craves an appeal & tenders James Allen Thompson as
security who acknowledges he is doubly bound to plaintiff for all
future cost & condemnation

24 Sept. 1832   Z. B. Hargrove, atty. for James Thompson
Test Oliver Strickland, Clk
Court adjourned til tomorrow morning at 8 o'clock

Page 11.   Grand jurors for next term:

169

1. William Baker
2. R. F. Daniel
3. Charles Harris
4. William H. Ray
5. James Tippens
6. George R. Glenn
7. Noble Timmons
8. Henry Holcomb
9. Edward Harrel
10. Simeon White
11. Thomas Willson
12. John B. Chastain
13. Green B. Durham
14. Samuel Means
15. Hoalmon F. Simmons

16. Hubbard Barker
17. John Jaim (James?)
18. William Smith
19. Reuben Thornton
20. William B. Malone
21. John P. Brook
22. Leroy Hammons
23. Charles Haynes
24. Henry Wircher
25. Ginnbeth Winn
26. James Hemphill
27. James Daniel
28. John Dossen
29. Soward Clayton

Petit Jurors for next term:

1. William Willis
2. John Holland
3. Joseph Keaton
4. William Grant
5. Edward Mays
6. Nimrod H. Penley
7. Charles Smith
8. Joseph H. Bradford
9. William Stancil
10. William Henderson
11. James Simmons
12. Uriah Holden
13. Lewis Ralston
14. Pleasant Henderson
15. James Chambers

16. Elisha Wellbourne
17. David Sims
18. Phillip Burns
19. Williabe Buending
20. George Freeman
21. Green Doss
22. Nathaniel Wofford
23. Jesse Day
24. Jesse Townsend
25. Ralph Smith
26. Ezekiel T. Henderson
27. John Defier
28. David Guthry
29. David Welchel
30. James Holsonback

Page 12.

31. William Nolin
32. Daniel Butler
33. James Bailey
34. Lewis Arthur
35. John T. James
36. George W. Gaddis
37. David Nickols
38. Wills Garrot
39. Jabez Holcomb
40. William Williamson

41. Henson Dempsey
42. Andrew Culwell
43. Robert Phillips
44. Lewis Blackburn
45. Jesse Thomas
46. David B. Ellington
47. Jesse Thompson
48. Andrew Wood
49. John Southard
50. William Warren

Robert Brazzil) Debt & Cost
    vs.) I confess judgement to the plaintiff for $60.00
Robert Denny) and cost with right of appeal.

Defendent being dissatisfied and claiming an appeal comes forward
and pays all costs and brings Ambrose Harnage as his security...
said Ambrose Harnage acknowledging bond to Robert Braziel for ____

25 Sept. 1832.   Robert (X his mark) LS
                    Ambrose Harnage   LS
  Oliver Strickland, Clk.

Page 13. Sept. term 1832

Stop   ) Certiorari - sustained to new trial ordered
vs   )
Edward Edwards)

Lautelake (Santetake?) or redcocke (Peacock?))Certiorari sus-
vs   ) tained & case
Shadericke Rogan   ) below dismissed

Sept. term 1832 whereupon it is considered & adjudged by the
court that the plaintiff do recover of the defendant the sum of
$12.25 for cost of suit in this behalf alid out & expended and
the defendent & he is mercy of the court.. Signed & dated 25
Sept. 1832. Thomas A. Laytham, dfft's atty.

John Kizer) Certiorari
vs   ) Certiorari sustained & a new trial ordered
William Fain) The defendant to have privelege of giveing
Wm. B. Malone) good security an appeal.

Ambrose Harnage) Attachment
vs   ) Dismissed at plf. cost
Joseph Lynch) Ordered by court that dft. recover

The State) Horse stealing
vs.   ) We Jury find verdict of guilty agst. deft.
John Kimble) Sept. 25, 1832 John T. Case, F.M. (Foreman)

The State   ) Negro Stealing
vs   ) True Bill
Joseph Waters &) Eli McConnell, F.M.
Robert Waters)

The State   ) Digging for gold
vs   ) True Bill
Andrew Arnold) Eli McConnell, F.M.

Page 14. Sept. term 1832

The State   ) Assault & Battery
vs   ) True Bill
James B. Waller) Eli McConnell, F.M.

The State   ) Digging for gold
vs   ) True Bill
Jane Dawning alias) Eli McConnell, F.M.
Blankall's wife &)
Levi Doghead)

The State   ) Digging for gold
vs   ) True Bill
Jeremiah Gibbs &) Eli McConnell, F.M.
Joseph B. Leather)

The State   )
vs   )
James Hempbill)
A. H. Johnston)
William Smith   ) Fales Imprisonment &
Alex. T. Harper) Assault & Battery
And. Cunningham)
Tenvil Mayo   ) True Bill

Alxr. Carroll   )
John Elliott   )
Ork. E. Henderson   ) Eli McConnell, F.M.
E. W. Henderson   )
John Wirte   )
Geo. Lemmons   )
Davis Lemmons   )
George Chambers   )
Bob   )

Page 15. Sept. Term 1832

The State   ) Tresspass & _fals_ Imprisonment
   vs   )
James Hempbell   ) True Bill
Wm. Smith   )
John Wirte   ) Eli McConnell, F.M.
Ezekiel Wirte   )
David Vann   )

The State   ) Cherokee Superior Court Sept. term 1832
   vs   ) The dft. having been recognized for his appear-
Richard Dennis   ) ance at this time of the Superior Court toget-
                        her with 4 negroes belonging to him upon a
charge of gould digging and no person appearing to prosecute for
sd supposed offense for therefore it is ordered that said dft. be
discharged from his said recognizance and from all further liability thereas.

The State   ) Hog Stealing
   vs   ) No Bill
Thomas Woodall   ) Malicious prosecution   Eli McConnell, F.M.

The State   ) Horse stealing
   vs   ) We jury find dft. guilty sept. 25, 1832
Butler Kimble   ) John T. Case, F.M.

The State   ) Hog Stealing
   vs   ) True Bill
Nevel S. Early   ) Eli McConnell, F.M.

Page 16.

Cherokee County - James Hemphill. And. Johnson, Wm. Smith and Wm.
H. Ray bound to....$800....having been indicted for false impris-
onment and assault and battery...to appear superior court... 25
Sept. 1832. James Hemphill, A. H. Johnston, Wm. Smith, Wm. H.
Ray. Oliver Strickland, Clk.

Calvin Young for the use of) Judgment at Sept. 1832 term:
P. J. Murray   ) Charles Haynes dft. came & gave
   vs   ) Ambrose Harnage...for security a
Charles Haynes   ) stay of execution who acknowledge
                               bound jointly for principal interest
and cost.   25 Sept. 1832

Oliver Strickland, Clk.

Page 17.

State	)	Indictment for horse stealing
vs	)	Verdict Gilty
John Kimball	)	Sept. term 1832 Cherokee Superior Court
Butler Kimball	)	

You: John Kimball & Butler Kimball shall be taken by the sheriff of said county from the bar of this court to some convenient place near the courthouse and then & there receive on your bare back 39 lashes each to be laid on by said sheriff with a cowskin or hickory and then kept in close custody until Wednesday 26 of Sept. when you shall again be taken by said sheriff and again receive 39 lashes each to be laid on as aforesaid and then kept in close custody until Thursday 27 of Sept. when you shall again be taken by said sheriff and again receive 39 lashes each in manner and form aforesaid and then to be confined in jail for space and time of 20 days from 27 day of Sept. This 15 Sept. 1832

Sept. term 1832:
We, the grand jury sworn, chosen and selected for county of Cherokee make the following presentments to wit: We present Ransom P. Boswell and Lucinda Cochran for living in a state of adultery...witnesses John Witcher and James M. Smith. On examination of the law for disposing of by seperate lottery of gold region in the country we find there is no reserve made of any fractional parts of surveys...neither is there any part of the law to authorise them to be drawn for...we: therefore recommend to our Senator and representative to use their influence in the next Legislature to have them deposited in the wheel and drawn for as other lots are, We cannot refrain for an expression of opinion in regard to the excitement created of late in regard to the "Tariff Act" and its effect we view the law passed at the last session of Congress as a small concession of the odious and unequal mode of taxation we also view said act as unjust in principal and unequal in its operation...yet cannot but express our decided disapproval...

Page 18. (continued)
...of a resort to nullification...cession or any other mode that will in the least have the tendency to weaken the bonds of our Federal Union. We, therefore, recommend to the citizens of this county to meet and appoint delegates to meet in Milledgeville on the 2nd Mon. in Nov. next for the purpose of taking into consideration the said act of Congress and to propose some mode of redress for its unequal bearing.

We present John Miles, Mitchel Childers, Russel Williams, Tyler Wade, ----- Doozenbery, Zach. Palmer, Dennis Sharp and ------ Welch for the crime of digging for gold on the mines of Cherokee County. Witnesses: Roland Beaden and Richard Wade. In taking leave of His Honor Judge Doughtery...presentments to be published in Federal Union and Southern Recorder. Eli McConnell, Foreman; John Witcher, John McConnell, Robert Osarr, Thomas W. Bolton, James Tippin, George R. Glenn, John B. Garrison, Elias Putnam, Randol McDonald, Isaac L. Parker, Robert Cuther, John Lay, Micajah Goodwin, Henry McConnell, Joseph McSherry, John P. Winn, William Baker and John Smith.

Page 19.

We the undersigned enter our protest to so much of the foregoing
presentments as relate to an expression of opinion as regards
nulification cessassion or any other mode that will in the least
have a tendency to weaken the bounds of our Federal Union because
we think the tariff extremely unjust and unconstitutional and
because we prefer the interest right and freedom of Ǥ̶ę̶ǫ̶ŕ̶ǥ̶ị̶ą̶
(marked through) the state of Georgia to all other interest
whatever.   T. W. Bolton, J. P. Winn, John Smith

Satetaker or Peacock)   Certiorari
       vs   )   Sustained and case below dismissed
Shadrach Bogan   )

(Written in another hand in pencil...which hand had already
numbered pages.."The above pages 1 to 19 are inclusion clasify the
record of the mcee & sentences of the Superior Court of Cherokee
Co., Ga. for the 1832.")

Page 20.   Minutes Superior Court Cherokee Court

Henry Morris by   )   Bill for relief and injunction
his gdn. oc.   )   Plf. in foregoing case comes forth pays all
   vs   )   cost and brings W̶i̶l̶l̶i̶s̶/̶J̶/̶/̶M̶i̶l̶n̶e̶t̶ (marked
Jason H. Wilson)   through) William Morris as his security and
et al   )   the said William Morris acknowledges bounded
                      with Henry Morris by his gdn. oc. for the
eventtual condemnation mony with all cost of court.....Henry (X)
Morris by his gdn.; Willis J. Milner & William Morris. 23 Jan.
1833

Alfred Livingston)   Bill for relief & injunction
     vs   )   Plf. in foregoing comes forward and pays all
Thomas J. Ruske   )   costs & brings Levi Mervecer and David
John C. Waters   )   Bishop as his security...bound with Alfred
George W. Keith   )   Livingston for the eventual condemnation...
26 Jan. 1833   )   money with all costs.   Alfred Livingston,
                      Levi Mercer, David Bishop by their attorneys
Alfred Livingston.   Oliver Strickland, Clk.

Page 21. Minutes - Feb. Term 1833
At Superior Court begun and holden at Cherokee Courthouse to wit:
near the house of John Lay in county of Cherokee on Monday the
11th of Feb. (2nd Monday) 1833 his honor John W. Hooper, Judge.

Hetty Vickery, admr.)   Mandammas in Cherokee Superior Ct. It is
       vs   )   agreed between Hitchins & Holt attys. for
Oliver Strickland   )   plff. and the dft. appointment of admr. of
                         estate of Harry Vickery dec'd be confirmed.
Hutchins & Holt attys. for Hattie Vickery. Oliver Strickland
Admr. for Harry Vickery, dec'd.

Superior Court Feb. Term 1833
Ordered that the clerk of Superior Court of said county be and he
is hereby authorized & directed to amend all processes made re-
turnabel to March term 1833 dated since the 3 day of Dec. last or
not served so as to make them returnable to August term 1833.

On motion ordered that ALL cases now pending in this court and
which may be pending at the organization be transferred to the
respective counties to which they properly belong...so soon as
the said counties are organized...and that the clerk deliver over

all papers relating to them to the clerk of the respective county
so soon as they shall be elected and qualified and that all persons may have notice of the transfer and to enable them to prepare
for trial at the next term of the Superior Court of the respective
counties of Cherokee circuit; It is further ordered that this
order be published in the Georgia Journal and Cherokee Intelligencer.

Page 22.
....To His Honor John W. Hooper, Judge Superior Court for Cherokee Circuit of Georgia...petition of Gaston M. Underwood...engag-
ed for some years in the study of law...last Legislature of said
state having passed an act that your applicant should be entitled
to admission to plead and practice law therein...after an eximan-
ination in court...prays...if your honor should think fit cause
him to be accepted...
11 Feb. 1833
This is to certify above applicant had been engaged in the study
of law under my direction for a considerable time that he is a
citizen of Georgia and hath been an inhabitant therof since his
birth and is of good moral character.
11 Feb. 1833   Wm. H. Underwood, Atty.

To Honorable John W. Hooper
Gaston W. Underwood having appeared in open court and been duly
examined in presence of the court by Mr. Robert Mitchell, Mr.
_____ Paschal and Gen. Wm. Ezzard and having satisfactorily...
he was according sworn to following oath, to wit:
Cherokee: I, Gaston M. Underwood do swear I will faithfully and
uprightly demean myself as an attorney counsellor and solicitor
and that I will support the Constitution of the State of Georgia
and United States...so help me God.
11 Feb. 1833   Oliver Strickland, Clk.

Page 23
.....John W. Hooper...affirm admittance of Gaston M. Underwood
"in several courts of law and equity in this state."
11 Feb. 1833
It appearing to court that Vinson Bowman and Sylvanus Walker have
been bound for the appearance of Nancy an Indian who has been
recognized as a witness for her appearance at the term of this
court & that they have produced the body of said Nancy in court
It is therefore ordered that exonerated be entered and said
parties be discouraged for their recognizance.
Court adjourned until court in course   John W. Hooper

Page 24
Venire of the Grand jury to serve in FORSYTH Superior Court of
August term 1833...drawn as grand jurors after a selection made
by the Honorable the Inferior Court Clerk and the Sheriff of said
county:
June 22, 1833.............Oliver Strickland, Clerk

1. Henry S. Campbell
2. John Tidwell, Senr
3. Eli Tanner
4. Thomas L. Garrott
5. John Gray
6. Henry Bagley Senr.
7. Daniel Willis
8. Joel Bramblet
9. Lemuel B. Jones
10. Richard Hayes
11. Thomas L. Garrott
12. Littleberry Hutchins
13. Denis Carrol
14. James Jones
15. George Cockburn
16. Joshua Holden

17. Robert McClure
18. James Middleton
19. James Hayes
20. William Hayes
21. William Hammond
22. Abner Philips
23. Alfred Hudson
24. Charles Haynes
25. John Shoemaker
26. William Mathis
27. Jacob Martin
28. Jacob M. Scudder
29. Isaiah McElhannon
30. John Jack
31. Greene Hudson
32. William Martin
33. Edward Hayes
34. Roderic McGwyre
35. Grief Williams
36. Leroy Hammond
37. Robert Nailor
38. James Edmondson Senr.
39. Joshua Martin
40. A. Landsdown
41. Jacob Rees
42. William Bennett
43. Jonathan Rollins
44. Jonathan Penley
45. John Armstrong
46. Osborn Haygood
47. John Wood
48. Isaac Penley

Page 25
Venire of Petit Jury to serve FORSYTH Superior Court at August
term 1833...following drawn...22 June 1833...Oliver Strickland,
Clk.

1. Robert Williams
2. Alfred Scudder
3. William Humphrey
4. Wm. Gravitt Senr.
5. Nicholas Crossnaw:
6. Isaac Holden
7. John Biddy
8. William Braylock
9. Jesse Carroll
10. John McBrayer
11. Wiley Bagley
12. Asa Garrott
13. Uriah Wilson
14. John Short
15. Abel Roberts
16. Absalom Thornton
17. Randolph Gravitt
18. John Hammond Jr.
19. Robert Mooney
20. Edward T. Howard
21. Samuel Edmonson
22. Elijah Willborn
23. Alfred McBrayer
24. John Southard
25. William Hope
26. Moses Ledbetter
27. William Penley
28. Rowland Williams
29. Edward Gilbert
30. Benjamin Jones
31. Owen J. Bowen
32. Fleming Bates
33. Nathaniel Vanable
34. Andrew Rousseau
35. Daniel Hammond
36. Harris Goodwin
37. William Jones
38. John Huggins
39. Jefferson Bond
40. Sion Burnett
41. John Webb
42. Charles Hawkins
43. Andrew Wood
44. Robert Johnston
45. Thomas Gravitt
46. John Aston
47. John Gravitt
48. Robert Gravitt
49. John Montgomery
50.
51. Benjamin Heath
52. James Edmonson
53. James Vanable
54. Jesse Howell
55. Bithel Bradley

Page 26
The Honorable the Inferior Court of county of Cherokee met at the
courthouse on 2nd Monday May 1833...following drawn as grand
jurors to serve August term.
Superior Court.....

1. Squire Herren
2. James Chambers
3. A. Bradhord
4. Ferninand Bailey
5. E. J. Maddox
6. Martin Evans
7. Ignatius A. Few
8. Lewis Winn

9. Stephen Harvey
10. John B. Garrison
11. Moses Perkins
12. Noble Timmons
13. A. C. Avery
14. Elias Putnam
15. James Willson
16. Henry Maddox
17. Jesse J. Leonard
18. Tilmon Chamlee
19. John M. Chambers
20. John P. Winn
21. William Lay
22. William Lawless

23. G. R. Glenn
24. John Waites
25. Emanuel Corbin
26. Angus McCormick
27. Valentine H. Cain
28. Pete C. Boger
29. John Cannon
30. John Daniel
31. Wiley King
32. George Brock
33. John G. Maddox
34. Wiley Hannet
35. John Nix
36. Felix Moss

.....Following drawn to serve Petit Jurors said term....

1. _____ Middleton
2. Larkin A. Ragsdale
3. Jabez J. Holcombe
4. Samuel Nelson
5. Aaron Moore
6. Hardy Moss
7. J. F. Brock
8. Seaborn Jones
9. William Priest
10. Rhea Paxton
11. John Timmons
12. Jona J. Johnson
13. James Couch
14. Joseph Bradford
15. John Blake
16. Jesse Stancil
17. John Nix
18. John Linley
19. Adam Barnett
20. Joel Leathers
21. George A. Bolch
22. William Aaron
23. Joseph Cagle
24. Seaborn Maddox

25. L. Peak
26. Lewis S. Langston
27. Joel Chandler
28. Martin Chambers
29. Philip McIntyre
30. Amos Chaffin
31. G. H. Trout
32. Ed Maddox
33. E. Dyer
34. James Fatze
35. George Cox
36. Surry Eaton
37. William Kinningham
38. William Nix
39. James Nailor
40. William Tate
41. F. M. Lumpkin
42. Edwin Mims
43. R. C. Blythe
44. R. T. Fowler
45. N. McInear
46. N. Moore
47. Albert A. Winn
48. John Lindley

Page 27
....Superior Court of county of Cherokee met...Monday the 12 day
of August, 1833...Present His Honor John W. Hooper, Judge...
following called and sworn and impannelled as Grand Jurors...

1. Archibald Bradford
2. Edward J. Maddox
3. Martin Evans
4. Ignatius A. Few
5. John B. Garrison
6. Noble Timmons
7. Elias Putnam
8. James Willson
9. William Lawless
10. John Waites
11. Emanuel Corbin
12. Valentine H. Cain

13. John Daniel
14. George Brock
15. John G. Maddox
16. John Nix
17. Jesse J. Leonard
18. Ferdinand Bailey
19. Moses Perkins
20. Squire Herren
21. Absalom C. Avery
22. Stephen Hervey
23. Felix Moss

Following also called...taken oath required by law organized as

Petit Jury for term of court....

1. George Cox
2. Jordan Brock
3. Jonathan J. Johnson
4. Edwin Mims
5. Adam Barnett
6. Joseph H. Bradford

7. Lewis S. Langston
8. Surry Eaton
9. John Wheeler
10. John Timmons
11. Hardy Moss
12. William Nix

Jabez J. Holcombe was sworn and impannelled in place of S. Eaton.

Thomas Haines for the)	Debt & C(costs)
use of P.J. Murray)	I confess judgment to the plaintiff for
vs)	$40 with interest & cost of suit
Charles Haynes)	Charles Haynes

Nicholas M. Ware)	Bill for discovery, relief, etc...
in right of his wife)	Settled and cost paid
Elizabeth Ware)	
vs)	
Joseph Doyle)	

Page 28.   Monday 12 August 1833 Cherokee County Superior Court
            Minutes

James J. Carter)	Debt and C(costs)
vs)	I confess judgment to plf. for $57.81 principal
Reuben Thornton)	with interest & cost of suit Aug. 12, 1833
	Underwood & Sims, Defts. Atty.

The State)	Assault & Battery
vs)	No Bill
Roger Greene)	Ignatius A. Few, Foreman

The State)	Assault & Battery
vs)	No Bill
Hardy Moss)	Ignatius A. Few, Foreman

The State)	Assault & Battery
vs)	True Bill
Simeon Rucker &)	Ignatius A. Few, Foreman
Archibald Bradford)	

Smith & Wright)	Debt and C(costs)
Vs)	I confess judgment to plf. for $76.96 principal
Reuben Thornton)	with interest & costs. Aug. term 1833
	Underwood & Sims, Defts. Atty.

Lewis Ralston)	Tresspass vi et armis & false
vs)	imprisonment and c(costs). We the
Joseph Lynch, Samuel Martin)	jury find for the plf. a verdict
Amos Richardson, Nugin Snip)	against the deft. $700
Ellis Beck, Nelson & Robert)	
Saunders)	J. J. Johnson, Foreman

Page 29

Wm. Sims & Williams)	Debt & C(osts)
vs)	I confess judgment to plf. for $381.66 2/3
Reuben Thornton)	prin. with interest & costs Aug. term 1833
	Underwood & Sims, Defts. Atty.

James W. Jones &) Debt & C(costs)
John R. Stanford) We the jury find verdict against the plf.
    vs   ) for costs.
Burten Mullens)   J. J. Johnson, Foreman

Lewis Ralston)
    vs   ) Trespass
Joseph Lynch   )
  a par   )
Verdict for the plf. $700
It is ordered by court that plf. shew cause on 1st day of next
term why the verdict should not be set aside and a new trial
granted on following grounds:
1. Because the trespass was proven to have been committed by
    defts, who were native Indians and Indian countrymen upon the
plf. who is also an Indian countryman, before the laws of Georgia
was in force in said nation where the trespass was committed.
2. Because Joseph Lynch and Walter Foster, 2 of the deft. reside
    out of the said county and did at the time of commencing said
action.
3. Because verdict is against law
4. Because damages are excessive and that the tule operate as a
    super sedeas.   Wm. H. Underwood

Wm. A. McMillan) Debt & C(osts)
    vs   ) I confess judgment to plf. for $250.77 &
John Ragsdale   ) interest cost.   John Ragsdale

The Honorable Superior Court adjourned until 8 o'clock a.m. Tues.
13 instant. Test: R. F. Daniel, Clk. John W. Hooper, J.S.C.C.C.

Page 30. Tuesday 13 August term Minutes.
....His Honor John W. Hooper, Judge....

Benjamin Goodwin) Assumpsit
    vs   ) We find for plf. $87.37½ principal with
Wm. T. Williamson) interest & cost. 13 Aug. 1833...J. J.
               Johnson, F.M.

A. Lawhon & Co. Fi Fa from Campbell County...ordered...Sheriff
pay over sum of $50 now in his hand sued out of the dft's proper-
ty....Downs Brewster...to the above fi fa.

E. L. Bryant) Scire Facias
    vs   ) Dismissed
M. M. Ham   )

Nelson Dickerson) Debt & C(osts)
    vs   ) I confess judgment to the plf. for $166 with
Martin Evans   ) interest & cost.   Robert Mitchell, Def.Atty.

The State   ) Digging for gold
    vs.   ) nol. prost. at Aug. term 1833
James Downign alias Blankets) Wm. Ezzard, Sol. Genl.
wife & Lucy Doghead   )

Simeon Walraven) Certiorari Cherokee Superior Court Aug. term
    vs   ) 1833. The magistrates in the above case fail-
James L. Adams &) ing to make any return to the above certior-
Richard Coleman) ari; it is ordered that they make a full re-
              turn to next Superior Court of said county to

CHEROKEE COUNTY SUPERIOR COURT MINUTES

shew cause to the contrary.   Wm. H. Underwood, Atty pro plff.

Page 31.

The State   ) Riot
  vs   ) We the jury find dft. George S. Bradford
Joseph H. Bradford   ) guilty.
Simeon Rucker &   )
George S. Bradford   )   J. J. Johnson, Foreman

The Governor on the) Sci Fa in Cherokee Superior Court Aug.1833
information of   ) It appears to court from return of sheriff
Wm. Martin   ) that the dft. is not to be found and by
  vs   ) the affadivit of the informant that he
Pyent E. Jackson   ) does not believe dft. resides in the state.
                       It is therefore ordered that service be
perfected by 3 months publication of this rule in 1 or more of the
public gazettes of this state...13 Aug. 1833

The Governor on the) Repeats the above case exactly except in
information of   ) the spelling of the name.
Wm. Martin   )
  vs   )
Pyant E. Jackson   )

The Governor on the   ) Sci Fa Cherokee Cup. Ct. Aug. term 1833
information of   ) It appears to court by return of sheriff
Henry Lightfoot Sims)   that dft. is not to be found and by
      vs   ) affadavit of the informant that he does
Michael Everett   ) not believe that the dft. resides in
                           state.   It is therefore ordered that
service be perfected by 3 mos. publication of the rule in 1 or
more of public gazettes of state.

Page 32
A duplicate Sci Fa on information of Jacob Martin vs Pyant E.
Jackson
2 duplicates Sci Fa on information of James Wood vs Pyant E. Jackson

John Conner   ) Case in assumpsit
    vs   ) Bail discharged on ground of defect in the
John Duncan   ) affadavit.

Page 33.
The following drawn to serve as grand jurors next term.....

 1. W. D. Menafee   16. Holman F. Simmons
 2. George W. Lumpkin   17. John Wheeler
 3. Sion House   18. John Dial
 4. James W. Dooly   19. William Baker
 5. Beverly Allen   20. Enoch Roper
 6. Elisha Dooly   21. John H. King
 7. Ignatius A. Few   22. Roger Greene
 8. James Tippens   23. David Dinemore
 9. Wm. W.B. Key   24. Harvey Small
10. Randol McDonald   25. Daniel Butler
11. Eli McConnell   26. Joseph Kelly
12. William King   27. Noble P. Bell
13. Edward Townsend   28. James Burns
14. William King   29. Benjamin Johnston
15. G. W. Jones   30. John Tate

180

31. Henry Holcombe
32. Solomon Peak
33. Henry Dobson

34. John McConnell
35. George R. Glenn
36. Angus McCormack

.....Petit Jurors next term.....

1. John Blake
2. James Holland
3. David Stansel
4. Isham King
5. James Kirkendoll
6. Wm. Jay
7. James Holcombe
8. S. Walraven
9. Robartus L. Sparks
10. John Pence
11. James Young
12. David Methvin
13. Charles Blythe
14. Isaac George
15. Joiner C. Bailey
16. Thomas Hance
17. Jacob Cagle
18. John F. Holcombe

19. James Barnett
20. Josephus L. Sparks
21. Lodowick Nix
22. Johnathan Gray
23. David Glaze
24. John Blair
25. Samuel C. Candler
26. John Ragsdale
27. Samuel Nelson
28. Seaborn Jones
29. Martin Chamlee
30. Adam Barnett
31. Wm. H. Kinningham
32. Surray Eaton
33. _____ Middleton
34. Aaron Moore
35. William Priest
36. Ray Paxton

The State) Aug. term 1833. It appears to court that
vs) deft. was recognized at this order of
Archibald Bardford) court on a peace warrant and the said
deft. appeared and prosecutor having
failed to appear to prosecute same on motion ordered the said
dft. be released from his recognizance.

Page 34. Cherokee County Superior Court Minutes
Jonathan J. Johnson) Rule Ni Si
vs) It appearing to the court herefore to wit.
Isaac D. Wall) on the --- of 1833 one Isaac D. Wall made
and executed to your petitioner Jonathan
J. Johnson his certain deed of mortgage without a date but which
in fact should have been dated about the 1st day of April 1833
where by he sold and conveyed unto your petitioner all that tract
and lot of land, lying and being in the 21st district of Cherokee
County #333 containing 40 acres...$43.75...whereby ordered by
court that said Isaac D. Wall do pay into clerk's office of this
county the sum of money aforesaid...with interest and cost...on
or before 1st day of next term of this court...or that the equity
of redemption in and to said lot of land be forever barred and
foreclosed and it is further ordered that this rule be published
in one of public gazettes of this state...or that the said Isaac
D. Wall be personally served with a copy of this rule 3 months
before the setting of the next term of court... R.D. Daniel, Clk.

Georgia: Cherokee County
We, the Grand Jurors, sworn, chosen and selected for county of
Cherokee, beg leave to make the following presentments. We have
nothing of a very special nature to present, We find the internal
affairs of our county to present a tolerable fair and auspicious
prospect for the time it has been in existence. We have one thing
which perhaps is a just cause of regret, to wit, the situation of
our courthouse, if indeed we might be said to have any...we,
therefore, recommend to our Inferior Court and hope they will
without further delay proceed and select a site.

Page 35.
......(continued)...for the town. We hope at the same time they
will have due regard to the beauty, elegibility and central
situation for the public buildings of our county. We cannot under
the present condition of our state refrain from an expression of
opinion upon the causes which have produced the excitement, we
allude particularly to the actings of the late convention for the
alteration of our Constitution we are decidely opposed to the
proceedings and the convention because instead of reducing and
equalizing the representation in our Legislature it changes the
principal of representation and renders it more unequal than it
is under the existing conditions we shall not presume to enter
into an aagruement upon the subject but barely state the 2 leading
facts as they actually exist and be content by an expression of
an opinion founded upon the undeniable truth of those facts. We
cannot refraim from expressing our approbation of the manner in
which his honor Judge Hooper has discharged the duties of the
court. The Sol-General also is entitled to our approbation.
We request that our presentments be published in the Cherokee
Intelligencer and Western Herrald..... Ignatius A. Few, Foreman.

We, the undersigned protest against the presentments as far as
relates to the Convention

Stephen Hervey	Emanuel Corbin
Archibald Bradford	George Brock
Squire Herren	Felix Moss
John G. Maddox	Ferninand Bailey
Valentine H. Cain	Jesse J. Leonard
Edward J. Maddox	Moses Perkins
Noble Timmons	James Willson

On motion of William Ezzard the Sol-General ordered that the
presentments be published in accordance with the requests of the
Grand Jury. Court adjourned until court in course, August 13,
1833.   R. F. Daniel, Clk.   John W. Hooper, J.S.C.C.C.

(Four blank pages, 36, 37, 38, 39)

Minutes of 10 March 1834 begin on unnumbered pages which shall be
numbered as (40)

Minutes of 10 March 1834....
At a Superior Court at Cherokee Courthouse on 2nd Monday in March
being 10 March 1834 in and for Cherokee County...present honorable
John W. Hooper, Judge...
Following persons having been selected, drawn and summoned to
attend this term of said court as grand jurors were empannelled
and sworn, to wit,

1. John H. King, Foreman	12. John Taite
2. Randol McDonald	13. Eli McConnell
3. James Burns	14. Ignatius A. Few
4. Elisha Dooly	15. William Watts Betty Key
5. James W. Dooly	16. Roger Green
6. Edward Townsend	17. Reuben F. Daniel
7. Noble P. Beall	18. William Lay
8. Daniel Butler	19. Holman F. Simmons
9. Benjamin F. Johnson	20. Blank
10. Enoch Rogers	21. Blank
11. John Wheeler	22. Blank 23 & 24 also blank

The following persons having been duly summoned and sworn were empannelled to serve on Jury #1 at present term:

1. Robartus L. Sparks, Foreman
2. Martin Chamlee
3. Joiner C. Bailey
4. William Jay (Lay?)
5. Charles Blythe
6. David Stancel
7. James Young
8. Jacob Kagle
9. Lodowick Nix
10. Samuel Nelson
11. William Priest
12. David Glaze

The following persons having been duly summoned and sworn were empannelled to serve as Jury #2 at present term:
        (No names here)

William Few, Constable was then sworn to attend the grand jury at this term, the usual oath by Wm. Ezzard, Sol. General: John Dejournette was sworn as constable to attend to Jury #1.

(Page 41) (page not marked)
across top of the page....of March 1834, Cherokee County, Ga.

Trueman Kellogg) March Term 1831
      vs   ) fi fa from Walton Superior Court...
Andrew Boyd   ) ...Former sheriff of Cherokee County levied
                    up and sold lot of land #328 district 21 of
said county as property of deft. for $120 and that purchaser has
failed to pay the money over...ordered that John P. Brooke, former
Sheriff of Cherokee County be directed now to make his entries
of the facts and that a Copy of this order be attached to said
fi fa.

Lewis Ralston   ) Trespass viet armies and false imprisonment
      vs   )
Joseph Lynch   ) Transferred fr : Superior Court: Gwinnett
Samuel Martin   ) County to Superior Court of Cherokee County.
William Martin)
Amos Richardson) Verdict at August term 1833 for plaintiff...
Nugan Snip   ) verdict in above case for plf. and a rule nisi
Ellis Beck   ) taken to show cause why a new trial should not
Ezekiel Beck   ) be granted on hearing of counsel...ordered by
Walter Foster   ) court that said rule be discharged.
Nelson Tennawd (?)
Robert Sanders)

A. R. Smith & Co.) Debts & Costs
      vs   ) I confess judgment to plff for $274.93
Ambrose Harnage   ) principal with interest & cost of suit.
                        Wm. Daniel, Deft. Atty.

The Governor on the   ) Seire facias
information of   )
Wm. P. Price   )
      vs   ) Dismissed
Nancy Holland, drawer)
of #114/14/2

183

Page 42.

✓Lewis Ralston) Trespass vi et armies
    vs) and
Joseph Lynch. Elis Beck. Samuel) false imprisonment
Martin, Ezekiel Beck, William) and verdict for the plff
Martin, Walter Foster, Amos Richard-) for $700 and cost the dfts
son, Nelson Tennuawa, Nugan Snip,) being dissatisfied with the
& Robert Sanders) verdict and the jury
                                                rendered in the above cause
and having paid all cost and demanded an appeal brings Holman F.
Simmons and James A. Thompson and tender them as their security
and...bound to Lewis Ralston the plft for the payment of the
eventual condemnation money in said cause...10 March 1834...
signed by: Joseph M. Lynch, Holman F. Simmons and James A.
Thompson (and none of the others)   Test: William Grisham, Clk.

The Governor on the Information) Sci fa not served
of William W. B. Key)
      vs) Dismissed
D. Holtzclaw)

Page 43.   ....10 March 1834 minutes.....

The State) Burgulary
    vs) True bill
William Nix) John H. King, Foreman

The State) Assault & Battery
    vs) No bill
Jonathan J. Johnson) John H. King, foreman

The State) Assault & Battery
    vs) No bill
Daniel Davis &) John H. King, Foreman
Alsey Harris)

John Conner) Case in assumpsit & bail. In this case Jabez
    vs) J. Holcombe having been taken as security and he
John Duncan) the said Holcombe having surrendered the body of
              said Duncan into hands of sheriff of Cherokee
County; ordered the said Holcombe be discharged from all liability
upon said bond.

The Governor on) Scire facias
the information of) I confess judgment to the defendent with
Benjmain F. Johnson) the right of appeal.
    bs)
Isaac Mayfield) Howard Cobb, dfts. atty.
937/2/2

Michael Prendergrast) Attachment in assumpsit...find for plf.
    vs) $200.14 with cost of suit...10 March
James Murray) 1834...R. L. Sparks, Foreman

The Governor on the) Scire Fa   lot #1049/21/2
information of)
Tumson Coryell) Dismissed
    vs)
Thomas Brown)

Page 44.

J. & J. McBryde	)	Debt
vs	)	I confess judgment to plf. for $83.67 with
Benj. F. Johnson	)	interest and cost of suit. Howell Cobb,
		defts. atty.

Smith, Booth & Ufford	)	Assumpsit...I confess judgment to plf.
vs	)	for $183.77 with interest & cost of
Benj. F. Johnson	)	suit. Howell Cobb, dfts. atty.

Eli S. Shorter	)	I confess judgment to plf. for $100 principal
vs	)	with interest & cost.
Howell Cobb	)	Howell Cobb, dft.

The Governor on   ) Scire Facias
information of   )
John Mattox   ) Dismissed
     vs   )
John Bowen, drawer of)
#63/16/2

The Governor on information) Scire Facias
of Thomas Haynes   )
     vs   ) Dismissed
Isaac Mayfield   )

The Governor on information) Sci fa
of P. W. Flynn   )
     vs   ) Dismissed
Daniel Holtzclaw   )

The Governor on info. of) Sci fa
Thomas Mehaffey   )
     vs   ) Dismissed
Augustus Hodge   )

Page 45.   Monday 10 March 1834

The Governor on info. of) Sci fa
John C. Miller   )
     vs   ) Dismissed
John Perry   )

Artemus Gold	)	Assumpsit & cost. I confess judgment to
vs	)	plf. for $410.83 principal with interest
Holman F. Simmons	)	and cost of suit. H. F. Simmons

Jonathan J. Johnson) Trespall upon the case.
     vs   ) Settled at dft. cost
Thomas Mehaffey   )

Jack Still, and Indian) Trespass vi et armies
     vs   )
Roger Green   ) Dismissed

Ephraim Downing, an Indian) Trespass vi et armies
     vs   )
Hardy Moss   ) Dismissed

Court adjourned until 8 o'clock tomorrow morning.
Wm. Grisham, clerk   John W. Hooper

Page 46.   .....11 March 1834

...Charley Clythe...having been empannelled and sworn to serve as
a petit juror at present term of court and having appeared in
court this morning so intoxicated as to be disqualified to serve
as a juror it is ordered that he pay a fine of $10 upon the pay-
ment of which he will be discharged.

John Ragsdale was summoned and sworn to serve on panel #1

Elisha W. Chester &	)	Assumpsit
James Hillyer	)	I confess to the plf. $324.00 with
vs	)	interest & cost of suit.
Ambrose Harnage	)	William Daniell, Defts. Atty.

The State	)	Assault
vs	)	True bill
David Rusk, Sr.	)	John H. King, Foreman

The State	)	Riot
vs	)	True bill
Hugh Rusk &	)	
David Rusk, Jr.	)	John H. King, Foreman

James Hudgins) Debt
     vs   ) It appearing to the court that the avove stated
John Williams) case was at the Feb. term 1833 of this court
               ordered to be transferred to county of Murray...
it can be hence be dismissed.

Nathaniel Blanchard et al) fi fa
          vs   ) Ordered by the court that the
Toliver Hicks   ) sheriff pay to the fi fas claiming
                          money according to their respective
dates.

Elijah Roberts   ) Trespass vi et armies
     vs   )
Wm. Smith, Ezekiel West, John   )
West, Andrew Johnson, Alex. T.   )
Harper, Orkney Henderson,   )
John Elliott, John Chambers   )

James Cartright   ) Trespass & cost
     vs   )
James Hemphill et al   )

Crawford Wright   ) Trespass &
     vs   )
James Hemphill et al   )

Willis Gilley   ) Trespass
     vs   ) It appearing to the court that the aforesaid
James Hemphill) cases were at the Feby. term 1833 ordered to
                be trans. to the county of Floyd ordered they
be dismissed.

Stephen H. Woodruff for   ) Debt   March term 1834
the use of Wm.B. Woodruff   ) I confess judgment to plf for $76.
          vs   ) 28 3/4 with interest from 4 Aug.
Benjamin F. Johnston   ) 1831 and cost. Howell Cobb, dft.atty

Page 47.

....Superior Court March term 1834...at present sitting of the
court Allen Dyer...made his application for leave to plead and
practice in the several courts of law and equity of this state...
therefore having given satisfactory evidence of good moral
character and having been examined in open court and being found
well acquainted and skilled in the law...admitted to court to
all privelege of an attorney, solictor and counsellor in the
several courts of law & equity in this state...in testimony whereof the presiding judge has hereunto set his hand and THERE BEING
NO SEAL OF THE COURT his private seal this 11 March 1834.

....Richard W. Jones...same application as above...admitted with
same words.

Sixkiller, an Indian) Trespass vi et armies
     vs   )
George Cox   ) Dismissed

James Brannon, appelant) Respd.
     vs   ) Appeal from the agents decision:
Charles Duncan   ) Dismissed

McJunkin & Smith, et al) Trespass vi et armies
     vs   ) Dismissed
John L. Doyal. dft.   ) Henry Fitzsimmons, claimant

The Governor for the use of) Debt
     vs   ) Confess to plf. for $81 with
A. Bradford, J. Sisner &) interest and costs
Geo. S. Bradford   ) Howell Cobb, defts. atty.

Page 50.

The State   ) Assault & Battery
     vs   ) Nol. Prov.
Simeon Rucher &   )
Archibald Bradford) William Ezzard, Sol. Gen'l.

Robert H. Brazil) Debt and cost on the appeal
    vs   ) Special Jury; to wit, John H. King; James
Robert Berry   ) W. Dooley; Ecward Townsend; Nobel P. Bell;
                Daniel Butler; Benjamin F. Johnson; Randal
McDonald returned with the following verdict...for plf. $60.00
for the principal with interest and cost of suit with 14% damage
for frivolous appeal...J. H. King, Foreman.

Wilson Lumpkin, Gov.) Sci fa
    vs   ) Appearing to court, that defendant
George S. Bradford &) George S. Bradford, one of defendants
Richard Coleman   ) in above case has been served with a
                copy of Sci fa in above slated case and
no sufficient cause having been shown to the contrary...therefore
ordered judgement be signed on the same for $200 amount of said
bond...on motion...ordered Sol. Gen. show cause at next term of
court why said order should not be set aside. It appearing that
prisoner was in court and was tried...John P. Winn became purchaser of #1210 district 15 section 2 of Cherokee...sheriff's sale...
during continence of J. P. Brooke as sheriff...said former
sheriff did not execute deed to said Winn for same...ordered S.C.
Candler to write...

Page 51.

The State	)	Cheating & swindling
vs	)	True Bill
John Velven	)	J. H. King, Foreman

The State	)	Horse stealing
vs	)	True Bill
Colemake, an	)	J. H. King, Foreman
Indian	)	

The State	)	Burglary
vs	)	dft. arraigned...plead not guilty...copy of
William Nix	)	bill & witness waived...William Ezzard, Sol.Gen.

The State   ) Burglary
vs   ) Sheriff required to summon a full pannell of
William Nix   ) 48 men and from that following chosen and sworn
                to try above traverse, to wit: William Lay;
John Ragsdale; David Stancil; James Young; Robartus L. Sparks;
Samuel Nelson; William Preast; William Whitaker; James Willson;
Samuel Timmons; John McCanless; John Timmons...we jury...not
guilty...and a malicious prosecuting...R. L. Sparks, Foreman

Court adjourned until tomorrow morning 8 oc'clock.   John W. Hooper

Page 52.   Court met Wednesday 12 March 1834.
        Following drawn as grand jury (Numbers only follow...
no names).   1-36.   Petit Jurors (numbers only...no names).   1-48

Page 53.

John Ragsdale   ) Certiorari
vs   ) Dft. has been served in above case and
Mark Castleberry, Jr.) has failed to render his answer...ordered
                        by court...that said dft. make his re-
turn...on or before 1st day of next term of this court or an
attachment for contempt be served against him.

John Lipper   ) Fi Fa
vs   ) Ordered by court that sheriff pay over all money
William Daniel) in his hands raised by sale of defendants pro-
                perty to fi fa's in favor of A. Abrams, agent
defendant after paying cost of sale and what is due on fi fa
from Justice Court in Madison Co. in favor of John Scott vs. said
William Daniel.

Abner Wellborn) Fi Fas
vs   ) From Lincoln Justice Court Sheriff having
James Gamble   ) presented for court sundry fi fas against dft
                ...for its direction and instruction in paying
out amount of money in his hands from sale of deft's property...
ordered sheriff pay to execution of Abner Wellborn amount in his
hand or as much as is sufficient to satisfy them after retaining
the cost.

Cherokee...March term 1834
Allen Dyer shows...his is and has been admitted as attorney in
all courts of law and equity in state of Tennessee...applies to
you by filing application for leave to plead and practice law
in...State of Georgia.   10 March 1834.   J. H. Stokes

Page 54.   Cherokee Superior Court Minutes 12 March 1834.

Ambrose Harnage   )   Trover and costs
    vs   )   Verdict for plf. for $500 and cost...the
Holman F. Simmons   )   dft. being dissatisfied with the verdict of
                         the jury rendered in the above case, and
having paid all costs and demanded an appeal brings Eli McConnell
and John McConnell and tender them as his security and they the
said F. S. Holman, J. McConnell and Eli McConnell bound to plff.
Ambrose Harnage for payment of the eventual condemnation money...
12 March 1834...Test: Wm. Grisham, CLK (Actual signature).

The State   )   Burglary
    vs   )   True Bill
James Whorton &   )   John H. King, Foreman
Elizabeth Whorton   )

John R. Stanford   )   In Inferior Court of Franklin Co. in said
    vs   )   state it appearing to court...
Wm. A. McMillon   )

The Governor on the)   Sci Fa
information of   )
John Elrod   )   Dismissed
   vs   )
Samuel Elrod   )

Page 55.

Artemus Gould   )   Assumpsit & costs
    vs   )   Came HFS, dft. and rendered Daniel R. Mitchell
Holman F. Simmons   )   as security on the stay of the levy of the
                         execution during the time allowed by law...
both of whom...bound to plf...full sum of principal & costs.
(original signature)

John R. Stanford, plf   )   In Inferior Court Franklin Co. in
    vs   )   said state...it appearing to court
William A. McMillon, dft.)   that John Ragsdale was garnisheed to
& John Ragsdale, garn.)   answer at this term of Superior Court
                         and has failed to answer it is ordered
that John Ragsdale do appear and answer in terms of law in such
cases made and proved...1st day of next term, or judgment will be
entered against him for amount due plff.

The Governor on info. of)   Sci fa
R. F. Johnson   )   Judgment confessed to the dft. and
    vs   )   for cost of suit. The informant
Isaac Mayfield   )   being dissatisfied with the confes-
                         sion in above cause and having paid
all costs and demanded an appeal brings Philip Krof as security...
and R. F. Johnston and Philip Krof bound to Isaac Mayfield the
defendant for payment of the eventual condemnation money...15
March 1834...Signatures of R.F. Johnston and Philip Krapt.

Page 56.   Presentments 12 March 1834.

...We, grand jurors...present Frances Jones and Elizabeth Welch
of the County for living in an open state of adultery. Wits:
R. F. Daniel, John Daniel, and John Conner.

...examined the books of county Treasurer and Clerk of Inferior

Court and find regular entries have been made...recommended a
moderate county tax to be levied for present year...We have seem
with much pleasure the notice our fellow citizens of Forsyth
County have taken of the Act of the last Legislature for the further government of the Cherokees remaining with us. We heartily
concur and agree with them in all their views relating to that act
and do hope that nothing will taken place by any of those engaged
in the administration of the laws to impede the progress of the
settlement of this country. We have learned with satisfaction of
the course of the Agent, and admire that firm and manly manner in
which he has gone into and continues the discharge of his ardious
duties (tho, from the nature and importance of the duties imposed
on the agent by the law under which he acts) it cannot be expected
that he can at once reconcile both parties claiming at the time
possession of land, but from the character and ability of our
agent we feel assured that the law will be fully administered, and
we here take occasion to express our wish that nothing may be
made to embarrass or interrupt him in the discharge of his duties.
In taking this view of the Indian subject we will further state
in our opinion the late law governing the Cherokees fully provided
for the Indians and was intended at the same time to relive the
state of a portion of that tribe who once sold their interest to
this country...
It cannot be doubted for a moment that those reserves have always
and still continue to be the most inveterate enimies of the
administration of its policy in the removal of the Cherokees. But
should the object of the late law be defeated it will fix down
upon us a people whose language and manners differ with those of
the whites: and should they remain a few years longer they will
be doomed to be draged out a miserable existence but should the
views of the government be advanced by the authorities of Georgia
it will eventually be a means of releaving the aborgines of our
country from a state of degradation to which they are fast
approaching. We return our report to his honor, Judge Hooper and
to the Sol. Gen. for their discharge of their duties druign this
present term of court...we request that so much of our presentments as are of a public nature be published in the Cherokee
Intelligencer.

John H. King, Foreman	James Burns
Elisha Dooley	James W. Dooley
Edward Townsend	Noble P. Beall
Daniel Butler	Benj. F. Johnson
Enoch Rogers	John Wheeler
John Tate	Eli McConnell
Ignatius Few	Wm. W. B. Key
Roger Greene	Holman F. Simmons
Reuben F. Daniel	William Lay
John McConnell	

We are opposed to the within presentment as far as that part of
it that relates to the conduct of the agent in the settlement of
Indian affairs...Ignatius A. Few; Wm. W. M. Kay; R. F. Daniel...
On motion of Wm. Ezzard, Sol. Genl. ordered presentments be
published. William Grisham, Clerk...John W. Hooper, Judge
(signatures)

Page 57.

...Superior Court met at the Cherokee courthouse...Tuesday 6 May
1834...for the purpose of drawing Grand and Special Jurors to
serve at next Sept. term of Superior Court of Cherokee Co., Ga.

when their Honors John Sarjeant, John McConnell and James H.
Chambers being present re-organized the jurbox of Superior Court
and following were drawn:

John P. Winn	Solomon Sowsberry
Peter C. Roger	William W. B. Key
Simeon R. Ricker	William Chambers
John Wagoner	Guilford W. Jones
John Wheeler	John Hamilton
Ignatius A. Few	Moses Perkins
Charles H. Nelson	William Reed
Robert L. Johnson	Holman F. Simmons
David Rusk	Samuel Jackson
James Tippen	Daniel Butler
Elisha Dyer	Edwin Mims
Joseph Naylor	John McConnell
Robartus L. Sparks	Thomas Townsend
John Waites	Charles Christian
James S. Elliott	James W. Dooly
James Burns	John McCanless

Following drawn to serve as Petit Jurors for next Sept. term.
From No. 1 to No. 2.

Adam Barnett	George S. Bradford
Samuel Nelson	Fred S. Lamb
Charles Sawyer	Caleb Sanders
Moses Whitsite	John Leathers
Jesse Greene	David Stancil
John Goodwin	Anderson Hicks
John Stancil	John Cannon
Richard Literal	Joel Chandler
Lewis Rhinehart	Jarrett Chamlee

continuing on page 58

Osborn Reeves	Nathaniel Harbin
Joseph Walker	William Wayne
Lindsey Peak	Thomas Johnson
Thomas Preast	David Dudley
James Kirdendoll	Andrew Cathey
Elias Chaffin	George Kitchens
Willis Weems	William McNair
William Ward	Abraham Harbin
William M. Bird	William Preast
Alsey Camp	Hardy Moss
George Cox	John L. Black
Thompson Tippins	John De journett
James Young	James Stewart
William A. Few	Dennis Miller
Joseph Fincher	Hiram Dimsdall

...6 May 1834, Signatures of James H. Chambers, John Sarjeant and
John McConnell...J.I.C.

A loose fragmented page gives Grand Jurors (96 names) at re-organ-
ization...reverse side of page is blank except for some figures
(not copied).

Grand Jurors:

James Waggoner	James H. Chambers
John McConnell	Daniel Bird
Simpson C. Dyer	John Wheeler

John P. Brooke
John Waites
Eli McConnell
Robartus L. Soarks
Noble P. Beall
James Tippen
Edwin Mims
William M. McAfee
William O. Bell
Samuel Jackson
John W. Leanard
William Whitaker
Holman F. Simmons
Edward Townsend
Enoch Rogers
John B. Bird
David Rusk
George Brock
John Taite
Noble Timmon
John Hamilton
William Reed
Archibald Bradford
George M. Smith
Elijah Chaffin
Martin Evans
Burton Mullins
Elias Putnam
Charles McGrady
James H. Bell
Daniel Butler
William Lay
James S. Elliott
Jacob Avary
Guilford W. Jones
James Wilson
Ignatius A. Few
William Lawless
John Edwards
John P. Winn
Jeremiah Wofford
Solomon Sowsberry
Joseph S. Doyle
Elisha Dyer
Ferdinand Bailey

William Chamlee
John Sarjeant
John Black
John Brewster
James Cooper
John G. Garrison
Felis Moss
James Barmore
Absolom C. Avary
Randol McDonald
John Epperson
Jesse Bates
Robert L. Johnston
Elisha Dooley
Thomas Townse (nd? torn)
Smith A. McCre(torn)
Simeon B. Rucker
John McCanless
Joseph Donaldson
William Tate junior
William May
Andrew Scott
Moses Perkins
Daniel Methvin
Jesse J. (?)eonard
Amos Chaffin
Jabez J. Holcomb
John M. Chambers
Joseph Naylor
Peter C. Boger
Benjamin F. Johnston
Tilmon Chamlee
Roger Green
Charles Christian
James Jordan
Squire Herren
James (blot) Burn (torn)
John H. King
James W. Dooley
Reuben F. Dan(iel? torn)
William W. B. Key
Lodourck Nix
John Y. Maddox
Charles H. Nelson
Robert T. Griffin

Page 59. Monday 8 Sept. 1834...Superior Court...Cherokee Court-
          house...2nd Monday Sept. 1834...John H. Hooper, Judge
of Cherokee Circuit, Ga.

Following Grand Jurors...
John McConnell, Foreman
Peter C. Bogar
Moses Perkins
James S. Elliott
Ignatius A. Few
Holman F. Simmons
James Tippen
John Wheeler
William Chamlee
Guilford W. Jones
Charles H. Nelson

Edward Mims
Daniel Butler
Robert L. Johnston
Elisha Dyer
David Rusk
John Waggoner
Thomas Townsend
John McCanless
John Waits
Simeon B. Rucker

Following are Petit Jury #1:

David Stancil
Charles A. Sawyer
Thomason Tippen
James Kirkendoll
John L. Black
Elias Chaffin

James Young
Hardy Moss
William Wayne
Hiram Dimsdale
Thomas Johnson
Joel Chandler

Emanuel Corbin, constable, was sworn to attend on Jury #1 during this term of court.

Dr. James Burns was sworn to attend on the Grand Inquest for this county during the present term of this court.

Page 60.

Turpin, G. &) Attachment
William II. Atwood) Dismissed
      vs   )
Henry Hammack   )

The State   ) Assault
      vs   ) With intent to murder as principal in
Wiley, alias Kante-) 2nd degree: No Bill
satee, a Cherokee) John McConnell, Foreman
Indian

The Governor on the info of) Sci fa
John P. Brooke   ) I confess judgment to cost of suit
      vs   ) reserving right of appeal as in
Milton M. Ham   ) case of verdict. D.R. Mitchell,
                             plff's. atty.

John Cannon, having hallowed at the court and to the officers of the court and when brought into court, disregarded the authority of the court and been guilty of profane swearing, whilst in court. It is ordered that he pay a fine of $10.00 and that he remain in the custody until paid with all costs that may acrue.

D. R. Mitchell   ) Debt and costs
      vs   ) confess judgment to plff for $50 with
Thomas Townsend   ) interest and cost of suit 8 Sept. 1834.
                    William Daniel, Dfts. atty.

Jarratt P. Moody) Fi Fa from Justice Court...
      vs   ) ordered by court to show cause tomorrow...
Henry G. Daniel)

Page 61. Morning at 8 o'clock and...why he does not pay over to
          the plff. or his atty...money due on said fi fa.

The Governor on the info.) Judgment conferred with liberty of
of John P. Brooke   ) verdict for dfts. for costs of suit.
      vs   ) Sci Fa Plff being dissatisfied with
Milton M. Ham   ) the verdict of the jury rendered in
                            above case, (or confession with
liberty of appeal) and having paid all costs and demanded an appeal, brings R. F. Daniel and tenders him as his security and
they...said John P. Brooke and R. F. Daniel...bond to Milton M.
Ham...the dft for payment of the eventual condemnation money...
13 Sept. 1834. Wm. Grisham, Clk. John P. Brooke & R. F. Daniel.
(signature)

193

The governor on info. of) Sci fa vs #131/14/2
Yancy Johnson   )
    vs   ) Dismissed...not served
Jesse Hodges   )

The Governor on info. of) Scire Facias on #60/13/2
William Martin   ) We, the jury find the return
    vs   ) fraudulent
Pyant E. Jackson   ) Hiram Dimsdale, Foreman

Page 62.

Following persons...Jury #2
Richard Literal   Joseph Fincher
John Leathers   William A. Few
Anderson Hicks   William Ward
Jarrett Chamlee   William M. Bird
Caleb Saunders   Jordan Brock
Curtis Saterfield   Pleasant H. Nix

The State   ) Simple Larceny...No Bill
    vs   ) Malicious prosecution
Tom Blanket, alias   ) John McConnell, Foreman
Tom Downing, an Indian)

The State   ) Larceny from the house
    vs   ) True Bill
Titus & Johnson)   John McConnell, Foreman
Cherokee Indian)

The State   ) Simple Larceny
    vs   ) True Bill
Elisha Atkerson)   John McConnell, Foreman

The State   ) Indictments & assault, with intent to murder as
    vs   ) principal in the 2nd degree...returned no bill by
Wiley, alias   ) grand jury... It appearing to court...no further
Kantesatee   ) cause of prosecution...appears against...ordered
) he be discharged for confinement and have leave
to go hence without cost or delay.

The Governor on info. of) Scire Facias of no. 108/4/2
William Martin   ) We, the jury find the return
    vs   ) fraudulent
Pyant E. Jackson   ) P. H. Nix, Foreman

Court adjourned till 8 o'clock tomorrow morning. William
Grisham, Clk. John W. Hooper, Judge SCCC

Page 63. 9 Sept. 1834

The Governor on the info. of) Two Sci fas in Cherokee Superior
Osborn Wallace   ) Court, Sept. term, 1834.
    vs   ) Verdict for the informant
Henry F. Cordery,   ) Rule Ni Si
alias H. F. Hitson   )

On the motion of Defendant's counsel, ordered that Informant's
counsel shew cause at the next term of this court why the verdicts
in the above cases should not be set aside and a non suit entered
in each case on the grounds:
1st That the court misconcieved the law

194

2nd That the jury found contrary to evidence
3rd That the sci fa does not negative the qualification of the
     drawer and further order, that this rule operate as a super
cedias to the judgment until discharged.

Jarrett P. Moody) Fi Fa from Justice Court
     vs   ) In answer to a rule Ni Si obtained on yes-
Henry G. Daniel   ) terday, why the sheriff should not pay over
                     the money due on said fi fa to plff or his
atty...the sheriff shows for cause that he rec'd said fi fa from
constable who stated to him that he had rec'd it from Daniel H.
Bird and that he raised the money thereon and paid it over to
said Bird and returned the fi fa to said Bird. M. J. Canden, D.
Sheriff.

The State   ) Assault & Battery
     vs   ) True Bill
Joseph Wofford   ) John McConnell, Foreman

Page 63.

William Thurmond) Fi Fa from Hall Superior Court
     vs   ) Cherokee Co. Superior Court Sept. 1834.
James R. Russell) It appearing to the court that the above
                     stated fi fa was levied on lot of land
#208 in dist. 9 or 3rd section, originally Cherokee now Murray by
the former sheriff of Cherokee County when the grant was not out
and that the entries of sale of said lot of land was made on said
fi fa and that the purchaser of said lot of land refuses to pay
over the purchase money, on motion of counsel for plff: It is
ordered by the court that the present Sheriff of Cherokee county
do correct the entries on said fi fa as to shaw that the money
was never paid to said fi fa so that said fi fa can proceed against defendant's property the same as though said entries had
never been made on said fi fa.

John Cannon, who having committed contempt, and having been
therefore fined by the court $10 which transpired on yesterday
and having made a suitable apology to the court on the subject,
ordered by the court that the said fine be remitted. 9 Sept. 1834.

William Loveless) Debt and costs
     vs   ) I confess judgment to plff for $69.37½ with
Bryant Ingram   ) interest and cost of suit. Howell Cobb,
                     dfts. atty.

A. R. Smith & Co.   ) Sci fa on Bail bond
     vs   )
Charles H. Nelson   ) Dismissed
Elias Henderson   )

Elisha W. Chester &   ) Sci fa on Bail bond
Junior Hillyer   )
     vs   ) Dismissed
Charles H. Nelson   )
Elias Henderson   )

Page 64.

...on written application of Solomon Morgan & Fenn Morgan, 2
mulatto free men and consent in writing of that consent having
been made to this court, and that they the said Solomon Morgan

and Fenn Morgan derived that David Qualls of said county of
Cherokee, should be appointed their guardian, the said David
Qualls having consented thereto and given Pleasant H. Nox as his
security in each bond...court...then ordered that said David
Qualls be appointed guardian of said free men of colour...

```
Saffold and Fears    )  Attachment Debt & costs
       vs            )  find for plff $37.36¼
Bazelle Rowland      )  Andrew Hicks, Foreman
with cost of suit    )
```

```
William Lay    )  Libel for divorce
    vs         )
Rebecca Lay    )  Dismissed
```

```
Elijah Robert   )  Assumpsit
    vs          )  Jury to plff doe(?) $251.50 with cost of suit
Joel Leathers   )  Joel D. (X) Leathers
```

```
The State        )  Simple Larceny
    vs           )  True Bill
George Heard     )  John McConnell, Foreman
```

✓
```
Lewis Ralston         )  Sci fa & cost
    vs                )  jury returns fraudulent
Joseph Lynch, et al   )  Anderson Hicks, foreman
```

Page 65. Tuesday...9 Sept. 1834...Minutes of Cherokee..

```
John Conner    )  Case in Assumpsit & cost
    vs         )  find for plff. $75 with interest and cost...
John Duncan    )  Sept. 9...Hiram Dimsdale, Foreman
```

```
John Larimore        )  Case & cost
    vs               )  find for plff $58.30 with cost of suit
Champ Taylor         )
John McCanless &     )  Hiram Dimsdale, Foreman
William K. McCanless )
```

```
The State        )  Simple Larceny...No bill...
    vs           )  Malicious prosecution
Elias Barnett    )  John McConnell, Foreman
```

```
The State                     )  Hog Stealing
    vs                        )  No Bill
Tagah-Togah, alias            )  John McConnell, Foreman
Stand, alias Standing up,     )
an Indian                     )
```

```
Hugh Rusk for John Lynch  )  Special writ for possession
       vs                 )  find the issue in favor of the
Daniel Butler             )  defendant.  Pleasant H. Nox, Foreman
```

```
Wilson Lumpkin, Governor  )  Debt for rent
       vs                 )  I confess judgment to plff for sum
Henry Holcombe, John S.   )  of $61 principal, $8.37½ interest &
Holcomb, & Elisah Dooley  )  cost of suit.  Howell Cob, dft.atty.
```

Court adjourned to 8 o'clock tomorrow morning...(signed) John W.
Hooper...Test: William Grisham, Clerk

The State   ) Horse Stealing
   vs   ) In Cherokee Superior Ct. it appearing to the
John Kimball &) sum of $25.00 is due by the annexed acct. to
Butler Kimball) D. R. Mitchell, as late Sol. Genl. pro tem. It
                  is ordered that the clerk pay to said D.R.M.
Sol. Genl. pro tem, said sum of $25 out of any money in his hand
arriving from fines and/or forfeiture not otherwise appropriated
12 Sept. 1834. John W. Hooper, J.S.C.C.C.

Page 66. Superior Court...Wed. 10 Sept. 1834

The State   ) Simple Larceny
   vs   ) dft arraigned and pled not guilty
Elisha Atkerson) William Ezzard, Sol. Genl....following person
                  were empanelled and sworn on the jury to try
traverse of the above case, to wit:

John Leathers	William E. Few
Anderson Hicks	William Ward
Jarrett Chamlee	William M. Bird
Caleb Sanders	Jordan Brock
Thompson Tippen	Curtis Satterfield
Pleasant H. Nix	William Wayne

who returned the following verdict...not guilty to this charge.
William Ward, Foreman

The State   ) Assault with intent to murder
   vs   ) The dft arraigned and pled not guilty
Log in the water, alias)
Teshatooskaa   ) William Ezzard, Sol. Genl.
a Cherokee Indian   )

Following sworn and empannelled to try above...

James Young	Charles A. Sawyer
Jell Chandler	Richard Literal
William Whitaker	John P. Winn
Joseph S. Dial	Thompson Tippen
Pleasant H. Nix	Joel Leathers
Samuel Roe	Robert Burns

...verdict...guilty...Sept. 10, 1834...John P. Winn, Foreman

Spencer Riley   ) Certiorari
   vs   ) Dismissed
Nobel P. Bell, J.P.)

Page 67.

The State   ) Assault with intent to murder
   vs   ) Dft arraigned and plead not guilty
Log in the Water, alias) William Ezzard, Sol. Genl.
Teshshotooskad, a   )
Cherokee Indian   )

...following...named jurors selected...sworn and empannelled...
as evidence was not recorded on last page in connection with the
verdict it is here recapitulated...)Repeats names of the 12 jurors
on preceding page).
....James Burns, the prosecutor, sworn....Witness was on the 11
day of May, 1834 riding on the Alabama road, about 5 miles from
Etowa in said county he saw 2 Indians, one whom presented a gun

at him and withdrew it...he then rode past them and being in some alarm, continued to look at them until he got about 40 yards when he put off at a pretty rapid rate when the gun fired and the ball passed through his hat grazing his head thought be some to have touched the skull...prisoner was one of the Indians, though not the one who presented the gun before he came up to where they were and passed them.

X Examination:

When he first saw Indians, they were coming meeting him (witness upon X examination showed particularly by putting on his hat how it was worn, when he was shot) also stated that his horse was a horse of ordinary size and explained the manner in which he rode. Witness did not which of the Indians it was who fired the gun. When he passed them and said good evening, the prisoner replied, Wah/ which was explained by the interpreter to mean "Well!". To question by Sol. Genl., witness was on less elevated ground when the gun fired than the Indians.

George Still, sworn:

Witness states that prisoner in making confess to him was not promised anything or threatened in any way but made the confession in answer to his questions...voluntarily...Witness asked prisoner if he shot Burns, who replied that he did, and gave as a reason for it that he was a little groggy. Prisoner said that he took the gun away from the little

Page 68. (continued)

Indian who was with him and shot.

X Examination:

Prisoner did not say that Burns had given him any reason to shoot him or that he disturbed him...The jury, after a few minutes retirement returned the following verdict...Guilty...Sept. 10, 1834.   John P. Winn, Foreman

The State	)	The dft arraigned and plead guilty of assault
vs	)	verdict...dft pay fine of $5.00 & cost
David Rusk	)	J. W. Hooper, J.S.C.C.C.

The State	)	Riot
vs	)	arraigned and plead guilty...pay fine of $10.00
Hugh Rusk &	)	each and costs.
David Rusk, Jr.)		J. W. Hooper, J.S.C.C.C.

Lewis Rawlston, Respd't	)	Trespass vi et armes and false
vs	)	imprisonment...Sept. term, 1834
Joseph Lynch, S. Martin	)	...appeal dismissed as to all the
William Martin, A. Robinson,	)	defendants who has appealed, the
Neugin Snip, Ellis Beck,	)	case suspended for advisement.
Ezekiel Beck, Walter Foster	)	
N. Tinuawa & R. Saunders	)	
appelants	)	

Court adjourned until 8 o'clock tomorrow morning. (signature) John W. Hooper

Page 69. Minutes Thursday 11 Sept. 1834

Turpin, G. & William H. Atwood	)	Attachment
vs	)	Dismissed on the 8th
Henry Hammack	)	

Thursday...11 Sept. 1834. Court met pursuant to adjournment

Ambrose Harnage   ) Bill for discovery, relief acct. and
     vs   ) settlement and costs
Holman F. Simmons) Dismissed

The State   ) Larceny from the house
    vs   ) Defendants arraigned and plead not guilty
Titus & Johnson   ) not guilty
2 Cherokee Indians) William Ezzard, Sol. Gen'l.

The State   ) Simple larceny....
    vs   ) Defendant arraigned and plead not guilty
George Heard) William Ezzard, Sol. Gen'l.

Isaac Gray   ) Debts and costs
    vs   ) Dismissed
Elizabeth Ragsdale)

James Brannon   ) Assumpsit and costs
    vs   ) Dismissed
Randol McDaniel)

Ambrose Harnage, Resp.) Trover on the appeal
       vs   )
Holman F. Simmons, Appt.)

Special jury trial:

John Waggoner	James Tippen
Daniel Butler	John Wheeler
Moses Perkins	John McCanless
Robert L. Johnson	William Chamlee
Guilford W. Jones	Simeon B. Rucker
David Rusk	Peter C. Boger

...following verdict...for plff...$194.40...11 Sept. 1834...G.
W. Jones, Foreman

Page 70.

The State   ) Simple Larceny
    vs   )
George Heard)

Following jurors on this case:

James Young	James Kirkendoll
Elias Chaffin	Richard Literal
Joseph Sturdivant	Noble P. Beall
William F. Bates	William Literal
Albert A. Winn	John Brewster
Overton Hitchcock	George Post

...persons sworn and testified as follows...For the Prosecution:

Joel Leathers, sworn, says that about the time mentioned in the
Bill of Indictment (4 June 1834) the Indian Wolf, had a black
horse pony about 12 years of age such as one as is described in
the bill of indictment. He met with Wolf who professed to have
lost his pony and went with him to hunt for him. He went with
the Indian upon the poney track and came across a hickory that
appeared to have been skinned for the bark apparently to tye

the poney...witness and Indian followed the track until it
reached within about 150 yards of Heard's house which was in this
county where the pony seemed to have been tied, they then followed
the track from the place where the pony seemed to have been tied
for about 20 miles in the direction of the Chattahoochee River.
It was in Cobb county where he left the track of the pony, not
pursuing it further...where he tracked the pony near the prisoners
house h̶e̶/̶w̶e̶n̶t̶/̶t̶o̶ (marked over) to the house and prisoner was not
at home...Prisoner's wife appeared to have recently confined in
childbed. Witness said he had never seen the pony in question
since that time or some short time before the tracking aforesaid.
X Examination
Witness did not know that the pony he tracked was the pony of
Wolf (the Indian) and prosecutor Charles McGrady, sworn says that
prisoner had been to DeKalb County and back, when he told him he
had purchased a pony of Tom Blanket (an Indian) and paid him $16
for it.

Page 71. (continued)

that it was enough, had sold him for $25. It was a black pony he
said he had purchased, they were in conversation about Wolf's
pony...which was the pony prisoner said he had purchased...
Prisoner left on the 4th June and his...(wife?) had been confined
in childbed the night before he left. It was not till after it
was said that prisoner had stoled the pony and that he was about
to be arrested that he told him he had bought the pony of Tom
Blanket. Witness was at prisoner's house speaking of Wolf's pony
when prisoner's wife said in his presence that she had no doubt
but that the pony had been stoled and prisoner made no reply.
X Examination
Did not recollect whether prisoner's wife said anything about the
pony's having been stoled by Tom Blanket, did not remember that
prisoner said anything about going for meal, or that it was
scarce, or anything about meal...Question by Sol. Gen'l...It was
2-3 days after Heard came back that he told him he had taken the
pony off and sold it.
Mrs. Temperance Jay, sworn, says That she was at Prisoner's
house the night his wife was confined, she got there a little
before night, prisoner came about dark and left there before
light in the morning, and this was about the 4th of June.
X Examination
The day before prisoner had borrowed meat and lard at her house,
did not recollect whether he borrowed meal. does not think he did.
Questions by solicitor general:
Mrs. Heard was delivered of a child a little before daylight or
between midnight and day, soon after which event prisoner left.
Charles H. Nelson, sworn says that prisoner testified during the
pending of a Bill of Indictment before the Grand Jury vs Blanket
for stealing the pony, 1st that he had purchased the pony of one
Blanket one evening and left early in the morning and sold him
that day in Cobb County...upon a subsequent examination he stated
that he carried the pony into DeKalb county, kept him 3-4 days
and sold him to his brother, remained absent 7 or 8 days and
returned and that it was not until some 5 or 6 more days after
his return that he heard anything about the stealing of the pony

Page 72. (continued)

William Few, sworn knows nothing admissible. Thomas Mchaffy,
sworn says that he saw prisoner pay Blanket a pair of pantoloons

and vest and they was to call that night and get 6 yards of northern homespun.
William F. Bates, sworn says that he saw between the 1st and 5th June, an Indian riding down the hill rapidly on a pony, did not know the Indian then nor since...nor did he know the pony suppos- ed from his conduct that he was either drunk or scared. Witness lives 3 miles from Wolf's...Indian was not from direction of Wolf's but from the other direction...pony was a dark pony, seemed to be tired had seen the pony before at Blyth's Cook who lived 1/2 or 3/4 of a mile from Wolf's.
Charles McGrady recalled and asked if Prisoner was at home all day on the 4 June, said he had no recollection of having seem him that day.
It was some 4, 5 or 6 days after Heard left home before returned.
William A. Few recalled had seen Heard on the 4 June going after an old woman.
Mr. Sturdivant sworn, saw him returning same evening, got sugar and coffee from him and perhaps spirits...believe that he came again and got spirits.
Prisoner lives 1½ miles from the Sixes. Wolf lives 4 or 5 miles from Heard...does not know exactly.
Mrs. Jay recalled...says it was the day before the child was born that Mrs. Bright came to prisoners house. Mr. Few, recalled that it is 6-7 miles from Heard's to Wolf's.
C. H. Nelson recalled. Says that prisoner on his examination before the grand jury said that the pony had not the appearance when he bought him of having been rode hard...was dry and presented no evidence of having been rode hard by the Indian. Return the following verdict, to wit the jury aforesaid returned. We, the jury find the prisoner guilty...Noble P. Beall, Foreman

The court then adjourned until 1/2 past 7 o'clock tomorrow .
John W. Hooper.

Page 73. Friday Cherokee County Superior Court Minutes court met
          the 12 Sept. 1834 pursuant to adjourment

George Welch et al   )   Bill for relief and Injunction
        vs   )   The equity in the above case has been
Jesse Leonard   )   sworn off by the answer. It is ordered
                         Injunction be dissolved

Edmund Duncan &)   Bill & C
Charles Duncan   )   Chambers 4 April 1834. The deft having filed
      vs   )   his answer and sworn off the equity of the
Emariah Popham   )   Bill & no cause to the contrary being shown,
                     etc...is ordered that the rule be discharged.
          John W. Hooper, J.S.C.C.C.

David Utley & Oma Utley)   Bill & c(osts)
           vs   )   Injunction dissolved
David Stancil   )

Nelly Ragsdale)   Bill for relief and injunction
     vs   )   Injunction dissolved
John Waggoner   )

Benjamin Ragsdale   )   Bill for relief & Injunction
      vs   )   Injunction dissolved
Daniel Pitman, et al)

201

Ephraim T. Shelton) Attachment on note
      vs   ) We, the jury, to wit:
Daniel Pitman, et al)

Hiram Dimsdale	Joseph Fincher
James Young	Caleb Saunders
Curtis Satterfield	John L. Black
Plesant H. Nix	Joel Chandler
Anderson Hicks	Jarrett Chamlee
Thompson Tippen	David Stancel

find for the plff sum of $240 with interest and cost. Hiram
Dimsdale, Foreman

Page 74.   Friday 12 Sept. 1834

The State   ) Simple Larceny
   vs   ) In Cherokee Superior Court Sept. term 1834.
George Heard) Verdict of guilty: Whereupon it is considered
                     ordered and adjudged by the court that you the
said George Heard be taken from the bar of this court by the
Sheriff of the county to the common jail of Gwinnett county in
said state where you will remain until you shall be applied for
by the penitentiary guard when you will be delivered to such
guard and by such guard conveyed to the penitentiary in said
state, within the walls thereof where you will remain at labour
for the term of 4 years from the time of your reception therein
and you the said George Heard be in mercy.

The State   ) Assault with intent to murder
   vs   ) In Cherokee Superior Court: Verdict guilty
Log in Water, alias) (Sentence same as above)
Teshalooskaw   )
A Cherokee Indian)

The State   ) Larceny from the house
   vs   )
Titus & Johnson)
Cherokee Indian   )

The following named jurors were selected:

James Young	Hardy Moss
Hiram Dimsdale	John L. Black
Joel Chandler	Joseph Fincher
Thompson Tippens	Anderson Hicks
Curtis Satterfield	Jarrett Chamlee
Caleb Sanders	Pleasant H. Nix

Page 75.

Upon the hearing of which the following evidence was given in...
William Lay, sworn says about the 26th April 1834, the time
charged, witness lost a pocket book and a $10 bill & 3 cotton
handkerchiefs, red stamped, price 25¢ each, 1 worsted vest price
$1.50 found 1 of the handkerchiefs in the bush. Johnson admitted
he had taken the things and went and showed the things where he
had hid them the handkerchief and vest, so soon as Titus was
charged he went off round the house, the goods, and ____ were
taken from the storehouse of witness in Cherokee county.
Cross:
The Indians were drinking...this was in the afternoon, got the
spirits from witness pranks had not been practiced of that

character.
Curtis Satterfield, sworn says
Saw Titus hide the handkerchief on the day alleged at the storehouse of the prosecutor hid it under another Indian, saw the other
articles, the vest and 2 handerchiefs, found and heard Johnson
acknowledge the taking of the things...Cross examined does not
think from the manner of the acts that the things were hid in a
jest...when the vest and 2 handkerchiefs were found Johnson said
he knew nothing of the pocketbook that the vest and handkerchiefs
were all he took. Johnson was asleep when Titus hid the 1st
handkerchief, Titus said Johnson had the pocketbook. After the
hearing the following verdict, to wit:
We, the jury returned the following prisoners guilty of the
charge. Sept. 12, 1834.   Hiram Dimsdale, Foreman

The State   ) Larceny from the house
    vs   ) In Cherokee Superior Court Sept. term 1834
Titus & Johnson   ) Verdict Guilty
Cherokee Indians   )

Whereupon it is considered ordered and

Page 76.   (continued) Friday 12 Sept. 1834

Adjudged by the court that you the said Titus and Johnson,
Cherokee Indians be taken from the bars of this court by the
sheriff of this county to the common jail of Gwinnett county in
said state where you will remain until you shall be applied for
by the Penitentary guard when you will be delivered to such guard
and by such guard conveyed to the pentitentary in said state
where you will remain at LABOUR for the term of 4 years from the
time of your reception therein, and you Titus and Johnson be in
mercy.

Wilson Lumpkin, Governor) Judgment of forfeited Recognizance
        vs   ) A rule ni si having been taken at
George S. Bradford   ) the last term of this court calling
                             on the Superior Court to show cause
why the judgment in the above case should not be set aside...and
sufficient cause having been shewn, it is therefore ordered that
the said rule be discharged and the judgment proceed.

The State   ) Cattle stealing
    vs   ) True Bill
George Heard) John McConnell, Foreman

The State   ) Malicious mischief
    vs   ) True Bill
Tagah Togah, alias   )
Stand alias   ) John McConnell, Foreman
Standing up, an Indian)

The State   ) Riot
    vs   ) True Bill against Roger Green,
Roger Green, Hardy Moss,   ) Hardy Moss & John Edwards. No Bill
John Edwards & William Lay) against William Lay...John McConnell,
                                 Foreman

Page 77. Minutes of Superior Court Cherokee County

203

Joseph Smith   )   The sheriff having raised a certain amount
    vs   )   of money on the above fi fa ordered that he
Joseph S. Doyle   )   pay over to the plff or his atty the sum of
                           $5.31¼

The State   )   Malicious Mischief
    vs   )   The deft arraigned and plead not Guilty
Tegah Togah alias   )   John J. Word, Sol. protem
Stand alias Standing,   )
an Indian

The following persons were drawn to serve at the next term of
this court as Grand Jurors, to wit:

1. Joseph S. Dial	2. Benj. F. Johnston
3. Daniel Methvin	4. Charles McGrady
5. Amos Chaffin	6. Burton Mullins
7. John Epperson	8. Smith A. McCracken
9. John W. Leonard	10. Jacob Avery
11. James Cooper	12. Lodowick Mix
13. John G. Maddox	14. Felix Moss
15. William Whitaker	16. Reuben F. Daniel
17. James Jordan	18. Noble P. Beall
19. Tilmon Chamlee	20. Edward Townsend
21. George Brock	22. William M. McAfee
23. Robert T. Griffin	24. Noble Timmons
25. Elisha Dooly	26. Joseph Donaldson
27. George M. Smith	28. William Tate, Jr.
29. John H. King	30. Andrew Scott
31. John Edwards	32. Absalom C. Avery

Page 78. Georgia, Friday 12 Sept. 1834

Following persons were drawn to serve at the next term of court
to serve as Petit Jurors

1. Jesse Wallis	2. John Miller
3. George A. Boalch	4. Abner Phillips
5. Simon Tate	6. Charles Blythe
7. John M. Mullens	8. William Tippens
9. John P. Wiley	10. Arch'd Cogburn
11. John Seamore	12. Bryant Ingram
13. Martin Chamlee	14. John Naylor
15. James Copeland	16. Elias Barnett
17. Tho. B. Wells	18. Henry Right
19. Blar Studard	20. Harley A. Sawyer
21. Wm. P. Nix	22. Emariah Popham
23. Reuben Harrison	24. Joho S. Bobo
25. James Ellard	26. Wm. Tribble
27. Alex. Miller	28. Eli Grimes
29. Steph. Bates	30. Wiley Barber
31. John Landrum	32. Saml' Timmons
33. Isaac George	34. Geo. McKaskle, Jr.
35. Wm. Holland	36. Geo. Hinkle
37. Augus McCormick	38. John Daniel
39. John Timmons	40. Stephen Kemp
41. Curtis Satterfield	42. Robert Blyth
43. John Pugh	44. Alfred Dickens
45. Jos. H. Bradford	46. John Robers
47. Tho. J. Bates	48. Jona. Crow

```
The State                    )  Malicious Mischief
     vs                      )
Tagah Togah alias Stand      )
alias Standing Up            )
an Indian                    )
```

We the Jury, to wit:

1. Richard Literal	2. Wm. Wayne
3. Wm. Ward	4. Jordan Brock
5. Elias Chaffin	6. Wm. Few
7. Wm. M. Bird	8. Charles A. Sawyer
9. Thos Johnson	10. Jas Kirkendoll
11. Robert Blythe	12. Carlton Ragsdale

find the prisoner guilty of killing one hog. Wm. Ward, Foreman.

```
F. C. Andoe      )  Debt & Costs
     vs          )  I confer to the plff for $40 principal with
W. W. B. Key     )  interest and costs of suit.  12 Sept. 1834
                        Howell Cobb, dft's atty
```

```
The State        )  Malicious Mischief
     vs          )  Verdict of guilty; whereupon it is considered
Tagah Togah      )  ordered and adjudged by court that prisoner pay
alias Stand      )  a fine of $10 and cost and upon payment of fine
                 )  & costs be discharged
```

Page 79. Minutes of Superior Court of Cherokee

```
Hardy Moss, plff in fi fa    )
        vs                   )
Ephraim Downing dft &        )
Lizzie Downing claimant      )
```

We the jury:

1. Hiram Dimsdale	2. Joseph Fincher
3. James Young	4. Caleb Saunders
5. Curtis Satterfield	6. John L. Black
7. Pleasant H. Nix	8. Joel Chandler
9. Anderson Hicks	10. Jarrett Chamlee
11. Thompson Tippens	12. Anderson Hicks

find the property subject...Joseph Fincher, Foreman

```
The State        )  Assault & Battery
     vs          )  True Bill
Roger Green      )  John McConnell, Foreman
```

```
A. Harnage       )  Trover & Costs
     vs          )  The dft after the appeal in this case was tried
H. F. Simmons    )  and verdict rendered comes forward and render.
                        John M. McConnell as security on the stay of
the levy of the execution of both the appelant security acknow-
ledge themselves bound to the plff for principal, interest &
costs.  (signed by John M. McConnell)    H. F. Simmons
```

```
John R. Standford            )  Plff in fi fa
        vs                   )  Dismissed
Wm. A. McMillan, dft &       )
John Ragsdale, a garnishee   )
```

205

Russell Shipley) Bill to acct & for discovery
   vs   ) Dismissed
Nelson Dickerson)

McJunkin & Smith) Fi Fa Illegality taken
   vs   ) Illegality dismissed
Henry Fitzsimmons)

Page 80. Co. Georgia Fri. 12th Sept. 1834

Presentment of the Grand Jury of Cherokee County Sept. term 1834
.....Grand Jury sworn.....make following presentments.....We
recommend to the Inferior Court of our county a more energetic
enforcement of the road laws, altho much has been done yet con-
sidering the mountainous situation of our county, we deem it
absolutely necessary for that body to make extraordinary exertions in the improvement of the publick roads, expecially those
necessary to make a safe communication of the different interests
of our citizens. We have noticed with regret the rapid increase
of cases upon the criminal docket of our county and we sincerely
hope that all good citizens of the county will act in concert in
the laudable undertaking of suppressing this state of immorality
so disgraceful to a civilized community. We preceive with the
highest approbation the determination of the people to protect
the Indians in the enjoyment of their rights secured to them by
law, the vicious white man is taught to know that injuries done
them are not to escape unpunished. That prosecutions will be
preferred and urged against all persons that do wrong to the
Indians, either in person or property. (Then follows an entire
page of discussion of the nullification of the United States
Bank).

Page 81.

We urge upon our next legislature the great necessity of adopting
some means calculated to meet the untiring efforts of Gen'l
Jackson for a speedy disposition of our Indian Difficulties at
least so far as to afford protection to the lives of our
Cherokee brethern who are willing to avail themselves of the
humane efforts of the general government by a removal to the
west, as under the existing Cherokee regulations, no Cherokee
dare advocate measure of the government without eminent peri or
loss of life. We would recommend to the legislature the creation
of some tribunal calculated to ensure an uniform administration
of the laws of this state. We would also recommend to the next
legislature the urgent necessity of a reorganizating of the
militia system of this state, placing it upon a more efficient
and respectable footing...so important an arm of our peculiar
government and our still more peculiar situation...from a mixed
population with interests at war with our rights, would admonish
any prudent people to cherish with peculiar care a bulwark so
necessary to their defence and security. We take much pleasure
in saying that the spirit of internal improvement that engages
the attention of the people of Georgia receives our highest approbation situated so far as we are from a common market we
anticipate gladly the time when Rome shall flourish and furnish
the benefits of a market to the people of this section of the
state by the use of the beautiful river upon which it is situated
and a railroad that we expect will be connected to pass through
it. We have examined the books of John B. Garrison, the Tax
Collector of year 1832 and have allowed him the sum of $6.62½ cts

for his unsolvent list of this county

Page 82.

also we have allowed him the sum of $352.93 the amount that is
not in his power to collect as it is due from other counties that
were originally included in the county of Cherokee. We have
examined the books of the Treasurer and find them fairly kept.
We present Jesse Greene for retailing spirits without license
and for retailing spirits on the Sabath, also for selling and
furnishing negroes with spirits in the county on the 10th of
July last, witnesses: Thomas Hendricks, Dozier Sutton, Dred
Patterson, Archibald Taylor, & Elam Boke. We present James
Minton and Elizabeth Lindsey for living in a state of adultery,
witnesses Wm. May and John Cannon. We present Roger Green and
David Utley for a breach of the peace on 9 Sept. Inst. Witnesses
Edwin Mims & R. L. Johnston. We Tender to His Honor John W.
Hooper and the Solicitor General Wm. Ezzard our thanks for their
zealour attention to business during this term. We request that
our presentments of a public nature be published in the Standard
Union and Southern Whig.
John McConnell, Foreman; Edwin Mims; R. L. Johnston; James S.
Elliott; Peter C. Boger; John Wheeler; James Tippen; C. H. Nelson;
Wm. Chambly; Thos. Townsend; Elisha Dyer; Daniel Butler; David
Rusk.   (Then follows a disavowal of the sentiments expressed
concerning national affairs as pouring fuel upon a fire and sign-
ed by follwoing): Holman F. Simmons; Robertus S. Sparks; G. W.
Jones; I. A. Few; John Waits; Moses Perkins; S. B. Rucker; John
McCanless; John Wagoner

Adjourment signed by Judge and Clerk of Court

Page 83.   Minutes of Superior Court...9 March 1835...John W.
            Hooper. Judge of Cherokee Circuit, Ga.

Following...grand jurors...this term

1. Noble P. Beall, Foreman	2. Noble Timmons
3. Andrew Scott	4. Lodowick Nix
5. Smith A. McCracken	6. James Cooper
7. William Whitaker	8. John Epperson
9. Burton Mullens	10. Elisha Dooly
11. John H. King	12. George Brock
13. Benjamin F. Johnston	14. Reuben F. Daniell
15. Charles McGrady	16. Amos Chaffin
17. John W. Leonard	18. Jacob Avery
19. Felis Moss	20. Robert T. Griffin
21. Joseph Donaldson	22. Absalom C. Avery

...Following...Petit Jury #1 at this term

1. Samuel Timmons	2. Stephen Bates
3. Curtis Satterfield	4. George Hinckle
5. John Miller	6. John Landrum
7. Stephen Kemp	8. John M. Mullens
9. Jesse Wallis	10. William P. Nix
11. Alexander Miller	12. Robert Blythe

(and C. F. Lay in pencil in different hand)

James A. Maddox, constable was sworn to serve as constable and
wait on grand jury this term...William Nix, constable sworn to
attend on Jury #1...

Page 84. .....9 March 1835

The State	)	Simple Larceny
vs	)	True Bill
Sequakes, an Indian	)	Noble P. Beall, Foreman

The Governor on the	)	Scire Facias on (land lot) #122/14/2
information of	)	I confess judgment to the dft for cost
William W. B. Key	)	9 March 1835
vs	)	D. R. Mitchell, Atty pro infr.
William A. Crombie	)	

The Governor on the	)	Scire Facias
information of	)	I confess judgment to dft for cost with
Minor S. Langford	)	liability of appeal.
vs	)	J. Choice, atty pro informant
Thomas Millican	)	

Wilson Lumpkin, Governor	)	Sci fa #86/14/2
on information of	)	We, the jury find the return fradulent
Reuben Cone	)	John T. Landrum, Foreman
vs	)	
Littleton Ivay alias Joy	)	

Following...Jury #2...this term

1. George A. Post
2. Lewis W. Reinhardt
3. Charles F. Lay
4. William K. McCanless
5. Thomas Copeland
6. Eli Grimes
7. Elias Narbett
8. John Timmon
9. George A. Balch
10. Roger Green
11. William Brooke
12. James Wilson

and thereupon Littleton C. Edwards was sworn to serve and wait on said jury...this term

The Governor on the	)	Scire facias on #1050/21/2
information of	)	We, the jury find the return
Jacob Martin	)	fradulent
vs	)	James Willson, Foreman
Pyent E. Jackson	)	

Page 85.   Minutes of Superior Court   Cherokee

The State	)	Simple Larceny
vs	)	True Bill
Tutleartah alias	)	Noble P. Beall, Foreman
Toothpick alias	)	
Two Pick	)	

The Governor on	)	Sci fa
information of	)	Dismissed
Jacob Martin	)	
vs	)	
Epps Moss	)	

Jonathan J. Johnston	)	Care and costs
vs	)	We find for plff $300 with cost of suit
Thomas Mehaffey	)	John T. Landrum, Foreman

In Cherokee Superior Court 9 March 1835, on motion ordered that the clerk have leave to enter the following order nunk pro tunk.

208

The State   ) Hog Stealing
   vs   ) In Cherokee Superior Court
John Kimbal and   )
Butler Kimbal   )

The State   ) Digging for gold
   vs   )
James Downing alias   )
Blanket's Wife &   )
Lucy Doghead   )

The State   ) Hog Stealing
   vs   )
Thomas Woodall   )

It appears to court that the sum of $25 is due by the annexed
account to Daniel R. Mitchell as late Solicitor General protem.
It is ordered that the.....clerk pay to said DRM said sum of $25
out of any money in his hands arising from fines and forfeiture
not otherwise appropriated...12 Sept. 1834...John W. Hooper,
J.S.C.C.C.

Page 86.   County...Ga...Monday...9 March 1835

Rec'd of William Grisham Clerk of Cherokee Superior Court $25 in
full payment of the within order...12 Sept. 1834...D.R. Mitchell

The State   ) Retailing Spirits, without license
   vs   ) Nol. Pros.
Jesse Green   ) William Ezzard, Solicitor General

William Nix) Malicious Prosecution
   vs   ) We, the jury find verdict of $300 with cost of
John Nix   ) suit in favor of plff. James Willson, Foreman

Governor of Georgia   ) Scire facias against drawer of #146/4/2
on information of   ) and judgment confessed to the dft for
Minor S. Lankford   ) cost of suit. The informant being dis-
   vs   ) satisfied with the confession of judg-
James Millican, exor   ) ment in above cause and having paid all
of Thomas Millican,   ) costs and demanded an appeal brings John
dec'd   ) H. King and tenders him as his security
                         and they the said Minor S. Lankford and
John H. King acknowledge themselves, jointly and severally bound
to James Millican, exor of Thomas Millican, dec'd the dft for
production of eventual condemnation money in hands and seal...
this 9 March 1835...(signature of John H. King and Josiah Choice
as attorney for Minor S. Lankford). Test. William Grisham, Clk.

Page 87.

Governor of Ga.   ) Sci fa against drawer of #114/14/2
on information of   ) Dismissed
Collier Foster   )
   vs   )
Nancy Holland   )

Governor on information of) Sci fa against drawer of #109/4/2
James S. Mitchell   ) Dismissed
   vs   )
William Townsend   )

209

Governor on information of) Sci fa
David C. Neal) Dismissed
   vs)
William Townsend)

Governor on information of) Sci fa
James Wood) Dismissed
   vs)
Pyent E. Jackson)

Court adjourned until half after 8 o'clock tomorrow morning
Signed: John W. Hooper....Test. William Grisham, clerk.

Page 88.   Court met...10 March 1835...

Governor on information of) Sci fa
John Wells) Dismissed
   vs)
Pyent E. Jackson)

Kellogg & Sanford) Debt & Costs
   vs) I confess judgment to plff for $123.53 3/4
Burton Mullens) with interest and cost of suit. 10 March
              1835...William Daniel, Dft. atty.

C. Squire & S. Rogers) Debt and costs
   vs) I confess judgment to plff for $135.58
Benjamin F. Johnston) with interest & cost. B.F. Johnston

John Miller was placed on Jury #2 and C. F. Lay on Jury #1

Israel Gilbert) Debt and Cost
   vs) I confess judgment to plff for $125.85
Benjamin F. Johnston) with interest & cost...B.F. Johnston

George R. Gilmer, governor) Case for rent
   vs) Settled
James Crow, Sam'l Tate and)
Edward Townsend)

Thomas A. Lathem) Assumpsit
   vs) I confess judgment to plff for $60.37½
William Daniel &) principal with interest & cost
John Burke, Indr.) William Daniel

Page 89. Tuesday...10 March 1835...

M. W. Perry & Co.) I confess judgment to plff for $1,010.87
   vs) with interest and cost of suit...10
Sanuel C. Candler) March 1835 against Samuel C. Candler &
Benjamin D. Chapman &) Abner Chapman
Abner Chapman) Howell Cobb, Dft's. atty.

Isaac Gilbert) Debt and costs
   vs) I confess judgment to the plff for
E. Henderson & Co.) $199.25 plus interest and cost...10 March
              1835...Wm. Daniell, Dft's. atty.

Lemuel Smith) Debt and costs
for the use of) I confess judgment for $110 and interest
William W. McKnight) and cost...10 March 1835
     vs) Wm. Daniell, Dft's atty.
Elias Henderson &)
Charles H. Nelson)

Wm. W. McKnight) Debt and cost
Indorsee) I confess judgment to plff for $110 and
    vs) interest and costs....10 March 1835
E. H. & C. Nelson)   Wm. Daniell, Dft's atty.

James W. Jones) Debt and costs
    vs) I confess judgment on within to plff for
Burton Mullens) $57.50 principal plus interest and costs.
                10 March 1835...Wm. Daniell, Dfts. atty.

Caleb Goodlittle, ex dem) Ejectant
Wm. Ward) After the case was submitted to
    vs) the jury it is ordered that
Peter Holdfast, camel ejector) Seaborn Woodcock be and he is
Wm. Ward, tenant) hereby made co-defendent in the
                     above case

Caleb Goodtitle, ex dem) Trespass and Ejectment
Wm. Ward) We, the jury find for the dft
    vs) with cost of suit
Peter Holdfast, casual ejector) James Willson, Foreman
Wm. Lay, tenant in possession)

Page 90. Superior Court...Tuesday...10 March 1835

Wm. Nix) Malicious prosecution
   vs) Verdict for plff for $300 and cost. The dft being
John Nix) dissatisfied with the verdict of jury rendered in
        the above case and having paid all costs and demanded
an appeal brings Charles Nix and tenders him as his security and
they the said John Nix and Charles Nix...bound to Wm. Nix, plff
for payment of the eventual condemnation money...10 March 1835.
John Nix (actual signature)...Charles X Nix (with his mark)

Robert Williams, admr of) Debt and cost
estate of Moses Whitsitt,) Settled
dec'd   vs)
Thomas R. Wells)

James Barmore, admr) Debt and cost
of Henry Dobson, decd) Settled
    vs)
Thomas B. Wells)

Felix Moss) Assumpsit
    vs) Settled
Lewsunday, Echa Archa, Soap)
Shuates & Lawny)
Cherokee Indians)

Luke Reed & Co.) Debt
    vs) Settled
Eli McConnell)
Court adjourned until 8 o'clock tomorrow morning....

Page 91.   Wednesday...11 March 1835...Cherokee Court met...

GA:)   To Honorable Superior Court...
Cherokee Co.   )   Petition of Jonathan Johnson shews that James
                             Gray on 13 April 1833 executed to your petitioner
a mortgage deed upon lot of land #272/14/2...securing the payment
of a promissory note made by the said James Gray...for sum of
$92.67...due 25 Dec. 1823 (should have been 1833)...said note is
due and wholly unpaid...therefore prays court to grant him an
order ni si for foreclosure...Z. B. Hargrove, atty for petitioner
...It is on motion ordered by court that said James Gray...the
entire amount of principal and interest due upon said note as
well as all costs...

Page 92.

...ordered that a copy of this rule be published in some one of
public gazettes of this state once a month for 4 months or
served upon said James Gray or his special agent or atty....

Daniel Butler   )   Trespass & cost
     vs   )   Settled
Davis Rusk, Senr   )

Daniel Butler   )   Trespass & cost
     vs   )   Settled
Davis Rusk, Jr. &   )
H. L. Rusk   )

Governor on information of)   Rule ni si
of Wm. Martin   )   2 cases of Sci fa
     vs   )   Rule discharged and judgment
Pyent E. Jackson   )   entered

Valentine Nash   )   Rule ni si requiring Wm. Daniel, atty to
     vs   )   shew case and cost
James Hawthorn   )   Rule discharged

Sam' McJunkin   )   Fi fa from a justice court of Walton Co....
     vs   )   having been levied upon lot #987/2/2 in
Griffin Owen   )   Cherokee County and...advertised for sale on
                         1st Tuesday in Oct. 1833 which was bid off by
Samuel McJunkin who failed to have a deed executed to him for
said lot by John P. Brooke who was at that time Sheriff...It is
ordered by court that Samuel Candler who is present Sheriff for
county of Cherokee execute a deed to said Samuel McJunkin for
said lot....R. M. Holt, plff's. atty.

Page 92.   Wednesday...11 March 1835...Minutes

Samuel Leathers having been bound for his appearance at this
term of court...upon a recognizance to keep the peace, and no
person appearing to prosecute said Samuel and no other matter or
things existing why said Samuel should not be discharged from his
said...ordered...discharged from liability

Jack Still   )   Judgment for cost
     vs   )   On motion of counsel for Jack Still it is ordered
Roger Green   )   that the attorney for Roger Green shew cause on
                   the 1st of July of next term or as soon as
counsel can be heard why the jury in above case should not be set

aside on the ground that Jack Still never commenced such action,
and if ever such as action was commenced it was done without
knowledge or consent of Jack Still and that all further proceedings be staid in the meantime...S. Rockwell, Baron & Irwin

Ga   ) To Honorable John W. Hooper, Judge of
Cherokee County   ) Superior Court, petition of undersigned
                               respectfully sheweth that he has read law
and desires to be admitted to plead and practice law in the several courts of law and equity in this state...10 March 1835...
Smith A. McCracken

I do certify that I am acquainted with Smith A. McCracken that
he is 21 years of age of good moral character and that he has
studied law....March term 1835.....Howell Cobb

(follows repition of above application & admittance of all
privledges of an attorney, solicitor and counsellor in several
courts of law & equity...)

In testimony whereof the presiding judge has hereunto set his
hand with the seal of the court in a private manner there being
no seal of court...this 11 March 1835...John W. Hooper

Page 93.

....I, Smith A. McCracken, do solemnly swear that I will justly
and uprightly demean myself, according to law as an attorney
counselor and solicitor and that I will support and defend the
Constitution of United States and Constitution of the state of
Georgia, so help me God....Smith A. McCracken
Sworn to and subscribed in open court his 11 March 1835...Test:
William Grisham, Clk.

The State   ) Malicious mischief
    vs   ) True Bill
William Priest   ) Noble P. Beall, Foreman

The State   ) Simple larceny
    vs   ) Defendent arraigned and pled not guilty
Tutleartah   ) Wm. Ezzard, Sol. Gen...We, the jury find deft.
alias toothpick   ) guilty
alias Two Pick   ) James Willson, foreman

The State   ) Riot
    vs   ) Defendant Roger Greene pled guilty...and
Roger Greene   ) considered by court that deft Roger Greene pay
Hardy Moss &   ) fine of $10 and cost and upon payment he be
John Edwards   ) discharged...John W. Hooper, J.S.C.C.C.

The State   ) Extortion
    vs   ) No bill & malicious prosecution
William Nix   ) Noble P. Beall, Foreman

The State   ) Assault & battery
    vs   ) Defendant arraigned and pled not guilty...We, the
Roger Green   ) jury find deft not guilty...John T. Landrum,
                    Foreman

Page 94.   Wednesday...11th March 1835...Cherokee Co. Superior
              Court

CHEROKEE COUNTY SUPERIOR COURT MINUTES

The State   ) Indian in Cherokee Superior Court
  vs   ) Simple larceny
Sequashee) The jury in the above case returned into court
               a verdict if not guilty, it is on motion ordered
that the saddle bridle and quilts be returned to the said Sequashee by the officer who has them in possession

Lewis Ralston   ) Fi Fa
  vs   ) Ordered that the affadavit of
S. Martin-Wm. Martin   ) illigality be dismissed and that
A. Robinson-Neugin Smith) the execution proceed
Ellis Beck-Ezekiel Beck)
Walter Foster-N. Tenuawa)
and Robert Saunders   )

The State   ) Simple larceny
  vs   ) Verdict of guilty Whereupon...it is considered,
Tutleartah   ) ordered and adjudged by the court that the
alias Toothpick) dft be confined and imprisoned in the common
alias two Pick) jail of Cherokee County for term of 30 days
                and upon the payment of cost at end of that
time the prisoner be discharged and the dft be in mercy

The State   ) Simple larceny
  vs   ) Copy of indictment and list of witnesses waived
Sequakee,   ) before arraignment 11 March 1835...Barron & Irwin,
an Indian   ) dfts. atty...The dft. arraigned and pled not
              guilty...William Ezzard, Sol. Gen.

The State   ) Simple larceny
  vs   ) Not guilty
Sequahee,   ) Wm. C. Brooke, Foreman
an Indian   )

...following jurors:

1. Curtis Satterfield   2. George Hinckle
3. John M. Mullens   4. Wm. P. Nix
5. Robert Blyth   6. George A. Post
7. John Miller   8. Wm. K. McCanless
9. Eli Grimes   10. John Timmons
11. Wm. Brooke   12. Pleasant H. Nix

Page 95.

The State   ) Riot
  vs   ) Nol. pros as to Hardy Moss and John Edwards
Roger Green) Wm. Ezzard, Sol. Gen.
Hardy Moss   )
John Edwards)

Caleb Goodtitle ex   ) Trespass & ejectment
dem: Wm. Ward   ) Verdict for dft and cost
    vs   )
Peter Holdfast, casual ejector)
Seaborn Woodcock, made Co-dft)

The plaintiff being dissatisfied with the verdict of the jury
rendered in the above case and having paid all costs and demanded
an appeal, brings Reuben F. Daniel and tenders him as his
security and they the said William Ward by his attorney at law
Samuel Rockwell and Reuben F. Daniel acknowledge themselves

214

jointly and severally bound to William Lay, tenant in possession and Seaborn Woodcock (made co-dft)...the dft for the payment of the eventual condemnation money in said case...In testimony thereof, they have hereunto set their hands and seals, this 12 March 1835...(Original signature of R. F. Daniel)...att: William Grisham, clerk

Young Johnson and) Distress warrant for rent
William Ward   ) Jury...find favor of dft.
    vs   ) John T. Landrum, Foreman
John P. Brooke   )

Court adjourned until 8:00 tomorrow morning...Test: Wm. Grisham, Clk...John W. Hooper, J.S.C.C.C.

Page 96. Thursday...12 March 1835...Cherokee County Superior Court

William Nix) Case & costs
    vs   ) Ordered by court that plff has leave to withdraw
John Nix   ) his interrogatories taken in above case, which
             are defectively executed and have them re-executed.

Young Johnson and) Distress warrant for rent
William Ward   ) Verdict for dft. for cost...the plff being
    vs   ) dissatisfied with verdict of jury rendered
John P. Brooke   ) ...and having paid all costs and demanded
                   an appeal beings (blank)____ and tenders
as their security and they, the said Young Johnson and William
Ward by S. Rockwell, his attorney at law and (blank) ask themselves jointly and severally bound to John P. Brooke for the deft
for the payment of the eventual condemnation money in said case...
this -- day of March 1835...

The Governor on the information of) Sci fa
James Wood   ) Dismissed
    vs   )
Pyent E. Jackson   ) Drawer of #108/4/2

William Ward   ) Case judgment confessed for the plff for
    vs   ) $750 with interest from 1st Feb. 1834 with
Joseph Donaldson   ) cost of suit...Joseph Donaldson

Ambrose Harnage   ) Bill for discovery, relief and account
    vs   ) Dismissed
Holm. F. Simmons   )

D. H. Bird, plff in fifa) Claim of negro boy, Jonathan
    vs   ) We, the jury find the property
Wm. W. B. Key, dft   ) John T. Landrum, Foreman
& T. W. Key, claimant   )

Page 97.

The State   ) Assault with intent to murder
    vs   ) True Bill
Edward Edwards) Noble P. Beall, Foreman
          (Repeats above twice)

The State   ) Assault with intent to murder
    vs   ) Copy of indictment and list of witnesses
Edward Edwards) before arraignment and the dft arraigned and
                 pled not guilty...Wm. Ezzard, Sol. Gen.
(Repeats the above twice)

215

The Governor on information of) Sci fa
John P. Brooke, appellant   ) Appeal
          vs   ) Dismissed
Milton M. Ham, respondent   ) Drawer of #167/14/2

Page 98. Thursday...12 March 1835...Superior Court

The State) Assault & Battery		$ 5.00	$ 3.75
vs) No Bill			
Roger Green)			
The State) Ass & Bett			
vs) No Bill			
Hardy Moss)		5.00	3.75
The State) Riot		10.00	
vs) Noe pros			
Jos H. Bradford) Geo S. G & Nulbona			
& G. S. Bradford)			
The State) Ass & Batt			
vs) Noe pros		5.00	
The State) Ass. with intent to murder		5.00	3.75
vs) nula pros			
Log in Water)			
The State) Larceny		10.00	3.75
vs) Guilty nul bona			
Titus & Johnson)			
The State) Horse stealing		5.00	3.75
vs) Not guilty			
E. Atkerson)			
The State) Horse stealing		5.00	3.75
vs) Guilty-nul bona			
Geo. Heard)			
The State) Malicious mischief		5.00	3.75
vs) Guilty-nul bona			
Tagahtogah)			
The State) Hog stealing		5.00	3.75
vs) No Bill			
Tagahtogah)			
The State) Assault & Battery		10.00	3.75
vs) No Bill			
Daniel Davis &)			
Alsey Harris)			
The State) Assault & battery		5.00	3.75
vs) No Bill			
Jona N. Johnson)			
The State) Horse stealing		5.00	3.75
vs) No Bill			
Tom Blanket)			

The State vs Wiley, an Ind.	) Assault with int. to murder) No Bill)	$ 5.00	$ 3.75
The State vs Roger Green	) Assault & Battery) Not guilty)	5.00	3.75
The State vs Sequahee, Ind.	) Simple larceny) Not guilty)	5.00	3.75
The State vs Two Prick, Ind.	) Simple larceny) Guilty)	5.00	3.75
		$100.00	$56.25

....$100 due to William Ezzard, Sol. Gen. and sum of $56.25 to
William Grisham, Clerk for fee in above cases therefore ordered
same be paid out of any monies arising from fines & forfeitures.

The State   ) Assault with intent to murder
  vs   )
Edward Edwards   )

...Following persons sworn for jury:

1. Samuel Timmons   2. Curtis Satterfield
3. John Landrum   4. John M. Mullins
5. Alexander Miller   6. John Miller
7. John Tunnious (?)   8. William Brooke
9. James Wilson   10. John F. Winn
11. Robert Blyth   11. Ferd. Bailey

...find defendent guilty of an assault and battery...March 12,
1835....John P. Winn, Foreman

Page 99.

Daniel H. Bird, plff   ) Fi fa
  vs   ) Claim and verdict for claimant for
William W. B. Key, dft. &   ) cost. Plff in Fi Fa being dis-
Tandy W. Key, claimant   ) satisfied with the verdict jury
                                rendered and having paid all cost
and demanded an appeal, brings Joseph Donaldson and tenders him
as security...to Tandy W. Key the claimant...13 March 1835.
(Original signature of Daniel H. Bird and Joseph Donaldson).

The State   ) (The same case as on bottom of last page)
  vs   ) Assault with intent to murder
Edward Edwards)

Following persons selected and sworn as jurors on this case, to
wit:

1. Samuel Timmons   2. Curtis Satterfield
3. John Landrum   4. John M. Mullens
7. John Timmons   8. William Brooke
9. James Willson   10. John P. Winn
11. Robert Blyth   12. Ferdinand Bailey

(Where are 5 & 6 ?)

217

The following was the evidence taken down by His Honor John W. Hooper, Judge of said court on the trial of said issue.

Indian Chevey says through sworn interpretters John Martin and George Still on yesterday there were some lightwood knots lying near the parties, prisoner took up one and struck the party alleged in the indictment to have been stricken and struck him upon the head and inflicted the wound upon Downing which is exhibited and is a severe wound, that prisoner and an Indian named Poor Shoat were quarrelling, the Indian was very drunk and spoke in English and, this witness does not know what they said, that Downing was not quarreling.

Cross examine-Question was any whiskey thrown in prisoner's face? Witness says he witness after prisoner had knocked down the Indian he threw some whiskey into the face of the prisoner.

Page 100.   Thursday...12 March 1835...Cherokee Co., Superior Court Minutes   (continued from previous page)

was not guns used by the Indian and attempts to use them upon the prisoner? Witness answers after prisoner had knocked down the Indians, he got a gun. Who had the whiskey? Blanket or Downing had whiskey-does not know how prisoner came there. Did he not go after his horse? Thinks he did his horse was there.

Jury returned following verdict, to wit...guilty of assault and battery...March 12, 1835...John P. Winn, Foreman (original signature)......Court adjourned until 8 o'clock tomorrow morning. John W. Hooper...Test: William Grisham, clerk

Friday...13 March 1835

The Gov. on information on) Sci fa on #122/14/2
of Wm. W. G. Key and   ) Judgment confessed to the dft for
Wm. A. Crombie   ) cost of suit. The informant being
                             dissatisfied with the confession
entered in the above case, and having paid all costs and demanded an appeal brings Tandy W. Key, William Grisham and tenders them as his security and they the said Wm. W. B. Key by Daniel R. Mitchell, his atty at law...acknowledge...bound to Wm. A. Crombie the dft for the payment of the eventual condemnation money in said case...Wm. W. B. Key by Daniel Mitchell...14th March 1835... Tandy W. Key (original signature)...William Grisham...Test: Wm. Grisham, clerk.

The Gov. on information of) Sci fa
James Wood   ) Dismissed
   vs   ) Drawer of #60/13/2
Pyent E. Jackson   )

Page 101.

John Conyer) Debt and cost
   vs   ) March term 1835 in Superior Court of said county
John Duncan) Whereas in the above case a bail process was
              issued against the dft and whereas Lewis Ralston
became bound as his security and judgment was afterwards rendered against the said dft and the said Lewis having failed to produce the body of the said dft after judgment, on motion it is ordered that the sheriff assign said bond to plff that a Scire Facias may be legally issued thereon.

Lewis Ralston   ) Trespass viet armies and
    vs   ) false imprisonment
Joseph Linch, Samiel Martin   )
William Martin, Amos Richardson,) In Cherokee Superior Court
Neugin Snip, Ellis Beck,   )
Ezekiel Beck, Walter Foster,   )
Nelson Tennwa

It is ordered on motion of dft <u>council</u>, who have not appealed
that the plff or his <u>counsel</u> show cause on or before the last
day of next term why the judgment in the above case should not
be set aside on the following ground:
1st because the judgment does not conform to the verdict rendered
in said case and the judgment entered against several dfts.
2nd That the verdict is uncertain and therefore no judgment can
be entered upon it...and in the meantime all further proceedings
be staid in said case and that a copy of this rule be served upon
plff's <u>council</u>...Service of above acknowledged March 13, 1835...
R. Mitchell by D. R. Mitchell, Plff's atty.

John Larrimore, plff in   ) Claim of a cow & heifer
execution   vs   ) Levy dismissed so far as to the
C. Taylor, J. McCanless,   ) property claimed
W. K. McCanless & Samuel   )
Thompson, claimant   )

Page 102.   Friday...13 March 1835...Minutes of Superior Court

We, the grand jury...presentments...examined the books of Tax
Collector and allowed him for his insolvent list $25 state tax...
Examined the books of the county treasurer and find them regularly
kept...books of clerk of Inferior Court and find them regularly
kept...and in good order...examined books of Clerk of Superior
Court...regularly kept and in good order...We would also request
Inferior Court of said county to strickly enforce the road laws
of the county as we find them in bad order. We present David
Quals of said county for the offence of retailing spiritous
liquors without license...on 18th day of Feb. 1835...did sell to
John Woodall a smaller quantity of whiskey than 1 quart...
witness...Lodowich Nix, Kellis Turner, Kader Stansell of Forsyth
county and William Nix...
We also present the said David Quals for the offence of keeping a
disorderly house for said David Quals on 5 Feb. 1835...did keep
and maintain a common ill governed and disorderly house to the
encouragement of idleness gaming drinking and other misbehavior
witnesses Wm. Nix, James W. (N) Dooly and John Woodall Killis
Turner and <u>Kedar Stancel</u>.
We also present Geroge M....for the offence of retailing liquor
without license for said George M.S. on 20 Feb. 1835...did sell
to Charles McGrady a smaller qualitity of whiskey than 1 quart
without a license so to do...Witness Charles McGrady and Amos
Chaffin.
We also present Jonathan J. Johnson for offense of...of selling
liquor without a lawful license...on 10 Oct. 1834...did sell
Nick Prscktor (?), an Indian a smaller quantity that 1 quart...
Witness Wm. McMahan...Morgan...We have learned with some degree
of satisfaction of an act which was passed at last legislature to
alter the court of the state so as to authorize or establish a
court for the correction of error in this state, we, therefore
recommend to our members in next legislature to use their influence
in the alternation of the constitutions so as to authorize the

establishment of such a court.

Following jurors chosen:

Noble P. Beall, foreman	George Brock
John H. King	Benj. F. Johnston
Noble Timmons	Reuben F. Daniel
Andrew Soctt	Charles McGrady
Lodowick Nix	Amos Chaffin
James Cooper	John W. Leonard
Wm. Whitaker	Jacob Avery
Elisha Dooly	Felix Moss
John Epperson	Robert T. Griffin
Burton Mullins	Joseph Donaldson

We, the grand jury...present a Cherokee Indian by the name of Mushsticks with the offence of accessory after the fact of an assault with intent to murder...said Mushsticks on 10 day of Oct. 1834 did harbour and conceal a certain Cherokee Indian by the name of Log in the Water...had been at last term of Superior Court...duly convicted of the offence of an assualt with intent to murder of which said Mushsticks had full knowledge...Witness, Charles McGrady

Following jury chosen:

Noble P. Beall, Foreman	Burton Mullins
Felix Moss	John H. King
George Brock	Robert T. Griffin
Noble Timmons	Benj. F. Johnston
Joseph Donaldson	Andrew Scott
Reuben F. Daniel	Lodowick Nix
Charles McGrady	James Cooper
Amos Chaffin	Wm. Whitaker
John W. Leonard	Elisha Dooly
Jacob Avery	John Epperson

Page 103.   Friday...13 March 1835...Minutes

Eleanor Ragsdale, appellant) Claim of #103/4/2
          vs   )
John Waggoner, Respondent   )

Special jury trial, to wit following grand jury empannelled:

1. Noble P. Beall	2. Noble Timmons
3. Andrew Scott	4. Lodowick Nix
5. James Cooper	6. John Epperson
7. Burton Mullins	8. Elisha Dooly
9. Benjamin F. Johnston	10. Charles McGrady
11. Amos Caffin	12. Jacob Avery

...returned following verdict according to issue: We find for the appellant...Noble P. Beall, Foreman

Robert Camp) fi fa
    vs   )
Moses Ellison)

Richard Gwinn   ) fi fa
     vs   )
Robert Ellison &   )
Moses Ellison   )

William George   )   fi fa
   vs   )
Moses Ellison &   )
Robert Ellison   )

C. M. Genning   )   fi fa
   vs   )
Moses Ellison &   )
Robert Ellison   )

S. McJunkin   )   fi fa
   vs   )
Moses Ellison   )

S. McJunkin   )   fi fa
   vs   )
Moses Ellison   )

Joseph N. James   )   fi fa
   vs   )
Moses Ellison &   )
Robert Ellison   )

Ira Segars   )   fi fa
   vs   )
Moses Ellison   )

The above fi fas from a justice court in Walton Co....sheriff has
COLLECTED $78.43 from sale of defendant Moses Ellison's property
...ordered by court that sheriff pay over said amount of money to
be applied to payment of above fi fas...according to their prio-
rity.

Jacob M. Scudder) Debt and costs
    vs   ) Settled
Francis Jones   )

Page 104.

The State   ) Assault with intent to murder
  vs   ) Deft pleads guilty to the above offense of
Edward Edwards   ) assault & battery...Wm. Ezzard, Sol. Gen.

...order by court...that deft Edwards be taken from bar of this
court to common jail of this county and there kept and imprisoned
for term of 10 days in the 4 walls there and upon the expiration
of that term upon the payment of the costs of this prosecution
and all future costs he be discharged and the deft be in mercy...
13 March 1835....J. W. Hooper, J.S.C.C.C.

Page 105.

179 dist 15 sec 2 was sold by John P. Brooke, late sheriff of
said county, as property of Hugh Roberts, and the money arising
therefrom applied through mistake to some young fi fas' on
motion it is ordered that I be permitted to erase the said entries
so made by mistake and apply the money to an older fi fa, in as
much as the said fi fas are all controlled by the one plaintiff,
the fi fa's that is to be erased is one in favour of John Jordan
for the use of Charles Hudspeth, the other in favour of J.
Culbertson for the use of Hop Good Grover and costs...

Wm. Daniel, Plffs. atty.

John Larrimore, plff in fi fa 　　　　　vs C. Taylor, J. McCanless, Wm. K. McCanless, deft. and Whitaker & Burns, claimants	) Claim of yoke of ox) Levy dismissed so far as) to the property claimed))
John Larrimore, Plff, in execution 　　　　　vs C. Taylor, John McCanless & W. K. McCanless & Wm. Lay, claimant	) Claim of a waggon and yoke) of oxen) Levy dismissed so far as) to the property claimed

The court then adjourned until court in course...Test: William Grisham, clerk...John W. Hooper

The following person were drawn to serve as grand jurors at the next term of this court, to wit...drawn on this 13th day of April 1835 by their Honors, the Justices of the Inferior Court of said county, present their honors John McConnell, William Lay, and Joseph Donaldson

1. John Brewster
2. Eli McConnell
3. John Black
4. John M. Chambers
5. Jesse Bates
6. James H. Bell
7. John P. Brooke
8. Enoch Rogers
9. William Lay
10. Jesse J. Leonard
11. Martin Evans
12. Jeremiah Wofford
13. Daniel H. Bird
14. James Willson
15. Ferdinand Bailey
16. Rand. McDonald
17. James Barmore
18. John B. Garrison
19. Jabez J. Holcombe
20. Elijah Chaffin
21. Simpson C. Dyer
22. John Tate
23. Wm. O. Bell
24. George M. Smith
25. Joseph Donaldson
26. William Lawless
27. Wm. May
28. Archd Bradford
29. Squire Herren
30. Noble P. Beall
31. Elias Putnam
32. James H. Chambers

Page 106.　...13 April

Following person were drawn for jurors by their Honors the said Justices of the Inferior Court to serve as petit jurors at next term of Superior Court to be held 2 Monday Sept. next viz:

1. William Nix
2. Bennett Morgan
3. William Jay
4. Thomas Hendricks
5. Zechariah Davis
6. Jordan Brock
7. Wiley A. Roberts
8. Lawson Fields
9. Richard Ragsdale
10. Henry Wilson
11. Levi Merritt
12. Henry G. Ellison
13. William Pitman
14. John Preast
15. Elijah Grayhorn
16. Joseph Kagle
17. James Conn
25. Charles F. Lay
26. John S. Holcombe
27. James T. Sutton
28. Berry Barnett
29. Joseph Chaffin
30. Joseph Watt
31. Thomas Smith
32. Robert Chandler
33. William Crow
34. Abram. Cros
35. Joiner C. Bailey
36. Pleasant Logan
37. John Hendricks
38. William P. Bates
39. Seaborn Jones
40. William B. Payne
41. Kinchen M. Thomas

18. William Townsend
19. John Williamson
20. Stephen Whitmire
21. George Post
22. Wiley Petty
23. James Bradford
24. John Nix

42. Hugh Rusk
43. John Blyth
44. Edward J. Maddox
45. Enock Vandiver
46. Wm. K. McCanless
47. David Qualls
48. Emanuel Corben

John McConnell, J.I.C.; Joseph Donaldson, J.I.C.; William Lay, J.I.C....(original signatures of Justices)

Page 107.   BLANK

Page 108.   Minutes of Cherokee Superior Court...Monday

At a Superior Court begun and holden at Canton in and for the county of Cherokee, which met persuant to its adjournment and according to law, this 14th day, being the second Monday in September in the year of our Lord 1835 and in the 60th year of the Independence of the United States of America...present his Honor John Word Hooper, Judge of said court and of the Cherokee circuit Georgia.

The following persons having been drawn, summoned and empannelled to attend this term of the court were sworn, to wit:

1. Jeremiah Wofford, Foreman
2. Eli McConnell
3. John Brewster
4. James H. Chambers
5. Elijah Chaffin
6. John M. Chambers
7. John Tate
8. Martin Evans
9. James Barmore
10. George M. Smith
11. William Lawless

12. Randal McDonald
13. John P. Brooke
14. James Willson
15. William O. Bell
16. John B. Garrison
17. Elias Putnam
18. William Lay
19. James H. Bell
20. Jesse Bates
21. Ferdinand Bailey
22. Jesse J. Leonard

James A. Maddox was duly sworn to serve as constable to the grand jury. The following persons having been drawn and summoned, were impannelled and sworn to serve as petit jury #1 at this term of the court, to wit:

1. William B. Payne
2. Kinson M. Thomas
3. Charles F. Lay
4. Hugh G. Rusk
5. Zechariah Davis
6. John Preast

7. Pleasant Logan
8. William Townsend
9. Wiley Petty
10. John Nix
11. Wm. K. McCanless
12. Joseph Kagle

Littleton C. Edwards, constable was sworn to wait and attend on the jury at this term of this court.

Page 109.   ...14th day of September 1835...

Chales McClain   ) Debt & cost
        vs   ) I confess judgment to plaintiff for forty-
John Tate Junior   ) five dollars with interest & cost of suit.
                        Jogn (X) Tate, Jr.

The following having been summoned to attend this court as petit jurors, and having failed to attend, the court ordered that they each pay a fine of ten dollars:

Bennett Morgan
William Jay
Joseph Chaffin
Thomas Smith
John Blythe

Thomas Hendrix
John S. Holcombe
Joseph Watt
Abram Crow
Edward J. Maddox

Green K. Cessna	)	Assumpsit
vs	)	I confess judgment to the plff for $500
John W. Leonard	)	with interest and cost...John W.Leonard

F. Logan & Co.	)	Debt
vs	)	I confess judgment to the plff on the within
Emanuel Corben	)	for the sum of $42.90 with interest and cost
		this 14th Sept. 1835...R. F. Daniel for Emanuel
Corbin		

Central Bank of Georgia	)	Case
vs	)	I confess judgment to the plff for
Nelson Dickerson, Prin.	)	$160 with interest and cost of suit
& Eli McConnell & John	)	Sept. 14, 1835....Howell Cobb, Dft's.
McConnell, endorsers	)	atty

Amaziah B. Middlebrooks	)	Debt
vs	)	I confess judgment to the plff on the
John P. Winn	)	within for the principal interest &
		cost this 14 Sept. 1835...John P. Winn

Page 110.

Reuben F. Daniel	)	Assumpsit & costs
vs	)	We confess judgment to the plff for the
Lewis Reinhardt	)	principal interest & cost this 14 Sept.
George Brock	)	1835...Lewis Reinhardt & George Brock

Z. B. Hargrove	)	Debt
John Martin	)	I confess judgment to the plff for $650
Tomlinson Fort &	)	with interest & cost of suit...Sept. 14,
William Salmon	)	1835
vs	)	
John Waiter	)	John Waites

The State	)	Simple larceny
vs	)	True Bill
Jim Skit, an Indian &	)	Jeremiah Wofford, Foreman
Jim Blanket, an Indian	)	
accessory after the fact	)	

Green K. Cessna	)	Judgment confessed for the sum of $500
vs	)	principal with interest and cost of suit.
John W. Leonard	)	The deft comes forward, brings Jesse J.

Leonard as security on the stay of the levy
of the execution in term of law, pays the cost and both of whom
acknowledge themselves bound for as in full terms as they can
bind themselves for the payment of the principal interest and
future cost...14th Sept. 1835...John W. Leonard & Jesse J.
Leonard (original signatures)

The State	)	Assault and battery
vs	)	True Bill
Thomas Copeland	)	John P. Brooke, Foreman pro tem

224

Page 111. ...14th Sept. 1835...Superior Court Minutes

Thos. R. Johnson, bearer)	Fi fa in Justices Court in Cherokee
vs)	County...it appearing to the court
John Tate)	that James S. Elliott one of the

justices in said county has collected
the money in the above stated case it is ordered that he do shew
cause on tomorrow morning or as soon thereafter as counsel can be
heard why he does not pay it over to the plff or his attorney...
it is further ordered that he be served with a copy of the foregoing order, and that he produce the above stated fi fa's in
court at the same time...Sept. 14th 1835

A. R. Smith & Co)	Scire Facias in debt on bond
vs)	We confess judgment to the plff for the
Charles H. Nelson &)	sum of $314 and 69 ½ cents with interest
Elias Henderson)	from 10th March 1834 and cost of suit.
	Wm. Daniel, Defts atty

Elisha W. Chester &)	Scire facias on bail bond
Junius Hillyer)	We confess judgment to the plff for the
vs)	sum of $375.37½ with interest from the
Charles H. Nelson &)	11th March 1834 and cost of suit
Elias Henderson)	Wm. Daniel, Defts atty

George Kellogg)	Debt
vs)	I confess judgment to the plff for the
R.F. Daniel, principal)	sum of $326 with interest & cost...
D.R. Mitchell, J.P.)	14th Sept. 1835
Brooke, securities)	Wm. Daniel, Defts atty

Jacob Page, endorser)	Assumpsit & c
vs)	Settled
Jabez J. Holcombe)	

Page 112.

John Burke)	Fi fa
vs)	It appearing the court that the sheriff has now
Isaac Moore)	in his hands $15.37½ raised from the sale of dfts
	property...whereupon it is ordered that the same

be paid to Z. B. Hargrove, plff. atty.

Jonathan Johnston)	A Rule Ni Si having been granted at the
vs)	last biding of this court requiring the
James Gray)	above named James Gray on or before the
	present term, to pay into said court the

entire amount of principal and interest due upon a note made by
said James Gray for $92.67...due the 20th of Dec. 1833 as well
as all the costs of the application for foreclosure...or that
the equity of redemption of the said James Gray in and to lot of
land #272 in 14th district of the 2nd section of said county...be
forever barred and foreclosed...and it was further ordered by the
court that a copy of said rule ni si should be published in some
one of the public gazettes of this state once a month for 4
months or served upon the said James Gray or special agent or
attorney at least 3 months before the money was directed to be
paid...and it now appearing to the court that the money has not
been paid according to its order...and it further appearing that
the said rule has been published as required...whereupon it is
now ordered that the prayer of the petition be granted and the

rule made absolute

The Governor on the information of   )   Sci fa
Wm. W. B. Key   )   Non suit
     vs
William A. Crombie   )   On motion of counsel for the
                                           informer it is ordered by
the court that the defts counsel shew cause on or before the last
day of the next term of this court why the nonsuit entered in the
above case should not be set aside and the case restored to the
docket, on the gollowing grounds, to wit:
1st that the solicitor general had no right to appear on the

Page 113. Georgia...Tuesday...15th Sept. 1835...(continued)

part of the defendant, nor he any right to appear on the part of
the state, unless the state was made co-defendant...
2nd That the Court erred in not permitting the plaintiff to prove
that there was an Indian improvement upon the said lot of land
in question...the scire facias charging that the said lot of land
was in the occupancy of an Indian and that there was Indian
improvement thereon...and also charging that the grant had
regularly issued for said lot...and also that the court erred in
not permitting the plaintiff to strike out the charge that said
lot had been granted after the case was submitted to the jury

The State   )   Adultery
     vs   )   Nol. pros'd
Elizabeth Welch   )   Wm. Ezzard, Sol. Gen.

The State   )   Simple Larceny
     vs   )   True Bill
George Still   )   Jeremiah Wofford, Foreman

The State   )   Simple Larceny
     vs   )   True Bill
Ned Van & Turnover,   )   Jeremiah Wofford, Foreman
Cherokee Indians   )

The State   )   Assault with intent to murder
     vs   )   True bill for an assault & battery
Joseph Wofford   )   John P. Brooke, Foreman, pro tem

The State   )   Riot
     vs   )   No Bill, Malicious prosecution
Thomas Copeland &   )   John P. Brooke, Foreman, pro tem
Daniel Copeland   )

The State   )   Assault with intent to murder
     vs   )   No Bill
James Copeland   )   John P. Brooke, Foreman

Page 114. Tuesday...15th Sept. 1835...Minutes of Cherokee

The State   )   Retailing spirituous liquors without license
     vs   )   The deft arraigned & pled not guilty
George M. Smith   )   Wm. Ezzard, Sol. Gen.

The Jury #2 sat on the trial of this issue...we, the jury find
the dft. guilty...William Nix, Foreman.

A. B. Middlebrooks) Debt
     vs   ) John P. Winn, being desirous to have the
John P. Winn   ) stay of the levy of the execution in this
                  case, entered, renders John Tate as security
both of whom acknowledge themselves bound in terms of the law for
the principal $270 with interest and cost in this case...witness
our hands and seal this 15 Sept. 1835...John P. Winn (original
signature)...John (X) Tate

Charles McClain) Debt
     vs   ) The defendant renders J.P. Winn as security
John Tate   ) in this case and both whom acknowledge them-
               selves bound to the plaintiff on the stay of
the levy of the execution in this case for the sum of $45 prin-
cipal with interest and cost...John (X) Tate, John P. Winn
(original signature)

Page 115.   ...Superior Court...15th Sept. 1835...Tuesday

R. F. Daniel   ) Debt
     vs   ) The deft being desirous of the benefit of the
Lewis Reinhardt) levy of the execution in this case, brings
George Brock   ) John Brewster and Eli McConnell and all of
                whom acknowledge themselves bound...15th day
of Sept. 1835...Lewis W. Reinhardt (orignial signature), John
Brewster (original signature) & Eli McConnell (original signature)

B. F. Patton) Debt & c
  vs   ) Settled
Jesse Bates)

The Governor on the information of) Sci Fa
F. C. Andoe   ) Dismissed
  vs   )
Isaac Mayfield   )

The Governor on the information of) Sci fa
Bennett Martin   ) Dismissed
  vs   )
James A. M. Glass   )

The Inferior Court of   ) No. 16 to March term 1835
Cherokee County   ) Debt & c
    vs   ) Settled
Burns & Whitaker   )

Wm. M. Roberts) Debt
   vs   ) Settled
John Brewster)

Page 116.   Tuesday...September 1835...

The Inferior Court of Cherokee Co. for use of) Debt & c
Wm. Hitchock   ) Settled
  vs   )
Burns & Whitaker & R. M. Holt   )

The court then adjourned until eight o'clock tomorrow morning.
John W. Hooper (original signature)...Test: William Grisham, Clk

Wednesday the 16th Sept. 1835...The court met pursuant to adjournment.

227

Page 117. Wednesday...16th September 1835...

The following named persons were drawn to serve as Grand Jurors at the next term of the Superior Court of this county, to wit:

1. James W.(?) Dooly
2. Daniel H. Bird
3. Wm. M. McAfee
4. David Rusk
5. William Lawless
6. Eli McConnell
7. Martin Evans
8. Peter C. Boger
9. John P. Winn
10. William Chamlee
11. Henry McConnell
12. Ben Elisha Dyer
13. James Barmore
14. Simeon B. Rucker
15. John P. Brooke
16. Ferdinand Bailey
17. John Tate
18. Guilford W. Jones
19. Noble P. Beall
20. Joseph Naylor
21. William Lay
22. John Waggoner
23. John Brewster
24. John Edwards
25. Edward Townsend
26. Jaben J. Holcomb
27. George Brock
28. John B. Garrison
29. Jesse Bates
30. Amos Chaffin
31. Charles McGrady
32. Elijah Chaffin
33. Joseph Donaldson

The persons whose names are herein after next numbered were than drawn to serve as petit jurors at the next term of this court, to wit:

1. Elisha Wright
2. Robert A. Winn (written over Albert)
3. Jonathan J. Johnson
4. Henry Wheeler
5. James Barnett
6. George McCorkey
7. Jacob Kagle
8. Robert T. Fowler
9. William Eeds
10. Andrew Boyd
11. Gideon H. Trout
12. Flemming Bates
13. Adam Bennett
14. Charles Sawyer
15. John Miller
16. George A. Boalch
17. Jesse Wallis
18. George Kitchens
19. Hardy Moss
20. William Ward
21. Lewis W. Reinhardt
22. David Stancil
23. George S. Bradford
24. Lindsey Peak
25. Jesse Green
26. William Wayne
27. David Dudley
28. Jarrett Chamlee
29. John Rodgers
30. James Bradford
31. Joseph Walker
32. Nathaniel Harbin
33. James Kirkendoll
34. Osborn Reeves
35. George A. Post
36. James T. Sitton
37. Berry Barnett
38. Joseph Watt
39. William Crow
40. Charles Blythe
41. Wm. M. Bird
42. Fred S. Lamb
43. John Hendrick
44. Joseph Chaffin
45. Robert Blythe
46. John Stancil
47. Thomas Smith
48. Edw. J. Maddox

Page 118. Wednesday...16th Sept. 1835...Minutes

The Governor on the info. of) Scire facias
Reuben Cone) And verdict for the deft for cost
  vs) of suit...the informant being
James Millican, exor) dissatisfied with the verdict of
of Thomas Millican, decd) the jury rendered in the above
                              case...and having paid all costs
and demanded an appeal, brings John H. King and tenders him as
his security...and they the said Reuben Cone by William Ezzard

his attorney at law and John H. King...bound to James Millican
the exor of Thomas Millican decd the deft...for the payment of
the eventual condemnation money in said case...16th Sept. 1835
...William Ezzard, atty for informer (original signature)...
John H. King (original signature)...Test: William Grisham, clerk

The State   ) Retailing spirits without license
vs   ) William Nix and Jordan L. Brock from Jury #2
David Qualls   ) sat with Jury #1 except Charles F. Lay and Hugh
                  G. Rusk who were absent...we the jury find the
dft. not guilty...Wiley, foreman

The State   ) Keeping disorderly house
vs   ) Nol. Pros't
David Qualls   ) Wm. Ezzard, Sol. Genl.

The State   ) Retailing without license
vs   ) Nol. pros'd
Jona. J. Johnson) Wm. Ezzard, Sol. Genl.

Page 119. Cherokee Superior Court...16 Sept. 1835

The State   ) Retailing spiritous liquos without license
vs   ) Whereupon it is considered by the court that
George M. Smith) the deft George M. Smith pay a fine of $50 and
                    the cost of this prosecution and on failure to
pay the said fine ordered that he be imprisoned in the common
jail of the county of Cherokee 30 days and that the said George M.
Smith be in mercy.

P. J. Murray   ) Debt & c
vs   )
Benjamin Herndon   )

Wm. Brewster   ) Debt
vs   )
Ambrose Harnage   )

S. Ballard for the use of) Debt
        vs   )
Asa May   )

Wm. McClure for the use of) Debt
Charles Haynes   )
     vs   )
Wm. S. McKenzie   )

John Sanders   ) Debt
vs   )
Samuel Allen   )

Isaac Grey   ) Assumpit
vs   )
Chewlow, an Indian)

Daniel Davis   ) Assumpit
vs   )
Joshua H. Newberry)

Joseph Daniel   ) Debt
vs   )
Seaborn Florence   )

229

Asa Keith) Care   Allman Chambers & Co.) Assumpsit
  vs   )   vs   )
John H.Stover)   Alford McBrayer   )

Bennett Bell,assgn)Assumpsit   Wm. P. King) Debt
  vs   )   vs   )
Thos. J. Douthet)   Jesse Day   )

Edward Daniel) Assumpsit   Samuel R. Hartsfield) Care
  vs   )   vs   )
Tho Petit   )   Tho Whitehead et alias)

Deveraux Jarrett) Assumpsit   Reuben Thornton) Debt
  vs   )   vs   )
Nath. Wofford   )   John Dial   )

John Patterson) Assumpsit   Lowery Rooker) Assumpsti
  vs   )   vs   )
Nancy Patterson)   John Jacobs   )

Charles Duncan) Certiorari   Leander Smith) Trespass
  vs   )   vs   )
Wm. Edgerton   )   Daniel DeBord   )

John Doe ex dem   )Eject- Crawford Wright) Ejectment
A. Livingston   )   vs   )
  vs   )   Jas Hemphill, etal)
Thos.J.Rusk et alias)

Crawford Wright   ) Eject- Michael Dearon   ) Tres. & c
  vs   ) ment   vs   )
Jas Hemphill, etal)   James Hemphill, etal)

Willis Gilly   ) Eject-
  vs   ) ment
Jas Hemphill etal   )

Page 120.   Cherokee Superior court minutes...

Michael Dearon   ) Tres. &c   Elijah Roberts   ) Tres. &c
  vs   )   vs   )
Jas Hemphill etal)   James Hemphill etal   )

Elijah Roberts   ) Tres. &c   McGee & McCarty   ) Debt
  vs   )   vs   )
James Hemphill etal)   Cabbin Smith   )

Jacob M. Scudder) Debt   Jona. J. Johnson   ) Fi fa
  vs   )   vs   )
Francis Jones   )   Tho. McHaffey   )

Jona. J. Johnson) Fi fa   William Lay   ) <u>Crim Con</u>
  vs   )   vs   )
Tho. McHaffey   )   Joseph Kelley   )

James Ligon   ) Assumpsit   Charles Day   ) Assumpsit
  vs   )   vs   )
Tho. McHaffey   )   S. C. Candler   )

Dannis Shay) Tres.   Felix Moss   ) (No charge)
  vs   ) & c   vs   )
Ezekiel McLaughlin)   Lusunday & 4 other)
                  Indians   )

James Barmore) (No charge)
  vs   )
Tho.B. Wells)

and the following cases wherein Wilson Lumpkin Governor on the information of:

Larkin Cleveland) Sci fa		H. F. Simmons) Sci fa	
vs)		vs)	
Elijah Davis)		Adolphus Dauvergne)	
Wm. Blalock) Sci fa		Thos. S. Tate) Sci fa	
vs)		vs)	
Isaiah Cheek)		James R. King)	
James Montgomery) Sci Fa		David C. Neal) Sci fa	
vs)		vs)	
Elisha Turner)		Isaiah Goulding)	
Wm. H. Underwood) Sci fa		Jeremiah Chitwood) Sci fa	
vs)		vs)	
Daniel Deal)		David Hudgins)	
Isaac R. Walker) Sci fa		Hamilton B. Gaither) Sci fa	
vs)		vs)	
Hudgins orphans)		Augustus Hudges)	
Daniel H. Bird) Sci fa		David Dyer) Sci fa	
vs)		vs)	
Teany Champman)		Noel Mixon)	
J. W. Jones) Sci fa		Wm. Lay) Sci fa	
vs)		vs)	
Richard Philpot)		John Saxon)	
Leroy Hammond) Sci fa		Felix Lewis) Sci fa	
vs)		vs)	
Wm. Pierce)		Samuel Williams)	
Joseph W.Andrews) Sci fa		David C. Neal) Sci fa	
vs)		vs)	
Samuel Williams)		Abraham Mallet)	
John Mattox) Sci fa		H. F. Simmons) Sci fa	
vs)		vs)	
John Bowen)		Cain Evans)	
Joseph W. Andrews) Sci fa		David C. Neal) Sci fa	
vs)		vs)	
Samuel Williams)		Thomas Turley)	

Page 121. Wednesday...16th day of September 1835...

David C. Neal) Sci fa		Holman F. Simmons) Sci fa	
vs)		vs)	
Jesse George)		Adolphus Dauvergne)	

Joseph W. Andrews vs James Bar	)))	Sci fa	William Lay vs John Roberts	))) Sci fa

Joseph W. Andrews) Sci fa   William Lay) Sci fa
vs)   vs)
James Bar)   John Roberts)

P. W. Flynn) Sci fa   W. W. B. Key) Sci fa
vs)   vs)
Daniel Holtzclaw)   Daniel Holtzclaw)

Henry Storment) Sci fa   John Waites) Sci fa
vs)   vs)
Pyent E. Jackson)   Sherwood Stroud)

Henry Hatchway) Sci fa   J. Mooney) Sci fa
vs)   vs)
Eliz. Clinch)   B. Keen)

John Wells) Sci fa   John Wells) Sci fa
vs)   vs)
Isaac Wheaton)   James Murray)
  (Whorton?))

John Wells) Sci fa   John H. Hines) Sci fa
vs)   vs)
Pyent E. Jackson)   Patrick Froley)

On motion it is ordered that the Clerk of the Superior Court of
Cherokee county be authorized to sign judgments and issue executions in the above and foregoing stated cases against the plffs
and their attornies wherein they are liable under the laws of
Georgia...William Grisham, Clerk

The State   ) Simple larceny
vs   ) The deft Jim Skit arraigned
Jim Skit, an indian &   ) and pled not guilty
Jim Blanket, an indian accessory)
  and c   )

The State   ) Simple larceny
vs   )
Jim Skit, an indian)

The following jury has been sworn to try this issue:

1. Wm. B. Pogue   7. Seaborn Jones
2. Hugh G. Rusk   8. Alsey Kemp
3. John Preast   9. Wm. Ellison
4. Wm. Townsend   10. John P. Wiley
5. Wm. K. McCanless   11. Cornelius Howell
6. Stephen Whitmire   12. Merrick H. Ford

We, the jury find the deft not guilty...William R. Pogue, foreman
...Nol. Pros'd as to Jim Blanket...Wm. Ezzard, Sol. Genl.

Page 122. Minutes of Cherokee Superior Court...Wednesday

The State   ) Recognizance to keep the peace
vs   ) The prosecutrix not appearing the deft having
James Eaton   ) regularly attended during the term to answer to
                 what might be objected to him by the court...it
is ordered that the deft and his securities be exonerated from
their recognizance

The State	)	Burglary
vs	)	Nol Pros'd
James Whorton &	)	Wm. Ezzard, Sol. Genl.
Elizabeth Whorton	)	

A. R. Smith & Co.) Sci fa against bail
vs) It appearing to the court that a scire
Charles H. Nelson &) facias has issued in the above case which
Elias Henderson) has been regularly served on the said
parties...it is therefore, on motion
ordered that the plffs have leave to sign judgment against the
said Charles H. Nelson & Elias Henderson for the sum of $314.69½
for their principal debt...with interest from the 10th of March
1834 and all cost of said suit.

Elisha W. Chester &) Scire facias against bail
Junius Hillyer) It appearing to the court that a scire
vs) facias has issued in the above case &
Charles H. Nelson &) that the same has been regularly served
Elias Henderson) on the said parties...therefore ordered...
that the plffs have leave to sign judg-
ment against the...for the sum of $375.07½...

(scire facias means a writ to enforce, annul, or vacate a judgment, patent, charter, or other matter of record)

Page 123. ...The 16th day of September 1835...

The Grand Jurors sworn, chosen and selected for the county of
Cherokee at Sept. term, 1835, make the following presentment,
viz:...We present to the consideration of the next legislature
the embarrasing situation of our citizens respecting the prosecution of insolvent indians the number of such presecutions
already in default, have become subject of vital importance to
the citizens of our county...we are taxed of considerable magni-
tude, and which appears to this body to be insurmountable...
unless resorting to the very unpleasant and oppressing necessity
of a high county tax, we therefore under this view of the care
feel that we are acting in good faith to our citizens to make
this appeal to the liberality of the next legislature in asking
for the passage of a law to relieve our citizens from the
burthen complained of...we earnestly request our representation
in the next legislature to use their exertions in having such a
law passed as will relieve our citizens from this unreasonable
burden...and we request the grand juries of the new counties for
an expression of their opinion on this subject...we earnestly
recommend to our next legislature to take into serious consideration the embarrassed situation of a considerable portions of the
Cherokee territory both in regard to the difficulty in obtaining
legal titles as well as to the unreasonable length of time they
have been kept out of the possession and enjoyment of lands in
which some have invested their all...We therefore recommend the
passage of a law to grant all lands now in the possession of
Indians and provide for the protection of such indians in the
enjoyment of what lands they may have in their immediate possession...We recommend to our next legislature the passage of a law
compelling resident indians to do road duty and also to tax their
slaves...we would respectfully call the attention of the legislature to that part of our penal code which provides for the
punishment of cattle and hog stealing where the amount does not
exceed $20 we hold that stealing of cattle and hogs should be

233

punished in the penitentiary without regard to value as a case
seldom occurs where the amount is sufficient under our present
code to punish the offender in the penitentiary...There is another
part of the penal code which we most earnestly submit for the
consideration of the next legislature which is the confinement in
the penitentiary for life for the crime of murder where the evidence is wholly circumstancial as we believe that most of murders
are committed where nothing but corrobarating

Page 124. Wednesday...16th September 1836...(continued)...

circumstances can be had to convict the murderer. We are of opinion that all murders should stand upon the same footing whether is
be made appear by positive or circumstancial evidence...We see
with regret that many of the grand juries throughout the state
drag into their presentments subjects of a political character, we
therefore refrain from any expression of opinion upon the subjects
that agitate the political world...we allow to Martin Chamlee,
the Tax Collector for the year 1834 the sum of $15.13½ as his
insolvent list. In taking into consideration the amendment of the
constitution of the state of Georgia for the establishment of a
court for the correction of errors, while we deplore the inequali-
ty of the administration of our laws, we consider that for the
poor man such a court will put suits out of his power to continue
them to a final decision we are therefore content with the present
judiciary as any amendment might prove worse than the evil of
which some complain...We present Pleasant H. Nix and Elizabeth
Ragsdale for living in a state of adultery and fornication is said
county, between the 1st of May and the 1st of September 1835...
Witnesses Viney Bean alias Viny Nelms and Eliza Crawford...
We present George A. Bolche for the offence of illegally trading
with slaves of Eli McConnell in the purchasing from 2 negroes Jim
and Mariah a quantity of bacon of over the value of one dollar the
said offence committed in Cherokee county between the 1st day of
June and the 1st day of October 1832. witness Eliza Grimes...
We present Middleton Story for the offence of bigamy, between the
20th day of August and the 10th day of September 1835 in the
county of Cherokee, by unlawfully and wilfully marrying according
to the form of law Maletha Ellison, having at the same time a
lawful wife, witnesses William Tate (redhead), William Priest,
Asa Tate and Noble P. Bell...In taking leave of His Honor Judge
Hooper...we return to the Sol. Genl...

Page 125...Minutes of Cherokee Superior Court 1835...Presentments

We request that our presentments of a public nature be published
in the Miners Recorder and Cassville Pioneer...Jeremiah Wooford,
F. M.

2. Eli McConnell
3. John Brewster
4. James H. Chambers
5. John Tate
6. Martin Evans
7. James Barmore
8. George M. Smith
9. William Lawless
10. Randal McDonald
11. John P. Brooke
12. James Willson
13. William O. Bell
14. John B. Garrison
15. Elias Putnam
16. Elijah Chaffin
17. John M. Chambers
18. William Lay
19. James H. Bell
20. Jesse Bates
21. Ferdinand Bailey
22. Jesse J. Leonard

234

On motion of Wm. Ezzard Sol. Genl. ordered the foregoing presentments be published in accordance with the request of the Grand
Jury

John May) Debt & c
vs) And verdict for the plff for $32 with interest
John P. Wiley) and cost of suit...the defts being dissatisfied
John Prease &) with the verdict of the jury rendered in the
John Black) above case brings John P. Brooke and renders him
as their security and they...bound to John May
the plff for payment...this 17th day of Sept. 1835...John Prest
(original signature), John P. Brooke (original signature)...Test:
William Grisham

Page 126. Minutes of Cherokee Superior Court...Wednesday

The State) Indictment, simple larceny
vs) And now at this term comes the deft into
George Still, Jr.) court and demands his trial in the above
case...there being a jury empannelled and
ready to try said case and prays to have his demand entered in
the minutes of court

William Nix, Respondent) Malicious prosecution
vs) Settled
John Nix, Appellant)

Page 127. Sept. 16, 1835...Cherokee County...To William Ezzard,
Sol. Genl. & to William Grisham, clerk...Dr.

The State) Assault & Battery 5 . . 3.87½
vs)
Edward Edwards)

The State) Convicted & unable 5 . . 3.75
vs)
Edward Edwards)

The State) To pay cost 5 . . 3.75
vs)
Edward Edwards)

The State) Larceny verdict 5 . .
vs)
Jim Skit)

The State) Nol. pros 5 . . 3.87
vs)
Jim Blanket)

The State) Retailing verdict 5 . . 4.87
vs)
David Qualls)

The State) Adultery 5 . . 4.50
vs) nol. pros
Eliz Welch)

The State) Asst. to kill 5 . . 6.25
vs) No Bill
James Copeland) ──────────
40 . .30.87

235

It appearing to the court that...due...ordered said sums of money be paid to them out of any moneys arising from fines and forfeitures.

The court then adjourned until the next regular term in course. test: Wm. Grisham...John W. Hooper, J.S.C.C.C.

Page 128. March Term...1836...Monday...14th March

At a Superior Court begun and holden at Canton in and for the county of Cherokee which met persuant to its adjournment and according to law, this 14th day of March. being the 2nd Monday in March....Presnet, His Honor Owen H. Kenan, Judge of said Superior Court and of the Cherokee circuit, Georgia

The following named persons having been selected, drawn and summoned to attend at this term of this court as Grand Jurors were empannelled and sworn as such, to wit:

1. Eli McConnell, foreman	13. Ferdinand Bailey
2. James W. Dooly	14. William Lawless
3. Peter C. Roger	15. Joseph Naylor
4. William Chamlee	16. John Edwards
5. Elijah Chaffin	17. Elisha Dyer
6. Charles McGrady	18. Guilford W. Jones
7. Henry McConnell	19. Jabez J. Holcombe
8. James Barmore	20. John Tate
9. George Brock	21. (Blank)
10. John P. Brooke	22. (Blank
11. Jesse Bates	23. (Blank)
12. John Wagnon	

William Nix, constable was then sworn according to law to serve said Grand inquest at this term of this court

The following persons having been drawn and summoned were empannelled and sworn to serve at this term as Jury #1

1. Henry Wheeler	7. George A. Boalch
2. Jacob Kagle	8. Jesse Wallis
3. Wm. Eads	9. William Ward
4. James Barnett	10. Gideon H. Trout
5. Charles Sawyer	11. Lindsey Peak
6. John Miller	

Page 129. Minutes of Cherokee Superior Court...Monday

Samuel Hillhouse constable was sworn to serve at this term of this court and wait on <u>pannel</u> of Jury #1

Thomas Smith   ) Having been summoned to attend this term of
    vs   ) this court were respectively sworn in regard
Joseph Walker   ) to their age, and it appearing that they were
) over 60 years of age were each discharged

George Kitchens was discharged from service on the jury at this term of court on account of the sickness of his family

The following persons having been drawn and summoned were empannelled and sworn to serve as Jury #2, to wit:

236

1. Edward J. Maddox	7. James Keykendoll
2. William Wayne	8. George A. Post
3. William M. Bird	9. John M. Mullins
4. Lewis W. Reinhardt	10. Osbern Reeves
5. Jarrett Chamlee	11. Joseph Watt
6. James Bradford	12. Thomas Hendricks

Joseph Fincher constable was then sworn to serve as constable to
wait on Jury #2

Jury #1

The Governor on the) Sci fa on fraudulent draw of lot #541/21/2
information of   ) We the jury find the return fraudulent
George W. Heard   ) 14th March 1836
     vs   )
William Smith   ) John Miller, Foreman

The State   ) Assault & Battery
     vs   ) True Bill
William Grisham   ) Eli McConnell, Foreman
                        The defendant arraigned and plead ń∮ŧ
(marked over) guilty...14 March 1836...William Grisham, Defendant

Joseph Fincher, Constable, being discharged from service at this
term, Joiner C. Bailey was sworn as constable in his stead

Page 130. Minutes of the Superior Court of Cherokee

Jury #1

Mayson Ezzell) Case for deceit & c
     vs   ) We the jury find for the plff $100 with cost
Alsey Camp   ) of suit...John Miller, foreman

Benj. Hagood) Trover & c
     vs   ) March term 1836
Daniel H. Bird) On motion of plffs counsel it is ordered that
                the plff be permitted to withdraw the inter-
rogatories now in the office in his behalf for the purpose of
amendment...Daniel & Hansell, plffs. attys.

Collins Brown) Debt
     vs   ) We the jury find for the plff the sum of $77.50
John Black   ) with interest and cost...John Miller, Foreman

Wm. Bailey   ) Lease
     vs   ) We, the jury find in favor of the plff $100 and
Eli McConnell) cost of suit...Joseph Watt, foreman

J. & J. McBride) Assumpsit
     vs   ) I confess judgment on the within for $39.58
Philip Kroft   ) with cost of suit this 14th March 1836...
                  Philip Kroft

Warren Akin, Indorsee) Assumpsit
     vs   ) I confess judgment to the plffs for the
Felix Moss &   ) sum of $200 with interest & cost of
William Lay, Indorsers) suit...Wm. H. Steelman, Dfts. atty

B. W. Force & Co.) I confess judgment to the plff for $338.69
     vs   )
Philip Kroft   ) Wm. Daniel, Defts atty

Page 131. County, Ga...Monday March 14th 1836...

Warren Akin, Indorsee   ) Assumpsit
     vs   ) And judgment confessed to the plff
Felix Moss &   ) for the sum of $200 with interest
William Lay, Indorsors   ) & cost...the dfts being dissatisfied
                             with their confession rendered in
the above cause, and having paid all cost and demanded an appeal
bring William Worley, and tenders him as their security...and the
said Felix Moss and William Lay acknowledge themselves...bound to
Warren Akin the plff for the payment...Felix Moss (original
signature), Wm. Worley (original signature)...Test: William
Grisham, clerk

George Kellogg   ) Debt and c & confession for $226.00
    vs   ) It appearing to the court that the plff
R. F. Daniel, pr   ) counsel in entering the judgment in the
D. R. Mitchell &   ) above case, made a mistake of $24.50 in
J. P. Brooke, securities) calculating the interest...ordered by
                         the Court that the plffs counsel have
leave to amend said judgment munc pro tunc

The Branch Bank of Darien & c) Assumpsit & c
          vs   ) We the jury find for the plff
Charles H. Nelson, William M.) the sum of $300 with interest
Varnum, Samuel McCarter, Asa) and protest & cost of suit
Johnston, H.L. Towns & H. M.) John Miller, foreman
Terrell   )

Page 132.   Minutes of the Superior Court of Cherokee

It appearing to Court that in pursuance of a writ of petition
issued out of said court for the purpose of dividing lot of land
#108 in 14th district of the second section Edward Townsend,
Charles F. Lay & James Eaton the partitioners therein named
together with the deputy sheriff of said county have entered upon
said lot of land and have made partition thereof and have assigned
the 1/2 to the state and the other 1/2 to the informer as will
more fully appear by reference to the annexed plat...it is therefore ordered that the return with the annexed plat be made the
judgment of the court.

William Christian, Admr & c) Debt & C
        vs   ) I confess judgment to the plff
Charles Christian   ) for $102 with interest and cost of
                        suit with liberty of appeal...
C. Christian

Louis Cress & Co.) Debt & c
     vs   ) We the jury find for the plff $252.60 with
Wm. Whitaker   ) interest and cost of suit...John Miller,
                  foreman

George R. Jessup) Debt & c
     vs   ) ..confess judgment to plff for $138.17 with
Philip Kroft   ) interest & cost of suit...Wm. Daniel, Defts
                atty

William Nix   ) Malicious Prosecution
     vs   ) ...the jury find in favour of the plff $100
Pleasant H. Nix) damage with cost of suit...John Miller, Foreman

Elijah Fuller) Debt & c
     vs   ) ...confess judgment to plff for $55 with interest
John P. Winn   ) and cost of suit...D. R. Mitchell, Defts atty

Page 133.   County, Georgia...Monday...March 14, 1836...

James H. Hill   ) Trover & c
     vs   ) Dismissed
George Still Junior)

                      Jury #2

Bears Paw, for the use of) Debt & c
Wm. M. Green   ) ...find for the plff...$42 with
     vs   ) interest and cost of suit...14 March
Jack Downing & Polly Proctor) 1836...Joseph Watt, foreman

                      Jury #1

John E. Brown, bearer) Debt & c
     vs   ) ...find for plff...$65 with interest
Ellis Beck   ) & cost...14 March 1836...John Miller,
                         foreman

William Ward) Assumpsit
     vs   ) Dismissed
William Lay   )

Wright, Van Antwerp & Co.) Assumpsit & c
     vs   ) Dismissed
John P. Winn   )

John W. Lowery) Debt & c
     vs   ) Settled
Wm. Daniel   )

John May, Respondent) Debt
     vs   ) Settled
John P. Willey,   )
John Preast &   )
John Black, appellants)

Court adjourned until 8 o'clock tomorrow morning...Test Wm.
Grisham, clk...O. H. Kenan, JSCCC

Page 134.   Tuesday...15th March, 1836...court met pursuant to
            adjournment

Wilson Lumpkin, Governor & c on the) Sci fa on #146/4/2
information of R. Cone, Appellant   ) Dismissed
              vs   )
James Millican, Exr of Tho Millican)
decd   )

Georgia) To the honorable Owen H. Kenan Judge of the Superior
         Court in and for the county of Cherokee...the peti-
tion of Warren Akin, respectfully showeth unto your honor by the

certificate of A. D. Shackleford atty at law that your petitioner
has read law, that he is of good moral character, and that he is
21 years of age, therefore, he prays to be examined according to
law and the rules of court in such cases made and provided and
admitted to plead and practice law in the several courts of law
and equity of this state...Warren Akin

Georgia) I do hereby certify that Warren Akin of the county of
Cherokee) Cass has read law, that he is of good moral character
            and I believe him to be 21 years of age...14 March
1836...Achilles D. Shackleford, atty

Wm. Ezzard, John W. Hooper, William Daniel & Henry L. Sims are
appointed to examine the applicant...having been examined in open
court and being found well acquainted and skilled in the laws, he
was admitted by the court...O. H. Kenan, JSCCC

Page 135.

Test William Grisham Clerk
I Warren Akin do solemnly swear that I will justly and uprightly
demean myself according to law as an attorney, counsellor and
solicitor...and that I will support and defend the Constitution
of the United States and the constitution of the state of Ga, so
help me God...Warren Akin...Sworn to in open court 15th March
1836...Willm Grisham clerk

Caleb Goodtitle, ex dem	)	Tresspass & Ejectment
William Ward, Appellant	)	Dismissed
vs	)	
Peter Holdfast, casual ejector	)	
William Lay, tenant in possession	)	
& Seaborn Woodcock, co-defendant,	)	
Respondants	)	

A. R. Smith & Co.	) Fi fa	Elisha W. Chester &	)	Fi fa
vs	)	James Hillyer	)	
Charles H. Nelson I	)	vs	)	
Elias Henderson	)	Charles H. Nelson &	)	
		Elias Henderson	)	

It appearing to the court that the above stated fi fas have been
placed in the hands of the sheriff for collection, it is ordered
that he do produce said fi fas into court and shew cause why he
does not pay over the money due on the same to the plffs atty.

Page 136. Minutes of Cherokee Superior Court...

The Governor on the information of	)	Sci fa on #15/14/2
Wm. M. Waites	)	$̸e̸t̸t̸l̸e̸d̸ (marked over)
vs	)	
Elijah B. Moseley	)	

The State	)	Assault & Battery
vs	)	In this case it is ordered and adjudged by the
William Grisham	)	court that the deft do pay a fine of $5.00
		with all costs...O. H. Kenan, JSCCC

CHEROKEE COUNTY SUPERIOR COURT MINUTES

The Governor on the information of) Scire facias on return of
Henry H. Cone   ) #197/22/2 sec. and a
    vs   ) verdict of a fraudulent
Elisha Sterling   ) return...in pursuance of a
                                      writ of partition issued
out of said court for the purpose of dividing lot of land #197 in
22 district of 2nd section...William Grisham, William B. Pogue,
Lewis W. Reinhardt & Joseph Donaldson together with M. J. Camden
deputy sheriff of said county have entered upon the said lot of
land and made partition thereof, and have assigned the south part
containing 52 acres to the state and the other part to the informer containing 108 acres on the north side or part of said lot...
reference to annexed plat...be made judgment of court...

The State   ) Simply larceny
    vs   ) True bill
Chicken   ) Eli McConnell, foreman
alias Takarkaluche)
alias Chaticar   )

Page 137. ...March 15, 1836...Tuesday...

The State   ) Horse stealing
    vs   ) Copy of the indictment and list of
Young Panther, an indian   ) witnesses waived, March term 1836...
                             David Irwin, Defts atty

The State   ) Horse stealing
    vs   ) The deft arraigned and plead not guilty March
Young Panther) term 1836...Henry L. Sims, Sol. Genl.

The State   ) Jury #2 sat on the trial of this issue and after
    vs   ) being sworn and hearing the evidence retd the
Young Panther) following verdict to wit...not guilty...Joseph
                 Watt, foreman

The State   ) Accessory after the fact of an assualt with
    vs   ) intent to murder
Mushstick   ) The deft arraigned and plead not guilty...
a Cherokee indian) March term 1836...H. L. Sims, Sol. Genl

The State   ) Peace Warrant
    vs   ) Harriet Hillhouse prosecution
Caroline Brock) Settled

The State   ) Bigamy, Superior Court
    vs   ) The deft in the above M. W. Story having
Middleton Story) appeared at this term of court and demanded a
                   trial and not being tried...there being a jury
empannelled...ordered therefore by the court that the said Story
be tried at the next term of this court or discharged from said
prosecution

Page 138.   Tuesday...March 15, 1836...Minutes...March term 1836

It appearing that lot of land No. 108 in the 4 district of the
2nd section of Cherokee county has been comdemned in this court
as a lot fraudulently drawn...that partitioners having been
appointed to make partition of said lot between the state of Ga
and the informer and said partition having been made and a return
thereof made to this term of this court...ordered moiety of said

241

lot assigned to the state by the pertitioners be sold by sheriff
of Cherokee county in pursuance...

William Bailey   ) and the verdict for the plff for $100 with
   vs   )   cost of suit...the deft being dissatisfied
Eli McConnell   )   with the verdict of the jury...having paid
                      all costs and demanded an appeal...brings
James Tippens and tenders him as his security...jointly bound...
Eli McConnell & James Tippens (original signatures)...Test:
William Grisham, clerk

George W. Winters, bearer) Debt & c Bail
   vs   ) Assumpsit
Edward Edwards   ) Settled

Page 139. Cherokee Superior Court...Tuesday...15 March 1836...
           Presentments...

The Grand Jurors sworn chosen and selected for the county of
Cherokee at March term 1836 make the following presentment viz,
We have examined the books of the Clerk of the Inferior Court, and
find that several estrays have been posted a sufficient length of
time to have received from the justices before whom such estrays
have been posted a return of the disposition or sale of such
estrays but it appears from the books that several justices are
in default or the Clerk has ommitted to make the proper entries
...we therefore recommend the present Clerk to all on all default-
ing justices to make a return as the law directs...
We have examined the books of the county treasurer and find them
kept in a manner highly creditable to that officer...
With regard to our county Tax we recommend the justices of the
Inferior Court to assess a moderate Tax...
We present the bad condition of our public roads, but hope the day
is not far distant when they will be greatly improved, as the work
in many parts of the county has been commenced that the justices
of the Inferior Court will take such measures as will enable them
to have bridges built across some of the largest water courses
where ferries are not kept...
We present Solomon Williams, John Burdett, Middleton Story and a
young man by the name of Wright his Christian name not known but
thought to be William Wright for being concerned in the murder of
Abraham Salomon of this county either as principal or accessories
which murder was committed in the county of Cherokee, between the
10th and 13th days of January 1836...
We present a Cherokee Indian by the name of George Blackwood for
the offence of horse stealing committed in the county of Cherokee
between the 1st and last day of April in the year 1835. The
property of Thomas Townsend, Senr...witness an Indian by the name
of Jackson...
We present Alexander Miller for the crime of perjury committed
in this county on the 13th of Feb. 1836...witnesses William Lawless, John Anderson, Charles Christian and William Hardman...
We present Joseph Walker for retailing of spirits without license
...witnesses Richard Otwell & Wiley Fowler...
In taking leave of His Honor Judge Kenan...thanks to Sol Genl
H. L. Sims...Eli McConnell, foreman...

John P. Brooke   Jabez J. Holcombe
James Barmore   John Edwards
William Lawless   Charles McGrady
James W. Dooly   John Wagnon

Elijah Chaffin	George Brock
John Tate	Jesse Bates
Elisha Dyer	Joseph Naylor
Henry McConnell	William Chamlee
Peter C. Roger	Ferdinand Bailey
Guildord W. Jones	

(Following seems to be in the handwriting of O. H. Kenan, judge)
It appearing to the court that lot of land #197 in 22 district
of 2nd section of Cherokee county has been condemned in this court
as a lot fraudulently drawn...that partitioners having been
appointed to make partition of said lot between the state of GA
and the informer and said partition having been made and a return
thereof made to this term of this court ordered that the monety of
said lot assigned to the state by the partitioners be sold by the
sheriff of Cherokee County in pursuance of the law in such cases
made and provided...O. H. Kenan, JSCCC

Page 141.   ...of Cherokee Superior Court...

William H. Williams)	Debt & c	Benjamin Ragsdale)	Bill for
vs)	Settled	vs)	relief &
Jabez J. Holcomb)		Daniel Pitman)	injunction
		Wm. Pitman &)	Dismissed
		Zech. Pitman.)	

The State)	Assault &	The State)	Assault &
vs)	battery	vs)	battery
Joseph Wofford)	Nol. pros'd	Thos. Copeland)	Nol. pros'd

George S. Matthews, bearer)	Debt
vs)	Dismissed
William Townsend)	

The Governor on the information of)	Sci fa
James H. Chambers)	Dismissed
vs)	
James A. M. Glass)	

The court adjourned until court in course...O. H. Kenan, JSCCC

Page 142.   ...Minutes of the Superior Court of Cherokee...

At a meeting of their honors John McConnell, William Lay and
Joseph Donaldson, Justices of the Inferior Court in and for
Cherokee county on Monday the 6th day of June for the purpose of
reorganizing the Jury Box for said court, after which the follow-
ing named were drawn to serve at the next Sept. term of the
Superior Court of said county as Grand jurors, to wit:

1. Abraham G. Avery	2. Joseph Harris
3. Thomas Hunt	4. James Cooper
5. William Eeds	6. Levi Merrett
7. William Lay	8. Noble Timmons
9. Charles F. Lay	10. John Waites
11. Burton Mullins	12. Thomas Johnson
13. Stephen Bates	14. William Bolin
15. Daniel Butler	16. Levi Hoyle
17. John T. Landrum	18. John McCanless
19. Jacob Avery	20. David E. Garrison
21. Amos Brasselton	22. John Holt
23. Elias Putnam	24. Abner Phillips

25. Isaac L. Sego	26. George M. Smith
27. George Cox	28. John P. Brooke
29. Jesse Wallis	30. James H. Bell
31. Manly Brown	32. William Worley
33. John M. Dorris	34. Jesse Bates
35. Charles Christian	36. Samuel Tate

The following person were then drawn to serve at said court at said term, to wit:

1. William Litteral	2. Joseph Conn
3. Dennis Miller	4. Dempsey Miller
5. Jo. A. Sturdivant	6. E. K. Davis
7. James Eaton	8. Barnabas Arthur
9. Samuel Ellison	10. William Holland
11. William Hunt	12. William A. McCurdy
13. Benj. Kennedy	14. Pleasant Worley
15. Henry Strickland	16. James Baker
17. George Hinckle	18. Wm. Young
19. Wm. Defreese	20. Josiah Thompson
21. Stephen Whitmire	22. John Melton
23. Wm. B. Page	24. John Morris
25. Gabriel Morris	26. Andrew Boyd
27. Solomon Hinckle	28. John C. Dejournette
29. Henry Wheeler	30. John M. Chambers
31. Richard Literal	32. Joseph Chaffin
33. Jona. Gamblin	34. Wm. Tate
35. John Heard	36. James Copeland
37. Fred. B. Lamb	38. Fred. B. Lamb
39. Phil. Foster	40. Jesse Young
41. Wm. K. McCanless	42. Lindsey Peak
43. Wm. F. Bates	44. James Young
45. Joseph Wofford	46. Wm. Pence
47. John Conn	48. Daniel Curbow

Page 143. ...County...Georgia...March Term 1836...

The above done as aforesaid...this 6th day of June 1836...William Lay, John McConnell & Joseph Donaldson (original signatures)...
Test: Wm. Grisham, clerk

Page 144. ...Monday...12th September 1836...Minutes

At a meeting of the Honorable, the Superior Court held in and for the county of Cherokee...in the town of Canton...2nd Monday ... 12th day of Sept. 1836...his honor Owen H. Kenan, Judge...

Following named persons having been selected and summoned, to attend this term of court as Grand Jurors, were empannelled and sworn, to wit:

1. John P. Brooke, Foreman	13. Amos Braselton
2. Thomas Hunt	14. John McCanless
3. Joseph Donaldson	15. John Waites
4. Jacob Avery	16. David Garrison
5. James Cooper	17. Daniel Butler
6. William Eeds	18. John Holt
7. Levi Merritt	19. Noble Timmons
8. Thomas Johnson	20. Manly Brown
9. Joseph Harris	21. John T. Landrum
10. John M. Dorris	22. Jesse Wallis

11. Absalom C. Avery   23. William Lay
12. Isaac L. Seago

Samuel Hillhouse, constable of said county was duly sworn to attend said Grand Inquest during this term of this court

Following named persons having been drawn and summoned were empannelled and sworn to serve as petit jury #1 at this term of
court...
1. William B. Pogue   7. Gabriel Morris
2. Stephen Whitmire   8. Solomon Morris
3. William Defreese   9. John M. Chambers
 4. Henry Strickland   10. Richard Literal
5. James Copeland   11. William Literal
6. William A. McCurdy   12. Henry Wheeler

Wm. Nix, constable was sworn to attend on said day...

Page 145. Of the Superior Court...Cherokee County...Georgia...

James Barnett   ) Debt
      vs   ) ...confess judgment to plff...$50 with
Ferdinand Bailey   ) interest and cost of suit 12th Sept. 1836
                      Ferdinand Bailey

The Governor on the information of) Sci fa on #114/14/2
John Wagnon   ) We, the jury find the
      vs   ) return fraudulent
Nancy Holland   ) Geo. M. Taylor, Foreman

Wilson Lumpkin, Gov. & c on information of) Sci fa on #215/3/2
Lewis J. Groce   ) Dismissed
      vs   )
Anna Abner an infant and Lucy Abner, her   )
mother & natural gdn   )

The Governor on information of) Sci fa on #60/13/2 & #108/4/2
Robert Henderson   )
      vs   ) Dismissed
Pyent E. Jackson   )

The Governon on the information of) Sci fa on #114/14/2
R. Mitchell   ) Dismissed
      vs   )
Nancy Holland   )

Benjamin Hagood) Trover and c
      vs   ) Nonsuit
D. H. Bird   )

              Sept. term   rule Nisi
Upon the petition of Everard Hamilton executor of the last will
and testament of William B. Rogers, decd praying the foreclosure
of the equity of Redemption of in and to a certain lot of land
lying and being in the 15th district of the second section of
Cherokee county and known in the plat of said district as lot
#284 containing 40 acres

Page 146. Monday...12th day of September 1836...(continued)

which was mortgaged by Ezekiel Smith to Isaac Harvey on 21 day of May 1833 for the better securing the payment of the sum of $853 and interest...which mortgage was assigned to the said Everard Hamilton by the said Issac Harvey on the 28th day of July 1834...it appearing to court that the sum of $331.60 principal with interest from the 25th day of June 1834 remains due and unpaid...ordered by the court that the said Ezekiel Smith do pay into the clerks office of this court the amount of principal interest and cost on or before the first day of the next term of this court or in default thereof that the redemption of in and to said mortgaged premises me from thenceforth and forever barred and foreclosed and that the mortgagor be served with a copy of this rule nisi in terms of the law

Page 147.

The following named jurors having been chosen for Jury #2

1. John G. Heard
3. George M. Taylor
5. Frederick Lamb
7. William Tate
9. John Morris
11. William K. McCanless

2. Robert Qualls
4. James Eaton
6. Eli Grimes
8. William Hunt
10. Dempsey Miller
12. Lindsey Peak

John R. Bates, constable was then sworn to attend said jury at this term of this court

The Bank of Darien) Assumpsit
    vs   ) ...confess judgment to plff for $175 with
William Worley   ) interest, protest and cost of suit with the
                        right of appeal...12 Sept. 1836...W. H.
Steelman, Defts atty

Sterling T. Austin) Assumpsit
    vs   ) We...find for plff for $55 principal and
George W. Winters) $17.60 with cost of suit...Geo. M. Taylor,
                        foreman

Peter B. Taylor) Debt
    vs   ) Confess judgment...$37.99 with interest and
Philip Kroft   ) cost of suit...12 Sept. 1836...Wm. Daniel,
                        Defts atty

William Bostick) Debt & c
    vs   ) ...confess judgment to plff for $244.31½ with
Philip Kroft   ) interest and cost...Wm. Daniel, Defts atty

James Mitchell) Assumpsit & c & bail
    vs   ) ...confess judgment to the plff for $50 with
Isaac Chue   ) interest and cost of suit...
an indian   ) Wm. Daniel, defts atty

Page 148. ...Monday 12th day of September 1836...Minutes

James R. Bishop   ) Assumpsit (Breach of Promise)
    vs   ) I confess judgement to the plff
William Tate, Jr., red head) for $35 with interest & cost of
                                   suit...William X Tate, his mark

Herrs, Graham & Hope) Debt
    vs   ) I confess judgement to the plff for the
Philip Kroft   ) sum of $663.00 with interest and cost

of suit...12 Sept. 1836...Philip Kroft

```
Farish Carter        )  Debt
     vs              )  We confess judgment to the plff for the sum
William Worley &     )  of $674 with interest & cost of suit, with
Samuel Tate          )  leave to appeal...W. H. Steelman, D. Atty...
Samuel Tate, security
```

```
The State       )  Simple larceny
     vs         )  True Bill
Sparrow Hawk &) John P. Brooke, foreman
Bark Chicken, )
Indians       )
```

```
The State     )  Assault & Battery
     vs       )  True Bill
George Brock  )  John P. Brooke, foreman
```

```
The State          )  Simple larceny
     vs            )  True Bill
Sdwny, Indian      )  John P. Brooke, foreman
```

```
The State                        )  Riot
     vs                          )  No Bill
Joiner Bailey & Caty Bailey      )  John P. Brooks, foreman
```

```
Philip Kroft       )  Attachment
     vs            )  Dismissed
Joel Chandler      )
```

Page 149. Minutes of the Superior Court...Cherokee County...Ga.

```
William Henson     )  Trover
     vs            )  We the jury find for the dedendant...
Samuel Tate        )  William Defreese, foreman
```

The Court then adjourned till tomorrow morning eight o'clock...
Test William Grisham, clerk...O. H. Kenan, J.S.C.C.

Tuesday...13th Sept. 1836. The court met according to adjournment

```
Z. B. Hargrove &   )...And judgment confessed to the plff for
Tomlinson Fort     )   $972 principal besides interest & cost...
     vs            )   the defendent being dissatisfied with the
William Worley &   )   confession rendered in the above cause and
Samuel Tate        )   having paid all cost and demanded an appeal
                       bring and tenders Samuel Tate as their
security and they...the said William Worley acknowledge themselves
jointly and severally bound of the eventual condemnation money in
said cause...in testimony whereof they have hereunto set their
hands and seal this 13th day of September 1836
```

Page 150. ...Minutes of the Superior Court of Cherokee County...

```
Jacob Capehart, plff )  Fi fa on claim #526/2/2
     vs              )  Dismissed
Amos Ellard, deft.   )
George M. Taylor, Claimant)
```

247

Jacob M. Johnson, plff) Attachment
    vs) Claim of negro girl & child...Jury
Joel Leathers, defendant &) #1 sat on the trial of this issue
Samuel Leathers, claimant) ...We the jury find for the claim-
                         ant generally...William DeFreese,
foreman

William Grisham, respondent) Claim of possession of #130/14/2
     vs) We the jury find for the appellant
Dinah, appellant) with cost of suit...John P. Brooke,
                         foreman

Special jury chosen for the above trial:

1. John P. Brooke   2. Thomas Hunt
3. Levi Merritt   4. Joseph Harris
5. John M. Dorris   6. Isaac L. Seago
7. Amos Braselton   8. Daniel Butler
9. John Holt   10. Manly Brown
11. John T. Landrum   12. Jesse Wallis

William Grisham, respondent) Claim of #131/14/2
     vs) We, the jury find that William
Jack Still, appellant) Grisham is entitled to the
                         possession of the premises in
dispute...John P. Brooks, foreman

Special trial jury to wit:

1. John P. Brooke   2. Thomas Hunt
3. Levi Merritt   4. Joseph Harris
5. John M. Dorris   6. Isaac L. Leago
7. Amos Braselton   8. Daniel Butler
9. John Holt   10. Manly Brown
11. John T. Landrum   12. Jesse Wallis

Page 151.   ...Tuesday...13th September 1836...

The State) Simple Larceny
    vs) the defendant arranged & plead not guilty
Chicken, alias) and copy of Bill of Indictment and list
Takarkaluche alias) of witnesses waived...Sept. term 1836...
Chatakar) H. L. Sims, Sol. Genl.

The State) Simple larceny
    vs)
Chicken alias)
Takarkaluchee alias)
Chaticar)

Jury #1 to wit:

1. William B. Pugne   2. Stephen Whitmire
3. William Defreese   4. Henry Strickland
5. James Copeland   6. William A. McCurdy
7. Gabriel Morris   8. Solomon Hinckle
9. John M. Chambers   10. Richard Literal
11. William Literal   12. Henry Wheeler

Benjamin Ragsdale, bring sworn as a witness on the part of the
state, testifys as follows...Eleanor Ragsdale...owned a large
steer red and white five years old marked with an underbit and
crop out of the right and underbit in the left, sometime in the

month of last November in search for the steer...I found in company with others partly barbacued...we saw the skin and it bore the marks of the steer...
crossexamined...
Says it was found in the woods two miles and a half from Chickens house...he did not find Chicken there he went and found Chicken and carried him to the beef...he told him he must go and show him where the beef was...he did not whip him nor threaten him but merely told him he must show him...
Rebuttel...
He found him about three hundred yards from the beef...making off from the point where the beef was deposited...Chicken told him that his son and another Indian had the beef and that he had no hand in killing of the steer...that occurrence was in this county ...James Timpson being sworn in behalf of the State...says that he went in company with Mr. Ragsdale and found the steer...it was partly barbacued...he saw Chicken the prisoner have an axe...it was bloody...

Page 152.   ...Tuesday...13th September 1836...(continued)

Ignatius A. Few, sworn says that he went with Timpson(Simpson ?) and Mr. Ragsdale from Mrs. Ragsdale's in pursuit of Mrs. Ragsdale's steer they tracked the steer carried off by some individual to the place where it was found two miles and a half beyond Chicken's house the steer he knew well...the spots and marks and he examined the mall and he believed it to be the same steer...
Cross examined...
says he measured the tracks and the steer was gentle and easily lead...sometimes he lead him sometimes he walked behind him...he knew it was Chicken's track for when he came upon him he examined his shoes he wore a peculiar shoe...a little worn off at the corner of the heel...they came upon Chicken before they found the steer...he saw the blood on the axe handle...Chicken told them he was in search of a board tree...Chicken asked them what they wanted within him they told him they did not intend to injure him ...they told him they wanted Mrs. Ragsdale's steer...he then carried them to where the steer was barbacued...not more than two hundred and fifty or three hundred yards distant...he saw signs of other Indians about the barbacued meal...he did not know them ...Chicken proffered to give them $60 to let him go free...he never heard Chicken say he stole the steer...We the jury find the prisoner guilty...William Defreese, foreman...

The State	)	Trading with slaves
vs	)	We, the jury find the prisoner guilty
George A. Boalch	)	William Defreese, foreman

The Court then adjourned until eight o'clock tomorrow morning.
Test. William Grisham, clerk...O. H. Kenan, I.S.C.C.C.

Page 153...Wednesday...14th Sept. 1836....

State of Georgia...Cherokee County...Wednesday morning 8 o'clock ...14 Sept. 1836...The Superior Court met persuant to adjournment

William Henson	)	Trover & c
vs	)	And verdict for the defendant for the cost...
Samuel Tate	)	the pltff being dissatisfied with the verdict
		of the jury rendered in the above case & having

paid all costs and demanded an appeal by his attorneys Shackel-

ford and Wright and David Irwin and R. D. Daniel acknowledge
themselves jointly and severally bound to Samuel Tate the defendant for the payment of the eventual condemnation money in said
cause...in testimony whereof they have hereunto set their hands
and seals this 14th day of September 1836...William Henson by his
attys at law...Shackleford & Wright (seal); David Irwin (seal);
R. F. Daniel (seal)...Test. William Grisham, clerk

The State   ) Bigamy
    vs   ) No. 1 pros'd
Middleton Story   )

The State   ) Accessory after the fact of an
    vs   ) assault with intent to murder
Mushstick, Cherokee Indian   ) No. 1. pros'd

The State   ) Assault & Battery
    vs   ) Arraigned & plead guilty...Sept. term 1836
George Brock   ) Henry L. Sims, Sol. Genl.

The State   ) Assault & Battery
    vs   ) ...and plea of guilty...whereupon it considered
George Brock   ) ordered and adjudged by the Court that the defen-
                   dant George Brock do pay a fine of $20...

Page 154.   ...Minutes of Superior Court...Tuesday...

The State   ) Horse stealing
    vs   ) The defendant having been bound over to
Chicken, an Indian   ) appear at this court...and...having been
                       rendered into court by his securities...it
is therefore ordered that the securities of said Chicken be hence
discharged and exhonerated from their liability on their bond

The State   ) The defendant having been bound over to
    vs   ) appear at this term of this court and having
Uchilla, Indian   ) been rendered to wit...the defendant appeared
                     and was put into jail and the defendant
securities are hence discharged from the liability on their
recognizance...

Russel Jones) Debt
    vs   ) I confess judgment to the pltff for $38 with
John P. Winn) interest and cost of suit...12 Sept. 1836...
                John P. Winn

The State   ) Simple larceny
    vs   ) True Bill
George A. Boalch   ) John P. Brooke, foreman

Warren Akin, endorsee   ) Assumpsit
    vs   )
Felix Moss & William   )
Lay, endorsers   )

It appearing to the court that the plaintiff in the above case
(at the March term of the said court 1836 recovered against the
defendants the sum of $200 with interest and cost of suit...and
Felix Moss having entered an appeal and William Lay having
refused to do so...it is on motion ordered that the Clerk for the
principal interest and cost...D. Irwin, Plffs atty

The State	)	Assault & Battery
vs	)	True Bill against Caty Bailey...
Joiner Bailey & Caty Bailey	)	No Bill against Joiner Bailey

Page 155.   ...13th September 1836...

Bear Paw for the use of	)	Fi fa
William M. Green	)	principal $42.50...Interest $12.46...
vs	)	and cost...returnable to Sept. term
Jack Downing & Polly	)	
Proctor	)	

Georgia   ) Personally appeared before me M. J. Camden
Cherokee County) who being sworn deposeth and saith that if
                   the above mentioned fi fa was ever in his
possession as sheriff of said county...that he has lost or mislaid
it...so that it cannot be found...sworn to and subscribed before
me this 13th Sept. 1836...Wm. Whittaker, J.P....M. J. Camden

It appearing to the Court that the above fi fa has been lost or
mislaid from the affidavits of the sheriff M. J. Camden & the
clerk Wm. Grisham...ordered that the clerk issue a new fi fa in
lue of the lost one...Sept. term 1836

Nelly Ragsdale	)	Bill for relief and Injunction
vs	)	Dismissed
John Waggoner	)	

Edmund Duncan & Charles Duncan	)	Bill & c
vs	)	Dismissed
Emariah Popham	)	

George Welch et al	)	Bill for relief & injunction
vs	)	Dismissed
Jesse Lenard	)	

David Utley & Oma Utley	)	Bill for relief & injunction
vs	)	Dismissed
David Stancel et al	)	

The State	)	Simple larceny
vs	)	Recognizance...forfeited
George Still	)	

Page 156.

The Bank of Darien	)	And judgment confessed to the pltff for
vs	)	the sum of $125 principal besides interest
William Worley	)	& cost...the defendant being dissatisfied
		with the confession of judgment rendered

in the above cause and having paid all cost & demanded an appeal
brings...and tenders...as his security and they the said William
Worley and...acknowledge themselves jointly and severeally bound
to the Bank of Darien the pltff for the payment of the eventual
condemnation money in said cause...in testimony whereof they have
hereunto set their hand and seals this 13th day of September...
(No signatures)

Farish Carter	)	And judgment confessed to the pltff for $674
vs	)	besides interest & cost...the defendants being
William Worley &	)	dissatisfied with the (verdict of the jury)
Samuel Tate	)	

251

rather the confession of the judgment in the above cause and having paid all cost and demanded an appeal bring Felix Moss... and tender him as their security...and they the said William Worley, Samuel Tate and their security Felix Moss acknowlege themselves jointly and severally bound to Farish Carter the pltff for the payment of the eventual condemnation money in said cause ...in testimony whereof they have hereunto set their hands and seals this 13th day of September 1836...William Worley; Saml. Tate, by his attys W. H. Hartman; Felix Moss (original signature) ...Test William Grisham, clerk.

The State	)	Trading with slaves
vs	)	Arraigned and plead not guilty
George A. Rolche	)	Henry L. Sims, Sol. Genl.

Page 157.

Jack Still	)	Affidavit of Illegality
vs	)	Illegality dismissed and the execution ordered
Roger Green	)	to proceed

Lewis Raulston, respondent) Trespass vi et armies & false
vs) imprisonment & cost
Joseph Lynch, Samuel Martin,)
William Martin, Amos Richard-)
son, Nugin Snip, Ellis Beck,)
Walter Foster, Nelson Tenu-)
awd, Robert Saunders &)
Ezekiel Beck, appellants)

Special jury trial, to wit:

1. John L. Brooke
2. Thomas Hunt
3. Levi Merritt
4. Thomas Johnson
5. Joseph Harris
6. John M. Dorris
7. Abasalom C. Avery
8. Isaac L. Seago
9. Daniel Butler
10. Manly Brown
11. John T. Landrum
12. Jesse Wallis

Members of the grand jury sat on the trial of this appeal and returned the following verdict, to wit: we, the jury find for the defendants with cost of suit...John P. Brooke, foreman

The State) Accessory after the fact of an assault
vs) with intent to murder
Mushstick, an indian) The defendant having been rendered into court by his securities in this case it is ordered therefore that the securities of the said Mushstick be and are henceforth discharged from the liability on their bonds or recognizance in this case

The State) Presentment by the Grand Jury at March term
vs) 1836 for being concerned in murder of A.
James W. Wright) Solomon...the defendant being bound over to appear at this term of this court...and having appeared & been delivered over to the Sheriff & confined in jail...it is theredore ordered that his securities be henceforth discharged from their liability on said bond

Page 158. Minutes of the Superior Court of Cherokee County...

At a meeting of their Honors the Justices of the Inferior Court

of Cherokee County on Monday the second day of January 1837 to
draw jurors for the Superior Court of said county to serve at
the next February Term thereof...present John McConnell, Joseph
Donaldson and William Lay...when the following named persons were
drawn to serve at the next term of the Superior Court of said
county as Grand Jurors, to wit:

1. Samuel Thompson	2. Israel Evans
3. Simeon R. Rucker	4. Nelson Dickerson
5. Jabez J. Holcomb	6. Hiram Dimsdale
7. Peter C. Boger	8. James W. Dooly
9. James S. Elliott	10. William Hardman
11. David Rusk	12. William Whitaker
13. James H. Chambers	14. Toliver Bostick
15. Joseph S. Dial	16. Eli McConnell
17. John McConnell	18. Jesse J. Leonard
19. Robert T. Griffin	20. R. F. Daniel
21. Caleb Jones	22. Burwell Dobbs
23. John Tate	24. Jesse Brown
25. Burwell Mobley	26. Andrew Scott
27. William Chamlee	28. Joseph Nelson
29. John Epperson	30. Randal McDonald
31. Felix Moss	32. Edward Townsend
33. Solomon Humphreys	34. George M. Taylor

The following named persons were drawn to serve at the next term
of Superior Court of said county as petit jurors, to wit:

1. James Keykendall	2. John Pence
3. James A. Gober	4. William Ward
5. Joseph Lamb	6. William Aaron
7. James M. Daniel	8. Jesse Padget
9. Elijah A. McMillion	10. James Bates
11. John R. Williamson	12. Ferdinand Bailey
13. Wiley Moody	14. Robert Hill
15. No name	16. James Owens
17. McKinney Lay	18. John Short
19. William Featherston	20. William Word
21. Killis Turner	22. Samuel Conn
23. Robert Ingram	24. John Black
25. Samuel Timmons	26. Charles McGrady
27. Adam Barnett	28. James Barnett
29. Wm. McAdams	

Page 159 ...(continued)

30. no name	31. Joseph Knox
32. John Dover	33. Wm. Nix
34. Toliver P. Martin	35. Pleasant Logan
36. Joel Robinet	37. Philip Kroft
38. William Bogs	39. John Nailor
40. John Pitman	41. Abraham Crow
42. Timothy Hunt	43. Abraham Wilson
44. Larkin A. Ragsdale	

Re-organized...drawn...and entered in the presence of us...
John McConnell, JIC; Joseph Donaldson, JIC; William Lay, JIC...
(original signatures)...Test William Grisham, clerk

Page 160. Minutes of the Superior Court of Cherokee County

CHEROKEE COUNTY SUPERIOR COURT MINUTES

Joseph Donaldson
James Cooper
Levi Merritt
Joseph Harris
Absalom C. Avery
John McCanless
David E. Garrison
John Holt
Manly Brown
Jesse Wallis

Jacob Avery
William Erds
Thomas Johnson
John M. Dorris
Isaac L. Seago
John Waites
Daniel Butler
Noble Timmons
John T. Landrum
William Lay

Bulfinch & Wetherow) Debt
    vs) We confess judgment to the pltff for the
Wm. K. McCanless &) sum of $37.50 with interest & cost of
John McCanless) suit...Wm. K. McCanless & John McCanless

Young Johnston) Debt & c
    vs) Settled
William Worley &)
Plesant Worley)

Page 161. ...Wednesday...14th day of September 1836...

The State) Horse stealing
  vs)
John Kembell &)
Butler Kembell)

The State) Digging for gold
  vs)
James Downing, alias Blanketts)
wife & Lucy Downing)

The State) Hog stealing
  vs)
Thomas Woodall)

The court adjourned until court in course...test William Grisham, clerk...O. H. Kenan, J.S.C.C.C.

Page 162. Minutes of the Superior Court...Wednesday...

The State) Horse stealing
  vs) Recognizance forfeited...Sept. term
Bark Chicken, an Indian) 1836...Henry L. Sims, Sol. Genl.

Milligan P. Quillian) Assumpsit & c
  vs) Dismissed
William Worley, Endor-)
ser & W.W. Chastain,)
Endr.)

Samuel B. Monroe) Libel for a divorce
  vs) It appearing to the court from the
Sarah Caroline Monroe) return of the sheriff...that the
defendant resides out of said county
and out of state of Georgia...on motion of counsel for the pltff
it is ordered by the court that service be perfected upon the
defendant by a publication of this rule once a month for ----
months and that said notice be published in some public gazette
of the state previous to the next term of said court the length

254

of time aforesaid

The State	)	Simple larceny
vs	)	True Bill
Chicken, alias Tarkarkalu-	)	Verdict...it is ordered and adjudged
chee, alias Chaticur	)	by the court, that the defendant be
		sentenced to two years confinment

in the Penitentiary at hard labour...that he be remanded to the
common jail of Cherokee county there to remain until demanded by
the keeper of the Penitentiary...O. H. Kenan, J.S.C.C.C.

The State	)	Trading with slaves
vs	)	True Bill
George A. Rolche	)	Verdict...guilty...whereupon it is consid-
		ered and adjudged by the court that George

A. Rolche be sentenced to confinment in the common jail of the
county for the space of six months...O. H. Kenan, J.S.C.C.C.

Page 163. ...14th September 1836...Presentments...

Georgia	)	We the Grand jurors sworn chosen and selected for
Cherokee	)	the county aforesaid at September term 1836 make the
		following presentment, viz:...

We have examined the tax collectors book for the year 1835 and
allow him the sum of $30.11 as his insolvent list...
We have also examined the books of the county treasurer and find
the books kept in a manner highly creditable to that officer...
We regret to have to say that our publick roads are in a situation truly alarming for the want of bridges and causeways and
shows almost a total neglect of the officers whose duty it is to
have them attended to...it has been a practice for several preceding grand jurors to strickly notice the bad state of the roads,
and nothing more was ever heard of it...but we do most earnestly
urge it upon our Inferior Court to use every lawful exertion in
their power to cause a more rigorous execution of the road laws
in this county and to cause good causeways to be constructed in
every case where it is absolutely necessary...and as much as the
county is able to bear to have good and sufficient bridges
elected (sic) across the large watercourses in this county...
We refrain from any interference with any questions that agitates
our political world...believing such questions as not coming
within the province of the guardians of the county...in taking
leave of his honor Judge Kenan we tender him our warmest approbation of the able and impartial manner with which he has discharged the duties of Judge during the present term of this Court...
To Solicitor Genl. H. L. Sims we return him our thanks for his
polite attention to this Body during the present term of the
Court...John P. Brooke, Forman...Thomas Hunt...

Page 164. Minutes of Cherokee Superior Court...

James Barnett	)	Action on the case & c
vs	)	and verdict for the pltff for $40 & cost
Ferdinand Bailey	)	of suit...the defendant being dissatisfied
		with the verdict of the jury rendered in

the above cause, and having paid all cost & demanded an appeal.
brings Moses Perkins and tender him as his security and they the
said Ferdinand Bailey and Moses Perkins acknowledge themselves
jointly and severally bound to James Barnett the pltff for the
payment of the eventual condemnation money in said cause...in
testimony whereof they have hereunto set their hands and seals,

this 25th day of February 1837...Ferdinand Bailey & Moses Perkins (original signatures)...Test. William Grisham, clerk...

At a meeting of their honors the Justices of the Inferior Court in and for Cherokee County, Georgia...in the courthouse at Canton in said county to draw grand and petit juries for the next August term of the Superior Court in said county...present their honors, John Waites, Joseph Donaldson & Levi Hoyl, Esquires when named persons were duly drawn to serve at said next term of said Superior Court as Grand jurors to wit, on the first day of March 1837. to wit:

1. Henry Fitzsimmons	2. William M. McAfee
3. Merick H. Ford	4. Wm. Ellie
5. John W. Leonard	6. Daniel H. Bird
7. Allen Gilleland	8. Fleming Bates
9. Austin C. Roberts	10. Joseph Donaldson
11. Elisha Kirby	12. Henry McConnell
13. Joseph Fincher	14. William H. Evans
15. Tilmon Chamlee	16. William B. Dean
17. John Anderson, Senr.	18. John Anderson
19. Hugh G. Rusk	20. Moses Perkins
21. Jesse Green	22. William Lawless
23. Elisha Dyer	24. Lewis W. Reinhardt
25. Stephen Kemp	26. John Waggoner
27. Wiley Petty	28. Henry Wilson
29. John H. King	30. James Jourdan
31. John P. Winn	32. Enoch Rogers
33. Guildord W. Jones	34. James McConnell
35. John Wheeler	36. (no name)

Page 165. February term 1837

And the following named persons were then duly drawn to serve at the next August term of said Superior Court as petit jurors, to wit:

1. Dixon Naler	2. Daniel Robbinette
3. Simpson C. Dyer	4. Thomas Priest
5. (no name)	6. William Harris
7. William Tate, r.h.	8. John Robbinett
9. William W. Worley	10. Robert Hawkins
11. Gallant Reynolds	12. Wm. W. Smithwick
13. Hiram Bennett	14. Toliver S. Carr
15. John Pew	16. Charles Horton
17. Michael Sims	18. George Brock
19. Allen Bolen	20. Allen King
21. Elias Chaffin	22. John S. Holcomb
23. Cornelius Howell	24. Lawson Fields
25. Calton Ragsdale	26. John Nix
27. James Wilson	28. Curtis Satterfield
29. William Foster	30. Garrison Cross
31. James Barmore	32. William Pitman
33. Hardridge Walker	34. John R. Bates
35. Lazarus Anderson	36. William Priest
37. Thompson Tippens	38. John A. Pannell
39. James Haines	40. Caleb Sanders
41. Andrew Phillips	42. William P. Nix
43. Bryant Ingram	44. James Ramsey
45. Elisha Dooly	46. James Land
47. Alpheus Phillips	48. William S. Johnson

CHEROKEE COUNTY SUPERIOR COURT MINUTES

Witness our hands this 1st of March 1837...Levi Hoyl, JIC: John
Waites, JIC & Joseph Donaldson, JIC (original signatures)...

Page 166. Minutes of the Superior Court, Cherokee County

At a sitting of the Honorable the Superior Court of Cherokee
county at Canton in and for the county of Cherokee, State of
Georgia on Monday the 20th day of February...being the third
Monday in Feby in the year of our Lord 1837...and of the American
Independence the 61st year...present His Honor Owen H. Kenan,
Judge of said court, and of the Cherokee circuit of said state...

The following named jurors being selected and summoned to attend
this term of this court as grand jurors were empannelled and
sworn, to wit...

1. Eli McConnell, foreman	2. James S. Elliott
3. Robert T. Griffin	4. Jesse Brown
5. William Whittaker	6. Andrew Scott
7. William Chamlee	8. Nelson Dickerson
9. Israel Evans	10. Peter C. Boger
11. Hiram Dimsdale	12. Jabez J. Holcomb
13. James W. dooly	14. David Risk, Senr.
15. John Tate	16. William Hardman
17. James H. Chamlee	18. Burwell Dobbs
19. Edward Townsend	20. Felix Moss
21. Toliver Bostwick	22. Solomon Humphries
23. (no name)	

Abraham Deveraus, Constable of said county was duly sworn to
attend said Grand Jury, during this term of this court...the
following named persons having been drawn and summoned were
empannelled and sworn to serve as petit jury #1 at this term of
this court, to wit:

1. William Nix	2. Joseph Knox
3. Philip Kroft	4. Larkin A. Ragsdale
5. Abraham Crow	6. Toliver P. Martin
7. Joel Robinnett	8. Henry Odum
9. Joiner C. Bailey	10. Pleasant Logan
11. John Williamson	12. John Nailer

Edward Edwards, Constable was sworn to attend on said jury.

Page 167. ...Georgia...Monday...20th February 1837...

The following named persons having been summoned were empannelled
and sworn to serve as petit jury #2 at this term of this court,
to wit...

1. William Ward	2. Elijah McMillion
3. Jesse Padget	4. John L. Black
5. John Pence	6. Joseph Lamb
7. William Aaron	8. Robert Ingram
9. Ferdinand Bailey	10. Jas. Barnett
11. Samuel Conn	12. James Keykendoll

Cader Stancill, Constable was sworn to attend on said jury #2...

James Barnett) Case & c
vs) We the jury find for the pltff $40 and cost
Ferdinand Bailey) of suit...Philip Kroft, foreman

George Kellogg) Debt & c
vs) Settled
John P. Winn)

The Central Bank of Georgia) Debt & c
vs) Settled
John Tate, Jr., E. McConnell &)
John McConnell)

John Jones) Debt & c
vs) We the jury find for the pltff the sum of
Daniel Reinhardt) $65 with interest & cost of suit...William
Ward, foreman

John P. McCormack) Trover & c
vs) Dismissed
William May)

John Epperson & Co. for the use of) Debt & c
Littleberry Underwood) I confess judgement to the
vs) pltff for $67.12 with
James Jordan, with right to appeal) interest & cost of suit...
Wm. Daniel, Dfts. atty.

Page 168.

Hand & Barton) Debt & c
vs) I confess judgment to the pltff for the
R. F. Daniel & Co.) sum of $235.70 with interest & cost of
suit...Andrew J. Hansell, Defts. Atty.

The State) Malicious mischief
vs) Nol. Pros.
William Preast)

Evan Howell) Case & c
vs) We the jury find for the pltff $100 with cost
A. G. Daniel) of suit...Wm. Ward, foreman

M. P. Quillian, bearer) Assumpsit & c
vs) I confess judgment to the plaintiff the
William Worley) sum of $150 principal...the sum of
$13.50 interest with cost of suit...
20th Feby 1837...Wm. H. Steelman, Defts. atty.

The State) Assault with intent to commit a rape
vs) True Bill
George M. Kilo) Eli McConell, foreman...Wm. H. Steelman, Defts.
atty.

The State) Assault & Battery
vs) True Bill
William R. Gappin) Eli McConnell, foreman

The State) Assault & Battery
vs) No Bill
Kizzy Pilgrim) Eli McConnell, foreman

D. H. Bird, plff) Fi fa
vs) Claim of a negro...dismissed
Wm. W.B. Key, deft)
& Ferdinand Bailey)

Page 169.

Georgia) February term 1837...It appearing to the Court
Cherokee County) that John B. Garrison Sheriff of said county
of Cherokee sold while he was late Sheriff,
lot of land #75 in the 15th district of said county for the sum
of $514 under some fi fas from a Justice Court of Baker county
issuing from Keel's district against John Smith, when Jeremiah
Fields became the purchaser for the sum aforesaid and it further
appearing that said lot of land was drawn by a different individual...to wit...John Smith of Hattons district of said county and
the Sheriff has still in his hands the said sum of money so improperly paid at said sale...on motion of Council for the said
Fields it is ordered by the court that the said John B. Garrison
shew cause tomorrow morning by nine o'clock or so soon thereafter
as counsel can be heard...why he should not pay back the whole
amount of said sum of money...there being no legal claimant for
the same and co...I acknowledge due and legal service of the within...this 20th Feby 1837...John B. Garrison, D.S.

William Bailey, respondent) Case & c
vs) We, the jury find for the pltff
Eli McConnell, appellant) $100 & cost of suit...David Rusk,
Sen., foreman

Special jury trial...jurors drawn:

1. James S. Elliott   2. Robert T. Griffin
3. Jesse Brown   4. Nelson Dickinson
5. Israel Evans   6. Hiram Dimsdale
7. Jabez J. Holcomb   8. James W. Dooly
9. David Rusk, Sen.   10. John Tate
11. Wm. Hardman   12. Jas. H. Chambers

William Henson, appelant) Trover & c
vs) Dismissed
Samuel Tate, respondent)

William Few) Debt & C
vs) Dismissed
(Illegible))

Page 170. ...Monday...20th February 1837...Minutes of...

John Doe, ex dem & Andrew Utt) Trespass & ejectment & c
vs) Dismissed
Richard Roe, casual ejector &)
John Waters, tenant in poss.)

Jacob M. Johnson) Attachment
vs) Dismissed
Joel Leathers)

The State) Simple larceny
vs) The securities of the defendant having produced
Bark Chicken) in open court...the body of the defendant...and
demanded an exhoneration to be entered on their

259

recognizance...it is hereby granted and they are hereby exhonerated from their liability on said recognizance...

The Court then adjourned until nine o'clock tomorrow morning...
Test William Grisham...O. H. Kenan J.S.C.C.C.

Page 171.   ...Tuesday...21 Feb. 1837...9 o'clock...The court met
            according to adjournment...

The State	) Six several executions for fine of
vs	) $10 each for non attendance as
John Blythe, Edward J. Maddox)	jurors at the term of said court
Abraham Crow, John S. Holcomb)	1836...on motion to have the
Joseph Watt & William Jay)	several fines remitted...on read-
	ing the several affidavits showing

the cause of their attendance...it is ordered that the several
fines be remitted

Richard M. Holt	) Debt & c
vs	) We confess judgment to the pltff for the
John C. Bailey &	) sum of $80 with interest & cost of suit
Ferdinand Bailey	) this 20th Feby 1837...Ferdinand Bailey
	& John C. Bailey

James Barnett	) Debt & c
vs	) Settled
Ferdinand Bailey	)

The State	) Misdemeaner
vs	) True Bill
David Still	) Eli McConnell, foreman

Warren Akin, respondent	) Debt & c
vs	) We the jury find for the
Felix Moss & William Lay, appellant	) pltff $200 with interest
	& cost with ten percent

Special jury trial...jurors drawn:

1. Jas. S. Elliott   2. Robt. T. Griffin
3. Jesse Brown   4. Andrew Scott
5. Wm. Chamlee   6. Nelson Dickerson
7. Israel Evans   8. Solomon Humphries
9. Hiram Dimsdale   10. James W. Dooly
11. David Rusk, Senr.   12. John Tate

Page 172.   ...Tuesday...21st February 1837...Minutes of...

Green K. Cessna	) Assumpsit & c
vs	) Dismissed
Jonathan Chastain &	)
William Worley, endorser	)

James Gilbert	) Assumpsit
vs	) Settled
John Brewster	)

David Brown, Assignee	) Assumpsit & c
vs	) Settled
John Dial	) O. H. Kenan, I.S.C.C.C.

Page 173. ...Minutes of the Superior Court, Cherokee Co., Ga...

CHEROKEE COUNTY SUPERIOR COURT MINUTES

M. P. Quillin, bearer   ) Assumpsit & c
    vs   ) Judgment confessed for the pltff for
William Worley   ) sum of $150 with interest & cost...
                      the defendant being dissatisfied with
the verdict...the confession of Judge rendered in the above cause
...and having paid all cost and demanded an appeal brings James
A. Maddox and tenders him as his security and they the said
William Worley and James A. Maddox, Samuel Tate acknowledge
themselves jointly and severally bound to M. P. Quillian bearer
...the pltff for the payment of the eventual condemnation money
in said cause...in testimony whereof they have hereunto set their
hands and seals this 24th day of February 1837...William Worley,
James A. Maddox & Samuel Tate (original signatures)...Test.
William Grisham, clerk.

John Epperson & Co. for the use of) Debt & c
Littleberry Underwood   ) Judgment confessed to the
        vs   ) pltff for the sum of $67.12
James Jordan   ) principal with interest &
                      cost of suit...with right
of appeal...the defendant being dissatisfied with the confession
of judgment rendered in the above case and having paid all cost
and demanded an appeal...brings Eli McConnell and tenders him as
his security and they the said James Jordan and Eli McConnell
acknowledge themselves jointly and severally bound to John Epperson & Co. for the use of Littleberry Underwood the pltff for the
payment of the eventual condemnation money in said cause...in
testimony whereof they have hereto set their hands and seals this
25th day of February 1837...James Jourdan & Eli McConnell (original signatures)...Test. William Grisham, clerk

Page 174.   Minutes of the Superior Court...Cherokee County...

Georgia   ) February Term 1837...The Grand Jurors sworn,
Cherokee Co.) chosen and selected for the county of Cherokee at
             the present term of the Superior Court, in addition
to the presentments already made by the grand jury...they also
present John Poor Dear, a Cherokee Indian for stabbing Rattling
Gourd and Walanetah on the 23rd January 1837 in said county of
Cherokee, witnesses Rattling Gourd and Walanetah...
We present Aaron Seamore, William Barker and Lewis Roberts for
malicious mischief committed by throwing down the chimney of
the house occupied by Eady Storey in said county...some time
about the last of January 1837...witness Eady Storey...

On examination of the condition of the jail, we find the lower
room to be kept in good order...the upper room is in a very bad
condition...we therefore request the Inferior Court to take it
into consideration and compel the Sheriff or Jailer to have it
cleaned...
Having gone through the ordinary business of the county...we beg
to take into consideration a matter in which the whole people of
Georgia are particularly interested...we consider the appointment
of Col. William N. Bishop of Murray county to the office of
Teller of the Central Bank of Georgia as calculated in a great
degree to paralize the confidence of the publick in the true
administration of its financial affairs...from the character of
Col. Bishop great distrust will arise in the management of the
bank...believe it to be our duty as citizens to demonstrate
against the appointment...

CHEROKEE COUNTY SUPERIOR COURT MINUTES

In taking leave of his Honor Judge Kenan...we tender to him our
warmest thanks for the able manner in which he has discharged the
ardeous duty of Judge during the present term...also to H. L.
Sims, solicitor for his polite attention to this body during the
present term...
We request that so much of our presentments as are of a publick
nature be published in the Miners Recorder...Eli McConnell, foreman...

James S. Elliott	Robert T. Griffin
William Chamlee	Nelson Dickerson
Jabez J. Holcomb	James W. Dooly

Page 175.   ...Tuesday...21st February 1837...(continued)...

Jesse Brown	William Whitaker
Andrew Scott	James H. Chambers
Toliver Bostick	Isreal Evans
Peter C. Boger	Hiram Dimsdale
Burwell Dobs	Solomon Humphries
David Rusk, Senr.	John Tate
William Hardman	Edward Townsend

F. Logan & Co.   ) Sci fa
       vs   ) The defendant having shown no cause in the
R. F. Daniel   ) foregoing case it is therefore ordered...
                   that judgment be entered against the defend-
ant for the principal interest & cost...R. M. Holt, Plff's atty

The State   ) Misdemeanor
    vs   ) As previously entered in Cherokee Superior Court
David Still   ) True bill...Eli McConnell, Foreman

The State   ) Trading with a slave without license & simple
    vs   ) larceny
G. A. Bolch) The defendant in the case first aforesaid having
                been convicted & sentenced by the court to 6 months
imprisonment...and which time has not yet expired and the case
last aforesaid being yet pending against the defendant...but the
prosecutor being willing that said Bloch be discharged from his
said confinement and the case last aforesaid continued and at the
term of this court #1...Pros. provided the said Boalch leaves
this county and never again appear in it...it is ordered by the
court that so much of said sentence as shall not have been
executed on the first day of March next be remitted and that at
that time the Sheriff be authorized and directed to release said
Bolch from confinement...February term 1837...

Page 176.   ...Tuesday...21st Feb. 1837...Minutes...

The State   ) Peace warrant
    vs   ) on payment of cost...the defendant was discharged
George Brock) from his recognizance...Samuel Hillhouse, pro-
                secutor

The Ignatius A. Few) Assumpsit
       vs   ) We the jury find for the pltff $50 with
W. B. Key   ) interest & cost of suit...Philip Kroft,
                      foreman

Georgia   ) February term 1837...The grand jurors sworn

262

Cherokee County) chosen & selected for the county of Cherokee
                       at the present term of the Superior Court beg
leave to make the following presentments...we present Aaron Downing and David Still, Cherokee Indians for a misdemeanor for having
in possession a quantity of stolen goods the property of William
Hammonds of the State of Tennessee...witnesses William Hammonds
& Samuel Hillhouse...
We also present Pidgeon Roost a Cherokee Indian for the crime of
murder committed on the 17th of February instant 1837 upon the
body of an Indian by the name of Hogshooter in Cherokee county...
witnesses John Uwana & Tinny...
We also present Joiner C. Bailey for an assault & battery committed upon the body of Amanda Thompson a female in said county on
the 3rd day of February 1837...witnesses Amanda Thompson & Curtis
Satterfield.

Special Jury sworn:

Eli McConnell, foreman	James S. Elliott
Robert T. Griffin	Jesse Brown
William Whitaker	Andrew Scott
William Chamlee	Nelson Dickerson
Israel Evans	Peter C. Boger
Hiram Dimsdale	Jabez T. Holcomb
James W. Dooly	David Rusk, Senr.
John Tate	William Hardman
James H. Chambers	Burwell Dobbs
Edward Townsend	Toliver Bostick
Solomon Humphries	

The State   ) Simple larceny
   vs   ) Nol. Pros.
George Still, Jr., an Indian)

Page 177.   ...Tuesday...21st Feb. 1837...Minutes...

The State   ) Murder
   vs   ) Whereas M. W. Story has attended at this
Middleton W. Story &) term and being ready for trial and a jury
others   ) being empannelled...and no trial had...
                        ordered that he be prosecuted at next
term or discharged.

Georgia   ) It appearing to the court that John B. Garrison
Cherokee County) Sheriff of said county of Cherokee sold while
                     he was late sheriff...lot of land #75 in the
15th district of said county for the sum of $514 under some fi fas
from a Justice Court of Baker County issuing from Keel's district
against John Smith...when Jeremiah Fields became the purchaser for
the sum aforesaid and it further appearing that said lot of land
was drawn by a different individual...to wit...John Smith of
Hattons district of said county and that the sheriff has still in
his hands the said sum of money so improperly paid at said sale...
on motion of counsel for the said Fields it is ordered by the
court that the said John B. Garrison show cause tomorrow morning
by nine o'clock or so soon thereafter as council can be heard why
he should not pay back the whole amount of said sum of money there
being no legal claimant for the same...by said Fields relinguish-
ing his title to said lot of land as aforesaid and filing the
same in the Clerks Office of the Superior Court of said county...
I acknowledge due and legal service of the within this 20th Feby

1837...John B. Garrison, D.A.

```
John McWhorter   )  Debt & c
     vs          )  I confess judgment in the within gor the sum of
G. W. Winters &  )  $75 principal with interest & cost of suit...
Joseph Wofford   )  21 Feb. 1837
```

```
The State   )  Simple larceny
    vs      )
Ned Van & ---)
```

Page 178. Minutes of the Superior Court...Cherokee County...

The court then adjourned until court in course...O. H. Kenan
(original signature), J.S.C.C.C....Test. William Grisham, clerk

Page 179.   Georgia...August term 1837...

```
Milligan P. Quillian            )  Assumpsit & c
     vs                         )  Verdict for the pltff for $300
William Worley, maker &         )  principal besides interes & cost
Elijah W. Chastain, Indorser    )  ...the defendant being dissatis-
                                   fied with the verdict of the
```
juryrendered in the above cause and having paid all costs and
edmanded an appeal...bring William W. Worley and tender him as
their security and they the said William Worley, Elijah W. Chastain and William W. Worley acknowledge themselves jointly and
severally bound to Millican P. Quillian, the pltff for the payment
of the eventual condemnation money in said cause...in testimony
whereof they have hereunto set their hands and seals this the
twenty sixth day of August 1837...Wm. Worley & W. W. Worley
(original signatures)...$10...cost sec. only...Test William
Grisham, clerk

Page 180. Minutes of the Superior Court of Cherokee County...

It appearing to the court that lot of land #75 in the 15th district
of the 2nd section of Cherokee county was heretofore levied on by
virtue of sundry fi fa against John Smith the drawer of said lot
of land by virtue of which levy John B. Garrison late sheriff of
said county sold said lot of land for the sum of $514...it is
therefore ordered that said sheriff show cause why he does not
pay over the said sum of money to the pltffs atty...I acknowledge
service of the within...John B. Garrison

```
James Burns, Resp.     )  Assumpsit
     vs                )  I confess judgment to the pltt for the
Wm. Whitaker, Appelant )  sum of $47.84 with interest & cost of
                          suit...Wm. Whitaker
```

```
John Nailer    )  Trover & c
     vs        )  Dismissed
Kader Stancel  )
```

```
Z. B. Hargrove, pltff       )  Claim
     vs                     )  Dismissed
Wm. Hanna, defendant &      )
Howard Smith, claimant      )
```

CHEROKEE COUNTY SUPERIOR COURT MINUTES

Farish Carter, Respondent) Debt
vs) We confess judgment to the pltff
William Worley & Samuel Tate) for the principal sum of $674 with
interest & cost...21 Aug. 1837...
W. H. Steelman, Defts. atty.

The State) Prejury
vs) No Bill
George A. Walker) Joseph Donaldson, foreman

Page 181. Georgia...Monday...21st of August 1837...

John Doe, ex dem & William Grisham) Ejectment
vs) We the jury find for the
Richard Roe, casual ejector &) pltff the possession in
Jack Still, tenant in possession) dispute and for the rent
$24 with cost of suit...
Wm. W. Smithwick, foreman

John Doe, ex dem & William Grisham) Ejectment & c
vs) We the jury find for the
Richard Roe, casual ejector & Jack) pltff that part of the
Still & Dinah, Cherokee Indians,) premises in dispute lying
tenants in possession) on the south side of the
river & the sum of $40 for
rent & cost of suit...Wm. W. Smithwick, foreman

R. B. Duncan) Debt
vs) Settled
John Tate)

Henry Albright) Assumpsit & c
vs) I confess judgment to the pltff for the sum
William Worley) of $62 with interest & cost of suit this
21st August 1837...Wm. Worley

William Kirkham) Debt & c
vs) I confess judgment to the pltff for the sum
William Worley) of $75 with interest & cost of suit...21st
August...Wm. Worley

The Inferior Court of Cherokee County) Debt
vs) I confess judgment to
Philip Kroft) the pltffs for the sum
of $80 with interest and
cost of suit this 21st Aug. 1837...Philip Kroft

The court then adjourned until eight o'clock tomorrow morning...
O. H. Kenan (original signature), J.S.C.C.C....Test. William
Grisham, clerk

Page 182. ...Third Monday in August 1837...Minutes of the court..

Wm. A. McMillion) Fi fa
vs) It appearing to the court that the above
John Ragsdale) fi fa is founded upon a judgment which was
entered up at the August term of this court
in the year 1833 upon a promissisory note made by John Ragsdale
and Elender Ragsdale and payable to Lydia McMillion or bearer in
favor of William A. McMillion who had become the bearer of said
note and that the name of Elender Ragsdale was not included in

265

the action upon which the said fi fa is founded...it is therefore
ordered that the pltff in said fi fa be permitted to take a copy
of said note in order to proceed against Elender Ragsdale the
other obligor...

It appearing to the court that Felix Moss has been compelled to
pay a note as an endorser upon William Worley, which was sued
upon and a recovery had in this court...ordered that the clerk
deliver said note to said Moss to enable him to collect the same
from said Worley...the clerk retaining a copy in his office...

COPY NOTE; Twelve months after date I promise to pay Felix Moss
or bearer $200 for the value rec'd...witness my hand & seal
January the 22nd 1834...Wm. Worley...Endorsed Felix Moss...Wm.
Lay...received the above described note this 22nd Aug. 1837...
Felix Moss (original signature)

James Jordan) Debt & c
     vs   ) I confess judgment to the pltff for the sum
A. C. Roberts) of $180 with interest & cost of suit this 21st
)   August 1837...A. C. Roberts

Page 183. Superior Court of Cherokee County, GA...21 Aug. 1837...

James Jordan) Judgment for the pltff for $180 principal
     vs   ) with interest & cost of suit...in this case
A. C. Roberts) the defendant comes forward and stays the same
)   in terms of the law...John Anderson Senr.
binding himself on the stay as fully as if herein more fully
stated for the principal interest & cost...witness our hands &
seal this 21 Aug. 1837...A. C. Roberts & John Anderson (original
signatures)

Truman Kellogg   ) Assumpsit & c
     vs   ) Judgment for the pltff for $500 principal
Austin C. Roberts &) with interest & cost...in this case the
John Anderson   ) the defendants comes forward to stay the
)   case and render Maj. John Anderson as
security all of whom acknowledge themselves bound to the plff
for the principal interest & cost of suit...21 Aug. 1837...A. C.
Roberts & John Anderson (original signatures)

It appearing to the court that John W. Leonard, former deputy
sheriff of the county of Cherokee under John P. Brooke former
sheriff of said county gave his receipt to Benjamin F. Williams
for a fi fa issued from a Justices court in the county of Habersham in favor of Calvin J. Hanks vs E. Jackson for $10.56 prin-
cipal with interest and cost...it is herefore ordered by the court
that John P. Brooke shew cause on tomorrow morning why he does
not pay over the money to the plantiff or his atty or produce the
fi fa in court with the proper entries thereon...J.A.R. Hanks,
plffs. atty.

Page 184. Minutes of Cherokee Superior Court, GA...

Milligan P. Quillian   ) Assumpsit & c
          vs   ) We the jury find for the pltff
William Worley, maker   ) $300 for his principal debt...
Elijah W. Chastain, endorser) with interest and cost of suit
)   James Wilson, foreman...21st
August 1837...

Page 1-3. Will of Stokes Pinyan. I, Stokes Pinyan, of advanced age...to my beloved wife Nancy Pinyan Lots #498 and 499, part of 497 in 4th Dist., 1st Sect...containing 80 acres more or less; to dau. Polly Barker, wife of Jeremiah Barker...to dau. Sally Pinion...to son William Pinyan...to son Jacob Pinyan ...to dau. Nancy Sluder, wife of William Sluder...to son Ellerson Pinyan...to dau. Rebecca Brown, wife of Andrew Brown...to son Thomas Pinyan...to dau. Elizabeth Brown, wife of William Brown...to son Jeptha Pinyan...to dau. Belinda Pinyan; at death of wife or end of widowhood, property to be sold and divided among children. Appt. Jacob Pinyan and Mathias Tally, Exers. Dated 11-19-1848. Signed Stokes Pinyan. Wit: Adam Thompson, Peter Weaver, John Cooper. Jacob Pinyan swore he was named Excr. 6-1-1857. Jas. R. Lawson, Ord. Will proven upon oaths of Adam Thompson and John Cooper 6-1-1857. Signed James R. Lawson, Ord. of Lumpkin Co. Jas. R. Lawson swore will to be true transcript and ordered to be recorded 6-4-1858. Recorded 6-4-1858 by H. K. Wikle, Ord. of Dawson Co.

Calvin J. Lawless, Samuel R. Findley, and James Sutton, Securities, bound unto H. K. Wikle, Ord. and Successors...$600.00...condition being that Calvin J. Lawless adm. of estate of Stokes Pinyan...make true and perfect inventory...just/ and true account...deliver legacies. Signed Calvin J. (X) Lawless, L.S., Samuel R. Findly, L.S., and James Sutton, L.S. H.K. Wikle, Ord. Calvin J. Lawless swore will was last true will of Stokes Pinyan 6-7-1858.

Pages 4-7. John L. Summerour, principal, and Efford Seay (pp.5-6 missing) are firmly bound unto Henry K. Wikle and Successors...$2500.00...7-5-1858...condition that John L. Summerour is adm. of est. of George Reid...true and just accounts...pay to persons entitled...signed, sealed and acknowledged in open court. John L. Summerour, L.S., Efford Seay, L.S. H. K. Wikle, Ord. John L. Summerour swore Geo. Reid died intestate...pay debts...make true return...7-5-1858. J. L. Summerour. Henry K. Wikle, Ord.

Page 7. Alfred Webb, principal, and David Hill and Asaph Hill, securities...held firmly bound to H. K. Wikle, Ord. and successors...$3000.00...condition that Alfred Webb appl. for Letters of Adm. in the estate of Reuben Hill, Sr., dec'd... make true and perfect inventory before 1st Mon. in Sept. Alfred Webb, L.S., David Hill, L.S., Asaph Hill, L.S. Tested and approved by H. K. Wikle, Ord. Recorded 7-28-1858. H. K. Wikle, Ord.

Page 8. We, Alfred Webb, principal, and David Hill and Asaph Hill, Securities...firmly bound unto D. P. Monroe, Ord. and successors...$3000.00...9-6-1858...condition that Alfred Webb is adm. of est. of Reuben Hill, Sr., dec'd...make true and perfect inventory...truly administer...make true account as required by Superior Court or Register of Probates...pay to persons entitled...obtain cert. of probate. Alfred Webb, L.S., David Hill, L.S., Asaph Hill, L.S., David P. Monroe, Ord.

Page 9. Alfred Webb swore Reuben Hill, Sr. died intestate... truly adm. goods and chattels...make true return. Sworn to in open court 9-6-1858. Alfred Webb, Adm. Daniel P. Monroe, Ord.
...we Calvin J. Lawless, principal, James Sutton and

Francis Findley, securities, are firmly bound unto John W.
Hughes, Ord. and successors...$600.00...12-6-1858...condition is
that Calvin J. Lawless appt. adm. of est. of Stokes Pinyan.
Calvin J. (X) Lawless, J.S., James (X) Sutton, F. F. Findley.
        Calvin J. Lawless, James Sutton and Francis Findley swore
they were worth $600.00 12-6-1858. Calvin J. (X) Lawless, James
(X) Sutton, F. F. Findley. John W. Hughes, Ord.

Page 10. ...we Daniel P. Monroe and James L. Baird are bound
        unto John W. Hughes Ord...$700.00...12-14-1858...con-
dition that Daniel P. Monroe has been appt. gdn. of the property
of minor children of Zachariah Wilkins (vix), Hill Wilkins, and
also Nathaniel D. Hall (vix), Malinda S.J. Hall, Sarah Ann E.
Hall and Albert H.W. Hall. Daniel P. Monroe, L.S., James L.
Baird, L.S., John Hughes, Ord.
        Daniel P. Monroe swore to perform duties of gdn. Daniel P.
Monroe. Subscribed and sworn to this 12-14-1858. John W.
Hughes, Ord.

Page 11. Georgia, Lumpkin County...we Stephen Cantrell and
        Robert B. McClure, security, are firmly bound unto
James B. Lawhorn, Ord. and successors...$6,000.00...condition
that Stephen Cantrell appl. for Temporary Letters of Adm. of
est. of Basil S. Cantrell, dec'd...make true and perfect inventory...surrender est. and effects with inventory unto proper
adm. on 1st Mon. in Jan. Stephen Cantrell, L.S., Robert B.
McClure, L.S. Attest: James R. Lawhorn, Ord.

Page 12. Lumpkin County...bond of Stephen Cantrell swore that
        Basil S. Cantrell. Signed Stephen Cantrell, L.S.,
Robert B. McClure, L.S., James R. Lawhorn.

Page 13. Lumpkin County...Stephen Cantrell swore that Basil S.
        Cantrell died intestate...adm. goods and chattels,
pay debts...make true return and perfect inventory...1-8-185(5?).
Stephen Cantrell. James R. Lawhorn, Ord.

Pages 14-15. State of Alabama, Jackson Co., 11-11-1858. David
        L. Hall applied to court for Letters of Gdnship of
Malinda S.J. Hall, Sarah A.E. Hall, and Albert Hall, minor ch.
of Nathaniel D. and Martha E. Hall...$396.00...bond with J. P.
Ledbetter and G. W. R. Larkin as securities...appt. David L.
Hall gdn. of sd. minors.
        I, John H. Norwood, Judge of the Ct. of Probate of sd. co.
swear the above is true and correct. Swore cert. is in due
form of law. 1-19-1859. John H. Norwood, Judge.
        Recorded 2-3-1859. John W. Hughes, Ord. of Dawson Co.

        I, David L. Hall of the Co. of Jackson and State of Ala...
Gdn. of minor children of M.E.B. Hall, dec'd of Forsyth Co. and
St. of Ga...have appt. Nathaniel P. Hall of the Co. of Jackson
and St. of Ala. my true and lawful atty...sue for $200.00 out
of est. of Reuben Hill, dec'd, which is left to dau. Belariah Wilkins, dec'd, which sum is now due to Malinda S.J. Hall, Sarah
A.E. Hall and Albert H.W. Hall, minor heirs of the above named
M.E.B. Hall, formerly M.E.B. Wilkins, dau. of Belariah Wilkins,
dec'd, and sd. N.P. Hall...11-13-1858...signed, sealed, and delivered in the presence of W.C. (X) Owen. David L. Hall, L.S.
        State of Ala., Jackson Co...I, John Norwood, Judge...
certify that David Hall, Gdn. executed same voluntarily...John
R. Norwood, Judge of Probate. Recorded 2-3-1859. John W.

DAWSON COUNTY, GEORGIA, WILLS AND BONDS 1857

Hughes, Ord. of Dawson Co.

Page 16.   ...we, J. J. Burt and John Hockenhull, Sr. are bound
        unto John W. Hughes, Ord. and successors...$300.00...
5-2-1859...condition is that J. J. Burt is appt. gdn. of John
Sheriff and Sarah Sheriff, minor ch. of Hinchy B. Sheriff, dec'd.
...5-2-1859...in presence of R. V. Wilson and James M. Hulsey.
J. J. Burt, L.S., Jon Hockenhull, L.S.

Pages 17-19. Will of Charles I. Thompson. I, Chas. I. Thompson,
        being of advanced age...bequeath to son Henry C.
Thompson all my land lying east of Robt. B. McClure in 13th
Dist., south half, 1st Sect...also bequeath to son Henry C.
Thompson slaves Julia and her four children, Amanda and her two
ch., Green Bob and Jo...to my two sons Andrew J. Thompson and
William W. Thompson, house place and land attached to same in
the 13th Dist., south half, 1st Sect...also bequeath to son
Andrew J. Thompson negro slaves Betsy, Lucy, John, Clark. Solomon, Roan, Bonaparte, Piety, Josaphien, Nancy and one small
Negro slave from out of Williams stock of Negroes...also to my
son William W. Thompson, Negro slaves Garrison, Eliza and her
five children, Allen, Harret and her child little Eliza and her
child...also to son William W. Thompson the land I hold in my
own name above Jeffery Becks on waters of Shoal Creek in the
4th Dist. and 1st Sect...to son Andrew J. Thompson land I hold
in my own name lying on waters of Hanging Rock Creek adj. Andrew
J. Logan in the 4th Dist., 1 Sect...to sons Henry C. Thompson,
Andrew J. Thompson and William W. Thompson lands lying in the
Hightower River including land in the big shoal of sd. river now
in the possession of Jackson Martin as tenant...to beloved wife
Sarah S. with whom I have lived in the strictest quiet for
thirty-nine years, slaves Harry, Kate, Cyntha, Mary and Jenny,
during her natural life...at her death, to be divided among
three sons...appt. Henry C. Thompson and Andrew J. Thompson,
Excrs...this 3-13-1857. Charles I. Thompson, L.S. Wit: James
Cantrell, James B. Anderson, Elias P. Bond, Andrew J. Logan.
        G., Lumpkin Co. Before me came Andrew J. Thompson and
James Cantrell, Elias P. Bond and Andrew J. Logan, witnesses of
the will of Chas. I. Thompson, dec'd, and produced last will
and test...said they saw Chas. I. Thompson sign voluntarily...
said testator was of sound and disposing mind...sworn to in open
ct. 10-5-1857. Jas. R. Lawhorn, Ord. Jas. Cantrell, Elias P.
Bond, Andrew J. Logan.
        I, Andrew J. Thompson, one of excrs. of will of Chas. I.
Thompson, swear writing contains last true will...will pay debts,
then legatees...will make true and perfect inventory. Sworn and
subscribed in open ct. 10-5-1857. Andrew J. Thompson. Jas. R.
Lawhorn, Ord.

Page 20. ...We Wm. P. Reynolds, principal, and Wm. L. Reynolds,
        G. B. Hudlowe and A. Beam, securities...bound unto
Ord. and successors...$2400.00...9-5-1859...condition that Wm.
P. Reynolds has perm. adm. of est. of Ransom P. Reynolds, dec'd
...true and perfect inventory...make just and true account...
pay to persons entitled...obtain Cert. of Probate...Wm. P. Reynolds, L.S., Wm. L. Reynolds, L.S., G. B. Hudlowe, L.S., A.
Beam, L.S. D. H. Logan.

Page 21. ...we Nancy Nix and Samuel Weaver, principal, and
        Reuben T. Burt and Daniel P. Monroe, securities...
bound unto Ord. and successors...$3,000.00...9-5-1859...condi-

269

tion that Nancy Nix and Samuel Weaver adm. est. of Thomas Nix,
dec'd...true and perfect inventory...true account...pay to persons entitled...obtain Cert. of Probate. Nancy Nix, L.S.,
Samuel Weaver, L.S., Reubin T. (X) Burt, D.P. Monroe, L.S.,
Samuel C. Johnson, N.P.

Pages 22-23. ...we, Andrew H. Hill and John W. Hill, principal,
          and James L. Harris, Jas. Hill, Samuel E. Taylor,
A. J. Taylor, D. H. Logan, securities...bound unto Ord. and
successors...$10,000.00...10-3-1859...condition that Andrew J.
Hill and John W. Hill have perm. adm. of est. of Asaph Hill,
dec'd...true and perfect inventory...make just and true account
...pay to persons entitled. Andrew H. Hill, L.S., John W. Hill,
L.S., J. L. Harris, L.S., James Hill, L.S., Samuel E. Taylor,
L.S., A. J. Taylor, L.S., D. H. Logan, L.S. ...John L. Summerour,
George R. Robinson.

Page 24. ...we David H. Logan, principal, L. J. Lefbetter,
          A. J. Logan, B. L. Logan...bound unto Ord. and suc-
cessors...$12,000.00...11-7-1859...condition that David H. Logan
appt. gdn. to Wm. H. Logan and Jas. M. Logan, orphans of James
Logan, dec'd. David H. Logan, L.S., Lewis J. Ledbetter, Andrew
J. Logan, L.S., Benj. L. Logan, L.S., David Hill, L.S., John W.
Hill, L.S. Lewis J. Ledbetter, Jacob Pinyan...approved John
W. Hughes, Ord.

Page 25. ...we, Rebecca Robinson, principal, and Moses M. Burt,
          security...bound unto Ord. and successors...$250.00...
12-5-1859...condition that Rebecca Robinson appt. gdn. to John
B. Robinson, Andrew J. Robinson, Sarah E. Robinson, and Wm. T.
Robinson, orphans of Wm. Robinson, dec'd. Rebecca Robinson,
L.S., Moses M. Burt, L.S. John W. Hill, Samuel Harben.

Page 26. ...we, John A. McClure and David J. Roe, principal,
          and Stephen Cantrell and Robt. N. McClure, securities
...bound unto Ord. and successors...$40,000.00...12-9-1859...
condition that John A. McClure and David J. Roe appt. temp.
adms. of Robt. B. McClure...make true inventory...surrender to
proper adm. John A. McClure, L.S., David J. Roe, L.S., Stephen
Cantrell, L.S., Robt. N. McClure, L.S. H.J. Whitmer, John
Burnett.

Page 27. ...we John A. McClure and Robt. N. McClure...bound unto
          Ord. and successors...$4,000.00...1-9-1860...condition
that John A. McClure is appt. gdn. of John C. Cantrell, orphan
of Basil S. Cantrell, dec'd...John A. McClure, L.S., Robert N.
McClure, L.S. ...W.J. Barrett, John Hockenhull, M.D.

          ..., Robt. N. McClure and John A. McClure...bound unto Ord.
and successors...$4,000.00...1-9-1860...condition that Robt. N.
McClure appt. gdn. to Robt. N. Cantrell, orph. of Basil S.
Cantrell, dec'd...Robt. N. McClure, L.S., John A. McClure, L.S.,
W. J. Barrett, John Hockenhull, M.D.

Page 28. ...we, Stephen Cantrell and David J. Roe, principal,
          and John A. McClure, security, bound unto Ord. and
successors...$8,000.00..2-6-1860...condition that Stepehn
Cantrell and David J. Roe appt. gdn. to Polly Ann Cantrell and
Martha Cantrell, orphans of Basil S. Cantrell. dec'd...Stephen
Cantrell, L.S., David J. Roe, L.S., John A. McClure, L.S.
Dennis Hyde, James J. Stone...tested and approved John W.

Hughes, Ord.

Pages 28-29.   ...John A. McClure and David J. Roe, principal,
               ...and Stephen Cantrell and Robert N. McClure,
security...bound unto Ord. and successors...$40,000.00...2-6-
1860...condition that John A. McClure...true and perfect inventory...just and true account...pay to persons entitled...obtain
cert. of probate...John A. McClure, L.S., David J. Roe, L.S.,
Stephen Cantrell, L.S., Robert N. McClure, L.S.   Dennis Hyde,
James A. Stone...test and approved John W. Hughes, Ord.

Page 30.   ...we Christopher Young, principal, and Horatio Tatum
           and Adam Thompson, securities...bound unto Ord. and
successors...$500.00...3-5-1860...condition that Christopher
Young has perm. adm. of est. of James Young, dec'd...true and
just account...pay to persons entitled...obtain cert. of probate
...Christopher Young, L.S., Horatio Tatum, L.S., Adam Thompson,
L.S.   S.C. Johnson, N.P. for Dawson Co...tested and approved
John W. Hughes, Ord.

Page 31.   ...we Robt. N. McClure, gdn. of Robt. N. Cantrell, and
           Stephen Cantrell, security bound unto John A. McClure
and David J. Roe, Adms. of Robt. B. McClure, dec'd...$1200.00...
3-21-1860...condition that John A. McClure and David J. Roe,
Adms. paid to Robt. N. McClure $1225.25 in full of the sd.
Robt. N. Cantrell distributive share, it being the one fourth
of one fifth of sd. estate...Robt. N. McClure, L.S., Stephen
Cantrell, L.S.

Page 32.   ...I, Robt. N. McClure and Stephen Cantrell, security,
           bound unto John A. McClure and David J. Roe, Adms. of
Robt. B. McClure, dec'd...$5,000.00...3-21-1860...condition that
John A. McClure and David J. Roe, Adms., delivered unto Robt. N.
McClure his distributive share of land and negroes valued at
$4901.00, it being one fifth.   Robt. N. McClure, L.S., Stephen
Cantrell, L.S.

Page 33.   ...we, Andrew H. Hill and A. W. Wilkins, William
           Barrett, John Hollingshead, David M. Hill and Martha
Hill...bound unto Ord. and successors...$1800.00...6-4-1860...
condition that Andrew H. Hill appt. gdn. of Martha J. Hill,
Barbray L. Hill and Clamentra D. Hill, minor children under
fourteen years of age of Asaph Hill, dec'd...Andrew Hill, principal, A. W. Wilkins, security...Wm. Barrett, sec....John
Hollingshead, sec., David M. Hill, sec., and Martha (X) Hill,
sec...approved by John W. Hughes, Ord. for Dawson Co.

Page 34.   ...we, Andrew H. Hill, principal, and Anonymus W.
           Wilkins, William Barrett, John Hollingshead, David M.
Hill and Martha Hill...bound unto Ord. and successors...$1800.00
...6-4-1860...condition that Andrew H. Hill is appt. gdn. to
Arabella E. Hill, Lucinda C. Hill and Reubin Hill, orphans of
Asaph Hill, dec'd.   Andrew H. Hill (seal), A. W. Wilkins (seal),
William Barrett (seal), John Hollingshead (seal), David M. Hill
(seal), Martha (X) Hill (seal).   Approved by John W. Hughes,
Ord. of Dawson Co.

Page 35.   ...we William P. Reynolds, principal, and William L.
           Reynolds, security...bound unto Ord. and successors...
$698.00...7-2-1860...condition that William P. Reynolds appt.
gdn. of Lurania Reynolds, Eliza A. Reynolds, Ransom P. Reynolds,

Margarett S. Reynolds and William E. Reynolds, orphans of Elijah H. Reynolds, dec'd...W. P. Reynolds, L.S., W. L. Reynolds, L.S. Samuel R. Findley...attested and approved John W. Hughes, Ord.

Page 36.   ...we, William M. Bearden and Leonard Bearden...bound unto Ord. and successors...$1,000.00...12-3-1860... condition that William M. Bearden is appt. gdn. to Patrick W. Fitzsimmons, orphan of Henry Fitzsimmons...William M. Bearden, L.S., Leonard Bearden, L.S.   L. H. Hope, J. E. Talley... approved John W. Hughes, Ord.

Page 37.   ...we A. M. Barrett, principal, and Wm. Kelley, William Anderson...bound unto Ord. and successors... $6,000.00...1-14-1861...condition that A. M. Barrett has perm. adm. of est. of Reuben Barrett...true and perfect inventory... just and true acct...pay persons entitled...obtain cert. of probate...A. M. Barrett, L.S., William Kelley, L.S., William Anderson, L.S....signed, sealed and acknowledged in open court before me John W. Hughes, Ord.

Page 38.   ...we Nancy Nix, and Pickins E. Willis and R. H. Moss, securities...bound unto John W. Hughes, Ord. and successors...$2400.00...3-4-1861...condition that Nancy Nix, natural gdn. to Susan E. Nix, Wm. J. Nix, Bethina C. Nix, John L. Nix, Rachel M. J. Nix, and Rutha M. P. Nix to whom there has lately come an estate by distribution from the est. of Thomas Nix of $1200.00...Nancy Nix, L.S., Pickens E. Willis, L.S., R.H. Moss, L.S.   John W. Hughes, Ord.

Page 39.   ...we James L. Heard, principal, and David Hill. sec... bound unto Ord. and successors...$7,000.00...4-2-1861 ...condition that James L. Heard appt. temp. adm. of Lewis J. Ledbetter...James L. Heard, L.S., David Hill, L.S.   Tested and approved by me John W. Hughes, Ord.

Page 40.   ...we James L. Heard, principal, and David Hill and Harrison Summerour, securities...bound unto Ord. and successors...$7,000.00...6-3-1861...condition that James L. Heard has perm. adm. of est. of Lewis J. Ledbetter...true and perfect inventory...just and true acct...pay persons entitled... obtain cert. of probate...James L. Heard, L.S., David Hill, L.S., Harrison Summerour, L.S.   Signed, sealed and acknowledged in open court this 6-3-1861.   John W. Hughes, Ord.

Page 41.   ...we E. P. Bond, principal, and James L. Baird, security...bound unto Ord. and successors...$120.00... 6-5-1861...condition that E. P. Bond appt. temp. adm. of James W. Reynolds, dec'd...true inventory...surrender property with inventory unto legal adm...E. P. Bond, L.S., James L. Baird, L. S.   Tested and approved by me John W. Hughes, Ord.

Page 42.   ...we E. P. Bond, principal, and James L. Baird, security...bound unto Ord. and successors...$132.00... 8-5-1861...condition that E. P. Bond has perm. adm. of est. of James W. Reynolds...perfect inventory...just and true account... pay persons entitled...obtain cert. of probate...E. P. Bond, L. S., James L. Baird, L. S.   Tested and approved John W. Hughes, Ord.

Page 43.   ...we, James Netherland and William Anderson and A. M. Barrett...bound unto Ord. and successors...$600.00...

4-7-1862...condition that James Netherland has perm. adm. of
est. of Mary M. Dooly...true and perfect inventory...just and
true account...pay persons entitled...obtain cert. of probate...
James Netherland (seal), Wm. (X) Anderson (seal), A. M. Barrett
(seal). Acknowledged in open court before me John W. Hughes,
Ord.

Page 44. ...we, Henry Howser, principal, and A. J. Logan,
security...bound unto Ord. and successors...$35.00...
4-7-1862...condition that Henry Howser has perm. adm. of est. of
Robt. Howser...true and perfect inventory...just and true acct...
pay persons entitled, obtain cert. of probate...Henry Howser
(seal), A. J. Logan (seal). Acknowledged in open court before
me John W. Hughes, Ord.

Page 45. ...we Wm. Kelley, Sr., principal, and Jordan Anderson,
security...bound unto Ord. and successors...$1,000.00
...6-31-1862...condition that Wm. Kelley, Sr. appt. temp. adm.
of est. of Wm. Kelley, Jr...perfect inventory...surrender property and inv. to legal adm...Wm. Kelley, Sr., L.S., Jordan (X)
Anderson, L.S. Tested and approved by John W. Hughes, Ord.

Page 46. ...we, John E. Rives, principal, and Raymond Sanford,
security...bound unto Ord. and successors...$7,000.00
...8-4-1862...condition that John E. Rives has perm. adm. of est.
true acct...pay to persons entitled...obtain cert. of probate
...Jno. E. Rives, L.S., Raymond Sanford, L.S. Tested and
approved by me John W. Hughes, Ord.

Page 47. ...we, Wm. Burt, principal, and James J. Burt, security
...bound unto Ord. and successors...$600.00...8-21-
1862...condition that Wm. Burt appt. temp. adm. of est. of David
Densmore...true inventory...surrender property with inv. to
legal adm...Wm. Burt, L.S., J. J. Burt, L.S. Tested and approved by me John W. Hughes, Ord.

Page 48. We Ransom Seay, Efford Seay, Lorenda Seay and Caroline
Gross was present yesterday morning 7-28-1862 at the
residence of Dempsey Seay before and at the time of his death.
About three hours before his death in perfect possession of his
mental faculties as appeared to us said Demsey Seay called upon
the bystanders and upon undersigned in particular to remember
and take notice of what he was about to say when he said that
it had been his intention for some time past to make his will in
writing thereby to dispose of his property but had neglected to
carry his intention into execution and that now it was not
practicable that he wished us to understand that his will and
desire was that Mrs. Caroline Seay, my wife, should have, take
and possess all my personal estate of every kind and description
to her own proper use, benefit and behoof and he desired and
requested that his brother Ransom Seay and his cousin Efford
Seay would see that his wishes and desires in this regard were
carried fully out immediately after which he died, this 7-29-
1862. Signed Ramson Seay, Efford Seay, Lorenda (X) Seay,
Caroline (X) Goss.

In person appeared before me John S. Holden, a Justice of
the Peace...Ransom Seay, Efford Seay, Lorenda Seay and Caroline
Goss, who being duly sworn say that this writing contains the
last request and disposition of the personal property of Demsey
Seay, dec'd...and is just and true in all its parts. Ransom

Seay, Efford Seay, Lorenda (X) Seay, Caroline (X) Goss. Sworn and subscribed before me this 7-19-1862.

Pages 49-50. Will of James Banister, Sr. I, James Banister, Sr. of advanced age...bequeath to beloved wife Martha Banister for and during her natural life all my land... Lots 796, 768, 837, 771, 797, lying in the Fourth Dist., First section of Dawson Co....also farming utensils, roan mare, mule, cows, etc...at her death property to be sold by excr...dau. Salina Phillips, wife of Wm. L. Phillips, $25.00 and her share of proceeds...proceeds to be divided equally among children Powell Banister, Deverix Banister, James Banister, Jr., Elizabeth Banister, Jarrett Banister, and Martha Stewart, wife of Clark Stewart...appt. son James Banister, Jr., adm. 7-14-1862. James (X) Banister, L.S.   Wit: Daniel P. Monroe, John Hollinshead, A. M. Barrett, James Netherland.

Before me John W. Hughes, Judge of the Ct. of Ord., came A. M. Barrett, Daniel P. Monroe and James Netherland, witnesses of will of Jas. Banister...saw him sign of his own accord... possessed sound mind...9-2-1862...Daniel P. Monroe, James Netherland, A. M. Barrett.

FORSYTH COUNTY WILL BOOK A - 1833-1844
Record of the Proceedings of the Court of Ordinary
Contributed by Mary Annette Schroeder, Cumming, Georgia

Abstracted by: Mary Annette Schroeder

Page 1: Aug. 26, 1833 Court of Ordinary adjourned term.
Present: Hon. WILLIAM MATTHEWS, ISAAC WHARTON and RICHARD
HAYES.

Ordered that the following will recorded and proven:

Pages 1-5: Aug. 21, 1833 Will of PARKER COLLINS...to my
eldest dau. SALLY HARRIS, my Negro girl Celia, age 13, and her
furture increase... to my second daughter ELIZA HARRIS, my Negro
girl Mary Ann and her future increase... to my third daughter
LUCINDA COLLINS, my Negro girl Rose and her future increase...
to my fourth daughter SUSAN HARRIS, my Negro girl Betsy and her
future increase... to my fifth daughter JANE COLLINS, my Negro
girl Louise and her increase... to my sixth daughter
NANCY COLLINS, my Negro girl Fanny and her increase... to my
seventh daughter KATHY COLLINS, my Negro girl Caroline and her
increase... to my eighth daughter MARY COLLINS, my Negro boy
Henry... to my ninth daughter MARTHA COLLINS, my Negro boy
Jacob... to my eldest son JOSEPH COLLINS, my Negro boy George...
to my second son PARKER COLLINS, my Negro boy Andy... for the
education of children JUNE COLLINS, NANCY COLLINS,
KATHY COLLINS, PARKER COLLINS and MARTHA COLLINS, custody of
tuition to my wife ANN COLLINS... to wife ANN COLLINS, Negro
slaves Sam and his wife Hannah, Celia, Molly, David and his wife
Riah; also 10 cows, calves, 10 two-year-old head of cattle, all
stock of hogs, household and kitchen furniture, plantation tools
and farming utensils, five horses and tract of land on which I
live... to daughter SUSAN HARRIS, land known as Collins Cowpens
whereon HENRY BAGLEY now lives... to my youngest son
PARKER COLLINS, $100 to purchase horse, saddle and bridle... to
daughters who have not received cows and calves and bed
furniture, $50. Appts: sons-in-laws CHARLES HARRIS,
RANCE B. HARRIS and WILLIAM HARRIS Executors.
PARKER (X) COLLINS. Wit: JAMES MCGINNIS, JOHN SMITH,
MAT J. WILLIAMS.

Sworn in open court Aug. 5, 1833. Signed:
WILLIAM MATTHEWS, J.I.C., ISAAC WHARTON, J.I.C., RICHARD HAYES,
J.I.C., MASON EZZELL, J.I.C.

Sworn in court Aug. 26, 1833. CHARLES (X) HARRIS,
RANCE B. (X) HARRIS, WILLIAM (X) HARRIS.

Recorded in open court Aug. 26, 1833.

JAMES MCGINNIS swore he saw PARKER COLLINS sign will. Dated
Aug. 5, 1833.

CHARLES HARRIS, RANCE B. HARRIS and WILLIAM HARRIS swore to
properly execute will of PARKER COLLINS. Dated: Aug. 26, 1833.

Pages 6-7: Will of PARKER COLLINS exhibited in court,
proved and admitted to record, Adm. of Estate granted to
CHARLEY HARRIS, RANCE B. HARRIS and WILLIAM HARRIS... required
to render inventory... Witnesses the Hon. WILLIAM MATTHEWS,
W. A. ROSS, C.C.O.

Page 7: DAVID BLACKWELL, JOHN ROGERS, MARTIN BRANNON,
JOHN ANDERSON and WILLIAM MATTHEWS authorized to make
appraisement of Estate of PARKER COLLINS.

Pages 8-10: Appraisement of Estate of PARKER COLLINS...
Negroes listed: David, Marcia, Celia, Mary Ann, George, Louisa,
Carolina, Molly, young Celia, Rose, Betsy, Andrew, Fanny, Henry,
Jacob, Sara,Hannah... Notes: A. R. SMITH, HENRY BAGLEY,
JOHN ROGERS, JOHN BREWSTER, WILLIAM HARRIS, Total
$9217.43-1/2... sworn before WILLIAM MSTTHEWS, J.I.C.
Sept. 3, 1833. Signed: JOHN ROGERS, DAVID BLACKWELL,
MARTIN (X) BRANNON.

Pages 11-13: Nov. 13, 1833. Account of the sales of the
personal property of the Estate of PARKER COLLINS. Buyers:
DAVID BLACKWELL, MARTIN BRANNON, THOMAS B. WELLS, DIXON NAYTON,
JAMES C. MARTIN, JAMES MIDDLETON, WILLIAM A. CAMERON,
EVAN HOWELL, NATHAN L. HUTCHINS, WILLIAM ROGERS, JOSEPH COLLINS,
JAMES MCGINNIS, JR., JOHN PRIEST, CHARLES HARRIS, BENJAMIN IVEY,
JOSEPH NAYTON, YOUNG P. POOL, MARTIN AYERS, ROBERT NAYTON,
S. F. ALEXANDER, WILEY BROGDON, ANN COLLINS, LOVELY ROGERS,
JOHN ROGERS, D. A. LANSDOWN, DAVID CORDRAY, EDWARD DANIEL,
THOMAS B. WILLS, SAMUEL PEDEN, HEZEKIAH MILLEN, ROBERT ROGERS,
H. TRAMMELL, JOSEPH WOTT(?), WILLIAM H. DRUMMOND, BENJAMIN
PRUITT, DAVIS WILLIAMS, HENRY BAGLY, JOHNSON B. LOWERY,
JOHN ANDERSON, WILLIAM FUQUA, HAMILTON TRAMMELL,
DAVID L. WORDLAW, REUBIN SAMS... Total $1014.75...
DAVID BLACKWELL, Auctioneer.

Page 13: Jan. 13, 1834. The Honorable the Court of
Ordinary met pursuant to adjournment. Present: Their Honors
ISAAC WHARTON, RICHARD HAYES and MASON EZZELL.

Examined Return of Estate of PARKER COLLINS which was
received and ordered to be recorded.

Page 14: Return on Estate of PARKER COLLINS... total
$5275... allowed and recorded by Court of Ordinary.

Page 15: PARKER Returns... Lists notes of JOHN BREWSTER,
A. R. SMITH, JOHN ROGERS, ELISHA WINN, WILLIAM HARRIS, HENRY
BAGLEY, MARTIN BRANNON, DIXON NAYTON, JAMES C. MARTIN,
JAMES A. MIDDLETON, WILLIAM A. CAMMERON, NATHAN L. HUTCHINS.

Pages 16-17 (cont.): WILLIAM ROGERS, JOSEPH COLLINS,
JAMES MCGINNIS, BENJAMIN PRUITT, CHARLES HARRIS, BENJAMIN IVEY,
JOSEPH NAYTON, Y. P. POOL, MARTIN AYERS, ROBERT NAYTON,
S. F. ALEXANDER, WILEY BROGDON, ANN COLLINS, LOVELY ROGERS,
D. A. LANSDOWN, DAVID CORDRAY, DAVID BLACKWELL, EDWARD DAVID,
SAMUEL REDDEN, HARDIN MILLER, ROBERT ROGERS, HAMILTON TRAMMELL,
JOSEPH WOTT, WILLIAM H. DRUMMOND, LEWIS WILLIAMS, HENRY BAGLEY,
SOLOMON R. LOWERY, JOHN ANDERSON, WILLIAM FUQUA, D. L. WORDLAW,
REUBEN SAMS. Balance on hand... $2794.16-1/2.

The above return sworn to in open court by CHARLEY HARRIS,
RANCE B. HARRIS and WILLIAM HARRIS, Executors of PARKER COLLINS
Estate... Jan. 13, 1834.

276

Page 17: Recorded Jan. 13, 1834. Examined and sanctioned Jan. 13, 1834. Signed: ISAAC WHARTON, J.I.C., RICHARD HAYES, J.I.C., MASON EZZELL, J.I.C.

Page 18: May 5, 1834. Court met agreeable to adjournment. Present: Their Hon. JAMES ROBERTS, MASON EZZELL and JOHN MIDDLETON.

Ordered that ISAAC WHARTON pay to MRS. SARAH ROBERTS seventy dollars for the relief of her distressed family.

Aug. 5, 1834 - Aug. Term 1834 - The Hon. the Court of Ordinary met agreeable to adjournment. Present: Hon. JAMES ROBERTS, ROBERT WILLIAMS, JOHN MIDDLETON, MASON EZZELL, JACOB MARTIN.

JOHN W. THOMPSON, having petitioned said court for leave to give bond and security as Guardian of GEORGE W. T. ALLEN and THOMAS M. ALLEN, orphans of THOMAS G. ALLEN, in order to removed the guardianship from Jackson County as the annexed certificate will show that he had complied with the law in such case, made approved... Ordered that Clerk take bond in the amount stated in said Certificate and good security.

Georgia, Jackson County... WILLIAM COWAN, Clerk of the Inferior Court of said County and state afsd... when sitting for Ordinary purposes do hereby certify that JOHN W. THOMPSON, guardian to GEORGE W. T. ALLEN and THOMAS G. ALLEN has given his bond with securities for the sum of $2000, as appears on record in my office. Given under my hand and seal... 30th day of July, 1834... WILLIAM COWAN, C.C.O. (L.S.)

Page 19: JOHN W. THOMPSON, ROBERT SMITHWICK and LEVEN HUDSON are bound unto the Ordinaries... and successors... in sum of $2,000. Dated Aug. 5, 1834. Agreement made to transfer guardianship to Forsyth County. Signed: JOHN W. THOMPSON, ROBERT SMITHWICK, LEVEN (X) HUDSON.

Examined and approved Aug. 5, 1834. JAMES ROBERTS, J.I.C., ROBERT WILLIAMS, J.I.C., JOHN MIDDLETON, J.I.C., JACOB MARTIN, J.I.C., MASON EZZELL, J.I.C.

Page 20: At a Court of Ordinary held for Jackson County Sept. 1, 1828. Present: WILLIAM D. MARTIN, SAM'L BARNETT and JOHN W. GLENN, Esqrs...

ROBERT ALLEN and LOUISA ALLEN having given the notice required by law that they should apply to this court for Letters of Adm. on the Estate of THOMAS G. ALLEN, dec'd and no objections being made -- ordered that said letters be granted.

ROBERT ALLEN, LOUISA ALLEN, DAVID L. KNOX and HORATIO WEBB... bound under judges of Court of Ordinary in the sum $3,000. Sept. 1, 1828.

Page 20-21: Court required ROBERT ALLEN and LOUISA ALLEN to make inventory and exhibit same in Court of Ordinary... required to obtain certificate of probate. EDWARD ADAMS, Clerk. Signed: ROBERT ALLEN, LOUISA (X) ALLEN, DAVID L. KNOX, HORATIO WEBB. Recorded Feb. 23, 1832.

Page 21: InVentory and appraisement of the Estate of
THOMAS G. ALLEN... Total personal property $2996.68-3/4.

Georgia, Jackson County... Swore that inventory above
contained true appraisement of the Estate of THOMAS G. ALLEN.
JOS. DAVIS, THOMAS A. NLOX(?), JAS. APPLEY, Appraisers.

I do certify that the above appraisers were sworn to perform
their duty as appraisers according to law... Oct. 30, 1828... W.
L. BRYANT, J.P.

Pages 21-23: Personal property of THOMAS G. ALLEN, dec'd
sold at public sale... total $530.77-1/4. Buyers: LOUISA
ALLEN, JOSEPH PRICE, H. WEBB, CHARLEY HUDSON, RALPH B. MCNEESE,
SOLOMON WOFFORD, SAM'L HUNTER, EPHRIAM BROWN, L. B. HOUSE, DAN'L
WHITEHEAD, R. ALLEN, JOSEPH LITTLE, J. YOUNG.

Pages 23-24: No. 1st Return of ROBERT ALLEN and
LOUISA ALLEN, Administrators of the Estate of THOMAS G. ALLEN.
Apr. 24, 1830 Amt. paid: $374.09-3/4. Paid to:
CHARLEY HUDSON, ORRS & WATSON, F. MERIWEATHER, L. DOSTER,
WILEY ROSS, Clerk Ct. of Ord., H. WEBB, D. L. KNOX,
JOSHUA ROBERTS, S. RIPLEY, G. R. DUKE, JAMES COCHRAN,
CHARLES BACON, HOBSON & PALMER.

Page 24: Return of ROBERT ALLEN, Administrator... monies
paid to L. KELLOGG, ISAAC RAWLS, GEORGE SHAW, H. WEBB,
J. L. CUNNINGHAM, CAMAK & RAGLAND, printers, O. P. SHAW,
printer, J. SHIELDS, L. ADAMS, J. RANDOLPH, for crying sale,
WILLIAM APPLEBY, WILLIAM COWAN, Clk. Total $459.92-1/2.

Return of ROBERT ALLEN, Adm. of Estate of THOMAS G. ALLEN...
at July Term, 1834. Paid to EDWARD ADAMS, THOMAS NIBLACK...
total $2.18-3/4

List of insolvent debts owed estate... notes on
ELIAS MCOLLUM, R. D. CASTER... total $66.27-1/2.

Page 25: Jan. 14, 1834. Court met according to
adjournment. Present: Hon. EDWARD ADAMS, JOHN G. PITTMAN,
N. C. JURRETT, SAMUEL BURNS.

Ordered by the Court that JAMES APPLEBY, WILLIAM MONTGOMERY
AND EZEKIEL RATCHFORD be appointed for the purpose of appraising
and distributing the property of THOMAS G. ALLEN, dec'd among
the legatees of said dec'd.

At the Inferior Court sitting for ordinary purposes in and
for the County of Jackson on Mon., Nov. 4, 1833. Present: Hon.
EDWARD ADAMS, NATHANIEL C. JURRETT, SAMUEL BURNS.

Ordered that JOHN W. THOMPSON be appointed Guardian for
GEORGE W. T. ALLEN and THOMAS M. LAYFAYETTE ALLEN, orphan
children of THOMAS G. ALLEN, dec'd... he giving bond and
security in terms of the law.

FORSYTH COUNTY WILL BOOK A - 1833-1844
Record of the Proceedings of the Court of Ordinary

Page 25-26: Georgia, Jackson County... JOHN W. THOMPSON,
HORATIO WEBB and WILLIAM E. JONES are firmly bound unto...
Judges of the Inferior Court... and their successors... in the
sum of $2,000. Dated Nov. 4, 1833. JOHN W. THOMPSON appointed
Guardian to GEORGE W. T. ALLEN and THOMAS M. LAYFAYETTE...
signed and acknowledged in open court... WM. COWAN, C.C.O.
Signed: JOHN W. THOMPSON, HORATIO WEBB, WILLIAM E. JONES.

Page 26: Recorded Nov. 26, 1833. Georgia, Jackson
County... I, WILLIAM COWAN, Clk. of the Inferior Court of said
county... do hereby certify the above... dated Sept. 4, 1834.
WILLIAM COWAN, C.C.O.

Clks fas. -
23 copy sheets @ 7-3/4 cts. per copy sheet   1.77-3/4
                 seal and certificate   .62-1/2
                                        $2.40-1/4

Georgia, Forsyth County, Clerks office of the Court of
Ordinary for said County, recorded Oct. 14, 1834.

November Term, 1834. The Hon. Court of Ordinary met
agreeable to adjournment. Present: Hon. JAMES ROBERTS,
JOHN MIDDLETON and ROBERT WILLIAMS.

Ordered that CHARLOTTE VICKERY be appointed Guardian for
CHARLES VICKERY, MARY VICKERY, SARAH VICKERY, JOHN VICKERY,
LUCY VICKERY and SUSAN VICKERY, orphans of HARRY VICKERY, dec'd
and that Letters of guardianship do issue.

Page 27: Georgia, Forsyth County... we CHARLOTTE VICKERY,
JOHNSON ROGERS, THOMAS CORDRAY are bound... unto Judges of the
Inferior Court... in the sum of $1500. Dated Nov. 3, 1834.

CHARLOTTE VICKERY appointed Guardian of CHARLES VICKERY,
MARY VICKERY, SARAH VICKERY, JOHN VICKERY, LUCY VICKERY and
SUSAN VICKERY, orphans of HARRY VICKERY. W. A. ROSS, C.C.O.
Signed: CHARLOTTE (X) VICKERY, JOHNSON ROGERS, THOMAS CORDRAY,
DAVID (X) CORDRAY. Recorded Nov. 7, 1834. W. A. ROSS, Clk.
Approved by Court W. A. ROSS, C.C.O.

Page 28: Georgia, Forsyth County... to CHARLOTTE VICKERY...
whereas CHARLES VICKERY, MARY VICKERY, SARAH VICKERY,
JOHN VICKERY, LUCY VICKERY and SUSAN VICKERY, orphans of
HARRY VICKERY... possessed of a considerable estate... more
ample maintenance and education of said orphans... do hereby
commit the tuition, education and Guardianship... to you the
said CHARLOTTE VICKERY... charging you that you maintain and
cause to be educated said orphans... a perfect account you shall
render to the 1st Term of the Court of Ordinary in every year...
CHARLOTTE VICKERY appointed Guardian of said orphaNs during
their minority. Witness the Hon. ROBERT WILLIAMS, one of the
judges of said Court of Ordinary. Dated Nov. 3, 1834. W. A.
ROSS, C.C.O. Recorded Nov. 7, 1834.

Page 29: Mon. Jan. 5, 1835. The Hon. Court of Ordinary met
agreeable to adjournment. Present: Their Hon. ROBERT WILLIAMS,
MASON EZZELL and JACOB MARTIN.

Page 29-30: Return of JOHN W. JOHNSON, Guardian of
G. W. T. ALLEN and T. M. L. ALLEN, orphans of THOMAS G. ALLEN,
dec'd. 1834 Sum of $117.91... for hire of Negroes $115. Sworn
to in open court Jan. 5, 1835. W. A. ROSS, C.C.O. Recorded
Jan. 5, 1835.

Page 30: At a court held for Forsyth County Jan. 5, 1835.
Present: ROBERT WILLIAMS, MASON EZZELL and JACOB MARTIN, esqrs.

RICHARD H. LESTER, having given the notice required by law
that he should apply for Letters of Adm. on the Estate of
LEWIS SIMS, dec'd and no objection being made, ordered that said
letters be granted.

Pages 30-31: Georgia, Forsyth County... we
RICHARD H. LESTER, WILLIAM P. ANDERSON and JOHN BOYD are held
bound to... Judges of the Court of Ordinary and successors...
for sum of $800. Dated Jan. 5, 1835... required to make true
and perfect inventory... shall pay debts of Estate... required
to obtain certificate of probate. Signed, sealed and
acknowledged in open court W. A. ROSS, C.C.O. Signed:
R. H. LESTER, JOHN L. BOYD, WM. P. ANDERSON. Recorded
Jan. 19, 1835, W. A. ROSS, Clk.

Page 32: Georgia, Forsyth County... whereas LEWIS SIMS died
intestate... having divers goods, chattels, lands and credits
within the County of Gwinnett... full power of adm. granted to
R. H. LESTER. Witness the Hon. MASON EZZELL, one of the Judges
of the said Court of Ordinary... this 5th day of Jan., 1835.
W. A. ROSS, C.C.O. Recorded Jan. 19, 1835.

Page 33: At a court held for the County of Forsyth, Jan. 5,
1835. Present: ROBERT WILLIAMS, MASON EZZELL and JACOB MARTIN,
Esqrs. JAMES GASTON, having given lawful notice that he should
apply for Letters of Adm. on the Estate of MESHACK DEAL of
Fayette Co., dec'd and there being no objection, ordered that
said letters be granted.

Pges 33-34: Georgia, Forsyth Co.... JAMES GASTON and
CULLEN DAVIS are held firmly bound... unto the Judges of the
Court of Ordinary and their successors.. sum of $600... dated
Jan. 5. 1835.

JAMES GASTON ordered to make a true and perfect inventory...
signed, sealed and acknowledged in open court. W. A. ROSS,
C.C.O. Signed: JAMES GASTON (L.S.), CULLEN DAVIS (L.S.).
Recorded Jan. 19, 1835. W. A. Ross, C.C.O.

Pages 34-35: Georgia, Forsyth Co... Whereas MESHACK DEAL,
late of Co. of Fayettte, dec'd died intestate... do hereby grant
unto JAMES GASTON, adm. of the goods, chattels, lands and
credits of said dec'd... JAMES GASTON having given bond and
security and having taken the oath and performed all other
necessities required by law... ordained, constituted and
appointed adm. Witness the Hon. MASON EZZELL, one of the Judges
of said Court of Ordinary. Jan. 5, 1835. W. A. ROSS, C.C.O.
Recorded Jan. 19, 1835. W. A. ROSS, C.C.O.

Page 36: Mar. 3, 1835. The Inferior Court met pursuant to
adjournment. Present: Hon. JAMES ROBERTS, JACOB MARTIN and
ROBERT WILLIAMS.

The Second Return of the Executors of the Last Will and
Testament of PARKER COLLINS, dec'd, being examined by the court
and received, ordered to be recorded.

Page 37: Second Return of the Estate of PARKER COLLINS,
dated Jan. 13, 1834 - March 3. Cash to legatees. H. SUTTON,
LUCINDA SUTTON, CHARLEY HARRIS, SARAH HARRIS, R. B. HARRIS,
ELIZA HARRIS, WILLIAM HARRIS, SUSAN HARRIS. Signed:
CHARLY HARRIS, R. B. HARRIS, WILLIAM HARRIS, Executors.
July 13, 1834.

Page 38: Dated 1834. Return on PARKER COLLINS Estate
(cont.) Names listed: WILLIAM HARRIS, JOHN ROGERS,
ELISHA WINN, WILLIAM FUQUA, S. MCGINNIS, ANN COLLINS,
H. TRAMMELL, PRUITT D. NAYTON, W. H. DRUMMOND, J. C. MARTIN,
N. L. HUTCHINS. L. T. ALEXANDER, J. MATT, T. B. WELLS,
D. BLACKWELL, E. HOWELL, H. MILLER, W. BROGDON, R. H. NAYTON,
P. L. WORDLAW, M. AYERS, (?) PEYDON, D. A. LANDSDOWN,
Y. P. POOL, S. NAYTON, T. & L. RAGEN, W. ROGERS, W. A. CAMERON,
R. B. HARRIS, CHARLY HARRIS, W. HARRIS.   Total $1020.86.

Page 39: The foregoing Return of the Executors of
PARKER COLLINS, dec'd., sworn to in open court this 3rd Mar.
1835. W. A. ROSS, C.C.O. Recorded March 3, 1835.

Received this 8 Jan. 1835 from the Exrs. of PARKER COLLINS a
certain Negro girl called Mary Ann left to my wife by her late
father. Signed: R. B. HARRIS, ELIZA (X) HARRIS. Recorded
Mar. 11, 1835. W. A. ROSS, C.C.O.

Received this 8 Jan. 1835 from the Excrs. of PARKER COLLINS
a Negro girl named Lila left to my wife by her late father. In
presence of ABRAHAM HARRIS. CHARLY (X) HARRIS,
SARAH (X) HARRIS. Recorded Mar. 11, 1835.

Rec'd this 8 Jan. 1835 from the Exrs. of PARKER COLLINS a
certain Negro girl called Betty left to my wife by her late
father. In presence of ABRAHAM HARRIS. WILLIAM (X) HARRIS,
SUSAN (X) HARRIS. Recorded Mar. 11, 1835.

Page 40: The Honorable the Inferior Court met for Ordinary
purposes. Present: Hon. JAMES ROBERTS, MASON EZZELL and
ROBERT WILLIMAS.

...the petition of WILLIAM CRUISE by his next friend
JOHN CRUISE... showeth that his father is insolvent and has no
pemanent place of abode and that he stands much in need of a
guardian to direct and control his course and to provide him
with a fixed and regular home... your Honorable Body will
proceed to appoint a Guardian as the premises required...
WILLIAM CRUISE by JOHN CRUISE.

Whereupon it is ordered by the court here and now present that the said WILLIAM CRUISE having appeared in open court and made choice of JOHN CRUISE as his Guardian that upon the said JOHN giving bond and security in terms of the law he shall receive of the clerk the appropriate letters.

Pages 40-41: Georgia, Forsyth Co... JOHN CRUISE and REUBIN SAMS are held firmly bound unto... the Judges of the Inferior Court for ORDINARY purposes... and successors... in sum $500. Dated Apr. 21, 1835.

Court appointed JOHN CRUISE the Guardian of WILLIAM CRUISE, minor son of JEREMIAH CRUISE. Signed, sealed and acknowledged in presence of W. A. ROSS, C.C.O. JOHN (X) CRUISE (L.S.), REUBIN SAMS (L.S.)

Pages 41-42: Georgia, Forsyth Co... to JOHN CRUISE greeting... whereas WILLIAM CRUISE, a minor... for the better education and maintenance of said WILLIAM CRUISE... we hereby commit the tuition, education and Guardianship... charging you that you maintain and cause to be educated said WILLIAM CRUISE during his minority... manage real and personal property to the best interest of said WILLIAM CRUISE... render a true and perfect account of property to first term of Court of Ordinary every year... app. you Guardian of WILLIAM CRUISE. Dated Apr. 21, 1835. W. A. Ross, C.C.O.

Examined and sanctioned: JAMES ROBERTS, J.I.C., MASON EZZELL, J.I.C., ROBERT WILLIAMS, J.I.C.

Page 43: May 17, 1835. The Hon. the Inferior Court met for Ordinary purposes. Present: ROBERT WILLIAMS, JOHN MIDDLETON and MASON EZZELL.

Ordered that R. H. LESTER, Adm. of LEWIS SIMS, dec'd having applied for leaf to sell nol Estate of said dec'd. Said application having been advertised agreeable to law and there being no cause shown why said leaf should not be granted. Therefore said Adm. has leaf to sell said nol Estate agreeable to law... ROBERT WILLIAMS, J.I.C., JOHN MIDDLETON, J.I.C., MASON EZZELL, J.I.C.

July 6, 1835. The Hon. the Inferior Court met for Ordinary purposes. Present: Hon. REUBIN SAMS, NIMROD H. PENDLEY and ELIAS FINCHER, not having accomplished all the business before the court at that time the said court was adjourned until Fri. the 17th of July, 1835.

July 17, 1835. The Hon. the Inferior Court met according to adjournment. Present: Hon. REUBIN SAMS, NIMROD H. PENDLEY, JACOB MARTIN and ELIAS FINCHER.

Page 44: Ordered that JAMES GASTON, Adm. of MESHACK DEAL, dec'd having applied for leave to sell the nol Estate of said dec'd... therefore the said Adm. has leave to sell nol Estate.

Pages 44-45: Ordered that the following will and probate be
recorded. I, ROBERT SMITHWICK of the State of Ga. and Co. of
Forsyth... this my last will and testament... my body to mother
dust and soul to God... to wife ELIZABETH SMITHWICK, all my nol
personal and perishable est. during her natural life... after
death of my wife, to ROBERT ALLEN one fourth of all my nol
personal and perishable est.; to BEVERLY ALLEN, one fourth; to
JOHN ALLEN, one fourth; to GEO. W. T. ALLEN and THOMAS MADISON
L. ALLEN, one fourth. Appts.: BEVERLY ALLEN and ROBT. ALLEN,
exrs. Signed, sealed this 9th June, 1835 in presence of
WILLIAM H. BACON, THOMAS EZZELL, J. T. GARNER, ROBERT SMITHWICK
(seal).

Page 45: Georgia, Forsyth County. Personally appeared
before us JOSEPH T. GARNER, one of the witnesses to the
foregoing will... said he saw ROBERT SMITHWICK sign will... and
saw WILLIAM H. BACON and THOMAS EZZELL sign as witnesses.
(Signed) JOSEPH T. GARNER.
Sworn to in open court this 17th day of July, 1835.
W. A. ROSS, C.C.O.
We do solemnly swear that this writing contained in the last
will... of ROBERT SMITHWICK, dec'd... believe will truly
executed by paying debts and legacies... we will make a true and
perfect inventory. Signed: BEVERLY ALLEN, ROBERT ALLEN.
Recorded July 17, 1835. W. A. ROSS, C.C.O.

Page 46: Dated July 17, 1835... last will and testament of
ROBERT SMITHWICK was exhibited in open court and proved in
common form... admitted to record... administration of good
chattels and credits granted to BEVERLY ALLEN and ROBERT ALLEN,
having taken oath and performed requisites by law... required to
render true and perfect inventory and make returns yearly.
W. A. ROSS, C.C.O. Recorded July 17, 1835.

Page 47: To WILLIAM A. CAMERON (?), JOSEPH T. GARNER,
ARTHUR ERWIN, ALEXANDER WHITE and SAMUEL BENTLY, Esq...
authorized and empowered to appraise estate of ROBERT SMITHWICK.
Wit. the Hon. REUBIN SAMS, one of the judges of said court.
Dated July 17, 1835. W. A. ROSS, C.C.O. Examined and
sanctioned. Adjournment of Court in Course. REUBIN SAMS,
J.I.C., NIMROD H. PENDLEY, J.I.C., ELIAS FINCHER, J.I.C.,
JACOB MARTIN, J.I.C.

Pages 48-49: Inventory and apprisement of estate of
ROBERT SMITHWICK... Slaves: Anthony, Charles, Judah... note on
MOSES LOTT... total $1858.75.

Page 49: Inventory sworn to July 23, 1835 by
JOSEPH T. GARNER, WM. A. CAMERON, ARTHUR ERWIN, appraisers.
Certified July 23, 1835 by SAMUEL BENTLY, J.P.
Recorded Nov. 2, 1835 by W. A. ROSS, C.C.O.
The Court of Ordinary met the 4th of Jan., 1836. Present:
IRA R. FOSTER and NIMROD H. PENDLEY. There being no business
ready to be transacted, adjourned til tomorrow ten o'clock.
W. A. ROSS, C.C.O., IRA A. FOSTER, J.I.C., NIMROD H. PENDLEY,
J.I.C., JOSEPH D. FOSTER, J.I.C.

Page 50: Tuesday, 5th day of Jan. 1836, the Court of
Ordinary met pursuant to adjournment. Present: REUBIN SAMS,
IRA R. FOSTER, JOSEPH D. FOSTER, ELIAS FINCHER.
Jan. Term, 1835. It being the term that Executors,
Administrators and Guardians should make their returns.

JOHN THOMPSON, Guardian of the orphans of THOMAS G. ALLEN
made... return. To MARY O. B. BACON for tuition... paid
WILLIAM MARTIN, JAMES BLACKSTOCK, IRA R. FOSTER... $129.48.
Hire of the Negroes... JOHN JOLLY for Moriah and child and
Jeff... $168. Balance due the estate $38.51. (Signed)
JOHN THOMPSON, Guardian.
Sworn to in open court. IRA R. FOSTER, J.I.C.

Page 51: January Term, 1836. An election having taken
place for Clerk of the Court of Ordinary -- on counting out of
the vote DAVID MCCOY was duly elected to fill that office.
DAVID PUTNAM, Adm. of Estate of WILSON PUTNAM, dec'd...
interest $37.96, misc. $250. Sworn in open court. W. A. ROSS,
C.C.O. Adjourned till Saturday 10 o'clock. IRA B. FOSTER,
J.I.C., REUBIN SAMS, J.I.C., ELIAS FINCHER, J.I.C.,
JOSEPH D. FOSTER, J.I.C.

Page 51-52: ...DAVID PUTNAM and HENRY TEDDER are held
firmly bound unto... Judges of the Court of Ordinary in sum of
$1,000... sesaled and dated Jan. 5, 1836... DAVID PUTNAM
required to make inventory of WILSON PUTNAM Estate... required
to give account of administration to court... signed and sealed
and acknowledged in open court. W. A. ROSS, C.C.O.,
DAVID PUTMAN Adm. (L.S.), HENRY TEDDER (L.S.)
Georgia, Hall County... DAVID PUTNAM (note spelling change)
and THOMAS PUTMAN are held firmly bound unto... Judges of the
Court of Ordinary... in sum $1,000... sealed and dated
Jan. 4, 1830.

Pages 52-53: Georgia, Hall County... DAVID PUTMAN, Adm. of
Estate of WILSON PUTMAN, dec'd... required to make true and
perfect inventory... required to give account of
administration... signed, sealed and acknowledged in open court.
GEO. HAWSSE(?), C.C.O., DAVID PUTMAN (L.S.), THOMAS PUTMAN
(L.S.)

Pages 53-58: Inventory and appraisement of the Estate of
WILSON PUTMAN, dec'd... notes due: NATHANIEL HARBIN, JACOB
ELROD, JAMES JOHNSON, HENRY ADAMS, LUTHER WALLIS, NEALY DOBSON,
RICHARD PIRRY... total $500... certified upon oath by
appraisers. JOHN PUTMAN, THOMAS MAYES, ROBERT TATE.
Certified that the above appraisers were sworn to perform
their duty as appraisers according to the law this 6th day of
March, 1830. F. WHELCHEL, J.P.
March 10, 1830. Sale of Estate of WILSON PUTMAN, dec'd...
Names of buyers: MOSES WATERS, MALESSA PUTMAN, WILLIAM K___(?),
THOMAS PUTMAN, DAVID PUTMAN, WM. J. GRIFFIN, BENJAMIN GOSS, JOHN
HOUSE, WILLIAM WOOD... total $324.18-1/2
Georgia, Hall County. DAVID PUTMAN swore that Bill of Sale
transacted March 10, 1830 is just. Sworn and subscribed before
me this 29th day of Dec., 1830. GEORGE HAWSSE, C.C.O., DAVID
PUTMAN.

To DAVID PUTMAN, Adm... $27.93-3/4
Balance of Estate of Putman... $19.87-1/2
Return of DAVID PUTMAN, Adm. of Estate of WILSON PUTMAN,
dec'd. to Dec. 31, 1831... $136.75.
Personally came DAVID PUTMAN, Adm. of WILSON PUTMAN, dec'd.
and being duly sworn saith the return he now has made is just
and true. Sworn and subscribed this third day of Jan., 1832.
GEORGE HAWSSE, C.C.O., DAVID PUTMAN.
The Estate of WILSON PUTMAN dec'd. in account current with
DAVID PUTMAN for the year 1832... $21.22-1/2.
Personally came in open court DAVID PUTMAN... swore above is
true... sworn and subscribed in open court July Term, 1833.
GEO. HAWSSE, C.C.O., DAVID PUTMAN, Adm.

Nov. 1, 1833. Received of GRIFFIN REEVES the interest of
note of hand $194.40. Int. 12 mos... $15.55.

Personally came DAVID PUTMAN, Adm. of WILSON PUTMAN, dec'd,
and saith on oath the within account is just and true. Sworn to
and subscribed this 7th day of Jan., 1834. DAVID PUTMAN,
GEO. HAWSSE, C.C.O.
Received of D. PUTMAN, Adm. $1.25 cost of a jury 1834.
GEO. HAWSSE, C.C.O.... Also 12-1/2 cents tax 1833... cost plat
of grant to Lot 98 $5. In open court came DAVID Putman, Adm....
within account just and true... sworn and subscribed this 5th
day of Jan., 1835. DAVID PUTMAN, GEO. HAWSSE, C.C.O.

Georgia, Hall County
Ordinary Court, Sept. Term, 1835... Ordered that
DAVID PUTMAN, Adm. of WILSON PUTMAN, dec'd. have leave to remove
his proceedings from this court and that the Clerk gives him a
copy of all the proceedings had in said case Minutes signed.
JOHN BATES, J.I.C., N. GARRISON, J.I.C., JOSEPH DUNAGAN, J.I.C.

Georgia, Hall County Clerks Office, Court of Ordinary
I do hereby certify that the foregoing is true copy of the
Bond Returns of DAVID PUTMAN, Adm. of WILSON PUTMAN, dec'd.
taken from the records of my office.
Given under my hand and seal of office this 3rd day of Dec.,
1835. E. M. JOHNSON, Clk. C.O. Recorded this 6th July, 1836.
W. A. Ross, C.C.O.

Pages 58-62: Sale of Property of the Estate of
PARKER COLLINS, dec'd. sold on Oct. 26, 1835. Buyers:
JOHN BROWN, ANN BRANON, ISAIAH WILLIAMS, ANN COLLINS,
JAS. ROGERS, JAS. BROWN, WILLIAM HARRIS, THOMAS FOSTER,
WILLIAM GRAHAM, H. H. SUTTON, ALEXANDER FLANAGAN, ELI COMPTON,
SAMUEL BROWN, BEVERLY ALLEN, JAMES OWENS, MARTIN BRANNON,
DAVID BLACKWELL, EDWARD S. HAYES, JAS. H. WILLIAMS,
JOHN ANDERSON, CHARLES HARRIS, WILLIAM MCGINNIS, GEORGE JAMES,
A. BRANNON, RICHARD HAYES, JAMES S. SHADBURN, YOUNG P. POOL,
JAMES H. CHAMBERS, R. B. HARRIS, WILLIAM A. CAMERON(?),
JAMES T. GARNER, LEROY HAMMON, NIMROD H. PENDLEY, CALEB JONES,
JAMES VENABLE, JAMES MILLER, JAMES MOTT, ROBERT H. NIALER,
ARTHUR ERWIN, EZEKIEL HARRIS, JAMES STONE, JOHN ROGERS,
JARRELL GRAY, ROBERT DUNCAN, PETER TERRY, BRESWELL COOK,
CLABORN BROWN, HENRY BELL, D. A. SANSDOWN, S. BROWN,
DAVID A. SANDSDOWN, JOHN P. DICKINSON, JOHN HARDIN,
WM. H. BACON, DOW WILLIAMS, S. B. RUCKER, JAMES MCGINNIS,
JAMES MIDDLETON... total $1002.17.

Page 62: Sale of Negroes first Tues. in Dec., 1835. Named Celia, Molly, David, Mariah and child... $2225.

Jan. 9, 1836. The Hon. the Court of Ordinary met pursuant to adjournment. Present: IRA R. FOSTER, JOSEPH D. FOSTER, ELIAS FINCHER and REUBIN SAMS.

The Return of the Estate of PARKER COLLINS received on the usual oath and ordered to be recorded.

Page 63: No. 3. The Estate of PARKER COLLINS, dec'd. in WILLIAM HARRIS, Exr... $71.12.

Page 64: Account with CHARLES HARRIS, R. B. HARRIS... March 31, to Dec., 1835... Sales of Negroes in Dec.: $3223.17. Cash received on above sale: $3223.35-1/2. Cash on hand and laons: $1084.00 Sworn to in open court, IRA FOSTER, J.I.C., CHARLES HARRIS, Exr., R. B. Harris, Exr. WM. HARRIS, Exr.

Page 64: ROBERT WILLIAMS and NANCY T. WHITSITT, Adms. of the Estate of MOSES WHITSITT, dec'd. apply for leave to give bond here in order to remove the proceedings from Cherokee Co. to this county. Ordered that they have leave.

Jan. Term. 1836... ROBERT WILLIAMS, NANCY T. WHITSITT, DAVID N. SMITH and JOHN H. RUSSEN(?) are bound unto the Judges of the Court... in sum $10,000. Dated Jan. 9, 1896... ROBERT WILLIAMS and NANCY WHITSITT, Adms. of MOSES WHITTSITT, required to make inventory... required to account to the Court of Ordinary... signed, sealed and acknowledged in open court. W. A. ROSS, C.C.O., ROBERT WILLIAMS (L.S), NANCY T. WHITSITT (L.S.), JOHN H. RUSSEN(?) (L.S.), DAVID N. SMITH (L.S.)

Page 65: Adjourned till Court in course, July 9, 1836. IRA R. FOSTER, J.I.C., JOSEPH D. FOSTER, J.I.C., ELIAS FINCHER, J.I.C., REUBIN SAMS, J.I.C.

Georgia Cherokee Co.... MOSES WHITSITT, late of said county, died intestate... temporary letters of Adm. granted ROBERT WILLIAMS... ROBERT WILLIAMS required to make true returns. Dated Dec. 27, 1834. B. F. JOHNSON, C.C.O.

Pages 65-66: Georgia, Cherokee County... Whereupon the foregoing appt. of ROBERT WILLIAMS as Temporary Adm. of Estate of MOSES WHITSITT, dec'd... NANCY WHITSITT and ELI WHITSITT acknowledge themselves bound with said ROBERT WILLIAMS... sum of $6,000.

Pages 66-67: Georgia, Cherokee Co. Mar. 2, 1835. It being the required time of the Court of Ordinary the Hon. the Inferior Court met pursuant to adjournment. Present: Their Hons. JOHN MCCONNELL, JOSEPH DONALDSON and WILLIAM SAG... Ordered that ROBERT WILLIAMS and NANCY WHITSITT be appointed Adms. of... MOSES WHITSITT... bound in sum $10,000 with JOHN KING. Rec'd. in office of Clerk of the Court of Ordinary. Also ordered that ELI MCCONNELL, JOHN H. KING, ARTHUR ERWIN, MARK CASTLEBERRY and ENOCH ROGERS be appointed appraisers.

Pages 67-69: Georgia, Cherokee County. Inventory and
Appraisal of the Estate of MOSES WHITSITT. Negro slaves: Jim,
Frankey, Becky, Hubbard, Ellen, Isaac, Mary, William, Harriett,
Elleck, Julia, Duncan, Rose. Balance due on: JOHN NAYLER,
JAS. STEWART, JOSEPH ROGERS, ROBERT VENABLE, EDWARD J. MADDOX,
NATHAN POOL, JOHN B. WILLIAMS, ENOCH ROGERS... $4346.50.

Page 69: Georgia, Cherokee County... Appraisal of Estate of
MOSES WHITSITT sworn under oath by appraisers March 13, 1835.
ELI MCCONNELL, ENOCH ROGERS, MARK CASTLEBERRY, ARTHUR ERWIN.
    I do hereby certify that the above appraisers were sworn to
perform their duty as appraisers according to law. Dated
March 13, 1835. ELI MCCONNELL, J.P. Recorded June 11, 1835.
B. F. Johnson, C.C.O.

Pages 69-71: Inventory of the personal property of
MOSES WHITSITT, dec'd. sold at public sale July 6, 1835.
Purchasers: NANCY WHITSITT, EZEKIEL HARRIS, L. D. HARRIS,
W. A. BACON, WM. H. BACON, W. W. VAUGHAN, ROBERT WILLIAMS,
SAM'L HOLBROOK, JESS(?) C. HOLBROOK, ALEXANDER WHITE,
M. H. FORD, JAMES HARRIS... $379.07-3/4... ROBERT WILLIAMS,
Adm... MASON EZELL, Auctioneer.

Page 72: Current Estate of MOSES WHITSETT, dec'd. Lists
ALEX MILLER, JOHN H. KING, JESS(?) C. HOLBROOK, D. R. MITCHELL,
JAMES STEWART, ELI MCCONNELL, WILLIAM COUDRY, WILLIAM AARON,
MASON EZELL, JOHN NAYLER, WILLIAM HAY, MARTIN CHAMBER. Balance
remaining: $428.45-3/4.

State of Georgia, Cherokee County. At a meeting of the Hon.
the Inferior Court of Ordinary at the adjourned time on this
second day of Feb., 1836. Present: Their Hons. JOHN MCONNELL,
WILLIAM TOWNSEND, WILLIAM SAG(?) and JOSEPH DONALDSON met on
ordinary business. ROBERT WILLIAMS, Adm. of Estate of
MOSES WHITSITT, dec'd. having filed his return and vouchers with
the clerk was now sworn to its correctery examined by the court
received and ordered to be recorded and the voucher returned and
a certificate showing that a bond was filed in the Ordinary
Office in Forsyth County, it is ordered that said Administration
be removed to Forsyth County.

Page 73: ROBERT WILLIAMS, Adm. and NANCY WHITSITT, Adm. up
to Dec. 29, 1835... total $428.45-3/4.

State of Georgia, Cherokee Co.... I WILLIAM GRISHAM, Deputy
Clk. of the Court of Ordinary for said county do hereby certify
that this and the two named ____?, contain true copies of the
proceedings had on the Estate of MOSES WHITSITT, dec'd. and are
now recorded in said office... 1836. Given under my hand and
seal. WILLIAM GRISHAM, Dept. C.C.O. Cherokee Co.

The Inferior Court of Cherokee County on examination believe
that ROBT. WILLIAMS will be entitled to $15 for extra services
in his trouble and attention to administration of said Estate
and recommend to the Inferior Court of Forsyth County that he be
allowed this amt. on this next settlement... Given under our
hands and seal Feb. 3, 1836... JOSEPH DONALDSON, J.I.C.,
EDWARD TOWNSEND, J.I.C., JOHN MCCONNELL, J.I.C. Recorded
Feb. 9, 1836, W. A. ROSS, C.C.O. F.C.

Page 74: March Term 7th 1836.
The Hon. the Court of Ordinary met according to adjournment.
Present: IRA FOSTER, NIMROD H. PENDLEY, REUBIN SAMS,
ELIAS FINCHER, JOSEPH D. FOSTER.

Ordered that ROBERT WILLIAMS be authorized to manage the
Estate of MOSES WHITSITT, dec'd. to the best advantage.

Ordered that MARY FIELDS be appointed Guardian of
SUSAN MATILDA CAROLINE FIELDS and SAMUEL E. FRANKLIN FIELDS, her
two children... condition of proper conduct.

Court adjourned till court in course March 7, 1836.
D. MCCOY, C.C.O., IRA FOSTER, J.I.C., REUBIN SAMS, J.I.C.,
NIMROD H. PENDLEY, J.I.C., ELIAS FINCHER, J.I.C.

Page 75: Georgia, Forsyth County... we MARY FIELDS,
STEPHEN NOBLE and RICHARD H. LESTER are firmly bound unto...
Judges of the Court... in sum $1,000. Dated March 7, 1836.
... Whereas MARY FIELDS is this day appointed Guardian for
SUSAN M. C. FIELDS and SAMUEL E. F. FIELDS... signed, sealed and
delivered in the presence of D. MCCOY, C.C.O....
MARY (X) FIELDS, STEPHEN NOBLE, R. H. LESTER.

Georgia, Forsyth County. May Term the 2nd 1836.
The Hon. Court of Ordinary met according to adjournment.
There being no business ready the Court adjourned till Friday
the 5th. D. MCCOY, C.C.O., I. R. FOSTER, J.I.C., E. FINCHER,
J.I.C.

Page 76: 5th May 1836 Adjourned Term
The Hon. Court of Ordinary met according to appointment.
Present: I. R. FOSTER. There being no business ready the court
was adjourned till court in course. I. R. Foster, J.I.C.,
D. MCCOY, C.C.O.

July Term 4th 1836
The Hon. the Court of Ordinary met according to adjournment.
Present: Nons. REUBIN SAMS, ELIAS FINCHER, WILLIAM MARTIN, Esq.
There being no business ready the Court adjourned until Sat. the
9th. D. MCCOy, C.C.O., REUBIN SAMS, J.I.C., WILLIAM MARTIN,
J.I.C., ELIAS FINCHER, J.I.C.

July the 9th Adjourned Term
The Hon. Court of Ordinary met according to adjournment.
Present: Hons. REUBIN SAMS, I. R. FOSTER, WILLIAM MARTIN,
ELIAS FINCHER, JOSEPH D. FOSTER.

Ordered that WILLIAM W. VAUGHAN be and is appointed Guardian
to sell all the real estate of MATTHEW PENDER, idiot son of
WILLIAM PENDER... Court adjourned till court in course.
D. MCCOY, C.C.O., REUBIN SAMS, J.I.C., I. R. FOSTER, J.I.C.,
WILLIAM MARTIN, J.I.C., ELIAS FINCHER, J.I.C.

FORSYTH COUNTY WILL BOOK A -- 1833-1844
Record of the Proceedings of the Court of Ordinary

Page 77: Georgia, Forysth County... we WILLIAM W. VAUGHAN,
BERRY HILL, CHAS. WILLIAMS are held and firmly bound unto...
Judges and successors... in sum $500. Sealed and dated July 9,
1836. WILLIAM VAUGHAN appointed Guardian of MATTHEW PENDER,
idiot son of WILLIAM PENDER... conditional upon proper behavior.
D. MCCOY, C.C.O., W. B. HUTCHENS, W. W. VAUGHAN (L.S.),
BERRY (X) HILL (L.S.), CHARLES (X) WILLIAMS (L.S.).

Page 78: Georgia, Forsyth Co.... To WILLIAM W. VAUGHAN of
said Co. Greeting. Whereas MATTTHEW PENDER, idiot son of
WILLIAM PENDER, is possessed in his own right of a certain
fortune of real estate by means whereof the power of granting
the guardianship of said MATTHEW PENDER to us manifestly known
to belong and for better securing the Estate... appoint you
Guardian of MATTHEW PENDER... required to render a true and
perfect account the first term of the court every year.
    Wit. the Hon. WILLIAM MARTIN one of the Justices of the said
Court of Ordinary this mo. of July 1836. D. MCCOY, C.C.O.

Page 79: Sept. Term Sept. 5, 1836.
    The Hon. Court of Ordinary met according to adjournment.
Present: Hons. ELIAS FINCHER, JOSEPH D. FOSTER, REUBIN SAMS.
There being no business before the Court the adjourned till
Court in course.

    Georgia, Forsyth Co.... To MARY FIELDS, Greetings... Whereas
SUSAN M. C. FIELDS and SAMUEL E. FIELDS, minors... for better
securing the righTs and more ample maintenance and education...
we do hereby commit the tuition, education and guardianship...
required to render true and perfect account first term of court
every year. Wit. the Hon. IRA R. FOSTER, one of the Judges of
said Court. March 7, 1836. D. MCCOY, C.C.O.

Abstracted by
Mary Annette Schroeder Bramblett (in 1977)

Cont'd from Issue #65-66

Page 80: November Term the 7th 1836
The Hon. Court of Ord. met according to adjournment.
Present their Hons. REUBIN SAMS, ELIAS FINCHER, WILLIAM MARTIN,
IRA R. FOSTER.
Ordered that JAMES HUTCHINS, orphan of JAMES HUTCHINS,
dec'd. be bound to JOSEPH HAMMOND until he is 21 yrs. by the sd.
Hammond complying with the terms of the law.
Ordered that ROBERT ROGERS be and is appointed Guardian of
the heirs of the estate of DAVID CORDERY, dec'd.
The Hon. Court of Ord. adjourned till the 1st Tues. in Dec.,
1836. D. MCCOY, C.C.O., WILLIAM MARTIN, J.I.C., REUBEN SAMS,
J.I.C., IRA R. FOSTER, J.I.C., ELIAS FINCHER, J.I.C.

Page 81: Georgia, Forsyth County... ROBT. ROGERS,
WILLIAM ROGERS, JOHN ROGERS are held and firmly bound unto...
the Inferior Court sitting as a Court of Ordinary... and
successors... sum of six thousand dollars... sealed with our
seals and dated this 7th Nov., 1836... condition being that
ROBERT ROGERS is this day appt. Gdn. to THOMAS CORDERY,
WILSON CORDERY, ANDREW CORDERY, SEBORN CORDERY, CHARLOT CORDERY,
NANCY CORDERY, orphans of DAVID CORDERY, dec'd. Signed, sealed
and delivered in the presence of D. MCCOY, C.C.O.,
ROBERT ROGERS,, L.S., WILLIAM ROGERS, L.S., JOHN ROGERS, L.S.

Page 82: Georgia, Forsyth County. By the Hon. Inferior
Court sitting for Ordinary purposes... to ROBERT ROGERS...
whereas THOMAS CORDERY, WILSON CORDERY, ANDREW CORDERY,
SEBORN CORDERY, CHARLOT CORDERY, NANCY CORDERY, possessed in
their own right of a considerable estate... for better securing
the estate and more ample maintenance and education of sd.
orphans... we hereby commit the tuition, education and
guardianship... to you ROBERT ROGERS... required to render a
true and perfect account to the first term of Ct. every year.
Wit. the Hon. WILLIAM MARTIN, one of the Justices of sd. Ct. of
Ord. this 7th day of Nov., 1836. D. MCCOY, C.C.O.

Page 83: Dec. 6th 1836 Adjourned term
The Hon. Court of Ord. met according to adjournment, there
being no business ready the Court adjourned till the 12th of
Dec., 1836. D. MCCOY, C.C.O., IRA R. FOSTER, J.I.C.

Dec. the 12th, 1836 Adjourned term
The Hon. Court of Ord. met according to adjournment.
Present: their Hons. IRA R. FOSTER, ELIAS FINCHER,
JOSEPH D. FOSTER.

JOSEPH HAMMOND gave notice he would apply for Letters of
Guardianship of JAMES HUTCHINS, orphan of JAMES HUTCHINS, dec'd.
There being no objection it was ordered by the Court that sd.
Letters should be granted.

Court adjourned till Court in course. D. MCCOY, C.C.O.,
IRA R. FOSTER, J.I.C., JOSEPH D. FOSTER, J.I.C., ELIAS FINCHER,
J.I.C.

Page 84: Georgia, Forsyth County... we JOSEPH HAMMOND and
CULLEN DAVIS are held and firmly bound unto the... Inferior
Court sitting as a Court of Ord... and successors... sum of one
thousand dollars... sealed and dated this 12th of Dec., 1836...
condition that JOSEPH HAMMOND is this day appt. Gdn. of
JAMES HUTCHENS, orphan of JAMES HUTCHENS, dec'd... Attest:
D. MCCOY, C.C.O., JOSEPH HAMMOND, L.S., CULLEN DAVIS, L.S.

Page 85: Georgia, Forsyth Co.... to JOSEPH HAMMOND... whereas
the power of granting the guardianship of JAMES HUTCHENS... for
the better maintenance and education of the sd.
JAMES HUTCHENS... we do hereby commit the tuition, education and
guardianship to you... render a true and perfect acct. to the
first term of the Court of Ord. in every year... appt. you the
sd. JOSEPH HAMMOND guardian of afsd. JAMES HUTCHENS during his
minority... wit. the Hon. IRA R. FOSTER, one of the Justices of
the sd. Court of Ord. this 12th of Dec., 1836. D. MCCOY, C.C.O.

Page 86: Georgia, Forsyth County... We WILEY B. HUTCHENS,
ARTHUR ERWIN are held and firmly bound unto... the Inferior
Court sitting for Ord. purposes... and successors sum of one
thousand dollars... sealed with our seals and dated this 12th
day of Dec., 1836... condition being that WILEY B. HUTCHENS,
adm. of the estate real and personal of WILLIAM D. HUNT, dec'd.
do make a true and perfect inventory... required to administer
estate by law and make a true acct... deliver and pay to persons
entitled by law... last will and testament be proved before the
court and executor obtain a certificate of probate thereof.
Attest: D. MCCOY, C.C.O. WILEY B. HUTCHENS, L.S.,
ARTHUR ERWIN, L.S.

Page 87: Georgia, Forsyth County, Justices of the Inferior
Court... whereas WILLIAM D. HUNT late of the County, dec'd, died
intestate... having divers estate real and personal... hereby
grant unto WILEY B. HUTCHENS, administrator, full power to adm.
the entire estate. Wit. the Hon. IRA R. FOSTER, one of the
Justices of the COURT of Ord. this the 12th day of Dec., 1836.
D. MCCOY, C.C.O., IRA R. FOSTER, J.I.C.

Page 88: Jan. Term 1837 Jan. 2nd.
The Hon. Court of Ord. met pursuant to adjournment there
being not a majority of the Court present they adjourned till
the 3rd of Jan. D. MCCOY, C.C.O., IRA R. FOSTER, J.I.C.

Jan. 3rd. Adjourned Term 1837
The Hon. Court of Ord. met pursuant to adjournment. Present
their Hons. IRA R. FOSTER, WILLIAM MARTIN, ELIAS FINCHER. This
being the term for general returns of administrators, executors
and guardians the follow returns were made.

The three returns of the executors of the last will and
testament of PARKER COLLINS, dec'd. were examined by the Court
and received and ordered to be recorded...

Page 89-90: The Fourth Return of the Estate of
PARKER COLLINS by CHARLES HARRIS, R. B. HARRIS and
WILLIAM HARRIS, Excrs... balance $30.87-3/4.

Return of DAVID PUTMAN, Adm. of the Est. of WILSON PUTMAN,
dec'd., up to the 1st of Jan., 1837.

CHARLES HARRIS, R. B. HARRIS and WILLIAM HARRIS, Excrs. of PARKER COLLINS, dec'd... 1836... balance $181.46-1/2. Sworn to in open court this 3rd of Jan., 1837. D. MCCOY, C.C.O.

Page 91: I as Adm. of the Est. of MESHACK DEAL, dec'd., do herewith render an account of my actings and doings and do hereby certify that all the effects that has come to my hands is Lot No. 107, 10th Dist., Carroll Co. and that I have solD the same for the sum of $5 and appropriated the same to the expenses incurred in Adm. Given under my hand this 3rd of Jan., 1837. Signed JAMES GASTON.

The above return was sworn to in open court this 3rd of Jan., 1837. D. MCCOY, C.C.O.

Page 92: The Est. of MOSES WHITTSITT, ROBT. WILLIAMS, Ad., Return No. 2, balance $165.84... named WM. GRISSOM, NATHAN POOL, YOUNG P. POOL, ENOCH ROGERS, JAMES BYRD, WILLIAM MCADAMS.

Page 93: In acct. current with NANCY WHITTSITT, adm. from 1st of Jan. 1836 to 31st of Dec., inclusive... balance $455.75-3/4... named JAMES STUART, NATHAN POOL, YOUNG P. POOL, EZEKIEL HARRIS, JOSEPH ROGERS, THOMAS EZZELL... sworn to in open court this 3rd of Jan., 1837. D. MCCOY, C.C.O.

Page 94: Return of JOHN W. THOMPSON... G. W. T. and M. L. T. ALLEN, minors... balance $39.55-1/2... sworn to in open court. D. MCCOY, C.C.O.

Page 95: Court adjourned till the first Tues. in Feb. next. WILLIAM MARTIN, J.I.C., ELIAS FINCHER, J.I.C., IRA R. FOSTER, J.I.C., D. MCCOY, C.C.O.

Feb. 7th 1837 Adjourned Term
The Hon. Ct. of Ord. met pursuant to adjournment. Present: their Hons. WILLIAM MARTIN, SAMUEL JULIAN, GEORGE WILLINGHAM, THOS. MCDONALD, WILLIAM WADSWORTH.

Ordered that LARKEN GREEN be and is hereby appt. Gdn. of Amsariah(?) Newton, illigitimate of LUCINDA GREEN.

1st Return of the Adm. of the est. of WM. D. HUNT, dec'd., N. L. HUTCHENS, gdn... notes on ELIZA M. HUNT and WILLIAM GILBERT... balance 3rd Feb., 1837, $363.94.

Court adjourned till Court in course. WILLIAM MARTIN, J.I.C., WILLIAM WADSWORTH, J.I.C., SAMUEL JULIAN, J.I.C., GEORGE WILLINGHAM, J.I.C., THOMAS MCDONALD, J.I.C., D. MCCOY, C.C.O.

Page 96: March 6th 1837
Regular Term of the Ct. of Ord. There being not a majority of the Court present the Court was opened and adjourned till Court in course. GEORGE WILLINGHAM, J.I.C., D. MCCOY, C.C.O.

May 1st 1837 Regular Term
The Hon. Ct. of Ord. met according to adjournment. Present: their Hons. SAMUEL JULIAN, THOMAS MCDONALD, WILLIAM WADSWORTH, GEORGE WILLINGHAM.

Ordered that DAVID HUGGINS be and ishereby appt. Gdn. of
RUTHY ISBEL STEGAL, orphan of NANCY STEGAL.

The Hon. Ct. of Ord. adjourned till Court in course.
THOMAS MCDONALD, J.I.C., WILLIAM WADSWORTH, J.I.C.,
GEORGE WILLINGHAM, J.I.C., SAMUEL JULIAN, J.I.C., D. MCCOY,
C.C.O.

Page 97: Georgia, Forsyth Co.... we DAVID HUGGINS and
CULLEN DAVIS are held and firmly bound... unto the Inferior
Court sitting for Ord. purposes... and successors... sum of five
hundred dollars... sealed and dated May 1, 1837... condition
being that DAVID HUGGINS is appt. Gdn. of RUTHY ISBEL STEGAL...
orphan of NANCY STEGAL, dec'd... signed, sealed and delivered in
the presence of D. MCCOY, C.C.O., DAVID (X) HUGGINS,
CULLEN DAVIS.

Page 98: ... to DAVID HUGGINS... whereas RUTHY ISBEL
STEGAL, orphan of NANCY STEGAL... for the better maintenance and
education of RUTHY STEGAL... we do hereby commit the tuition,
education and guardianship of RUTHY STEGAL during her
minority... required to render true and perfect account to the
1st Term of the Ct. of Ord. every year... Wit. the Hon.
WILLIAM WADSWORTH, one of the Justices of the sd. Ct. of Ord.
this 1st of May, 1837. D. MCCOY, C.C.O.

Page 99: July Term July 6th 1837
The Hon. Ct. of Ord. met according to adjournment. Present:
The Hons. THOMAS MCDONALD, GEORGE WILLINGHAM, WILLIAM WADSWORTH.

Ordered that JAMES GASTON be appt. Gdn. of a certain female
infant, the child of EVALINE SMALLWOOD of Forsyth County upon
his complying with the terms of the law.

The 1st Return of WILLIAM W. VAUGHAN, Gdn. of
MATTHEW PINDER, idiot son of WILLIAM PINDER... signed
W. W. VAUGHAN.

Court adjourned till Court in course. GEORGE WILLINGHAM,
J.I.C., WILLIAM WADSWORTH, J.I.C., THOMAS MCDONALD, J.I.C.,
D. MCCOY, C.C.O.

Page 100: Return No. 1 The Est. of ROBERT SMITHWICK,
dec'd, in account current with BEVERLY ALLEN and ROBERT ALLEN,
Excrs. from the 17th July 1835 to the 3rd July 1837 inclusive...
balance $66.60-1/4. D. MCCOY, C.C.O.

Page 101: ... we SOLOMON CARROLL and WILLIAM P. ANDERSON
are held and firmly bound... unto DANIEL MCCOY and successors...
sum of five hundred dollars... sealed and dated Aug. 10, 1837...
condition being that SOLOMON CARROLL appt. Adm. of EST. of
JAMES R. BEPPLE... required to make a just and true acct...
required to deliver and pay to persons entitled... required to
prove any last will and testament before the Court and obtain a
certificate of probate. SOLOMON (X) CARROLL, L.S., WILLIAM
P. ANDERSON, L.S. Attest: D. MCCOY, C.C.O., ABSALOM FOSTER.

Page 102: Georgia, Forsyth County... by Clk of Ct. of
Ord... whereas JAMES R. BEPPLE died intestate... do hereby grant
unto JACOB CARROLL Temporary Letters of Adm... to ask, demand
and receive and to pay the debts... to pay over to the legal
heirs... ordained, constituted and appointed Temporary
Administrator... Aug. 10, 1837. D. MCCOY, C.C.O.

Page 103: Sept. 4th 1837 Regular Term
The Hon. Ct. of Ord. met according to adjournment. Present:
their Hons. GEORGE WILLINGHAM, J.I.C., D. MCCOY.

There being not a majority of the Court present Court was
adjourned till the 1st Tues. in Oct. GEORGE WILLINGHAM, J.I.C.,
D. MCCOY, C.C.O.

Oct. the 4th, 1837 Adjourned Term
The Hon. Ct. of Ord. met according to adjournment. Present:
their Hons. GEORGE WILLINGHAM, WILLIAM MARTIN, SAMUEL JULIAN,
WILLIAM WADSWORTH, THOMAS MCDONALD.

Ordered that NANCY (?) GUTHRIE be and is hereby appt. Gdn.
to JOHN F. GUTHRIE, ROBERT M. GUTHRIE, MARY ANN GUTHRIE,
NANCY GUTHRIE and LUCINDA GUTHRIE.

Ordered that SOLOMON CARROLL be and is hereby appt. Adm. of
the Est. of JAMES BEPPLE, dec'd. GEORGE WILLINGHAM, J.I.C.,
SAMUEL JULIAN, J.I.C., WILLIAM WADSWORTH, J.I.C.,
WILLIAM MARTIN, J.I.C., THOMAS MCDONALD, J.I.C., D. MCCOY,
C.C.O. Court adjourned till Court in course.

Page 104: Georgia, Forsyth Co... we NANCY GUTHRIE,
JAMES GUTHRIE and ASA GARRET are held and firmly bound unto...
Inferior Court sitting as a Court of Ord... and successors...
sum of five hundred dollars... condition being that
NANCY GUTHRIE is this day appt. Gdn. to JOHN F. GUTHRIE,
ROBERT M. GUTHRIE, ELISA GUTHRIE, ANDREW W. GUTHRIE,
MARY ANN GUTHRIE, NANCY GUTHRIE and LUCINDA GUTHRIE, orphans of
ROBERT GUTHRIE, dec'd... attest D. MCCOY, C.C.O., NANCY GUTHRIE,
Seal; JAMES (X) GUTHRIE, Seal; ASA (X) GARRET, Seal.

Pages 104-105: Georgia, Forsyth Co. By the Ct. of Ord. to
NANCY GUTHRIE... whereas JOHN F. GUTHRIE, ROBERT M. GUTHRIE,
ELISA GUTHRIE, ANDREW W. GUTHRIE, MARY ANN GUTHRIE,
NANCY GUTHRIE and LUCINDA GUTHRIE, orphans of ROBT. GUTHRIE,
dec'd... for better maintenance and education... commit to
tuition, education and guardianship... render a true and perfect
acct. to the 1st term of Ct. of Ord. every year... appt. gdn.
during their minority... Wit. the Hon. SAMUEL JULIAN, one of the
Justices of the Ct. of Ord. this 4th of Oct. 1837. D. MCCOY,
C.C.O.

Pages 106-107: Will of John Ivie
I, JOHN IVIE... weak in body, perfect in mind... soul to
God... body to be buried in a Christianlike manner... all just
debts and funeral charges to be satisfied... to wife NANCY...
all money, land, farming tools, household and kitchen furniture,
all stock property, hogs and cattle... to be sold at her
death... to wife NANCY, my negro boy Dick during her natural
life or widowhood... to son STEPHEN, one dollar... to daughter
NANCY, one dollar... to daughter WINNEFORD, one dollar... to son
ABLE, one dollar... to daughter SUSANNA, one dollar... to son
HUGH, one dollar... to daughter RODA, one dollar... to daughter
FRANCES, one dollar... to son THOMAS at death of my wife NANCY
my Negro boy Dick... none of the legatees to get afsd. estate
until after the death of my my wife NANCY... I appt. NANCY IVIE
Executor. Dated 24th of Aug. 1837. JOHN (X) IVIE, L.S. Wit:
SAMUEL M. REESE, CHRISTOPHER WHITMIRE, JOHN H. MASHBURN.

Georgia, Forsyth County. This day came before me, an acting
Justice of the Peace, SAMUEL M. REESE and JOHN H. MASHBURN...
deposeth and saith that they saw JOHN IVIE assign this will and
they were subscribing witnesses... and they saw the other
CHRISTOPHER WHITMIRE do likewise. Sworn to and subscribed
before me this 30th of Aug., 1837. SAMUEL M. REESE, JOHN H.
MASHBURN. Attest: JAMES M. BLACK, J.P.

Page 108: Nov. the 5th, 1837 Regular Term of the Court of
Ordinary
The Hon. Ct. of Ord. met according to adjournment. There
not being a majority of the Court present, the Court adjourned
till Court in course. GEORGE WILLINGHAM, J.I.C., D. MCCOY,
C.C.O.

Jan. 1, 1838 Regular Term
The Hon. Ct. of Ord. met according to adjournment. Present:
their Hons. SAMUEL JULIAN, GEORGE WILLINGHAM, WILLIAM MARTIN.
Court adjourned until Tues. the 2nd day of Jan., 1838.
GEORGE WILLINGHAM, J.I.C., SAMUEL JULIAN, J.I.C.,
WILLIAM MARTIN, J.I.C., D. MCCOY, C.C.O.

The Hon. Ct. of Ord. met according to adjournment. Present:
their Hons. SAMUEL JULIAN, GEORGE WILLINGHAM, WILLIAM MARTIN,
WILLIAM WADSWORTH. Jan. 2, 1838.

Ordered that WILLIAM W. VAUGHAN have leave of the court to
sell lots of land...

Ordered by the Court that ELIAS FINCHER be and is hereby
appointed Guardian of a certain Negro man Peter.

Page 109: Georgia, Forsyth County... Whereas ALLEN WIGLEY
in his lifetime and just before his death did make a nuncupative
will... all that I have I want my mother to have. If there is
anything left at her death, let the daughter have it... ordered
by the Ct. that the Clk. of sd. Ct. issue processed directed to
WILLIAM WIGLEY, AMOS H. CHAPMAN and wife ELIZABETH (blank) and
wife SARAH and NANCY WIGLEY to be and appear at the next
Inferior Court sitting for Ordinary purposes on the 1st Mon. in
March next... to show cause why will of ALLEN WIGLEY should not
be established as last will and testament... copy of order be
posted at least thirty days before the Court.

Court adjourned till Court in course, SAMUEL JULIAN, J.I.C.,
WILLIAM MARTIN, J.I.C., WILLIAM WADSWORTH, J.I.C.,
GEORGE WILLINGHAM, J.I.C., D. MCCOY, C.C.O.

THE 1834 STATE CENSUS OF FORSYTH COUNTY

From the county files, Telamon Cuyler Collection, Special
Collections, University of Georgia Libraries. Reproduced with
permission.

Heads of Households and number of white persons per family.

Bithel Bradley-2
Isaiah McElhannon-5
Henry Bagley-8
Mashack Biddy-8
John McGreer-6
James Carr-6
William Gravett-3
Seward Clayton-9
John Coleman-5
John Crews-2
Noah Langley-9
James Gray-6
Edward Gilbert-4
Austin Wilborn-2
David Steward-4
Samuel Edmanson-8
John Holland-7
Robert Williams-5
John Middleton-5
Robert McCluer-7
Joshua Martin-9
Z. M. Sample-5
James Edmanson-3
R. H. Lester-8
Cooper McElhannon-5
Sion Bennett-4
William Hammond-6
Levi Pendley-5
R. H. Nailer-6
Joseph Hammond-4
A. F. Richards-7
John Gravett-7
Beremin Foster-3
William Scott-8
Thos. Cordrew-5
Robert Johnson-2
Abner Coleman-3
Thos. Burford-9
J. R. Light-3
John Barker-8
Wm. Bennett-7
Jessee Thomas-7
James Daniel-10
John McCleur-3
Lewis Sames-5
Charles Darby-10
Benjamin Bradley-4
Willis Garrett-4
Littleberry Hutchens-5
Greef Williams-8
J. G. Austin-7
Ruthy Short-10

Jonathan Rolins-3
William Pain-5
Adensan Smith-6
Elijah Wellborn-9
Christopher Baker-7
J. C. Holbrook-11
Samuel Holbrook-11
H. S. Campbell-5
Riley Willson-6
James Gravett-4
Culen Davis-9
Evin Thomas-6
William Middleton-2
Jesse Sample-5
L. D. Harris-4
W. A. Comron-7
Moses Cantrell-6
G. G. Witherspoon-5
Green Collett-9
Jacob Martin-8
John Dickson-3
Wiley Bagley-8
Aaron Fowler-8
John Hutson-10
Johugh Howel-6
Edward Harrell-7
W. W. Vaughn-6
Luke Gravett-3
John Montgomery-3
Sally Tidwell-5
John Tidwell Sr.-3
Freelan Shorter-2
Obediah Gravett-8
James Williams-11
John Williams-3
John Tidwell Jr.-2
Anderson Tidwell-8
John Rectr-8
Green Huggins-6
Charles Ferrell-8
McKinsey Smallwood-5
D. F. Mooney-3
B. B. Hatt(Holt?)-9
William Humphrey-4
Solomin Kemp-5
David Humphrey-4
Mary Baker-5
Lincy Young 6
Berry Hill-7
William Anderson-5
N. H. Pendley-6
John Blalock-4

John Jolly(Golly?)-7
James Edmansons-5
Alexander Pugh-7
William Jones-12
John Shumaker-12
William Wood-10
J. B. Sudworth-7
James Jones-9
Lewis Prides
(Brides?)-9
Peter Raly-6
Edward Pellom-6
James Cockrun-7
Philip Coleman-4
Simeon White-10
John Armstrong-5
Emanuel Hendrix-6
John Rogers-6
William Ethrige-4
William Thomas-7
JamesPierce(Purce?)-4
Anderson Carrell-3
Solomon Tailor-6
Barns Crow-6
Sterling Goodwin-5
Gli Waldrip-7
Ira Waldrip-7
Isaac Wharton-8
John Crow-8
James Crow-11
Warren Clayton-6
Jesse Carrell-4
Isaac Smithey-9
U. W. Pain-6
Samuel Pain-8(2?)
John Pitmon-3
Jesse Howel-6
John Adams-5
William McCoy-7
Barney Braden-4
Enoch Erley-6
James Cogborn-5
John McCrary-3
John Wood-7
William Hope-3
J. G. Hope-2
Robert Mooney-6
Green King-9
John Woodliff-3
William Stoveall-8
George Woodliff-6
Pendleton Hutchins-4

John Leach-3
Nely Molen-7
Christey Oglesby-4
William Gravett-6
John Hammond Sr.-2
Mily Hammond-4
Leroy Hammonds-6
Henry Bell-5
Thomas Meaders-6
Simeon Oliver-6
Joseph Hambleton-8
Abram Harris-4
George Hammonds-12
Philip Coleman Sr.-10
Joshua Baker-3
William Martin-10
Iby Herst-6
Jonathan Pendley-6
Robert Rolen-2(8?)
Thos. Pendley-8
Archibald Lindsey-8
Oliver Strickland-6
James Davis-5
James Pendley-2
D. A. Landsdown-4
James Hays-8
Amos Elard-5
Zachariah Day-8
Joel Bramlet-6
Enoch Bramlet-3
Thomas Pain-3
Abe Roberts-8
Abner Smith-5
Jesse Hendrix-4
Jacob Carrell-10
Denis Carrell-9
Charles Haines-7
Denis Shay-6
John Bird-5
William Bird-3
John Biddy-4
L. B. Jones(James?)-7
Jacob Scuder-4
Alfred Scuder-1
Hubbard Barker-3
John Sample-5
William Fincher-4
Charles Sample-4
Reubin Sams-6
Esquire Sames-4
Thos. Gravett-9
John Hammond Sr.-4
David Huggins-7
John Huggins-7
Samuel Brooks-2
Berry Stone-6
Randol Gravett-6
Benjamin Heath-14
Isaac Pendley-3
Asa Baggett-5

Joshua Estis-4
Joel Estis-4
Abner Philips-10
Henry Todder-7
Robert Venible-7
James Venible-3
Thos. Rogers-3
Isaac Sanders-13
A. Bungarner-8
Larkin Green-11
E. T. Howard-3
Mathew Queen-7
Martin Caliway-2
Alen Winn-5
Hyram Boen-5
John Anderson-5
George James-7
John Miller-5
John Fowler-6
James Miller-5
Jonathan Barnett-9
Alexander Flanigan-4
James Westmoreland-2
Wm. Westmoreland-11
J. A. Meddleton-8(?)
Henry Bramlett-7
Alexander Redman-8
Solomon Carrell-9
Wyatt Farrent-8
John Sharp-4
Robert Harden-8
Madison Hutson-3
Isaac Tinsley-3
James Hutson-10
Westly Kemp-5
William Willson-4
Peniny Blakhorn-4
Alfred Hutson-1
Lewis Blackborn-2
Benjamin Jones-7
Ezekiel Harris-2
Alen Cook-7
Mark Castleberry-3
Bevely Allen-11
Robert Smithwick-3
Wm. Rutherford-5
Livin Hutson-2
J. W. Thompson-6
Thos. Ezell-7
W. H. Bacon-7
Isaac Freehand-4
Nicholas Crosno-2
Abraham Acles-10
William Fields-5
William Pinder-2
Edward Hays-2
Richard Hays-9
T. L. Cox-4
Lewis Long-11
John Gray-6

John Russell-3
Jesse Coffee-7
William Blackstock-9
William Hays-7
John Hays-3
William Mathes-8
Martin Brown-6
William Harmon-2
Abden Jesture-6
John Simpson-4
John Hambleton-7
Elijah Tippens-6
Garet Gray-5
Milton Worthy-7
Alfred Webb-7
John Webb-3
Ephraim Willson-6
David Blackwell-9
Cary Games-9
William Gradue-5
Bird Harris-1
William Harris-1
Charles Harris-1
Hyram Trammell-7
Christin McGines-4
John Rogers Sr.-1
James Roberts-6
Susan Flanigan-4
Clynton Webb-4
William Walraven-8
Simeon Walraven-3
Samuel Brown-3
John Brown-2
James Stone-8
Jonathan Stone-8
Nathan Pool-9
William Hammond Sr.-6
Elias Fincher-8
James Cogins-8
Moses Ledbeder-3
Joseph Williams-2
Henry Bagley, Jr.-9
Valitine Cain-3
Toliver Reed-8
James Jorden-8
Uriah Hubbard-8
Jeremiah Hubbard-4
Elijah Bennett-12
Luke Wood-6
John Holcon-2
Elias Henderson-4
Green Henderson-2
George Gellogg-5
Edy Hurden-3
H. M. Willis-3
T. T. Garrett-3
T. L. Garrett-4
Asa Garrett-3
Curtis Green-6
James Haywood-8

298

THE 1834 STATE CENSUS OF FORSYTH COUNTY

William Haywood-2
A. M. Reece-6
Thos. Hitts-6
Larkin Whitmore-4
Christophe Whitmore-6
Jacob Reece-2
John Sherat-3

David Vistell-5
John Wallis-6
William Wallis-4
Jesse Jay-5
Joshua Garner-3
Joshua Holder-6
Joab Ashworth-4

Osborn Haywood-11
Moses Martin-8
Ely Tanner-10
Mason Ezell-7
Isaac Holder-6
Abram Smith-6

GROOM	BRIDE	MARRIED	PAGE
Johnston, John	Young, Bethany	9/ 8/1833	1
Higg, John	Lowery, Elizabeth	10/ 3/1833	1
Bradley, Bethal	Williams, Ann	11/ 3/1833	1
Henderson, Nathaniel G.	Bradley, Margaret	11/14/1833	2
Cruse, John L.	Sams, Syntha	1/12/1834	2
Williams, Joseph	Bagley, Elisa	12/ 4/1833	2
Harmon, William	Venable, Harriett	2/ 6/1834	3
Barker, Hubbard	Henderson, Elizabeth	2/11/1834	3
Westmoreland, James	Downey, Abigail	2/16/1834	3
Henson, James W.	White, Rebecca	1/ 8/1834	4
Miller, Joseph	Delk, Tempy	1/12/1834	4
Goodwin, Harris	Dogin (Doogan?), Emily	2/13/1834	4
Richards, Josophus	Beck, Anna	7/31/1834	5
Roach, Ulet (?)	McGullion, Elizabeth Ann	8/19/1834	5
Pendley, James T.	Easter, Harriett	3/20/1834	5
Howell, William F.	Martin, Mary E.	9/25/1834	6
Howell, Pinkney	Haygood, Eliza	7/13/1834	6
Duyck (Duke?), Timothy	Cox, Celia	8/10/1834	6
Sutton, Henry H.	Collins, Lucinda	10/ 7/1834	7
Cockburn, Russell	Carroll, Celia	10/26/1834	7
Parris, George	Hubbard, Matilda	1/ 8/1835	7
Hardin, Joshua H.	Garrett, Nancy	2/ 3/1835	8
Bennett, Samuel C.	Vickery, Mary	2/22/1835	8
Coleman, Phillip	Bridges, Matilda	3/22/1835	8
Guthrie, James	Biddle, Sarah	1/11/1835	9
Holbrook, William B.	Tallant, Nancy	6/11/1835	9
Wellborn, Aaron G.	Wellborn, Mary B.	3/ 6/1835	9
Williams, Isaiah	Venable, Judith	7/21/1835	10
Lindsey, Ransom	Smallwood, Lanty	8/30/1835	10
Bradford, James	Smallwood, Renie (?)	8/ 3/1835	10
Morgan, Fen	Bean, Mary (Col.)	9/ 5/1835	11
Sims, William B.	Campbell, Isabella D.	11/ 8/1835	11
Brown, William R.	Gravitt, Sarah	9/24/1835	11
Boyd, John L.	Anderson, Celia	11/15/1835	12
Evans, William	Willingha, Obedience	12/17/1835	12
Brannon, Martin	Collins, Nancy	8/30/1835	12
Ray, William H.	Whitsitt, Mrs. Nancy T.	2/21/1836	13
Fergerson, Edmond	Lester, Julia Ann	3/20/1836	13
Sanders, Johnson	Hawkins, Mary	4/28/1836	14
Thornton, Isaac	Nuckolls, Clarinda	2/ 4/1836	14
Pike, Ransom	Holeyfield, Rosannah	4/21/1836	15
Heath, William	Darby, Icy	4/10/1836	15
Offutt, Jesse	Sisson, Siphia	5/ 5/1836	16
Holeyfield, Bryson	Pike, Calven (?)	7/ 7/1836	16
Pugh, Sampson	Heath, Mary	7/12/1836	17
Goodard, Jesse (or Jefrey)	Gravitt, Sally	8/19/1836	17
Mullins, Andrew J.	Daniel, Martha P.	9/25/1836	18
Coleman, Collinton	Campbell, Nancy	9/19/1836	18
Hudson, William J.	Tarrent, Licetry C.	11/24/1836	19
Wadsworth, William	Martin, Tempy	11/ 7/1836	19
Whitney, Teni (?)	Evans, Rithy	11/ 1/1836	20
Davis, Joshua	McKay, Susan	12/22/1836	20
Ellison, Dudley	Stone, Polly	10/19/1836	21
Collett, John	Darby, Jane	12/ 7/1836	21
Tallant, Thomas C.	Collett, Nancy	12/28/1836	22
Samples, Thomas C.	Davis, Sarah	1/10/1837	22
Davis, James	Samples, Rachel	1/ 9/1837	23

FORSYTH COUNTY MARRIAGES, BOOK A (1833-1848)

GROOM	BRIDE	MARRIED	PAGE
Lester, Jerman M.	Born, Sarah	9/13/1836	23
Bennett, Merrel C.	Ellison, Milly	9/22/1836	24
Goodwin, James J.	Henson, Rebecca	1/ 8/1837	24
Blackburn, Ambrose	Hudson, Elizabeth	9/22/1836	25
Fewell, Thaddeus M.	Eaton, Margaret	8/ 8/1836	25
Stone, William	Baker, Mary	12/22/1836	26
Brown, John	Mason (?), Rebecca	12/15/1836	27
Dudley, John W.	Pruitt, Malinda	3/16/1837	27
Shaw, David C. T.	Wickett, Mary	4/18/1837	28
Collins, Joseph B.	Miller, Ann	2/18/1837	28
Brooks, Richard	Fowler, Neata	1/ 8/1837	29
Harris, Charles	Collins, Jane	2/ 2/1837	29
Davis, James	Samples, Rachel	1/ 9/1837	30
Stone, James	Bailey, Charlotte	2/ 5/1837	30
Dunahoo, James M.	Monday, Lucy	1/ 5/1837	31
Baty, James N.	Rawlins, Elizabeth	1/23/1837	31
Anderson, Daniel	Venable, Martha	1/17/1837	32
Parris, Malorey	Martin, Mahala	3/23/1837	32
Langley, John	McClure, Susannah	7/30/1837	33
Duncan, Robert S.	Smith, Armetta	8/20/1837	33
Owens, John	James, Emily	6/19/1837	34
		(or 29)	
Hunter, Thomas	Martin, Nancy	9/12/1837	34
Wellborn, Chapley B.	Foster, Mary A.	9/10/1837	35
Gaston, James	Foster, Jane H.	11/21/1837	35
Harris, Thomas P.	Jay, Rebecca	11/14/1837	36
Castleberry, Benjamin W.	Harris, Caron	10/12/1837	36
Bagley, Harmon	Strickland, Anna	11/22/1837	37
Clayton, Reuben M.	Poor, Emily	10/ 8/1837	37
Gravitt, Alfred	Tidwell, Lucy	9/14/1837	38
Anderson, Eilliam P.	Pendley, Temperance	10/18/1837	38
Tidwell, James	Bowman, Nancy	9/10/1837	39
Weems, Darisu R.	Sewell, Ritha	10/26/1837	39
Aaron, William	Bradford, Lucy	10/ 9/1837	40
Stricland, Talbot	Young, Celia	12/28/1837	40
Jenkins, John	Bradford, Rosea (?)	12/14/1837	41
Chamblee, Washington	Martin, Rebecca	12/21/1837	41
Murray, John	Orr, Martha	12/19/1837	42
Thomas, William	McDonald, Caroline	12/28/1837	42
Lummus, William	Bentley, Mary A.	12/31/1837	43
Vickery, Charles	Clements, Malinda	1/16/1838	43
Torrence, William B.	Jackson, Martha	1/30/1838	44
McRight, William	Coggins, Caroline	2/ 1/1838	44
Williamson, William	Jones, Eliza	2/ 4/1838	45
Vaughan, Willis	Carlisle, Elizabeth	2/10/1838	45
Perry, Lewis	Martin, Martha	2/15/1838	46
Davis, William B.	Poor, Frances	3/30/1838	46
Anderson, James	James, Calinder	4/ 8/1838	47
Agerton, James P.	Wood, Emily	3/ 8/1838	47
Dacus, Arthur	Tatum, Peggy	2/28/1838	48
Whitmire, James M.	Hollins, Carry	5/14/1838	48
Robbins, Levi	Dickerkey, Jane	5/ 3/1838	49
Mayfield, Battle	Bobo, Martha	4/ 1/1838	49
Ellis, Joshua	Kelly, Sarah	2/28/1837	50
Ashby, Level	Blackburn, Jerrusha	2/16/1837	50
Haygood, L. D.	Holbrook, Mary	5/10/1838	51
Gravitt, Alfred	Langley, Jane	7/26/1838	51
Davis, William	Huggins, Sally	7/19/1838	52
Bradford, Moses	Aaron, Nancy	7/31/1838	52

FORSYTH COUNTY MARRIAGES, BOOK A (1833-1848)

GROOM	BRIDE	MARRIED	PAGE
Owens, William W.	Owens, Elizabeth	8/ 8/1838	53
Willingham, Jackson	Montgomery, Elizabeth	8/ 6/1838	53
Holbrook, Lewis	Yancey, Sarah	8/22/1838	54
Tribble, Joel B.	Coffey, Jane	7/26/1838	54
Bowen, Hiram	Stewart, Caroline	9/19/1838	55
Woodall, John	Holcomb, Ann	6/ 2/1838	55
Fendley, Elisha B.	Watson, Martha	10/ 7/1838	56
Bagley, Edmond	Strickland, Sarah	11/ 1/1838	56
James, Sherrod	Lindsey, Sarah	11/ 9/1838	57
Fendley, Emanuel	Whitmire, Malinda	10/21/1838	57
Hulsey, Isaiah	Thomas, Amanda	11/ 8/1838	58
Landrum, William R.	Bush, Elisa	11/ 1/1838	58
Johnson, John H.	Reece, Mary	11/25/1838	59
Light, Pleasant G.	Jones, Annie	12/18/1838	59
Cary (Casy?), Barrabas	Hutchins, Harriet P.	1/ 2/1839	60
McHugh, Wilson	Cox, Elizabeth	12/23/1838	60
Holbrook, John F.	Hudson, Amanda	12/ 6/1838	61
Jackson, James	Terry, Rebecca	12/21/1838	61
Landsdown, David A.	Martin, Julie Ann	2/ 7/1839	62
Coleman, Hosea	Brannon, Betsy	11/ 8/1838	62
Tanner, James	Jay, Mary	1/10/1839	63
McCleskey, George W.	Bell, Angeline	1/31/1839	63
Holland, Samuel	Bennett, Melissa	5/31/1838	64
Cruse, William	Hawkins, Emaline	1/15/1839	64
Green, Newton	Gazaway, Malinda C.	1/10/1839	65
Hadder, John	Williams, Elisa	2/19/1838	65
Owens, Owen	Edwards, Susan	3/ 5/1839	66
Sneed, Absalom	Sneed, Dianna	5/16/1839	66
Dickson, Edley P.	Holden, Milly	3/ 6/1839	67
Martin, Henry	Langley, Rebecca	3/13/1839	67
McGinnis, Osborn	Foster, Nancy	3/19/1839	68
Bobo, Silas	Autrey, Minerva	2/ 7/1839	68
Lindsey, Anderson	Cruse, Mary Ann	4/21/1839	69
Davenport, John	Hendrix, Susan	3/12/1839	69
Stewart, Andrew M.	McCall, Mary	6/ 6/1839	70
Light, Gilford	Bib, Margaret	11/21/1839	70
Gravitt, Gilford	Hendrix, Inder	4/ 4/1839	71
Langley, James	Sanders, Artilla (or Artitia)	7/25/1839	71
Crow, Isaac J.	Bewry, Elly	8/ 7/1839	72
Martin, Hezekiah	Sloan, Parthena	8/ 8/1839	72
Pannell, Thomas	Delk, Mary	9/ 9/1839	73
Hadder, Solomon	Scott, Matilda	9/22/1839	73
Casey, Washington	Casey, Patsy	11/11/1839	74
Blackburn, Thomas	Barett, Lucinda	12/24/1839	74
Rice, Benjamin J.	Burford, Susan	12/19/1839	75
Dunn, Ezekiel	Cameron, Mrs. Ann E.C.	12/19/1839	75

NOTE ON FORSYTH COUNTY: Immediately after the Lottery of 1832 was held, which made available for distribution and settlement that part of the Cherokee Indian Nation which was in Georgia, the whole area of Cherokee County was divided into ten counties, one of which was Forsyth County. This former Cherokee land was a large area generally north of the Chattahoochee River in the north west and north central parts of the state. Forsyth County is situated at the eastern most side of the former Cherokee country bordering Hall County to the east, Gwinnett to the southeast, Fulton to the southwest and Cherokee on its western side.

FORSYTH COUNTY MARRIAGES, BOOK A (1833-1848)

GROOM	BRIDE	MARRIED	PAGE
King, Robert A.	Gober, Mary E.	1/ 2/1840	76
Kelly, George W.	Wickett, Sarah	12/24/1839	76
Julian, George H.	Webster, Adaline	10/ 3/1838	77
Whorton, Isaac	Julian, Rebecca M.	3/ 6/1838	77
Moor(e), Alvin	Norris, Elizabeth	11/24/1838	78
Hardin, Alfred	Perry, Nancy	12/ 5/1839	78
Dooly, R. J.	Hudson, Parmela	12/22/1838	79
Mashburn, Elisha J.	Wellborn, Sarah Ann	12/ 8/1839	79
Aaron, William	Bradley, Polly	8/ 8/1839	80
Lester, Harrison	Parks, Sarah Amanda	12/21/1830	80
Sewell, Milton N.	Davis, Sarah Ann	12/29/1839	81
Guthery, Robert M.	Wadkins (Watkins), Frances	12/17/1839	81
Terry, Stephen	Parkinson, Martha	2/20/1840	82
Leach, James W.	Wadkins (Watkins), Sarah	1/ 2/1840	82
Milford, James	Thornton, Elender	2/20/1840	83
Dooley, James	Wadkins (Watkins), Martha	2/ 9/1840	83
Garrett, John	Bennett, Elizabeth	1/16/1840	84
Hudson, Madison E.	Blackburn, Frances H.	1/ 2/1840	84
Caldwell, Hiram J.	Blankenship, Elisa	1/22/1840	85
Barker, William	Russell, Elisa	3/ 5/1840	85
Bentley, Jerry (Jeremiah H.)	Pool, Emily C.	3/12/1840	86
Lenoir, John W.	Rogers, Ann C.	4/ 3/1840	86
Farris, John	Drennon, Nancy Ann	3/31/1840	87
Monroe, Thomas L.	Kelly, Elizabeth	4/ 7/1840	87
Sloan, Samuel	Tidwell, Sussanah	4/15/1840	88
Bates, Antony W.	Nuckolls, Ann T.	7/12/1836	88
Campbell, Elias	Carroll, Jane	11/21/1839	89
Hays, William F.	Bagley, Anna	4/ 1/1840	89
Terry, John	Perkinson (Parkinson), Mary	3/22/1840	90
Castleberry, Timothy	Bacon, Agnes	4/26/1840	90
Killian, A. J.	Sanders, Mahala	4/29/1840	91
Sneed, Samuel S.	Pugh, Mary	5/10/1840	91
Cheek, Gazaway	Pike, Terrisa	5/19/1840	92
Bagley, Nathan F.	Hays, Melissa C.	6/25/1840	92
Drennon, John N.	Brannon, Arcadias	7/ 5/1840	93
Martin, William	Pruett (Pruitt), Letty	7/ 9/1840	93
Saugers, John R. (or K.)	Matin (Martin?), Martha	7/22/1840	94
Waldrop, Partilla	Morrow, Polly	8/27/1840	94
Higgins, James	Bramblett, Polly	9/ 4/1840	95
Lott, Enoch	Randall, Elizabeth	11/15/1840	95
McDow, Thomas B.	Conley, Elizabeth	9/16/1840	96
Oslin, Reubin C.	Randall, Martha A.	9/ 3/1840	96
Bonner (?), Benjamin F.	Haynes, Sarah Elizabeth	10/ 1/1840	97
Sharp, William	Hudson, Matilda	9/17/1840	97
Goin, Dillard	Conley, Permelia C.	10/14/1840	98
Green, James A.	Woodliff, Nancy Jane	10/15/1840	98
Foster, William P.	Pirkle, Zelfa (or Tilfa)	11/19/1840	99
Collett, Archibald	Holbrook, Pernessa	9/ 7/1840	99
Patterson, George W.	Morris, Sinther	11/17/1840	100
Hill, Isaac W.	Ellis, Nancy	10/27/1840	100
Thompson, Benjamin O.	Swilling, Matilda M.	12/24/1840	101
Bramblett, James K.(R?)	Roberts, Margaret	2/ 7/1841	101

FORSYTH COUNTY MARRIAGES, BOOK A (1833-1848)

GROOM	BRIDE	MARRIED	PAGE
Kown, David	Huggins, Polly Ann	2/11/1841	102
Echolls, Elias L.	Strickland, Elizabeth	2/ 7/1841	102
Burtz, Joshua	McCormack, Christian	1/24/1841	103
Howell, George W.	Huggins, Fanny	1/12/1841	103
Tidwell, William	Gravitt, Caroline	1/ 7/1841	104
Hendrix, James W.	Compton, Jane Alvira	4/ 5/1840	104
Wilson, James	Light, Pernela Ann	12/11/1840	105
Stone, Thomas	Holbrook, Prudence	12/23/1840	105
Jones, Hiram	Hammond, Elizabeth Ann	3/18/1841	106
Redd, Josiah	Holbrook, Elizabeth	3/25/1841	106
Pendley, Thomas	Howell, Mahala	3/30/1841	107
Pirkle, William	Dollar, Delitha (Tolitha?)	4/15/1841	107
Compton, William C.	Doster, Bency (?)	5/23/1841	108
Burtz, James B.	Fowler, Emily A.	5/ 9/1841	108
Madden, Robert J.	Segars (Sagers),Sarah N.	4/ 1841	109
Montgomery, James N.	Compton, Nancy Emily	5/ 6/1838	109
Tribble, Thomas C.	Fendley, Elizabeth	8/19/1841	110
Smith, Albert G.	Morris, Eliza F.	(no date)	110
Watson, Hampton F.	Malden, Hannah M.	8/19/1841	111
Burton, Elias	Dodd, Mary Ann	8/19/1841	111
Owens, Gabriel T.	Stovall, Nancy T.	6/17/1841	112
Crow, Shadrack A.	Cazey (Casey),Elviny(?)	8/ 5/1841	112
Thompson, James R.	Garner, Martha	7/19/1841	113
Matin (Martin?), Elias	Thompson, Malinda	8/19/1841	113
Kitchens, James H.	Davis, Frances R.	8/26/1841	114
Casey, Ellison	Waldrup, Sarah	8/ 5/1841	114
Garrett, Hendrick	Foster, Louisa	9/30/1841	115
Gravitt, Charles	Taylor, Rebecca	9/ 9/1841	115
Garner, Aaron	Conner, Catharine	10/24/1841	116
Reaves, John P.	Harris, Rosannah C.	11/18/1841	116
Brown, James H.	Haney (Honey,Honea?), Abigail	11/18/1841	117
Haynes, Hiram	Farrow, Susannah	12/ 1/1841	117
Armstrong, John	McGinnis, Mary	11/ 7/1841	118
Daniel, William	Osburn, Rachael	12/30/1841	118
Horton, Daniel D.	Vaughan, Cynthia	1/ 6/1842	119
Austin, James G.	Bennett, Mary Ann	12/25/1841	119
Harris, Benjamin	Sharp, Martha	8/19/1841	120
Bates, George	Lawless, Jane	12/26/1841	120
Allen, William	Biddy, Rutha	12/22/1841	121
Nuckolls, Joel T.	Bryant, Irana	2/ 1/1842	121
Hawz (Howz?),Ezekiel P.	Martin, Elinder	1/30/1842	122
Hughes, Russell	Bennett, Lucinda	1/20/1842	122
Pool, Street	Autrey, Frances	1/ 7/1842	123
Segars, Zachariah	McDow, Tempy	2/ 1/1842	123
Smith, Obed	King, Lucinda	2/17/1842	124
King, Ebenezer	Smith, Margaret C.	2/17/1842	124
Hockenhull, John	Kemp, Mary	2/ 5/1842	125
Bailey, Thomas T.	Yancy, Lucinda	2/13/1842	125
Gates, William	Mobley, Mary	3/23/1842	126
Langley, Jackson	Howell, Mary Ann	3/24/1842	126
Powell, Allen	Garrett, Slaterli (?)	2/18/1841	127
Hughes, Andrew O.	Watters, Louesa Fountain	2/18/1841	127
Chadwick, Benjamin	Eaton, Lucinda	4/ 8/1842	128
Nunn, William H.	Langley, Delilah	4/19/1842	128
Orr, Emaziah	Porter, Hannah	4/24/1842	129
Barnett (Barrett?), Nathan	Johnson, A.M.Frances	5/ 1/1842	129

GROOM	BRIDE	MARRIED	PAGE
Lewis, Major John	Lenoir, Evalina Jane	5/10/1842	130
Lowrey, Isaac P.	Vestal, Nancy Jane	5/22/1842	130
Hunt, Thomas W.	Burruss, Lucy Ann E.	5/17/1842	131
Williams, Lewis	Wimms, Ibby	5/15/1842	131
Matthews, James	League, Nancy E.	6/12/1842	132
Owen, Oliver P.	League, Betsy Ann	6/12/1842	132
Brumbelow, Joel	Snead, Nancy	6/23/1842	133
Tribble, James W.	Holbrook, Nancy	6/28/1842	133
Wallis (Wallace), Jesse B.	Edwards, Sarah	7/18/1842	134
McLelon (McLeland?), James	Motes, Elizabeth	7/29/1841	134
Compton, John T.	Scruggs, Nancy E.	7/28/1842	135
Brumbelow, Isaac	Snead, Leddy (Letty?)	7/28/1842	
Terry, Martin	Dodd, Mary	8/18/1842	136
Bagley, Wesley S.	Bagley, Caroline	9/28/1842	136
Lindsey, Henderson	Redd, Appy (Azzy?)	8/ 7/1842	137
Hauser, James C.	Spruce, Rebecca	8/25/1842	137
Tallant, David, Jr.	Scruggs, Rachael R.	9/11/1842	138
McGinnis, Osborn	Dougherty, Lavinia E.	9/15/1842	138
Pendley, Jesse	Gravitt, Polly Ann	10/23/1842	139
Coffey, Thomas W.	Roper, Eliza	10/23/1842	139
Williams, Charles	Samples, Polly Ann	10/30/1842	140
Fowler, William	Balote, Rachael	9/ 4/1842	140
Blankenship, William	Boyd, Irana	12/18/1842	141
Rutledge, Joseph	McCoy, Melissa Ann	10/ 1/1839	141
Harris, William	Whitsitt, Jane	12/18/1842	142
McAfee, Elijah C.	Thompson, Emily C.	12/11/1842	142
Conner, Reubin T.	Falcher (Fulcher?), Sarah	12/27/1842	143
Boyd, Samuel	Wood, Prissy	5/ 8/1842	143
Harvey, George M.	Martin, Mursylea	9/11/1842	144
Johnson, John W.	Davis, Sarah Ann	11/13/1842	144
Davis, Robert F.	Baker, Obedience	11/13/1842	145
Cole, Caswell N.	Holbrook, Sarah	12/ 1/1842	145
Jones, Azariah	Hendrix, Cynthia	12/22/1842	146
Martin, Joel J.	Langley, Cynthia	12/22/1842	146
Edmondson, Andrew J.	Jeffreys, Mary	12/29/1842	147
Light, Wiley	Phillips, Allethia E.	11/22/1842	147
Harkless, Robert W.	Bacon, Evalina	12/22/1842	148
Haygood, Henry	Foster, Malissa	1/ 1/1843	148
Hitt, Henry	Staver, Hannah	11/ 9/1842	149
Leonard, Jesse J.	McAfee, Mary L.	12/25/1842	149
Garmon, Matthew	Yancy, Martha	12/26/1842	150
Wright, William W.	Mann, Franky H.	1/ 4/1843	150
Lee, Henry	Carr, Rody A. M.	1/19/1843	151
Nicholson, Neamon C.	Edmondson, Pantsy(?)	1/31/1843	151
Day, Andy L.	Key, Rebecca W.	2/ 2/1843	152
Waldrup, William C.	Owen, Sarah	2/ 5/1843	152
Yancy, James	Garmon, Barbara	2/ 5/1843	153
Gravitt, Reuben	Langley, Amy	2/16/1843	153
Fitten (Felton?), Isaiah C.	McCoy, Kezia A.	2/20/1843	154
Simmons, James	Bannister, Mary Ann S.	2/ 4/1843	154
Foster, Ira Row	Haynes, Milly A. C.	10/ 9/1842	155
Blackwell, William B.	Carver, Martha	9/28/1842	155
Long, Hiram	Procter, Mary Ann	9/11/1842	156
Webb, Toliver	Logan, Mary	2/28/1841	156
Brannon, James R.	Martin, Sarah C.	12/22/1842	157

FORSYTH COUNTY MARRIAGES, BOOK A (1833-1848)

GROOM	BRIDE	MARRIED	PAGE
Osborn, Joseph	Morris, Sarah	12/ 5/1841	157
Townley, Zachariah	Watters, Zelpha Caroline	3/6/1842	158
Martin, James H.	Cantrell, Thompsy (?)	9/18/1842	158
Tippens, Dennis S.	Anderson, Matilla	1/29/1843	159
Miller, John	Johnson, Cesley Ann	2/12/1843	159
Prater, Loyd	Ashworth, Nancy	3/19/1843	158
Cantrell, Wilson	Hutchins, Elizabeth M.J.	3/12/1843	158
Bennett, Cooper	Brooks, Catharine	4/ 6/1843	159
Blackwell, David	Green, Lucinda	5/11/1843	159
Reon (Roan?), Berry	Henderson, Milly	5/30/1843	160
Harrison, Jason C.	McGinnis, Sarah Ann	5/ 4/1843	160
Foster, William T.	Haynes, Abi A.	5/16/1843	161
Ashworth, James	Stoball (Stovall?), Nancy	5/ 8/1843	161
Jenkins, Bartlett M.	Barnett, Mary	5/ 4/1843	162
Blackstock, Richard W.	Whitsitt, Cornela (Corneta?)	7/ 2/1843	162
Wilson, Laven	Killingsworth, Eliza-beth R.	6/15/1843	163
Sharp, William	Hackstt, Mary C.	4/21/1843	163
Rogers, John	Buckner, Lotty (Charlotte-DLS)	6/13/1843	164
Boring, Thomas W.	Barnett, Mahala	6/15/1843	164
McCoy, William P.	Coleman, Jane	7/25/1843	165
Aaron, Russel D.	Darby, Minerva	7/16/1843	165
Arthur, William	Hammond, Elizabeth	7/10/1843	166
Mashburn, Elisha	Wallace, Mary Ann	8/ 3/1843	166
Autry, William H.	Collins, Katharine	3/16/1841	167
Seale, Benezar H.	Foster, Jemima C.	11/17/1840	167
Campbell, Henry J.	McAll (McCall?),Eliza	2/18/1841	167
Blackburn, John	Wood, Malissa	1/12/1843	168
Mann, James M.	Jenkins, Sarah	7/30/1843	168
Boring, James H.	Miller, Thenery (?)	10/15/1843	169
Parker, Jeremiah	Brumbelow, Sarah	9/ 3/1843	169
Woodliff, Josiah H.	Burruss, Mary Jane	9/14/1843	170
Lawson, Sion (Cyrus?)	Brumbelow, Caroline	11/20/1843	170
Shatten, Nelson T.	Langley, Katharine	10/ 1/1843	171
Smith, James M.	Redd (Reed?), Emily	11/25/1843	171
Yancy, Stephen	Holbrooks, Polly Ann	11/ 9/1843	172
Harris, Abraham	McCall, Elizabeth	12/24/1843	172
Echols, Mason P.	Yancy, Nancy	12/13/1843	173
Park, Andrew H.	Tryson, Delitha W.	12/28/1843	173
Taylor, David	McDonald, Maranda L.	2/19/1843	174
Rainwater, Sidney	McSimms, Martha	10/10/1843	174
Warden, James	Blaylock, Mary	11/12/1843	175
Wadkins (Watkins), Nathan C.	Buchanan, Sarah C.	11/15/1843	175
Hughes, Thomas D.	Hendrix, Virginia Esther	12/10/1843	176
Kelpin, William	Towrence (Torrence), Mary Ann	12/10/1843	176
Chatham, William C.	Holbrooks, Annie D.	12/21/1843	177
Otwell, William	Tidwell, Sarah	1/22/1844	177
Jones, Gilford W.	Bell, Lavenia Y.	1/31/1844	178
Mulky, James J. (I.?)	Vaughan, Margaret A.	2/ 5/1844	178
Rogers, Jackson (Cherokee-DLS)	Blackburn, Sarah G. (Cherokee-DLS)	2/ 7/1844	179
Boring, Alexander	Roberts, Roady	1/18/1844	179
Howell, Fendley J.	Pugh, Elizabeth	1/24/1844	180

GROOM	BRIDE	MARRIED	PAGE
Porter, John S.	Dixon, Martha K.	3/ 7/1844	180
Harris, Zachariah N.	Harden, Louisa	2/18/1844	181
Davis, Calvin W.	Ledbetter, Sarah	2/ 1/1844	181
Harris, Alfred (Lic.) Alexander (Cert.)	Malden, Kezia	3/ 3/1844	
Parmer (Palmer?), Edmond T.	Dollar, Sarah	3/ 3/1844	182
McClure, James	Howell, Rebecca	3/17/1844	183
Yarborough, Walter G.	Phillips, Mary T.	4/ 7/1844	183
Ashworth, Joab	Woodall, Sarah	4/28/1844	184
Thompson, Joseph J.	Jackson, Sarah	4/ 2/1844	184
Cantrell, Wilson	Hudson, Elizabeth	4/18/1844	185
Fowler, William	Landsdown, Adaline	5/16/1844	185
Swanagen, Thomas	Davis, Eliza	5/21/1844	186
Honea, Henry	Fendley, Margaret	6/16/1844	186
Mitchell, Wm. Bennett	Watters, Jane	8/10/1843	187
Pridges (Bridger?),Lewis	Christopher, Oliviat	1/25/1843	187
Sartin, John	Smith, Mary	10/ 5/1843	188
Payne, Elias	Orr, Elizabeth	1/16/1843	188
McDonald, Alexander	Mooney, Caroline	11/ 5/1843	189
Wilson, Anderson	Wellborn, Civella S.	1/14/1844	189
Martin, Hix	Casey, Margaret	1/ 7/1844	190
Jackson, Samuel	Naler (Nailor?),Adaline	3/13/1844	190
Morris, Henry M.	Cantwell, Emily	6/ 9/1844	191
Williams, Thomas W.	Byram, Rebecca	5/30/1844	191
Delk, Jackson	York, Isabella C.	7/30/1844	192
Wilder, Jonathan	Jorden, Fanny	7/28/1844	192
Anglin, Henry B.	Cobb, Nancy	7/18/1844	193
Edwards, Thomas	Offutt, Sophia	7/28/1844	193
Brooks, Richard B.	Hadder, Martha	8/22/1844	194
Reese (Reece?), Henry	Martin, Matilda	4/26/1844	194
Brannon, William B.	Pool, Mahala F.	8/15/1844	195
Smithy, George W.	Scott, Jane	8/15/1844	195
Red, Archibald H.	Holbrooks, Martha M.	9/26/1844	196
Morris, David	Thompson, Dorcas	9/ 3/1844	196
Mooney, Eli	Mashburn, Mary A.	10/ 3/1844	197
Allred, Jerry	Strickland, Sarah	10/28/1844	197
McGinnis, Stephen W.	Staggs, Hester Ann	10/ 1/1844	198
Wynn, John R. (K.?)	Dodd, Clarissa	11/21/1844	198
Weems, George	Echols, Margaret	11/22/1844	199
Caldwell, Andrew	Matthews, Sarah	11/17/1844	199
Floyd, Gallent	Davis, Nancy	12/12/1844	200
Smith, Alhpa	Segars, Mary	12/17/1844	200
Adkins, James	Crow, Sarah	12/23/1844	201
Simmons, Wm. H.	Allen, Adaline E.	12/26/1844	201
Conley, Wilson S.	Allen, Louisa	12/29/1844	202
Lummus, James M.	Harris, Margaret M. (F., Cert.)	1/ 5/1845	202
Parmer (Palmer), Abner	Fisher, Mary	1/ 9/1845	203
Lowe, John	Rogers, Cynthia (Cherokee-DLS)	1/30/1845	
Martin, Zachariah	James, Eliza	1/19/1845	204
Phillips, David	Estes, Tabitha	2/13/1845	204
Echols, James M.	Thomas, Mary	1/16/1845	205
Whitworth, William K.	Roberts, Mary Eliza	1/16/1845	205
Strickland, Henry	Smith, Ann E.	1/22/1845	206
Queen, Timothy	Russell, Eliza	1/26/1845	206
Daniel, John	Brooks, Clarinda	1/27/1845	207
Bailey, William B.	Bennett, Elizabeth E.	1/29/1845	207

GROOM	BRIDE	MARRIED	PAGE
Conner, William J.	Watters, Sarah	2/23/1845	208
Leonard, Starling	McAfee, Martha	2/23/1845	208
Stone, Jonathan	Bailey, Sussanah	2/10/1845	209
Stone, Allen, Sr.	Holbrooks, Alefore (?)	2/13/1845	209
Driskell, Mark	Grant, Milly	2/ 6/1845	210
Barrett, John W.	Gates, Elizabeth	3/ 6/1845	210
Chamblee, Lewis	Payne, Susan	3/14/1845	211
Naramon, Jackson	Rawlins, Nancy Jane	3/24/1845	211
Pate, Butler	Blackwell, Elizar	3/ 2/1845	212
McGinnis, Elijah	Jenks, Mary	4/20/1845	212
Shaw, James A. J.	Sanders, Jane	5/ 4/1845	213
Langley, John	Sanders, Martha C.	5/ 4/1845	213
Taylor, Abel	Slatin, Lucinda E.	5/28/1845	214
Naler (Nailor?), Stephen C.	Strickland, Susannah	5/18/1845	214
Stone, Jonathan	Stone, Rebecca	5/19/1845	215
Roper, Henry F.	Holbrooks, Evaline	6/ 1/1845	215
Blankenship, William	Rouse, Ann	7/ 3/1845	216
Scott, William	Jones, Rosa	7/20/1845	216
Payne, David H.	Jones, Juliann F.	7/13/1845	217
Deal, George	Thomas, Cynthia Caroline (Thompson written over surname)	7/13/1845	217
Taylor, Nicholas H.	Jenkins, Carity (?) G.	7/27/1845	218
Bryant (?), Clark H.	Butler, Elizabeth	7/27/1845	218
Howell, Evan D. (May be Evan P. Howell)	Knox, Margaret D.	8/19/1845	219
Holden, Elias E.(C.?)	Tatum, Winnie	8/23/1845	219
Blanton, Charles S.	Henson, Sarah Ann	8/31/1845	220
Cain, Francis M.	Bell, Sarah Ann	9/11/1845	220
Jones, Thomas J.	Tippins, Minerva	9/11/1845	221
Bradley, Joel	McPherson, Ardallia(?)	9/ 1/1845	221
Brumbelow, Lindsey	Simmons, Jane	9/20/1845	222
Wilder, Silas	Buchanan, Amanda	9/30/1845	222
Ford, John J.	Harrell, Lavina	10/ 2/1845	223
Jones, Seaborn	Allen, Agnes	10/ 2/1845	223
Welch, Lemuel	Harris, Mary Ann	10/ 8/1843	224
Carter, Henry C.	Breeder, Eliza	10/ 9/1845	224
Fitts (Felts?), Wm. H.	Mason (Mesona?), Minty Ann	10/23/1845	225
Segars, William H.	Welborn, Sarah C.	10/23/1845	225
Weems, Isaiah B.	Holbrook, Frances	11/ 6/1845	226
Stephens, Ephraim	Estes, Elizabeth	11/ 4/1845	226
Thornton, Andrew	Hendrix, Webby L.	11/20/1845	227
Echols, Benjamin	Fields, Caroline	11/30/1845	227
Samples, Jesse	Jeffreys, Elizabeth	12/14/1845	228
Lewis, Thomas	Jones, Lula B.	12/ 7/1845	228
Lewis, William A.	Gordon, Eleanor J.	12/23/1845	229
Hawkins, John S.	Kemp, Minerva	12/14/1845	229
Tate, Evan P.	Foster, Margaret J.	12/18/1845	230
Huggins, David J.	Sams, Mary	12/21/1845	230
Terrell, Joshua W.	Hadder, Frances M.	12/22/1845	231
Patterson, Joshua	Cockburn, Darcus	12/25/1845	231
Pruett, William H.	Wilcox, Martha	9/18/1844	232
Hughes, Francis H.	Crow, Sarah S.	2/ 7/1845	232
McFarlin, Richard	Wilkins, Margaret H.	3/11/1845	233
Moor, Jerry	Crow, Nancy	9/ 1/1845	233
Rhodes, Reubin P.	Tailor, Martha	10/23/1845	234
Brooks, John	Biddy, Louisa	10/24/1845	234
Jones, Caleb P.	Bird, Martha Adaline	12/23/1845	235

GROOM	BRIDE	MARRIED	PAGE
Wilkie, Andrew H.	Tailor, Mary	12/23/1845	235
Potts, James	McLelon, Elizabeth	1/ 8/1846	236
Owens, Wiley W.	Brown, Elizabeth Ann	1/14/1846	236
Cain, Samuel	Bell, Emily	1/16/1846	237
Bramblett, Reubin	Swilling, Harriet H.	1/21/1846	237
Fowler, John	Wiley, Sarah	1/22/1846	238
Martin, Archibald	Pool, Lucinda	1/25/1846	238
Brownlow, James A.H.	Austin, Jane Ann	1/27/1846	239
Kemp, Marvel L.	Ezzard, Mary	2/ 5/1846	239
Jenkins, Reuben M.	Reed, Malinda A.	2/19/1846	240
Bell, Anderson S.	Rogers, Albina M. (Cheorkee)	2/16/1846	
Harris, Henry A.	Redmon, Frances	2/26/1846	241
Guthery, Andrew N.	Gravitt, Polly	3/ 7/1846	241
Hutchins, Livingston	Harrison, Malissa Ann	3/25/1846	242
Jones, Thomas M.C.	Tallant, Lucinda	5/ 7/1846	242
King, Joseph D.	Figgins, Lucinda	4/ 7/1846	243
Wilcox, David S.	Hutchins, Nancy Ann	4/13/1846	243
Bagley, Fletcher	Nailor, Susan M.	4/26/1846	244
Hall, Nathaniel D.	Wilkins, Martha A.E.B.	4/30/1846	
Swilling, Berry B.	Bramblett, Malinda A.	6/ 7/1846	245
Robbs, William	Jordon, Parthena	6/15/1846	245
Anderson, William W.	Brown, Arminda (Amanda?)	7/ 5/1846	246
Comer (Conner?),Wiley	Pharrar, Mary Ann	7/ 5/1846	246
Walker, David	Welborn, Theodocia C.	7/ 7/1846	247
Parker, Weston	Gates, Sarah W.	7/17/1846	247
Ramsey, Richard	Echols, Nancy M.	7/30/1846	248
Ratford, Giles	Pettyjohn, Nancy	10/23/1844	248
Gravitt, Luke	Parris, Celia	3/29/1846	249
Holland, William	Chaplin, Nancy	7/22/1846	249
Thompson, Graham	Thompson, Mary	8/30/1846	250
Bagley, Henry S.	Williams, Annie (Amy)	9/15/1846	250
Tollison, Russel A.	Blankenship, Frances	9/ 6/1846	251
Owen, Powell	Johnson, Emaline	9/27/1846	251
Fisher, James	Terry, Nancy	10/ 1/1846	252
P9lgrim, Petty	Otwell, Susan	10/ 7/1846	252
Southard, John B.	Strickland, Sally	10/29/1846	253
Daniel, James W.	Westbrooks, Winnie	11/11/1846	253
Coffey, Larkin	Gravitt, Tempy	11/19/1846	254
Holbrook, John W.	Dummer, Elizabeth	11/29/1846	254
Miller, Green	Pendergrass, Susan	11/ 8/1846	255
Biddy, Watts	Brooks, Polly	12/24/1846	255
Vaughan, Jeremiah	Tidwell, Susan	12/24/1846	256
Jones, Benjamin W.	Brown, Mary Ann	12/27/1746	256
Morris, Andy	Wynn, Sattavery	12/29/1846	257
Palmer, Edmond T.	Holbrooks, Arnill	12/28/1846	257
Blaylock, John J.	Martin, Mahala	12/ 6/1846	258
Martin, Samuel	Nix, Sarah	1/ 3/1847	258
Holbrooks, Asberry	McDonald, Sarah Ann	3/23/1845	259
Davis, James M.	McDonald, Lucinda	12/19/1845	259
Brannon, Hiram E.	Bagley, Mary E.	7/ 9/1846	260
Blanton, John J.	McBrayer, Amelia R.	7/29/1846	260
Vaughan, William B.	Coggins, Polly Ann	7/31/1846	261
Hays, Harmon	Roberts, Elizabeth	10/23/1846	261
Bagley, Richard H.	Hays, Martha Jane	11/10/1846	262
Fendley, Henry R.	Geer, Louise K.	1/24/1847	262
Crow, William	Stovall, Betsy Ann	1/24/1847	263
Hardage, William C.	Howard, Malinda	1/27/1847	263
Rowland, Robert	Heath, Elizabeth	2/ 4/1847	264

FORSYTH COUNTY MARRIAGES, BOOK A (1833-1848)

GROOM	BRIDE	MARRIED	PAGE
Bennett, Berry	Martin, Emily	2/10/1847	264
Monroe, Theron E.	Kelly, Mary S.	3/24/1846	264
(exec. in Cherokee Co.)			
McClure, John A.	Henderson, Roxy Ann	11/10/1846	265
Clayton, John M.	Clayton, Amarilus A.	3/ 2/1847	265
Thomas, Joseph	Bridges, Margaret	9/23/1846	265
Chapman, John	Russell, Catharine	8/20/1846	266
Kell, James	Wallis, Jane	7/ 5/1846	266
(Lumpkin Co.)			
Cobb, Enoch	Holland, Margaret	10/29/1846	266
(Cherokee Co.)			
Chastain, Madison	Owen, Frances	7/26/1846	267
Bramblett, Henry N. H.	McEntire, Tillitha	2/18/1847	267
Hawkins, Henry B.	Lewis, Harriett M.	3/11/1847	267
Powell, Oliver C.	McCrary, Eliza	2/28/1847	268
Person (Pearson?), Joel	Darby, Arminta	3/25/1847	268
Lewis, Wiley H.	Pearson, Deanny	4/18/1847	268
Bramblett, Enoch	Roberts, Catharine	4/25/1847	269
Bennett, Elisha	Rowland, Sarah	5/ 2/1847	269
Whitmire, James W.	Hadder, Catharine	5/20/1847	269
Gravitt, Charles	Beshears, Winnie	6/ 6/1847	270
Tumlin, William	Green, Elizabeth	6/ 9/1847	270
Gravitt, John	Brooks, Susan	7/25/1847	270
Cobb, Jackson	Vickery, Susannah	8/13/1847	271
(Cherokee Co.)			
McGinnis, Elijah	Jenks, Catharine	8/22/1847	271
Steagall, Richard	James, Mary Ann	8/23/1847	271
Hendricks, Russell	Howard, Zeruah A.	9/16/1847	272
Yancy, Francis	Fitspatrick, Mary	9/19/1847	272
Keller, Cane	Anderson, Sarah Ann	9/30/1847	272
Wilson, Benjamin	Stone, Ellender	10/ 3/1847	273
Stovall, Lewis	Malden, Grace G.	11/ 1/1847	273
Gravitt, James Pickney	Beshears, Jane	11/14/1847	273
Owens, Alfred	Stone, Elizabeth Jane	11/14/1847	274
Bagwell, Berry E.	Johnston, Mary Ann	11/18/1847	274
Fowler, John M.	Vaughan, Delilah	12/ 2/1847	274
Thomas, John	Bridges, Dicy Ann	12/13/1846	275
Flenn, Joseph	Huggins, Sally	8/24/1842	275
		(no return made)	
Light, Young K.	Munday, Susan	3/ 9/1847	275
Pool, John	Brannon, Mary C.	4/11/1847	276
Taylor, David	Gant, Betsy	1/ 5/1847	276
Crompton, Perry	Mosley, Martha	1/28/1847	276
Holbrook, Samuel A.	Roper, Hulda C.	4/29/1847	277
Powell, Allen	Bennett, Easter	1/25/1847	277
Figgin, Adam	Barnett, Marchel	3/21/1847	277
Nalley, Barksdel	Barrett, Miram	4/ 6/1847	278
Otwell, Benjamin	Vaughan, Nancy Jane	7/24/1845	278
Townley, Thomas M.	Morris, Serena	3/28/1847	278
Anglin, Henry F.	Tedder, Catharine	3/14/1847	279
McKay, Harrison	Guthery, Elisa	9/27/1845	279
Thompson, William	Adkins (Atkins?), Mary	2/ 3/1847	279
Gage, Ransom A.	Redmon(d?), Jane E.	12/20/1846	280
Sutton, Orsama	Blackstock, Adaline	1/ 3/1847	280
Eaton, Reuben	Aldridge, Mary	1/ 4/1847	280
Hardage, William C.	Howard, Malinda	1/27/1847	281
Fendley, Henry R.	Geer, Louisa K.	1/24/1847	281
Witherspoon, Charles W.	Foster, Mary Ann	3/25/1847	281
Fowler, S. W.	Davis, Mary	9/ 5/1847	282

FORSYTH COUNTY MARRIAGES, BOOK A (1833-1848)

GROOM	BRIDE	MARRIAGE	PAGE
Connally, William	Harkness, Elizabeth Ann	6/29/1847	282
Chatham, Joshua	Cobb, Sarah	11/25/1847	282
Hammon(d), Hiram	Thomas, Emily	10/21/1847	283
Martin, William	Martin, Martha	12/30/1847	283
Lindsey, Lawson C.	Hix, Elizabeth	12/23/1847	283
Grier, John F.	Thompson, Nancy E.	12/21/1847	284
Allen, William G.	Swilling, Georgia Ann	9/ 9/1847	284
Walraven, Isaac	Solomon, Mary	11/17/1847	284
Martin, William P.	Barrett, Nancy	2/ 5/1848	285
James, Mahlon Henry	Butler, Lucinda	12/ 9/1847	285
Terry, Byrd	Barton, Arminda(Aminda?)	3/18/1847	285
Rogers, Henry C.	Thompson, Louisa J.	12/28/1847	286
(Cherokee - DLS)	(nee Blackburn)		
Rowland, Robert	Heath, Elizabeth	2/ 4/1847	286
Childers, John	Jourdan, Anna	8/26/1847	286
Money (Mooney?), Francis	Jenkins, Elizabeth J.	12/ 9/1847	287
Barrett, John R.	Coston, Hannah C.	8/ 2/1848	287
Worley, Pleasant	Mills, Margaret C.	4/29/1847	287
Scott, William R.	Smithey, Nancy	8/27/1848	288
Spence, Calvin	Mashburn, Cynthia Ann	10/26/1848	288
Seagours, William G.	Waters, Cynthia A.M.	1/ 9/1848	288
Venable, Sanford	Bagley, Adaline	10/19/1848	289
Kemp, Andrew J.	Killingsworth, F.M.	2/20/1848	289
Tenly (Fendley),			
Benjamin F.	Jones, Amanda C.	1/ 2/1848	289
Hughes, James E.	Bennett, Isabella	1/ 6/1848	290
West, John W. C.	Bowls, Elizabeth	9/29/1848	290
Tallant, Benjamin C.	Collett, Narcissa	5/31/1848	290
Dobson, Washington P.	Evans, Margaret	3/ 2/1848	291
(Lumpkin County)			
Wallis, William W.	Harris, Martha	4/13/1848	291
Fitzgiles, William	Mitchell, Abashaba	11/ 5/1848	291
(Lumpkin County)			
Mashburn, Henry T.	Atkinson, Eliza N.	2/10/1848	292
Glover, Jarrett W.	Nash, Elizabeth	4/20/1848	292
McGinnis, Elijah	Waldrup, Jane	8/20/1848	292
Rowlin (Rowland,			
Rawlin?), Tilman	Gravitt, Patsy	4/ 2/1848	293
Strickland, Samuel J.	Blaylock, Philadelphia	8/ 3/1848	293
Echols, Eber B.	Gant, Emaline	8/18/1848	293
Cawdrey (Cordery),	Carrell (Carroll),		
Thomas (Cherokee-DLS)	Sarah	5/14/1848	294
Reay (Ray?), William	Allen, Jane	3/ 8/1848	294
Phillips, Reuben F.	Burtz, Nancy	8/11/1848	294
Vaughan, Clabourn	Bo(w)man, Frances	9/28/1848	
	Avaline		
Bond, Henry	Johnston, Martha Jane	9/15/1848	295
Bennett, Ransom	Rowland, Matilda	12/14/1848	295
Terry, John	Jackson, Martha	11/23/1848	296
Williams, William	Bennett, Sarah F.	8/27/1848	296
Steagal, Peter	Kelly, Elizabeth	5/14/1848	296

End of Book A.

GROOM	BRIDE	DATE	PAGE	BOOK
Aaron, Russel D.	Darby, Minerva	16 July 1843	165	A
Aaron, William	Bradford, Lucy	9 Oct 1837	40	A
Aaron, William	Bradley, Polly	8 Aug 1839	80	A
Abbott, Albert N.	Roberts, Sarah J.	14 May 1854	23	C
Addington, Thomas L.	Ripley, Martha A.E.	5 Nov 1854	30	C
Adkins, James	Crow, Sarah	23 Dec 1844	201	A
Agerton, James P.	Wood, Emily	8 Mar 1838	47	A
Alexander, James	Hale, Jane	23 Nov 1851	120	B
Allen, William	Bagley, Agnes	2 Mar 1854	13	C
Allen, William G.	Swilling, Georgia Ann	9 Sep 1847	284	A
Allred, Jerry	Strickland, Sarah	28 Oct 1844	197	A
Anderson, Daniel	Venable, Martha	17 Jan 1837	32	A
Anderson, James	James, Calinder	5 Apr 1838	47	A
Anderson, William P.	Pendley, Temperance	15 Oct 1837	38	A
Anderson, William W.	Brown, Amandy	16 June 1846	246	A
Andrews, James W.	Thompson, Mahulda Ann	10 Nov 1853	17	C
Anglin, Henry B.	Cobb, Nancy	18 July 1844	193	A
Anglin, Henry F.	Tedder, Catherine	14 Mar 1847	279	A
Armstrong, John	McGinnis, Mary	7 Nov 1841	116	A
Arthur, William	Hammond, Elizabeth	10 July 1843	166	A
Ashby, Level	Blackburn, Jerrusha	16 Feb 1837	50	A
Ashworth, James	Stoball (Stovall), Nancy	8 May 1843	161	A
Ashworth, Joab	Woodall, Sarah	28 Apr 1844	184	A
Austin, James G.	Bennett, Mary Ann	25 Dec 1841	117	A
Autry, William H.	Collins, Katharine	16 Mar 1841	167	A
Bagley, Edmond	Strickland, Sarah	1 Nov 1838	56	A
Bagley, Fletcher	Nailor, Susan M.	26 Apr 1846	244	A
Bagley, Harmon	Strickland, Amma	22 Nov 1837	37	A
Bagley, Henry T.	Williams, Annie	15 Sept 1846	250	A
Bagley, Nathan F.	Hays, Melissa C.	25 June 1840	92	A
Bagley, Richard H.	Hays, Martha Jane	10 Nov 1846	262	A
Bagley, Wesley S.	Bagley, Caroline	28 Aug 1842	134	A
Bagley, William H.	McGinnis, Jemina	19 Mar 1854	22	C
Bagwell, Berry E.	Johnston, Mary Ann	18 Nov 1847	274	A
Bailey, Thomas T.	Yancy, Lucinda	13 Dec 1842	123	A
Bailey, William B.	Bennett, Elizabeth E.	29 Jan 1845	207	A
Baker, Samuel H.	Compton, Ann	13 Apr 1854	26	C
Banister, Powel	Dooley, Elizabeth	15 Dec 1853	15	C
Bannister, Dearix	Dooley, Mary Ann	21 Dec 1854	41	C
Barker, Hubbard	Henderson, Elizabeth	11 Feb 1834	3	A
Barker, William	Russell, Elisa	5 Mar 1840	85	A
Barnett, Nathan	Johnson, A.M. Frances	1 May 1842	127	A
Barrett, John R.	Coston, Hannah C.	2 Aug 1848	287	A
Barrett, John W.	Gates, Elizabeth	6 Mar 1845	210	A
Barrett, Warren	McBrayer, Margaret E.	12 June 1850	107	C
Barrett, William J.	Hockenhull, Ann	11 Oct 1855	62	C
Bates, George	Lawless, Jane	26 Dec 1841	118	A
Baty, James N.	Rawlins, Elizabeth	23 Jan 1837	31	A
Beall, Wesley C.	Staggs, Rosy J.	18 May 1854	31	C
Beaver, Francis M.	Doss, Emily C.	15 Mar 1853	147	B
Beaver, Thomas M.	Doss, Elizabeth A.	8 May 1853	147	B
Bell, Anderson S.	Rogers, Albina M.	16 Feb 1846	240	A
Bennett, Berry	Martin, Emily	10 Feb 1847	264	A
Bennett, Cooper	Brooks, Catharine	6 Apr 1843	159	A
Bennett, Elisha	Rowland, Sarah	2 May 1847	269	A
Bennett, Merrel C.	Elison, Milly	22 Sep 1836	24	A
Bennett, Ransom	Rowland, Matilda	14 Dec 1848	296	A
Bennett, Samuel C.	Vickery, Mary	22 Feb 1835	8	A
Bennett, William	Crow, Elizabeth	4 Aug 1859	158	C
Bentley, Jerry	Pool, Emily C.	12 Mar 1840	86	A
Bertz, L. W.	Hughes, Mary	16 Oct 1855	58	C
Biddy, Watts	Brooks, Polly	24 Dec 1846	255	A
Blackburn, Ambros	Hudson, Elizabeth	22 Sept 1836	25	A
Blackburn, John	Wood, Malissa	12 Jan 1843	168	A
Blackburn, Thomas	Barrett, Lucinda	24 Dec 1839	74	A
Blackstock, Allen	Rogers, Nancy	1 Oct 1853	4	C

GROOM	BRIDE	DATE	PAGE	BOOK
Blackstock, John L.	McGinnis, N. E.	1 Jan 1854	146	C
Blackstock, Richard W.	Whitsitt, Cornelia	2 July 1843	162	A
Blackwell, David	Green, Lucinda	11 May 1843	159	A
Blackwell, William B.	Carver, Martha	28 Sept 1842	153	A
Blankenship, William	Rouse, Ann	3 July 1845	216	A
Blankenship, William	Boyd, Irana	18 Dec 1842	139	A
Blanton, Charles S.	Henson, Sarah Ann	31 Aug 1846	220	A
Blanton, John J.	McBrayer, Amelia R.	29 July 1846	260	A
Blaylock, John J.	Martin, Mahala	6 Dec 1846	258	A
Bobo, Silas	Autry, Minerva	7 Feb 1839	68	A
Bond, Henry	Johnston, Martha Jane	15 Sept 1848	296	A
Bonner, Benjamin F.	Haynes, Sarah Elizabeth	1 Oct 1840	97	A
Boring, Alexander	Roberts, Roady	18 Jan 1844	179	A
Boring, Francis M.	Harris, Parmilia	16 Oct 1853	19	C
Boring, James H.	Miller, Thenay	15 Oct 1843	169	A
Boring, Thomas W.	Barnett, Mahaly	15 June 1843	164	A
Born, Elbert G.	Pool, Rachel F.	2 Jan 1853	144	A
Boseman, John	Darby, Sarah G.	27 Sept 1855	54	C
Bowen, Hiram	Stewart, Caroline	19 Sept 1838	55	A
Bowls, Henry J.	Sanders, Anna	30 Oct 1853	152	B
Boyd, John L.	Anderson, Celia	15 Nov 1835	12	A
Boyd, Samuel	Wood, Prissy	8 May 1842	141	A
Boyle, Joseph H.	Terry, Susanna	10 Oct 1852	126	B
Bradford, James	Smallwood, Renie	30 Aug 1835	10	A
Bradford, Moses	Aron, Nancy	31 July 1838	52	A
Bradley, Bethal	Williams, Ann	3 Nov 1833	1	A
Bradley, Charles C.	Gravitt, Louisa	1 May 1853	133	B
Bradley, Joel	McPherson, Ardallia	1 Sept 1845	221	A
Bramblett, Enoch	Roberts, Catharine	25 Apr 1847	269	A
Bramblett, Henry N.H.	McEntire, Tillitha	18 Feb 1847	267	A
Bramblett, James R.	Roberts, Margaret	7 Feb 1841	101	A
Bramblett, Reubin	Swilling, Harriet H.	21 Jan 1846	237	A
Bramblett, W. H.	Eddleman, Rutha M.	3 Apr 1855	46	C
Brannen, Martin	Collins, Nancy	30 Aug 1835	12	A
Brannon, Hiram E.	Bagley, Mary E.	9 July 1846	260	A
Brannon, James R.	Martin, Sarah C.	22 Dec 1842	155	A
Brannon, Reuben W.	Spruce, Nancy	14 Dec 1854	27	C
Brannon, William B.	Pool, Mahaly F.	15 Aug 1844	195	A
Briant, Clark H.	Butler, Elizabeth	27 July 1845	218	A
Bridges, Lewis	Christopher, Olivet	25 Jan 1843	187	A
Brooks, John	Biddy, Louisa	24 Oct 1845	234	A
Brooks, Richard	Fowler, Neata	8 Jan 1837	29	A
Brooks, Richard B.	Hadden, Martha	22 Aug 1844	194	A
Brooks, William T.	Spence, Amanda	25 Dec 1851	16	C
Brown, James H.	Honea, Abigail	18 Nov 1841	117	A
Brown, James W.	Barnett, Sarah	13 Jan 1853	141	B
Brown, John	Masons, Rebecca	15 Dec 1836	27	A
Brown, John T.	Cunningham, Fleta F.	27 Dec 1855	59	C
Brown, Thomas	Naylor, Frances	19 Mar 1854	20	C
Brown, William R.	Gravitt, Sarah	24 Sept 1835	11	A
Brownlow, James A.H.	Austin, Jane Ann	27 Jan 1846	239	A
Bruce, George	Cain, Nancy	14 Apr 1853	20	C
Brumbelow, Isaac	Snead, Leddy	28 July 1842	133	A
Brumbelow, Joel	Snead, Nancy	23 June 1842	131	A
Brumbelow, Lindsey	Simmons, Jane	20 Sept 1845	222	A
Burford, Thomas A.	Brown, Nancy E.	1 Jan 1855	38	C
Burton, Elias	Dodd, Mary Ann	19 Aug 1841	111	A
Burtz, James B.	Fowler, Emily A.	9 May 1841	108	A
Burtz, Joshua	McCormack, Christian	24 Jan 1841	103	A
Cain, Francis M.	Bell, Sarah Ann	11 Sept 1845	220	A
Cain, Samuel	Bell, Emily	16 Jan 1846	237	A
Caldwell, Andrew	Mathews, Sarah	17 Nov 1844	199	A
Caldwell, Hiram J.	Blankenship, Elisa	22 Jan 1840	85	A
Caloway, James	Martin, Sarah Ann	8 May 1853	139	B
Campbell, Elias	Carroll, Jane	21 Nov 1839	89	A
Campbell, Henry J.	MCall (McCall), Eliza	18 Feb 1841	167	A
Cantrell, Wilson	Hutchins, Elizabeth M.J.	12 Mar 1843	158	A

GROOM	BRIDE	DATE	PAGE	BOOK
Cantrell, Wilson	Hudson, Elizabeth	18 Apr 1844	185	A
Carter, Henry C.	Breeder, Eliza	9 Oct 1845	224	A
Casey, Barnabas	Hutchins, Harriet R.	2 Jan 1839	60	A
Casey, Ellison	Waldrup, Sarah	5 Aug 1841	114	A
Casey, Washington	Casey, Patsy	11 Nov 1839	74	A
Castelberry, Benjam-				
in W.	Harris, Caron	12 Oct 1837	36	A
Castleberry, David	Williams, Nancy Matilda	4 Nov 1853	18	C
Castleberry, Timothy	Bacon, Agnes	26 Apr 1840	90	A
Cawdrey, Thomas	Carrell, Sarah	14 May 1848	294	A
Chadwick, Benjamin	Eaton, Lucinda	8 Apr 1842	126	A
Chadwick, Ephraim	Smith, Hannah M.	2 Oct 1853	5	C
Chamblee, Lewis	Payne, Susan	14 Mar 1845	211	A
Chamblee, Washington	Martin, Rebecca	21 Dec 1837	41	A
Chapman, Isaac	Manning, Elizabeth Ann	13 Dec 1849	59	D
Chapman, John	Russell, Catharine	20 Aug 1846	266	A
Chastain, Madison	Owen, Frances	26 July 1846	267	A
Chatham, Joshua	Cobb, Sarah	25 Nov 1847	282	A
Chatham, Stephen M.	Estes, Tempy	29 Dec 1853	11	C
Chatham, Thos. M.	Davis, Sarah Jane	26 Nov 1854	88	C
Chatham, William C.	Holbrooks, Anny D.	21 Dec 1843	177	A
Cheek, Gazaway	Pike, Terrisa	19 May 1840	92	A
Childers, George W.	Daniel, Sariannas	15 Sept 1849	331	C
Childers, John	Jourdan, Anna	26 Aug 1847	286	A
Christenberry, Silas				
G.	Edwards, Nancy	29 Dec 1855	46	C
Christopher, Henry	Congo, Narcisis	4 Nov 1852	143	B
Clayton, John M.	Clayton, Amarilus A.	2 Mar 1847	265	A
Clayton, Reuben M.	Poor, Emily	8 Oct 1837	37	A
Coats, Reuben	Terry, Emaline	1 Jan 1854	17	C
Cobb, Enoch	Holland, Margaret	29 Oct 1846	266	A
Cobb, Jackson	Vickery, Susannah	13 Aug 1847	271	A
Cobb, Peter	Harris, Sarah	20 Jan 1853	130	B
Cockburn, Russell	Carroll, Celia	26 Oct 1834	7	A
Coffey, Larkin	Gravitt, Tempy	19 Nov 1846	254	A
Coffey, Thomas W.	Roper, Eliza	23 Oct 1842	137	A
Cole, Caswell N.	Holbrook, Sarah	1 Dec 1842	143	A
Coleman, Hosea	Brannon, Betsy	8 Nov 1838	62	A
Coleman, Phillip	Bridges, Matilda	22 Mar 1835	8	A
Coleman, Volenten	Campbell, Nancy	19 Sept 1836	18	A
Collett, Archibald	Holbrook, Peressa	7 Sept 1849	99	A
Collett, John	Darby, Jane	7 Dec 1836	21	A
Collins, Joseph B.	Miller, Ann	18 Feb 1837	28	A
Compton, Henry M.	Bennett, Mary Jane	23 Apr 1854	87	C
Compton, John T.	Scruggs, Nancy E.	28 July 1842	133	A
Compton, William C.	Doster, Bency	23 May 1841	108	A
Conley, Wilson S.	Allen, Louisa	29 Dec 1844	202	A
Connally, William	Harkness, Elizabeth Ann	29 June 1848	282	A
Conner, Lindsey	Ravins, Barbary A.E.	24 Aug 1854	46	C
Conner, Reubin T.	Fulcher, Sarah	27 Dec 1842	141	A
Conner, William J.	Watters, Sarah	23 Feb 1845	208	A
Cornelison, Burrell	Barrett, Martha A.R.	25 Oct 1855	63	C
Cowen, Wiley	Pharrar, Mary Ann	5 July 1846	246	A
Creamer, Raleigh W.	Waters, Martha F.	20 July 1854	141	C
Crocker, Berry H.	Holcomb, Mary	7 Apr 1853	7	C
Crompton, Perry	Mosley, Martha	28 Jan 1847	276	A
Cross, Garrison	Compton, Sophriah			
	Eveline	8 July 1849	62	D
Cross, Gideon	McCrary, Frances L.	27 Mar 1855	44	C
Crow, Eli	Hughes, Mary A.	14 Mar 1854	15	C
Crow, Isaac J.	Bewry, Elly	7 Aug 1839	72	A
Crow, Shadrack A.	Casey, Edny	5 Aug 1841	112	A
Crow, William	Donaldson, Milley	14 Sept 1854	32	C
Crow, William	Stovall, Betsy Ann	24 Jan 1847	263	A
Cruse, John L.	Sams, Cintha	12 Jan 1834	2	A
Cruse, Pinckney	Williams, Melissa	3 Apr 1853	136	B

FORSYTH COUNTY MARRIAGES 1832-1855

GROOM	BRIDE	DATE	PAGE	BOOK
Cruse, William	Hawkins, Emaline	15 Jan 1839	64	A
Curbow, James N.J.	Horton, Martha C.	25 Mar 1855	42	C
Dacus, Arthur	Tatum, Peggy	25 Feb 1838	48	A
Daniel, James W.	Westbrooks, Winnie	11 Nov 1846	253	A
Daniel, John	Brooks, Clarinda	27 Jan 1845	207	A
Daniel, William	Osburn, Rachael	30 Dec 1841	116	A
Davenport, John	Hendrix, Susan	12 May 1839	69	A
David, Simon B.	Harris, Frances E.	1 Mar 1855	40	C
Davidson, Aswell	Terry, Mary	14 Aug 1855	52	C
Davis, Benjamin W.M.	Bagwell, Lavina	9 Oct 1851	147	C
Davis, Calvin W.	Ledbetter, Sarah	1 Feb 1844	181	A
Davis, Hezakiah N.	Anderson, Martha E.	29 Mar 1853	134	B
Davis, James	Samples, Rachel	9 Jan 1837	23	A
Davis, James M.	McDonald, Lucinda	19 Dec 1845	259	A
Davis, Joshua	McKay, Susan	22 Dec 1836	20	A
Davis, Robert F.	Baker, Obedience	13 Nov 1842	143	A
Davis, William	Huggins, Sally	19 July 1838	52	A
Davis, William B.	Poor, Frances	20 Mar 1838	46	A
Day, Andy L.	Key, Rebecca W.	2 Feb 1843	150	A
Deal, George	Thomas, Cynthia Caroline	13 July 1845	217	A
Delk, Jackson	York, Isabella C.	30 July 1844	192	A
Dickson, Edley P.	Holden, Milly	6 Mar 1839	67	A
Dobson, Washington P.	Evans, Margaret	2 Mar 1848	291	A
Dodd, George W.	Dollar, Caroline	7 Aug 1855	50	C
Dollar, John G.	Holbrook, Sarah	28 June 1855	59	C
Doneyhue, James M.	Monday, Lucy	5 Jan 1837	31	A1
Dooley, James	Wadkins, Martha	9 Feb 1840	83	A
Dooly, R.J.	Hudson, Parmela	22 Dec 1838	79	A
Dooly, Wesley	Phillips, Cleopatry	22 Feb 1855	42	C
Drennon, John N.	Brannon, Arcadias	5 July 1840	93	A
Driskell, Mark	Grant, Milly	6 Feb 1845	210	A
Dudly, John W.	Pruet, Malinda	16 Mar 1837	27	A
Dun, Ezekiel	Cameron, Mrs. Anny E.C.	19 Dec 1839	75	A
Dunking, Robert S.	Smith, Armetta	20 Aug 1837	33	A
Duyck (Duke), Timothy	Cox, Celia	10 Aug 1834	6	A
Eaton, Reuben	Aldridge, Mary	4 Jan 1847	280	A
Echols (Achols), Mason P.	Yancy, Nancy	13 Dec 1843	173	A
Echols, Benjamin	Fields, Caroline	30 Nov 1845	227	A
Echols, Eber B.	Gant, Emaline	18 Aug 1848	293	A
Echols, Elias L.	Strickland, Elizabeth	7 Feb 1841	102	A
Echols, Elija P.	Cape, Mississippi	13 Oct 1853	4	C
Echols, James M.	Thomas, Mary	16 Jan 1845	205	A
Echols, James M.	Brown, Elizabeth J.	3 Sept 1854	29	C
Eddelman, Joseph	Bramblett, Mary M.	2 Sept 1852	118	B
Edmondson, Andrew J.	Jeffreys, Mary	29 Dec 1842	145	A
Edmondson, Thomas	Davis, Frances L.	4 Dec 1854	37	C
Edwards, Benjamin F.	Johnston, Caroline C.	2 Sept 1849	44	B
Edwards, Thomas	Offutt, Sophia	28 July 1844	193	A
Elison, Dudley	Stone, Polly	19 Oct 1836	21	A
Ellis, Joshua	Kelly, Sarah	28 Feb 1837	50	A
Estes, Cicero	Mills, Adela E.	18 Oct 1855	57	C
Eunersom, William	Bettis, Eliza	5 Sept 1853	5	C
Evans, William	Willingham, Obedient	17 Dec 1835	12	A
Evans, Willis	Evans, Mary	26 Oct 1848	106	C
Evatt, William P.	Roper, Sarah Adaline	10 Mar 1853	131	B
Fendley, Elisha B.	Watson, Martha	7 Oct 1838	56	A
Fendley, Emanuel	Whitmire, Malinda	21 Oct 1838	57	A
Fendley, Henry R.	Geer, Louise K.	24 Jan 1847	281	A
Fergerson, Edmond	Lester, Julian	209(?) Mar 1836	13	A
Fewell, Thadias M.	Eaton, Margret	8 Aug 1836	25	A
Fields, William R.	White, Katherine	9 Sept 1855	68	C
Figgin, Adam	Barnett, Marchel	21 Mar 1847	277	A
Fincher, James C.	Evans, Sarah Ann	30 Oct 1853	81	C
Fincher, Jesse C.	Kemp, H. M.	27 Mar 1853	146	B
Fincher, John W.	Hallman, Rody	15 May 1853	3	C
Fisher, James	Terry, Nancy	1 Oct 1846	252	A

315

GROOM	BRIDE	DATE	PAGE	BOOK
Fitten, Isaiah C.	McCoy, Kezia A.	20 Feb 1843	152	A
Fitts, William H.	Mason, Minty Ann	23 Oct 1845	225	A
Fitzgiles, William	Mitchell, Abashaba	5 Nov 1848	291	A
Fitzpatrick, Stephen W.	Yancy, Sarah F.	20 Dec 1853	14	C
Fitzpatrick, Thomas D.	Yancey, Sarah	3 Aug 1855	52	C
Fleen, Joseph	Huggins, Sally	24 Aug 1842	275	A
Fleming, George W.	Goodwin, Sarah M.	18 July 1852	124	B
Floyd, Gallent	Davis, Nancy	12 Dec 1844	200	A
Ford, John J.	Harrell, Lavina	2 Oct 1845	223	A
Foster, Green B.	Hays, Martha F.	31 Dec 1851/57	110	C
Foster, Ira Row	Haynes, Milly A.C.	9 Oct 1842	153	A
Foster, Ransom E.	James, Kindness	20 Dec 1853	7	C
Foster, William P.	Pirkle, Zelfa	19 Nov 1840	99	A
Foster, William T.	Haynes, Abi A.	16 May 1843	161	A
Fowler, John	Wiley, Sarah	22 Jan 1846	238	A
Fowler, John	Walls, Caroline	19 Feb 1857	271	C
Fowler, John M.	Vaughan, Delilah	2 Dec 1847	274	A
Fowler, Phillip K.	Ledbetter, Nancy Jane	18 Feb 1855	141	C
Fowler, S.W.	Davis, Mary	5 Sept 1847	282	A
Fowler, William	Landsdown, Adaline	16 May 1844	185	A
Fowler, William	Balote, Rachael	4 Sept 1842	138	A
Francis, Thomans H.	Tinsley, Georgia Ann	15 Aug 1855	53	C
Freeland, Isaac	Key, Elizabeth	20 Sept 1855	54	C
Freeman, John	Craus, Melinda	15 Nov 1851	120	B
Friedley, George, Jr.	McCanna, Bridget Ann	29 Aug 1853	150	B
Gage, Ransom A.	Redman, Jane E.	209? Dec 1846	280	A
Garmon, Matthew	Yancy, Martha	26 Dec 1842	148	A
Garner, Aaron	Coinner, Catherine	24 Oct 1841	116	A
Garrett, Hendrick	Foster, Louisa	30 Sept 1841	115	A
Garrett, John	Bennett, Elizabeth	16 Jan 1840	84	A
Garrett, Thomas T.	Overby, Eliza	23 Dec 1855	71	C
Gaston, James	Foster, Jane H.	21 Nov 1837	35	A
Gates, William	Mobley, Mary	23 Mar 1842	124	A
Gault, Jefferson	Lummus, Frances	20 Feb 1853	135	B
Gentry, William	Hood, Melinda	4 Jan 1855	37	C
Giton, John W.	Terry, Rebecca	26 July 1855	52	C
Glass, James A.	Howard, Mary J.	29 Nov 1855	70	C
Glover, Jarrett W.	Nash, Elizabeth	20 Apr 1848	292	A
Gober, Henry E.	Robinson, Mary J.	25 Nov 1852	128	B
Goddard, Jesse	Gravitt, Sally	19 Aug 1836	17	A
Godsey, James P.	Echolls, Milley	19 Apr 1854	31	C
Goin, Dillard	Conley, Permelia C.	14 Oct 1840	98	A
Goode, Joshua M.	Croy, Margaret M.	19 Sept 1852	140	B
Goodwin, Harris	Dogin, Emily	13 Feb 1834	4	A
Goodwin, James J.	Henson, Rebecca	8 Jan 1837	24	A
Gravitt, Alfred	Langley, Jane	26 July 1838	51	A
Gravitt, Alfred	Tidwell, Lucy	14 Sept 1837	38	A
Gravitt, Charles	Beshears, Winnie	6 June 1847	270	A
Gravitt, Charles	Tailor, Rebecca	9 Sept 1841	115	A
Gravitt, Gilford	Hendrix, Juda	4 July 1839	71	A
Gravitt, James Pinkney	Beshears, Jane	14 Nov 1847	273	A
Gravitt, John	Brooks, Susan	25 July 1847	270	A
Gravitt, Luke	Parris, Celia	29 Mar 1846	249	A
Gravitt, Reuben	Langley, Anny	16 Feb 1843	151	A
Green, Foris	Beaver, Casandra	30 Aug 1855	55	C
Green, George W.	Samples, Sarah A.	5 Feb 1854	2	C
Green, James Addison	Woodliff, Nancy Jane	15 Oct 1840	98	A
Green, John	Mooney, Rachel M.	12 Aug 1852	119	B
Green, Newton	Gazaway, Malinda C.	10 Jan 1839	65	A
Grier, John F.	Thompson, Nancy E.	21 Dec 1847	284	A
Griffin, James J.	Bramblett, Elizabeth	27 Sept 1855	53	C
Grizzell, James	Terry, Joicey	27 Sept 1853	3	C
Guthery, Andrew N.	Gravitt, Polly	7 Mar 1846	241	A

GROOM	BRIDE	DATE	PAGE	BOOK
Guthery, Robert M.	Wadkins, Frances	17 Dec 1839	81	A
Guthrie, James	Biddle, Sarah	11 Jan 1835	9	A
Guthrie, John F.	Southard, Caroline M.	19 Oct 1854	44	C
Hadder, John	Williams, Elisa	19 Feb 1839	65	A
Hadder, Solomon	Scott, Matilda	22 Sept 1839	73	A
Hall, William	Singleton, Darcus	16 June 1854	26	C
Hames, Presley	McCrary, Nancy Ann	31 Aug 1854	31	C
Hamilton, William G.	Shin, Elizabeth A.	25 Sept 1853	18	C
Hammon, Hiram	Thomas, Emily	21 Oct 1847	283	A
Hammond, Daniel	Rollin, Mary	5 Apr 1855	48	C
Hammond, Daniel J.	Benson, Druscilla	13 Feb 1853	139	B
Hammond, William	Pearson, Mahala	9 Mar 1854	21	C
Hammond, William N.	Benson, Elizabeth M.	25 Dec 1853	9	C
Hansard, George	Davenport, Eliza Jane	2 Sept 1855	50	C
Hansard, James C.	Spruce, Rebecca	25 Aug 1842	137	A
Hardage, William C.	Howard, Malinda	27 Jan 1847	263	A
Hardin, Joshua H.	Garrett, Nancy	3 Feb 1835	8	A
Hardin, Jourdan	Hulsey, Joannah	17 Jan 1854	12	C
Hardin, Robert	Singleton, Sarah E.	27 Dec 1853	10	C
Harkless, Robert W.	Bacon, Evalina	22 Dec 1842	146	A
Harmon, William	Venable, Harriett	6 Feb 1834	3	A
Harris, Abraham	McCall, Elizabeth	24 Dec 1843	172	A
Harris, Alfred	Malden, Kezia	3 Mar 1844	182	A
Harris, Benjamin	Sharp, Martha	19 Aug 1841	118	A
Harris, Charles	Collins, Jane	2 Feb 1837	29	A
Harris, Henry A.	Redmon, Frances	26 Feb 1846	241	A
Harris, James C.	Brown, Elizabeth	26 Feb 1854	22	C
Harris, Overton	Bennett, Mary E.	14 Dec 1854	47	C
Harris, Parker	Little, Elizabeth	27 Dec 1853	2	C
Harris, Smith C.	Garner, Rachel Caroline	18 Nov 1852	131	B
Harris, W.W.	Julian, Martha A.	14 Dec 1854	104	C
Harris, William	Whitsitt, Jane	18 Dec 1842	140	A
Harris, Zachariah N.	Harden, Louisa	18 Feb 1844	181	A
Harris, Thomas P.	Jay, Rebecca	14 Nov 1837	36	A
Harrison, Jason C.	McGinnis, Sarah Ann	4 May 1843	160	A
Harvey, Ezekiel P.	Martin, Elinder	30 Jan 1842	120	A
Harvey, George M.	Martin, Mursylea	11 Sept 1842	142	A
Hawkins, Henry B.	Lewis, Harriett M.	11 Mar 1847	267	A
Hawkins, John L.	Lewis, Nancy E.	29 Jan 1854	2	C
Hawkins, John S.	Kemp, Minerva	14 Dec 1845	229	A
Hawkins, Robert L.	Brannon, Samantha A.	10 Dec 1854	28	C
Haygood, Henry	Foster, Malissa	1 Jan 1843	146	A
Haygood, L. D.	Holbrooks, Mary	10 May 1838	51	A
Haynes, Hyram	Farrow, Susannah	1 Dec 1841	117	A
Hays, Harmon	Roberts, Elizabeth	23 Oct 1846	261	A
Hays, William F.	Bagley, Anna	1 Apr 1840	89	A
Heath, William	Darby, Icy	10 Apr 1836	15	A
Henderson, Nathaniel G.	Bradley, Margarett	14 Nov 1833	2	A
Hendricks, Russell	Howard, Zeruah A.	16 Sept 1847	272	A
Hendrix, James W.	Compton, Jane Alvira	5 Apr 1840	104	A
Henson, Hiram L.	Gravitt, Nancy A.	21 Dec 1852	135	B
Henson, James W.	White, Rebecca	8 Jan 1834	4	A
Herring, Alexander	Brown, Louisa E.R.	12 Aug 1855	54	C
Higg, John	Lowery, Elizabeth	3 Oct 1833	1	A
Higgins, James	Bramblett, Polly	4 Sept 1840	95	A
Higgins, James D.	Tribble, Elizabeth C.	10 Oct 1852	127	B
Higgins, John	Dacus, Ann	6 Oct 1854	33	C
Hightower, Thomas G.	Henderson, Eliza E.	14 May 1854	102	C
Hill, Isaac W.	Ellis, Nancy	22 Oct 1840	100	A
Hill, James	Hollinshead, Narcissa	13 Mar 1854	24	C
Hill, John W.	Logan, Martha Jane	4 Apr 1854	20	C
Hitt, Henry	Staver, Hannah	9 Nov 1842	147	A
Hix, William W.	Honea, Elizabeth	10 July 1853	149	B
Hockenhull, John	Kemp, Mary	5 Feb 1842	123	A
Holbrook(s), Asberry	McDonald, Sarah Ann	23 Mar 1845	259	A

GROOM	BRIDE	DATE	PAGE	BOOK
Holbrook(s), John F.	Hudson, Amanda	6 Dec 1838	61	A
Holbrook(s), John W.	Dummer, Elizabeth	29 Nov 1846	254	A
Holbrook(s), Lewis	Yancey, Sarah	22 Aug 1838	54	A
Holbrook(s), Samuel A.	Roper, Hulda C.	29 Apr 1847	277	A
Holbrook(s), William B.	Tallant, Nancy	11 June 1835	9	A
Holbrook, Elijah L.	Hudson, Lavada M.	17 Apr 1855	43	C
Holbrook, John W.	Hadder, Sarah J.C.	11 Oct 1855	56	C
Holbrook, Russell J.	Chamblee, Mary C.	11 Jan 1855	40	C
Holbrook, William B.	Scott, Lucinda	22 Nov 1855	59	C
Holbrooks, Wilson L.	Kennedy, Rachel Sylvester	13 Dec 1852	123	B
Holden, Elias E.	Tatum, Winnie	23 Aug 1845	219	A
Holeyfield, Brison	Pike, Calven (?)	7 July 1836	16	A
Holland, William	Chaplin, Nancy	22 July 1846	249	A
Hollinshead, Burdine	Waters, Sarah Ann E.	5 Nov 1854	39	C
Holshowser, Wiley	McGinnis, Margaret H.	21 Oct 1855	56	C
Honea, Henry	Findley, Margaret	16 June 1844	186	A
Hope, Benjamin J.	Barrett, Eliza A.	23 Aug 1855	62	C
Hopkins, Joseph	Hays, Milly	14 Oct 1855	57	C
Horton, Daniel D.	Vaughan, Syntha	6 Jan 1842	117	A
Howell, Evan D.	Knox, Margaret D.	19 Aug 1845	219	A
Howell, Fendley J.	Pugh, Elizabeth	24 Jan 1844	180	A
Howell, George W.	Huggins, Fanny	12 Jan 1841	103	A
Howell, Pinkney	Haygood, Eliza	13 July 1834	6	A
Howell, William F.	Martin, Mary E.	25 Sept 1834	6	A
Hudson, Madison E.	Blackburn, Frances H.	2 Jan 1840	84	A
Hudson, William J.	Tarrent, Licetry C.	24 Nov 1836	19	A
Huggins, David J.	Sams, Mary	21 Dec 1845	230	A
Huggins, William N.	Nuckelreath, Elizabeth P.	12 Aug 1852	118	B
Hughes, Andrew O.	Watters, Louesa	18 Feb 1841	125	A
Hughes, Francis M.	Crow, Sarah S.	27 Feb 1845	232	A
Hughes, James E.	Bennett, Isabella	6 Jan 1848	290	A
Hughes, John	Cannon, Elizabeth	19 Feb 1855	38	C
Hughes, Russell	Bennett, Lucinda	20 Jan 1842	119	A
Hughes, Thomas D.	Hendrix, Virginia Easter	10 Dec 1843	176	A
Hulsey, Isaiah	Thomas, Amanda	8 Nov 1838	58	A
Hunt, Thomas W.	Burress, Lucy Ann E.	17 May 1842	129	A
Hunter, Thomas	Martin, Nancy	12 Sept 1837	34	A
Hutchins, Livingston	Harrison, Malissa Ann	25 Mar 1846	242	A
Jackson, Alfred M.	Hughes, Arminda K.	22 Oct 1853	45	C
Jackson, James	Terry, Rebecca	21 Dec 1838	61	A
Jackson, Jasper N.	Bond, Eliza J.	8 Oct 1854	34	C
Jackson, Samuel	Naler, Adaline	13 Mar 1844	190	A
Jackson, William C.	Bond, Nancy E.	15 Apr 1855	62	C
James, George W.	Moore, Mary I.	3 Feb 1853	132	B
James, John	Sims, Elizabeth A.	7 Oct 1852	145	B
James, John A.	Mahu, Clarinda	13 Mar 1855	51	C
James, Mahlon Henry	Butler, Lucinda	9 Dec 1847	285	A
James, Sherod	Lindsey, Sarah	9 Nov 1838	57	A
James, Thomas	Osborn, Elizabeth	22 Aug 1852	122	B
Jenkins, John	Bradford, Karen	14 Dec 1837	41	A
Jenkins, Reuben M.	Reed, Malinda A.	19 Feb 1846	240	A
Jinkins, Bartlett M.	Barnett, Mary	4 May 1843	162	A
Jinks, James M.	Gant, Margaret Ann	17 July 1855	73	C
Johnson, John	Johnson, Susan E.	20 Feb 1853	138	B
Johnson, John H.	Reece, Mary	25 Nov 1838	59	A
Johnson, John W.	Davis, Sarah Ann	13 Nov 1842	142	A
Johnson, Martin V.	Baker, Nancy	9 Oct 1853	141	C
Johnston, John	Young, Bythany	8 Sept 1833	1	A
Jones, Azariah	Hendrix, Synthia	22 Dec 1842	144	A
Jones, Benjamin W.	Brown, Mary Ann	27 Dec 1846	256	A
Jones, Berryman	Bennett, Mary	16 Dec 1852	-	F

GROOM	BRIDE	DATE	PAGE	BOOK
Jones, Caleb P.	Bird, Martha Adaline	11 Dec 1845	235	A
Jones, Gilford W.	Bell, Lavenia Y.	31 Jan 1834	178	A
Jones, Hyram	Hammond, Elizabeth Ann	18 Mar 1841	106	A
Jones, Seaborn	Allen, Agnes I.A.	2 Oct 1845	223	A
Jones, Thomas J.	Tippins, Manerva	11 Sept 1845	221	A
Jones, Thomas M.C.	Tallant, Lucinda	7 May 1846	242	A
Jones, W.E.	Leister, Sarah Ann	21 Dec 1854	36	C
Jones, William R.	Murray, Josephine	19 Jan 1854	12	C
Josephson, Julius	Young, Agnes	25 Mar 1855	42	C
Karr, Jesse M.	Samples, Frances	23 Aug 1855	49	C
Karr, John B.	Clifton, Mahala J.	5 July 1853	8	C
Karr, John C.	Brown, Elizabeth	31 Sept 1855	55	C
Kell, James	Wallis, Jane	5 July 1846	266	A
Keller, Cane	Anderson, Sarah Ann	30 Sept 1847	272	A
Kelpin, William	Towrence, Mary Ann	10 Dec 1843	176	A
Kemp, Andrew J.	Killingsworth, Miss F.M.	20 Feb 1848	289	A
Kemp, Marvel L.	Ezzard, Mary	5 Feb 1846	239	A
Keon, Berry	Henderson, Milly	30 May 1843	160	A
Keon, David	Huggins, Polly Ann	11 Feb 1841	102	A
Killian, A.J.	Sanders, Mahala	29 Apr 1840	91	A
Killingsworth, Or- lando	Lazenby, Catherine	13 Oct 1853	151	B
King, Ebenezer	Smith, Margaret C.	17 Feb 1842	122	A
King, Joseph D.	Figgins, Lucinda	7 Apr 1846	243	A
King, Robert A.	Gober, Mary E.	2 Jan 1840	76	A
Kisinger, John	Golesby, Minerva	20 Jan 1853	130	B
Kitchens, James H.	Davis, Frances R.	26 Aug 1841	114	A
Landrum, William R.	Bush, Elisa	1 Nov 1838	58	A
Landsdown, David A.	Martin, Judy Ann	7 Feb 1839	62	A
Langley, Jackson	Howell, Mary Ann	24 Mar 1842	124	A
Langley, James	Sanders, Artilla	25 July 1839	71	A
Langley, John	Sanders, Martha C.	4 May 1845	213	A
Langley, John	McClure, Susannah	20 July 1837	33	A
Lawson, Lesal	Hayne, Julia Ann	24 Feb 1855	45	C
Lawson, Sion	Brumbelow, Caroline	20 Nov 1843	170	A
Leach, James W.	Wadkins, Sarah	2 Jan 1840	82	A
Leadbetter, Charles	Hagood, Hannah E.	13 Oct 1853	152	B
Ledbetter, Daniel	Fowler, Mary Caroline	6 May 1855	117	C
Lee, Henry	Carr, Rody A.M.	19 Jan 1843	149	A
Lenoir, John W.	Rogers, Ann C.	3 Apr 1840	86	A
Leonard, Jesse J.	McAfee, Mary L.	25 Dec 1842	147	A
Leonard, Starling	McAfee, Martha	23 Feb 1845	208	A
Lesley, Alvin	Hawkins, Martha A.	21 Oct 1855	87	C
Lessley, Warren D.	Blankenship, Mary A.	29 Sept 1853	6	C
Lester, Harrison	Parks, Sarah Amanda	21 Dec 1839	80	A
Lester, Terman H.	Born, Sarah	13 Sept 1836	23	A
Lewis, Elsey W.	Hawkins, Martha Ann	5 Sept 1852	142	B
Lewis, Major John	Lenoir, Evalina Jane	10 May 1842	128	A
Lewis, Thomas	Jones, Lula B.	7 Dec 1845	228	A
Lewis, Wiley H.	Pearson, Deanny	18 Apr 1847	268	A
Lewis, William A.	Gordon, Eleanor J.	23 Dec 1845	229	A
Light, Gilford	Bibb, Margaret	21 Nov 1839	70	A
Light, Newton F.	Cross, Margarett	11 Mar 1854	23	C
Light, Pleasant G.	Jones, Annie	18 Dec 1838	59	A
Light, Wiley	Phillips, Elizabeth A.	22 Nov 1842	145	A
Light, Young K.	Munday, Susan	9 Mar 1847	275	A
Lindsey, Anderson	Cruse, Mary Ann	21 Apr 1839	69	A
Lindsey, James H.	Huggins, Nancy J.	5 June 1853	148	B
Lindsey, Lawson C.	Hix, Elizabeth	23 Dec 1847	283	A
Lindsey, Ransom	Smallwood, Lanty	30 Aug 1835	10	A
Linzay, P.H.	Sanders, Catherine	8 Sept 1853	153	B
Logan, Andrew J.	Thompson, Sarah Ann	8 Feb 1853	151	B
Long, Hyram	Procter, Mary Ann	11 Sept 1842	154	A
Lott, Enoch	Randall, Elizabeth	15 Nov 1840	95	A
Low, Addison C.	Jackson, Frances	9 Nov 1854	89	C
Lowe, John	Rogers, Cynthia	30 Jan 1845	203	A
Lowrey, Isaac P.	Vestal, Nancy Jane	22 May 1842	128	A

GROOM	BRIDE	DATE	PAGE	BOOK
Lummus, James M.	Harris, Margaret M.(F.)	5 Jan 1845	202	A
Lummus, William	Bentley, Mary A.	31 Dec 1837	43	A
Madden, Robert J.	Segars, Sarah M.	7 Apr 1841	109	A
Major, Richard	Waters, Matilda	27 Oct 1854	33	C
Mann, James M.	Jenkins, Sarah	30 July 1843	168	A
Martin, Archibald S.	Pool, Lucinda	25 Jan 1846	238	A
Martin, Henry	Bagley, Mary	24 Dec 1852	132	B
Martin, Hezekiah	Sloan, Parthena	8 Aug 1839	72	A
Martin, Hix	Casey, Margeret	7 Jan 1844	190	A
Martin, James H.	Cantrell, Thomsey	18 Sept 1842	156	A
Martin, James L.	Hood, Mary	2 Feb 1854	3	C
Martin, Joel J.	Langley, Synthia	22 Dec 1842	144	A
Martin, John	Fowler, Oliffan	26 Aug 1852	128	B
Martin, John	Osborn, Mary Ann	7 Sept 1855	53	C
Martin, Peter Burdine	Johnson, Elizabeth J.	1 Sept 1855	61	C
Martin, Samuel	Nix, Sarah	3 Jan 1847	258	A
Martin, Samuel	Martin, Tabitha E.	19 Dec 1852	140	B
Martin, William	Pruett, Letty	9 July 1840	93	A
Martin, William	Hix, Elizabeth	15 June 1855	48	C
Martin, William	Martin, Martha	30 Dec 1847	283	A
Martin, William P.	Barrett, Nancy	5 Feb 1848	285	A
Martin, Zachariah	James, Eliza	19 Jan 1845	204	A
Mashburn, Elisha	Wallace, Mary Ann	3 Aug 1843	166	A
Mashburn, Elisha J.	Wellborn, Sarah Ann	8 Dec 1839	79	A
Mashburn, Henry T.	Atkinson, Eliza N.	10 Feb 1848	292	A
Mashburn, John H.	Pain (Payne), Martha	19 Jan 1854	12	C
Matthews, Ephraim	Mahaffey, Celestia E.A.D.	1 Oct 1854	33	C
Matthews, James	League, Nancy E.	12 June 1842	130	A
Matthews, John J.	Traylor, Mary E.	10 Nov 1853	58	C
Mayfield, Battle	Bobo, Martha	1 Apr 1838	49	A
McAfee, Elijah C.	Thompson, Emily C.	11 Dec 1842	140	A
McClelon, James	Motes, Elizabeth	29 July 1841	132	A
McCleskey, George W.	Bell, Angeline	31 Jan 1839	63	A
McClure, James	Howell, Rebecca	17 Mar 1844	183	A
McClure, John A.	Henderson, Roxy Ann	10 Nov 1846	265	A
McClure, Robert N.	Hockenhull, Emma	1 Feb 1855	39	C
McCoy, William P.	Coleman, Jane	25 July 1843	165	A
McDonald, Alexander	Mooney, Caroline	5 Nov 1843	189	A
McDow, Thomas B.	Conley, Elizabeth	16 Sept 1840	96	A
McFarlin, Richard	Wilkins, Margaret H.	11 Mar 1845	233	A
McGinnis, Elijah	Waldrup, Jane	20 Aug 1848	292	A
McGinnis, Elijah	Jenks, Mary	20 Apr 1845	212	A
McGinnis, Elijah	Jenks, Catherine	22 Aug 1847	271	A
McGinnis, John	Owens, Mrs. Casandra	17 Feb 1855	81	C
McGinnis, Osborn	Foster, Nancy	19 Mar 1839	68	A
McGinnis, Osborn	Dougherty, Lavinia E.	15 Sept 1842	136	A
McGinnis, Stephen W.	Staggs, Hester Ann	1 Oct 1844	198	A
McGinnis, William	Bowlin, Martha J.	14 Feb 1853	6	C
McHugh, Wilson	Cox, Elizabeth	23 Dec 1838	60	A
McIntire, Phillip	Mullican, Molly E.	19 Aug 1854	27	C
McKay, Harrison	Guthery, Elisa	27 Sept 1845	279	A
McNight, William	Coggins, Caroline	1 Feb 1838	44	A
Milford, James	Thornton, Elender	20 Feb 1840	83	A
Miller, Green	Pendergrass, Susan	8 Nov 1846	255	A
Miller, John	Johnson, Cesley Ann	12 Feb 1843	157	A
Miller, John	Cruse, Adaline	19 Feb 1854	7	C
Miller, Joseph	Delk, Tempey	12 Jan 1834	4	A
Millwood, William	Davis, Jane	19 Mar 1854	24	C
Milwood, Jackson	Davis, Mary	8 Apr 1855	44	C
Mitchener, H.E.	Shields, Mary H.E.	1 Jan 1855	36	C
Money, Francis	Jenkins, Eliza J.	9 Dec 1847	287	A
Monroe, Theron E.	Kelly, Mary L.	24 Mar 1836	264	A
Monroe, Thomas L.	Kelly, Elizabeth	7 Apr 1840	87	A
Montgomery, James N.	Compton, Nancy Emily	6 May 1838	109	A
Montgomery, James P.	Bulls, America	3 Apr 1853	1	C
Montgomery, R.C.	Brogdon, Frances	13 Nov 1853	9	C

GROOM	BRIDE	DATE	PAGE	BOOK
Mooney, Eliary A.	Mashburn, Mary A.	3 Oct 1844	197	A
Mooney, Robert A.	Owen, Nancy E.	22 Oct 1853	6	C
Moor, Alvin	Norris, Elizabeth	24 Nov 1838	78	A
Moor, Jerry	Crow, Nancy	1 Sept 1845	233	A
Moor, William F.	Rogers, Sarah A.	22 Dec 1853	10	C
Moore, Reubin J.	Rogers, Martha J.	13 Dec 1855	61	C
Morgan, Fen	Bean, Mary	5 Sept 1835	11	A
Morris, Andy	Wynn, Sattavery	29 Dec 1846	257	A
Morris, David	Thompson, Dorcas	3 Sept 1844	196	A
Morris, Henry M.	Cantwell, Emily	9 June 1844	191	A
Morris, Sanford M.	James, Hannah	17 May 1855	47	C
Moten, Elias	Thompson, Malinda	19 Aug 1841	113	A
Moten, Henry	Langley, Rebecca	13 Mar 1839	67	A
Mulkey, James J.	Vaughan, Margaret A.	5 Feb 1844	178	A
Mullins, Andrew J.	Daniel, Martha P.	25 Sept 1836	18	A
Murry, John	Orr, Martha	19 Dec 1837	42	A
Naler, Stephen C.	Strickland, Susannah	18 May 1845	214	A
Nalley, Barksdale	Barrett (Barnett), Miram	6 Apr 1847	278	A
Naramone, Jackson	Rawlins, Nancy Jane	24 Mar 1846	211	A
Nash, W. P.	Webb, Manda C.	25 Dec 1855	73	C
Nicholson, Francis M.	Karr, Sarah M.	10 Dec 1854	28	C
Nicholson, Namon C.	Otwell, Jane	10 Sept 1854	30	C
Nicholson, Neamon G.	Edmondson, Parthy	31 Jan 1843	149	A
Nuckolls, J.G.L.	Moore, E.E.	1 Nov 1853	13	C
Nuckolls, Joel T.	Briant, Irana	1 Feb 1842	119	A
Nunn, William H.	Langley, Delilah	19 Apr 1842	126	A
Orr, Emaziah	Porter, Hannah	24 Apr 1842	127	A
Osborn, Joseph	Morris, Sarah	5 Dec 1841	155	A
Osfet, Jessee	Sissan, Sophia	5 May 1836	16	A
Oslin, Reubin C.	Randall, Martha A.	3 Sept 1840	96	A
Otwell, Benjamin	Vaughan, Nancy Jane	24 July 1845	278	A
Otwell, Cullin	Blankenship, Elizabeth A.	8 May 1854	22	C
Otwell, William	Todwell, Sarah	22 Jan 1844	177	A
Owen, Sanford	Wheeler, Jane	7 Sept 1854	28	C
Owens, Alfred	Stone, Elizabeth Jane	14 Nov 1847	274	A
Owens, Gabriel T.	Stovall, Nancy T.	17 June 1841	112	A
Owens, John	James, Emmaly	19 June 1837	34	A
Owens, Oliver P.	League, Betsy Ann	12 June 1842	130	A
Owens, Owen	Edwards, Susan	5 Mar 1839	66	A
Owens, Powell	Johnson, Emaline	27 Sept 1846	251	A
Owens, Wiley W.	Brown, Elizabeth Ann	14 Jan 1846	236	A
Owens, William W.	Owens, Elizabeth	8 Aug 1838	53	A
Pace, H.J.	Hansard, Minnie B.	21 Apr 1901	154	G2
Palmer, Edman T.	Holbrooks, Anney	28 Dec 1846	257	A
Pannell, Thomas	Delk, Mary	9 Sept 1839	73	A
Park, Andrew H.	Tyson, Delitha W.	28 Dec 1843	173	A
Parker, Jeremiah	Brumbelow, Sarah	3 Sept 1843	169	A
Parker, Weston	Gates, Sarah W.	17 July 1846	247	A
Parmer, Abner	Fisher, Mary	9 Jan 1845	203	A
Parmer, Edmond T.	Dollar, Sarah	3 Mar 1844	182	A
Parris, George	Hubbard, Matilda	8 Jan 1835	7	A
Parris, Maliga	Morten, Mahala	23 Mar 1837	32	A
Pate, Butler	Blackwell, Elizar	2 Mar 1845	212	A
Patterson, George W.	Morris, Sinther	17 Nov 1840	100	A
Patterson, Joshua	Cockburn, Darcus	25 Dec 1845	231	A
Payne, David H.	Jones, Juliann F.	13 July 1845	217	A
Payne, Elias	Orr, Elizabeth	16 Jan 1843	188	A
Pearson, William	Christenberry, Martha	11 Aug 1854	32	C
Pendergrass, John T.	Green, Mary	6 Aug 1854	26	C
Pendley, James T.	Easters, Harriett	20 Mar 1834	5	A
Pendley, Jesse	Gravitt, Polly Ann	23 Oct 1842	137	A
Pendley, Thomas	Howell, Mahala	30 Mar 1841	107	A
Perry, Lewis	Martin, Martha	15 Feb 1838	46	A
Person, Joel	Darby, Arminta	25 Mar 1847	268	A
Petet, Benjamin H.	Milton, Minerva C.	4 July 1854	34	C
Phillips, David	Estes, Tabitha	13 Feb 1845	204	A

GROOM	BRIDE	DATE	PAGE	BOOK
Phillips, Edward W.	Childress, Margaret A.	27 Nov 1853	19	C
Phillips, F.M.	Bennett, Jane	14 Feb 1854	25	C
Phillips, Reuben F.	Burtz, Nancy	11 Aug 1848	294	A
Phillips, William L.	Banister, Torlina	29 Dec 1853	10	C
Pierce, John C.	Harvey, Ludia C.	5 Feb 1854	16	C
Pike, Ransom	Holeyfield, Rosanah	21 Apr 1836	15	A
Pilgrim, Perry	Otwell, Susan	7 Oct 1846	252	A
Pirkle, William	Dollar, Delitha	15 Apr 1841	107	A
Pirkle, Willis	Shadburn, Martha J.	31 Dec 1854	36	C
Pool, John	Brannon, Mary C.	11 Apr 1847	276	A
Pool, Street	Autrey, Frances	7 Jan 1842	121	A
Pool, Washington F.	Chamblee, Frances E.	23 Feb 1854	8	C
Porter, John S.	Dixon, Martha R.	7 Mar 1844	180	A
Pots, James	McClelon, Elizabeth	8 Jan 1846	236	A
Powell, Allen	Bennett, Easter	25 Jan 1847	277	A
Powell, Allen	Garrett, Slatnah	2 Apr 1842	125	A
Powell, Oliver C.	McCrary, Eliza	28 Feb 1847	268	A
Prater, Loyd	Ashworth, Nancy	19 Mar 1843	158	A
Pruett, William H.	Wilcox, Martha	18 Sept 1854	232	A
Pruitt, J.T.	Redman, Nancy	7 May 1854	41	C
Pruitt, John W.	Rogers, Hannah M.	26 Jan 1854	40	C
Pugh, Abner	Samples, Mary	11 Feb 1855	48	C
Pugh, John P.	Hawkins, Josephine	21 Oct 1855	56	C
Pugh, Phillip	Fields, Mary Ann	2 Aug 1855	49	C
Pugh, Sampson	Heath, Mary	12 July 1836	17	A
Qualls, Jesse	Martin, Mary	10 Nov 1853	16	C
Queen, Timothy	Russell, Eliza	26 Jan 1845	206	A
Rainwaters, Sidney	McGinnis, Martha	10 Oct 1843	174	A
Ramey, William	Conner, Divinity	23 Dec 1854	45	C
Ramsey, Richard	Echols, Nancy M.	30 July 1846	248	A
Ratford, Giles	Pettyjohn, Nancy	23 Oct 1844	248	A
Ray, William	Allen, Jane	8 Mar 1848	294	A
Ray, William H.	Whitsitt, Mrs. Nancy T.	21 Feb 1836	13	A
Reaves, John P.	Harris, Rosannah C.	18 Nov 1841	116	A
Red, Archibald H.	Holbrooks, Martha M.	26 Sept 1844	196	A
Redd, Josiah	Holbrooks, Elizabeth	25 Mar 1841	106	A
Reece, Henry	Martin, Matilda	26 Apr 1844	194	A
Reed, M.K.	Wallis, S.E.	8 July 1855	50	G
Revis, Francis M.	Harris, Sarah Jane	6 Dec 1855	58	C
Rhodes, Reubin P.	Tailor, Martha	23 Oct 1845	234	A
Rice, Benjamin J.	Burford, Susan	19 Dec 1839	75	A
Richards, Josephus	Beck, Anna	31 July 1834	5	A
Richardson, John C.	Moore, Emily	26 Feb 1854	21	C
Rider, William A.	Lindsay, Mary	20 Mar 1853	146	B
Roach, James B.	Perry, Mary Ann	2 July 1854	34	C
Roach, Ulet	McGullian, Elizabeth Ann	19 Aug 1834	5	A
Robbins, Levi	Dickenkey, Jane	3 May 1838	49	A
Robbs, William	Jordan, Parthena	15 June 1846	245	A
Roberts, Jessey C.	Anderson, Mary Ann	6 Dec 1853	18	C
Rogers, Henry C.	Thompson, Louisa J.	28 Dec 1847	286	A
Rogers, Jackson	Blackburn, Sarah G.	7 Feb 1844	179	A
Rogers, John	Buckner, Lotty(Charlotte)	13 June 1843	164	A
Rogers, John	Harden, Sophrona	15 Nov 1855	69	C
Rogers, John N.	Ezzard, Nancy	3 Nov 1852	129	B
Roper, Hamilton	Cape, Missey Ann	29 June 1854	25	C
Roper, Henry F.	Holbrooks, Evaline	1 June 1845	215	A
Roper, Jason	Talant, Dorcas	1 Mar 1853	134	B
Roper, William A.	Tallant, Sarah	9 Sept 1855	51	C
Rowland, Robert	Heath, Elizabeth	4 Feb 1847	264	A
Rowlin, Thomas	Crane, Mary	23 Jan 1855	38	C
Rowlin, Tilman	Gravitt, Patsy	2 Apr 1848	293	A
Runnells, John	Stagg, Louisa J.	5 Aug 1855	51	C
Russell, William	Vaughan, Mary Ann	26 Dec 1852	121	B
Rutledge, Joseph	McCoy, Melissa Ann	1 Oct 1849	139	A
Samples, Jesse	Jeffrey, Elizabeth	14 Dec 1845	228	A

GROOM	BRIDE	DATE	PAGE	BOOK
Samples, Monroe M.	Phillips, Elizabeth Jane	26 Dec 1854	37	C
Samples, Thomas O.	Green, Sarah J.	22 Apr 1855	43	C
Samples, William V.	Blake, Sarah Jane	9 Aug 1855	49	C
Sams, Reubin J.	Wallace, Emaline J.	6 Oct 1853	4	C
Sams, William N.	Baker, Emily	17 July 1853	149	B
Sanders, Jonson	Hawkins, Mary	28 Apr 1836	14	A
Sangers, John R.	Morten, Martha	22 July 1840	94	A
Sartin, John	Smith, Mary	5 Oct 1843	188	A
Scoggins, Drury S.	Kelly, Mary Ann	17 Oct 1852	121	B
Scott, William	Jones, Rosa	20 July 1845	216	A
Scott, William R.	Smithey, Nancy	27 Aug 1848	288	A
Seagours, William G.	Waters, Cynthia A.M.	9 Jan 1848	288	A
Seale, Benyan H.	Foster, Jemina C.	17 Nov 1840	167	A
Segars, William H.	Welborn, Sarah C.	23 Oct 1845	225	A
Segars, Zachariah	McDow, Tempy	1 Feb 1842	121	A
Setzer, Evan A.	Blankenship, Nancy E.	19 Oct 1852	124	B
Sewell, Simeon	Buice, Mary	9 Dec 1852	142	B
Sharp, William	Hackett, Mary C.	21 Apr 1843	163	A
Sharp, William	Hudson, Matilda	17 Sept 1840	97	A
Shatten, Nelson T.	Langley, Katharine	1 Oct 1843	171	A
Shaw, David C.T.	Wickett, Mary	18 Apr 1837	28	A
Shaw, James A.J.	Sanders, Jane	4 May 1845	213	A
Simmons, James	Bannister, Mary Ann S.	4 Feb 1843	152	A
Simmons, William H.	Allen, Adalisa E.	26 Dec 1844	201	A
Simpson, Jackson	Simpson, Martha Ann	2 May 1853	137	B
Sims, William B.	Campbell, Isabella D.	8 Nov 1835	11	A
Sisson, George W.	Harris, Narcissa	21 Jan 1855	81	C
Sloan, Samuel	Tidwell, Susannah	15 Apr 1840	88	A
Smith, Albert G.	Morris, Eliza F.	14 Dec 1840	110	A
Smith, Alpha	Segars, Mary	17 Dec 1844	200	A
Smith, James M.	Redd, Emily	25 Nov 1843	171	A
Smith, Obed	King, Lucinda	17 Feb 1842	122	A
Smith, Uriah W.	Day, Amy	1 Sept 1854	29	C
Smithy, George W.	Scott, Jane	15 Aug 1844	195	A
Sneed, Absolom	Sneed, Dianna	16 May 1839	66	A
Sneed, Samuel S.	Pew (Pugh), Mary	10 May 1840	91	A
Southard, John B.	Strickland, Sally	29 Oct 1846	253	A
Spence, James	Thompson, Mary Jane	24 Apr 1853	148	B
Spruce, Calvin	Mashburn, Cynthia Ann	26 Oct 1848	288	A
Steagal, Peter	Kelly, Elizabeth	14 May 1848	295	A
Stegall, Richard	James, Mary Ann	23 Aug 1847	271	A
Stephens, Ephraim	Estes, Elizabeth	4 Nov 1845	226	A
Stone, Allen, Sr.	Holbrooks, Alafara	13 Feb 1845	209	A
Stone, David	McDonald, Margaret	4 Oct 1854	32	C
Stone, James	Bailey, Charlot	5 Feb 1837	30	A
Stone, Jonathan	Stone, Rebecca	19 May 1845	215	A
Stone, Jonathan	Baley, Susana	10 Feb 1845	209	A
Stone, Thomas	Holbrooks, Prudence	23 Dec 1840	105	A
Stone, Wesley	McDaniel, Elizabeth	16 June 1853	1	C
Stone, William	Baker, Mary	22 Dec 1836	26	A
Stovall, John M.	Crow, Louisa	1 July 1853	5	C
Stovall, Lewis	Malden, Grace G.	1 Nov 1847	273	A
Streetman, John M.	Bagley, Gilian	21 Apr 1853	133	B
Strickland, Hardy	Hammond, Ann E.	13 Oct 1850	102	C
Strickland, Henry	Smith, Ann E.	22 Jan 1845	206	A
Strickland, Samuel J.	Blaylock, Philadelphia	3 Aug 1848	293	A
Strickland, Talbot	Young, Celia	28 Dec 1837	40	A
Sutton, Henry H.	Collins, Lucinda	7 Oct 1834	7	A
Sutton, Miles W.	Hutchins, Harriett	18 Mar 1855	43	C
Sutton, Orsama	Blackstock, Adaline	3 Jan 1847	280	A
Swanagen, Thomas	Davis, Elisa	21 May 1844	186	A
Swilling, Berry B.	Bramblett, Malinda A.	11 June 1846	245	A
Tallant, Benjamin C.	Collett, Narcissa	31 May 1848	290	A
Tallant, David, Jr.	Scruggs, Rachael R.	11 Sept 1842	136	A
Tallant, Thomas C.	Collett, Nancy	28 Dec 1836	22	A
Tanner, James	Jay, Mary	10 Jan 1839	63	A

FORSYTH COUNTY MARRIAGES 1832-1855

GROOM	BRIDE	DATE	PAGE	BOOK
Tapp, Elijah D.	Red, Catherine	14 July 1850	57	B
Tate, Evan P.	Foster, Margaret J.	28 Dec 1845	230	A
Tatum, Elisha	Owens, Julian	21 July 1850	59	B
Tatum, Moses	Daniel, N.P.	15 Jan 1851	335	C
Taylor, Abel	Slatin, Lucinda E.	28 May 1845	214	A
Taylor, David	Gant, Betsy	5 Jan 1847	276	A
Taylor, David	McDonald, Maranda L.	19 Feb 1843	174	A
Taylor, Jacob	Saxton, Charity Emaline	11 Dec 1853	14	C
Taylor, Nicholas H.	Jenkins, Carity G.	20 July 1845	218	A
Teasley, Silas	Dodds, Julia	15 Jan 1850	42	B
Tedder, John W.	Lord, Arminda	1 Oct 1854	35	C
Tenly, Benjamin F.	Jones, Amanda C.	2 Jan 1848	289	A
Terrell, Joshua W.	Hadder, Frances M.	22 Dec 1845	231	A
Terry, Byrd	Barton, Arminda	18 Mar 1847	285	A
Terry, John	Jackson, Martha	23 Nov 1848	295	A
Terry, John	Parkinson, Mary	22 Mar 1840	90	A
Terry, Martin	Dodd, Mary	18 Aug 1842	134	A
Terry, Stephen	Parkinson, Martha	20 Feb 1840	82	A
Thally, Andrew J.	Montgomery, Anna	10 Nov 1850	61	B
Thomas, John	Bridges, Dicey Ann	13 Feb 1846	275	A
Thomas, Joseph	Bridges, Margaret	23 Sept 1846	265	A
Thomas, William	McDonald, Caroline	28 Dec 1837	42	A
Thompson, Benjamin O.	Swilling, Matilda M.	24 Dec 1840	101	A
Thompson, Clark	Gunnells, Mary Ann B.	10 Feb 1853	136	B
Thompson, Graham	Thompson, Mary	30 Aug 184(?)	250	A
Thompson, James R.	Garner, Martha	19 July 1841	113	A
Thompson, Joseph J.	Jackson, Sarah	2 Apr 1844	184	A
Thompson, Joseph J.	Foster, Sarah	17 Oct 1852	127	B
Thompson, Lewis	Webb, Angaline	29 July 1849	35	B
Thompson, William	Adkins, Mary	3 Feb 1847	279	A
Thornton, Andrew	Hendrix, Mebby L.	20 Nov 1845	227	A
Thornton, Isaac	Nuckolls, Clarinda	4 Feb 1836	14	A
Tidwell, Henry	Fowler, Sarah Susannah	28 May 1852	150	B
Tidwell, James	Boman, Nancy	10 Sept 1837	39	A
Tidwell, Meredith R.	Munday, Jane E.	1 June 1854	25	C
Tidwell, William	Gravitt, Caroline	7 Jan 1841	104	A
Tinsley, Miles W.	Hays, Elinor	27 July 1854	27	C
Tippins, Dennis S.	Anderson, Matilda	29 Jan 1843	157	A
Tolbert, Joel	McGinnis, Martha	16 June 1850	52	B
Tollison, Russel A.	Blankenship, Frances	6 Sept 1846	25	1A
Torrence, William B.	Jackson, Martha	30 Jan 1838	44	A
Townley, Thomas M.	Morris, Serena	28 Mar 1847	278	A
Townley, Zachariah	Watters, Zelpha Caroline	6 Mar 1842	156	A
Trammell, Albert O.	Sanders, Malinda	19 Feb 1854	17	C
Tribble, James W.	Holbrooks, Nancy H.	28 July 1842	131	A
Tribble, Joel B.	Coffy, Jane	26 July 1838	54	A
Tribble, Thomas C.	Fendley, Elizabeth	19 Aug 1841	110	A
Tribble, Sandford K.	Tapp, Elizabeth A.	19 Nov 1850	58	B
Tumlin, William	Green, Elizabeth	9 June 1847	270	A
Turner, Drewary	Bolton, Elizabeth	26 Dec 1852	125	B
Vaughan, Clabourn	Boman, Frances Avaline	28 Sept 1848	296	A
Vaughan, James E.	Naylor, Melinda	19 Mar 1854	21	C
Vaughan, Jeremiah	Tidwell, Susan	24 Dec 1846	256	A
Vaughan, John	Wiggins, Patchey	21 Dec 1848	8	B
Vaughan, William B.	Coggins, Polly Ann	31 July 1846	261	A
Vaughan, William W.	Powell, Sarah	8 Jan 1853	138	B
Vaughan, Willis	Carlile, Elizabeth	10 Feb 1838	45	A
Venable, Sanford	Bagley, Adaline	19 Oct 1848	289	A
Vernon, Josiah C.	Reed, Eliza H.	12 Oct 1852	145	B
Vickery, Charles	Clemmens, Malinda	16 Jan 1838	43	A
Vickory, T.N.	Sanders, Mary A.	25 Dec 1853	13	C
Wadkins, Nathan C.	Buchanan, Sarah C.	15 Nov 1843	175	A
Wadkins, Nathan C.	Griffin, Sarah A.	25 Nov 1854	24	C
Wadsworth, William	Martin, Tempy	7 Nov 1836	19	A
Waldrop, Partilla	Morrow, Polly	27 Aug 1840	94	A
Waldrup, William C.	Owen, Sarah	5 Feb 1843	150	A

FORSYTH COUNTY MARRIAGES 1832-1855

GROOM	BRIDE	DATE	PAGE	BOOK
Walker, David	Wellborn, Theodocia C.	7 July 1846	247	A
Wallace, Jesse B.	Edwards, Sarah	18 July 1842	132	A
Wallis, David J.	Newton, Sarah C.	19 Jan 1854	15	C
Wallis, John M.	Barnwell, Sarah A.	23 Jan 1853	141	B
Wallis, William W.	Harris, Martha	13 Apr 1848	291	A
Walraven, Isaac	Solomon, Mary	17 Nov 1847	284	A
Warden, James	Blaylock, Mary	12 Nov 1843	175	A
Watson, Ansel	Ivy, Sarah A.	5 Sept 1852	144	B
Watson, Hampton F.	Chapman, Mahulda	5 Jan 1854	14	C
Watson, Hampton F.	Malden, Hannah M.	19 Aug 1841	111	A
Webb, Jesse	Thompson, Sophronia	8 Dec 1853	23	C
Webb, Toliver	Logan, Mary	28 Feb 1841	154	A
Weems, Darius R.	Sewell, Ritha	26 Oct 1837	39	A
Weems, George	Echols, Margaret	22 Nov 1844	199	A
Weems, Isaiah B.	Holbrook, Frances	6 Nov 1845	226	A
Welch, Lemuel	Harris, Mary Ann	8 Oct 1843	224	A
Wellborn, Aaron G.	Wellborn, Mary B.	6 Mar 1835	9	A
Wellborn, Chapley B.	Foster, Mary A.	10 Sept 1837	35	A
Wellborn, Johnson D.	Shadburn, Sarah O.	11 Dec 1853	9	C
West, John W.C.	Bowls, Elizabeth	29 Sept 1848	290	A
Westmoreland, James	Downy, Abigal	16 Feb 1834	3	A
Wetherford, Alfred	Willis, Partheny	5 Oct 1855	331	C
White, C.H.	Angelly, Frances A.V.	4 Jan 1855	35	C
Whitmire, James M.	Cagle, Hannah Jane	25 Dec 1853	8	C
Whitmire, James M.	Hollins, Casey	14 May 1838	48	A
Whitmire, James W.	Hadder, Catherine	20 May 1847	269	A
Whitny, Zeno	Evans, Ruthy	1 Nov 1836	20	A
Whitworth, William K.	Roberts, Mary Eliza	16 Jan 1845	205	A
Whorton, Isaac	Julian, Rebecca M.	6 Mar 1838	77	A
Wilcott, David S.	Hutchins, Nancy Ann	13 Apr 1846	243	A
Wilder, Jonathan	Jordan, Fanny	28 July 1844	192	A
Wilder, Silas	Buckanan, Amanda	30 Sept 1845	222	A
Wilkins, Charles S.	Bradwell, Adaline L.	25 Oct 1855	57	C
Wilkins, J.G.	Phillips, Louisa A.	23 Aug 1855	68	C
Wilkins, J.W.	Barrett, M.E.	16 Mar 1851	103	C
Williams, Charles	Samples, Polly Ann	30 Oct 1842	138	A
Williams, Isaiah	Venable, Judith	21 July 1835	10	A
Williams, Joseph	Bagley, Eloisa	4 Dec 1833	2	A
Williams, Lewis	Wimms, Ibby	15 May 1842	129	A
Williams, Matthew K.	Roper, Rachel E.	2 Jan 1852	123	B
Williams, Thomas C.	Stovall, Sarah E.	19 Jan 1854	11	C
Williams, Thomas W.	Byram, Rebecca	30 May 1844	191	A
Williams, William	Bennett, Sarah F.	27 Aug 1848	295	A
Williamson, William	Jones, Elisa	4 Feb 1838	45	A
Willingham, Jackson	Montgomery, Elizabeth	6 Aug 1838	53	A
Wilson, Anderson	Wellborn, Civella S.	14 Jan 1844	189	A
Wilson, Benjamin	Stone, Ellender	3 Oct 1847	273	A
Wilson, J.W.	Moor, Mary E.	28 Feb 1855	39	C
Wilson, James	Light, Pernela Ann	11 Dec 1840	105	A
Wilson, Laben	Killingsworth, Eliza-beth	15 June 1843	163	A
Wingo, Thomas W.	Baldwin, Elizabeth	28 Aug 1853	11	C
Wingo, William P.	Foster, Mary A.	6 Mar 1854	30	C
Witherspoon, Charles W.	Foster, Mary Ann	25 Mar 1847	281	A
Wofford, Elijah	Burford, Pacific	10 Feb 1853	137	B
Wood, John J.	Harris, Francis E.	26 Dec 1852	143	B
Wood, Martin B.	Hollinshed, Elizabeth	16 Apr 1854	41	C
Woodall, John	Holcom, Ann	2 June 1838	55	A
Woodliff, Augustin L.	Low, Chester L.D.	25 Jan 1854	19	C
Woodliff, Josiah H.	Burruss, Mary Jane	14 Sept 1843	170	A
Worley, Pleasant	Mills, Margaret C.	29 Apr 1847	287	A
Wright, Joseph	Edwards, Christina	18 June 1854	35	A
Wright, William W.	Mann, Franky H.	4 Jan 1843	148	A
Wynn, John R.	Dodd, Clarissa	21 Nov 1844	198	A
Yancy, Francis	Fitspatrick, Mary	19 Sept 1847	272	A

28

GROOM	BRIDE	DATE	PAGE	BOOK
Yancy, James	Garmon, Barbara	5 Feb 1843	151	A
Yancy, Stephen	Holbrooks, Polly Ann	9 Nov 1843	172	A
Yarborough, Walter G.	Phillips, Mary T.	7 Apr 1844	183	A

GROOM	BRIDE	MARRIED	PAGE
Thomas W. Allen	Francis M. Bruice	9/ 8/1853	1
William Allen	Agnes Bagley	3/ 2/1854	13
James W. Andrews	Mahulda Ann Thompson	11/10/1853	17
Albert N. Abbott	Sarah Roberts	5/14/1854	23
Thomas Addington	Martha A.E. Rippley	11/ 5/1854	30
Leroy P. Allen	Winnie A. Dodd	4/27/1856	65
Wells G. Austin	Sarah A.E. Bell	10/26/1856	78
Henry G. Adams	Mary D. Pool	11/22/1856	84
Eli Armstrong	Elizabeth King	11/25/1856	86
Thomas A. Autrey	Samantha E. Green	7/14/1857	95
James G. Anglin	Mary G. Doss	1/28/1858	122
John F. Allen	Amanda Prudence Gober	5/23/1861	186
Carey Anderson	Susan Julian Brosell	12/16/1860	194
Samuel R. Autry	America Ann Lee	1/ 5/1861	206
John Ashworth	Martha Bruton	8/25/1862	207
James C. Anglin	Clerinda V. Wilson	12/13/1860	212
William Ashworth	Martha A. Collins	1863	222
James Austin	Jane Speer	3/ 8/1864	227
Balis Atkins	Mrs. Malinda C. Holtzclaw	12/22/1864	233
James Anglin	Mrs. Hannah McGinnis	7/11/1864	234
John V. Asbell	Martha A. Samples	12/27/1864	240
Virgil A. Armstrong	Mary L. Hunt	11/22/1866	333
John L. Anglin	Permelia E. Yarbrough	11/28/1866	365
John W. Anglin	Lety Harris	10/ 1/1867	369
Allen Blackstock	Nancy Rogers	10/ 1/1853	4
Powel Banister	Elizabeth Dooly	12/15/1853	15
William Brooks	Amanda A. Spence	12/25/1851	16
Francis M. Boring	Permelia Harris	10/16/1853	19
Thomas Brown	Francis Naylor	3/19/1854	20
Willism H. Bagley	Jamima McGinnis	3/19/1854	22
Samuel H. Baker	Anne Compton	4/13/1854	26
Reuben W. Benson	Nancy Spruse	12/14/1854	27
Wesly C. Beall	Rosy J. Staggs	5/18/1854	31
Thomas A. Burford	Nancy E. Brown	1/ 1/1855	38
Devily (?) Banister	Mary A. Dooly	12/21/1854	41
W. H. Bramblett	Rutha M. Eddleman	4/ 3/1855	46
John Boseman	Sarah C. Darby	9/27/1855	54
L. W. Berts	Mary Hughs	10/16/1855	58
John T. Brown	Fleeta F. Cunningham	12/27/1855	59
William J. Barrett	Ann Hockenhull	10/11/1855	62
William E. Bacon	Mary J. Sharp	2/26/1856	63
Asberry P. Bell	Celia Strickland	3/25/1856	64
J. J. Boyle	Sarah Jane Hawkins	10/ 9/1856	76
Richard B. Brooks	Martha D. Burriss	5/21/1856	82
John H. Burress	Sarah J. E. Reeves	5/27/1856	92
Benjamin J. Brown	Saira Garrett	3/31/1857	93
James J. Benefield	Chancy Bagbey	11/12/1857	97
Warren J. Barrett	Margaret E. McBryer	6/12/1850	107
William Bailey	Gileyan E. Bennett	2/ 7/1858	109
James R. Bramblett	Elizabeth Stewart	11/ 5/1857	112
Andrew Bennett	Kansada Crow	1/14/1858	115
Wilson Brooks	Mary Brooks	11/12/1857	115
Jeremiah Bentley	Julia L. Pool	1/25/1859	116
John G. Bond	Delila A. Phillips	10/11/1857	123
Alexander L. Bull	Zilpha A. Pruit	8/15/1858	128
R. M. Barrett	Lucy Weaver	3/ 4/1858	128
Robert Buice	Marcena Buice	7/ 5/1858	133
Samuel G. Bruce	Mary A. Henson	5/30/1858	134

GROOM	BRIDE	MARRIED	PAGE
Joshua Brown	Eliza Huggins	8/11/1858	136
John K. Blake	Elizabeth Blackston	8/12/1858	137
Toliver Bettis	Martha Vickary	7/22/1858	138
William H. Brashears	Charcissa E. McGinnis	1/ 1/1854	144
John W. Branon	Caroline E. Major	4/17/1859	146
Thomas G. Branon	Chancy J. Pool	12/12/1858	146
Augustus C. Bell	Martha C. Little	10/19/1859	152
Leroy Brannon	Matilda Bona	12/27/1859	153
William Bennett	Elizabeth Crow	8/ 4/1859	158
James R. Bramblett	Sinda Bowlin	7/31/1859	160
William D. Bently	Drucilla Harris	1/26/1860	163
Robert Brown	Mary E. Smith	11/ 3/1859	165
W. B. Branon	Phoebe D. Edmanson	10/ 7/1858	167
Francis M. Blackston	Catherine E. Mashburn	9/20/1860	169
T. R. Bennett	Polly M. Crow	12/10/1860	173
James M. Bagley	Eliza Chatham	10/25/1860	175
William T. Broadwell	Mary A. Willingham	10/ 4/1860	176
William R. Boyle	Nancy Boyle	2/ 2/2860	177
Jeremiah Bently	Elizabeth Sanders	8/29/1860	178
William A. Beecham	H. P. Harris	9/ 9/1860	180
Joshua Bruce	Ataline Vandike	9/18/1859	183
Nathan L. Bruce	Milly Hall	12/21/1859	184
James Bruce	Safronia Johnson	3/25/1860	185
Robert S. Branon	Martha J. Ezzard	4/ 3/1861	190
Harrison T. Bell	Emily M. Grambling	9/10/1861	191
W. E. Bacon	E. L. Hutchins	9/ 5/1861	194
Isaac M. Brownlow	Delilah C. Cruse	8/26/1860	203
William P. Bruce	Martha Doss	2/10/1861	213
Wislon Barnett	Margatet Stone	9/30/1864	232
A. W. Barrett	Martha Walls	1/10/1865	238
Enoch W. Bruton	Mary A. Ellis	5/ 7/1863	238
Hiram N. Bently	Sarah J. Hughes	3/12/1865	245
Jesse H. Bently	Eliza A. Garrett	10/20/1865	245
M. C. Beavers	Florence Hutchins	6/26/1865	260
J. J. Bettis	Hester A. Red	6/26/1865	267
G. M. Bennett	Jane F. Chambers	7/ 1/1861	267
S. J. Bagly	Julia A. Bennett	7/19/1865	268
Ross A. Bagley	Maranda C. Preist	11/16/1864	276
James T. Blake	Nancy A. Blackston	12/19/1865	284
Thomas A. Bales	Sarah L. Dooly	10/ 5/1865	288
G. L. Blanton	M. E. Moorehead	2/15/1866	291
John B. Boyed	Elizabeth Rice	8/21/1866	301
James A. Bramblett	Arminta Red	3/11/1866	305
William M. Bannister	Mary A. McGuire	9/13/1866	307
James Boyle	Margaret Burnett	5/28/1865	311
R. P. Brown	M. H. Leonard	10/21/1865	312
Joseph D. Boyle	Mary Wilder	2/ 3/1867	319
James W. Brooks	Matilda Gilbert	2/14/1867	322
Obediah Brownlow	Lucinda C. Guthrie	3/22/1854	327
J. R. Birse	Mirey Henson	11/18/1866	329
James Beck	T. A. White	10/14/1866	337
James H. Beecham	Susan W. Gravitt	11/ 1/1867	356
George G. Bowman	R. A. Light	10/28/1867	357
J. M. Bennett	Mahuldah A. Jordan	9/ 8/1867	358
John T. Broadwell	Riziah Rice	7/20/1867	362
James A. Boggs	Frances Patterson	1/20/1867	367
J. S. Bond	Martha R. Edmonson	12/18/1867	379
Noble J. Buice	Sarah F. Gilbert	1/ 5/1868	381
W. H. Brogdon	Ophelie Strickland	2/ 4/1868	397
J. M. Blake	T. C. McDonnel	2/20/1868	

GROOM	BRIDE	MARRIED	PAGE
Ephriam H. Chadwick	Hannah M. Smith	2/10/1853	5
Berry M. Crocker	Mary Holcomb	4/ 7/1853	7
Stephen M. Chatham	Tempy Estes	12/29/1853	11
Reuben Coats	Emaline Terry	1/ 1/1854	17
David Castleberry	Mary Matilda Williams	11/ 4/1853	18
William Crow	Milley Donaldson	9/14/1854	32
N. J. Curbow	Martha E. Horton	3/25/1855	42
Gidean Cross	Francis L. McCrary	3/27/1855	44
Lindsey E. Conner	Barbarey A.E. Ravens	8/24/1854	46
Burrell Cornelison	Martha A.R. Barrett	10/25/1855	63
William J. Childers	Seabil A. Austin	8/18/1856	74
Henry M. Compton	Mary Jane Bennett	4/23/1854	87
Thomas M. Chatmon	Sarah Jane Davis	11/26/1854	88
John B. Crow	Mary A.D. Wilkins	11/20/1856	90
Oliver P. Childres	Mary Evaline Hutchins	2/ 8/1857	91
William Castleberry	Grace G. Wood	11/22/1857	99
John Comer	Nancy Read	12/ 6/1857	113
Levi R. Clayton	Nancy A.L. Henson	12/21/1858	117
Smith F. Cottrell	Hannah Terry	3/16/1858	136
William P. Christian	Catherine Garum	12/26/1856	140
Raleigh W. Creamer	Martha F. Waters	7/20/1854	141
Thomas T. Crow	Nancy C. Kemp	5/ 3/1859	143
N. H. Cockran	Elizabeth Creamer	5/19/1859	145
Hiram Cain	Mary Wallis	5/13/1859	148
Alphonsay Connally	Mary A. Bruse	10/ 9/1859	150
Philbon H. Cumpton	Elizabeth Gravitt	10/30/1859	151
Charles C. Christian	Mary C. Holbrook	10/13/1859	151
Henry Christenberry	Samantha White	10/18/1859	152
James J. Chatham	Elizabeth Phillips	8/25/1859	156
Sampson Clayton	Nancy Bagwell	9/23/1860	168
Ross A. Corruth	Georgia A.F. Bell	5/10/1860	172
Joseph A. Cain	Mary E. Auston	2/12/1861	173
William Clement	Mentorey Hutchins	10/18/1866	176
Roley Colbert	Elizabeth Hutson	10/28/1860	176
James S. Carter	Martha Gault	3/29/1860	181
Charles W. Collins	Mary A. Foster	7/12/1860	182
Milton L. Clark	Diannah E. Almon	4/10/1860	186
Isaac S. Clement	Arminta O. Bell	7/21/1861	188
William Collins	Amanda Dunahoo	3/24/1861	189
B. W. Clark	Mary C. McCormack	7/ 4/1861	191
James M. Chatham	Mary J. Wallis	4/15/1862	197
Marion Cope	Kesiah Mullinax	2/29/1862	198
William Carver	Mary Thacker	1/ 8/1862	200
James Crow	Lucretia Couch	1/12/1860	203
John H. Castleberry	Frances D. Wood	5/25/1862	205
William C. Copeland	Sarah Jane Dunlap	6/ 5/1862	211
John Craine	Mary Reese	11/21/1861	214
William M. Castleberry	Martha F. Fagins	4/ 5/1863	216
J. C. Cantrell	E. E. Jackson	1863	221
E. M. Chatham	----- Pool	1863	222
William H. Castleberry	Mary A. Anglin	10/13/1864	233
Henry Cooper	Nancy Jones	7/ 7/1864	235
William Collins	Deliliah Tidwell	1/22/1865	240
James P. Clark	Nancy L. Bottoms	3/ 9/1865	242
Henry L. Cunningham	Lucinda Garrett	1/31/1865	247
Simean B. David	Francis E. Harris	3/ 1/1855	40
Wesley Dooly	Cleopatry Phillips	2/22/1855	42
George W. Dodd	Caroline Dollar	8/ 7/1855	50
Aswell W. Davidson	Mary Terry	8/14/1855	52

GROOM	BRIDE	MARRIED	PAGE
John G. Dollar	Sarah Holbrook	6/28/1855	59
Jacob Driver	Nancy A. Townley	8/31/1856	76
James M.C. Durham	Josephine Dooly	11/11/1856	78
Jesse Dooley	Michel Bulls	1/ 1/1857	88
Thomas W. Dooly	Sarah A. Julian	10/22/1851	106
William F. Davenport	Sarah Boman	11/15/1857	119
John L. Delaney	Mary M. Harris	2/ 9/1858	120
James T. Dougharty	Elizabeth A. Bentley	9/13/1857	123
Isaac Right Duncin	Luisa F. Anderson	11/18/1858	130
Benjamin W.M. Davis	Lavina Bagwell	10/ 9/1851	147
Hawkins Dacus	Sarah Childres	10/10/1858	180
Thomas H. Daniel	Sarah Woodliff	10/10/1861	207
Reuben Denton	Permelia Garrett	5/ 4/1862	211
Day	Majors	(faded)	223
Lewis Dooly	Malissa C. Gravitt	1/ 5/1865	236
James M. Dodd(Milton Co.)	Sarah M. Dodd	4/21/1864	242
James F. Dollar	Louiza Brown	10/25/1864	250
Nelson Dollar	Emily Burton	6/28/1864	252
E. S. Dodd	A. Priest	1/ 7/1866	287
James Dooly	Susanah Smith	10/18/1866	313
Van W. Davis	Fanny E. David	12/ 2/1866	336
Josiah P. Dougherty	Synthia C. Allen	2/19/1867	351
Eli H. Davis	G. E. Merrett	3/14/1867	360
George W. Daniel	Harriett Singleton	5/12/1867	363
William Dacus	Elvira Hall	3/ 5/1868	385
John N. Duncan	Mary M. Tidwell	1/19/1868	394
Elija P. Echols	Mississippi Cape	10/12/1853	4
William Emmerson	Eliza Bettis	9/ 5/1852	5
James M. Echols	Elizabeth J. Brown	9/ 3/1854	29
Thomas Edmundson	Francis L. David	12/24/1854	37
Cicero Estes	Adela E. Mills	10/18/1855	57
Willis Evans	Mary Evans	10/21/1848	106
John L. Ezzard	Mahala E. Bettis	2/24/1858	108
Whitman Elder	Mary Diskert	7/20/1857	119
Joshua Estes	Mary E. Vaughan	12/ 2/1858	131
Robert A. Ekes	Nancy Sims	9/ 2/1858	136
Hutson Estes	Margaret Pruitt	12/15/1859	148
John Edmondson	Nancy E. Samples	9/ 2/1859	156
John Edwards	Daleyann Taylor	12/ 8/1859	159
Harrison Estes	Martha A. Sexton	2/12/1860	165
John W. Ellis	Sarah J. Milford	11/11/1860	177
Wesley Estes	Mary Fagans	3/10/1861	187
Joshua Echols	Sarah Purcell	8/30/1861	210
Jasper Estes	M. M. Reid	5/11/1865	253
Thomas J. Ellis	Joyce Bruton	7/23/1865	260
Samuel J. Ellis	Sallie E. Hughes	10/12/1865	261
Robert E. Ellison	Eliza E. Leach	10/17/1865	265
W. A. Edwards	Mary A. Broadwell	4/29/1866	291
J. W. Edwards	M. E. Phillips	10/24/1866	302
M. H. Eakes	Almyra D. Johnston	8/14/1866	305
Noah Edmonson	Nancy J. Stephens	1/24/1867	319
Charles Estes	Margaret Estes	5/13/1866	330
L. B. Edwards, Jr.	Rosalee Chamblee	11/28/1867	369
Leroy Edmonson	Sarah J. Windows	11/19/1867	374
William T. Ezzard	Eloira Finley	10/ 6/1867	377
W. P. Elliott	Harriet M. Purcell	4/ 9/1868	387
John W. Fincher	Rody Hallman	5/15/1853	3
Ransom E. Foster	Kindness James	12/20/1853	7

GROOM	BRIDE	MARRIED	PAGE
Stephen W. Fitzpatrick	Sarah L. Yancy	12/20/1853	14
Thomas D. Fitzpatrick	Sarah Yancy	8/ 3/1855	52
Isaac Freeland	Elizabeth Key	9/20/1855	54
William R. Fields	Katherine White	9/ 9/1855	68
James C. Fincher	Sarah Ann Evans	10/30/1855	81
Matthew C. Fowler	Cornelia A. Goolsby	1/31/1856	96
Green B. Foster	Martha F. Hays	12/31/1857	110
Green B. Foster	Martha F. Hays	12/31/1857	118
Nathaniel Forman	Colendar A. Chapman	1/17/1858	122
E. W. Fincher	Nancy David	7/15/1858	137
Phillip K. Fowler	Nancy Jane Ledbetter	2/18/1855	141
G. W. Frix	G. E. Nuckolls	8/19/1858	148
Joshua Fowler	Margaret Chadwick	12/ 8/1859	154
William J. Freeland	Sarah Rey	9/18/1859	156
A. J. Fowler	Martha J. Gravitt	1/29/1859	162
Ira R. Foster	Amanda Samples	3/22/1860	182
George W. Fowler	Martha J. Pool	2/24/1861	198
William W. Foster	C. J. Martin	10/25/1864	242
Benjamin F. Foster	Josephine Williams	7/19/1865	248
John W. Fincher	Emily J.J. McAfee	4/30/1865	251
John Fowler	Caroline Walls	2/19/1857	271
Charles W. Fitts	Loniza M. Owens	1865	280
James W. Fowler	Mrs. Mary Delany	11/28/1865	285
Joseph D. Foster	Eveline M. McAfee	4/29/1866	290
Nelson Fowler	Fannie Huggins	4/12/1866	291
James D. Fagans	Virginia Strickland	7/22/1866	304
Augustus Flesh	Malinda Owens	9/ 2/1866	327
John G. Flinn	Drucilla Pugh	12/25/1866	336
George W. Green	Sarah A. Samples	2/ 5/1854	2
James Grizzell	Joicy Terry	9/27/1853	3
Cicero M. Gravitt	Mary C. Brooks	9/20/1854	29
James P. Godsey	Milly Echols	4/19/1854	31
William Gentry	Melinda Hood	1/ 4/1855	37
John F. Guthrie	Caroline M. Soughard	10/19/1854	44
John W. Giton	Rebecca Terry	7/26/1855	52
James J. Griffin	Elizabeth Bramblet	9/27/1855	53
Faris Green	Cassandra Beaver	8/30/1855	55
Augustus W. Gilmer	Mary James	3/27/1856	65
James A. Glass	Mary J. Howard	11/29/1855	70
Thomas T. Garrett	Eliza Overby	12/23/1856	71
John J. Garrett	Mary Jane Fowler	7/ 6/1856	71
James M. Gravitt	Nancy M. Gravitt	5/25/1856	78
Bluford Gant	Rebecca Ann Jane McGinnes	12/ 7/1856	81
Thomas E. Green	Melissa Pearson	2/12/1857	92
John M. Green	Mary A. Buchannan	8/23/1857	98
Ambrose Green	Eveline White	5/ 2/1858	105
James D. Graham	Virginia E. Nuckolls	4/ 6/1858	107
Obadiah W. Gaddis	Mary E. Shands	1/12/1858	109
Robert M. Galloway	Mrs. Mahala Hammond	12/21/1857	112
Mancil Garrett	Matilda C. Street	1/19/1858	112
Roger Green	Francis Jordan	6/ 6/1858	120
John W. Gossett	Mary E. Hansard	8/20/1857	123
Elija Green	Francca A.E. Brooks	9/22/1858	133
William Gant	Martha L.E. Jackson	8/22/1858	134
Thomas M. Goodwin	E. A. Sheets	10/26/1856	140
Isham H. Gilbert	Nancy C. Braswell	1/13/1859	144
Edwin S. Grimmett	Adeline W. Kellogg	9/27/1859	149
Presly Gantt	Milly S. Hadden	11/18/1860	172

GROOM	BRIDE	MARRIED	PAGE
Asa Gantt	Sibella Gravitt	12/20/1860	173
Albert G. Green	Frances Samples	3/15/1861	187
Thomas N. Gravitt	Narcissa M. Compton	9/ 8/1861	188
W. Gossett	Narcussus Hansard	6/ 2/1861	192
Hosea Garrett	Emily Bolton	7/ 2/1861	193
Nathan A. Garrett	Elizabeth Pugh	5/15/1862	196
John F. Gentry	Rody Ann Pugh	11/16/1862	208
John Goswick	Margaret Castleberry	2/ 4/1864	226
B. F. Gilmer	Mary J. Bagby	9/15/1863	227
Daniel A. Garrett	Charity Ellison	9/12/1864	243
H. M. Goss	Sarah C. McGinnis	7/22/1865	256
Andrew J. Gravitt	Mrs. Lucinda C.Brownlow	9/30/1865	265
William G. Gravitt	Louissa Gravitt	2/ 1/1866	285
Gaston Green	Eveline Phillips	4/26/1866	292
James Gravitt	Elizabeth Reese	1/26/1866	293
P. P. Gray	M. E. E. Mitchiner	10/25/1865	297
W. P. Garrett	J. A. Red	9/20/1866	308
L. F. Gober	L. C. Maness	9/19/1866	309
John L. Goolsby	Martha C. Taylor	8/ 5/1866	310
Nathaniel G. Garrett	Louisa A. Woodliff	1/ 2/1867	321
M. M. Gentry	M. L. Roach	1/28/1866	326
T. J. Grogan	Mary E. Lummus	10/11/1866	338
Isaac V. Gravitt	Francis Patterson	9/ 9/1866	339
L. T. Green	E. J. Hutchins	9/12/1867	340
Thomas Grogan	Mary E. Lummus	10/11/1866	352
George W. Garrett	Prissella Sanders	11/25/1866	364
J. P. Gallagher	L. C. Pool	11/24/1867	371
S. C. Gunter	Margaret E. Edwards	12/22/1867	383
Squire Gober	Sarah Holbrook	3/19/1868	386
Henry C. Garmony	Nancy E. Taylor	11/15/1866	392
Henry Greenle	Rachel Kellogg	1/16/1868	396
Parker Harris	Elizabeth Little	9/27/1853	2
John L. Hawkins	Nancy E. Lewis	1/29/1854	2
William N. Hammond	Elizabeth M. Benson	1/25/1853	9
Robert Hardin	Sarah E. Singleton	12/27/1853	10
William G. Hamilton	Elizabeth A. Skin	9/28/1853	18
John W. Hill	Martha Jane Logan	4/ 4/1854	20
James C. Harris	Elizabeth E. Brown	2/26/1854	22
James Hill	Narcissa Hollingshed	3/13/1854	24
William Hall	Darcus Singleton	6/16/1850	26
Robert L. Hawkins	Samantha A. Brannon	12/10/1854	28
Pressley Homes	Nancy Ann McCrary	8/31/1854	31
John Higgins	Ann Dacus	10/ 6/1854	33
John Hughs	Elizabeth Cannon	2/19/1854	38
Burdine Hollingshead	Sarah Ann E. Waters	11/ 5/1854	39
Russell J. Holbrook	Mary C. Chamblee	1/11/1855	40
Elijah L. Holbrook	Lucinda Mournin Hudson	4/16/1855	43
Overton Harris	Mary E. Bennett	12/14/1854	47
Daniel Hammond	Mary Rollin	4/ 5/1855	48
George Hansard	Eliza Jane Davenport	9/ 2/1855	50
Alexander Herring	Louise E.R. Brown	8/12/1855	54
Wiley Holshowser	Margaret H. McGinnis	10/21/1855	56
John W. Holbrook	Sarah J.C. Hadder	10/11/1855	56
Joseph Hopkins	Milley Hays	10/14/1855	57
William B. Holbrook	Lucinda Scott	11/22/1855	59
Golson M. Hook	Gabriella A. Anglin	1/27/1856	60
William T. Holbrook	Mrs. Elmian Nelson	1/23/1856	60
James Walker	Letty Ann Powel	2/10/1856	62

FORSYTH COUNTY MARRIAGE RECORD C (1853-1868)

GROOM	BRIDE	MARRIED	PAGE
Wilson F. Haselett	Susan Amanda Brooks	2/10/1856	63
Tilmon D. Hagood	Nancy E. Red	6/10/1856	67
James M. Herndon	Mary E. Fry	9/28/1856	74
William Hood	Saphrona Moor	11/23/1856	79
Elijah Hayes	Adaline Pucket	12/28/1856	85
James L. Hunnicut	Martha Ann Jinks	2/ 3/1856	88
Balis M. Hubbard	Elizabeth Tidwell	10/22/1856	89
Jacob Hollingshead	Nancy Hamby	12/26/1856	91
Ballard Hays	Drucilla Hopkins	12/ 9/1857	94
John Holtzclaw	Elizabeth Whitmire	5/ 3/1857	95
Foster Hutchins	Kindness Cruse	7/16/1857	95
Bluford Holcomb	Irana Hendrix	4/19/1857	97
A. C. Harris	R.J.K. Williams	10/18/1857	99
Green J. Holbrook	Mary A. Rogers	2/25/1858	101
W. W. Harris	Martha A. Julian	12/14/1854	103
Samuel G. Higgins	Sarah Ann E. Higgins	5/23/1858	105
Isaac Harden	Harriet Wallace	9/10/1857	111
James Hunter	Elizabeth Goss	12/31/1857	114
Ira R. Holbrook	Sarah A. Jefferson	1/30/1859	117
William L. Hardin	Mary J. Martin	4/20/1858	118
Newton Harrell	Mary E. Harris	2/11/1858	120
John F. Harrison	Athalinda Merritt	12/30/1858	124
John L. Hudson	Elizabeth C. Moor	12/23/1858	125
James Harrell	Ann Holbrook	10/ 5/1858	126
John W. Holbrook	Sarah N. Bruce	12/23/1858	126
James A. Holbrook	Nancy Tinsley	9/10/1858	129
Drury B. Hutchins	Nancy Jane Light	7/18/1858	129
J. P. Heard	Rachel Martin	11/14/1858	130
Asberry Holbrook	Hannah Townly	11/21/1858	131
Daniel Horton	Melinda Blankinship	8/13/1858	132
John Henson	Rebecca Bruce	8/22/1858	135
M. D. Harris	Sarah Trammel	12/30/1856	140
Lafayette Hardin	Jane Garrett	1/ 4/1859	143
Meriman Holbrooks	Elizabeth Allen	11/13/1859	150
William Hendrick	Zeeda Compton	10/25/1859	151
William O. Hammond	Adeline Kemp	10/ 6/1859	152
C. J. Henderson	Martha Jane Phillips	1/12/1860	163
Thomas I. Hopkins	Eliza B. Puckett	1/17/1860	164
William B. Harris	Nancy C. Harris	1/19/1860	164
William N. Hammond	Frances Milwood	9/20/1860	168
Andrew J. Hardeman	Leonora A. Hutchins	9/30/1860	168
William Holbrook	Julia H. Weems	1/24/1861	170
N. G. Henderson	L. M. Moon	1/ 7/1861	171
Thomas Holdbrook	Jane Edwards	7/25/1860	178
H. M. Harris	R. A. Crow	2/ 9/1860	184
James L. Hagood	Elizabeth Roper	1/17/1860	186
Benjamin A. Huff	Mary E.J. Cox	5/30/1861	188
Samuel L. Hays	Mary J. Hawkins	9/ 5/1861	189
James O. Hughs	Martha E. Davis	3/ 9/1862	197
James A. Hagood	Susan L. Francis	4/11/1862	200
M. D. Hughs	M. A. Henderson	10/27/1861	205
G. N. Holbrook	Sissy G. Cooper	8/17/1862	207
Thomas W. Hunt	Martha Bryant	9/16/1862	208
James H. Holbrook	Mary E. Jefferson	4/27/1862	216
Thomas W. Hawkins	Eveline J. Hawkins	3/27/1863	218
W. H. Hawkins	Easter Kemp	1863	221
Howell	Mahee	(faded)	222
Andrew W. Hughes	Margaret J. Austin	6/30/1860	224
John Higgins	Julia Green	(faded)	228
David Harris	----- Smith	1864	229

GROOM	BRIDE	MARRIED	PAGE
James M. Hughes	Nancy M. Parks	4/28/1864	229
Isaac L. Hendrix	Elizabeth Gravitt	1/12/1865	234
Thomas D. Hawkins	Martha C. Fagans	1/15/1865	236
Ruben Hill	Mary A. Roach	1/26/1865	237
Joseph B. Harrison	Sarah A.P. Stuart	9/13/1863	239
Luke Hendrix, Dawson Co.	Elizabeth Wood	2/ 5/1865	240
William Hunter	Martha Ezzard	3/17/1864	241
W. H. Hagood	M. A. Red	11/20/1864	246
William E. Hansard	Lucinda A. Bensen	7/14/1864	247
Thomas W. Hunt	Martha J. Red	7/14/1864	249
Abijah Holbrook	Mary J. Compton	8/15/1865	258
J. M. Hammon	Mary A. Martin	7/20/1865	261
John Lewis Holbrook	Mary Elizabeth Kelly	1865	264
Thomas H. Hood	Charley Ann M.Sanders	12/31/1865	269
G. W. Holbrook	Nancy A. McDaniel	1/21/1866	286
Major Holbrooks	Senia A. Sherly	2/ 8/1866	288
Plesant T. Hulsy	Jane Phillips	5/ 9/1866	293
Ira W. Hansard	T. E. Barker	10/24/1866	303
Robert Hood	Susan C. Garrett	4/22/1866	303
Alfred G. Harrison	Flora A. Hope	9/ 4/1866	314
Isaiah Hubbard	Elizabeth Owen	7/31/1866	321
Samuel L. Hansard	C. H. Roberts	1867	323
M. T. Harris	Ellen Cole	12/25/1866	325
Leroy Harrison	Sarah J. Henson	11/ 6/1866	328
Andrew J. Hawkins	Mary C. White	10/29/1866	328
Richard D.B. Henderson	Julia A. Miller	8/ 3/1856	331
Thomas J. Hernden	Mary E. Neisler	(no cert.)	331
James C. Harris	Elisabeth Jones	11/20/1866	332
Ezekiel Henderson	Mary E. Hope	(not dated)	333
William W. Hubbard	Syntha E. Hendrix	3/11/1866	334
Isaac N. Henderson	Martha C. Light	12/20/1866	335
Thomas J. Herndon	Mary E. Neisler	10/18/1866	336
J. H. Henderson	Nancy Strickland	8/ 9/1867	342
Jesse M. Holbrook	Mrs. Darcus C. Carter	2/14/1867	348
John T. Holbrook	Elizabeth J. Elliott	9/26/1867	358
Thomas J. Herndon	Mary E. Neisler	(cert.not dated)	359
James W. Hudson	Maggie Wilson	11/ 7/1867	360
John F. Hawkins	Ruth Westbrooks	10/10/1867	370
James Hansard	L. E. Samples	11/21/1867	372
William B. Hood	Sarah Orr	12/ 5/1867	382
William T. Hawkins	Lucy V. Bennett	5/14/1868	384
W. B. Hawkins	Mary V. Westbrook	9/14/1865	272
General M. Holbrook	Mary J. Cooper	10/29/1865	275
John H. Hubbard	Manurva Bennett	12/24/1865	276
Thomas P. Hopkins	Silvey C. Pilgrim	11/30/1865	282
W. C. Holbrook	Mary A.S. Brannon	10/15/1865	284
Hardin Jourdan	Joannah Hulsey	1/17/1854	12
William R. Jones	Josephine Murray	1/19/1854	12
Alfred M. Jackson	Arminda K. Hughs	10/22/1853	15
Jasper N. Jackson	Eliza J. Bond	10/ 8/1854	34
W. E. Jones	Sarah Ann Leister	12/21/1854	36
Julius Josephson	Agnes Young	3/25/1855	42
John A. James	Clarinda Mahee	3/13/1855	51
William C. Jackson	Nancy E. Bond	4/15/1855	62
James M. Jinks	Margaret Ann Gaunt	7/19/1855	73
Makagel Monroe Johnson	Mary Ann Williams	7/17/1856	84
C. W. Jackson	Polly E. McAfre	3/25/1858	101
Bailey F. Julian	Stella J. Clement	3/19/1857	104

GROOM	BRIDE	MARRIED	PAGE
William M. Jones	Jane Cross	1/ 6/1859	116
Benjamin Jones	Sarah Garrett	2/ 2/1858	119
Martin V. Johnson	Nancy Baker	10/ 9/1853	141
William J. Jones	Lucinda E.F. Fowler	9/13/1860	170
John L. Jones	Didama Cross	10/11/1860	179
Bassel Jefferson	Cintha E. Crow	6/28/1860	184
John W. James	Margaret Phillips	1/17/1861	193
Russell Jones	Eliza Ann Rogers	2/16/1862	197
Jessup L. Johnston	Sarah S. Delenport	5/21/1865	255
M. C. Jackson	M. S. Westry	5/ 3/1866	302
Baswell Jefferson	Mrs. Frances Staggs	7/ 8/1866	311
Samuel B. Julian	Sarah Hood	4/ 1/1866	317
J. L. Johnson	Taliena E. Garrett	2/24/1867	322
Jesse T. Johnson	Mary E. Jackson	1866	324
(Milton Co.)			
Harden Jordan	Martha A. Perce	4/14/1867	368
James M. Jett	Lewsenda Green	11/17/1867	370
Starling B. Jones	Eliza Jane Hope	1/27/1867	375
Isaac L. Jackson	S. L. Hope	3/12/1868	391
John B. Karr	Mahala Clifton	7/ 5/1853	8
Jesse M. Karr	Francis M. Samples	8/23/1855	49
John C. Karr	Elizabeth Brown	9/31/1855	55
Matthew Karr	Mary Nicholson	4/27/1856	86
H. G. Karr	Milly C. Pugh	7/27/1856	86
T. M. Kemp	Feba A. Fincher	7/29/1858	137
S. V. Kelly	Harriet M. Benson	7/20/1858	138
Augustus M. Kemp	Amanda J. Samples	10/27/1859	150
James F. Karr	Frances Long	4/14/1860	182
James Kelly	Mary E. Johnson	5/11/1861	194
Greenberry King	Mary C. Anderson	8/11/1861	213
Stephen Kile	Margaret M. Barker	8/20/1863	217
Collumbus T. Kemp	Susan M. Gravitt	8/22/1865	257
Dr. J.R.G. McDouell Knox	Martha Jane McAfee	1/30/1866	287
Benjamin Kelly	Mary Jane Chatham	2/15/1866	286
William Key	Arminda Ingram	8/20/1866	309
W. W. Kemp	M. A. Thornton	8/27/1867	343
Lewis Kellogg	Issalellor Baly	2/23/1863	398
Warren D. Lesley	Mary A. Blankinship	9/29/1853	6
Newton F. Light	Margaret Cross	3/11/1854	23
Lesal Lawson	Julia Ann Hayne	2/24/1855	45
Levi Lancaster	Mariah Davis	6/19/1856	84
Alvin Lesley	Martha A. Hawkins	10/21/1855	87
Addison C. Low	Francis Jackson	11/ 9/1854	89
Thomas C. Langley	Nancy Beevers	4/ 3/1858	108
Pleasant G. Light	Flora E. Mooney	2/28/1858	110
Daniel Ledbetter	Mary Caroline Fowler	5/ 6/1855	117
John H. Lamb	Mary H. Major	1/ 2/1859	125
William Lawson	Sarah Callahan	9/ 9/1858	130
Stephen S. Lee	Elizabeth J. Braswell	7/13/1858	138
Henry B. Light	Amanda S.L. Bowman	11/ 7/1858	139
Isaac J. Lafarm	Harriet L. Reese	5/13/1858	144
Daniel F. Light	Martha E. King	10/ 5/1859	153
William Lamb	Josephine Cruse	1/ 1/1860	158
William H. Lamb	Nancy E. Dunaway	1/11/1859	162
Elias Lazenberry	Amanda Hagood	8/ 3/1860	177
Lewis G. Logan	Elizabeth Chapman	11/26/1857	180
Cyrus N. Little	Nancy M. Rogers	1/ 5/1861	201
Ell. Lummus	Francis M. Tidwell	9/22/1863	219

FORSYTH COUNTY MARRIAGE RECORD C (1853-1868)

GROOM	BRIDE	MARRIED	PAGE
Ell. Lummus	Francis M. Tidwell	9/22/1863	220
Sanford Lindsey	Georgia A.O. Blake	12/29/1864	230
Charles Ledbetter	Martha A. Wallis	8/31/1865	259
Henry Low	Mary E. Bottoms	4/22/1865	262
Thomas W. Lazenby	Catherine Green	4/ 1/1865	259
Lewis J. Ledbetter	Nancy H. Jackson	12/14/1865	273
Ruchin Ledbetter	Mary Petty	2/16/1866	289
Horain Low	Suntha C. Higgins	3/22/1866	290
Isaac N. Lamb	Manerva Carns	9/23/1866	314
Benjamin Lamb	Edny Norrel	9/20/1866	315
Isaac Lindsey	Mary Wallace	11/25/1866	339
William J. Lockamy	Amanda A.K. Christian	5/ 3/1866	346
Davis Lemans	Martha Davis	1/ 7/1868	382
James T. Montgomery	America Bulls	4/ 3/1853	1
James L. Martin	Mary Hood	2/ 2/1854	3
Robert A. Moony	Nancy E. Owen	9/22/1853	6
John Miller	Adaline Cruse	2/19/1854	7
R. C. Montgomery	Frances Brogdon	11/13/1853	9
William F. Moor	Sarah A. Rogers	12/22/1853	10
John H. Mashburn	Martha Pain	1/19/1854	12
William Millwood	Jane Davis	3/19/1854	24
Ephraim Matthews	Celestia E.A.D.Mahaffy	10/ 1/1854	33
E.E.C. Mitchiner	Mary H.E. Shields	1/ 1/1855	36
Jackson Millwood	Mary Davis	4/ 8/1855	44
Sanford M. Morris	Hannah James	5/17/1855	47
William Martin	Mrs. Elizabeth Hix	6/14/1855	48
John Martin	Mary Ann Osbon	9/ 7/1855	53
John J. Matthews	Mary E. Traylor	11/10/1853	58
Bird Martin	Nancy Nix	2/ 6/1856	60
Peter Burdine Marti	Elizabeth Johnson	9/ 1/1855	61
Reubin J. Moor	Martha J. Rogers	12/13/1855	61
William M. Monroe	Elizabeth T. Wingo	4/10/1856	65
John T. Mays	Levicy E. Lummus	4/ 3/1856	66
John W. Merrett	Mary Elizabeth Davis	9/11/1856	74
Tidwell P. Martin	Polly Ann Hughs	9/ 8/1856	80
Reuben Matthews	Amanda Buice	1/ 7/1857	82
John Mangum	Eliza Thornton	12/27/1856	87
Hillyard L. Martin	Mary E. Howard	1/21/1858	114
William C. Milton	Emily E. Gloss	3/ 9/1858	124
Joseph F. Mashburn	Lucretia M. Blake	12/30/1858	125
Daniel G. Mize	Elvira M. Reavice	11/21/1858	132
Hugh Martin	Sarah E. Wofford	5/ 4/1858	135
Wiley W. Mangum	Frances Tidwell	12/16/1858	161
John W. Mahaffy	Mary E. Williams	2/22/1860	166
Joseph L. Moor	Jane O. Carter	3/28/1860	172
Josiah F. Merritt	Eliza A. Pilgrim	11/29/1860	175
John B. Monday	Elizabeth E. Shadburn	11/25/1860	179
Jessy Millwood	Marthy E. McGee	3/ 1/1860	183
Charles B. Martin	Easter Ellison	8/24/1862	209
Hiram Mathis	Mary Collins	10/ 9/1862	215
Jesse B. Monroe	Mariah A. Lott	3/17/1864	231
Joseph L. Moor	Sarah L. Rogers	4/14/1864	234
Seaborn Moor	Sarah M. Hawkins	5/ 7/1865	254
James Ervin Mashburn	G. Ann Harwell	10/12/1865	262
Benson E. Martin	Malissa Hammen	10/ 8/1865	266
F. H. Mullins	Sarah Moore	11/28/1865	270
G.T.(?) Mitchell	Mariah Roach	2/14/1864	283
Severe Martin	Nancy Jane Holland	3/17/1866	299
William P. Millford	Nancy Kelly	8/28/1866	310

GROOM	BRIDE	MARRIED	PAGE
Absolom Martin	Nancy Wallis	6/24/1866	316
John A.J. Martin	Mary Ann R. Foster	9/ 5/1867	341
Leonader B. Monrow	Sarah Willingham	3/ 7/1867	354
Jacob Moulder	Anna A. Pirkle	6/20/1867	362
Andrew P. Moor	Savannah C. Lott	12/10/1867	375
Singleton Moulder	Arminda P. Pirkle	12/19/1867	377
Samuel Morris	Elizabeth Mays	9/ 8/1867	382
Lenard Monroe	Artimisa Holland	1/18/1868	399
Robert A. Moony	Nancy E. Owen	9/22/1853	6
Phillip McIntire	Milley E. Mullican	8/19/1854	27
Robert N. McClure	Emma Hockenhull	2/ 1/1855	39
John McIntire	Sarah F. Eddleman	3/ 2/1856	64
James McDill	Nancy Ann Wilson	10/ 1/1856	75
John McGinnis	Mrs. Cassandra Owens	2/22/1855	80
Samuel R. McBrayer	Luvenia E. Milford	2/ 1/1857	90
James D. McGinnis	Justina Howard	2/10/1857	93
Jesse McGee	Mary Gault	3/ 1/1857	93
William A. McBryer	Mary L. Logan	2/13/1859	104
Augustus C. McGinnis	Martha Estes	2/13/1859	116
W. W. McAfee	A. L. Freeze	5/ 8/1859	142
Augustus C. McCormack	Adaline McGrier	11/19/1857	159
James D. McGinnis	Sarah A. Pettyjohn	12/11/1859	159
Randall M. McDonald	Parmelia N. Conn	1/28/1858	169
Daniel F. McCormack	Luisa C. Tidwell	2/28/1861	174
Nathaniel C. McGinas	Nancy Yancy	3/22/1860	185
H. H. McClure	Sarah J. West	3/21/1861	204
William R. McGinnis	Cyntha Garrett	10/29/1863	219
McCormack	Harrison	9/22/1863	220
Augustus C. McGinnis	Sarah Estes	12/24/1863	235
James McDaniel	Mary Reid	3/14/1864	244
Joseph M. McAfee	Mary Cain	2/ 8/1866	288
R. H. McCoy	A. L. Garrett	9/20/1866	307
Robert N. McGuire	Nancy E. Priest	12/28/1865	317
Dr. James W. McFaull	Mary C. Peers	8/18/1867	344
William F. McCrary	Missouri V. Pearce	7/20/1867	351
Frederick N. McKinny	Sallie J.E. Waller	12/ 8/1866	354
John B. McBreyer	Harriet Blanton	1/ 2/1868	395
Nathaniel McClure	Eliza E. Williams	1/15/1868	398
Stephen P. McKinny	Polly A. Singleton	3/18/1868	398
I.G.L. Nuchols	E. E. Moore	11/ 1/1853	13
Francis M. Nickolson	Sarah M. Karr	10/10/1854	28
Namon C. Nickolson	Jane Otwell	9/10/1854	30
W. P. Nash	Manda C. Webb	12/25/1855	73
Thomas Newton	Nancy Burnett	12/30/1857	113
William H. Newton	Lucretia Graham	11/19/1861	202
C. H. Nuckolls	Rachel A. Beard	9/30/1862	211
Yerba Norrell	Jane Hammond	8/ 3/1862	212
Robert D. Naler	Francis A. Wilson	12/13/1860	212
F. H. Nichols	Menerva Rogers	6/26/1862	214
James H. Nickolson	Arabella A.H. Winders	11/ 6/1864	250
W. J. Nix	R. A. Tatum	5/ 4/1865	254
John Norrell	Susan C. Martin	7/17/1865	255
Barksdel Nally	Sarah J. McAfee	8/23/1865	258
W. B. Nicholson	Sallie Long	6/22/1865	263
Cunningham M. Nally	Mary A. Stephens	12/28/1865	287
Nathan Pool	Sylvania Chatham	6/23/1861	204
James J. Pendley	Francis Davis	12/ 1/1861	205
James Pugh	Elender Fowler	8/22/1862	210

GROOM	BRIDE	MARRIED	PAGE
Thomas J. Pilgrim	Catherine N. Merrit	6/ 3/1863	218
Harvy M. Pruitt	Sarah M. Pery	9/3(?)/1863	228
John N. Pace	Nancy Killingsworth	1/21/1864	228
Benson F. Pugh	Mrs. Mary A. Pugh	1/ 9/1865	231
J. C. Phillips	Narcissa M. Holbrook	6/ 9/1864	232
James J.P. Perry	Arbella Hill	11/ 8/1864	237
E. J. Puett	Mary A. Johnston	9/21/1865	268
William C. Purkle	Margret Otwell	11/19/1865	270
Isaac S. Pirkle	Harriet V. Phillips	4/22/1866	292
John Pendley	Emily Martin	4/ 5/1866	295
George W. Powell	Laura S. Clement	1/19/1866	296
Moses Pirkins	California Light	1/28/1866	296
Richard N. Phillipps	Cansada G. Edmondson	3/ 1/1866	298
W. L. Pearce	Cyntha Bell	3/ 1/1866	298
Jesse M. Pirkle	Sarah Samples	8/ 9/1866	302
Richard H. Pruett	Adaliza Estes	9/12/1866	303
Albert N. Pilgrim	Nancy E. Tate	8/ 7/1866	304
George K. Porter	Clarisa A. Sanford	1/27/1867	317
Hugh Porter	Harriett Higgins	1/27/1867	320
A. W. Perry	Mary Glass	10/ 7/1866	335
F. A. Parker	Martha A. Crow	9/19/1867	348
Green B. Parks	Mrs. Martha A. Steple	9/12/1867	353
William Patterson	Sarah Brown	5/26/1868	386
Jesse Qualls	Mary Martin	11/10/1853	16
Moses Qualls	Sarah Hollinshead	1/29/1859	91
Jesse C. Roberts	Mary Ann Anderson	12/ 6/1853	18
John C. Richardson	Emily Moore	2/26/1854	21
Hamilton Roper	Nepsey Ann Cope	6/29/1853	25
James B. Roach	Mary Ann Perry	7/ 2/1854	34
Thomas Rolin	Mary Crame	1/23/1855	38
William Ramey	Divinity Conner	12/23/1854	45
M. K. Reed	S. E. Wallis	7/ 8/1855	50
John Runnels	Louiza J. Staggs	8/ 5/1855	51
William A. Roper	Sarah Talent	9/ 9/1855	51
Francis M. Revis	Sarah Jane Harris	12/ 6/1855	58
Joseph Robertson	Sarah C. Lindsey	5/ 4/1856	66
John Rogers	Sophrona Hardin	11/15/1855	69
George W. Red	Harriet W. Wingo	7/ 6/1856	70
Samuel M. Reese	Elizabeth Howard	2/28/1856	72
David M. Rogers	Mary J. Strickland	2/ 3/1856	72
William B. Red	Mary Angeline E. Moor	8/14/1856	76
James J. Red	Permelia Pearson	8/ 3/1856	77
Pinckney W. Roberts	Mary E. Samples	12/ 9/1856	79
George C. Roper	Elizabeth Hockenhull	9/18/1856	79
John Roper	Amy Elizabeth Reid	12/16/1856	83
Thomas B. Rogers	Judy Ann Cawley	1/18/1857	85
Joseph Rogers	Martha Shands	1/25/1857	90
James A. Rollins	Catherine P. Branon	8/ 6/1857	96
John P. Rogers	Pattie M. Crawford	11/18/1857	100
Thomas Nix	Nancy A. Hamby	10/23?/1866	300
W. G. Nailer	Francis Holbrook	12/23/1866	325
William Norris	Margaret A. Nations	9/12/1867	376
Benjamin Nuckolls	Polly Mannon	(no cert.)	
Cullin J. Otwell	Elizabeth A. Blankenship	5/8/1854	22
Sanford Owen	Jane Wheeler	9/ 7/1854	28
Solomon M. Otwell	Adaliza A. Bryant	8/ 7/1856	75
Cullen J. Otwell	Mrs. Maranda H. Cook	2/25/1858	108
Asa Owen	Emily M. Hutchins	8/22/1858	127

GROOM	BRIDE	MARRIED	PAGE
Oswell Owen	Malinda Beaver	1/13/1859	147
Benjamin Otwell	Elizabeth Karr	9/ 5/1859	155
John Orr	A. E. Jones	3/22/1860	181
William S. Owens	Mrs. Martha Tatum	11/23/1864	259
John R. Owens	Amanda A. Wood	9/10/1865	255
F. M. Owens	Sarah M. Whitmire	1(?)/17/1865	281
Howell Cobb Owens	Margret E. Garrett	9/20/1866	308
James M. Owen	Mary M. Hutchins	12/ 5/1867	373
William Owen	Harriet P. Armstrong	6/23/1867	376
Washington F. Pool	Francis E. Chamblee	2/23/1854	8
William L. Philips	Salens(?) Banister	12/29/1853	10
John C. Pierce	Lydia C. Harvy	2/ 5/1854	16
Edward W. Philips	Margaret A. Childress	11/27/1853	19
F. M. Philips	Jane Bennett	2/14/1854	25
John T. Pendergrass	Mary Green	8/ 6/1854	26
William Pearson	Martha Christenberry	8/10/1854	32
Benjamin H. Petit	Minerva C. Milton	7/ 4/1854	34
Willis Pirkle	Martha J. Shadburn	12/31/1854	36
John W. Pruitt	Hannah M. Rogers	1/26/1854	40
J. T. Pruitt	Nancy C. Redman	5/ 7/1854	41
Abner Pugh	Mary Samples	2/11/1855	48
Philip Pugh	Mary Ann Fields	8/ 1/1855	49
John P. Pugh	Josephine Hawkins	10/21/1855	56
William T. Pruitt	Frances E. Edmonson	3/10/1856	66
John F. Pendly	Permelia H. Cross	12/28/1856	96
Young P. Pool	Mrs. Mary A. Shields	12/24/1857	100
William Pugh	Angeline Karr	12/23/1857	100
Elias Pain	Mary C. Pain	1/14/1858	118
Henry W. Parris	Martha Webb	6/14/1856	139
William Pain	Eliza Orr	5/12/1859	142
William Putman	Harriet M. Hawkins	3/28/1859	145
Caleb W. Pierce	Martha A. Williams	8/ 3/1859	157
S. A. Pruitt	C. A. Estes	1/ 5/1860	162
Marshal A. Philips	Elizabeth Hays	1/19/1860	164
John Pugh	Nancy Pugh	5/22/1860	167
James C. Powell	S. Harris	10/28/1860	179
William H. Perry	Sarah A. Hope	8/14/1861	190
Andrew Perkle	Mary E. Philips	1/17/1861	192
Albert Pirkle	Caroline Philips	4/27/1861	192
Benjamin F. Pruett	Mary H. Readmand	1/27/1861	195
John W. Pruett	P. Pain	/29/1861	196
Richard W. Propes	Sarah J. Carroll	11/14/1861	199
J. M. Phillips	Elvira Cox	12/15/1861	203
William J. Rogers	Susan Chatham	10/22/1857	111
Larkin H. Roberts	Debby Goolsby	1/26/1858	124
Josiah Roberts	Malinda Edwards	7/18/1857	129
Warren B. Rackley	Esther Red	11/11/1858	131
James F. Russell	Margaret Hutchins	12/22/1858	132
Burwell E. Rieves	Elizabeth A. Taylor	12/22/1859	153
James D. Ramsey	Mary J. Castleberry	9/29/1859	155
Allen W. Rey	Sarah Ellard	10/ 2/1859	155
William P. Red	Caroline Porter	3/ 6/1860	166
Benjamin F. Roberts	Laura A.F. Bell	4/26/1860	167
Meshiae Red	Malita Rackley	1/30/1861	169
James Red	Nancy F. Edwards	1/13/1861	171
Henry Russell	Minerva C. Rackley	1/20/1861	187
Peter B. Rogers	Nancy J. Cape (Cope?)	1/16/1862	200
James Rakestraw	Daliah Raines	8/16/1862	209
F. M. Roberson	Martha M. Hammond	8/12/1863	217

GROOM	BRIDE	MARRIED	PAGE
Thomas J. Rusk	Jane C. Killingsworth	5/ 1/1864	231
J. H. Reese	Nancy E. Holland	6/29/1865	253
E. M. Roberts	Mary E. McAfee	6/13/1865	253
J. M. Red	Luvina D. Monroe	7/21/1865	267
W. H. H. Rogers	Vianna Cawley	11/ 5/1865	277
J. G. Red	M. C. Walls	12/31/1865	281
R. P. Roper	Mary E. Purcell	12/ 3/1865	293
Charles F. Roper	Rebecca A. Henson	10/ 9/1866	300
Thomas J. Reynolds	Mary J. Williams	7/29/1866	301
Robert N. Rogers	Sarah E. Jones	5/24/1866	316
R. P. Rogers	Eliza Jane Estes	12/23/1866	318
Lewis Roach	M. M. Martin	10/18/1866	332
Claiborn T. Roper	Martha Tallant	10/18/1866	353
M. B. Robert	M. E. Hughes	11/19/1867	371
Thomas C. Tribble	Sarah A. Green	11/28/1867	372
Wesley Stone	Elizabeth McDaniel	6/16/1853	1
Reuben Sams	Emaline Wallace	10/ 6/1853	4
John M. Stovall	Louisa Crow	7/21/1853	5
Micah W. Smith	Amy Day	9/ 1/1854	29
David Stone	Margaret McDonald	10/ 4/1854	32
Monroe M. Samples	Elizabeth Jane Phillips	12/26/1854	37
Miles M. Sutton	Harriet Hutchins	3/18/1855	43
Thomas O. Samples	Sarah J. Green	4/21/1855	43
William O. Samples	Sarah Jane Blake	8/ 7/1855	49
Alvin Snipes	Clerinda Chamblee	1/ 3/1856	61
John Smith	Martha Ann Childers	1/31/1856	63
William T. Shoemaker	Ann Stidham	1856	69
John H.C. Shirley	Sency (?) Johnson	3/ 9/1856	72
George W. Sisson	Narcissa Harris	1/21/1855	81
Samuel P. Sayler	Elizabeth Eleanor Buice	6/17/1856	83
John Samples	Mary A. Foster	5/ 1/1856	85
Joel Strickland	Sarah Taylor	4/14/1857	94
Elijah Smith	Caroline Robinson	1/22/1857	94
John N. Salter	Nancy Nelson	5/ 7/1857	97
Almasine Shands	Mary Francis	5/24/1857	99
Hardy Strickland	Ann E. Hammond	10/18/1850	102
Harrison Summerour	Mary Ann Henderson	3/11/1849	102
Asberry F. Stone	Davida C. Thompson	3/ 5/1858	111
Isaac Southern	Amanda Pearson	12/ 3/1857	113
Aaron J. Sewel	Rutha Ann Chatham	10/22/1857	114
John C. Spruce	Sarah E. Hampton	12/31/1857	121
Newton J. Shoemaker	Sarah Ashworth	1/21/1858	121
Archibald Starns	Kassy Hyde	12/26/1857	122
George W. Stovall	Rosetta Owen	1/ 6/1859	126
Jesse Samples	Jane Grimes	3/21/1858	127
Warren F. Smith	Narcis Collett	10/14/1858	128
Edward Smith	Arminda Herndon	1/14/1858	135
Calvin H. Spruce	Sarah Bailey	4/10/1859	143
J. H. Stephens	Eliza M. Parks	10/18/1859	149
Alvin Snipes	Frances E. Westbrook	8/ 2/1859	157
Alexander Smith	Sarah Millwood	3/13/1859	161
Oliver V. Strickland	Frances T. Fagan	12/ /1860	174
John M. Streetman	Emely Bagley	11/28/1860	175
Wade Smith	Elizabeth Ann Hawkins	7/ 8/1860	181
Calvin J. Sparks	Elizabeth O. Boyle	7/10/1860	185
Irvin Sewell	Mary A. Phillips	4/17/1862	196
Hardy W. Strickland	Amanda J. Right	12/12/1861	201
Lewis A. Sams	Mary Connon (Connor?)	6/16/1861	215

GROOM	BRIDE	MARRIED	PAGE
John C. Samples	Amanda A. Poss	3/11/1864	225
Lenor W. Spearman	Sarah A. Major	10/ 9/1864	233
James P. Stovall	Mary E. Owens	3/14/1865	241
Daniel Stephens, Jr.	Martha A. Rider	3/ 2/1865	244
Thomas J. Stanly	Martha A. Lummus	10/ 9/1864	246
Robert M. Simpson	Elizabeth J. Blake	8/29/1865	260
Robert P. Stokes	Mary J. Johnston	7/11/1865	264
John R. Smith	Sarah M. Whitmire	3/ 2/1865	266
William Smith	Sarah A. Westbrook	11/15/1865	269
Henry Stedmon	Mary Collins	8/24/1865	274
Francis N. Strong	Margaret Puckett	9/21/1865	279
John A. Sims	A. D. Hutchins	1/16/1866	285
John Strayhorn	Elisabeth Gravitt	5/20/1866	312
John Stone	Aleaza Strahorn	5/28/1866	315
Nathaniel A. Smith	Margret Bishop	3/20/1866	315
W. B. Strickland	Lucinda Smith	9/18/1866	318
A. N. Swinney	Nancy Burton	5/12/1865	320
Shadburn	Light	(faded)	323
W. C. Swinney	Eugenie M. Hutchins	12/27/1866	332
James Samples	Adaline Karr	11/15/1866	334
R. T. Smith	M. A. Talent	9/16/1866	338
Joel M. Sherly	Drucilla A. Lawrence	9/ 9/1866	345
Henry Clay Strickland	Nancy McAfee	8/13/1867	347
Solomon Smith	Martha Martin	10/31/1867	349
James Swinney	Eliza Hays	8/ /1867	358
John A. Shadburn	Martha A. Mashburn	6/ /1867	361
Amos Stapler	Sarah Stone	5/30/1867	361
Isaac Strickland	Mary Nichols	6/18/1866	363
Pyrenus Singleton	Mary E. Patterson	4/14/1867	366
Henry L. Shadburn	Amanda Light	2/24/1867	366
Robert N. Speer	Emly Phillips	10/12/1867	379
Jacob F. Sanders	A. C. Hutchins	1/ 5/1868	380
Samuel Stokes	H. B. Bice	3/22/1868	384
Isaac N. Samples	Frances Green	3/10/1868	388
Jacob Taylor	Charity Emaline Sexton	12/11/1853	14
Albert O. Trammel	Malinda Sanders	2/19/1854	17
Meridith R. Tidwell	Jane E. Monday	6/ 1/1854	25
Miles W. Tinsley	Eleanor Hays	7/27/1854	27
John W. Tedder	Arminda Lord	10/ 1/1854	35
Andrew J. Thomas	Martha Martin	1/10/1856	63
William J. Thrasher	Francis A. Cole	6/11/1856	67
Andrew J. Thompson	Eliza J. Dollar	5/31/1856	69
James M. Thackston	Emily E. Horton	9/21/1856	73
Francis M. Terry	Rebecca Jackson	8/26/1856	77
Josiah J. Tribble	Susan J. Tapp	2/ 8/1857	92
Wisdom Tucker	Mary Adaline Parks	8/27/1857	98
Washington Tinsley	Linney Caroline Holbrook	12/20/1857	101
Thomas J. Tinsley	Elvira Roberts	1/18/1859	142
Ransom F. Tinsley	Mary Henderson	12/ 6/1859	154
William Toney	Irena Cole	8/18/1859	160
E. B. Torrence	E. A. Black	2/ 2/1860	163
Henry Tidwell	Mrs. Judah Gravitt	11/21/1860	170
William Tidwell	Mary Jane Gravitt	7/27/1860	171
Alexander B. Thornton	Catherine V. Nicholls	8/ 2/1860	183
William C. Thornton	Martha Jane Wheeler	7/18/1861	189
William Thrasher	Winney Creamer	2/16/1862	198
Marion J. Townley	Susan A. Reid	12/18/1861	199
Newport C. Thackston	Celia A. Cockran	6/16/1861	199

GROOM	BRIDE	MARRIED	PAGE
James B. Thomas	Luisa Sutton	6/15/1862	210
John C. Tidwell	Louisiana Tate	9/27/1863	217
Joseph R. Thompson	Mrs. Mary Harris	2/24/1864	225
R. F. Tinsley	Arcadi Trible	10/ 6/1864	247
Anderson Tidwell	Mrs. Nancy Martin	3/26/1865	251
Isaac Thornton	Mary J. Otwell	6/24/1865	271
Alexander Tate	Dulcina J. Thornton	3/ /1865	251
Alfred R. Thompson	Elizabeth Hallmon	10/25/1865	272
Obdiah Tidwell	E. E. Youngblood	11/ 9/1865	275
W. J. Thompson	Martha Hunt	11/ 9/1865	278
Thomas Terry	Julia Cawley	11/12/1865	294
James P. Thompson	Mary L. Lott	8/14/1866	302
William N. Tribble	Cansady Sams	8/19/1866	306
Benjamin F. Townley	Mariah White	6/ 7/1866	309
William B. Tipp	Martha J. Wills	2/21/1867	322
John Terry	Elizabeth Cawly	3/ /1866	324
Moses Tatum	N. P. Daniel	1/15/1857	335
Francis M. Tribble	Harriet E. White	6/10/1867	337
Edmond S. Turner	Josie A.F. Edwards	2/28/1867	350
William Josephus Turner	Mary E. Thompson	3/31/1867	355
John Tolbert	Georgia Ann Cantrell	6/ 6/1867	359
Robert A.H. Thompson	Lucinda Manness	2/20/1867	364
John Tiner	Martha C. Bell	4/20/1867	368
Thomas C. Trible	Sarah A. Green	11/28/1867	372
Stephen Terry	Virginia Rogers	1/ 5/1868	380
Nathaniel E. Tuell	Adaline M. Monroe	12/25/1867	384
Wiley Thompson	----- Brown	12/25/1867	388
T. B. Tallent	Martha Pearson	2/20/1868	399
F. F. Turner	Harriet F. Owens	12/26/1867	401
John H. Thornton	Sarah C. Hammonds	3/10/1864	401
T. N. Vickory	Mary A. Sanders	12/25/1853	13
James E. Vaughan	Melinda Naylor	3/19/1854	21
Leland F. Vaughan	Martha E. Chamblee	6/ 3/1860	166
Hamilton Vaughn	Charlotte Jackson	11/23/1865	274
J. M. Whitmire	Hannah Jane Cagle	12/25/1853	8
Johnson D. Welborn	Sarah O. Shadburn	12/11/1853	9
Thomas W. Wingo	Elizabeth Baldwin	8/28/1853	11
Thomas C. Williams	Sarah E. Stovall	1/19/1854	11
David Wallis	Sarah C. Newton	1/19/1854	15
Augustin L. Woodliff	Chester L. D. Law	1/26/1854	19
Jesse Webb	Sophronia Thompson	12/ 8/1853	23
Nathan Wadkins	Sarah A. Griffin	3/25/1854	24
William P. Wingo	Mary A. Foster	3/26/1854	30
Joseph Wright	Christina Edwards	6/18/1854	35
C. H. White	Francis A.V. Angelly	1/ 4/1855	35
J. W. Wilson	Mrs. Mary E. Moor	2/28/1855	39
Martin B. Wood	Elizabeth Hollinshed	4/16/1854	41
Charles S. Wilkins	Adaline L. Broadwell	10/25/1855	57
James Walker	Letty Ann Powel	2/10/1856	63
Martin L. Wallace	Martha Ann Jefferson	5/ 4/1856	67
J. G. Wilkins	Louisa A. Philips	8/23/1855	68
James P. Wallis	Mary Green	7/ 6/1856	70
Benjamin Wofford	Martha T. Hurt	7/10/1856	71
John Williams	Margaret Croft	7/14/1856	75
Green B. Wallace	Eveline Cope	11/17/1856	77
Joel Webb	Sarah Terry	10/22/1857	98
Andrew H. Wilkie	Elizabeth J. McClure	1/ 3/1858	103
A. W. Wilkins	M. E. Barrett	3/16/1851	103

GROOM	BRIDE	MARRIED	PAGE
Jesse Wingo	Elizabeth Red	5/ 9/1858	105
John W. Wilkins	Lucy C. Cook	8/ 7/1856	106
Benjamin W. Weems	Jane Holbrook	12/27/1857	109
Pierce M. Welborn	Harriet J. Baily	12/24/1857	110
A. H. Williams	Ann Armstrong	1/10/1858	115
John L. Williams	Susan Buice	10/ 3/1858	134
William W. Webb	Eveline Miller	9/14/1856	139
R. B. Whitmire	Sarah M. Perry	3/20/1859	145
Wesley E. Westbrook	Mary Ann Garrett	5/10/1859	147
Thomas W. Wilson	M. J. Bennett	11/13/1859	149
Thomas G. White	Martha A. Pool	7/31/1859	157
John J. Wallis	Keziah K. Bruce	9/22/1859	158
Milton Westbrook	Elizabeth Holbrook	1/ 3/1858	160
John L. White	Risiah McCurley	10/14/1857	161
George F. Woodliff	Sarah E. Boyd	9/10/1858	165
Oliver Weems	Caroline Holbrook	12/20/1860	174
David M. Wilson	Manerva Tedder	1/13/1860	178
James B. White	Frances Caroline Shadburn	8/22/1861	
William S. Wood	Angeline Blankenship	8/11/1861	193
William Wade	----- M. Townley	12/11/1861	202
Eli Waldrip	Malissa A. Hendrix	12/12/1861	204
Lightner West	Sarah E. Moor	1/10/1862	206
Evin Watson	Mary E. Wiggins	2/22/1863	213
Jesse Williams	Frances A. Gravitt	8/16/1863	214
Jesse T. Wallis	Sarah Collett	8/16/1863	216
Jacob Wofford	Jane Hays	8/14/1863	217
A. P. Whitmire	Elizabeth Knight	3/ 5/1863	218
William E. Willingham	Mary A. Mashburn	12/29/1863	224
John Wallis	Manervia Martin	12/25/1864	230
Madison Williams	Mary E. Compton	11/10/1864	238
Harvy C. Wallis	Mary A. Blanton	1864	243
Thomas C. Walker	L. A. F. Brown	7/ 9/1865	248
W. R. Williams	Fannie J. Boyd	8/23/1864	256
Isaac White	Nancy A. Samples	7/31/1864	263
J. B. Wilson	Sarah A.R. Burton	4/ 9/1865	264
John A. Wilson	Mary Pruitt	10/23/1865	270
David Watts	Elizabeth Sparks	11/ 5/1865	273
James C. Whitmire	Sarah J. Stone	9/ 2/1857	277
Wiley H. Westbrook	Martha Rogers	1/21/1866	278
John W. Wright	Sarah J. Holbrook	9/28/1865	283
William P. Wheeler	Margarett A. Youngblood	2/15/1866	286
F. M. Williams	Martha Ashworth	2/ 8/1866	295
John E. Wills	Sarah Jane Thompson	3/ 1/1866	299
Elisha M. Whitmire	Mary J. Barnwell	12/21/1865	300
Marion T.W. Wallis	Martha A. Red	8/13/1866	306
William T. Walls	Mary Jane Nix	8/23/1866	306
Marvel L. Wallis	Mary A. Holbrook	9/ 9/1866	308
D. M. Walls	Louesa Glass	9/ 6/1866	314
Elias Waldrup	H. J. M. Crow	8/12/1866	316
William R. White	Mary J. Pearson	10/21/1866	318
James W. Walker	Sarah Jane Burrell	(no cert.)	320
Clinton W. Webb	Martha C. Terry	9/ /1866	324
James W. Walker	Sallie J.E. Burrell	7/ 1/1865	330
Alfred Wetherford	Partheny Willis	10/ 5/1855	331
Patrick S. Westmoreland	Malinda Edwards	12/26/1866	337
John M. Webb	Francianna P.A.Shields	8/25/1867	341
James D. Westbrook	Arillia H. Gober	8/28/1867	343
James C. Wellborn	Mary J. Shadburn	7/ 6/1866	344
William C. White	Elizabeth Bryan	9/12/1867	345

GROOM	BRIDE	MARRIED	PAGE
William R. Westbrook	Mary J. Emerson	12/23/1866	346
John A. Whitmire	Mrs. Sarah E. West	7/ 7/1867	350
William E. Westbrooks	Abia A. Read	9/ 8/1867	370
Richard R. Whitmire	Mary Susanah Thompson	1/27/1867	375
Samuel R. Whitmire	Martha E. Heard	2/10/1867	375
John W. Wooton	Sarah Ann Rolon	12/26/1867	381
Hardy W. White	Sarah C. Fincher	2/ 6/1868	394
Newton Yancy	Matilda Holbrook	6/ 8/1856	68
Robert L. Yancy	Jane Holbrook	11/29/1857	121
Elechsander Yancy	Emily Owens	11/19/1859	154
J. W. Yarber	F. A. Thornton	10/ 3/1865	255

NOTE: Only those marriages with applications have been included.
Other marriages (approximately half of book) will be abstracted
later.

Page 136
Name of Groom: Isaac M. Anderson   Date of Marriage: 9-14-1878
Residence: Bartow Co.   Name of Bride: Mary E. Hawkins
Age: 24   Residence: Forsyth Co.
Occupation: Farmer   Age: 23
Place of Birth: Union Co.   Place of Birth: Forsyth County
Father's Name: F.W. Anderson   Father's Name: Uriah Hawkins
Mother's M. Name: Mary Holiway   Mother's M. Name: Margaret Cox

Page 162
Name of Groom: John J. Anderson   Date of Marriage: 1-29-1880
Residence: Forsyth Co.   Name of Bride: Julie E. Gilbert
Age: 20   Residence: Forsyth Co.
Occupation: Farmer   Age: 18
Place of Birth: Forsyth Co.   Place of Birth: Forsyth Co.
Father's Name: James Anderson   Father's Name. S.P. Gilbert
Mother's M. Name: Calender James   Mother's M. Name: Sarah C.Riden

Page 172
Name of Groom: Olive Adams   Date of Marriage: 4-29-1880
Residence: Forsyth Co.   Name of Bride: Sarah J. Holbrook
Age: Residence: Forsyth Co.
Occupation: Farmer   Age:
Place of Birth: Walton Co.   Place of Birth: Forsyth County
Father's Name: Adams   Father's Name: Hiram Holbrook
Mother's M. Name: Mathews   Mother's M. Name: (not given)

Page 179
Name of Groom: Asberry Angling   Date of Marriage: 2-5-1880
Residence: Forsyth County   Name of Bride: Sallie J.Angling,
                                                      Wid.
Age: 23   Residence: Forsyth Co.
Occupation: Farmer   Age: 23
Place of Birth: Milton Co.   Place of Birth: Mississippi
Father's Name: H.F. Angling   Father's Name: William Parker
Mother's M. Name:Catherine Tedder Mother's M. Name: Millie _____

Page 22
Name of Groom: James I. Bennett   Date of Marriage: 6-21-1877
Residence: Forsyth Co.   Name of Bride: Julia A. Patterson
Age: 23   Residence: Forsyth Co.
Occupation: Farmer   Age: 19
Place of Birth: Forsyth Co.   Place of Birth: Forsyth Co.
Father's Name: James M. Owens   Father's Name: Hiram Patterson
Mother's M. Name: Teria Bennett   Mother's M. Name: Louisa Singleton

Page 32
Name of Groom: Isaac M. Brownlow   Date of Marriage: 4-2-1877
Residence: Forsyth Co.   Name of Bride: Caroline Huggins
Age: 50   ResidenceL Forsyth Co.
Occupation: Farmer   Age: 40
Place of Birth: Place of Birth: Jackson Co.
Father's Name: John Brownlow,Dec.   Father's Name: Green Huggins, dec.
Mother's M. Name: Susan Wimpy   Mother's M. Name: Letty Pugh

Page 86
Name of Groom: Geo.W.Bennett
Residence: Forsyth Co.
Age: 23
Occupation: Farmer
Place of Birth: Forsyth Co.
Father's Name: Sam Bennett
Mother's M. Name: Mary Bagley

Date of Marriage: 4-22-1877
Name of Bride: Francis A.Samples
Residence: Forsyth Co.
Age: 19
Place of Birth: Forsyth Co.
Father's Name: A.G.Samples
Mother's M. Name: E. Dooley

Page 37
Name of Groom: Asbury C.Blackburn
Residence: Dawson Co.
Age: 18
Occupation: Farmer
Place of Birth: Dawson Co.
Father's Name: John C.Blackburn
Mother's M. Name: Mary Reynolds

Date of Marriage: 11-18-1877
Name of Bride: Nancy Brownlow
Residence: Forsyth Co.
Age: 18
Place of Birth: Forsyth Co.
Father's Name: Obed. Brownlow
Mother's M. Name: Lucinda Guthrie

Page 41
Name of Groom: Wesley D.Benson
Residence: Forsyth Co.
Age: 20
Occupation: Farmer
Place of Birth: Forsyth Co.
Father's Name: Reuben W.Benson
Mother's M. Name: Nancy Spence

Name of Bride: Asilee Phillips
Residence: Forsyth Co.
Age: 19
Place of Birth: Forsyth Co.
Father's Name: King.D.Phillips
Mother's M. Name: Tibitha Estes
Date of Marriage: 1-31-1877

Page 59
Name of Groom: William H.Buice
Residence: Fulton Co.
Age: 22
Occupation: Merchant
Place of Birth: Cobb Co.
Father's Name: Elisha Buice
Mother's M. Name: Parker

Date of Marriage: Jan. 1878
Name of Bride: Amanda E.Buice
Residence: Forsyth Co.
Age: 25
Place of Birth: Calhoun Co., Ga.
Father's Name: Henry B.Buice
Mother's M. Name: Nancy Thouson

Page 72
Name of Groom: Monroe Bennett
Residence: Forsyth Co.
Age: 24
Occupation: Farmer
Place of Birth: Forsyth Co.
Father's Name: Berry Bennett
Mother's M. Name: Emily Adeline Martin

Date of Marriage: 1-31-1878
Name of Bride: Sarah Carrie Wallis
Residence: Forsyth Co.
Age: 19
Place of Birth: Forsyth Co.
Father's Name: Jessee Wallis
Mother's M. Name: Eliza Whitmire

Page 55
Name of Groom: Richard W. Branon
Residence: Forsyth Co.
Age: 23
Occupation: Farmer
Place of Birth: Forsyth Co.
Father's Name: Wm.R.Branon
Mother's M. Name: Mahala Pool

Date of Marriage: 10-28-1877
Name of Bride: Mrs.Victoria Smith
Maiden Name: Victoria Langley
Residence: Forsyth Co.
Age: 21
Place of Birth: Gwinnett Co.
Father's Name: William Langley
Mother's Maiden Name: Malinda __

Page 75
Name of Groom: Noah Bagly
Residence: Murray Co., Ga.
Age: 21
Occupation: Farmer
Place of Birth: Forsyth Co.
Father's Name: Wm.H.Bagly
Mother's M. Name: J. McGinnis

Date of Marriage: 1-6-1878
Name of Bride: Matilda Bagley
Residence: Forsyth Co.
Age: 19
Place of Birth: Forsyth Co.
Father's Name: Fletcher Bagley
Mother's M. Name: Susan Naler

Page 48
Name of Groom: Alonzo Buice
Residence: Forsyth Co.
Age: 24
Occupation: Farmer
Place of Birth: Spartanburg, SC
Father's Name: Elista Buice
Mother's M. Name: Margaret Hall

Date of Marriage: 2-24-1878
Name of Bride: Rebecca C.Martin
Residence: Forsyth Co.
Age: 20
Place of Birth: Forsyth Co.
Father's Name: Hesakiah Martin
Mother's M. Name: Prathenes
            Stone

Page 81
Name of Groom: J.H. Barrett
Residence: Forsyth Co.
Age: 21
Occupation: Farmer
Place of Birth: Forsyth Co.
Father's Name: William Barrett
Mother's M. Name: Martha Phillips

Date of Marriage: 5-2-1878
Name of Bride: S.E. Williams
Residence: Forsyth Co.
Age: 17
Place of Birth: Forsyth Co.
Father's Name: A.H. Wilkey
Mother's M. Name: L.A.Armstrong

Page 82
Name of Groom: William S.Butler
Residence: Forsyth Co.
Age: 21
Occupation: Med. Student
Place of Birth: Cobb Co., Ga.
Father's Name: W.T. Butler
Mother's M. Name: C.L. Wood

Date of Marriage: 6-2-1878
Name of Bride: Nancy E. Jones
Residence: Forsyth Co.
Age: 17
Place of Birth: Hall Co., GA
Father's Name: John L.Jones
Mother's M. Name: Susanah Stokes

Page 95
Name of Groom: James B.Beaver
Residence: Forsyth Co.
Age: 21
Occupation: Farmer
Place of Birth: Forsyth Co.
Father's Name: Thomas Beaver,dec.
Mother's Name: Elisabeth Thompson

Date of Marriage: 8-25-1878
Name of Bride: Mary Angaline
            Wills
Residence: Forsyth Co.
Age: 28
Place of Birth: Forsyth Co.
Father's Name: Mastive Wills,dec.
Mother's M. Name: Susan M.Spruce

Page 97
Name of Groom: J. E. Brooks
Residence: Forsyth Co.
Age: 24
Occupation: Farmer
Place of Birth: Forsyth Co.
Father's Name: Wm.Thomas Brooks
Mothers M. Name: Adaline Spence

Date of Marriage: 10-24-1878
Name of Bride: Lunie Azlee Riden
Residence: Forsyth Co.
Age: 18
Place of Birth: Gwinnett Co,Ga.
Father's Name: Hiram Parks Riden
Mother's M. Name: Lucinda A.
            Haynill

Page 114
Name of Groom: John W.Brannon
Residence: Forsyth Co.
Age: 54
Occupation: Farmer
Place of Birth: Butts Co., Ga.
Father's Name: Thos. Brannon
Mother's M. Name: Mary Wilder

Date of Marriage: 1-8-1879
Name of Bride: Martha J.Brannon
Residence: Forsyth Co.
Age: 34
Place of Birth: Forsyth Co.
Father's Name: Wm.B. Brannon
Mother's M. Name: Mahala F.Pool

Page 127
Name of Groom: Charles Banister
Residence: Forsyth Co.
Age: 18
Occupation: Farmer
Place of Birth: Forsyth Co.
Father's Name: Reason Banister
Mother's M. Name: P. Rakestraw

Date of Marriage: 9-9-1877
Name of Bride: Francis Henderson
Residence: Forsyth Co.
Age: 18
Place of Birth: Cherokee Co.
Father's Name: Enoch Henderson
Mother's M. Name: Emeline Martin

Page 134
Name of Groom: C.E. Butler
Residence: Forsyth Co.
Age: 21
Occupation: Farmer
Place of Birth:
Father's Name: John Butler
Mother's M. Name: Butler

Date of Marriage: 8-24-1879
Name of Bride: L.A. Galile
Residence: Forsyth Co.
Age: 19
Place of Birth: Habersham Co.
Father's Name: G.W. Galile
Mother's M. Name: Elizabeth
                  Hardon

Page 148
Name of Groom: J.H. Banister
Residence: Forsyth Co.
Age: 23
Occupation: Farmer
Place of Birth: Forsyth Co.
Father's Name: Powell Banister
Mother's M. Name: Eliza Dooly

Date of Marriage: 12-11-1879
Name of Bride: Rosie V.Pruett
Residence: Forsyth Co.
Age: 19
Place of Birth: Forsyth Co.
Father's Name: Enoch E.Pruett
Mother's M. Name: M.C.Albridge

Page 152
Name of Groom: Cicero C. Byrd
Residence: Forsyth Co.
Age: 23
Occupation: Farmer
Place of Birth: Hall Co.
Father's Name: John F.M. Byrd
Mother's M. Name: Mary A.Eakes

Date of Marriage: 12-21-1879
Name of Bride: Mary A. Gilbert
Residence: Forsyth Co.
Age: 21
Palce of Birth: Cherokee Co.
Father's Name: Sidney H.Gilbert,
                dec'd.
Mother's M. Name: Naricssa C.
                Gilbert

Page 149
Name of Groom: Joseph Brown
Residence: Forsyth County
Age: 17
Occupation: Farmer
Father's Name: Robert Brown
Mother's M. Name: Emeline Rogers

Date of Marriage: 12-18-1879
Name of Bride: Lueller Cannon
Age: 18
Place of Birth: Dawson Co.
Father's Name: Moses C.Cannon
Mother's M. Name: Disey Smith

Page 157
Name of Groom: James Bettis
Residence: Forsyth Co.
Age: 19
Occupation: Farmer
Place of Birth: Forsyth Co.
Father's Name: Toliver Bettis
Mother's M. Name: Martha Vicery

Date of Marriage: 1-11-1880
Name of Bride: Harret A.Patterson
Residence: Forsyth Co.
Age: 20
Place of Birth: Forsyth Co.
Father's Name: Josiah B.
              Patterson, dec'd.
Mother's M. Name: Mary B. McNeal

Page 159
Name of Groom: H.P. Bell, Jr.
Residence: Forsyth Co.
Age: 22
Occupation: Farmer
Place of Birth: Forsyth Co.
Father's Name: W.H.Bell, dec'd
Mother's M. Name: Samuella Burrell

Date of Marriage: 1-2-1880
Name of Bride: E.C. Hutchins
Residence: Forsyth Co.
Age: 20
Place of Birth: Forsyth Co.
Father's Name: Drury B.Hutchins
Mother's M. Name: Nancy J.Light

Page 178
Name of Groom: John Blake
Residence: Forsyth Co.
Age: 18
Occupation: Farmer
Place of Birth: Forsyth Co.
Father's Name: John K. Blake
Mother's M. Name: Elizabeth Blackstock

Date of Marriage: 5-30-1880
Name of Bride: Eveline Bennett
Age: 22
Place of Birth: Forsyth Co.
Father's Name: Grief Bennett
Mother's M. Name: Elisabeth H____

Page 180
Name of Groom: Francis M.Bagley
Residence: Forsyth Co.
Age: 20
Occupation: Farmer
Place of Birth: Forsyth Co.
Father's Name: Henry T.Bagley
Mother's M. Name: Annie Williams

Date of Marriage: 3-11-1880
Name of Bride: Mary L.Brannon
Residence: Forsyth Co.
Age: 16
Place of Birth: Forsyth Co.
Father's Name: Seaborn Brannon
Mother's M. Name: Nancy J.Pool

Page 183
Name of Groom: Joseph F.Barrett
Residence: Forsyth Co.
Age: 22
Occupation: Farmer
Place of Birth: Dawson Co.
Father's Name: Nandy Barrett
Mother's M. Name: Whitmire

Date of Marriage: 7-21-1878
Name of Bride: Mentoria R.Owen
Residence: Forsyth Co.
Age: 19
Place of Birth: Atlanta, Ga.
Father's Name: Jaction Owen,dec'd.
Mother's M. Name: M. Hutchen

Page 160
Name of Groom: B.F. Byrs
Residence: Dawson Co.
Age: 19
Occupation: Farmer
Place of Birth: Dawson Co.
Father's Name: John Byrs,dec'd
Mother's M. Name: Crissy Roper, dec'd

Date of Marriage: 9-2-1879
Name of Bride: Mattie Hammons
Residence: Forsyth Co.
Age: 15
Place of Birth: Dawson Co.
Father's Name: Daniel Hammons
Mother's M. Name: Mary Rolin

Page 161
Name of Groom: Robt.B.J.Burrell
Residence: Forsyth Co.
Age: 21
Occupation: Farmer
Place of Birth:
Father's Name: John H.Burress,dec
Mother's M. Name: Jane Riaves

Date of Marriage: 1-14-1880
Name of Bride: Susan E.Tatum
Residence: Forsyth Co.
Age: 18
Place of Birth: Forsyth Co.
Father's Name: Elisha Tatum
Mother's M. Name:

Page 167
Name of Groom: Geo.W.Bagwell
Residence: Forsyth Co.
Age: 22
Occupation: Farmer
Place of Birth: Forsyth Co.
Father's Name: M. Bagwell
Mother's M. Name: Harriet Stone

Date of Marriage: 1-1-1880
Name of Bride: Samantha Brooks
Residence: Forsyth Co.
Age: 17
Place of Birth: Forsyth Co.
Father's Name: Wm. T. Brooks
Mother's M. Name: Amanda Spence

Page 179
Name of Groom: Edward S.Baggely
Residence: Forsyth Co.
Age: 19
Occupation:
Place of Birth: Forsyth Co.
Father's Name: Harmon Baggely
Mother's M. Name: Anna Strickland

Date of Marriage: 4-1-1880
Name of Bride: Mrs.Callie Baggely
Residence: Forsyth Co.
Age: 23
Place of Birth:
Father's Name: Albert T____
Mother's M. Name: Sindey Sanders

Page 170
Name of Groom: P.B. Bruice
Residence: Forsyth Co.
Age: 23
Occupation: Farmer
Place of Birth: Blunt Co., AL
Father's Name: Benjamin B.Bruice
Mother's M. Name: Nancy Thompson

Date of Marriage: 2-1-1880
Name of Bride: Martha A.Moulder
Residence: Forsyth Co.
Age: 26
Place of Birth: Forsyth Co.
Father's Name: Hutson W.Moulder
Mother's M. Name: Caroline Bagley

Page 187
Name of Groom: J.T. Boling
Residence: Forsyth Co.
Age: 18
Occupation: Farmer
Place of Birth: Pickens Co,, SC
Father's Name: John Boling
Mother's M. Name: Margrate White

Date of Marriage: 10-10-1880
Name of Bride: M.J. Fowler
Residence: Forsyth Co.
Age: 17
Place of Birth: Forsyth Co.
Father's Name: W.B. Fowler
Mother's M. Name: R. Baley

Page 60
Name of Groom: John L.Cruis, Sr.
Residence: Forsyth Co.
Age: 65
Occupation: Farmer
Place of Birth: Jefferson Co.,GA
Father's Name: Jeremiah Cruis,dec'd
Mother's M. Name: Delilah Higgins, dec'd.

Date of Marriage: 11-4-1879
Name of Bride: Malinda Green
Age: 25
Place of Birth:
Residence: Forsyth Co.
Father's Name: G.W. Green, Sr.
Mother's M. Name: Page

Page 104
Name of Groom: Levi Cox
Residence: Milton Co.
Age: 21
Occupation: Farmer
Place of Birth: Milton Co.
Father's Name: Isaac Cox
Mother's M. Name: Elisabeth Morris

Date of Marriage: 12-29-1878
Name of Bride: Amanda Stephens
Residence: Forsyth Co.
Age: 17
Place of Birth: Spartanburg, SC
Father's Name: John Stephens
Mother's M. Name: Elisabeth Low

Page 135
Name of Groom: W.T. Castleberry
Residence: Forsyth Co.
Age: 24
Occupation: Farmer
Place of Birth: Forsyth Co.
Father's Name: David Castleberry
Mother's M. Name: Nancy Williams

Date of Marriage: 7-29-1879
Name of Bride: Melzone L.Reeves
Residence: Forsyth Co.
Age: 24
Place of Birth: S.C.
Father's Name: Levi Reeves
Mother's M. Name: Mily Young

Page 137
Name of Groom: Wm.J. Carter
Residence: Forsyth Co.
Occupation: Farmer
Age: 22
Place of Birth: Cherokee Co.
Father's Name: Martin Carter,dec'd
Mother's M. Name: D.C. Wain

Date of Marriage: 9-7-1879
Name of Bride: E.B. Holbrooks
Residence: Forsyth Co.
Age: 18
Place of Birth: Forsyth Co.
Father's Name: F.M. Holbrooks
Mother's M. Name: Catherine
                              Briant

Page 140
Name of Groom: James O.Cantrell
Residence: Forsyth Co.
Age: 23
Occupation: Farmer
Place of Birth: Forsyth Co.
Father's Name: Wm.H.Cantrell
Mother's M. Name: Sarah Butler

Date of Marriage: 10-9-1879
Name of Bride: Catherine Morgan
Residence: Forsyth Co.
Age: 18
Place of Birth: Gwinnett Co.
Father's Name: C.C. Morgan
Mother's M. Name: Elizabeth Davis

Page 141
Name of Groom: John Collett
REsidence: Forsyth Co.
Age: 66
Occupation: Farmer
Place of Birth: S.C.
Father's Name: Green Collett
Mother's M. Name: Caroline Red

Date of Marriage: 10-9-1879
Name of Bride: Caroline Red(?)
Residence: Forsyth Co.
Age: 36
Place of Birth: Forsyth Co.
Father's Name: Hugh Porter, dec'd
Mother's M. Name: Elizabeth
                              Garrett

Page 146
Name of Groom: Sylvestus T.
                Chamblee
Residence: Forsyth Co.
Age: 22
Occupation: Farmer
Place of Birth: Forsyth Co.
Father's Name: W.L. Chamblee
Mother's M. Name: Pool

Date of Marriage: 11-6-1879
Name of Bride: Evlie Bennett
Residence: Forsyth Co.
Age: 18
Place of Birth: Forsyth Co.
Father's Name: Jas.M.Bennett
Mother's M. Name: Mary H.Bacon

Page 149
Name of Groom: Henry Carnes
Residence: Forsyth Co.
Age: 24
Occupation:
Place of Birth: Forsyth Co.
Father's Name:
Mother's M. Name: Mary A.Carnes

Date of Marriage: 12-21-1879
Name of Bride: Emily Lamb
Residence: Forsyth Co.
Age: 21
Place of Birth: Forsyth Co.
Father's Name: Robert Lamb
Mother's M. Name: Mary Patterson

Page 150
Name of Groom: Wm. S. Crey
Residence: Forsyth Co.
Age: 22
Occupation: Farmer
Place of Birth: Forsyth Co.
Father's Name: Johnathan Crey
Mother's M. Name: Sallie Perry

Date of Marriage: 12-11-1879
Name of Bride: Mary F.Holcomb
Residence: Forsyth Co.
Age: 19
Place of Birth: Forsyth Co.
Father's Name: Harrison Edwards
Mother's M. Name: Mary Holcomb

Page 158
Name of Groom: Wm.H.Chadwick
Residence: Forsyth Co.
Age: 20
Occupation: Farmer
Place of Birth: Forsyth Co.
Father's Name: Hezkiah Shadwick
Mother's M. Name: Elizabeth Wooten

Date of Marriage: 12-18-1879
Name of Bride: Emeline Chatham
Residence: Forsyth Co.
Age: 19
Place of Birth: Forsyth Co.
Father's Name: James Chatham
Mother's M. Name: Jane Phillips

Page 181
Name of Groom: Jesse Collett
Residence: Forsyth Co.
Age: 18
Occupation: Farmer
Place of Birth: Forsyth Co.
Father's Name: John Collett
Mother's M. Name: Jane Darby

Date of Marriage: 8-12-1880
Name of Bride: Mary E. Glass
Residence: Forsyth Co.
Age: 18
Place of Birth: Dawson Co, GA
Father's Name: Wm. F. Glass
Mother's M. Name: Nancy McKeny

Page 184
Name of Groom: James O. Cawly
Residence: Faulkner Co., Ark.
Age:
Occupation: Farmer
Place of Birth: Forsyth Co.
Father's Name:
Mother's M. Name: Elizabeth Terry

Date of Marriage: 10-14-1880
Name of Bride: Mary F. Terry
Residence: Forsyth Co.
Age: 28
Place of Birth: Forsyth Co.
Father's Name: John Terry
Mother's M. Name: Martha Jackson

Page 194
Name of Groom: John M. Carter
Residence: Forsyth Co.
Age: 20
Occupation: Farmer
Place of Birth: Cherokee Co.
Father's Name: Martin Carter
Mother's M. Name: Hayne

Date of Marriage: 12-7-1880
Name of Bride: Eliza A. Hunter
Residence: Forsyth Co.
Age: 15
Place of Birth:
Father's Name: Thomas Hunter
Mother's M. Name:

Page 27
Name of Groom: Henry H.Davidson
Residence: Fulton Co.
Age: 23
Occupation: Farmer
Place of Birth: Forsyth Co.
Father's Name: Dec'd
Mother's M. Name: Mary Terry

Date of Marriage: 7-13-1877
Name of Bride: A.F. Smith
Residence: Forsyth Co.
Age: 19
Place of Birth:
Father's Name: Alpha Smith
Mother's M. Name: Mary Rogers

Page 47
Name of Groom: Henry A.Dooly
Residence: Forsyth Co.
Age: 20
Occupation: Farmer
Place of Birth: Dawson Co.
Father's Name: Wesley Dooly
Mother's M. Name: Cleopatre Phillips

Date of Marriage: 12-16-1877
Name of Bride: Martha E.Wallis
Residence: Forsyth Co.
Age: 16
Place of Birth: Forsyth Co.
Father's Name: Jesse Wallis
Mother's M. Name: Eliza Whitmire

Page 52
Name of Groom: H.C. Davis
Residence: Pickens Co, GA
Age: 22
Occupation: Farmer
Place of Birth: Pickens Co.
Father's Name: Benjamin Davis
Mother's M. Name: Nancy Blackstock

Date of Marriage: 12-9-1877
Name of Bride: Mary S.Blackstock
Residence: Forsyth Co.
Age: 16
Place of Birth: Forsyth Co.
Father's Name: Wilson N.Blackstock
Mother's M. Name: Huldah Strick-
                                    land

Page 60
Name of Groom: William H.Davidson
Residence: DeKalb Co., GA
Age: 21
Occupation: Farmer
Place of Birth: White Co., GA
Father's Name: John B.Davidson
Mother's M. Name: Amanhah Elliott

Date of Marriage: 11-27-1877
Name of Bride: Martha A.Mashburn
Residence: Forsyth Co.
Age: 21
Place of Birth: White Co.
Father's Name: John H.Mashburn
Mother's M. Name: Martha Payne

Page 66
Name of Groom: William F.Dover
Residence: Lumpkin Co., GA
Age: 23
Occupation: Horses
Place of Birth: Lumpkin Co.
Mother's M. Name: Nancy Chambers
Father's Name: William Dover

Date of Marriage: 2-24-1878
Name of Bride: Margaret E.Evans
Residence: Forsyth Co.
Age: 16
Place of Birth: Whitfield Co, GA
Father's Name: William Evans
Mother's M. Name: Betsey Willing-
                                    ham

Page 91
Name of Groom: John Dover
Residence: Lumpkin Co.
Age: 22
Occupation: Farmer
Place of Birth: Lumpkin Co.
Father's Name: William Dover
Mother's M. Name: Samanthy Chambers

Date of Marriage: 7-25-1878
Name of Bride: Elizabeth Foster
Residence: Forsyth Co.
Age: 26
Place of Birth: S.C.
Father's Name: John Foster
Mother's M. Name: Nancy G. Page

Page 102
Name of Groom: James D.Driskell
Residence: Forsyth Co.
Age: 23
Occupation: Farmer
Place of Birth: Forsyth Co.
Father's Name: Washington Driskell
                            ded'd
Mother's M. Name: Aellin Hensin

Date of Marriage: 12-1-1878
Name of Bride: Mary White
Residence: Forsyth Co.
Age: 17
Place of Birth: Anderson Co.,SC
Father's Name: John Taylor White
Mother's M. Name: Lucinda Elrod

Page 115
Name of Groom: Franklin Davis
Residence: Forsyth Co.
Age: 27
Occupation: Farmer
Place of Birth: Alabama
Father's Name: Daniel G.Davis
Mother's M. Name: Margaret Ganney(?)

Date of Marriage: 1-9-1879
Name of Bride: Cornelia Pearce
Residence: Forsyth Co.
Age: 19
Place of Birth: Forsyth Co.
Father's Name: Caleb C.Pearce
Mother's M. Name: Martha Williams

Page 122
Name of Groom: John F. Dikes
Residence: Forsyth Co.
Age: 21
Occupation: Farmer
Father's Name: John Dikes
Mother's M. Name: Sarah Daniel

Date of Marriage: 1-7-1879
Name of Bride: Sarah E.McKiney
Residence: Forsyth Co.
Age: 18
Place of Birth: Forsyth Co.
Father's Name: Lewis McKiney
Mother's M. Name: Mary Woodliff

Page 134
Name of Groom: W.J. Dean
Residence: Forsyth Co.
Age: 26
Occupation: Farmer
Place of Birth: Anderson Co., SC
Father's Name: Zariah M. Dean
Mother's M. Name: Elizabeth Cherokee

Date of Marriage: 8-31-1879
Name of Bride: M.E. Wallace
Residence: Forsyth Co.
Age: 18
Place of Birth: Forsyth Co.
Father's Name: Jessy B.Wallace
Mother's M. Name: Sarah Edwards

Page 154
Name of Groom: M.T. Dooly
Residence: Forsyth Co.
Age: 24
Occupation: Farmer
Place of Birth: Dawson Co.
Father's Name: Wesley Dooly
Mother's M. Name: Cleopatra Phillips

Date of Marriage: 11-9-1879
Name of Bride: Ellen M. Hope
Residence: Forysth Co.
Age: 18
Place of Birth: Forsyth Co.
Father's Name: James A. Hope
Mother's M. Name: Hannah Caleb

Page 170
Name of Groom: Allen Y. Day
Residence: Forsyth Co.
Age: 18
Occupation: Farmer
Place of Birth: Forsyth Co.
Father's Name: Andy Day
Mother's M. Name: Rebecca Key

Date of Marriage: 2-26-1880
Name of Bride: Elizabeth Pugh
Residence: Forsyth Co.
Age: 21
Place of Birth: Forsyth Co.
Father's Name: David Pugh
Mother's M. Name: L. Brown

Page 48
Name of Groom: Pinkney Edmonson
Residence: Forsyth Co.
Age: 22
Occupation: Farmer
Place of Birth: Forsyth Co.
Father's Name: Jas.O.Edmonson
Mother's M. Name: Mary Barker

Date of Marriage: 8-16-1877
Name of Bride: Lutitie Phillips
Residence: Forsyth Co.
Age: 18
Place of Birth: Forsyth Co.
Father's Name: Lewis B.Phillips
Mother's M. Name: Hele H.Pirkle

Page 56
Name of Groom:Cicero Columbus Elliott
Residence: Forsyth Co.
Age: 30
Occupation: Farmer
Place of Birth: White Co., GA
Father's Name: James Jackson
                        Elliott
Mother's M. Name: Matilda Freeman

Date of Marriage: 2-5-1878
Name of Bride: Sarah Dooly
Residence: Forsyth Co.
Age: 19
Place of Birth: Forsyth Co.
Father's Name: James Michael
                        Dooly
Mother's M. Name: Elizabeth
                        Taylor

Page 114
Name of Groom: E.M. Echols
Residence: Forsyth Co.
Age: 21
Occupation: Farmer
Place of Birth: Forsyth Co.
Father's Name: Eber Echols
Mother's M. Name: Francis Gant

Date of Marriage: 1-9-1879
Name of Bride: Harriet E.Terry
Residence: Forsyth Co.
Age: 21
Place of Birth: Forsyth Co.
Father's Name: John Terry
Mother's M. Name: Martha Jack-
son, dec'd

Page 42
Name of Groom: James M. Fowler
Residence: Cherokee Co.
Age: 25
Occupation: Farmer
Place of Birth: Cherokee Co.
Father's Name: James A.Fowler
Mother's M. Name: Elizabeth A. Miligan

Date of Marriage: 8-5-1877
Name of Bride: Lou V. Harris
Residence: Forsyth Co.
Age: 24
Place of Birth: Forsyth Co.
Father's Name: James G.Harris
Mother's M. Name: Martha Fowler

Page 59
Name of Groom: William J.Flowery
Residence: Forsyth Co.
Age: 19
Occupation: Farmer
Place of Birth: Cobb Co., GA
Father's Name: Geo.W. Flowery
Mother's M. Name: Emily C.Griffin

Date of Marriage: 8-5-1877
Name of Bride: Nancy J.Owens
Residence: Forsyth Co.
Age: 21
Place of Birth: Forsyth Co.
Father's Name: S.L. Owens
Mother's M. Name: Elizabeth
Griffin

Page 67
Name of Groom: Benjamin Fincher
Residence: Forsyth Co.
Age: 18
Occupation: Farmer
Place of Birth: Forsyth Co.
Father's Name: Joseph L.Fincher
Mother's M. Name: Edny F.Phillips

Date of Marriage: 8-9-1877
Name of Bride: Mary L.Edmonson
Residence: Forsyth Co.
Age: 17
Place of Birth: Forsyth Co.
Father's Name: Andrew J.Edmonson
Mother's M. Name: Mary C.Jeffers

Page 92
Name of Groom: Franklin M.Floyd
Residence: Cherokee Co.
Age: 26
Occupation: Farmer
Place of Birth:
Father's Name: Thomas Floyd
Mother's M. Name:

Date of Marriage: 8-15-1878
Name of Bride: Amanda Young
Residence: Forsyth Co.
Age: 35
Place of Birth: Cherokee Co.
Father's Name: William Young,dec.
Mother's M. Name: Rebecca Growler

Page 108
Name of Groom: Franklin C.Fiendley
Residence: Milton Co.
Age: 27
Occupation: Farmer
Place of Birth: Forsyth Co.
Father's Name: Benjamin C.Fiendley
Mother's M. Name: Julia P. Martain

Date of Marriage: 11-17-1878
Name of Bride: Amand C. Jones
Residence: Forsyth Co.
Age: 16
Place of Birth: Forsyth Co.
Father's Name: John C.Martain
Mother's M. Name: Lucy C. Dodd

Page 108
Name of Groom: Joel M.Fowler,Jr.
Residence: Forsyth Co.
Age: 23
Occupation: Farmer
Place of Birth: Forsyth Co.
Father's Name: William A.Fowler
Mother's M. Name: Eliza King

Date of Marriage: 12-17-1878
Name of Bride: Columbia C.Julian
Residence: Forsyth Co.
Age: 17
Place of Birth: Forsyth Co.
Father's Name: Baily F.Julian
Mother's M. Name: Stella Clement

Page 119
Name of Groom: Thomas E.Foster
Residence: Forsyth Co.
Age: 20
Occupation: Farmer
Place of Birth: Union Co., SC
Father's Name: William A.Foster
Mother's M. Name: Clemintin Kerr

Date of Marriage: 10-24-1878
Name of Bride: Martha M.Kemp
Residence: Forsyth Co.
Age: 25
Place of Birth: Forsyth Co.
Father's Name: Label Kemp,dec'd
Mother's M. Name: Mary Ann Ezzard

Page 151
Name of Groom: Joseph Fowler
Residence: Forsyth Co.
Age: 21
Occupation: Farmer
Place of Birth: Cherokee Co.
Father's Name: William Fowler
Mother's M. Name: Lucy Nix

Date of Marriage: 12-7-1879
Name of Bride: Lettie M. Odum
Residence: Forsyth Co.
Age: 16
Place of Birth: Forsyth Co.
Father's Name: Bery A.Odum
Mother's M. Name: Elizabeth
                          Fowler

Page 28
Name of Groom: Andrew J.Green
Residence: Forsyth Co.
Age: 23
Occupation: Farmer
Place of Birth: Forsyth Co.
Father's Name: Geo.W.Green
Mother's M. Name: Sarah A.Samples

Date of Marriage: 3-17-1877
Name of Bride: Missouri E.Rolins
Residence: Forsyth Co.
Age: 19
Place of Birth: Forsyth Co.
Father's Name: James A.Rollins
Mother's M. Name: Catherine
                          Brannon

Page 67
Name of Groom: Dr. Samuel Glover
Residence: Forsyth Co.
Age: 20
Occupation: Farmer
Place of Birth: Whitfield Co, GA
Father's Name: Milz W. Glover
Mother's M. Name: Agnes Bagley

Date of Marriage: 1-20-1878
Name of Bride: Georgia A.Fagan
Residence: Forsyth Co.
Age: 18
Place of Birth: Forsyth Co.
Father's Name: Geo.W. Fagan
Mother's M. Name: Elizabeth
                          Bagley

Page 69
Name of Groom: Jasper Gravitt
Residence: Forsyth Co.
Age: 24
Occupation: Farmer
Place of Birth: Forsyth Co.
Father's Name: John B.Gravitt
Mother's M. Name: Anna Gravitt

Date of Marriage: 4-15-1877
Name of Bride: Martha Youngblood
Residence: Forsyth Co.
Age: 20
Place of Birth: Forsyth Co.
Father's Name: James W.Youngblood
Mother's M. Name: Ellener Allen

Page 74
Name of Groom: Joseph F.Garner
Residence: Cherokee Co., GA
Age: 23
Occupation: Farmer
Place of Birth: Meron Co., GA
Father's Name: Geo.Washington
                          Garner
Mother's M. Name: ____Jane Osborn

Date of Marriage: 1-22-1878
Name of Bride: Frances Rosalee
                          Holbrook
Residence: Forsyth Co.
Age: 21
Place of Birth: Forsyth Co.
Father's Name: William T.Holbrook
Mother's M. Name: Elmander
                          Wheeler

Page 77
Name of Groom: William M.Glover
Residence: Forsyth Co.
Age: 26
Occupation: Farmer
Place of Birth: Whitfield Co., GA
Father's Name: Wily Glover
Mother's M. Name: Azzie Bagley

Date of Marriage: 11-6-1879
Name of Bride: Susanah Bagley
Residence: Forsyth Co.
Age: 18
Place of Birth: Forsyth Co.
Father's Name: G.W. Fagan
Mother's M. Name: Lucy Bagley

Page 78
Name of Groom: Newton S.Gravitt
Residence: Forsyth Co.
Age: 21
Occupation: Farmer
Place of Birth: Forsyth Co.
Father's Name: John B.Gravitt
Mother's M. Name: A. Gravitt

Date of Marriage: 11-8-1877
Name of Bride: Columbia S.Samples
Residence: Forsyth Co.
Age: 21
Place of Birth: Forsyth Co.
Father's Name: Thomas C.Samples
Mother's M. Name: Sarah J.Green

Page 93
Name of Groom: Alford G.Gravitt
Residence: Forsyth Co.
Age: 64
Occupation:
Place of Birth: Jackson Co., GA
Father's Name: William Gravitt
Mother's M. Name: Mary Hammond

Date of Marriage: 9-1-1878
Name of Bride: Sarah Tallant
Age: 39
Place of Birth: Forsyth Co.
Father's Name: Thomas Tallant
Mother's M. Name: Nancy Collett

Page 118
Name of Groom: W.R. Gazaway
Residence: Forsyth Co.
Age: 22
Occupation: Farmer
Place of Birth: Forsyth Co.
Father's Name: John G.Gazaway
Mother's M. Name: Ritha A.Attison

Date of Marriage: 1-26-1879
Name of Bride: Mary M.Pilcher
Residence: Forsyth Co.
Age: 21
Place of Birth: Fannin Co., GA
Father's Name: Geo. Pilcher
Mother's M. Name: Sallie Woodall

Page 194
Name of Groom: Lawrence Gobbe
                    (Gable?)
Residence: Forsyth Co.
Age: 24
Occupation: Farmer
Place of Birth: Habersham Co., GA
Father's Name: Geo. W.Gob-e(?)
Mother's M. Name: Elizabeth Horton

Date of Marriage: 10-7-1880
Name of Bride: Addie Mullis
Residence: Forsyth Co.
Age: 20
Place of Birth: Union Co., NC
Father's Name: James Mullis,
                    dec'd
Mother's M. Name: Alice Moor

Page 24
Name of Groom: Eli S. Harris
Residence: Forsyth Co.
Age: 21
Occupation: Farmer
Place of Birth: Forsyth Co.
Father's Name: Wm.Wesly Harris
Mother's M. Name: Martha Adalizer
                    Julian

Date of Marriage: 8-20-1876
Name of Bride: Sarah Pauline
                    Bruton
Residence: Forsyth Co.
Age: 18
Place of Birth: Forsyth Co.
Father's Name: Alberry Bruton
Mother's M. Name: Elmina Caruth

Page 32
Name of Groom: Thomas A.Holland
Residence: Forsyth Co.
Age: 21
Occupation: Farmer
Place of Birth: Hall Co., GA
Father's Name: Arch B.Holland
Mother's M. Name: Anna Luther

Date of Marriage: 3-23-1877
Name of Bride: Mary A.Martin
Residence: Forsyth Co.
Age:
Place of Birth: Forsyth Co.
Father's Name: Absalom Martin,
                 dec'd
Mother's M. Name:

Page 38
Name of Groom: L.L. Harwell
Residence: Forsyth Co.
Age: 22
Occupation: Farmer
Place of Birth: Jackson Co., GA
Father's Name: Frederick Harwell
Mother's M. Name: Jane Hodges

Date of Marriage: 3-7-1877
Name of Bride: Margaret Secret
Residence: Forsyth Co.
Age: 17
No other information

Page 40
Name of Groom: James R.Henderson
Residence: Forsyth Co.
Age: 23
Occupation; Farmer
Place of Birth: Hall Co., GA
Father's Name: Albert H.Henderson
Mother's M. Name: Charlott Black

Date of Marriage: 12-16-1877
Name of Bride: Allie Ezzart
Residence: Forsyth Co.
Age: 18
Place of Birth: Forsyth Co.
Father's Name: John L.Ezzard
Mother's M. Name: Mahaly Bettis

Page 45
Name of Groom: Henry L.Hawkins
Residence: Forsyth Co.
Age: 26
Occupation: Teacher
Place of Birth: Forsyth Co.
Father's Name: Frederick H.Hawkins
Mother's M. Name: Elizabeth Brannon,dec'd

Date of Marriage: 12-9-1877
Name of Bride: Martha A.Foster
Residence: Forsyth Co.
Age: 18
Place of Birth: Forsyth Co.
Father's Name: Ransom E.Foster
Mother's M. Name: Kindness E.
                Jones

Page 46
Name of Groom: William E.Henderson
Residence: Forsyth Co.
Age: 21
Occupation: Farmer
Place of Birth: Dawson Co., GA
Father's Name: Alfred H.Henderson
Mother's M. Name: Lettie Black

Date of Marriage: 1-9-1878
Name of Bride: Harret A.E.Taylor
Residence: Forsyth Co.
Age: 16
Place of Birth: Dawson Co., GA
Father's Name: John M. Taylor
Mother's M. Name: Frances E.
                Stripland

Page 51
Name of Groom: Lewis J. Hurt
Residence: Forsyth Co.
Age: 22
Occupation: Farmer
Place of Birth: Forsyth Co.
Father's Name: Thomas W.Hurt
Mother's M. Name: Lucy A. Burris

Date of Marriage: 11-29-1877
Name of Bride: Georgia A.Otwell
Age: 21
Residence: Forsyth Co.
Place of Birth: Forsyth Co.
Father's Name: Joseph C.Otwell
Mother's M. Name: Samples

Page 62
Name of Groom: Nathan S.Higgins
Residence: Forsyth Co.
Age: 18
Occupation: Farmer
Place of Birth: Forsyth Co.
Father's Name: James D.Higgins
Mother's M. Name: Caroline L.Tribble

Date of Marriage: 9-23-1877
Name of Bride: Victoria B.Wingo
Residence: Forsyth Co.
Age: 18
Place of Birth: Forsyth Co.
Father's Name: William P.Wingo
Mother's M. Name: Mary Foster

Page 63
Name of Groom: H.H. Howard
Residence: Dawson Co., GA
Age: 21
Occupation: Farmer
Place of Birth: Forsyth Co., GA
Father's Name: Thomas B.Howard,dec
Mother's M. Name: Martha E.Crane

Date of Marriage: 12-20-1877
Name of Bride: Julia A.Bennett
Residence: Forsyth Co.
Age: 20
Place of Birth: Forsyth Co.
Father's Name: Berry Bennett
Mother's M. Name: Emily Martin

Page 80
Name of Groom: Hiram K.Hughes
Residence: Forsyth Co.
Age: 23
Occupation: Farmer
Place of Birth: Forsyth Co.
Father's Name: Kenedy Hughes,dec'd
Mother's M. Name: M.A. Burtz

Date of Marriage: 6-19-1878
Name of Bride: Epsey C.Wheeler
Residence: Forsyth Co.
Age: 23
Place of Birth: Forsyth Co.
Father's Name: James Wheeler
Mother's M. Name: R.A.Davenport

Page 85
Name of Groom: Ancel Hide
Residence: Forsyth Co.
Age: 22
Occupation: Farmer
Place of Birth: Pickens Co., GA.
Father's Name: Ancel W. Hide
Mother's M. Name: Elizabeth Holland

Date of Marriage: 4-11-1878
Name of Bride: Rebecca Garrett
Residence: Forsyth Co.
No other information

Page 89
Name of Groom: James J. Heard
Residence: Forsyth Co.
Age: 21
Occupation: Farmer
Place of Birth: Pickens Co., SC
Father's Name: William R.Heard
Mother's M. Name: Lettie Alexander

Date of Marriage: 4-9-1878
Name of Bride: Samantha J.Fowler
Residence: Forsyth Co.
Age: 19
Place of Birth: Forsyth Co.
Father's Name: D.H. Fowler
Mother's M. Name: Drucilla L.
                              Smith

Page 98
Name of Groom: Mathew Brooks Hooper
Residence: Forsyth Co.
Age: 61
Occupation: Farmer
Place of Birth: Habersham Co., GA
Father's Name: Mathew B.Hooper,Sr
                dec'd.
Mother's M. Name: Gincy Laine

Date of Marriage: 9-8-1878
Name of Bride: Sarah Elizabeth
                              Williams
Residence: Forsyth Co.
Age: 40
Place of Birth: Rabun Co., GA
Father's Name: Thomas C. Williams
Mother's M. Name: Malinda Jones

Page 107
Name of Groom: James A.Hutchins
Age: 24
Occupation: Farmer
Place of Birth: Forsyth Co.
Father's Name: Josiah Hutchins,
                dec'd
Mother's M. Name: Lillie Nelson,
                dec'd

Date of Marriage: 12-19-1878
Name of Bride: E.Ema Hutchins
Residence: Forsyth Co.
Age: 22
Place of Birth: Forsyth Co.
Father's Name: Almon G.
                Hutchins, dec'd
Mother's M. Name: Adaline M.
                Swilling

Page 113
Name of Groom: John W. Henson
Residence: Forsyth Co.
Age: 70
Occupation: Farmer
Place of Birth: Benford Co., NC
Father's Name: Jones Miller
Mother's M. Name: Sarah Hanson

Date of Marriage: 11-24-1878
Name of Bride: Elizabeth Aascen
Maiden Name: Manning
Age: 45
No further information

Page 120
Name of Groom: Walker D.Hughes
Residence: Forsyth Co.
Age: 21
Occupation: Farmer
Place of Birth: Pickens Dist.,SC
Father's Name: Andy Hughes
Mother's M. Name: Lucinda Ellis

Date of Marriage: 2-2-1879
Name of Bride: Augusta O.Carouth
Residence: Forsyth Co.
Age: 18
Place of Birth: Forsyth Co.
Father's Name: Ross A.Carouth,
                     dec'd
Mother's M. Name: Georgia A.Bell

Page 126
Name of Groom: Wm.Davis Humphrey
Residence: Forsyth Co.
Age: 41
Occupation: Brick mason
Place of Birth: Forsyth Co.
Bather's Name: William Humphrey
Mother's M. Name: Ruth Davis

Date of Marriage: 3-27-1879
Name of Bride: M.A.Francis Bagley
Maiden Name: Medlock
Residence: Forsyth Co.
Age: 18
Place of Birth: Forsyth Co.
Father's Name: James M.Medlock
Mother's M. Name: Are.Strickland

Page 133
Name of Groom: Leander Hood
Residence: Forsyth Co.
Age: 20
Occupation: Farmer
Place of Birth: Forsyth Co.
Father's Name: William Moor
Mother's Name: Francis Moor

Date of Marriage: 7-31-1879
Name of Bride: A.L. Martin
Residence: Forsyth Co.
Age: 28
Place of Birth: Forsyth Co.
Father's Name: Jeptha Martin
Mother's M. Name: Rachel Kelly

Page 138
Name of Groom: Lewis F. Hill
Residence: Dawson Co.
Age: 24
Occupation: Farmer
Place of Birth: Dawson Co.
Father's Name: Anderson H.Hill
Mother's M. Name: Marcell Barrett

Date of Marriage: 11-15-1877
Name of Bride: Martha Frances
                     Roach
Residence: Forsyth Co.
Age: 19
Place of Birth: Forsyth Co.
Father's Name: William Roach
Mother's M. Name: Nancy Cook

Page 138
Name of Groom: Lawson G.Hawkins
Residence: Forsyth Co.
Age: 19
Occupation: Farmer
Place of Birth: Forsyth Co.
Father's Name: F.M. Hawkins
Mother's M. Name: Brannon

Date of Marriage: 9-8-1879
Name of Bride: Martha J.Wingo
Residence: Forsyth Co.
Age: 15
Place of Birth: Forsyth Co.
Father's Name: William P.Wingo
Mother's M. Name: Mary A.Foster

Page 143
Name of Groom: Elijah Holland
Residence: Forsyth Co.
Age: 45
Occupation: Farmer
Place of Birth: Hall Co.
Father's Name: Arch Holland,dec'd
Mother's M. Name: Nancy Puckett

Date of Marriage: 10-21-1879
Name of Bride: Renia Garrett
Residence: Forsyth Co.
Age: 21
Place of Birth: Forsyth Co.
Father's Name: Asa Garrett
Mother's M. Name: Gutherie

Page 144
Name of Groom: Andrew C.Hughes
Residence: Forsyth Co.
Age: 55
Occupation: Farmer
Place of Birth: Pickens Co., SC
Father's Name: James W.Hughes
Mother's M. Name: Jane Smith

Date of Marriage: 6-22-1879
Name of Bride: Mary Jane Hope
Residence: Forsyth Co.
Age: 35
Place of Birth: Forsyth Co.
Father's Name: James A. Hope
Mother's M. Name: Nancy Cobb,
                            dec'd

Page 147
Name of Groom: S.O.C. Hood
Residence: Forsyth Co.
Age: 22
Occupation: Farmer
Place of Birth: Dawson Co.
Father's Name: Jessy Hood, dec'd
Mother's M. Name: Mary A.Howard

Date of Marriage: 11-16-1879
Name of Bride: Francis C.Whitmire
Residence: Forsyth Co.
Age: 21
Place of Birth: Forsyth Co.
Father's Name: Elias Whitmire
Mother's M. Name: Elzia Owen

Page 154
Name of Groom: Wady T. Hyde
Residence: Forsyth Co.
Age: 35
Occupation: Farmer
Place of Birth: Pickens Co., SC
Father's Name: Ancil Hyde
Mother's M. Name: Holland

Date of Marriage: 11-9-1879
Name of Bride: Mary Stephens
Residence: Forsyth Co.
Age: 23
Place of Birth: Spartanburg, SC
Father's Name: John Stephens
Mother's M. Name: Elizabeth Low

Page 168
Name of Groom: George W.Hendrix
Residence: Forsyth Co.
Age: 20
Occupation: Farmer
Place of Birth: Cherokee Co.
Father's Name: James W.Hendrix
Mother's M. Name: Mary A. Ledbetter

Date of Marriage: 2-22-1880
Name of Bride: Celia Galaway
Residence: Forsyth Co.
Age: 18
Place of Birth: Forsyth Co.
Father's Name: Robt. Galaway
Mother's M. Name: Mahalia Pierson

Page 172
Name of Groom: Robt.O.Harrison
Residence: Forsyth Co.
Age: 19
Occupation: Farmer
Place of Birth: Franklin Co., GA
Father's Name: Martin Harrison,dec
Mother's M. Name: Nancy Jenkins

Date of Marriage: 3-11-1880
Name of Bride: Mary M.M. Reed
Residence: Forsyth Co.
Age: 15
Place of Birth: Forsyth Co.
Father's Name: A.H. Reed
Mother's M. Name: Martha Holbrook

Page 174
Name of Groom: James W.Hardian
Residence: Forsyth Co.
Age: 22
Occupation: Merchant
Place of Birth: Fulton Co.
Father's Name: James W.Hardian
Mother's M. Name: Mary F. Bacon

Date of Marriage: 4-23-1880
Name of Bride: Mary E.Clinkscales
Residence: Forsyth Co.
Age: 18
Place of Birth: Gordon Co.
Father's Name: W.Clinkscales
Mother's M. Name: M.E. Walker

Page 177
Name of Groom: H.J. Hood
Residence: Forsyth Co.
Age: 20
Occupation: Farmer
Place of Birth: Dawson Co.
Father's Name: Winchester Hood
Mother's M. Name: Jane Shelton

Date of Marriage: 2-23-1880
Name of Bride: Martha Chastain
Residence: Forsyth Co.
Age: 20
Place of Birth: Gilmer Co.
Father's Name: James W.Chastain
Mother's M. Name: E.C. Clayton

Page 179
Name of Groom: Julious W.Howell
Residence: Milton Co., GA
Age: 27
Occupation: Merchant
Place of Birth: Macon Co., NC
Father's Name: W.M. Howell
Mother's M. Name: Sarah Love, dec'd

Date of Marriage: 5-2-1880
Name of Bride: Norah Strickland
Residence: Forsyth Co.
Age: 16
Place of Birth: Forsyth Co.
Father's Name: Joel Strickland
Mother's M. Name: Sarah Taylor

Page 182
Name of Groom: Marcus L.Hacker
Residence: Forsyth Co.
Age: 23
Occupation: Merchant
Place of Birth: Cherokee Co.
Father's Name: Larken Hacken
Mother's M. Name: Martha E.Freeman

Date of Marriage: 7-7-1880
Name of Bride: Martha Satterfield
Residence: Forsyth Co.
Age: 19
Place of Birth: White Co., GA
Father's Name: W.T. Satterfield
Mother's M. Name: S.C. Huff

Page 164
Name of Groom: John W. Ivy
Residence: Forsyth Co.
Age: 18
Occupation: Farmer
Place of Birth: Hall Co.
Father's Name: Samuel J.Ivy, dec'd
Mother's M. Name: Sarah Butler, dec'd

Date of Marriage: 11-30-1879
Name of Bride: Mary A.Mayfield
Residence: Forsyth Co.
Age: 18
Place of Birth: Forsyth Co.
Father's Name: Balis Mayfield
Mother's M. Name: Harriett H.
                                    Wingo

Page 47
Name of Groom: John Henry Jones
Residence: Forsyth Co.
Age: 26
Occupation: Farmer
Father's Name: John Jones, Sr.
Mother's M. Name: Susanna Stokes

Date of Marriage: 12-6-1877
Name of Bride: Hannah Foster
Residence: Forsyth Co.
Age: 20
Place of Birth:
Father's Name: John Foster
Mother's M. Name: Nancy Page

Page 124
Name of Groom: Homer V. Jones
Residence: Gwinnett Co., GA
Age: 21
Occupation: R.R. Fireman
Place of Birth: Gwinnett Co.
Father's Name: Thomas H.Jones
Mother's M. Name: Susan E.Hoyle

Date of Marriage: 2-25-1879
Name of Bride: Mary E. James
Residence: Cumming, GA
Age: 17
Place of Birth: Forsyth Co.
Father's Name: John W. James
Mother's M. Name: Margaret J.
                                    Phillips

Page 163
Name of Groom: J.W. James
Residence: Forsyth Co.
Age: 18
Occupation: Farmer
Place of Birth: Forsyth Co.
Father's Name: Robt.James, dec'd
Mother's M. Name: Clarinda May____

Date of Marriage: 2-12-1880
Name of Bride: Mollie Holbrook
Residence: Forsyth Co.
Age: 16
Place of Birth: Forsyth Co.
Father's Name: Rae Allen
Mother's M. Name: Margaret
                                    Holbrook

Page 182
Name of Groom: Ervin Johnston
Residence: Forsyth Co.
Age: 21
Occupation: Miner
Place of Birth:Trancilvaine Co.,NC
Father's Name: William Johnson
Mother's M. Name: Sally Jones

Date of Marriage: 7-14-1880
Name of Bride: Malinda Padgett
Residence: Forsyth Co.
Age: 21
Place of Birth: Pickens Co., GA
Father's Name: Cary G. Padgett
Mother's M. Name: Mary Jones

Page 186
Name of Groom: John L.Johnson
Residence: Forsyth Co.
Age: 26
Occupation: Farmer
Place of Birth: Gwinnett Co.
Father's Name: Jasper Johnson,dec'd
Mother's M. Name: Drucilla Kyle

Date of Marriage: 10-3-1880
Name of Bride: Lousa N.Monday
Residence: Forsyth Co.
Age: 18
Place of Birth: Hall Co., GA
Father's Name: B. Monday
Mother's M. Name: E.Shadburn

Page 197
Name of Groom: L.A. Jones
Residence: Forsyth Co.
Age: 20
Occupation: Farmer
Place of Birth: Forsyth Co.
Father's Name: John L. Jones
Mother's M. Name: Dawnkoss (?)

Date of Marriage: 11-13-1880
Name of Bride: Mary L. Crow
Age: 18
Place of Birth: Forsyth Co.
Residence: Forsyth Co.
Father's Name: Isaac Crow
Mother's M. Name: Alsy Stovall

Page 33
Name of Groom: Nathaneal Key
Residence: Forsyth Co.
Age: 17
Occupation: Farmer
Place of Birth: Forsyth Co.
Father's Name: William Key,Sr.dec
Mother's M. Name: Arminda Smith

Date of Marriage: 8-8-1877
Name of Bride: Eveline Barrett
Residence: Forsyth Co.
Age: 17
Place of Birth:
Father's Name: Jack Barrett
Mother's M. Name: Henrietta
                              Garmany

Page 51
Name of Groom: James E.Keith
Residence: Cherokee Co.
Age: 20
Occupation: Farmer
Place of Birth: Cherokee Co.
Father's Name: Martin Keith
Mother's M. Name: Sarah Wilbanks

Date of Marriage: 12-28-1877
Name of Bride: Elizabeth A.
                              Sizemore
Residence: Forsyth Co.
Age: 23
Place of Birth: Forsyth Co.
Father's Name: John L.Cartright
Mother's M. Name: Abby Sizemore

Page 53
Name of Groom: Jackson Kemp
Residence: Forsyth Co.
Age: 32
Occupation: Farmer
Place of Birth: Forsyth Co.
Father's Name: Maswell Kemp,dec'd
Mother's M. Name: Mary Ezzard

Date of Marriage: 3-14-1878
Name of Bride: Margret E.Roges
Residence: Forsyth Co.
Age: 29
Place of Birth: Forsyth Co.
Father's Name: Simeon P.Roges
Mother's M. Name: Margret Pickens

Page 54
Name of Groom: James A. Kelly
Residence: Forsyth Co.
Age: 20
Occupation: Farmer
Place of Birth: Cherokee Co., GA
Father's Name: A.J. Kelly
Mother's M. Name: Julia Holbrook, dec'd

Date of Marriage: 1-31-1878
Name of Bride: Frances Hawkins
Residence: Forsyth Co.
Age: 20
Place of Birth: Forsyth Co.
Father's Name: F. Hawkins
Mother's M. Name: Elizabeth
                              Brannon

Page 121
Name of Groom: John W.Kemp
Residence: Forsyth Co.
Age: 19
Occupation: Farmer
Place of Birth: Forsyth Co.
Father's Name: A.M. Kemp
Mother's M. Name: A.J. Kemp

Date of Marriage: 2-13-1879
Name of Bride: Luella M.Major
Residence: Forsyth Co.
Age: 19
Place of Birth: Forsyth Co.
Father's Name: Dannal P.Major
Mother's M. Name: Martha Rain-
                              Water

Page 33
Name of Groom: Leroy P.Lockhart
Residence: Cumming
Age:
Occupation: Merchant
Place of Birth:
Father's Name: B.J. Lockhart
Mother's M. Name: Sarah M. McEatchen

Date of Marriage: 2-23-1877
Name of Bride: Rutha A.McAfee
Residence: Cumming
Age:
Place of Birth: Forsyth Co.
Father's Name: Elijah C.McAfee
Mother's M. Name: Emily C.
                              Thompson

Page 41
Name of Groom: Joseph B.Lewis
Residence: Forsyth Co.
Age: 19
Occupation: Farmer
Father's Name: Elsy W.Lewis
Mother's M. Name: Martha A.Hawkins
Place of Birth: Forsyth Co.

Date of Marriage: 2-25-1877
Name of Bride: Ellen McGinley
Residence: Forsyth Co.
Age: 19
Place of Birth: Forsyth Co.
Father's Name: Barney McGinly
Mother's M. Name: Suzan Fitzibon

Page 42
Name of Groom: Dr. Thomas Lipscomb
Residence: Forsyth Co.
Age: 25
Occupation: Physician
Place of Birth: Hall Co.
Father's Name: Smith Lipscomb
Mother's M. Name: Nancy Pool. dec'd

Date of Marriage: 10-18-1877
Name of Bride: Mary A. Sams
Residence: Forsyth Co.
Age: 16
Place of Birth: Forsyth Co.
Father's Name: Wm.N. Sams
Mother's M. Name: Emily Baker

Page 68
Name of Groom: James F.Lummus
Residence: Forsyth Co.
Age: 21
Occupation: Farmer
Place of Birth: Forsyth Co.
Father's Name: Andrew J.Lummus
Mother's M. Name: Charity Baker

Date of Marriage: 1-20-1877
Name of Bride: Lenora Barrett
Residence: Forsyth Co.
Age: 19
Place of Birth:
Father's Name: John A.Barrett
Mother's M. Name: Malinda Walker

Page 96
Name of Groom: Daniel Ledbetter
Residence: Forsyth Co.
Age: 38
Occupation: Farmer
Place of Birth: Forsyth Co.
Father's Name: Moses Ledbetter
Mother's M. Name: Pollie Harmon

Date of Marriage: 9-5-1878
Name of Bride: Mary J. Smith
Residence: Forsyth Co.
Age: 25
Place of Birth: S.C.
Father's Name: James M. Smith
Mother's M. Name: Hulday Skelton

Page 105
Name of Groom: J.B. Lewis
Residence: Forsyth Co.
Age: 21
Occupation: Farmer
Place of Birth: Forsyth Co.
Father's Name: L.W. Lewis
Mother's M. Name: Martha Hawkins

Date of Marriage: 12-8-1878
Name of Bride: Minnie Hawkins
Residence: Forsyth Co.
Age: 19
Place of Birth: Forsyth Co.
Father's Name: John S.Hawkins
Mother's M. Name: Nancy E.Lewis

Page 110
Name of Groom: Joseph C.Light
Residence: Forsyth Co.
Age: 29
Occupation: Farmer
Place of Birth: Forsyth Co.
Father's Name: John Russell Light
Mother's M. Name: Christian Morgan

Date of Marriage: 12-12-1878
Name of Bride: Leah S. Rolin
Residence: Forsyth Co.
Age: 19
Place of Birth: Forsyth Co.
Father's Name: Tilmon R.
Mother's M. Name: Mahalah Bennett

Page 133
Name of Groom: Franklin P.Lewis
Residence: Forsyth Co.
Age: 22
Occupation: Farmer
Place of Birth: Forsyth Co.
Father's Name: Elsey W. Lewis
Mother's M. Name: Martha Hawkins

Date of Marriage: 7-20-1879
Name of Bride: Mattie Neise
Residence: Forsyth Co.
Age: 18
No further information

Page 146
Name of Groom: Charles A.Lowe
Residence: Forsyth Co.
Age: 22
Occupation: Farmer
Place of Birth: Forsyth Co.
Father's Name: Joseph Lowe
Mother's M. Name: Virginia Jones

Date of Marriage: 1-22-1879
Name of Bride: Mintoria E.Petyjohn
Residence: Forsyth Co.
Age: 22
Place of Birth: Forsyth Co.
Father's Name: Jacob Petyjohn
Mother's M. Name: Mary Whitner

Page 158
Name of Groom: E.C. Loggin
Residence: Forsyth Co.
Age: 23
Occupation: Farmer
Place of Birth: Banks Co., GA
Father's Name: James Loggin
Mother's M. Name: Rebecca E. Edward

Date of Marriage: 1-19-1880
Name of Bride: J.O. Hope
Residence: Forsyth Co.
Age: 19
Place of Birth: Forsyth Co.
Father's Name: Ira G.Hope
Mother's M. Name: Mary A.
                                Holland

Page 168
Name of Groom: Western E.Leach
Residence: Forsyth Co.
Age: 21
Occupation: Farmer
Place of Birth: Gilmer Co., GA
Father's Name: John Leach
Mother's M. Name: Darcus Suggs

Date of Marriage: 1-4-1880
Name of Bride: Addis Jane Gravett
Residence: Forsyth Co.
Age: 22
Place of Birth: Forsyth Co.
Father's Name: Ruben Gravett
Mother's M. Name: Nancy Tidwell

Page 169
Name of Groom: Benjamin Lamb
Residence: Forsyth Co.
Age: 21
Occupation: Farmer
Place of Birth: Forsyth Co.
Father's Name: Robert Lamb
Mother's M. Name: Mary Patterson

Date of Marriage: 2-22-1880
Name of Bride: Emly C.Holtzclaw
Residence: Forsyth Co.
Age:
Place of Birth: Forsyth Co.
Father's Name: John Holtzclaw
Mother's M. Name: Elizabeth
                                Whitmire

Page 181
Name of Groom: Lewis J.Ledbetter
Residence: Forsyth Co.
Age: 29
Occupation: Farmer
Place of Birth: Dawson Co.
Father's Name: Lewis J.Ledbetter
Mother's M. Name: Martha Hill

Date of Marriage: 7-25-1880
Name of Bride: Martha Doly
Residence: Forsyth Co.
Age: 16
Place of Birth: Forsyth Co.
Father's Name: Josiah M.Doly
Mother's M. Name: Elizabeth
                          Taylor

Page 36
Name of Groom: Absalom Martin
Residence: Dawson Co.
Age: 63
Occupation: Farmer
Place of Birth: S.C.
Father's Name: Benjamin Martin
Mother's M. Name: Paline Cantrel

Date of Marriage: 12-27-1877
Name of Bride: Mary Botanna Ellis
Residence: Forsyth Co.
Age: 22
Place of Birth: Pickens Co., SC
Father's Name: Benj.Ellis, dec'd
Mother's M. Name: A.L. Hughes

Page 44
Name of Groom: Green Wells McCollum
Residence: Milton Co.
Age: 22
Occupation: Farmer
Place of Birth: Milton Co.
Father's Name: John B.McCollum
Mother's M. Name: Saphrona Wells

Date of Marriage: 12-6-1877
Name of Bride: Mary E.Bennett
Residence: Forsyth Co.
Age: 17
Place of Birth: Forsyth Co.
Father's Name: William Bennett
Mother's M. Name: Elizabeth
                          Crane

Page 53
Name of Groom: Crosby Miller
Residence: Dawson Co.
Age: 23
Occupation: Farmer
Place of Birth: Pickens Co., SC
Father's Name: Samuel Neal Miller
Mother's M. Name: Emily Arnold

Date of Marriage: 12-20-1877
Name of Bride: Mary R. Ando
Residence: Forsyth Co.
Age: 17
Place of Birth: Hall Co., GA
Father's Name: Robt. E. Ando
Mother's M. Name:

Page 57
Name of Groom: Wm.B.Millwood
Residence: Forsyth Co.
Age: 23
Occupation: Farmer
Place of Birth: Union Co., SC
Father's Name: Abraham J.Millwood
Mother's M. Name: Mary Davis

Date of Marriage: 3-1-1877
Name of Bride: Ella Martin
Maiden Name: Christian
Residence: Forsyth Co.
Age: 29
Place of Birth: Georgetown, ___
Father's Name: Nicholas Christian
Mother's M. Name: Margaret Wilson

Page 61
Name of Groom: James I.Milford
Residence: Forsyth Co.
Age: 25
Occupation: Farmer
Place of Birth:
Father's Name: James Milford,dec'd
Mother's M. Name: Elenor Thornton

Date of Marriage: 5-5-1877
Name of Bride: Nancy Owens
Maiden Name: Stovall
Residence: Forsyth Co.
Age: 53
Place of Birth: Franklin Co.
Father's Name: William Stovall
Mother's M. Name: Mary Burgess

Page 64
Name of Groom: Charles W.Mashburn
Residence: Forsyth Co.
Age: 47
Occupation: Farmer
Place of Birth: Busk C.M.
Father's Name: James Mashburn
Mother's M. Name: Jane Finly

Date of Marriage: Nov., 1877
Name of Bride: Martha E.Orr
Residence: Forsyth Co.
Age: 18
Place of Birth: Forsyth Co.
Father's Name: Samuel Orr
Mother's M. Name: Elizabeth ___

Page 120
Name of Groom: Henry P.Mayfield
Residence: Forsyth Co.
Age: 26
Occupation: Farmer
Place of Birth: Franklin Co.,GA
Father's Name: William Mayfield,
               dec'd
Mother's M. Name: M.J. Richerson,

Date of Marriage: 10-24-1878
Name of Bride: Patience A.Wingo
Residence: Forsyth Co.
Age: 26
Place of Birth: Hall Co., Ga.
Father's Name: Zachriah Wingo,
               dec'd
Mother's M. Name; Jane H. Foster
dec'd

Page 122
Name of Groom: Peter F.McKiney
Residence: Forsyth Co.
Age: 26
Occupation: Farmer
Place of Birth: Pickens Co., SC
Father's Name: Mack McKiney
Mother's M. Name: Ma Rawley

Date of Marriage: 11-17-1878
Name of Bride: Eliah Martin
Residence: Forsyth Co.
Age: 19
Place of Birth: Forsyth Co.
Father's Name: Elijah Martin
Mother's M. Name: Jane Moorhead

Page 131
Name of Groom: Darrell Martin
Residence: Forsyth Co.
Age: 27
Occupation: Farmer
Place of Birth: Forsyth Co.
Father's Name: John C. Martin
Mother's M. Name: Lucy Dodd

Date of Marriage: 1-26-1879
Name of Bride: Josephine Stone
Residence: Forsyth Co.
Age: 21
Palce of Birth: Forsyth Co.
Father's Name: Alen Stone
Mother's M. Name: Halfrah Holbrook

Page 141
Name of Groom: William C.Mooney
Residence: Forsyth Co.
Age: 20
Occupation: Farmer
Place of Birth: Forsyth Co.
Father's Name: Elie Mooney
Mother's M. Name: Alline Mashburn

Date of Marriage: 10-19-1879
Name of Bride: Dacus E.Bennett
Residence: Forsyth Co.
Age: 19
Place of Birth: Pickens Co., SC
Father's Name: Andrew Mauldin
Mother's M. Name: Nancy Campbell

Page 148
Name of Groom: Isaac N. McGhee
Residence: Dawson Co.
Age: 35
Occupation: Merchant
Place of Birth: Russell Co., Ala.
Father's Name: Isaac McGhee,dec'd
Mother's M. Name: Martha Cannon

Date of Marriage: 10-30-1879
Name of Bride: Mary E. Roach
Residence: Forsyth Co.
Age: 25
Place of Birth: Forsyth Co.
Father's Name: William Roach
Mother's M. Name; Nancy Cook

Page 155
Name of Groom: James E.Massy
Residence: Forsyth Co.
Age: 21
Occupation: Farmer
Place of Birth: Pickens Co., SC
Father's Name: Ezekiel Massy,dec'd
Mother's M. Name: Emily C.Mauldin

Date of Marriage: 12-16-1879
Name of Bride: Jane Byrd
Residence: Forsyth Co.
Age: 18
Place of Birth: Dawson Co., GA
Father's Name: Byrd, dec'd
Mother's M. Name: Amanda Lowry

Page 162
Name of Groom: Berry Mathis
Residence: Forsyth Co.
Age: 21
Occupation: Farmer
Place of Birth: Forsyth Co.
Father's Name: Reuben Mathis
Mother's M. Name: Amanda Bruice

Date of Marriage: 2-8-1880
Name of Bride: Lucy E.Jordan
Residence: Forsyth Co.
Age: 23
Place of Birth: Cherokee Co.
Father's Name: James Jordan,decd
Mother's M. Name: Nancy Epperson

Page 164
Name of Groom: James E.Mauldin
Residence: Forsyth Co.
Age: 22
Occupation: Farmer
Place of Birth: Pickens Co., SC
Father's Name: John Mauldin
Mother's M. Name: Carolin McAlister

Date of Marriage: 1-8-1880
Name of Bride: Mary Ann Ellis
Residence: Forsyth Co.
Age: 23
Place of Birth: Forsyth Co.
Father's Name: Balis Ellis,decd
Mother's M. Name: Margaret Martin

Page 167
Name of Groom: Daniel H.B.Moulder
Residence: Forsyth Co.
Age: 26
Occupation: Farmer
Place of Birth: Forsyth Co.
Father's Name: Hutson M.Moulder
Mother's M. Name: Caroline Bagley

Date of Marriage: 2-15-1880
Name of Bride: Victory Bagley
Residence: Forsyth Co.
Age: 20
Place of Birth: Forsyth Co.
Father's Name: Fletcher Bagley
Mother's M. Name: Susan Nailer

Page 173
Name of Groom: John H.Major
Residence: Forsyth Co.
Age: 21
Occupation: Farmer
Place of Birth: Forsyth Co.
Father's Name: Richard Major,decd
Mother's M. Name: Matilda Pruett,decd

Date of Marriage: 3-7-1880
Name of Bride: Sarah C.Barker
Residence: Forsyth Co.
Age: 19
Place of Birth: Forsyth Co.
Father's Name: W.H.H. Barker
Mother's M. Name: Mandy Davis

Page 188
Name of Groom: J.G. Morgan
Residence: Forsyth Co.
Age: 17
Occupation: Farmer
Place of Birth: Forsyth Co.
Father's Name: George B.Morgan
Mother's M. Name:

Date of Marriage: 10-28-1880
Name of Bride: N.C. Steel
Residence: Forsyth Co.
Age: 17
Place of Birth: Cherokee
Father's Name: H.J. Steel
Mother's M. Name: M.J.M. Johnson

Page 189
Name of Groom: N.B. Mathis
Residence: Forsyth Co.
Age: 19
Occupation: Farmer
Place of Birth: Forsyth Co.
Father's Name: R.H. Bice
Mother's M. Name: Amanda M.Bice

Date of Marriage: 10-24-1880
Name of Bride: Amanda C.Bice
Residence: Forsyth Co.
Age: 28
Place of Birth: Blunt Co., AL
Father's Name: Berry Bice
Mother's M. Name: Nanch Thomson

Page 198
Name of Groom: William A.Mashburn
Residence: Forsyth Co.
Age: 27
Occupation: Farmer
Place of Birth: Forsyth Co.
Father's Name: H.T. Mashburn
Mother's M. Name: Eliza A.Adkinson

Date of Marriage: 12-21-1880
Name of Bride: Huldah D.Cockran
Residence: Forsyth Co.
Age: 21
Place of Birth: Banks Co, GA
Father's Name: dec'd
Mother's M. Name: Malinda Shery(?)

Page 199
Name of Groom: Plesant L.Mathis
Residence: Forsyth Co.
Age: 20
Occupation: Farmer
Place of Birth: Forsyth Co.
Father's Name: James Mathis
Mother's M. Name: P. Sara Jordan

Date of Marriage: 12-7-1880
Name of Bride: Frances C.Pearce
Residence: Forsyth Co.
Age: 23
Place of Birth: Hall Co.
Father's Name: James J.Pearce
Mother's M. Name: P. Deale

Page 205
Name of Groom: George W.Moony
Residence: Forsyth Co.
Age: 20
Occupation: Farmer
Place of Birth: Hall Co.
Father's Name: Jonithan Moony
Mother's M. Name: Anna Tumlin

Date of Marriage: 1-6-1881
Name of Bride: Martha J.Hughes
Residence: Forsyth Co.
Age: 19
Place of Birth: Hall Co., GA
Father's Name: T. Hughes
Mother's M. Name: M. Whitmir

Page 70
Name of Groom: Hardy Mauldin
Residence: Pickens Co., SC
Age: 62
Occupation: Farmer
Place of Birth: Pickens Co., SC
Father's Name: Claburn Mauldin
Mother's M. Name: Charlott Hamby

Date of Marriage: 9-27-1877
Name of Bride: Mrs.Elizabeth
                           Brooks
Maiden Name: Williams
Residence: Forsyth Co.
Age: 43
Place of Birth: Hall Co.
Father's Name: John Williams
Mother's M. Name: Issabelle Wilson

Page 75
Name of Groom: Elija F.Mason
Residence: Forsyth Co.
Age: 21
Occupation: Farmer
Place of Birth: Pickens Co., SC
Father's Name: Washington Mason
Mother's M. Name: Emily Hide

Date of Marriage: 11-29-1877
Name of Bride: Lou Danniel
Residence: Forsyth Co.
Place of Birth: Pickens Co., SC
Father's Name: James Daniel
Mother's M. Name: Eliza Honey

Page 103
Name of Groom: George M.Martain
Residence: Forsyth Co.
Age: 21
Occupation: Farmer
Place of Birth: Forsyth Co.
Father's Name: James N.Martain
Mother's M. Name: Milly Brown

Date of Marriage: 1-2-1879
Name of Bride: Sarah E. Fowler
Residence: Forsyth Co.
Age: 21
Place of Birth: Forsyth Co.
Father's Name: William B.Fowler
Mother's M. Name: Rachell Betote

Page 109
Name of Groom: Levi Martain
Residence: Forsyth Co.
Age: 38
Occupation: Farmer, merchant
Father's Name: Jacob Martain
Mother's M. Name: Susan Martain

Date of Marriage: 1-8-1879
Name of Bride: L.A. Barrett
Residence: Forsyth Co.
Age: 18
Place of Birth: Forsyth Co.
Father's Name: John Barrett
Mother's M. Name: H.C.Caster

Page 106
Name of Groom: Madison J.J.
                McElreath
Residence: Forsyth Co.
Age: 27
Occupation: Farmer
Place of Birth: Forsyth Co.
Father's Name: Alexander McElreath
Mother's M. Name: Harriett C.Heath

Date of Marriage: 12-15-1878
Name of Bride: Amanda J.
                Vaughn
Residence: Forsyth Co.
Age: 21
Place of Birth: Forsyth Co.
Father's Name: Robin Mayhew
Mother's M. Name: Fagans

Page 31
Name of Groom: Joel Thos.Nuckolls,
                Jr.
Residence: Forsyth Co.
Age: 18
Occupation: Farmer
Place of Birth: Forsyth Co.
Father's Name:Joel T.Nuckolls,Sr.
Mother's M. Name: Irene Bryant

Date of Marriage: 5-20-1877
Name of Bride: Gabrillia
                Phillips
Residence: Forsyth Co.
Age: 15
Place of Birth: Forsyth Co.
Father's Name: Gabriel E.
                Phillips
Mother's M. Name: Mary Clifton

Page 54
Name of Groom: Joseph E.Neese
Residence: Forsyth Co.
Age: 20
Occupation: Farmer
Place of Birth: Cobb Co., GA
Father's Name: Jacob Neese
Mother's M. Name: Minerva Sewell

Date of Marriage: Aug., 1877
Name of Bride: Shasta H.Monroe
Residence: Forsyth Co.
Age: 16
Place of Birth: Forsyth Co.
Father's Name: Wilber F.Monroe
Mother's M. Name: Susan Clayton

Page 81
Name of Groom: Phillip L.Niece
Residence: Forsyth Co.
Age: 26
Occupation: Farmer
Place of Birth: Cobb Co.
Father's Name: Lewis Niece
Mother's M. Name: Betsey Allbrooton

Date of Marriage: 5-12-1878
Name of Bride: Mary H. Kemp
Residence: Forsyth Co.
Age: 28
Place of Birth: Forsyth Co.
Father's Name: Marvel Kemp
Mother's M. Name: Mary Ezzard

Page 127
Name of Groom: Joseph Milton
                Neisler
Residence: Forsyth Co.
Occupation: Farmer
Place of Birth: Lumpkin Co., GA
Father's Name: David Neisler
Mother's M. Name: Catherine Denning

Date of Marriage: 9-25-1877
Name of Bride: Ellen A. Andoe
Residence: Forsyth Co.
Age: 15
Place of Birth: Hall Co.
Father's Name: Robt.E.Andoe
Mother's M. Name: Margaret O.
                Conner

Page 178
Name of Groom: R.T. Nash
Residence: Forsyth Co.
Age: 26
Occupation: Physician
Place of Birth: Forsyth Co.
Father's Name: Frank Nash
Mother's M. Name: Liney Haley

Date of Marriage: 3-7-1880
Name of Bride: Lou E. Brown
Residence: Forsyth Co.
Age: 21
Place of Birth:
Father's Name: B.J. Brown
Mother's M. Name: Sarah Garrett

Page 200
Name of Groom: Jefferson D.Neise
Residence: Forsyth Co.
Age: 20
Occupation: Farmer
Place of Birth: Cobb Co., GA
Father's Name: William Neise
Mother's M. Name: Addy Bryant

Date of Marriage: 12-19-1880
Name of Bride: Rebecca A.Hood
Residence: Forsyth Co.
Age: 19
Place of Birth: Forsyth Co.
Father's Name: W.Hood, dec'd
Mother's M. Name: Unknown

Page 129
Name of Groom: James Odum
Residence: Forsyth Co.
Age: 24
Occupation: Farmer
Place of Birth: Forsyth Co.
Father's Name: Berry A. Odum
Mother's M. Name: Elizabeth Fowler

Date of Marriage: 3-16-1879
Name of Bride: Hester Ann Kemp
Residence: Forsyth Co.
Age: 26
Place of Birth: Forsyth Co.
Father's Name: Andrew J.Kemp
Mother's M. Name: Faithey
                         Killingsworth

Page 150
Name of Groom: Guilford F.Otwell
Residence: Forsyth Co.
Age: 26
Occupation: Mechanic
Place of Birth: Forsyth Co.
Father's Name: Solomon Otwell.decd
Mother's M. Name: Alsey Davis

Date of Marriage: 12-16-1879
Name of Bride: Mary Ann R.Bentley
Residence: Cumming
Age: 17
Place of Birth: Forsyth Co.
Father's Name: William D.Bentley
Mother's M. Name: Drucilla A.
                         Harris

Page 29
Name of Groom: William Pardon
Residence: Forsyth Co.
Age: 35
Occupation: Farmer
Place of Birth: Eason, Tenn.
Father's Name: Rily Pardon
Mother's M. Name: Polly Day

Date of Marriage: 4-18-1877
Name of Bride: Elisabeth Cochran
Residence: Forsyth Co.
Age: 26
Place of Birth: Hall Co., GA
Father's Name: Robt.Cochran,decd
Mother's M. Name: Sheridon, decd

Page 30
Name of Groom: Elijah M.Pilgrim
Residence: Forsyth Co.
Age: 36
Occupation: Teacher
Place of Birth: Pickens Co., SC
Father's Name: Elijah Pilgrim,decd
Mother's M. Name: Elizabeth Perry,decd

Date of Marriage: 1-24-1877
Name of Bride: Lucretia L.Merrett
Residence: Forsyth Co.
Age: 19
Place of Birth: Forsyth Co.
Father's Name: Jas.H.A.Merrett
Mother's M. Name: Lucretia
                         Willingham

Page 30
Name of Groom: Rusus E.Padgett
Residence: Forsyth Co.
Age: 21 (?)
Occupation: Farmer
Place of Birth: Union, SC
Father's Name: Padgett
Mother's M. Name:

Date of Marriage: 3-8-1877
Name of Bride: Sarah Gault
Residence: Forsyth Co.
Age: 16
Place of Birth: Forsyth Co.
Father's Name: Presly Gault
Mother's M. Name: Milly Hadder

Page 36
Name of Groom: Newton S.Phillips
Residence: Forsyth Co.
Age: 23
Occupation: Farmer
Place of Birth: Forsyth Co.
Father's Name: Gabrel Phillips
Mother's M. Name: Mary Horton

Date of Marriage: 9-23-1877
Name of Bride: E.J. Hunt (Hurt?)
Residence: Forsyth Co.
Age: 18
Place of Birth: Forsyth Co.
Father's Name: Thos.W.Hurt
Mother's M. Name: Lucy M.Burress

Page 45
Name of Groom: John M.Pugh
Residence: Cherokee Co., GA
Age: 22
Occupation: Farmer
Place of Birth: Cherokee Co.
Father's Name: Frances Pugh
Mother's M. Name:Gadsey Chamblee,
                      dec'd

Date of Marriage: 12-23-1877
Name of Bride: Lori M.Jefferson
Residence: Forsyth Co.
Age: 17
Place of Birth: Forsyth Co.
Father's Name: Boswell Jeffer-
                      son, dec'd
Mother's M. Name: Cyntha Pool

Page 43
Name of Groom: Samuel B.Patterson
Residence: Forsyth Co.
Age: 29
Occupation: Farmer
Place of Birth: Abbeville Dist.,SC
Father's Name: Josiah B.Patterson
Mother's M. Name: Mary B.McNeal

Date of Marriage: 11-13-1877
Name of Bride: Margret E.McAfee
Residence: Forsyth Co.
Age: 18
Place of Birth: Forsyth Co.
Father's Name: Elijah C.McAfee
Mother's M. Name: Elizabeth K.
                      Thompson

Page 44
Name of Groom: William Y.Pool
Residence: Forsyth Co.
Age: 21
Occupation: Farmer
Place of Birth: Forsyth Co.
Father's Name: William Y.Pool.decd
Mother's M. Name: Julia A.Chamblee

Date of Marriage: 12-19-1877
Name of Bride: Lucretia C.
                      Pilgrim
Residence: Forsyth Co.
Age: 20
Place of Birth: Forsyth Co.
Father's Name: Thos.J.Pilgrim
Mother's M. Name: Elizabeth A.
                      Atkinson,decd

Page 50
Name of Groom: David C.Phillips
Residence: Forsyth Co.
Age: 21
Occupation: Farmer
Place of Birth: Forsyth Co.
Father's Name: Lewis B.Phillips
Mother's M. Name: Hele H.Pirkle

Date of Marriage: 8-16-1877
Name of Bride: Ophelia H.Samples
Residence: Forsyth Co.
Age: 23
Place of Birth: Forsyth Co.
Father's Name: Charles Samples
Mother's M. Name: Rebecca Scott

Page 56
Name of Groom:Benjamin L.Pirkle
Residence: Forsyth Co.
Age: 23
Occupation: Farmer
Place of Birth: Forsyth Co.
Father's Name: Nathaniel Pirkle
Mother's M. Name: Elizabeth Bryant

Date of Marriage: 1-24-1878
Name of Bride: Ruth A.Banister
Residence: Forsyth Co.
Age: 17
Place of Birth: Forsyth Co.
Father's Name: Powell Banister
Mother's M. Name: Elizabeth
                      Dooly

Page 57
Name of Groom: Barry Potes
Residence: Forsyth Co.
Age: 24
Occupation: Farmer
Place of Birth: Forsyth Co.
Father's Name: Phillip Potes
Mother's M. Name: Delilah Cheshare

Date of Marriage: 11-29-1877
Name of Bride: Rebecca A.Westbrook
Residence: Forsyth Co.
Age: 19
Place of Birth: Forsyth Co.
Father's Name: Samuel Westbrook
Mother's M. Name: Mary J.White

Page 69
Name of Groom: Riley Phillips
Residence: Forsyth Co.
Age: 20
Occupation: Farmer
Place of Birth: Forsyth Co.
Father's Name: Washington Phillips
Mother's M. Name: Margaret Childers

Date of Marriage: 10-25-1877
Name of Bride: Mary N.McGinnes
Residence: Forsyth Co.
Age: 18
Place of Birth: Forsyth Co.
Father's Name: James McGinnes
Mother's M. Name: Cyntha Lollis(?)

Page 71
Name of Groom: James Padgett
Residence: Forsyth Co.
Age: 21
Occupation: Farmer
Place of Birth: Pickens Co., SC
Father's Name: Terrell Padgett
Mother's M. Name: Mary Edmonson

Date of Marriage: 8-16-1877
Name of Bride: Lidda Bettis
Residence: Forsyth Co.
Age: 16
Place of Birth: Forsyth Co.
Father's Name: Tolbert Bettis
Mother's M. Name: Martha Vickery,
                          dec'd

Page 86
Name of Groom: Noah Pirkel
Residence: Forsyth Co.
Age: 24
Occupation: Farmer
Place of Birth: Forsyth Co.
Father's Name: Ambrose Pirkel,decd
Mother's M. Name: Sarah A.Pirkel,decd

Date of Marriage: 4-29-1878
Name of Bride: Harriet Deaton
Residence: Forsyth Co.
Age: 20
Place of Birth: Forsyth Co.
Father's Name: John Blanton
Mother's M. Name: Martha Orr,decd

Page 104
Name of Groom: Juvanill(?) Page
Residence: Cherokee Co.,GA
Age: 40
Occupation: Engineer
Place of Birth: Lincoln Co., NC
Father's Name: James M.Page
Mother's M. Name: Sopha Sample,(?), decd.

Date of Marriage: 12-29-1878
Name of Bride: Elise E.Wilson
Residence: Forsyth Co.
Age: 23
Place of Birth: Forsyth Co.
Father's Name: Robt.T.Wilson
Mother's M. Name: L. Jinkens

Page 137
Name of Groom: J.G. Parker
Residence: Forsyth Co.
Age: 21
Occupation: Farmer
Place of Birth: Pickens Co.
Father's Name: Abe Parker
Mother's M. Name:

Date of Marriage: 9-14-1879
Name of Bride: Margarett M.Lively
Residence: Forsyth Co.
Age: 21
Place of Birth: Cherokee Co.
Father's Name: Bartholemew
                          Lively
Mother's M. Name: Mary Ray

Page 139
Name of Groom: Crawford B.Page
Residence: Forsyth Co.
Age: 23
Occupation: Farmer
Place of Birth: Forsyth Co.
Father's Name: Wm.J.Page
Mother's M. Name: Mahalah Brooks

Name of Bride: Mary M. Summer
Residence: Forsyth Co.
Age: 18
Place of Birth: Gwinnett Co.
Father's Name: G.H. Summer
Mother's M. Name: P.A. Scrumly
Date of Marriage: 9-21-1879

Page 150
Name of Groom: George L.Phillips
Residence: Forsyth Co.
Age: 23
Occupation: Farmer
Place of Birth: Forsyth Co.
Father's Name: King D.Phillips
Mother's M. Name: Tabiatha Estes

Date of Marriage: 12-24-1879
Name of Bride: Lena Strickland
Residence: Forsyth Co.
Age: 18
Place of Birth: Chattooga Co,GA
Father's Name: Jacob C.Strickland
Mother's M. Name: Melita Gilbert

Page 156
Name of Groom: Enoch E.Pruett
Residence: Forsyth Co.
Age: 51
Occupation: Farmer
Place of Birth: Spartanburg Co.,SC
Father's Name: Washington H.
                    Pruett, dec'd
Mother's M. Name: Zelpher Early

Date of Marriage: 12-30-1879
Name of Bride: R.J. Moorhead
Residence: Forsyth Co.
Age: 54
Place of Birth: Anderson Co.,SC
Father's Name: Whitaker Smith,
                    dec'd
Mother's M. Name: Mary Irvin

Page 156
Name of Groom: Presley Payne
Residence: Forsyth Co.
Age: 18
Occupation: Farmer
Place of Birth: McDonnell Co.,NC
Father's Name: Thomas Payne
Mother's M. Name: Amanda Walker

Date of Marriage: 12-23-1879
Name of Bride: Francis E.Jordan
Residence: Forsyth Co.
Age: 19
Place of Birth: Forsyth Co.
Father's Name: Harden Jordan
Mother's M. Name: Jermia Hulsey

Page 157
Name of Groom: Emanuel Page
Residence: Forsyth Co.
Age: 24
Occupation: Farmer
Place of Birth: Forsyth Co.
Father's Name: William J.Page
Mother's M. Name: Mahala Brook

Date of Marriage: 12-28-1879
Name of Bride: Sarah M.Holland
Age: 17
Place of Birth: Hall Co., GA
Residence: Forsyth Co.
Father's Name: Samuel B.Holland
Mother's M. Name: Luther

Page 185
Name of Groom: J.S.Phillips
Residence: Forsyth Co.
Age: 19
Occupation: Farmer
Place of Birth: Forsyth Co.
Father's Name: K.D. Phillips
Mother's M. Name: Tabitha Estes

Date of Marriage: 10-7-1880
Name of Bride: Sarah E.Benson
Residence: Forsyth Co.
Age: 20
Place of Birth: Forsyth Co.
Father's Name: R.W. Benson
Mother's M. Name: Nancy Spence

Page 188
Name of Groom: Joshua Potts
Residence: Forsyth Co.
Age: 62
Occupation: Farmer
Place of Birth: Jackson Co., GA
Father's Name: William Potts
Mother's M. Name: Nancy Thomason

Date of Marriage: 8-17-1880
Name of Bride: Mary F. Martin
Residence: Forsyth Co.
Age: 34
Place of Birth: Forsyth Co.
Father's Name: Hezekiah Martin
Mother's M. Name: T. Stone

Page 201
Name of Groom: James K.Pritchett
Residence: Forsyth Co.
Age: 29
Occupation: Blacksmith
Place of Birth: Buttes Co., Ohio
Father's Name: Joseph Pritchett
Mother's M. Name: Flora S.Mullins

Date of Marriage: 1-7-1881
Name of Bride: Hester A.C.Red
Residence: Forsyth Co.
Age: 19
Place of Birth: Forsyth Co.
Father's Name: Mashack Red
Mother's M. Name: Malina Rack___

Page 202
Name of Groom: Sisco Puckett
Residence: Forsyth Co.
Age: 22
Occupation: Farmer
Place of Birth: Forsyth Co.
Father's Name: J.A. Puckett
Mother's M. Name: May

Date of Marriage: 1-10-1881
Name of Bride: Elisabeth Neese
Residence: Forsyth Co.
Age: 17
Palce of Birth: Cook Co.
Father's Name: W.J. Neese
Mother's M. Name: Ader Bryant

Page 204
Name of Groom: John Benjamin Page
Residence: Forsyth Co.
Age: 28
Occupation: Farmer
Place of Birth: Madison
Father's Name: Thos.Page,dec'd
Mother's M. Name: Margrett Shader

Date of Marriage: 12-26-1880
Name of Bride: Marietta Phillips
Residence: Forsyth Co.
Age: 19
Place of Birth: Forsyth Co.
Father's Name: Lewis B. Phillips,
                        dec'd
Mother's M. Name: Hela Pirkle

Page 34
Name of Groom: Joshua L. Red
Residence: Forsyth Co.
Age: 19
Occupation: Farmer
Place of Birth: Forsyth Co.
Father's Name: James Red
Mother's M. Name: Mahulda Sewell

Date of Marriage: 7-19-1877
Name of Bride: Cassanda A.A.
                        Brooks
Residence: Forsyth Co.
No further information

Page 35
Name of Groom: John F. Roper
Residence: Forsyth Co.
Age:
Occupation: Farmer
Place of Birth: Forsyth Co.
Father's Name: John Roper, dec'd
Mother's M. Name: Annie Red

Date of Marriage: 12-16-1879
Name of Bride: Mary E.Tinsley
Residence: Forsyth Co.
Age: 18
Place of Birth: Spartanburg, SC
Father's Name: Mils W.Tinsley
Mother's M. Name: Elener Hays

Page 61
Name of Groom: Jeter J. Ried
Residence: Forsyth Co.
Age: 18
Occupation: Farmer
Place of Birth: Forsyth Co.
Father's Name: Archobold H.Ried
Mother's M. Name: Elizabeth Holbrook

Date of Marriage: 11-11-1877
Name of Bride: Laura Venable
Residence: Forsyth Co.
Age: 17
Place of Birth: Forsyth Co.
Father's Name: Robert R.Venable
Mother's M. Name: Eliza Bacon

Page 82
Name of Groom: John L. Red
Residence: Forsyth Co.
Age: 19
Occupation: Farmer
Place of Birth: Forsyth Co.
Father's Name: James Red
Mother's M. Name: Mahulda Sewell

Date of Marriage: 7-19-1877
Name of Bride: C.A.A. Brooks
Residence: Forsyth Co.
No further information

Page 93
Name of Groom: Thomas Red
Residence: Forsyth Co.
Age: 52
Occupation: Farmer
Place of Birth: Gwinnett Co., GA
Father's Name: James Red, dec'd
Mother's M. Name:

Date of Marriage: 8-15-1878
Name of Bride: Lucy Terry
Residence: Forsyth Co.
Age: 27
Place of Birth: Forsyth Co.
Father's Name: Martin Terry
Mother's M. Name:

Page 107
Name of Groom: James A. Rily
Residence: Hall Co., GA
Age: 21
Occupation: Farmer
Place of Birth: Hall Co.
Father's Name: Isaac Rily
Mother's M. Name: Harriet Bell

Date of Marriage: 11-28-1877
Name of Bride: Americus Light
Residence: Forsyth Co.
Age: 21
Place of Birth: Forsyth Co.
Father's Name: Guilford B.Light
Mother's M. Name: Margaret Bibbs,
                              dec'd

Page 123
Name of Groom: George W.Robbs
Residence: Forsyth Co.
Age: 25
Occupation: Farmer
Father's Name:
Mother's M. Name:

Date of Marriage: 12-27-1878
Name of Bride: Narcissa E.Gable
Residence: Forsyth Co.
Age: 20
Place of Birth: Habersham Co.,GA
Father's Name: George W.Gable
Mother's M. Name: Elizabeth
                              Wharton

Page 128
Name of Groom: Frederick F.Reed
Residence: Forsyth Co.
Age: 23
Occupation: Farmer
Place of Birth: Forsyth Co.
Father's Name: A.H. Reed
Mother's M. Name: Martha Holbrook

Date of Marriage: 5-4-1879
Name of Bride: Henrietta Samples
Age: 21
Place of Birth: Forsyth Co.
Father's Name: John Samples
Mother's M. Name: Mary Ann Foster

Page 183
Name of Groom: John L.Reed
Residence: Forsyth Co.
Age: 20
Occupation: Farmer
Place of Birth: Forsyth Co.
Father's Name: G.W. Red
Mother's M. Name: H. Wingo

Date of Marriage: 7-20-1880
Name of Bride: P.A. Holdbrook
Residence: Forsyth Co.
Age: 23
Place of Birth: Forsyth Co.
Father's Name: S.H. Holbrook
Mother's M. Name: M. C. Roper

Page 185
Name of Groom: George B.Rice
Residence: Forsyth Co.
Age: 23
Occupation: Teacher
Place of Birth: Forsyth Co.
Father's Name: Benjamin J.Rice
Mother's Name: Susan Buford

Date of Marriage: 10-20-1880
Name of Bride: M.J. Chatham
Residence: Forsyth Co.
Age: 21
Place of Birth: Forsyth Co.
Father's Name: J.Chatham, decd
Mother's M. Name: E. Castleberry

Page 196
Name of Groom: Joseph Read
Residence: Forsyth Co.
Age: 24
Occupation: Blacksmith
Place of Birth: Winston Co., AL
Father's Name: John Read
Mother's M. Name: Matilda Roper

Date of Marriage: 12-19-1880
Name of Bride: Lucinda E.Perry
Residence: Forsyth Co.
Age: 23
Place of Birth: Forsyth Co.
Father's Name: Lewis Perry
Mother's M. Name: Martha Martin

Page 199
Name of Groom: John W.H.Robertson
Residence: Forsyth Co.
Age: 34
Occupation: Seaman
Place of Birth: Rutherford Co.,NC
Father's Name: John Robertson
Mother's M. Name: Martha Byrd

Date of Marriage: 11-23-1880
Name of Bride: Martha F.Bottoms
Residence: Forsyth Co.
Age: 22
Place of Birth: Forsyth Co.
Father's Name: John B.Bottoms
Mother's M. Name: Frances Young(?)

Page 201
Name of Groom: William W.Ried
Residence: Forsyth Co.
Age: 19
Occupation: Farmer
Place of Birth: Forsyth Co.
Father's Name: Hampton Ried
Mother's M. Name: Martha Holbrook

Date of Marriage: 12-23-1880
Name of Bride: Martha C.Perry
Residence: Forsyth Co.
Age: 19
Place of Birth: Forsyth Co.
Father's Name: Lewis Perry
Mother's M. Name: Mary Martin

Page 211
Name of Groom: Joseph Brown Roach
Residence: Forsyth Co.
Age: 23
Occupation: Farmer
Place of Birth: Forsyth Co.
Father's Name: James B.Roach,decd
Mother's M. Name: Mary A. Perry

Date of Marriage: 1-16-1881
Name of Bride: Amanda S.McDaniel
Residence: Forsyth Co.
Age: 18
Place of Birth: Forsyth Co.
Father's Name: George W.McDaniel
Mother's M. Name: Amanda Montgomrey

Page 39
Name of Groom: Samuel A.Shoemaker
Residence: Dawson Co.
Age: 21
Occupation: Farmer
Place of Birth: Dawson Co.
Father's Name: Jackson Shoemaker
Mother's M. Name: Dorcas A.Chastain

Date of Marriage: 10-21-1877
Name of Bride: Georgia S.Whitmire
Residence: Forsyth Co.
Age:
Place of Birth:
Father's Name: Elias E.Whitmire
Mother's M. Name:

Page 50
Name of Groom: William P.Stevens
Residence: Forsyth Co.
Age: 24
Occupation: Farmer
Place of Birth: Forsyth Co.
Father's Name: Ephram Stevens
Mother's M. Name: Caroline Estes

Date of Marriage: 5-1-1877
Name of Bride: Nancy E.Phillips
Residence: Forsyth Co.
Age: 17
Place of Birth: Forsyth Co.
Father's Name: William Phillips
Mother's M. Name: Jane Edwards

Page 63
Name of Groom: James G.Samples
Residence: Forsyth Co.
Age: 18
Occupation: Farmer
Place of Birth: Forsyth Co.
Father's Name: Andrew A.Samples
Mother's M. Name: Sarah A.Dollor

Date of Marriage: 4-4-1878
Name of Bride: Kesiah Pruett
Residence: Forsyth Co.
Age: 19
Place of Birth: Forsyth Co.
Father's Name: Elias Pruett
Mother's M. Name: Margaret Payne

Page 65
Name of Groom: William A.Southard
Residence: Forsyth Co.
Age: 25
Occupation: Farmer
Place of Birth: Forsyth Co.
Father's Name: John B.Southard
Mother's M. Name: Polly Smith

Date of Marriage: 4-17-1877
Name of Bride: S.J. Youngblood
Residence: Forsyth Co.
Age: 25
Place of Birth: Forsyth Co.
Father's Name: James W.Youngblood
Mother's M. Name: Elvira Allen

Page 80
Name of Groom: Marcus A.Smallwood
Residence: Cherokee Co., GA
Age: 21
Occupation: Farmer
Place of Birth: Forsyth Co.
Father's Name: Marke Smallwood
Mother's M. Name: Hyde

Date of Marriage: 7-6-1878
Name of Bride: Annie Ellington
Residence: Forsyth Co.
Age: 19
Place of Birth: Pickens Co., GA
Father's Name: Peter Ellington
Mother's M. Name: Hutchins

Page 97
Name of Groom: Thomas N.Steel
Residence: Forsyth Co.
Age: 21
Occupation: Farmer
Place of Birth: Cherokee Co., GA
Father's Name: Henry J.Steel
Mother's M. Name: Mary Holland

Date of Marriage: 9-15-1878
Name of Bride: Martha Manassas
                       Blackston
Residence: Forsyth Co.
Age: 16
Place of Birth: Forsyth Co.
Father's Name: James H.Blackston
Mother's M. Name: Joannah Pilgrim

Page 100
Name of Groom: William H.Sanders
Residence: Cherokee Co.
Age: 20
Occupation: Farmer
Place of Birth: Forsyth Co.
Father's Name: Moses Sanders
Mother's M. Name: Diannah E.Jones

Date of Marriage: 9-8-1878
Name of Bride: Evlin Ledbetter
Residence: Forsyth Co.
Age: 22
Place of Birth: Forsyth Co.
Father's Name: William Ledbetter
Mother's M. Name: Catherine
                       Gravitt

Page 100
Name of Groom: Alston Mahaffy
                       Secrest
Residence: Forsyth Co.
Age: 23
Place of Birth: Cherokee Co., AL
Father's Name: Jacob S.Secrest,decd
Mother's M. Name: Susan Boyd

Date of Marriage: 10-3-1878
Name of Bride: C.A. Mashburn
Residence: Forsyth Co.
Age: 19
Place of Birth: Forsyth Co.
Father's Name: Henry T.Mashburn
Mother's M. Name: Eliza Atkinson

Page 101
Name of Groom: James B.Smith
Residence: Forsyth Co.
Age: 17
Occupation: Farmer
Place of Birth: Anderson Co.,SC
Father's Name: James Smith, dec'd
Mother's M. Name: Nancy Nally

Date of Marriage: 9-29-1878
Name of Bride: Francis L.G.
                       Castleberry
Residence: Forsyth Co.
Age: 14
Place of Birth: Forsyth Co.
Father's Name: David Castleberry
Mother's M. Name: Nancy M.Williams

Page 110
Name of Groom: Millard F.Scoggins
Residence: Forsyth Co.
Age: 22
Occupation: Farmer
Place of Birth: Hall Co., GA
Father's Name: D.S. Scoggins
Mother's M. Name: Mary Ann Kelly, dec'd

Date of Marriage: 1-23-1879
Name of Bride: Syntha C.Cruse
Residence: Forsyth Co.
Age: 23
Place of Birth: Forsyth Co.
Father's Name: John Losson Cruse
Mother's M. Name: Synthia Sams

Page 112
Name of Groom: John K.Strickland
Residence: Gwinnett Co., GA
Age: 20
Occupation: Farmer
Place of Birth: Gwinnett Co.
Father's Name: Tolver Strickland
Mother's M. Name: Sarah King

Date of Marriage: 11-21-1878
Name of Bride: Caroline Rolins
Residence: Forsyth Co.
Age: 18
Place of Birth: Forsyth Co.
Father's Name: James H.Rolins
Mother's M. Name: Catherine
                                    Brannon

Page 115
Name of Groom: William H.Smith
Residence: Forsyth Co.
Age: 20
Occupation: Farmer
Place of Birth: Jackson Co., GA
Father's Name: John H.Smith
Mother's M. Name: Nancy M.A.Gober, dec'd

Date of Marriage: 1-30-1879
Name of Bride: Lew Johnston
Residence: Forsyth Co.
Age: 20
Place of Birth: Hall Co., GA
Father's Name: Phillip Johnston
Mother's M. Name: Nancy Rankley

Page 117
Name of Groom: C.V. Smith
Residence: Forsyth Co.
Age: 19
Occupation: Farmer
Place of Birth: Cobb Co., GA
Father's Name: E.J. Smith
Mother's M. Name: S.E. Young

Date of Marriage: 8-11-1878
Name of Bride: Evelin Cates
Residence: Forsyth Co.
Age: 16
Place of Birth: Forsyth Co.
Father's Name: Jackson Cates
Mother's M. Name:

Page 125
Name of Groom: Cicero M.Sams
Residence: Forsyth Co.
Age: 26
Occupation: Farmer
Place of Birth: Forsyth Co.
Father's Name: William N. Sams
Mother's M. Name: Emily Baker

Date of Marriage: 3-6-1879
Name of Bride: Lenie Red
Residence: Forsyth Co.
Age: 17
Place of Birth: Forsyth Co.
Father's Name: George W. Red
Mother's M. Name: Wingo

Page 132
Name of Groom: Dr. H.S.Stanford
Residence: Milton Co.
Age: 36
Occupation: Physician
Place of Birth: Gwinnett Co., GA
Father's Name: Stephen Stanford
Mother's M. Name: Millie J. Harris

Date of Marriage: 4-9-1879
Name of Bride: J.E. Jones
Residence: Forsyth Co.
Age: 22
Place of Birth: Forsyth Co.
Father's Name: Seaborn Jones
Mother's M. Name: R.E. Allen

Page 132
Name of Groom: Johnathan A.Stone
Residence: Forsyth Co.
Age: 22
Occupation: Farmer
Place of Birth: Forsyth Co.
Father's Name: Thomas Stone
Mother's M. Name:

Date of Marriage: 7-24-1879
Name of Bride: Laura A.M.Harminy
Residence: Forsyth Co.
Age: 17
Place of Birth: Forsyth Co.
Father's Name: Alexander Harminy
Mother's M. Name: Louisa Brown

Page 139
Name of Groom: Ancil Strickland
Residence: Forsyth Co.
Age: 21
Occupation: Physician
Place of Birth: Cherokee Co.
Father's Name: Henry Strickland,decd
Mother's M. Name: Elizabeth Smith

Date of Marriage: 9-30-1879
Name of Bride: Julia Hockenhull
Residence: Forsyth Co.
Age: 19
Place of Birth: Dawsonville, GA
Father's Name: Dr.John Hockenhull
Mother's M. Name: Mary Hutchins

Page 140
Name of Groom: William Scoggins
Residence: Forsyth Co.
Age: 23
Occupation: Miller
Place of Birth: Dawson Co.
Father's Name: John Scoggins
Mother's M. Name: Rosa Millsap

Date of Marriage: 9-21-1879
Name of Bride: Frances B.Williams
Residence: Forsyth Co.
Age: 18
Place of Birth: Forsyth Co.
Father's Name: Thomas C.Williams
Mother's M. Name: Elizabeth
                          Stovall

Page 142
Name of Groom: Monroe Smallwood
Residence: Cherokee Co.
Age: 23
Occupation: Farmer
Place of Birth:
Father's Name: John Smallwood
Mother's M. Name:

Date of Marriage: 11-29-1879
Name of Bride: Sarah Tippins
Residence: Forsyth Co.
Age: 21
Place of Birth:
Father's Name: Jackson Tippins
Mother's M. Name:

Page 143
Name of Groom: Danial A.Samples
Residence: Forsyth Co.
Age: 19
Occupation: Farmer
Place of Birth: Forsyth Co.
Father's Name: Thomas C.Samples
Mother's M. Name: Sarah A. Davis

Date of Marriage: 12-11-1879
Name of Bride: Mary E.Samples
Residence: Forsyth Co.
Age: 16
Place of Birth: Forsyth Co.
Father's Name: Andrew G.Samples
Mother's M. Name: Sarah E.Dollor

Page 145
Name of Groom: Danial W.Stephens
Residence: Forsyth Co.
Age: 22
Occupation: Farmer
Place of Birth: Forsyth Co.
Father's Name: Ephame Stephens
Mother's M. Name: Caroline Phillips

Date of Marriage: 10-30-1879
Name of Bride: Martha J.Phillips
Residence: Forsyth Co.
Age: 17
Place of Birth: Forsyth Co.
Father's Name: William Phillips
Mother's M. Name: Jane Edwards

Page 145
Name of Groom: Alford K. Smith
Residence: Forsyth Co.
Age: 29
Occupation: Farmer
Place of Birth: Pickens Co., GA
Father's Name: Barthy J.Smith
Mother's M. Name: Lucinda Burt

Date of Marriage: 10-23-1879
Name of Bride: Mary A. Hooper
Residence: Forsyth Co.
Age: 20
Place of Birth: Banks Co.
Father's Name: Brooks Hooper
Mother's M. Name: Mary Perrele)?)

Page 14
Name of Groom: William N.Smith
Residence: Dawson Co.
Age: 19
Occupation: Farmer
Place of Birth: Dawson Co.
Father's Name: Harvy Smith
Mother's M. Name: Eliza Miney

Date of Marriage: 11-13-1879
Name of Bride: Mary A. Harden
Residence: Forsyth Co.
Age: 17
Place of Birth: Forsyth Co.
Father's Name: Isaac Harden
Mother's M. Name: Harrett Wallis

Page 153
Name of Groom: Noah Strickland
Residence: Forsyth Co.
Age: 16
Occupation: Farmer
Place of Birth: Forsyth Co.
Father's Name: Tolbert Strickland, Dec'd
Mother's M. Name: Celia Young

Date of Marriage: 1-1-1880
Name of Bride: Catherine Dean
Residence: Forsyth Co.
Age: 18
Place of Birth: Pickens Co., SC
Father's Name: Josiah M. Dean
Mother's M. Name: Elizabeth Chamblee

Page 159
Name of Groom: William R.Settle
Residence: Forsyth Co.
Age: 25
Occupation: Farmer
Place of Birth: Elbert Co., GA
Father's Name: James S.Settle,decd
Mother's M. Name: Senie Mathis

Date of Marriage: 1-20-1880
Name of Bride: Martha E.Terry
Residence: Forsyth Co.
Age: 22
Place of Birth: Forsyth Co.
Father's Name: Martin Terry
Mother's M. Name: Mary Dodd

Page 166
Name of Groom: Andrew H.Stewart
Residence: Forsyth Co.
Age: 22
Occupation: Farmer
Place of Birth: Pickens Co., SC
Father's Name: A.P. Stewart
Mother's M. Name: Malinda A.Stapler

Date of Marriage: 2-15-1880
Name of Bride: Martha J.Roper
Residence: Forsyth Co.
Age: 20
Place of Birth: Forsyth Co.
Father's Name: Jones H.Roper, dec'd
Mother's M. Name:Nepsian Cape (Cope?)

Page 166
Name of Groom: George M.C.Scott
Residence: Forsyth Co.
Age: 22
Occupation: Farmer
Place of Birth: Forsyth Co.
Father's Name: William R.Scott
Mother's M. Name: Nancy E.Terial

Date of Marriage: 2-4-1880
Name of Bride: Harriett E.Cope
Residence: Forsyth Co.
Age: 22
Place of Birth: Forsyth Co.
Father's Name: Jackson Cope
Mother's M. Name: Eliza Mullinax

Page 163
Name of Groom: George T.Settle
Residence: Forsyth Co.
Age: 21
Occupation: Farmer
Place of Birth: Elbert Co.
Father's Name: James S.Settle,dec'd
Mother's M. Name: Cenie Mathis

Date of Marriage: 12-18-1879
Name of Bride: Sarah E.Cantrell
Residence: Forsyth Co.
Age: 18
Palce of Birth: Forsyth Co.
Father's Name: Smith Cantrell
Mother's M. Name: Hannah Terry

Page 171
Name of Groom: Alonzo Scoggins
Residence: Forsyth Co.
Age: 19
Occupation: Farmer
Place of Birth: Forsyth Co.
Father's Name: D.S. Scoggins
Mother's M. Name: Elender Huggins

Date of Marriage: 3-11-1880
Name of Bride: Mary A.Medlock
Residence: Forsyth Co.
Age: 18
Place of Birth: Gwinnett Co.
Father's Name: W.H. Medlock
Mother's M. Name: Permelia Wood

Page 180
Name of Groom: Louie E.Samples
Residence: Forsyth Co.
Age: 18
Occupation: Farmer
Place of Birth: Forsyth Co.
Father's Name: Thos.Calvin Samples
Mother's M. Name: Sarah A.Samples

Date of Marriage: 8-10-1880
Name of Bride: Ema O.Hawkins
Residence: Forsyth Co.
Age: 15
Place of Birth: Forsyth Co.
Father's Name: Thos.W.Hawkins
Mother's M. Name: Evie O.Hawkins

Page 196
Name of Groom: George Sweatman
Residence: Forsyth Co.
Age: 61
Occupation: Farmer
Place of Birth: Jones Co., GA
Father's Name: John Swetman
Mother's M. Name: Nelly Wallis

Date of Marriage: 11-21-1880
Name of Bride: Martha J.Martin
Residence: Forsyth Co.
Age: 32
Place of Birth: Lincoln Co., GA
Father's Name: Heziah Martin
Mother's M. Name: Stone

Page 195
Name of Groom: John R.Stovall
Residence: Forsyth Co.
Age: 18
Occupation: Farmer
Place of Birth: Forsyth Co.
Father's Name: John W.Stovall
Mother's M. Name: Louisa Crow

Date of Marriage: 11-13-1880
Name of Bride: Lucy A. Morgan
Residence: Forsyth Co.
Age: 18
Place of Birth: Jackson Co.
Father's Name: Jesse Morgan
Mother's M. Name: E. Rogers

Page 210
Name of Groom: William C.Stone
Residence: Forsyth Co.
Age: 25
Occupation: Farmer
Place of Birth: Forsyth Co.
Father's Name: Thomas Stone
Mother's M. Name: Prudy Holbrook

Date of Marriage: 10-6-1880
Name of Bride: Alvarina Whitmire
Residence: Forsyth Co.
Age: 18
Place of Birth:
Father's Name: dec'd
Mother's M. Name: dec'd

Page 38
Name of Groom: Marion Tanner
Residence: Forsyth Co.
Age: 27
Occupation: Mechanic
Place of Birth: Carroll Co.
Father's Name: James R. Tanner
Mother's M. Name: Malisa Hembree

Date of Marriage: 11-22-1877
Name of Bride: Anna Virginia
                    Phillips
Residence: Forsyth Co.
Age: 14
Place of Birth: Forsyth Co.
Father's Name: Isaac Phillips
Mother's M. Name: Elvira Cox

Page 72
Name of Groom: George W.Tumblin
Residence: Forsyth Co.
Age: 26
Occupation: Farmer
Place of Birth: Hall Co., GA
Father's Name: James Tumblin
Mother's M. Name: Delilah Mooney

Date of Marriage: 2-9-1878
Name of Bride: Georgia A.Leage
                    (Teage?)
Residence: Forsyth Co.
Age: 18
Place of Birth: Forsyth Co.
Father's Name: Dennis M.Leage
Mother's M. Name:

Page 58
Name of Groom: Jesse Treadway
Residence: Forsyth Co.
Age: 21
Occupation: Farmer
Place of Birth: Andrews Co., SC
Father's Name: Oliver Treadway
Mother's M. Name:

Date of Marriage: 2-3-1878
Name of Bride: Octavia Potts
Residence: Forsyth Co.
Age: 18
Place of Birth:
Father's Name: Jinatha Potts
Mother's M. Name: Teassely Brown

Page 70
Name of Groom: Willis Thompson
Residence: Forsyth Co.
Age: 24
Occupation: Farmer
Place of Birth: Ala.
Father's Name: Moses Thompson
Mother's M. Name: Adaline Bice

Date of Marriage: 11-11-1877
Name of Bride: Salena Bice
Residence: Forsyth Co.
Age: 18
Place of Birth: Forsyth Co.
Father's Name: Joshua Bice
Mother's Name: Adaline Bagley

Page 85
Name of Groom: Simeon A. Tutton
Residence: Forsyth Co.
Age: 28
Occupation: Farmer
Place of Birth: Floyd Co., GA
Father's Name: William Tutton, decd
Mother's M. Name: Mary E. Berry

Date of Marriage: 7-12-1878
Name of Bride: Nancy Strickland
Residence: Forsyth Co.
Age: 23
Place of Birth: Forsyth Co.
Father's Name: Tolbert Strickland
Mother's Name: Celia Young

Page 112
Name of Groom: John W. Thompson
Residence: Forsyth Co.
Age: 22
Occupation: Farmer
Place of Birth: Calhoun Co., GA
Father's Name: Moses Thompson
Mother's M. Name: Adline Bruice

Date of Marriage: 10-20-1878
Name of Bride: Carinder Bruice
Residence: Forsyth Co.
Age: 18
Place of Birth: Forsyth Co.
Father's Name: Nathan L. Bruice
Mother's M. Name: Mily Hall

Page 113
Name of Groom: Thomas P. Tedder
Residence: Forsyth Co.
Age: 21
Occupation: Farmer
Place of Birth: Forsyth Co.
Father's Name: Ransom Tedder
Mother's M. Name: Susan C. Whitmire

Date of Marriage: 1-9-1878
Name of Bride: Manervia D. Echols
Residence: Forsyth Co.
Age: 19
Place of Birth: Forsyth Co.
Father's Name: Eber Echols
Mother's M. Name: Francis E. Gant

Page 119
Name of Groom: William M. Tritton?
Residence: Forsyth Co.
Age: 27
Occupation: Farmer
Place of Birth: Cavespring, Floyd
          Co., GA.
Father's Name: William Tritton
Mother's M. Name: Mary C. Berry

Date of Marriage: 2-6-1879
Name of Bride: Manervia C. Barker
Residence: Forsyth Co.
Age: 22
Place of Birth: Forsyth Co.
Father's Name: William Baker(?)
Mother's M. Name: Eliza C. Russell

Page 121
Name of Groom: Willis F. Tumlin
Residence: Forsyth Co.
Age: 21
Occupation: Farmer
Place of Birth: Hall Co., GA
Father's Name: Samual P. Tumblin
Mother's M. Name: Sarah Morris

Date of Marriage: 2-2-1879
Name of Bride: Nancy C. Shoomake
Residence: Forsyth Co.
Age: 18
Place of Birth: Dawson Co., GA
Father's Name: Jackson Shoomake
Mother's M. Name: Adline Chastain

Page 123
Name of Groom: E.S. Tinsley
Residence: Forsyth Co.
Age: 20
Occupation: Mechanic
Place of Birth: Spartanburg Co.,SC
Father's Name: Isaac Tinsley
Mother's M. Name: Mahala Nolen

Date of Marriage: 11-7-1878
Name of Bride: E.A. Prewett
Residence: Forsyth Co.
Age: 14
Place of Birth: Jackson Co., GA
Father's Name: John P.Prewett
Mother's Name: Mary C.Nunie

Page 125
Name of Groom: Ransom Tinsley
Residence: Forsyth Co.
Age: 19
Occupation: Farmer
Place of Birth: Forsyth Co.
Father's Name: Wash Tinsley
Mother's M. Name: Nelly Hays

Date of Marriage: 3-9-1879
Name of Bride: Ellen Bolland
Residence: Forsyth Co.
Age: 17
Place of Birth: Forsyth Co.
Father's Name: John Bolland
Mother's M. Name: Margaret White

Page 136
Name of Groom: John A. Tallent
Residence: Forsyth Co.
Age: 25
Occupation: Farmer
Place of Birth: Forsyth Co.
Father's Name: Thomas C.Tallent
Mother's M. Name: Nancy Collett

Date of Marriage: 9-4-1879
Name of Bride: Mary Jane Taylor
Residence: Forsyth Co.
Age: 21
Place of Birth: Forsyth Co.
Father's Name: John M.Taylor
Mother's M. Name: Francis
                            Stripling

Page 186
Name of Groom: D.A. Tinsley
Residence: Forsyth Co.
Age: 22
Occupation: Farmer
Place of Birth: Forsyth Co.
Father's Name: W.W. Tinsley
Mother's M. Name: Nelly Hays

Date of Marriage: 9-30-1880
Name of Bride: Nancy White
Residence: Forsyth Co.
Age: 18
Place of Birth: Hall Co., GA
Father's Name: John White, dec'd
Mother's M. Name: Francis Coon

Page 49
Name of Groom: James E.Vaughn
Residence: Forsyth Co.
Age: 20
Occupation: Farmer
Place of Birth: Forsyth Co.
Father's Name: Andy G.Vaughn
Mother's M. Name: Martha A.Chopeale

Date of Marriage: 12-6-1877
Name of Bride: Frances S.Major
Residence: Forsyth Co.
Age: 17
Place of Birth: Forsyth Co.
Father's Name: James T.Major
Mother's M. Name: Marcena Brannon

Page 31
Name of Groom: William N.Willson
Residence: Cherokee Co., GA
Age: 33
Occupation: Merchant
Place of Birth: Cherokee Co., GA
Father's Name: Lee Roy Willson
Mother's M. Name: Mourning Colile

Date of Marriage: 4-29-1877
Name of Bride: Mary Jane James
Residence: Forsyth Co.
Age: 20
Place of Birth: Forsyth Co.
Father's Name: Mahlin H.James
Mother's M. Name: Lucinda Butler

Page 40
Name of Groom: Hiram Wright
Residence: Fulton Co., GA
Age: 23
Occupation: Farmer
Place of Birth: Forsyth Co.
Father's Name: Joseph Wright
Mother's M. Name: Charistianna Edwards

Date of Marriage: 9-6-1877
Name of Bride: Mary Treadway
Residence: Forsyth Co.
Age: 21
Place of Birth: Pendleton, SC
Father's Name: Toliver Treadi-
                            way, dec'd
Mother's M. Name:Arminda
                            Isbelle

Page 43
Name of Groom: Richard A.Williams
Residence: Forsyth Co.
Age: 19
Occupation: Farmer
Place of Birth: Forsyth Co.
Father's Name: Charles Williams, dec'd
Mother's M. Name: Mary Ann Samples

Date of Marriage: 3-26-1878
Name of Bride: Hulda Issabella Benson
Residence: Forsyth Co.
Age: 18
Place of Birth: Forsyth Co.
Father's Name: Reuben W.Benson
Mother's M. Name: Nancy Spruill

Pagr 58
Name of Groom: Jesse M.Williams
Residence: Forsyth Co.
Age: 19
Occupation: Farmer
Place of Birth: Yadkin Co., NC
Father's Name: John M.Williams
Mother's M. Name: Lucinda C.Broadwell

Date of Marriage: 8-15-1877
Name of Bride: Frances Tinsley
Residence: Forsyth Co.
Age: 16
Place of Birth: Forsyth Co.
Father's Name: Isaac T.Tinsley
Place of Birth: Spartanburg Co., SC

Page 64
Name of Groom: James H.Watt
Residence: Forsyth Co.
Age: 31
Occupation: Mechanic
Place of Birth: Russell Co., AL
Father's Name: James M. Watt
Mother's M. Name: Thersa McCrary

Date of Marriage: 12-11-1877
Name of Bride: Elizabeth H.Harris
Residence: Cumming
Age: 20
Place of Birth: Forsyth Co.
Father's Name: Benjamin J.Harris
Mother's M. Name: Martha Sharp

Page 76
Name of Groom: Wily R.Westbrook
Residence: Forsyth Co.
Age: 23
Occupation: Farmer
Place of Birth: Forsyth Co.
Father's Name: Samuel Westbrook
Mother's M. Name: Jane White, dec'd

Date of Marriage: 3-19-1877
Name of Bride: Eva Wallis
Residence: Forsyth Co.
Age: 15
Place of Birth: Forsyth Co.
Father's Name: David Wallis
Mother's M. Name: Johanna Roach

Page 76
Name of Groom: Robert P.White
Residence: Forsyth Co.
Age: 24
Occupation: Farmer
Place of Birth: Forsyth Co.
Father's Name: Ransom White
Mother's M. Name: Parthena Tapp

Date of Marriage: 12-2-1877
Name of Bride: Sarah T.Roper
Age: 17
Residence: Forsyth Co.
Place of Birth: Forsyth Co.
Father's Name: Henry F.Roper
Mother's M. Name: Evaline Holbrook

Page 92
Name of Groom: John B. Woods
Residence: Forsyth Co.
Age: 22
Occupation: Farmer
Place of Birth: Dawson Co., GA
Father's Name: Winchester Woods
Mother's M. Name: Jane Shelton

Date of Marriage: 5-19-1878
Name of Bride: Mary Wilkins
Residence: Forsyth Co.
Age: 17
Place of Birth: Forsyth Co.
Father's Name: Hesekire Wilkins
Mother's M. Name: Malinda Whitmire

Page 99
Name of Groom: Joseph C.Waters
Residence: Decatur, DeKalb Co.
Age: 40
Occupation: Railroad Clerk
Place of Birth: Floyd Co., GA
Father's Name: Joseph Waters
Mother's M. Name: Elizabeth Acock

Date of Marriage: 10-10-1878
Name of Bride: Mrs. Addie Webster
                              Grimmett
Residence: Forsyth Co.
Age: 40
Place of Birth: Forsyth Co.
Father's Name: George Kellogg
Mother's M. Name: Carolin _____

Page 116
Name of Groom: Claibon A.Wallis
Residence: Forsyth Co.
Age: 21
Occupation: Farmer
Place of Birth: Forsyth Co.
Father's Name: William W.Wallis
Mother's M. Name: Martha Harris

Date of Marriage: 11-28-1879
Name of Bride: Sarah Martin
Residence: Forsyth Co.
Age: 22
Place of Birth: Forsyth Co.
Father's Name: William R.Martin
Mother's M. Name: Nancy Barrett

Page 117
Name of Groom: William B.Wallis
Residence: Forsyth Co.
Age:
Occupation: Farmer
Place of Birth:
Father's Name: John Wallis,dec'd
Mother's M. Name:

Date of Marriage: 1-5-1879
Name of Bride: Susan A. Cox
Residence: Forsyth Co.
Age: 24
Place of Birth:
Father's Name: Phillis Cox
Mother's M. Name:

Page 128
Name of Groom: William L.Walls
Residence: Forsyth Co.
Age: 38
Occupation: Farmer
Place of Birth: Forsyth Co.
Father's Name: Nath Walls
Mother's M. Name: Nancy Roach

Date of Marriage: 4-3-1879
Name of Bride: Marieas Monday
Residence: Forsyth Co.
Age: 29
Place of Birth: Forsyth Co.
Father's Name: Samuel D.Monday
Mother's M. Name: Martha J.Crump

Page 131
Name of Groom: George L. Wallis
Residence: Forsyth Co.
Age: 27
Occupation: Farmer
Place of Birth: Forsyth Co.
Father's Name: William Wallis
Mother's M. Name: Eliza Wofford

Date of Marriage: 5-11-1879
Name of Bride: Laura B.Hughes
Residence: Forsyth Co.
Age: 17
Place of Birth: Pickens Co.,SC
Father's Name: Andrew Hughes
Mother's Name: Lucinda Ellis

Page 153
Name of Groom: J.F. Watson
Residence: Hall Co.
Age: 23
Occupation: Farmer
Place of Birth: Forsyth Co.
Father's Name: H.F. Watson
Mother's M. Name: Hulda Chatman

Date of Marriage: 9-11-1879
Name of Bride: D.E. Bennett
Residence: Forsyth Co.
Age: 21
Place of Birth: Forsyth Co.
Father's Name: G.J. Bennett
Mother's M. Name: Elizabeth
                              Hammon

Page 160
Name of Groom: John T.Wooten
Residence: Forsyth Co.
Age: 28
Occupation: Mechanic
Place of Birth: Pickens Co., SC
Father's Name: Jessy Wooten
Mother's M. Name: Sarah McKinney

Date of Marriage: 1-15-1880
Name of Bride: Mary A.Martin
Residence: Forsyth Co.
Age: 27
Place of Birth: Forsyth Co.
Father's Name: Burd Martin
Mother's M. Name: Nancy Nix

Page 161
Name of Groom: George E.Whitmire
Residence: Forsyth Co.
Age: 19
Occupation: Farmer
Place of Birth: Forsyth Co.
Father's Name: Boon Whitmire
Mother's M. Name: Sarah Perry

Date of Marriage: 1-5-1880
Name of Bride: Eliza C.Hubbard
Residence: Forsyth Co.
Age: 20
Place of Birth: Forsyth Co.
Father's Name: Isiah Hubbard
Mother's M. Name: Nancy Childress

Page 169
Name of Groom: E.M. Welborn
Residence: Forsyth Co.
Age: 23
Occupation: Farmer
Place of Birth: Jackson Co., GA
Father's Name: Aaron T.Welborn,decd
Mother's M. Name: Mary B.Welborn

Date of Marriage: 2-26-1880
Name of Bride: Mary L.Beaver
Residence: Forsyth Co.
Age: 21
Place of Birth: Forsyth Co.
Father's Name: Alsey D.Beaver
Mother's M. Name: Agnis

Page 171
Name of Groom: William A.White
Residence: Forsyth Co.
Age: 21
Occupation: Farmer
Place of Birth: Pickens Co., SC
Father's Name: B. F. White
Mother's M. Name: Annie Morgan

Date of Marriage: 3-11-1880
Name of Bride: Margarett Jordan
Residence: Forsyth Co.
Age: 23
Place of Birth: Forsyth Co.
Father's Name: James Jordan
Mother's M. Name: Nancy Booker

Page 174
Name of Groom: James M. Vaughn
Residence: Forsyth Co.
Age: 16
Occupation: Farmer
Place of Birth: Forsyth Co.
Father's Name: James M.Vauthn,decd
Mother's M. Name: Harrit Estes

Date of Marriage: 4-5-1880
Name of Bride: M. E. Wallace
Residence: Forsyth Co.
Age: 15
Place of Birth: Forsyth Co.
Father's Name: J. B. Wallace
Mother's M. Name: S.B. Edwards

End

THE 1834 STATE CENSUS OF GILMER COUNTY, GA.

From the county files, Telamon Cuyler Collection, Special Collections, University of Georgia Libraries. Reproduced with permission.

To the Executive of the State of Georgia I do herby Certify that the above Statement maid out By me is a Just and true Return of the Whit Cityzns of Gilmer Coty. Given under my hand and Sele. June 7th 1834--Nobrs pursons-369-- /s/ James Kell

Clemand Quillion-7
Cornealir Cooper-10
Robert Smith-9
Robert Kincaid-8
William P. King-2
Ralph Smith-10
Luther Walas-8
Henry McNeail-10
Lurkeen Halt-8
John Drum (Deed?)-5
Jemar Woody-9
Milton Danise-14
Joshua H. Newbery-8
Josiah Holden-6
Newnan Oasbun-9
William R. King-2
Rubun Fasett-5
David Z. Colb-5
Francis Haiz-7
William Tucker-3
Alexander Kell-10
Gidien Smith-4
Isom Ponder-6
T. C. King-2
George W. Barker-1
John Barton-2
John T. Baly-6
Thomas W. Smith-5
Elegoh Eller-6
Wely Ballard-6

Elijah Chatur-5
John Steph-4
Eligh Serton-4
B. L. Goodm-4
William Allen-2
Robert Bery-1
Mark Corbety-9
John Harrss-6
James Smen-4
Weler Handrix-1
Polly Peak-2
Roehill Morris-1
Elizabeth Lumkin-1
Sareh Lumkin-1
Lew Clark-15
Wm. Ellegton-7
Bryon Griffth-9
B. M. Griffth-5
Stephen Griffth-6
H. R. Quillion-5
A. Y. Demond-4
Josiah Gerer-8
Mass Gnen-8
Ruben Holly-7
William Cox-7
Sula Cox-3
Welechud Barac-8
Meldeik M. Chart(?)-8
John Mills-1

(The above census shows heads of households and number of persons)

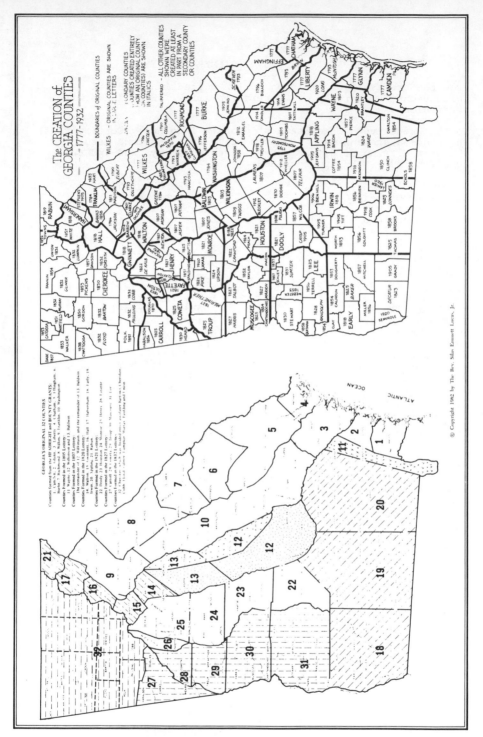

MAPS SHOWING THE CREATION OF GEORGIA'S COUNTIES

Page 1: 12 April 1850. George Gilbert to Osborn R. Johnson (Gordon County a part of Murray County until 1852, that is, North section). Lot 234, 8th dist. 3rd section (234-8-3) South of the Coosawattee River. 20 A. more or less $600. Wit: William E. Wellborn, D. W. Chase, J.P.

Page 1: 31 Aug. 1850. Bazzel Lowrey from Joseph H. Pritchard. Lots 39 & 40-7-3. Formerly Cherokee County, now Gordon County - 160 A. $1550.00. Wit: William Akin, Meredith Collier, J.P.

Page 2: 10 Feb. 1853. George A. Robbins from David G. King, for copyright of James L. Bonham improved garment cutter of Virginia, to teach and sell in all counties of said State and to convey the copyright to others for any or all the counties in the State of Virginia. Warrant same is unimcumbered, that I have the legal right to convey the same to said G. W. Robbins with 200 copies of Bonham Garment Cutter to be delivered at Knoxville, Tenn. - $400. I bind myself to furnish from 100 to 200, at 35 cents a copy to be sold only in above described territory. Wit: W. P. Fain, Joab Lewis, J.P.

Page 3: 8 Jan. 1850. Thomas W. Miller from Williamson Zuber Lot 61-24-4 $66.66-2/3 160 A. Wit: James B. Black, John W. Robertson, Wm. M. Peeples, Clerk.

Page 4: 2 Oct. 1851. William F. Miller from Thomas W. Miller of Floyd Co. Lot 61-24-3 originally Cherokee Co. now Gordon Co. $600. Wit: William Zuber, John Thomas, Wm. M. Peeples, Clerk.

Page 5: Armstead Abbott from W. P. Fain, 2 July 1852. Lot 180-15-3. $1200. Wit: Wm. Printup, Wm. P. Rainey J.I.C.

Page 5: 20 April 1852. Daniel R. Mitchell from Wm. F. Miller part Lots 27-15-3 and 61-24-3. Miller trustee from Mary Mann, of Floyd Co. $1500. NW half of Lot 27, 80 A. except 1/4 A. for the church. Wit: Asa S. Davis, Samuel T. King, J.P., Wm. M. Peeples, Clk.

Page 7: 1853. Young Scott from William M. Connors, part Lot 142-24-3. $37.45. Commence at a stake SW corner to a pine stake, commencing to a rock to the West line. Wit: Terence M. A. Guise, William J. Knight, Erasmus Bearden, acting J.P., Wm. M. Peeples, Clk.

Page 8: 5 December 1849. John Williamson of Emmanuel County to Andrew J. Williamson of Montgomery County, power of attorney to sell Lot 137-14-3 in the Cherokee purchase. Original was signed by John Williamson before John McIntosh. Copy was certified by William M. Peeples, Clk. before James Lay and Duke H. Hodge, J.P., 14 March 1853.

Page 8: 18 December 1849, John Williamson of Emanuel County to Michael Ficks of Cass, Lot 137-14-3 in the Cherokee purchase for $500. Recorded 14 March 1843 and original was signed by William M. Peeples, Clk. before James Lay and Duke H. Hodge, J.P.

Page 9: 27 Dec. 1850. Michael Fricks from James Lay, Lot 151-14-3, $2,000. Wit: A. N. Hargrove, W. W. Wall, J.I.C., W. M. Peeples, Clk. (Wall St. Calhoun named for Dr. W. W. Wall).

Page 10: Michael Fricks from John Higginbotham 1851. Lot 152-14-3, $1,000. Wit: John Baugh and Osborn Reeves. Wm. Peeples, Clk.

Page 11: 2 March 1851. Harrison Turner of Gordon Co. from Benjamin H. Jones of Early Co., Lot 115-23-2, $150. Wit: S. N. Lewis, Joshua Terry, J.P., W. M. Peeples, Clk.

Page 11: 9 Feb. 1852. Eli T. Haynes from Blair R. Mays (big slave dealer) S. half of lot 64-14-3, 80 A. $45. Wit: L. P. Hunt and John B. Rooker. W. M. P., Clk.
8 March 1851. Andrew B. Calhoun from Martha Wellborn, Lot 287-8-3, $1,000. Martha of Wilkes Co., Calhoun of Coweta. Wit: Jane X Murphy, Wilks X R. Wellborn, J.P., W. M. P., Clk.

Page 12: 13 March 1852. Martha Wellborn from legatees of Abner Wellborn, Lot 287-8-3 & 18-6-3. Signed by: Andrew B. Calhoun, William G. Hill, A. R. Wellborn, L. M. Hill of Wilkes Co., (1st three of Coweta Co.), L. R. Wellborn and Ann M. Simmons of Lincoln Co. Martha Wellborn of Wilkes. $237, Quit claim to lots of land bequeathed by Abner Wellborn, dec'd. to said Martha Wellborn to have and to hold during her natural life. (A long list of lots in several counties.) Wit: James H. Brown, W. M. Gordon, W. M. P., Clk. (The above is actually two deeds consolidated into one)

Page 14: 8 Feb. 1853. Humphrey W. Cobb, Cass Co. from James L. Eubank, Lincoln Co. Lot 153-6-3, 160 A., $300. Wit: Levi Baugh. Benjamin S. O'Neal, J.P., W. M. Peeples, Clk.

Page 15: 29 March 1853. Claiborn J. Butler, Gordon Co. from Lewis Tumlin, Cass Co. Lot 285-7-3, 160 A. $500. Wit: E. Barker (Hotel Manager) Robert N. White, J.P., W. M. P., Clk.

Page 15: 25 March 1853. Alfred B. Coulter, Floyd Co. from Homer Miller, Floyd. Lots 320, 293 & 294-14-3. $4000. Wit: Henry A. Gartrelle, F. I. Sweenall(?), J.P., W. M. P., Clk.

Page 16: Washington City, D.C. 3 March 1853. James H. Powell from Virginia Ann Powell-James in Gordon Co. In consideration of love and affection for beloved brother and $1 to her paid - Lot 289-24-2-160A. Land granted to V. A. Powell. 13 Sept. 1845. Wit: P. Daggy (?), J. W. Chastain. Robert A. White, acting J.P., W. M. P., Clk.

Page 17: 15 Dec. 1852. William E. Johnson from Pleasant Watts, Lot 322-7-3, $100. Wit: W. E. Carter, Isaac Lowe. Isaac Wofford, N. P., W. M. P., Clk.

Page 18: 15 Dec. 1852. Malinda Robinson from Pleasant Watts, Lot 323-7-3. $175. Wit: W. E. Carter, Isaac Lowe, Isaac Wofford, N. P.

Page 19: 12 Oct. 1838. Richard Jones of Muscogee Co. from Murdock Chisholm of Stewart Co. Lot 167-7-3, $300. 160 A. John Taylor, Michael N. Clardy, J.P., W. M. P., Clk.

Page 20: State of South Carolina, Charleston District; Seymour R. Bonner of Muscogee Co. from Richard Jones, Lot 167-7-3, 160 A. $600. Wit: T. B. Swift, B. C. Presley, J.P.

Page 20: 15 Sept. 1850. Samuel Franklin of Cass Co., from Sarah Striplin, of Cherokee Co. Lot 138-23-3. $112. Wit: Augustus F. Hubbard. John J. Dickinson, J.P., W. M. P., Clk.

Page 21: 1 Oct. 1848. Wiley C. Ballard of Walker Co. from Joshua S. Carpenter of Floyd Co. Lot 94-25-3, 80 A. $125. Commencing at SW corner running the original line West unto the branch to the fork and up the ridge to the S. line running to the East corner. Wit: Joel C. M. Carpenter. Jno. W. Medcalf, J.P., W. M. P., Clk.

Page 23: 11 Feb. 1850. John C. Roswell of Floyd Co. from Darius E. Keel, Cass Co. Lot 94-25-3. $160. 80 A. Same lot sold 3 times.

Page 24: 11 Dec. 1851. Joseph H. Jones, Gordon from John C. Boswell of Cass Co. Lot 87-25-3. $450. In Floyd Co. 160 A. Wit: W. F. Tracey, David S. Law, J.I.C., W. M. P., Clk.

Page 24: 11 Dec. 1850. Joseph H. Jones of Cass Co., from J. C. Boswell. Lot 94-25-3. 80 A. $160 Wit: N. P. Tracey, David S. Law, N. P., W. M. P, Clk.

Page 25: 21 Feb. 1835. William Montgomery of Gwinnett Co. from Amelia Ramey. Lot 8-6-3. $1,000. Wit: John C. Perry (Remy?). John Hammond, W. M. Davis, J.P., W. M. P., Clk.

Page 26: 9 Sept. 1851. John C. Boswell from John R. Alexander of Floyd, Lot 87-25-3. 160 A. $350. Wit: John A. Johnson, Wm. C. Price, J.I.C., W. M. P., Clk.

Page 27: 17 Feb. 1837. Hiram Moore of Baldwin Co. from William Montgomery of Gwinnett. Lot 8-6-3. $100. Wit: Joseph Evins, James McAuber, J.I.C., W. M. P., Clk.

Apr. 4, 1853. Agreement S. D. Everett with Webster and Palmer. Joseph Webster and George S. Palmer, city of Savannah. Said Webster and Palmer agree to furnish said S. D. Everett groceries, wares and merchandise at the Savannah prices and that the said S. D. Everett agrees on his part to sell the goods and use the profits only and also the said goods belong to said Webster and Palmer and are subject to their order until sold. W. M. Peeples, Clk.

391

Page 28:   4 August 1851. Wilkinson Co. Elizabeth Rozer, Robert A. Rozer and others to John W. Allen. Lot 132-6-3. Elizabeth Rozer, wife of Anderson Rozer; Robert A. Rozer, John Mason, in the right of his wife, Fanny Rozer formerly, now Fanny Mason, Dexter Rozer and Susan Rozer and Theophilus Rozer of Wilkinson Co. To John Allen of Twiggs Co. 100 A. in Cass Co. $200. Robert Rozer, William A. Rozer. Signed by all above named. Willis Allen, J.P., W. M. Peeples, Clk.

Page 29:   John W. Allen sold same lot to John T. Harrison, $100, 1852. Wit: Ira E. Perry, Willis Allen.

Page 31:   Same lot: John F. Harrison of Texas to Evan C. Pearson of Baldwin Co. 8 Oct. 1853. Wit: J. M. Patton, William Latimer, J.P. Cass Co., W. M. Peeples, Clk. Gordon Co.

Page 31:   6 Apr. 1853; Evan Pearson, Canton from Tarelton Lewis, Cass Co. Lot 157-6-3, $1000. Wit: Ruth A. M. Holden, N.C. Wyley, J.I.C., W. M. P., Clk.

Page 32:   26 Jan. 1837. Hentry Allbright Floyd Co. from Hiram Moore Baldwin Co. Lots 8 & 19-6-23, 325 A. $500. Wit: Benjamin Cleveland, James Ransom, J.P. Henry Co.

Page 33:   11 March 1853. R. J. Penn, Cafs Co. from Henry Allbright, Walker Co., no lot number given, 160 A., $160. Wit: Isaac Morrison, Ephraim Parker, J.P.

Page 33:   Thomas Hamilton vs. Augustus Crawford, principal and Joel Crawford, indorsee, Madison Co., Ga. Sheriff of said State and County. We command you that the goods and chattels, lands and tenements of Augustus Crawford, principal, and Joel Crawford, indorser, you cause to be made the sum of $3070, principal, and also the further sum of $149.40 int. up to the 14th day of March, 1842, and also the further sum of $6.75 for costs with interests on principal sum from 14 March, 1842 which Thomas M. Hamilton indorses lately in our superior court of said Co. recoverable against said Augustus Crawford, principal, and Joel Crawford, indorsee -- you have several sums of money before the Judge of said court in Sept. 1843. William Penn Sheriff. Page and a half follow, itemized -- sales of lots and property. J. N. Miller, Sheriff, Gordon County, 1853.

Page 36:   5 April 1853. Lewis Tumlin Cafs Co. from Jefse Miller Sheriff, Lot 129-6-3, Crawford Estate, 160 A, $170. Wit: P. L. Kay, Geo. Ranson, J.P.

Page 37:   31 Jan. 1851. Roger Murphy from William S. Murphy, both Cafs Co., Lot 187-6-3, 160 A., $400 Wit: William Stevens and S. I. Pinion. Henry M. Crany, J.P., Wm. M. Peeples, Clerk Gordon Co.

Page 38:   20 June 1851. William M. Denman, Cafs, from Felix Denman Gordon Co. Lots 198-199 & 219-6-3 in consideration of affection he has and bears to his son William M. Denman, 480 A. $5 cash. John A. Wilks, J.P., A. M. Covington, J. G. Denman. W. M. Peeples, Clk. David G. King, J.P. Gordon Co.

Page 39: 10 Sept. 1851. Albert Rich Gordon Co. from
W. C. Wyley Cafs, Lot 228-6-3, 160 A., $400. Wit:
James D. Terrell, Henry M. Crany (?), J.P., W. M. P, Clk.

Page 40: Rec'd. Apr. 16, 1853, Capt. Andrew Orr, highest
bidder from Justices of Inferior Court, Lot 9 - 22nd section
town of Calhoun, $75 - Long preamble to all these first town lot
deeds -- land lots 205 & 206 owned by John P. King of Augusta.
He donated lots for 3 churches and all county bldgs. Wit:
John Baugh, Isaac Wofford, J.P., W. M. Peeples, Clk. Justices.
George Lumpkin, David G. King, S. T. Mays, G. F. Swaggerty.

Page 41: D. G. Hunt from Inf. Court 18 Apr. 1853.
William Baley purchaser at public outcry, Jan. 10, 1853, $150.
Justices deeded it to D. Granville Hunt, $150. Wit:
T. M. Ward, John Baugh, J.P., W. W. Wall, Wesley Kinman and
David B. Barrett, J.I.C.'s.

Page 42: James W. Trippe, Atty. Eatonton Mfg. Co. 28 March
1853, sold to William H. Black, Lot 143-14-3, 160 A., $100.
Wit: W. C. Jones, Samuel I. King, J.P., W. M. P., Clerk.

Page 43: 30 Nov. 1850. Matthew Patrick, Murray Co. from
Isaac Justice Pulaski, Lot 162-13-3, 160 A, $300. Wit:
John Monroe, James Henson, W. M. P., Clk.

Page 44: Matthew Patrick from Joseph Monroe. Bill of Sale
$800. 2 certain negroes, 1 a boy named Malcolm, 6 or 7 years
old, dark complexion and a girl, Eliza, about 13, dark
complexion - warrant them to be sound and well in body and mind
and to be slaves for life. Wit: L. W. McAbee, Thos. O. Austin,
W. M. P., Clk.

Page 44: 18 Apr. 1853. Daniel Johnson and
William R. Chandler, Admins. Abraham Chandler Estate to
Jefse N. Miller, Sheriff. Lots 168 & 182-14-3; long detailed
account. Wit: Thomas M. Compton, W. M. P., Clk.

Page 46: 17 Dec. 1838. Reuben Phillips from
Dennis C. McClendon, Russell Co., Ala. Lot 172-7-3, $100. Wit:
J. A. J. Phillips W--x Phillips, W. M. P., Clk.

Page 47: 1 Nov. 1852. Jonathan Phillips, Cafs Co. from
James R. Brock, Gordon Co. Lot 72-7-3, 81 A. S. half, $150.
Wit: A. D. Shackelford, F. M. Gibbs, David Morrow, J. .P.,
W. M. P., Clk.

Page 48: 8 Dec. 1852 E. R. Kiker from Wm. J. Gartrell.
Lot 149-7-3 mortgage, F. Tate, C. Tate, Wm. Douglas, J.P.

Page 49: 18 March 1852. John C. Phillips from Nathan Land
Lot 228-7-3, 160 A., $300. Wit: R. H. Clardy,
Joseph N____?, J.I.C.

Page 50: 3 Nov. 1852. Lorenzo D. Wyatt from
Robert M. Gunby, Muscogee Co. Lot 20-14-3, 160 A., $1500. Wit:
William B. Langdon, Robert H. Green, N. P.

Page 50: 7 Apr. 1853, William H. Dabney from Sheriff Miller. Property of John T. Thweatt, Inf. Ct. Pike Co. -- in favor of Charlie Campbell and Asher Ayers, merchants, using name of C. Campbell against John T. Thweatt and James P. Shackelford -- sold at courthouse to W. H. Dabney, $51. Wit: Thomas M. Compton, W. M. P., Clk.

Page 51: 21 Apr. 1853 Agreement between Wm. G. Bonner & Capt. Samuel McSpadden - Bonner agrees to allow McSpadden the free use and cultivation of lot of land 67-7-3 for the rest of the year 1848 and all of 1849. A comfortable log cabin 18' x 18', to clear 15 A. of land and give up possession quickly. Wit: A. L. Boncher.

Page 52: March 1853 term of court. William N. Peeples vs. Samuel McSpadden and Ellisha L. Boncher - $86.26 on goods and chattels of McSpadden, also $4.85 int. up to 16 Oct. 1852 - $12.87 costs levied this fi fa on one lot of land - David G. Wylie Sheriff. Sold above property J. H. B. Shackelford $81.

Page 55: 7 Apr. 1853. Hiram C. Roe from James Lay, Lot 99-15-3. 160 A. $225. Wit: James W. Seten, G. W. Ransom, J.P.

Page 55: 11 Sept. 1852. Joshua King from Jonathan King, both of N. C. Rutherford Co. 160 A., $4500. Wit: Jonas King. Samuel T. King, J.P.

Page 56: 9 Sept. 1852. Jonathan King from Joseph H. Jones. Lots 23 and 38-14-3, 160 A. each, $2000. Wit: William Whitesides, Samuel King, J.P.

Page 57: 21 Jan. 1853 - J. M. Field, Gordon Co. from George W. Harrison, Baldwin Co., Lot 120-14-3, $100. John H. Hatcher, N. I. Jones, J.P.

Page 57: 25 Dec. 1839. Fi Fa - Daniel Fulford vs. Zack Wallace and James H. Cotten Security, Marion Co. To Constables, greetings - you are hereby authorized to levy on goods and chattels, lands and tenements of Zachariah Wallace and James Cotten security - levy and sale - $1.25 cost - 430(?) 808 Dist. Ga. Militia - Randall W. Raston, J.P. Settled in Gordon Co. 1851 - David Wylie Sheriff.

Page 58: 23 Apr. 1853. M. C. Ownings from M. C. Bewley, Lot 280-14-3, 160 A., $1600. Wit: M. Fricks, Isaac Wofford, J.P., W. M. P., Clk.

Page 59: 2 May 1853. Thomas Binion and R. F. Conoway. Lot 159-14-3, granted to George Damson, Green Co, 160 A., $400, James Sams Test. W. P. Fain, J.I.C., W. M. Peeples, Clk.

Page 59: 7 March 1848. Addison B. Scott, Marion Co. from Seaborn I. Collins of Covington Co., Ala., Lot 275-7-3, 160 A., $70. Wit: J. I. Halley, L. S. Peacock. Wm. Doud, J.P. On back of deed. Recorded in the office of the clerk, Murray Co. Sup. Crt. Bk. G. P. 350. Robert McCamy, Clk. Rec. in Gordon Co. 1853, W. M. P. Clk.

Page 61: 3 May 1853. A. V. Edmondson from J. M. Field, Lots 82, 63 and part of 99-7-3. Wit: (could not read), W. M. P., Clk.

Page 62: 3 May 1853. Nathaniel N. Baxter from Hiram McGontgomery (?) Adm. Lot 42-14-3 Estate of Thomas Montgomery - sold before the courthouse door Gordon Co. $2000, commence at stake 50 poles East of SW corner of Lot 42 running E. to S.E. corner Lot 43, W. to Van's Creek, S. with meanderings of said creek to within 50 poles of W. line of Lot 42 thense due S. to beginning. Wit: William H. Dabney, Wm. P. Fain, J.I.C., W. M. P., Clk.

Page 63: 7 May 1853. Warren Akin of Cafs Co. from Humphrey W. Cobb(?), Lot 155-6-3, 160 A., $150. Wit: John W. Burke, T. H. Gilbreath, J. C., W. M. P., Clk.

Page 65: 7 May 1853. Robert Russell of Walker Co. to James Burch of Gordon Co., Lot 259-14-3, 160 A., $2100. Wit: J. H. Arthur, W. P. Fain, J.I.C., Thomas M. Compton, Clk.

Page 66: 10 July 1852. James S. Bryant from John Malone. Lot 321-13-2, $200, reserved 5 A. in S.E. corner, containing 8 A. Sold E. half of Lot 321-13-3. Wit: M. H. Miller, Thos. P. Austin, J.P., W. M. P., Clk.

Page 67: 7 Jan. 1851. S. B. Reeves from A. W. Reeves, Lot 4-14-3. Asbury W. Reeves & Strawberry W. Reeves of Murray Co., 80 A., $400. Wit: Jesse Miller, David B. Barrett, J.I.C., T. M. Compton, Clk.

Page 67: 24 Dec. 1851. Ezekiel T. Henderson from S. R. Reeves, Lot 48-14-3, $450. Wit: Thomas O. Austin, James Ratchford, T. M. Compton, Clk.

Page 68: 19 Jan. 1853. E. T. Henderson from Miller & Echols, Lot 41-14-4 between Jesse Miller and A. B. Echols. Wit: J. C. Butler, John Baugh, J.P., R. S. Thompson (wit), Thos. M. Compton, Clk.

Page 69: 16 May 1853. William H. Dabney to Thomas M. Compton. Lot 10, 2nd section town of Calhoun, $250. Lot lies between house now occupied by John Braswell, which was formerly occupied by J. B. Richards as a store - West of that portion of said Lot 10 sold by Duke and Mims to D. Johnson - said Johnson to Comptom - 20' front, 50' back, W. M. P., Clk.

Page 70: Wm. P. Fain from Inf. Court - Lot 4 - Section 5 - town of Calhoun, 200' front, 150' back - 19 May 1853. Wit: David W. Neel. Wm. J. Fuller, J.P., W. W. Wall, David B. Barrett, Wesley Kinman, J.I.C.'s, T. M. Compton, Clk.

Page 71: 2 April 1836. Elijah Roberts from Francis Wilson, both of Screven Co., $500. Land in Gordon Co. Cherokee Lottery - Lot 110 14-3. wit: Alfred Routh, Henry Buford, J.P., T. M. C., Clk.

Page 72: 18 May 1853. Thomas M. Compton from Wm. P. Fain, Lot 4, Section 5, town of Calhoun except 8' across the N.E. side of lot adjoinging lot of Wm. H. Dabney to be used as a lane or street. Wit: W. H. Brown, W. M. P., Clk.

Page 72: 25 May 1853. Hiram Montgomery from Nathaniel N. Baxter - 2_-7-3, $2000. Wit: Hugh P. Montgomery, J. R. Montgomery, J.P., W. M. P., Clk.

Page 73: 7 June 1853. Robert Beasley of Macon Ga. from J. N. Miller. Sheriff seized and levied on certain town lots - Lots 9 & 2 - 100' front, 150' back - was property of Reuben Scott of Dekalb Co. William H. Riley sec. $559. Wit: William H. Dabney, Isaac Wofford, N.P., W. M. P., Clk.

Page 75: 4 June 1853. W. B. Thomas from John C. Butler, part of Lot 1-6 section, town of Calhoun, 25' front, 150' back, $21. Wit: Thomas Compton, W. M. P., Clk.

Page 75: 23 March 1853. Christopher Garlington from John Robinson of Carroll Co., Lot 291-14-3, 160 A, $1600 cash. Wit: A. M. Sloan, W. M. P., Clk.

Page 76: 12 March 1852. Charlie Kiker for use of Nancy Pittman from Thomas B. Barnwell, Lot 2-23-2, $5 cash and natural affection for his sister, Nancy E. Pittman, wife of Henry H. Pittman, in trust for her children, 100 A. taken from S. part of lot adjoining lands of J. H. Butler, J. M. Field, Wm. Townsend and others. Wit: John Townsend and Arvina Davis. Robert N. White, J.P., W. M. P., Clk.

Page 77: Copyright John O'Neil, Green Co. Ohio did obtain letters patent of U.S. for certain improvements on Atmospheric Lever Churns, date 30 July 1850. I, Edward C. Quiet (?) of Kingston Ulster Co., did obtain of John O'Neil the right and interest in said invention in State of Tennessee. Wm. M. Baren of county of Gordon is desirous of acquiring an interest therein. For $300, I have sold and set over all rights in said invention in the counties of Hamilton, Meigs, Dekalb, Marion, Cannon, Van Buren, Baldwin and Rhea in the State of Tennessee to Wm. M. Baren for his use and his legal representatives for 14 years. Wit: James E. Brown, G. W. Ransome, J.P., W. M. P., Clk.

Page 79: Acheson Findley of Chambers Co., Ala. to James M. Harlan of Gordon County. Lots 73, 108, 107, 37 and 38-7-3, $8000. Wit: Evan G. Richards, Jefferson Faulkner, N.P. 12 May 1853. Rec. Gordon Co. 21 June 1853. W. M. Peeples, Clerk.

Page 80: 7 May 1851. Robert C. Smith from James H. Bailey, part Lot 122-15-3. Wit: W. H. Dabney, David S. Law, J.I.C. commencing at a pile of rock, East to a certain free stone rock, West line. Part of said Lot, 95 A.

Page 80: 30 Dec. 1852 Wiley Johnson from Jefse Waddell, S. portion Lot 124-15-3, 100 A. $500. Wit: H. W. Barnett, David Morrow, J.P., W. M. Peeples, Clk.

Page 81:   29 June 1852.   Clifford Woodruff from Harden
Woodruff and others, Power or Attorney, Wilkes County.
John D. Reaves, Harden Woodruff and David Woodruff appointed
Clifford Woodruff of Meriwether Co. Lots 5-25, 2, 9-7-3, drawn
by Richard Woodruff, dec'd. and willed to us. Wit: John ____?,
Lewis J. Brown, J.I.C., W. M. P., Clk.

Page 82:   17 June 1853.   Elijah Dillard from
Clifford Woodruff, Atty. in fact for J. D. Reaves and others,
Lot 96-7-3, $135. Hardin & David Woodruff and J. D. Reaves.
Wit: George A. Hall, Thomas Benson. James I. Holland, J.P.

Page 83:   1 April 1853.   William H. Bailey to Robert
C. Saxon, Lot 173-15-3, 1 A. S. side known as the old
Adairsville town lot. Wit: John C. Aycock, W. P. Fain, J.I.C.,
Thomas M. Compton, Clk. (Mr. Saxon built an 8-sided house on
land at present Gordon-Bartow line. Furious battle took place
here during Civil War -- house known as the Octagon House.
Federals had heard that there was a fort here. House was left
in ruins.)

Page 84:   9 July 1853.   Thomas Benson from Sheriff Wylie,
Lot 159-14-3, 8 A. Property of B. F. Conaway, in favor of
Martin Duke against B. F. Conaway. Sold at the courthouse.
Wit: William H. Dabney, Wylie Roberts, J.P., T. M. Compton,
Clk.

Page 85:   24 Dec. 1852.   Daniel Johnson and
William B. Chandler, Adms. Abraham Chandler Estate to
John P. Phillips, town lots adjoining town of Calhoun. Lot 36,
sold at courthouse 1851, $16, 1 A. Wit: E. V. Ammons,
James M. Strange, J.P., T. M. C., Clk.

Page 86:   2 July 1853.   Inferior Court to John P. Phillips,
Lots 8 & 1, Section 17, town of Calhoun, Lot 8 in 2nd. Section.
Wit: S. T. Mayes, W. M. Peeples, Clk. Inf. Court $196.

Page 87:   17 June 1853.   William H. Howard of Augusta from
William H. Culpepper, Floyd Co. Mrtg. Lot 52-24-3, Floyd Co.
William H. Culpepper on 16 July 1852, $736 promissory note.
Rec. Gordon Co. 1853. Wm. P. Fain, J.I.C., T. M. Compton, Clk.

Page 89:   14 June 1853.   George C. Selman from
W. L. Baldwin, Lot 4, Section 1, town of Calhoun, undivided 1/2
part, N. half of lot, 25' front, 65' back, all rights and
buildings, etc. Wit: William H. Dabney, Wm. P. Fain, J.I.C.,
T. M. C., Clk.

Page 107:   6 Aug. 1853.   S. G. L. Chandler from
W. H. Bailey, Lot 9, Section 2, town of Calhoun, $300.
Robt. White, J.P.

Page 109:   21 Dec. 1850.   Obdiah Miller from David Miller,
Lot 326-14-3, $150. David Morrow, J.P., Thos. M. Compton, Clerk
(hereafter listed as T.M.C.)

Page 111:   30 Nov. 1852.   William O. Cleveland from
Joseph Watters (Floyd Co.) 136-24-3. T. M. C., Clk. J. Watters,
J.P.

Page 112: 23 Aug. 1833. Taliafario Witcher, Floyd Co. from John Robinson, Carroll Co. 283-14-3, 160 A., $500, Wit: Osborn Reeves, Joel Fain, J. P., T. M. C., Clk.

Page 113: 19 Jan. 1853. William I. Witcher, Floyd, Co., from John Robinson, Carroll Co. 284-14-3, 160 A., $1500. Wit: Osborn Reeves, Joel Fain, J.P.

Page 114: 18 Feb. 1853. James W. Strange from Daniel Johnson and Wm. P. Chandler, Lot No. 15 of 192-14-3 Chandler estate, run off into town lots, 44 A. adjoining town of Calhoun, Lot 15 sold to highest bidder at courthouse, $51. Wit: Thos. M. Evins, G. W. Ransom, J.P., T. M. C., Clk.

Page 117: 24 March 1853. Ephraim Strickland from Matthew Davis, 323-24-3, 160 A, $2000. Wit: James H. Powell, Henry H. Pittman, J.P., T. M. C., Clk.

Page 118: 25 Aug. 1853. J. L. Gregg from William C. Rawlston, 92-6-3, $85. Wit: O. P. Heath, Robert M. White, J.P., T. M. C., Clk.

Page 119: 5 Aug. 1853. W. C. Pendley from Nancy Tracey, Lot 12, Section 15, town of Calhoun, $90. Wit: James F. Kinman, Henry Cooper, J.P., T.M.C., Clk.

Page 120: 25 June 1853. William F. Jones and/or The Wesley Chapel Church from James Gannaway. Lot 317-7-3 for love and desire he has for the cause of God. Wit: E. J. Holcombe, O. C. Campbell, J.P.

Page 121: 17 July 1852. Inf. Court to R. B. Spears, Lot 10, Section 8, town of Calhoun, $158. Wit: S. T. Mayes, W. M. Peeples, Clk. Rec. 1853, T. M. C., Clk.

Page 122: 25 Aug. 1853. Spears sold same lot to James M. Orr, $185. Wit: S. T. Mayes, John Baugh, J.P., T. M. C., Clk.

Page 123: 20 Jan. 1853. James M. Orr and Bros. from Andrew Orr and Mary P. Orr, 274-14-3. James M. Orr, Robert Orr, John Orr, S. M. Jones (bro.-in-law) $500. Wit: James R. Wylie, David G. Wylie, T. M. C., Clk.

Page 126: 24 July 1844. W. S. McSpaden from William Bagley, Murray Co., 167-7-3, $300. Wit: Charles A. Grisham.

Page 124: 2 Feb. 1853. James M. Orr from Daniel Johnson and Wm. B. Chandler, Lots 192 and 168-14-3, No. 4 4, 1 A. town of Calhoun, $22. Wit: Hugh Davison, G. W. Ransom, J.P., T. M. C., Clk.

Page 125: 15 March 1842. The Republic of Texas, County of Harmon, William Bagley from John S. Wray, both of Republic of Texas, Lot 167-7-3, land in the county of Cafs in State of Georgia, $50, 160 A. on Pine Log Creek. Wit: Edward C. Bagley, Henry Bagley.

Page 127: 29 Dec. 1853. Cafs Co., Benj. Tally from Stephen Talley, N.E. side Lot 32-15-3, $225. Wit: Samuel Hodges, David Morrow, J.P., T. M. C., Clk.

Page 128: 11 Jan. 1853. Robert Boyd from Lanchlin McKinnon, both of Telfair Co., Lot 5-15-3, 160 A., $375. John McKinnon, J.I.C., T. M. C., Clk.

Page 129: 4 March 1839. William F. Bond and Co. Wilkinson Co., from Robert T. Boyd, Telfair Co., Lot 5-15-3, Cafs Co., $300. Wit: William Espey, James A. Rogers. Rec. 9 Sept. 1853. T. M. C., Clk.

Page 131: 2 May 1853. Gabriel M. Clements of Montgomery Co. to Lanchlin McKinnon, Lot 5-15-3, $170. Wit: Jabob C. Clements, D. M. Rose, A. Campbell, J.P., Rec. 10 Sept. 1853.

Page 131: Jan. 1853. Andrew J. Watters of Floyd Co. to Joseph Watters, Lot 5-15-3, 160 A., $700. Wit: John Mathis, William Watters, J.P., T. M. C., Clk.

Page 133: 15 March 1853. John G. Scales from William Harris, mrtg. Lot 264-13-3, $134. Wit: James A. Sloan, A. S. Sloan, J.I.C., W. M. P., Clk.

Page 135: 22 Sept. 1852. Israel P. Bowen from Olive Hampton, Hamilton Co. Tenn. & Thomas W. Hampton, Lot 192-7-3, $75. Wit: George Julian. William Varnell, J.P.

Page 136: 15 March 1853. Solomon Roe from Samuel McDow, 175-7-3, $300, 160 A. Wit: David G. Wylie, G. W. Ransome, J.P., T. M. C., Clk.

Page 137: 20 April 1853. Robert R. Orr from Joseph L. Neel, Lot 6, Sect. 2, town of Calhoun, $375. Wit: J. Braswell. George Lumpkin, J.I.C., T.M.C., Clk.

Page 137: 13 July 1852. Henry H. Dobson from Nathan Calderbank of Richmond Co., Lot 5-15-3, $1000. Wit: David Ward (?), J. W. Meridith, J.P.

Page 138: 13 Sept 1852. David Black from Henry H. Dobson, Lot 5-15-3, 160 A, $1200. Wit: James Lay, James B. Black, James ___?, David G. King, J.I.C., T. M. C., Clk.

Page 139: 10 Nov. 1851. Lewis R. Hunt, Murrary Co. from John Stewart, Walker Co., Lot 12, -14 district, town of Resaca, $275. Wit: George Watters, A. Stewart, W. M. P., Clk.

Page 140: 3 Feb. 1853. Enoch Humphries and David W. Humphries of Murray Co., from James C. Morris 29-7-3, 160 A. Gordon Co. $218.70. Wit: Dawson A. Walker, F. B. Morris, C.S.C., W. M. P., Clk.

Page 141: 12 Sept. 1853. Thomas M. Compton from John G. B. Andrews, Lot 3, Sect. 10, town of Calhoun, $300. Wit: John A. Hopper, W. M. P., Clk., T. M. C., Clk.

Page 142: 30 Sept. 1853. Lot 1, Sect. 10, town of Calhoun, Stephen M. Jones to James M. Orr, $500. Wit: J. H. Arthur. W. M. P., Clk., T. M. C., D. Clk.

Page 143: 13 Sept. 1853. Thomas Aiken of Gordon from Allen May of Walker, 24-25-3, $500. Wit. W. O. Fincher, John W. Medcalf, J. P.

Page 144: 4 June 1854, Cafs Co., M. M. Blalock, Adm. to Alexander Cameron, 29-14-3, Estate of James Connally. 8 Jan 1844, Court appointed adms. $115.50. Wit: George _____, David Morrow, J.P., T. M. C., Clk.

Page 145: 7 April 1849. Alexander Cameron, Cafs from Daniel Morrison, Adm. estate John Morrison, Richmond Co., Lot 25-14-3, advertised in Augusta Chronicle, 160 A, $300. Wit: Samuel Kinman, David Morrow, J.P., T. M. C., Clk.

Page 146: 6 May 1852. Pickett Shifflett from Felix Mofs, 178-15-3, except 4 acres, $2000 - in the S.W. Corner, the 4 acres - Mary R. Barrett, Joseph R. Barrett, David B. Barrett, J.I.C., T. M. C., Clk.

Page 147: 24 Aug. 1849. Mary Harden of Murray Co., from John McClure, 31-7-3, 160 A., $400. Wit: Ablsalom Homcomb, Perry Harden, Gordon Co., Willie Roberts W. J., T. M. C., Clk.

Page 148: 23 Feb. 1850. Matthew Robertson, Cafs to McKinney Scott, 41-23-2, $150, 80 A. Wit: Thomas C. Robertson, Robert N. White, H. H. Pittman, J.P., T. M. C., Clk.

Page 149: 15 Sept. 1853. Jesse N. Miller from James W. Abernathy of Bibb Co., 240-13-3, granted to H. V. Johnson, Armstrong from Johnson. Wit: R. B. Mayes, Isaac N. Buckner, J.P., T. M. C., Clk.

Page 150: 6 Oct. 1853. A. E. Vandiver from Jesse N. Miller, 37-14-3, 160 A., $600. Wit: A. B. Echols, Robert White, J.P., T. M. C., Clk. (A. B. Echols was Clerk of Court during the 1860's. Was shot and killed in front of his house at dusk, Oct. 10, 1866, by a horse thief, because Mr. E. asked the man "What are you doing here at this time of day, bareheaded and barebacked?" -- the horse was barebacked, no saddle)

Page 150: 18 Oct. 1853. Henry G. Morris of Cherokee Co. from Michael C. Kirkham, 278-14-3, $1760, 160 A. Wit: Richard W. Cain, Isaac Wofford, N.P., T. M. C., Clk.

Page 151: 3 Nov. 1853. J. D. Phillips and D. G. Wiley from Ruth A. M. Nelson (widow Gen. Charles Haney Nelson) 24-7-3, $2000, 160 A. Wit: James Rogers (Quarter-master under Gen. Nelson) G. W. Ranson, J.P., T. M. C., Clk.

Page 152: 9 Nov. 1853. David S. Law from Inf. Court, Lot 5 Section 10, town of Calhoun, sold at public outcry, $201. Wit: Washington Lawson, W. M. P., Clk. (First train to Dawsonville (Calhoun) pulled by engine Texas, stopped by Wash Lawson's store)

Page 153: 10 Aug. 1852. Robert R. Orr, John Orr, James M. Orr, Samuel D. Wylie (wife an Orr), S. M. Jones (wife an Orr) from William Orr of Henry Co., 277-14-3, $850, lot West of Oothclaga Creek. Wit: Isaac M. McBride, G. W. McMillan, J.P., T. M. C., Clk.
Also Lot 27-14-3, 5 Dec. 1852, 160 A., $600. Wit: David White, G.W. McMillan, J.P., T. M. C., Clk.

Page 155: 21 Jan. 1853. Williamson Zuber of Floyd Co. from Beaufort Randolph of Whitfield Co., 3 & 4-15-3, $900. Wit: Houston Adcock, Joseph Waters, J.P., T. M. C., Clk.

Page 155: 10 Nov. 1853. William M. Peeples from David S. Law, Adm. Gabriel T. Moore, 21-7-%00 (?), 160 A. Wit: James F. Kinman, G. W. Ransome, J.P.

Page 156: 22 Oct. 1853. William M. Peeples from Richard W. Jones, bill of sale, boy Joe, 15 years old, dark complexion, slave for life, $900, T. M. C., Clk.

Page 158: 11 July 1842. John Shepherd of Gwinett Co. from Jesse Lowe, Troup Co., 33-6-3, $100, 160 A., Gordon Co. Wit: P. H. Wildman, Jesse Murphry, J. P., T. M. C., Clk. Same lot sold 1843 by Shepherd to John H. Fox.

Page 159: 25 May 1849. Wm. Rich, D. G. Wylie and Phillip McEntire of Cafs Co., from Francis Holden, Lots 44, 78 & 103 07-3. Said Francis Holden hath this day been arrested for assault and battery - 1 warrant for keeping a disorderly house, 1 warrant for selling spiritouse liquors to slaves. These men were security. 3 several bonds. Holden was to appear at next court at Cafsville. -1 bond $100 -2 for $150 each. Case against Merrill Collier, larceny from the house; Jacob Capehart, giving liquor to a slave without the consent of his overseer -- total bonds $700. Wit: James R. Brock, Jarrett Addington. Rec. 1853. T. M. C., Clk.

Page 160: 28 April 1852. Elias Putnam of Floyd Co. from Richard Phillips of Forsyth Co. 103-24-3, 160 A., $50. Wit: John W. Fincher, R. D. Mullins, N.P., T. M. C., Clk. Elias sold same lot 3 Nov. 1852 to John C. Bowell. Wit: _____ Tomlinson, George W. Walker, J.P.

Page 162: 6 Feb. 1851. Martin Duke from Joseph D. Shumate, $1000, Lot 225-14-3. Wit: B. F. F. ____?, Samuel F___, T. M. C., Clk.

Page 163: 10 Oct. 1853. William Scott from John Boswell, 1/2 lot, 103-24-3, 80 A., $150. Wit: G. M. Cropley, Samuel C. King, J.P., T. M. C., Clk.

Page 164: 20 Sept. 1853. James Freeman from J. G. Wylie Dep. Shrff, 160 A. Property John J. Thweatt, Spalding Co., favor Joseph Goddard, $76. Wit: William H. Dabney, Robert N. White, J.P., T. M. C., Clk.

Page 165: 6 Sept. 1853. Wiley Kinman, William Curtiss, David B. Barrett from Jesse N. Miller, Shrff. 39-6-3, 160 A. property of John Thweatt, Spalding Co., $96. Wit: Ely P. Howell, Henry Cooper, J.P., T. M. C., Clk.

Pge 166: Sept. 1853. Robt. C. Saxon from Alex. G. Powers, 177-15-3, 160 A, $5002 (?). Henry Cooper, J.P., H. S. Gardner, T. M. C., D. Clk.

Page 167: 12 June 1853. Richard Peters, City of Atlanta, from James M. Orr - 276 & 277-14-3 East of Oothcaloga Creek, 50 A. on 277, 160 A. on 276, $4200. From: James M. Orr, Robert Orr, John Orr, Stephen M. Jones & Jane W. Jones (Orr); Samuel D. Wylie & Margaret Wylie (Orr). Wit: David G. Wylie, Robt. N. White, J.P., Margaret & Jane, privately signed a statement that they joined in the sale of their own free will (This is the noted Peters Farm, now mostly residence section.)

Page 169: 6 Sept. 1853. Kinman, Curtiss, Barrett from Jessee N. Miller Shrff. 96 & 97-15-3, each 160 A. -- prop. James Day $6.75. Wit: Eli P. Howell, Henry Cooper, J.P., T. M. C., Clk. (Deputy Clerk)

Page 170: 11 Nov. 1853. Cafs Co. T. L. Stanford from L. B. Roberson, 63-6-3, 160 A., $465. Wit: David Porter, Ephraim Porter, J. P., T. M. C., D. Clk.

Page 171: 19 Nov. 1852. Jame P. Kinman from James M. Orr, 248-14-3, $300, 80 A. Wit: A. B. Thomas, James M. Strange, J.P., T. M. C., C. Clk.

Page 171: 10 Nov. 1853. John C. Butler and Martin Duke from Allen May, 24-25-3, $300, 80 A. John Malone, J.P., T. M. C., D. Clk.

Page 172: 11 Feb. 1853. Cafs Co. Littleberry B. Roberson from Augustus Wright & Warren Akin, 43-6-3, $100, 160 A. Wit: N. Gilreath, J. H. Gilreath, J.I.C., T. M. C., D. Clk.

Page 173: 4 Oct. 1853. John G. McKenzie, Floyd Co. from Joshua Knowles, Baldwin Co., 101-24-3, $50, 160 A. Wit: David G. Lowe, F. I. Sullivan, J.I.C., T. M. C., D. Clk.

Page 174: 4 June 1853. W. M. Peeples from J. P. King, 138-14-3, $200.

Page 174: 20 Nov. 1853. Jesse N. Miller Shrff. from William N. Peeples, 158-14-3, 160 A., $300. Wit: Isham K. Arnold. G. W. Ransom, J.P., T. M. C., D. Clk.

Page 175: 5 Nov. 1853. W. M. Peeples from Jessee N. Miller Shrff. Lot 66, Chandler Survey, town of Calhoun, from Land Lot 192-14-3, $100. Wit: Isham R. Arnold, G. W. Ransom, J.P., T. M. C., D. Clk.

Page 176: 5 Dec. 1852. Robt. B. Bandy from Jesse N. Miller, 319-13-3 West half of lot, 80 A, $6. Prop. James Morrow. Wit: Thos. M. Compton, William M. Peeples, Clk. T. M. C., D. Clk.

Page 177: 12 Nov. 1853. W. P. Christopher from
Daniel Johnson & Wm. B. Chandler, Abraham Chandler Estate, Lots
43 & 44, Chandler Survey, town of Calhoun, from Land
Lot 192-14-3, 1 A. each, $49. Wit: Will H. Morris,
G. W. Ranson, J.P., T. M. C., D. Clk.

Page 178: 29 Oct. 1842. Richard Bowen from
Ezekiel S. Miller, both of Ware (?) Co., $200 for Lot 154-6-3,
Cherokee Co., 160 A. (Gordon Co. was formed from part of
Cherokee) (later Cass, now Bartow) Wit: John F. Clough,
Samuel I. Norman. Rec. 1853, W. M. Peeples, Clk.

Page 179: 2 Feb. 1844. George Wilcox from Richard Bowen,
Lot 154-6-3, Cherokee Co., 160 A., $100. Wit: N. J. ?,
Joshua I. Kemp, Rec. Dec. 1853, W. M. P., Clk.

Page 180: 14 Feb. 1845. Appling Co., James Wilcox from
George W. Wilcox, 154-6-3, $120, 160 A. Cherokee Co. Wit:
Thomas Wilcox, Nathaniel I. Holton (?), J.P. Rec. 5 Dec. 1853,
W. M. P., Clk.

Page 181: 6 Dec. 1845, Ware Co. ?, John F. Clough from
James Wilcox, 154-6-3, $150, 160 A. Wit: Caylor Hilliard,
David I. Miller, J.P., Rec. 5 Dec. 1853, W. M. P., Clk.

Page 182: 1 Aug. 1851. Ware Co., George B. Williamson from
John I. Clough, 154-6-3, $200, 160 A. Wit: P. McDonald,
William A. McDonald, J.P. Rec 1853. W. M. P., Clk.

Page 182: 1 Sept. 1851. Same lot Raleigh Hall from
George Williamson, $200. Wit: William Hays, Riley Gofs, J.P.
Rec. 1853, W. M. P., Clk.

Page 183: Daniel M. Keith and others - Relinquishment to
Lot 132-7-3; Thomas James Keith, dec'd, late of Gordon Co.,
owner of lot. Settlement and division of the estate; Levi Todd
& Elizabeth, his wife, one of the children; James, another of
said children, gave receipts and settlement of full and entire
interest in said Estate, relinquishing all claim upon same;
also, Sarah Keith and David A. Keith and David M. Keith and
Mary Ann Keith Chastain and Cynthia Keith, now Cynthia Prince
agreed to divide said lot between them, the two girls having
choice and taking the East and undeveloped half. David and
Daniel have improved their half. Daniel purchased interest of
David. Wit: James Hopkins, Bazzel Lowery, J.P. Signed:
Sarah Keith, D. A. Keith, Daniel M. Keith, Mary Ann Chastain,
Cynthia Prince, Obadiah Chastain, K. Prince. Rec. Dec. 1853,
W. M. P., Clk.

Page 189: 31 March 1843. Aspasia Earle from Joseph Watters,
Floyd Co., S. half 134-24-3, $100, 80 A. Wit: B. Aycock,
William Watters, J.P. Rec. 5 Dec. 1853. W. M. P., Clk.

Page 185: 13 Feb. 1850. R. M. Carter from Inf. Court,
Lots 6 & 7, 22nd Section, town of Calhoun, $108. Rec. 1853.

Page 186: David S. Law from Inf. Court No. 39, 22 Section,
town of Calhoun, $30. W. M. P., Clk.

Page 516: 1856 Deed of gift from Wm. A. Hooper to
Mary Burt, wife of L. E. Burt, to my beloved daughter, a negro
girl, named Missouri, aged 7 and past.

Page 210: 1853. W. J. & Spivey Fuller to J. A. Mims, Lot
199-14-3, 80 A.

Page 461: John T. Malone to William A. Greene, 1854,
Lots 321 7 322-13-3.

Page not given: John P. King to Elders of Mt. Zion
Presbyterian Church, Lot 24th Section, town of Calhoun. Elders:
Matthew Thompson (father of Maurice and Will Thompson),
William Gaston, William B. Chandler and Robert Orr.

Page 187: 10 March 1853. Nicholes Mofs from
Toliver S. Saxon Lot 16, Chandler Saweytown of Calhoun land
Lot 192-14-3. E. 210', N. 132', W. 198', S. 210', $350.
S. T. Mays, J.I.C., Isaac Wofford, T. M. C., D. Clk.

Page 188: 6 April 1842. Kinchen Carr from Lewis Tumlin,
189-6-3, $1750, 160 A. Wit: Wm. Clark Wyly, John H. Starr.
Rec. 1853. T. M. C., D. Clk.

Page 189: 19 Jan. 1852. Charles F. Walters from
William A. Dawson, 220-6-3, $17, part of lot. Wit:
R. M. Waters, P. M. Pearson.

Page 191: 30 Dec. 1848. Andrew Dorsey from Clark Co.,
William H. Dorsey, $1000, 189-6-3. Wit: William Phillips,
John Kirkpatrick. Rec. Dec. 1852. T. M. C., D. Clk.

Page 191: 18 Nov. 1853. Jaboc Tate from Walker Co.,
John Tate, 36-6-3, $200. Wit: David Woodall, Amos Griffin,
J.P., W. M. P., Clk.

Page 191: 5 May 1855. Habersham Co. William H. Dorsey
from Ezekiel McCravey. 189-6-3, $2000. Wit: Illegible,
T. M. C., Clk.

Page 192: 7 March 1850. Oliver C. Wyley from
Andrew Dorsey, Habersham Co., $100, 189-6-3, 160 A. Casey Cox,
J.I.C., T. M. C., Clk.

Page 193: 17 April 1840. Puloksi Co., Shadrack Floyd from
Thomas I. Floyd, 31-24-2, $50, 160 A. in Cherokee Co. Wit:
Charley Lowe, James Smith, Rec. Dec. 1853, W. M. P., Clk.

Page 194: 5 May 1847. Houston Co. Curtiss Daniel from
Shadrach Floyd, 31-24-2 (same as above). Wit:
Phillip F. Woodson, Wilson Smith. Rec. Dec. 1853. W. M. P.,
Clk.

Page 195: 7 Aug. 1850, Henry Irby from Nook Daniel, Dovey
Co., 31-24-2. $150, 160 A. Wit: James J. Lock, J.P. Rec.
1852. T. M. C., D. Clk.

Page 195: 19 Aug. 1850, Oliver Wyley from Wm. O'Neel and
others, State of Ala. 197-6-3, $275. Wit: John C. Hancock,

Hogan Wadsworth, T. M. C., D. Clk.

Page 196: 14 April 1851, Clark Co. Oliver C. Wylie from William Murray, 190-6-3, $600, 160 A. Wit: Thomas Booth, Thomas S___ton, J.P., T. M. C., D. Clk.

Page 197: 4 Nov. 1852, Oliver C. Wiley from Ely P. Howell adms. 144-6-3, Estate Phillip McEaton, $1050, 160 A. Wit: J. H. Murdock, Lewis G. Walker, T. M. C., C. Clk.

Page 275: Both Clark Co. 4 Jan. 1853. W. I. Carlton from H. H. Hancock, $35, 40 A. Wit: illegible. Robert Higden, Gordon Co., J.I.C., W. M. P., Clk.

Page 199: 31 Jan. 1838. John Millican, Cafs Co. William Aiken, Butts Co. 257-24-2, $150, 160 A. Wit: Douglas Waters, Charles B. Cuby, J.P. Rec. 1853, W. M. P., Clk.

Page 200: 2 Jan. 1848. Cafs Co. William C. Watts from John Milliam, 257-24-2, $300, 160 A. A. J. Covington, J.P. Rec. 1853, W. M. P., Clk.

Page 201: 15 July 1834. Amelia Ramsey (?) to Stephen C. Ruce, $50, 8-6-3, Cafs Co. Wit: John M. Thompson, John _____, J.P. Rec. 1853, W. M. P., Clk.

Page 201: 31 Dec. 1853. E. B. Mosley to Andrew Adams, 297-7-3, $250, 40 A. Wit: J. P. B., O. C. Campbell, J.P., T. M. C., D. Clk.

Page 202: 3 Nov. 1853. Ruth A. M. Nelson from Jonathan D. Phillips & Daniel G. Wylie. Mitg. 240-7-3, $2000, 160 A. Wit: James Rogers, G. W. Raneon, J.P., T. M. C., D. Clk.

Page 203: 2 Jan. 1854. Hugh R. Mofs. from Daniel M. Keith, 132-7-3, one half of lot, $600. Wit: T.R. Marshall, Bozzel Lowery, J.P., T. M. C., D. Clk.

Page 204: 26 May 1853. William A. Beall, Baldwin Co. from W. H. Mitchell, Richmond Co. and George W. Crawford, 104-14-3, $1600. Wit: James M. Davis, George M. _____, N.P. R.C., T. M. C., D. Clk.

GORDON COUNTY, GEORGIA, MARRIAGE AND DEATH NOTICES

Gordon County and Environs Residents Included in
Marriage and Death Notices from the Southern Christian Advocate
1837-1860 Vol. I, 1861-1867 Vol. II, by Brent Holcomb

Issue of March 19, 1847
Died on the 19th January, 1847, in Cass co., Ga., Louisa A. Trimble,
wife of Augustus C. Trimble, and daughter of Wiley and Sarah
Brogdon in the 23rd year of her age...

Issue of November 24, 1848
Died in Murray oo., Ga., Sept. 4, Mrs. Leah Campbell, wife of
Robert H. Campbell, and daughter of George and Elizabeth Lutes of
Lincoln, N. C...left a husband and 11 children....

Issue of December 22, 1848
Married in Cassville, Ga., on the 13th inst., by Rev. J. Knowles,
Mr. Jno. A. Erwin to Miss Jane E., daughter of Hon. J. W. Hooper.

Issue of February 2, 1849
Died in Cass co., Ga., on the 18th inst., at the residence of his
brother, Mr. Aaron Puckett, in the 27th year of his age...left mother
and sister and brothers. W. J. G.

Issue of February 16, 1849
Married on the 6th inst., by the Rev. Wm. A Simmons, Isaac M. Teig
to Miss Isabella P. Crews, all of Spring Place, Ga.

Issue of November 16, 1849
Married at Thistle Dale, Cass co., Ga., Nov. 1, by the Rev. J.
Knowles, Mr. John R. Freeman of Jones co., to Miss Mary T. daughter
of Dr. Thos. Hamilton, of Cass co., Ga.

Issue of December 14, 1849
Married on the 22nd ult., by the Rev. J. Knowles, Mr. G. W. Waters,
to Miss Martha L., daughter of the Rev. G. Winn, all of Floyd co., Ga.

Issue of March 22, 1850
Died, in Rome, Ga., Feb. 13, Richard Sawrie, in the 35th year of his
age...a native of Marion co., Tenn., moved to Alabama and married
in 1838.... J. Knowles.

Issue of April 12, 1850
Married, March 28th, 1850, near Ellijay, Ga., by the Rev. B. B.
Quillian, the Rev. Levi Brothertin of Dalton, Ga., to Miss Martha
A. Gudger, daughter of Wm Gudger, Esq., of the former place.

Issue of April 19, 1850
Married on the morning of the 6th inst., by Rev. W. G. Parks,
Col. William T. Trammel, of Rome, Ga., to Miss Eliza H. Wyley,
daughter of Clarke Wyley, Esq., Cass county, Ga.

GORDON COUNTY MARRIAGE AND DEATH NOTICES

Issue of April 26, 1850
Died, in Rome, Ga., on the 2d inst., Mrs Nancy C. Underwood, wife
of the Hon. W. H Underwood, in the 64th year of her age...a native
of Wake co., N C., but in early life removed to Ga...J. Knowles.

Issue of August 9, 1850
Married July 25, by Rev. J. L. Gibson, W. M Peeples, to Miss
Mira M. Erwin, all of Gordon co., Ga.

Issue of October 25, 1850
Married in Murray co., Ga., Oct. 8th, by Rev Levi Brotherton,
Wm. W. West, Esq. of Ellijay, Ga., to Miss Elizabeth C. Roberts.

By the Same, Oct. 10, Thomas T. Christian, Editor of the Dalton
Times, to Miss Caroline M. Roberts, all of Dalton.

Issue of December 13, 1850
Married near Rome, Ga., Nov. 26, by Rev. J. Knowles, Dr. T. J. Word,
to Miss Georgia, eldest daughter of D. R. Mitchell, Esq.

Minerva Ann Hughes, consort of James H. Hughes, and daughter of
Lewis and Sarah Kirby, died in Floyd co., Ga., on the 17th of
August in the 23 year of her age, leaving a husband and infant
child... J. E. Cook.

Issue of January 10, 1851
Married, Dec. 26, by Rev. Thos. H. Whitby, Rev. W. B. Moss, of the
Ga. Conf., to Mrs. Miry T. Scott, of Rome, Ga.

Issue of September 5, 1851
Married in Gilmer co., Ga., Aug. 19, by Rev. G. R. Edwards, Mr.
Daniel E Slagle, of Franklin co., N C., to Miss Priscilla Ann,
daughter of Rev. B. B. Quillian.

Issue of October 31, 1851
Died, in Murray co., Ga., Sept. 27th, 1851, Polly Ann King, consort
of J. C. King, and eldest daughter of Clemmons and Anna Quillian,
aged 31 years and 11 months... S. C. Quillian.

Issue of November 21, 1851
Married on the 5th inst., in Gordon co., A. F. Hurt, of Columbus,
Ga., to Miss Ann E., daughter of Major James Freeman.

Married, Oct. 6th, in Gilmer co., Ga., by Rev. B. B. Quillian,
Wm. F. Hopper, to Miss Louisiana Caroline Winkle.

Issue of December 26, 1851
Married in Rome, Ga., on the 13th inst., by the Rev. J. Knowles,
A. E. Ross, to Miss M. L. Tuggle, all of Rome, Ga.

Issue of February 6, 1852

Married in Dalton, Ga., Jan. 8, by the Rev. Levi Brotherton, Green B. Mathena to Miss A. R. Ford.

Issue of February 20, 1852

Married, Jan. 1., by the Rev. J. Paty, David Derrick, son of the Rev. W. Fleming, of Cherokee co., Ala., to Miss Mary Ann Comer, daughter of A F. Comer, of Floyd co., Ga.

Issue of July 2, 1852

Syndonia B. Cook, consort of the Rev. J. E. Cook, and daughter of brother Miles Scarborough, died in Rome, Ga., 11th June...left husband and one little daughter. J. B. Smith.

Issue of August 13, 1852

Died, in Calhoun, Ga., on the 10th of July, Mrs. Sarah E. Fain, wife of Wm. P. Fain, and daughter of U. D. and J. Cornett, aged 18 years and nearly 12 months. S. D. Everett.

Issue of August 27, 1852

Died, in Rome, Ga., on the 27th of July, Mrs. Mary Frances, wife of the Rev. J. Knowles, and daughter of Col. N. C. and Mrs. M. J. Barnett, in the 24th year of her age...

Died in Cartersville, Ga., August 12, 1852, William Ellington, son of Watson R. and Salina H. Coleman, aged 5 years, 11 months and 18 days.

Issue of September 3, 1852

Died in Cartersville, Cass co., Ga., May 14, in the 33rd year of her age, Miss Sarah John Trimble, daughter of Mr. John Trimble, formerly of Covington, Ga., but many years since, deceased...A.M.

Issue of November 26, 1852

Mrs. Anna Quillian, wife of Clemonds Quilliam, died on the 18th of Oct., in Whitfield co., Ga., aged 67 years 5 months and 18 days

Issue of December 3, 1852

At Elmwood, Ga., on the 9th inst., by the Rev. G. F. Pierce, James C. Longstreet of Calhoun, to Miss Mary Ann, daughter of Judge L. Q. C. Lamar, deceased, of Milledgeville.

Issue of March 4, 1853

Died in Murray co., Ga., January the 21st, Jeremiah Harrison in the 68th year of his age, born in Rutherford co., N. C...left a large family. G. H. Clark.

Died in Vann's Valley, Floyd co., Ga., 6th Feb., Mrs. Sarah D. Ware..
born 5 Feb. 1805, married 20 Dec. 1821 to Edward Ware, whom she has
left.... D. P. Jones.

Died, on the 12th inst., near Cartersville, Sarah Jane Elizabeth,
infant daughter of W. W. and R. B. Leake, aged 7 days. W. W. Leake.

Issue of March 18, 1853
On the 30th Jan., by Rev. J. Strickland, Samuel E. Binion, to Miss
Emlia M. Mays of Gordon co., Ga.

Died in Gordon co., Ga., Oct. 16, 1852, W. E. Willborn, in his
46th year... J. Strickland.

Issue of April 1, 1853
On the 17th March, by the Rev. G. H. Clark, William A. Reagan to
Miss Agnes E. Reed, all of Murray co., Ga.

Issue of April 8, 1853
Married on the 8th of March, by Rev. A. Smith, Wm. Etter of Whitfield co., to Miss Mary E. Johnson of Walker co., Ga.

Issue of April 22, 1853
Married on the 23d of March, by Rev. Josiah H. Clark, Mr. Richard
P. Tyson of Cherokee co., to Miss Tabitha Leonard, of Murry co., Ga.

Issue of May 13, 1853
Married on the 21st April, by Rev. D. D. Cox, James W. Langston
to Miss Eliza Jane Lambeth, all of Rome, Ga., Also on the 28th
April, by the same, Marcus A. Higgs, of Cassville, Ga., to Miss
Mary E. Butler, of Rome, Ga.

Issue of May 20, 1853
At Tunnell Hill, Ga. 3rd of May, by Rev. J. M. Richardson, Dr. C. J.
Emerson to Miss Matilda Caroline, daughter of Rev. C. Austin.

On the 8th of May, by Rev. J. Brotherton, Dr. J. R. McAfee, to
Miss Mary R. Ranver, all of Dalton, Ga.

Issue of June 24, 1853
On the 15th inst., by Rev. L. Brotherton, Junius J. Jones of
Elberton, to Miss Ann E., daughter of Judge W. Hammond of Whitfield co.

Issue of September 2, 1853
August 18th, by the Rev. A. Neese, Reuben J. Mulkey to Mary J.
Stephens, all of Floyd co., Ga.

Issue of September 23, 1853
Died at his brother's, in Gilmer co., Ga., Aug. 27, 1853, David M.
Slagle, in his 21st year...son of J. and B. Slagle of Macon co.,
N. C., had been living in Cartersville, Ga., for the last year...

Issue of October 14, 1853

William R. Gartrell, son of W. J. and E. A. Gartrell, was born in Gordon co., Ga. 28th June, 1852, and died in Rutherford co., N. C., 21st Sept. 1853.

Issue of October 21, 1853

Died in Rome, Ga., Sept. 29, Sister Mary A. B., wife of Judge Wm. Johnson and daughter of Col. Wm. and N. Hardin...born in Henry co., Ga., Jan. 10, 1828... D. D. Cox.

Issue of November 4, 1853

Married on the 20th Sept., by the Rev. C. B. Wellborn, W. Y. Amos, of LaGrange, Troup co., to Miss Mary C., daughter of Rev. J. S. P. Powel, of Murray co, Ga.

Issue of December 16, 1853

Married on the 7th Dec., by Rev. G. E Smith, John Harkins, of Rome, Ga., to Miss Permelia R. Persons of Coweta co.

On Dec. 8th, by the Rev. M. A. Clounts, L. P. Higgs to Miss Sarah Dillard of Cass co.

Issue of December 23, 1853

Died on the 7th Dec., James Burch, of Gordon co., Ga.... G. J. S.

Issue of April 14, 1854

In Thomaston, March 16, by Rev. J. M. Marshall, John Burkhalter of Cartersville, to Miss Fanny Weaver.

Issue of May 26, 1854

Died in Floyd co., Ga., April 19, 1854, George Metts in the 87th year of his age...born in Lexington Dist., S. C., where in early life he joined the Lutheran Church... A Neese.

Issue of August 4, 1854

Died, in Murray co., Ga., June 7th, in her 19th year, Altha Caroline McFarland, daughter of James and Elizabeth McFarland

Issue of October 27, 1854

Sep. 25, by the Rev. J. M. Richardson, J. W. Patterson of Dalton to Miss E. N. Ducket, all of Whitfield co., Ga.

Issue of December 22, 1854

Dec. 14, by the Rev Levi Brotherton, A. C McAfee to Miss Sarah J. Tyler, all of Dalton, Ga.

Issue of May 4, 1855

Died in Calhoun, Ga., on the 7th April, Mrs. Frances Gray, at the residence of her son, Dr. W. W. Wall, in her 63d year... R. M. Carter

Died at Cartersville, Ga., Jan. 10, Sarah Florence, oldest daughter of Uriah and Hannah A. Stephens, aged 8 years and 7 days... preceded but a day by her sister Cornelia Antoinette...

Issue of June 14, 1855

Died in Gordon co,, Ga., Feb. 28th, Milton Parks, infant son of Nancy and Rev. W. F. Jones, aged 3 years, 4 months and 4 days. J.J.

Issue of July 19, 1855

Died, in Whitfield co., Ga., on the 1st of May, James W., son of Theophilus and Rebecca Lewis, in the 27th year of his age.. J. Lewis.

Issue of September 27, 1855

On Sept. 11, by Rev. A Neese, Rev. Thos. T. Christian of the Ga. Conf., to Miss Cornelia McClendon, of Floyd co., Ga.

Issue of November 8, 1855

On 24th Oct., by Rev. J. M. Richardson, William A. Anderson, of Chattanooga, Tenn., to Miss Harriet W. Edmondson, of Spring Place, Ga.

Issue of November 29, 1855

On Nov. 1st, by Rev. D. D. Cox, Dr. J J. Harris, of Washington co., to Miss Roxana Mitchell, of Rome, Ga.

Issue of January 3, 1856

Died in Whitfield co., Ga., Oct. 20, 1855, Wm. Vastine Haigler, aged 28 years, son of sister Margaret Haigler, who moved in 1852 from Orangeburg Dist., S. C., to Ga. Daniel Johnson.

Issue of January 10, 1856

Died, near Red Clay, Whitfield co., Ga., Dec. 4, 1855, John Pitner, in his 55 year...one of the first settlers of this part of Ga., then Cherokee... J. H. H.

Died, at Red Clay, Ga., Dec. 4, 1855, John G. Starret, born in Guilford co., N. C., June 1, 1810, thence he emigrated to Tenn. in 1839, and thence to where he died in 1851 (sic)...raised by Presbyterian parents... J. H. H.

Issue of March 13, 1856

In Dalton, Ga., March 2nd, 1856, by Rev. M. A. Clontz, Mr. S. S. Turner, and Miss Mary Elizabeth Senter.

Issue of May 15, 1856

Mary U. Hopper, daughter of John and Priscilla Kilian, died in her 30th year. (Actual death date 2 October 1855 -J.B.G.)

Issue of August 7, 1856
Henry Dozier was born 23rd April 1771, in Prince (sic) Ann co., Va., lived subsequently in Roanoke and Surrey Cos., N C., and Campbell Co., Ga., and died June 22nd, at John Foster's in Floyd Co., Ga.

Issue of September 18, 1856
By Rev. A. Neese, Mr. John M. W. Camp, of Campbell Co., Ga., to Miss Margaret V. Winn, of Gordon Co., Ga.

Issue of November 13, 1856
In Atlanta, Ga., on the 4th Nov., by Rev. A. Neese, Dr. James T. Bond, to Miss M. L. Tutt, both of Floyd Co., Ga.

Issue of December 4, 1856
Benjamin Kiker was born May 15th, 1794, in Mecklenburg Co., N.C., moved to Habersham Co., Ga., in 1821, afterwards removed to Cass, now Gordon Co., and lived there until his death 6th Oct. 1856...

Issue of January 8, 1857
Julia Ann Humphreys, wife of D. W Humphreys, and daughter of Samuel and Charlotte Harian, was born in Jackson Co., Ga. March 31, 1837, and died at Tilton, Ga., Dec. 5, 1856...

Issue of July 23, 1857
Mrs. Elizabeth Terrell, daughter of Peter Hoff, died in Gordon Co., Ga., May 5th, 1857, aged 70 years, 5 months and 27 days...a native of Virginia. She moved to Oglethorpe Co., Ga., there married Joseph R. Terrell, and from thence moved to S.C., and from thence removed to Georgia again... J. R. Terrell

Issue of July 30, 1857
On the 23rd, 1857, at the residence of the bride's father, by Rev. M. A. Clontz, J. H. Martin, of Dalton, Ga., to Miss M. E. Thornton, of Whitfield Co., Ga.

Issue of August 20, 1857
David Black, son of James Black, dec'd, was born and raised in Abbeville Dist., S.C., and died in Gordon Co., Ga., June 22nd, 1857, aged 67 years, 8 months and 2 days... J. D. Anthony

Issue of October 8, 1857
On Sunday night, the 20th September, by Rev. H. P. Pitchford, Rev. F. W. McCurdy, to Miss Rhoda Ann Hamilton, both of Whitfield Co.

Issue of November 12, 1857
On the 6th Sept., in Gordon Co., Ga., Lizzie H., daughter of J. H. and Mrs. R. Starr, aged 5 years, 10 months and 20 days.

Issue of December 10, 1857

On the 25th Nov., by Rev. M. A. Clontz, Mr. John M. Bridges of
Athens, Tenn., to Miss Mary M. Holt, of Dalton.

On the 24th Nov., by Rev. Joab Humphreys, Rev. H. H. McHan of the
Ga. Conf., to Miss Margaret Jane, only daughter of Jonathan
Lassater, Esq. of Murray county, Ga.

Issue of August 5, 1858

Rev. Wm. M. McClain, died near Dalton, Ga., on the 2nd July, in
his 35th year.

Issue of August 12, 1858

Mrs. Nancy Y. Senter died at the residence of her son-in-law S. S.
Turner, on the 21st July, in her 59th year...born in Roan Co., Tenn.,
and was the daughter of Adam and Margaret Carson, who were among
the first settlers of East Tennessee. In 1817 she was married to
Seaborn Senter, with whom she removed to Spring Place, Murray co.,
Ga. After the death of her husband in 1845, she removed with her
family to the vicinity of Dalton...

Issue of August 19, 1858

By Rev. J. H. Mashburn, on the 27th July, Dr. Marcus M. Green, of
Gordon co., Ga., to Miss Ann E Johnson, of Floyd county, Ga.

Issue of September 2, 1858

Married on the 12th August, by Rev. A. W. Rowland, Rev. Wiley T.
Hamilton of Walker county, to Miss Pairzade Ware, of Gordon co., Ga.

Issue of October 21, 1858

On 7th Sept. in Gordon co., Ga., Aaron Hogan, infant son of J. M.
and M. A. Harlan, aged one month.

Mrs. Myra M. Peeples, wife of Wm. M. Peeples, of Calhoun, Ga., died
Sept. 11th, 1858...daughter of Jas. S. and Elizabeth D. Erwin, of
Cassville, Ga., and was born Feb. 10th, 1833...J. H. Mashburn.

Issue of November 25, 1858

Loanny Adaline Trimble, wife of Augustus C. Trimble, of Octhcaloga,
and daughter of Rev. W. Fain, dec'd and Karon Happuck, his wife,
of Cass county, was born April 23d, 1832 and died Oct. 13th, 1858..
married on 21st May 1851... J. H. Mashburn.

Issue of February 24, 1859

Married on February 6th, by Rev. J. M. Richardson, Mr. William H.
Brotherton, of Tilton, to Miss Parale Williams, of Dalton.

Issue of March 3, 1859

On 16th Feb., in Dalton, Ga., by Rev. John W. McGehee, Mr. John F. Rennels to Miss Jane J. Thompson, both of Dalton, Ga.

Issue of October 13, 1859

Mrs. Josephine L. Erwin, wife of Mr. Samford Erwin, and daughter of Col. Lewis Turnlin, was born Aug. 24th, 1836, and died in Cartersville, Ga,, Sept. 9, 1859...

Mrs. Jane E. Erwin, wife of John A. Erwin, and daughter of Hon. John W. Hooper, was born Sept. 22d, 1829, and died in Cartersville, Ga., Sept. 16t, 1859...

Issue of January 19, 1860

On the 20th Dec., by Rev. W. M. D. Bond, Rev. James D. Freeman of the Ga. Conf., to Miss Fannie S. Ware, of Floyd co., Ga.

Issue of February 9, 1860

George W. Mealer, Jr., son of Isham R. and Elvira Mealer, was born im Murray co., Ga., and died in Monroe co., Miss., on 16th January, in his 18th year... J. D. Tatum

Issue of March 15, 1860

Married on March 1st, in Dalton, Ga., by Rev. Wesley P. Pledger, Mr. B. C. Waddaill to Miss Mary E. McCrary.

Issue of July 5, 1860

On Monday morning, the 18th inst., by Rev. John W. Reynolds, Mr. Henry Kingsberry, of Adairsville, to Miss Julia L. Curtis, of Carrollton, Ga.

Issue of November 8, 1860

Mrs. Anne Gillespie, aged 86 years, 1 month and 27 days, died in Gordon co., Ga., at the residence of her son-in-law, Rev. W. F Jones, the 6th of August last...My mother was born in Guilford co., N.C., in the days of the revolution, joined the Presbyterian Church, later the M. E. Church... R. M. Jones.

Issue of January 31, 1861

By C. A. Crowell, January 9th, 1861, Mr. Milton C. Jackson, of Calhoun, Gordon co., to Miss Emily Milican, of Cass co., Ga.

Issue of February 7, 1861

Mrs. Mary E. Johnson, daughter of Thos. E. and Martha Zuber, was born in Oglethorpe co., Ga., died Dec. 22nd, 1860, near Floyd Springs, Floyd co., in her 19th year... R. H. Jones

North West Georgia

The "Cherokee Strip," "Cherokee Country," "Original Cherokee County," or "Pioneer Georgia."

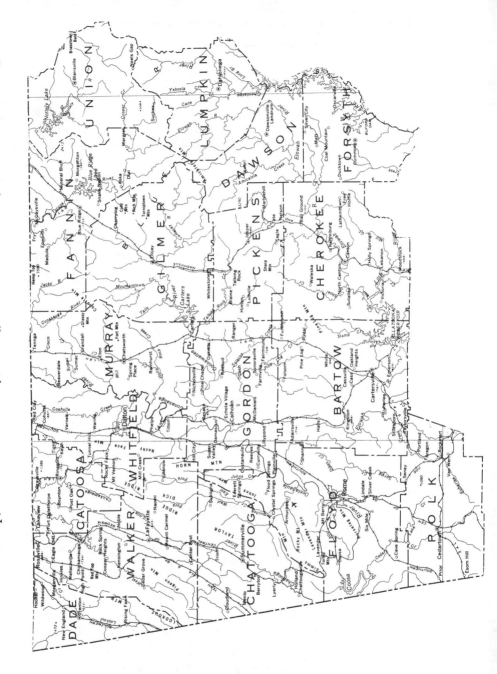

413 b.

GORDON COUNTY, GEORGIA, MARRIAGE AND DEATH NOTICES

Abstracted by Jo Bailey Gladney

Issue of March 21, 1861

On the 26th Feb., by W. R. Branham, Mr. Isham H. Branham of Floyd
co., Ga., to Miss Mollie Mathews, only daughter of Dr. Wm. A.
Mathews, of Ft. Valley, Ga.

Issue of April 4, 1861

By the Rev. C. B. Webborn on 25th inst., Mr. E. W. Bond, of Whitfield co., Ga., to Miss Mary L. McClain of Murry co., Ga.

Issue of May 30, 1861

By Rev. C. A. Crowell, Mar. 28th, Mr. T. S. Strickland, second son

of Rev. J. Strickland, of the Ga. Conf., to Miss L. C. Ellis, all
of Gordon co., Ga.

Issue of June 20, 1861

On June 4th, by Rev. C. A. Drowell, Mr. B. D. Clarke, and Miss
Mary R. Barrett, all of Gordon co., Ga.

Issue of August 15, 1861

Married July 18th, 1861, by Rev. J. M Richardson, Thos. J. Simmons
to Miss Nancy C. King, both of Whitfield co., Ga.

Issue of September 26, 1861

On the 18th inst., by Rev. D. J. Myrick, Col. James W. Harris, of
Cartersville, Cass co., Ga., to Miss Julia Florence Candler, of
Villa Rica, Carroll co., Ga.

Died in Calhoun, Gordon co., Ga., on 2d Sept., Hannah Altoe(?),
only daughter of Z. T. and Elizabeth Gray, aged 2 years and 4 months.

Issue of January 23, 1862

Miss Eliza Jane, daughter of George W. and S. A. Hill was born in
Cass co., Ga., Sept. 9th, 1845, and died in Dalton, Ga. Dec. 19th,
1861... L. D. Palmer.

Issue of March 6, 1862

W. S. Wimpy died Jan. 13th, in the Potomac Army, Va., a member of
the "Miller Rifles", Capt. J. R. Towers, Floyd co., Ga....age 22...

Issue of July 17, 1862

Charles W. Bridges, son of Rev. J. W. Bridges, and Bethany Bridges,
was born in Floyd co., Ga., July 30th, 1845, and died at Corinth,
Miss., May 2nd...   E. L. King

Issue of August 14, 1862
Mrs. Sarah Ford, wife of Joseph Ford, sen., died in Floyd co., Ga., 21 July in her 56th year.

Lt. Edwin S. Gwinnett of Capt. Haney's cavalry company, Floyd co., Ga., died June 28, in his 25th year...

Issue of August 21, 1862
W. H. Saxon, 1st Regt. Ga. Cavalry, son of Lewis and Caroline Saxon, died in Bartow co., Ga., July 1st, aged nearly 24 years.

Issue of September 18, 1862
Rev. D. M. Keith was born in Merriwether co., April 3, 1828, and died in Gordon co., Ga. on 1st July 1862...

Issue of October 2, 1862
Mrs. Martha Hurt, widow of the late Col. Joel Hurt, of Ala., died 3 July, at the residence of Maj. James Freeman, of Gordon co., Ga., aged 73 years...

Issue of October 30, 1862
At the residence of Rev. Joshua Bowdon, Gordon co., Ga., on 10th Oct., Pickett, son of Stephen and Ann F. Sikes, aged 2 years and 9 months.

Issue of November 13, 1862
Mrs. Catherine Watts, wife of Rev. Hope Watts, died near Cave Spring, Ga., Oct. 15, 1862, in the 74th year of her age.

Issue of February 5, 1863
Died in Gilmer co., Ga., Jan. 15, 1863, Hellena Emogene, daughter of D. E. and Priscilla Ann Slagle, aged 4 years, 5 months, and 16 days.

Issue of February 19, 1863
Mr. Samuel Woodruff was born in Surry co., N.C., and died Jan. 26th, 1863, near Silver Creek, Floyd co., Ga., aged 70 years....While his father was lying a corpse in the house, his son M. Woodruff died, aged 30(?) years...John W. Reynolds.

Issue of April 30, 1863
Catherine E. Davis, wife of Archibald Davis, Esq., died near Rome, Ga., February 7th, in her 42d year...

Issue of May 7, 1863

Catharine Bowen, wife of J. R. Bowen, and daughter of Charles and Elizabeth Christian, died in Gordon co., Ga., April 15, 1863...

Issue of July 9, 1863

Henry H. Hay, son of W. P. Hay of Bartow co., Ga., died June 18th, 1863, aged 17 years and 7 months...entered the 28th Miss. Regt., with his uncle...

Issue of October 15, 1863

Louisa Augusta, youngest daughter of G. M. and Sarah J. McDonald, died near Tilton, Ga., July 2, 1863, aged 13 months and 13 days.

Issue of December 3, 1863

Mrs. Sallie Leake died in Cartersville, Ga., Nov. 4, 1863, aged 64 years, 9 months and 20 days...

Issue of December 17, 1863

On 26th Nov., near Dalton, by Rev. J. M. Richardson, Col. J. W. Avery of the 4th Ga. Cavalry, to Miss Sallie H. Morris, daughter of Judge Morris of Whitfield co.

Issue of January 28, 1864

Elizabeth A. Weems, wife of A. J. Weems, of Bartow co., Ga., died Jan. 8, 1863, in her 49th year...

Issue of March 17, 1864

Mr. John Patterson died near Stilesboro, Bartow co., Ga., 20th Jan., aged 53 years...born in Henry co., Va....

Mrs. R. Ann Helvenstein, wife of the late Capt. Jos. E. Helvenstein, who was killed 17 Sept. 1863, died in Whitfield Co., 12th Dec., 1863, in her 27th year...

Issue of May 12, 1864

Bro. Jas. L. Carpenter, died near Stilesboro', Bartow Co., Ga.... left wife and children.

Issue of November 10, 1864

Alfred H. Hammond, son of Wm and Lucy Hammond, late of Whitfield co., Ga. (now refugees) was born 31st March 1833, and died in Anderson Dist., S.C., 16th Oct. 1864....

Issue of April 13, 1866

On the 23d ult., by Rev. B. J. Johnson, Mr. Turplin Gregory of
Murray co., Ga., to Miss Susan Terry, daughter of Rev. Jos. Terry
of Whitfield co., Ga.

Issue of October 5, 1866

On August 28th, by Rev. W. C. Dunlap, Mr. George H. Hues to Miss
Lucinda H. Vincent, both of Bartow co., Ga.

Issue of October 12, 1866

In Whitfield co., near Dalton, Sept. 27th, by Rev. J. M. Richardson,
Mr. Henry Conkin, to Miss Mattie Morris.

In Dalton, Ga., Sept. 27, by Rev. J. M. Richardson, Mr. Robert S.
Rushton and Miss C. E. Sims.

Issue of November 23, 1866

On the 3d Oct., at the residence of W. B. Ellington, by Rev. B. B.
Quillian, Col. James G. Browne, of Murray co., Ga., to Miss
Rachel P. Ellington, of Gilmer co., Ga.

Issue of November 30, 1866

By Dr. W. H. Felton, in Cartersville, Ga., Nov. 6, Dr. David H.
Ramsaur and Miss Cordelia S. Erwin.

GORDON COUNTY, GA. MARRIAGE LICENSES (1864-1870)

1864

Jan. 17	C.A. Anderson to Margaret H. Wood, I.N. Buckner, J.I.C. (Justice Inferior Court).
Jan. 24	Emerson Overlock to Eliza Norman, John N. Adams, J.P. (Justice of Peace).
Jan. 28	J. H. Gammon to Martha A. Mathis, Henry Cooper, JP.
Jan. 31	James Coleman to Mahala Phillips, Rev. S. Hoyle, MG.
Dec. 9	Joseph H. Willingham to Miss E. A. Harlan, Andrew Adams, MG (Minister Gospel).
Dec. 5	William Lively to Elizabeth Collier, Robert H. Nesbitt, JP.
Dec. 31	Thomas N. Stancel to Malana S. Keele, Elisha Lowery, JP.
Dec. 17	Rufus Owens to Miss S. Wilson, Robert H. Nesbitt, JP.
Dec. 27	B.E. Moon to Miss C.J. Underwood, Miles J. Abernathy, MG.
Feb. 29	W.A. Sloan to Miss M.M. Greeson, I.N. Buckner, JIC.
April 10	F.M. Smith to Susannah Bolding, J.D. Tinsley, JP.
April 19	Solomon J. Goode to Martha Ann Bandy, Miles J. Abernathy, MG.

1865

Jan. 1	W. C. Terry to Miss J. E. Miller, G. M. Thompson, MG.
Jan. 5	Charles Lay to Margaret Gunthrop, W.J. Fuller, JP.
Jan. 27	James B. Lane to Susan T. Lane, A. Templeton, MG.
July 20	David Hubbard to Elizabeth Dempsey, Burton Bradley, MG.
June 23	A.J. Fletcher to M.C. Reeves, Thos. A. Foster, JIC.
Feb. 1	Gilbert T. Thompson to Josephine A. King, A. Templeton, MG.
Feb. 3	John Norrell to Malinda Taylor, Miles Abenathy, MG.
Aug. 1	J.L. Hayes to Elizabeth Stewart, Burton Brady, MG.
Feb. 7	T.P. Aycock to Miss C.A. Durham, G.M. Thompson, MG.
March 11	W.F. Slaton to Miss M.E. Campbell, William F. Jones, LD.
March 23	Dennis Miller to Margaret A. Pickard, J.H. McCoole, JP.
March 27	W.B. Pippin to Miss F.A. Henderson, Thomas A. Foster, JIC.
April 25	Van B. Hill to Mary J. Adams, Benton Bradley, Minister.
April 15	G.T. Tate to Rebecca C. Covington, I.N. Buckner, JIC.
June 1	L.M. Knight to Miss F.E. Inlow, A. Chastain, MG.
June 4	M.V. Eaves to Mrs. H.E. Woolbright, S.W. Stallings, MG.
Feb. 26	A.J. Sular to Miss J.B. Mathis, Andrew Adams, MG.
Aug. 25	J.R. Bagley to Mrs. Melinda Wylie, William A. Simmons, MG.
Aug. 13	W.E. Covington to Miss M.J. Cannon, E.M. Lowry, MG.
Sept. 3	A.P. Black to Miss W.D. Groover, William A. Simmons, MG.
Aug. 17	J.A. McClain to Martha J. Fuller, H.M. Hunter, JP.
Aug. 2	B.F. Holland to Miss M.J. Wilson, C.G. Grammell, JP.
Aug. 6	John Free to Miss M.A. Lewis, Burton Bradley, Minister.
Sept. 4	Jacob Powell to Mildred Todd, E.M. Lowry, Minister.
Aug. 27	J.S. Garett to Miss M.C. Dempsey, William F. Jones, JP.
Sept. 28	N.M. Garner to Mary J.E. Long, Thomas A. Foster, JIC.
Oct. 1	William E. Myers to Martha A.O. Anglin, Miles J. Abenathy, MG.
Sept. 17	Henry M. Walker to Molly J. Hutson, J.L. Camp, JP.
Sept. 23	John T. Warren to Sarah A. Turner, T.M. Ward, JP.
Sept. 20	Thomas Tudor to Miss M. Cooper, T.M. Ward, JP.
Sept. 11	John B. Mitchell to Sarah C. Nix, Thomas A. Foster, JIC.

GORDON COUNTY, GA., MARRIAGE LICENSES (1864-1870)

1865

Sept. 10	William Keys to Precious Elizabeth Hill, J.L. Camp, JP.
Sept. 14	J.F. Brown to Miss R.L. Butler, William S. Johnson, MG.
Sept. 7	F.A. Weems to Miss J.E. Ramsaur, William A. Simmons, MG.
Oct. 12	W.D. Timmons to Susan Atkins, William A. Simmons, MG.
Oct. 3	Willis Tate to Sarah A. Heifner, T.M. Ward, JP.
Sept. 28	Larkin J. Craft to Jane Greeson, Elisha Lowry, JP.
Sept. 24	Monroe Hooper to Eliza Borders, E.M. Lowry, MG.
Oct. 2	William Moore to Anna Blalock, Elisha Lowry, JP.
Oct. 2	J.C. Bond to Miss Susan Maulden, Thomas A. Foster, JIC.
Oct. 15	Oliver J. Garrett to Frances S. Higginbotham, Elisha Lowry, JP.
Oct. 26	A.J. King to Miss A.C. Dover, Thomas A. Foster, JIC.
Oct. 29	Daniel Kegens to Mary Holland, John W. Bowdoin, JP.
Oct. 31	William A. Duckett to Mary A. Harkins, Thomas A. McDaniel, MG.
Oct. 25	F.M. Knight to Mary Boon, John N. Andrews, JP.
Oct. 8	D.S. Anglin to Miss M.E. Tate, Miles J. Abernathy, MG.
Oct. 23	P. Wilson to Miss M.R. King, Thos. A. Foster, JIC.
Oct. 5	J.B. Henry to Martha Brock, Burton Bradley, Minister.
Oct. 10	Harrison Howell to Catherine Jackson, Thomas A. Foster, JIC.
Oct. 9	H. Erwin to Mary Morgan, Thomas A. Foster, JIC.
Oct. 8	J.W. Morgan to Frances R. Anglin, Miles J. Abernathy, Minister.
Oct. 13	Wm. Mason to Mary Ann Wickett, Thos. A. Foster, JIC.
Oct. 24	Martin Cooley to Mary O'Conner, Thos. A. Foster, JIC.
Oct. 26	George Hefner to Miss S. Holcomb, Levi Nix, JP.
Oct. 10	George W. Howard to Clara Mathis, Thos. A. Foster, JIC.
Oct. 24	M.S. Cooley to Hulda Kay, D.W. Neel, Ordinary.
Nov. 2	James M. Douglass to Mary E. Smith, William S. Johnson, MG.
Nov. 9	J.P. Kinman to Laura A. Stewart, Thos. A. Foster, JIC.
Nov. 30	J.J. Wood to Mary Owens, Miles J. Abernathy, MG.
Nov. 17	C.M. Turner to Mary E. Brock, Wm. F. Fleming, MG.
Nov. 9	G.B. Smith to Sarah Roebuck, T.F. Jones, MG.
Nov. 30	L.S. Oats to Miss M.J. Lewis, A. Templeton, MG.
Nov. 30	G.L. Roberts to Mary E. Jones, A. Templeton, MG.
Nov. 21	A.J. Wigley to Emma E. Moore, Elisha Lowry, JP.
Nov. 14	H.A. Wigley to Sarah A. Gartrell, Elisha Lowry, JP.
Nov. 8	D.C. Jackson to Mary Anglin, Robert H. Nesbitt, JP.
Nov. 22	Edward Thorn to Miss Candes Wofford, Burton Bradley, MG.
Nov. 9	James F. Dickerson to Miss E. Putnam, Wm. B. McCain, Minister.
Dec. 14	M.A. Brantley to Mrs. J.A. Henderson, S.D. Wylie, JP.
Dec. 20	Alexander S. Puryear to Mrs. Nancy Dye, Osborn Reeves, MG.
Dec. 25	C.H. Barrett to Olin Lynn, Thos. A. Foster, JIC.
Dec. 6	S.W. Alexander to Miss S.J. Adams, S.D. Wylie, JP.
Dec. 20	Perry Walraven to Miss L.J. Chamblee, J.L. Camp, JP.
Dec. 5	S.R. Redmon to Sarah Watts, Wm. F. Fleming, MG.
Dec. 19	Warren D. Stewart to Susan A. Neel, Thos. A. Foster, JIC.
Dec. 21	Thomas Bird to Miss A.J. Ballew, Wm. F. Fleming, MG.
Dec. 19	Charles Dragon to Amelia C. Monroe, Thos. A. Foster, JIC.
Dec. 24	William S. Greeson to Miss M.E. Freeman, Bird Wilson, JP.

GORDON COUNTY, GA., MARRIAGE LICENSES (1864-1870)

1865

Dec. 30   J.J. Keene to Miss S.E. Fite, E.T. Hanes, JP.
Dec. 26   William Ennis to Nancy C. Jones, E.T. Hanes, JP.
Dec. 11   W.E. Gardner to Martha C. King, A. Templeton, MG.

1866

Jan. 10   G.T. Fite to Miss S.L. Defoor, J.J. Martin, Minister.
Jan. 7   W.I. Holmes to Rebecca Varice, Z.F. Wilson, JP.
Jan. 9   Singleton Decker to Melissa Ballard, T.A. McDaniel, MG.
Jan. 9   L. Green to Mary A. Ballard, T.A. McDaniel, MG.
Jan. 17   Perry L. McCutchen to Mary A. Chandler, E.T. Hanes, JP.
Jan. 24   A.G. Holcomb to Miss M.E. Taylor, E.T. Hanes, JP.
Jan. 28   John Wood to Nancy Wood, A. Chastain, MG.
Jan. 3   R. Brock to Jane Haney, Eli T. Hanes, JP.
Jan. 2   W.J. Hooper to Sarah M. Holmes, Bird Wilson, JP.
Jan. 3   W.A. Witcher to Martha S. Wright, Osborn Reeves, MG.
Jan. 4   William Wright to Sarah J. Beggs, W.C. Eads, JP.
Jan. 18   E.J. Adams to Nancy Kay, Andrew Adams, MG.
Jan. 17   J. Roberts to Jane John, Thomas A. Foster, JIC.
Jan. 26   G.B. Hunter to Nancy E. McClain, J.L. Camp, JP.
Jan. 28   J.H. Malone to Miss A.E. Ward, Elisha Lowry, JP.
Jan. 18   C.P. Hubanks to Miss M.C. Cox, Bird Wilson, JP.
Jan. 4   John Tucker to Sarah J. Hooper, Bird Wilson, JP.
Jan. 31   Michael Enty to Miss E. Ray, Andrew Adams, MG.
Feb. 1   Timothy S. Strickland to Mary W. Burt, Bird Wilson, JP.
Feb. 1   A.P. Walker to Miss M.W. Morrow, W.M. Isham, MG.
Feb. 13   Z.L. Water to Anna Humphries, Thomas A. Foster, JIC.
Feb. 13   John L. King to Martha J. Dover, G.M. Thompson, MG.
Feb. 22   Calvin G. Sheppard to Martha J. Smith, A. Chastain, MG.
Dec. 25   T.J. Pryor to Miss P.E. White, W.T. Fleming, MG.
Feb. 8   Jesse J. Roberts to Jane Jones, Thomas A. Foster, JIC.
Feb. 6   John Skillern to Rebecca Carlton, John W. Bowdoin, JP.
March 1   William Walraven to Mary Fisher, G.W. Brogdon, JP.
March 15   W.L. Holbrook to Matilda Robertson, Burton Bradley, MG.
March 29   S.B. McBee to Mary C. Alton, Miles J. Abernathy, MG.
March 27   D.A. Norton to Julia A. King, I.N. Buckner, JP.
March 31   J.E. Brooks to Mary Eaves, Elisha Lowry, JP.
April 8   T.G. Jones to Helen Davenport, Thomas A. Foster, JIC.
April 16   Wadson Lawless to Lucinda Platt, Thomas A. Foster, JIC.
May 17   John T. Nix to Miss M.A. Montgomery, Bird Wilson, JP.
May 20   Willis Hendricks to Mrs. M.L. Tate, Jacob Tate, MG.
June 20   Matthew B. Barron to Mary D.G. Watts, A. Thompson, MG.
June 7   J.A. Collins to Miss T.A. Moss, E.M. Lowry, MG.
June 28   R.H. Welchel to Sarah H. Callahan, G.M. Thompson, MG.
June 14   John Higginbotham to Mary Donaldson, S.D. Wylie, JCCGC.
June 10   John Parrott to Melissa Hannah. J.N. McCool, JP.
July 17   C.B. Roe to Frances Rogers, S.C. Gold, MG.
-----   J.C. Strickland to Martha Owens, G.M. Thompson, MG.
-----   W.J. Thompson to Mrs. M.E. Johnson, G.M. Thompson, MG.
May 31   B.A. Robertson to Mary E. Smith, Isaac Rutherford, MG.
July 26   R.M. Presley to Miss M. Lard, J.D. Tinsley, JP.
Feb. 8   Adolphus R. Johnson to Miss C.E. Thomlinson, J.L. Camp, JP.
July 19   W.J. Alexander to Emma Bray, Z.M. McGhee, MG.
July 1   W.F. Rolls to Mary Crossley, W.L. McDaniel, JP.
July 26   James Haney to Mrs. E. Gibson, W.L. McDaniel, JP.

420

1866

Aug. 7   M.M. Scott to Frances Hannah, J.H. McCoole, JP.
Aug. 21   James Black to Mary A. Stone, I.D. Neal, JP.
Aug. 23   F.P. Mathis to Miss M. Dickson, Burton Bradley, MG.
Aug. 5   Nathan L. Stone to Mary J. Lowry, John R. Green, JP.
Sept. 30   G.S. Wright to Fanny Lumbus, John L. Camp, JP.
Sept. 23   Pleasant A. Butler to Catherine M. Carter, M. Watts,
            JP.
Sept. 26   T.A. Vandiver to Miss M.A. Roe, I.N. Buckner, JP.
Sept. 13   William R. Spears to Miss M.J. Foote, G.W. Brogdon,
            JP.
Oct. 4   W.H. Terry to Miss M.E. Harbor, T.M. Ward, JP.
Oct. 9   John H. Dodd to Jane Hudgins, G.M. Thompson, MG.
Oct. 3   J.A. Johnson to Miss M.A. Barnett, I.N. Buckner, JP.
Oct. 1   Z.F. Wilson to Mrs. Kay Ann Johnson, James Miller,
            JSCCC.
Oct. 21   I.A. Roe to Barthelma Gideon, Thomas A. Foster, JIC.
July 29   B.F. Brown to Mrs. Frances E. West, A. Chastain,
            Minister.
Sept. 6   W.H. Eedes to Miss S.M. Terrell, Z.M. McGhee, MG.
Aug. 30   A.G. Stidman to Mrs. Susan Harden, Jas. H. McCoole,
            JP.
Aug. 19   W.P. Langley to Mary S. Scoggins, William A. Simmons,
            MG.
Sept. 20   E.D. Tate to Mrs. F.C. Hendricks, T.M. Ward, JP.
Aug. 21   N.H. McGinnis to Miss N.A. Simpson, Thomas A. Foster,
            JIC.
Aug. 30   David Miller to Martha Neel, Elisha Lowry, JP.
Aug. 21   Joseph Tate to Miss L. Hefner, T.M. Ward, JP.
May 20   Dr. A.H. Sessions to Mary E. Johnson, I.N. Buckner,
            JP.
Aug. 2   James W. Smith to Caroline Adcock, A. Chastain, MG.
July 26   W.C. Adams to Mary E. Smith, A. Chastain, MG.
Aug. 16   J.M. Bennett to Miss E.C. Kay, A. Chastain, MG.
July 23   Rev. A. Templeton to Mary King, William A. Simmons,
            MG.
Sept. 5   J.W. Nabers to Miss M.C. Strain, T.M. Ward, JP.
Aug. 12   Stephen Cowart to Elizabeth A. Covington, A. Chastain,
            MG.
Sept. 13   A.W. Taylor to Cynthia C. Roe, A. Chastain, MG.
Oct. 14   Alfred L. Grogan to Phoebe Ann Tate, Jacob Tate, MG.
Nov. 1   Jonathan G. Boyd to Mrs. Mary Stewart, Jacob Tate, MG.
Nov. 1   J.W. Woods to Nicy Miller, J.H. McCoole, JP.
Oct. 22   Geo. W. Payne to Permelia Potts, Wm. A. Simmons, MG.
Nov. 7   Louis Putney to Julia A. Bowdoin, Z.M. McGhee, MG.
Oct. 25   Cornelius Bowman to Mary Ann Nesbit, A. Chastain, MG.
Nov. 21   B.G. Boaz to Bessie Fain, H.C. Carter, VDM.
Nov. 8   H.M. Goss to Nancy Patterson, Jacob Tate, MG.
Nov. 20   A.J. Bryson to Miss F.A. Goodman, Jacob Tate, MG.
Nov. 22   Andrew J. Love to Mary Dawson, Jacob Tate, MG.
Nov. 15   A.R. Bates to Sarah A. Brown, T.M. Ward, JP.
Oct. 21   William D. Tate to Frances Neel, T.M. Ward, JP.
Aug. 8   J.H. Shaw to Mrs. A.E. Miniard, J.N. Andrews, JP.
Oct. 4   H.A. Terrell to Margaret E. Scott, John N. Andrews, JP.
Nov. 24   W.M. Harris to Clarinda Cowan, G.M. Thompson, MG.
Dec. 6   G.W. Ware to Miss S.A.C. Capehart, C.M. Thompson, MG.
Nov. 29   W.W. Oats to Miss J.L. Cox, B.J. Johnson, MG.
Dec. 5   J.A. Matthius to Emma Gardner, John W. Kaigler, DD.
Oct. 23   N.J. Brogdon to Miss A.O. Johnson, Bird Wilson, JP.
Sept. 16   James P. Tucker to Emma E.L. Maulden, Bird Wilson, JP.
Dec. 2   George Bunn to Molly S. Kinser, Bird Wilson, JP.

1866

Dec. 9	A.B. Taylor to Mary Watts, A. Chastain, MG.
Dec. 9	J.H. Ellis to Mrs. C.F. Floyd, E.M. Lowry, MG.
Dec. 18	Marion Floyd to Miss R.E. Scoll, W.J. King, MG.
Dec. 20	John J. Abbott to Miss M.F. Burch, G.M. Thompson, MG.
Dec. 23	David M. Watson to Sarah A. Harbor, T.M. Ward, JP.
Dec. 23	James J. Medcalf to Nancy A. Ward, Elisha Lowry, JP.
Dec. 20	G.R. Smith to Miss E.F. Spencer, Burton Bradley, MG.
Dec. 20	A.G. Willingham to Miss S.E. Cantrell, James Miller, JSCCC.
Dec. 27	R.S. Pritchett to Lucinda Miller, T.M. Ward, JP.
Dec. 20	T.W. Miller to Jane Hill, J.H. McCoole, JP.
Dec. 23	William B. Zuber to Rachel Miller, W.L. McDaniel, JP.
Dec. 20	J.W. Dawson to Lussaphine Hill, Jacob Tate, MG.
Dec. 13	Thos. B. Mobley to Miss M.A.V. Lowry, S.C. Gold, MG.
Dec. 20	J.T. Morgan to Miss T.A. Waters, A. Chastain, MG.
Dec. 12	E.H. Davis to Miss L.J. Jackson, A. Chastain, MG.
Dec. 13	W.J. Hutchips to Sarah A. Collier, A. Chastain, MG.
Oct. 4	John Mathis to Miss C.L. Blalock, Burton Bradley, MG.
Dec. 27	H.C. Horton to Miss I.P. Deal, Osborn Adams, JP.
Feb. 8	Henry L. Cook to Martha I. Shellhorse, William T. Fleming, MG.
Feb. 14	Charles Bennett to Eda Hill, Jacob Tate, MG.
Aug. 16	F.S. Garrett to Miss S.A. Smith, William T. Fleming, MG.
Sept. 16	P.M. Bird to Mary M. White, William T. Fleming, MG.
Oct. 11	J.F. Stewart to Miss J. Hayes, John Slaten, JP.
Oct. 18	A.B. Shellhorse to Miss G.A. Adams, Wm. T. Fleming, MG.
Nov. 25	T.R. Dodd to Miss E.E. Blalock, Wm. T. Fleming, MG.
Jan. 22	F.M. Frisby to Miss M. Johnson, W.A. Ellis, MG.
Dec. 20	C.F. Horton to Miss N.E. Smith, W.T. Fleming, MG.
Dec. 23	H.H. Burke to Elizabeth Ponder, Wm. T. Fleming, MG.
Dec. 31	John Moss to Sarah A. Webster, Wm. T. Fleming, MG.

1867

Sept. 15	P. Hewett to Nancy Gurtrie, J.M. Harlan, JIC.
Sept. 28	John Cogan to Mary Kilgore, J.W. Buckner, JP.
Sept. 12	F.A. Ray to Miss M. Bennett, S.C. Gold, MG.
Sept. 19	W.H. Alexander to Victory Russell, Jno. N. Andrews, JP.
Oct. 6	J.C. Dew to Miss J.P. Dodd, Wm. J. King, MG.
Oct. 8	A.M. Kay to Miss M.C. Bowles, Jacob Tate, MG.
Oct. 8	Francis Whitemore to Miss M.E. Stancel, E.J. Underwood, JP.
Oct. 10	G.W. Crane to Hulda Cannon, Jacob Tate, MG.
Oct. 13	Jno. R. Dorsey to Sarah A. Miller, Z.M. McGhee, MG.
Oct. 3	G.W. Littlefield to Fannie Beal, Jas. S. Harkins, MG.
Oct. 9	A.J. Darnell to Miss C.L. Blalock, Burton Bradley, MG.
Oct. 13	J.R. Baugh to Miss G. Miller, T.M. Ward, JP.
Jan. 1	L. Justice to Mary A. Barrentine, W.L. McDaniel, JP.
Jan. 2	R.F. Orr to Miss S.A. Pearson, W.L. McDaniel, JP.
Jan. 9	J.A. Bradford to Mary M. Farmer, T.W. Ward, JP.
Jan. 27	Jesse H. Thornbrough to Savannah Pass, J.D. Tinsley, JP.
Feb. 7	W.H. Talley to Nancy E. Jones, Z.M. McGhee, MG.
Feb. 7	J.M. JOnes to Rachel E. Fricks, Z.M. McGhee, MG.
Feb. 21	Francis M. Boaz to Martha E. Malone, D.W. Moncrief, MG.
March 6	Wh. H. Darnall to Mrs. M.A. Cobt, Z.M. McGhee, MG.

1867

March 13	C.R.A. Harris to Eugenia M. Harkins, Atticus G. Haygood, MG.
March 21	L.B. Stowers to Miss E.A. Cleghorn, Elisha Lowry, JP.
March 10	William Parris to Mary Campbell, Osborn Adams, JP.
March 23	William Goss to Martha Butler, T.A. Foster, JIC.
May 30	W.H. Williams to Miss S. Chrisman, Z.M. McGhee, MG.
March 14	C.D. Harris to Miss A.D. Cowan, A. Chastain, MG.
Jan. 11	Samuel B. Green to Nancy C. Stone, Wm. T. Fleming, MG.
Feb. 19	S.R. Watts to Miss C.E. Stanton, Wm. T. Fleming, MG.
Feb. 14	W.W. Whitsett to Mary Ballew, Wm. T. Fleming, MG.
Feb. 17	Wm. F. Wood to Josephine Zuber, J.H. McCoole, JP.
Feb. 17	Isaac Ezell to Martha Hughey, I.N. Buckner, JP.
April 25	Riley Goss to Miss M.E. Smith, John Slaten, JP.
April 20	R.P. Kiker to Elizabeth Johns, W. Roberts, JP.
May 19	Henry H. Woodall to Louisa Tate, T.M. Ward, JP.
Sept. 25	Chas. Thomas to Amanda Hopper, Osborn Adams, JP.
June 2	Alfred Wylie to Harriet Nelson, W.S. Johnson, MG.
June 12	W.A. Nix to Elizabeth Gastin, Andrew Adams, MG.
June 23	James Blair to Sarah Bennett, J.M. Harlan, JIC.
June 23	W.W. Dunn to Miss M.J. Williams, J.D. Tinsley, JP.
July 25	A.P. Bailey to Rosalie Moss, Z.M. McGhee, MG.
July 23	W.J. Clark to Miss B. Cook, G.M. Thompson, MG.
Aug. 1	L. Bennett to Milly Ellis, Jacob Foster, MG.
July 20	L.M. White to M.M. Harkins, J.D. Tinsley, JP.
Aug. 29	R.J. Fields to Anna Cook, Thos. A. Foster, JIC.
Sept. 4	Robert Gresham to Miss M.A. Gresham, Thos. A. Foster, JIC.
Aug. 6	L.S. Long to Miss Y.J. Moon, Elisha Lowry, JP.
Aug. 20	D.H. Littlefield to Miss S. Bosmon, A. Templeton, MG.
Aug. 11	Augustus Lowery to Mary Joiner, S.D. Wylie, JIC.
Aug. 4	G.W. Perkins to Miss M.M. Perking, A. Templeton, MG.
Aug. 13	J.C. Quinn to Martha Black, J.M. Harlan, JIC.
Nov. 9	Absalom Hughey to Sarah A. Adams, I.N. Buckner, JP.
Nov. 21	Ellis Dempsey to Mary McInton, John Stanton, JP.
Dec. 17	W.C. Smith to Miss M.M. Nesbit, A. Chastain, MG.
Dec. 8	J.R. Garrett to Miss M.A. Woodard, John Slaten, JP.
Dec. 11	J.C. King to Elizabeth Moss, I.N. Buckner, JP.
Dec. 3	W.S. Barton to Miss S.A. Gold, A. Chastain, MG.
June 16	J.W.T. Jones to Emily C. Jones, I.N. Buckner, JP.
Sept. 8	Josephus Trimble to Elizabeth Brown, Bird Wilson, JP.
April 5	Sandford H. Cox to Miss A.A. Gideon, I.N. Buckner, JP.
July 18	W.F. Montgomery to Mary J. Brogdon, Bird Wilson, JP.
July 3	George Smith to Miss Julia McConnell, James S. Harkins, MG.
July 28	George Anderson to Joycey Anderson, John W. Bowdoin, JP.
Aug. 1	J.W. Bennett to Miss S.C. Hewett, A. Chastain, MG.
July 25	L.J. Bailey to Miss M.J. Huston, J.L. Camp, JP.
Aug. 22	W.L. Strain to Miss M.E. Ray, L.M. Ward, JP.
Oct. 6	W.A. Allbritten to Miss M.W. Gober, Elisha Lowry, JP.
Oct. 8	R. Borders, M.D. to Lucy Pulliam, J.E. D____, MG.
Oct. 6	M. Fuller to Miss S.F. Burns, J.L. Camp, JP.
Oct. 27	A. Littlefield to Mary Stanton, Burton Bradley, MG.
Oct. 6	James Hunt to Miss M. Stokes, Osborn Adams, JP.
Oct. 19	A.W. Ballew to Lizzie Gresham, Thos. A. Foster, JIC.
Oct. 20	William Lovejoy to Mary Bryson, J.M. Harlan, JIC.
Nov. 7	P.F. Groover to Miss E.C. Little, Elisha Lowery, JP.
Dec. 1	D.F. Adams to Miss A.A. Evans, L.D. Wyatt, MS.
Dec. 8	B.E. Putman to Miss S. Putman, J.M. Barnes, MG.
Dec. 1	Daniel Croft to Nancy C. Walker, Elisha Lowery, JP.

1867

Nov. 29	James H. Glanton to Miss M.F. Winter, Z.M. McGhee, MG.
Nov. 20	George G. Adams to Miss A.E. Smith, Osborn Adams, JP.
Nov. 23	James W. Armster to Amanda Newton, S.D. Wylie, JIC.
Nov. 17	Henry O. Higginbotham to Dessie Copeland, J.H. Aderhold, MG.
Nov. 19	J.H. Arthur to Susan Lane, Z.M. McGhee, MG.
Nov. 7	N.M. Russell to Miss F.J. Bates, T.M. Ward, JP.
Dec. 22	A.T. Roe to Miss R.D. Borders, E.J. Andrews, JP.
Dec. 24	Isaac Aples to Miss E. Henderson, Z.M. McGhee, MG.
Dec. 5	R.B. Gartrell to Mary L. Ward, T.M. Ward, JP.
Dec. 22	S.H. Griffin to Miss L.M. Gardner, Jno. W. Kaigler, JP.
Dec. 15	J.A. Parks to Mary Turner, Bird Wilson, JP.
Dec. 25	John Walraven to Emily Taylor, Samuel Pulliam, JP.
Dec. 20	H.C. Hunt to Miss M.E. Dobbins, Thos. A. Foster, JIC.
Dec. 25	W.L. Williams to Miss E.M. Martin, B.J. Johnson, MG.
Dec. 11	G.M. Stone to Linda Dudley, J.R. Green, JP.
July 22	James E. Lewis to Miss S.A. Goodwin, W.T. Fleming, MG.
Sept. 28	S.J. Crook to Miss G.A.A. Bradley, W.T. Fleming, M.G.
July 5	W.C. Bates to Miss C.L. Lewis, W.T. Fleming, MG.
April 16	John H. Goodman to Miss M.E. Cannon, John Andrews, JP.
May 11	H.W. Wooten to Sarah Smith, O.B. Adams, JP.
June 20	M.H. Sanders to Miss S.A. Scott, W.J. King, MG.
July 28	Hiram Moss to Julia Tatum, Sam Pulliam, JP.
Jan. 29	Thos. Wheat to Cynthia Holcomb, I.N. Buckner, JP.
July 23	James McBrayer to Miss M.E. Akins, B.J. Johnson, MG.
July 27	Vandiver Johnson to Harriet Sheppard, G.W. Brogdon, JP.
July 17	T.M. McKown to Miss A.E. Drake, T.M. Ward, JP.
July 25	William Sutton to Miss A.A. Gray, Jacob Tate, MG.
July 16	G. Holden to Rebecca Borders, J.M. Harlan, JIC.
Sept. 3	C.L. Bray to Miss J.S. Hamilton, Z.M. McGhee, MG.
Sept. 13	P.B. Keeter to Miss P.L. Akin, B.J. Johnson, MG.

1868

Sept. 5	Jesse B. Thornbrough to Miss O.A. Walker, B. Johnson, MG.
Sept. 10	F.I. Bray to Miss M.L. Alexander, Z.M. McGhee, MG.
Sept. 10	H. Mathis to Elizabeth Hughes, J.D. Tinsley, JP.
Sept. 15	J.A. Rooker to Susan Reynolds, J.W. Buckner, JP.
Sept. 23	Richard F. Ford to Mary M. Lane, Z.M. McGhee, MG.
Sept. 29	O. Pinkerton to Miss M.R. Starr, F.G. Brown, MG.
Sept. 27	Wm. M. Robertson to Miss M.E. Warren, Burton Bradley, JP.
Oct. 3	R. Butler to Ellen Smith, G.W. Ransom, JP.
Oct. 11	W. Tate to Eliza Bailey, M.J. Abernathy, MG.
Oct. 15	R.S. Abbott to Miss S.E. Adams, Burton Bradley, MG.
Oct. 15	S.C. Drake to Miss S.E. Flody, T.M. Ward, NP.
Nov. 5	William M. Parker to Miss M.E. Barton, J.L. Camp, JP.
Nov. 26	M.Y. Scott to Sarah Floyd, W.L. McDaniel, JP.
Nov. 16	Berry Fricks to Jane Wise, John W. Bowdoin, JP.
Nov. 26	C.L. Gober to Mary E. Dorsey, J.D. Tinsley, MG.
Dec. 10	G.W. Burch to Miss S.G. Conaway, D.H. Moncrief, MG.
Dec. 9	W.C. Sparks to Miss M.M. McCaul, Elisha Lowery, JP.
Dec. 17	B. Hughes to Miss N.E. Alexander, John Slaten, JP.
Dec. 17	G.R. Thompson to Miss M.E. Cameron, Z.M. McGhee, MG.
Dec. 22	Moses Black to Miss C. McGurney, Bird Wilson, JP.
Dec. 31	J.H. Fox to Miss L.E. Dempsey, Burton Bradley, MG.
Dec. 24	E.H. Stephens to Miss P. Morrow, J.D. Tinsley, NP.
Dec. 27	J.C. Bradley to Miss F.L. Tillery, J.R. Green, JP.

GORDON COUNTY, GA., MARRIAGE LICNESES (1864-1870)

1868
Dec. 29   David Russell to Miss M. Gordon, J.M. Davidson, JP.
Dec. 27   John F. Gamling to Miss S. Gideon, J.W. Buckner, JP.
Jan. 23   T.H. Elrod to Miss M.A. Blalock, Burton Bradley, MG.
Jan. 16   Wm. Green to Mary Richards, W.L. McDaniel, JP.
Feb. 9   Gilbert Wiley to Hannah Moore, J.L. Camp, JP.
Jan. 5   H.B. Herrington to Miss C.C. Dobbins, B.J. Johnson,
       MG.
Jan. 16   J.J. Morrow to Octabia Moore, Z.M. McGhee, MG.
Jan. 16   J.E. Fallin to Miss B.A. Lowery, T.M. Ward, JP.
Jan. 16   O.M. Taylor to Miss M.J. Darnell, E.J. Anderson, JP.
Jan. 16   Geo. W. Sparks to Miss S.J. Turner, Jacob Tate, MG.
Jan. 28   William Nealy to Miss L.M. Underwood, Jacob Tate, MG.
Feb. 23   C.J. Thayer to Mary F. Davenport, A. Templeton, MG.
March 26   J.L. Campbell to Miss C.R Wylie, J.D. Tinsley, JP.
March 22   J.R. Cooper to Miss S.R. McIntyre, Burton Bradley, MG.
March 5   J.H. Craig to Miss M.M. Scott, M.V. Watts, JP.
March 15   William G. Durham to Miss M. Moncrief, A.L. Moncrief,
       MG.
March 1   G. Adams to Rebecca Kiker, M.V. Watts, JP.
April 2   Lewis B. Knowles to Martha A. Hughes, W.A. Hickey.
April 11   George Dorsett to Jane Young, Jas. S. Harkins, MG.
July 12   James W.V. Findley to Miss A.C. Holden, B.J. Johnson,
       MG.
June 14   G. Gazaway to Miss A.L.A. Ledbetter, Andrew Adams, MG.
May 31   Samuel Eizel to Miss C. Abernathy, T.M. Ward, JP.
June 30   J.L. Hughes to Miss S. Hunt, Thos. A. Foster, JIC.
Jan. 1   John Phillips to Martha Parker, E.J. Underwood, JP.
Jan. 1   David Smith to Miss M. Henderson, Z.M. McGhee, MG.
Dec. 18   B.P. Franklin to Laura Adams, W.T. Fleming, MG.
Nov. 18   G.P. Dodson to Miss M.E. Fleming, W.T. Fleming, MG.
Dec. 22   J.M. Ballard to Miss A. Horton, W.T. Fleming, MG.
July 9   James Cochran to Josephine Holmes, W.T. Fleming, MG.

1869
Jan. 23   J.M. Henson to Miss M.J. Elmore, J.L. Camp, JP.
Jan. 7   D.D. Walraven to Miss E.F. Scott, J.L. Camp, JP.
Jan. 28   James J. Carney to Miss H.A. Haynes, D.H. Moncrief,
       MG.
Jan. 3   William Murphey to Miss H.M. George, Thos. J. Simmons,
       MG.
Jan. 10   J.R. Chastain to Mary Jarrett, A. Chastain, MG.
Jan. 23   John Gibbs to Miss L.A. Findley, Samuel Pulliam, JP.
Jan. 28   G.N. Brogdon to Miss S.J. Harlan, W.P. Harrison, DD.
Feb. 18   James Brock to Miss M.A. Massengale, T.M. Ward, NP.
Feb. 9   George Fields to Mary Fricks, J.D. Tinsley, JP.
Feb. 4   W.M. Lute to Miss M.E. Wood, J.W. Buckner, JP.
Feb. 14   W.J. Morgan to Miss A. Robbins, Jno. W. Kaigler, LD.
Feb. 3   A.D. Bailey to Miss A. Croft, T.M. Ward, NP.
Feb. 25   M. Wylie to Miss J.D. Ferguson, J.D. Tinsley, NP.
Feb. 18   A.C. Rich to Miss A.T. Powell, John N. Andrews, JP.
Feb. 4   H.M. Goss to Miss B.V. McDonald, Jno. W. Bowdoin, JP.
Feb. 28   Henry Scoggins to Matilda Bird, M.V. Watts, NP.
Feb. 29   Wesley Pryor to Frances Lay, John W. Bowdoin, JP.
Feb. 3   A. Greeson to Miss C.C. Dillard, J.B. Sloan, NP.
March 25   James B. Fuller to Miss M.F. Jones, James M. Barnes,
       MG.
March 7   A.J. Pulliam to Miss S. Owens, Samuel Pulliam, JP.
April 1   S.D. Roe to Miss A.E. Moss, E.J. Underwood, JP.
Feb. 7   James R. Bird to M.A. Ballew, W.T. Fleming, MG.
March 17   M.E. Ward to Miss G.A. Ward, J.D. Tinsley, NP.

1869

April 18	David Garner to Elizabeth Free, Andrew Adams, MG.
April 26	A.P. Pulliam to Sarah Baxter, John B. Nesbitt, NP.
April 18	Jackson Carpenter to Miss M.A.H. Pierce, Laban Pilkerton, MG.
April 22	R.B. Headden to Mary Dyer, A.W. Bayard, MG.
April 22	J.M. Fields to Miss N. Dyer, R.B. Headden, MG.
May 2	C.M. Murphey to Miss M.F. Bozeman, Burton Bradley, MG.
April 15	E.G. Mulkey to Miss T.M.H.E. Gaddis, J.R. Green, JP.
April 18	Harrison Norrell to Miss R.L. King, Laban Pilkerton, MG.
May 2	J.W. Boyd to Ann Covington, Ezekiel Ables, MG.
May 6	L.C. Greeson to Harriet Green, J.W. Buckner, JP.
May 6	C.H.B. Simpson to Miss D.E.C. McAdams, M.H. Sanders, MG.
June 15	W.M. Curtis to Miss A.M. Houk, A.B. Wilson, MG.
Aug. 1	W.W. Wright to Miss M.A. Robertson, W.M. Isham, MG.
July 31	A.V. Quinn to Mary Carter, W. Roberts, JP.
July 24	T.J. Dodd to Miss S.F. Wilkey, M.V. Watts, NP.
July 22	C.L. Walker to Miss J.H. Jackson, J.M. Barnes, MG.
Aug. 29	Asa Tate to Alpha Tate, J.B. Sloan, NP.
Aug. 19	Dabney Bennett to Miss N.E. Dempsey, Andrew Adams, MG.
Aug. 5	W.H. Stewart to Miss F.M. Patterson, J.M. Barnes, MG.
Aug. 5	C.L. Burns to Miss M.J. Thompson, Z.M. McGhee, MG.
Aug. 19	J.E. Rogers to Sarah Armstrong, Z.M. McGhee, MG.
Sept. 30	J.W. White to Miss M.J. Cox, James M. Barnes, MG.
Sept. 30	Wm. S. House to Miss S.E. Miller, T.M. Ward, JP.
Sept. 19	Robert Pursley to Miss C. Morehead, T.M. Ward, NP.
Sept. 19	J.W. Morrow to Miss M.E. Seales, J.D. Tinsley, JP.
Sept. 21	J.H. Humphrey to Sarah E. Cox, James M. Barnes, MG.
Sept. 12	Wm. C. Duffen to Miss M.E. Gaines, J.D. Tinsley, JP.
Sept. 9	W.R. Mardeman to Miss T.E. Fuller, J.L. Camp, NP.
Sept. 26	H.A. Reed to Sarah Rogers, William A. Hooper, NP.
Oct. 12	W.A. Roberts to Mattie A. Franklin, Jno. W. Kaigler, JP.
Oct. 17	D. Miller to Louisa McDaniel, J.L. Camp, JP.
Oct. 8	John H. Armstrong to Susan M. Perry, Osborn Reeves, MG.
Oct. 13	Samuel Pulliam to Betty Ballew, John B. Nesbitt, NP.
Oct. 28	John T. Gober to Sarah Downs, Joshua Bowdoin, MG.
Oct. 7	Robert P. Bush to Emma Buckner, Z.M. McGhee, MG.
Oct. 18	J.L. Hill to Nancy Adams, Burton Bradley, MG.
May 2	J.W. Boyd to Ann Covington, Ezekiel Ables, MG.
May 6	L.C. Greeson to Harriet Green, J.W. Buckner, JP.
May 6	C.H.B. Simpson to Miss D.E.C. McAdams, M.H. Sanders, MG.
June 15	W.M. Curtis to Miss A.M. Houk, A.B. Wilson, MG.
Aug. 1	W.W. Wright to Miss M.A. Robertson, W.M. Isham, MG.
July 31	A.V. Quinn to Mary Carter, W. Roberts, JP.
July 24	T.J. Dodd to Miss S.F. Wilkey, M.V. Watts, NP.
July 22	C.L. Walker to Miss J.H. Jackson, J.M. Barnes, MG.
Aug. 29	Asa Tate to Alpha Tate, J.B. Sloan, NP.
Aug. 19	Dabney Bennett to Miss N.E. Dempsey, Andrew Adams, MG.
Aug. 5	W.H. Stewart to Miss F.M. Patterson, J.M. Barnes, MG.
Aug. 5	C.L. Burns to Miss M.J. Thompson, Z.M. McGhee, MG.
Aug. 19	J.E. Rogers to Sarah Armstrong, Z.M. McGhee, MG.
Sept. 30	J.W. White to Miss M.J. Cox, James M. Barnes, MG.
Sept. 23	Wm. S. House to Miss S.E. Miller, T.M. Ward, JP.
Sept. 19	Robert Pursley to Miss C. Morehead, T.M. Ward, NP.
Sept. 19	J.W. Morrow to Miss M.E. Seals, J.D. Tinsley, JP.
Sept. 21	J.H. Humphrey to Sarah E. Cox, James M. Barnes, MG.

1869

Sept. 12	Wm. C. Duffen to Miss M.E. Gaines, J.D. Tinsley, JP.
Sept. 9	W.R. Mardeman to Miss T.E. Fuller, J.L. Camp, NP.
Sept. 26	H.A. Reed to Sarah Rogers, William A. Hooper, NP.
Oct. 12	W.A. Roberts to Mattie A. Franklin, Jno. W. Kaigler, JP.
Oct. 17	D. Miller to Louisa McDaniel, J.L. Camp, JP.
Oct. 8	John H. Armstrong to Susan M. Perry, Osborn Reeves, MG.
Oct. 13	Samuel Pulliam to Betty Ballew, John B. Nesbitt, NP.
Oct. 28	John T. Gober to Sarah Downs, Joshua Bowdoin, MG.
Oct. 7	Robert P. Bush to Emma Buckner, Z.M. McGhee, MG.
Oct. 18	J.L. Hill to Nancy Adams, Burton Bradley, MG.
Nov. 18	D.L. Reeves to Miss M.D. Gray, J.D. Tinsley, NP.
Nov. 3	D.H. Collins to Miss R.A. Phillips, John B. Nesbitt, JP.
Nov. 30	David Tanner to Adeline Frix, James S. Harkins, MG.
Dec. 26	Rufus Moss to Miss M. Hogan, Preston C. Moss, JP.
Dec. 30	John Conaway to Susan Redman, G.W. Ransom, JP.
Dec. 19	G.M. Collier to Sarah Dickerd, Preston C. Mays, JP.
Dec. 23	E.C.M. Jones to Miss M. Gresham, J.D. Tinsley, JP & NP.
Jan. 9	L.A. Bryson to Miss L.J. Scott, M. Moony, NP.
May 17	William Silks to Savannah Hayes, M. Moony, NP.
Oct. 20	E.M. Wilkie to Miss M.A. Warnick, M.V. Watts, NP.
Nov. 3	I.C.C. Armstrong to Miss G.M. Morrow, T.M. Ward, NP.
Dec. 16	Augustus Palmer to Sarah I. Powell, M.V. Watts, NP.
Dec. 14	Wilson Adcox to Nancy Watts, M. Mooney, NP.
Oct. 12	W.R. Miller to Miss M.A. Miller, T.M. Ward, NP.
Dec. 20	F.W. Center to Miss S.B. Horton, L.L. Luper, MG.
Dec. 23	W.A. Longley to Miss E.C. Coley, John W. Bowdoin, JP.
Nov. 22	J.L. Payne to Miss S.J. Meler, W.T. Fleming, MG.
Dec. 17	E.J. Dillard to Mary Adcox, A. Chastain, MG.
Nov. 28	J.J. Cox to Miss Casey Hewett, A. Chadwick, MD.

1870

Jan. 30	W.D. Green to Amanda Austin, I.N. Buckner, JP.
Jan. 6	David Darnell to Mary Dawson, Ezekiel Ables, MG.
Jan. 5	S.V. Roe to Miss C. Warren, T.M. Ward, NP.
Jan. 5	Moses Morrow to Harriet Reynolds, I.N. Buckner, JP.
Jan. 7	Joseph T. Starr to Sarah Freeman, M.V. Watts, NP.
Jan. 8	W.L. Liles to Miss H.M. Bird, T.M. Ward, NP.
Jan. 13	S.M. Ellison to Miss M.A. Aker, Bird Wilson, JP.
Jan. 19	O.C. Campbell to Fannie Stewart, Ezekiel Ables, MG.
Jan. 23	J.T. Black to Miss M.F. Kimbrought, L.D. Wyatt, MG.
Feb. 6	Henry Lokey to Miss E.J. Johnson, E. Ables, MG.
Jan. 27	James D. Wyatt to Miss F.L. Johnson, Preston E. Moss, JP.
Jan. 30	F.M. Rolls to Nancy L. Eaves, E. Ables, MG.
Feb. 1	Robert Liles to Josephine Kay, M.V. Watts, NP.
Feb. 5	Allen Towns to Susan Bennett, I.N. Buckner, JP.
Feb. 6	P.C. Darnell to Sarah Floyd, E. Ables, MG.
Feb. 9	L.C. Fields to Polly Fuller, Jas. S. Harkins, MG.
Feb. 10	W.N. Stevens to Miss J.A. Brownlow, J.D. Tinsley, JP.
Feb. 15	W.H. Moss to Miss Malvin Haynes, M.H. Sanders, MG.
Feb. 16	J.N. White to Miss E.F. Fowler, T.M. Ward, NP.
Feb. 20	Peter Miller to Eliza Betton, Jefferson Bell.
March 3	Augustus Talley to Margaret Kemp, J.L. Camp, NP.
March 3	M.J. Hunnicutt to Miss M.A. Ware, M.H. Sanders, MG.
March 12	John Austin to Susan Jones, G.W. Ransom, JP.
March 15	A.J. Noles to Susan Pate, B.M. Hipp, MG.

GORDON COUNTY, GA., MARRIAGE LICENSES (1864-1870)

1870
March 27   James Roberts to Mattie Green, Burton Bradley, MG.
March 12   D.F. Smith to Elizabeth Hutchens, G.W. Ransom, JP.
March 20   Dempsey Findley to Miss S.A. Holden, Thos. M. Pledger, MG.
March 22   J.H. Bailey to Miss E.P. Crossly, Osborn Reeves, MG.
April 7   W.T. Hall to Miss J.C. Neel, Z.M. McGhee, MG.
April 10   J.S. Callahan to Miss M. Helton, I.N. Buckner, JP.
April 14   W.E. McDaniel to Ann Smith, C.J. Oliver, MG.
April 14   J.F. Eaves to Jane Roberts, G.W. Ransom, JP.
April 16   F. Pinion to Amanda Sloan, I.N. Buckner, JP.
May 8   G.V. Crisman to Molly Crisman, Washington Johnson, MG.
May 23   A.P. Phillips to Jane Campbell, Preston C. Moss, JP.
June 7   Wm. S. Long to Sarah Wood, G.W. Ransom, JP.
June 11   W.W. Blassingame to Miss C.M. Reeves, Thos. M. Pledger, MG.
Aug. 4   J.F. Lont to Frances Hunter, G.W. Ransom, JP & NP.
Aug. 14   M. Wyatt to Lindy Burgess, L.D. Wyatt, MG.
Aug. 21   G.M.J. Ford to Miss S. Ford, A.B. Wilson, MG.
Aug. 21   Nicholas Moss to Amanda Buren, Preston C. Moss, NP.
Aug. 21   T.B. Andrews to Miss D. Lackey, J.S. Milburn, MG.
Aug. 31   J.L. Mosteller to Miss M.R. Robertson, A.B. Wilson, MG.
Sept. 1   W.N. Richards to Miss D.E. Scroggins, G.W. Ransom, JP.
Sept. 15   R.L. McWhorter to Miss F. McDaniel, W.T. Brash, MG.
Sept. 4   Jas. M. Covington to Sarah Carter, J.H. Parker, MG.
Sept. 18   J.C. Townsend to Miss M.A. Lewis, S.M. Gore, MG.
Sept. 18   W.T.C. Johnson to Miss Sidney Eeds, J.D. Tinsley, JP.
Sept. 12   Joseph McConnell to Julia Morris, T.M. Pledger, MG.
Sept. 15   A.H. Hulsey to Miss E.V. Hulsey, T.M. Ward, NP.
Sept. 27   R.W. Thornton to Miss A.E. Phillips, A.B. Wilson, MG.
Oct. 1   E.M. Cobb to Miss C. Hanks, G.W. Ransom, JP.
Oct. 20   A. Holsomback to Frances Lanier, T.M. Ward, NP.
Oct. 20   S.S. Puryear to Miss E. Hursten, T.M. Ward, NP.
Dec. 23   W.A. Hardy to Miss M.A. Nichols, T.M. Pledger, MG.
Nov. 9   J. Ponder to Miss J. Coker, J.L. Evans, JP.
Nov. 22   J.E. Beavers to Miss A.J. Fricks, A.W. Wilson, MG.
Dec. 1   M.H. Jackson to Fannie Kiker, G.W. Ransom, JP.
Dec. 8   James B. Barton to Elizabeth Tate, Preston C. Moss, JP.
Dec. 15   H.J. Mooney to Miss M.E. Parr, Burton Bradley, MG.
Dec. 14   J.W. Ballew to Miss F.E. Walraven, Z.F. Wilson, JP.
Dec. 11   M.G. Scott to Miss M.M. Orr, M.H. Sanders, MG.
Dec. 26   J.A. Barday to Miss S.P. Jones, I.N. Buckner, JP.
Dec. 30   H.F. Shellhorse to Miss M. Cochran, W.T. Fleming, MG.
Dec. 28   J.T. Gastin to Miss M. Adams, Andrew Adams, MG.
Dec. 29   Henry Martin to Eliza Wilkey, M.M. Dillar, JP.
Dec. 29   Ben Clemmons to Miss H. Mann, G.W. Ransom, JP.
Dec. 29   W.S. Bower to Miss G.A. Johnson, Burton Bradley, MG.
Feb. 20   J.H. Silber to Miss E. Holmes, W.T. Fleming, MG.
Oct. 15   S.C. Murphey to Elizabeth Hogins, M.M. Dillard, NP & JP.
Nov. 28   G.M. Hunt to Mary C. Freeman, T.M. Pledger, MG.
Oct. 20   William Cochran to Lucinda Shellhorse, W.T. Fleming, MG.
Sept. 1   B.F. Greeson to Miss M.E. Foster, I.N. Buckner, JP.
May 12   J.M. Shellhorse to Adeline Mealor, W.T. Fleming, MG.
Dec. 11   A.L. Keys to Emily Robnett, Osborn Reeves, MG.

Jan. 8, 1882 - Columbus Hutchinson & Julia An Pulliam (black),
Z. F. Wilson, JP.

Jan. 5, 1882 - H. M. Penn & Miss Ann Weber, J. L. Bennett, MG.

Jan. 11, 1882 - L. A. Stone & Miss Lawranceville Helton, W. S.
Ellis, MG.

Jan. 19, 1882 - J. M. Harkins & Sarah Pulley, Z. F. Wilson, JP.

Jan. 24, 1882 - E. T. Talley & Fannie Jones, W. M. Bridges, MG.

Jan. 23, 1882 - James J. Measell & Miss Judith Pittman, W. M.
Smith, JP.

Feb. 3, 1882 - Jesse Hughes & Miss Mollie Copeland, T. J. Simmons, MG.

Feb. 16, 1882 - J. A. Smith & Miss Victoria Jones, J. S. Harkins,
MG.

Feb. 16, 1882 - R. G. Robertson & Miss Edith A. Helton, T. J.
Simmons, MG.

Feb. 18, 1882 - R. P. Hill & Miss Abigail Stanton, T. J. Simmons,
MG.

Feb. 22, 1882 - Benjamin Butler & Mamie Bowdoin (black), Benjamin
Newton (his mark), MG.

Feb. 18, 1882 - Thomas Huckabee & Miss Sultana Harkins, J. D.
Huckabee, MG.

Feb. 22, 1882 - George E. Scott & Betsey J. Fuller, J. A. Mims,
MG.

Feb. 26, 1882   James A. Norrell & Maudia Massey, J. A. Johnson,
MG.

Mar. 7, 1882 - S. D. Cornwell & Miss S. A. Ables, J. L. Camp,
NP & JP.

Mar. 8, 1882 -   John Bailey & Miss Edna Jane White, A. R. Bates,
NP & JP.

Mar. 12, 1882 - G. T. Crowell & Miss Delai Hill, J. B. Hillhouse,
MG.

Sept. 4, 1882 - Alvin Murphy & Lula Bell (Black), A.J. Kinman, JP.

Apr. 9, 1882 - Willburn Humber & Miss Amanda Blankenship, G.L.
King, JP.

Apr. 17, 1882 - W. N. Brock & Miss A. N. Shaw, J. M. McBrayer, MG.

Apr. 23, 1882 - Joe Bird & Frances Barnwell (black), W.A. Nix, MG.

Apr. 23, 1882 - William Stevens & Miss Lizzie Baker, J. H.
Bennett, NP & JP.

May 7, 1882 - W. P. Morris & Miss Mary J. Hunter, A. R. Bates,
NP & JP (Floyd Co.).

May 1, 1882 - John Couch & Elizabeth Hilley, C. J. Ballew, MG.

Sept. 4, 1882 - J. C. Sampler & Marietta Austin, W. M. Bridges,
MG.

May 20, 1882 - Milton Lackey & Martha Coggins, W. M. Smith, JP.

May 31, 1882 - W. B. Robertson & Alice M. Blalock, Burton Bradley, MG.

May 21, 1882 - Wm. S. Glenn & Julia A. Shaw, B.E.L. Timmons, MG.

May 23, 1882 - Alonzo W. Johnson & Ida J. Reddick, E. B. Rees, MG.

May 28, 1882 - Cicero J. Ray & Margaret Cox, J.C. Martin, NP & JP.

June 25, 1882 - Lawrence N. Jones & Jane Tomlinson, J.L. Bennett,
MG.

June 11, 1882 - Lucien Johnson & Josephine Mason (black), C.L.
King, JP.

June 11, 1882 - Henry F. Powell & Miss Lucy Roach, W.J. McDaniel,
NP & JP.

June 2, 1882 - Tole Foster & Martha Folds (black), W.J. McDaniel,
NP & JP.

July 9, 1882 - Wm. C. White & Laura Eulalia Smith, W. K. Hopper,
NP.

Sept. 4, 1882 - Hamilton Green & Celia Ann Kinney, J. C. Johnson,
MG.

June 21, 1882 - Harvey Ellis & Lizzie Waters (black), J. C.
Johnson, MG.
Sept. 4, 1882 - Thomas D. Brock & Lorena Shaw, J. M. McBrayer,
MG.
July 15, 1882 - Silas Montgomery & Lizzie Jackson (black), J. D.
Tinsley, NP & JP.
Sept. 4, 1882 - Augustus Stearnes & Claudia Ann Hopper (black),
Ben Newton (his mark), MG.
Aug. 24, 1882 - V. H. Bentley & Miss Katie Brown, R. A. Eaks, MG.

Jan. 7, 1883 - A. F. Wofford & Miss Mary M. Taylor, E. J. Under-
wood, NP & JP.
Jan. 14, 1883 - Washington Baxter & Lucy Kimbrough (col), J. A.
Johnson, MG.
Jan. 7, 1883 - Alonzo Little & Miss Georgia Montgomery, O. G.
Harris, JP.
Jan. 11, 1883 - J. L. Burch & Miss Lillie May Brooks, J. D.
Huckabee, MG.
Jan. 14, 1883 - William Mulkey & Miss Margaret M. Lackey, R. M.
Pittman, NP.
Jan. 15, 1883 - W. M. Stone & Miss Nancy Powell, Z. F. Wilson,
JP.
Jan. 25, 1883 - Wheeler Smith & Caroline Butler (col), R. E.
Newton, XMG.
Feb. 1, 1883 - James N. Shinholder & Miss A. F. Lewis, E. J.
Underwood, NP.
Feb. 4, 1883 - W. J. D. Johnson & Miss Octavia Brogdon, John H.
Philips, MG.
Feb. 16, 1883 - William Humphrey & Matilda Offutt, J. A. Johnson,
MG.
Feb. 14, 1883 - Samuel C. Dodd & Charlotte Dodd, J. L. Barnett,
MG.
Feb. 22, 1883 - J. H. King & Miss Vienna Green, J.D. Huckabee,
MG.
Feb. 26, 1883 - Parry Davis & Miss Fannie Wade, Samuel Pulliam,
JP.
Mar. 1, 1883 - C. E. Sexton & Miss Annie Bowles, A.S. Tatum, MG.
Mar. 1, 1883 - W. F. Ellis & Miss Fannie A. Hogan, J. M. McBrayer,
MG.
Mar. 1, 1883 - John K. Strain & Miss Camassa Copeland, V. H.
Haynes, JP & NP.
Mar. 8, 1883 - Thomas White & Martha L. Mashburn, Joab Lewis,
NP 7 JP.
Mar. 11, 1883 - John P. Page (William?) & Miss Sue Lister, John
A. Bradley, MG.
Mar. 15, 1883 - J. T. Benson & Miss Sallie Hunt, A.S. Tatum, MG.
Mar. 14, 1883 - H. C. Nesbitt & F. C. Walraven, Daniel Taylor,
NP & JP.
Mar. 14, 1883 - Abraham Philips & Suckie Bennett, J.D. Tinsley,
NP & JP.
Mar. 15, 1883 - P. T. Kimbrough & Miss Mary Carter, J. D. Tinsley,
NP & JP.
Mar. 20, 1883 - William Philips & Miss Julia Corbin, Samuel
Pulliam, NP & JP.
Mar. 25, 1883 - Monut Greason & Miss Sarah Ann Keene, J. A.
Johnston, Minister.
Mar. 25, 1883 - P. D. King & Miss Amanda E. Powell, E. J. Under-
wood, NP & JP.
Apr. 1, 1883 - J. H. Lanham & S. E. Morris, A. J. Kinman, JP.
Apr. 8, 1883 - Thomas Wood & Lidia Smith, J. L. Barnett, MG.
Apr. 8, 1883 - Nathan Holt & Miss Sallie Keigh, Z.F. Wilson, JP.

Apr. 17, 1883 - T. F. Harkins & Miss Amelia Boisclair, J. D.
        Tinsley, NP & JP.
Apr. 29, 1883 - William B. Anglin & Miss Mary Brooks, E. J.
        Underwood, NP & JP.
May 13, 1883 - Thomas Green & Miss Emma Cook, W. J. McDaniel, JP
May 17, 1883 - Thomas Jefferson & Caroline Mills (col), Ben (X)
        Newton, MG.
May 23, 1883 - John G. Ledbetter & Clara M. Cox, W.M. Bridges,
        MG.
May 13, 1883 - John W. Adams & Mariah L. Lanier, John W. Swain,
        NP & JP.
May 23, 1883 - B. M. Pack & Miss Alice Norrell, W. M. Bridges,
        MG.
June 3, 1883 - R. B. Bray & Minnie Stancil, A. J. Kinman, NP & JP.
(No date) - Daniel Boone Curtiss & Frances L. Harden, W. M. Cur-
        tiss, MG.
July 15, 1883 - Joseph Ware & Marietta Henderson, A. R. Bates,
        NP & JP.
July 15, 1883 - W. A. McCrary & Nancy Jane McElroy, R. M. Pitt-
        man, NP.
July 22, 1883 - J. H. Nicholson & Martha A. Bridges, A. J. Kinman,
        JP.
July 19, 1883 - Albert Harper & Alice Lake (col), J.B. Bedens, MG.
Aug. 26, 1883 - Henry Curtiss & Sally Kaigler, W.J.M. McDaniel,
        NP & JP.
Aug. 19, 1883 - T.R. Philips & Miss Missouri Stanton, J.A. Col-
        lins, JP.
Sept. 2, 1883 - Nathaniel Robertson & Miss Rosa Noble, T. J.
        Simmons, MG.
Aug. 26, 1883 - James Holcomb & Miss Nancy Pritchard, J. A.
        Johnson, MG.
Sept. 2, 1883 - Edmund Wiley & Alsey Baxter, Daniel Taylor, NP &
        JP.
Aug. 16, 1883 - J. J. Mooney & Miss S.J. Brogdon, J.L. Huckabee,
        MG.
Aug. 9, 1883 - W.T. Nation & Miss Jane McGhee, R.S. Pritchett,
        MG.
Aug. 12, 1883 - John R. Wood & Miss Eliza Parker, John M. Swain,
        NP & JP.
Aug. 22, 1883 - James Peoples & William Griffin (col), W. J.
        McDaniel, NP & JP.
Sept. 5, 1883 - Joe M. Barrett & Miss Sallie Weber, John E.
        Bennett, MG.
Sept. 5, 1883 - A. J. Wadkins & Miss Mary V. Alverson, William
        Barton, JP.
Sept. 9, 1883 - A. W. Fields & Miss Clara Buckner, J. A. Johnson,
        MG.
Sept. 2, 1883 - Pinkney Lanham & Miss Sallie Ray, V. H. Haynes,
        NP & JP.
Sept. 19, 1883 - W. A. Stanton & Lilla G. Fite, W. M. Bridges,
        MG.
Sept. 24, 1883 - John C. Bolding & Miss Alice Roberts, Z. M.
        McGhee, MG.
Oct. 7, 1883 - Columbus Burch & Miss Sarah A.E. Green, F. E.
        Chase, MG.
Oct. 12. 1883 - Knox Conley & Cynthis Baxter (col), Daniel
        Taylor, NP & JP.
Nov. 6, 1883 - Sylvanus Hamrick & Miss Jane Smith, W. M. Smith,
        JP.
Nov. 11, 1883 - E. J. Greason & Miss Fannie M. Freeman, J. M.
        McBrayer, MG.

Nov. 1, 1883 - Andrew Clint & Mrs. Martha Holcomb, T. J. Simmons, MG.
Nov. 4, 1883 - D. E. Greene & Miss Florence C. Stagg, T. J. Simmons, MG.
Nov. 4, 1883 - Henry Jackson & Minerva Liles, W. M. Smith, JP.
Nov. 18, 1883 - Lee Foster & Laura Treadaway, C.L. King, JP.
Nov. 22, 1883 - Lee Hearing & Miss Josephine Mooney, R. T. Teese, JP.
Nov. 25, 1883 - James R. Green & Miss Frances-Viola Kay, J.D. Harris, MG.
Nov. 19, 1883 - Stephen Smith & Cherokee Alexander (col), Samuel Pulliam, JP.
Dec. 1883 - W. B. Hayes & Miss Henrietta Morrow, J. H. Huckabee, MG.
Dec. 20, 1883 - J. A. White & Sarah Ann Dugger, Wm. R. Hopper, NP & JP.
Dec. 20, 1883 - John Wesley Penden & Sallie Gardner, A. J. Kinman, JP.
Dec. 16, 1883 - W. D. Jackson & Miss Annice Howard, A. J. Kinman, JP.
Dec. 21, 1883 - Frank Adams & Mattie Hendrick, C.L. King, JP.
Dec. 23. 1883 - Cicero Blalock & Miss Louisianna A. Jarrett, H.G.B. Turner, MG.
Dec. 26, 1883 - Andrew J. Kirby & Miss Matilda S. Hendrick, John W. Swain, NP & JP.
Dec. 27. 1883 - J. A. Horton & Miss Ruth V. Ashworth, H.G.B Turner, MG.
Dec. 20, 1883 - J. H. Rice & Miss Addie Gresham, J.D. Tinsley, NP & JP.
Dec. 26, 1883 - George Freeman & Miss Tatie Gentry, Wm. Barton, JP.
Dec. 27. 1883 - J.D. Baxter & Mrs. J.L. Robertson, J.M. McBrayer, MG.
(No date) - John Mangum & Delia Wiley (col), Joab Lewis, NP & JP.

Jan. 3, 1884 - John Hopper to Carrie Harper, Sam Pulliam, JP.
Jan. 10, 1884 - John Holcomb to Miss Rosetta Pritchard, J. A. Johnson, MG.
Jan. 19, 1884, W. R. Kinnamon & Miss Florence L. Keys, Samuel Pulliam, JP.
Jan. 24, 1884 - Thomas Wood & Miss Mary E. Garrett, Jno. A. Bradley, MG.
Jan. 20, 1884 - S. M. Fuller & Miss Mary Mansell, H.F. Smith, MG.
Jan. 20, 1884 - Andrew W. Barnes & Miss Josie Arnold, Joab Lewis, NP & JP.
Jan. 22. 1884 - S. M. Wood & Miss Lizzie Ray, R.S. Pritchett, MG.
Feb. 17, 1884 - R.D. Lanier & Miss Lucy Adams, J.S. Harkins, MG.
Feb. 21, 1884 - J.J. Padgett & Miss G.L. Mooney, Z.T. Wilson, JP.
Feb. 24, 1884 - John L.B. Porch & Miss Amanda Fox, J.A. Mims, MG.
Feb. 21, 1884 - J.B. Ashworth & Miss Georgia B. Horton, H.G.B. Turner, MG.
Mar. 9, 1884 - John Lea & Miss Nellie Cooley, W.M. Bridges, MG.
Mar. 11, 1884 - Robert Goodnight & Miss Alice Abbott, W.N.N. Curtiss, MG.
Mar. 13, 1884 - F.C. Blankenship & Miss Theodosia Chastain, M.M. Smith, MP.
Mar. 15. 1884 - Jack Wilson & Miss Jane Russell, C.L. King, JP.
Mar. 15. 1884 - Simon Printup & Laura Mann (col), J. Betton (col), MG.
Mar. 27, 1884 - Nelson Bray & Miss Georgia Ann Fossett, Erwin P. Price, MG.

Mar. 30, 1884 - D.C. Barton & Miss Mary F. Dillard, E. Borders,
     NP & Ex-officio, JP.
Mar. 30, 1884 - E.A. Sutherland & Miss Rebecca M. Reeves, B.R.
     Bray (?).
Apr. 5, 1884 - J.C. Huckabee & Miss Mahala J. Harkins, Z.F.
     Wilson, JP.
Apr. 9, 1884 - G.W. Holdenby & Testy Taylor, Z.F. Wilson, JP.
Apr. 27, 1884 - Edwin Giles & Miss Sallie Orr, M.M. Scott, JP.
May 1, 1884 - Robert Jackson & Judy McDenman (col), Robert T.
     Wilkinson (?).
May 11, 1884 - E.P. Dempsey & Miss Fanny Land, J.D. Tinsley, NP
     & JP.
May 26, 1884 - Emanuel D. Barrett & Miss Nancy Roe, E. Borders,
     NP & JP.
June 1, 1884 - George A. Hollingsworth & Miss Martha J. Cook,
     Samuel Pulliam, JP.
June 1, 1884 - Thaddeus B. Pye & Louisa Grant, J.S. Harkins, MG.
June 15, 1884 - G.W. Treadaway & Miss Sarah E. Ables, A.P. Bates,
     NP & JP.
June 15, 1884 - S.R. Ables & Miss Sarah G. Treadaway, A.P. Bates,
     NP & JP.
June 15, 1884 - B.T. Stokes & Miss Lucinda Treadaway, NP & JP (?).
June 25, 1884 - George L. Chastain & Mattie L. Kiker, W.H. Hickey,
     M.E.C.S.
July 7, 1884 - Janos H. Hollingsworth & Mrs. S.C. Dowdy, Samuel
     Pulliam, JP.
July 13, 1884 - L.M. Dorsey & Miss Elizabeth Dorsey, J.B. Hill-
     house, MG.
July 10, 1884 - Hezekiah Watkins & Miss Mary M. Darnell. J.D.
     Tinsley, NP & JP.
July 27, 1884 - J.A. McArthur & Miss Martha K. Coggins, A.
     Chadwick, MG.
July 23, 1884 - J. W. Mi--- & Mariah T. Riley, W.M. Bridges, MG.
Aug. 1, 1884 - Samuel B. Dover & Miss Frances Fossett, M.M.
     Scott, JP.
Aug. 21, 1884 - Joseph Jones & Janie Adams (col), J.J. Merrill.
     O.MG.
Aug. 24, 1884 - John King & Miss Annie Jones, J.M. McBrayer, MG.
Sept. 2, 1884 - Middleton M. Rosson & Martha M. Kinney, J.H.
     Bennett, NP & JP.
Sept. 7, 1884 - W.A. Davis & Miss Emily Green, William Stone, MG.
Sept. 11, 1884 - Simon Stephens & Miss Annie Gardner, M.H.
     Edwards, MG.
Sept. 2, 1884 - A.P. Hill & Mrs. B.F. Copeland (Miss Betty),
     W.M. Bridges, MG.
Sept. 14, 1884 - B.F. Fuller & Miss Julia A. Parker, A.J. Kinman,
     JP.
Sept. 14, 1884 - Benjamin Reel & Maggie Hutcherson, Daniel
     Taylor, NP & JP.
Sept. 25, 1884 - W.F.M. Cudd & Miss Lavinia Massey, J.A. Johnson,
     MG.
Sept. 30, 1884 - John Dean & Miss Sallie Greason, J.A. Johnson,
     MG.
Oct. 9, 1884 - J.L. Paine & Miss Sallie Costain, Rev. M.D.
     Burgess.
Oct. 9, 1884 Alfred Hopper & Alice Baxter, W.H. Hooper, NP & JP.
Oct. 12, 1884 - R.J. Chandler & Miss Nora Hardy, Joab Lewis, NP &
     JP.
Oct. 12, 1884 - Benny Carder & Miss Susan Helton, W.H. Black,
     Ordinary.
Oct. 19, 1884 - W.C. Talley & Miss Lula Perry, R. F. Wilkerson,

L. (licensed) Preacher.

Oct. 19, 1884 - William Kemp & Miss Lula Touchstone, A. R.
         bates, NP & JP.

Oct. 23, 1884 - Thomas A. Frierson & Miss Annie E. Gedard, E. H.
         Bennett, Pastor First Presbyterian Church,
         Atlanta, Ga.

Oct. 31, 1884 - George Evans & Nellie Malone (col), Rev. J.B.
         Betton (col).

Oct. 15, 1884 - J.F. Adams & Miss Jennie Mullens, J.H. Bennett,
         JP & NP.

Nov. 2, 1884 - Julius Jones & Miss Minnie Bray, A.S. Tatum, MG.

Nov. 2, 1884 - William Davis & Mattie Lay (col), J.H. McCoole,
         MG.

Nov. 6, 1884 - E.H. Shields & Miss Laura Jones, B.F. Bright, MG.

Nov. 9, 1884, C.A. Neel & Miss Alice Cooley, M.M. Scott, JP.

Nov. 9, 1884 - John P. Davis & Miss Effie T. Camp, T.S. Edwards,
         MG.

Nov. 12, 1884 - William D. Sloan & Miss Susan L. Helton, J.M.
         McBrayer, MG.

Nov. 16, 1884 - M.F. Batterson & Miss Julia M. McCool, John A.
         Auprelds, MG.

Nov. 16, 1884 - James T. Bates & Miss Martha F. Bridgerman, A.S.
         Tatum, MG.

Nov. 23, 1884 - B.D. Todd & Miss Texanna Reynolds, J.L. Barnett,
         MG.

Nov. 23, 1884 - Charles Graves & Miss Mary Ward, J.S. Harkins,
         MG.

Nov. 25, 1884 - J.S. Underwood & Miss Mary E. Whitsett, A.J.
         Kinman, JP.

Nov. 27, 1884 - Carlton Curtiss & Fannie Garson, Joab Lewis, NP
         & JP.

Nov. 28, 1884 - H.H. Harriman & Samantha Ray, Joab Lewis, NP & JP.

Dec. 3, 1884 - Vincent V. Harlan & Miss Maggie M. Borch, D. J.
         Weems, MG.

Dec. 3, 1884 - James W. Hudgins & Miss Charlotte B. Bowdoin, A.S.
         Tatum, MG.

Dec. 11, 1884 - T.J. Merritt & Miss Ann A. Holland, Z.F. Wilson,
         JP.

Dec. 11, 1884 - J.W. Sisk & Miss Lula Dodd, J.L. Bennett, MG.

Dec. 14, 1884 - Benjamin F. Tate & Miss Eva Hill, A.S. Tatum, MG.

Dec. 18, 1884 - William F. Trimmier & Mamie Willingham, A.S.
         Tatum, MG.

Dec. 18, 1884 - Jack Beaven & Laura Mann (col), J.M. Miller,
         NP & JP.

Dec. 18, 1884 - J.D. Fox & Miss Emily Abbott, J.A. Mims, MG.

Dec. 21, 1884 - R.W. Dillard & Miss Lillie Wilson, J.D. Huckabee,
         MG.

Dec. 25, 1884 - Joseph Gilbreath & Miss Tiny Curtiss, J.M. McBary-
         er, MG.

Dec. 25, 1884 - William H. Williams & Miss E.A. Davis, F.T.
         Powell, JP.

Dec. 24, 1884 - J.A. Porch & Mollie Jones, J.A. Mims, MG.

Dec. 25, 1884 - O.W. Campbell & Miss Mariah J. Hill, M.H. Edwards,
         MG.

Dec. 25, 1884 - Marvin Fite & Miss Leola Borders, M.H. Edwards, MG

Dec. 25, 1884 - James F. Thomas & Emma J. Williams, A.S. Tatum, MG.

Dec. 20, 1884 - Elias D. Neel & Willie F. Green, William Stone,
         MG.

Dec. 32(?), 1884 - Mr. Willis Whitsett Harris & Bettie Stewart
Nesbitt, J.J.S. Callaway, MG (prominent Minister, Principal
Ryals HS at Sugar Valley & Calhoun Coll. Inst. at Calhoun).

Each year the tax collector of every Georgia county was required
to submit to the county grand jury the names of all "insolvents,"
or people who were subject to pay a tax, but had not done so.
To my knowledge, none of the Gwinnett County tax digests survived
the courthouse fire of 1871, other than one dated 1866. For
some reason, three "insolvents" lists survived, dated 1822, 1824,
and 1826. This is the first of these lists. The original list,
located at the Georgia Department of Archives and History, File
II, Gwinnett County, includes the amount of tax that each person
owed.

Capt. Worsham's Dist.

John Lawson
do. agent Sarah Lawson
Robert Cameron
James W. Sikes
John Bridges
Axom Pearce
Etheldred Wilder
Benjamin Whitehead
Thomas Jones
James Hill
William H. Worsham
Isaac Gray
Matthew T. Hamilton
James McBride
David Spence
Betsy B. McCaul
William McBride
Vincent Timms
Edward Lee
William White
John Maddox
do. agent Sebron Maddox
Edmon Pearce
Amos Speller
William Bradford
Ansen Williams
Richard Bass, Sen.
James Wheeler
Sabird Beauchamp
Archabald Hamilton

Capt. Dunlap's Dist.

Burdy Howel
James Mehaffee, agent
  Wm. Smith
Henry Woody
Reddick Smith
Zimma (?) McGuire
Westley Yancey
Edward Wade
Charles Yancey
Sollomon Johnston
Blany Meeks
Shaderic Bogan
Zachariah Thompson
do. agent Henry Thompson
agent Martha Thompson

Capt. Dunlap's Dist. cont.

John Torrence

Capt. Pendley's Dist.

Michael Roach
John Brown
Charles King
Robert Montgomery
Charles Randol
Nimrod Pendley
William Cash
Joseph Trimble
Jacob Thomas

Capt. Ware's Dist.

Mathew Goss
Wiley Goss
William Walraven
William Wallace
Joseph Roberts
Thomas Faulk
James B. Huckabe
Isaac Goss
Robert Kenedy
Tilman Bobo
Philip Coleman
William Spencer
Laughlen Arnall
William Cox
Thomas Matthews
William Woodall
John Cook
Peter Salter
William B. Tate(?)
James Riggs

Capt. Gazaway's Dist.

Calvin Mimms
James Barnett
  by J. Barnett
James Collum
Tomas Hudson
Benjamin Harres
Wiley Nicholds
do. agent David Nicholds
Edward Harres

Capt. Gazaway's Dist. cont.

Lincey Elsberry
Hubard A. Rowden
George Bornes
Daniel Price
Sarah Bankston
Crofford Bagwell
James White, agent
    Jesse Williams
William Fendley
Austin Bryant
Benjamin Mirill
do. agent James Chappel
George Heard
James Loller

Capt. Ellison's Dist.

Francis Ellison, agent
    Samuel Ellison
Samuel Lard
Jerimiah McGlawn(?)
James Swords
William Nicks
David Sayes(?)
Nathan Ward
James Camp
Thos. Minchew
do. agent Martha Minchew(?)
John Britt
William Camp
John Laurence, agent
    Silas Laurence
Nathan Spence
Elisha Minchew
Isham Thornton
William Killgore
Russel Rutledge, agent
    Elias G-----(?)
Joseph Stinson
John McLung
Barton Smith
Jas. Taylor, agent
    Andrew Bonds
Vardy Bonds
John Wester

Capt. Baker's Dist.

Joseph Barnett
Wells Thompson
Hardy Benton
Paschal Brooks
Richard Austin
David Daniel
John McLane
Thomas Cargill
Richard Benson
John Doss
N. L. Sturges

Capt. Baker's Dist. cont.

William Matthews
Frederic Bagwell
John Locke
Michael Cupp
Levi Dempsey
John Buck
Elias Miller
James Donaldson
William McLane
Samuel Dukes agent Gray
    Roberts

Capt. Bailey's Dist.

Joseph Hill
William Hawkins
Willis Jinks
Reuben Higgins, Jur.
William Johnston
Samuel Key
Curry (?) Butler
Henry Butler
William Morris
David Spay
William Jinks
Edward Turner
do. agent Elisha Turner

Default List, Capt. Fendley's Dist.

Jesse Sorrows
Josiah Johnston
James Lockibee
Harbard Cook
Bishop Wilkins

Capt. Ware's Dist.

Benjamin Green
Simeon Sheridon
Asa Coker
William Heard
Allen Heard
John Usra
Daniel Glaze
William Clarke
William Watson
John Williams
William Scott

Capt. Gazaway's Dist.

Sandford Raimey
Redden Blocker
William Leverett
Jeremiah Corley
Tobias Honey
John Terry

GWINNETT COUNTY, GEORGIA TAX DEFAULTERS, 1824-1826

"List of Defaulters allowed John Boring, tax collector for the year 1824 by the Grand Jury of Gwinnett County at September of Superior Court 1825."

Capt. Gazaway's Dist.

Elijah Cochran
Joseph Springer
Nathaniel Cooper
  agent for Martha Weems
Pleasant Craft
Drury M. Boman

Capt. Ellison's Dist.

David Funderburg
Jacob Bankston
John Rutledge
Uriah Casey
  Do agent for Isaac Casey
Danville Mitchel
edward Gilbert
Thomas Richards
John R. Jenkins
John N. Cargill
John Chandler
James Smith
Isham Thornton
James L. Bonds
Andrew Jester
Asa L. Scoggins
Francis Ellison
Moses Ellison
Samuel Rollings
Robert Phillips
Jonathan Langford
Edward Langford
Valentine Braswell

Capt. Bradbury's Dist.

James Donley
John W. Beachum
Ira Segars (crossed out)
Nathaniel Harris (crossed out)
Daniel M. Jakcson
Joseph Higgins
Burrel Higgins
Milton Acock
Mason Davis
Jeremiah George
Richard Holcom
James Higgins
James George
John Vinyard

Capt. Pierce's Dist.

Edward Morgan
William Crawford
William S. White

Capt. Pierce's Dist cont.

Howard Robertson
Levi Beauchamp
John Wright
Phillip Blanchet
  agent for Ezekiel Fuller
John Strayhorn
Mathew Sparks
Etheldrid Wilder
William Sikes
  agent for Wm. G. Sikes
Hugh Perry
Robert Hairston
Benjamin Mosely
David Ballard
Richard Bass, Senr.
James Camp

Capt. Gray's Dist.

Wiley M. Carr
William Grady
John Boman
John Wade
Zachariah A. Thompson
Littleton Hunt
Joseph Hill
Thomas Fuller
Ephraim Britt
Solomon Johnson
John James
Vincent Timms
James Smith
James Phillips
James Perry

Capt. Dunlap's Dist.

Isaac Gray
William Campbell
Renney Colman
  agent for Abner Colman
Mathew T. Hamilton
Thomas Cooper
John Loyd
Van Davis
Alexander Hamilton
James Gray
John Baskin
Henry Benson

Capt. Moore's Dist.

Aaron Kemp
John Barber
Cyrus Dobbs

Capt's Moore's Dist. cont.

Bryant Bailey
Christopher Longcrier
James Smith
Thomas Pendley
  agent for Jonathan Pendly
William Davis
Zimma McGuire
Samuel Edmonson
  agent for Wm. Pendley
  agent for Robert Defur?
Nimrod Pendley
John Rogers
James Caruthers
William Merriman
Christopher Conelly
Warren Young
Owen Humphrey
Wiley Barber
John Black
Theopholus Gailer
Cullen Davis
Frederick Taylor
Harben Moore
Jessee Warren
Lewis Stewart
Reuben Warren
Thomas Mayo
William Nealy
Thomas Gravette
Archibald Thomas
Thomas Calhoun
John Lockabay
Josiah Stewart
John Pinder
Benjamin Pendley
James Walker

Capt. Brandon's Dist.

George James
Samuel Knoles
Davis Vowel
Hicks Spurling
Warner Hubbard
Christopher Baker
Thomas Connell
William E. Williford

Capt. Caruther's Dist.

Joseph Barnett
Joel Walker
John Oakley
William Camp (snip?)
Bird Womack
James A. Reid
Jessee Collins
Robert Jones
Ansel Hudjens

Capt. Caruther's Dist. cont.

Arthur McLain
Samuel M. Wilson
Hubbard Williams
Reddin Robertson
William B. Chamley
James Brasell
John M. Thompson
James Beardin
John Reid
John Palmer

Capt. Atwell's Dist.

P. L. W. Brooks
David Wright
Asa A. Turner
William Green
William McLain
David Spence
James B. Hairston
Andrew Barr
Drewry Thompson
Thomas Nations
Ezekiel Thomas
Robert M. Hogg
Nathaniel Nuchols
Hardy Burrell
Littleberry Harbour
Frederick Baldwin
Do. Administrator for H.
  B. Greenwood, dec'd.
Phillip H. Alston
Thomas Campbell
Reace Pruet
Silas Taft
G. W. F. Lampkin
Benjamin Lampkin
Reddin Massey
Gilbert Austin
John Williams
James B. Bourn
Robertson Asborn
William Greenwood
Thompson Austin
Martin Law
Thomas S. Glen
John Spence
James Law
Phillip Barnes
Wm. P. Hall
Wm. Phillips

Capt. Baker's Dist.

Zachariah Wimberly
John Wallace
Asa Coker
Briton Davis
John Garret

GWINNETT COUNTY, GEORGIA TAX DEFAULTERS, 1824-1826

Capt. Baker's Dist. cont.

Christopher Sewel
Jeremiah Webb
George W. Owens
James Miller
Edward Brombelo
Archibald Dean
William Raney
James Spurlings
John Collett

Capt. Baker's Dist. cont.

Robert Beasley
Dennis Cook, agent for
  John Cook
H. F. M. M. Lipford
William Spencer
Randle Dalton (marked out)
John Armer
John Williams
George Horsbern

Georgia
Gwinnett County

"We the undersigned Grand Jurors for Sept. term of the Superior Court Gwinnett County 1825 do allow John Boring tax collector for 1824 as his insolvent list the sum of $147.68½ cts."

Joseph Morgan, foreman

Young Moore
Robert S. Adair
Washington Chamblee
James M. Moore
James F. Rucks
George M. Gresham
Mathias Bates
William Hall
Henry Dunn

Pleasant R. Lyle
Shadrack Morris
Hardy Stricklin
Isham Medlock
Thomas Wood
Thompson Moore
Josephus Harrison
Reubin McLung
Hope H. Watts

Georgia
Gwinnett County, 27th September 1827

A list of persons who have not paid their Tax due for the year 1826.

Capt. Cupp's Dist.

Jason Bennett
Nathan Bankston
Michael Cupp
Joseph Hisaw
Henson Harriss
Thomas Head
William Hawkins
John Loyd
Joseph Morrow
Robert Pritchitt
Peter Rawlings, Sr.
Peter Rawlings, Jr.
Joseph Stinson
Claiborne Vaughan
James Wilson
John L. Wilson
Thomas Williamson
George Latham

Found good by the Grand Jury

Jason Bennett

Found good by the Grand Jury

Joseph Hinsaw
Henson Harriss
Joseph Stinson
Claiborne Vaughan
Thomas Williamson

Capt. Caruther's Dist.

William Cruce
John Dempsey
Tolbert Sims
Robert Jones
James Lee
John McClane
Flemming B. Nance
D. W. Holder (non-res.)
Nathan Caler
Moses W. Robinson
William Say
Lewis Sims
David Spence
Alexander Stinson

GWINNETT COUNTY, GEORGIA TAX DEFAULTERS, 1824-1826

Capt. Caruther's Dist. cont.

Randol Williams
John Meachum
John Eaton
Ansel Hudgens
George Lawrence
Warner Cupp
Benjamin Sims
George Steen
James White
Barnett J. Dempsey
Dennis Dilda

Found good by the Grand Jury

William Cruce
Flemming B. Nance
Alexander Stinson
Warner Cupp
Barnett J. Dempsey

Capt. Davis's Dist.

Dunken Campbell
Thomas Garner
Solomon Johnson
Thomas Kercus
William McDowell
John Tanner
James Crew
Henry B. Thompson
Zachariah Thompson
Gilbert Hays
Robert Phillips
Alexander C. Hamilton

Found good by the Grand Jury

Thomas Garner

Capt. Evans's Dist.

John Bass
Richard Bass
Andrew Boyd, agent
  Ann Cowen
William Black
James Hill
William Hamilton
James Kemp
Thomas McLendon
George Moore
John McGuffey, Sr.
John M. McGuffey, Jr.
John Bruister
James Mayo
Jourdan Odam
Britain Osborne
Jessee Osborn

Capt. Evans's Dist. cont.

Do. agent for William
  Osborn's Orphans
Jesse Ponder
Gadwell Pearce
William G. Sikes
Rebecca Shaw
Jonathan Sell
Do. agent Phillip Blanchett
James Thompson
John M. Stewart
Etheldred Wilder
William Yancey
James Burton
John Bridges
Thomas Chriswell
Benjamin Mannin
Wiley Mosley
William Sikes
Matthew McNight
Amos Spillers
Vincent Timms
Joseph Hill
William Beddenton

Found good by the Grand Jury

Andrew Boyd agent Ann Cowen
James Hill
Thomas McLendon
Etheldred Wilder
Thomas Chriswell

Capt. Green's Dist.

Joel Casey
James Carson
John Defoor
Jacob Dennis
Elijah Foster
William Gragg
Obadiah Glasgow
George Isley
Josiah Johnson
Alexander Johnson
Charles Lowery
James Lockabey
John Underwood
Elie Miller
James D. Peadon
William A. Pearce
James F. Rucks
John Toney
James V. White
William Walraven
Isaac Walraven
Levi Taylor
William Goderth
John Barnes
Ezekiel Yancy

GWINNETT COUNTY, GEORGIA TAX DEFAULTERS, 1824-1826

Capt. Green's Dist. cont.

John Foster
John Barnes
Lewis Cooper

Found good by the Grand Jury

James Carson
John Defoor
Elijah Foster
George Isley
Elie Miller
James F. Rucks
John Toney

Capt. Harper's Dist.

Andrew B. Bonds
Daniel Camp
William Gilbert
Edward Gilbert
Austin Hide
Alexander Hughett
Richard Holt
Asa Newborn
Samuel Paschal
Thomas Richards
William Simmons
Wyley Scoggins
Jonathan Swan
Archibald York
Nathan Posey
Jacob Gilbert

Found good by the Grand Jury

William Gilbert
Richard Holt

Capt. Hill's Dist.

Elijah Barber
James Campbell
Robert Campbell
Frederick Hart
Benton Cannon
Zimma McGwire
Prestley Norrard
Charles Randal
John Randal
John Red
Moses Rhice
William Rucks
Ezekiel Warren
Edward Wing
James Phillips
Archibald Hamilton
Joseph Red, Sr.
Joseph Red, Jr.
Andrew Clemments

Capt. Hill's Dist. cont.

Jeremiah Russell
Arireal Red
Nancey Man
Abner Coleman (no poll)
John Strayhorn
William Yates
John Brown
Renny Coleman
William Campbell
Harmon Davis

Found good by the Grand Jury

James Campbell
William Rucks
Edward Wing
Archibald Hamilton
Jeremiah Russell
Nancy Man
Abner Coleman (no poll)
Renny Coleman

Capt. Hay's Dist.

Mark Anthony
David Brogdon
Hardy Burwell
Thomas Compton
Robert Curbo
Simeon Congo (?)
Henry Haygood
Ezekiel Curbo
William Davis
Mourman Dobbs
Cyrus Dobbs
Charles Deavenport
Samuel Edmonson
    agent James Edmonson, Sr.
    agent James Edmonsin, Jr.
Joseph Fincher
John Gilbert
William Hays
Jackson Hatcher
Joseph Higgins
Richard Hays
Edward Kent
Bailey Kerby
Joseph Kerby
Andrew Kile
John Lamb
Michael Moore
William Merryman
John Martin
Benjamin Moseley
John Pendley
Michael Pruett
John Pruett
Thomas Pendley
Isaac Pendley

Capt. Hay's Dist. cont.

William Pendley
John Pendley
William Pinder
Matthew Parr
Jonathan Rawlings
Reddin Robinson
Alexander Right
John Strayhorn
Thomas Smith
  agent for Robert Brinn
Jessee Umphrey
David Vowell
Stephen Williford
Amos Wellborn
David Wimborn
Reubin Warren
James Williamson
Harmon Bagley (no poll)
Wiley Bagley
Alexander Nuckolds
Thomas Pendley, agent
  Jonathan Pendley
Do agent Robert Rowland
Shadrack Bogan
Samuel Fee
Israel Nations
Josiah Stewart
Robert Venable
James Walker

Found good by the Grand Jury

Mark Anthony
Thomas Compton
Simeon Congo (?)
William Davis
Mourman Dobbs
Cyrus Dobbs
Samuel Edmondson
William Hays
Richard Hays
Bailey Kerby
Andrew Kile
Michael Moore
Jesse Umphrey
James Williamson
Alexander Nuckolds
Shadrack Bogan
Israel Nations

Capt. Hunnycut's Dist.

Philo P. Atwell
Thomas Allen
George Allen
Martin Adams
Ransome Cooper
David Daniel, Jr.
Benjamin Davis

Capt. Hunnycut's Dist.

William Drummond
Elie (?) Frost
Isaac Funderburgh
John Greene
Richard Holman
Reubin Jordan
John Landers
Michael Macken
Edward Macken
Arthur McLane
Thomas Porter
Nathaniel Austin
Samuel Slate
Sims Smith
John S. Smith
Allen B. Strong
Zachariah Stedham
Drewrey Thompson
Silas Vickus (no poll)
William Williamson
Thomas Monk
Peter Wallace
Richard Wilson
J. L. Cunningham
John R. Strickland
Benjamin H. Lampkin
Charles Lavender
Murdock Martin
William Hunnycut
Frederick Baldwin
William Brewster
Murdock Martin

Found good by the Grand Jury

Thomas Allen
George Allen
Martin Adams
William Drummond
Richard Holman
Edward Macken
Thomas Monk
William Bruister

Capt. Whorton's Dist.

Benjamin Abbott
Ira (?) Bishop
Henry C. Butler
Jessee Ball
John Carr
James Cochran
William Cochran
William Cochran, Jr.
Nathan Fowler
Sanford Hagans
Newton Hagans
Silas Hagans
James Hagans

Capt. Whorton's Dist. cont.

Reubin Hagans
Nathaniel Harriss
John Harriss
John Holderfield
Benjamin Johnston
John Kerk
Edmond Pearce
Laban P. Poole
John Raven
Allen Willson
William Scott (no poll)
John Seagus (?)
William Terry
William Yearley

Found good by the Grand Jury

Jessee Ball
John Carr
Nathaniel Harriss
Edmond Pearce

Capt. Shippy's Dist.

George Dalton
Richmond Baker
do Admr. Charles Baker,
  desed.
do agent Sarah A. Baker
do agent Sarah Baker
(Richmond Baker)
do agent Osbon W. Baker
  (non-age)
Joshua Baker
Benjamin Carroll
Alexander M. D. Cawley
William Clarke
John Dunn
Britton Davis
William Higginbothom
John Lyle
James B. Lions
John McCormmack
  do agent James McComack
John R. Medlock
John Sims
Simeon Sheridon
John Terry
Bartley Whorton
Bird Wammack
Phillip Coleman
Jessee J. Hawkins
Jeffrey Pittman
Hamlet Fuller
William Spencer
James Holbrooks
John Gardner
William Fortune
Write Smith

Capt. Shippys's Dist. cont.

James Pogue
Asa A. Phillips
William Brumbelow
William J. Childres
Kellet(?) Sims
James Thompson
Mr. J. Pickens
Larkin Simpson
William Pickens
William Lain
John Pogue
Washington Norman
  half tax remitted
William McCarley
John Ware

Found good by Grand Jury

John Terry
Jeffrey Pittman
John Gardner
William McCarley
John Ware

Capt. Woodruff's Dist.

William Bass
James Brumley (?)
Pleasant Craft
John Cochran
Elijah Cochran
Robert Carter
Thompson Dickerson
William Fendley
James Garner
Joseph C. Hunter
Ambrose H. Jones
Jonathan Luallen
William Miller
Hiram McLung
William Peadon
Benjamin Price
Moses Stron
Thomas W. Wood
Thomas Weems
Pinson McDaniel
Saml. D. Peadon
John Elsberry
Benjamin Sims

Found good by the Grand Jury

James Garner
Jonathan Luallen
William Peadon
Benjamin Price
Moses Stron
Thomas Weems
Pinson McDaniel

Found good by the Grand Jury cont.
    Capt. Woodruff's Dist.

Samuel D. Peardon

We, the Grand Jury for the county of Gwinnett for September term
1827 do pass to the credit of the tax collector his Insolvent
list hereunto us returned $164.54 3/4 cents of State tax with
the exception of those seventy four persons whose names are
thus marked / / opposite to. He is required to issue his
Executions and lodge the same in the hands of the Collection
Officer and return that officers receipt or the money for each
persons tax to the clerk of the Inferior Court of this County.
Elisha Winn, Form., William Montgomery, Benjamin W. Maddox,
Matthias Bates, Richd. J. Wates(?), James Baskin, William H.
Cole, Charles McHugh, Richard Plunkett, Isaac Rutherford, William
Baskin, Joshua Ballard, Lewis Williams, James McGinness, Sr.,
Benjamin Gholston, E. Bagby, H. B. Watkins, Thomas J. Stell,
Cliffo___ Woodruff, George M. Grisham, James McGinness, Jr.

GWINNETT COUNTY, GEORGIA, MARRIAGES (1835-1838)

These records were compiled from old original marriage records
that had been recorded in Gwinnett County Marriage Book No. 3,
which along with books Nos. 1 & 2, were destroyed during a fire
in the Gwinnett County Court House in 1871. These few loose
papers survived the fire and are on file in the Ordinary's
Office of the Court House.

Gwinnett County was created by legislative act, Dec. 15, 1818.
out of treaty land acquired from the Cherokee in the same year.
Named for Button Gwinnett, one of the signers of the Declaration
of Independence, from Georgia, Lawrenceville, the county seat
was named for Capt. James Lawrence of the Chesapeake, who fell
mortally wounded on board his ship on June 1, 1813.

Page
149   Alred, James and Polly Leach, married 25 January 1838 by
      Silas King, MG.
155   Allen, Lovick P. and Sarah Thompson married 26 April 1838
      by Kinchen Rambo, MG.
152   Allen, Thomas H. and Harriet Gilbert married 20 March 1838
      by Joseph W. Baxter, JP.
131   Athy, Elijah C. and Eliza Salter married 18 August 1837 by
      John P. Hutchins, JP.
134   Atkinson, William E. and Martha C. Nelms married 27 August
      1837 by John Clower, JP.
142   Ballard, Andrew J. and Jane Drummond married 17 December
      1837 by William Rakestraw, JP. (Recorded 20 Feb. 1838).
139   Beadles, Joseph and Miss Wiley Austin married 13 November
      1837 by Edwin Dyer, MG. (Recorded 2 December 1837).
150   Brandon, Moses A. and Elizabeth Adair married 15 February
      1838 by Joseph W. Baxter, JP.
130   Broadwell, Jesse and Sophronia M. Jackson married 6 August
      1837 by John Wayne, MG.
153   Brown, Larkin and Jane Weems married 27 March 1838 by John
      Clower, JP.
115   Brown, William H. and Irena Mathews married 6 December 1836
      by Elijah Moore, MG. (Recorded 20 February 1837).
(?)   Buckelew, James M. and Drucilla Blake married 4 February
      1837. (Recorded 23 September 1837).
161   Butler, John and Temperance Bridges married 31 May 1838 by
      John C. Whitworth, JP.
119   Cain, John and Martha Anders married 20 July 1836 by Lot
      Rowden, JP. (Recorded 7 April 1837).
145   Camp, Johnson and Emily T. Lacy married 11 January 1838 by
      John C. Whitworth, JP.
143   Camp, Walton and Nancy Hardin married 21 December 1837 by
      John C. Whitworth, JP. (Recorded 20 February 1838).
156   Carr, William A. and Ann Morgan married 3 May 1838 by
      Andrew Anthony, MG.
137   Cates, John and Martha Y. Moore married 12 October 1837 by
      Henry W. Inges, JP. (Recorded 2 December 1837).
154   Clarke, Archibald and Elizabeth Hill married 25 April 1838.
139   Couch, Chaney and Elizabeth Jackson married 23 November
      1837 by Kinchen Rambo, MG. (Recorded 2 December 1837).
150   Crawford, Hambree and Clarrisa T. Williams married 13
      February 1838 by Kinchen Rambo, MG.
120   Crow, Norman M. and Polly Hansford married 8 January 1835
      by Silas King, MG. (Recorded 8 April 1837).
131   Demby, James W. and Matilda W. Cameron married 18 May 1837
      by Daniel Sanford, JP. (Recorded 26 August 1837).
141   Dillard, Edmund and Margaret Thurmond married 16 December

GWINNETT COUNTY, GEORGIA, MARRIAGES (1835-1838)

1837 by William Rakestraw, JP. (Recorded 20 February 1838).

137 Drummond, Mathew and Lydia M. Fincher married 5 November 1837 by John C. Whitworth, JP.

151 Fee, Samuel and Isabella Spraggins married 11 March 1838 by Silas King, MG.

121 Garmon, James and Caroline Yancy married 21 February 1837 by Daniel Sanford, JP. (Recorded 8 April 1837).

133 Gordon, Nathaniel H. and Elizabeth C. Page married 27 July 1837 by John Sanders, MG. (Recorded 25 October 1837).

140 Graham, Moses W. and Malinda Crumley married 12 November 1837 by J. W. Pharr, MG. (Recorded 19 February 1838).

166 Gresham, Edmond C. and Lucinda Stone married 30 August 1838 by Daniel Sanford, JP.

163 Harris, Clark M. and Nancy Garner married 10 July 1838 by J. R. Thompson, JP.

117 Harville, Thomas H. and Sarah Sell married 23 February 1837 by M. Rakestraw, JP.

153 Haynes, Richard L. and Martha M. Tate married 7 January 1838 by William Gober, MG.

159 Henry, George W. and Emeline Minor married 26 March 1838 by James Millican, JP.

129 Henson, William and Anna Kilpatrick married 9 May 1837 by James Maudlin, JP.

148 Higgins, Sanford and Lucinda Bramlett married 18 January 1838 by N. Bramlett, JP.

143 Hunt, Isaac L. and Diama Rutledge married 21 December 1837 by Mathew Henry, JP. (Recorded 20 February 1838).

142 Jackson, John and Charlotte R. Terry married 21 December 1837 by N. Bramlett, JP. (Recorded 20 February 1838).

132 James, Joseph and Jemima Cook married 20 February 1838.

156 Johnston, Robert D. and Nancy Pittard married 7 September 1837 by James Hale, MG. (Recorded 26 September 1838).

161 Jones, John C. and Eliza Hyde married 6 June 1838 by William Gober, MG.

165 Jordan, William and Elizabeth Langley married 9 August 1838 by James Hale, MG.

121 Kemp, Burrell and Permelia Henson married 15 July 1835 by Silas King, MG. (Recorded 8 April 1837).

166 Landreth, William P. and Emily L. Maxwell married 30 August 1838 by Jesse Murphey, JP.

162 Leach, John W. and Nancy Hopkins married 8 July 1838 by William Gober, MG.

134 Lucas, William W. and Polly Gordon married 8 June 1837 by Mathew Henry, JP.

136 Martin, Rance B. and Milly Ford married 16 November 1837 by John Clower, JP.

140 Mauldin, Absalom and Trecy Otwell married 9 November 1837 by Windsor Graham, MG. (Recorded 19 February 1838).

136 Mayer, John F. and Juletta Pharr married 21 August 1837 by Jesse Murphey, JP.

135 Mayfield, Elisha M. and Elizabeth Blackwell married 21 September 1837 by Jesse Boring, MG.

115 McCully, Barnett and Elizabeth Wade married 25 December 1836 by Elijah Moore, MG. (Recorded 11 February 1837).

145 McDaniel, Eli J. and Martha Mathews married 25 March 1838 by Kinchen Rambo, MG.

132 McKern, Edward and Rebecca Garmon married 4 July 1837 by Daniel Sanford, JP.

162 McKinney, Samuel and Missouri Huggins married 12 June 1837.

GWINNETT COUNTY, GEORGIA, MARRIAGES (1835-1838)

GWINNETT COUNTY, GEORGIA, MARRIAGES (1835-1838)

HALL COUNTY, GA. - MARRIAGES

First Marriage License Record, 1819-1840, unpaged.

GROOM	BRIDE	MARRIED
John Martin	Elender Collum	7/29/1819
Griffin Reed	Mary Phinasee	12/ 4/1819
John Denman	Elizabeth Carlton	11/ 9/1819
Jonathan West	Nancy Holliday	12/28/1819
		(License dated)
Alexander Caven	Maria Pennell	1/ 2/1820
John Hardridge	Margaret Kerr	8/20/1819
		(Date of License)
Isaac York	Drusilla McClung	11/ 4/1819
Noah Langley	Sarah Rains	1/ 3/1820
Alexander Spence	Jane Wilson	12/14/1819
Hugh McKay	Millissa Black	11/16/1819
James Thompson	Sibbey Kindrick	12/22/1819
Pennell Qualls	Elizabeth Blalock	9/22/1819
James Morris	Eliza Jones	10/13/1819
James Hogue	Cynthia Pate	10/27/1819
Hugh Kerr	Sarah Wilson	3/18/1820
John Porter	Elizabeth Martin	10/20/1819
Isaac Mitchell	Elendor Tankersley	3/ 4/1820
Bruell Boy	Tempey Hulsey	1/10/1820
Samuel Smith	Elizabeth Ritch	2/11/1820
Luke Hendricks	Cynthia Hubbard	1/ 4/1821
William Pirkle	Patsey Tallant	3/ 1/1821
Mark McCutchen	Patsey Christian	12/15/1820
James Young	Willey Cuttery	2/ 5/1821
Cullin Davis	Frances Hammons	6/ 8/1820
Joseph G. Davis	Mary Baxley	12/26/1820
Thomas Venable	Patsey Still	4/20/1820
John M. Stringer	Isabel Blythe	10/22/1820
Zimri Thomason	Jannett Montgomery	7/27/1820
Irwin Strickland	Mary Maynor	12/16/1820
Jacob Mires	Ann Stewart	12/21/1820
Joseph F. Comer	Frances Venable	5/ 4/1820
Cornelius Cooper	Ruth Weems	9/26/1820
Allen Cook	Ellendor Lowry	9/ 5/1820
Henry Walker	Patsey Head	11/30/1820
Jesse Hulsey	Mary Baxwell	11/ 5/1820
William Morris	Milly Ballard	2/11/1820
Isaac Henson	Mary Kimball	10/26/1820
Thomas Byrd	Martha Russell	12/28/1820
John Conn	Ann Smith	1/18/1820
Joel C. Chandler	Mary Frost	11/ 2/1820
Mark Casselberry	Mary Warren	11/12/1820
Goldman Biffle	Elizabeth Boyd	3/ 6/1821
✓Isaac Head	Kitty Cavender	9/14/1820
William Clark	Ann Cooper	6/29/1820
Robert Black	Nancy Barber	6/ 8/1819
Ezekiel Buffington	Nancy Gilmore(date Lic.)	4/ 5/1820
John Dunn	Elizabeth Hill (Kell?)	6/17/1819
Edmund Harp	Pattey Combs	1/ 5/1823
John Wilkerson	Nancy Mattocks	8/ 7/1821
Robert Guthrey	Sarah Williams	11/11/1821
Warren Keaton	Mary Brown	12/10/1821
David Barton	Hannah Thomason	9/ 6/1820
Thomas Buffington	Elizabeth Gilmore	11/27/1822
Pressley Powell	Nelly Casselberry	11/14/1822
John M. Blagg	Charlotte Eaton	8/27/1822

HALL COUNTY, GA. - MARRIAGES

GROOM	BRIDE	MARRIED
James Rise	Sarah Weaver	8/ 1/1822
Daniel O'Neal	Susannah Griggs	9/15/1821
John Wharton	Elizabeth Willie	9/30/1821
Gary Davis	Sarah Floyd	12/ 6/1821
John Richards	Nancy Herndon	4/11/1822
Thomas Montgomery	Mahaly Maulden	9/ 7/1820
Phillip Wade	Catherine Moor	11/21/1822
Joseph Martin	Elizabeth Reece	6/ 4/1822
George Barnwell	Ann Warren	6/24/1819
Moses Martin	Delilah Bennett	10/17/1821
Lewis Smith	Susannah Trout	12/ 3/1819
Samuel B. Landrum	Kerenhappuck Casselberry	7/ 5/1821
Thomas A. Fenn	Lydia Otwell	10/10/1822
Henry Bell	Elizabeth Kendrick	3/18/1823
William Hulsey	Jennett Cooper	1/17/1822
John Martin	Margaret Hendrick	9/23/1823
Robert Smith	Rachel Anderson	7/13/1823
	(date of License)	
William Stewart	Morning Mullins	4/20/1823
Middleton Blare	Rebecca Hulsey	7/15/1823
Rowland Johnson	Nancy Diffey	7/17/1823
William Cowen	Elizabeth Reed	7/22/1819
Isaiah Hollis	Elizabeth Stringer	2/27/1823
Johnston Pate	Rebecca Hurt	6/26/1822
Thomas Horton	Nicey Nelson	12/16/1821
Stephen Garner	Judith Edwards	3/25/1821
John Thompson	Pamely Keaton	4/ 3/1823
Francis Gilmore	Nancy Buffington	11/14/1822
Dempsey Miller	Sarah Walravens	7/19/1821
William Thacker	Susannah Rice	8/ 4/1819
Micajah Walker	Mary Nicks	12/27/1822
Noah Smith	Nancy Hulsey	1/30/1823
William Goddard	Hannah McCollum	10/15/1822
	(date of License)	
Thomas V. Scott	Mary Murray	5/31/1823
David Jackson	Clericy Harlow	10/ 8/1822
Jesse Dodd	Jane Hulsey	3/15/1821
Yarby Osburn	Jane Otwell	2/10/1820
John Hill	Catherine Barnwell	2/20/1822
Mark McCutchen	Patsey Christian	12/15/1820
Wiatt Moor	Mary Casselberry	11/22/1821
Permenus Pilkington	Ruth Bradford	7/29/1821
William P. Reed	Lucinda Reynolds	11/21/1821
Charles Hawkins	Sally Davis	1/19/1823
Garrison Thomason	Louisa Gibson	10/ 6/1822
William B. Box	Sarah Whitehead	3/14/1822
William Dowdy	Margaret Myres	3/27/1823
Robert Pritchett	Margaret Dawson	6/23/1822
George Woodliff	Isabell Henderson	9/26/1822
Phillip M. Byrd	Mary Russell	6/21/1821
Lazarus Wood	Rebecca Dalrymple	11/28/1822
Worthy Lewallen	Elizabeth Burt	11/16/1821
Josiah Clayton	Edith Reed	8/ 2/1821
Brian W. Nowlin	Mary Wade	11/ 7/1822
Thomas Gravett	Lindsey Hammons	8/ 2/1821
William Moor	Sophia Chambers	4/ 3/1821
Nicholas Derifield	Sally Gorman	4/22/1821
Clabourn Gorman	Wallias (Elizabeth)	4/18/1820
James Young	Milly Guttery (date lic.)	2/ 5/1821

GROOM	BRIDE	MARRIED
Roger Green	Mary Nelson	7/31/1821
Wm. Washington Fleming	Elizabeth Putman	4/13/1823
William Southerland	Delilah Hubbard	12/20/1821
Merrell Patterson	Biddy Wood	1/ 5/1823
Jonathan Williams	Ann Guttery	5/10/1821
Robert D. Inzer	Elizabeth Levell	7/ 3/1822
Kineil Pipkins	Elizabeth Whitley	1/ 6/1823
Joseph Raper	Mahaly Box	1/16/1823
Madison Henderson	Jemimah Williams	9/10/1822
John Brown	Elizabeth Crow	4/30/1823
Moren Moore	Abigail Gravett	3/10/1822
William Hendrix	Nancy Clements	12/20/1821
Joshua Cox	Elizabeth Hawkins	6/15/1823
John Halloway	Darky Beck	8/11/1823
William Thompson	Mary Teadwells	8/ 6/1823
Gideon Land	Asenith Hembell	8/ 9/1823
Isaac Prichard	Temperance Wyley	9/ 8/1823
	(date of License)	
David Casselberry	Ceny Casselberry	7/29/1823
John O'Bryant	Rhuhama Russell	6/27/1823
Burrell Thompson	Pheby Watson	9/25/1823
Rowland Gentry	Nancy Mattocks	6/30/1823
Nathan G. Newton	Sally Byrd	1/ 9/1823
Paton Wade	Elizabeth Cox	9/11/1823
Reuben Barrett	Loamy Rogers	12/11/1823
Archibald Harris	Anna Langley	1/ 5/1824
Rowell Durham	Lucy Woodliff	1/29/1824
Peter Wiatt	Louisa Kelly	5/ 9/1823
Robert Miller	Susanna Broadnax	1/14/1824
Joel Briant	Elizabeth Briant	5/13/1823
John Dowie	Mary Ann Jones	2/ 9/1823
William S. Rogers	Araminta Boyd	5/22/1823
Toliver Riggins	Roda Walker	12/ 4/1823
James Tippins	Sarah Trout	4/27/1823
Wiley Pearn	Sally Mills	9/25/1823
Henry Sinyard	Dicy Hulsey	11/26/1823
Isaac Pugh	Anna Winter	11/ 6/1823
Abraham Cox	Cinthy Stewart	11/19/1823
William Shipley	Sarah Danforth	11/27/1823
William Barnwell	Lether Greenway	12/30/1823
William York	Nancy Pitman	10/30/1823
Robert Mooney	Levyna Hope	12/23/1823
Jacob Wickram	Ellender Board	11/19/1822
John Williams, Jr.	Margaret Marks	1/ 8/1824
John E. Reeves	Elizabeth Warren	4/30/1824
Nathaniel Smith	Ruth Hawkins	7/ 9/1822
Asa Whitley	Claracy Wigley	2/ 7/1824
William Willis	Mary Dougherty	11/20/1823
William Sims	Rhoda House	9/29/1823
John W. Elit	Sarah Scaggs	10/26/1823
James McConnill	Sarah Putman	12/11/1823
Jesse Clayton	Mary Woodliff	5/ 4/1824
William Neel	Rebecca Slaton	2/15/1824
William Carver	Elizabeth Staniell(?)	4/18/1824
Andrew Wood	Charity Langely	2/19/1824
John Thompson	Nancy Feels	9/ 7/1823
Ezekiel Cerbo	Elizabeth Parker	2/16/1824
Isaac Butterworth	Parky P. Hix	12/23/1820
William Harris	Elizabeth Evans	6/ 3/1823

GROOM	BRIDE	MARRIED
John Webster	Rachel McCay	9/ 7/1823
Sion How	Nancy Lowry	12/23/1824
John Dorsey	Elizabeth Brice	1/13/1825
John Greenway	Mahala Everett	2/ 3/1825
Bennett Pettygrew	Betha Coddle	1/27/1825
Thomas Garner	Jemimah Charles	7/25/1824
Humphrey Tarbutton	Eley Lord	6/19/1824
Sirrah Eaton	Susannah Beck	3/11/1824
Enoch Severn (?)	Cynthia Griffith	1/25/1824
Joseph Kizer	Sarah Wirt	9/ 2/1824
Joseph C. Doss	Mahaly Thornton	2/18/1824
James J. Conner	Elizabeth Swalford	6/20/1824
William Coffey	Delila Trantham	3/17/1822
Moses Imtry	Milly Hammons	3/28/1824
Jesse Jay	Ann Yarborough	8/10/1824
Isham Snow	Ann McGloughlin	7/ 8/1824
Thomas Terrell	Ester Kemp	6/10/1824
John Clark	Lucy Morris	10/31/1822
Samuel Viles	Alsey Head	7/15/1824
Silas Dobbs	Nancy Barnwell	5/ 6/1824
Alfred Yancey	Elizabeth Dobbs	8/ 1/1822
James Davis	Nancy Floyd	7/21/1824
Hugh Whiteman	Keziah Blalock	11/19/1824
James Leathers	Elizabeth Faine	9/ 2/1824
William Cockram	Nancy Sellers	8/14/1824
Hiram Cope	Nancy Cagle	1/15/1824
Isham Poole	Tripema H. Garrison	6/ 3/1824
Moses M. Cantrell	Elizabeth A. Wooly	10/26/1824
Samuel K. Oliver	Marthy Waits	12/30/1824
Richard Miller	Letty Guttery	12/ 9/1824
Henry Whiteman	Sophia Kidd	12/23/1824
John W. Leavell	Mary Wood	1/16/1825
Jacob Elrod	Linney Boyd	1/ 6/1825
Thomas Moore	Sefie(?) Doan	2/ 6/1825
Joseph Hubanks	Tempy Bearden	4/27/1821?
	(Lic. 4/23/1821)	
John G. Byrd	Nancy Garner	11/18/1824
Thomas W. Blaney	Zelpha Woolley	11/ 1/1824
Wyett Van	Rachel Moore	11/27/1824
Lock Langley	Margaret Hubert	1/27/1825
William S. Miller	Milbery T. Herren	1/ 9/1823
Isaac Johnson	Levina Kenom	11/ 2/1824
Edward Hawkins, Jr.	---------	2/10/1825
Julius King	Elizabeth Wingay	3/ 4/1825
Thomas Covington	Frances Byrd	6/22/1825
David Patman	Nancy M. Connel	9/ 8/1825
John Thomas	Polly Thomas	7/21/1825
James Young	Molly Guttery	2/ 5/1825
John Smith	Barbery Ketter	7/18/1825
John Greenway	Mahala Everett	2/ 3/1825
Elijah Pinson	Lovey Herren	8/21/1825
Joel Leathers	Mary Mucklerath	2/17/1824
John Wigley	Polley Wisner	5/25/1825
Pleasant Chitwood	Anna Brannon	11/25/1824
Solomon Reece	Susannah Brannon	3/28/1825
Martin Camp	Delilah Wisner	4/21/1825
Jonathan Loven	Susannah Bridgeman	10/ 6/1825
James J. McClesky	Ann Dunnagan	11/21/1823
William Fain	Kery Lumpkin	3/ 5/1825

GROOM	BRIDE	MARRIED
Reuben Harrison	Margaret Miller	6/ 6/1825
William Duncan	Polly Barnwell	12/23/1824
Uriah Posey	Mary Hammett	8/15/1825
John Lancaster	Hannah F. Driskell	3/ 3/1825
Elijah Brown	Cinderella Slaughter	12/26/1824
Zachary Hutchins	Peggy Majors	3/16/1825
Henry B. Cobb	Rebecca Putman	11/18/1824
James B. Roberson	Emeline Adrian	8/18/1825
Joel H. Bryner	Elizabeth Martin	9/ 8/1825
John Cook	Hannah Moor	3/20/1825
William Norris	Permelia Kunom	10/28/1824
Lemuel R. Tankersly	Kizza Skene	1/27/1825
Noah Strong	Elizabeth B. Noble	9/ 6/1824
Ezekiel Gaily	Ruth Henderson	4/ 7/1825
James C. Doss	Fanny Fowler	5/25/1824
John Evans	Milly Blackstock	3/30/1825
Jonathan Crow	Susan Crow	Lic. 7/28/1824
	(No certificate)	
James Whitmore	Malinda Lochridge	12/24/1824
Henry Brooks	Locky McWire	2/ 7/1825
Samuel Edmondson	Martha Karr	3/16/1825
Dugal Monroe	Nancy Jones	2/24/1824
William Jones	Dorcey Garrett	Lic. 6/30/1824
	(No Certificate)	
Alford Manor	Polly Berry	7/ 2/1824
Allen Bradley	Susannah Harbin	6/23/1825
John Tuggle	Nancy Griggs	11/ 3/1824
William B. Colwell	Sary Haise	7/ 7/1825
Blueford McRight	Rebecca Curbo	7/29/1825
Jacob Pirkle	Nancy Lawless	9/15/1825
John Wadkins	Elizabeth Barnwell	11/11/1824
Banjamin Parks	Sally Henderson	2/10/1825
John Padon	Sarah Cox	11/12/1824
Henry Tedder	Sarah Cassleberry	9/26/1824
John West	Jane Fulton	9/25/1825
Wiley Prince	Delilah Piedman	11/10/1825
For-- W. Otwell	Aley Davill	10/13/1825
Thomas Gentry	Rachel Gentry	12/11/1825
Uriah Davis	Ellinder Headrick	1/23/1823
Elijah Martin	------------	10/ 9/1825
Uriah Hubbard	Nancy Norris	8/18/1825
Eli Lofton	Susan Woodliff	12/21/1825
George Elrod	Elizabeth Shockley	12/29/1825
Charles T. Hulsey	Susannah Hulsey	10/10/1821
John Wilson	Elizabeth Bates	12/22/1825
James L. Coleman	Matilda Williams	3/ 4/1826
Dan Gilmore	Matilda Red	3/23/1826
Richard Thomas	Susannah Franklin	8/14/1825
Wilson Putman	Malissa Goss	1/12/1826
Cinnaka Deadman	Bede Pool	2/19/1826
Tiptin W. Cotton	Clarissa Davis	5/ 7/1826
John Furr	Jenny Wakefield	4/17/1826
William Vavender	Cresy Pearce	4/ 9/1826
Daniel Moore	Elizabeth Davis	6/15/1826
Hiran Lisle	Martha Blalock	4/ 6/1826
Daniel Herrin	Mary Prisnell	2/22/1826
Jeremiah Fell	Ruthe Payne	2/14/1826
Robert C. Cain	Winiford Bates	1/ 5/1826
William Chambers	Peggy Eaton	2/ 2/1826

HALL COUNTY, GA. - MARRIAGES

GROOM	BRIDE	MARRIED
William M. Otwell	Malinda Bond	6/20/1823
Matthew Kuth (Keeth)	Betsy Tallant	1/ 5/1826
John Say	Elizabeth Eberhart	1/12/1826
Thomas Green	Mary Jackson	2/ 3/1826
John Thomason, Jr.	Easter Grindle	10/ 5/1825
John Gorman	Lutitha Christian	1/27/1826
John Pugh	Nancy Wheeler	10/12/1825
James Gossett	Kiza Reed	7/ 6/1826
Cain Evans	Elizabeth Garner	6/ 3/1826
John Pearce	Sarah Dean	9/28/1826
John Smith	Caty M. Woods	8/20/1826
Alexander Miller	Polly Hulsey	7/20/1824
Hezekiah Panter	Susan Hagwood	9/17/1826
William Cain	Margaret McCormack	8/27/1826
David Greenway	Mary Thurmond	7/16/1826
David M. Gilliam	Margaret S. Grady	7/20/1826
Aaron Slaton	Susan Colbert	7/ 2/1826
Granvill Thompson	Sarah Collins	11/18/1825
Martin P. Pool	Lucinda Gaily	7/20/1826
Silas Gratton	Nancy McKay	8/13/1826
Jeremiah Wisnor	Nelly Wigley	8/21/1826
Jesse D. Hardridge	Mahala Cook	8/15/1826
Philip Chambers	Elizabeth Baker	10/10/1826
Thomas Bangus	Tabitha Dunaway	11/ 5/1826
William Bolen	Mary Bowls	11/29/1826
Gabriel Fulton	Willey Statton	12/20/1826
John King	Keziah Smith	11/ 9/1826
Jesse Thomas	Delilah Rains	1/ 2/1827
David Durham	Betsy Young	8/13/1826
William H. Pepnell	Dowely (Elizabeth)	2/15/1827
William F. Trout	Mary Barziel	1/11/1827
Ange Delaperriere	Mary Ann Thurman	11/14/1826
James T. Payne	Elizabeth Lampkin	12/21/1826
Ransom Foster	Martha Milner	2/ 8/1827
Vincent Garner	Polly Wood	3/ 1/1827
Sharp S. Reynolds	Nancy Bates	1/25/1827
Thaddeus H. McClesky	Asenith Smith	2/ 1/1827
Thomas Powell	Caroline Robbins	3/15/1827
Patrick G. Denham	Didimay Trout	1/ 2/1827
Moses Wright	Polly Bein	2/ 4/1827
John I. Lask	Elizabeth Jay	2/11/1827
Isaiah Whitlock	Frances Wolley	3/18/1827
Nelson Padgett	Seeneth Padgett	2/13/1827
John Wallace	Semmia Jackson	2/13/1827
Lemuel B. Jones	Susan White	10/12/1826
Lewis Whitehead	Searberry Westkinon	2/ 4/1827
William Going	Violet Jackson	4/12/1827
James Martin	Melinda Sarton	4/17/1827
Emanuel Cox	Mary Ballard	3/25/1827
Alexander Robertson	Catherine Kelton	6/ 5/1827
John Watson	Mary O'Bare	6/ 6/1827
John B. Garrison	Pamelia Dogan	5/15/1827
Charles Colling	Louisa Pannell	11/ 1/1826
Richard Major	Mourning Heath	12/27/1825
Thomas Nations	Huldah Thompson	2/28/1827
John Ogle	Sarah Walker	7/19/1827
John Massey	Nancy Starr	7/22/1827
Aaron Paris	Celia Tidwell	5/13/1827
Jesse Paris	Elizabeth Blag	5/13/1827

GROOM	BRIDE	MARRIED
Ambrose Brown	Clara Dunkin	5/27/1827
Stephen Camp	Nancy Hunt	2/25/1827
William Lareton (?)	Temperance Mortain	7/31/1827
Edward Doss	Selicia Parker	8/ 1/1827
William Hammon	Sirenia Gentry	4/ 6/1823
Riley Wilson	Rebecca Fowler	12/22/1825
James Karr	Polly Orr	10/14/1824
James Pugh	Frances Whitworth	12/23/1824
John Wheeler	Mahala Doss	5/10/1827
Wiley Fowler	Nicy House	9/12/1822
William Pane	Elizabeth Fowes	10/21/1825
Henry S. Campbell	Mary Mercks	4/13/1827
Tilman Driskell	Patsey Stone	9/ 6/1827
Daniel McCay	Caroline B. Spence	7/12/1827
Lewis Miller	Nancy Johnston	7/25/1827
Samuel Martin	Ann Colley	8/ 7/1827
James Carlisle	Rebecca Hamby	8/19/1827
Adley Hulsey	Sally Caigle	2/23/1827
Jeremiah Creswell	Mary Colley	9/13/1827
William Wells	Nancy Shelton	1/17/1827
Thomas Bearden	Anny East	5/ 6/1827
Thomas Guthrie	Elizabeth Cape	8/19/1827
Morgan Guthrie	Frances Cape	1/ 4/1827
James Landrum	Patsey Castleberry	9/15/1827
William Tapp	Margaret Savage	8/26/1827
Coleman Bruce	Margaret Nowill	10/ 3/1827
Ford Butler	Rachel Williams	12/23/1827
James A. Head	Sarah Cain	11/29/1827
Benjamin F. Johnston	Joannah Dobson	6/ 8/1827
William Morgan	Nancy Shepherd	11/ 8/1827
Amos Brown	Jane Taylor	12/ 6/1827
William Gorman	Sarah Furr	10/ 7/1827
John Vines	Franky Robert	9/30/1827
William B. Dennis	Narcissa Williams	3/15/1827
James T. Barrett	Sarah Mabry	10/10/1827
Jesse Jay	Rachel Charles	6/26/1827
Thomas Whitehead	Elizabeth McElreath	12/30/1827
William Grissom	Nancy Pucket	1/14/1828
Joel Fain	Nancy Lay	12/ 9/1827
Berry Hutchins	Sarah Burford	11/22/1827
John B. Nichols	Priscilla Burford	1/27/1828
Nathan H. Goss	Millicent Whitten	1/10/1828
John Puckett	Elizabeth Wood	12/21/1827
Burton Mullins	Susan Wilson	11/12/1827
Ashworth McBrayer	Barbary Wigley	1/27/1828
Johnston Sarter	Elmina Roberts	3/27/1828
Stephen Barton	Sarah Ann Thomason	4/27/1828
James Wilson	Mary Saunders	11/11/1827
Joel Bennett	Elizabeth Pain	1/29/1828
Elijah Pucket	Nancy Grissome	2/24/1828
John G. Fenn	Matilda Pierson	2/28/1828
David W. McWhorter	Elizabeth Nichols	4/21/1828
Elisha C. Barrett	Mary Mabry	1/15/1828
Hamilton Hutchins	Frances Bates	3/11/1828
George Laythem	Jane Roark	3/ 4/1828
John Wallis	Susan Parmer	7/ 1/1827
William P. Pool	Amanda Hamilton	12/29/1827
James Edmison	Susannah Carr	1/31/1828
Absolom McSturgen	Sarah Evans	3/ 4/1828

GROOM	BRIDE	MARRIED
William Clemens	Terrecy Crafford	3/ 5/1828
Ransome Tader	Milly Baker	12/20/1827
Stephen Whitmire	Frances Bradley	6/28/1828
William Broadwell	Martha Kidd	3/ 3/1828
Midam Broadwell	Kity Hemay	2/ 1/1827
James Miller	Sarah Saunders	7/17/1826
Sheard Knowling	Matilda Duncan	1/17/1828
Tirey Jackson	Susannah Dawes	7/31/1827
William Danill	Rhoda Jay	2/23/1826
Elijah Wade	Rebecca Hames	12/30/1823
Pleasant Thomas	Nelly Harris	5/21/1826
John Hames	Martha Pierce	8/17/1826
John Y. Hardage	Jane Robeson	4/ 3/1828
Jacob McDonald	Macenda Broadwell	3/23/1828
William Wallace	Susannah Watson	11/25/1826
Samuel H. Wilson	Jane McCoy	7/31/1828
Etic Pruit	Polly Payne	7/16/1828
Sherwood Hatley	Ecarilla Dickerson	7/ 8/1828
John Chalmers	Betsy Broadman	8/24/1828
William B. Braziele	Eliza M. Christian	1/ 3/1828
Greenberry Sarnes	Peggy Ross	8/ 2/1828
John Dickerson	Mary Garrison	4/27/1828
David G. Cobb	Mariah Goddard	10/10/1827
John Patterson	Jane Chapman	10/ 6/1828
Wade Parsons	Kesiah Combs	11/16/1828
Richard F. Archer	Prudence Pinson	12/11/1828
Moses Bryan	Mary Buffington	11/ 6/1828
John O'Barr	Elizabeth Kelton	1/19/1829
Enoch Mills	Courtney Meuse	1/29/1829
Isaiah Dunagan	Susannah Eberhart	1/17/1828
John Chambers	Nancy King	12/13/1828
Lorenzo D. Wood	Louise McClusky	1/24/1828
David Hyde	Rosetta Redman	10/12/1828
James Vann	Sally Edwards	3/20/1828
Joseph Guyton	Zemily McClusky	3/13/1828
James Donneldson	Sarah Pessnel	4/ 9/1829
Bazil Gowen	Varrah Downs	3/26/1829
Bluford Foster	Nancy Dellafield	2/26/1829
James Norris	Jane Moss	2/17/1829
Fielding Thurmond	Hannah Rogers	2/26/1829
Caleb Clark	Polly Mullins	9/14/1828
Henry Huff	Martha Pewes	11/27/1828
Jeremiah Hubbard	Eliza G. Moss	3/19/1829
James Barton	Delilah Boyd	2/25/1829
William Hubbard	Margaret Morgan	12/18/1828
Jacob Beasley	Jemimah Guthrie	12/21/1827
Carlisle B. Crow	Nancy Whitworth	2/21/1829
Bryant B. Bradley	Malinda Eaton	8/21/1828
Robert Gravett	Nancy Tidwell	7/16/1828
Asa Puggeth	Polly Vilyard	3/12/1829
William Castleberry	Sarah Wallice	4/17/1828
Thomas W. Williams	Mary Ann Tallant	3/23/1828
William Tedder	Nancy Baker	11/25/1828
James Wigley	Polly Gorman	3/ 9/1828
Armsed Whitlock	Drusilla Ayres	2/ 3/1829
Wesley Parrett	Narcissa Austin	4/26/1828
Pleasant Logan	Sarah Cash	11/ 2/1828
James R. Sparks	Susan Harben	4/ 5/1829
Archibald Whitehead	Mary Thomas	1/ 4/1829

GROOM	BRIDE	MARRIED
Peter Raby	Sarah Hubbard	8/13/1828
Burwell G. Reeves	Anny Jay	3/ 1/1829
William Glass	Mahala Porter	2/17/1829
John Wiley	Elizabeth Priest	8/16/1828
Thomas J. Thurmond	Caroline Robinett	1/ 1/1829
James Hawkins	Sarah Kittle	3/ 8/1829
William M. McCutchen	Lucinda Major	9/14/1828
Abraham Wood	Betty Hubbard	7/24/1828
Benjamin Bracket	Susan Hubbard	6/25/1830
William Bailey	Mary Bailey	3/ 9/1830
James Liles	Rhody Guthrie	8/ 6/1829
Archibald Whitehead	Mary Thomas	1/ 6/1829
Samuel S. Crews	Mary Stringer	1/ 7/1830
Isaac G. West	Cintha Hulsey	4/ 1/1830
Benjamin Pollard	Rachel Parks	12/ 6/1829
William Head	Sarah Thompson	11/23/1829
William Jay	Tempy Brock	8/19/1828
William Armour	Melinda Dodd	12/31/1829
James B. White	Elizabeth Jones	3/ 2/1830
James Baley	Elizabeth Grissom	3/ 8/1830
Joseph P. Pool	Rebecca Hinkle	12/21/1828
Thomas S. Tate	Mariah L. Reed	8/ 9/1829
Lasking Johnston	Nancy Morgan	1/26/1829
John Smethy	Melinda Kittle	5/19/1829
Joseph Barton	Matilda Kelly	2/ 2/1830
James Jordan	Nancy Epperson	2/16/1830
Silas Cross	Elizabeth Wilson	12/27/1829
George Bond	Melinda Hulsey	5/11/1830
John Fowler	Sarah Alexander	11/18/1829
Michael C. Wood	Polly Hubbard	12/17/1829
Martin Preast	M. Bradley	3/25/1830
John Armstrong	Melinda Burford	12/ 2/1829
Ebert G. Andrew	Frances Ellington	1/16/1829
Benjamin C. Stephens	Elizabeth Colley	5/10/1829
John Barnes	Myram Barker	3/15/1827
Berry Hill	Melinda Simmonds	10/ 6/1829
Bazil Cowin	Sally Dowis	3/26/1829
James Norris	Jane Moss	2/17/1829
John Cockrum	Elizabeth Cockram	2/ 7/1830
Asa Lanford	Katherine C. Hanson	5/30/1830
Thomas Robins	Polly Bates	2/ 2/1830
Russell Mabry	Ann Champion	12/31/1829
Drury A. Martin	Ellender Holly	10/ 4/1829
Gadwell Ayres	Rachel Hill	7/30/1829
John Leach	Sarah Jay	2/25/1830
John Leslie	Margaret Evans	8/29/1829
David Stuart	Elizabeth Lindsey	7/16/1829
Amos Patterson	Elizabeth Wilson	9/21/1829
Reuben Mullins	Rebecca Powers	10/ 4/1829
Hector D. McCormack	Mary A. Cain	3/22/1829
Samuel Redman	Jemima Shelton	11/23/1829
William Stuart	Nancy Thomas	2/18/1830
James Williams	Barbery Myers	11/19/1829
Martin Chamlee	Polly Guthrey	12/11/1828
Charles Hawkins	Jane Gravett	3/30/1830
John Clayton	Nancy Crafford	3/18/1830
Joseph Patterson	Agnes Wilson	3/25/1830
Andrew Presley	Mary Strickland	1/13/1830
James Chambers	Ally Miller	9/21/1829

GROOM	BRIDE	MARRIED
Elisha Eubanks	Rebecca Williams	12/20/1827
Rice Smith	Mary Welchell	10/27/1829
Robert Alexander	Elizabeth Shirley	8/13/1829
Benjamin G. McClesky	Haldak Boyd	3/18/1830
Henry H. Maddox	Elizabeth Welchel	2/12/1829
William Byrd	A. B. Thompson	10/14/1829
		(Date of License)
Drury Duncan	Eliza Dodd	1/21/1830
Henry Hinkle	Anna Thomas	8/11/1829
William Hendrix	Lucinda Crow	12/10/1828
David Putman	Lucy Castleberry	1/ 7/1830
John McCoy	Nancy Wiley	1/22/1829
James D. Hardage	Mary B. Clements	10/24/1829
Philip Coleman	Mary Mason	6/15/1830
Martin Roberts	Mary Fann	3/25/1827
		(Date of license)
William Kelly	Nancy Heath	3/ 7/1830
Sterling Goodwin	Elizabeth Carter	3/ 9/1829
Joel Bramblet	Elizabeth Keith	3/23/1830
Syrus Henderson	Tempy McKenzie	3/18/1830
William Davis	Elizabeth Johnson	6/ 5/1831
Geo. W. Wacason	Eliza Reynolds	8/ 8/1830
Edmund Johnson	Mary Hackett	5/30/1831
Samuel Waits	Ann Eaton	5/19/1822
Arthur Warren	Sarah Baber	6/28/1831
William C. Hope	Penelope Saunders	10/ 1/1829
Martin Dobbs	Rosalinda Hulsey	1/ 9/1831
John Garmon	Nancy Wheeler	11/ 4/1830
Zedeck H. Robeson	Celia Holt	7/31/1831
W. H. Wood	Mariah Lane	4/23/1830
Levi Wates	Elizabeth Bailes	6/21/1831
Dennis Night	Sarah Ashworth	6/15/1831
John B. E. Roberts	Mary A. Roberts	11/ 6/1831
William Wilson	Martha Pool	10/24/1831
William Webb	Nancy Whitlock	9/28/1830
Lewis W. Rinehart	Jane Harben	7/ 5/1831
Jacob Robertson	Mariah Norris	11/11/1830
W. L. Duke	Sarah Ann Murray	11/29/1831
Pendleton Hutchins	Elizabeth Barrett	5/19/1830
Reuben Daniel	Delila Right	9/25/1830
John Pirkle	Jane Ezell	11/14/1830
Sion Adkinson	Mary Carroll	5/26/1831
Henry L. Sims	Emily Clements	3/31/1831
James Head	Katherine Miers	8/23/1831
Simeon Terrell Jr.	O. Camp	11/29/1829
William Reeves	Hannah Champion	4/14/1831
Moses Banks	Rebecca Jay	1/ 2/1831
Joseph Carson	Margaret Stephens	12/27/1830
Oliver Wilson	Ridley Saunders	10/14/1830
James Jackson	Matilda H. Chastain	11/24/1831
David Utley	Oma Martin	10/ 7/1830
Moses Brooks	Slater Dperson	5/12/1831
James A. Johnson	Nancy M. Moore	9/25/1831
William Anderson	Emily Gravett	2/21/1828
Lewis Sams	Margaret Biddy	1/30/1831
John Vilyard	Jane Williams	9/16/1830
William Fields	Melissa Thornton	9/26/1830
William Goddard	Nancy Guthrie	8/ 5/1830
Stephen Pruitt	Margaret Low	9/25/1821

GROOM	BRIDE	MARRIED
Luke Gravitt	Sarah Goddard	9/22/1831
Ezekiel Bonds	Nancy Redman	12/ 5/1830
William Blake	Elizabeth Thurmond	5/ 8/1831
Squire Herron	Lucinda Fowler	10/10/1830
Robert Tedder	Elizabeth Keenum	12/21/1830
Edward Gilbert	Abbitha E. Pugh	12/16/1830
David Allen	Amelia Terrell	12/26/1830
Hiram Patterson	Elizabeth Cantrell	8/26/1830
Martin Davis	Jemima Barnett	9/12/1830
Zebulon Savage	Jincy Loggan	12/30/1830
Neavel Bennett	Nancy Smith	8/26/1830
Hiram Thomason	Rebecca Montgomery	2/10/1831
William Champion	Elizabeth Kenaday	2/19/1831
Cain Wade	Mary Edwards	2/10/1831
James Cantrell	Sarah Thurmond	1/ 2/1831
Nathaniel Watson	Sarah Bates	8/14/1831
Moses Langley	Amy Harris	9/ 4/1831
John Tidwell	Elizabeth Grant	9/ 4/1831
James Waugh	Susan Cook	1/ 6/1831
John Mullins	Vicey Whitehead	5/ 4/1830
Andrew S. Wilson	Elizabeth Ann W.Wilson	12/21/1830
A. B. Harden	Mary Barnwell	10/19/1830
James Bailey	Phebe McDow	2/24/1831
Nathaniel Y. Carr	Sarah A. Kennedy	9/ 6/1831
Osburn Reeves	Lucy Hawking	8/28/1831
William Tucker	Elizabeth Fossett	4/25/1830
Granville Tuggle	Shewrett (Ann)	9/24/1830
William Byrd	Mary Jones	12/ 4/1830
Jeremiah Nix	Annis Howard	9/30/1830
John Starnes	Rebecca Carter	11/11/1830
Benjamin Ragsdale	Rebecca Terrell	1/11/1831
George W. Hardage	Mary Ann Cook	9/ 1/1831
Rolly Gentry	Elsey Greavitt	11/ 3/1830
Merrell Cantrell	Elizabeth Cantrell	2/13/1831
Thomas Eubanks	Elenora Thompson	1/30/1831
Joshua Nicholson	Rachel O'Barr	8/23/1831
William Cogswell	Peggy McCay	10/21/1830
Stephen Cowen	Sarah Russell	1/13/1831
John Collins	Jincy Saxon	3/ 5/1831
William Frost	Helay Waide	6/26/1832
Seaborn Palmer	Mary Blake	12/31/1829
Oliver Hackett	Ruth Sellers	7/10/1831
Henry G. King	Mary Christopher	11/17/1831
James M. Reed	Frances C. Tate	2/14/1832
Tilman Shamblee	Kindness Breedlove Light	12/22/1830
Thomas M. Johnston	Mica M. Johnston	12/27/1831
William H. Lyon	Lucinda Mauldin	2/13/1832
James Say	Elizabeth Eberhart	2/14/1832
Samuel M. Fleming	Eliza C. Robeson	3/22/1832
William D. Lumpkin	Esther Hudgins	1/13/1831
Redding Pinson	Nancy Whitehead	3/ 6/1832

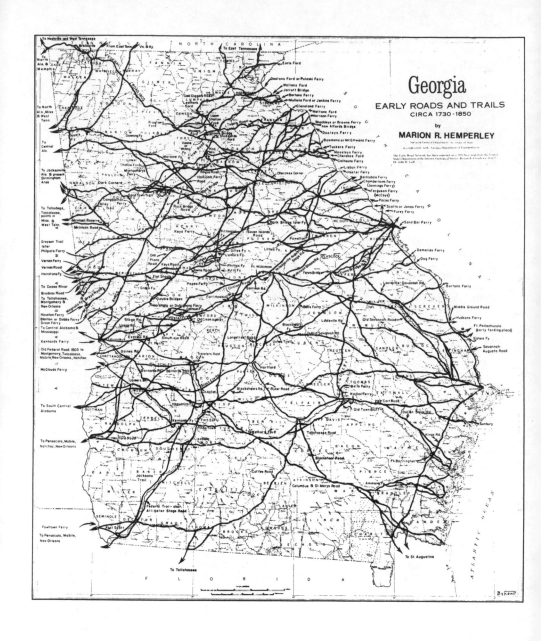

EARLY ROADS AND TRAILS, Ca. 1730-1850

THE 1834 STATE CENSUS OF LUMPKIN COUNTY

From the county files, Telamon Cuyler Collection, Special Collections, University of Georgia Libraries. A fragment of the 1838 state census of Lumpkin County was discovered by Madeline Anthony of Dahlonega and published in the R. J. Taylor, Jr., Foundation, Census For Georgia Counties (Atlanta, 1979).

"The amount of Free white population of Lumpkin County taken by John Oxford"

1834

John Oxford-7 (white persons)
James Davis-13
Andrew Flowers-3
Solomon Sebolt-6
John Ledford-5
Rolly Patterson-10
George Bowers-1
Peter Flowrrs-6
Peter Sebolt-3
Abram Sebolt-10
John Owenby-7
John Johnson-6
Sarah Jones-3
David Oxford-7
Jonathan Oxford-2
John W. Mcaffee-7
Thos. Mcaffee-5
William Mcaffee-8
Jesse Turner-3
Polly Miller-3
Hugh Swim-2
Levy Swim-7
James Franklin-8
Benjamin Winkler-6
Josiah Daniel-6
William Daniel-4
Henry Jenings-6
John Elrod-7
Frederick Dover-10
Thos. Holcomb-3
John Sitton-2
A.B. Baker-4
George Hedrick-5
Casper Hedrick-5
Nepoleon Lion-5
William Saxton-10
Moses Link-5
Thomas Ash-6
Caleb Spencer-6
James Corban-4
Henry Ash-2
John Pursel-9
James Pursel-8
Stephen Palmor-7
Benjamin Hester-9
James D. Sutton-7
Jacob Hetten-5
Elisha Freshawers-5
Samuel Jones-8
John Frazure-3

Enoch Swim-7
Jesse Stancel-4
James C. Hetten-6
Sally Hetten-4
James Hetten-8
Henry Wisenhunt-4
Seborn Shed-4
John Boyd-9
Ransom Whiteworth-7
Samuel Bright-4
William Carpenter-6
James Cochran-4
Willis Mcdaniel-4
William Cochran-7
John Rider-9
Rachel Brown-5
Rober McCaary-4
Sampson Vickery-4
Thos. Barnett-1
Thos. Pilgrim-8
Thos. Carder-4
Iverson Carder-4
James Mahan-2
Samuel Tate-9
John Frohawk-2
Robert W.P. Moor-6
Elender Bond-5
Goodman Hughs-2
John Ravan-9
Berry Turner-9
Samuel Atres-3
Joseph Atres-5
Henry Atres-4
Jonathan Rider-6
Michael Pilgrim-2
Peter Atres-7
Jonas Nix-9
William McCrary-8
Tilmen Jarrett-4
Elias Turner-6
Joel Stephens-9
John Baker-12
Levi Holmon-10
John D. Field-3
Solomon Hinkle-8
Jonsey Parker-8
Archibald Gaddis Sr.-4
Archibald Gaddis-4
John Hudson-3
Lewis Terry-5

Martin Keith-8
Edwerd Burgess-9
Racheal Reace-3
Jefferson Logan-5
William Reaves-8
Jeffrey Beck-4
John C. Carter-11
E. J. Carter-2
James Grindle-11
Lot Warren-7
Daniel Killian-6
Robert A. Holt-6
John O. Glover-7
Mathew Marable-8
Francis Howard-4
John Mcfarlin-3
Melinda Sutherland-5
Nathaniel Swancy-6
William O. Boman-9
John Sutherland-6
Polly Shaffet-5
Robert Sexon-2
Edward Carnes-9
Elejah Chaffin-6
John Martin-8
Stephen Martin-2
John Grizzel-14
Absalem Martin-6
Lewis Brady-8
Thos. Garrison-5
James Payne-2
Charles Runals-7
John Grindle-5
William Cockran-5
Hezekiah Cockran-5
Philip Mulkey-2
Philip Mulkey-2
James C. Mulkey-3
Marke Mulkey-5
Averett Shuffield-2
Darkey Parker-2
Abram Powel-9
Isem Shuffield-8
Benjamin Martin-2
James Gailey-8
John Rider-4
Ephraim Harris-1
John Anderson-5
Wm. Anderson-5
Shadrick Jenson-5
Jerry Frieland-2
Howel Frieland-2
Sarda Sissen-7
Solomon Barnes-8
John Barnes-6
Daniel S. Mary (Macy?)-11
William R. King-2
Carter Evans-6
Christopher Rider-4
Wm. H. Lion-3
John Holenshed-2

William Rider-6
John Kunam (Keenam?)-14
Richard Perry-11
William Jackson-2
Barnett Sims-7
John Nix-2
Amos Bayzmen-9
Philip Collins-6
Reuben Emery-5
William Pool-4
Rachael King-6
Willis Prince-7
William G. Foster-4
William Wallis-6
William Hughs-7
Jacob Cochran, Sr.-2
Richard Wilsen-2
Jacob Cochran, Jr.-11
Henry Cochran-7
Turner Conaway-3
Hiram Privet-3
Jessee Thomas-2
John Conaway-8
Burgess Princeon-5
William Pinchback-1
Jesse Bagwell-1
Ambras K. Blackwell-3
William Ragan-16
Henry H. Ware-8
P. Thomas-4
Thos. W. Blaney-4
George Wallis (Walles?)-7
Hannah Clemons-3
Roswell Hall-9
Jacob Elrod-5
A. H. Kee-3
William Stocks-13
William Porter-5
Robert Childres-2
Harper Pare-4
James S. Morris-6
Thos. Gramen-5
Hensen Chapman-7
Christopher Chapman-6
John Patterson-4
Rachael McGulleon-5
Dempsey Hill-6
Edmond Tilly-9
Lot Day-3
Jesse Martin-2
John Ashly-1
John Rose-1
Obediah Gravit-10
Hiram Moss-3
Robert Carr-7
William Lindsey-6
Lewis Chandler-1
Elihue Creswell-1
John Moss-1
Nancy Hulsey-5
John Walraven-5

THE 1834 STATE CENSUS OF LUMPKIN COUNTY

Jarvis Tramel-9
Samuel Day-1
Benjamin Parks, Sr.-4
Benjamin Parks, Jr.-7
James Stephens-8
Ransen Wilson-11
William Thompson-5
Elizabeth Sims-6
Thos. Hughbanks-3
Mark B. Robson-1
William R. Johnson-7
William Lindsey-6
David H. Porter-6
William Egington-10
John Langston-12
Samuel H. Smith-8
Joshua Dunagan-7
Thos. Reaves-1
Elejah Edwards-1
Jediah Blackwell-13
Bolling W. Field-2
Philip Keller-11
Azriah Denny-1
Elheed Denny-5
David Jackson-2
Henry Adams-7
Aren Mincy-7
Jane Powell-4
Reufus Barker-2
Mary Slatton-2
Plesant Powell-7
Emsely Gaddis-3
Aron Mincy Snr.-8
Isaac Mincy-6
Henry Adams Snr.-8
William Step-10
Thos. Davis-7
Jesse Camel-10
Jacob Glaze-1
Austin McDaniel-5
Joseph Glaze-5
David Adams-6
Ambrose Christopher Jr.-11
Ambrose Christopher Sr.-2
William Christopher-11
Hinry King-3
John Cantrell-10
James Baty-4
John Lollis-7
James Lollis-6
Sarah Roberds-3
Hiram Croney-4
Benjamin Long-11
William Townsend-3
James Bradberry-1
George Kelly-6
James Jonsen-6
Benjamin Hatfield-5
Rawland Berdin-9
Joseph Right-3
James Sutton-10

Jacob Bardin-11
Robert Ray-10
Alexandria Kennum-5
Dingham Ray-6
John Ray-8
Josiah Shaw-3
James Woody-7
Menoah Person-7
Elejah McCrary-3
John S. Walters-5
Andrew Nickoles-2
David Nickoles-8
James Olear-5
Joseph Lothlin-7
Johnson Hargett-2
Barthalomew Greeven-5
Charles Spillers-3
Abram Smith-5
Tilmon Cox-4
Lewis Dobbs-8
Edward D. Petetgrew-6
William Deaten-6
James Meeler (Maler?)-13
William Forister-7
William Patterson-7
Hiram Patterson-4
John R. Cochran-1
Mordaca Brown-4
Alen Galaspa-9
Allen Mathews-12
Charles H. Nelson-4
Thomas Potete-3
Willis Parks-1
Thos. Hutchinson-4
Adam Carson-1
Orval Ayres-6
Joseph Rutlege-4
Jourdan Gilly-5
Ecca Rafer-4
John D. Chapman-13
Willis Milliner-5
John N. Howell-3
Merida Bowen-12
William Bradford-2
William Brooks-2
Mathew McDaniel-9
Dulphas Rutherford-4
Bartly Jones-8
Zealous Miller-8
Nathaniel B. Harben-6
John Lowrey-5
Thos. Williams-1
Andrew Tancasley-6
William Wheeler-4
Martin Blake-3
P. Caldwell-3
John Surcy-2
Mary Baldwin-3
Johnathan Smith-4
Ansolem Bugg-10
A. N. Baird-13

William Worley-8
Jonathan Chastain-9
Hiram Harris-1
Elejah McMillon-8
James McCartney-1
Acil Smith-1
John Noblit-3
James Barington-1
Jeremiah Chastain-3
William B. Jones (?)-7
Abreham Jensen-3
Jeremiah Payne-3
Alexandria Duncan-2
John Donalson-10
William Rogers-4
William H. Robinson-3
John Choice-7
M. F. Cannon-6
Menoah Felton-1
Jeremiah Murphey-5
John H. Ware-1
Richard Thompson-1
H. C. Tatum-12
E. P. Hale (Hall?)-6
Garland Caldwell-9
William A. Slaton-2
Ezra Sanloon-3
Harrison W. Riley-6
R. S. Brashears-15
Mark Littleton-8
Isaac Hunter-1
William H. Riley-3
Jemima Brown-7
Francis Darter-2
J. F. Steel-3
Henry Huff-4
William Eaton Snr.-3
Quiller Bruce-7
Samuel Eaton-5
Jonas Melton-4
John Eaton-8
William Eaton Jnr.-6
John Broadaway-6
John Armstrong-5
John Coacher-7
John Warters-5
John Hall-1
Sarah Smitell-1
Asa Reaves-7
Daniel Reaves-7
William Green-2
John L. Cox-5
William B. Woody-9
Gilbert Falls-6
David Watters-8
Tolaver L. Hicks-6
John O. Brackin-3
Robert Sharp-2
Joshua Holcomb-6
William Carson-8
Asa Keith-8

Alexandria Brown-4
John S. Miller-10
Isaac Hill-2
John Humphries-10
Brice Howard-9
Elisha Reese-1
George Whisenant-4
George Couch-3
John Corn-9
Elijah B. Smith-2
Thos. J. Calbert-5
Asbury Curtis-6
James Killgo-4
William Price-7
William Kunurn(Keenum?)-5
Samuel Bradford-4
James Branam-10
William Larance-3
Charles Unruh-1
Green K. Seisna-7
Joseph R. Horth-4
Uriah Holden-9
William Findley-6
James Logan-8
James Reder-5
John Grerdner(Gardner?)-9
Cornelius Townsend-6
Howard S. Counsel-6
James Akales-7
David Smith-8
Ransom Bennett-10
Zeboder Shetton(Stetton?)-7
Henry Sumerand-9
Benjamin Flemin-3
Ann Watters-2
Isaac Wood-4
Isom R. Call(Hall?)-8
Thos. Nutiaris-5
Jacob Mathews-7
William Thompson-12
William Gilmer-15
Micajah Hornby(Hemby?)-7
Samuel Clence-7
Michael Obar-5
Ira Obar-3
George C. Terry-3
William Head-2
John Chapman-11
Henry M. Clay-5
Samuel Rutherford-2
Zachariah Samuel-3
Wallis Park-1
Samuel Shoemakre-9
D. C. Gibson-8
Clemon Parks-10
William Swepman-9
E. C. Lane-5
William Rail-7
Archebald McCollum-3
William Wilson-11
Richard Moor-9

Allen Downs-7
Jerry Nix-4
J. C. Calhoun-5
Jacob Nix-6
Thos. Nix-3
James Smith-2
J. Williams-3
William Spears-4
Mathias Gaswick-6
Barge Lane-4
Barna West-7
D. Elmor-2
Samuel Towler(Fowler?)-2
Jesse Rail-9
Jn. (?) D. Smith-3
Sherwood Howlin (Nowlin?)-9
James E. Herd-5
Edmond H. Dryer-4
Michael Shoar-3
Wade Edwards-6
G. W. Lindsey-7
G. H. Fuller-5
John Mooney-7
John Shaw-1
James Cantrell-7
Joseph Rogers-8
Martin Malueph-9
James Mahafphy-5
John B. Morison-5
William Jack-3
Samuel Jack-3
Edward Wing-8
William Lard-8
Joshua Welch-5
James Flecher-9
J. C. Bradford-3
John Wing-5
J. H. Thomas-4
H. Green-5
William Wilky-7
James Prater-5
Abel Winingham-5
Andrew Howell-7
Joshua Stewart-10
William Stewart-3
Cornelieus Stewart-2
Farrow Mcgaee (Stegall?)-5
Nancy Wheeler-9
Gelbert Mooney-4
B. Love-2
Micajah McCravey-5
Thos. Westbrooks-13
Jesse Mills-13
James G. Cleveland-6
Jacob Husus (Hupus?)-8
Mary Obrnion-3
J. C. Welch-5
Michael Smith-8
John Martin-8
R. A. Watkins-18
William Didman-7

Susanah Prater-7
Oliver Wilson-4
Alfred Harris-5
James S. Tucker-3
Jesse Harbin-6
William Banks-5
Reuben Hutchinson-3
H. L. Towns-5
Johnson Davis-1
Charles A. Ely-4
Agness Paschal-18
Henry Lewis-2
Roswell King-2
G. A. Parker-4
A. D. Wildes-5
William Bun-4
Jefferson Officer-9
Henry Kenady-10
John Davis-2
Thos. Dotson-3
Henry McNeal-9
William Thomas-4
Thos. Reese (Ruse?)-4
Hannah Kelly-9
Tensey Kelly-3
John Hills-1
Daniel Merida-2
Samuel King-5
Richard Dennis-2
J. Garnett-5
Jonathan Mooney-4
John Muckalray-5
John Odam-12
Uriah Gaton-9
E. Levingston-3
Christopher Rider-4
Robert Ligon-1
John F. Raulston Sr.-9
James H. Braden-3
Isaac Cropley (Crosley?)-3
Mary Dalrimple-2
William Champion-4
James Canddy-1
Hugh Bruce-5
James Rimington-6
Robert Anderson-8
Daniel Price-4
Francis Nerrill-5
Thos. F. Turner-9 (7?)
Gabrail McCoal-8
Peter Oliver-8
Abram McCorke-4
Elsabeth Manin-2
Mary Mannin-6
Thos. Norton-5
David Hall-5
George W. Cilow-3
Thos. Cantrell-3
Philip Wade-6
William Hall-8
James Patterson-5

John Patterson-3
John Hubbard-10
William Tumberlin-5
Joseph Roberson-9
George Hall-8
Horatio Bruce-3
William Moor-8
John Moor-5
Wiatt Sass-6
Thos. Moor-7
Joshua Smith-4
Morgan Colly-5
Roling Orsburn-5
John Greens-7
Luke Hendrix-9
Asa Padgett-5
Abraham Padget-7
John Nations-9
Rebecca Morgan-3
John Stroud-2
Thomas Jonsen-3
Burttin Lowlis-8
Elias Bruce-2
George Bruce-4
William Tailor-8
James Neal-7
Joseph Merois (Morris?)-3
Butler Turner-6
Nancy Childres-4
Thomas God-5
Edward Tatum-5
John Tatum-5
Robert Byers-10
John Bruce-7
Samuel Byers-3
Gideon Smith-5
Barter Lawless-8
Aaron Roper-6
Susan Roper-7
Rachael Ward-2
Elisha Murphey-5
Thomas Norrill-5
William Glass-5
Marry Johnson-7
Solomon Rowe (?)-4
Hugh Tatum-7
John Palmour-6
Silas Palmour-4
Solomon Palmour Jr.-3
Solomon Palmour Sr.-4
Lewis Barker-7
Henry Edwards-7
Mathias Tally-8
Samuel Thomas-3
A. K. Craig-4
John Clayton-2
J. C. Lothridge-1
Jane Ratty-5
William Ratty-3
William Lacky-6
John Stowers (Flowers?)-6

Robert B. McCleur-6
Charles J. Thompson-5
Osten Banister (Barrister?)
  -9
Caleb Herington-3
J. Herington-3
David Carroll-3
William Barrett-3
Elias Braden-4
William G. Harris-9
Samuel Fain-5
John W. Hughs-7
Richard Blackstocks-3
Jesse Evett-5
Benjamin Jones-4
William Jones-3
Henry Jones-9
William Barrett-3
Reuben Barrett-7
David Carrol-6
Samuel Hunly(Hemly?)-3
Andrew Wood-6
Uriah Hawkins-2
Charles Hawkins-4
Jason Johnson-10
Samuel Hamby-3
William Jackson-5
Tire Jackson-4
Alexandria Smith-8
Clark Alumas (?)-5
John Wallis-6
James Mills-4
Pleasent Hulsey-8
Charles Hawkins-4
Uriah Hawkins-2
Samuel Hainby-3
P.G. Garmen(Garner?)-5
Nathaniel Goss-7
Neely Dobson-8
Jonathan Hughbanks-4
Benjamin Goss-10
Elisha Kinse-6
Nathaniel Harben-10
Ansel Berdin-11
Robert Obar-4
Ashle Obar-3
Thomas Berdin-6
William Berdin-5
James Rice-8
William Burtt-6
Henry Mcneal-9
John Turner-5
Richard Berdin-7
Moses Watters-11
James Watters-9
Abraham Cochran-10
John Thompson-7
Henry Clark-6
John N. Wisenant-5
William Clark-8
Lemuel Roberson-4

THE 1834 STATE CENSUS OF LUMPKIN COUNTY

Demps Rice-2
Barnett Parker-5
Patsy Pool-7
Henry Carver-6
Joseph Rice-3
Henry Watkins-6
Lewis Arthur-7
George Lowman-11
Albert Hoss-3
John C. Jones-8
Williamson Turner-3
Richard Wade-6
Charles Dowda-4
Plesent Worley-8
William Dowda-3
Balum Dowda-6
Amos Dowda-7
James Kizer-4
Robert Dowda-7
N. H. Erley-4
W. Rice-5
Thomas Howell-5
Stephen Bird-2
Thompson Eperson-6
Wisley Walker-7
William Wheeler-11
Washington Greer-4
Uel Watkins-2
David Alerson-12
James Barlowe-6
Memmary Walker-8
Jerry Stover-7
David Caldwell-6
James Bryan-7
Phillip Whitter-2
George Durham-11
Major Sutherland-3

John Sutherland-8
William Sutherland-3
Abner Watkins-6
Colman Ferguson-9
Martin Lance-12
Charles Arthur-6
Barnabus Arthur-7
William Arthur-10
Mathew Arthur-2
Riley Goss-3
William Keenum-5
Vincent Garner-4
Hiram Proctor-6
Jerry Gibbs-9
William Proctor-6
Sutten Yong-6
Reuben Warren-3
John Coner-6
James Poteete-4
James R. Rusel-7
J. Nowlin-8
Stephen Edwards-8
Tarzen Bryant-8
Canada Kemp-10
Robert Freeman-5
William Norris-3
John Alexandria-2
Zim Mcguire-7
Lackston Crow-7
Jacob Holinshead-9
Wiley Nix-9
Jonathan Howard-4
William Smith-3
Harris Huchons-3
William Wooton-10
Joseph Boyd-8
Marion Linton-3

The foregoing Statement of 787 is a true Statement of the Number of Families in Lumpkin County and 4393 is a true Statement of the whole free white population of said County-taken by me since the 19th of February 1834 to this 22d March 1834.

/s/ John Oxford

467

Savannah. Circa 1825, Courtesy the Georgia Historical Society

THE 1834 STATE CENSUS OF MURRAY COUNTY, GEORGIA

From the county files, Telamon Cuyler Collection, Special
Collections, University of Georgia Libraries. Reproduced with
permission.

Georgia)   We, James Edmondson, James Kincannon & Eli
Murray County) Bowlin, Justices of the Inferior Court for said
                 County do hereby certify that we did on the 3rd
day of March 1834 Appoint Meddleton Blalock to take the census
for said county, which the said Blaylock has performed in Terms
of the statute, -- a certified copy is hereinto annexed--this
1st day of april 1834--

                   /s/ James Edmondson JIC
                       Eli Bolan JIC
                       James Kincannon JIC

March 29th 1834   (Heads of Families & Number of White Persons)

Francis Burk-6
James Nicholson-8
William J. Tarvin-6
Thomas Menamee-4
George Upton-8
John A. Upton-5
Robert Murphy-6
Littleton Baker-4
Martin Saxon-6
Jacob Wallis-2
John Saxon-10
David Shields-3
Alexander Saxon-4
James Quinton-4
Osamus Camp-9
Frederick Thompson-6
David M. Coley-7
James Edwards-6
David McNab-7
John Greenwood-9
Renne Fitzpatrick-4
William Hancock-8
Moses Neal-3
James C. Barnett-12
William Smith-10
Johal Holton-7
John V. Cotter-7
John Stancel-9
Nathaniel Wafford-1
John G. B. Adams-9
John Johnstun-5
Charles Horton-5
Nathaniel Adams-6
M. M. Blalock-6
Daniel Anderson-9
James Kincannon-6
John Trigg-7
Joseph Youngblood-5
Jessey Casey-10
Enoch Higgins-10
Jack Morris-4
W. S. Oats-9
Edmund Smith-4
Saml. McGauhey-8

Littleberry Jackson-6
Nathan Ward-6
Samuel Johnstun-10
M. W. Johnstun-2
Casey W. Jackson-8
Matthew Kincannon-5
James McGhee-9
Morgan Hampton-3
William May-3
Elijah King-9
Moses Dunn-8
J. R. Smedley-6
J. S. Cornwell-3
Larkin Satterfield-3
George Wilson-1
Robert Reed(Reece?)-10
Eli Bolin-8
Wm. W. Tankesly-3
James Whittenberg-5
James Rose-6
Jerry Cloud-8
Madison Nicholass-3
James Ellard-7
Stephen Hay-3
Amos Ford-10
Mitchel Beasly-2
Armsted Thornhill-6
Moses Cantrel-4
John Staunton-6
James Whittenberg-3
John B. McMillian-7
Jonathan Akin-5
Samuel Miller-8
Michael Wacafer-8
Elijah Mays-3
Martha Mays-2
John Gillehan-7
Andrew Pickins-2
Nelson Dickerson-6
George Rollins-4
Archibald Sloan-7
Wilson B. Young-7
John B. Martin-2
Hilory Stoker-9

469

THE 1834 STATE CENSUS OF MURRAY COUNTY, GEORGIA

Terrell Cantrell-1
John J. Humphreys-3
James Donohoo-2
James Edmundson-10
Daniel (David?) N. Henry-5
R. T. Banks-4
William N. Bishop-6
Martin Keith-9
Lewis Terry (Tersy?)-3
Daniel Cornwell-6
Warren Sams-5
Moses Gillehan-4
James S. Crumwell-3
Geo. W. Wacaser-4
Samuel B. Campbell-8
Peter Fry-7
Henry Davis-15
T. J. Davis-8
Hugh Weathers-9
Jonathan Freadel-6
John Schrimsher-3
Jerry Gentry-2
Moses Johnstun-2
Sarah Berry-6
Thomas Simmons-3
Edward Jackson-4
Moses Shirp-2

Benjamin Clark-12
Amos Cook-3
William Blalock-5
Boos Still-7
James Head-4
Joel Lanair-5
Christopher Ramey-5
Mr. Gentry-2
Mr. Felton-2
Greenville Davis-4
Paten Wade-6
John Cooper-6
William Grant-8
Philip McIntyre-4
Pickens Howel-2
Hiram Runion-3
Absalom Waits-6
John Waits-7
Mary Murray-1
Elijah Cursling-1
William Conner-(?)
Leroy May-1
James May-1
Asa May-1
James Cruse-1
Richard Humn-1

Whole No. of Whites - 763 ----- Families - 142

SOME MURRAY COUNTY JURORS, 1837 AND 1839

The following jury lists for Murray County are on microfilm at the Georgia Department of Archives and History. For more on the history and pioneers of Murray County see Tim Howard, Murray County Heritage (1989), available from him at Rt. 3, Box 480, Chatsworth, GA 30705.

Grand Jurors January 17, 1837

1. H. D. Boyd
2. Carter Byas
3. John Burk
4. Absalom Bishop
5. John S. Beall
6. Julius Bales
7. Isaac Baker
8. Eli Bolan
9. Robert Black
10. Dennis Carroll
11. Andw Cathey
12. George Chappel
13. (skipped)
14. Martin Casaday
15. Martin Casaday
16. Wm. L. Conally
17. Leander G. Caldwell
18. Greenville Davis
19. Grief Felton
20. David J. Casaday
21. Henry Davis Sr.
22. William S. Jones
23. Jahial Hilton
24. Brooks Harper
25. Stephen Barton
26. Earter-B.-King
27. William-Kelly
28. John W. Laymance
29. John Lemming
30. William F. McCord
31. James Barton
32. James McGhee
33. Ambers McGhee
34. Harrell Felton
35. John K. Mears
36. Solomon Mcmurray
37. George Fagle

38. Russel Cogburn
39. Hiram Gillelean
40. Caswell Ramsey
41. Thomas Montgomery
42. Samuel Miller
43. John Sloan
44. Burton McGhee
45. William J. Oates
46. Anderson Watt
47. John Oates
48. Stephen Paxson
49. Israel Nations
50. George Rollins
51. Daniel-G.-Stafford
52. William Neil
53. Nathan Ward
54. Lewis Arter
55. Jackson Fitzpatrick
56. Bennett Stringfield
57. John Slegar
58. Barny Stewart
59. George W. Wacasa
60. Griffin Heath
61. John Hawkins
62. Lewis Terry
63. Joel Wagner
64. William-B.-Swain (Swason?)
65. Riley Wilson
66. Barney B. Whaley
67. James Kincannon
68. Thomas Walker
69. Robert Browne
70. James Prater
71. Seaborn Senter
72. James Sample
73. Warren Sams
74. Jacob Shoopman

Petitt Jurors January 17, 1837

1. Thomas O. Austin
2. Willis Bobo
3. Jesse Bookout
4. Richard Butler
5. John Brookshear
6. James Cloud
7. Elijah-Cirson
8. Isaac Cloud
9. Charnie L. Cox
10. George Cloud
11. Wesley Casaday

12. James Cardin
13. Daniel Cornwell
14. David-M.-Coleg
15. Harrison Davis
16. Littleton H. Davis
17. Walton Davis
18. Surray Davis
19. James Ellard
20. William Ellard
21. Thomas-Edmondson
22. Peter Etter

471

23. Beverly Greenwood	84. William Gerry (Terry?)
24. Hudson Greenwood	85. James Ledford
25. Joseph Housley	86. John A. J. Upton
26. William Holcomb	87. Joseph Burks
27. Vinson Jones	88. Thomas Cooper
28. Thomas F. Lowrey	89. James S. Cromwell
29. William Lemming	90. Eli Cates
30. James Mcnamee	91. William Cawley
31. Alexander Martin	92. Jeremiah Cloud
32. John S. Martin	93. John Cocks
33. John Mac Key	94. Silas Cook
34. Larkin Myers	95. John S. Cotter
35. Moses Neal	96. Joseph Cain
36. Wesley Reins	97. John Cook
37. Joseph Richardson	98. James Donaldson
38. Obediah Abels	99. Ira A. Douglas
39. P. N. Black	100. Hiram Douglas
40. David Barton	101. Jesse Douglas
41. Aleab Barton	102. Baylas Donaldson
42. Hughs Burk	103. David Douglas
43. Robert G. Banks	104. James Edmondson
44. Andrew J. Bates	105. Joseph McClure
45. Wilson Browne	106. Wilson Norton
46. Simpson Bearfield	107. Norman Norton
47. John Broadrick	108. Jefferson Officer
48. George Black	109. Alexander Officer
49. Moses Black	110. William P. Poole
50. Henry Browne	111. Thomas Payne
51. James M. Bates	112. Robert Reed
52. John Browne	113. George Ramy
53. James Barnett	114. Thomas Ramy
54. John Baxter, Sr.	115. John Ross
55. John Baxter, Jr.	116. Calvin Rollins
56. Michael Wacaser	117. Alexander Rogers
57. William Wilbanks	118. John Rollins
58. John Williams	119. James M. Sellers
59. Paten Wade	120. William Smith
60. Barney West	121. William Shamlin
61. Thomas Wacaser	122. John Stancil
62. Joseph Youngblood	123. William Stoker
63. J. H. Kimbro	124. Hilory Stoker
64. John Brookshear	125. Leonard Speeks
65. William Brumbelo	126. Elijah Shamlin
66. Wilson Watson	127. Robert Sloan
67. Adam W. Caldwell	128. Archibald Sloan
68. John S. Larkey	129. Brooks Sparks
69. L. W. Runion	130. Nehemiah Sparks
70. John Rogers	131. A. M. Turner
71. John Ransom	132. John B. Tipton
72. William Sweatman	133. William Walker
73. George Simmons	134. A. B. Weir
74. John F. Sams	135. Hugh Weathers
75. Jackson Snow	136. Benjamin West
76. Dozier Sutton	137. James Whittenberg
77. John D. Sutton	138. Alexander Williams
78. Langston S. Springfield	139. James H. Williams
79. John Starnton	140. Wilson R. Young
80. Hugh Springfield	141. Joseph Edmondson
81. Thomas B. Simmons	142. Amos Ellard
82. Jesse Snow	143. Amos Ford
83. Duncan Terry	144. Stephen Graves

145. Morgan Hampton
146. Thomas Hancock
147. James Hansucker
148. ~~Thomas J. Harper~~
149. William Hancock
150. Thomas Hall
151. Jeremiah Hamby
152. John D. Holbrooks
153. Joab Humphreys
154. Daniel N. Henry
155. James Holder
156. ~~Archibald Harris~~
157. Carey W. Jackson
158. Littleberry Jackson
159. Samuel Johnston
160. A. H. Johnston
161. James Johnston

162. Elijah King
163. John King
164. Samuel H. Keith
165. Martin Keith
166. Asa Keith
167. W. R. Keith
168. William Leadford
169. Absalom Leadford
170. ~~Mark Lacey~~
171. ~~John Lacey~~
172. Isaac Laymance
173. William B. Malone
174. Samuel B. McCamey
175. James McCaslin
176. John B. Marston
177. Robert McCamey

Grand Jurors March 1, 1839

1. George Rollins
2. Samuel Miller
3. Thomas Mcnamee
4. John Limming
5. Martin Cassada
6. Luois Terry
7. John Stansell
8. James Strawn
9. John K. Meares
10. William F. McCoard
11. John D. Holbrooks
12. George Cloud
13. Absalom Bishop
14. Leander G. Coldwell
15. Joseph Terry
16. David Blackwell
17. Smith Treadwell
18. John McElroy
19. Joseph McLure
20. Jason Johnson
21. Samuel C. Fane
22. Lewis Tremble
23. Joseph Tremble
24. H. D. Boyde
25. Hiram Montgomery
26. William McEntire
27. James McEntire
28. John McEntire
29. John Oates
30. William L. Connelly
31. John S. Martin
32. John Stanton
33. Dixon Nailer
34. Langly B. Camp
35. Nathaniel Cox
36. Greenville Davis
37. John T. D. Park
38. William Bennett
39. Thomas Black

40. Barney B. Whaley
41. Anderson Watt
42. William White
43. Allen George
44. David Barton
45. Moses Widner
46. James Mcnamee
47. John Cockburn
48. Jacob Hollifield
49. Robert Teid
50. Thomas Hall
51. David Carroll
52. Carter Byers
53. John Sutherland
54. Jacob Reagan
55. Levi Miller
56. Wilson Norton
57. James Whittenburger
58. Clark T. Cockburn
59. James Johnson
60. Dennis Carroll
61. Russell Cockburn
62. Thomas Montgomery
63. Jacob Shoopman
64. Robert Patrick
65. Thomas Walker
66. Bennet Springfield
67. William Hassler
68. Seburn Senter
69. Nathan Ward
70. Jacob Laymance
71. John R. Rollins
72. Eli Bolan
73. David Douglass
74. James Sample
75. Jahile Helton
76. Manley Nations
77. Israel Nations
78. Jackson Strawn

Pettit Jurors March 1. 1839

1. William B. Sutherland
2. John Pritchard
3. William Shamblin
4. Tobe Tyre
5. William Walker
6. John W. Laymance
7. Isaac Laymance
8. Walton H. Davis
9. Daniel Boatright
10. Samuel R. McCamey
11. William Whitton
12. Anderson F. Cromwell
13. Jeremiah Hamby
14. John F. Moreland
15. William McGill
16. James M. Cloud
17. Anthony Smith
18. Calvin Rollins
19. James Ellis
20. Dean W. Chase
21. John Gordan
22. Joel Waggenor
23. James McCasland
24. A. B. Weir
25. James C. Cromwell
26. Rucker Mauldin
27. John Broadrick
28. Gideon Jackson
29. William Ledford
30. J. B. Officer
31. Anderson White
32. William Richardson
33. Osborn Love
34. William Paslen
35. Samuel H. Keith
36. Thomas Payne
37. Jesse Brookout
38. Abel Edwards
39. James Donaldson
40. Williford Chapman
41. Clem Quillian
42. Barney Stewart
43. Franklin B. Morris
44. Ralph Ellison
45. Thomas T. Mcmullan
46. Randolp Mcmullan
47. F. L. Blair
48. Asa Keith
49. John Hutchison
50. William Terry
51. Thomas J. Burnes
52. George Terry
53. Duncan Terry
54. Brition Williams
55. Thomas J. Robins
56. James Kincannon
57. Benjamin West
58. John G. Park
59. James Hutchison
60. Harrison Davis.
61. Abel Jackson
62. Wesley Cassada
63. Anderson Putnam
64. John Harralson
65. James Buckhannon
66. Brooks Harper
67. Nathaniel Anderson
68. Thomas O. Austin
69. A. J. Bates
70. Carey W. Jackson
71. D. J. Cassada
72. Asa Douglass
73. Martin Keith
74. William Neal
75. James Barton
76. Stephen Barton
77. James C. Rogers
78. William Green
79. William Green
80. Osborn R. Johnson
81. A. M. Turner
82. Joseph Kimbrough
83. John M. Real
84. Enoch Humphreys
85. Shaderach Lowery
86. William Johnson
87. Thomas Davis
88. William Lowery
89. Jesse Snows (?)
90. Asa Thompson
91. William B. Malone
92. James Tedford
93. Thomas W. Smith
94. Malone Cox
95. William Burk
96. Cyrus Smith
97. Stephen McCurdy
98. Thomas Nichols
99. Krief Felton
100. George H. Ramey
101. Hezekiah Felton
102. William Brumbelo
103. Charles Cook
104. Silas Cook
105. George Chappell
106. Deaton Mobley
107. William Douglass
108. Aleb Barton
109. George W. Davis
110. William Sweatman
111. Griffin Heath
112. John Mays
113. James Tate
114. Archibald Stone
115. Balis Donalson
116. Richard Hill
117. Absalom Smith
118. William A. Robbins

THE LOST MARRIAGE RECORDS OF PICKENS COUNTY

by Marvis Dilbeck and Robert S. Davis, Jr.

The Pickens County, GA courthouse burned in 1947. Of the few records lost in the fire was the second book of marriages. However, the loose original marriages recorded in that book were saved although they eventually ended up in private hands. Marvis Dilbeck compiled the following list of those marriage records and the Marble Valley (Pickens County) Historical Society has microfilmed the original records with a grant provided by County Commissioner Bill Quinton. The microfilm is available for use by researchers at the Pickens County Library in Jasper.

Adams, Nathaniel S. to Adeline C. Ashworth, 5 Aug. 1860, by William Stone, MG.

Akens, Elias to Rachel Cowart, 1 Aug. 1880, by John Darnell, JP.

Akins, Ezekiel to Catherine V. Satterfield, T. Pickett, MG.

Akins, James A. to Martha Ann Cook, 2 Mar. 1874, by H.G.B. Turner, MG.

Atkins, J.P. to Nancy Carver, 24 June 1880, by E.J. Watson, JP.

Allen, Albert L. to Georgia Wanic, 12 Nov. 1888, by Wm. Cagle, MG.

Allen, Lafayette (col.) to Lucy Kirby, 10 Oct. 1875, by Sidney Roberds, MG.

Allen, W.A. to Mary C. Winterbottom, 20 July 1887, by T.J. Warlick.

Allen, Judge to Ellen Johnson, 22 Sept. 1887, by Jeremiah Sosebee, NP.

Allred, Elias J. to Laura J. Taylor, 2 September 1876, by E.W. Allred.

Anderson, Abraham to Narcisa E. Ivey, 5 Jan. 1859, by Caswell L. Corbin.

Anderson, George W. to Nancy Elizabeth Cape, 1 De. 1870, by L.C. Ivey, MG.

Anderson, James M. to Isabella C. Burlison, 4 February 1879, D.W. Burlison, JP.

Anderson, John N.J. to Sarah Elizabeth Turner, 14 June 1867, by James Turner, JP, Cherokee County.

Anderson, William to Sarah Morris, 13 February 1868, by B.C. Hitt, MG.

Anderson, W.W. to Medora Manous, 17 Apr. 1888, by Isaac Grant, JP.

Arnold, George E. to Lucinda E. Van Horn, 2 Feb. 1879, Josiah Reese, JP.

Arthur, C.W.N. to Julia Ann Beavers, 11 Apr. 1869, by Josiah Reese, JP.

Arwood, J.E. to Louisa Arwood, 29 Mar. 1885, J.P. Worley, JP.

Baker, G.A. to Susan Hanes, 19 Nov. 1882, by Rev. Daniel C.P. Carter.

Bailey, William J. to Mary T. Roe, 14 Apr. 1872, by W.A. Chambers, JP.

Barnett, J.W. to I.J. Godfrey, 24 July 1876, by James Sharyer, JP.

Barnett, Luther L. to Mary Jane Godfrey, 5 Feb. 1876, by James Sharyer, JP.

Barrett, C.C. to Alta Lindsey, 11 Feb. 1883, B.F. Warlick, JP.

Barrett, J.A. to M.F. Tatum, 23 Jan. 1887, by J.O. Harris, MG.

Barrett, William J. to Sarah E. Pack, 20 Dec. 1885, by Elder J.A. McDaniel.

Barron, Robert to Donea Taylor, 5 Dec. 1886, H.P. Sheffield, MG.

Barton, Joseph B. to Mary E. Tate, 26 Jan. 1875, by Elias W. Allred, MG.

Bearden, J.A. to Mary E. Caisel, 27 Jan. 1875, by A. Chadwick, MG.

Beaver, Milton M. to Sarah J. Groover, 22 Jan. 1873, by James W.
    Grogan, NP.
Bell, James B. to Mary Willis, 13 Feb. 1866, by Thomas A. McDan-
    iel, MG.
Bennett, John S. to Mary Hales, 22 Jan. 1876, by S. Hamrick, NP.
Bennett, M.A. to Mary E. Taley, 23 Oct. 1870, by S. Hamrick.
Biddy, John to Elizabeth Blackwell, 18 Oct. 1874, by John Holbert.
Biddle, John to Jula (Jola?) Bradford, 27 Feb. 1887, by Jeremiah
    Sosbee, NP.
Bishop, Henry to Martha Dooley, 23 June 1872, by John Darnell,
    Jr., NP.
Blackstock, William to Mary Ann Blackwell, 14 Mar. 1884, by
    Jeremiah Sosebee, NP.
Blackwell, Francis M. to Caroline Hays, 10 Oct. 1869, by F. M.
    Williams, MG.
Blackwell, Marion to Coldona Harris, 7 Sept. 1884, by J. C.
    Padget, MG.
Blackwell, Newton to Wenney Cowart, 16 Nov. 1884, by W.J. Wilson,
    JP.
Blalock, Thomas K. to Emma A. Brown, 15 Nov. 1883, by T. D.
    Harris, MG.
Blackwell, William D. to Louisa Evans, 10 Dec. 1875, by W. J.
    Hyde, MG.
Bolin, Cicero to Sarah C. Crain, 20 Sept. 1877, by A. Crow, JP.
Bowen, W.P. to India Holmes, 4 Feb. 1875, by William Stone, MG.
Bowers, Stephen Grffin to Licenia Mayfield, 24 Sep. 1874, by John
    Darnell, JP.
Bozeman, Link to Lidda Ingram, 20 Dec. 1885, by Josiah Bagwell,
    JP.
Bozeman, Sherman to Arminda M. Stanfield, 28 Oct. 1883, by Wm.
    Westbrook, MG.
Bradley, Andrew J. to Augustine E. Wheeler, 5 Mar. 1871, by R. G.
    Allen, NP. License bought 22 January 1868.
Bradley, Augustus B. to Mary A. Thompson, 10 Mar. 1878, by A.V.P.
    Jones, JP.
Bradley, Joseph H. to Hazela C. Weaver, 15 Aug. 1869, by Bethel
    Q. Disharoon, NP.
Bramblett, William to Elizabeth Blalock, 14 Mar. 1869, by James
    Sharyer, JP.
Bramlett, Sampson to Nancy Blaylock, 25 Nov. 1869, by Thomas
    Ray, NP & JP.
Brand, David to Lucy Jane McPherson, 2 Mar. 1874, by James
    Sharyer, JP.
Branon, J.A. to Mary Ann Lambert, 18 Dec. 1884, by William Stone,
    MG.
Brown, Joseph to Nancy Jane Anderson, 9 Jan. 1870, by A.F. Honea,
    MG.
Brown, M. to H.A. Woodall, 4 Feb. 1874, by B.F. Warlick, NP.
Brown, W.M. to Mary A.V. Willson, 22 Nov. 1885, by A.W. Patterson,
    gosepl ministry.
Bruce, James to Mary Padget, 10 Jan. 1887, by A.V.P. Jones, JP.
Bryant, Calvin P. to Mary Jefferson, 29 May 1887, by Isaac Grant,
    JP.
Bryant, John to Mary Mealer, license bought 11 August 1868.
Bryant, John to Sarah E. Mealer, 2 May 1880, by John Holbert.
Bryant, John to Elizabeth Murphy, 26 Jan. 1886, by L.H. Triplett,
    OMG.
Bunch, John to Evory F. Bryant, 22 Dec. 1870, by Silvanus Hamrick,
    JP.
Bunch, Henry C. to Jane E. Anderson, 5 Aug. 1869, by T. A.
    McDaniel, MG.

Burges, D.F. to Mary Francis Manly, 16 Feb. 1879, by Thomas I. Stancil, JP.

Burgis, James C. to Lourana Mooney, 30 July 1868, by Wm. Westbrook, MG.

Burren, Jasper to Mary Ann Carver, 30 April 1876, by James Sharyer, JP.

Burrell, Joseph to Martha Burlison, 19 Feb. 1870, by J.M. West, MG.

Butler, James E. to Martha J. Bradford, 14 Aug. 1874, by E.T. King, JP & NP.

Cagle, John W. to Emma W. Addington, 16 Sep. 1880, by A. Crow, JP.

Calahan, W.G. to Mary Norton, 4 Oct. 1876, by William R. Allen, NP.

Call, E.J. to Susan Chilson, 4 Dec. 1887, by L.M. Taylor, MG.

Cantrell, John to Mossella Johnson, 27 Nov. 1870, by W.H. Simmons, Ord.

Cantrell, Sherman to Rhoda Ann Presley, 5 January 1886, by Jeremiah Sosebee, JP.

Carnes, Wilborn W. to Olevia C. Lawson, 10 Aug. 1874, by James P. Groover, JP.

Carney, Spartan G. to Martha A. Evans, license bought 6 Aug. 1868.

Cape, William D. to Mariah Ivie, 30 July 1868, by T.A. McDaniel, MG.

Cape, W.L. to M.D. Yancy, 11 Aug. 1886, by R.B. Striplin, MG.

Carr, T.S. to Caldona Striplin, 19 June 1886, by Isaac Grant, JP.

Carrol, Thomas T. to Emer Long, 7 Dec. 1885, by Parson Chadwick.

Carter, Elijah N. to Lavada Puckett, 7 Oct. 1880, by Samuel A. Ralston.

Carter, Miller to Thetos, Jordan, 16 Aug. 1885, by E. Wofford, NP.

Carver, Lewis C. to Marietta Lowery, 6 Oct. 1867, by R.B. Fulton, MG.

Carver, Manuel B. to Laura Ann Pearson, 15 Nov. 1868, by Jesse Padget, MG.

Carver, William D. to Susan Holder, 3 May 1868, by John A. Heard, JIC.

Chadwick, John to Georgia Ann Bell, 22 Apr. 1885, by A.B. Chadwick.

Chadwick, J.S. to L.A. Ganus, 6 Dec. 1883, by F.D. Harris, MG.

Chadwick, Lewis to Cinda Goss, 8 Nov. 1886, by H.L. Coffey, NP.

Chadwick, Thomas to Cleracy Carter, 2 Mar. 1884, by M.C. McClain, CSC.

Chambers, David to Margaret Wilson, 6 Mar. 1884, by J.P. Worley, JP.

Champion, Benjamin to Elizabeth Rich, 8 June 1868, by James Sharyer, JP.

Champion, Martin to Mary Hamby, 22 Feb. 1871, by E.P. King, JP.

Champion, Thomas C. to Rebecca Blackwell, 16 Sep. 1874, by S.M. Morton, JP.

Champion, William to Sarah Quinton, 29 Mar. 1868, by M.V. Coffey, JP.

Charles, W.B. to Amanda Taylor, 28 Jan. 1883, by James Sharyer, JP.

Chastain, F.M. to Sarah N. Chastain, 17 Jan. 1875, by Elder T.A. McDaniel.

Chastain, W.D. to Mary P. Anderson, 29 dec. 1887, by David anderson.

Chastain, William H. to Mary A. Gravley, 23 Dec. 1866, by J.D. Neal, JP.

Chasteen, Eligra to Cordelia Young, 31 Aug. 1873, by H.S.

Holbert, JP.

Chasteen, Joseph R. to Mandey Bunch, 23 Dec. 1858, by Caswell L. Corbin, JP.

Chumlee, James M. to Barbara M. Pendley, 22 Feb. 1878.

Chumbler, John to Salia Brooks, 3 Nov. 1885, by Thomas Honea, NP & JP.

Childers, Dolphus to Georgia Ann Jordan, license bought 18 October 1884.

Clark. J. Thaddeous to Catherine Rice, 16 Oct. 1873, by S. Hamrick, JP.

Clark, William G. to Mary Young, 19 Aug. 1877, by Elder J.J. Keeter, MG.

Cochran, James J. to Sarah Herreon, 3 Sept. 1885, by H.I. Ingram, MG.

Coffey, Henry L. to Rosle Arwood, 1 Jan. 1888, by Enoch S. Carr.

Coffey, William J. to Margaret Roe, 18 Oct. 1881, by J.B. Blackwell, MG.

Coffey, William L. to Nancy A. Drayman, 6 August 1865.

Collett, John to Callie Huggins, 20 Nov. 1879, by W.J. Wilson, JP.

Collins, A.G. to Nancy Ann Thompson, 5 Nov. 1868, by J.D. Neay, JP.

Collins, Giles (freedman) to Josephine Tate (freedwoman), 24 Oct. 1868, by Jeremiah Lambert, MG.

Compton, James N. to Arminda Wigington, 22 Oct. 1876, by James Sharyer, JP.

Compton, Thomas J. to Nancy Patterson, 24 July 1872, by Patterson Head (?), JP.

Cook, Isaac R. to Martha J. Turner, 4 June 1874, by J.J. Land, MG.

Cook. John G. to Martha Jane Nations, 13 Aug. 1876, by William M. Bearden, JP.

Cook, William P. to Amanda J. Moss, 22 Aug. 1880, by William Stone, MG.

Cook, William R. to Elizabeth J. Addison, 5 Feb. 1869, by Wm. M. Bearden, NP.

Cook, Worth to Margaret Turner, 25 Dec. 1873, by Rev. Joshua Cantrell, MG.

Corbin, Benjamin F. to Sarah E. King, 29 December 1866, by B.C. Hitt, MG.

Corbin, J.H. to Caroline Bruce, 19 July 1874, by W.B. Chambers, NP.

Corbin, John Henry to Arminda King, 15 August 1865.

Covington, J.T. to A.C. Duncan, 20 August 1886, by Elijah Roper, MG.

Cowart, A.W. to Mary Ann Burrell. 19 August 1872, by James W. West, MG.

Cowart, Merrit R. to Martha C. Ellingberg, 18 March 1872, by B.D. Cowart, MG.

Cowart, Peter to Malinda (E.) Swinford, 25 October 1877, by John Holbert, MG.

Cowart, Stephen D. to Eliza Compton, 19 September 1872, by John Holbert, MG.

Cox, J.H. to Martha Pendley, 2 November 1884, by John Darnell, JP.

Cox, James M. to Nancy E. Vaughn, 28 December 1871, by E.P. King, MG.

Craig, George T. to Mary Thomason, 26 July 1884, by Wm. M. Jones, MG.

Crite, Lige to Nancy Goss, 14 February 1885, by Silas Smith.

Crow, Ezekiel to Caroline Evans, 11 June 1876, by Thomas J.

Stancil, JP.
Crow, James A. to Amanda Pesley, 7 March 1869, by W.B. Chambers, JP.
Crow, James H. to E.E. Cook, 5 August 1886, by Wm. Jones, MG.
Crow, John M. to Nancy Tarbutton, 23 December 1866, by T.C. Whitfield, JP.
Crow, Kimsey to Lorrie Brock, 1 March 1888, by Enoch S. Carr, MG.
Crowder, James M. to Elizabeth M. Pendley, 22 September 1873, by S. Hamrick, NP.
Cross, Robert to Ophalia Eaton, 10 October 1875, by S. Hamrick, NP.
Day, Joshua Denny to Brelley West, 15 October 1858, by J. Lambert, MG.
Darnell, James P. (S.?) to Florence Johnson, 2 February 1888, by G.W. Fitts, JP.
Darnell, J.W. to Josie Fitzsimmons, 28 August 187-?, by L.T. Padget, MG.
Darnell, J.W.R. to Nora Reaves, 22 October 1886, by Rial B. Striplin, MG.
Darnel, Levi J. to Mary E. Barton, 6 June 1880, by George King, MG.
Darnell, Manson W. to Mary Jane Padget, 30 December 1869, by John Darnell, JP.
Darnell, W.J. (L.?) to Larenia Vincent, 14 September 1884, J.G. Chase, MG.
Darnell, William J. to Catherine Dover, 18 October 1866, by John Darnell, JP.
Davis, Ancil B. to Martha C. Cox, 22 February 1874, by A. Crow, JP.
Davis, Ancel B. to Mary C. Gozeman, 23 April 1885, by J.P. Worley, JP.
Davis, G.W. to Eby Fundy, November 19, 1857, by C.L. Corbin, JP.
Davis, James to Martha Somes, 29 July 1883, by W.W. Wright, JP.
Davis, Joseph to Louisa Chadwick, 18 February 1888, by Isaac Grant.
Dozey, Joseph Denny, see Day, Joseph Denny.
Dean, John M. to Harriett Chadwick, 23 June 1868, by Wm. C. Thompson, JP.
Dean, John J. to Tressa Corbin, 29 December 1858, by Caswell L. Corbin, JP.
Dean, W.H. to Mary Carver, 22 November 1876, by A.V.P. Jones, JP.
Dearing, Jeremiah to Sarahan R. Akins, 7 November 1875, by J.B. Harris, MG.
Dearing, R.B. to Martha Jane Fulton, 31 August 1883, by N.W. Blalock, O.M.G.
Dearing, Robert to Lucinda Evans, 18 August 1881, by E. Wofford, NP.
Derby, James B. to Margaret Pendley, 4 July 1876, by W.J. Wilson, JP.
Derby, James S. to Caldonia D. Wolley, 17 February 1886, by Jeremiah Sosebee, JP.
Derby, Henry to Margaret Sams, 11 October 1887, by Jeremiah Sosebee, NP.
Dillingham, Jehue M. to Martha E. Lemons, 2 August 1868, by A.P. Mullinax, JP.
Dimsel, Smith to Mary E. Wilson (b. 1851, daughter of W.J. Wilson), 21 June 1867.
Dimsdale, W.S. to Sarah L. Holcomb, 29 January 1888, by J.E.B. Lyon, JP.
Disharoon, Ervin C. to Sis Chumley (no dates, torn, signed 16 May 1880), by Thomas Honea, JP.

Disharoon, Ervin C. to Abby Brooks, 25 April 1880, by Dolphus
Gaddis, JP.

Disharoon, John H. to Martha Pendley, 17 February 1887, by Leroy
T. Padget, MG.

Dobson, W.M. to Martha Blackwell, 9 January 1887, by J.B. Blackwell, JP.

Dodd, Monroe to Lucinda Goss, 13 February 1886, by Rev. Silas
Smith.

Dorsey, Benjamin F. to Betty Ray, 30 May 1885, by J.A. Mewberry,
MG.

Dover, David H. to Eliza Manus, 5 January 1879, by John Darnell,
JP.

Dowda, James T. to Beedy Whitfield, 6 August 1865, by J.P. Worley, JP.

Duck, William to Manerva A. Westbrook, 3 November 1886, A.V.P.
Jones, JP.

Duckett, John W. to Jane Dunn, 21 May 1885, William J. Westbrook,
MG.

Duncan, John B. to Larah E. Partin, 12 February 1888, by L.T.
Padget, MG.

Dunlap, William to Mary Moss, 16 December 1868, by William C.
Thompson, JP.

Eaton, Jesse W. to Zilphia Dobson, 8 October 1874, by Jesse
Padgett, Minister of the Gospel.

Eaton, T.I. or Z.J. to Elizabeth Tolbert, 14 October 1875, by S.
hamrick, NP.

eller, William H. to Malinda A. Bramlett, 9 March 1871, by R.G.
Allen, NP.

Ellington, S. Robert to Lizza Ann Ledbetter, 16 October 1883, by
R.G. Woodall, JP.

Ellis, Andrew R. to Sarah M. Whisenant, 28 December 1868, by J.D.
Neal, JP.

Emory, Charles W. to Roxanah L. Dorsey, 19 July 1867, by R.B.
Fulton, MG.

Elrod, Alfred to Martha Godfrey, 2 April 1868, by James Sharyer,
JP.

Elrod, John T. to Elizabeth Bryant, 8 October 1869, by James
Sharyer, JP.

Elrod, Levie to Narcisse Bryant, 8 April 1869, by James Sharyer,
JP.

Elrod, Thomas to Mandy C. Dorsey, 1 February 1867, by John M.
Gaddis, JP.

Eubanks, Edward M. to ------- Sosebee, 31 August 1881, by E.W.
Allred, MG.

Eubanks, H.L. to Octabia Townsend, 2 January 1887, by Jeremiah
Sosebee, NP.

Eubanks, Reuben A. to Mary M. Ray, 3 September 1885, by Jeremiah
Sosebee, NP.

Eivens, George to Harriett McArthur, 2 February 1873, by James C.
Mulkey, GM.

Eivans, Harvey to Mary P. Langford, 29 December 1870, by Lemuel
S. Ivey, MG.

Evans, Benjamin F. to Eller C. Orr, 3 December 1871, by R.G.
Allen, JP.

Evans, J.A. to Liney Hightower, 13 January 1887, by William
Stone, MG.

Evans, M.D. to Elizabeth J. Chilson, 20 May 1883, by Rial B.
Striplin, MG.

Fann, George to Mary Taburaiux, 12 September 1875, by A.W.
Richards, MG.

Farmer, James F. to Nancy J. Simmons, 19 December 1886, by E.P.

Watson, JP.

Farmer, J.F. to Mary E. Cannon, 20 December 1885, by James P. Tauze, JP.

Farrell, William H. to Belle M. Teague, 21 February 1886, by Baxter D. Reid, MG.

Fawsett, James to ---------- ------------, 15 August 18--.

Fields, Eli to Easter Watkins, 30 December 1886, by J.A. Newberry.

Fields, J.M. to M.E. Coffey, 31 March 1887, by J.B. Blackwell, MG.

Fields, William L. to Susan D. Buchanon, 5 September 1872, by John Darnell, JP.

Findley, A.M. to L.M. Stoveall, 12 March 1886, by J.A. Newberry, MG.

Findley, Henry L. to Luseny Smith, 22 September 1858, by C.L. Corbin, JP.

Findley, Marion to Frances Jane Martin, 15 March 1858, by Caswell L. Corbin, JP.

Ferguson, James L. to Martha C. Hopkins, 26 December 1875, by H.G.B. Turner, MG.

Fitts, William E. to Callie Tatum, 29 March 1885, by Stephen Griffeth, NP.

Fleming, Charlie C. to Martha D. Allen, 10 October 1886, by A.W. Smith, minister of the gospel.

Fossett, Albert to Rosetta Ward, 23 January 1886, by Josiah Bagwell, JP.

Fossett, Chappel to Sarah A. Evans, 22 October 1871, by R. G. Allen, JP.

Fossett, George W. to Lucy Allen, 14 September 1876, by George T. King, MG.

Fountain, James F. to Amanda A. Caylor, 3 January 1872, by Jeremiah Lambert, MG.

Fouts, W.S. to Emma a. Morrison, 24 March 1875.

Fuller, Jesse to Sarah Turner, 25 September 1870.

Fuller, Z.T. to Amanda Catherine Talley, 17 December 1874, by W.B. Chambers, NP.

Fulton, Thomas J. to Mary D. Dearing, 7 August 1870, by Jeremiah Lambert, MG.

Fulton, William to Teresa Johnson, 30 December 1874, by William Westbrook, MG.

Gaddis, James W. to Martha Fosett, 23 December 1880, by Elder Thos. A. McDaniel.

Gaddis, John M. to Elizabeth Watkins, 20 December 1871, by R.G. Allen.

Gamboling, Isick Newton to Manervy Haselfing Forrester, 30 January 1877, by B.V.P. Jones.

Garied, Matthew T. to Feland Sams, 20 March 1878, by W.J. wilson, JP.

Garner, Joseph to Nancy Cagle, 24 August 1876, by John Holbert.

Gibson, J.H. to S.C. Clark. 29 April 1886, by James P. Tawzer, JP.

Goble, Henry to Milly Smith, 27 August 1868, by S. Hamrick, JP.

Godfrey, Francis M. to Manergy Reese, 3 October 1878, by Ing Wingington.

Goode, Joseph J. to Cary Vaughn, 15 April 1869, by John Darnel, JP.

Goss, John F. to Canzada Champion, 20 December 1885, by J.A. Newberry, MG.

Gravley, C.C. to Mandia Moss, 14 March 1875, by S. Hamrick, NP.

Gravley, Luke W. to Lovy Mime Swan, 27 October 1872, by H.S. Tolbert, JP.

Gravley, Samuel to Martha J. Moss (Bunch), 10 August 1868, by C.N. Trible, LD.

Greenwood, Frederick to Leah Lovicia Cantrell, 10 September 1872, by Jesse Padget, MG.

Griffeth, Caleb to Margaret A. Disharoon, 20 January 1884, by E.W. Allred, MG.

Grogan, George W. to Manervy Elrod, 11 August 1866, by A.P. Mullinax, JP.

Grogan, James W. to Teresa C. Smith. 1 February 1874.

Groover, James R. to Susannah A. Falkner, 8 July 1877, by John A. Darnell.

Groover, Thomas P. to Rebecca Ledbetter, 17 December 1871, by Doctor W. Padget, NP & JP.

Groover, William to Nancey Simmons, 18 April 1874, by E.T. King, JP.

Guyton, Joseph to Amanda Bell. 2 August 1874, by Abraham Chadwick, Minister.

Guring, William to Mary Jane Collins, 1 April 1888, by A. Murphy, MG.

Hagood, M.T. to Cordelia Anderson, 13 November 1887, by H.E. Ingram, MG.

Haygood, Zachariah T. to Mary J. Beavers, 19 December 1867, by Wm. F. Cantrell, MG.

Hales, Drayton C. to Sarah J. Cason, 8 August 1880, by John Darnell, JP.

Hales, Isaac to Sarah A.E. Reese, 29 September 1875, by Wm. Westbrook. MG.

Hall, Calvin to Mary A. Hayes, 23 February 1873, by John Holbert, MG.

Hammett, D.B. to A.J. Westbrook, 24 December 1885, by Rev. L.J. McArthur.

Hamilton, Willie to Savannah Townsend, 9 January 1887, by William Padget, MG.

Hammontree, George W. to Delilah J. Tabereaux, 6 January 1887, by J.A. Newberry, MG.

Hammontree, William N. to Mrs. Susan Swafford, 1 November 1885, by J.B. Blackwell, MG.

Hammontree, Sylvester to Nicy Eveline Howell, 16 December 1869, by Thomas Ray, NP & JP.

Hampton, G.C. to Callie Smith. 29 December 1882, by B.F. Warlick, NP (Gilmer County).

Harbin, Samuel M. to A.T.A. Edwards, 4 September 1887, by Jeremiah Sosebee.

Hardin, D.A. to H.A. Roper, 25 December 1872, by Sylvanus Hamrick, JP.

Hardin, Caleb to Sarah Hutchens, 27 September 1874, by W.B. Chambers, NP.

Harden, Calep to Sarah M. Carver, 15 August 1880.

Hardy, M.C. to Roxie Harris, 31 October 1886, by William Padget, MG.

Harris, J.F. to Josa Mann, 13 September 1885, by William Stone, MG.

Harris, Singleton C. to Hannah Waldrop, 17 August 1876, by W.B. Chambers, JP.

Hazelwood, John F. to Mary Duck. 5 April 1877, by W.B. Chambers, JP.

Heath, Jospeh P. to Ellender J. Turner, 7 January 1872, by W.B. Chambers, NP.

Heath, Robert to Elizabeth Colbert, 4 August 1868, by W.T. Cantrell, JP.

Henderson, A.P. to Callie Loveless, 29 October 1881, by E.R. Allred, NP.

Henderson, John W. to Amanda Taylor, 21 October 1869, by W.B.

Chambers, JP.

Hendrix, Andrew J. to Mary Pendley, 23 January 1879, by John Darnell, JP.

Hensley, W.J. to M.J. Cowart, 21 October 1877, by John Holbert, MG.

Herren, Augustus to Angeline D. McArthur, 30 May 1869, by R.G. Allen, NP.

Herren, Martin to Mary Nelson, 1 February 1872, by W.B. Chambers, NP.

Herrin, William to Nancy E. Brown, 25 August 1872, by G.D.L. Green, JP.

Hethcock, John N. to Mary L. Spence, 26 November 1876, by T.J. Stancil, JP.

Hightower, Columbus to Rebecca Young, 3 April 1879, by Elder Thomas A. McDaniel.

Hightower, George to Martha J. Williams, 28 September 1871, by W.B. Chambers, JP.

Hightower, George W. to Mary Evins, 7 November 1872, by Silvanus Hamrick, JP.

Hightower, J.N. to Samantha Palmer, 29 December 1887, by A.V.P. Jones, JP.

Hill. George to Caroline Jefferson, 13 February 1871, by J.D. Neal, JP.

Hitt, John L. to Nancy Cochran, 29 August 1879, by H.T. Ingram.

Hitt, David R. to Martha Jane Ray, 30 October 1873, by Thomas J. Stancil.

Hodgens, Wm. H. to Sarah C. Dobson, 22 August 1880, by A.P. Dobson, MG.

Hogan, Joseph to Sallie Eubanks, 5 October 1885, by Jeremiah Sosebee, NP.

Hogan, William to Sarah Corbin, 31 December 1882, by H.P. Sheffield, MG.

Holbert, Isaac to Amiller Hambrick, 31 August 1879, by John Holbert, PJ.

Holbert, James L. to Malinda Ingram, 30 November 1876, by John Holbert, PJ.

Holcomb, Isiac to Lucinda Reynolds, 5 February 1879, by Wm. Blackwell, NP & JP.

Holcomb, Jackson to Rebecca Ann Cook, 6 March 1873, by william M. Bearden, JP.

Holcomb. John to Nancy E. Sams, 4 January 1877, by W.J. Wilson, JP.

Holcomb, Josiah to Lucinda Reynolds, 5 February 1879, by William Blackwell, JP.

Holcomb. Mac to Annise Padget, 17 February 1867, by R.B. Fulton, MG.

Holcomb. Thomas F. to Adeline Lambert, 1 September 1872, by Jeremiah Lambert, MG.

Holmes, C.W. to Mary Jane Puckett, 17 September 1885, by A.W. Patterson, MG.

Holmes, David to Lucinda Chadwick, 15 October 1875, by A. Chadwick.

Holmes, J.M.F. to Mary E. Gravley, 27 September 1866, by Thomas A. McDaniel, MG.

Holmes, Marion to Caldonia A. Dunkin, 27 September 1873, by B.F. Warlick. NP & JP.

Holt, Cicero to Zalona A. Price, 20 August 1882, by E.P. Watson, NP.

Honea, James F. to Mary M. Canady, 8 August 1869, by A.F. Honea, MG.

Honea, James T. to Lila Bozeman, 5 December 1869.

Hood, Samuel to Malisa Corbin, 29 December 1858, by Caswell I.
    Corbin, JP.
Howard, Samuel to Martha Darnell, 12 January 1869, by Jesse
    Padgett, minister.
Howard, Thomas to Mary Watkins, 25 November 1883, by T. Pickett,
    MG.
Howell, Russel to Maryan Disharoon, 21 November 1878, by A.W.
    Richards.
Howell, E.W. to M.C. Anders, 19 March 1887, by Jeremiah Sosebee,
    NP.
Hudgins, William B. to Lizer J. Bozeman, 12 January 1882, by
    Josiah Bagwell, JP.
Huggins, William R. to Margie Bozeman, 15 September 1880, by
    William Blackwell, JP.
Hudlow, Andrew J. to Elvira Padgett, 9 February 1871, by Doctor
    W. Padgett, NP.
Hurlick, Stephen to Betsey Tate, 26 January 1888, by Isaac Grant,
    JP.
Hutcherson, Willie to Emmet McClure, 10 December 1887, by Aaron
    Murphy, MG.
Hyde, Jasper to Mary Chastain, 1 July 1886, by B.B. Bradley.
Ingram, I.N. to Sarah Pinyen, 27 January 1876, by E.P. King, JP.
Ingram, Samuel to Martha J. Aiken, 20 November 1870, by Thomas
    Ray, NP & JP.
Ingram, William A. to D.C. Smith, 16 April 1887, by William
    Padgett, MG.
Ivie, W.H. to Disa Evans, 23 June 1867, by Lemuel S. Ivey, JP.
Jackson, Gral. A. to Nancy H. McCloud, 2 February 1879, by Elder
    Thomas A. McDaniel.
Jackson, W.F. to Isabel Kelley, 22 April 1875, by Elder T.A.
    McDaniel.
James, Erwin M. to Huida C. Sharyer, 22 August 1880, by J.B.
    Harry, MG.
James, J.H. to Linda Eubanks, 4 December 1887, by Jeremiah Sose-
    bee, NP.
Jefferson, Jonas (black) to Larra Blackwell (black), 20 December
    1883, by Aaron Murphey, MG.
Jefferson, Samuel (black) to Elsey McHan (black), 29 July 1883,
    by A. Murphey.
Jefferson, Samuel to Hanah McHan, 29 May 1887, by Isaac Grant, JP.
Johnson, Albert to Martha Jane Hamilton, no dates, permission by
    father Wm. J. Hamilton.
Johnson, Edward to Eliza Scote, 27 May 1877, by Wm. Westbrook.
Johnson, John B. to Hannah Kimmons, 27 January 1879, by John
    Holbert, PG.
Johnson, Robert to Margaret Smith, 15 March 1866, by Thomas A.
    McDaniel, MG.
Jones, Andrew V. to Violet McCutchens, 1 October 1871, by E.L.
    King, JP.
Jones, G.A. to Nancy H. McCloud, 2 February 1879, by Thomas A.
    McDaniel.
Jones, J.B. to Lizzie James, 6 February 1887, by J.R. Allen, MG.
Jones, Thomas to Sarah A. Dooley, 2 January 1870, by John Darnel,
    Jr., JP.
Jones, William B. to Elizabeth Evans, 5 September 1875, by Rev.
    Joshua Cantrell, MG.
Jones, W.E. to Clementine Pact, 23 October 1870, by T.A.
    McDaniel, MG.
Jones, W.N. to Martha J. McHan, 16 March 1873, by Silvanus
    Hamrick, JP.
Jones, William N. to Rebecca Willis, 4 December 1874, by T.A.

McDaniel, MG

Jones, William M. to Sarah E. Adair, 10 September 1885, by A.V.P. Jones, JP.

Jones, Rial T. to Elizabeth Thompson, 24 December 1875, by A.V.P. Jones, JP.

Kirby, Henry to Frances Jones, 28 December 1874.

Keeter, Carter T. to Mary C. Eubanks, 23 December 1883, by E.R. Allred, NP.

Keeter, John G. to Mary J. Morris, 22 August 1880, by E.B. Allred, JP.

Kell, John A. to Martha M. Wilson, 13 January 1878, by Elder T.A. McDaniel.

Kelley, Andrew J. to Emily J. Johnson, 20 February 1877, by E.P. Watson, JP.

Kenedy, W.A. to Sallie Evans, 22 September 1886, by H.G.B. Turner, MG.

Key, Newton to Catherine Key, 30 June 1867, by James Sharyer, JP.

Kimmons, James J. to Malinda Lansdown, 5 November 1885, by john M. Gaddis, JP.

Kirby, Stephen to Mary Mann, 3 October 1869, by Ebenezer P. King, JP.

Knot, Walt to Sophia Davis, 4 September 1887, by Isaac Grant, JP.

Lambert, Joseph A. to Voletia S. Mulkey, 8 May 1884, by William Stone, JP.

Langley, Albert to Elizabeth Ann Mathis, 13 October 1874, by B.F. Warlick, NP.

Langley, Locke to Jane Taylor, 11 July 1869, by J.C. Goble, NP.

Langston, M.S. to R.L. Wickett, 1 January 1886, by B.B. Bradley, NP.

Lankston, Jacob to Sallie McHan, 27 November 1881, by Aaron Murphey, MG.

Lawing, E.W. to Lucinda Burrell, 3 November 1882, by Rev. D.C.P. Carter.

Lawson, Franklin (black) to Nancy Townsend (black), 30 June 1872, by John Darnell, JP.

Lewis, John H.L. to Nancy Jane Jones, 14 December 1886, by David Anderson.

Linkenfelt, James to Mandy Fricks, 22 April 1886, by E.P. Watson, NP.

Little, Martin E. to Julian Whitfield, 1 August 1869, by B.C. Hitt, MG.

Logan, Jacob to Canzady Allen, 15 November 1885, by W.J. Pool, JP.

Long, Charlie to Miss Maggie Day, 15 January 1888, by M.S. Williams, MG.

Long, John M. to Clarisa M. Griffin, 8 September 1878, by E.P. Watson, NP.

Long, John N. to Ariey Wigdon, 24 December 1883, by B.F. Warlick, NP.

Low, Hiram to Elizabeth Huggins, 14 October 1877, by T. Pickett, MG.

Lowman, Martin B. to Ellender Thomas, 12 September 1869, by Sylvanus Hamrick, JP.

Loveless, Barton to Susan M. Ferguson, 25 December 1872, by W.B. Chambers, JP.

Loveless, J.M. to Ellen Presley, 12 October 1881, by E.R. Allred, NP.

Lyon, Albert Redden to Kincy Finley, 4 October 1881, by James P. Tanzer, JP; permission given by N. Finley.

Mahan, Cage (black) to Harriett McClure (black), 5 March 1876, by Aaron Murphey, MG.

Mahall, John E. (black) to Melinda E. Jefferson (black), 22 April 1868, by Jeremiah Lambert, GM.

Manley, A.C. to Mary Ann Burgess, 13 August 1885, by W.B. Allred, MG.

Manley, William G. to Margaret O. Nicholson, 6 February 1876, by A.F. Honea, MG.

Mann, Calvin A. to Julia F. Anderson, 5 January 1873, by A.F. Honea.

Martin, Berryman H. to Martha A. Pence, 8 December 1876, by Wm. Westbrook, MG.

Martin, John S. to Lansy Rice, 12 July 1873.

Martin, Juland M. to Lula Mullins, 15 February 1886, by Wm. M. James, MG.

McArthur, A.G. to Darkes Jane Teague, no dates.

McArthur, Rugus V. to Mary A. Burrell, 25 March 1888, by A.M. Johnson, JP.

McCall, E.J. to Susan Chillson, 4 December 1887, by L.M. Taylor, MG.

McCloud, William to Roxey Pack, 31 January 1876, by Elder J.A. McDaniel.

McCluer, Brag to Alverda Herlick, 8 November 1883, by Aaron Murphy, MG.

McClare, Dan to Louisa McHan, 20 September 1885, by Aaron Murphy, MG.

McCollum, James R. to Ruthy Roe, 14 September 1868.

McCollum, Robert to Frances Gravley, 31 July 1866, by J.D. Neal, JP.

McCue, George to Archa Ash, 22 August 1880, by Ezekiel Akins, MG.

McCutchens, J.R. to Catherine Loveless, 23 January 1870.

McDaniel, Jackson M. to Malinda Chastain, 19 February 1874, by H.S. Tolbert, JP.

McDaniel, Jonathan H. to Mary C.J. Holmes, 13 May 1869, by Wm. E. Thompson, JP.

McDaniel, W.H. to Ida Ellis, 8 January 1888, by David Anderson, MG.

McElroy, Alphanus to Sophroney C. Blaylock, 23 October 1884, by J.G. Chastain, MG.

McFarland, John H. to Adeline Childers, 6 October 1868, by William E. Thompson, JP.

McGaha, Wm. P. to Margaret Norton, 15 February 1874, by Stephen Griffeth, JP.

McGaha, Wm. S. to Minerva A. Lewis, 21 February 1886, by J.A. Newberry, MG.

McHan, Abe to Georgia Ann McClure, 19 October 1884, by A. Murphy, MG.

McHan, Alanson to Sarah C. McHan, 28 October 1869, by F.M. Williams, MG.

McHan, Alfred W. to Arminda Roe, 23 January 1869, by H.B. Johnson, MG.

McHan, Barnabus to Cynthia Ferguson, 16 December 1866, by F.M. Williams, MG.

McHan, Henry M. to Mary A. Bearden, 4 September 1867. by F.M. Williams, MG.

McHan, Lewis T. to Mary F. Thomas, 4 August 1878, by W.B. Chambers, JP.

McKinney, Willis to Ketter Larman, 27 July 1874, by Aaron Murphy, MG.

McMillen, Franklin L. to Salina Gartrell, 11 October 188e, by Wm. Cagle, MG.

McPherson, G.R. to Amanda Godfrey, 18 October 1883, by L.J. McArthur, MG.

Mealor, Robert to Catherine Cowart, 4 November 1866.
Mealor, R.M. to Drusilla Cowart, 14 July 1874, by Isaac Burlison,
    JP.
Medlin, C.H. to Martha Hales, 6 February 1887, by David Anderson.
Meddlin, James F. to Mary M. Yancy, 30 January 1879, by Q.V.P.
    Jones, JP.
Mills, Joseph L. to Mary Hitt, 10 August 1879, by H.T. Ingram,
    MG.
Monroe, Thomas P. to Martha Pendley, 29 May 1879, by John Darnel,
    JP.
Mooney, William C. to Rebecca Blalock, 3 March 1869, by T.A.
    McDaniel, MG.
Moore, William to Mary Ann Moss, 12 August 1866, by H.J. Mills,
    JP.
Morgan, Henry to Larra Gilstrap, 5 March 1888, by Jeremiah
    Sosebee, JP.
Morris, Jessie to Rozilla Dorsey, 23 July 1883, by A.F. Honea,
    MG.
Morris, Joseph B. to Sarah L. Morris, 8 September 1880.
Morris, Henry F. to Emmeline Nelson, 9 August 1866, by B.C. Hitt,
    MG.
Morris, Perry H. to Sarah L. Tapp, 4 April 1869, by B.C. Hitt,
    MG.
Morris, Samuel K. to Phedonia Smith, 1 August 1866, by H.J.
    Mills, JP.
Morris, Thomas C. to Margaret Andrews, no date.
Moss, Robert M. to Manda T. Bruce, 3 February 1886, by A.V.P.
    Jones, JP.
Moss, Pinckney to Hester Roper, 5 December 1886, by A.V.P.
    Jones, JP.
Mullins, Alfred W. to Elizabeth Dunnegan, 4 November 1866, by
    Jeremiah Lambert, GM.
Mullins, D.B. to C.L. Jones, 6 November 1879, by W.B. Chambers,
    JP.
Mullins, Elias L. to Samantha Williamson, 17 December 1878, by
    R.B. Fuller, MG.
Mullins, Martin Z. to Phala A. Corbitt, 2 December 1866, by
    Silvanus Hamrick, JP.
Mullinax, Manual to Elsey McCutchens, 1 March 1885, by Aaron
    Murphy, MG.
Murphy, A. to Effie Blackwell, 29 December 1887, by L.M. Taylor,
    MG.
Neal, Isaac to Martha Ann Evans, 30 December 1875, by William
    Stone, MG.
Neal, M.P. to Sarah Baily, 18 August 1879, by A.V.P. Jones, JP.
Nichols, thomas J. to Martha J. Evans, 22 September 1869.
Micholson, George C. to Salenia Hearren, 26 January 1886, by
    Jacob Holbert, minister of the gospel.
Norton, William Thomas to Julia Pendley, 14 July 1867, by James
    Sharyer, JP.
Padget, Allison Alonzo to Mrs. Mary Hitt (?), 21 June 1868, by
    Jeremiah Lambert, MG.
Padget, Columbus to Mary M. Hendrix, 1 May 1880, by E.W. Allred,
    MG.
Padget, Henry to Rhoda Smith. 17 February 1870, by A.W. Richards,
    MG.
Padget, Ire to Frances Evans, 13 October 1872, by W.B. Chambers,
    JP.
Padget, Jacob A. to Melissa E. Blackwell, 14 October 1875, by
    Jesse Padget, MG.
Padget, Peter A.D. to Martha E. Darnell, 22 February 1869, by

B.B. Disharoon, JP.

Padget, Sanford W. to Mary Fitts, 13 December 1875, by S. Griffeth, NP.

Padgett, William to Malinda Dillbeck. 4 October 1886, by R.B. Striplin, MG.

Pack, James to Altha Griffeth. 28 October 1876, by Elder T.A. McDaniel.

Parker, Francis to Mary Cardell, 11 April 1873, by E.L. Chadwick.

Parker, Samuel to Josephine Norton, 15 December 1886, by A.W. Richards, MG.

Parris, Joseph S. to Sarah E. Killian, 28 July 1880, by S. Hamrick, NP.

Patten, Samuel Anthony (black) to Cunia Ann Jefferson (black). 29 December 1875, by E.D. Jefferson, JP.

Payne, C.W. to Nancy J. Cook, 13 February 1876, by William M. Bearden, JP.

Pearce, Floyd A. to Eliza L. Cayler, 2 March 1871, by Wm. J. Thompson.

Pearce, William T. to Eliza Curtis, 1 November 1866, by Thomas P. Manning, JP.

Pearson, Ephraim to Mary Revis, 8 May 1867, by W.T. Cantrell.

Pearson, Lafayette to Rebecca Reavis, 16 March 1872, by John Holbert.

Pendley, Alfred W. to Nancy E. Moss, 1 January 1874, by John Darnel, Jr., JP.

Pendley, Barnabus to Jane Edwards, 18 September 1876, by Elias W. Allred.

Pendley, Carter to Mary Stegall. 29 December 1878, by John Darnell, JP.

Pendley, Elias W. to Rhoda P. Hales, 29 August 1880, by John Darnell, JP.

Pendley, Henry I. to Esther H. Cathlin, 25 October 1874, by John Darnel, JP.

Pendley, John L. to Mary Seay, 14 February 1876, by Jeremiah Sosebee, NP.

Pendley, J.M. to George Ann Ledford, 25 September 1879, by John M. Gaddis, JP.

Pendley, Thomas to Catherine Darnell, 11 September 1879, by E.W. Allred, MG.

Pendley, T.E. to Martha M. Disharoon, 11 September 1887, by L.T. Padgett, MG.

Pendley, T.M. to M.E. Coffey, 21 December 1884, by William Stone, MG.

Pendley, William to Missouri Arena Chumbley, 4 July 1874.

Pendley, Samuel to Martha E. Bruce, 24 September 1874, by W.B. Chambers, NP.

Pharr, Gabriel A. to Mary A. Harris, 20 September 1874, by H.G.B. Turner, MG.

Perry, B.A. to Martha L. Davis, November (the rest of the document is torn).

Perry, John H. to Artemesie Partin, 1 April 1880, by E.B. Allred, MG.

Pettigrew, Wm. M. to Arranda M. Woodring, 25 July 1880, by W.B. Chambers, NP.

Pettett, C.G. to B.V.D. Moss, 1 December 1887, by William Padget, MG.

Pettit, Benjamin M. to Theodosia West, 17 December 1878, by T. Pickett.

Pettit, Christopher Columbus to Missouri E. Fields, 22 November 1868, by S.M. Norton, JP.

Pettit, Perry W. to Billy Louisa Lansdown, 3 October 1872, by

John Darnel, Jr., JP.

Pickett, Joseph to T. Millison Glenn, 23 December 1866, by James C. Mulky, MG.

Pierce, Henery Jonas to Luguesy Wilson, 28 November 1875, by B.F. Warlick, NP.

Pike, Andrew J. to Mary J. McKinney, 5 September 1886, by J.S. Wigington.

Pinyan, D.S. to Mary Texaner Worley, 1 October 1885, by L.T. Padget, MG.

Pinyan, John to Sarah J. Waldroup, 28 August 1872, by W.B. Chambers, JP.

Powel, D.S. to Rhoda Ann Moss, 24 August 1884, by Elder T.A. McDaniel.

Powell, James R. to R.A. Godfrey, 6 July 1883, by B.F. Warlick, JP.

Prater, John Daniel to Martha Barrett, 29 January 1874, by T.A. McDaniel, MG.

Prater, Thomass to Amanda A. Barrett, 7 September 1873, by H.S. Tolbert, NP.

Prather, Henry W. to Alice Barrett, 28 September 1879, by Elder Thomas A. McDaniel.

Presley, Cicero to Emily C. McCrary, 21 March 1869, by A.F. Honea, MG.

Presley, Robert T. to Mary Hopkins, 18 February 1872, by A.F. Honea, MG.

Presley, W.T. to R.J. Cook, 14 September 1884, by William Stone, MG.

Presley, Zachariah to Elizabeth Ann Hopkins, 21 June 1874, by A. Crow, JP.

Price, Calvin J. to Georgia Johnson, 23 November 1876, by William Stone, MG.

Price, Charles to Catherine Brown, 11 April 1869, by William Westbrook, MG.

Prince, A.W. to Emiline Tatum, 22 July 1887.

Pool, Samuel T. to Julian Carver, 5 March 1868, by James Sharyer, JP.

Pool, William to Elizabeth Dearing, 18 August 1874, by H.G.B. Turner, MG.

Pool, W.W. to Caroline Elrod, 19 April 1874, by James Sharyer, JP.

Qualls, Robert to Elizabeth Ledbetter, 17 March 1871, before Doctor W. Padget, NP.

Quinton, J. to Mollie Ray, 21 December 1884, by Rial B. Striplin, MG.

Raper, J.W. to Rosety McLeod, 28 December 1883.

Raines, G.B. to J.M. Hales, 4 November 1883. by William Stone, MG.

Ray, Augustus to Amanda Mann, 24 September 1882, by Wm. Westbrook, MG.

Ray, John F. to Lucinda Carver, 22 July 1883, by William M. Bearden, JP.

Ray, J.W. to Georgian Ward, 21 October 1886, by J.A. Newberry.

Reeves, William to Julia Halk, 20 May 1883, by William Stone, MG.

Reese, Solomon K. to Catherine E. Taylor, 25 December 1873, by Wm. Westbrook, MG.

Reese, W.H. to M.J. Evans, 21 December 1869, by A.F. Honea, MC.

Renedy (Kenedy?), W.A. to Sallie Evans, 21 September 1886, by H.G.B. Turner, MG.

Revis, William to Louisa Darnell, 2 November 1879, by H.G. Holbert, NP.

Rice, Cansel L. to Angeline Keith, 15 December 1872, by Silvanus

Hamrick, NP.

Ridings, Charles to Margaret Stephens, 10 May 1876, by W.J. Wilson, JP.

Rider, Evan B. to Lourana Crow, 9 July 1876, by Thomas J. Stancil, JP.

Ridings, Hosea to Dicy Grenshaw, 24 March 1871.

Ridings, Jeptha to Sarah Jane Hearden, 16 April 1868, by F.M. Williams, MG.

Richards, F.C. to Octavia Allen, 22 December 1887, by Isaac Grant, JP.

Richards, Stephen C. to Mary J. Barbers, 29 August 1869, by Thomas Hudlow, JP.

Richards, William A. to Samantha Cornellson, 3 October 1879, by A. Crow, JP.

Rippy, Thomas E. to Louisa Jane Crenshaw, 1 October 1867, by Wm. Tate, JIC.

Roe, Ancil to Eveline Cantrell, 14 December 1873, by Wm. Bearden, JP.

Roe, Horatio V. to Mary J. Bozeman, 7 August 1870, by W.B. Chambers, JP.

Rolen, Thomas to Mary Parker, 30 December 1883, by John Darden, JP.

Roling, Robert to Jane Johnson, 21 April 1875, by H.G.B. Turner, MG.

Roper, A.H. to Nannie Smith, 28 June 1885, by A.V.P. Jones, JP.

Roper, Benjamin F. to Martha Martin, 7 November 1867, by F.M. Williams, MG.

Roper, J.W. to Roseyty Mcleod, 28 December 1883, by A. Chadwick.

Ross, William N. to Mary L. Collis, 5 February 1885, by E.W. Wofford, NP.

Rowlan, Robert to Malinda Palmour, 19 February 1867, by J.D. Neal, JP.

Sams, Christopher to Susan A. Mills, 22 January 1874, by F.M. Williams, MG.

Sams, James C. to Nancy Derby, 3 January 1886, by Jeremiah Sosebee, JP.

Sams, Samuel T. to Martha M.E. Hogan, 31 October 1878, by E.W. Allred, MG.

Samuels, Theodore J. to Zilphia Emmerlissa Reese, 23 June 1873, by Wm. Westbrook, MG.

Sauges, James C. to Susannah Taylor, 20 December 1875, by J.B. Harris, JP.

Scott, John to Aliza Reese, 21 October 1881, by J.D. Harris, MG.

Shellhorse, Henry to Elizabeth Bryant, 22 June 1872, by Silvanus Hamrick, JP.

Shelton, Andrew J. to Nancy Mae Payne, 5 February 1871, by W.B. Chambers, JP.

Silvers, James to Nancy Ann Wilson, 9 August 1869, by Henry W. Head, MG.

Silvers, Samuel to Maranda Holmes, 16 October 1866, by T. McDaniel, MG.

Silvers, S. to Janie Silvers, 30 January 1876, by J.N. Parker, MG.

Sims, William B. to Rebecca Blackwell, 10 June 1883, J.A. Newberry, MG.

Simmons, James to Jane Wilson, 21 November 1876, by John H. Mashburn, MG.

Simmons, James A. to Nancy Shelley, 2 March 1876, by James Sharyer, JP.

Simmons, James E. to Mary Hayne, 15 August 1886, by A.W. Johnson, JP.

Simmons, John F. to S.E. Forrester, 20 November 1879, by Geo. T. King, MG.

Simmons, Robert R. to Ida V. Jones, 18 January 1880, by T. Pickett, MG.

Simmons, Samuel W. to Martha Seay, 11 September 1876, by A.W. Richards, MG.

Simmons, T.G. to L.A. Chapman, 17 November 1886, by Isaac Grant, JP.

Slagle, W.F. to Ella Haley, 18 May 1886, by B.B. Quillion, MG.

Smith, Alfred to Elizabeth A. Potts, 27 November 1870, by A.W. Richards, MG.

Smith, Charley to Eveline Allen, 16 January 1886, by E. Hood (?), ordinary. Also written on the license are the names George Allen, Charley Smith, and Noah Lawson.

Smith, D.W. to Eliza Sharptior, 5 March 1873, by S. Hamrick. NP.

Smith, Georga to Vina Padget, 5 December 1869, by Jeremiah Lambert, MG.

Smith, Joel K. to Emalina D. Fuller, 5 June 1878, by W.B. Chambers, JP.

Smith, Moses to Mary Larmon, 10 April 1872, by W.B. Chambers, JP.

Smith, S.C. to Eveline Yancy, 30 March 1873, by Silvanus Hamrick, NP.

Sosebee, John to Mary Ann Densmore, 20 October 1885, by John P. Worley, JP.

Sosebee, William G. to Catherine Edwards, 16 July 1876, by John Darnell, JP.

Southern, Robert to Catherine Hamrick, 11 December 1876, by John Russell, JP.

Stancil, U.L. to Mary Whitfield, 1 February 1877, by T.G. Stancil, JP.

Stanfield, E.L. to Barbara Tabriuax, 28 January 1885, by J.A. Newberry, MG.

Stearns, A.H. to R.E. Stephens, 13 October 1874, by J.J. Harris, MG.

Stearns, L.G. to L.V. James, 1 April 1877, T. Pickett, MG.

Steel, James M. to Harriett L. Godfrey, 3 February 1875, by L.H. McArthur, JP.

Stegal, Andrew H. to Amanda Swafford, 11 February 1877, by John Darnell, JP.

Stegal, Sherman to Malinda Pendley, 1 November 1885, by H.P. Sheffield, MG.

Stephens, James M. to Telitha McLeod, 17 January 1884, by A. Chadwick.

Stokes, Andrew J. to Mary D. Ganus, 23 February 1886, by J.R. Allen, MG.

Stone, Marion to Sarah Carpenter, 28 February 1886, by Elder T.A. McDaniel.

Stone, David A. to Martha C. Grogan, 20 November 1883, by Samuel Roper, MG.

Stoner, Andrew A. to Laura D. Cornelison, 27 February 1876, by Thomas J. Stancil, JP.

Strickland, John W. to Harriett Darnell, 13 March 1870, by John Darnell, Jr., JP.

Striplin, John A. to Martha L. Ivey, 10 November 1868, by L.S. Ivey, JP.

Sudduth, William to Martha Fossell, 5 November 1871, by R.G. Allen, JP.

Sumner, William T. to Dora A. Baley, 25 November 1877, by B.F. Warlick. NP.

Sutton, James A. to Florence P. Mullins, 8 May 1874, by Jeremiah Lambert, MG.

Swafford, Miles to Susan Patterson, 23 February 1868. by John
    Darnell, Jr., JP.
Swan, James M. to Tabitha E. Renney, 12 January 1873, by L.S.
    Ivey, MG.
Tate, Caleb R. to Winney Pendley, 23 November 1874, by E.W.
    Allred, MG.
Talley, Newton M. to Georgia Ann Norrell, 17 October 1869, by
    J.B. Harris, MG.
Tatum, Edward M. to Sarah J. Bryan, 18 March 1880, by B.F.
    Warlick, NP.
Tatum, Horatio to Nancy M. Darnell, 9 February 1879, by John T.
    Chapman.
Tatum, J.C. to Angeline Ammons, 11 February 1883, by L.J.
    McArthur.
Tatum, John W. to Lula Duckett, 30 June 1887, by J.R. Allen, MG.
Tatum, W.R. to Margaret Selena Long, 27 August 1878. by I.G.
    Chase, MG.
Taylor, G.N. to Mary Tatum, 8 January 1888. by J.R. Allen, MG.
Taylor, J.W. to Melissa E. Smith, 10 October 1871, by Thaddeus
    Pickett, MG.
Taylor, William to Nellie Griffeth, 29 August 1868, by A.P.
    Mullinax, JP.
Taylor, William R. to Callie Biddy, 30 September 1882, by James
    P. Grover, NP.
Thacker, Dock to Tinie Standfield, 19 December 1886, by Wm.
    Cagle, MG.
Thacker, F.N. to Olive Standfield, 7 April 1887, by Wm. Cagle,
    MG.
Thomas, Thomas F. to Sophronia Bradley, 4 March 1886, by A.W.
    Richards, MG.
Thomason, George W. to Ida Simmons, 30 August 1865, by Shrayer,
    JP.
Thompson, Clark to Rosannah Williams, 8 October 1871, by W.B.
    Chambers, JP.
Thompson, Hugh L. to Nancy Ann Kell, 7 September 1868, by Wm.
    Westbrook, MG.
Thompson, James to Nancy Jones, 30 November 1887, by A.V.P.
    Jones, JP.
Thompson, John W. to Cintha T. Moss, 11 January 1874, by H.G.B.
    Turner, MG.
Thompson, W.B. to Julia Ann Waldroup, 6 April 1873, by A.W.
    Honea, MG.
Tomberlin, Harvey C. to Roxanna Darnell, 9 February 1871, by John
    Darnell. Jr., JP.
Tomblin, James A. to Mary Ann Gaddis, 26 August 1883, J. A.
    Newberry, MG.
Townsend, Elias Carter to Martha Carney, 5 August 1866, by B.C.
    Hitt, MG.
Townsend, J.H. to Margaret L. Cole, 15 July 1883, by William
    Stone, MG.
Turner, B.W. to Juleyan M. Corbin, 25 March 1872, by Silvanus
    Hamrick.
Turner, George T. to Penelope J. Henderson, 30 September 1865, by
    William W. Bearden, JP.
Turner, George T. to Adeline Murdock. 29 August 1886, by W.B.
    Chambers, JP.
Turner, James M. to Susan Virginia Thomason, 2 September 1881,
    by W.B. Chambers, JP.
Turner, Memory to Martha Adoline Larmon, 12 September 1872, by
    W.B. Chambers, JP.
Ward, Wesley to Emiline Tatum, 5 January 1888, by L.T. Padget, MG.

Warlick, W.H. to E.A. McMillan, 13 August 1874, by Thaddeus
Pickett, MG.

Warren, Monroe T. to Nancy Nicholson, 19 October 1876, by Thomas
J. Stancil, JP.

Washington, James H. (black) to Eliza Murphey (black), 30
September 1868, by L.S. Ivey, JP.

Watkins, G.H. to Nancy E.V. Ledford, 3 Janaury 1883, by J.D.
Harris, MG.

Watkins, Joseph to Martha Quinton, 24 November 1866, by A.P.
Mullinax, JP.

Watkins, William A. to Ellen King, 10 October 1887, by Jordon
Presley, NP.

Watson, E.P. to Harriett E. Groover, 30 April 1868, by Wm. Westbrook.

Wehunt, H.L. to M.C. Richards, 23 December 1883, by H.P. Sheffield, MG.

West, Lovan to Mary Lucinda Berry, 2 September 1869, by E.P.
King, JP.

West, Mordica F. to Ann Chatham, 15 March 1868, by William C.
Thompson, JP.

West, Samuel to Mary Jane Murphy, 2 January 1873, by S. Hammrick,
NP.

Westbrook, Alfred to Sarah Ann Pool, 24 December 1873, by R.B.
Fulton, MG.

Westbrook, Cicero to Martha Ganus, 4 November 1883, by J.A.
Newberry, MG.

Westbrook, James W. to Margaret A. Reeves, 20 August 1874.

Whisenant, Thomas to Lucinda C. Striplin, 9 August 1868, by H.
Tribble.

White, Ira to Luisa Jane Bennett, 13 January 1876, by S. Hamrick,
NP. (Ira White was born in Gwinnett County, GA and lived in
Bartow County, the son of William White and Poley Fendley.
Luisa Jane Bennett was born in Forsyth County, the daughter
of Ransom Bennett and Matilda Rolling.)

White, Jacob Z. to Harriett Cowart, 10 September 1873, by Stephen
Griffeth, JP.

White, Jesse to Francis C. Hogan, 29 January 1874, by Stephen
Griffeth, JP.

White, Jesse to Lizzie Maryo, 17 January 1886, by Jeremiah
Sosebee, NP.

Whitfield, Thomas to Emily M. Cox, 13 December 1874, by A. Crow,
JP.

Whitley, Robert to Mary Duncan, 4 September 1887, by Elijah
Roper, MG.

Wigington, James N. to Sarah M. Pinyan, 20 March 1872, by E.P.
King, JP.

Wigington, James M. to Malissa Landsdowne, 2 December 1883, by
J.C. Newberry, MG.

Wingington, Joseph to Sharo Quinton, 24 November 1866, by A.P.
Mullinax, JP.

Wiggington, Mageor M. to Mary M. Bozeman, 2 November 1866, by
A.P. Mullinax, JP.

Wigginton, R.B. to Sarah J. Dorsey, 28 September 1886, by J.G.
Newberry, MG.

Wilbanks, William Edgar to Mary M. Taylor, 6 January 1867, by
J.C. Whitfield, JP.

Wilder, William to Julia A. Wilson, 30 April 1888, by W.B.
Allred.

Willis, Daniel to Lizzie Smith, 28 July 1872, by R.B. Fulton, MG.

Willis, T.J. to Kisiah Caylor, 29 April 1869, by Abraham Chadwick, MG.

Wilson, J.R. to Hattie Lewis, 20 March 1887, by J.P. Worley, JP.

Wilson, James H. to Sarah L. Hammontree, 24 December 1877, by T. Pickett, MG.

Willson, Thomas to Jane Collins, 18 November 1883, by Abraham Chadwick, MG.

Wilson, William L. to Susan E. Cline, 16 June 1887, by J.R. Allen, MG.

Williams, Levi J. to Mary J. Lovelady, 6 January 1870.

Williams, Zachariah I. to Mary A. Fuller, 1 January 1867, by Wm. T. Fleming, MG.

Winkle, Benjamin to Tisha Hall, 26 May 1867, by Wm. F. Cantrell, JP.

Winter, Charles L. to Mary Hastey, 30 July 1876, by William M. Bearden, JP.

Winters, Joseph M. to Sarah Jane Boling, 14 March 1867, by B.C. Hitt, MG.

Winters, Noah J. to Elizabeth Townsend, 29 November 1885, by W.B. Allred, MG.

wofford, Cicero to Caroline E. Cowart, 3 January 1875, by H.C.B. Turner, MG.

Wofford, Doctor to Sophronia Cowart, 24 August 1873, by A.W. Cowart, JP.

Wofford, Thomas G. to Hattie Elizabeth Cagle, 1 February 1885, by J.F. Kelley, MG.

Wooten, Nute to Lucinda Chastain, 12 September 1886, by R.D. Ellis, NP.

Worley, Jason W. to Emily D. Derby, 10 February 1870, by Jesse Padget, MG.

Worley, Joel W. to Julian Holcomb, 15 December 1870, by A.W. Richards, MG.

Worley, John T. to Nancy A. Bozeman, 10 February 1885, by William M. Bearden, JP.

Worley, J.W. to Emily Derby, permission to marry from James Derby.

Wright, Jesse to Mary Cagle, 17 July 1876, by A. Crow, JP.

Vaughn, Virgil P. to Martha Gravley, 23 April 1874, by James Sharyer, JP.

Voyles, J.E. to Manervy Creige, 20 November 1873, by William Stone, MG.

Yancy, Jasper to Mary Bowden, 25 February 1884, by A.V.P. Jones, JP.

Yancy, John L. to Mary Rice, 4 June 1873, by S. Hamrick, NP.

Young, D.M. to Sarah C. Palmour, 25 January 1884, by A.V.P. Jones, JP.

Young, Samuel to Anner Barrett, 12 February 1871, by Thomas A. McDaniel, MG.

THE 1838 PAULDING COUNTY STATE CENSUS

From the county files, Telamon Cuyler Collection, Special Collections, University of Georgia Libraries. Reproduced with permission.

Heads of Households and Number of White Persons

Jesse(?) Philpot-5
Puler(Peeler?) Bryant-7
Jerrimaiah Cockburn-7
William Philpot-11
Michael L. Andrews-6
Leonard Lulbrite-2
William Easterling-2
Samuel Jentry-4
John Jentry-4
Obediance Easterling-8
Mary Hensen-6
Hugh Wilson-11
John Wilson-4
William L. Philips-8
Lewis Eavs-4
Ledford B. Eaves-6
Tacomah Rentfroe-10
W. H. Adair-11
M. S. Adair-5
John Hilburn-10
Allen Hilburn-5
Nelson Porterfield-4
Royal Clay-9
Thomas Reynolds-6
Micajah Hulsey-11
Nathan Butler-2
William B. Box-8
Samuel Dickson-11
Wiley Jones-2
D. D. Heslep-7
George Swain-1
William S. Hogue-8
William Taylor-5
Mary Swinney-3
John Wilcher-5
Larkin D. Powell-12
Henry Fuller-9
Stephen Sanders-9
Thomas Crumpton-5
John Orsborne-10
Alpha Eliot-6
Deskin H. Wilcher-2
William Rollins-3
Levi C. Blair-6
Martin Jones-8
James Forsyth-7
Henry Curbow-5
Samuel C. Hannon-3
Martin Dodd-5
Israel P. Davis-8
Jonathan Langford-6
Curtis C. Bowman-3
Gilbert Bowman-2
Joseph McBrayer-5
William Rowel-6

Martin Kerby-2
David Griffin-5
Thomas Hogan-3
Elizabeth Carter-3
Jonathan Box-9
James A. Collum-4
William B. Heddrick-11
Turman Walthall-8
Crawford Wright-6
Hiram Wright-10
Thomas Carter-11
William L. Kerby-3
Henry Camron-4
John Barber-3
John Owens-3
Ethelbert Williamson-8
Thomas Dorrough-8
Wordsen Hubbard-11
William Shipley-7
John Wright-6
James Phelpot-8
James Johnson-6
Reuben Phelpot-7
Jesse Morrison-2
William Wood-5
Allen York-5
William N. Henson-3
James Cleghorn-4
Micajah Deason-9
L. B. McMillion-6
John Alexander-6
Joshua Lilly-3
J. C. York-11
James Tollerson-5
Presley Powell-6
Stephen King-2
George M. Nest-6
Jackson Prior-3
Wilson Watley-4
W. N. Williams-4
R. W. Pollard-5
C. C. Wilkerson-2
Nathan Gann-1
Martin Ayres-10
William Tollerson-3
Thomas C. Dunlap-8
John Hackney-13
Elizabeth Sparks-3
Carter W. Sparks-7
F. W. Paterson-6
John Pollard-11
Joseph Hobbs-8
Alexander Bryant-5
George F. Shepherd-9
A. E. McBrayer-3

Henry Hulsey-8
Richard Phelpot-3
John Mahaffey-6
Henry McAdams-11
Keader Keaten-7
Pecter Wood-5
John C. Rasberry-4
Ephraim Thompson-9
John Y. Allgood-5
John P. Lyle-3
Lewis L. Clark-8
James H. Bryson-1
A. W. McBrayor-6
Gilford Smith-3
Elisha Wright-3
Jacob Parlier-6
George Lawrence-6
James Lawrence-3
Benjamin Carver-11
Varge Nettles-4
Barnabas Pace-6
John C. Davitte-7
Norman McRae-10
Joseph James Sr.-2
Joashley James-4
Heartwell Lee-4
Edwin Anderson-5
John Murfry-5
John C. Smith-3
John M. C. Smith-11
Williamson Rollins-6
Tueneal Quarles-10
John H. Veazey-4
Jacob Scott-8
John Brooks-11
Micajah Brooks-2
Elisha Brooks-11
John H. McBrayor-3
William Hicks-6
John Colwell-6
Mark Williams-7
Permelia Dodd-4
John E. Davis-6
Archabel Holland-7
Richard Crumpton-5
Asa Prior-9
Jesse Mayfield-5
James Witeher-6
Augustin Young-7
James Kearly-8
James Walker-5
William Parker-13

Puter Thiess(Hiess?)-7
William Adair-10
David H. Blaylock-4
Joseph Roper(Raper?)-5
Joel M. Weaver-4
Mitchell S. Roberts-3
John L. Sencard-2
William Clayton-7
Middleton Clayton-10
Jesse Johnson-6
David C. Eidson-9
Tarah Wilkerson-2
Nathaniel Hull-6
Isaac A. Swords-5
Alexander Wetcher-5
Henry Sweard(Smeard?)-7
John Muckleroy-10
Leroy Hulsey-2
U. S. Crosby-4
John Stephenson-7
Mary Gilley-4
Mansel Tidwell-2
John Lyle-3
Joseph Gallemore-5
Joel D. Crumpton-7
W. A. Roberts-1
Thomas J. Douthit-3
Anderson Dudley-8
Martin Forsyth-3
Evan Parsons-8
Daniel Butler-9
William A. Smyth-4
William Allgood-4
Clalom Camp-2
John C. Blair-4
Jacob Cagle-6
John A. Jones-1
Mary Hicks-2
Henry Richards-2
Lacy Witcher-6
Daniel Witcher-3
Joseph C. Dunlsp-4
Ornon Pollard-2
Nancy Maberry-7
Baley Cameron-8
Margaret Savington-5
William Wood-6
John Morris-7
W. V. B. Watley-2
Paschael H. House-2
William Malone-3
Melborne Cameron-3

Total amount - 1248

Georgia   ) I do hereby Certify that the above return is
Paulding County) Correct to the best of my knowledge and belief
                  Given under my hand this 6th of November 1837.

/s/ Nathaniel Hull

VITAL STATISTICS FROM PAULDING NEW ERA
1883-1893

The Paulding New Era is available on microfilm from the University of Georgia at Athens.

...This newspaper is really a chronicle of its times. There were correspondents from many of the communities in the county. Politics were often argued in letters from readers... Disasters from all over the world played a big part in the front page news selections, and weather was of constant concern. There was continuing interest throughout the years as to who would bring in the season's first cotton blossom, the biggest cabbage, the best watermelon. The editors reported the names of their subscribers. Schools and businesses and churches were reported. Anyone who wants to know more about life in Georgia during the period would find this worthwhile reading.

...I have not extracted the deaths of people who lived away from the area, since someone from, say Savannah, would not be looking in a book about Paulding County to find out about his relatives. But if there was a clear Paulding County connection I did extract the item... There are births, deaths, marriages, divorces, and items which detail relationshps. I hope this will be helpful to those who are searching for roots in this time and place.

Lou Pero

Jones, J R--Died of gunshot wound.
Dockings, Gilbert--Died of typhoid last Thursday.
Swanson, John--Guilty in Hicks murder case. Colored.
      Sentenced for life.
Slaughter, Bill--Guilty in Hicks murder case. Colored.
      Sentenced for life.
Jennings, Martha M--Granted divorce from John C.
      Jennings.
Brock, G W--Granted divorce from Sarah F Brock.
Hunt, Stephen B--Son of William J Hunt of Atlanta.
      Nephew of J Meigs Hunt (of Dallas?) Foot
      crushed by train.
      2/22/83
Hunt, Charles--Colored. Killed in train wreck.
Kidwell, R P--Killed in train wreck.
Cox, John--Stepson of Harrison Wade. Killed in train
      wreck.
Langley, J W--W H. Crew appointed admr of estate.
Veal, Alexander--S R. McBrayer appointed admr of estate.
Manley, S C--L M McBrayer appointed admr of estate.
      3/1/83
      History of county, long account.
Hamilton, C A--Visited Decatur, his wife's late home.
Connally, Mary Lee--Cousin of Emmie Shackleford.
Shelton, Martha--John Shelton appointed admr of estate.
Carroll, A B--E S Carroll appointed admr of estate.
Mason, T C--Wife a sister of S L Strickland.
      3/8/83
Campbell, Thomas N--Age 14, commited suicide near
      Smyrna.
Cole, George--Son of Jesse M Cole, confined with
      consumption.
      3/15/83
Springer, John E--Married Minnie Benedict at residence

of Rev Mr Springer of Marietta last Friday.

Shaw, Pauline--Niece of Mrs W A Christian.

Day, Mrs--Died last Thursday, age 73.

Rainwater, James--His 15 year old son very sick and expected to die.

Ragsdale, Sauk--Died Thursday night.

Smith, J F--J M Watson, executor, files for dismission.

3/22/83

Adair, Thomas--Brother-in-law of John Cox lately killed in train wreck. Had epileptic fit, fell into fire and burned badly. Rescued by aged grandmother.

3/29/83

Cleghorn, Jimmie--Died on election day. Claimed to be kin of Cleghorn-Herring & Co of Augusta.

Allen, Stephen--Married last Thursday at Southern Hotel, Atlanta to Miss Tennie G Caldwell of West End. Esq Pitchford officiated.

Fisher, W H--Killed in train accident. Body forwarded to kin in KY.

Gray, Garrett--Lists first settlers of the county.

Frazier, Henry--His son age 16 buried Mar 14 at New Canaan.

4/5/83

Davis, Pete--Visit to Toomsboro, GA, his former home.

Foote, Charles--His father is George W Foote.

Foote, J B--Uncle of Millie Tidwell of Atlanta.

Perkinson, Thomas--Late of Cobb Co, W H and Mary Perkinson, appointed admrs of estate.

4/12/83

Bullock, Willie--Of Rollins, son of N H Bullock.

Rollins, W L--Mother is Martha Rollins of Rollins.

Cason, Wool--Infant died Mar 22.

Cason, George--Infant died Mar 22. Both Cason infants died in the same house, buried same grave yard.

Paris, Oliver--Formerly of Paulding Co, died Clayton Co last Friday. Buried New Canaan on Sunday. Leaves wife and one child.

4/19/83

Palmer, William Carter--Died last Wednesday, buried Nebo Church. Son of W F and Ella Palmer

Timmons, Prof A M--"It's a boy."

Clonts, J M--a girl born.

4/26/83

Snell, W M--of Orange Co, FL. 8th Ga Reg Vet.

Baker, Amanda--Memorial service Sunday the 13th at Mt Zion Baptist Church.

George, Jack--Inf son died Wednesday at residence of Mrs. Alexander Bullock.

Hamilton, Charles H--Father, from Montezuma in Macon Co, visited.

5/4/83

Brooks, William--and wife Catherine mentioned in legal notice.

5/13/83

Foster, Carrie--Daughter of Dr T J Foster visiting in Fairburn.

Carter, W K--Moved to Atlanta

Ritch, Lizzie--Daughter of H C Ritch of Weddington.

Cobb, Miss Bershie--Married Perry Turner of Atlanta on

Sunday, May 6.
5/17/83
Poore, Mrs J J --Died, leaving 2 weeks old infant.
Busby, Elias--of Mt. Zion, 80 years old, very ill,
    has made will.
Baker, Mrs--Funeral preached by Rev J S Reynolds.
5/24/83
Story, John--Only son age 13 drowned near County Line
    Church in Story and Lewis' gin pond. He and
    Charley Brooks tried to save some boys who
    couldn't swim.
McGarrity, Sanborn S--Of 19th Dist, one of County's
    oldest settlers, buried at Pleasant Grove
    Church.
5/31,83
Carter, Charley--Son of E M Carter, first reported
    dangerously ill with typhoid, now reported
    recovering.
6/7/83
Mayson, James L--Graduated from Vanderbilt University
    in Nashville.
Turner, Mrs--At Point of death, dau of Burnt Hickory
    citizen B J Penn.
McGregor, S R--as largest creditor of Martha McCollors,
    appointed admr of estate.
McGregor, C D--Appointed admr of James Cleghorn estate.
Cooper, Nathan--Admr of estate of Moses Cooper, letters
    of dimission.
    Also letter of dismission from estate of
    James Cole.
Turner, Mrs--Died, buried at Burnt Hickory Church yard.
Golden, Mrs Lucy--Daughter of David Austin, wife of
    John Golden of California District, died
    Tuesday morning, leaves husband and mother.
Carter, Charley--Died of Typhoid.
Poore, J J--Who lost young wife recently, died last
    Sunday.
6/14/83
McCollum, Dixon--Died last week of flux.
Hogue, Billie--Of 19th Dist, near 90.
Embry, C C--Visited children in Texas.
Lawrence, Newton--Died last Saturday of consumption.
Cooper, J N--Delighted father of a baby girl.
6/21/83
Matthews, J M--Son of ex-Sheriff Matthews, died, and
    sermon preached at New Hope on Sunday June
    10th by Rev J R T Brown and Zedekiah Land.
Burns, Berry--Married last week to Miss Sarah J. Wix of
    Pumpkinville Dist.
Foote, Will F--Married to Miss Annie Peek.
Robertson, Snowden--Daughters are Nettie and Fannie,
    returned from college at Gainesville.
6/28/83
McBrayer, W E--Visiting from Haralson Co.
7/5/83
Hamilton, C A--His sister Ida passed away at residence
    of her father in Montezuma, Ga.
Westbrook, Ella--Wife of John Westbrook of 20th
    District, aged 24 years 6 months and her
    baby, Birty, 8 months and 21 days, both died.
Roberts, Marian (Mr)--Tried to commit suicide.

VITAL STATISTICS FROM PAULDING NEW ERA

7/12/83

Smith, A C--Of Bowden, GA and W J Smith of Birmingham,
          AL, brothers of Wesley W Smith are visiting
          at home of Prof P M Duncan, their
          brother-in-law.

Kennedy, Clarence Eugene--age 15, and sisters Alica
          Melville and Mamie Florida Kennedy are
          visiting their uncle, Dr Connally, from
          Clay Co., AL.

Roberts, Marion--Died last Saturday, buried High Shoals
          Church, age 50.

Pace, Dick--In altercation after Sunday School
          celebration, was stabbed by Bill Neal,
          now in jail.

7/26/83

Brown, Mark--Of Cherokee, knocked down and kicked
          step mother, who is in critical condition.
          Sheriff searching for fugitive.

8/2/83

Brown, Elizabeth--and Frank Wills and O W Pickett
          offered reward for the capture of Mark
          Brown, age 25.

Ragsdale, Mrs.--Died July 29, wife of John F Ragsdale
          of California District. Died of consump-
          tion. Two little boys. Daughter of
          Daniel White of Marietta.

Ogletree, Charles--Was passing through town to live
          with a Mr Hulsey with wife and invalid
          mother. Charley Tilton, a runaway boy from
          Atlanta, accused Ogletree of kidnapping him.

Cochran, Mr--Was away from home on July 26 and someone
          used the rope from his well to let himself
          down the chimney and rob the house.

Badgett, Minnie--has her cousin Lula Treadwell of
          Atlanta visiting her.

Turner, Will--Son of J H Turner of Acorntree, killed
          horn snake.

Foote, J B--and J R Green appointed admrs of S J
          Tidwell, deceased.

8/16/83

Puckett, J R--Guilty of public indecency.

8/23/83

Duval, Major Eugene--died last Saturday at Villa Rica,
          born in Franca, served in French Armies,
          has relative in Charleston, SC.

Cooper, Nathan--appointed admr of Moses Cooper.

Ellmore, Rev--of Macon Co is visiting brother-in-law Dr
          S Robertson.

Robertson, Dr S--no

McGuire, Mrs J M--Died of consumption last Sunday the
          12th, at Burnt Hickory. Buried Mars Hill,
          Cobb Co.

Moore, Stephen S--To be tried for murder of Boss
          Jones (not guilty).

Freeman, Addie May--Died last Tuesday the 14th of
          diphteria, daughter of Joe Freeman.

Echols, Elizabeth--Step daughter of John Earwood
          adjudged insane and sent to asylum.

8/30/83

Haygood, Dr--An interesting character sketch.

Wilkins, W W--of Babcock Co, Ala, appointed admr of

B H Wortley.

Holland, Mrs Wash--Died last Monday at home of her
    father, Rev Burrell Camp. Buried High
    Shoals Church.

Hagan, Mrs Newt--Her daughter is Mrs Bob Moon.

Freeman, Joe--Infant child died last Sunday.

Turner, Perry--Died at ETV & GA RR Station near Macon.
    Returned to Dallas for burial last Monday.
    9/6/83

Turner, Perry--Masonic resolution commemorating his
    death.

Camp, Ben--An odd series of accidents involving aged
    couple.

Pearson, Spartin--Married Miss Parker of Acorntree
    last week.

Camp, James--Married to Miss Nancy Camp of Acorntree.
    9/13/83

Moon, Mrs Mattie--Wife of Z R Moon of Atlanta police
    dept died in Atlanta Monday of typhoid
    fever. Sister-in-law of Bob Moon of Dallas.

Cole, James W--Admr of Sarah Cole, deceased.

Pope, Emma--Visiting her sister Mrs A S Pitman.

Bankston, Mr--erected tombstone over grave of S B
    McGregor, father of C D McGregor, a
    Dallas attorney.

Parker, Glenn and Pat--Will locate in Gainesville.

Ogletree, Mr--Tried to kidnap another boy.

Branham, Judge--Opened and closed court that morning
    because his daughter was getting married
    that evening. (No other names given).

Rakestraw, C--Admr of M W Porter
    9/20/83

Furman, Farish--Died Friday the 14th of malaria.

Payne, Mrs H W--of Tocca is visiting her parents
    Mr & Mrs W A Christian.

Hay, Freeman--Son of H W Hay, age 12, picked 250
    pounds of cotton.

Paris, Dillard--Son of N D Paris of California Dist,
    picked 162 pounds of cotton.

Hope, Mamie--age 1 year 2 months 10 days, died.
    Daughter of Rm and S O Hope.

Connally, Dr D H--Wishes to sell farm in Tyler, Texas.
    9/27/83

Ogletree, Chas--The kidnapper is still at large.

Weaver, J H (Jr)--Died last Monday. Son of Col and
    Mrs. Weaver. Typhoid.
    10/4/83
    There are about 104 names mentioned in a
    legal notice advertising the sale of wild
    lands for which taxes are due.

Brown, George W--Fell out of hotel window while
    walking in sleep.

Shelton, John--admr of Martin Shelton.
    10/18/83

Woodall, M H--of Campbell Co has joined brother W H
    Woodall in Dallas business.

Martin, John--Charged with carrying concealed weapon,
    has gone to Texas.
    11/8/83

Lewis, Fredrick T--Married to Miss Laura Kirk at
    home of bride's father H L Kirk at

Draketown. George N Allgood married
Lewis and Kirk.

Butts, John D--of Augusta killed in RR accident.
About 22 years old.

Roberts, Willis--Deceased, M Lee appointed admr.

Bussey, E W--Has bound Pat Bankston, colored, age 10.

Cook, J F--appointed admr of Dolphus Mahaffley,
deceased.

Dean, J B--Deceased. Mary Dean appointed guardian of
L E, Ally, E B, & Daniel Dean, minor
children of J B Dean.

Ellsberry, Mrs--Wife of Co Treasurer, A B Ellsberry
died last Monday.
11/15/83

Hudson, Wesley--Father of George and Dock Hudson is
moving from Atlanta to Paulding County.

Chastain, Oscar--Age seven months, died Nov 7th.
Son of Mr and Mrs J K Chastain.
11/22/83

Bone, Monroe--Child, age 2, died last Saturday.
11/29/83

Landon, John H--Married Mollie O Bates of Dawson.

Posey, Benjamin--Died recently near Cassville.

Langford, H S--of Alabama married Nov 21 to Dora
Haney, only daughter of Captain Haney,
near Cartersville.

Spillman, Harry--of Marietta married Maggie
Bissner. (Marietta Journal).

Miller, Ed F--married Martha Butler of new
Powder Springs (Marietta Journal).

Cox, A J--of Chickamauga, TN married Susie Moon
(Marietta Journal).

Howell, Lula--(from Douglasville Star), dau of H P
Howell, drowned in Love's gin pond.

Owen, John A--(from Cartersville Free Press), the son
of John Owens was killed by William Lawrence
Simpson in a fight. Simpson took off for
parts unknown.

Earwood, John--his two sons, Henry and Serrling,
killed a wildcat.

Blalock, William--until recently lived near Acorntree,
was arrested earlier for illicit distilling.
Swore illegal warrant against S S Moore.

Payne, Rev B F--Interesting personal article about him.

Campbell, William--Died last Thursday morning a week at
asylum in Milledgeville. Buried Dallas with
Masonic honors.
12/20/83

Rawls, J Ira--Died at age 24 last Monday. Typhoid.
Born Wilkinson County and came to Dallas 10
months ago. Buried at Stephensville.
Leaves Mother and 5 brothers, including
Robert I Rawls and B H Rawls.

Hurst, Lula--Daughter of B H Hurst has astonishing
powers-from Cedartown. (Seems like they
are talking of psychic powers, she toured
around area for several years.)

Jushan, Dr D H--of Carroll Co died Dec 12.

Wallace, Maj Frederic--Chief Engineer of Marietta and
No GA RR married Lottie Whitmore of Canton.

Hagan, Ned--age 70, married Miss Margaret Farr, age

59 near Acworth.

Walsh, Joseph--Cut his throat and died.

Marshman, Mr--of LaGrange, GA will marry today Miss
Ida Marshman of Powder Springs.

Smith, Thomas--age 22, died at Mrs Able's residence
of typhoid last Monday. Buried Dallas
Cemetery. Nephew of Rev F M Smith of
Dallas. His father was Rev James Smith
who died in Confederate service.

Brand, William--Married to Bettie Williams last
Sunday at home of bride's father, Rev
J M Williams.

McBrayer, J L--applies to be discharged as guardian
of P H Whitehead.
12/27/83

Chappell, William--Died at Milledgeville on Nov 20,
1881. Tribute by Dallas lodge. This was
earlier reported as Campbell.

Phillips, Katie--Daughter of Colonel Chas D Phillips
of Marietta married G Phillips of Habersham
County last Tuesday week.

Brown, Ed--Colored boy died of train wreck injuries.

Foote, Will--and wife are spending holidays with
her family in Polk County.

Holland, G W--Married Dec 20 to Mary Ellsberry.

Bone, Rich--Died last Wednesday at home of thphoid
fever, buried Dallas Cemetery. 35 years
old, wife and several children.
2/24/84

Ragsdale, J F--and William F and C F, guardians of
heirs of Daniel White.

McLarty, George W--Brother of Wm T McLarty of Garfield,
Polk County.

Blanchard, Mrs Mary A--Died Mon Jan 14 near line of
Douglas.

Weddington, A G--is son-in-law of Mrs. Blanchard.

Allen, S N--father of Bob Allen, who got into
difficulty with Ransey Carter, colored.

Christian, W A--of Atlanta visiting son, J A Christian.

Bullock, Miss Alice--Daughter of N T Bullock climbed
out window and escaped on north bound train.
Married Charlie Wells on Monday at Rome.

McMicken, Mrs--age 75 years, mother of J J McMicken.
Mother of 13 children, 9 now living. 102
grand children. 16 gr grandchildren.
1/31/84

Furr, Charles W--Died of pneumonia last Monday a few
miles from Dallas.

Adair, Adeline--Admx of W S Adair.
2/7/84

Hagan, George T--Father of bouncing boy.
1/21/84

Dunn, May--Applied for personalty and homestead.

Portwood, Old Man--His grandchild killed in storm
at Burnt Hickory.

Clonts, J D--First report of a phenomenon reported
over several months, sighted a buzzard
wearing a bell.

Weaver, M M--Died last Tuesday, youngest son of
J H Weaver, buried Dallas.

Hudson, Mrs Elizabeth--Died last Saturday the 16th.

Wife of Wesley Hudson.

Henderson, Mrs J W--Died last Tuesday.

Goss, John--Aoubt 60 years old, married Miss Mary
        Paythress. They were lovers in their
        youth.

Bishop, Mrs--Whose husband was killed last year
        by falling off trestle was awarded
        $4000.

Butler, Henrietta--Accidentally shot in leg at
        dance. Daughter of Mr Marion Butler.

Echols, W S--Deceased. Land to be sold at auction.
        3/6/84

Flowers, W M--and S J Ward both of Dalton killed
        by train.

Hudson, Paul C--Died in Texas.

Howder, John--of Indianapolis killed last Monday
        in wreck of ETV & GA RR between Juliet
        and Macon.

Busby, Elias--Died last Tuesday, 80 years old, had
        been minister of Methodist Church.

Hogue, William B--Died on Tuesday the 20th of
        pnuemonia. About 85 years old. First
        sheriff of County. Member of Primitive
        Baptist Church.

Harris, Mrs Jane--Is 101 years old. Widow of Charles
        Harris who was in War of 1812. Formerly
        of Paulding Co and now Haralson Co.
        400 descendants.

Gann, F M--A grandson of Mrs Harris (above). Has
        lived in Dallas 40 years. S Gann, Sr
        in her son-in-law.
        3/20/84

Allen, Bob--In jail at Fairburn for murder of
        Andrew Lively.

Lane, G W--formerly of Dallas, visited from DeKalb
        Co, AL.

Benton, Benny--Married Miss Hill at Sand Mountain, AL.
        Son of Rev James Denton who moved to Sand
        Mountain.

Williams, W W--Father of Hans and B W Williams.

Christian, William--Visited his father W A Christian.

Jordan, May--of Tunnel Hill is visiting her sister Mrs
        R A Wyatt.
        3/27/84

Wright, D G--Personal article about him.

Cochran, W L--Postmaster of Huntsville, Paulding Co has
        madstone made by his grandfather in Dawson
        Co 40 or 50 years ago.

Cooper, ------Killed in tornado.
        This issue is full of the tornado which
        swept through the area, and went on
        through Gainesville and on into SC.

Parris, N D--Mentions his daughter Lou and a gold
        piece that was lost and found, this might
        be one of the editor's jokes.

Tatum, Clay--Killed with wife and child in cyclone
        in Dade Co.

Crowley, William--Entire family killed in cyclone
        (Dade Co?).

Kirk, T W--Applied for personalty.

Furr, Mrs Georgia--Applied for letters of Admin on

estate of O W Furr.
McCurry, B--Married last Sunday to Melissa Kitchens.
Pace, Mrs Adeline--Found to be a lunatic.
Mobley, John--A brother of Mrs Pace will take her
    to asylum.
Ogletree, Charles--Finally caught and convicted and
    sentenced to life in penitentiary in
    Mississippi.
Austin, Michael--Died near Nebo, about 70 years old,
    buried Nebo with Masonic honors.
Kemp, J G--father of Starling Kemp.
    4/10/84
Pool, Johnny--Died Apr 7 at home of his father, C A
    Pool of California District.
McLarty, Dr G A--Married Sallie Umphries last Sunday.
    Both of Brownsville.
Langford, Bud--Killed by tree he was falling Tuesday,
    son of Berry Langford.
Bone, Bailey--Took Adeline Pace to asylum and brought
    his wife home, recovered.
Moody, Retinsa--Aged widow died last Monday.
Wigley, John--Died last Sunday near New Hope of measles.
Howard, Capt S W--Married at Hiram to Eliza Farlow at
    home of her mother.
Pool, John C--Died on the 7th, leaves wife and
    two children.
    4/17/84
    Destructive storm, 14 inches of rain, most
    bridges washed out. Reynolds Bridge over
    Pumpkinvine is only one still standing.
    Ownes mill on Pumpkinvine still in running
    order. Had 7 ft of water in mill house.
Merrell, Mr--Burned to death in train accident (part
    of storm damage).
McDonald, Zink--RR engineer killed in RR accident above
    Marietta.
Alford, Lee--of Troup Co killed in cyclone.
Smith, Elijah Bunion--2½ year old son of Mr & Mrs
    H E Smith died Saturday, buried Sunday
    at Dallas Cem.
Crew, E W--Married to Mrs Antinet Crew on Apr 13 at
    bride's residence. Rev B M Camp officiating.
Pool, John C--Trubute--Son of Squire C A & Rachel
    Bookout Pool. (Her father Dr Charles
    Bookout). John born Oct 30, 18-0. Raised in
    Paulding Co. At age 20 married Miss M J S
    Vaughn, dau of Randolph Vaughn. Age 24 at
    death. Two small children.
    4/24/84
Upson, J D--Moving to Cartersville.
Matthews, Mrs--Died Tuesday, buried Dallas Cemetery.
    Mother of W C Matthews.
White, James B--Daughter died recently from
    consumption, third to die from this disease.
Forsyth, Elijah--Veteran of Mexican War.
    Also John Foote, Monroe McGuire, and B H
    Smith.
Bingham, William--& wife oldest two people living
    together in district.
    5/1/84
Woodall, Mrs--Died Tuesday, wife of Willie.

Finch, Mrs--80-9- years old, mother of Terrell Finch,
    died near Braswell Station Wednesday night.
Brannon, Carrie--is visiting cousin May Ashworth in
    Atlanta.
Worthan, John--Youngest son of Rev Duncan Worthan of
    Nebo died Thursday. About 22 years of age.
Camp, Alford--Little child died Sunday.
Payne, Eliza--Aged lady resided with her son-in-law Mr
    Brown. Died of pneumonia last Saturday.
    5/8/84
Smith, Thomas--of Cartersville, killed by train
    recently.
Waldrop, W C--Admr of Milton Waldrop estate.
Turner, Robert A--Filed will of Elias Busby.
Wigley, O M--admr of John Wigley estate.
Turner, John H--Admr of estate of Martin Shelton.
Matthews, Mrs Terry--Baptized into Baptist Church by
    Rev J R T Brown.
Wigley, Mrs Fox--Died last Wednesday of measles.
    Leaves husband and two children.
Dale, W R--Will be ordained a minister at Baptist
    Church.
Monk, J T--Married last Sunday by Mr Camp to Miss
    Georgia Nolund.
Elsberry, J W--Married last Sunday by Mr Camp to Miss
    Delilah Hubbard. Rev Camp had a busy day.
Worthan, John--of Dallas, youngest son of Rev D and
    Melinda Worthan died 30 Apr at age 22.
    Interred Bethany Church Cemetery.
Tatum, Mercer L--Age 4, can answer 65 Bible questions.
    Son of James Tatum.
    5/15/84.
Connally, Taylor--of Rome, visited his brother Dr
    W C Connally.
Furr, Charles--Died recently (Oval).
Newton, Rev R M--Died May 1.
Meadows, Jacob--Is 81 years old.
Badgett, Mrs--and Mrs Penn have gone to see their
    sick mother in Newton County.
Gray, J M--Died Feb 28, 1884, 34 years of age. Widow
    living with her only brother, Charley
    Badgett.
    5/23/84
Connally, Dr--A boy born Thursday.
Landmond, John N--Died last Sunday evening at age
    34 of typhoid.
Scoggins, H C--and wife have gone to Floyd Co to see
    Mrs Scoggins sick mother.
Davis, Jimmy--Nearly 89 and feeble.
Upton, Mrs Eli--Died last Friday and buried at Mt Moriah.
    5/30/84
Young, Mrs E E--Died last Monday, age 76, mother of
    P M Young.
Ragsdale, John F--of Paulding Co married May 18th to
    Fannie Biggers of Draketown.
Parker, C W--is visiting his brother Dr Parker of
    Dallas.
Barber, George--Married last Sunday to Miss Kaylor.
Rattaree, John--Baby girl born.
Hagin, B F--Daughters Bertha and Ludelia, ages 12 and
    10, have woven 25 yards of carpet.

6/6/84

Kennard, Rev I R--of Cedartown to be taken to asylum.

Moody, S H & J M--admrs of Thomas Moody.

Bone, John--Daughter age 9 died last Tuesday.

Camp, Carl--Injured last Feb in fall from Raccoon
        trestle has recovered enough to get around
        with a staff but will be crippled for life.
        Brought suit against RR in Fulton Co.

Powers, S H--of Rome will leave for England (his old
        home) tomorrow.

6/13/84

Shirah, Michael--Accidentally shot himself with musket
        last Saturday. About 21 years of age.
        Shooting occurred at residence of John Wood.
        Buried Berry Gann Cemetery near
        Pumpkinvine Church.

Childers, Mrs Abi--Wife of Mr Henry Childers and
        daughter of S P Spinks died Monday at her
        home near Mr Ellsberry's saw mill and will
        be buried at High Shoals Church.

McEver, Joseph--Gives list of old people at Harmony:
        J N Sligh-about 80, William Kennedy-81, W K
        Goss-89. John Brown-78, John Brock-87, Levi
        Bowman-80, Sarah Cochran-74, Nancy Carnes-72,
        Divinity Goss-70, Margaret McEver-87.

Austin, Josephine--(Paid matter) A long account of a
        journey to Alabama and her separation for
        her husband. Possibly 8 children. Her
        parents of Paulding County received her, her
        husband's brother Jim Austin.

Buford, J L--New baby girl this week.

Moore, Mrs Laura--of Draketown visiting her brother
        Col. Weaver.

Shaw, Sallie--Died last Sunday near Antioch church.

Dorris, Rev John M--Died May 12, 1884. Born Abbeville
        Dist SC in 1806. Orphaned young and lived
        with Rev Robt L Edwards. Sleeps beside his
        companion. Obituary written by J B C
        Quillian.

Williams, Lula and Doris--Daughters of W W Williams
        have pneumonia. Dr Dean of Hiram is
        treating them.

Allgood, John T--Settled in this county on 12 Nov 1830.

Smith, Guy W--Ran off (surveyed?) lot in Paulding Co.

Hicks, Joel D--Elected first Clerk of Superior Court in
        Jan 1834.

Hogue, W S--First Sheriff.
        Other names mentioned in sketch of early
        Paulding County: L M Walthall, Wodson
        Hubbard, John Brooks, James Johnson, Emsley
        P Hogan, Martin Jones, Mitchell Adair, Owen
        R Kenon, Wilson Whatley, Woodson Hubbard,
        William Allgood, John Brooks, William
        Malone, Old Man Rollins, Lucy Witcher, David
        Griffin, John T Allgood.

Bullock, Walter--Five month old son of N T Bullock died
        last Friday.

Parris, Dover--Has twins.

Thompson, Belle-Of Rockmart is visiting her brother W
        E Thompson.

Wade, Homer--Son of Harris Wade cut arm with scythe.

Parris, William--Died on 13th this month in Arkansas.
    Was born and raised in California Dist and
    moved to Arkansas about 5 years ago. Leaves
    wife and 5 living children and 5 dead.
Ables, John--Has twin boys.
Twilley, James--Nine year old daughter died last
    Thursday.
Ellis, John R--Who was born in Paulding Co, died at
    Fish in Polk Co on the 20th. Buried in
    Polk Co.
McBrayer, James--Died of dysentery on 19th. Interred
    at Pine Log Church.
Smith, B H--Father was Benjamin Smith of Anderson Co SC.
    Article about his old horse.
Brown, G W--A bouncing boy.
McBrayer, T J & J W--applied for admr of estate of
    James McBrayer.
    7/4/84
Clayton, Johnnie--who died in Athens recently while
    bathing in Oconee River. Connected with J B
    Toomer. Engaged to Octavia Kenney who died
    last Wednesday of a broken heart. He had
    been adopted by Richard Boggs.
Rymer, Jo--of Candy Ridge and Mrs McDole of Raccoon
    were married at Groom's residence last
    Saturday by Rev J G New.
Smith, Fletcher--Married to Miss Lena D. Williford on
    June 14 at Gadsden, AL. Maj W J Williford
    is bride's father. Both raised in
    Cartersville.
    --Number two in series of pen and ink
    sketches:
Gray, Garrett--Involved in cutting of Paulding from
    Cobb Co.
Cornett, Hardy--Had contract to build log courthouse.
Irwin, David--Judge of Superior Court in 1852? Charged
    grand jury to investigate a nest of
    gamblers. Gamblers took revenge on grand
    jury. Those on grand jury:
    Sander Ragsdale, Joseph Ragsdale, Robert
    Harper, Mack Matthews, Hiram Whitworth,
    Seaborn Gann, W B Miller, Duncan Bohanon.
Tibbitts, Green--One of his children died.
    7/11/84
Hogue, H W--and Callie Hogan married. They played a
    trick on their friends by being married in
    town.
Carter, J F--Died in train accident last Friday. About
    age 23. Got on train with two brothers and
    3 sisters. Children of Pinson Carter.
    Buried Dallas Cemetery. (This was an
    excursion. Body brought back on same train.)
Moon, Charley--Married Miss Georgia Knox last Thursday
    at W B Knox's.
    Third Pen and Ink Sketch, E Guild was
    contractor to build first courthouse instead
    of Cornett. More about conflict between
    grand jury and gamblers. A town/country
    dispute. Disrespect for sheriffs. Mrs
    Seleta Drake has oldest Bible in county.
    7/11/84

Monks, Dennis--Died Wednesday.

Green, B--of Texas visited relatives.

Moon, Robert--Daughter died Sunday, age 10 months.

Howard, Fannie--Sister of Mrs Alonzo Foote, came for
        concert, escorted by John Smith.

Phillips, Lewis--Died near New Hope Monday, buried at
        New Hope with Masonic honors.

Holland, Mrs G W--and Mrs J S Spinks joined High Shoals
        Church, baptized by Rev Camp.

Stegall. Lewis--It's a boy.
        7/25/84

Pen & Ink Sketches No 4 Judges Irwin and
        Brown. Also gives list of people killed
        in the County, no dates.--

Bowman, Edward--Killed John Thompson. Justifiable
        homicide.

Harper, Thornton--Struck and killed James Torrance with
        hoe. Penitentiary 20 years.

Compton, S P--Killed Absolom Jones, acquitted.

Bone, William--Killed Wylie Jones, acquitted.

LaRue, Thomas--Killed in riot by persons unknown.

Jones, Sep & Brud--Killed by parties unknown.

Gann, Seaborn (Jr)--Shot by soldier in discharge of
        duty.

Jones, Wylie (Jr)--Killed William Steggall. Convicted
        and pardoned by governor.

Brown, J M--Killed David Gorman. Tried and acquitted.

Carter, J R-- Killed Shepart Kincannon.
        Carter pardoned by Governor.

Adair, Willis--Colored. Killed Bruce Tilman, Colored.
        Case not pressed and Adair released.

Allen, N C--Killed by persons unknown.

Shelton, J K P--Killed Bud Puckett. Convicted. Served
        two years and pardoned by Governor.

Jackson, George--Killed Jackson Moss. Both colored.
        Jackson was hanged by Sheriff Henry
        Braswell. Only legal hanging in county.

Jones, Boss--S S Moore acquitted of murder.

Hicks, John M--Killed by colored men (work gang) at
        Tunnel in 1882. 30 men implicated. Became
        offended by Hicks actions and rioted. Miles
        Jackson still to be tried.

Hyde, Mr--killed Mr Shaw. No arrest because people did
        not blame Hyde. Northern men employed by RR.
        Long article about Sunday School celebration.

Bowman, J G--Married Miss Susan Roberts on 26th by Rev.
        J. N. Cooper.

Upson, Dr J D--Died in Cartersville Wed the 16th.

Gann, Polk--Married Mrs Emma George last Sunday at
        residence of Uncle George McLarty, the
        bride's father, by Rev J R T Brown.

Root, Coroner--held inquest for murdered child of
        Adeline Holleman (colored).

Veach, J S--It's a girl.

Hagin, G F--Has sick child not expected to live.

Florence, Billy--Died Friday the 18th. Buried at
        Pleasant Hill Church. Leaves wife and
        children. Two sons Mason J and I B Florence.

Quillion, Uncle--Preached John Dorris' funreal Not
        clear when Dorris died.

Hendricks, Aca--Pen & Ink Sketches remembers another
        murder, Hendricks killed by persons unknown.
        Pen & Ink Sketches gives a long list of
        first settlers of the County, last names
        only, no additional data. Two long funny
        stories about gambling.
Farmer, Lafayette--Little daughter killed by lightening
        last Saturday.
McGee, William--It's a boy.
Rainwater, John--One year old child died last Wednesday.
Wilkins, Major--Died at Poor House last Monday.
        Stricken with paralysis few years ago and
        had no means of support.
Hagin, Floyd--5 year old son of G W & Jennie Hagin
        died on the 27th. First born.
Shipp, Joseph--10 lb guest.
Hardin, R S--married Lillie Penn Tuesday night. Left
        for Newton Coor Alabama.
        8/8/84
Summers, Elias--of Coweta raised eleven children, ten
        are married.
Jackson, Miles--Guilty of murder, life in penitentiary.
Moore, William--once of Paulding Co and now of Tenn is
        visiting his mother aged 93.
Jorman, T R--Going to Texas.
Jacobs, Thomas--Infant died while visiting at Acworth.
Willingham, William--12 lb boy.
Whitfield, William--It's a girl.
        Can't resist one joke: "Waiter, I saw your
        thumb in the soup." "Oh, I thank you for
        your concern, sir, but it wasn't hot enough
        to hurt."
        8/15/84
        Pen & Ink Sketches remembers 5 more murders:
Marable, Bill--Killed Larkin Wormock during war.
        Pardoned by Governor.
Linsey, Marion--Killed John L Martin. Justifiable
        homicide, not bound for court.
Echols, Charles L--Killed Jack Edwards. Both colored.
        Justifiable.
Buffington, David--Killed Anson Ables. Acquitted.
Hall, Old Man--Killed by party unknown (19th Dist).
        Then Pen & Ink Sketches names some men of
        Co C, 7th Ga Vols, CSA.
Jenkins, Capt C S--Carried off first company of
        volunteers, at first for 12 months, at end
        of time all between 18 & 35 were conscripted
        "for the war". Then ages were extended to
        include more men.
        Officers were J H Weaver, 1st Lieut, L B
        Andrews, 2nd Lieut, S P Compton, 3rd Lieut,
        J N Cooper, 1st Sergeant, F M Gann, 2
        Sergeant, W S Wright, 3rd Serg, W S Turner,
        4th Serg.
        Then tries to name all the men, which will
        not be listed here.
Moody, William--Died Friday.
Edmondson, Bill--Stabbed by Tom Jackson on work gang.
        Both colored. Edmondson later died.
        There is a list of marriageable young men in

Edomonson, Bill--Stabbed by Tom Jackson on work gang.
　　　　　　　Both colored. Edmonson later died.
　　　　　　　There is a list of marriageable young men in
　　　　　　　the county drawn by lady reporters. No
　　　　　　　names given, but for someone familiar with
　　　　　　　various families might be able to infer
　　　　　　　identity.
　　　　　　　A bit in the same paper refers to five of
　　　　　　　cleverest old bachelors who attended a
　　　　　　　meeting at High Shoals: Tom Sanders, Tony
　　　　　　　Hill, Charley Turner, Will Spinks.
　　　　　　　8/22/84
McLarin, R P--Returned from Campbell Co with wife's
　　　　　　　mother Mrs W B Swan.
Bradley, John--Went to Texas
Head, W H--Died last Friday, leaves wife and child.
　　　　　　　Buried at Wilner.
　　　　　　　The fire on South side of the tracks should
　　　　　　　be mentioned. Hotel of Dr T J Foster
　　　　　　　burned, Ables and Turners store burned.
　　　　　　　Depot saved. W C Matthews store lost. Benny
　　　　　　　Smith Store. O P Cooper had damage to goods.
　　　　　　　Tenants of hotel were Mr & Mrs F M
　　　　　　　Smith--she got out of fire and then became
　　　　　　　confused and returned, had to be carried
　　　　　　　out. Mrs Perry Turner--lost all she owned.
　　　　　　　F J Pentecost, James Howell.
Pentecost, F J--Howell, James
Moore, S S--Reported as having killed Boss Jones. It
　　　　　　　is said that Jones threatened Moore and he
　　　　　　　saved his own life. Moore gave himself up
　　　　　　　to judge but was never arrested.
Cooper, D--Son of J N Cooper convalescing.
Rogers, John--married Eva McBrayer on the 10th by J N
　　　　　　　Cooper.
Davis, James--of Hiram age 89.
Parker, Mrs Frank--Died, no children.
Reid, Alice--of Cedartown is visiting brother G W Reid.
　　　　　　　Pen & Ink Sketches tells humorous story of
　　　　　　　passwords used by guards in Civil War. No
　　　　　　　one expected fighting.
　　　　　　　9/5/84
Pierce, George F--died at Sparta Ga. last Wednesday.
　　　　　　　Distinguished Methodist divine.
Ewings, J E--Is visiting aunt Mrs. J D Reed.
Pope, Mrs Fannie--of Cobb Co. is visiting her sister Mrs
　　　　　　　A S Pittman.
Head, J B--Brother of W H Head, deceased, has taken
　　　　　　　charge of business.
　　　　　　　8/29/84
Simmons, Terrell E--Of Norcross, son of C James Simmons
　　　　　　　of Gwinnett and Ida Henry of Chattanooga
　　　　　　　married in Atlanta. Eloped anticipating
　　　　　　　objections because they are cousins.
Dobbins, Thomas--Son of George Dobbins died Thursday.
Weisner, Joseph--Child died Wednesday.
Briley, Capt.--Moved to Indian Springs.
Carter, Nancy--Colored, about 70 years old, died
　　　　　　　Wednesday.
Head, W H--Had life insured for 3000 dollars.

Foster, Mrs. Missouri--Died last Thursday. Wife of T J
        Foster. Dau of Dr C L LeSeur. Born Monroe
        Co, Ga on 15 Dec 1835. Married 10 Nov 1857.
        Nine Children with 5 living. Died of
        consumption.
Noland, W A--Died Friday morning.
Porter, T R--Trying to commit suicide.
Moon, Mrs. M J--Feneral to be preached Sunday at Powder
        Springs by Rev. John Eubanks.
Head, Mrs. Eula L--Granted temporary letters on estate
        of W H Head.
Bullock, Albert--Died last Wednesday, son of Sherman
        Bullock, Buried at Mt Olive.
Phillips, Lewis--Died 11 July 1884. Removed to the
        Supreme Grand Lodge above.
Moore, Sally--Died last Sunday, age 93.
McBrayer, Elizabeth--Has applied for exemption of
        personalty.
Cole, T F V--HAS APPLIED FOR PERSONALTY.
Smith, Andrew J--Died last Sunday at Gainesville.
Henson, Jesse--Little son of James Henson of Nebo died
        of typhoid 6 Sept 1884. Age 4 years.
Ewing, Mr--Has returned to Tennessee accompanied by his
        cousin Miss Tempa Reed.
Howard, Pearl--Little girl of S W Howard died Thursday.
        To be buried at Dallas Cemetery.
Lane, G W--of DeKalb Co., Ala., is visiting his father's
        family in Paulding Co.
        9/19/84
Chestnut, Thomas--Has been sick at his brother's, D R
        Chestnut.
Morgan, Mrs William--Died Thursday near Mt Zion Church.
Casey, Mrs--Wife of Bob Casey and daughter of J M
        Griggs is very sick.
Bookout, John L--and Miss Eula Meadows were married
        last Sunday.
        9/26/84
Cobb, Howell--was born in Athens, Sketch about him.
Pittman, James A--of Douglasville and Miss Marion A
        Kennedy of Fulton Co married last Tuesday.
Hudson, Allen--and Miss Fannie Turner both of
        Douglasville were married last Sunday.
        Bride is daughter of George Turner formerly
        of this County.
Cooper, Emma--Gave ice cream festival on her father's
        birthday last Wednesday.
Johns, Doc--Married Josie Moon last Sunday.
Ferguson, Mrs--Dau of Dan Clonts died Friday the 19th.
Colquitt, Walter T--(the late) of Milledgeville Ga,
        interesting sketch.
Hay, Park L--11 year old son of Henry W Hay picked 304
        pounds of cotton.
Head, W H--Eulogy given. He died 15 Aug 1884 age 32
        years. Leaves widowed mother, young wife,
        little daughter.
Turner, Mrs M L--Deceased, Admr B J Penn
        10/10/84
Fielder, W K--Married 7 Oct 1884 to May Jordan. At
        residence of Bride's father at Tunnell Hill
        by Rev James L Hillhouse.

Adams, James--Killed by train near Hiram last Sunday,
          about 19 years old.
Henderson, Mrs Parks--Buried at Sweetwater Church
          cemetery the 6th.
Bearden, Maize--about 16 years old, died of typhoid
          last Thursday, burried Dallas Cemetery.
Rogers, J C--and fireman and a man named Partin were:
          killed in explosion of sawmill boiler near
          Tallapoosa Thursday. His son John Rogers
          not expected to live.
Willis, Brewster--Applied for Personalty.
Echols, R W--Applied for admin of W S Echols estate.
Hanson, John--Who lived at Marietta for two years was
          arrested for murder of a Crawford Co negro
          man in June, 1881.
Matthews, Ben--plays violin, Tony Hill plays banjo, and
          Frank Gann plays bones.
Williams, Johnson--of Lost Mountain is reported to have
          five children weighing 1100 pounds.
Mitchell, Ella--Colored--had a child 8 mos old which
          she bound to Will Graham. Ella Simmons to
          take care of child. Rambling story.
Starnes, Perry--A boy.
Baker, W J--A girl.
Furr, Adeline--Has applied to be guardian of minor
          heirs of Wilson Furr: John F, Alonzo, R E, F
          B, M P, L V Furr.
Sheffield, Martha C--applied for guardianship of Mary F
          Pickett, lunatic.
Minning, Thomas--Appointed admr of P Turner
Little, Penelope--Applied for personalty.
Fannin, James--Who moved to St Clair Co Ala four years
          ago, returned last Tuesday, feeble from
          fever.
McLarin, R P--& family returned from visit to Campbell.
          Accompanied by Alice McLarin, R P's sister.
Ritch, Lizzie--Died Saturday.
Reed, Rev J D--Born Buncomb Co, N C, 1 Jan 1822 and
          died 3 Nov 1884. Lived in Tennessee until
          1846. Married 1844 to Nancy Murphy, still
          living. Moved to Alabama 1846. Became
          Minister in 1859. Buried Dallas Cemetery.
          11/14/84
Wilson, R W--Went to California in 1848. Left wife and
          newborn son. Returned to Acworth last week.
          Wife had remarried at last and then died.
Furr, Wilson--Personal property to be sold,.
Bearden, Mazie--Died 9 Oct 1884, Daughter of Richard
          and Mattie Bearden, age 16.
Clay, Maj John C--Died 25 Aug 1884 in Cobb Co. Age 94.
          Father of Thomas Clay of Paulding and W P
          Clay of Cobb.
Land, Bud--Married Emma Washington Thursday.
Gallidge, Drew--Married Miss Stipe of Carroll Co Sunday
          a week.
Cooper, Henry--Married Alice Caster daughter of Pinson
          Carter Saturday two weeks since.
Griffin, Mattie--Daughter of John Griffin died last
          monday. Buried Dallas.
Dupree, Mrs Mary Jane--Wfie of Rev Wm A Dupree died
          near Etta, 1 Nov 1884. Born Union Co S C 29

Dec 1834. Married 26 Dec 1852. Leaves
Husband and son.

Kirk, H L--Applied for admr of William S Hogue estate.

Davis, F M--Applies for Admr of estate of J C Rogers
11/28/1884

Cooper, Jane--Died at residence of her son Nathan
Cooper on 9th. Age 75.
12/5/84

McBrayer, Henrietta-Died on 25th Nov near Oval Post
Office.

Hipps, H L--Married Lizzie Hunt 23 Nov. Dau of J Meigs
Hunt.
12/19/84

Brown, Tilman--of Yorktown died last Friday.
12/26/84

Nolund, B J & S J--Applied for Admr of estate of W A
Naland.

Bullock, Frank--Died near Dallas last Friday. Age
about 50 years. Eccentric in character.

Cole, Jimmy--Wife died last Friday.

Carter, Mrs Pinson--Invalid for many years died last
Monday.

Chestnur, Dave--Marshall of Dallas injured in street
fight. Hit over left eye hit with pistol
and stabbed in left side. May lose eye.

Hunt, Mrs Ella--Wife of Henry Hunt died 11 Jan 1885.
Age 29. Married Mr. Hunt one year ago.

McLarty, George W--Born in Mecklenburg N C 30 Aug 1804
and died in Dallas 15 Jan 1885. Came to Ga
in 1832 and settled near Douglasville.
Lived there 41 years and then moved to
Dallas. Married on 24 Jan 1833 to Charity
Bates.
Lived with her 50 years and survived her by
two years. Eleven children, 6 sons and 5
daughters. 5 sons and 1 daughter are
deceased. Presbyterian, and after coming to
Ga M E Church.
Mason for 40 years having joined at Villa
Rica. Buried at old family burying ground
at Villa Rica.
1/23/85

Prewett, G W--Has baby girl.

Freeman, Meturis--Wife of James L Freeman and daughter
of John McMickens, died on 2nd. Age 24
years and 2 days. Leaves husband and 2
children.

Wheeler, Nancy--Has applied for personalty.

Owens, E B--Has applied for personalty.

Howard, William--of ETV and Ga RR and Dora Lawrence of
Dallas married Wednesday.
1/30/85

Williams, Wm--Who was wanted in Marietta was arrested
in Chattanooga.

Jones, Albert--Wife gave birth to deformed child.

Adams, Henry--It's a girl.
2/13/1885

Moore, Z C--Applied for personalty.

Parris, Isaac--Married Miss lula Helms on the 5th.
Both of Paulding.

Foster, Lela--The fourteen year old daughter of Dr T J

Foster died last Sunday. Buried Dallas
Cemetery. Funeral by REv W R Dale.
2/27/85
Causey, Samuel--Died at Hiram 4th Feb of typhoid.
Morgan, Rev Benj--of Polk Co died last Sunday.
Rakestraw, Mr Ivey--Died last wek of something like
            meningitis.
Pate, Samuel B--old citizen died at Hiram.
Foote, Charley--Son of Mr and Mrs J B Foote died last
Sunday. Age ten months. Buried Dallas Cem.
Anderson, James A--One of the deputy sheriffs of this
            County and Miss Sarah Lindley of Cobb Co
            were married at residence of Bride's mother.
Camp, Mrs Mabry--Wife of Luther Camp, dau of G F
            Turner, died last Monday. Aged 30 years.
            Member Methodist Church. Leaves parents,
            brother, husband, and one child. Rev W W
            Brinsfield. Buried Dallas Cem.
Hitchcock, Cuma--burned in fire used to burn off
            ground. Sister Lee and her mother both
            badly injured trying to save her. Cuma died
            Wednesday. 14 years old. Lee age 16.
Lee, Mr.--Married Fannie Rusk 1 Mar 1885 at Rev Dr
            Armstrong's house.
Rustk, Fannie--Armstrong, Rev
Gore, Thomas--married Taddy Pace, daughter of Isaac
            Pace. 19th Feb.
Adair, William--Married Lucy J Pace last Thursday.
Florence, M E--Applies for letters on estate of M J
            Florence.
            3/20/85
Turner, Babe--Moved to Douglasville
            3/27/85
Cooper, Mark A--of Cartersville died the 17th.
George, Jack--It's a girl.
McLarty, G W--It's a girl.
Fults, Callie--Formerly of Dallas is now living with W
            N Edwards family at Marietta.
Smith, Matilda--Burned to death (Haralson Co.)
Davis, Pete--and Bob Rawls and Jesse Clay have begun
            keeping bachelors hall.
Hammer, Jacob--Letters on estate of Henry Jones.

George, Jack--It's a girl.
McLarty, G.W.--It's a girl.
Fults, Callie--Formerly of Dallas is now living with W.N.
            Edwards family at Marietta.
Smith, Matilda--Burned to death (Haralson Co.)
Davis, Pete--and Bob Rawls and Jesse Clay have begun keep-
            ing bachelors hall.
Hammer, Jacob--Letters on estate of Henry Jones.
Hulsey, Taylor--Married Miss Nancy Glower last Sunday
            at home of bride's father, Mr. Aleck Glower.
            (Pumpinvine Dist.)
Strickland, Mrs. G. W.--Daughter of Rev. J. B. C. Quillian
            died at Chattahoochee last Saturday and is
            buried at Douglasville. Typhoid. Two little
            boys are recovering.
Durham, L.E.--of Candy Ridge, it's a girl.
Kennedy, Billy--Has been on his place since the Indians
            left it.

515

Warner, R.--It's a girl.
Rogers, Alf--Lost a child last Saturday.
     4/17/85
Rogers, Jack--It's a girl.
     4/24/85
English, James--Married Lula McDonald of Dalton last
     Tuesday. Surprised everyone.
McLeary, Mrs.--Living on Gary Spinks place, died Wednesday,
     buried Dallas.
Osborne, Dr. J. J.--a cousin of Dr. J. C. Osborne is leav-
     ing for Indiana.
Latham, S. P.--and H. P. McCollum have quit batching
     because the dishes got too sticky.
Barnes, Nathan--It's a girl.
Ellison, D. A.--Has 16 year old son seven feet tall.
Reed, Mrs. Louisa--Died in Marietta Sunday. Lula Brintle
     is her niece.
Walker, Mrs. Newt--Died last Wednesday.
Gentry, G. W.--It's a boy.
Thompson, Z. T.--Has been ill, recovering. His brother
     Henry of Covington has been visiting.
     5/8/85
Hitchcok, Lee--burned in fire reported earlier, can now use
     hands.
Taylor, J. L.--and Marcy Cole married on the 26th. Elder
     J. N. Cooper officiating.
McBrayer, P. P.--Arrival of 10th daughter.
Green, Mrs.--Widow of James Green died Thursday, buried
     Dallas Cemetery.
McDuffie, Malcom--Died last Monday.
Ragsdale, T. J.--Fine girl.
Hunt, Ella--Funeral to be preached at Flint Hill.
Moore, Minnie Lee--Niece of J. H. Weaver from Limestone
     Tenn is visiting.
Robins, George--Son of James M. Robins of Weddington died
     of eating wild parsnip. 18 years old.
     5/22/85
Weaver, Col. M. M.--Died at Douglasville.
Williams, Savannah--Daughter of widow Williams died Monday
     of dropsy.
Moon, Mary--(Colored) Died Tuesday.
Watkins, Dick--The Dallas barber and Fannie Carter
     married Thursday. Both colored.
Maulding, Thomas--and wife have separated.
     5/29/85
Echols, T. J.--of Dallas and wife and dau Alice visited
     Douglasville.
Morris, Benjamin--Letters of Admin on estate of Enoch
     Morris.
Sheffield, Isom--Child (Junior) very sick.
     6/19/85
Trezevant, Elizabeth--And Frederick Hunt, Luke S. Northcutt,
     and Mrs. Mary Barnes all died in Marietta last
     week.
Osborne, J. B.--of Atlanta and Maggie Byrd of Marietta
     married this week.
Davenport, Arthur E.--of New York married Mary Lou Check
     this week (Marietta).
Payne, Mrs. B. F.--Her novel "Psyche" was published.
Bullock, N. T.--Visited daughter in Danville, VA
     6/26/1885

McWorter, Rev. Harvey--of Douglasville died.
McBrayer, A. W.--Deceased, William McBrayer letters of admin
   of estate.
Phillips, Mac--of Calhoun Co., Ala visiting his mother
   Mrs. Emeline Phillips.
Smith, Jennie--Daughter of Henry Smith died in Atlanta last
   Wednesday, buried Dallas.
Mason, William--of Draketown struck by lightning. Age 40.
   (Dead)
Leathers, Noah--of Draketown died--age 13. There was an
   error in reporting this but the full name is
   in next week's paper.

Brown, John--Son of William Brown.
   I think Leathers drowned in William Fuller's
   millpond. Aleck Sinyard tried to rescue
   John Brown. Richard Bass was pulled under.
   Luke New saved the others with a fence rail.
Gammell, W. B.--Died last Friday.
   7/3/1885
Echols, Catharine--Died. Age 80 years 5 mo 3 days. T. R.
   Echols wrote tribute. 5 children mourn her.
   T. R. is the baby, age forty.
Hardwick, Thomas & Cecilia--Are visiting relatives, the
   G. F. Turner family.
Reynolds, Rev. J. S.--To preach funeral of James D. Craton.
Phillips, Mrs. Emeline--Died last Sunday, age about 65.
   Her sister, Miss Elizabeth Hogan age 62,
   died Monday.
Sheffield, Tom--Child died last week.
   8/7/85
Boston, Mr.--and Martha Moody married last Sunday.
Camp, H.--Crazy about his little son. (I don't know what
   this meant.)
   List of Pauper Farm Inmates
   Ozbourn Thommasson, age 82; Martha Jackson,
   age 71 bowel disorder; Christopher Griffin,
   age 86; heart disease; Martha Matilda Griffin,
   age 45 rheumatism; Annie Johns, age 77, asthma;
   Mary Buff, age 70, generally diseased; David &
   Elizabeth Aldridge. The grand jury inspected
   the farm regularly and reported on its condition.
   Only those who needed help were there, but care
   for the needy was a serious obligation.
   8/14/85
Sanders, A. C.--Wife of A. C. Sanders, died last Sunday.
   Sister of Mrs. Phillips and Miss Hogan who died
   recently.
Cole, Susana E.--vs. James Cole. Settled. (Not clear if
   they got the divorce.)
Cagle, Sarah E.--vs. William B. Cagle. Divorce granted.
Wheelen, Amanda J.--vs. P. D. Wheelen. Divorce granted.
Adair, J. K.--vs. Nancy Adair. Divorce granted.
   8/21/85
Quarles, Jessie--of Marietta killed by train.
Lewis, Mrs. George m--Aged lady died.
Chupp, Lizzie--Visiting her aunt, Mrs. Braswell.
Gibson, Bayless--Married Susie Bron, age 14, at Bowden
   Lithia Spring, by Rev. Starnes.
Spears, John--Child died last Sunday, buried Shady Grove.
Briley, Bersheby--Petitions to be executrix of will of

T. C. Dunagan. Heirs are herself as a sister
of deceased, Martha Dunagan as sister-in-law,
Elizabeth Dunagan and T. G., A. F., and Reubin
Underwood.
9/11/85
Seals, John A. G.--Legal notice, deceased.
Wigley, John--Legal notice, deceased. These are probably
estate admr notices. Don't know why I copied
them like this.
Russom, R. W.--Leave to sell land of Lewis Phillips, dec.
Florence, Obediah--Legal notice, deceased.
Green, John W.--Son of M. L. Green married in Texas.
Robinson, John C.--Married Miss Mattie Caylor last Sunday,
Squire Henderson officiating.
Brown, Walker--Little son died Thursday.
10/16/85
Edwards, Fred--Murdered in Haralson Co. Farm of Green
Barnwell. Jonas Windbach suspected.
Bulloch, James A.--Admr of R. J. Smith.
Thompson, Nancy--Wife of John Thompson, died last Thursday,
age 30 years.
Bomar, Miss Tommie--of Douglas Co. visited her cousin
Carrie Foster.
10/30/85
Collins, Elizabeth--Estate of H. Collins, deceased.
Morries, Robert Lee--born 3 May 1880, son of A. J. and
Nancy R. Morris of Paulding Co. Died. "Jesus
has come for me," he said.
Hammer, Jacob--Admr of Henry Jones estate.
Green, J. L.--Admr of Mrs. M. L. Green estate.
11/27/85--All national news and ads.
11/27/85
Hipps, Miss Maggie--Visiting her sister, Mrs. O. P. Cooper.
Hulsey, Joseph--Shot by a man named Campbell in Bridges'
photograph gallery in Rockmart. Wounded in the
ribs. (He did die.)
Bullock, C. H. S.--Deceased, minor children are J. Homer
and S. Catherine Bullock.
12/25/85
Attaway, W. M.--& James Carrol admr of F. Thompson.
Parker, Rachel--years support from estate of L. M. Parker.
Portwood, G. W.--Admr of T. M. Campbell, land sale.
Breckinridge, Sally--of Walhalla SC is visiting her brother
in Dallas.
Nealy, William--It's a girl.
McEachern, S. C.--of Atlanta, and T. J. Babb of Bonham
Texas visited.
Rogers, Thyrza--of Fort Smith, Ark, visiting her sister
Mrs. W. E. Thompson.
Moon, Walter--Son of Capt. Z. B. Moon of Atlanta has been
living with his uncle, J. R. Moon in Dallas and
is visiting his father in Atlanta.
Gann, E.--Son of Frank Gann was scalded severely.
1/1/86
Owen, L. E.--Gave sociable at home of his father G. A.
Owens.
Carter, Robert--Is visiting his father E. M. Carter.
1/29/86
Bobo, Hiram--Of Douglas Co. and Fannie Robinson of Carroll
Co. married in Waco by Rev. S. M. Garrett.
Mann, J. C.--His wife and son died of typhoid.

Hollingsworth, Tracy--of Gadsden married Julie Parrott
            of Newnan (Cartersville Courant).
Seals, Alma--applied for 12 months support on estate of
            J. A. G. Seals.
McBrayer, Elizabeth--Applied for 12 months support on
            estate of James McBrayer.
Hogue, Elizabeth--Applied for 12 months support on estate
            of William Hogue.
Newton, Mrs. Sallie Morgan--Died at home of her father.
            John W. Morgan near Embry on 11 Dec 1885.
            Born Sep 3, 1850. M. E. Church. Married
            15 Dec 1875 to Rev. H. M. Newton
            2/12/86
Pool, Tom--of Douglasville, age 13, accidentally shot
            himself.
Chandler, Mrs.--Died on Thursday.
Cooper, Emma--Visiting her grandfather at Lost Mountain.
Nichols, Robert J.--Died last night.
            2/26/86
Maret, David--Married Mettie Lou Russell on Feb 11 at
            Cedartown. Her father D. M. Russell.
Matthew, Erastus--Married Ella Bradley of Cartersville.
Hipps, Mrs. Oscar--of Atlanta died. Late of Powder
            Springs.
Root, Mrs. Wm.--of Marietta died.
Parker, G. T.--Admr of Lucinda Porter.
Hays, Dicy--Year's support on estate of R. G. Hays.
Haynie, M. A.--Guardian of W. E., E. M., and Carrie White,
            minor children of A. D. White.
            3/5/86
Head, M. J.--of Buchanan married Jennie Young, daughter of
            a Young.
Payne, Warren--and Miss Beulah Williams eloped.
            Married at home of Bud House by F. A. Bell.
Bentley, John--of Cobb Co. and Miss Claude Roberts of
            Cherokee Co. married 24 Feb.
Glasscock, Thomas--of Cherokee Co. died in Fulton Co.
            jail.
            3/26/86
Lee, Mrs.--Mother in law of William Rouche of Marietta
            died.
Price, Green P.--Married Rosa C. Rivers on 18th.
            (Haralson Co.)
Spinks, J. M.--It's a girl.
Hayes, John--Age 71 to marry Harriet Rogers.
            4/2/86
Camp, Penn--It's a girl.
Holland, William--age 21, died last Thursday.
            4/9/86
Cooper, R. J.--Died at Cartersville.
            4/16/86
Ragsdale, W. G.--and Laura Denson of Roxana were married
            last Sunday.
Pickett, Malley--Died Thursday. Buried New Hope Church.
Price, G. W.--It's a boy.
Vaughn, Mrs. J. T.--nee Pickett was visiting her sick
            father.
Winn, Matt--and Bisey Wigley eloped last Sunday.
Austin, James--and Fannie Croker married Sunday.
Weatherby, Aaron--age 75 and Mrs. Mary Driver age 30 of

Haralson wer married on the 21st.

5/7/86

Simms, Mrs. George--Visiting relatives in New York State.

Ray, J.--Child burned fatally (colored).

Hill, Mrs. Benjamin--of Cherokee Co. is visiting her
daughter Mrs. Thompson.

Pickett, Mrs. M.--is visiting her daughter Mrs. Vaughn.

5/14/86

King, Lum--Of Summerville and Emma Smith of Dallas married
last Wednesday.

Matthews, J. B.--of Atlanta married Maggie Chocran of
Paulding Co. at residence of her father last
Wednesday.

5/21/1886

Davis, E.--of Dallas married Miss Mollie Tidwell of Atlanta
last Wednesday.

5/28/86

Rawls, N. B.--Visiting brother Robert Rawls.

Hagan, Miss Mandy--of Braswell is visiting her sister Mrs.
Robert Moon.

Hogan, James--Died from cancer on 25th. Interred New Hope,
Masonic honors.

Duncan, J. B.--of Douglas Co. visited his brother Prof.
F. M. Duncan. History of Co D, 7th Ga Reg CSA.

Rhymer, Angelina--known as Old Mrs. McDole, and daughter
Mary McDole has left employ of Wiley Jones.

Earwood, Mrs. Allen--of Big Shanty died last Sunday
evening. Several children.

6/4/86

Pickette, Malachi--Will probated.

Williams, Mrs. Uriah--Died near Nebo of Dropsy on 31st.
Interred Bethany Church.

Williams, Jacob--Died Tuesday night of consumption. Lived
Jasper Clay's place.

Williams, W. R.--of Cotton, "gained possession of his two
boys."

6/11/86

Thompson, W. E.--A son born Sunday the 6th died the 9th.

Hilburn, Bud--Died last Tuesday. Boiler explosion at saw-
mill of Lewis Thompson and Dick Lawrence.

Parris, Phoebe--Died at residence of her daughter Mrs.
Louiza Calley in Ark on May 25. Cause was
poisoned honey. Had lived in Paulding Co. 40
years, move to Arkansas a year ago.

6/25/86

Neal, Maj. S. H.--of Carroll Co. is 82 years old. 100
grandchildren.

Mathews, Lucy--daughter of M. C. Mathews was taken suddenly
ill.

Hogan, James--Died 25 May (?). Born Union Co. SC. Moved
to Paulding Co. several years before the war.
Near 73 years at death. One wife deceased, one
living. M. E. Church. Buried New Hope Cem
26 May (Masonic tribute.)
A kite ought to made of fly paper (to prove
there are no new jokes, L. P.)

7/2/86

Vernon, L. L.--to probate will of James Hogan.
"How to Cook Husbands", a delightful article.

Leathers, P. K.--Has a mica-kaolin-gold mine.

Allgood, Mrs. Pat--Died last Thursday, stricken with
                paralysis.
Smith, B. H.--gives editor list of Captain Nelson's Co. of
                Mexican War who are still living. John R.
                Winters, Elisha Knight, B. H. Smith, James
                McGuire, John Foote, Joel Shed, G. W. Phillips.
Winters, J. R.--McGuire, J.
Foote, J.--Shed, J.
Phillips, G.--Coursey, John
Coursey, John--and wife killed in train accident.
                (Lurid details.) Wife had been married to John
                Baker, She and Coursey just married in Atlanta.
                She was Nancy Taylor, reared by Mr. Henderson
                near Stilesboro. From Polk Co.
McLarty, G. W.--Child died.
                7/16/86
Fite, Mrs.--Visiting her mother's family at Big Shanty.
Meeks, Jas J.--Married Nancy J. Baker Tuesday night.
Land, Esther--Staying with her sister Mrs. F. M. Gann.
Wimpy, B. R.--Succeeded George Sims at telegraph office.
                George has gone to Morristown NY.
Vaughn, Randall--Was wounded by minie ball on 22 Dec 1864,
                while serving in 2nd Ga. cavalry. Ball removed
                recently.
                7/23/86
Puckett, William--Night marshal at Cartersville killed
                Bryant Strickland age about 30 years, unmarried.
Parramore, Mrs. M. E.--of Chattanooga visited her mother
                Mrs. Smith.
Matthews, Lucy--Recovering at her brother Jerry's.
Roberts, Dan--Colored. Died on farm of J. T. Henderson
                where he had lived 30 years. Buried 9 July
                1886 at Mt. Vernon.
Meadows, Jacob--Oldest man in county.
                9/6/86
Fite, B. A.--Visiting his mother in Cartersville.
Fullmore, Mr.--of Memphis is visiting his cousin Mrs. Dr
                Robertson.
                8/13/86
Earwood, Mrs. Allen--Funeral to be preached by Rev. J. S.
                Reynolds.
Doyal, Mary E.--Wife of J. G. Doyal has applied for
                personalty exemption.
                8/20/86
Rogers, Adie Lee--Poem commemorating her death was written
                10 Aug 1886. Lived Ft. Smith, Ark. Sister of
                Mrs. W. E. Thompson.
Wix, Addison--Died last Monday.
Babb, Mr. Jessie--Twin girls.
Sanders, T. M.--A girl.
McLarty, Dr. Tom--Has set up practice at Hope, Ark.
Denson, Brooks--A girl.
                8/27/86
Tomason, Martin--Judged Lunatic.
Verner, S. S. or I. S.--of Paulding Co. was present at the
                bedside of his sick brother, James M. Verner,
                who died last Tuesday.
Smith, W. M.--of Paulding Co. and Maud C. Tanner of Acworth
                were married by Rev. F. A. Bell on 19 Aug.
Robertson, Mr.--of Five Points was married to Ella Green
                near Villa Rica last Sunday. (Carroll Free
                Press.)

Williams, Eva--died at her home near Villa Rica last Sunday.
Thompson, Belle--Married M. L. Satterfield of Rome on 21st.
        Residence of her father Thomas J. Thompson near
        Rockmart.
Spinks, Gary H.--Died 30 Aug 1886. Born Clark or butts Co.
        16 June 1820. Moved to Newton Co. at age 2.
        Came to Paulding Co. 1843. Married 26 Aug.
        1844 to Elizabeth Ann Matthews, daughter of
        C. J. and Sallie Matthews. Buried Dallas
        Cemetery.
Brooks, James--vs. Lizzie Brooks. Libel for divorce.
        Since she does not live in county notice to be
        published for four months.
Wommack, J. M.--Applied for guardianship of Adaline
        Richards, minor child of W. B. Richards late of
        Polk Co.
Winne, A. H.--applies for discharge as guardian of James
        D. Middlebrooks and Laura A. Entrekin nee
        Middlebrooks.
        9/10/86
Pickett, Matilda--12 months support from estate of Malachi
        Pickett.
Vaughn, J. T.--of Roxana plans to move to late father-in-
        law's homestead near Owen Mill (Malley Pickett.)
        9/17/86
Ables, John--Moved to Silver Creek.
Morris, Dorthulia--of Acworth Died Friday and buried at
        Roxana Cemetery. Daughter of Ambrose Morris.
Williams, Rev. Henry--Died at Cross Plains, Ala the 14th.
        Brought to Dallas and buried New Hope Church.
        Father of H. S. Williams.
        9/24/86
Conner, Mrs. Fannie--wife of J. E. Conner died last Tuesday
        at Villa Rica. Daughter of John Floyd.
Ragan, Frank--of Villa Rica died and buried same day as
        Conner.
Compton, Mrs. Mintie--age 85 is very low.
Parris, Octavia--Age seven died last Wednesday. Daughter
        of N. D. Parris of Branch.
Rainwaters, J. M.--house burned. Mrs. Rainwater's father
        is N. D. Parris.
        10/1/86
Pardue, Will--Four year old daughter died. (Carroll Co.)

Dimmock, T. W.--Infant son died (Carroll Co.)
Bayles, D. E.--Married Miss Lyle last Sunday (Wheeling),
        residence of bride's father D. E. Bayles.
        (S/B Groom's father).
Nix, A. E.--Married Flora Strain last Monday. (Carroll Co.)
Johnson, Will--married Fanny Worthy (Carrollton.)----
Broadnax, John H.--married Belle Sims on Wednesday
        (Carrollton.)
Bradley, Newt--Married Katie Smith in Gainesville. Sis of
        F. R. Seaborn of Cartersville.
Holcombe, J. M.--Infant child died (Haralson.)
Speight, John--and Mary Harper married on 16th. (Haralson.)
Glover, Ned--formerly of Marietta was married in Texarkana,
        Tex.
Hirsch, Samuel R.--of Marietta will marry Hettie Lindheimer
        on Oct 12.
Hill, Wilson--Six year old son of John Hill died last
        Friday--Cedartown.

McMillian, Mrs. R. H.--Died last Wednesday.
Whitlock, Mr.--Two month old infant died last Saturday.
Powell, James--Married Dora Forsyth, Sept 26.
Prather, J. M.--married Mollie Truett of Douglas Co.
        10/3/86
Cowley, John W.--of Milner buried his wife on Saturday and
        he died Monday.
Bradley, W. A.--of Charleston SC will marry Lilly Johnson
        on Oct 6. She is dau of late Abba Johnson.
Killon, Thomas--killed by train. Wife is suing RR.
Barnes, C. M.--and Alada C. Root were married Tuesday by
        Rev. G. S. Tumlin.
Rainwater, John--Child died Saturday.
Hollis, J. A.--Married Lula Pace on Oct. 3.
Brintle, Lula--Married on Sept 29 to B. F. Carrie. Married
        in Marietta at residence of her uncle Humphrey
        Reed.
Parker, Mary L.--Wife of Dr. Geo T. Parker died at her home
        near Dallas on Sept 30. Born SC Sept 1832.
        Maiden name was Anderson. Half sister of W. P.
        Anderson of Marietta, who died less than a year
        ago. Married at Powder Springs Nov 1851.
Hightower, John W.--formerly of Rockmart now lives Seden
        Ala.
        10/15/86
Terry, Noah--Died Tuesday.
Morris, Sallie--Wife of Milton Morris died Oct 4.
Maddox, Henry--baby girl dead.
Wayland, Mrs. Harriett--of Marietta died Saturday.
Jackson, Jas N.--of Waco. His wife died last Wednesday.
Hardeman, S. I.--Died last Tuesday at Waco.
Jackson, Elizabeth--Died at home of her sister Mrs. E. H.
        Burden. Wife of Joe Jackson (Haralson.)
Awtrey, Eldridge--Married Mattie Wigley Sept 26.
        (Haralson)
Spinks, Elizabeth--Widow of G. H. Spinks has applied for
        12 months support.
Cochran, W. C.--admr of William Cochran.
Fuller, William--Admr of Harriet W. Gore.
Dill, J. M.--and son charged with murder of John Allen are
        being tried today in Dallas.
Allen, John--Died Wednesday. Leaves wife and 4 children.
        Allen got drunk in Atlanta, came home to Dallas.
        He hit Mr. Whitlock with a stick and Whitlock
        got the Misses Archer to sit up with him.
        J. N. Dill and son lived with the Archers.
        They went to town to get doctor. Met Allen
        near Foote house. It was found that Allen was
        seriously stabbed and he died.
        10/22/86
Goldin, Wesley--of Haralson died Friday.
Brown, William J.--of Haralson died 12 Oct. Father of Jasper
        Brown.
McGregor, Mr.--A boy.
Fain, Mr.--A girl
Carter, Bartow--Accidentally killed Will Richards at Broken
        Arrow, Ala. (Cedartown paper).
McLarty, Dr. Thomas--Visiting his sister Mrs. R. P. Gann.
Pritchett, Capt. M. L.--Married Miss S. S. Kingsbury at home
        of James Ramsauer on 18 Nov 1886.

Parris, N. J.--Daughter found Masonic badge of J. H. Harris
    who died in 1872.
    11/26/86
Anderson, D. S.--Died at Marietta on Wednesday week.
Murray, Dr. Robert--Married Georgia Lindley in Powder Springs
    on last Wednesday. (Marietta)
Good, Evelyn--Died last Sunday, age 2. Daughter of Mr. &
    Mrs. J. E. Good. (Cedartown)
Horn, F. W.--Twins died. (Cedartown)
Lumpkin, H. P.--(Jr) brother of Mrs. W. J. Hall of Forest-
    ville died in Cedartown on Nov 10. Age 19.
Mitchell, Nancy--Wife of James W. Mitchell has applied for
    personalty.
Earwood, Annie--Wife of G. W. Earwood has applied for
    personalty.
Spinks, Lucius--Age 26, died Sunday, Nov 21.
McLarty, Dr. Tom--of Hope, Ark, is visiting John Mables of
    Villa Rica. Hopes to have eyesight restored by
    Dr. Calhoun.
Cantrell, Mattie A.--of Cartersville died Tues. Sister
    of late Mrs. B. C. Rowan.
Ford, Annie--10 year old daughter of Henry Ford died Satur-
    day. (Cartersville)
Coogler, G. W.--of Bremen has died.
Attaway, J. C.--and family went to Hunt Co, Tex.
    (Cartersville)
Morgan, Columbus--and Minda Elliot were married Nov 21
    in Marietta.

Alston, William--and Mrs. Ida Christian were married at
    home of the brides father, Dr. G. W. Cleland.
    (Marietta)
Peek, Mattie--of Cedartown died last Saturday. Wife of
    Julius A. Peek. Methodist Church.
Baker, Sammie Gilbert--Son of Tom Baker died 21 Nov 1886
    at Birmingham and brought to Cedartown for
    burial.
Hawkins, Judge W. A.--died at home in Americus last Sunday.
Mitchell, Mrs.--Wife of James W. Mitchell applied for
    exemption of property.
Allen, Lizzie--Applied for 12 months support. Widow of
    J. H. Allen.
Douthit, Mrs.--and daughter Alice of Huntsville visited.
Reese, Mellita--of Rome married J. H. Reed of Marietta.
Hill, Tony--and Bob Hill killed each other in Atlanta.
    Only children of Col. D. P. Hill of Dallas.
Spinks, Elizabeth--12 month support.
Sewell, Dr. George--Married Sallie Downer (Cedartown)
Jarrett, Nannie L.--and Frank H. Jarrett married of Blue
    Ridge Ga (Marietta)
Roberts, Joshua--of Cherokee Co, GA, died last Tuesday.
Dutton, John C.--Married Malissa C. Moon last Sunday.
Seals, Eudora--Married W. Y. Wyatt of Atlanta. Her father
    J. R. Seals.
Lovelace, Milton--Died at Cartersville last week.
Winn, John--son of A. H. Winn got a pistol ball in thigh.
    12/17/86
Ryals, Walter--Formerly of Cartersville died at Birmingham,
    Ala on Dec 10.
Price, Lillie--Died at Bremen 3 Dec 1886, daughter of late
    I. J. Price.

Bunn, William C.--and Annie Knight were married last Thurs-
        day at Methodist Church in Cedartown.
Casey, James H.--Died near Cedartown last Thursday. Lime
        Branch Cemetery.
Dill, J. N.--and son were charged with murder, found guilty
        of manslaughter.
        12/24/86
Montgomery, Will--Married Mary E. Fite. His mother Mrs.
        J. G. Montgomery. (Cartersville)
Wigle, Mrs. I. F.--Died at home of her father R. A.
        McMillan in Talladega, Ala on Dec 8. Leaves
        two little boys.
Thorton, R. B.--Married A. C. Woodham (Carroll Co.)
Rawls, Robert L.--Married Emana Cooper on 19 Dec at M. E.
        Church. Daughter of T. J. Cooper.
Nichols, L.--Married Sallie Tidwell of Atlanta on 20 Dec.
        Sallie is a sister of Mrs. E. Davis and a niece
        of Mrs. J. B. Foote of Dallas.
        12/31/86
England, Mrs.--Left for McLemore's Cove to join husband who
        has charge of that circuit.

Breckinridge, W. A.--Going to Polk Co.
Hitchcock, Jessie--Wife died last Sunday. Maiden name
        Adair.
        1/14/87
Christian, P. A. & J. A. & C. S.--Not guilty of assault
        with intent to murder.
        1/21/87
Ramsauer, Rev. James--Moved to Cedartown.
Reed, Tempa--and J. H. Washington were married Jan 16.
        Bride's mother Mrs. J. D. Reed.
Jordan, Florence--Married Dr. T. J. Foster at Tunnel Hill
        at residence of bride's father W. W. Jordan.
        Bride is sister of Mrs. W. K. Fielder.
        1/28/87
Corn, John C.--To serve 1 year on chain gang.
Witts, John--Married Mary Woodall near New Hope last Thurs-
        day. Her father John W. Woodall.
Weaver, Eula--Married John S. Lamm of Braswell last Wednes-
        day. Col. J. H. Weaver her father.
Christian, Mrs. S. J.--applied for personalty.
        2/11/87
Oglesby, Isaac--of Powder Springs died.
Young, A. J.--Funeral held Sunday.
Smith, F. M.--guardian of Francis and Jackson Smith, minor
        children of R. J. Smith Jr.
Owen, J. C.--petition for estate of Milesberry Owen to be
        placed in hand of County Administrator W. L.
        Rollins.
Dodd, Henry--Applied for personalty.
Davis, L. F.--12 months support from estate of F. M. Davis.
Petty, J. R.--Admr of estate of F. Thompson Sr.
Mullins, Frank--Died at Marietta.
Gibbs, A. J.--Child died of measles.
Culpepper, Mr.--of Atlanta visited his sister Mrs. G. P.
        Roberts of Dallas.
Wright, Mrs. Dr. B. F.--Died in Polk Co.
Barron, Dora--Married B. F. Waver Jan. 1. (Carroll Co.)
Fleming, Eula--Married Jas Gaston Jr, Jan 30. (Carroll Co.)
Bass, Minnie--of Carrollton married Howard Harwell of
        Newburn on Jan 3. Her father J. A. Bass.

Fain, Johnson--of Atlanta married Miss Tommie Green of
        Carrollton.
Cantrell, Callie--of Temple married Mr. Sheridan.
Milan, Charles--Married Nelia Jones, on Leak St. Bride
        is youngest sister of Rev. Sam Jones (a well-
        known crusader.) Courant-American.
        2/18/87
Rogers, William--Killed while playing on trains last
        Wednesday. (Gory details.)
Eaves, W. T.--Married Shady Brown Jan 30 at home of bride's
        father, Joseph E. Brown. (Haralson)
Steward, C. B.--Married Cordelia Dean "last Sunday".
        (Haralson)

Strickland, C. B.--Married Hettie Hazleton several days
        ago.
McLendon, Mrs.--Mother of John, James, Moses McLendon.
        Died Feb 12. Very old.
McEachern, Samuel C.--Married at Marietta on the 2nd to
        Eula Stanley. Bride's father is William
        Stanley.
Gilham, Emma--Died on 5th of consumption.
Collie, James G.--Married Fanny B. Hamby at home of
        bride's father, Leonard Hamby (Mableton)
Alexander, J. M.--of Roopville married Myrtie Green.
        Bride's father Dr. J. D. Green. (Carrollton)
        2/25/87
Hay, David G.--Died last night (Tax Collector) leaves
        wife and several children.
Fults, Maggie--Married Mr. Hutchin at Tallapoosa.
Carter, Robert and Bartow--visiting their father, E. M.
        Carter.
Matthews, Miss Lou--Married Frank Wills of New Hope last
        Sunday. Will live at Rome.
Waters, John--Wife had twins, a boy and a girl.
Simpson, Mrs. Annie--Died last Wednesday of Apoplexy.
        Married one week before. (Rockmart).
Martin, Rube--Wife died Saturday (Carroll Co.)
        No
        3/4/87
Compton, D. C.--and family of Collier Creek, Ala visiting
        relatives in Dallas.
Roberts, W. G.--Baby girl born yesterday.
Cook, Violet--Wife of Isaac Cook died in Birmingham Ala
        on 25th. Remains interred New Hope Church.
Cochran, Mrs. W. C.--Died last Thursday from burns.
Hay, H. W.--Filed to fill his brother's office of tax
        collector.
Cooper, Bertie--Died last Monday of Meningitis. 8 year old
        daughter of C. or O. P. Cooper.
Martin, Mrs. Mary Ann--of Carrollton died on Feb. 13, age
        43.
        3/11/87
McCurry, William--His son age 10 or 12 left home near
        Bowan to visit neighbor on Feb 19. Hasn't been
        seen since.
Furr, Bob--of Villa Rica, brother of H. Furr of Douglas-
        ville died last Thursday.
Maxwell, J. G.--and M. C. Polk married last Sunday.
        (Douglasville)
Chambers, J. T.--Married Maggie Burns at home of Samuel
        Burns, the bride's father. (Carroll Co.)

VITAL STATISTICS FROM PAULDING NEW ERA

Cole, Dr. and Mrs.--Child died, buried Concord Church.
    (Carroll Co.)
Power, D. P.--3 year old John died Tuesday.
Alley, Fannie--of Paulding visiting sister Mrs. J. W.
    Hamling of Douglasville.
Cates, Laura--of Newnan died last week, daughter of A.
    B. Cates, age 19. (Douglasville)

Odon, ----- was Killed at Charles Vines saw shop Thursday
    (Haralson).
Cotton, Mrs. P.F.--Died at home of her father A.H. Daniel
    (Carroll Co.).
Beall, N.N.--Vistied his brother Col. J.B. Beall (Carroll Co.).
Voss, Phillip J.--of Atlanta married to Olive Gann of Cobb Co.
Washington, J.D.--His store house burgled. Goods found in yard
    of old lady Rogers by her brother John Dowdy.
    4/1/87
McLendon, Bettie--Died yesterday, sister of Mrs. N.W. Roberts of
    this place.
    4/8/87
Turner, Mrs. G.F.--Too sick to be moved home from Atlanta.
    4/22/87
Satterfield, J.H.--Died in Ft. Smith, Ark. on the 20th. Notified
    by telegram.
Neely, Wm.--Moved to Atlanta.
Turner, Mrs. G.F.--Died in Atlanta, buried at Concord in Henry
    Co. Member of M.E. Church, leaves husband, son
    and granddaughter.
Christian, Mrs. S.J.--Applied for personality.
    4/29/87
Orr, Florence--of Carroll Co. died Apr. 9, aged 17 yrs., 9 mo.,
    9 days.
Malone, Rev. J.D.--Died Monday (Villa Rica).
Hudgins, Earnest--age 7, died Tues. Son of T.J. Hudgins (Villa
    Rica).
Gable, W.B.--Married Barret, Alice on April 19 at home of bride's
    father, M.C. Barrett. Married by Rev. Joseph Galbe.
    (Marietta).
Crumley, Rev. W.M.--Died at Atlanta (Marietta).
Braswell, John--of Sardis died Saturday. (Marietta).
Beckwith, Mrs.--Died in Atlanta on Tues. Wife of Rev. Bishop
    Beckwith. (Marietta).
Malone, D.J.--Married Sallie Love at home of her father Seaborn
    B. Love in Atlanta last Tues eve. (Marietta).
Turner, R.M.--Has boy and girl twins.
Gray, Garrett--Died yesterday, buried family grave yard. Once
    represented Cobb and Paulding Cos. in legislature.
    5/13/87
Zuber, R.S.--of Floyd Co. died in Rome Sunday.
    5/20/87
Robertson, Fannie--of Dallas married Jas. L. Mason of Atlanta.
    Daughter of Dr. S. Robertson.
    6/3/87
Holland, Kate B.--admx. of E.W. Holland of Fulton Co., land sale.
Austell, W.W.--and W.J. Garrett, admrs. of Alfred Austell of
    Fulton Co., land sale.
    6/3/87
Hogan, Mrs. Sarah--12 months support.
Foote, Author--Son of Charles Foote sick.
    6/10/87

Walker, Jerry--of Cobb Co. will be released from penitentiary.
         (Marietta).
Phillips, Duval--Died on the 28th. Grand child of C.D. Phillips.
         (Marietta).
Heaton, Mrs. Mary Ann-Died May 25 two miles from Rockmart--age 71.
Johns, Pierce--Died last Sunday.
Compton, D.C.--Infant died Saturday of hives.
Volantine, Bob--Colored, died in copper mine fall.
Grist, Rev. John--Married Sarah Zebuner the 29th at home of T.J.
         Parsons.
Norton, Milton--Married Miss Amanda Norton at residence of W.R.
         Owen last Sunday.
Shockley, Rhoda--from Nebo visiting her brother A.B. Shockley
         near Senoy.
Nichol, T.J.--of Cedartown has moved to Nachez, Miss.
Jones, A.T.--and Janie E. Wofford married Tues. by Mr. Cooper.
         Bride is daughter of E.E. Wofford.
Wright, Jas. H.--2 year old child died Sunday. (Cedartown)
Reed, W.G.--Child died Saturday.
;No,--6/17/87
Hicks, Eunice--Died Monday--wife of David Hicks of Timel Ranch.
         (Cedartown).
Reed, Mrs.--Died, (I think). Mother of Mrs. I.F. Thompson, and
         A.R. Reed of Anniston, Ala. (Cedartown).
Hamrick, R.A.--Child age 7, or 8 died. (Cedartown).
Parks, R.B.--of Atlanta married Lorena Yound on the 7th.
         (Cedartown).
Chambers, Will--formerly of Marietta died last Sunday at
         Chattanooga.
Burk, Rev. Thornton--Died on June 6 at Powder Springs. Born
         Elbert Co. in 1794, ordained Baptist preacher in
         1833. (Marietta).
Carroll, J.F.--Married Mrs. O.C. Robertson on 5th June. (Carroll
         Co.).
Croft, David--Died last Sunday at residence of son D.W. Croft.
         (Carroll Co.).
Richardson, Mrs.--wife of Maj. John Richardson of Texas and
         mother of Mrs. L.C. Mandeville of Carroll Co. died
         in Texas on 31st. (Carroll Co.).
Hagin, George--of Morgan Co. died 2nd. Leaves wife and 2 or 3
         small children. Son of H.N. Hagin of Braswell.
         9/2/87
Jones, Manning--Little daughter died. (Yorkville).
Ferguson, James--Funeral to be preached at Methodist Church
         Sunday.
Williams, Mrs. J.J.--Wife of Mr. George Williams died Nov. 8.
         Daughter of O.I. & Eliza Winn.
Durham, Jacob O.--Died at Marietta. Injured in train accident
         on Oct. 19.
Kirkpatrick, John C.--formerly of Cartersville, killed by Dr.
         Ford of Shreveport, LA. Kirkpatrick stole Ford's
         wife.
Hutchings, Bat J.--Child died.
         9/16/87
Cole, J.B.--Admr. of John M. Duffey.
         9/23/87
Clonts, John A.--Exec. of will of R.E. Kiker.
Foote, T.A.--Daughter born.
Foote, Byrd--a boy born.
Roberts, G.P.--A girl born, died within a few days.
Fite, Mrs.--has been visiting her son B.A. Fite.

528

Arrington, Beda--and Miss Willie York of Rockmart were married at
    Reed House in Dallas yesterday by A.J. Morgan.
Smith, Elyzabeth--Wife of Z.Z. Smith died at Lost Mountain on
    the 21st. Buried at Vernon.
Harrison, C.F.--vs A.J. Harrison, divorce. Defendant has left
    state.
    9/3/87
Rollins, W.I.--Admr. of I.C. Hix.
Wells, M.L.--Admr. Thos. Gore.
Rawls, R.L.--Nine pound boy.
Bishop, Wm. Henry--of rock gang for ETV and GA RR was struck by
    train at Hamlet. Brain surgery at Atlanta but he
    died Monday night. Son of Mr. Izzy Bishop of
    Pumpkinvine. Age about 21. Buried at New Canaan
    Baptist Church.
Barnett, John--A boy last Sunday at Braswell.
Norton, Mr.--Responsible for two pound newcomer.
    10/7/87
Griffith, Thomas--and Olivia Jordan were married at residence of
    Jonathon Williams in Buchanan. (Haralson).
Hawling, Jack--of Bremen died Monday of typhoid.(Haralson).
Holcombe, Mrs. Reuben--Sister of Seab and Robt. Reed died last
    Tuesday. (Haralson).
Ritch, H.C.--exec. of George K. Williams.
Reed, Mr.--age 17 of Haralson County killed in syrup mill
    accident.
Brintle, Nancy--Wife of O.F. Brintle applied for exemption of
    personalty.
    10/21/87
Spearman, Mr.--of Anderson, NC visited relatives in Dallas.
Helms, G.W.--Died last Wed. Buried Shady Grove.
Reynold, Mrs. Mary--is sick at Spinks hotel, had been assisting
    G.W. Helms family.
Penn, William--Married Miss Douthitt of Huntsville on the 18th
    by Rev. S.B. Ledbetter.
Palmer, John W.--Applied for personalty.
Osborne, Louisa--Applied for personalty.
    11/4/87
Elders, A.A.--left for lower GA.
Cochran, W.L.--Exec. Jerry Wood. (Word? Ward?)
Scott, Matthew--and Mary Rose were married recently by G.W. Cole.
Ferguson, Mack--and Nancy Brown ran off to Texas. He is married.
    They were arrested.
    1/20/88
Phillips, Charles D.--Grand Jury of Paulding Co. found a true
    bill of assault with intent against him.
Bullock. Nat--also indicted by grand jury of assault with intent
    to murder. Case will be tried by Judge Maddox who
    will not be influenced by Bullock's friends and will
    see that Bullock made an unprovoked attack on
    Phillips. (Marietta Journal).
Bowden, John--Fired shots at his father-in-law Judge John James
    near Salt Springs. James not hurt. (Marietta
    Journal).
Cobb, Ollie--Died Monday last age 21. (Villa Rica Gold Leaf).
    4/26/89
Webb, Tol--Stepson killed at Anniston, Ala. in saw mill explosion.
    Buried Yorkville.
Watts, William--Married Lizzie McBrayer last week. (Yorkville).
O'Neal, Mr.--Not able to do any work and his wife is following
    the plow. (An appeal for help by California Dist.

correspondent.)

Davis, James--Now past 94 years, confined to bed. (California).

Embry, J.M.--is travelling and writes from Texas. Says land is
          better but water not good. Has travelled also
          through Indian Territory, left Georgia first Monday
          in December.

Holland, Elizabeth--Admx. of Parthena Anderson.

Alley, P.A.C.--Admr. is W.L. Rollins.

McWhorter, Sammie--is visiting her uncle Dr. G.P. Underwood.

Baxter, Mrs.--Wife of Nat Baxter, died last Tuesday. Buried
          Pumpkinvine Church. J.M. Spinks conducted funeral.
          Over 74 years of age, lived in Paulding County over
          40 years.

Nix, R.J.--Fell dead at a spring near A. Mauldings. Leaves wife,
          three sons and one daughter to mourn departure.
          (Embry--written Apr. 29, 1889.)

Vaughn, R.--Guardian of Blanche Pool, minor heir of J.C. Pool.

Pool, C.A.--Guardian of Kate Pool, and J.S. Vaughn, guardian of
          T.L. Pool, also minor heirs of J.C. Pool.

Lewis, Mrs. John D.--Funeral to be....

Lewis, George--Age 82 was in town.

Tomlin, Taylor--is father of twins.
          5/10/89

House, W.R.--Looking around in Texas.

Reed, Andy--Wife of John Carter died. Funeral last Sunday con-
          ducted by Rev. Thomas Powell.

Carter, Julia--Is wife of John, reported above. Andy Reed re-
          ported for California Dist..

Norton, Mr.--No. 2 has arrived, weights 12 pounds.

Williams, G.W.--tried by Judge Scoggins for lunacy.

Cain, Henry--Baby died last Thursday. Buried New Georgia.

Ables, Mrs. John M.--Showing off twin girls at picnic.
          5/17/89
          There is a long article about Potash "army"
          which I didn't understand so don't know if
          it was vital or not.

Gentry, G.W.--Funeral to be preached by Rev. J.M. Williams 5th
          Sunday in June at Shady Grove Church.

Hagan, B.F.--Sec. of Daisy Dale Alliance (Farmer's Alliance?)
          writes in honor of J.J. Forsyth, lately deceased.

Bone, J.M.--Baby boy.

Shockley, B.F.--Lost eyeglasses on way to Dallas. His son is
          W.F. Shockley.

Hanson, Green--Interred at Bethany Church last Tuesday.
          5/24/89

Foster, T.J.--His mother died in Campbell Co. last week, over 80
          years old.
          5/31/89

Waldrop, J.R.--Left Georgia 5 years ago and lives at Hice, Tex.

Rainey, Pitman--of Embry died the 21st.

Matthews, B.F.--It's a boy.

Cagle, Ben--Wife tried to drown herself in well.

Foster, Mrs.--Died 16 May, "Grandmama", 82 years old.
          6/7/89

Houk, W.E.--Letter about his trip to Texas.

Hall, Mrs. Nannie--Visiting her parents Mr. & Mrs. N.W. Roberts.

Roberts, Mrs. Dr.--Visiting her daughter Mrs. J.L. Mason of
          Atlanta.

Weaver, Watt--and wife visited parents, from Gate City.

Horton, Catie--of Missouri is visiting her uncle, Col. J.H.
          Weaver.

McDonal, Mrs. Margaret--To be sent to her children in Arkansas
        by people of Liberty Hill Section. Lady of unsound
        mind.
        6/14/89
Wood, Dan--Has moved to Lovejoy, Ga.
Cagle, Mrs. Ben--is subject of application to be confined in
        Asylum. Formerly the widow Carroll.
Brown, Ella--of Atlanta, daughter of L.L. Brown, visiting in
        Dallas.
        6/21/89
Midwell, Pleas--Daughter died. Buried Mt. Mariah.
Marshall, Prof.--Died in Cartersville last week.
Lane, G.W.--Child died.
Tibbits, Mr.--Died Sunday. Farming with G.A. Owen.
Baxter, Mrs. Nathaniel--Funeral to be preached at Mt. Olivet 1st
        Sunday in July.
Smith, Dr.--of Dallas went to visit his sister Mrs. Ward at Lost
        Mountain.
        7/5/89
Hooper, Hiram--has sold farm near Yorkville to Isaac Pace who is
        returning from Arkansas.
Gordon, Singer--son of J.B. and M.E. Gordon departed this life on
        the 27th. Remains to Collins Springs church ten
        mile north of Atlanta. Wife and babe. Consumption.
Kiser, Mrs.--of Harmony Grove not expected to recover.
Baxter, Orena--Died last Tuesday, interred at Mt. Zion on
        Thursday morning. Lived in this county since it
        was settled.
Holland, S.D.--spent several days with her daughter Mrs.
        Matthews at Yorkville.
Ragsdale, Parsha Ann--Daughter of Mr. & Mrs. G.W. Ragsdale, born
        26 Jan. 1880 and died 26 May 1889. Mother's only
        child. Memorial written by Mary Rochester of Hiram,
        her aunt.
Reeves, J.A.--Married Lena Barr last Sunday.
Meek, Moses--of Cain Dist. died 4th July. Interred Nebo.
Johnson, Mrs. Charles--of Hiram buried Flint Hill last Sunday.
McBrayer, William--and Rebecca Mobley received marriage license.
        7/26/89
McBrayer, William--and Rebecca Mobley were married on the 18th.
        He is the son of J.L. McBrayer.
Moody, J.M.--Received letter from J.R. Waldrop of Hico, Tex.,
        reporting times are good.
Smith, B.J.--Died last Wed. Interred Dallas Cemetery. Heart
        trouble. Wife and 4 children.
Miller, Mrs. L.A.--and children of De Kalb Co., Ala., visiting
        her father Levi Cooper.
Girley, Robert--Married Mary Harrison last Sunday.
Bowlen, B.Y.--of Cobb Co. married Minnie Tant at Braswell.
Wood, Frank--arrived home from Texas.
        8/2/89
Cawley, Mrs. G.W.--of Burnt Hickory not expected to recover.
Matthews, Zack--Son of Mack Matthews in from west on visit to
        his sister, Mrs. James Elsberry.
Cooper, T.J.--Son Talmage cut his head.
McCheaner, Mr.--Son-in-law of J.E. Carter arrived from Mexico
        where he has been running train engine.
Denton, George--of Ala. visiting relatives.
        8/9/89
Cole, Noah--and Joe Morris of Allalia, Ala. vistited.
Hanie, Julia--Wife of F.A. Hanie, died Aug. 5, buried New Hope.

one 2 weeks old child.

Willis, J.M.--and Miss Fracis Bowman were married last Sunday in
    Burnt Hickory Dist. (This was from Aug. 2, missed
    it).

Cason, Mrs. G.W.--Died Monday night. Buried Pine Log. Husband
    and five children. Also from Aug. 2 paper.

Bowen, S.E.--Widow of R.M. Bowen applies for year's support.

Thompson, Louise--Visiting her sister Mrs. Hagan.

Strickland, J.C.--Granted total divorce.

Bell, J.H.--of McPharson has gone to KY.

Lee, James--and family of Clay Co., Ala., visiting father-in-law
    Wm. Ganell of Paulding.

Robertson, Clabe--grandson of Clabe Bishop visiting from
    Columbus, Miss.

Tant, Mr.--One month old child died.

        8/16/89

Orr, Cornelia--of Atlanta visiting her brother Rev. G.J. Orr.

Harris, Elicia--of Liberty Hill died on Aug. 6. Interred Whie

Harden, J.D.--of Cherokee Co., Ala., G.W. Cole and wife, Mr.
    Adair and Wife and their mother Mrs. Elizabeth
    Sinyard took dinner with their uncle, Wm. Clark.

Robertson, Oliver H.--and son Clabe returned home to Columbia.

        8/23/89

Brown, W.W.--Father of 11 pound boy.

Chamber, Mrs.--Adjudged insane.

Turner, Will--Shot himself, died instantly.

Youman, J.B.--Depot agent resigned, went to Jackson, Ga.

Ronman, E.--Night operator resigned also, leaving for Atlanta.

Grant, W.F.--of Stockbridge is new agent.

        8/30/89

Paris, Homer--of California Dist., cut himself with a knife and
    died in a few minutes.

Adair, M.R.--New daughter.

Johnson, D.H.--admor. of Mariweather Johnson.

Caldwell, Andrew--Deceased. Can't read admr.

Cole, Joseph--admr. William Cole.

Buttler, Mary F.--Guardian of Jacob and William Tidwell.

Pace, Isaac--All the families that went west last year will
    return.

Foster, W.A.--and Georgie Griffin were married Sunday. Rev.
    J.M. Spinks.

Meek, Mrs.--Mother of R.A. Meek died last Sunday.

Campbell, Tom--Accused in Polk Co. of murder of Joe Hulsey
    several years ago, arrested in lower part of state.

Lane, J.C.--Returned from visit to son in Laneburg, Ark.

        9/13/89

Meek, Moses--Born in Mecklenburg Co., NC on March 16, 1809 and
    died Paulding Co. July 4, 1889. His wife Margaret
    Brown born Lancaster Dist., SC Aug. 11, 1811, died
    Paulding Co., Ga. Aug. 26, 1889. Married 5 Feb.
    1829 Henry Co., Ga.(?). 12 Children, 8 living now.
    32 grandchildren, 11 gr. grandchildren, all children
    but 1 belonged to Methodist Church. Joined Presby-
    terian Church in Henry Co. Moved to Cobb Co. in
    1839, lived 19 there 19 years. To Paulding Co. in
    1857. Joined Meth. Church in 1860. Buried Nebo
    Church.

Matthews, Henry--of Yorkville visited his aunt Mrs. E.B. Carter
    of Atlanta. She gave him fine shotgun.

Johnson, Sarah--Wife of William Johnson died 6th at Mt. Olivet.
    Husband, six children. Member Mt. Olivet Church.

Gore, Arch--New baby daughter.
Sewell, Litt--of Cains Dist. died last week.
Levell, A.J.--returned from trip west.
Gore, Arthur--Son of Arch Gore died last Thursday.
  9/27/89
Shelton, Polk--Child died last week.
Baxter, Rev. John--Will be ordained at Mt. Olivet on Saturday.
Carter, Mrs. Rufus--and her children Frank and Steve Pace the two
  oldest sons of Isaac Pace have returned from Arkan-
  sas. All hve chills. Rest of family will return
  as soon as can sell crops.
Lester, Mrs. Leon--Died last Monday.
  10/11/89
Gip, Mr.--is happy, it's a girl. Hope this isn't a nickname--
  it's from Braswell.
Owens, Lee--Little boy died last Sunday, buried Dallas just
  seven weeks after his brother was buried.
Phillips, F.P.--vs Ollie A. Phillips for divorce. Defendent does
  not reside in state so notice to be published for
  four months.
Turner, N.C.--Admr. of Henry Lester.
Looney, D.M.--has left Dallas.
Cole, Henry--Baby died last Wednesday.
Armstrong, Mrs. Dr.--of Braswell departed this life last week.
Cagle, Mrs.--of Calif. Dist. died a few days ago.
Trapp, Mrs. Jilia--of Cain's Dist. departed this life last
  Saturday night. Interred Pine Log Church.
Williams, Henry S.--Will move to Middle Ga.
  10/18/89
Story, Mrs. Frank--Not expected to live.
Osborn, Mrs. Green--died last Sunday.
  10/25/89
Matthews, Mrs. Thomas--from Texas visiting Robert Fann (Gann?)
  and Henry Matthews families likes Texas. Mrs. Clark,
  her mother-in-law, will return to Texas with her.
Moody, J.A.--Prettiest little boy.
Hagin, Fannie--Little daughter of Wm. Hagin of Braswell, died
  last Saturday night. Buried Braswell.
Spriggs, Mr.--of Atlanta has purchased Head house and is coming
  to live in Dallas. Has made his fortune and will
  have no business.
Wilson, Mrs. Bob--of Rockmart is visiting her brother-in-law
  H. Wilson of Dallas.
Hudson, Wesley--Died last Wednesday night. Fell against a fence
  and had cut head, was interred at Lane grave yard.
  Over 80 years old.
Winn, Judge Will J.--Died last Sunday.
Denton, Mrs. J.G.--of Ala. is visiting her son-in-law, Lee Owen
  of Dallas.
Wood, John--visited his father, Jno. G. Wood.
Turner, Linard--of Polk Co. visited his father, J.H. Turner of
  Paulding Co.
Ragsdale, Sanders--of Calif. Dist. is 80 years old, raised large
  family, citizen of Paulding Co. for 50 years.
Story, Mrs. Frank--of New Hope died last week.
Sisk, Mr.--and wife of Texas are visiting their father, Mr.
  Joseph Wood.
Barber, Mrs.--Died 23 last month, 5th wife of Richard Barber.
Cooper, T.J. (Jr.)--Moved to Chattanooga.
  1/9/91 (Issues were missing)
East, Emily--died during Christmas week.

Parks, John--Died during Christmas week.
Lockler, Bill--Married Miss Lou Gore on the 25th.
Gann, Robert--and family left for Snyder, Tex. on Dec. 30.
Maulding, Albert--Admr. of A. Coldwell.
Kennedy, David--Admr. of estate of Wm. Kennedy.
Cantrell, M.F.--Moving to Floyd Co.
Dewberry, William--Died last Tuesday. (Another place spells it
        Duberry.) Interred New Hope with masonic honors.
Hitchcock, James Q.--Married Miss Minnie Bone, dau. of John
        Bone, Sr.
Baker, Jack--Died near Braswell. Citizen of this county thirty
        years.
Forsyth, E.R.--80 years old.
        1/16/91
Hagin, Wm. F.--Born Dec. 22, a851, died Sep. 24, 1890. Born and
        reared Paulding Co. Married Ellen Davis of Polk
        Co. at age of 21. Five sons and 2 daus. All living
        except Fanny.
Adair, Mrs. James K.--of Snider, Tex. is dead.
Bullock, Henry--married Ada Dean at residence of J.M. Spinks,
        date not legible.
Phillips, John L.--Little girl age 7 months died. Buried Poplar
        Springs.
Hitchcok, James Q.--Married Miss Minnie Bone, dau. of John Bone,
        Sr.
Baker, Jack--Died near Braswell. Citizen of this county thirty
        years.
Barber, Mrs.--Died 23 last month. 5th wife of Richard Barber.
Cooper, T.J. (Jr.)--Moved to Chattanooga.
        1/9/91
East, Emily--(or Foot?) died during Christmas week.
Parks, John--Died during Christmas week.
Lockler, Bill--Married Miss Lou Gore on the 25th.
Gann, Robert--And family left for Snyder, Tex. on Dec. 30.
Maulding, Albert--Admr. of a Coldwell.
Kennedy, David--admr. of estate of Wm. Kennedy.
Cantrell, M.F.--Moving to Floyd Co.
Dewberry, William--Died last Tuesday. (Another place spells it
        Duberry.) Interred New Hope with Masonic honors.
        1/23/91
Compton, E.W.--Died last Thursday at Hiram. Served 7th Ga. Reg.
        Newly re-elected tax receiver.
Leathers, Mary Jane--of Woodland, TX married to Charly Selby
        last week.
Adair, James K.--Lost his wife (Texas).
Compton, George--Son of E.W. Compton, also died last Tuesday, the
        other boy is not expected to live.
Smith, Robert--Child died Monday.
McGregor, Mrs. C.D.--Visited by her sister Ada Flynt of Sharron,
        Ga.
Turner, Mrs. R.A.--Died last Tuesday.
Hays, Ben--Son of widow Hays near Remous.
Carter, Jesse--A boy 24 hours old.
Lowry, E.--Brother of James Lowry died of consumption this week.
Pool, Charley--Son of Enoch and Winnie Pool of Hiram. Died Jan.
        1. Born 29 Jan. 1860. At age 20 married Nannie
        Thompson. Missionary Baptist Church at Poplar
        Springs. Wife and 4 children.
Weaver, J.H.--and Laura left for Asheville, NC to visit scenes
        of his boyhood.
        1/30/91

VITAL STATISTICS FROM PAULDING NEW ERA

Wilson, R.L.--Little girl age one year and four months died at
        Cedar Bluff, Ala. Buried Braswell Cemetery on the
        22nd.
Moon, E.T.--Admr. of Tilmon E. Porter.
Rakestraw, Grover T.--Minor child of J.M. Rakestraw, 12 months
        support.
Lester, A.R.--Guardian of Effie Howard minor child of S.W. Howard.
Snyder, George N.--Shot his wife (Jan. 25?) at San Marcos, Tex.
        Daughter of late Judge Underwood. Her brother Chas.
        Underwood. The couple resided at Remous, separated
        and then reconciled. Moved to Texas two years ago.
        3 Children.
Smith, Catharine--Died last Wednesday.
Matthews, B.M.C.--His daughter, Mrs. W.B. Nealy of Atlanta came
        to see him.
        2/6/91
Williams, J.J.--Married Sunday to Cora Cheek of Polk Co..
Brock, E.--Moving to Cobb Co..
Wilson, John--Married Lizzie Brocks, Feb. 1 at residence John A.
        Moody. Raised nearly in sight of each other, he
        was 34 and she was 33. He took this long to get
        tired of being single.
Trentham, J.D.--Lost child last week.
Henderson, Gen. Robert--Died in Atlanta Tuesday.
Moon, J. Robert--Baby weights 12 lbs.
Ragsdale, Berry--His daughter Addie is better.
        2/27/91
Mobley, Allen--Adjudged insane.
Hicks, Buck--Died last Sunday.
Pinkard, Noah--Returned from Texas with son James whose mind has
        become a little unbalanced.
Lane, Rev. W.A.--Died at Atlanta last week. Well-known Baptist
        minister.
Cassady, Eugene--Married Mary Hardy.
Brown, Oscar--of Carroll Co. and Ola Kirk of Paulding married
        last Tuesday.
Allgood, J.F.--is 6½ ft. tall, courting a girl who "is very low".
        makes it unhandy for courting, "he has to set down
        to talk to her."
Michael, J.S.--Says he want to marry. Wants a girl 5½ ft. tall,
        150 lbs., fair complexion, black hair and eyes. Any
        girl interested write him.
Smith, W.J.--Personalty to be set aside.
        3/6/91
Rickerson, E.F.--and Decia Norton married at residence of W.R.
        Owen.
Jones, Dick--and Sallie Nichols married at residence of Mrs. S.A.
        Weldon.
Womack, Mathey--A boy.
Dudley, Marion--A girl.
Weaver, Ida--Visiting her father J.B. Gordan of Pumpkinvine.
Rawls, Robert--Child died, will be buried in former home.
Prewett, Anderson--Moved back from Dooly Co.
Hill, D.P.--Moved to Atlanta.
        3/13/91
Sinyard, Bud--and Ada Parks married.
Owens, Matt--and Lena Wood both of Paulding married in Atlanta
        last Tuesday.
Horton, Will--Child Hattie, age 3 or 4, burned to death at
        Atlanta. Buried Mt. Olivet. Their oldest child.

Moxley, Will--Moved to Lumber City below Macon.
        3/20/91
Ragsdale, Bob--Writes letter from Margaret, TX. (Age 15).
Lawrence, George--Born Paulding Co. Aug. 14, 1862, died at Fort
        Payne, Ala. 4 Mar. 1891. Wife, one child. Father,
        sister and babe in heaven. Mother, four sisters,
        two brothers remain.
Neal, W.M.--Letters of dismission as guardian of Jossie Moore.
Allgood, P.P.--Died last Tuesday.
Hunt, Thos. B.--Married Miss Georgie Furgerson.
Ragsdale, J.--Died 28 Dec. 1890. Born Jackson Co., Ga., on 20
        Jan. 1811. Married Lucinda Carter in 1831. Moved
        to Paulding 1844. Baptist Church Poplar Springs,
        buried there. Stone placed by R. Davis.
        3/27/91 Nothing extracted.
        4/3/91
Gentry, George--and Mrs. Brewster Wilkins were married last
        Sunday.
Cooper, J.B.--A girl.
Davis, Ephraim--Went to Temple on business Wednesday and dropped
        dead. Son of Jimmie Davis.
Stokely, N.E.W.--of Acworth and Ella Brown of Paulding married
        last Sunday in Atlanta at residence of S.S. Moor.
Wright, A.R.--Fell dead this week at home in Rome.
        4/10/91
Lawrence, J.F.--of Rome, visiting his mother Amanda Lawrence at
        Oak Hill.
Baty, Mr.--Daughter, age 14, who got burned died Wednesday.
Whitfield, Thomas--Died Sunday.
Foster, W.A.--A Girl, last Monday.
Foote, J.B.--Married Soonie Parker. Her father is George T.
        Parker.
Carmichael, William--and Addie Embry were married on the 5th.
Griffin, Old Man--Died at pauper farm last Tuesday.
Hendrix, G.D.--of Atlanta and Minnie Badgett of Acworth were
        married last Sunday at M.E. Church. (Description
        of event.).
Taylor, R.F.--Married Saidie Hicks last Sunday. (Braswell).
Cooper, Thomas J.--Of Chattanooga visiting his father Mayor T.J.
        Cooper.
Robertson, Dr. S. and Judge Scoggins represented Dallas at
        reception given in Atlanta for President Harrison.
        Judge Scoggins bought new blue suit for the event.--
        4/24/91
Owen, Fannie--Is visiting her sister Mrs. L.E. Haisten in Fort
        Payne, Ala..
Newton, Carrie--of Atlanta visiting her brother Rev. H.M. Newton
        of Dallas.
Owens, Dr.--and wife left for Texas to live.
Matthews, Thomas--of Columbus, GA not expected to live. His
        sister Mrs. A.G. Bullock has gone to see him.
        5/1/91
Ogle, Mrs.--Mother of Jno. H. Ogle, died Apr. 26 with measles.
Ragsdale, G.W.--Writes from Margaret, TX. No cotton where he
        is. He settled in Hardeman Co. but is now in Ford
        Co. which was newly formed. Wants to hire a hand
        from Paulding at $150 year.
Rataree, Alexander--Buried at High Shoals next Friday.
Cooper, Katie--Dau. of T.J. Cooper died Apr. 23. Buried County
        Line.
Camp, Mr.--of New Hope--it's a girl.
Carter, Green--Lost an infant four days old.

        5/8/91
Smith, J.H.--of Buchanan, GA and Jessie Beall of Embry married
        last Sunday.

Barnett, Marshall--and Mattie Blalock married in Braswell last
   Thursday.
Willingham, Mrs. William--Died Monday. Buried New Hope. Husband
   and several children.
Nealy, Dedie--Dau. of E.D. Nealy of Atlanta received a prize at
   school, got first instruction at Dallas.
Jones, Wiley W.--Died last Monday. Buried with Masonic honors
   at family grave yard. Leaves aged wife.
   5/15/91
Welch, Gus--I think this is announcing birth of a baby. Some-
   times they are so "funny" it's hard to tell.
Turner, Mrs. Robert--Funeral at Mt. Zion.
Holton, W.T.--Child's funeral at Mt. Olivet.
Bone, John Jr.--Died last Sunday at his father's home. Age 25,
   not married. Fever and heart trouble. Buried at
   Dallas Cemetery.
Stanley, John--Found baby at his door. Mrs. James Lowry has
   taken it to raise. (In a later issue it said they
   thought they knew who the mother was.)
Hay, J.W.--Writes from Bowden, Ga.
   7/3/91
Payne, J.J.--Writes from San Diego, California.
Kennedy, Wm.--Admr. of W.L. Rollins.
Smith, Robert--Died near Mt. Olivet Church last Friday.
Harris, J.B.--Another girl.
   7/10/91
Dooly, Henry--Another girl.
Prance, George--and Ella Forsyth married last Thursday.
White, Ella--Died June 26. Age 18. Nice obituary but no other
   facts.
Ables, John M.--Another boy.
Bryant, Rachel--Colored, died Tuesday.
Green, Dave--Son, age 14 drowned in a pond near Atlanta while
   Swimming last Sunday. Buried Villa Rica.
Howell, Ben--Died 18 June, age 19. Mt. Olivet Cemetery. Son of
   Thomas J. Howell. Wife and Child.
   7/17/91
Cole, James--of Ind.(?) son of Jacob Cole married Mary Fuller,
   the widow of Abram Fuller last Sunday.
Cole, G.W.--Liberty Hill Correspondent has interesting Civil
   War tales.
Wix, Zody--Age 2, dau. of Ben Wix died Jul. 1. Sister Dovey
   died 3 years ago.
Matthews, B.F.--Shot and killed Marshal L.M. Phillips. Indicted
   for murder. Phillips was buried New Hope.
Mote, W.C.--Applied for personalty.
   11/21/91
Tamlin, Will--Left for Anniston to work in a foundry.
   7/31/91
   List of divorces at next term of court:
   Picket, Bundrum, Norman, Melts, Wisener,
   Gann, Whitfield, Coldwell
Hagin, Ella--Baby passed away at Braswell on 28th.
Russom, R.W.--Youngest child died Sunday. Buried New Hope.
Cooper, Sallie--Died last Sunday. Daughter of T.J. Cooper.
   Buried Dallas Cemetery. Born Mar. 1873. M.E.
   Church. Memorial in next issue.
Verner, Isaac--his 4 month old babe died Sunday. Buried Yorkville.
   8/7/91

Adair, J.B.--and Miss M.J. Talley married Aug. 2.
      8/14/91
McGregor, S.R.--of Huntsville visiting his daughter Mrs. R.M.
      Moon.
Moon, H.T.--Died Wednesday. Run over by train. Interred Moon
      burying ground on Thursday. Mother, five brothers,
      one sister.
Elsberry, James--Died Monday. Over 60 years old. Buffered for
      3 years. Buried Shady Grove.
      8/21/91
Anderson, J.A.--Died Friday. Buried Dallas Cemetery.
Green, Mrs. Anderson--Died Monday. New Hope Cemetery.
      9/18/91
Hix, Henry--Married Matilda Smith last Sunday.
Aldredge, David--Age 85. Married Miss Liza Maddres, age 30.
Anderson, Sarah J.--Admr. of J.A. Anderson. Guardian of Emma,
      his minor child.
      9/25/91
Parris, Warner--Married Addie Austin last Sunday.
Pearson, Mrs.--Mother of John Pearson, died near New Hope a few
      days ago.
      10/2/91
Pinkard, Alexander--Five sons.
Wyatt, J.E.--Died, buried Holly Springs. Two weeks to a day that
      his brother-in-law was laid to rest at same place.
      10/9/91
Singletch (?), E.J.--Babe buried the 7th.
Furgerson, M.J.--vs M.C. Furgerson, divorce, and also Lillie
      Hardie vs J.J. Hardie. Neither defendant lives in
      state.
Medows, Will--Daughter died of fever.
Kingsbery, Wm. C.--Married Mrs. Frank Leslie Sunday.
Owens, Matt--Moved back from Texas.
      10/16/91
Norton, W.S.--Another boy.
Baxter, Nat--Age 88 on 3rd of next month. Interesting article.
Pinkard, Alexander--Babe died, buried Mt. Olivet.
Osborn, John--Went to join army.
      10/23/91
Meadows, Bettie--Died Oct. 4 of typhoid fever. Would have been
      17 on the 25th Jan. Nice memorial.
Cooper, William D.--Died last Sunday at his fathers. Fever.
      Buried New Hope. Sounds like one of his children
      had also died of fever.
Sanford, William--Died Wednesday.
      10/30/91
Parris, Cal--Child died (Hiram).
Anderson, Noah--Died last Friday. Buried Dallas. 80 years old.
      Baptist Church.
Arnold, J.H.--and Lucy Prickett married last Sunday.
Sandford, Lucy--Died 21st. Buried New Hope.
      11/6/91
Howell, Joe--Killed while working on RR last Friday. Buried Mt.
      Olivet. Wife and several children. Younger brother
      killed by same road 4 or 5 months ago.
Matthews, B.F.--Guilty, prison for life.
      11/13/91
White, Barnett--Died last Friday, Yorkville Cem. M.E. Church
      member.
Cooper, Mollie--Died. Daughter of Levi Cooper. Born Sept. 15,

1874. Three weeks ago her brother died. Nice
    memorial.
Hollis, George--Died last Friday. Son of J.W. Hollis. Age 15.
    Youngest child. Buried at Gann graveyard near
    Pumpkinvine Church. Long obituary.
        11/20/91
Elsbery, Z.B.--Admr. Thomas Whitfield.
Bowman, Larkin--Married Lizzie Stancel(?).
Keever, Birthia--4 month old child of George Keever.
        11/27/91
Wells, Charley--Married a Miss McPherson of Temple.
Adams, James--of Vanwert, Ga. died Thursday. Buried Holly
    Springs.
Garner, George--18 year old son of G.W. and Martha Garner died
    of typhoid Sunday. Buried Bethany Church.
Chambless, T.M.--and Mrs. Edia Parris married last Sunday.
Hughes, Warren--Married Miss Rosa Mosley on the 19th.
        12/4/91
Ragsdale, Mary Alice--Died Nov. 4 at Ford Co., TX. Age 15
    months, 4 days.
Campbell, W.M.--Applied for personalty.
Cobb, Ned--Vs Francis Cobb--divorce. She does not live in state.
Wyatt, Mrs. M.E.--Years support on estate of J.E. Wyatt.
Davis, M.E.--Married Laura Hipps of Hiram, Ga. on the 29th.
        12/11/91
Coalson, John--Son of Thomas Coalson, and Alice Robins, dau. of
    John Robins married on the 6th.
Brown, T.J.--Guardian of Lizzie and Lucy Brown, minor children
    of T.P. Brown.
        12/18/91
Burhan, A.W.--Died Saturday. Took morphine for "gravel" and
    died of overdose. Buried Braswell.
Cole, James W.--and Margaret Talley married last Sunday.
Adair, Thomas--Died near Salt Springs. Beaten with a club.
Cooper, W.D.--Widow and little boy moved to Texas.
Wyatt, Joseph--Born SC Sept. 18, 1855. Baptised Holly Springs
    church Aug. 1872. Married Martha Coalson Dec. 13,
    1872, she was daughter of Wm. and Harriet Coalson.
    Died from typhoid Sept. 24, 1891. Wife and seven
    children.
        12/25/91
Harris, Eli--Married Alice Ragsdale last Sunday.
Argrow, Pete--Married Ida Summerhill, daughter of W.A. Summerhill.
Percer, Will--Married Miss Denson, daughter of James Denson.
Dale, W.R.--Long poem this issue. He is in prison.
        1/8/92
Spears, J.B.--A girl.
McLendon, J.L.--A boy.
Hight, James L.--Moved to his farm near Rome to teach his two
    sons how to farm.
Matthews, Thomas--Son of G.P. Matthews.
Jordan, Mr.--of Tunnell Hill, father of Mrs. Dr. Foster is
    visiting.
Foote, J.B.--Buried infant boy only a few days old.
Rogers, Levi--Married Sibbie Daniel last Sunday.
        1/15/92
Hagan, J.H.--Newly married.
Camp, Mary--Died 23 Dec. at New Hope, Ga. Age 40. Daughter of
    Nancy Camp. Buried New Hope. Leaves mother, 6
    brothers and 3 sisters. Obit written by "her
    Niece, Martha Camp."

1/22/92

Elsberry, Fletcher--Died last Sunday. Son of G.R. Elsbery, he
          was 15 years and 3 months old. Buried New Hope.
          Six brothers and 2 sisters. Long obituary.
Sinyard, Lud--It's a boy.
Moody, E.S.--A girl.
Gore, Mrs.--Widow of Sam Gore died Sunday. Buried Yorkville.
Cole, Alice--18th birthday party on the 6th.
Baggett, Steeve--Little girl died last Saturday.

1/29/92

Eaves, T.M.--Married Miss M.L. Ford, both of Cartersville,
          married last Sunday.
Prewett, Mrs. J.R.--Died Monday. Interred New Hope.

2/12/92

Little, Jake--Married Mary Pace last Thursday.
Allgood, Mrs. John V.--Died last Wednesday.
Hogue, W.J.--Admr. John Shelnutt.
Tanner, W.J.--(Jr.) Married last Sunday to A.S. Gladden.
Carter, William--Child two years old died last Tuesday.
Cole, John F. to Ella McDuffie. Married last Wednesday.
Russom, R.W.--Another little girl.
Wix, Zack--Infant died on the 26th.
Moody, E.S.--Child died Thursday.

2/19/92

Hicks, Gip--13 lb. boy.

2/26/92

Dale, W.R.--Out of jail on bond, went to Atlanta where his wife
          had started a divorce, had no place else to go.
Davis, R.W.--Writes from Bartahatchie, Miss. Letters in several
          different issues would be of interest to family.

3/4/92

Gann, J.R.--of Snyder, Tex. married Mrs. Bettie Thompson, a widow
          of 33 with a son age 14.

3/11/92

Forsythe, Lizzie--Died Jan. 10, 1892. Born 21 Feb. 1876. Long
          obituary.
Thompson, Fed--Fine girl.
Walker, Mrs. John--Died last Sunday. Buried New Hope.
Foote, G.W.--(Jr.) Died last Sunday. Buried Dallas Cemetery.
Billings, J.S.--Writes from Huntsville.

3/18/92

Walker, Littie P.--Wife of J.O. Walker, born Dec. 15, 1848.
          Married 5 May 1872. Died Mar. 7, 1892. Eleven
          children. Some of this too pale to read.

3/25/92

Trammell, Mrs. Elizabeth--Died in Jefferson Co., Ala., on 22 Jan.
          1892. Born 18 May 1808. Mother of three children,
          one the late Robert Trammell of Paulding Co..

4/1/92

Nothing extracted.

4/8/92

Wheeler, Mrs. A.C.--Died last Wednesday. Buried Nebo Church.
Moody, J.A.--A Daughter on the 1st.
Hollis, James--A Girl on the 1st. Later it says not James but
          some other Hollis I can't read.
Matthews, Ben--Died Wednesday. Buried Dallas Cenetery.
Gogins, Maryane--Colored, died Monday.
Whitehead, Mrs. Missouri--Died on the 1st. Buried Old Antioch.
Ramsey, Lula--Died Scurry Co., Tex. Mar. 12, 1892. Buried Snyder
          Cemetery by the side of her mother who died 20 Apr.
          1891. Oldest Daughter of Robert Gann. Born 5 Sep.

1864, Paulding Co. Married Henry Ramsey 29 Sep. 1891 at Snyder.

Prewett, Martha--Died Saturday. Buried New Hope. 4/15/92

Hay, Gus--A girl.

Boggs, Mrs.--Aged lady died at her son's near New Canaan last week.

Walker, John--Child interred New Hope.

Rawls, Bob--A girl.

Matthews, Sam--Son of G.E. Matthews died Friday? Buried High Shoals. Young wife.

Howell, Mrs. T.C.--Died last Tuesday. Heart trouble. Interred Mt. Olivet. 4/29/92

Wood, J.T.--A boy.

Land, Thomas--A girl. Now has one boy and one girl.

Moody, J.A.--A daughter on the 1st.

Carter, Mrs. Jasper--Died last night a week ago.

Hay, Mrs. P.J.--Died near Hiram on Mar. 23. Buried New Harmony Primitive Baptist.

Hipps, R.E.--Father of eleven children. Oldest is twenty, the youngest fifteen days and will be named either Henry Newton or Lovejoy.

Freeman, Mr.--Died Last Saturday. Buried Dallas Cemetery. 5/6/92

Foote, Amanda--Died last Friday. Wife of G.W. Foote Sr. Long obit but no other facts.

Hulsey, Henry--A girl. (Braswell).

Clay, William--12 lb. brick mason. 5/13/92

Parris, J.S.--and John Rainwater and Billy Taylor all have baby girls.

Watson, James B.--Married Georgie Hooper of Cobb Co. last Sunday.

Matthews, Mrs. Nancy died Wednesday. Widow of B.M.C. Matthews who died 5 weeks ago. Dropsy. Buried Dallas Cemetery.--No, 5/20/92

Trentham, Jim--I think this means a baby.

Henderson, William--Married to Georgie Wade yesterday.

Holland, W.E.--Died on the 12th. Buried High Shoals.

Matthews, Eddie--Died last Saturday. Son of B.F. Matthews Age 7. Dallas Cemetery. The father was allowed to come from prison but arrived too late to see his child. Two little new-made graves. 5/27/92

Drake, Mrs. B.S.--Died Atlanta on May 6.

Baker, J.O.--Died Saturday. Buried Baker graveyard.

Smith, W.J.--A boy.

Little, Jacob--Died last Tuesday. Son of Joseph Little of Nebo. Buried Mt. Zion.

Turner, Mrs. Daniel--Buried High Shoals on the 19th.

White, Henry C.--Died last Saturday. Buried Pleasant Grove. 6/3/92

Baxter, John--Married last Sunday to Dockie Craton.

Russom, R.W.--Youngest child died Monday, a few months old. Buried New Hope.

Matthews, Charlie--Son of B.F. Matthews, six years old. Brother Ed preceded him in death by only 2 weeks.

Clay, Sony--Little boy died, age 6. Buried Cedartown. 6/10/92

Hart, Doll--Twin boys.

Walker, Frank--Son of John Walker adjudged insane.
Moon, George--Died last Wednesday. Son of Chas. C. Moon. Buried
           Poplar Springs.
Arnold, Hattie--Wife of H.E. Arnold, died May 30. Daughter of
           Jonathon P. and Aseenath Lindley.
           6/17/92
Robertson, Gertrude--Died last Saturday, Daughter of Dr. S.
           Robertson. Dallas Cemetery. A later issue said he
           had had all his family graves moved to a better
           location.
O'Neil, Mrs. R.H.--Gave birth to an infant only born for burial.
Nix, William--Died on the 8th of apoplexy.
Hitchcock, Mary Jane--Was Mary Jane Toler. Born Bibb Co., Ala.,
           Jan. 17. 1845. Married Jesse Hitchcock May 12, 1861,
           Polk Co., GA. Eleven children, 9 living as follows:
           William Oscar, John Oliver, Leona Madora, Louise
           Estell, Jesse Glenn, Henry Gresham, Charles Toler,
           Lucy Elizabeth, Jabez Cornelius. Died on the 10th,
           buried White Oak Springs. A long obituary.
           6/24/92
Carter, R.--Fine boy.
Denton, George R.--of Luna, Ala. married Julia Parker, daughter
           of Dr. G.T. Parker of Paulding.
Lane, B.T.--Writes from Clarendon, Tx..
Henley, Newtie--Died June 16, buried New Harmony.
           7/8/92
Black, Catherine--Died last Saturday. Buried Watson grave yard,
           Douglas Co..
Graham, J.D.--Twin girls.
Moore, Mr. J.D.--and Miss Jennie Sewell were married last Sunday.
Braswell, W.T.--Married Bella Gray on June 30.
Garner, John--and Maggie Wheeler married last Sunday. He is
           about 80 and she is 20.
Rataree, Will--Baby died.
Walker, Mrs. J.O.--Funeral at New Hope on 5th Sunday.
Johnson, J.M.--Died June 7 at Viola, Ala.
           7/15/92
Coalson, Ida Mary--Daughter of Rev. A.J. Coalson, died July 7.
Cooper, T.J. (Jr.)--Died last Monday, buried at Dallas Cemetery.
           Joined Methodist Church last week.
Cooper, A.J. (Dr.)--and Alice House married yesterday.
Baggett, John W.--A 10 lb. boy.
           7/22/92
Cantrell, James--Died Sunday, June 19. A Memorial on front page.
Henderson, Calvin--Visiting in Dallas, is principal of school at
           Waldron, Ark..
Hitchcock, Overton--Child died on July 10, buried White Oak
           Spring on the 11th.
           7/29/92
Caldwell, Susan--Died Wednesday the 26th. Cancer of the face.
           Age 54. Daughter of Andrew Caldwell. Buried
           Smyrna Church.
           8/5/92
Lewis, J.A.--and Frank visited their sister Mrs. T.J. Cooper.
Little, G.M.--Son adjudged insane.
McGarrity, J.W.--Nominated for Congress. Born Paulding Co. 7 Jan.
           1854.
Norton, Emma--Died July 25, buried Sweet Water.
           8/12/92
Wilson, Charlie--Married at Huntsville on last Sunday to Miss
           Emma (can't read).

Lane, J.W.(?)--Married Nora Colbert last Tuesday.
Cole, Jacob--Died on July 23. Buried White Oak Springs.
  8/19/92
Tant, N.S.--New father of a boy.
Matthews, L.F.--Tells of his narrow escape from a panther on
    Foster's Ranch in Texas.
Maulding, Mrs. Willie--Year's support from estate of D.L. Maulding.
Tidwell, J.S.--Babe died last Sunday.
Glore, Elliot--Died Aug. 19 at Atlanta. Born near Dallas 24 Oct.
    1864. Wife and several children, one died about 8
    months ago.
  8/26/92
Morrow, Alsey--of near Fish Creek died of consumption on the
    14th. Buried Holly Springs.
Lenard, Bailas--Married Leoner Hitchcock, daughter of Jesse
    Hitchcock on the 14th.
Looney, Mattie--was murdered a week ago at Cobb Co. Will Ellis
    charged with the crime.
Wallace, Joe--Was killed in Cobb Co. also a week ago, age 40.
    Tryed to protect his father-in-law, Jim Jacobs from
    assault by Walter Millwood and Sattie Cosey. Mill-
    wood shot Jacobs. Wallace leaves a wife and three
    children. Millwood is son of Rev. S.W. Millwood of
    Atlanta, age 20. John Cosey is the father of Sattie
    Cosey and owns the farm where Millwood and Cosey
    were living.
Gammell. William--Was 81 years old in June and still does general
    farm work.
Barrett, Manuel--and Annie Lyle married on Second Sunday.
Robertson, Sidney--of Pumpkinvine and Jane Mosley of Yorkville
    married first Sunday.
9/9/92
Bullock, George--and Lula Elliott were married last Sunday.
Griggs, A.P.--Infant boy died. California Dist. Eleven days old.
McLendon, Mose--Married Mrs. Robert Hughes "last night one week."
Guy, William--and family have moved back to Dallas from Alabama.
    Also Job Miller and family.
Mitchell, Mr.--Now of Leesburg, Fla., is visiting his brother-in-
    law W.J. Grogan.
Norton, Emma J.--Died July 25, 1872. Daughter of Andrew J. and
    Mary Norton. Consumption. Interesting obituary.
  9/16/92
Elsberry, W.T.--A new girl.
Elsberry, Ann--Colored, wife of Ike Elsberry, died Tuesday.
Mable, Mrs. John--Died last Tuesday. Buried Villa Rica.
Blalock, Mrs. J.R.--Died the 10th at Brawell. Buried New Hope.
    Came here from Buchanan three weeks ago. Leaves
    husband and four children.
  9/23/92
Brooks, Dr.--Died Tuesday, buried County Line.
  9/31/92
Wade, Mr.--Baby died Monday.
Bobo, Mrs.--Died at her daughter's Mrs. W.R. Griffin. Consump-
    tion. New Canaan Church.
Atkinson, Mr.--Died Sunday, buried Atlanta.
  10/7/92
Davis, Susan W.--Died Sep. 26. Born Putnam Co., Ga., Apr. 28,
    1818. Married Carroll Co., Ga., Dec. 24, 1830.
    Died Monroe Co., Miss. Buried Pleasant Grove Church.
Dupree, William--of Other, Ga., died last Thursday. Buried Mt.
    Zion.

Postell, Joseph--Married Leoler Palmore of Cains Dist., last
      Sunday.
Cole, Thomas--and Emma Morgan married on 4th Sunday last month.
Davis, E.--Applied admr. of A.J. Atkerson.
Alexander, Mrs. S.E.--Admr. of W.C. Estes.
Twilly, Mrs. A.C.--and Alice Barber, admrs. of B.L. Pace.
Marchman, Alvah B.--and Annie Fain married last Wednesday.
      Daughter of W.I. Fain. Nice story.
Rakestraw, Mr.--12 lb. girl.
Clark, F.B.--Baby died.
      10/14/92
Rataree, Mary--12 month support on estate of E.L. Rataree.
Dudley, Gennett--Personalty. Wife of David Dudley.
Land, Arthur--Married Miss Austin last Sunday.
Washington, L.M.--I think, a boy.
Broadwell, Phillip--And Martha Williams married last Sunday.
Shelton, Warner--And Della Brand married last Sunday.
McCord, J.F.--and Francis Coalson married at her father's, J.F.
      Coalson.
Bass, W.D.--and Mary Cornett married yesterday.
Elsberry, Mrs. Linsey--Age 93 (or 98?), oldest person in the
      county.
      10/21/92
Bussey, E.W.--11 lb. girl.
Bullock, Mrs. Juda--(I can't read rest of it.)
Boswell, Mr.--of Hiram died last Friday. Buried Poplar Springs.
Hay, James P.--Died Tuesday. Buried New Harmony. Father of
      H.W. and J.R. Hay.
Elsberry, Mrs. Linsey--Died last Sunday, 98 years old.
      10/28/92
DeFrese, Mrs. Mollie--Wife of Charlie, dau. of John W. Palmer,
      died Sunday. Buried Bethany Church.
Butler, H.W.--Babe died. Buried Mt. Olivet.
Pool. F.L.--and Miss Clyde Wolf of Candy Ridge in Henry Co. were
      married last Sunday.
Gann, Ella--Writes from Snyder, Texas. Her Grandma Mrs. M.A.
      Clark returned to Dallas two weeks ago.
      11/4/92
Brown, John--Died in the Indian Nation on Oct. 15.
Matthews, George--Son of B.F. Matthews died yesterday.
Wix, Zack--Buried White Oaks at Nov. Fever. Young wife, 4 daus.
      Four brothers and sisters and mother.
      11/11/92
Langston, J.M.--of Gordon Co. married Mrs. Alexander Rataree.
Moon, Monk--Died last week. Son of J. (or I.) N. Moon.
Pool, E.W.--Married Winnie ------ of Henry Co., Ga. in the year
      1851 (4?). His son F.L. Pool married Miss Clyde
      Wolf standing on the exact same spot.
      11/18/92
Carter, Robert--Died of wounds fighting off robbers in SC on Nov.
      8. Son of E.M. Carter.
      11/25/92
Partin, Samuel--and Ida Wells married, can't read rest.
Tumlin, Virgil--Moved to Gadsden, Ala.
Camp, A.J.--Married Miss Perkerson of Villa Rica on the 22nd.
      12/9/92
Wills, John--Died Saturday. Buried New Hope. Wife and 3 small
      children.
Harper, Mrs. Rod--Died last Friday. Buried Cass station.
Bussey, E.W.--Moved to Moulton, Ala.
      12/23/92

Wells, William--Infant died the 14th, buried Yorkville.
Williams, Willie--Married Edna Carlton on the 8th.
Gann, Robert F.--Married Annie Thompson last Tuesday in Atlanta.
    12/30/92--Nothing extracted.
    1/20/93
McBrayer, W.A.--Married to Etta Coleman of Carrollton.
Adair, Adeline--Died last Monday.
Williams, Wyatt--Died a few weeks ago and was buried at Bethany
    Church. Six year old son died last Wednesday,
    buried at side of his father.
Griggs, John--Died last Wednesday. Buried Norton's Chapel.
    2/3/93
Butler, John--Married Mrs. J. Howell. His father J.M. Butler.
Spinks, J.T.--Married Dora Anderson on Feb. 1. Son of John W.
    Spinks.
Williams, Grover--Died on 11 Jan. Son of J.E. & Martha Williams.
    Age 5. Two brothers, two sisters. Buried family
    cemetery near residence of the widow Lawrence.
    2/10/93
Wilson, G.W.--New daughter.
Wix, Carrah--Died on 6 Feb. Age 16 months. Has lost wife and
    three little girls in 5 years.
George, J.L.--Infant child buried at family burying ground.
Thompson, Fed--Married last Wednesday to Caroline Bragg.
    2/17/93
Forsyth, Rev. L.L.--Married.
Gann, Millie--Died last Sunday. Wife of Robin Gann. Buried
    Gann's Cemetery.
Carter, Joseph--Married Mattie Gray of Temple. Son of P.M. Car-
    ter.
Womack, Mrs.--Mother of G.W. Womack, died Sunday.
Henderson, James--Oldest son of John Henderson died the 13th,
    age 21.
Wilson, Siphronia--Died on the 10th. Born May 5, 1857, married
    Jan. 10, 1872 to G.W. Wilson. Gave her babe to the
    wife of her brother, Mrs. John W. Moody before she
    died.
    2/24/93
Moon, Joseph B.--Died Feb. 11, 1893 age 29 years, 8 months, 29
    days. Son of I.N. Moon of Cobb Co.. Consumption.
    Wife and 4 children.
Fuller, Mrs. Ann--Mother of Z.B. Fuller died of heart disease
    last Monday. Buried Friendship.
Bomar, A.R.--Is visiting his nephew, Dr. T.J. Foster. Mr. Bomar
    age 82.
Cornett, W.D.--Married Lizzie McBrayer last week. Parental ob-
    jections so they got married before old folks knew
    what was up. His father Sam Cornett, her father
    James McBrayer.
Garrett, M.J.--Married Bettie Elsberry last Sunday.

End

-A-

262 Ables, Ezekiel
42 Adams, Richard A.
14 Allen, Jas.
294 Allen, Robert
283 Allen, Wm.
301 Anderson, John
228 Anderson, Joseph
347 Anderson, Moss G.
151 Anderson, Noble
127 Anderson, William
78 Arnol, Thomas

-B-

327 Ballard, Wyly
124 Beck, Harmon
217 Barnett, Calvin
279 Barrett, Jas.
161 Beck, Beverly
269 Beck, James
180 Beck, Samuel
241 Beck, Solomon
46 Bent, Wm.
309 Bishop, Job
120 Birch, Jarrett
122 Birch, John Jr.
123 Birch, John Sr.
47 Black, John
62 Blackston, Richard
235 Blair, George
33 Bleckley, Jas.
39 Boling, Thomas
223 Brand, Elijah
99 Bramblett, Jesse
98 Bramblett, Reuben
351 Brown, Joseph
144 Brown, Robert
27 Bruce, Eddy
328, Bryant, Caleb B.
267 Byers, Robt.

-C-

260 Calahan, Josiah
203 Campbell, Robert
244 Cannon, Ellis
247 Cannon, Henry
60 Cannon, Hiram
31 Cannon, Issac F.
257 Capehart, Jacob
352 Capps, Thompson
344 Carnes, Hubbard
359 Carnes, Ruth
165 Carnes, Thos.
160 Carnes, Wm.
282 Carson, John
302 Carter, Edward
287 Carter, Isnish
303 Carter, Jesse

-C- cont.

118 Carter, Joseph
213 Cason, Jas.
226 Chastain, Edward
107 Chastain, Elijah
106 Chastain, Hannah
281 Chester, Eslingh
65 Clardy, Elliott
248 Clark, William
245 Cleveland, Wm.
209 Cline, Dan'l
220 Cline, Joe
278 Cody, Jas.
103 Coffee, Cleveland
305 Coffee, Edward
90 Coffee, Elijah
129 Coffee, Elisha
21 Coffee, Joel
96 Coffee, Joel
104 Coffee, Nathan
182 Collins, George
94 Collins, Watson
9 Cook, Wm.
337 Copeland, Wm.
326 Cornett, Cullen
310 Coward, Elizabeth
70 Crane, Elijah
308 Crane, Jesse
256 Crawford, Margaret
95 Credleton, Eleanor
317 Crow, Jas.
318 Crow, Lawrence
52 Culberson, Martin

-D-

193 Darnol, Gerald
293 Dawson, Abel
268 Dawson, Bery
271 Dawson, Enoch
188 Dawson, Jonas
44 Dawson, Jonas
163 Dawson, Wm. A.
72 Davis, Green
25 Davis, Wm.
53 Denton, Jonas
56 Denton, Elijah
340 Dedman, Wm
198 Derrick, John
208 Dickerson
3 Dilda, Polly
285 Dildy, Elias
280 Dilingham, Hiram
291 Dillard, Jas.
289 Dillard, John
259 Dolson, Thos.
12 Dover, Bailey
196 Dun, John
38 Dunn, John
334 Dunlap, Jonathan

-D- Cont.

253 Dunlap, Mathew

-E-

310 Ebord, Dewry
 67 Ellard, Amos
 68 Ellard, Jas. Jr.
307 Ellard, Jas. Sr.
295 Ellard, Joseph
261 Elliot, Ephraim
224 Ellis, Elijah
204 Ellis, Wm.
251 Evans, David

-F-

 41 Fariss, Sam'l
 49 Fitzgerald, Ambrose
342 Forister, Amos
184 Forister, John
178 Forister, Thos.
 24 Foster, George
115 Foster, Thomas (no home)
190 Fowler, David
345 Fowler, Elizabeth
246 Fowler, Jeremiah
167 Fowler, John
 92 Fowler, Moses
219 Fricks, Michael

-G-

 40 Galaspie, William
 13 Galiway, Wm. L.
 93 Gassaway, Obedience
212 Gains, Alen R.
110 Gains, Elizabeth
111 Gains, Henry S.
108 Gains, Hiram
174 Gains, Jas.
141 George, Arthur
 87 George, Isaac
134 George, Jas.
252 George, Jesse
255 Gilleland, Allen
197 Gilleland, Elizabeth
 15 Ginn, Ruffin
187 Goble, Cornelius
168 Goble, John
157 Godfrey, Ansel
 43 Godfrey, Thos.
164 Goldy, Orstin
232 Gooch, Tilman
 97 Grantham, Wm. M.
350 Green, John
  6 Grice, Idealir

-H-

149 Ham, Ezekiel
172 Hamby, Wm.
242 Harris, John L.
341 Hayes, Wm.
173 Hayes, Wm. Sr.
179 Haynes, Thos.
300 Heady, George
254 Hed, John
264 Henson, Andrew B.
296 Henson, Isaac
286 Henson, James B.
312 Henson, Thompson M.
265 Henron, W. N.
315 Hicks, Henry
 48 Hide, Isaiah
189 Hide, Reuben
 63 Higginbotham,Francis G
 19 Holbrook, Alexander
316 Holden, Isaac
249 Hopkins, Wm.
276 Hunter, Richard
191 Hunter, Robet

-I-

None

-J-

 16 Jackson, Wm
 81 Jarrett, Jos.
210 Johnson, John
 18 Johnson, Thos.
 37 Jones, Jas. N.
 71 Jones, Joseph
 51 Jones, Martin
 82 Jones, William
 80 Jones, William

-K-

117 Keener, Abraham
320 Kelly, George
166 Kelly, John
333 Kelly, John
284 Kelly, John L.
329 Kelly, Rev. Thomas
335 Kelly, Thos.
234 Kelly, Wm.
170 King, Isaac

-L-

322 Langston, John
332 Ledbetter, Jas.
 30 Lilly, Lewis
221 Loots, Joseph
202 Loots, George
270 Lovelady, Davis

-L- cont.

258 Lovelady, Solomon
199 Lovelady, Thos.
 36 Lovell, Isaac
 10 Lunceford, George
105 Lunceford, Wm.
 85 Lynes, Joseph

-Mc-

 11 McClain, David
 35 McClain, Ephraim E.
 34 McClain, Jas. N.
 22 McClain, John
  5 McClain, John C.
325 McConl, Thos. (McConnell?)
220 McClure, Andrew
236 McDaniel, David
114 McDaniel, David L.
298 McGleny (?), Thos.
297 McGramy (?), Wm.
299 McGuire, William
 79 McKenzie, Charley

-M-

207 Martin, Jas.
 57 Middleton, Thos.
 50 Miler, Sally
  1 Miller, Andrew
  2 Miller, John C.
126 Mines, Elizabeth
324 Moody, Martin
 83 More, Eli
263 More, John B.
277 More, Wm.
 89 More, Jordan
306 Morgan, Rebecca
101 Morris, John
 54 Morris, Thomas
192 Moss, Jas.
200 Mozley, David

-N-

154 Nevele, Jas. B.
272 Norris, Wm.
201 Norton, Messer

-O-

 26 Oakes, James
 45 Odell, Benjamin
117 Oliver, Michael
100 Owenby, Wm.

-P-

 88 Page, Cary
146 Page, David
 17 Parker, John

-P- cont.

109 Patterson, George
237 Patterson, John
339 Patterson, Joseph
142 Patterson, Roley
227 Pell, Wm.
233 Pemoy, John
121 Penson, Curtice
119 Penson, Joseph
 28 Powell. Jas. B.
 32 Powell. Jefferson
112 Powell, Pleasant
102 Powell, Tilman
  7 Price, Ervin
131 Price, Jas. B.
132 Price, John B.

-Q-

128 Quarles, Davis
 64 Quarles, Hubbard
314 Quarls, Robert

-R-

219 Ramy, Elenor
177 Ramey, Isaac
155 Ramey, Jas.
140 Ramy, Thos
153 Ramey, Thomas Sr.
156 Ramey, Wm.
113 Redmon, Richard
150 Richards, Wm.
137 Roach, Jas.
211 Roberts, John
183 Roggers, Jas
145 Roper, Thos.
  8 Russell, Elisha
275 Russell, George

-S-

274 Samon, George
311 Sanders, Isaac
338 Scarlet, Lewis D.
266 Scoggins, Charles
186 Scruggs, Jas.
185 Selney, Joel
 66 Sharley, Benjamin
254 Shaw, Wm.
295 Shelton, Benjamin
135 Singleton, Henry
330 Singleton, Jas.
136 Singleton, William
323 Smith, George
169 Smith, Hampton
239 Smith, Jas
353 Smith, Joshua
 59 Smith, John C.
 29 Smith, Robert

-S- cont.

231 Smith, William
304 Spivy, Wm.
 77 Staten, Zebedee
205 Steel, Richard
158 Stone, Aaron
148 Stone, Thos.
 23 Steonecypher, Jas.
181 Strother, Jas.
218 Stroud, John
290 Sutton, Ambrose

-T-

176 Tally, Evan
348 Taylor, Robert
 58 Taylor, William
248 Tilly, Lafite
220 Tredaway, Wm.
321 Turpin, Elias
125 Turpin, Jas.

-U-

None

-V-

230 Visage, Wm.

-W-

250 Wadts, Joseph
 55 Walker, John
175 Wall, Drewry
313 Wall, Etheld
 84 Wall, Jesse
171 Wall, Wm.
 86 Warnock, Elizabeth
331 Watkins, Thos.
214 Watts, Pleasant

-W- cont.

292 Webb, Jeremiah
162 Wever, Koonrod
346 Wever, Martha
143 Williams, Amos
 61 Williams, Caliway
130 Williams, Edward
147 Williams, Etheld
152 Williams, Jonathan
139 Williams, Joseph
243 Williams, Martin
133 Williams, William
138 Williams, Wm. Sr.
343 Willy, John
194 Wilson, Robt.
  4 Wilson, William
240 Wimpy, Daniel
273 White, John
 73 Woodall, Drewry
 91 Woodall, Joseph
 69 Woodall, Morgan
 76 Woodall, William
288 Woods, Robert
222 Woods, Thomas
 75 Wooten, Dudley
 74 Wooten, John
159 Wootten, Charley
266 Word, Saml'd D.
 20 Worley, Wm.

-X-

None

-Z-

None

-Y-

225 York, Jeffrey
238 York, Jeremiah
336 York Seymore

WALTON COUNTY LOOSE MARRIAGES

By Robert Scott Davis, Jr.

The following inventory of the loose original Walton County, Ga.
marriages was found in Record Group 247-2-11 at the Georgia Department of Archives and History. Additional Walton County
loose, original, marriages can be found for the 1850s-1880s in
Record Group 247-1-12. These marriages and the microfilm copies
of the bound Walton County records are available for use by researchers at the Georgia Department of Archives and History.
These will be listed as groom, bride and date of marriage.

Abercrombie, Hugh to Eliza Blasingame; March 18, 1829
Adams, Elijah to Moriah Lewis; August 6, 1835
Adams, Samuel to Susan Statam (Statum); November 12, 1829
Adcock, Joseph to Lucey Odam (Odom); March 6, 1829
Adcock, Seaborn to Sarah A. Peeters; October 25, 1843
Addison, Charles to Eliza McGraw; May 31, 1832
Agnew, Samuel to Mrs. Mary Jones; December 25, 1832
Albertson, Edward to Permelia Reynolds; April 14, 1831
Allen, Earley to Jane Dial; April 16, 1844
Allen, Gideon H. to Lucinda Mayo; January 24, 1832
Allen, John to Hester Ann Cason; March 25, 1833
Allen, John to Mrs. Elizabeth Little; September 25, 1844
Allen, John to Catherine Tomison; January 10, 1844
Anderson, Edward to Thena James; November 4, 1830
Anderson, John J. to Mrs. Elizabeth Humphrey; July 18, 1844
Armstead, Virgil H. to Lucy N. Cheak; October 9, 1844
Arnold, Elijah B. to Susannah Ware; August 4, 1829
Arnold, Jesse H. to Mary Jackson; November 24, 1831
Arnold, Joshua P. to Nancy F. Morgan; January 12, 1847
Atcherson, Jesse H. to Jane Blair; August 4, 1831
Austin, Isaac to Syntha Campbell; December 20, 1842
Austin, James to Mary Sorrells; July 2, 1832
Austin, William to Nancy Brannon; March 11, 1829
Awtry, Henry S. to Elizabeth A. Hanson; July 22, 1842
Aycock, Joel to Neta Lackey; February 13, 1842

Bailey, Tatan W. to Amanda Tullum; March 6, 1844
Baker, James M. to Priscilla English; July 23, 1829
Baldwin, Jefferson Jackson to Mary Ann Watson; October 7, 1846
Banks, Joseph to Mrs. Mary Sheppard; April 29, 1829
Banks, William to Sobrina Childers; July 1, 1829
Barker, Rufus to Sophia N. Craven; March 23, 1843
Barnett (Bennett), Joseph to Ernestine (Eveline) Studdard;
    October 15, 1846
Barnett, John to Mary Bird; October 4, 1842
Barron, David A. to Amanda Brimbury; January 20, 1835
Barron, David A. to Mary E. Walker; January 3, 1833
Batchelor, Nathaniel M. to Alsey Cox; June 7, 1835
Batchelor (Bachelor), William H. to Elizabeth Baggett; June 27,
    1830
Bauner (Bonner), Allen to Elizabeth Ann Ivy; December 29, 1846
Baxley, Asa to Sarah Ann E. Baker; August 14, 1845
Baxly, Aron to Martha Benett; December 23, 1830
Beall, Elias (M.D.) to Ann B. Jennings; December 16, 1830
Beard (Beaird), William to Sarah Easterling; January 20, 1829
Bearden, Elisha to Polly Whitley; January 11, 1824
Bell, James M. to Emily Wilson; September 26, 1843
Benefield, Caleb C. to Lucinda Stone; October 13, 1831
Benefield, William to Dibley (Decley) Stone; September 6, 1831

551

Bennett, James A. to Lanrey (Lara) Ann Davis; December 20, 1844
Bennett, William B. to Martha Ann Barker; October 8, 1846
Bentley, Eligah to Luoisa Kilgore; September 23, 1831
Benton, Andrew J. to Sina Simanton; January 4, 1838
Betts, John to Permelia Lancaster; March 14, 1833
Bilboe, William G. to Susan Hughey; August 16, 1829
Bird, Thomas to Evalina Jones; March 12, 1829
Blasingame, James to Martha Laws; February 25, 1833
Bledsoe, Thomas to Ann F. Martin; November 23, 1830
Boice, Charles W. to Jane Moore; August 11, 1831
Balis (Boles), James H. to Elizabeth Ward; October 29, 1831
Bolt, Beremon to Punmelia Dial; May 4, 1831
Bowman, Miles A. to Mouring Sturdivant; March 12, 1843
Bonds, James M. to Tabitha Whitlow; December 30, 1830
Booker, Richardson to Rebeccah Harvey; September 1, 1829
Bookout, Charles L. to Sandal Moon; November 6, 1828
Boswell, Josiah to Emaline Presley; January 14, 1845
Bowling, John W. D. to Mary Fletcher; March 17, 1829
Brantley, John M. to Elrutha McCulloughs; February 18, 1846
Braswell, Larkin to Susannah McCulloughs; December 20, 1846
Broach, Henderson H. to Mrs. Sarah C. Harrison; October 23, 1842
Brooks, Bradford to Jane P. Hood; November 7, 1831
Brooks, James to Margarett Chandler; October 3, 1842
Brooks, Joel to Cyntha Ann Irwin; May 8, 1820
Brooks, Larkin to Delilah Jones; February 16, 1832
Brown, Asbury to Elizabeth Parker; December 23, 1832
Brown, George to Elizabeth Studley; September 22, 1844
Brown, William L. to Elizabeth Bullock; May 30, 1844
Bruster, John D. to Sally H. Guinn; November 22, 1829
Bryan, Jesse to Nancy Tidwell; June 14, 1821
Buchamon, Charles W. F. to Lovey B. Anderson; January 25, 1832
Bullard, John to Matilda Reynolds; April 27, 1831
Bullock, William to Nancy Edwards; August 23, 1832
Burke, John to Christian Allen; April 17, 1842
Burnes, Wilson to Lucy Coker; May 10, 1835
Burnham, Elisha B. to Mary L. Willingham; May 19, 1829

Callahan, Jacob J. to Sarah M. Herndan; November 18, 1845
Camp, Avery to Nancy May Whitlow; March 6, 1830
Camp, Ira to Nancy Palmore; January 26, 1829
Camp, Merrit to Frances Echison; January 24, 1833
Carden, James to Mary Branon; June 13, 1830
Carpenter, Jacob to Margarett Blair; March 11, 1830
Carr, Jesse G. to Piety Brantley; January 26, 1832
Carr, John to America Carr; January 12, 1832
Carter, Robert M. to Susan Ann C. Robertson; November 20, 1844
Chandler, Waltan to Mary Elizabeth Gre; January 6, 1846
Chappel, Jefferson to Elizabeth Carter; December 13, 1829
Chappel, John to Lucy Mullins; June 13, 1830
Chesteen, John to Mary Shivey; March 21, 1830
Clark, Aaron to Martha Harbuck; February 4, 1830
Clark, Elijah to Sarah Janis (Jones); May 8, 1831
Clark, Nathan to Ally Pool; February 11, 1833
Clybon, Britton to Polly Pike; February 15, 1831
Cochral, Robert to Cathrine Kelgore; October 4, 1820
Coker, Hiram to Elizabeth Whitten; December 17, 1829
Coker, John to Martha E. Doval; November 25, 1830
Coker, Solomon to Keziah McDonald; February 4, 1830
Coker, William to Martha Holloway; December 25, 1834
Colley (Colly), Francis S. to Mary Ann Richardson; April 7, 1830

Collins, Abraham to Frances Speller; October 15, 1829
Conner, Ganaway to Nancy Lewis; December 18, 1828
Cookey (Cooksey), John to Mary Tamislin; April 3, 1831
Cooper, James K. to Temperance J. Shellnutt; October 11, 1846
Crouch, George to Aletha Norris; December 24, 1834
Crawley, Charles to Talither C. Phillips; December 29, 1831
Cronie, Valentine to Peggy Reynolds; January 10, 1832
Crow, Isam to Mrs. Elizabeth Arnold; June 27, 1835
Culbutson, Washington C. to Sarah Hinton; March 14, 1835
Cullins, Elyah to Lilis Ford; January 16, 1842
Cumby, Pleasant A. to Martha McMicheal; December 12, 1830

Darby, Julius G. to Nancy C. Hambleton; July 3, 1830
Darby (Darbry), William L. to Jane Taylor; June 25, 1830
Davenport, Richard to Mahala McGraw; October 16, 1831
Davis, Alford B. to Alice (Allice) Rosser; December 3, 1823
Davis, James to Julia Ann Mathins (Mathews); January 17, 1844
Davis, John to Polley Malcom; September 12, 1822
Daughety, Mason to Catharine Few; August 25, 1823
Dennis, Henry to Comfort Parker; October 4, 1831
Depreist, Green to Deborah Jones; February 12, 1835
Dickerson, Welborn T. to Nancy Ann Malcom; March 7, 1841
Dismuke, Jesse H. to Nancy Brown; October 24, 1832
Dley (?), Hiram H. R. to Louisa Vandiford; April 8, 1835
Doster, James C. to Susan Ann Armsted; December 17, 1846
Drake, William A. to Mahala Hill; March 2, 1831
Duke, Charles E. to Martha Cotton; December 16, 1832
Duke, James to Minerva Hightower; February 22, 1829
Duke, Thomas to Mary Ann White; August 2, 1829
Duren, Samuel to Polly Vann; October 1, 1829

Early, Richard S. to Sarah E. Guthry; December 8, 1846
Easterling, Joel C. to Cordelia A. Greene; October 3, 1843
Edgar, John to Polly Holloway; August 26, 1827
Edmonds, Burwell to Nancy Beardin; August 22, 1832
Edwards, Thomas to Mary Fletcher; November 28, 1833
Edwards, Thomas P. to Nancy Allin; November 24, 1831
Elliott, Cornelius to Burgett McCarty; March 22, 1842
Elliott, Cornelius to Mrs. Burchett McCarty; April 29, 1841
Ellis, John to Sytha Lassetoer; December 1, 1831
Ellis, Joshua to Sarah Ann Hughes; September 5, 1833
Ellison, Watson to Elizabeth Stone; July 1, 1830
Elutt, William to Mary Mullins; November 10, 1831
Ethridge, William to Sarah Williams; July 31, 1831
Evans, James M. to Dicey Carter; September 20, 1829
Everett, John G. to Addaline Hogans; November 24, 1846
Evins, Thomas L. to Nancy B. Prince (Pierce); October 10, 1845
Ewing, Thomas to Elizabeth Pattillo; September 8, 1829
Farrar, George W. to Susannah Bunkley (Brinkley); September 13,
    1829
Fletcher, Nathan A. to Sarah Bennett; February 5, 1833
Ford, Edward to Eliza Reynolds; April 21, 1831
Forister, Alex to Anna Willis; January 25, 1831
Forister, Joseph T. to Lucy M. Greeson; January 12, 1843
Freeman, Thomas to Elizabeth Hinton; November 8, 1843
Freeman, William Henry to Sarah Elizabeth Hughes; March 8, 1846
Fullilove, Seaborn J. to Frances W. Selman; January 13, 1831

Garner, George to Mary Howell; February 15, 1844
Giles, James to Marthy (Martha) Christopher; January 11, 1824

WALTON COUNTY LOOSE MARRIAGES

Glass, Joseph to Mary Ann E. Heald; January 30, 1842
Glore, George to Emily Bostwick; July 6, 1834
Goodson, Thomas B. to Martha J. Hogan; December 19, 1833
Goolsby, George to Matilda Goolsby; March 28, 1844
Grainger, Stephen to Lucy Jones; February 20, 1831
Grainger, William B. to Margarett Norton; December 8, 1831
Gray, Benoni to Martha Speller; December 27, 1827
Gray, Jehu to Mrs. Elizabeth Wallace; January 15, 1829
Greason, Green to Mary Boman; May 10, 1846
Green, John to Mary Addison; January 20, 1831
Greer, Henry to Mrs. Lucy Bonner; April 2, 1835
Gregory, Reubin to Cecilda Duren; September 19, 1833
Gresham, John L. to Mary E. Kilsey; December 26, 1841
Griffin, Richard to Mary Ansley; April 4, 1833
Grubbs, Thomas to Jane Sophia Wilson; September 7, 1843
Guinn, Richard R. to Margaret Matilda Bruster; July 30, 1829
Gunn (Guinn), George W. to Mary Ann Willis; July 3, 1832
Gunn, Jesse to Tabitha C. Hill; June 3, 1830
Guthery, Robert M. to Mary Hardin; August 13, 1835

Hagerman, Asa F. to Margrett Louisa Steel; March 4, 1830
Hails, Allen J. to Nancy Wright; October 19, 1828
Hale, William to Lucy Jane Stroud; April 13, 1842
Halliday, Dickerson T. to Mary Ann Hill; January 19, 1832
Hammoch, Asa to Sarah E. Flynt; September 20, 1832
Hammock, Benjamin F. to Frances M. Shepherd; April 20, 1842
Hand, Edmund to Nancy S. Crow; June 24, 1830
Harbuck, James to Sally Thurmon; December 13, 1831
Hardy, John to Sarah Benson; March 21, 1832
Hardy, Thomas to Elizabeth Swords; January 14, 1835
Harper, Asa to Carolina Odom; April 21, 1830
Harris, Lewis to Nancy Strong; October 6, 1831
Harris, Tyrie S. to Hannah L. T. Glenn; July 26, 1831
Harris, William to Cynthia Adams; August 12, 1835
Harris, Willis to Lucinda Micheal; December 25, 1834
Harvey, Pinkethman to Mrs. Charlotte Flynt; June 11, 1829
Hayes, James to Matilda Hadaway; October 15, 1846
Hayes, Leonard B. to Louisa Sorrells; December 9, 1830
Head, B. A. to Mary Rosilla Cosby; May 14, 1846
Hearn, Stephen to Mary Glasson; October 3, 1830
Hendricks, James M. to Emily Person; November 6, 1843
Herndon, Francis M. to Mary Ann Mayo; April 30, 1846
Hester, John to Armenia Adcock; April 11, 1830
Higginbotham, Joseph to Elizabeth Broach; December 20, 1829
Hightower, Thomas to Kizere Armstead; January 13, 1835
Hinton, William to Susannah Richardson; January 22, 1824
Hitchcock, John to Talitha C. Herren; September 17, 1833
Hogan, Wiley to Martha Freeman; February 15, 1844
Holly, John J. to Elizabeth Ann Morgan; September 9, 1830
Hopson, William B. to Susan Roe (Rowe); December 15, 1831
House, Paschal G. to Susan Melton; August 2, 1829
Hubbard, William to Mrs. Sarah Ann Bramblett; December 15, 1846
Hudson, Anderson C. to Bethany Lane; December 6, 1832
Hughes, Rufus J. to Nancy Snow; February 9, 1843
Humphrey, John to Mary Jane Meredith; November 4, 1830
Hunter, John to Martha Jane Thomas; February 10, 1846
Huston, David R. to Mary O'Kelly; February 12, 1829

Ivey, Seaborn to Eliza Adcock; December 11, 1834
Ivey, Wilkins S. to Jane Herrin; April 2, 1835

Ivy, Elbirt to Emily Upshaw; April 7, 1842
Ivy, James to Sarah Ann Upshaw; October 24, 1843

Jack, Samuel S. to Elizabeth Ann Meredith; December 22, 1831
Jackson, John M. to Manerva Adams; December 16, 1845
Jacobs, Elisha to Mary Meador; October 1, 1829
Jean, Daniel B. to Mary Carmichael; April 23, 1829
Jenkins, Grafton to Rebecca Smith; December 1 (5), 1831
Johns, William to Mary Hightower; February 10, 1831
Johnston, Nathaniel to Margaret Pharr; December 8, 1829
Johnston, Robert H. to Delila Ellison; January 5, 1831
Johnston, William T. to Sarah Smith; March 17, 1842
Jones, Absalom to Nancy B. Anderson; September 16, 1834
Jones, Eli to Martha Smith; March 11, 1830
Jones, Thomas to Marina Harris; June 25, 1835
Jones, Thomas M. to Eliza Sturdivant; May 4, 1830
Jones, Warrenton to Clare Ann Giles; December 20, 1842
Jones, Wiley to Susan Miller; January 8, 1835
Jones, William to Mary Lewallen; December 8, 1829
Jourdan, Charles to Fanny Harden; October 19, 1832

Kelly, John to Nancy Howell; January 18, 1844
Kimbrell, David T. to Mary Elisabeth Peters (Preston), December
     10, 1840
Kirklin, Calvin to Celia McCarty; September 20, 1846
Knight, Henry to Lucretia Brown; December 24, 1829
Knight, Thomas to Elizabeth A. Ragan; October 6, 1842
Knott, Franklin to Mary A. A. Freeman; November 17, 1844

Lake, Elisha to Nancy Fuller; July 8, 1832
Lane, James S. to Annah J. C. Jones; August 25, 1844
Lee, David to Nancy Brewer; December 23, 1830

Mahafey, Kelly to Martha A. M. Peeters; August 13, 1846
Mahen, William A. to Emily Barnett; August 2, 1842
Malcom, Daniel to Elizabeth Gather; December 15, 1831
Malcom, James to Catharine Peters; March 17, 1835
Malone, Maranday C. to Nancy Drummond; February 19, 1833
Marable, Christopher to Eliza Perry; May 3, 1832
Martin, Martin to Nancy Dial; February 7, 1833
Mattox, Early J. to Mary Wooten; January 29, 1835
Mattox, Martin to Clara Wooten; December 22, 1831
Maughon, Francis M. to Selita Barrett; June 16, 1846
Maxwill, J. R. to Sarah Ann Reeder; November 27, 1846
Mayho, John to Sarah Harrell; November 29, 1829
McAdams, Blaford to Elizabeth Hughes; December 5, 1843
McCannon, William to Sarah Jarvis; February 5, 1835
McCarty, James A. to Peity Whitley; April 14, 1844
McCarty, Larkin to Leah Funderburg; April 22, 1835
McCaskill, Murdock to Elizabeth McKinnon; April 9, 1823
McCord, Samuel to Margaret Griffin; December 7, 1840
McCuller, _____ to Hannah Howard; August 25, 1842
McIntosh, Milas C. to Talitha Jones; October 6, 1844
McKinnon, Alexander to Sarah Cameron; May 12, 1831
McMahan, Woodward to Mrs. Melissa Glass; April 7, 1830
McMichaeal, Richard to Karenhapp (?) Millian; September 22, 1833
Meadars, Abram to Sarah E. Ogilby; August 6, 1835
Means, John S. to Eliza N. Buchanan; May 10, 1831
Medlin, Bartlett W. to Maryann Tatter (Sathy); February 20, 1842
Medlin, James A. to Luisa W. Grubbs; August 21, 1843

Melton, William N. to Agnes Arnold; May 17, 1840
Mersa, Aron to Mary Stephens; October 14, 1830
Millsaps, John M. to Coutney Whitley; December 20, 1840
Mitchel, Jordan H. to Julia Ann F. Hardin; December 28, 1831
Mitchell, Samuel P. to Sarah Smith; December 31, 1843
Mitchell, William T. to Jedida T. Perkins; June 22, 1843
Mitchell, W. T. to Desire Palmer; February 10, 1842
Mobly, William to Sarah Roper (Rosser); January 6, 1831
Moon, Daniel to Ellinor Francis Bullard; August 19, 1834
Moon, Elijah to Elizabeth McClurg; August 12, 1830
Moon, William E. to Susan J. Willingham; December 19, 1844
Moore, David S. to Juda Ann Boothe; March 23, 1842
Moore, Fredrick to Matilda Braswell; November 11, 1830
Morrow, James M. to Elizabeth L. Kennon; September 19, 1833
Morrow, John T. to Lucy Ann Bonner; September 26, 1833
Morrow, Richardson M. to Caroline Crow; January 26, 1832
Mosley, David M. to Nancy Floyd; December 13, 1827
Motley, John to Jane Ragan; May 11, 1828
Mullins, John to Nancy Bostwick; December 24, 1829
Mullins, Price J. to Elizabeth Beasley; April 7, 1831
Mynard, Nathaniel T. to Lucinda Horch (Hush); January 30, 1844
Myres, James B. to Mary Williams; November 7, 1832

Needham, Charles to Rebecca Griffin; November 27, 1845
Nichols, John to Sarah Rogers; April 28, 1831
Nix, Harrison to Catharine Ford; September 6, 1837
Nix, Williamson to Nancy Carter; June 5, 1825
Norris, James F. to Rachel Young; January 18, 1835
Norris, William J. to Susannah R. Malcom; January 6, 1846
Nowell, John W. to Mrs. Elizabeth Smith; November 30, 1843
Nunnelly, James A. to Margaret Pinson; October 2, 1832

Oakes, Isaac F. to Caroline Dickens; September 10, 1846
Odom, Jennings to Alcey Terrey; February 15, 1832
Odom, Livingston to Rebeccah Swords; February 2, 1830
O'Kelley, Overton to Tabither D. Phillip; November 8, 1832
O'Neal, William to Mary Fuller; December 12, 1831
Owen, Griffin L. to Mary Ann Allen; March 31, 1829
Owens, James H. to Catharine Roan; December 26, 1830
Owens, Coleman P. to Charlotte Allen; November 25, 1830

Palmer, Augustus H. to Sarah Jones; December 30, 1830
Palmer, John to Mary Camp; June 11, 1829
Park, Moses to Martha P. Paxton; December 14, 1829
Parker, Luke to Ann Brown; May 28, 1829
Parker, Rease C. to Harriett Hutchins; November 21, 1831
Parks, James to Lucy Formby; May 8, 1831
Partin, Allen to Adaline Melton; January 22, 1832
Partin, Robert to Margarett Meltone; August 23, 1832
Partrick, Paul to Matilda Smith; October 11, 1826
Paterson, Robert to Elinor Meredith; October 11, 1827
Paxson, Benjamin F. to Sarah Carter; January 23, 1844
Pearce, Austin R. to Matilda Hunt; December 24, 1829
Perry, James H. to Catharine Hunton; May 31, 1832
Peters, John to Sarah Williams; January 6, 1830
Peyton, Robert to Mary Studdard; March 10, 1835
Phillips, Singleton to Charity Jones; January 10, 1830
Pool, Elzy (Elijah) to Elizabeth Coleman; December 2, 1841
Pratt, George N. to Martha J. Peeters; December 23, 1846
Prince, Joseph to Luisa Rogers; January 12, 1832

Ray, James to Martha Barbara Allgood; March 7, 1831
Reed, Elliot to Elvira Lee; February 11, 1829
Reed, S. Wilbom to Frances Chandler; July 2, 1846
Reeves, Sidney to S. C. Nicholson; July 23, 1829
Reynolds, Jefferson M. to Elizabeth A. Bullard; April 25, 1830
Reynolds, John D. to Elizabeth Upshaw; December 22, 1844
Rhodes, William to Martha Moon; May 13, 1835
Richardson, John M. to Mary L. Christopher; October 22, 1844
Richardson, William H. to Effiah S. Frost; December 22, 1831
Roberts, James T. to Cyntha Moore; December 20, 1827
Robertson, Benjamin E. to Martha Furguson; December 29, 1844
Robinson, Bedford to Susan Reynolds; January 1, 1833
Rogers, David to Malinda Mayo; April 24, 1834
Rogers, James to Lucinda Malcom; September 10, 1829
Rogers, Jonathan M. to Dicey Sydes; January 4, 1831
Rogers, Joseph to Amanda M. Wooten; August 5, 1830
Rush, John to Mary Johnston; January 7, 1830

Samples, Charles to Polly Patrick; February 16, 1823
Sarells (Sorrells), Charles J. to Salley Still; November 18, 1830
Scears, Freeman to Rebecca Ann Freeman; February 6, 1843
Sewell, L. W. to Mary Weatherford; January 25, 1846
Seymour, Vardin to Jincey Segars; March 17, 1831
Shaw, Bryant to Lucretia Willingham; October 16, 1834
Shields, John B. to Eliza Ann Suddath; November 17, 1831
Shipp, Joseph R. to Elizabeth Wamach; January 31, 1833
Shipp, Mark to Cynthia Chappell; December 23, 1830
Simmons, James to Viney Calvary; December 28, 1830
Simmons, John to Mary Acock; December 23, 1834
Simms, Henry to Mrs. Peninah Cox; December 6, 1829
Simpson, William R. to Jane Mayhan; July 29, 1831
Sims, Waltan to Vilett Thompson; October 25, 1846
Slocumb, Joseph to Nancy Diggs; October 11, 1829
Smedley, John to Nancey Beardin; February (?), 1831
Smith, Benajer to Elisabeth Mullins; January 15, 1824
Smith, Haley to Martha Benefield; November 17, 1830
Smith, Isham to Biddy Smith; August 23, 1829
Smith, James to Francis Ivey; May 12, 1830
Smith, James to Rebecca Smith; August 12, 1830
Smith, John P. F. to Frances Day; February 18, 1841
Smith, John P. to Syntha Ivy; September 5, 1833
Smith, Joshua to Susan Smith; February 10, 1842
Smith, Madison to Carolina Patton; December 21, 1843
Smith, Miles to Elizabeth Wammock; January 2, 1845
Smith, Nathaniel to Edith Brown; November 21, 1830
Smith, Parnell (Pamell) to Eliza Thompson; January 13, 1835
Smith, Tryon to Mary Hilton (Helton); August 9, 1829
Smith, William to Nancy Carmichael; March 20, 1828
*Smith, Thomas to Martha E. Pendergrass; November 19, 1844
Sorrels, William to Jane Tanner; March 3, 1842
South, William to Elizabeth Main; March 26, 1829
Stanford, Stephen to Milley G. Harris; April 20, 1831
Stephens, Benjamin to Nancy Davis; February 14, 1832
Stephens, Jeptha K. to Levisa M. Jackson; February 26, 1846
Stewart, John M. to Polly Velvin; February 24, 1824
Stewart, John T. to Dicy Meredith; January 20, 1831
Stewart, Parkerson to Isabela Henderson; August 13, 1832
St. Johns, James to Louisa Stewart; May 26, 1842
Stokes, M. B. to Nancy Matthis; November 26, 1832
Stone, James to Rachel Ellison; February 8, 1829

Stome, James R. to Nancy Natt (Nott); October 1, 1844
Stroud, Manson to Lucy Thompson; July 15, 1832
Stroud, Sherwood E. to Elizabeth Haynes; March 24, 1842
Studdard, Joseph to Christy Dial; December 30, 1830
Studdard, William to Elizabeth Hoggans; December 10, 1844
Sturdivant, Joel to Mary Moore; January 16, 1844
Swords, John W. to Frances M. Whitehead; October 10, 1843

Tenney, Isaac P. to Mary Ann Mitchell; March 31, 1842
*Thomas, Andrewson to Matilda Webb; October 3, 1828
Thomas, Howard P. to Mary Thompson; November 9, 1843
Thomason, Orsmus to Elizabeth Price; February 26, 1835
Thompson, Charles to Tempsy Philups; November 22, 1831
Thompson, Richard to Peggy Ann Reid; June 27, 1829
Thompson, Richard to Peggy Ann Reed; January 7, 1832
Thompson, William to Rebecca Smith; January 17, 1844
Thorn, Ephraim to Lotium Reynolds; November 21, 1833
Titshaw, Stephen to Elizabeth Lackey; October 23, 1849
Titshaw, Anderson H. to Mary Cronie; October 20, 1846
Treadwell, William to Lucinda Lewallen; March 8, 1835
Tunner, James to Martha Spivy; August 24, 1841

Upshaw, George F. to Frances E. Edwards; August 19, 1842
Upshaw, Tinsley to Frances Bird; September 25, 1831
Upshaw, William to Mary Gibbs; December 12, 1830

Varner, John to Rebeccah Grubbs; September 22, 1842
Vickers, Charles D. to Martha G. Edwards; October 13, 1831
Vickery, John W. to Eliza Ann Allen; March 22, 1844

Walker, Edwin A. to Martha Winn; December 23, 1834
Walker, James S. to Sarah Adams; October 18, 1832
Wallace, Mitchell C. to Rachel Gresham; December 1, 1831
Walkins, William M. to Amanda F. Hinton; November 5, 1846
Watson, James to Lucinda Brewer; July 29, 1846
Watson, Joshua N. to Mary Hataway; December 15, 1844
Watson, Paris to Nancy Brewer; August 9, 1829
Watson, William to Malinda Mahaffy; September 16, 1846
Weaver, Gravis H. to Margarett Brown; September 1, 1846
Webb, James W. to Martha Moon; February 5, 1843
West, Milton P. to Cyntha Meadows; November 11, 1830
White, Caleb to Cenith Ivy; September 5, 1833
White, Edward H. to Susan Rogers; June 16, 1830
White, James T. to Mary Nix; June 19, 1842
White, Jeremiah to Dicey Nix; November 3, 1829
Whitworth, Charles H. to Susan Kilgore; December 14, 1843
Widner, Rubin to Nancy Greeson; June 10, 1841
Williams, Berrien to Nancy Moore; June 30, 1830
Williams, Hampton to Delila Peters; November 9, 1830
Williams, Hansill J. to Susan A. Peters; December 21, 1843
Willingham, Riley to Lucinda Wiley; June 23, 1833
Willis, Paul T. to Elizabeth Harden; April 1, 1832
Winn, William A. to Sarah Ann Walker; December 26, 1830
Wood, Cary to Mary Billups; October 14, 1823
Wood, Richard to Elizabeth Whitley; February 26, 1835
Woodruff, Joseph T. to Eliza Ann Ragan; November 25, 1829
Wright, Asa B. to Mary E. Morgan; July 21, 1835
Wright, Moses to Sophiah Swinney; January 10, 1832
Wright, William to Jennett M. Winn; March 4, 1832
*Date marriage license issued.   END

The list of ordinaries and their deputies is as follows:
William Gordon, Ordinary; Winston Gordon, Ordinary, John
S. Beall, C.C.O., Murray County; C. E. Broyles, Ordinary, Murray
County; Wm. K. Moore, Deputy Ordinary; Jno. W. Anderson, Ordinary
Ex Officio; Jesse P. Freeman, Ordinary; and J. E. Shumate,
Ordinary.

Page
1. McNabb, George to Perkepile, Hannah, Mar. 23, 1852, Jesse
   Wade, J.P.
1. Broaderick, John to Strickland, Eliza, Apr. 1, 1852,
   Edward McAbee, M.G.
1. Spann, Joseph K. to Blair, Hannah E., Apr. 4, 1852. John S.
   Martin, J.P.
2. Williams, Joel W. to McMurray, Nancy D., Apr. 8, 1852,
   Z. D. Clark, M.G.
2. Langhcld, Julius to Jeschke, Emilie, Apr. 18, 1852,
   William B. Malone, J.P.
2. Haynes, Francis C. to McDaniel, Elizabeth, Apr. 9, 1852,
   Wm. B. Malon, J.P.
2. Smith, J. N. to Carpenter, Mary, Apr. 29, 1852, Wm. W.
   Green, M.G.
3. Smith, Marvel L. to Parret, Eliza, June (no day, 1852,
   G. W. Selvidge, M.G.
3. Rauschenburg, Frederick to Ramy, Louisa M., July 18, 1852,
   James A. Ault, J.P.
3. Roberts, A. P. to Berry, Josephire T., July 31, 1852. W.
   Gordon, J.I.C.
4. Mcdonal, M. W. to Parks, Elisa A., Aug. 13, 1852, Wm. B.
   Malone, J.P.
4. Worthington, A. G. H. to Taley, Ann E., Sept. 9, 1852,
   Wm. B. Malone, J.P.
4. Stuart, James L. to Latch, Mariann, Aug. 18, 1852.
5. Springfield, William F. to Jinks, Linna Frances, June 26,
   1852.
5. Hebrenston, Joseph E. to Davis, K. A., Sept. 23, 1852,
   W. H. Vandever, M.G.
5-6. Bell, Sulivan E. to Davis, Elizabeth A., Aug. 24, 1852,
   A. D. Clark, M.G.
6. Carter, James to Davis, Martha, Sept. 2, 1852. Z. D. Clark,
   M.G.
6. Dees, Marion to Moore, Elizabeth, Sept. 12, 1852, Z. D.
   Clark, M.G.
6-7. Hardcastle, William to Scoggins, Mary A., June 24, 1852,
   Z. D. Clark, M.G.
7. Hess, Joseph to McAbee, Mary, July 22, 1852, Z. D. Clark,
   M.G.
7. Teague, Thomas to Cornish, Mary, Oct. 2, 1852, A. G.
   Johnson, M.G.
8. Johnson, W. R. to McDonald, Louisa, Oct. 21, 1852, E. H.
   Edwards, J.I.C.
8. McDonald, William B. to Crumbly, Sarah A., Aug. 1, 1852,
   A. McHand, L.D.
8. Atwood, Samuel J. to Lego, Mahalia A., Oct. 11, 1852,
   E. H. Edward, J.I.C.
9. Crawford, William to McDune, Martha, Aug. 1, 1852, F. W.
   McCurdy, J.I.C.
9. McKinney, M. P. to Martin, Rebecca, Oct. 5, 1852, John S.
   Martin, J.P.
9. McKinzie, W. A. to Shields, Mary, Aug. 22, 1852, John S.
   Martin, J.P.

PAGE
1-10. Gideon, Galson B. to Lacey, Larana F., Oct. 21, 1852, Wm.
B. Malone, J.P.
10. Mobley, L. C. to Tharn, Lucinday, Nov. 15, 1852, J. W.
Ramsey, M.G.
10. Hall, Thomas J. to Clark, Susanah, Dec. 5, 1852, James B.
Ault, J.P.
11. Jourdon, Robert to Lane, Malinda, Nov. 15, 1852, Wm. East,
J.P.
11. Carpenter, Jed to Glover, Narcissa J., Dec. 21, 1852, M. W.
Vandiver, M.G.
11. Bluminstoks, Gotlab to Jacobs, Haneretha, Jan. 12, 1853,
Wm. B. Malone, J.P.
12. Jaurdan, Robert to Lane, Malindand, Dec. 19, 1852, Wm. East,
J.P.
12. Hall, Thomas J. to Clark, Susanah, Dec. 18. 1852, James A.
Ault, J.P.
12. White, Robert H. to Fletcher, Nancy C., Dec. 23, 1852, Wm.
Nutt, M.G.
13. Fletcher, E. C. to Peck, Nancy A., Jan. 5, 1852. J. H.
Cawood, M.G.
13. Anderson, John W. to ?chister, Jane, Feb. 1, 1853, A. G.
Johnson, M.G.
14. Case, Bradly to Rose, Sarah Jane, Feb. 20, 1853, William
Whitten, J.P.
14. Brown, Benjamin to Cahaon, Elizabeth, Mar. 10, 1853, Levi
Brotherton, M.G.
14. Critenstan, Henry J. to Martain, Besy Ann, Jan. 13. 1853,
Wiley Catrell. M.G.
15. Fielder, W. to Crompton, Jane, Mar. 3, 1853, Wiley Cantell.
M.G.
15. Johnson, Henry to Creekmore, Nancy A., Mar. 27, 1853, D.
Johnson, J.P.
15. Davis, G. W. to Smith, Sarah Ann, Apr. 4, 1853, John
Anderson, J.P.
16. MCafee, J. R. to Tarver, Mary R., May 8, 1853, Levi
Brotherton, M.G.
16. Reed, Hugh J. to Crow, Narcissa E., Jan. 13. 1853, John S.
Martin, J.P.
16. Cook, Daniel to Keith, Frances, May 22, 1853, James A.
Ault, J.P.
17. Moore, William K. to Field, Elizabeth M., July 15, 1853.
A. G. Johnson, M.G.
17. Childers, Wiley to Johnson, Lucy, July 3. 1853, (?) Johnston, M.G.
17. Bridges, J. S. to Ellis, M. E. M., July 21, 1853, G. W.
Selvidge, M.G.
18. Steal?k, James B. to Roberts, Eliza J., July 21, 1853, John
B. Bell, M.G.
18. Broome, F. Callaway to Coamings, Emma, July 28, 1853, James
A. Ault, J.P.
18. Kincannon, George to Manis, Nancy, Apr. 28. 1853, J.
Gerthra(?), J.P.
19. Johnston, Blackborn to Harris, Rody, July 4, 1853, William
Whittin, J.P.
19. Clark, Joseph to Bick, Martha W. J., July 24, 1853, John B.
Bell, M.G.
19. Mulkey(?), David to Page, Jane, Aug. 10, 1853, Martin P.
Berry, J.P.
20. Looper, J. H. to Staam(?), Mary, Apr. 5, 1853, Z. D. Clark
M.G.

PAGE
20. Queen, Joseph L. to Bedingfield, Frances, Aug. 20, 1853,
    Bej. F. King, M.G.
20. Firestone, Robert A. to Hays, Isabella, Sept. 4, 1853,
    John Andersen, J.P.
21. Bridges, William to Webb, Sarah Ann, June 27, 1853, W. M.
    East, J.P.
21. Smith, James to Ray, Jane, Sept. 3, 1853, Alfred M.
    Gooeteykoontz, M.G.
21. May, Ruben to Stricklan, Elizabeth, Sept. 8, 1853, E.
    MCabee, M.G.
22. Walker, Dan F. H. to Pittman, Rebeca, Sept. (no day), 1853.
    M. W. Vandifer, M.G.
22. Pierce, Willis S. to Benton, Adeline, Sept. 22, 1853, J. A.
    Ault, J.P.
22. Williams, Enves(?) to Hood, Elizabeth, Sept. 29, 1853, E.
    MCabee, M.G.
23. Cook, Abel to Carmon, Jane, Sept. 15, 1853, J. Guthry, J.P.
23. Emerson, C. J. to Austin, M. C., May 5, 1853, J. M.
    Richardson, M.G.
23. Culver, Hardy G. to McDonold, Martha H., Dec. 5, 1853, John
    Anderson, J.P.
24. Johnson, D. C. to King, Emily, Oct. 16, 1853, Gilbert
    Randolph, M.G.
24. Green, Web to Gaddy, Elizabeth, Dec. 4, 1853, J. C. Bates,
    M.G.
24. Hendrus(?), William H. to Bates, Loiza, Dec. 7, 1853, J. C.
    Bates, M.G.
24-25. Forester, Jess to Dunn, Margaret, Nov. 3, 1853, W. I.
    Gustinn, J.P.
25. Burk, James A. to Hide, Mary, Oct. 4, 1853, J. Guthrie,
    J.P.
25. Crow, William S. to Neal, Mary, Dec. 8, 1853, J. Guthrie,
    J.P.
25. Perrot, William L. to Dobbs, Martha, Dec. 22, 1853, E. H.
    Edwards, J.I.C.
26. Rice, J. W. to Smallwood, Eliza J., Sept. 20, 1852, John
    Howard, J.P.
26. Kincanan, Samuel to Spann, Lucinda, Nov. 15, 1853. Young
    L. M'Lemore.
26. Martin, William to Marris, Elizabeth, Oct. 15, 1853, Young
    L. McLemore.
27. Odum, Oliver to Brooks, Fannie, Aug. 5, 1853, E. H.
    Edwards, J.I.C.
27. Cross, Jacob to Laurance, Louiza, Dec. 6, 1853, Young L.
    McLemore.
27. Neal, M. W. to Howard, Mary Jane, Dec. 22, 1853, Robert S.
    Smith, J.P.
28. Robeson, John M. to McBurk, J. A., Nov. 29, 1853, Young L.
    McLemore.
28. Smith, Alfred to White, Margaret J., Jan. 1, 1854, J. D.
    Anthony, M.G.
28. Weaver, Andrew J. to Pete, Lucretia H., Dec. 13, 1853,
    Wiley Cantrell, M.G.
29. Lewis, Miles W. to Moore, Anny M., "Nocto." 20, 1853,
    Wiley Cantrell, M.G. (The license was issued Oct. 12,
    1853).
29. Smith, Fillmond to Burin, Eliza, Dec. 29, 1853, J. W.
    Ramsey, M.G.
29. Heath, Preston to Black, Carolin, Feb. 5, 1854, Drury
    Johnson, M.G.

PAGE
30   Firestone, Robert A. to Hays, Barbara (Isabella), Sept. 4, 1853, John Anderson, J.P.

30   Minis, William to Norton, Margaret A., Nov. 17, 1853, William Whittin, J.P.

30-31. Hammack, R. B. to Williams, Sarah, Feb. 5, 1854, William Whitten, J.P.

31.   Sloan, Archibald to Carpenter, Permelia Arrenva, Apr. 12, 1854, J. W. Ramsey, M.G.

31.   Sanson, James L. to Johnson, Josephene, Apr. 20, 1854, James A. Ault, J.P.

31.   Dunnigan, B. S. to Edwards, Mary E., Feb. 27, 1854, Richard Cruce, J.P.

32.   Smith, Drewry R. to Gordy, Missourie, May 28, 1854, J. D. Anthony, M.G.

32.   Glover, William M. to Cantrel, Mary, Feb. 23, 1854, L. W. Baity, J.P.

32.   Phillips, Roberson to Wilden(?), Mary, May 28, 1854, L. W. Baty, J.P.

32.   Whitson, Jos. W. to Green, Sarah E., May 18, 1854, D. F. Smith, M.G.

33.   Cochran, Charles to Smith, Mary, July 18, 1853, L. W. Baty, M. G.

33.   Frost, John M. to Burnet, Nancy, May 7, 1854, J. Guthrie, J.P.

33.   Hilton, E. R. to Duncan, Nancy, May 18. 1853, J. P. Garner, J.P.

33.   Huffacre(Huffaker), Isaac A. to Foster, Martha A., June 1, 1854, J. Guthrie, J.P.

34.   Williams, Egbert C. to Bell, Mary M., May 7, 1854, J. Guthrie, J.P.

34.   McCarny, Wm. C. to Rushton, Annie, June 4, 1854, C. (?) Wellborn, M.G.

34.   Nations, James to McNair, Mary, Dec. 18, 1853, Britain Williams, M.G.

34-35. Overby, William B. to Bence, Martha L., Mar. 24, 1853, Robert Ware, M.G.

35.   Springfield, James M. to Bell, Sarah, June 7, 1854, J. Guthrie, J.P.

35.   Wrinkle, Andrew N. to Dover, Martha, June 11, 1854, E. H. Edwards, J.I.C.

35-36. Bridges, Thomas to Murrphy, Carolin, May 20, 1854, W. C. Norris, M.G.

36.   Snow, Jessee to Smith, Sarah, June 11. 1854, John B. Bell, M.G.

36.   Haggard, James to McDonald, Mary H., Dec. 8. 1853, John Anderson, J.P.

36-37. James, Lane to Keith, Sarah Ann, Jan. 8, 1854, Wm. East, J.P.

37.   Stephenson, William to Jarrett, Fanny, Mar. 9, 1854, J. P. Garner, J.P.

37.   Abels, Jeremiah to White, Julim H., Mar. 26, 1854, E. H. Edwards, J.I.C.

38.   Jolly, William W. to Shields, Elisabeth Ann, Apr. 17. 1854, E. H. Edwards, J.I.C.

38.   Evans, Henry to Smith, Nancy, July 4, 1854, J. D. Anthony, M.G.

38-39. Bradley, Felix to Chapman, Sarah E., July 13, 1854, John B. Bell, M.G.

39.   Stephenson, James S. to Hoyle, Mary J., Aug. 3, 1854, J. M. Kenner, M.G.

PAGE

39. McGhee, William M. to Smith, Sarah E., Aug. 15, 1854,
Raleigh Cupp, J.P.

40. Duggan, William J. to Johnson, Minerva A., Aug. 17, 1854,
Raleigh Cupp, J.P.

40 Swanson, John to Ponder, Harriet, Aug. 30, 1854, Robert
Ware, M.G.

41. Smith, Arter C. to Gordy, Mahaly, July 24, 1854, J. D.
Anthony, M.G.

41. Dycus, James G. to Hayle, Sarah A., Aug. 13, 1854, J. D.
Anthony, M.G.

42. Oneal, Willis to Smith, Tylons, Aug. 13, 1854, J. D.
Anthony, M.G.

42. Edwards, William T. to Dunnegan, Julia Ann Elisabeth,
Aug. 20, 1854, D. T. Fulton, M.G.

43. Durham, O. D. (C. D.) to Johnson, Unicy, Aug. 20, 1854,
John Anderson, J.P.

43. Bridges, Louis to Bolin, Crecy, Oct. 5, 1852, John J.
Gilbert, M.G.

44. Whaley, P. J. to Thorn, Mahaley A., Nov. 18, 1852, John
J. Gilbert, M. G.

44. Reid, Elijah T. to Jackson, Margaret E., Dec. 12, 1852,
John J. Gilbert, M.G.

45. Sartain, William to Hawkins, Sarah A., June 6, 1853,
John J. Gilbert, M.G.

45. Miller, Rusell to Davis, Mary, Sept. 8, 1853, John J.
Gilbert, M.G.

46. Carrel, Absalem J. to Card, Martha C., Dec. 22, 1853,
John J. Gilbert, M.G.

46. Sutherland, Ransom to Alexander, Lucy J., Jan. 26, 1854,
John J. Gilbert, M.G.

47. Smith, Joseph to Tucker, Mary Ann, July 18, 1854, William
Whitten, J.P.

47. Davis, Jackson to Bowing, Sarah, Aug. 6, 1854, James W.
Ramsey, M.G.

48. Dycus, David to Moore, Nancy, Aug. 15, 1854, Wm. East,
J.P.

48. Bates, Wilson H. to Miller, Nancy, Aug. 23, 1854, B. M.
Clark, J.P.

49. Johnson, Calep to McCormick, Caroline, Aug. 31, 1854,
William Whitten.

49. Seay, William J. to Brock, Almarena, Sept. 19, 1854,
James W. Ramsey, M.G.

50. Burns, James W. to Anderson, Mary A., Sept. 24, 1854,
Raleigh Cupp, J.P.

50. Stockberger, William G. to Everett, Mary L., Oct. 12,
1854, C. R. McAlister, J.P.

51. Jewell, Adison T. to Page, Martha, Oct. 19, 1854,
Raleigh Cupp, J.P.

51. Tucker, George W. to Smith, Elisabeth, Oct. 24, 1854,
Raleigh Cupp, J.P.

52. Brawdrick, Jessee to Webb, Frances, Oct. 15, 1854, Wm.
East, J.P.

52. Harris, Richard to Franklin, Elisabeth, Aug. 24, 1854,
D. T. Fulton, M.G.

53. Austin, William C. to Ellis, Mahalia, Sept. 25, 1854,
D. T. Fulton, M.G.

53. Treadwell, Smith to Mobley, Nancy Ann Elisabeth, Nov.
12, 1854, L. W. Batey, J.P.

54. Ault, Robert Sm. to Bearden, Nancy, Nov. 12, 1854, Milton
C. Smith, M.G.

PAGE

54. Davis, J. B. to Arnold, Sarah E., Nov. 14, 1854, Raleigh Cupp, J.P.

55. Webb, William to Cash, Lucy, Nov. 9, 1854, Drury Johnson, M.G.

55. Brown, James A. to Gasp, Martha, Nov. 11, 1854, C. T. Fulton, M.G.

56. Patterson, J.W. to Ducket, Ester N., Sept. 25, 1854, J. M. Richardson, M.G.

56. McGee, Andrew C. to Tyler, Sarah J., Dec. 14, 1854, Levi Brotherton, M.G.

57. May, Samuel to Duncan, Millia A., Nov. 23, 1854, Raleigh Cupp, J.P.

57. Williams, John T. to Webb, Sarah, Dec. 21, 1854, E. H. Edwards, J.I.C.

58. Wood, Isham to Calhoun, Amanda, Dec. 21, 1854, John B. Bell, M.G.

58. Strickland, H. F. to Broadwick, Mary I., Dec. 21, 1854, Edward McAbee, M.G.

59. Crute (Crite), John M. to Riddle, Mary A., Dec. 24, 1854, John Crawford, M.G.

59. Faith, Abraham to Owens, Sarah Jane, July 31, 1854, H. Rogers, J.I.C.

60. Harris, D. D. to Tipton, Mary Ann, Oct. 29, 1854, Jas. L. Capehart, J.P.

60. Ware, Alfred to Roach, Martha Jane, Aug. 3, 1854, Britain, Williams, M.G.

61. Manis, Jacob D. to Jarrett, Sally, Nov. 21, 1854, J. P. Garner, J.P.

61. Head, Alfred M. to Haynes, H. L., Dec. 24, 1854, Joshua Harlan, J.I.C.

62. Franklin, L. E. to Gamble, Narcissia, Jan. 11, 1855, C. B. Helborn, M.G.

62. Ducket, Jessee R. to Mooreland, Nancy, Dec. 24, 1854, J. M. Richardson.

63. Boyd, Martin to Cox, Sarah C., Feb. 15, 1855, John B. Bell, M.G.

63. Jolly, Thos. B. to Tye, Eliza, Feb. 14, 1855, E. H. Edwards, J.I.C.

64. Rouse, Joseph to Moreland, Margaret, Feb. 9, 1855, John Anderson, J.P.

64. Shaw, John to Burks (Burke), Sarah Ann, Feb. 22, 1855, L. W. Batey, J.P.

65. Fisher, Gustav to Sutterlin, Carolina, Mar. 5, 1855, Rufus S. E. Ford, J.P.

65. Maxwell, Caldwell to Caldwell, Frances, Mar. 27, 1855, D. F. Smith, M.G.

66. Oneill (O'Niell), John to Gavan (Gavin), Mary J., Apr. 1, 1855, E. H. Edwards, J.I.C.

66. Dunbar, James P. to Ennis, Minerva Ann, Apr. 1, 1855, John J. Gilbert, M.G.

67. Mitchell, David W. to Brumbelow, Mary, Apr. 8, 1855, John J. Gilbert, M.G.

67. Finch, James B. to Justice, Rhuamy, Dec. 11, 1853, W. C. Norris, M.G.

68. Burk, Hugh H. to Crow, Sarah A., Dec. 21, 1853, J. Guthrie.

68. Stevenson, David to Vandike, Harriet, Jan. 22, 1854, John B. Bell, M.G.

69. Bachman, S. Wilson to Sims, Virginia M., Sept. 8, 1854, Jno. Bachma, D.D., past Luth. Church, Charleston, SC.

PAGE
69. Williams, James I. to Drennan, Margaret E., Dec. 31,
1854, James L. Capehart, J.P.
70. Stewart, Thomas to Stricklin, Harriet, Apr. 1, 1855,
Edward McAbee, M.G.
70. Moreland, James M. to Hall, Araminta E., Feb. 15, 1855,
James A. Ault, J.P.
71. Bartels, William W. to Boman, Mary E., May 1, 1855, John
J. Gilbert, M.G.
71. Kirkpatrick, Jesse M. to Long, Julia A., Nov. 2, 1854,
William Whitten, J.P.
72. May, Berry to Dyer, Mary, Dec. 13, 1854, William Whitten,
J.P.
72. McCall, William L. to Ellis, Elisabeth M., May 13, 1855,
C. B. Wellborn, M.G.
73. Hawks, W. R. R. to Parret, Sarah E., June 28, 1855, Levi
Brotherton, M.G.
73. Douglas, William S. to Rogers, Martha E., May 8, 1855,
D. F. Smith, M.G.
74. Greenfield, John to Caststell. Sarah Ann, July 12, 1855,
R. F. Jones, M.G.
74. Odell, James A. to Chapman, Martha C., Aug. 2, 1855, L.
M. Richardson.
75. Wilson, Samuel to Constine, Sarah Jane, Aug. 15, 1855,
E. H. Edwards, J.I.C.
75. Gillian, Franklin to Torbet, Margaret, Feb. 16, 1855,
Y. L. McLenor, M.G.
76. Pollard, Joshua to Stone, Sarah, Aug. 16, 1855, Edward
McAbee, M.G.
76. King, Silas H. to Vandivere, Emerline, Aug. 12, 1855,
John B. Bell, M.G.
77. Callahan, William to Siglar, Cynthia, Aug. 26, 1855,
E. H. Edwards, J.I.C.
77. Long, William R. to Underwood, Ann Jane, Sept. 5, 1855,
C. B. Wellborn, M.G.
78. Alexander, William W. to Turner, Martha E., Aug. 30,
1855. M. C. Martin, M.G.
78. Jarvis, John to Hodge, Mary, Aug. 16, 1855, Z. D. Clark,
M.G.
79. Esskew, William to Parks, Elizabeth Ann, Sept. 13, 1855,
Levi Brotherton, M.G.
79. Gilbert, John I. to Shipp, Penelope, Oct. 11, 1855, H.
Rogers, J.I.C.
30. Anderson, Isaac T. to Nailor, Amanda, Oct. 14, 1855,
Raleigh Cupp, J.P.
80. Johnson, Jacob C. to Rodgers, Mary E., June 21, 1855,
D. F. Smith, M.G.

MURRAY COUNTY   GEORGIA

81. Steel, George to Robert, Elizabeth, Nov. 4, 1850, Wm. B.
Malone, J.P.
81. Tally, Thomas to Snow, Elizabeth Ann, Oct. 27, 1851,
Wm. B. Malone, J.P.
82. Rauchenberg, Emil to Wirth, Pauline, Feb. 19, 1852, Wm.
B. Malone, J.P.
82. Knorr, Charles to Suterlin, Elizabeth, Nov. 29, 1851,
Wm. B. Malone, J.P.

WHITFIELD COUNTY - GEORGIA

83. Rogers, Samuel M. to Hatcher, Elizabeth, Oct. 21, 1855,
Raleigh Cupp, J.P.
83. Dover, Anderson M. to Smart, Hester A., Jan. 10, 1856,
E. H. Edwards, J.I.C.
83. Johnson, Nelson to Cavender, Rebecca, Dec. 14, 1855,
Brizzel (?) Lervy, J.P.
84. Camp, Alfred to Lewis, Margaret A., Dec. 20, 1855, W. C.
Richardson, M.G.
84. Scott, James M. to Corigan, Catherine, Dec. 9, 1855, G.
W. Selvidge, M.G.
84. Fulton, F. M. to L-----n, Mary E., Dec. 29, 1855.
85. Cooper, Marion C. to Simmons, Mary, May 20. 1855, D. F.
Fulton, M.G.
85. Gordon, Jacob to Smith, Elizabeth, Dec. 22, 1855, Edward
McAbee, M.G.
85. Crow, Jeptha C. to Ault, Armidia, Dec. 20, 1855, C. R.
McAllister, J.P.
86. Rogers, Samuel L. to Haynes, Almina, Jan. 25, 1855, D. F.
Smith, M.G.
86. Shell, Jackson to Cline, Elmina, May 6, 1855, Wm. East,
J.P.
87. Lergmorance, E. M. to Austin, A. D., Feb. 7, 1856, Robt.
Ware, M.G.
87. Stenson, Samuel to Crow, L. H., Feb. 8, 1856, James A.
Ault, J.P.
87. Pritchard, Anderson to Howard, Ellen, Feb. 17, 1856, W.
W. Green, M.G.
88. Roberts, John to Wilkins, Mary A., Mar. 18, 1855, Mills
J. Abernathy, M.G.
88. Turner, Samuel S. to Senter, Mary Elizabeth, Mar. 2,
1856, M. A. Clonts, M.G.
88. Laymance, E. M. to Austin, A. D., Feb. 7, 1856, Robert
Ware, M.G.
89. Mote, John Q. A. to Lynch, Mary A., Mar. 2, 1856, John P.
Love, J.P.
89. Austin, J. C. to Haralson, M. C., Mar. 20, 1856, Robt.
Ware, M.G.
90. Emerson, R. C. to Austin, E. R., Mar. 4, 1856, F. Bird,
M.G.
90. Walker, William D. to White, Harriet Caroline, Mar. 6,
1856, M. C. Martin, M.G.
91. Jackson, John E. W. to Whitaker, Louemna, Mar. 29, 1856,
M. C. Martin, M.G.
91. Harp, Andrew J. to Cruse(Cruce), Sarah Jane, Sept. 26,
1855, James L. Capehart, J.P.
92. Farrell. Jasper to Croxton, Sarah, Mar. 9, 1856, James
L. Capehart, J.P.
92. King, Wiley A. to Carter, Milly, Mar. 8, 1856, James A.
Ault, J.P.
93. Greenwood, Wiley to Peterson, Mary Jane, Apr. 13, 1856,
John B. Bell.
93. Mylins, Henry to Armstrong, Silvia, Apr. 16, 1856, Levi
Brotherton, M.G.
94. Alton, Geo. W. to Tailors, Lucinda, Apr. 13, 1856, Haley
G. Fuller, M.G.
94. Mangum, Willaim C. to Chester, L. V., May 1, 1857, G. W.
Selvidge, M.G.
95. Boling, William T. to Parrot, Mary C., May 29, 1858,
Bredenbrough Thompson, J.P.
95. Maston, John B. (G.) to Whittle, Nancy, Feb. 3, 1856,

PAGE

Britain Williams, M.G.

95. Tally, Isham H. to Jones, Elizabeth M., Apr. 24, 1856, S. W. Adams, J.P.

96. Sebastian (Sebastine), Elisha I. to Boling, Nancy I., Apr. 20, 1856, S. W. Adams, J.P.

96. Shelton, John R. to Reese, Nanie, Feb. 27, 1856, G. F. Swaggerly, J.I.C.

96. Laymance, E. M. to Austin, A. D., Feb. 7, 1856, Robt. Ware, M.G.

97. Roberts, John to Wilkins, Mary A., Mar. 18, 1855, Mills J. Abernathy, M.G.

97. Turner, Samuel S. to Senter, Mary Elizabeth, Mar. 3, 1856, M. A. Clontz, M.G.

97-98. Nichols, W. L. to Wood, Rebecca J., June 1, 1856, Edward Mcabee, M.G.

98. Carr, William L. to Carden, Sarah, June 6, 1856, Charles D. Adair, J.P.

98-99. Helton, John F. to Fortune, Caroline, June 28, 1856, Edward Harper Edwards, J.I.C.

99. Hardcastle, J. G. L. to Cash, Louisa, July 3, 1856, Edward McAbee, M.G.

99-100. Greenwood, Hutson to Hall, Jurissa, May 24, 1856, E. H. Edwards, J.I.C.

100. Master, John A. to Worthy, Sarah A., May 25, 1856, J. W. Adams, J.P.

101. Henry, Ephraim L. to Blanton, Mary Ann, June 17, 1856, Griffin A. McAllester, J.P.

101. Thogmartin, Benjamin to Philips, Mary, July 10, 1856, C. R. McAllester, J.P.

102. Ponder, A. J. to Duncan, Elizabeth C., Aug. 14, 1856, Z. D. Clark, M.G.

102. Hall, William to Hall, Emily, Aug. 26, 1856, James A. Ault, J.P.

102. McCurdy, S. C. M. to Smith, Amanda A., Sept. 11, 1856, M. A. Clontz, M.G.

103. Creekmore, George to Jordan, Mary, July 20, 1856, Raleigh Cupp, J.P.

103. Harkins, James to Holder, Julian (Julia?), Aug. 24, 1856, E. H. Edwards, J.I.C.

103. Smith, Alfred A. to Torbitt, Nancy, July 8, 1856, Z. D. Clark, M.G.

104. George, William K. to Burns, Aley Melsiner (Melsine?), Aug. 14, 1856, E. M. Amos, M.G.

104. McDaniel, Francis M. to Stephenson, Martha M., May 30, 1855, S. C. Quillian, M.G.

105. Walker, James H. to Henderson, Hannah, June 28, 1855, S. C. Quillian, M. G.

105. McCurdy, S. C. M. to Smith, Amanda A., Sept. 11, 1856, M. A. Clouts, M.G.

106. Whaley, William A. to Pope, Mary B., Sept. 4, 1856, John L. Henton.

106. King, John to Strickland, Mary Ann, Oct. 16, 1856, Vredenburgh Thompson, J.P.

107. Loyd, Benjamin to Jurell, Sarah Jane, Oct. 23, 1856, S. C. Quillian, M.G.

107. King, Thomas W. to Cox, Bethena F., Oct. 20, 1856, Vrendenburgh Thompson, J.P.

108. Crane, Leonard L. to Johnson, Mary Ann, Nov. 16, 1856, Vredenburgh Thompson, J.P.

103. Guice (Guire?), William to McDonal, Eliza Ann, Dec. 21,

PAGE

1856, S. C. Quillian, M.G.

109. Cash, Peter C. to Girdy (Gordy?), Rebecca A., Jan. 1, 1857, Wm. East, J.P.

109. Keith, B. A. to High, Mary A., Jan. 3, 1857, E. H. Edwards, J.I.C.

110. Hopper, Zachariah to Henton, Mary E., Dec. 23, 1856, William W. Green, M.G.

110. Dana, William M. to Bishop, Annie E., Jan. 1, 1857, Robt. Ware, M.G.

110. Nance, William T. to Robertson, Nancy E., Dec. 30, 1855, John J. Gilbert, M.G.

111. Williams, A.C. to Head, Magee Ann, July 31, 1856, James L. Capehart, J.P.

111. Pierce, Thomas to Bryant, A. M. J. S., Feb. 3, 1857, C. B. Wellborn, M.G.

112. Hibberts, John M. L. to Hamilton, Martha, Aug. 15, 1856, Brendburgh Thompson, J.P.

112. Davis, William to Ward, Mary, Dec. 14, 1856, James W. Ramsey, M.G.

113. May, James to Cagle, Harriet, Dec. 11, 1856, G. A. McAllister, G.M.

113. Riley, Thomas to Cleaveland (Cleveland), Mary Ann, Feb. 11, 1857, J. O. O'Neill, Cath. Past., Atlanta.

114. Maffett, R. G. W. to Carpenter, Mrs. N. G., Feb. 19, 1857, G. W. Selvidge, M.G.

114. Boring, Rufus M. to Thompson, Mary J., Feb. 18, 1857, Hugh McDonald, J.P.

115. Boatwright, W. C. to Orear, Susan E., Feb. 19, 1857, Hugh McDonald, J.P.

115. Cash, Thomas to Harrison, Anna A., Apr. 15, 1857, G. M. Selvidge, M.G.

116. Blaylock, Robert C. to Harris, Margaret E., Nov. 27, 1856, Joshua Harlan, J.I.C.

116. Connally (Conally), Edwin, to Falks, Elizabeth Jane, Mar. 22, 1857. Raleigh Cupp, J.P.

117. Shaefer, Max to Haker, Henriette, Apr. 6, 1857. W. -- Chester, J.I.C.

117. Bearden, Richard to Hunt (?), Phebe, Apr. 26, 1857, G. G. Witherspoon, M.G.

117-118. Woodall, Martin E. to Kennemon, Ellen, May 31, 1857, J. L. Anthony, M.G.

118. Carpenter, Mitchel C. to McGuire, Elizabeth, June 4, 1857, James W. Ramsey.

118. Oxford, John to Austin, Mahalia, Jan. 29, 1857, Jacob Tate, M.G.

119. Keown, Wm. J. to Davis, Sarah A., Feb. 12, 1857, A. E. Vandiver, M.G.

119. Hooper, John W. to Worthy, Sarah, May 10, 1857, Jesse T. Freeman, J.P.

120. Davis, Charles C. to Varnell, Adelaid (Adelaide), June 14, 1857, Levi Brotherton, M.G.

120. Runells, John W. to George, Caroline, June 14, 1857, Z. N. Davis, J.P.

121. Cleveland, Benjamin F. to Martin, Eliza Ann, Oct. 20, 1855, Daniel Johnson.

121. Boatwright, N.C. to Harp, Sarah J., Jan. 6 (8), 1857, Daniel Johnson.

122. Dougherty, Solo F. to Patterson, Amanda, Jan. 20, 1857, Daniel Johnson.

122. Eslinger, J. S. to Smith, E. J., Jan. 22, 1857, D. T. Fulton.

PAGE
123. McClure, George to Roach, Francis Caroline, Mar. 24, 1857, D. T. Fulton.

123. Calwell (Caldwell), James L. to Roach, Elizabeth Jane, Mar. 25, 1857, D. T. Fulton.

124. Chapman, E. E. to Talley, N. G., Aug. 16, 1857, M. W. Vandiver, M.G.

124. Martin, Joseph H. to Thornton, M. E., July 23, 1857, M. A. Clouts, M.G.

125. Hardy, I. H. to Slay, Margaret, Aug. 25, 1857, C. B. Wellborn, M.G.

125. Cunningham, W. M. to Coffee, Sarah C., May 25, 1856, V. W. Wilson, M.G.

126. Smith, Micagah to Bailey, Elenora (Elnora), June 22, 1856, V. W. Wilson, M.G.

126. Giles, William C. to Long, Nancy, June 26, 1856, V. W. Wilson, M.G.

127. Ledford, Morris to Daniel, Elisabeth, Sept. 25, 1856, V. W. Wilson, M.G.

127. Jarret, Thomas to Manus (McManis), Margaret M., Nov. 13, 1856, Elder V. W. Wilson, M.G.

128. Rose, John to Stewart, Elisabeth I., Jan. 4, 1857, Elder V. W. Wilson, M.G.

128. Howard, Lafayette to Brown, Martha Jane, Aug. 23, 1857, Robert W. Ault, J.P.

129. Cross, Jesse to Brown, Nancy Ann, Sept. 3, 1857, Robert W. Ault, J.P.

129. Gordon, N. C. to Keith, Mary, Aug. 13, 1857, G. W. Selvidge, M.G.

130. Hamby, T. J. to Masters, M. E., Nov. 7, 1852, Jacob Tate, M.G.

130. Hawkins, Ephraim to Blalock, Elisabeth A., Apr. 18, 1856, John J. Gilbert, M.G.

131. Walker, Henry A.T. to Jones, Mary E., Feb. 22, 1857, L. W. Adams, J.P.

131. Pickens, John A. to Minnis (Minis), Latitia J., Aug. 5, 1857, Thomas Turner, M.G.

132. Petty, John R. to Thomas, Margaret E., Sept. 20, 1857, Vredenburgh Thompson, J.P.

132. Ward, Stephen D. to Vardivere, Hannah, Oct. 4, 1857, Jacob Tate, M.G.

133. Swift, T. G. to Carswell, C. V., Sept. 24, 1857, W. C. Richardson, O.M.

133. Hicks, James J. to Redwine, S. A. E., Oct. 15, 1857, Wm. Green, M.G.

134. Horne, Samuel D. to Bell, Harriet, Oct. 20, 1857, James M. Kenner, M.G.

134. Barnett, Joseph A. to Step, Lucinda Jane, Aug. 23, 1857, H. T. Holland, M.G.

135. Henkel, Frederick to Kreischer, Mary K., Nov. 26, 1857, J. P. Freeman, J.P.

135. Bridges, John M. to Holt, Mary M., Nov. 25, 1857, M. A. Clouts, M.G.

136. Cavender, William G. to Holland, Catherine (Catharine) K., Nov. 27, 1857, G. W. Selvidge, M.G.

136. Grubbs (Grubb), David M. to Dyke, Eliza, Nov. 30, 1857, W. P. Chester, J.I.C.

137. Schweizer, John C. to Togler, Anna, Oct. 19, 1857, W. P. Chester, J.I.C.

137. Fagala, John to Taliaferro, Sarah, Nov. 15, 1857, C. B. Wellborn, M.G.

PAGE

138.   Dooley, James to Wilson, Louiza, Feb. 10, 1856, Z. D.
Clark, M.G.

138.   Hollman, Israel to Meek, Fanny I., Nov. 27, 1857, Levi
Brotherton, M.G.

139.   Caneister, Alexander to Ward, Labelia, Nov. 29, 1857,
Z. D. Clark, M.G.

139.   Leak, A. C. to Harlin, M. J., Dec. 23, 1857, Levi
Brotherton, M.G.

140.   Head, J. M. to Masters, Elisabeth, Oct. 27, 1857, John
M. Richardson, M.G.

140.   Wilson, Willis to Johns, Mary, Dec. 24, 1857, Raleigh
Cupp, J.P.

141.   Oxford, David to Sweatman, S. J., Dec. 29, 1857,
Vredenburgh Thompson, J.P.

141.   Gordon, James to Evans, Mary Jane, Dec. 31, 1857,
Raleigh Cupp, J.P.

142.   Davies, Francis B. to Simmons, Mary E., Feb. 9, 1858,
L. J. Davies, M.G.

142.   Strickland, John W. to Holland, Ruth, Feb. 28, 1858,
G. W. Selvidge, M.G.

143.   Evans, H. T. to Fincher, Sarah M., Mar. 10, 1858, C. B.
Wellborn, M.G.

143.   Wilson, Daniel N. to Stockton (Stockten), Nancy L. Mar.
21, 1858, W. C. Richardson, M.G.

144.   Henson, Virgil to Masters, Mary Ann, Apr. 16, 1856, L. W.
Adams, J.P.

144.   Johnson, Alfred A. to Whittaker, Livonia, Nov. 19, 1857,
M. C. Martin, M.G.

145.   Shehan (Shahan), Lewis to Brown, Sarah Amanda, Feb. 28,
1858, Constantine Wood, J.P.

145.   Stone, Lewis S. to Howard, Annie, June 2, 1858, Wm. W.
Green, M.G.

145.   Worthy, Thomas N. to James, Mary J., July 29, 1858, Perry
E. Hawkins, M.G.

145.   Gaeker, John N. to Singleton, A. D., July 20, 1858, G.
Hughes, M.G.

146.   Sullivan, John to Linder, Jane, July 6, 1858, G. Selvidge,
M.G.

146.   Fortner, David F. to Romines Luticia M., July 30, 1858,
W. H. Stansell, J.P.

146.   Romines, Joseph to Crews, Mary H., July 30, 1858, W. H.
Stansell, J.P.

146.   Leconte, James N. to Gordon, Mary B., Apr. 22, 1858,
R. M. Baker, M.G.

147.   Wooten, J. L. to Henderson, Margaret, July 6, 1858, J. M.
Richardson.

147.   Burnell, Zachariah N. to Whittle, Harriet M., Dec. 9,
1857, John Forester, M.G.

147.   Wrinkle, Elisha to Cratty, Bridgett C., July 15, 1858,
Vred Thompson, J.P.

147.   Collins, G. B. to Hancock, Mary Ann, Jan. 21, 1858, J. J.
Gilbert, A.M.G.

148.   Chandler, Joseph C. to Riley, Adeline L., July 4, 1858,
E. M. Amos, M.G.

148.   Hall, J. Thomas (Thompson) to Bennett, Francis E., June
21, 1858, John J. Gilbert, M.G.

148.   Arnold, Cherly (?) to Jarrett (?), Nancy, July 29, 1858,
William Cole, J.P.

148.   Yarberry, Elias to McDonald, Martha E., Aug. 3, 1858.
William Cole, J.P.

PAGE

149. Stansberry, Albert G. to Carlisle, Susan, July 29, 1858, G. G. Witherspoon, O.M.G.

149. Adams, John S. to Hibberts, Isabella O., Apr. 1, 1858, Vredenburgh Thompson, J.P.

149. Dycus, Edward H. to McDune, Nancy, Aug. 19, 1858, Edward McAbee, M.G.

150. Green, Columbus to Thogmorton, Mira, Sept. 2, 1858, Edward McAbee, M.G.

150. Fulks, Joseph to Hicks, Jane, Sept. 6, 1858, Vredenburgh Thompson, J.P.

150-151. Strickland, R. C. to Duckett, Elisabeth, Sept. 12, 1858, William Cole, J.P.

151. Saunders, Robert to Fox, Mary, Sept. 13, 1858, W. H. Stansell, J.P.

151. Broyles, W. L. to Ruthe, Mary, Sept. 16, 1858, Wm. McNutt, M.G.

151-152. Scoville, E. to Roberts, A.M.F., Sept. 21, 1858, C. B. Wellborn, M.G.

152. Ember, William A. to Caldwell, Jane, Oct. 6, 1858, C. B. Wellborn, M.G.

152. Reed (Reid), Jordan to Odem, L. (Sabriney), Sept. 2, 1858. T. M. Henson, J.F. acting Gordon County, Ga.

153. Bohannan John H. to Smith, Louisa, Sept. 5, 1858, G. W. Selvidge.

153. Fuller, James H. to Johnson, Martha, Oct. 12, 1858, William Hammond, J.I.C.

153-154. McClain, W. M. to Brotherton, Catharine E., Oct. 25, 1858, Jno. C. Simmons, M.G.

154. Metts, Hugh C. to Richardson, Frances M., Nov. 25, 1858, G. Hughes, M.G.

154. Bridges, John H. to Jones, Dicey A., Nov. 28. 1858, E. M. Amos, M.G.

155. Turner, R. L. to Chapel (Chappell), Angenetta, Dec. 22, 1857, S. L. Hamilton.

155. Nations, James to Connally, Tyrena, Dec. 13, 1858, W. H. Stansell. J.P.

155-156. Roach, Henry to Colwell. Eliza, Apr. 13, 1857, George M. Lacy, J.P.

156. Walker, Charles to Stroup, Sarah E., Mar. 10, 1857, George M. Lacy, J.P.

156. Crow, Thomas J. to Reid (Reed), Nancy J., Nov. 21, 1857, George M. Lacy, J.P.

157. Roach, Elijah to Ponder, Sarah, Mar. 21, 1858, G. M. Lacy, J.P.

157. Bearden, Andrew A. to McWherter, Mary A., June 27, 1858, George M. Lacy, J.P.

157-158. Glass, W. R. to Minis (Minnis), Elisabeth J., Dec. 20, 1858, W. B. Brown, V.D.M.

158. Stevenson, W. B. to Willmutt, Nancy A., Dec. 2. 1858, Francis Bird, M.G.

158. Wilson, John to Hyfield, Mary Ann, Dec. 23, 1858. J. W. Green, M.G.

159. Fagin, W. T. to Dooley, Nancy L., Oct. 24, 1858, Z. D. Clark, M.G.

159. May, John to Cline, Naomi, Nov. 18, 1858, Wm. East, J.P.

159-160. Alexander, Lafayette W. to Guinn, Nancy G., Dec. 23, 1858, James W. Ramsey, M.G.

160. Sumner, William R. to Shehan, Mary J., Dec. 28, 1858, Z. D. Clark, M.G.

PAGE
160.   Lynch, William R. to Martin, L.A.E., Jan. 3. 1858(9?),
        Z. D. Clark, M.G.
161.   Manus, John C. to Cole, Martha, Jan. 16, 1859, Raleigh
        Cupp, J.P.
161.   Dowell, W. W. to Hooper, Mary C., Jan. 27, 1859, W. C.
        Richardson, M.G.
161-162. Ford, John W. to Williamson, Martha A., Feb. 3, 1859.
        W. J. Underwood, J.I.C.
162.   Faith, Early H. to Thomas, Milly, Jan. 10, 1859, W. W.
        Gordon, M.G.
162.   Ford, John W. to Williamson, Martha A., Feb. 3, 1859,
        W. J. Underwood, J.I.C.
163.   Gazaway, David to Bennet, Margaret, Feb. 20, 1859, W. W.
        Green, M.G.
163.   Dillard, Thos. P. to Hicks, Margaret, Feb. 3, 1859, W. W.
        Green, M.G.
163.   Boswell, W. M. to Henderson, E. I., Feb. 23. 1859, W. M.
        Shrospshire, J.I.C.
164.   Hannah (Hanna), Isaac S. to Hanna, Hepsy, Feb. 6, 1859,
        John D. Farrer, J.P.
164.   Hinecke, Earnest to Bender, Mary C., Mar. 6, 1859,
        E. M. Amos, M.G.
164.   Malone, Wm. B. to Fulks, Parmela (Permelia?) F., Jan.
        13, 1859, Vredenburgh Thompson, J.P.
165.   Varnell. F. M. to Whittle, Martha, Mar. 10, 1859. John
        Foster, M.G.
165.   Pierce, Alfred Q. to Condre, Margaret E., Mar. 13, 1859,
        John W. Cain, J.P.
165.   Turner, Thomas to Cook, Levisa, Mar. 8, 1859, Robert W.
        Ault, J.P.
166.   Dantzler, Jacob to Mailon, Mary, Mar. 17, 1859, Edward
        Mcabee, M.G.
166.   Sitton, Andrew J. to Brewer, Mary A. H., Apr. 5, 1859,
        W. H. Stansell, J.P.
166.   May, John to Arnold, Jane, Apr. 7, 1859, Raleigh Cupp,
        J. P.
167.   Dooley, Martin H. to Lauracy, Meita M., Feb. 22, 1859,
        Patrick J. Kirby, Catholic.
167.   Brotherton, William H. to Williams, Parale, Feb. 6, 1859,
        J. M. Richardson, M.G.
167.   Caldwell, Robert to Hulsey, Eliza E., Apr. 21, 1859,
        J. M. Richardson, M.G.
168.   Shoemake, G. W. to McNabb, Mary, Apr. 28, 1859, W. P.
        Chester, J.I.C.
168.   Reece, Jarred to Davis, Nancy, May 1, 1859, W. H. Stan-
        sell, J.P.
168.   McGaugha, Samuel to Only, Elizabeth, May 15, 1859, J. P.
        Cawood, M.G.
169.   Shelton, R. S. to Guinn, Mary, Apr. 15. 1859, Jesse
        Wade, J.P.
169.   Whisenant, David H. to Blake, Jane, May 25, 1859,
        Raleigh Cupp, J.P.
169.   Stewart, John to Hall, Sarah. June 2. 1859, Jesse Wade,
        J.P.
170.   Smith, E. J. to Parks, E. F., Mar. 31, 1859, J. J.
        Gilbert, M.G.
170.   Bohanan, William L. to Smith, Debby Ann, June 19, 1859,
        J. J. Gilbert, M.G.
170.   Bowman, James A. to Curd, Salina (Selina) A., Jan. 28,
        1855, John J. Gilbert, M.G.

PAGE
171.   Short, Richard T. to Yarberry, Elizabeth, May 4, 1859,
       A. J. Whitten, J.P.
171.   Aalam(?), George to Corder, Virginia, July 4, 1859,
       W. P. Chester, J.I.C.
171.   Patrick, Peter to Holland, Rhoda, July 14, 1859. J. J.
       Gilbert, M.G.
172.   McHan(?), T. M. to Longly, E. C., Sept. 2. 1859, W. H.
       Stansell. M.G.
172.   Wells, Rufus D. to Callahan, Levista C., Sept. 18, 1859,
       J. J. Gilbert, M.G.
172.   Ducket, Nathan A. to McClain, M. E., Aug. 20, 1859,
       H. P. Pitchford, M.G.
173.   Davidson, W. C. to Foster, M. J., Aug. 11, 1859, James
       M. Keener, M.G.
173.   Tapp, Hugh to Samples, Phebe A., July 26, 1859, C. B.
       Wellborn, M.G.
173.   Longly, J. E. (L.?) to Bell, M. E., July 31, 1859, J. J.
       Gilbert, M.G.
174.   Clark, William to Copp, Nancy A., Aug. 5, 1859, James
       Green, J.I.C.
174.   Vandivere, S. W. to Henderson, M. S., Aug. 16, 1859,
       W. W. Green, M.G.
174.   Bender, Charles to Gillmire, Mary, Sept. 4, 1859, E. M.
       Amoss, M.G.
175.   Dunn, J. W. to Love, Lou L., Aug. 22, 1859, G. W.
       Selvidge, M.G.
175.   Smart, Marcus to Talley, Sarah, Aug. 30, 1859,
       Vredenburgh Thompson, J.P.
175.   Caldwell, John to Tyler, Rohetta C., Sept. 20, 1859,
       James M. Kenner, M.G.
176.   Dupree, C. C. to Green, Jane, Sept. 8, 1859, J. D.
       Farrer, J.P.
176.   Long, Robert to Pepper, Mahaly C., June 2, 1859, John D.
       Farrer, J.P.
176.   Highfield, Marion L. to Murphy, Elizabeth J., Sept. 6,
       1859, John D. Farrer, J.P.
177.   Jordan, Greenberry (Green Berry) to Greenfield, Elizabeth,
       Aug. 15, 1859, W. H. H. Duggan, M.G.
177.   Reynolds, John F. to Thompson, Jane Judson, Feb. 16,
       1859, Jno. W. McGehee, M.G.
177.   Millirons, Henry to Owens, Margaret E., Feb. 7, 1859,
       John D. Farrer, J.P.
178.   Neal, William J. to Davis, Sarah E. (J.?), May 31, 1859,
       John D. Farrer, J.P.
178.   Brown, Henry to Lawrence, Mary, Oct. 16, 1859, Jesse
       Wade, J.P.
178.   Moorelock, David A. to Wood, Nancy E., Oct. 29, 1859,
       Wm. P. Chester, J.I.C.
179.   Lester, William C. to Smith, Fannie C., Oct. 27, 1859,
       J. W. McGehee, M.G.
179.   Davis, Richard M. to Holcomb, Martha J., Aug. 18, 1859,
       A. J. Whitten, J.P.
179.   Smith, J. J. to Crow, Polly Ann, Sept. 5, 1859, Wm.
       East, J.P.
180.   Radaway, James to Broughton, Melissa, Oct. 25, 1859,
       C. B. Wellborn, M.G.
180.   Sutherland, Amos L. to Fitzgerald, N. A., Oct. 26, 1859,
       G. F. Cooper, M.G.
180.   Manning, Marge to Thornton, Harriet E., Jan. 23, 1859,
       Jacob Tate, M.G.

PAGE

181 Pilgrim, William to Spence, Elizabeth, Nov. 3. 1859, J. J. Martin, J.P.

181. Miller, J. R. to Hardcastle, M. E., Oct. 20, 1859, John P. Compton, M.G.

181. Jones, Richard W. to Gordon, Mrs. M. A., Nov. 22, 1859, James A. Wallace, M.G.

182. Naler, George W. to Johnson, Martha Ann, Apr. 7. 1859, Elder V. W. Wilson.

182. Hambleton, James A. to Fulton, M. C., Dec. 22, 1859, F. W. McCurdy, M.G.

182. Collum, Sterling (Starlin) to Everett, Elizabeth, Dec. 15. 1859, J. D. Farrows, J.P.

183. Zaunt, James S. to Smoke, Margaret E., Dec. 22, 1859, Vredenburgh Thompson, J.P.

183. Bennett, M. C. to Dodd, Susan, Jan. 5, 1860, J. B. Martin, J.P.

183. Carlisle, Bery H. to Dooly, Rutha, Aug. 16, 1859, J. L. Capehart, J.P.

184. Adams, J. J. to Lacy, Mary E., Dec. 29, 1859, J. J. Martin, J.P.

184. Mulkey, Geor F. to Evans, Cath. A., Dec. 29, 1859, Raleigh Cupp, J.P.

184. Love, James to Clark, Mary E., Nov. 20, 1859, James Green, J.I.C.

185. McCutchins, B. A. to McCean (McKean), Ann, Nov. 20. 1859, James L. Capehart, J.P.

185. Babb, Joel to Everett, Mary, Dec. 1, 1859. Jacob Tate, M. G.

185. Denton, B. W. to Campbell, E. J., Jan. 9. 1860, W. H. Stancel, J.P.

186. Oxford, Jonathan L. to Pool, Mary B., Dec. 28, 1859, Levi Brotherton, M.G.

186. Hughes, Thomas R. to Williams, Mariah, Jan. 1, 1860, Edward Mcabee, M.G.

186-187. Massongill. John to Brown, Elizabeth, Feb. 5, 1860, Wm. Cole, J.P.

187. Hall, George W. to Seay, Sarah E., Jan. 3, 1860, John W. Cain, J.P.

187. Hicks, John B. to Bowan, Alvirah. Jan. 27, 1860, Vred. Thompson, J.P.

187. Sloan, Felix A. to Hoskins, Mary J., Jan. 26, 1860, Wm. Brown, J.P.

188. Pittman, Jabuz P.M. to Adams, M.A., Feb. 14, 1860, Levi Brotherton, M.G.

188. Stone, James to Roberts, Mary, Jan. 19, 1850, J. D. Farrow, J.P.

188. Waddail, B. C. to McCrary, Mary E., Mar. 7, 1860, Wesley P. Pledger, M.G.

189. Bender, John L. to Nailen, Martha M., Mar. 22. 1860, W. P. Pledger.

189. Morrison, William H. to Glaze, Caroline H., Feb. 8, 1860, W. H. Russell. M. G.

189. Whitman, J.F. to Brown, C.B., Feb. 23, 1860, J. Madison Gambrell. M.G. (J.F. Whitman and C.B. Brown were joined in matrimony at the house of G.R. Brown the brides father in the presents of several witnesses.)

190. Freeman, G.W.L. to Suttles, Jane M., Mar. 15, 1860, D. F. Fulton, M.G.

190. Guthrie, W. R. to Alexander, Sallie M., Apr. 8, 1860, James A. Wallace, M.G.

PAGE
190. Mosley, Peter G. to Treadwell, Susan, Apr. 22, 1860,
      W. J. Underwood, J.I.C.
191. Mcdaniel, Strawder to Haynes, Amanda, May 6, 1860.
      Wesley P. Pledger, M.G.
191. Mote, Charles T. to Spiva, Josephine A., May 3. 1860,
      W. J. Underwood, J.I.C.
191. Bryant, Jesse to Sweatman, Caroline, May 6, 1860, J. D.
      Farrow, J.P.
192. Bolin, Robert to Burges (Burgess), Susan, Sept. 15, 1859,
      Charles Tolleferro, M.G.
192. Gentry, C. T. to Potter, S. A., May 31, 1860, Ved
      Thompson, J.P.
192. Holden, James J. to Head, Mary F., Apr. 17, 1860, J. M.
      Richardson, L.P.M.E.C.
193. Burges, Henry C. to Burges, Sarah, May 17, 1860, Charles
      Tolliferror, M.G.
193. Higdon, L. to Jordan, Sarah, May 17, 1860, Raleigh Cupp,
      J.P.
193. Cox, Robert D. to Roberts, Louisa C., May 31, 1860, Geo.
      F. Cooper, M.G.
194. Cook, William H. to Williams, Effa M., June 7, 1860, J.
      J. Martin, J.P.
194. Threllkill, Isaac to Smith, Evaline, June 14, 1860, Levi
      Brotherton, M.G.
194. Davis, H. O. to Robbins, Elizabeth J., July 19, 1860,
      Charles Tolliferro, M.G.
195. Thrailkill, W. H. C. to Smith, Sarah Ann, July 22, 1860,
      Levi Brotherton, M.G.
195. Heughs (Hughes), Henry P. to Jarrett, Elinor C., July 27,
      1860, Jesse Wade, J.P.
195. Williams, Richard to Williams, Nancy, July 24, 1860,
      Jesse Wade, J.P.
196. McDonald, Stephen H. to Rollins, Mary M., Aug. 19, 1860,
      James Green, J.I.C.
196. Wilson, Wm. to Anderson, Martha, June 25, 1860, Jesse
      Wade, J.P.
196. Head, A. M. to Swofford, Hannah (Hanah) A., Aug. 9, 1860,
      Dawson H. Walker, J.I.C.C.C.
197. Word, E. A. to Lynch, Caroline, Jan. 19, 1860, Z. D.
      Clark, M.G.
197. Whitfield, S. T. to Dunn, V. A., Oct. 18, 1859, Z. D.
      Clark, M.G.
197. Nance, Larkin R. to Cudd, Anni P., Sept. 13, 1860, James
      M. Landers, O.D.M.
198. Kreischer (Kreicher), Peter to Bennett, Arminda, Oct.
      26, 1860, Levi Brotherton, M.G.
198. Nardin, Waller H. to Hammond, Lucy E., Oct. 24, 1860,
      Wesley P. Pledges, M.G.
198. Roberts, Lafayett L. to East, Nancy, Nov. 6, 1860, Benj.
      Wiggins, J.P.
199. Lam, J. F. to Keith, Rosa A., Sept. 19, 1858, Daniel
      Johnson, M.G.
199. Stewart, Edward A. to Keith, Sarah Ann, Oct. 2, 1860,
      Geo. F. Cooper, M.G.
199. Tate, William to Bowin (Bowan), Elizabeth, Oct. 4, 1860,
      E. M. Amos, M.G.
200. Shelton, R. S. to Vandyke, Rosante (Rosanth), Aug. 25,
      1857, A. Varnell, J.P.
200. OGlesby (Oglesby), W. A. to Blankenship, Sousan (Susan),
      Oct. 10, 1857, A. Varnell, J.P.

PAGE

200.   Stancipher, P. J. to Messemore, Louisah, Mar. 4, 1858,
A. Varnell, J.P.

201.   Staford, Henry M. to Dycus, Narcisis (Narcissus) E.,
Aug. 30, 1860, Edward Mcabee, M.G.

201.   Harris, C. G. to Boatright, Eliza A., Sept. 20, 1860,
Vred Thompson, J.P.

201.   Hughes, Henry to Smith, Mary C., July 25, 1860, James M.
Kenner, M.G.

202.   Sloan, James A. to Martin, Sarah F., Nov. 15, 1860,
William Richardson, O.D.M.

202.   Jarrett, John to Ledford, Arsena, July 26, 1860, J.
Madison Gambrell, M.G.

202.   Kiker, Charles P. to Martin, Elizabeth R., Jan. 10, 1861,
J. J. Martin, M.G.

203.   Cain, Robert C. to Blackburn (Blackborn), Eady C., Aug.
7, 1860, James L. Caphart, J.P.

203.   Green, E. Wilson to Hamilton, Rachel. Dec. 20, 1860, Jas.
A. Wallace, M.G.

203.   Collins, Martin to Booker, Martha A., Dec. 20, 1860,
George F. Cooper.

204.   Terry, Chapion to Carden, Catharine, Dec. 20, 1860,
Benj. Wiggins, J.P.

204.   Sparks, John to Hancock, Elisabeth, Dec. 13, 1860, Wm. W.
Green, M.G.

204.   Parson, Rubin P. to Dill, Margaret, Sept. 30, 1860, John
J. Gilbert, M.D.

205.   Crow, James to Ault, Eliza, Dec. 7. 1860, J. J. Gilbert,
M.G.

205.   Cardon, Anonymos (Anonimos) to Smith, Darah, Nov. 29,
1860, Benjamin Wiggins, J.P.

205.   Brendle, D. C. to Wilson, Hannah, Nov. 15, 1860, Benj.
Wiggins, J.P.

206.   Blanton, J. W. to Crow, Fatina D., Nov. 22. 1860, J. J.
Gilbert, M.G.

206.   Philips, William to Wren, Rhoda A., Oct. 21, 1860, J. J.
Gilbert, M.G.

206.   Babb, F. M. to Bridges, M. C., Nov. 1. 1860, Jacob Tate,
M.G.

207.   Denman, Chapley to Spear, Caroline, Dec. 27, 1860, W. C.
Richardson, O.M.

207.   Mcfarland, John to Drakeford, Mary, Jan. 2. 1861, James
A. Wallace, M.G.

207.   Sullivan, William to Pratt, Emina, Dec. 30, 1860, Vred
Thompson, J.P.

208.   Williams, William(s) to Morehead, Margaret, Dec. 16,
1860, Jas. L. Capehart, J.P.

208.   Gamble, William to Ballantine, Mary, Jan. 5, 1861, A. J.
Whitten, J.P.

208.   Hopper, John S. to Thomas, Sarah E., Feb. 6, 1861, J. J.
Martin, Minister.

209.   Taylor, William to Henderson, Georgia Ann, Mar. 22, 1861,
B. B. Brown, J.I.C.

209.   Kile, Newton to McDonald, Sarah C., Feb. 21, 1861, A. J.
Whitten, J.P.

209.   Riker, Wm. R. to Sloan, Mary M., Jan. 10, 1861, M. C.
Martin, M.G.

210.   Bond, Elisha W. to McLane, Mary L., Mar. 22, 1861, C. B.
Wellborn, M.G.

210.   Easterling, J. M. to Meridith, Mrs. Georgia, Feb. 27,
1861, Saml. L. Hamilton, M.G.

PAGE
210. Engelhardt, John B. to Bender, Mary C., Mar. 28, 1861,
     B. B. Brown, J.I.C.
211. Whaley, Ambrose V. to Alexander, Martha E., Jan. 24, 1861,
     J. A. R. Hanks, M.G.
211. Thompson, William to Dunagan, Louisa J., Mar. 27, 1861,
     John Wood, Local Preacher.
211. Thomas, Richard to Strickland, Jerusha, Mar. 7, 1861,
     Edward McAbee, M.G.
212. Henderson, Jesse B. to Nicholson, Pelina A., Mar. 25,
     1860, J. J. Gilbert, M.G.
212. Keith, George to Treadwell, Mary A., Mar. 18, 1860, J. J.
     Gilbert, M.G.
212. Sampson (Sapson), John to Burgess, Dedema (Didema),
     Mar. 13, 1860. J. J. Gilbert, M.G.
213. Bennet, R. B. to Howard, Nancy, Feb. 14, 1861, J. J.
     Gilbert, M.G.
213. Cook, Daniel to Ault, Frances, Mar. 14, 1861, J. J.
     Gilbert, M.G.
213. Mullins, Lafayette to Cudd, Martha Jane, Apr. 9, 1861,
     James M. Landers, O.D.M.
214. Pearce, William to Clark, Elizabeth, Apr. 29, 1861,
     Hervey McHan, M.G.
214. Tucker, William to Staned(?), Sarah, Feb. 10, 1861. W. D.
     Bussey, M.G.
214. Lee, B. F. to Duncan, Polly, Sept. 14, 1858, D. F. Fulton,
     O.M.G.
215. Rouse, Joseph to Daniel, Mary J., May 21, 1861, Thos. C.
     Davis, J.I.C.
215. Giles, Samuel to Hatch (Thatch?), Margarett, May 12.
     1861, Jesse Wade, J.P.
215. Messinger, Peter K. to McDonald, Jane, Aug. 15. 1861,
     E. S. Dean, J.P.
215-216. Turner, Francis M. to Richardson, Martha E., Sept. 12,
     1861, Edward Mcabee, M.G.
216. David, Thos. C. to Burroughs, Lodicy M., July 18, 1861,
     J. J. Gilbert, M.G.
216. King, John H. to Denton, Ema, July 18, 1861, James A.
     Wallace, V.D.M.
217. Martin, Wm. C. to Watson, Mary J., July 2, 1861, J. J.
     Martin, Minister.
217. Cummins, Samuel to Burgess, Nancy, May 19, 1861, Thos. C.
     Davis, J.I.C.
217. Bohanan, Robt. to Shipp, Nancy, June 23, 1861, Thos. C.
     Davis, J.I.C.
218. Kilpatrick, Wm. M. to Bohanan, Roda, June 30. 1861,
     Jonathan Green, J.P.
218. Simmons, Thos. G. to King, Nancy C., July 18, 1861, J. M.
     Richardson, J.P.
218. Mcalister, W. B. to Mcallister, Elizabeth, Aug. 9, 1861,
     Jonathan Green, J.P.
219. Horne, F. C. to Whitten, Susan M., Sept. 26, 1861, James
     M. Kenner, M.G.
219. Whitten, Isaac A. to Bartell, M. E., Sept. 22, 1861,
     James M. Kenner, M.G.
219-220. Clark, C. W. to Rollins, Maria E., June 30, 1861, G. G.
     Witherspoon, M.G.
220. Loughridge, William to (No name given), Aug. 7, 1861,
     A. Fitzgerald.
220. Innman, Carson to Leats, Sarah Ann, Feb. 21, 1861, W. J.
     Walls, J.P.

PAGE
220-no #.Hillborn, Robert M. to Anderson, Lou E., Nov. 12, 1861,
         A. ?. Lockridge, M.G.
no #.   Pearce, R. M. to Howard, Sarah J., Feb. 14, 1861, Levi
         Brotherton, M.G.
no. #.   Dougan, Wetson to Giles, Elizabeth, Feb. 28, 1861, Jesse
         Wade, J.P.
220.   Hill, A.S. to Chastain, June E., Nov. 28, 1861, Harvey
         McHann, M.G.
220.   Chastain, M. R. to Treadwell, R. F., Dec. 19, 1861, W. J.
         Underwood, J.I.C.
220.   Moody, Andrew J. to Jennings, Henrietta W., Feb. 14,
         1861, W. J. Walls, J.P.
221.   Bruce, W. G. to Morgan, Arulla, Oct. 3. 1861, S. Morgan,
         M.G.
221.   Bohanan, Thomas to Swanson, Julina, Sept. 12, 1861,
         Jonathan Green, J.P.
221-222. Richardson, Benjamin L. to Evans, Delia, Nov. 14, 1861,
         Jonathan Green, J.P.
222.   Loggins, Wm. A. to Hubbard, Frances M., Dec. 19, 1861,
         Jonathan Green, J.P.
222.   Short, John L. to Richardson, Caroline H., Jan. 1, 1862,
         Levi Brotherton, M.G.
223.   Wilson, Thomas P. to Whitton, Mary M., Dec. 29, 1861,
         Jesse Wade, J.P.
223.   Griffin, A. M. to Varnell, Nancy J., Dec. 10, 1861, J. H.
         Cawood, M.G.
223.   Queen, James M. to Stone, Cynthia S., Jan. 9, 1862,
         Edward Mcabee, M.G.
224.   Fincher, Elias to Chastain, Malissa, Jan. 5, 1862, Hervey
         McHan, Methodist Minister.
224.   Baker, E. P. to Dyer, Hannah D., Jan. 26, 1862, Thos. C.
         Davis, J.I.C.
224-225. Gordon, Charles P. to Bittings, Mary H., Jan. 30, 1862,
         James A. Walace, Minister.
225.   Morgan, M. to Staton, Falby, Jan. 14, 1862, Jonathan
         Green, J.P.
225.   Woodruff, Joseph P. to McNabb, Margaret Jane, Feb. 6,
         1862, Vred Thompson, J.P.
226.   Blair, Calvin M. to Jestice, Mary C., Sept. 27, 1860,
         Brittain Williams, M.G.
226.   Tidwell, William M. to Kelly, Georgianna, Feb. 28, 1862.
         S. J. Ward, J.P.
226-227. Goodson, John L. to Whittle, Sarah A., Feb. 2, 1862,
         Elder W. Hill.
227.   Jarrett, Drewry R. to Steaverson, Mary C., Jan. 30,
         1862, J. P. Anderson, J.P.
227.   Anderson, James A. to Winkle (Winkele), Rosana, Mar. 14,
         1862, Henry McHan.
228.   Robins, Henry A. to Adams, Augusta A., Jan. 19, 1862.
         James M. Landrege, M.G.
228.   Dyer, James to Philips, Susan E., Feb. 4, 1862. T. C.
         Davis, J.I.C.
228-229. Bromlette, Harrison to Milirons, Sarah E., Mar. 20,
         1862, T. J. Pope, M.G.
229.   Bucher, George B. to Horne, Anirick(?), Mar. 20, 1862,
         Samuel Benedict, Rector of St. James Church, Marietta,
         Ga.
229.   Frank, Jackson to Brown, Amanda, Mar. 20, 1862, D. F.
         Fulton, O.M.G.

PAGE
229-230. Earnest, Q. T. to Click, Mahala, Apr. 13, 1862, E. S.
Dean, J.P.
230.   Risener, J. M. to Ellison, S. C., May 8, 1862, B. B.
Brown, J.I.C.
230.   Bohanan, James to Province, Minerva, May (torn), 1862,
Z. C. Davis, J.I.C.
231.   Russell, A. B. to Adams, M.A.Q., Apr. 8, 1862, Wm. J.
Underwood, J.I.C.
231.   Riddle, M. S. to Newman, A. F., May 15. 1862, G. W.
Selvidge, M.G.
231.   Tyson, S. G. to Sitton, S. C., May 22. 1862, G. W.
Selvidge, M.G.
 (Pages 230 and 231 are repeated).
232.   Mauldin, William to Crouch, Malinda, Aug. 24, 1862, S. T.
Anderson, J.P.
232.   Burchfield, Wm. F. to Tony, Susan, Sept. 7, 1862, B. B.
Brown, J.I.C.
232.   Carlisle, Nathan to Dooly, Latitia(?), Nov. 18, 1862,
G. W. L. Freeman, J.P.
No #.   Shaw, Joseph Henry to Wood, Narcissie N., June 1, 1862,
Jas. A. Wallace, R.O.M.
No. #. Owen, Thadius C. to Turket(?), Isabella, Oct. 18, 1862,
Wm. T. Campbell, J.I.C.
No. #. Shields, Martin V. to Haras, Eliza A., Oct. 30, 1862,
J. J. Martin, Minister.
 (No page is numbered 233 or 234.)
235.   Hanks, S. M. to Wrinkle, N. J., June 15, 1862. B. B.
Brown, J.I.C.
235.   Ashworth, Lindsay to Bohanan, Martha, Dec. 25. 1862,
J. C. Davis, J.I.C.
235.   Gilbert, John J. to Dyer, Hulda A., Dec. 21, 1862. J. C.
Davis, J.I.C.
235-236. Joinen, Andrew S. to Shields, Margaret, Dec. 25, 1862,
J. J. Walls, J.P.
236.   Cooper, George A. to Printess, Mary, Nov. 9, 1862, G. W.
Selvidge, M.G.
236.   Kent, G. R. to Stevenson, Amanda, Dec. 14, 1862, J. P.
Anderson, J.P.
236.   Happwest, A. M. to Hopkins, Octavia C., Oct. 2, 1862,
James P. Wallace, V.D.M.
237.   Smith, John to Ross, Mary, Sept. 12, 1862. E. S. Dean,
J. P.
237.   Jones, William to Duckett, Jane, Sept. 12, 1862, E. S.
Dean, J.P.
237.   Dobson, Starritt W. to Evans, Sarah A., Nov. 27, 1862,
John N. Cain, J.P.
237-138. Arnold, James J. to Brawneh, Arminda C., Sept. 11, 1862,
S. J. Ward, J.P.
238.   Mote, Wm. A. to Roach, Emily A., Jan. 22. 1862, W. T.
Campbell. J.I.C.
238.   Daly, Rude to Griffin, Margaret, Mar. 8, 1863, W. J.
Walls, J.P.
238.   Horrocks(?), Samuel to Fry, Julia E., Feb. 10, 1863,
James A. Wallace, Minister.
239.   Moore, Daniel to Sigler, Eliza, Mar. 9, 1863, B. B.
Brown, J.I.C.
239.   McLellan, David to Boyd, Mary, Mar. 16, 1863, W. J.
Walls, J.P.
239.   Carver, C. C. to Boran, Mary J., June 8, 1862, J.
Madison Gambrell, M.G.

PAGE
240.   Martin, Wm. A. to Ellison, E. C., Mar. 30, 1863. J. H. B.
       Shackelford.
240.   Anderson, George W. to Jolly, Adaline, Apr. 1, 1863,
       W. J. Walls, J.P.
240.   Worthy, John C. to Holland, Nancy E., Apr. 5, 1863. W. J.
       Walls, J.P.
241.   Lacy, Joseph to Stone, Ann, Apr. 6, 1863, James M.
       Landress, M.G.
241.   Meadows, John H. to Thrailkill, Nancy Ann, May 3. 1863,
       W. J. Underwood, J.I.C.
241.   Dover, William M. to Whitice, Mary T., May 7. 1863, B. B.
       Brown, J.I.C.
242.   Mitchell, M. M. to Lucas, Mrs. Mary D., June 10, 1863.
       Wm. J. Walls, J.P.
242.   Cappice, Adam to Duckett, Margaret A., June 9, 1863.
       W. C. Richardson, O.M.
242.   Halcomb, Ambrose to Bridges, Eliza, Dec. 8, 1361, W. J.
       Walls, J.P.
243.   Ward, John to Reeves, Mary Ann, May 27. 1863, W. J.
       Walls, J.P.
243.   Gaskey, J. W. to Smith, Fany, May 28, 1863, J. M.
       Stansberry, M.G.
243.   Moore, Martin to Holbrook, Eliza A., June 23, 1863, W. J.
       Walls, J.P.
244.   Russell, J.P. to Riden, Elizabeth, June 22, 1863, W. J.
       Walls, J.P.
244.   McAllister, C. R. to Gitchel, Sarah, June 27. 1863,
       Jonathan Green, J.P.
244.   Steen, Samuel G. to Dooly, Elizabeth, June 24, 1863,
       G. W. Freeman, J.P.
245.   Thompson, W. J. to Pally, Mary M., July 7, 1863. J. M.
       Stansberry, M.G.
245.   McKendree, James N. to Harris, Georgia, July 3. 1863,
       Levi Brotherton, M.G.
245.   Bagwell, H. D. to Jones, L.(?) C., July 5, 1863, J. M.
       Gambrell, M.G.
246.   Bruve, B. B. to McClure, Melvina V., July 22, 1863, Jos.
       Wade, J.P.
246.   Smith, W. H. to Mathews, Mary C., Aug. 16, 1863. Jonathan
       Green, J.P.
246.   Davis, W. M. to Croft, Caroline, Sept. 3, 1863, Benjamin
       Wiggins, J.P.
247.   Cupp, Raleigh to Connally, Jane, Aug. 23, 1863, Isaac P.
       Anderson, J.P.
247.   Kile, M. M. to Adams, Lucy H., Aug. 30, 1863. James M.
       Landress, M.G.
247.   Jones, Stephen J.S. to Lowe(?). E. C., Aug. 11. 1863,
       J. J. Martin, M.G.
248.   Dunlap, R. H. to Pharis(?), Mary C., Aug. 18, 1863.
       J. M. Gambrell, M.G.
248.   Naler, Columbus to Cox, Sarah Ann, Aug. 9, 1863, J. P.
       Anderson, J.P.
248.   Whittemore, S. F. to Lee, Mary, Sept. 31 (30?), 1863.
       J. P. Anderson, J.P.
249.   Strickland, R.C. to Hubbard, Margarete, Sept. 6, 1863,
       Jonathan Green, J.P.
249.   Delk, David to Cox, Olympia, Sept. 15, 1863. Levi
       Brotherton, O.M.G.
249.   Williams, George W. to Pilgrim, Nancy A., Sept. 10, 1863,
       W. J. Walls, J.P.

PAGE

250. Cox, Thomas L. to Edge, Mary Ann, Oct. 13. 1863, G. W. Welvidge, M.G.

250. Fuller, S. B. to Roberts, Elizabeth, Oct. 28, 1863. W. J. Walls, J.P.

250. Wade, Jno. to Walston(?), Matilda, Oct. 3. 1863, W. J. Walls, J.P.

251. Avery, J. W. to Morris, Sallie H., Nov. 25, 1863. J. M. Richardson, local minister M.E. Church.

251. Sumner, Joshua to Miller, R. A., Dec. 25, 1863, B. B. Brown, J.I.C.

251. Jones, Richard J. to Snow, Elizabeth, Dec. 24, 1863, B. B. Brown, J.I.C.

252. Howell, H. E. to Nailor(?), Isabella, Dec. 21, 1863, Lewis Ball, M.G.

252. Tucker, George to Whittemore, A., Dec. 10, 1863.

252. Cooly, P. to Daniel, Martha Margaret, Dec. 17, 1863.

252. Henderson, J. H. to Snow, Susan, Jan. 10, 1864, O. J. Fitzgerald, O.M.

253. Hager(?), J.R. to Jenkins, Elizabeth, Jan. 31. 1864, W. J. Underwood, J.I.C.

253. Dowdy, Jno. W. to Tate, Margaret W., Jan. 28, 1864, W. J. Underwood, J.I.C.

253. Seton, James to Pendergrast, Martha E., Jan. 28, 1863, Jno. M. Richardson, M.M.E. Church.

254. Cobb, William S. to Leatherwood, Mary A., Jan. 25, 1864, P. S. Arther, M.G.

254. Bohanan, J.A. to Minar(?), L. A., Jan. 8, 1864, (?) C. Davis, J.I.C.

254. Huff, J.S. to Prince, Malissa, Feb. 22, 1864, B. B. Brown, J.I.C.

255. Boyd, Wm. E. to Hurt, Amanda, Feb. 10, 1864, Rev. J. P. White.

255. Kilpatrick, W. M. to Perry, Frances, Jan. 13, 1864, Jonathan Green, J.P.

255. Roach, Samuel to Rhodes, Mary, Feb. 16, 1864, G. W. L. Freeman, J.P.

256. Kendrick, Frank B. to Williams, Qunarthy, Feb. 4, 1864, T. K. Paersley, M.G.

256. Williams, H. P. to Freeman, Amanda S., Feb. 5, 1864, T. K. Prirsley.

256. Wilfield, Obediah to Cooper, Frances, Feb. 9, 1864, W. J. Walls, J.P.

257. Stewart, Thomas J. to Davis, Susan, Feb. 23, 1864, B. B. Brown, J.I.C.

257. Robertson, A. J. to Worthy, Mollie, Feb. 24, 1864, James L. Landress.

257. Morris, W. H. to Bromblett, Laura M., Feb. 24, 1864, J. J. Martin, M.G.

258. England, R. P. to Tammers, Ellen, Feb. 14, 1864, T. R. Espy, Chln. 31 Ala. Vols.

258. Earnest, John to Smith, Sallie, Feb. 23, 1864, B. B. Brown, J.I.C.

258. Forter, Robert to Bonnett, Martha, Feb. 14, 1864, T. R. Espy, Chaplin 31st Ala. Vols.

259. Thomas, John to Cathy, Margaret, Jan. 4, 1863, J. M. Stansberry, M.G.

259. White, B. F. Jr. to Ballard, Fannie O., Jan. 19, 1864, J. M. Schirrar, Chaplin 4th Regt. Tenn. Vols.

259. Best, T. C. to Dyer, Pauline, Jan. 23. 1864, Jno. A. Ellis, M.G.

PAGE
260.   Higgins, Jno. D. to Wordon, Mary E., Jan. 7, 1864, B. B. Brown, J.I.C.

260.   Watts, Jno. H. to Good, Bettie, May 1, 1864, B. B. Brown, J.I.C.

260.   Holland, B. F. to Mitchel, Mary Ann, Mar. 29, 1864, L. W. Earnest, J.I.C.

261.   Scott, Daniel to Bennett, Anna, Mar. 13. 1864, H. H. Kavanaugh, M.G.

261.   Pegg, John to Carrol. Eliza Jane, Mar. 14, 1864, Charles Hooper, J.P.

261.   Gazaway, Berry to Blalock, Martha M., Mar. 27, 1864, Charles Hooper, J.P.

262.   Williams, James C. to Cooper, Allice, Apr. 23, 1864, B. B. Brown, J.I.C.

262.   Lee, A. S. to Swenney, Mary E., Apr. 2, 1864, B. B. Brown, J.I.C.

262.   Tate, William to Carroll. Susa, Apr. 3, 1864, B. B. Brown, J.I.C.

263.   Tutwell, T. N. to Robins, J.S.N., Apr. 25, 1864, W. A. Cumbie, M.G.

263.   Carroll, W. W. to Whaley, Caroline, May 5, 1864, E. J. Hamill, M.G.

263.   Crorly, William to Misanger, Mary, May 6. 1864, A. Carrins, Cath. Priest, Chaplin A.T.

264.   Smith, John to Porter, Martha, Jan. 16. 1866, Benjamin Wiggins, J.P.

264.   McMahan, W. B. to Benton, Caroline, Jan. 16, 1866, J. M. Kenner, M.G.

264.   Croys, G. W. to Singletary, Dilla, Jan. 30, 1866, Anthony Smith, M.G.

264.   Elliot, Richard J. to Robertson, Elizabeth, Jan. 4, 1866, G. W. Selvidge, M.G.

265.   Fox, R. H. to Laymance, S. C., Dec. 23, 1865, S. J. Ward, J.P.

265.   Scott, Franklin A. to Baker, Elzavan, Sept. 30, 1863, John J. Gilbert, M.G.

265.   Anderson, David to Wilson, Martha A., Dec. 8, 1865, William Pullen, M.G.

265.   Freeman, Green H. to Smith, Martha B., Jan. 3, 1866, W. C. Richardson, O.M.

266.   Hersman, John to Couch, Julia, Jan. 16, 1866, John T. Compton, M.G.

266.   Dyer, Saml. G. to Alexander, Martha E., Sept. 24, 1865, James C. Mitchell, M.G.

266.   James, Pulaska D. to Ducket, Arminda J., Sept. 20, 1865, H. R. Swisher, M.G.

266.   Ganz, A. C. to Carrell, Sophia S., Sept. 28. 1865, G. W. Selvidge, M.G.

267.   Stribling, F. B. to Doyle, C. E., Dec. 18. 1865, T. M. Lane, M.G.

267.   McNab, Lafayett to Love, Sarah, Oct. 26, 1865, G. M. Selvidge, M.G.

267.   Word, Chas. B. to Pearce, Mahaly, Nov. 28. 1865, J. M. Richardson, M.G.

267.   Cardon, William M. to Cantrell, Martha, Sept. 7, 1865. Edward Mcabee, M.G.

268.   Moore, Joseph H. to Dobson, Laura S., Feb. 28, 1866, Z. D. Clark, M.G.

268.   Stone, Joel to Bowman, Sarah A., Sept. 23. 1865, G. Hoyle, M.G.

PAGE

268. Mesplay, Charles to Bearden, Martha, Dec. 6, 1865, James
C. Mitchell, M.G.

268. Burckle, Martin to Kruscher, Lessett, Nov. 30, 1865,
J. M. Richardson, Elder in M.E. Church South.

269. Guthery, William R. to Ford, A.A.M., Feb. 12. 1866, J.M.
Stansberry, M.G.

269. Dyens, T.L. to Wood, Biddy, Sept. 30, 1865, John M.
Richardson, M.G.

269. Dobson, William S. to Manning, Mrs. Harrit E., Dec. 11,
1865. Joseph Rogers, J.P.

269. Long, Charles T. to Ketchem, Sarah J., Sept. 26, 1865.
John M. Richardson, Elder in M.E. Church South.

270. Long, W. R. to Underwood, Elizabeth, Feb. 26, 1866,
G. W. Selvidge, M.G.

270. Tate, Jonathan to Langston, Susan E., May 16, 1866,
Robert W. Ault, J.P.

270. Carr, John to Swansen(?), Ruth A., (no date), John T.
Compton, M.G.

270. Thogmartin, Benj. W. to Prichett, Martha, Oct. 2, 1865,
Edward Mcabee, M.G.

271. Davis, Thom. C. to Ray(?), Nancy A., Nov. 3, 1865, J. P.
Anderson, J.P.

271. Niel, Benjamin A. to Brakebill. Mary M., Sept. 4, 1865,
Z. D. Clark, M.G.

271. Harris, Francis M. to Rouch, Clarinda, Oct. 20, 1865,
G. W. Selvidge, M.G.

272. Huff, James D. to Brook, Sallie J., May 9, 1866, J. J.
Martin, M.G.

272. Davis, R. A. to McMahan, Julia A., June 5. 1866, B. B.
Brown, J.I.C.

272. Gordon, Dr. Chas. P. to Manly, Maggie, July 18, 1866,
H. C. Carter, V.D.M.

273. Cate, J. A. to Baggiss, Texas S., June 12, 1866, W. A.
Nelson, M.G.

273. Blanton, Jacob N.(?) to Blanton, Mrs. F. D., June 20,
1866, J. P. Freeman, Co. Judge.

273. Wade, W. S. to Clark, Sidney A., May 11, 1866, Augustin
Harris, J.P.

274. Haddock, David C. to Russell, Eliza C., June 5, 1866,
Elder T. H. Wilson.

274. Neal, George R. to Crumley, Josephine, Apr. 24, 1866,
H. R. Swisher, M.G.

274. Heath, Alexander S. to Roberts, Malinda J., May 17, 1866,
Augustin Harris, J.P.

275. Blackburn, B. F. to McGaughy, Elizabeth A., Oct. 21,
1863, Joseph Rodgers, J.P.

275. Abner, James J. to Tisher, Elizabeth A., Dec. 23, 1863,
Elder L. W. Wilson.

275. Bowman, Thadeus C. to Whitten, Sarah E., Mar. 15, 1866,
Elder L. W. Wilson.

276. Hubbard, Isaah to McAllister, Emaline, Dec. 11, 1865.
Elder L. W. Wilson.

276. Robers, Patrick W. to Duckett, Sarah, June 8, 1866,
Elder L. W. Wilson.

276. Fuerstenick, Evon Entriss to Grempler, Clara, July 9.
1866, John T. Compton, M.C.

277. Stone, Hezakiah to McAbee, Leathy C., Dec. 11, 1865,
Benjamin Wiggins, J.P.

277. McCarty, William T. to Scott, Laura G., Mar. 1, 1866,
J. A. R. Hanks, M.G.

PAGE
277.　York, Andrew J. to Cruce, Mary E., Dec. 18, 1865.
　　　　Anthony Smith, M.G.
278.　Mitchell, Thomas M. to Buffington, Sarah A., Jan. 15,
　　　　1866, J. A. R. Hanks, M.G.
278.　Warmack, John W. to Jones, Fannie Ann, Feb. 9, 1866,
　　　　Edward McAbee, M.G.
278.　Parrott, Josiah to Clark, Emily, Mar. 6, 1866, Wm. C.
　　　　Maloy, Preacher in charge M.E. Church South, Dalton,
　　　　Georgia.
279.　Bandy, Josiah to Bates, Mary J., Jan. 2, 1866, Edward
　　　　McAbee, M.G.
279.　Stevenson, Benjamin F. to Bates, Elizabeth M., Sept. 2,
　　　　1865, S. J. Ward, J.P.
279.　Gregory, Topley to Terry, Susan L., Mar. 21, 1866, B. J.
　　　　Johnson, J.P.
280.　Hill, Henry to Wright, Mary, Apr. 5, 1866, S. J. Ward,
　　　　J.P.
280.　Fincher, H. C. to Whaley, Mrs. Mary, Jan. 23, 1866,
　　　　Harry McHan, Methodist Elder.
280.　Simmons, James B. to McGaughy, Margarit E., Mar. 26,
　　　　1866, J. M. Richardson, Elder in the M.E. Church South.
281.　Bell, John S. to Swift, Lizzie, Jan. 25, 1866, W. C.
　　　　Maloy, Georgia Conference, Pastor M.E. Church, Dalton,
　　　　Georgia.
281.　Leaptrot, Joseph H. to Robbins, Augusta A., Jan. 2, 1866,
　　　　J. J. Martin, M.G.
281.　Bohanan, D. J. to Sinas (Sims), Sarah J. Feb. 24, 1866,
　　　　Thomas Renfro, J.P.
282.　Pfannkucher, Adam to Canington, Susie, May 21, 1866,
　　　　G. W. Selvidge, M.G. ("I hereby give my consent to
　　　　the marriage of my daughter Susie Cannington with Mr.
　　　　Adam Pfannkircke this 21st May 1866." Signed S.
　　　　Cannington.)
282.　Fraker, Caleb S. to Tye, Sarah J., Apr. 5, 1866, J. M.
　　　　Richardson, Elder in the M.E. Church South.
282.　Gladden, James to Roberts, Mary, Jan. 2, 1866, Thomas
　　　　Renfro, J.P.
283.　Chastain, Raney to Richardson, Malissa, Mar. 7, 1866,
　　　　Levi Brotherton, O.M.G.
283.　Haffner, Frank to Cobb, Maria Louisa, Feb. 5, 1866, Wm.
　　　　C. Maloy, Preacher in charge M.E. Church South,
　　　　Dalton, Ga.
283.　Arnold, Jesse to Harmon, Francis, Jan. 3, 1866, J. P.
　　　　Anderson, J.P.
284.　Roberts, David J. to Wood, Louisa A., Jan. 2, 1866,
　　　　J. M. Richardson, Elder in the M.E. Church South.
284.　Hill, Wm. D. to Roberts, Louisa A., Jan. 2. 1866, J. M.
　　　　Richardson, Elder in the M.E. Church South.
284.　Carver, Samuel S. to Sams, America, Dec. 23, 1865, Jas.
　　　　C. Mitchell, M.G. ("I hereby give my authority for
　　　　my daughter America Sams who is under 18 years of age
　　　　to be joined in wedlock with Samuel S. Carver this
　　　　23rd day of December 1865." Signed Asa A. Sams.)
289.　Parker, William H. to Aldridge, Louisa Jane, June 28,
　　　　1866, S. J. Ward, J.P.
289.　Lamb, Derrick to Chester, Ella, Jan. 4, 1866, J. A. R.
　　　　Hanks, M.G.
289.　Hackney, Marcus L. to Wrinkle, S. E., Jan. 20, 1866,
　　　　J. M. Richardson, Minister of M.E. Church.

PAGE

290.   Barnett, J. M. to Click, C. M., June 21, 1866, J. M. Gambrell, M.G.

290.   Bowman, Alfred D. to McAbee, Martha J., Aug. 8, 1866, Thos. Renfro, J.P. ("I hereby give my consent for my daughter Martha J. who is under 18 years of age to be joined in matrimony with A. D. Bowman this 8th day of August 1866." Edward McAbee)

290.   Bomar(?), William P. to Horn, Mrs. Hattie, Aug. 13, 1866, J. M. Kenner, M.G.

289.   Sims, Henry L. to Selvidge, Lizzie, May 23, 1866, W. A. Nelson, M.G.

289.   Hartmann, B. to Wiggin, Elizabeth, Aug. 14, 1866, J. J. Gilbert, M.G.

289.   Rogers, Joseph A. to Springfield, Mrs. Sarah A., Aug. 8, 1866, J. M. Kenner, M.G.

PAGE

1. White, James A. to Coffee, Mary A., June 15, 1866, Benjamin Wiggins, J.P.

1. Friedman, Benhardt to Schwarz, Adele, Aug. 9, 1866, J. P. Freeman, Co. Judge.

1. Manis, Owen H. to Ortrey, Mary E., Aug. 8, 1866, C. R. McAllister, J.P.

2. Neal, A. J. to Neal, Elizabeth, July 5, 1866, C. R. McAllister, J.P.

2. Eddleman, Geo. W. to Williams, Nancy, July 14, 1866, Robert W. Ault, J.P.

2. Brodwell, William J. to McCoy, Clency A., Aug. 16, 1866, Robert W. Ault, J.P.

3. Jones, George to McClain, Susan, Sept. 1866, Robert W. Ault, J.P.

3. Wilburn, Francis G. to Sims, Sarah, Sept. 15, 1866, John Faith, J.P.

3. Wood, John H. to Burton, Miley E., Aug. 2, 1866, Augustin Harris, J.P.

4. Floyd, Allen F. to Anthony, Hannah J., Sept. 13, 1866, Levi Brotherton, M.G.

4. Fowler, Joseph to Dowdy, Emily J., Aug. 23, 1866, Jacob Tate, M.G.

4. Sailers, George W. to Reese, Nancy, Sept. 19, 1866, John P. Love, J.P.

5. Konkur, Henry to Morris, Martha, Sept. 26, 1866, J. M. Richardson, Elder in M.E. Church South.

5. Rushton, Robert S. to Sims, C. E., Sept. 27, 1866, J. M. Richardson.

5. Ducket, Thomas to Bennet, Martha, Sept. 21, 1866, J. P. Bailey, M.G.

6. Renfro, William to Parks, Rutha C., Sept. 19, 1866, J. P. Bailey, M.G.

6. Mulky, Francis M. to Sweeney, Lucinda, Sept. 22, 1866, C. R. McAllister, J.P.

6. Ray, James T. to Wood, Elvira, Oct. 1, 1866, Benjamin Wiggins, J.P.

7. Meredith, Alonzo H. to Oscar, Lucinda, Sept. 19, 1866, Benjamin Wiggins, J.P.

7. Aughtry, William to Gitchell, Clarinda, Sept. 12, 1866, J. M. Gambrell, M.G.

7. Howard, Samuel to Martin, Victoria, Nov. 29, 1866, F.(?) M. Sam, M.G.

8. Bates, Robt. B. to Hammock, Louisa, Nov. 16, 1866, Thomas Renfro, J.P.

8. Renfro, Henderson to Stone, Nancy, Nov. 14, 1866, J. P. Baily.

8. Bowen, William M. to Evans, Martha M., Oct. 8, 1866, Z. D. Clark, M.G.

9. Davis, Richard D. to Jackson, Harriet J., Oct. 15, 1866, Levi Brotherton, M.G.

9. Molloy, John to Wran, Mede (Mide), Oct. 17, 1866, Thomas Renfro, J.P.

9. Poe, E. M. to Fisher, Margaret R., May 7, 1864, S. M. Cherry, M.G.

10. Thompson, Richard to Love, Mary E., Oct. 18, 1866, G. W. Selvidge, M.G.

10. Cuso, Richard J. to Martin, Lucy A., Aug. 11, 1866, J. J. Martin, M.G.

10. Leonard, John R. to Harris, Eliza, Oct. 26, 1866, Levi Brotherton, M.G.

PAGE
11. McAllister, C. R. to Gitchell, Mrs. Sarah, Oct. 8, 1866,
J. M. Gambrell, M.G.

11. Roberts, A. J. to Gazaway, Mary O., Dec. 1, 1866, G. W.
Selvidge, M.G.

11. Robbins, Samuel H. to Osborn, Mary A., Oct. 19, 1866,
John M. Richardson, Elder in M.E. Church South.

12. Gilbert, J. W. to Barnett, Margaret, Oct. 19, 1866,
John Faith, J.P. (A. J. Barnett gave consent for his
daugher, Margaret, under 18 to marry.)

12. Faith, Josiah G. to Flemon, Eliza J., June 23, 1866,
J. J. Martin, M.G.

12. Massingill, Riley to Leatherwood, Martha A., June 20,
1866, Harvey McHan, M.G.

13. Hicks, Napolien B. to Renfro, Eliza J., Nov. 18, 1866,
J. P. Freeman, Co. Judge.

13. King, Wm. H. to Wood, Sabra A., Oct. 27, 1866, Augustin
Harris, J.P.

13. Roper, Nelson to Mitchell, Martha F., Dec. 1, 1866, J. J.
Martin, M.G.

14. Collins, Martin to Batson, Sarah J., Dec. 26, 1866,
J. A. R. Hanks, M.G.

14. Thompson, John W. to Walker, Mary L., Nov. 5, 1866,
Augustin Harris, J.P.

14. Gamble, Andrew to Fletcher, Sarah M., Dec. 15, 1866,
H. R. Swisher, M.G.

15. Lance, Washington to McNabb, Sarah, Nov. 23, 1866, Harvey
McHan, M.G.

15. Cleveland, David D. to McClure, Sarah C., Nov. 26, 1866,
J. M. Gambrell, M.G.

15. Thornton, A. N. to Sloan, Mary E., Dec. 22, 1866, J. P.
Freeman, Co. Judge.

16. Crumpton, Robt. to Hurst, Eliza, Dec. 21, 1866, H. McHan,
M. G.

16. Richardson, J. R. to Whitener, Sarah A., Dec. 3, 1866,
J. T. Compton, M.G.

16. McDonald, Noble W. to Smith, Narcissy C., Jan. 1, 1867,
H. C. Carter, V.D.M.

17. McConnell, Joseph C. to Swift, Jennie, Dec. 20, 1866,
H. C. Carter, V.D.M.

17. Burns, Geo. W. to Black, M. J., Jan. 6, 1867, H. C.
Carter, V.D.M.

17. Thompson, George H. to Warmack, Mary E., Dec. 4, 1866,
C. R. McAllister, J.P.

18. Croxton, E. H. to Singletary, Mary P., Dec. 8, 1866,
Z. D. Clark, M.G.

18. McCarson, Wm. B. to Whitener, Marther R., Nov. 9, 1866,
Benjamin Wiggins, J.P.

18. Springfield, H. G. to Fleoffre, Flora, Dec. 24, 1866,
Benjamin Wiggins, J.P.

19. Richardson, Columbus W. to Whitener, Mevaline, Nov. 21,
1866, Benjamin Wiggins, J.P.

19. Russell, W. N. to Young, Rebecca A., Jan. 16, 1867,
J. M. Kenner, M.G.

19. Russell, Harry A. to Wood, M. J., Jan. 9, 1867, J. M.
Stansbury, M.G.

20. Cargile, Lewis B. to Odell, Emma, Jan. 15, 1867, G. M.
Selvidge, M.G.

20. Eslinger, David L. to Fagala, Eliza A., Jan. 12, 1867,
James M. Hall, M.G.

PAGE

20. Martin, W. H. to Davis, Julia E., Jan. 14, 1867. J. M. Richardson, Minister M.E. Church South.

21. Leatherwood, T. T. to Prince, Margaret, Jan. 2, 1867. J. M. Richardson, Minister M.E. Church South.

21. Pursley, J. G. to Kirkpatrick, W. S., Oct. 13, 1866, J. M. Stansberry, M.G.

21. Love, John W. to Harris, Mary E., Dec. 18, 1865, J. M. Stansberry, M.G.

22. Collins, Moses O. to Carroll, Louisa C., Oct. 25, 1866, John M. Richardson, Minister M.E. Church.

22. Holden, James J. to Kizer, Elizabeth, June 9, 1866, J. M. Richardson, Minister M.E. Church.

22. Thornton, B. M. to Sloan, Minerva A., Feb. 21, 1867, J. T. Deck, J.P.

23. Orr, Chas. F. to Pearce, Mrs. Margaret, Jan. 22, 1867, Anthony Smith, M.G.

23. Bohanan, William L. to Kettle, Elizabeth A., Feb. 19, 1867, Thomas Renfro, J.P.

23. Glover, Henry P. to Chastain, Annis H., Feb. 15, 1867, Harvey McHan, M.G.

24. Howel, Elcaner to Parks, Tulitha E., Feb. 18, 1867. J. P. Freeman, Co. Judge.

24. Brooker, John W. to Quillian, Rebeca L., Nov. 29, 1866, N. C. Richardson, O.M.

24. Davis, Francis I. to Martin, Amelia J., Jan. 14, 1867, J. A. R. Hanks, M.G.

25. Mitchell, John F. to Riley, Margaret L., Feb. 26, 1867. E. M. Lowry, M.G.

25. Philips, George W. to Rodgers, Sallia(?) A., Mar. 13, 1867, J. W. Ramsey, M.G.

25. Crozier, Samuel C. to Pharis, Helen, Mar. 12, 1867. J. M. Gambrell, M.G.

26. Cox, Philip E. A. to Miller, Frances B., Mar. 7, 1867, E. M. Lowry, M.G.

26. Roper, Bennet to Adams, Mary Jane, Mar. 16, 1867, E. M. Lowry, M.G.

26. Ratcliff, Andrew to Philips, Bettie, Mar. 22, 1867. Thomas Renfro, J.P.

27. Crouch, Archibald F. to Oscar, Martha, Mar. 15, 1867, Benjamin Wiggins, J.P.

27. Whitener, Marcus L. to Whitener, Jane, Feb. 9, 1867. Benjamin Wiggins, J.P.

27. Bates, Albert to Ault, Meriline, May 4, 1867, Thomas Renfro, J.P.

28. Routh, William F. to Gambrell, S. Emily, Mar. 25, 1867, J. M. Gambrell, M.G.

28. Martin, John W. to Petit, Martha J., Apr. 22, 1867, Thomas Renfro, J.P.

28. Buff, Daniel to Phillips, Caroline, Apr. 3, 1867, Thomas Renfro, J.P.

29. Warmack, Jesse to James, Winnie, Mar. 19, 1867, C. R. McAllister, J.P.

29. Baker, W. W. to Dyer, E. E., Apr. 18, 1867. J. T. Compton, M.G.

29. Brinkley, Sterling to Shelton, Sarah M., Feb. 1, 1867, A. Varnell, J.P.

30. Cry, John to Shelton, Winny E., Nov. 17, 1866, A. Varnell, J.P.

30. Armstrong, Henry C. to Parker, Sallie M., Nov. 17, 1866, A. Varnell, J.P.

WHITFIELD COUNTY, GA. - MARRIAGE BOOK B(1)

PAGE
30. Bridges, W. L. to Lanham, M. E., Feb. 1, 1867, Augustin
Harris, J.P.

31. Caldwell, Thos. to Fraker, Mrs. Margaret, May 14, 1867,
John M. Richardson, Minister M.E. Church.

31. Sloan, Samuel B. to Killinger, J. C., June 1, 1867, W. C.
Richardson, M.G.

31. Rollins, John F. to McGaughy, A. J., June 17. 1867,
C. R. McAllister, J.P.

32. Dycus, Stephen B. to Compton, Annis, May 25, 1867. A.
Varnell, J.P.

32. Hays, Melvin to Caldwell. Elizabeth J., July 15, 1867.
J. T. Deck. J.P.

32. Smith, William to Lackey, Nancy Ann, May 29, 1867, J. P.
Freeman, Co. Judge.

33. Wadkins, Abraham (C) to Tatham, Ann (C), July 28. 1866,
J. P. Freeman, Co. Judge.

33. Wilson, Jefferson (C) to Clopston, Ann (C), Aug. 11,
1866, J. P. Freeman, Co. Judge.

33. Franklin, Benjamin (C) to Bodwell. Ann (C), July 31,
1866, B. B. Brown, J.I.C.

34. Clark, Felix (C) to Groves, Fanny (C), Feb. 10, 1866,
T. P. Jay, M.G.

34. Scott, Isaac (C) to Wright, Josephine (C), July 20, 1866,
S. J. Ward, J.P.

34. Eason, Joh (CF) to Russel, Judah (C). Jan. 15, 1866,
J. P. Anderson, J.P.

35. Dickinson, Perry (C) to Johnson, Charlotte (C), July 28,
1866, Andrew Brown, M.G.

35. Brown, Joshua (C) to Manning, Gracia (C), June 23, 1866,
Andrew Brown, M.G. (his mark)

35. Palmer, Robert (C) to Mills, Mitty (C), July 28, 1866,
Andrew Brown, M.G.

36. Cook, Anthony (CF) to Adams, Abby (CF). Jan. 6, 1866,
J. P. Anderson, J.P.

36. Cox, Wiley (C) to Forsyth, Miriah (C). May 1, 1866, B. B.
Brown, J.I.C.

36. Austin, Jefferson (C) to Lynch, Mary A. (C). July 7.
1866, J. A. R. Hanks, M.G.

37. Myers, Ezekiel (C) to Camp, Narcissa (C), July 19, 1866,
J. P. Freeman, Ordinary.

37. Bunch, Wm. S. (C) to Sheppard, Mahala (C), July 23, 1866,
B. B. Brown, J.I.C.

37. Jones, Miles (C) to Benham, Nancy (C). July 23, 1866,
J. P. Freeman, Co. Judge.

38. Henry, Madison (C) to Coleman, Ann (C). May 19, 1866,
B. B. Brown, J.I.C.

38. Underwood, George (C) to Worley, Martha (C), Feb. 25,
1867, F. A. Raushenberg, J.P.

38. Wells, Charles (C) to Bagget, Sulana (C). July 24, 1866,
Joseph Rodgers, J.P.

39. Brock, Solomon (CF) to Haynes, Anne (CF), Jan. 27. 1866,
Joseph Rodgers, J.P.

39. Cherry, David (C) to White, Amanda (C), Dec. 22. 1866,
J. P. Mitchell. M.G.

39. English. Dock (C) to Harland, Missouri (C), Dec. 26,
1366, Jos. Rodgers.

40. Loney, James (C) to Thompson, Daffny (C), Jan. 26, 1867,
Andrew Brown, M.G.

40. Harlin, Riley (C) to Walker, Cartwhite(?). (C), Feb. 20,
1867, J. P. Freeman, Ordinary.

PAGE
40.   Thomas, Isaac (C) to Wimpie, Julia (C), Jan. 15. 1867,
        B. B. Brown, J.I.C.

41.   Tatum, Lewis (C) to Bailey, Cluny (C), Feb. 12, 1867,
        Andrew Brown, M.G.

41.   Hamilton, Warren (C) to Moyers, Ellen (C), Feb. 23,
        1867, Andrew Brown, M.G.

41.   Donaldson, Samuel (C) to Hancock, Martha (C), July 28,
        1866, Andrew Brown, M.G.

42.   Jackson, John (C) to Jackson, Katy (C), Aug. 4, 1866,
        B. B. Brown, J.I.C.

42.   Lany, William H. (C) to Haynes, Mattie (C), Jan. 4, 1867,
        B. B. Brown, J.I.C.

42.   Gaither, Harry (C) to Henderson, Ellen (C), Dec. 24, 1866,
        C. R. McAllister, J.P.

43.   Russell, Henson (C) to Russell, Lodice (C). Dec. 24,
        1866, C. R. McAllister, J.P.

43.   Duner, Isaac E. (C) to Branner, Jane (C), Jan. 2, 1867,
        G. W. Selvidge, M.G.

43.   Pullium, William (C) to Bloon, Eliza (C), Dec. 26, 1866,
        B. B. Brown, J.I.C.

44.   Green, Alonzo (C) to Harris, Adaline (C), Dec. 15. 1866,
        B. B. Brown, J.I.C.

44.   Brock, Solomon (CF) to Haynes, Ann (CF), Jan. 27, 1866,
        Joseph Rodgers, J.P.

44.   Scott, David (C) to Wilka, Milla (C), Apr. 13, 1867,
        J. P. Freeman, Co. Judge.

45.   Pitner, William (C) to Reeves, Jennie (C), 19(?) Jan.
        19, 1867. C. R. McAllister, J.P.

45.   Rollins, Addison (C) to Morris, Phebe (C), July 3, 1867.
        W. J. Underwood, J.I.C.

45.   Homes, Henry (C) to Quillian, Adaline (C), Mar. 7, 1867,
        John P. Love, J.P.

46.   Thomas, Cuffie (C) to Givens, Lucy (C), Apr. 9, 1867.
        J. P. Freeman, Co. Judge.

46.   Kemp, Israil (C) to Street, Rebecca Jane (C), Jan. 23.
        1866, T. P. Jay, M.G.

46.   Morgan, John (C) to Gilbert, Mrs. Mariah (C), July 27,
        1867, J. J. Martin, M.G.

47.   Jentry, William to Freeman, Harriet A., July 20, 1867,
        S. J. Ward, J.P.

47.   Vance, Richard to Brown, Mary, July 27, 1867, Robert
        W. Ault, J.P.

47.   Simms, James to Pritchett, Mary, Aug. 2, 1867. Thomas
        Renfro, J.P.

48.   Rouch, James M. to Douglass, Sabina L., May 25, 1867,
        S. J. Ward, J.P.

48.   Johnston, Jacob H. to Anderson, Sarah E., Aug. 1, 1867.
        Thomas Renfro, J.P.

48.   Jentry, G. W. to Dillahunt, Mrs. Margaret, July 13, 1867,
        S. J. Ward, J.P.

49.   Bartenfeld, Henry A. to Nichols, Katherine C., Aug. 1,
        1867. Joseph Terry, M.G.

49.   Weatherly, Robt. W. W. to Haskins, Margaret A., July 29,
        1867. A. K. J. Hambright, M.G.

49.   Gazaway, Miles J. to Hubard, Catherine, Sept. 4, 1867,
        Thomas Rendro, J.P.

50.   Boyd, Richard (C) to Small, Lydia (C), Aug. 20, 1867,
        J. T. Deck, J.P.

50.   Swinton, John (C) to Fisher, Eliza (C), Sept. 5, 1867,
        B. B. Brown, J.I.C.

PAGE

50.   Kanaster, Henry R. to Neil, Eliza J., Sept. 2, 1867,
F. A. Raushenberg, J.P.

51.   Graham, William J. to Small. Lou J., Sept. 11, 1867,
A. J. Leet(?), M.G.

51.   Lane, Joseph M. to Hardcastle, Mrs. Louisa, July 8, 1867,
Benjamin Wiggins, J.P.

51.   Massengill. E. to Calhoun, Ellen E., Oct. 13, 1866,
Elder L. W. Wilson.

52.   Lasater, Wm. H. to Bradley, Susan A., Mar. 30, 1867,
Harvey McHan, M.G.

52.   Bradley, Croyton to Tally, Nancy E., Oct. 10, 1867.
Harvey McHan.

52.   Nichols, W. L. to Bradley, Mariah P., Oct. 3, 1867.
Harvey McHan, M.G.

53.   Jones, Humphrie M. to Warmack, Lucy, Oct. 23, 1867, T. M.
Lane, M.G.

53.   Roach, William to Pinder, Adaline, Oct. 8, 1867, Robert
W. Ault, J.P.

53.   Johnson, Zachariah to Burns, Elizabeth V., Aug. 21, 1867,
J. H. Aderhold, M.G.

54.   Winkle, William to Hawkins, Josephine, Sept. 20, 1867,
Harvey McHan, M.G.

54.   Roper, R. A. to Wier, Sarah L., Oct. 22, 1867, Thomas
Rendro, J.P.

54.   Calhoun, James K. P. to Bryant, Mary E., Aug. 15, 1867,
C. R. McAllister, J.P.

55.   Connally, James to Connally, Mary E., Oct. 23, 1867,
J. A. R. Hanks, M.G.

55.   Reeves, Peter (C) to Brown, Ada (C), Oct. 24, 1867, F. A.
Raushenberg, J.P.

55.   Henry, Marion to Mitchell. Elizabeth, July 11, 1867,
J. J. Martin, M.G.

(Pages 56 and 57 are blank)

58.   Hogwood, Wm. R. to Faith, Sarah J., Oct. 23, 1867, J. J.
Martin, M.G.

58.   Bagwell, Andrew J. to Thompson, Margaret, Oct. 16, 1867,
C. R. McAllister, J.P.

58.   Williams, S. R. to Moore, Mrs. Susan, Oct. 16, 1867,
Joseph Rodgers, J.P.

59.   Fulks, Joseph to Farmer, Susan, Aug. 17, 1867, Elder
W. W. Wilson.

59.   Bradley, Jasper P. to Winkle, Mary J., Sept. 25, 1867,
Harvey McHan, M.G.

59.   Mayfield, George W. to Carpenter, Louler E., Nov. 4,
1867, Z. M. McGee, M.G.

60.   Gire, James D. to Gilbert, S. A. L., Nov. 6, 1867, J. M.
Gambrell, M.G.

60.   Quinn, John to Whaley, Martha E., Oct. 30, 1867, Eld.
Joseph Perry, M.G.

60.   White, Benjamin to James, Nancy A., Oct. 1, 1863, Elder
L. W. Wilson.

61.   Rogers, William (C) to Durrooh, Adaline (C), Nov. 2,
1867, J. A. R. Hanks, M.G.

61.   Hambleton, Dennis (C) to King, Martha (C), Dec. 2, 1867,
J. M. Gambrell, M.G.

61.   Hambright, B. F. to Hoskin, Martha J., Mar. 15, 1866,
Wm. B. Brown, V.D.M.

62.   Gravis, Samuel G. to Brotherton, Martha, Dec. 12, 1867.
H. C. Carter, V.D.M.

PAGE
62. Delaney, John B. to Moffett, Narcissa B., Dec. 24, 1867,
Dawson A. Walker, Judge Supreme Court.
62. Tarver, John R. to Burson, Mattie A., Oct. 29, 1867,
T. M. Lane, M.G.
63. Parks, S. J. to Fowler, C. A., Nov. 16, 1867, Thomas
Rendro, J.P.
63. Rogers, Samuel (C) to Wilson, Patsy (C), Dec. 19, 1867,
J. A. R. Hanks, M.G.
63. Bilting, Nicholas to Nichols, Mary J., Dec. 31, 1867,
J. A. R. Hanks, M.G.
64. Avery, Isaac W. to Bivings, Emma, Jan. 1, 1868, J. A. R.
Hanks, M.G.
64. Davis, Warren R. to Bird, Malissa A., Dec. 31, 1868(67?),
J. A. R. Hanks, M.G.
64. Hopkins, R. B. to Mulkey, Lizzie, Dec. 10, 1867, C. R.
McAllister, J.P.
65. McGaughy, William G. to Page, Huldah L., Apr. 3, 1867,
H. R. Swisher, M.G.
45. Quillian, William C. to Tye, Sarah J., Nov. 20, 1867,
J. M. Richardson, Minister in M.E. Church South.
45. Mitchell, William F. to Holland, Alice C., Jan. 3, 1868,
John T. Compton, M.G.
66. Bramblette, E. W. to Haley, Sarah L., Dec. 23, 1867,
John T. Compton, M.G.
66. Henderson, Thomas J. to Lowery, Hattie C., Dec. 19, 1867,
H. C. Carter, V.D.M.
66. Cain, William O. to Cruce, Margaret V., Dec. 16, 1867,
Joseph Rodgers, J.P.
67. Walker, Hilliard (C) to Harlan, Elmina (C), Nov. 24,
1867, Joseph Rodgers, J.P.
67. Cash, Howard to Onar, Sarah J., Jan. 21, 1868, William
Hardcastle, J.P.
67. Bodmand, Henry C. to Mack, Martha Ann, Nov. 28, 1867,
J. T. Davis, J.P.
68. Kirf, Isaac S. (C) to Walker, Sallie (C), Nov. 21, 1867,
J. T. Deck, J.P.
68. Smith, James M. to Conley, Jennie Ann, Jan. 25, 1868,
Thomas Renfro, J.P.
68. Martin, Fletcher to Holder, Josephine, Jan. 25, 1868,
Jos. Terry, M.G.
69. Dugan, John C. to Ferington, Frances, Oct. 18. 1867,
Eld. F. M. Avans, M.G.
69. Holland, Jackson to Mitchell, Frances, Nov. 4, 1867,
Eld. Joseph Terry, M.G.
69. Leadferd, M. to McAllister, Mrs. Rachel U., Jan. 6, 1868,
C. R. McAllister, J.P.
70. Wofford, Richard (C) to Jackson, Eliza (C), Feb. 6, 1868,
J. P. Freeman, Co. Judge.
70. Mote, Silas W. to Simmons, Sarah A., Jan. 25, 1868, John
M. Richardson.
70. Hair, George W. to Cady, Emily L., Jan. 21, 1868, J. M.
Richardson.
71. Head, William to Sams, Georgia, Feb. 13. 1868, J. M.
Richardson.
71. Davis, John D. to Brooker, Martha K., Oct. 28, 1867,
W. J. Underwood, J.I.C.
71. Thomas, Alfred to McEntire, Martha E., Dec. 19, 1867,
John P. Love, J.P.
72. Moore, John N. to Davis, Mrs. Jane, Dec. 1, 1867, J. P.
Love, J.P.

PAGE
72. Burton, James D. to Davis, Sarah, Aug. 10, 1867. John P. Love, J.P.
72. Waller, William to Fowler, Lavinia, Nov. 29, 1867, John P. Love, J.P.
73. Smith, T. W. to Cantrell, Julia, Nov. 11, 1867, Augustin Harris, J.P.
73. Walker, Joseph M. to Bridges, Nancy E., Feb. 17, 1868, Augustin Harris, J.P.
73. King, Joseph to Murphey, Mrs. Lizzie, Feb. 24, 1868, J. A. R. Hanks, M.G.
74. Hawkins, David to Craig, Mrs. Susan, Feb. 13, 1868, Thos. J. Simmons, Minister M.E. Church South.
74. Panniel, William T. to White, Nancy D., Dec. 26, 1867, Thos. J. Simmons, Minister M.E. Church South.
74. Bird, Thos. D. to Rogers, Laura, Mar. 4, 1868, A. G. Johnson, M.G.
75. Bailey, John C. to McDonald, Sarah J., Mar. 17, 1868, Thomas J. Simmons, Minister M.E. Church South.
75. Whaley, Samuel A. to Brumbelow, Mary A., Mar. 25, 1868. Thomas J. Simmons, Minister M.E. Church South.
75. Talley, Moses to Bradley, Evaline, Mar. 24, 1868, Harvey McHan, M.G.
76. Williams, Joel J. (C) to Nelson, Mrs. Mary E. (C), Jan. 18, 1868, Samuel Brice, M.G.
76. Camp, George (C) to Southerland, Laura (C), Apr. 5, 1868, John T. Compton, M.G.
76. Hillsun, James (C) to Sprowl. Candus (C), Mar. 28, 1868, Willis Love, M.G.
77. Baxter, Ervin (C) to Graves, Harriet (C), Jan. 4, 1868, F. D. Clayton, M.G.
77. Baker, Hezekiah (C) to Jones, Martha (C), Apr. 4, 1868, F. A. Raushenberg, J.P.
77. Night, Austin to Peterson, Catharine, Apr. 22, 1868, Augustin Harris, J.P.
78. Lauderdale, Samuel H. to Kirkpatrick, Mary, Dec. 31, 1867, F. A. Raushenberg, J.P.
78. Rumsey, Joseph to Burchfield, Elvira, Dec. 23. 1867, F. A. Rausenberg, J.P.
78. Bartlette, L. G. to Whitener, Theresy, Mar. 25, 1868. Benjamin Wiggins, J.P.
79. Crowel. William D. to Neal, Mrs. Ann E., Nov. 9, 1867, John P. Love, J.P.
79. Little, James V. to Easterling, Mary J., Mar. 4, 1868, Levi Brotherton, M.G.
79. Graham, John (C) to Street, Emma (C), July 13, 1867, F. A. Raushenberg, J.P.
80. Burns(?), J. L. to Williams, S. M., May 16, 1868, Thos. J. Simmons, M.G.
80. Redwine, Lewis S. to Dupree, Emily J., May 2, 1868, Thos. J. Simmons, M.G.
81. Headrick, Lewis B. to Dickson, Maggie J., May 26, 1868, A. J. Lockridge, M.G.
81. Raney, Edward to Morehead, America, Jan. 28, 1868, J. J. Martin, M.G.
82. Bagwell, John Q. to Ridley, Mary L. (No date), T. M. Love, M.G.
82. Pritchet, Anderson to Tate, Ana E., Feb. 4, 1868, J. J. Martin, J.G.
83. Pucket, William to Vandvere, Mrs. Malany S., Mar. 30, 1868, J. J. Martin, M.G.

PAGE
83.   Mince, Thos. W. to McJunken, Eliza, June 24, 1868, Thos.
Renfro, J.P.

84.   Jackson, James M. to Anderson, Laura F., Dec. 16, 1867,
A. S. Leet, M.G.

84.   Faster, James R. to Morgan, Tabitha C., Nov. 27. 1867,
J. M. Stansberry, M.G.

85.   Williamson, J.A. to Ford, Laura J., Mar. 17, 1868. J. M.
Stansberry, M.G.

85.   Griffin, Wm. H. to Wamick, Mary R., July 3. 1868, Joseph
Rodgers, J.P.

86.   Griffin, Adam to Richards, Sallie, July 7, 1868, J. M.
Stansberry, M.G.

86.   Young, Robt. A. to Moore, Mary C., July 28, 1868.
Hewlett S. Moore, O.M.G.

86-7. Rice, James to Cox, Martha A., July 8. 1868, J. M.
Stansberry, M.G.

87.   Routh, Robt. F. to Bunson, Tebitha, June 29, 1868. J. M.
Gambrel. M.G.

87.   Robertson, James M. to Roper, Rebecca E., July 29, 1868.
(No record of marriage)

88.   Comming, Montgomery (of Savannah) to Wade, Rasalia M.,
Sept. 7. 1868, D. L. Bultolph.

88.   Forix, John R. to Sparks, Martha E., July 21, 1868, J. P.
Freeman, Co. Judge.

88-9. Caldwell, John to Clark, Elizabeth, Dec. 23, 1867. Robt.
W. Ault, J.P.

89.   Vann, James B. to Fannin(?), Elizabeth, July 16, 1868,
Thos. Renfro, J.P.

89.   Bell, Isaac (C) to Green, Mrs. (C), Aug. 8, 1868, J. B.
Bell, M.G.

90.   Stone, John to Parker, Mary, July 18. 1868, J. M.
Brittain, M.G.

90.   Glenn, Joseph to Thomson, Martha P., June 16, 1868,
Hewell S. Moore, M.G.

90-1. Smith, Eligah W. to Crow, Rebecca, May 16, 1867, J. J.
Gilbert, M.G.

91.   Dyre, John to Smith, Susan A., June 27, 1868, John J.
Gilbert, M.G.

91.   Minc, Wm. R. to Linder, Elizabeth M., June 16, 1868,
John J. Gilbert, M.G.

92.   Cowles, William F. to Wyche, Camelia D., Aug. 18, 1868,
John M. Richardson, M.G.

92.   Summerford, James E. to Carder, Martha J., Oct. 20, 1866,
Joseph Terry, M.G.

92-3. Russel, Wm. to Wright, Fannie, Sept. 14, 1867, J. Terry,
M.G.

93.   Duckett, E. J. to Dycus, Mary J., Sept. 17. 1868, J. P.
Bailey, J.P.

93.   Carden, J. A. to Gentry, Mrs. Frances A., Sept. 22,
1868, John M. Richardson, M.G.

94.   Longley, W. J. to O'Tyson, Mary, Sept. 18. 1868, J.A.R.
Hanks, M.G.

94.   King, J. L. to Fraker, Mary O., Sept. 19, 1868, J. M.
Richardson, M.G.

94-5. Dyre, Wm. to Baker, Elzevan, Sept. 23, 1868, J. J.
Gilbert, M.G.

95.   King, George to Compton, Edna Jane, Sept. 17, 1868, J.J.
Gilbert, M.G.

95.   Graves, John B. to Anderson, Mrs. Jane S., Oct. 5, 1868,
J.A.R. Hanks, M.G.

PAGE

96. Fitspatrick, John S. to Waugh, Mattie E., Oct. 1, 1868, J. A. R. Hanks, M.G.

96. Perry, James M. to Neal, Mrs. Sarah E., Oct. 3, 1868. John J. Gilbert, M.G.

96-7. Scruder, Harmon to Hume, Mrs. Mary, Oct. 2, 1868, J. J. Gilbert, M.G.

97. Moore, Thomas J. to Dobson, Mary L., July 17, 1867, Z. D. Clark, M.G.

97. Richardson, Robert to Worthy, Mary, Sept. 1, 1868, J. M. Gambrel, M.G.

98. Harris, J.P. to Messincer, Caroline, Oct. 8, 1868, J. M. Gambrel, M.G.

98. Sebastian, James P. to Robins, Mary L., Sept. 26, 1868, Thos. J. Simmons, M.G.

98-9. Masters, James to Scales, R. M., Oct. 12, 1868, Thos. J. Simmons, M.G.

99. Scales, John G. to Worthy, C., Oct. 15, 1868, Thos. J. Simmons, M.G.

99-100. Mack, James K.P. to Tiffins, Mary E., Oct. 17, 1868, Thos. Rendro, J.P.

100. Ketcham, Daniel to Kenester, Mary, Aug. 12, 1868, F. A. Raushenberg, J.P.

100. Cline, Samuel to Worthy, Louizia, Oct. 21, 1868. F. A. Raushenberg, J.P.

101. Randolph, John (C) to Williams, Julia (C), Aug. 7, 1868, J. J. Martin, M.G.

101. Brilton, William F. to Autery, Emolene, Sept. 25, 1868, J. T. Compton, M.G.

101. Morgan, John F. to Smith, Laura E., Dec. 21, 1868. J. J. Harris, M.G.

102. Hilton, E. M. to Pierce, Lugenea, Sept. 12, 1868. J. C. Mitchell, M.G.

102. Bromlett, Wesley to Towers, Sarah J. F., Aug. 11, 1868, Joseph Rodgers, J.P.

102-3. Long, Wiley to Petty, Ann, Nov. 11, 1868, Thos. Renfro, J. P.

103. Thomas, Alison to Cantrel, Mrs. Jane, Oct. 30, 1868, Hamilton Young, J.P.

103. Lane, James A. to Mitchell, Jenettie, Oct. 25, 1868. Thos. J. Simmons, M.G.

104. Varnell, Wm. M. to Creswell, Harriet J., Nov. 14, 1868. J. W. Brittain, M.G.

104. Knight, Elderad to Harben, Matilda, Nov. 12, 1868, Harvey McHan, M.G.

105. Hooper, James A. to Spruce, Mrs. Sarah J., Oct. 7, 1867, E. M. Lowry, M.G.

105. Davis, Leroy W. to Edwards, Mary E., Jan. 21, 1868, E. M. Lowrey, M.G.

106. Oxford, David J. to Bender, Catharine, July 15, 1868, E. M. Lowery, M.G.

106. Hicks, B. K. to Bird, Mollie, Mar. 18, 1868. E. M. Lowrey, M.G.

107. Talley, Alx. G. to Noblett, Harriet C., Feb. 8, 1868. E. M. Lowrey, M.G.

107. Smithey, R. A. to Pritchet, Susan, Sept. 7, 1867, E. M. Lowrey, M.G.

107-8. Masters, William to Roberts, Martha E., Aug. 6, 1867. E. M. Lowrey, M.G.

108. Cahoun, T. B. to Dugan, M. J., Sept. 12, 1868, Thos. D. Claytow, M.G.

PAGE
108. Routh, Saml. H. to Bursow, Nannie V., Nov. 11, 1868,
J. M. Gambrel, M.G.
109. Henry, J. A. to Kopkins, K. A. D., Oct. 27, 1868, C. R.
McAllester, J.P.
109. Hall, David S. to Grogan, Sarah S., Sept. 22, 1868,
Augustin Harris, J.P.
109-10. Sloan, R. P. to Owen, Tampy, Oct. 20, 1868, Thos. J.
Simmons, M.G.
110. Glover, H. P. to Cantrell, Caroline, Aug. 8, 1868, Benj.
Wiggins, J.P.
110-11. Cain, A. S. to Cruce, F. P., Dec. 21, 1868, A. Fitzgerald,
M.G.
111. Rogers, S. C. to Witzel, Frances, Dec. 12, 1868, Thos.
Renfro, J.P.
111. Gocio, William R. to Sims, Ann M., Dec. 11, 1868, John
T. Norris, M.G.
112. Dugan, D. R. to Rose, Mary Ann, Dec. 5, 1868, Thos. D.
Clayton, M.G.
112. Jones, Amos to Campbell, Cany V., Dec. 26, 1868. J.A.R.
Hanks, M.G.
112-3. Boyd, C. H. to Louer, Mollie, Dec. 3, 1868. Hamilton
Young, N.P.
113. O'Neal, J. W. to Deshayes, Mrs. Caroline, Dec. 3, 1868,
A. J. Barnett, N.P.
113. Boyle(?), Joseph to Langley, Louiza, Dec. 9, 1868, Levi
Brotherton, M.G.
114. Boyce, John M. to Hall, M. J., Dec. 16, 1868, Augustin
Harris, J.P.
114. Wiggins, James to Gibbert (Gilbert?), Miland, May 8,
1867, J. J. Gilbert, M.G.
115. Wheeler, George to Stinsan, Hannah, Dec. 20, 1868, J. J.
Gibbert (Gilbert?), M.G.
115. Justice, James D. to Thomas, Martha, Dec. 19, 1868,
Joseph Rodgers, J.P.
115-6. Summers, Geo. to Bromlet, A., Dec. 31, 1868, Joseph
Rodgers, J.P.
116. Plumer, J. C. to Rodgers, E. J., Jan. 6, 1869, J. J.
Gibbert (Gilbert?), M.G.
116-7. Owens, J. C. to Parmer, E., Jan. 7, 1869, L. N. Spier,
N.P. & J.P.
117. White, J. F. to Allums, S. E., Jan. 21, 1869, W. H.
Brooker, Ordinary.
117. Rogers, Hugh to Howard, Susan E., Dec. 22, 1868, T. M.
Lane, M.G.
118. Neal, Wm. F. to Keith, Sarah J., Dec. 30, 1868, T. M.
Lane, M.G.
118. Williams, J. L. to Chastain, Emily, Jan. 21, 1869,
Harvey McHan, M.G.
119. Anderson, John H. to Anderson, M.J., Jan. 2. 1869,
Raleigh Cupp, N.P. & Ex officio J.P.
119. Nailor, J.C. to Bagley, C. E., Dec. 14, 1868, Raleigh
Cupp, N.P. & J.P.
119-20. Dantzler, R. F. to Lockard, Sarah E., Dec. 17, 1868,
Raleigh Cupp, N.P. & Ex officio J.P.
120. Wells, John to Tate, A. E. F., Dec. 19, 1868, Z. D.
Clark, M.G.
121. Boatright, A. J. to Green, A. M., Dec. 21, 1868, Laban
Pilkenton, M.G.
121. Cartrel, John M. to McCurdy, A. J., May 18, 1867, J. P.
Baily, M.G.

596

PAGE
121.   McCollum, W. J. to Chastain, Mrs. Matilda, Feb. 11,
       1869, Wm. C. Richardson, M.G.
122.   Stofford, George W. to Mench, Katie, Feb. 4, 1869, W. C.
       Richardson, M.G.
122.   Tebbs, John J. to Galze, Phoeba, Jan. 28, 1869, J.A.R.
       Hanks, M.G.
123.   Burk, John H. to Cryer, Mrs. L.M.E., Mar. 3, 1869, J.J.
       Gilbert, M.G.
123.   Craig, R. M. to Gladden, Mrs. M.A., Mar. 13, 1869, John
       P. Love, J.P.
124.   Harris, C.N.P. to Evans, Rebecca C., Aug. 24, 1868,
       Rev. H. H. Poter.
124.   Coker, Wm. G. to Dobson, Josephine, Feb. 22, 1869,
       Joseph Rodgers, J.P.
125.   Fagala, Lewis to Varnell, Sarah, Nov. 29, 1866, J. W.
       Ramsey, M.G.
125.   Esskew, W. J. to Jones, Sarah A., Apr. 13, 1869, Levi
       Brotherton, M.G.
126.   Byars, H. N. to Miller, Mrs. E.C., Apr. 15, 1869, J. L.
       Bletch, M.G.
126.   Furgerson, George W. to Rose, Malissa J., Feb. 1, 1868,
       A. Varnell, J.P.
127.   Hamontree, Mr. to Brown, Millie, Feb. 6, 1869, C. R.
       McAllister, J.P.
127.   Arnold, Daniel to James, Martha, Mar. 2, 1869, C. R.
       McAllester, J.P.
128.   Fields, J. R. (C) to McCarrel(?), Harriet, Apr. 14,
       1869, Laban Pilkerton, M.G.
128.   Bivins(?), J. F. to Bell, L. P., Nov. 11, 1869, J.A.R.
       Hanks, M.G.
129.   Baggett, J.D. to Odell, Sallie, Oct. 18, 1869, John M.
       Richardson, M.G.
129.   Paxton, John T. to Brinkley, N. E., Sept. 28, 1869, John
       M. Richardson, M.G.
130.   Bradford, J. A. to Simson, M. W., July 31, 1869, Andrew
       J. Barnett, N.P.
130.   Pierce, John to Carpenter, Virginia, Aug. 7, 1869, L.
       Pilkerton, M.G.
131.   Stone, Esau to Autrie, Millie E., Aug. 7, 1869, C. R.
       McAllister, J.P.
131.   Leadford, J. L. to Haddock, Elizabeth, Sept. 21, 1869,
       C. R. McAllister, J.P.
132.   Belton, James (C) to Smith, Lou (C), July 28, 1869,
       J. J. Gilbert, M.G.
132.   Calhoun, W. H. C. to Slaten, Sara, July 12. 1869, J.J.
       Gilbert, M.G.
133.   Robins, William E. to Sloan, Elizabeth, Aug. 21, 1869,
       W. W. Sebastian, J.P.
133.   Hooker, Drury to Rogers, Catherine, Aug. 24, 1869, T. M.
       Lane, M.G.
134.   Lane, F. L. to McClure, Elizabeth, Sept. 9, 1869, T. M.
       Lane, M.G.
134.   Dean, Elbert J. to Gladen, Naomi L. E., Aug. 28. 1869,
       T. M. Lane, M.G.
135.   Moore, J. A. to Carpenter, M. A., Sept. 14, 1869, Z. M.
       McGhee, M.G.
135.   Lacy, James W. to Parks, Francis, Sept. 16, 1869, J. L.
       Bletch, M.G.
136.   Lanhan, O. A. to Harris, Eliza C., Aug. 12, 1869, Z. D.
       Clark, M.G.

PAGE
136. Denton, J. F. to McCrary, Ella C., Sept. 2, 1869, Levi
      Brotherton, M.G.
137. Wiggins, J. C. to Hardcautt, Julia A., July 10, 1869,
      T. M. Lane, M.G.
137. Lynch, Henry C. to Strickland, T. M., Aug. 19, 1867,
      W. C. Richardson, M.G.
138. Wood, Thomas K. to Gore, Nancy, July 19, 1867, W. C.
      Richardson, M.G.
138. Cox, Daniel to Smith, Salina J., Oct. 7, 1869, Wm. Pullen,
      M.G.
139. Bellheuer(?), Henry M. to Love, Eva, Sept. 2, 1869,
      J. L. Bletch, M.G.
139. Bowen, T. H. to Beardell, Cruthia A., Aug. 26, 1869,
      R. S. Carr, J.P.
140. Lane, G. T. to Dawn, Emma C., Aug. 25, 1869, W. C.
      Richardson, M.G.
140. Callaway, Jesse to Quinn, Frances, Nov. 16, 1869, J. J. S.
      Callaway, M.G.
141. Stone, Geo. W. to Julian, Piety, Oct. 27, 1869, E. F.
      King, J.P.
141. Richardson, Abel to Kown, Sarah A., Aug. 10, 1869,
      W.H.C. Freeman, N.P. & Ex J.P.
141-2. Calwell, J.T. to Burns, Mary J., July 31, 1869, Rev.
      Laban Pilkenton.
142. Redwine, Henry T. to Nations, Misiririe, Feb. 28, 1870,
      Wm. W. Sebastian, J.P.
142. Rucken, Sandy (C) to Banks, Martha (C), Feb. 3, 1870,
      Laban Pilkenton, M.G.
143. Page, Jasper N. to Henry, Ruthy J., Mar. 3, 1870, C. P.
      McAllister, J.P.
143. Whelcher, Maj. to Leroy, Mrs. Eliza, Mar. 16, 1870,
      John P. Love, J.P.
144. Hair, Nathan C. to Whitener, Jane, Mar. 8. 1870, R. N.
      Varnell, N.P.
144. Davis, Willis (C) to Tarver, Malinda (C), Mar. 17, 1870,
      John P. Love, J.P.
145. Earnest, M. M. to Mitchel, M. L., Mar. 27, 1869, S. H.
      Henry, M.G.
145. Kincaid, S. C. to Baggett, Mary, July 16, 1869, Levi
      Brotherton, M.G.
146. Scout, Joshua (C) to Swift, Jenny (C), Sept. 3. 1870,
      J.A.R. Hanks, M.G.
146. Johnson, O. H. to Nailor, M.J., Jan. 30, 1869, Raleigh
      Corp (Cupp), N.P. & J.P.
147. Baker, Morris (C) to McDonald, Allis, Dec. 23, 1868.
      Benj. Wiggins, J.P.
147. Neal, George (C) to Grubb, Frances (C), Nov. 27, 1869,
      John P. Love, J.P.
148. Barnett, A. J. to Faith, Sarah E., Feb. 24, 1869, T. J.
      Simmons, M.G.
148. Roberts, John T. to Palmer, Mary A., July 2, 1870, John
      Oates, M.G.
149. Jones, Wm. B. to Stone, Ossie T., Nov. 29, 1869, Elder
      J. W. Wilson.
149. Lanier, Madison to Ray, Josephine, Nov. 11. 1869, R. C.
      Carr, J.P.
150. Pitner, John (C) to Loudon, Emaline (C), Nov. 20, 1869,
      F. A. Raushenberg, J.P.
150. Duke, Jessee to Vaughn, Lucy, Nov. 3, 1868, Henry McHan,
      M.G.

PAGE

151. Cole, Wm. to Humphreys, Nancy, Aug. 9, 1869, F. A. Raushenberg, J.P.

151. Thornton, F. (C) to Nichols, Betty (C), Dec. 26, 1868, Joseph Rodgers, J.P.

152. Drue, Jefferson (C) to Fauster, Mandy (C), Feb. 21, 1870, T. A. Pharr, M.G.

152. Duckett, E. A. to Dunson, Caroline, Aug. 9, 1869, F. A. Raushenburg, J.P.

153. Masters, James A. to Englass(?), Loueson, Nov. 18. 1869, T. J. Simmons, M.G.

153. Bearden, F. L. to Law, Rebecca, July 20, 1870, H. Young, Notary Public & Ex. of J.P.

154. Solomons, Robert (C) to Evans, Dolly (C), July 22, 1868, J. J. Gilbert, M.G.

154. Wade, James (C) to Smith, Eliza (C), Dec. 20, 1869, Henry Reddin (C), M.G. (His mark)

155. Head, Frank to McCurdy, Sarah, Nov. 25, 1869, J. Richardson, M.G.

155. Height, Dempsey to Long, Alice, Oct. 19, 1868, John B. Bell, M.G.

156. Morris, Joe (C) to Williams, Lee (C), Dec. 16, 1869, John P. Love, J.P.

156. Tapp, Lamuel to Willson, Mary, Nov. 18, 1869, T. J. Simmons, M.G.

157. Bridges, W. L. to Springfield, W. A., Dec. 30, 1869, Z. D. Clark, M.G.

157. Brown, Geo. R. to Rogers, Mrs. M. H., Dec. 24, 1869, J.A.R. Hanks, M.G.

158. Green, Wash (C) to Harling, Jane (C), Nov. 3, 1868, J. T. Deck, J.P.

158. Bruce, Jesse (C) to Wilborn, Lu (C), Dec. 28, 1869, (No record of marriage).

159. Horn, Lewis to Gitchel, Mary, Jan. 11, 1870, C. R. McAllester, J.P.

159. Williams, David to Dawn, Josephine, Sept. 22, 1870, Edward Mabee, M.G.

160. Echols, Henry to Ivey, Sarah E., Apr. 28, 1869, L. M. Richardson, M.G.

160. McKenrie, S. W. to Scott, Paulina A., Oct. 4, 1870, J.A.R. Hanks, M.G.

161. Cook, Z. T. to Gordon, O. T., Dec. 22, 1869, W.H.C. Freeman, N.P.

161. Russel, Wm. to McClure, Addie, Dec. 27, 1869, Martin Tebill, M.G.

162. McCurdy, G.T. to Brinkley, C., Dec. 29, 1869, John M. Richardson, M.G.

162. Dempsey, Wm. to Caphort, Queen, Aug. 25, 1869, G. W. Green, J.P.

163. Shettlesworth, J.B. to Strickland, M.E., Sept. 30, 1860, Elder J. W. Wilson.

163. Kittle, W. A. to Park, Sarah A., Aug. 20, 1870, John P. Love, J.P.

164. Hill, Robert to Shields, Louise, June 10, 1869, John P. Love, J.P.

164. Taylor, Nelson to Denman, Nancy, June 6, 1870, John P. Love, J.P.

165. Wofford, Nathan to Rogers, Ella E., Jan. 10, 1870, J. M. Richardson, M.G.

165. Bramblett, Elisha to Head, Mary, Sept. 18, 1869, G. M. Green, J.P.

PAGE
166. Grogin, Tinsley to Grogin, Amanda, Jan. 22. 1870, Z. D.
      Clark, M.G.
166. Dickson, W. M. to Faulks, E., Oct. 21, 1870, J.A.R.
      Hanks, M.G.
167. Sinyard, Thomas to Stancett, Mary, Feb. 8, 1870, R. N.
      Varnell, N.P.
167. Cole, O. H. to Headrick, Jane, Oct. 23, 1870, J. D.
      Holcomb, M.G.
168. Swift, James (C) to Teag, Frances (C), Oct. 26, 1860,
      J. R. Hanks, M.G.
168. Wilson, Willis H. to Quillian, Maggia R., Oct. 15, 1870,
      W. S. Hamilton, M.G.
169. Mitchel, T. M. to Buffington, Elisabeth, Nov. 2, 1870,
      T. J. Simmons, M.G.
169. Wilson, Bird to Reid, Mary Jane, Oct. 24, 1870, J. J.
      Martin, M.G.
170. Weaver, Robert to Thomason, Sarah E., Aug. 30, 1870,
      T. J. Simmons, M.G.
170. Ransome, William to Huff, Mary E., Feb. 22, 1870, W. T.
      Hamilton, M.G.
171. Gasaway, John to Talley, Sallie, Mar. 2, 1879, T. J.
      Simmons, M.G.
171. Chamble, John to Barnett, E. A., Sept. 24, 1869, E.
      Mabee, M.G.
172. Brun(?), G. W. to Hanks, Mollie E., Aug. 7. 1870, J.A.R.
      Hanks, M.G.
172. Underwood, George to Underwood, Caroline (C), Aug. 19,
      1868, T. D. Clayton, M.G.
172-3. Glover, John J. to Moore, P. J., May 21, 1869, Harvey
      McHan, M.G.
173. Baldridge, Joseph to Cobb, Lizzie (C). Sept. 18, 1870,
      Hamilton Young, N.P.
173-4. Harris, Josiah F. to Grogan, Clarissa J., Aug. 4, 1870,
      W. M. Bridges, M.G.
174. Lebel, Charles to Davis, Anna A.R., Aug. 25, 1870, W. M.
      Bridges, M.G.
174. Howington, John to Whitner, Julia A., Aug. 2, 1870, R.N.
      Varnell, N.P.
175. Cowart, Charles to Barnwell, Mrs. Georgia, Aug. 11, 1870,
      Levi Brotherton, M.G.
175. Sansond, George to Boyd, Linda, Apr. 20, 1870, C. R.
      McAllester, J.P.
175-6. Kenner, Joe H. to Tibbs, Mary, Aug. 24, 1870, Geo. W.
      Yarbrough, M.G.
176. Clark, G. W. to Hicks, Louesia A., Nov. 2. 1870, S. J.
      Ward, J.P.
176-7. Riley, James to Wrench, Alice, Mar. 26, 1870, G. H.
      Loflon, M.G.
177. Quinn, James to Murdock, Laura, June 11, 1869. H. H.
      Porter, M.G.
177. Whisenaht, C. C. to Weaver, Elizabeth, Dec. 10, 1870,
      Wm. Pullen, M.G.
178. Moore, Fred. W. to Rogers, Lou Annie, Oct. 1, 1870,
      S. J. Ward, J.P.
178. Ried, Huston to Israel, Louisa, Oct. 17. 1868, H. H.
      Porter, L.D.
178-9. Adams, John J. to Spinks, Malvina, Nov. 26, 1870, T.J.
      Simmons, M.G.
179. Kenon, Warren to Timmier(?), Kate, May 15. 1871, J.A.R.
      Hanks, M.G.

PAGE
179. Newton, J.J. to Neal, Ann, Dec. 23. 1870, T. A. Raushenberg, J.P.
180. Sansom, J.C. to Bearden, Sarah, Jan. 5, 1870, S. J. Ward,
J.P.
180. Walker, Thos. J. to Johnson, L. J., May 9, 1870, T. D.
Halcomb, M.G.
181. La Bel. Andrew to Cady, Lauretta F., July 10, 1869,
Thomas M. Pledges, M.G.
181. Alexander, F. C. to Pilkenton, L. A., June 13, 1870,
John P. Love, J.P.
181. Adams, Sherwood to White, Sarah, Nov. 5, 1870, Thomas J.
Simmons, M.G.
182. Bridges, J. M. to Calhoun, Julia, Nov. 30, 1870. R. S.
Carr, J.P.
182. Beshiers, John to Morgan, Harriet, Dec. 29, 1870, John
P. Love, J.P.
182-3. Click, George W. to Nailor, Mary A., Apr. 29, 1870, Wm.
Pullen, M.G.
183. Redwine, John S. to Black. Martha, Nov. 21, 1870, Wm.
Sebastian, J.P.
183. Yeager, M. M. to Noblet, Charlot V., Mar. 30, 1870,
T. J. Simmons, M.G.
184. Straker, G. D. to Hair, M. A., Oct. 2. 1869, Thomas M.
Pledger, M.G.
184. Ledford, W. H. to Gitchel. Sarah, Oct. 17, 1870, C. R.
McAllester, J.P.
184-5. Arnold, Pink to Creekmore, Mary, Nov. 16, 1870, C. R.
McAllester, J.P.
185. Burns, W. T. to Lacy, Annie E., Dec. 19. 1870, Wm. M.
Sebastian, J.P.
135. Henderson, John W. to Jackson, Adaline, Sept. 2. 1869,
Thomas M. Pledger, M.G.
186. Dempsy, T. to Dobson, S.A., Nov. 24, 1868, T. M. Pledger,
M.G.
186. Wood, W. T. to Bridges, Jane, Aug. 24, 1870. W. M.
Bridges, M.G.
187. Hulsy, John W. to Gazaway, M.A.M., May 11. 1871, T. D.
Halcomb, M.G.
187. Bearden, J. N. to Sousom, Lucy E., July 27. 1870,
Hamilton Young, N.P.
188. Bomaw, Jas. A. to Redwine, Thersie M., Aug. 6, 1870,
T. J. Simmons, M.G.
188. Smith, William to Cox, Sarah, July 2, 1870. J. T. Compton, M.G.
189. Nailor, R. W. to Anderson, S. E., Apr. 28, 1870, T. A.
Raushenberg, J.P.
189. Bare, W. D. to Bare, Mrs. Susan, Dec. 18, 1869, T. A.
Raushenberg, J.P.
190. Williams, John to Patty, Susannah, Dec. 10, 1870, Wm.
Pullen, M.G.
190. Kaghn, J.J. to Eslinger, Mary L., Dec. 21, 1870, B. F.
Smith, J.P.
190-1. Love, R. R. to Roberts, R. O., May 26, 1870, Geo. A.
Lofton, M.G.
191. Roach, John H. to Roach, Mary, Jan. 6, 1870, S. J. Ward,
J. P.
191. Smith, J. H. to Longly, Sallie, Apr. 14, 1870, J.A.R.
Hanks, M.G.
192. Massengale, A.J. to Wilkie, Francis, Apr. 8, 1870, A.J.
Barnett, N.P. & Ex J.P.

PAGE
192.   Sparks, Richard to Roberts, Emma, Apr. 9, 1870, John P. Love, J.P.

192-3. Deck, Jacob to Anderson, Alice, May 17, 1870, J.J.S. Calaway, M.G.

193.   Millisons, J.A. to Pots, Margret, Mar. 31, 1870, Thomas J. Simmons, M.G.

193.   Grogan, William to Harris, Amanda, Feb. 17, 1870, Z.D. Clark, M.G.

194.   Woods, J. W. to Henderson, Jennie, Mar. 22, 1870, A. W. Gaston, M.G.

194.   McEntire, D.B.F. to Waters, Hellen, May 16, 1870, J.M. Gambrell, M.G.

194-5. Allen, D.E. to Harris, Susie R., Mar. 23, 1870, J.A.R. Hanks, M.G.

195.   Barnette, John W. to Cox, India S., Dec. 25, 1869, Wm. Pullen, M.G.

195.   Richard(?), James to Stone, Rachel, Mar. 29, 1870, T.J. Simmons, M.G.

196.   Heninger, John H. to Flinn, Mary L., Apr. 8, 1871. F.D. Halcomb, M.G.

196.   Adams, S.R.C. to Mitchell, N.C., Mar. 14, 1870, T.J. Simmons, M.G.

196-7. Nance, James to Jestus, Matilda, Oct. 29, 1870, S.J. Ward, J.P.

197.   Inman, T.J.J. to Boatright, Mary E., Mar. 26, 1870, J.L. Compton, M.G.

197.   Irwin, J.L.M. to Surratt(?), Endora(?) C., Mar. 2, 1870, A. W. Gaston, M.G.

198.   Orr, H.H. to Casaely, Lou J., Apr. 20, 1869, Anthony Smith, M.G.

198.   Tranthum, W.C. to Trammell, Mrs. C.T., Sept. 18, 1869, W. H. Porter, M.G.

198.   Miller, David to Gray, Rebecca, May 21, 1870, R. N. Varnell, N.P.

199.   Adams, John (C) to Foster, Jane (C), Feb. 26, 1370, John P. Love, J.P.

199.   Cormiels(?), John (C) to Curry, Caroline (C). Nov. 12, 1869, S. J. Ward, J.P.

199.   Craig, Frank (C) to Glenn, Annie (C), July 21, 1870, S.J. Ward, J.P.

200.   Kingsly, Henry (C) to Russell, Harriet (C), Apr. 6, 1870, T. A. Raushenberg, J.P.

200.   Kieth, Elias (C) to White, Matilda (C), Dec. 20, 1869, W. W. Parker, G.L.(?)

200.   Johnson, Frank (C) to Hawkins, Susan (C), July 28, 1860, M. Gassel, M.G.

201.   Shelton, Wm. (C) to Low, Mariah (C), Jan. 5, 1871, John P. Love, J.P.

201.   Brown, Washington (C) to Chastain, Lou (C), Jan. 12, 1871, Hamilton Young.

201.   Green, Thomas (C) to Rogers, Mary (C), Dec. 19, 1870, J.P. Love, J.P.

202.   Nations, David to Kineaster, Susan G., Oct. 6, 1870, J.J. Harris, M.G.

202.   Killion, Stephen to Eastland, Sallie, Jan. 11, 1872, Andirew(?) Hawkins.

202.   Hoard, A.J. to Mitchell, Charlotte E., Nov. 25, 1871, T. J. Simmons, M.G.

203.   Mitchell, Wiley P. to Mitchell, Ann, Dec. 8, 1871, T.J. Simmons, M.G.

PAGE
203. Green, Amos to Harlan, Caroline, Nov. 23, 1871, George Harlan, M.G.
203. Tappens, John to Bearden, Rosa, Sept. 23, 1871, M.L.C. Clouts, M.G.
204. Copehiot(?), J.E. to Strickling, Nancy, Sept. 8, 1871, W.H.C. Freeman, N.P.
204. Bird, J.W. to Wrinkle, Elisabet, May 3, 1871, G. A. Smith, M.G.
204. Parker, Samuel to Guinn, Sarah, Oct. 21, 1871, Anderson Hawkins.
205. Perry, Robert to Ketchum, Martha, Apr. 13, 1871, W. C. Richardson, M.G.
205. Reid, James to Brooks(?), Elisabeth, Nov. 29, 1870, James Mitchell, M.G.
205. Ran, Lock to Dantzler, Mary Ann, Oct. 29, 1870, J.M. Gambrell, M.G.
206. Mitchell, G.W. to Dowdy, Sarah, July 26, 1871, T.J. Simmons, M.G.
206. Wilson, A. to Dowdy, Margaret, July 24, 1871, T.J. Simmons, M.G.
206. Wimpey, D.H. to Short, Catherine, June 16, 1871, T.J. Simmons, M.G.
207. Brison, James M. to Sloan, Lenora, Feb. 27, 1871, T.J. Simmons, M.G.
207. Pitts, S.B. to Robison, Mrs. Sarah, July 29, 1871, John Wood, TMMES.
207. Jenings, John to Walston, S.J., Aug. 31, 1871, John P. Love, J.P.
208. Buffington, G.W. to Morgan, Kitty, Sept. 23, 1871, T.J. Simmons, M.G.
208. Bryant, J.L. to Boyd, Julia A., Sept. 19, 1871, C.R. McAlister, J.P.
208. White, James to Hardin, Mary J., Apr. 18, 1871, J.J. Harris, M.G.
209. Pogue, James M. to Fraker, Mrs. S.J., Dec. 2, 1871, R.A. Giddins, M.G.
209. Cathey, S.C.R. to Sellers, Nellie, Jan. 23, 1872, G.A. Lofton, M.G.
209. Quin, Wm. R. to Harris, Virginia, Nov. 1, 1871, J.M. Stansbury, M.G.
210. Ellison (Elison), R. to Jolly, E., Mar. 27, 1871, John P. Love, J.P.
210. Huffaker, S. L. to Phipps, Sarah A., Mar. 22, 1871, L.N. Spear, J.P.
210. Parker, R. A. to Kirkpatrick, L.J., Mar. 29, 1871, L.N. Spear, Ex J.P.
211. Satliff, J.P. to Dover, Nora O., Mar. 30, 1871, G.A. Lofton, M.G.
211. Campbell, M.M. to Mitchell, Sallie, Feb. 28, 1871, T.M. McGee, M.G.
211. Worthy, W.T. to Brombow, M.A., Feb. 25, 1871, J.T. Compton, M.G.
212. Gasaway, Almanne to Toller, Winnie, July 21, 1871, T.J. Simmons, M.G.
212. Shepard, J.M. to Richard, Mollie O., Jan. 28, 1871, W.W. Sebastian, J.P.
212. Stephenson, Nathan to Cagle, Eliza, Nov. 3, 1871, Elder J.W. Wilson.
213. Swanson, James to Cook, Frances, Nov. 21, 1870, J.M. Stansbury.

WHITFIELD COUNTY, GA. - MARRIAGE BOOK B(1)

PAGE

223. Lowry, John A. to Richardson, Ann E., Oct. 12, 1871, W.C. Richardson, M.G.

223. Hammontree, L.T. to Murphy, Emma J., Dec. 21, 1871, M.L. Clouts, M.G.

223. Swick, J.P. to Lowery, Fannie E., July 1, 1869, H.C. Carter, M.G.

224. Calhoun, Adam to Montgomery, Mrs. Sarah, Oct. 12, 1871, C. R. McAllister, J.P.

224. McClure, Thomas to White, Mollie, Nov. 20, 1871, J. C. Mitchell, M.G.

224. Wright, H.C. to Henton, Piety E., Nov. 5, 1870, Joseph Terry, M.G.

225. Thompson, J.W. to Stencel(?), Nancy(?), Sept. 7, 1871, Wm. Hardcastle, N.P.

225. Whelchel, B.F. to Sheperd, Sallie, Sept. 16, 1871, A.M. Sharger(?), M.G.

225. Cagle, E. to Johnson, M.E.L., Oct. 23, 1871, C.R. McAllester, J.P.

226. Bell, J.J. to Smith, Mary, Jan. 20, 1872, J.J. Martin, M.G.

226. Jones, C.C. to Taylor(?), Lucinela, Feb. 25, 1871, A.J. Barnet, N.P.

226. Frylock, E.W. to Cox, M.E., June 21, 1871, G.A. Lofton, M.G.

227. Carroll, Richard to Farrington, Collie, Nov. 4, 1871, Z. L. Manis, M.G.

227. Wells, John S. to Lowery, P.E., Feb. 21, 1871, A.W. Gaston, M.G.

227. Davis, L.W. to Edwards, Mary E., Oct. 25, 1871, A.J. Barnett, N.P.

228. Murphy, Joseph C. to Cahoon, Martha A., Oct. 29, 1869, A.R.P. Hambright, M.G.

228. Shuford, E.L. to McKey, Catherine, June 29, 1870, A.W. Gaston, M.G.

228. Strickland, S.J. to Sweeny, S.P., Dec. 21, 1870, Elder J.W. Wilson.

229. Varnell, Wm. E. to Harris, Naerruce(?) J., July 22, 1867, J.M. Stansberry, M.G.

229. Dowdy, M.L. to Milleions, Nancy, Jan. 31, 1872, Z.J. Martin, M.G.

229. Ogledy, F.A. to Tucker, Martha J., Jan. 31, 1871, J.W. Wilson, M.G.

230. Fry, W.D. to Couch, Martha Jane, Sept. 1, 1871, Wm. Hardcastle, N.P.

230. Sleig(?), Daniel to Millner, Jeanette, Oct. 21, 1871, Andrew Warekins.

230. Leach, Charles to Clark, Lucella, Aug. 3, 1870, W.C. Richardson, M.G.

231. Wood, W.H. to Blair, Mrs. Sarah, Apr. 19, 1871, John T. Compton, M.G.

231. Stewart, Henry to Hamilton, Amanda, June 1, 1871, John P. Love, J.P.

232. Smith, Henry (C) to Anderson, Jane (C), Feb. 10, 1871, W.H. Brooker, Ord.

232. Smith, John (C) to Hogie, M.A. (C), Apr. 13, 1871, John P. Love, J.P.

232. Beaver, Jordan (C) to Foster, Sallie, Oct. 19, 1871, Ken M. Cassel.

North West Georgia

The "Cherokee Strip," "Cherokee Country," "Original Cherokee County," or "Pioneer Georgia."

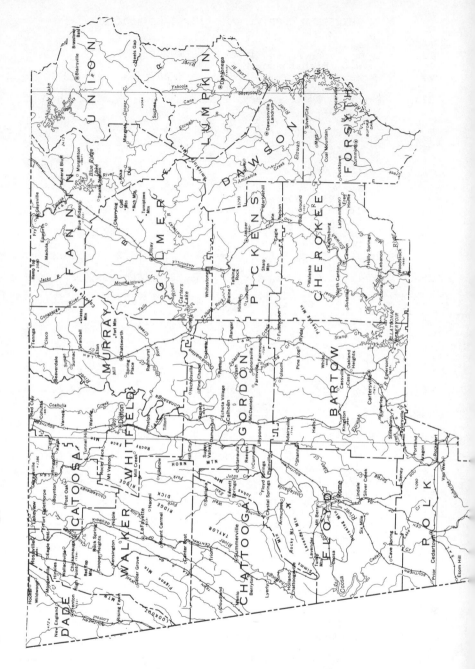

INDEX

607

608

610

611

613

. 422;MARTHA E. MALONE
. 422
BOBO,543;CALLABAT E.,53
. FANNIE ROBINSON,518
. HIRAM,518;JOHN S.,204
. MARTHA,53,301,320
. MINERVA AUTREY,302
. MINERVA AUTRY,313
. SILAS,302,313;TILMAN
. 435;WILLIS,471
BODMAND,HENRY C.,592
. MARTHA A. MACK,592
BODWELL,ANN,589
BOEN,HYRAM,298
BOGAN,SHADERIC,435
. SHADRACH,174;SHADRACK
. 442
BOGER,DANIEL C.,161
. PETE C.,177;PETER C.
. 151,192,199,207,228
. 253,257,262-263
. TERRISSA MOSS,161
BOGGS,541;FRANCES
. PATTERSON,328;JAMES
. A.,328;RICHARD,508
BOGS,WILLIAM,253
BOHANAN,D.J.,584
. DEBBY ANN SMITH,572
. ELIZABETH KETTLE,588
. J.A.,581;JAMES,579
. JULINA SWANSON,578
. L.A. MINAR,581;MARTHA
. 579;MINERVA PROVINCE
. 579;NANCY SHIPP,577
. ROBERT,577;RODA,577
. SARAH J. SIMS,584
. SARAH J. SINAS,584
. THOMAS,578;WILLIAM L.
. 572,588
BOHANNON,
. DEMARY F. HARRIS,9
. JOHN H.,571;LOUISA
. SMITH,571;WILLIAM F.,9
BOHANON,DUNCAN,508
BOICE,CHARLES W.,552
. JANE MOORE,552
BOISLCAIR,AMELIA,431
BOKE,ELAM,207
BOLAN,ELI,471,473
BOLCH,G.A.,262;GEORGE
. A.,151,177
BOLCHE,GEORGE A.,234
BOLDEN,AMANDA MANOR,20
. E.V. DANFORTH,11
. JAMES J.,20;MARY A.,19
. THOMAS E.,11;WILLIAM
. 53
BOLDING,
. ALICE ROBERTS,431
. JOHN C.,431;SUSANNAH
. 418
BOLEN,ALLEN,256;MARY
BOWLS,454;WILLIAM,454
BOLES,ELIZABETH WARD,552
. JAMES H.,552
BOLIN,CICERO,476;CRECY
. 563;ELI,469;ROBERT,575
. SARAH C. CRAIN,476
. SUSAN BURGES,575
. WILLIAM,243
BOLING,J.T.,350;J.W.,70
. JOHN,350;M.J. FOWLER
. 350;MARGRATE WHITE,350
. MARY C. PARROTT,566
. NANCY I.,567;SARAH
. JANE,494;THOMAS,34,547
. WILLIAM T.,566
BOLLAND,ELLEN,383;JOHN
. 383;MARGARET WHITE,383
BOLT,BEREMON,552
. PUNMELIA DIAL,552
BOLTON,ELIZABETH,324
. EMILY,332;JOHN,1;T.W.
. 174;THOMAS W.,149,166

. 173
BOMAN,DRURY M.,437
. FRANCES A.,324;JOHN
. 437;MARY,554;WILLIAM
. O.,462
BOMAR,HATTIE HORN,585
. TOMMIE,518;WILLIAM P.
. 585
BOMAW,JAMES A.,601
. THERSIE M. REDWINE,601
BOMER,A.R.,545
BONA,MATILDA,328
BONCHER,A.L.,394
. ELLISHA L.,394
BOND,
. DELILA A. PHILLIPS,327
. E.P.,272;E.W.,414
. ELENDER,461;ELIAS P.
. 269;ELISHA W.,576
. ELIZA J.,318,334
. FRANCIS,27;GEORGE,457
. HENRY,311,313;J.C.,419
. J.S.,328;JAMES T.,412
. JEFFERSON,176;JOHN G.
. 327;M.L. TUTT,412
. MALINDA,454;MARTHA J.
. JOHNSTON,313
. MARTHA M. JOHNSTON,311
. MARTHA R. EDMONSON,328
. MARY L. MCCLAIN,414
. MARY L. MCLANE,576
. MELINDA HULSEY,457
. NANCY E.,318,334
. SUSAN MAULDEN,419
. T.B.,53;THOMAS,53
. W.M.D.,413;WILLIAM F.
. 399
BONDS,ANDREW,436,441
. CAROLINE,447;EZEKIEL
. 459;JAMES L.,437
. JAMES M.,552;NANCY
. REDMAN,459;TABITHA
. WHITLOW,552;VARDY,436
BONE,BAILEY,505;J.M.,530
. JOHN,507,534,537
. MINNIE,534;MONORE,502
. RICH,503;SARAH,41
. WILLIAM,509
BONHAM,JAMES L.,389
BONNER,ALLEN,551
. BENJAMIN F.,303,313
. ELIZABETH ANN IVEY,551
. LUCY,554;LUCY ANN,556
. SARAH E. HAYNES,303
. SARAH ELIZ. HAYNES,313
. SEYMOUR R.,391
. WILLIAM G.,394
BONNETT,MARTHA,581
BOOKER,MARTHA A.,576
. MARTHA K.,592;NANCY
. 386;PHOEBE,9;REBECCA
. HARVEY,552;RICHARDSON
. 552
BOOKOUT,CHARLES,505
. CHARLES L.,552;EULA
. MEADOWS,512;JESSE,471
. JOHN L.,512;RACHEL,505
. SANDAL MOON,552
BOON,BRUNETTA,156;MARY
. 155,419;SUSSENAH,96
BOONE,R.W.,72
BOOTH,JOHN A.,144
. MARGARET,2;THOMAS,405
BOOTHE,JUDA ANN,556
BORAN,MARY J.,579
BORCH,MAGGIE M.,434
BORDERS,E.,433;ELIZA,419
. LEOLA,434;LUCY
. PULLIAM,423;R.,423
. R.D.,424;REBECCA,424
BOREN,JOHN,160;ROSANNA
. YOUNG,160;SUSANNAH,97
BORING,ALEXANDER,306,313
. ALEXANDER N.,17

. CASSIE A.E. JOHNSON,17
. FRANCIS M.,313,327
. JAMES H.,306,313
. JESSE,446;JOHN,437,439
. JOHN P.,53,134;MAHALA
. BARNETT,306;MAHALY
. BARNETT,313;MARY J.
. THOMPSON,568;MARY M.
. 53;PARMILIA HARRIS,313
. PERMELIA HARRIS,327
. ROADY ROBERTS,306,313
. RUFUS M.,568;THENAY
. MILLER,313;THENERY
. MILLER,306;THOMAS W.
. 306,313
BORN,ELBERT G.,313
. J.AL.,58,83
. RACHEL F. POOL,313
. SARAH,301,319
BORNES,GEORGE,436
BOROUGHS,H.H.,101
BORTLEY,B.H.,501
BOSEMAN,JOHN,313,327
. SARAH C. DARBY,327
. SARAH G. DARBY,313
BOSMON,S.,423
BOSTICK,C.C.,113;ROBERT
. B.,113;TOLIVER,253,262
. 263
BOSTON,JOHN H.,55
. MARTHA MOODY,517
BOSTWICK,ANNY,152;C.C.
. 53;EMILY,554;NANCY,556
BOSWELL,544;ADALINE,33
. E.I. HENDERSON,572
. EMALINE PRESLEY,552
. JOHN,401;JOHN C.,391
. JOSIAH,552;NANCY,11
. RANSOM P.,173;W.M.,572
BOTTOM,THOMAS M.,168
BOTTOMS,
. FRANCES YOUNG,376
. JOHN B.,376;MARTHA F.
. 376;MARY E.,336;NANCY
. L.,329
BOULTON,BENSON O.,37
. LULA WINN,37
BOURN,JAMES B.,438
BOWAN,ALVIRAH,574
BOWDEN,JOHN,529;JOHN C.
. 13;MARY,494
BOWDOIN,CHARLOTTE B.,434
. JOHN W.,419-420,423
. 424-425;JOSHUA,426-427
. JULIA A.,421;MAMIE,429
BOWDON,JOSHUA,415
BOWELL,JOHN C.,401
BOWEN,115;CAROLINE
. STEWART,302,313
. CATHERINE CHRISTIAN
. 416;CRUTHIA A.
. BEARDELL,598;HIRAM,302
. 313;INDIA HOLMES,476
. ISRAEL P.,399;J.F.,36
. J.R.,416;JOHN,185,231
. MARTHA M. EVANS,586
. MERIDA,463;OWEN J.,176
. R.M.,532;RICHARD,403
. S.E.,532;T.H.,598
. W.P.,476;WILLIAM M.
. 586
BOWER,G.A. JOHNSON,428
. W.S.,428
BOWERS,GEORGE,461
. LICENIA MAYFIELD,476
. STEPHEN GRIFFIN,476
BOWIE,ELIZA L.,21;JOSIE
. H.,30
BOWIN,ELIZABETH,575
BOWING,SARAH,563
BOWLEN,B.Y.,531;MINNIE
. TANT,531
BOWLES,ANNIE,430
BOWLIN,ELI,469;MARTHA

. J.,320;SINDA,328
BOWLING,JOHN W.D.,552
. MARY FLETCHER,552
BOWLS,ANNA SANDERS,313
. ELIZABETH,311,325
. HENRY J.,313;MARY,454
BOWMAN,ALFRED D.,585
. AMANDA S.L.,335
. CORNELIUS,421;CURTIS
. C.,495;EDWARD,509
. FRANCES A.,311
. FRANCIS,532;GEORGE G.
. 328;GILBERT,495;J.G.
. 509;JAMES A.,572
. LARKIN,539;LAWSON,149
. LEVI,507;LIZZIE
. STANCEL,539;MARTHA J.
. MCABEE,585;MARY ANN
. NESBIT,421;MARY E.,565
. MILES A.,552;MOURING
. STURDIVANT,552;NANCY
. 324;R.A. LIGHT,328
. SALINA CURD,572;SARAH
. 330;SARAH A.,582
. SARAH C. WHITTEN,583
. SHERWOOD,149;SUSAN
. ROBERTS,509;THADEUS
. C.,583;VINCENT,149
. VINSON,175
BOX,MAHALY,451;SARAH
. WHITEHEAD,450;WILLIAM
. B.,450,495
BOY,BRUELL,449;TEMPEY
. HULSEY,449
BOYCE,JOHN M.,596;M.J.
. HALL,596
BOYD,AMANDA HURT,581
. ANDREW,152,183,228,244
. 440;ANN COVINGTON,426
. ARMINTA,451;C.H.,596
. CELIA ANDERSON,300,313
. DAVID,53;DELILAH,456
. ELIZABETH,449;FANNIE
. E.,5;FANNIE J.,343
. H.D.,471;HALDAK,458
. HESTER ANN,34;IRANA
. 305,313;ISERAL,53
. ISRAEL P.,83;J.W.,426
. JOHN,280,461;JOHN L.
. 300,313;JONATHAN G.
. 421;JOSEPH,467;JULIA
. A.,603;LEVINA,53
. LINDA,600;LINNEY,452
. LYDIA SMALL,590
. MAGGIE,27,516;MARTIN
. 564;MARY,579;MARY A.
. 53;MARY STEWART,421
. MOLLIE LOUER,596
. PRISSY WOOD,305,313
. RICHARD,590;ROBERT,399
. ROBERT M.,53;ROBERT
. T.,399;SAMUEL,305,313
. SARAH C. COX,564
. SARAH E.,343;SUSAN,377
. WILLIAM E.,581
BOYDE,H.D.,473
BOYED,ELIZABETH RICE,328
. JOHN B.,328
BOYLE,CARRIE LEROY,37
. ELIZABETH,340;J.J.,327
. JAMES,328;JOSEPH,596
. JOSEPH D.,328;JOSEPH
. H.,313;LOUIZA LANGLEY
. 596;MARGARET BURNETT
. 328;MARGARET MITCHELL
. 9;MARTIN,9;MARY
. WILDER,328;NANCY,328
. NANCY BOYLE,328
. SARAH JANE HAWKINS,327
. SUSANNA TERRY,313
. WILLIAM R.,37,328
BOZEMAN,
. ARMINDA M. -
. STANFIELD,476;LIDDA

. INGRAM,476;LILA,483
. LINK,476;LIZER J.,484
. M.F.,426;MARGIE,484
. MARY J.,490;MARY M.
. 493;NANCY A.,494
. SHERMAN,476
BRABETT,M.,150
BRACKET,BENJAMIN,457
. SUSAN HUBBARD,457
BRACKETT,BENJAMIN,167
BERRY,167
BRACKETTS,BENJAMIN,149
BRACKIN,JOHN O.,464
BRADBERRY,JAMES,463
BRADBURY,437;BYTHEL,149
BRADEN,BARNEY,297;ELIAS
. 466;JAMES H.,465
BRADFORD,A.,176,187
. ARCHABALD,151
. ARCHIBALD,166,177-178
. 181-182,187,192,222
. ELIZ. J.,160;ELLA T.
. 53;FANNIE,44;G.S.,216
. GEORGE S.,180,187,191
. 203,228;J.A.,422,597
. J.C.,465;JAMES,223,228
. 237,300,313;JOSEPH,149
. 177;JOSEPH H.,170,178
. 180,204,216;JULA,476
. KAREN,318;LUCY,151,301
. 312;M.W. SIMSON,597
. MARTHA J.,477;MARY,447
. MARY M. FARMER,422
. MOSES,301,313;NANCY
. AARON,301;NANCY ARON
. 313;RENIE SMALLWOOD
. 300,313;ROSEA,301
. RUTH,450;SAMUEL,464
. WILLIAM,149,435,463
BRADHORD,A.,176
BRADLEY,ALLEN,453
. ANDREW J.,476;ANN
. WILLIAMS,300,313
. ARDALLIA MCPHERSON,308
. 313;AUGUSTINE E.
. WHEELER,476;AUGUSTUS
. B.,476;B.B.,484-485
. BENJAMIN,150,297
. BENTON,418;BETHAL,300
. 313;BETHEL,167-168
. BITHEL,176,297;BRYANT
. B.,456;BURTON,418-422
. 424-426;CHARLES C.,313
. CROYTON,591
. ELIZABETH S. DONEHOO
. 40;ELLA,519;EVALINE
. 593;F.L. TILLERY,424
. FELIX,562;FRANCES,456
. G.A.A.,424;GEORGE M.
. 40;HAZELA C. WEAVER
. 476;J.C.,424;JASPER
. P.,591;JOEL,308,313
. JOHN,511;JOHN A.,430
. 432;JOSEPH H.,476
. KATIE SMITH,522;LILLY
. JOHNSON,520;LOUISA
. GRAVITT,313;M.,457
. MALINDA EATON,456
. MARGARET,300,317
. MARIAH,591;MARY A.
. THOMPSON,476;MARY J.
. WINKLE,591;MELISSA,162
. NANCY E. TALLY,591
. NEWT,522;POLLY,303,312
. SARAH E. CHAPMAN,562
. SOPHRONIA,492;SUSAN
. A.,591;SUSANNAH
. HARBIN,453;W.A.,523
BRADLY,JOHN,604;NANCY
. HILL,604;SUSAN,9
BRADWELL,ADALINE L.,325
BRADY,BURTON,418;LEWIS
. 462
BRAGG,CAROLINE,545

BRAKEBILL,MARY M.,583
BRAMBLET,ELIZABETH,331
. ELIZABETH KEITH,458
. JOEL,175,458
BRAMBLETT,
. ARMINTA RED,328
. CATHARINE ROBERTS,310
. 313;ELISHA,599;ELIZ.
. 316;ELIZABETH BLALOCK
. 476;ELIZABETH STEWART
. 327;ENOCH,310,313
. HARRIET H. SWILLING
. 313;HARRIET SWILLING
. 309;HENRY F.,108
. HENRY N.H.,310,313
. JAMES A.,328;JAMES K.
. 303;JAMES R.,303,313
. 327-328;JESSE,547
. MALINDA,309,323
. MARGARET ROBERTS,303
. 313;MARY A. SCHROEDER
. 290;MARY HEAD,599
. MARY M.,313;POLLY,303
. 317;REUBEN,547;REUBIN
. 309,313;RUTHA M.
. EDDLEMAN,313;SARAH
. ANN,554;SINDA BOWLIN
. 328;TILLITHA MCENTIRE
. 310,313;W.H.,313
. WILLIAM,476
BRAMBLETTE,E.W.,592
. SARAH L. HALEY,592
BRAMLET,ENOCH,298;JOEL
. 298;N.,447-448
BRAMLETT,H.F.,102;HENRY
. 298;HENRY F.,102,108
. LUCINDA,446;MALINDA
. A.,480;N.,446;NANCY
. BLAYLOCK,476;RUTHA M.
. EDDLEMAN,327;SAMPSON
. 476;SARAH S.,604;W.H.
. 327
BRANAM,JAMES,464
BRANAN,SARAH,53
BRAND,
. BETTIE WILLIAMS,503
. DAVID,476;DELLA,544
. ELIJAH,547,ELISHA,53
. FRANCES,12;LUCY JANE
. MCPHERSON,476;WILLIAM
. 503
BRANDON,438;ELIZABETH
. ADAIR,445;LUCINDA,448
. MOSES A.,445
BRANGFORD,JOHN B.,105
BRANHAM,501;EVA,53
. ISHAM H.,414;JOWELL,74
. MOLLIE MATHEWS,414
. W.R.,414
BRANNEN,
. CINTHIA L. GREEN,47
. HIRAM E.,313;JAMES R.
. 313;MAHALY F. POOL,313
. MARTIN,313;MARY E.
. BAGLEY,313;NANCY
. COLLINS,313;NANCY
. SPRUCE,313;REUBEN W.
. 313;SARAH C. MARTIN
. 313;W.J.,47;WILLIAM
. B.,313
BRANNER,JANE,590
BRANNON,359;ANNA,452
. ARCADIAS,303,315
. BETSY,302,314;CARRIE
. 506;CATHERINE,355,378
. ELIZABETH,357,362
. HIRAM E.,309;JAMES,157
. 158,187,199;JAMES R.
. 305;JANE MANN,157
. JOHN A.,157;JOHN W.
. 347;LEROY,328
. MAHALA F. POOL,307,347
. MARCENA,383
. MARIAN S.T. MAN,158

. MARTHA M.,347
. MARTHA M. BRANNON,347
. MARTIN,276,285,300
. MARY A.S.,334;MARY C.
. 310,322;MARY E.
. BAGLEY,309;MARY L.,349
. MARY MANN,157;MARY
. WILDER,347;MATILDA
. BONA,328;NANCY,551
. NANCY COLLINS,300
. NANCY J. POOL,349
. SAMANTHA,317;SAMANTHA
. A.,332;SARAH C.
. MARTIN,305;SEABORN,349
. SUSANNAH,452;THOMAS
. 347;WILLIAM B.,307,347
BRANON,ANN,285
. CAROLINE E. MAJOR,328
. CATHERINE P.,338
. CHANCY J. POOL,328
. ELIZ. ANN CHAPMAN,33
. J.A.,476;JOHN,33;JOHN
. W.,328;MAHALA POOL,346
. MARTHA J. EZZARD,328
. MARY,552;MARY ANN
. LAMBERT,476;PHEOBE D.
. EDMANSON,328;RICHARD
. W.,346;ROBERT S.,328
. THOMAS G.,328
. VICTORIA LANGLEY,346
. VICTORIA SMITH,346
. W.B.,328;WILLIAM R.
. 346
BRANTLEY,
. ELRUTHA -
. MCCULLOUGHS,552;J.A.
. HENDERSON,419;JOHN M.
. 552;JOHN Q.,53;M.A.
. 419;MARY A.,45;PIETY
. 552;O.L.,54;SARAH,54
. WILLIAM R.,53
BRANTLY,THOMAS R.,92,94
BRASELL,JAMES,438
BRASELTON,AMOS,248
. ELISIAH,160;SARAH,161
BRASH,W.T.,428
BRASHEARS,
. CHARCISSA MCGINNIS,328
. R.D.,464;WILLIAM H.
. 328
BRASLETON,AMOS,244
BRASSELTON,AMOS,243
BRASWELL,533
BRASWELL,517;BELLA FRAY
. 542;CLIFFORD,54;D.L.
. 32;E.L.,67;ELIZABETH
. 335;ELIZABETH GUESS,32
. EPHRIM L.,83;HENRY,27
. J.,399;J.W.,54;JOHN
. 395,527;LARKIN,552
. MARY J.,9;MATLIDA,556
. MATTIE L.,54;NANCY A.
. CLANTON,27;NANCY C.
. 331;SUSANNAH
. MCCULLOUGHS,552;ULEA
. 54;VALENTINE,437;W.T.
. 542
BRAWDRICK,
. FRANCES WEBB,563
. JESSE,563
BRAWNEH,ARMINDA C.,579
BRAY,B.R.,433;C.L.,424
. EMMA,420;F.I.,424
. GEORGIA A. FOSSETT,432
. J.S. HAMILTON,424
. M.L. ALEXANDER,424
. MINNIE,434;MINNIE
. STANCIL,431;NELSON,432
. R.B.,431
BRAYLOCK,WILLIAM,176
BRAZIEL,ROBERT,170
BRAZIELE,
. ELIZA M. CHRISTIAN,456
. WILLIAM B.,456

BRAZIL,ROBERT H.,187
BRAZZIL,ROBERT,170
BRECKINRIDGE,SALLY,518
. W.A.,525
BREDWELL,HENRY,2
BREEDER,ELIZA,308,314
BRENDLE,D.C.,576;HANNAH
. WILSON,576
BRESWELL,EPHRIM L.,83
BREWER,EMELINE,160
. LUCINDA,558;MARY A.H.
. 572;NANCY,555,558
BREWSTER,DOWNS,179;JOHN
. 152,192,199,222-223
. 227-228,234,260,276
. MARGARET,155;MARY J.
. 162;SARAH S.,156
. WILLIAM,229,442
BRIANT,CATHERINE,350
. CLARK H.,313
. ELIZABETH,451
. ELIZABETH BRIANT,451
. ELIZABETH BUTLER,313
. IRANA,321;JOEL,451
BRICE,ELIZABETH,452
BRID,MALISSA A.,592
BRIDES,LEWIS,297
BRIDGEMAN,MARTHA F.,434
. SUSANNAH,452
BRIDGER,LEWIS,307
. OLIVIAT CHRISTOPHER
. 307
BRIDGES,BETHANY,414
. CAROLINE MURRPHY,562
. CHARLES W.,414;CRECY
. BOLIN,563;DICEY A.
. JONES,571;DICEY ANN
. 324;DICY ANN,310
. ELIZA,580;J.W.,414
. J.S.,560;J.W.,414
. JANE,601;JOHN,435,440
. JOHN H.,571;JOHN M.
. 413,569;JULIA CALHOUN
. 601;LEWIS,313;LOUIS
. 563;M.C.,576;M.E.
. LANHAM,589;M.E.M.
. ELLIS,560;MARGARET,310
. 324;MARTHA A.,431
. MARY M. HOLT,413,569
. MATILDA,300,314;NANCY
. E.,593;OLIVET
. CHRISTOPHER,313
. SARAH ANN WEBB,561
. TEMPERANCE,445;THOMAS
. 562;W.A. SPRINGFIELD
. 599;W.L.,589,599;W.M.
. 429,431-433;WILLIAM
. 561
BRIDGMAN,
. CATHERINE L. -
. TAYLOR,157;DANIEL,157
BRIGHT,B.F.,434;HENRY
. 149;SAMUEL,461
BRILEY,511;BERSHEBY,517
BRILTON,
. EMOLINE AUTERY,595
. WILLIAM F.,595
BRIMBURY,AMANDA,551
BRIMER,ANDERSON,39;MARY
. NEWTON,39;W.W.,53
BRINER,MARY BLYTHE,16
. WILLIAM W.,16
BRINKLEY,ADDIE,599;E.F.
. 54;J.F.,54;N.E.,597
. S.L.,55;SUSANNAH,553
BRINN,ROBERT,442
BRINSFIELD,W.W.,515
BRINTLE,LULA,516,523
. NANCY,529;O.F.,529
BRIRNER,
. ANALINE RUTHERFORD,37
. SIMEON B.,37
BRISON,JAMES M.,603
. LENORA SLOAN,603

BRITT,EPHRAIM,437;JOEL
. 136;JOHN,436
BRITTAIN,J.M.,26,49
BRITTON,J.M.,48
BROACH,ELIZABETH,554
. HENDERSON H.,552
. SARAH C. HARRISON,552
BROADAWAY,JOHN,464
BROADERICK,
. ELIZA STRICKLAND,559
. JOHN,559
BROADMAN,BETSY,456
BROADNAX,BELLE SIMS,522
. JOHN H.,522;SUSANNA
. 451
BROADRICK,JOHN,472,474
BROADWELL,ADALINE L.,342
. JESSE,445;JOHN T.,328
. KITY HEMAY,456
. LUCINDA,384;MACENDA
. 456;MARTHA,156;MARTHA
. KIDD,456;MARTHA
. WILLIAMS,544;MARY A.
. 330;MARY A.
. WILLINGHAM,328;MIDAM
. 456;NANCY,155;PHILLIP
. 544;RIZIAH RICE,328
. SARY ANN,156
. SOPHRONIA M. JACKSON
. 445;WILLIAM,456
. WILLIAM T.,328
BROADWICK,MARY I.,564
BROCK,A.N. SHAW,429
. ADALINE,161;ALMARENA
. 563;ANN HAYNES,590
. ANNE HAYNES,589
. CAROLINE,241;E.,535
. G.W.,497;GEORGE,151
. 177,182,192,204,207
. 220,224,227-228,236
. 243,247,250,256,262
. J.E.,177;JAMES R.,393
. 401;JANE HANEY,420
. JOHN,160,507;JORDAN
. 178,194,197,205,222
. JORDAN L.,229;LEACY
. TEDDER,160;LORENA
. SHAW,430;LORRIE,479
. MARTHA,419;MARY E.,419
. NANCY,155;R.,420
. SARAH F.,497;SOLOMON
. 589-590;TEMPY,457
. THOMAS D.,430;W.N.,429
BROCKMAN,91;C.M.,103
. E.F. JOHNSON,29;J.B.
. 148;J.P.,34;JAMES P.
. 71,101,103,108;JOHN
. B.,3,54,101,103,108
. L.M.,29;S.E. GOBER,34
BROCKS,LIZZIE,535
BRODWELL,
. CLENCY A. MCCOY,586
. WILLIAM J.,586
BROGDIN,DAVID,1
BROGDON,A.O. JOHNSON,421
. DAVID,441;FRANCES,320
. 336;G.N.,425;G.W.,421
. 424;LOUISA A.,406
. MARY J.,423;N.J.,421
. OCTAVIA,430;OPHELIE
. STRICKLAND,328;S.J.
. 431;S.J. HARLAN,425
. SARAH,406;W.,281;W.H.
. 328;WILEY,276,406
BROMBELO,EDWARD,439
BROMBLETT,LAURA M.,581
BROMBOW,M.A.,603
BROMLET,A.,596
BROMLETT,
. SARAH J.F. TOWERS,595
. WESLEY,595
BROMLETTE,HARRISON,578
. SARAH E. MILIRONS,578
BRON,SUSIE,517

BROOK,JOHN P.,151,165
. 168,170;MAHALA,373
. SALLIE J.,583
BROOKE,J.P.,187,225,238
. JOHN L.,252;JOHN P.
. 192-193,215-216,221
. 222-224,226,228,234
. 235-236,242,244,247
. 248,250,255,266;MARY
. ANN,161;WILLIAM,208
. 214,217;WILLIAM C.,214
BROOKER,JOHN W.,588
. REBECCA L. QUILLIAN
. 588
BROOKOUT,JESSE,474
BROOKS,543;ABBY,480
. ADALINE SPENCE,347
. AMANDA A. SPENCE,327
. AMANDA SPENCE,313,349
. BRADFORD,552;C.A.A.
. 374;CASSANDRA A.A.,374
. CATHARINE,306,312
. CATHERINE,498;CHARLES
. A.,54;CHARLEY,499
. CLARINDA,307,315
. CYNTHIA ANN IRWIN,552
. DELILAH JONES,552
. DRUCILLA,161;ELIJA N.
. 34;ELISHA,496
. ELIZABETH,368,603
. ELIZABETH G. MOSS,155
. ELIZABETH STEGALL,155
. ELIZABETH T. TRIPP,163
. FANNIE,561;FRANCES
. GEORGE,115;GEORGE F.
. 54;HENRY,453;J.E.,347
. 420;JACOB S.,3;JAMES
. 522,552;JAMES M.,155
. JAMES W.,328;JANE P.
. HOOD,552;JOEL,552
. JOHN,21,98,308,313,496
. 507;JOHN F.,155;JOHN
. P.,149,183;JOSEPH G.
. 19;JOSEPHINE,54
. LARKIN,552;LILLIE MAY
. 430;LIZZIE,522,535
. LOCKY MCWIRE,453
. LOUISA BIDDY,308,313
. LOUISE N.,54;LUNIE A.
. RIDEN,347;M.J.,54
. M.L.,54;MAHALA,372
. MARGARET CHANDLER,552
. MARTHA HADDEN,313
. MARTHA HADDER,307
. MARTHA KIRK,21
. MARTHA S. BURRISS,327
. MARTHA WILLIAMS,19
. MARY,327,431;MARY
. BROOKS,327;MARY C.,331
. MARY EAVES,420;MARY
. L.,54;MATILDA GILBERT
. 328;MICAJAH,496;MOSES
. 458;NANCY A.,19
. NANCY J. PRICE,34
. NANCY TATE,5
. NATHANIEL,163;NEATA
. FOWLER,301,313;P.L.W.
. 438;PASCHAL,436;POLLY
. 309,312;RICHARD,301
. 313;RICHARD B.,307,313
. 327;ROBERT A.,54
. SALIA,478;SAMANTHA,349
. SAMUEL,298;SLATER
. DPERSON,458;SUSAN,54
. 310,316;SUSN AMANDA
. 333;WILLIAM,94-95,327
. 463,498;WILLIAM F.,5
. WILLIAM S.,54;WILLIAM
. T.,313,349;WILLIAM
. THOMAS,347;WILSON,327
BROOKSHEAR,JOHN,471-472
BROOME,EMMA
. COAMINGS,560

. F. CALLAWAY,560
BROSELL,SUSAN J.,327
BROTHERTIN,LEVI,406
. MARTHA A. GUDGER,406
BROTHERTON,CATHERINE,571
. LEVI,407-410,560,564
. 565-566,568,570,574
. 575,578;MARTHA,591
. PARALE WILLIAMS,413
. 572;WILLIAM H.,413,572
BROUGHTON,MELISSA,573
BROWN,136-137,342,506
. A.A.,4;A.C.,54;A.E.,54
. ABIGAIL HANEY,304
. ABIGAIL HONEA,304,313
. ABIGAIL HONEY,304;ADA
. 591;ALEXANDRIA,464
. AMANDA,309,312,578
. AMANDA J. BELL,19
. AMBROSE,455;AMOS,3,89
. 90,455;ANN,556;ANN E.
. CROMER,45;ARMINDA,309
. ASBURY,552;B.B.,577
. 579;B.F.,421;B.J.,370
. BENJAMIN,560;BENJAMIN
. J.,327;BENJAMIN N.,43
. C.B.,574;CAROLINE R.
. TANNER,15;CATHERINE
. 489;CHARLOTTE CHAFFIN
. 157;CINDERELLA
. SLAUGHTER,453;CLABORN
. 285;CLARA DUNKIN,455
. CLAYBORN,54;COLLINS
. 237;DANIEL,260;E.J.,54
. E.W.,54;ED,503;EDITH
. 557;ELIJAH,453;ELISHA
. 157;ELIZA,155;ELIZA
. HUGGINS,328;ELIZABETH
. 309,317,319,335,423
. 500,574;ELIZABETH A.
. 321;ELIZABETH BULLOCK
. 552;ELIZABETH CAHAON
. 560;ELIZABETH CROW,451
. ELIZABETH E.,332
. ELIZABETH J.,315,330
. ELIZABETH PARKER,552
. ELIZABETH PHARR,159
. ELIZABETH PINYAN,267
. ELIZABETH STUDLEY,552
. ELIZABETH WINGO,48
. ELLA,531,536;EMELINE
. ROGERS,348;EMMA A.,476
. EPHRAIM,278;EULA,54
. F.G.,424;FLEETA F.
. CUNNINGHAM,54
. FRANCES,13;FRANCES E.
. WEST,421;FRANCES
. NAYLOR,313;FRANCIS
. G.W.,508;GEORGE,552
. GEORGE R.,599;GEORGE
. W.,3,501;GRACIS
. MANNING,589;H.A.
. WOODALL,476;HEMSBERRY
. 158;HENRY,57,573
. HIRAM,86,109;HIRMA,54
. IRENA MATHEWS,445
. J.C.,112;J.F.,419
. J.H.,86;J.M.,509
. J.R.T.,499,506,509
. JAMES,54,162,285
. JAMES A.,564;JAMES E.
. 396;JAMES H.,54,142
. 304,313,390;JAMES M.
. 136;JAMES R.,54;JAMES
. W.,54,313;JANE R.,10
. JANE TAYLOR,455;JANE
. WEEMS,445;JASPER,523
. JASPER N.,19;JEMIMA
. 464;JENNIE,34;JESSE
. 253,257,259-260,262
. 263;JOHN,15,96-97,100
. 127,285,298,301,435
. 441,451,507,517,544

. JOHN C.,54;JOHN D.,31
. JOHN E.,239;JOHN R.,29
. JOHN T.,327;JOSEPH,45
. 348,476,547;JOSHUA,328
. 589;JUNIUS CORNELIA,43
. KATIE,430;L.,353
. L.A.F.,343;L.L.,531
. LARKIN,445;LEWIS J.
. 397;LIZZIE,539;LOU
. CHASTAIN,602;LOU E.
. 370;LOUISA,378;LOUISA
. E.R.,317,332;LOUIZA
. 330;LUCRETIA,555;LUCY
. 539;LUDDIE,54;LUELLER
. CANNON,348;LUTIE,54
. M.,476;M.A.E.,54;M.H.
. LEONARD,328;M.H.
. ROGERS,599;M.J.
. BENNETT,31;M.L.,54
. MANLY,244,248,252,254
. MARGARET,532,558;MARK
. 500;MARTHA A. MERRITT
. 158;MARTHA GASP,564
. MARTHA J.,569;MARTHA
. R.C.,28;MARTHA R.C.
. BROWN,28;MARTIN,298
. MARY,28,34,449,590
. MARY A.V. WILLSON,476
. MARY ANN,309,318
. MARY ANN JOHNSON,162
. MARY E. SMITH,328
. MARY J. BAKER,29;MARY
. LAWRENCE,573;MATILDA
. 54;MATTIE,31
. MATTIE J. EATON,38
. MILLIE,597;MILLY,368
. MORDACA,463;NANCY,155
. 529,553;NANCY ANN,569
. NANCY BROWN,155;NANCY
. E.,313,327,483
. NANCY J. ANDERSON,476
. NANCYVILLE,155;OLA
. KIRK,535;OSCAR,535
. P.A.,54;R.E.,54;R.L.
. BUTLER,419;R.P.,328
. RACHEL,461;REBECCA
. MASON,301;RENA E.,447
. ROBERT,28,54,328,348
. 547;S.,285;S.M.,54
. SAIRA GARRETT,327
. SAMUEL,285,298;SARAH
. 338;SARAH A.,421,570
. SARAH BARNETT,313
. SARAH GARRETT,370
. SARAH GRAVITT,300,313
. SARAH J.,20;SARAH L.
. HAMMETT,43;SHADY,526
. SILAS,54,97-98;T.J.
. 539;T.P.,539;TEASSELY
. 381;THOMAS,1,108,184
. 313,327;TILMAN,514
. W.B.,571;W.H.,396
. W.J.,38;W.L.,54,70,86
. W.M.,476;W.S.,52,54,69
. W.W.,48,532;WALKER,518
. WASHINGTON,602;WILDS
. 159;WILLIAM,124,267
. 517,574;WILLIAM F.,54
. WILLIAM G.,54;WILLIAM
. H.,155,445;WILLIAM J.
. 523;WILLIAM L.,18,552
. WILLIAM R.,300,313
. WILLIAM S.,4,10,12,15
. 16,20,23,49;WINNIE,54
BROWN,B.B.,576
BROWNE,HENRY,472;JAMES
. G.,417;JOHN,472
. RACHEL P. ELLINGTON
. 417;ROBERT,471;WILSON
. 472
BROWNLOW,
. CAROLINE HUGGINS,345
. DELILAH C. CRUSE,328
. ISAAC M.,328,345;J.A.

616

. 427;JAMES A.H.,309,313
. JANE ANN AUSTIN,309
. 313;JOHN,345;LUCINDA
. C.,332;LUCINDA
. GUTHRIE,328,346;NANCY
. 346;OBED,346;OBEDIAH
. 328;SUSAN WIMPY,345
BROYLES,C.E.,559;MARY
. RUTHE,571;W.L.,573
BRUCE,ARULLA MORGAN,578
. ATALINE VANDIKE,328
. BURTON,159;CAROLINE
. 478;COLEMAN,455;EDDY
. 547;ELIAS,466
. ELIZABETH MAYFIELD,159
. GEORGE,313,466
. HORATIO,466;HUGH,465
. JAMES,328,476;JESSE
. 599;JOHN,466;JOSHUA
. 328;KEZIAH K.,343;LU
. WILBORN,599;MANDA T.
. 487;MARGARET NOWILL
. 455;MARTHA DOSS,328
. MARTHA E.,488;MARY A.
. HENSON,327;MARY
. PADGET,476;MILLY HALL
. 328;NANCY CAIN,313
. NATHAN L.,328;QUILLER
. 464;REBECCA,333
. SAFRONIA JOHNSON,328
. SAMUEL G.,327;SARAH
. N.,333;W.G.,578
. WILLIAM P.,328
BRUDALL,P.H.,93
BRUICE,ADLINE,382
. AMANDA,367;BENJAMIN
. B.,349;CARINDER,382
. DANIEL,1;FRANCIS M.
. 327;MARTHA A. MOULDER
. 349;MILY HALL,382
. NANCY THOMPSON,349
. NATHAN L.,382;P.B.,349
BRUISTER,JOHN,440
BRULISON,MARTHA,477
BRUMBALOW,JACKSON,54
. ROBERT M.,7;SUSAN J.
. BULLARD,7;WILLIAM,1,3
BRUMBELO,EZEKIEL,92
. WILLIAM,89,91,472,474
BRUMBELOE,EZEKIEL,91
BRUMBELOW,CAROLINE,306
. 319;ISAAC,305,313
. JANE SIMMONS,308,313
. JOEL,305,313;LEDDY
. SNEAD,305,313;LETTY
. SNEAD,305,LINDSEY,308
. 313;MARY,564;MARY A.
. 593;NANCY SNEAD,305
. 313;SARAH,306,321
. SOPHIA J.,39;WILLIAM
. 443
BRUMBL,WILIA,91
BRUMBOLO,JACKSON,82
BRUMBY,CARIE L. CASON,39
. CARRIE C.,55;EPHRAIM
. R.,28;JAMES,77;JAMES
. R.,7;JOHN G.,39
. LAURA M. SMITH,7;MARY
. MCPHERSON,28;T.M.,54
BRUMLEY,JAMES,443
BRUN,G.W.,600;MOLLIE E.
. HANKS,600
BRUNTLY,WILLIAM R.,98
BRUSE,MARY A.,329
BRUSTER,JOHN D.,552
. MARGARET M.,554
. SALLY H. GUINN,552
BRUTON,ALBERRY,356
. ELMINA CARUTH,356
. ENOCH W.,328;JOYCE,330
. MARTHA,327;MARY A.
. ELLIS,328;SARAH P.,356
BRUTZ,M.A.,358
BRUVE,B.B.,580

. MELVINA V. MCCLURE,580
BRYAN,CHLOE ANN,164
. ELIZABETH,343
. GEORGIA HUNT DODGINS
. 30;JAMES,467;JESSE,552
. JOHN P.,49;MARY
. BUFFINGTON,456;MOSES
. 456;NANCY TIDWELL,552
. R.H.,30;ROBERT R.,131
. SALEMA MITCHELL,49
. SARAH J.,492
BRYANT,A.M.J.S.,568
. ADALIZA A.,338;ADDY
. 370;ADER,374
. ALEXANDER,495;AUSTIN
. 436;CALEB B.,547
. CALVIN P.,476
. CAROLINE SWEATMAN,575
. CHLOE ANN,164;CLARK
. H.,308;E.L.,179
. ELIZABETH,371,480,490
. ELIZABETH BUTLER,308
. ELIZABETH MURPHY,476
. EVORY F.,476;FRANCES
. A.,39;FRANCIS PENDLEY
. 43;HARRIETT F.T.,43
. IRANA,304;IRENE,369
. J.L.,603;JAMES,43
. JAMES S.,395;JESSE,575
. JOEL M.,150;JOHN,476
. JULIA A. BOYD,603
. MARTHA,333;MARY E.,591
. MARY JEFFERSON,476
. MARY MEALER,476
. NARCISSA,480;PEELER
. 495;PULER,495;R.R.,54
. RACHEL,537;S. TABITHA
. CHAPEL,32;SARAH E.
. MEALER,476;SUSAN,54
. T.J.,54;TARZEN,467
. THOMAS F.,32;W.L.,278
BRYNER,
. ELIZABETH MARTIN,453
. JOEL H.,453
BRYSON,A.J.,421;F.A.
. GOODMAN,421;GERTRUDE
. J.,49;JAMES H.,496
. L.A.,427;L.J. SCOTT
. 427;MARY,423
BUCHAMON,
. CHARLES W.F.,552
. LOVEY B. ANDERSON,552
BUCHANAN,157;AMANDA,308
. EDNA A.,34;ELIZA N.
. 555;JOSIE H. BOWIE,30
. MARY A.,331;SARAH C.
. 306,324;SOPHIA,43
. THOMAS J.,30
BUCHANON,
. FRANCES J. GANN,34
. JAMES B.,34;SUSAN D.
. 481
BUCHER,ANIRICK HORNE,578
. GEORGE B.,578
BUCK,JOHN,436
BUCKANAN,AMANDA,325
BUCKANNON,H.F.,48
BUCKELOW,
. DRUCILLA BLAKE,445
. JAMES M.,445
BUCKHANNON,JAMES,474
BUCKNER,CLARA,431;EMMA
. 426-427;I.N.,418,420
. 421,423-424,427-428
. ISAAC N.,400;J.W.,424
. 425;JOSEPHINE POPE,50
. LOTTY,306,322;WILLIAM
. 144;WILLIAM E.,50
BUENDING,WILLIABE,170
BUFF,MARY,517
BUFFINGTON,A.V. TEACH,34
. A.V. TEAL,34;DAVID,510
. ELIZABETH,600
. ELIZABETH GILMORE,449

. EZEKIEL,449;G.W.,603
. J.A.,144;J.T.,34;JOHN
. A.,95;KITTY MORGAN,603
. MARY,456;NANCY,450
. NANCY GILMORE,449
. SARAH A.,584;THOMAS
. 449
BUFORD,HENRY,395;J.L.
. 507;SUSAN,375
BUGG,ANSOLEM,463
BUGGETTAS,BURTON,97
BUICE,ALONZO,347;AMANDA
. 336;AMANDA E.,346
. AMANDA E. BUICE,346
. ELISHA,346;ELISTA,347
. ELIZABETH E.,340
. HENRY B.,346;JAMES D.
. 54;LOUIE,54;MARCENA
. 327;MARCENA BUICE,327
. MARGARET HALL,347
. MARY,323;MINNIE L.,54
. NANCY THOUSON,346
. NOBLE J.,328
. REBECCA C. MARTIN,347
. ROBERT,327;SARAH F.
. GILBERT,328;SUSAN,343
. WILLIAM H.,346
BUISE,ELISHA,111-112,119
. J.,111;JUSH,112
BUISHOP,CLABORN,95
BULFINCH,254
BULL,ALEXANDER L.,327
. ZILPHA A. PRUITT,327
BULLANGER,M.S.,98
BULLAR,BENJAMIN,15
BULLARD,BENJAMIN,4,6,9
. 11,13-15,19,21,24,26
. 35,42,47,49,52,54,75
. 105,108;DANIEL,41
. E.P.,42;ELIZABETH A.
. 557;ELLINOR F.,556
. JASPER,26;JOHN,552
. MARGARET,54;MARTHA F.
. LEE,41;MATILDA
. REYNOLDS,552;MICAJAH
. 54;NANCY MCCAIN,26
. ROBERT,54;RUBY,54
. SUSAN J.,7;WILLIAM,1
. 54,105,108
BULLOCH,JAMES A.,518
BULLOCK,A.G.,536;ADA
. DEAN,534;ALBERT,512
. ALEXANDER,498;ALICE
. 503;C.H.S.,518
. ELIZABETH,552;FRANK
. 514;GEORGE,543;HENRY
. 534;J. HOMER,518
. JAMES,86;JOSEPH S.,94
. JUDA,544;LULA ELLIOTT
. 543;N.H.,498;N.T.,503
. 507,516;NANCY EDWARDS
. 552;NAT,529;RUFUS B.
. 132;S. CATHERINE,498
. SHERMAN,512;WALTER,507
. WILLIAM,552;WILLIE,498
BULLS,AMERICA,320,336
. MICHEL,330
BUN,CATHERINE,54
. WILLIAM,465
BUNCH,
. EVORY F. BRYANT,476
. HENRY C.,476;JANE E.
. ANDERSON,476;JOHN,476
. MAHALA SHEPPARD,589
. MANDEY,478;MARTHA J.
. MOSS,481;WILLIAM S.
. 589
BUNDRUM,537
BUNGARNER,A.,298
BUNKLEY,SUSANNAH,553
BUNN,ANNIE KNIGHT,525
. GEORGE,421;M.H.,54
. MOLLY S. KINSER,421
. WILLIAM C.,525

BUNSON,TEBITHA,594
BURCH,COLUMBUS,431;G.W.
. 424;J.L.,430;JAMES,395
. 410;LILLIE MAY BROOKS
. 430;M.F.,422;REBECCA
. 155;S.G. CONAWAY,424
. SARAH A.E. GREEN,431
BURCHFIELD,ELVIRA,593
. SUSAN TONY,579
. WILLIAM F.,579
BURCKLE,
. LESSETT KRUSCHER,583
. MARTIN,583
BURDEN,E.H.,523;EMMA F.
. WHITE,14;SIDNEY M.,14
BURDETT,JOHN,242
BURDIN,SAMUEL,101
BURDINE,ELIZA,162
BUREN,AMANDA,428
BURFORD,MELINDA,457
. NANCY E. BROWN,313,327
. PACIFIC,325;PRISCILLA
. 455;SARAH,455;SUSAN
. 302,322;THOMAS,297
. THOMAS A.,313,327
BURGE,H.A.,54;J.B.,54
. THOMAS,17
BURGES,D.F.,477;HENRY
. C.,575;MARY F. MANLY
. 477;SARAH,575;SARAH
. BURGES,575;SUSAN,575
BURGESS,DIDEMA,577
. EDWARD,462;LEMUEL,38
. LINDY,428;M.D.,433
. MARY,365;MARY ANN,486
. MARY BARTON,38;NANCY
. 577;NANCY E.,25
BURGIS,JAMES C.,477
. LOURANA MOONEY,477
BURHAN,A.W.,539
BURIN,ELIZA,561
BURK,FRANCIS,469;HUGH
. H.,564;HUGHS,472
. JAMES A.,561;JOHN,471
. JOHN H.,597;L.M.E.
. CRYER,597;MARY HIDE
. 561;SARAH A. CROW,564
. THORNTON,528;WILLIAM
. 474
BURKE,
. CHRISTIAN ALLEN,552
. ELIZABETH PONDER,422
. H.H.,422;JOHN,210,225
. 552;JOHN W.,395;SARAH
. ANN,564
BURKHALTER,
. FANNY WEAVER,410;JOHN
. 410
BURKHOLTER,J.T.,77
BURKS,JOSEPH,472;SARAH
. ANN,564
BURLISON,D.W.,475;ISAAC
. 487;ISABELLA,475
BURN,JAMES,192
BURNAP,ANNIE S.,54;C.C.
. 54;GEORGE S.,54
BURNELL,
. HARRIET M. WHITTLE,570
. ZACHARIAH N.,570
BURNES,112;JAMES,151
. LUCY COKER,552;THOMAS
. J.,474;WILSON,552
BURNET,HIRAM,2;NANCY,562
BURNETT,BENJAMIN,98
. JOHN,270;L.,136
. LEMUEL,131;MARGARET
. 328;NANCY,337;S.J.,148
. SION,176;SUSAN ANN,33
BURNEY,ELIZABETH D.,40
. I.H.,54;J.H.,145
. SARAH,447
BURNHAM,ELISHA B.,552
. MARY L. WILLINGHAM,552
BURNS,198,222,227;ALEY

. 139;MABRY TURNER,515
. MARGARET A. LEWIS,566
. MARGARET V. WINN,412
. MARTHA,539;MARTIN,452
. MARY,539,556;MARY C.
. 55;MARY E.,30;MARY L.
. HENDERSON,604;MAUD,55
. MERRIT,552;NANCY,501
. 539;NANCY CAMP,501
. NANCY HARDIN,445
. NANCY HUNT,455;NANCY
. MAXWELL,155;NANCY MAY
. WHITLOW,552;NANCY
. PALMORE,552;NARCISSA
. 589;O.,458;OSAMUS,469
. PAUL,55;PENN,519
. ROBERT,220;SARAH,55
. SARAH J.,55;STEPHEN
. 455;T.A.,55;THOMAS,55
. THOMAS L.,55;WALTON
. 445;WILLIAM,436,438
CAMPBELL,97,112,117,518
. A.,399;A.K.,105;ALICE
. 55;AMELIA M. KEMP,18
. C.R. WYLIE,425
. CHARLIE,394;DUNKEN,440
. E.J.,574;ELIAS,303,313
. ELIZA MCALL,306;ELIZA
. MCCALL,306,313;ELLA
. SAMS,604;FANNIE
. STEWART,427;G.B.,55
. H.S.,297;HARRIET L.,14
. HENRY J.,306,313
. HENRY S.,175,455
. ISABELLA,323;ISABELLA
. D.,300;J.B.,63,74,84
. J.G.,82,112;J.L.,425
. J.V.,122;JAMES,441
. JANE,428;JANE CARROLL
. 303,313;JOHN,55;JOHN
. B.,56,65,80;JOHN BELA
. 145;JOHN G.,4-23,25,42
. 50,69,111,132,145
. JOHN N.,118;LEAH
. LUTES,406;M.E.,418
. M.G.,7;M.M.,603
. MARIAH J. HILL,434
. MARY,423;MARY A.,55
. MARY M.,19;MARY
. MERCKS,455;MONROE F.
. 18;N.,117;NANCY,300
. 314,366;NANCY E.,55
. O.C.,398,405,427;O.W.
. 434;PORTER,55;ROBERT
. 441,547;ROBERT H.,406
. S.A.,55;S.J.,604
. SALLIE MITCHELL,603
. SAMUEL B.,470;SARAH
. E.,53,55;SYNTHA,551
. T.M.,518;THOMAS,438
. THOMAS N.,497;TOM,532
. W.H.,8,12,14-15,19,21
. 24,26,28,32-35,44-45
. 48,50;W.M.,539;W.T.
. 579;WILLIAM,437,441
. 502;WILLIAM H.,6,8,11
. 141;WILLIAM T.,579
CAMPTON,
. TEMPERANCE S. DAVIS,23
. THOMAS,23
CAMRON,HENRY,495
CANADA,DAVID,2;WILLIAM,2
CANADY,MARY M.,483
CANDDY,JAMES,465
CANDEN,M.J.,195
CANDLER,SAMUEL C.,152
. 154
CANEISTER,ALEXANDER,570
LABELIA WARD,570
CANINGTON,SUSIE,584
CANNINGTON,S.,584;SUSIE
. 584
CANNON,BENTON,441;DISEY
. SMITH,348;ELIZABETH

. 318,332;ELLIS,547
. HENRY,547;HIRAM,547
. HULDA,422;ISAAC F.,547
. JOHN,152,177,191,193
. 195,207;LUELLER,348
. M.F.,464;M.J.,418
. MARTHA,366;MARY E.,481
. MOSES C.,348;SARAH J.
. BROWN,20;WILLIAM J.,20
CANON,MARY,32
CANTON,165
CANTREL,JANE,595;MARY
. 562;MOSES,469;PALINE
. 365
CANTRELL,55;BASIL S.,268
. 270;C.F. EATON,40
. CALLIE,526;CAROLINE
. 596;CATHERINE MORGAN
. 350;E.A.,410;E.E.
. JACKSON,329
. ELIZ. M.J. HUTCHINS
. 306;ELIZABETH,459
. ELIZABETH A. WOOLY,452
. ELIZABETH CANTRELL,459
. ELIZABETH HUDSON,307
. 314;ELIZABETH
. HUTCHINS,313;EVELINE
. 490;GEORGIA A.,342
. HANNAH TERRY,380;J.C.
. 329;JAMES,149,269,459
. 465,542;JAMES O.,350
. JOHN,463,477;JOHN C.
. 270;JOHN H.,20;JOHN
. O.,105;JOSHUA,478,484
. JULIA,593;LEAH L.,482
. M.F.,534;MARTHA,270
. 582;MATTIE A.,524
. MERRELL,459;MOSES,150
. 297;MOSES M.,452
. MOSSELLA JOHNSON,477
. POLLY ANN,270
. RHODA ANN PRESLEY,477
. ROANCY L. EATON,20
. ROBERT N.,271;S.E.,422
. SARAH BUTLER,350
. SARAH E.,380;SARAH
. THURMOND,459;SHERMAN
. 477;SMITH,380;STEPHEN
. 268,270-271;T.B.,40
. TERRELL,470;THOMAS,465
. THOMPSY,306;THOMSEY
. 320;W.J.,410;W.T.,482
. 488;WILEY,560-561
. WILLIAM F.,482,494
. WILLIAM H.,350
. WILLIAM R.,410;WILSON
. 306-307,313-314
CANTRIL,JAMES,165,167
. MOSES,166;THOMAS,166
. 169
CANTWELL,EMILY,307
CAPE,ELIZABETH,455
. FRANCES,455;FRANCES
. C.,12;HASELTINE
. WILSON,12;J.R.,55
. LOUIS B.,12;M.D.
. YANCY,477;M.L.,55
. MARIAH IVIE,477
. MARTHA E.,21;MISSEY
. ANN,322;MISSISSIPPI
. 330;NANCY ELIZ.,475
. NANCY J.,339;NEPSIAN
. 380;SARAH E.,35;W.L.
. 477;WILLIAM D.,477
CAPEHART,JACOB,247,401
. 547;JAMES L.,564-566
. 568,574,576;S A C ,421
CAPELAN,THOMAS,1
CAPER,NANCY C.,9
CAPHORT,QUEEN,599
CAPPICE,ADAM,580
. MARGARET A. DUCKETT
. 580
CAPPS,THOMPSON,547

CARD,MARTHA C.,563
CARDELL,MARY,488
CARDEN,CATHERINE,576
. FRANCES A. GENTRY,594
. J.A.,594;JAMES,552
. MARY BRANON,552;SARAH
. 567
CARDER,IVERSON,461
. MARTHA J.,594;THOMAS
. 461
CARDIN,JAMES,471
CARDON,ANONYMOS,576
. DARAH SMITH,576
. MARTHA CANTRELL,582
. SARAH SMITH,576
. WILLIAM M.,582
CARE,MALISSA,156
CARGILE,EMMA ODELL,587
. LEWIS B.,587
CARGILL,JOHN N.,437
. THOMAS,436
CARIE,G.T.,134
CARLILE,JAMES,55;JAMES
. H.,55;WILLIAM,1
CARLISLE,BERY H.,574
. ELIZABETH,301,324
. JAMES,455;LATITIA
. DOOLY,579;NATHAN,579
. REBECCA HAMBY,455
. RUTHA DOOLY,574;SUSAN
. 571
CARLTON,EDNA,545
. ELIZABETH,449;JAMES
. W.,99;REBECCA,420
. W.I.,405
CARMICHAEL,
. ADDIE EMBRY,536
. ELIZABETH,1;EVELINE
. FINCHER,161;H.R.,161
. J.T.,55;J.W.,55;M.J.
. 55;MARY,555;NANCY,557
. WILLIAM,536
CARMON,JANE,561
CARNES,C.T.,55,137
. CHARLES T.,24;EDWARD
. 462;EMILY LAMB,351
. GREEN,2;HENRY,351
. HUBBARD,547;HUBBARD
. P.,159;JAMES,2;JAMES
. D.,39;JOHN J.,106
. JOSEPH,2;LOU E. SMITH
. 39;LYDIA,2;MARY A.,351
. NANCY,507;NANCY A.
. BATSON,24;OLEVIA C.
. LAWSON,477;RICHARD,95
. RUTH,547;SINDEY WELCH
. 159;THOMAS,547;W.B.,55
. 135;WILBORN W.,477
. WILLIAM,547
CARNEY,H.A. HAYNES,425
. JAMES J.,425;MARTHA
. 492;MARTHA A. EVANS
. 477;SPARTAN G.,477
CARNS,MANERVA,336
CAROUTH,AUGUSTA O.,359
. GEORGIA A. BELL,359
. ROSS A.,359
CARPENTER,
. ARTAMINA MATHIS,160
. ELIZABETH D. BURNEY,40
. ELIZABETH MCGUIRE,568
. HATTIE,27;J.O.,54
. JACKSON,426;JACOB,552
. JAMES L.,416;JAMES O.
. 40;JED,560;JOEL C.M.
. 391;JOSHUA S.,391
. E.,591;M.A.,597
. M.A.H. PIERCE,426
. MARGARET BLAIR,552
. MARY,559;MITCHEL C.
. 568;N.G.,568;NARCISSA
. GLOVER,560;PERMELIA
. A.,562;SARAH,491

. VIRGINIA,597;WILLIAM
. 461
CARR,AMERICA,552
. AMERICA CARR,552;ANN
. MORGAN,445;CALDONA
. STRIPLIN,477;ENOCH S.
. 478-479;JAMES,160,297
. JEPTHA P.,163;JESSE
. G.,552;JOHN,442-443
. 552,583;KINCHEN,404
. LAURESSA,160;LAURESSA
. CARR,160;LOARER,158
. MARY A.,55
. NARCISSA M. DOSS,163
. NATHANIEL Y.,459
. PIETY BRANTLEY,552
. R.S.,598;ROBERT,462
. RODY A.M.,305,319
. RUTH A. SWANSEN,583
. SARAH A. KENNEDY,459
. SARAH CARDEN,567;SARY
. BATES,158;SUSANNAH,455
. T.S.,477;TOLBERT,55
. TOLIVER S.,256;WILEY
. M.,437;WILLIAM A.,445
. WILLIAM L.,567
CARREL,ABASLEM J.,563
. MARTHA C. CARD,563
CARRELL,ANDERSON,297
. DENIS,298;JACOB,298
. JAMES R.,38;MARY
. WILSON,38;SARAH,311
. 314;SOLOMON,298
. SOPHIA S.,582;W.W.,13
. 16,27,33,47,49,76,96
. 97,100;WILLIAM W.,97
CARRIE G.T.,27
CARRIE,B.F.,523;B.H.,61
. 70;C.T.,17,28;G.F.,23
. G.T.,5,10,12,17,24,28
. 29-30,34,36-37,39,46
. 48-50,145,148;J.
. THEODORE,30;LULA
. BRINTLE,523;SUSIE,25
. WILLIAM W.,96;YENOBIA
. HARRIS,30
CARRINS,A.,582
CARRIO,G.T.,129;Z.T.,129
CARROL,DAVID,466;DENIS
. 175;JAMES,518
CARROLL,531;A.B.,497
. ALEXANDER,172
. BENJAMIN,443;CAROLINE
. WHALEY,582;CELIA,300
. 314;COLLIE FARRINGTON
. 606;DAVID,466,473
. DENNIS,471,473;E.S.
. 497;ELIZA JANE,582
. EMER LONG,477;J.F.,528
. JACOB,294;JANE,303,313
. JESSE,176;LOUISA C.
. 588;MARY,458;MARY ANN
. 23;O.C. ROBERTSON,528
. RICHARD,606;SARAH,311
. SARAH J.,339;SOLOMON
. 293-294;SUSA,582
. THOMAS,477;W.W.,4-5,9
. 14,23,42-43,70,80-81
. 100,127-130,133,145
. 582
CARRUTH,JAMES D.,16
. S.M.,103-104,106-107
. SIDNEY,101;SIDNEY M.
. 103;SUSAN F. KEMP,16
CARSON,ADAM,413,463
. CALVIN H.,161;J.P.,25
. JAMES,440-441;JOHN,547
. JOHN C.,92;JOSEPH,458
. MARGARET,413;MARGARET
. STEPHENS,458;MARY A.
. BATY,25;NANCY SUDEATH
. 161;NANCY Y.,413
. WILLIAM,464
CARSWELL,C.V.,569

CARTER,ARCHIBALD,102
. BARTOW,523,526
. CATHERINE,421;CHARLEY
. 499;CLERACY,477;D.C.
. WAIN,350;D.C.P.,485
. DANIEL C.P.,475
. DARCUS C.,334;DICEY
. 553;E.B.,532;E.B.
. HOLBROOKS,350;E.J.,462
. E.M.,499,518,526,544
. EDWARD,547;ELIJAH N.
. 477;ELIZA A. HUNTER
. 351;ELIZA BREEDER,308
. 314;ELIZABETH,458,495
. 552;FANNIE,516;FARISH
. 247,251-252,265;GREEN
. 536;H.C.,421,591
. HENRY C.,308,314
. ISNISH,547;J.E.,531
. J.F.,508;J.R.,509
. JAMES,559;JAMES J.,178
. JAMES S.,329;JANE O.
. 336;JASPER,541;JESSE
. 534,547;JOHN,530;JOHN
. C.,462;JOHN M.,351
. JOSEPH,545,547;JULIA
. 530;LAVADA PUCKETT,477
. LUCINDA,536;MARTHA
. DAVIS,559;MARTHA
. GAULT,329;MARTIN,350
. 351;MARY,426,430
. MATTIE GRAY,545
. MILLER,477;MILLY,566
. NANCY,511,556;P.M.,545
. PINSON,508,514;R.,542
. R.M.,403,411;RANSEY
. 503;REBECCA,459
. 544;ROBERT M.,552
. RUFUS,533;SARAH,428
. 556;SUSAN A.C.
. ROBERTSON,552;THETOS
. JORDAN,477;THOMAS,495
. W.E.,390;W.K.,498
. WILLIAM,540;WILLIAM
. J.,350
CARTREL,A.J. MCCURDY,596
. JOHN M.,596
CARTRIGHT,JAMES,186
. JOHN L.,362
CARUTH,ELMINA,356
. ROBERT,2
CARUTHER,438
CARUTHERS,440;JAMES,438
CARVER,AMERICA SAMS,584
. BENJAMIN,496;C.C.,579
. ELIZABETH STANIELL,451
. HENRY,467;JULIAN,489
. LAURA ANN PEARSON,477
. LEWIS C.,477;LUCINDA
. 489;MANUEL B.,477
. MARIETTA LOWERY,477
. MARTHA,305,313;MARY
. 479;MARY ANN,477
. MARY J. BORAN,579
. MARY THACKER,329
. NANCY,475;SAMUEL S.
. 584;SARAH M.,482
. SUSAN HOLDER,477
. WILLIAM,329,451
. WILLIAM D.,477
CARY,BARRABAS,302
. GEORGIA E.,55
. HARRIET P. HUTCHINS
. 302
CASADAY,DAVID J.,471
. MARTIN,471;WESLEY,471
CASAELY,LOU J.,602
CASE,BRADLY,560;JOHN T.
. 171-172;SARAH ROSE,560
CASEY,BARNABAS,314;BOB
. 512;EDNY,314;ELLISON
. 304,314;ELVINY,304
. HARRIET T. HUTCHINS

. 314;ISAAC,437;JAMES
. H.,525;JESSEY,469
. JOEL,440;JOHN A.,12
. LOUISA,10;MARGARET,307
. 320;NANCY M.,33;PATSY
. 302,314;PATSY CASEY
. 302,314;REBECCA MCKEY
. 17;SARAH WALDRUP,304
. 314;URIAH,437
. WASHINGTON,302,314
. WILLIAM,17
CASH,
. ANNA A. HARRISON,568
. GEORGE W.,95;HOWARD
. 592;LOUISA,567;LUCY
. 564;PETER C.,568
. REBECCA A. GIRDY,568
. REBECCA A. GORDY,568
. SARAH,456;SARAH J.
. ONAR,592;SARAH J.
. RAGSDALE,50;SARAH R.
. 111;THOMAS,568
. WILLIAM,435;WILLIAM
. P.,50
CASON,BESSIE S.,64
. CARIE L.,39;G.W.,532
. GEORGE,498;HESTER ANN
. 551;JAMES,547;MYRTIS
. 55;R.E.,51,55;SARAH
. J.,482;WALTER,55;WOOL
. 498
CASSADA,D.J.,474;MARTIN
. 473;WESLEY,474
CASSADY,EUGENE,535;MARY
. HARDY,535
CASSEL,
. MARY A.M. MULLINS,49
. W.W.,49
CASSELBERRY,CENY,451
. CENY CASSELBERRY,451
. DAVID,451;KERENHAPUCK
. 450;MARK,449;MARY,450
. MARY WARREN,449;NELLY
. 449
CASSLEBERRY,SARAH,453
CASTER,ALICE,513;H.C.
. 369;R.D.,278
CASTLEBARY,CATHERINE,32
CASTLEBERRY,
. AGNES BACON,303,314
. BENJAMIN W.,301,314
. CARON HARRIS,301,314
. CLARISSA,156;DAVID,314
. 329,350,377;E.,375
. ELIZABETH,34
. ELIZABETH A. DOSS,159
. FRANCES D. WOOD,329
. FRANCIS L.G.,377
. GRAVE G. WOOD,329
. H.C.,55;JOHN H.,329
. LUCINDA,160;LUCY,458
. M.T.,106;MARGARET,332
. MARK,188,286-287,298
. MARTHA F. FAGINS,329
. MARY,339;MARY A.
. ANGLIN,329;MARY M.
. WILLIAMS,329
. MELZONE L. REEVES,350
. NANCY M. WILLIAMS,314
. 377;NANCY WILLIAMS,350
. PATSEY,455;SARAH
. WALLACE,456;TIMOTHY
. 303,314;W.T.,350
. WILLIAM,159,329,456
. WILLIAM H.,329
. WILLIAM M.,329
CASTSTELL,SARAH ANN,565
CASY,BARRABAS,302
. HARRIET P. HUTCHINS
. 302
CATE,J.A.,583;TEXAS S.
. BAGGISS,583
CATES,A.B.,527;ELI,472
. EVELIN,378;JACKSON,378

. JOHN,445;JULIA WAITS
. 21;LAURA,527
. MARTHA Y. MOORE,445
. THOMAS B.,21
CATHEY,ANDREW,151,191
. 471;NELLIE SELLERS,603
. S.C.R.,603
CATHLIN,ESTHER H.,488
CATHY,MARGARET,581
CATRELL,WILEY,560
CATTELL,J.C.,55;JANE C. 55
CAULDEN,N.M.,104
CAURTH,SIDNEY W.,104
CAUSEY,ISRAEL,55,97
. MARGARET,55;MILLY M.
. PRUETT,48;SAMUEL,515
. THOMAS S.,48;WILLIAM
. M.,55
CAVEN,ALEXANDER,449
. MARIA PENNELL,449
CAVENDER,
. CATHERINE HOLLAND,569
. KITTY,449;REBECCA,566
. WILLIAM G.,569
CAWDREY,
. SARAH CARRELL,311,314
. THOMAS,311,314
CAWLEY,
. ALEXANDER M.D.,443
. G.W.,531;JUDY ANN,338
. VIANNA,340;WILLIAM,472
CAWLY,ELIZABETH,342
. ELIZABETH TERRY,351
. JAMES O.,351;MARY F.
. TERRY,351
CAWOOD,J.H.,560,578;J.P.,572
CAYLER,ELIZA L.,488
CAYLOR,AMANDA A.,481
. KISIAH,493;MARTHA A.
. 44;MATTIE,518
CAZEY,ELVINY,304
CENTER,F.W.,427;S.B.
. HORTON,427
CERBO,
. ELIZABETH PARKER,451
. EZEKIEL,451
CESSNA,GREEN K.,224,260
CHADWIC,MARTHA,36
CHADWICK,A.,427,433,475
. 483,490-491;A.B.,477
. ABRAHAM,482,493-494
. BENJAMIN,304,314
. CINDA GOSS,477
. CLERACY CARTER,477
. E.L.,488;ELIZABETH
. SMITH,40;ELIZABETH
. WOOTEN,351;EMELINE
. CHATHAM,351;EPHRAIM
. H.,329;EPHRIAM,314
. GEORGIA ANN BELL,477
. HANNAH M. SMITH,314
. 329;HARRIET,479
. HEZKIAH,351;J.S.,477
. JAMES D.,40;JOHN,477
. L.A. GANUS,477;LEWIS
. 477;LOUISA,479
. LUCINDA EATON,304,314
. MARGARET,331;PARSON
. 477;THOMAS,477
. WILLIAM H.,351
CHADZY,H.A.,55
CHAFFIN,AMOS,177,192,204
. 207,219,228;CHARLOTTE
. 157;ELEJAH,462;ELIAS
. 191,193,199,205,256
. ELIJAH,192,222-223,228
. 234,236,243;JOSEPH,222
. 224,228,244;SARAH M.
. 160
CHAFIN,AMOS,153;ELIAS
. 153;ELIJAH,153;JOSEPH
. 153
CHALBLE,E.A. BARNETT,600
. JOHN,600

CHALKER,EMILY HILL,40
. J.C.,55;J.M.,40;J.T.
. 55,145;M.V.,49;MATTIE
. 27;PHILLIP,55
CHALMERS,
. BETSY BROADMAN,456
. JOHN,456
CHALMORE,ANDREW,157
. PEGGY LANDRUM,157
CHAMBER,532;MARTIN,287
CHAMBERLIN,AUGUSTUS,55
. C.R.,55
CHAMBERS,ALLMAN,230
. ALLY MILLER,457
. BARBARY SAWYERS,159
. DAVID,477;E.L.,43
. ELIZABETH BAKER,454
. GEORGE,172;J.,26;J.T.
. 526;JAMES,151,170,176
. 457;JAMES B.,130
. JAMES H.,191,222-223
. 234,243,253,259,262
. 263,285;JANE F.,328
. JOHN,186,456;JOHN M.
. 151,192,222-223,234
. 244-245,248;MAGGIE
. BURNS,526;MARGARET
. WILSON,477;MARTIN,177
. NANCY,352;NANCY KING
. 456;PEGGY EATON,453
. PHILIP,454;REBECCA,55
. SAMANTHY,352;SOPHIA
. 450;W.A.,475;W.B.,478
. 481-483,485-492;W.H.
. 479;WILL,528;WILLIAM
. 191,453;WILLIAM B.,159
CHAMBLE,
. MARY E. HALEY,161
. ROBERT,161
CHAMBLEE,CLERINDA,340
. ELIZABETH,380;EVLIE
. BENNETT,351;FRANCES
. E.,322;FRANCIS E.,339
. GADSEY,371;JULIA A.
. 371;L.J.,419;LEWIS,308
. 314;MARTHA E.,342
. MARTIN,152;MARY C.,318
. 332;REBECCA MARTIN,301
. 314;ROSALEE,330;SUSAN
. PAYNE,308,314
. SYLVESTUS T.,351
. TARRETT,152;W.L.,351
. WASHINGTON,301,314,439
. WILLIAM,152
CHAMBLESS,
. EDIA PARRIS,539;T.M.
. 539
CHAMBLY,WILLIAM,207
CHAMLEE,
. ELIZABETH A. PEW,155
. JAMES H.,257;JARRETT
. 191,194,202,205,228
. 237;JERRETT,197
. MARTIN,181,183,204,457
. POLLY GUTHREY,457
. TILMON,177,192,204,256
. WILLIAM,155,192,199
. 228,236,243,253,257
. 260,262-263
CHAMLEY,L.J.,92;WILLIAM
. B.,438
CHAMPION,ANN,457
. BENJAMIN,477;CANZADA
. 481;ELIZABETH KENADAY
. 459;ELIZABETH RICH,477
. HANNAH,458;MARTIN,477
. MARY HAMBY,477
. REBECCA BLACKWELL,477
. SARAH QUINTON,477
. THOMAS C.,477;WILLIAM
. 459,465,477
CHAMPMAN,MAHULDA,325
. TEANY,231
CHANDLER,519;ABRAHAM,397

. 403;ADELINE L. RILEY
. 570;FRANCES,34,557
. JELL,197;JOEL,177,191
. 193,202,205,247;JOEL
. C.,449;JOHN,437
. JOSEPH C.,570;JULIA
. F.,414;LEWIS,462
. LUCINDA,447;LYDIA,156
. MARGARET,552
. MARTHA E. HANNON,15
. MARY A.,420
. MARY ELIZ. GRE,552
. MARY FROST,449;NORA
. HARDY,433;R.,86;R.J.
. 433;ROBERT,55,82-83
. 153,222;S.C.,187,230
. S.G.L.,397;SAMUEL C.
. 181,210;THOMAS M.,15
. 63;WALTAN,552;WILLIAM
. B.,397-398,404
. WILLIAM P.,398
. WILLIAM R.,393
CHANEY,A.J.,86
CHANNELL,MARY C.,18
. PENELOPE L. ADAMS,30
. THOMAS J.,30
CHAPEL,ANGENETTA,571;S.
. TABITHA,32
CHAPLIN,NANCY,309,318
CHAPMAN,ABNER,210;AMOS
. H.,295;BENJAMIN D.,210
. CATHARINE RUSSELL,314
. CATHERINE RUSSELL,310
. CHRISTOPHER,462
. COLENDAR A.,331;E.E.
. 569;ELIZ. ANN,33
. ELIZA. A. MANNING,314
. ELIZABETH,295,335
. ELIZABETH KUKYKENDALL
. 5;HENSEN,462;ISAAC,314
. JANE,456;JOHN,310,314
. 464;JOHN B.,5;JOHN D.
. 463;JOHN T.,492;L.A.
. 491;MARTHA,565;MARY
. 163;N.G. TALLEY,569
. SARAH,295;SARAH E.,562
. WILLIFORD,474
CHAPPEL,
. ELIZABETH CARTER,552
. GEORGE,471;JAMES,436
. JEFFERSON,552;JOHN,552
. LUCY MULLINS,552
CHAPPELL,ANGENETTA,571
. ARENA,56;CYNTHIA,557
. GEORGE,474;JOHN,56
. NANCY,56;WILLIAM,503
. WILSON,56,95
CHARLES,
. AMANDA TAYLOR,477
. JEMIMAH,452;RACHEL,455
. W.B.,477
CHART,MELDEIK M.,387
CHARUT,ELIJAH,387
CHASE,D.W.,389;DEAN W.
. 474;F.E.,431;GENLEY
. B.,4;GURLEY B.,4;I.G.
. 492;IDA MAE,56;J.G.
. 479;MARTHA E. DRENNAN
. 4;MARY O.,56
CHASTAIN,A.,418,420-422
. 427;ADLINE,382;ANNIS
. H.,588;DORCAS A.,376
. E.C. CLAYTON,361
. EDWARD,547;ELIJAH,90
. 547;ELIJAH W.,264,266
. ELIMIRA,15;EMILY,596
. Γ.,133;F.M.,477
. FRANCES OWEN,310,314
. G.B.,139;GEORGE L.,433
. GREEN B.,75,133
. HANNAH,547;J.F.,137
. J.G.,486;J.H.,56;J.K.
. 502;J.R.,425;J.W.,390
. JAMES M.,26;JAMES W.

. 361;JEREMIAH,464
. JEREMIAH S.,149;JOHN
. B.,170;JOHN D.,149
. JONATHAN,260,464
. JOSEPH,1,56,78,89,99
. JUNE E.,578;LOU,602
. LOUSANNE E. DODGEN,26
. LUCINDA,494;M.R.,578
. MADISON,310,314
. MALINDA,486;MALISSA
. 578;MALISSA
. RICHARDSON,584;MARTHA
. 361;MARY,484;MARY A.
. GRAVLEY,477;MARY ANN
. KEITH,403;MARY
. JARRETT,425;MARY P.
. ANDERSON,477;MATILDA
. 597;MATILDA H.,458
. MATTIE L. KIKER,433
. NANCY,56;O.,125
. OBEDIAH,403;OSCAR,502
. R.F. TREADWELL,578
. RANEY,584;SARAH N.,477
. SARAH N. CHASTAIN,477
. THEODOSIA,432;W.D.,477
. W.W.,254;WILLIAM H.
. 477
CHASTEEN,
. CORDELIA YOUNG,477
. ELIGRA,477;JOSEPH R.
. 478;MANDEY BUNCH,478
CHASTIAN,J.B.,166;JOHN
. S.,166
CHASTINE,JOSEPH,66
CHATHAM,ANN,493
. ANNIE D. HOLBROOKS,306
. ANNY D. HOLBROOKS,314
. E. CASTLEBERRY,375
. E.M.,329;ELIZA,328
. ELIZABETH PHILLIPS,329
. EMELINE,351;G.L.,52
. J.,375;JAMES,351
. JAMES J.,329;JAMES M.
. 329;JANE PHILLIPS,351
. JOSHUA,311,314;M.J.
. 375;MARY J. WALLIS,329
. MARY JANE,335;NAOMI,56
. RUTHA ANN,340;SARAH
. COBB,311,314;SARAH J.
. DAVIS,314;STEPHEN M.
. 314,329;SUSAN,339
. SYLVANIA,337;TEMPH
. ESTES,314;TEMPY ESTES
. 329;THOMAS M.,314
. WILLIAM C.,306,314
CHATICAR,241,248
CHATMAN,HULDA,385
. MATTIE,36
CHATMON,
. SARAH JANE DAVIS,329
. THOMAS M.,329
CHEAK,LUCY N.,551
CHEATHAM,ELLIN,50;G.B.
. 23;NANNY ADAMS,23
CHECK,MARY LOU,516
CHEEK,CORA,535;GAZAWAY
. 303,314;ISAIAH,231
. JAMES S.,109;TERRISA
. PIKE,314;TERRISSA
. PIKE,303
CHENEY,A.J.,56,66;CORA
. 56;J.N.,56;JAMES B.,56
. JOHN,57;JOHN P.,56,75
. W.S.,56
CHEROKEE,ELIZABETH,353
CHERRY,AMANDA WHITE,589
. DAVID,589
CHESHARE,DELILAH,372
CHESTEEN,JOHN,552;MARY
. SHIVEY,552
CHESTER,CHARLES,604
. ELIJAH W.,195;ELISHA
. W.,186,225,233,240
. ELIZABETH L.,56;ELLA

. 584;ESLINGH,547;L.V.
. 566;LULA J. GUTHRIE
. 604;N.L.,56,108
. NORMAN L.,109-110;W.
. 568;W.P.,569,572-573
. WILLIAM P.,573
CHESTNUR,DAVE,514
CHESTNUT,D.R.,512;DAVE
. 514;THOMAS,512
. WILLIAM,104;WILLIAM
. R.,105-107
CHEVEY,218
CHEWLOW,229
CHICKEN,241,248-250,255
. BARK,247,254,259
CHILDERS,ABI SPINKS,507
. ADELINE,486;ANNA
. JOURDAN,311,314
. DOLPHUS,478;GEORGE W.
. 314;GEORGIA ANN
. JORDAN,478;HENRY,507
. JOHN,311,314;LUCIA D.
. 17;LUCY JOHNSON,560
. MARTHA A.,340;MITCHEL
. 173;SARIANNAS DANIEL
. 314;SEABIL A. AUSTIN
. 329;SOBRINA,551;WILEY
. 560;WILLIAM J.,329
CHILDRES,MARGARET,372
. MARY E. HUTCHINS,329
. NANCY,466;OLIVER P.
. 329;ROBERT,462
. WILLIAM,131
CHILDRESS,JOHN M.,157
. MARGARET,322,339
. MARTHA CRANDALL,157
. NANCY,386;SARAH,330
. W.A.,140;WILLIAM A.
. 132,142;WILLIAM J.,443
CHILLSON,SUSAN,486
CHILSON,ELIZABETH J.,480
. SUSAN,477
CHISHOLM,MURDOCK,391
CHISM,SOPHRONIA,447
CHITWOOD,
. ANNA BRANNON,452
. JEREMIAH,231;PLEASANT
. 452
CHOICE,JOHN,464;JOSIAH
. 209
CHOPEALE,MARTHA A.,383
CHRISMAN,S.,423
CHRISTAIN,HOMER,56
CHRISTENBERRY,HENRY,329
. MARTHA,321,339;NANCY
. EDWARDS,314;SAMANTHA
. WHITE,329;SILAS G.,314
CHRISTIAN,AMANDA,336
. ANN,157;C.S.,525
. CALIFORNIA,160
. CAROLINE M. ROBERTS
. 407;CATHERINE,416
. CATHERINE GARUM,329
. CHARLES,152,191-192
. 238,242,244,416
. CHARLES C.,329
. CORNELIA MCCLENDON,411
. ELIZA M.,456
. ELIZABETH,416;ELLA,365
. IDA,524;J.A.,503,525
. LUTITHA,454;MARGARET
. WILSON,365;MARY C.
. HOLBROOK,329;NICHOLAS
. 365;P.A.,525;PATSEY
. 449-450;S.J.,525,527
. THOMAS T.,407,411
. W.A.,498,501,503
. WILLIAM,238;WILLIAM
. P.,329
CHRISTOPHER,AMBROSE,463
. CAROLINE MCKINNEY,158
. EILLIAM,463;HENRY,314
. JOHN,158;JOHN Q.A.,161
. MARGARET,161;MARGARET

. CHRISTOPHER,161
. MARTHA,553;MARY,459
. MARY L.,557;MATHEW,158
. MATHEW W.,37;NANCY,158
. NANCY CHRISTOPHER,158
. NARCISIS CONGO,314
. OLIVET,313;OLIVIAT,307
. ROBERT,161
. SAMANTHA A. HANEY,37
. SUSAN BATSON,161;W.P.
. 403
CHRISWELL,THOMAS,440
CHRISWILL,FRANCES,66
CHUE,ISAAC,246
CHUMBLER,JOHN,478;SALIA
. BROOKS,478
CHUMBLEY,MISSOURI A.,488
CHUMLEE,
. BARBARA M. PENDLEY,478
. JAMES M.,478
CHUMLEY,SIS,479
CHUPP,LIZZIE,517
CILOTEIN,
. ELIZABETH EMMA,82
. LOUISA GABLE,82
CILOW,GEORGE W.,465
CLACKUM,ELIZABETH,56
CI ADER,N M ,103
CLAK,THOMAS B.,99
CLANTON,CAROLINE,22
. ELISHA E.B.,40;JULIA
. CULP,8;LUCINDA
. DICKERSON,44;M.E.,44
. NANCY A.,27;NANCY
. TUMMIS,38;PINCKNEY,8
. SARAH J.,25;SARAH J.
. SMITH,40;THOMAS,38
CLARCK,ELLIAND,604
CLARDY,ELLIOTT,547
. MICHAEL N.,391;R.H.
. 393
CLARK,A.D.,559;AARON,552
. ALLY POOL,552;ANN
. COOPER,449;B. COOK,423
. B.M.,563;B.W.,329
. BENJAMIN,470;CALEB,1
. 456;CATHERINE RICE,478
. DIANNAH E. ALMON,329
. ELIJAH,552;ELIZABETH
. 577,594;EMILY,584;EVA
. 56;F.B.,544;FANNY
. GROVES,589;FELIX,589
. G.H.,408-409;G.W.,577
. 600;HENRY,466;J.
. THADDEOUS,478;JAMES
. F.,56;JAMES P.,329
. JANE,56;JOHN,452
. JOSEPH,560;JOSIAH H.
. 409;LEW,387;LEWIS L.
. 496;LOUISA A. HICKS
. 600;LUCELLA,606;LUCY
. MORRIS,452;M.A.,544
. MARIA E. ROLLINS,577
. MARTHA HARBUCK,552
. MARTHA W. BICK,560
. MARY C. MCCORMACK,329
. MARY E.,574;MARY
. YOUNG,478;MILTON L.
. 329;NANCY COPP,573
. NANCY L. BOTTOMS,329
. NATHAN,552;POLLY
. MULLINS,456;S.C.,481
. SARAH JANIS,552;SARAH
. JONES,552;SIDNEY A.
. 583;SUANNAH,560;SUSAN
. S.,56;W.J.,423
. WILLIAM,449,466,532
. 547,573;WILLIAM G.,478
. Z.D.,559-560,565,567
. 570-572,575
CLARKE,ARCHIBALD,445
. B.D.,414;ELIZABETH
. HILL,445;MARY R.
. BARRETT,414;WILLIAM

622

CROKER,FANNIE,519
CROMBIE,WILLIAM A.,208
. 218,226
CROMER,ANN E.,45
CROMIELS,
. CAROLINE CURRY,602
. JOHN,602
CROMPTON,JANE,560
. MARTHA MOSELY,314
. MARTHA MOSLEY,310
. PERRY,310,314
CROMWELL,ANDERSON
. F.,474
. JAMES C.,474;JAMES S.
. 472
CRONEY,HIRAM,463
CRONIE,MARY,558;PEGGY
. REYNOLDS,553
. VALENTINE,553
CROOK,G.A.A. BRADLEY,424
. S.J.,424
CROPLEY,ISAAC,465
CRORLY,MARY
. MISANGER,582
. WILLIAM,582
CROS,ABRAHAM,222
CROSBY,U.S.,496
CROSLEY,ISAAC,465
CROSNO,NICHOLAS,298
CROSS,DIDAMA,335
. ELIZABETH WILSON,457
. FRANCES L. MCCRARY,314
. 329;GARRISON,256,314
. GIDEAN,329;GIDEON,314
. JACOB,561;JANE,335
. JESSE,569;LOUIZA
. LAURENCE,561;MARGARET
. 319,335;NANCY ANN
. BROWN,569;OPHALIA
. EATON,479;PERMELIA H.
. 339;ROBERT,479;SILAS
. 457;SOPHRIAH E.
. COMPTON,314
CROSSLY,E.P.,428
CROSSNAW,NICHOLAS,176
CROUCH,ALETHA NORRIS,553
. ARCHIBALD,588;GEORGE
. 553;MALINDA,579
. MARTHA OSCAR,588
CROW,A.,476-477,479,489
. 490,493;ABRAHAM,151
. 253,257,260;ABRAM,224
. ALSY STOVALL,362
. AMANDA PESLEY,479
. ARMIDIA AULT,566
. BARNS,297;BETSY A.
. STOVALL,309,314
. CARLISLE B.,456
. CAROLINE,556;CAROLINE
. EVANS,478;CINTHA E.
. 335;E.E. COOK,479
. E.M.,49;EDNY CASEY,314
. ELEANOR D. LEADFORD,49
. ELI,314;ELIZA AULT,576
. ELIZABETH,312,328,451
. ELIZABETH ARNOLD,553
. ELLY BEWRY,302,314
. ELVINY CASEY,304
. ELVINY CAZEY,304
. EZEKIEL,478;FATINA D.
. 576;GEORGE H.,57
. H.J.M.,343;ISAAC,362
. ISAAC J.,302,314;ISAM
. 553;JACOB,2;JAMES,210
. 297,329,547,576;JAMES
. A.,479;JAMES H.,479
. JEPTHA C.,566;JOHN,297
. JOHN B.,329;JOHN M.
. 479;JONATHAN,151,204
. 453;KANSADA,327
. KIMSEY,479;L.H.,566
. LACKSTON,467;LAWRENCE
. 547;LORRIE BROCK,479
. LOUISA,323,340,381

. LOURANA,490;LUCINDA
. 458;LUCRETIA COUCH,329
. MARTHA A.,338;MARY,39
. MARY A. HUGHES,314
. MARY A.D. WILKINS,329
. MARY L.,362;MARY NEAL
. 561;MILLEY DONALDSON
. 314,329;NANCY,308,321
. NANCY C. KEMP,329
. NANCY S.,554;NANCY
. TARBUTTON,479;NANCY
. WHITWORTH,456
. NARCISSA E.,560
. NORMAN M.,445;POLLY
. ANN,573;POLLY
. HANSFORD,445;POLLY M.
. 328;R.A.,333;REBECCA
. 594;SARAH,307,312
. SARAH A.,564;SARAH S.
. 308,318;SHADRACK A.
. 304,314;SUSAN,453
. SUSAN CROW,453;THOMAS
. T.,329;WILLIAM,151,222
. 228,309,314,329
. WILLIAM S.,561
CROWDER,
. ELIZABETH M. -
PENDI FY,479;JAMES M.
. 479
CROWEL,ANN E. WARD,593
. WILLIAM D.,593
CROWELL,C.A.,413-414
. DELAI HILL,429;G.T.
. 429
CROWLEY,WILLIAM,504
CROXTON,E.H.,587;ELIJAH
. 1,89;MARY P.
. SINGLETARY,587;SARAH
. 566
CROY,MARGARET M.,316
CROYS,
. DILLA SINGLETARY,582
. G.W.,582
CROZIER,HELEN PHARIS,588
. SAMUEL C.,588
CRUCE,F.P.,596;MARGARET
. V.,592;MARY E.,584
. RICHARD,562;SARAH J.
. 566;WILLIAM,439
CRUIS,
. DELILAH HIGGINS,350
. JEREMIAH,350;JOHN L.
. 350;MALINDA GREEN,350
CRUISE,JEREMIAH,282
. JOHN,281-282;WILLIAM
. 281-282
CRUMBLY,SARAH A.,559
CRUMLEY,JOSEPHINE,583
. MALINDA,446;W.M.,29
. 527
CRUMP,MARTHA J.,385
CRUMPTON,ELIZA HURST,587
. JOEL D.,496;RICHARD
. 496;ROBERT,587;THOMAS
. 495
CRUMWELL,JAMES S.,470
CRUSE,ADALINE,320,336
. CINTHA SAMS,314
. DELILAH C.,328
. EMALINE HAWKINS,302
. 315;JAMES,470
. JEREMIAH,149;JOHN L.
. 300,314;JOHN LOSSON
. 378;JOSEPHINE,335
. KINDNESS,333;MARY ANN
. 302,319;MELISSA
. WILLIAMS,314;PINCKNEY
. 314;SARAH J.,566
. SYNTHA C.,378;SYNTHA
. SAMS,300;SYNTHIA SAMS
. 378;WILLIAM,302,315
CRUTE,JOHN M.,564
. MARY A. RIDDLE,564
CRUTHERS,439

CRY,JOHN,588;WINNY E.
. SHELTON,588
CRYER,L.M.E.,597
CUBB,JOHN,89
CUBY,CHARLES B.,405
CUD,JOHN,89
CUDD,ANNI P.,575;CARTER
. 101;JOHN,3,90;LAVINIA
. MASSEY,433;MARTHA
. JANE,577;W.F.M.,433
CULBERSON,MARTIN,547
CULBERTSON,J.,221
. MARTIN,150
CULBUTSON,
. SARAH HINTON,553
. WASHINGTON C.,553
CULLINS,ELYAH,553;LILIS
. FORD,553
CULP,JOSEPH,91;JULIA,8
. WILLIAM,91
CULPEPPER,525;WILLIAM
. H.,397
CULVER,HARDY G.,561
. MARTHA H. MCDONALD,561
. MARY,447
CULWELL,ANDREW,170
CUMBIE,W.A.,582
CUMBY,
. MARTHA MCMICHAEL,553
. PLEASANT A.,553
CUMMING,E.R.,57
. MONTGOMERY,57,594
. RASALIA M. WADE,594
. W.H.,57
CUMMINS,
. NANCY BURGESS,577
. SAMUEL,577
CUMPTON,
. ELIZABETH GRAVITT,329
. PHILBOW H.,329
CUNCAN,J.B.,86
CUNNINGAN,MATILDA,31
CUNNINGHAM,ANDREW,171
. F.,57;FLEETA F.,327
. HENRY L.,329;J.L.,278
. 442;JOHN,72;LEOLA,57
. LUCINDA GARRETT,329
. SARAH C. COFFEE,569
. W.M.,569
CUPP,439;HENRY,1;JANE
. CONNALLY,580;MICHAEL,1
. 436,439;RALEIGH,563
. 564-567,570,572,575
. 580;THOMAS,3;WARNER
. 440
CUPPS,111
CURBO,EZEKIEL,441
. REBECCA,453;ROBERT,441
CURBOW,DANIEL,162,244
. HENRY,495;JAMES N.J.
. 315;JOSEPH M.,159
. MARTHA BECK,159
. MARTHA C. HORTON,315
. MARTHA E. HORTON,329
. MELISSA BRADLEY,162
. N.J.,329
CURD,SALINA,572
CURMERSON,B.H.,53
CURRY,CAROLINE,602
. REBECCA,57
CURSLING,ELIJAH,470
CURTIS,A.M. HOUK,426
. ASBURY,464;ELIZA,488
. W.M.,426
CURTISS,402;CARLTON,434
. DANIEL BOONE,431
. FANNIE CANSON,434
. FRANCES L. HARDEN,431
. HENRY,431;SALLY
. KAIGLER,431;TINY,434
. W.M.,431;W.N.N.,432
. WILLIAM,402
CUSO,LUCY A. MARTIN,586
. RICHARD J.,586

CUTLER,R.R.,77
CUTTERY,WILLEY,449
CUYLER,TELAMON,1,297,387
. 461,469,495;TELMON,151
DABBS,JULIA,4
DABIS,C.C.,43
DABNEY,W.H.,394;WILLIAM
. H.,394-397,401
DACUS,ANN,317,332
. ARTHUR,301,315;ELVIRA
. HALL,330;HAWKINS,330
. PEGGY TATUM,301,315
. SARAH CHILDRESS,330
. WILLIAM,330
DAGGY,P.,390
DALE,STEPHEN,1,167;W.R.
. 506,515,539-540
DALRIMPLE,MARY,465
DALRYMPLE,REBECCA,450
DALTON,GEORGE,443
. LEANDER EDWARDS,28
. MITCHEL,28;RANDLE,439
DALY,
. MARGARET GRIFFIN,579
. RUDE,579
DAMSON,GEORGE,394
DANA,ANNIE E. BISHOP,568
. WILLIAM M.,568
DANFORTH,E.V.,11;SARAH
. 451
DANIEL R.F.,193
DANIEL,237;A.G.,258
. A.H.,527;ATLAS A.,16
. BEATON,8;BEVERLY,151
. CLARINDA BROOKS,307
. 315;CURTISS,404;DAVID
. 436,442;DELILA RIGHT
. 458;EDWARD,230,276
. ELIZA HONEY,368
. ELIZABETH,155,569
. EMELINE SIMPSON,16
. GEORGE M.,129;GEORGE
. W.,8,330;H.J.,57
. HARRIET SINGLETON,330
. HENRY G.,193,195;J.,5
. J.B.,57;J.M.,8,63
. J.S.,57;JAMES,149,166
. 170,297,368;JAMES M.
. 253;JAMES W.,309,315
. JEREMIAH,5,57;JESSE
. 107,115;JOHN,150,177
. 189,204,307,315
. JOSEPH,229;JOSIAH,461
. LOU,368;MACY S.,462
. MARTHA C. JOHNSON,8
. MARTHA M.,35,581
. MARTHA P.,300,321
. MARY J.,577;MARY S.
. 462;MARYAN PUGH,158
. N.C.,112;N.P.,324,342
. NOOK,404;R.,15;R.D.
. 181,250;R.F.,167,170
. 179,189,224-225,227
. 238,253,258,262;R.P.
. 57;RACHAEL OSBURN,304
. 315;REUBEN,150,458
. REUBEN F.,150,182,190
. 192,204,214,220,224
. REWBEN F.,151;ROBERT,9
. 25,31,34-36;SARAH,353
. SARAH WOODLIFF,330
. SARIANNAS,314;SIBBIE
. 539;THADDOUS C.,158
. THOMAS H.,330;WILLIAM
. 183,188,193,210,212
. 222,225,238-240,246
. 258,304,315,461
. WINNIE WESTBROOK,315
. WINNIE WESTBROOKS,309
DANIELL,A.A.,57;ALICE
. SHEFFIELD,43;BEATON,17
. 29;BERTON,21
. CATHARINE M.,48;CLARA
. C.,37;E.T. HAMBY,29

. EMMA WALLACE,26;G.B.
. 57;G.L.,29;GEORGE M.
. 57;H.V.,57;HENRIETTA
. 57;INEZ N.,57;J.M.,13
. 26,43;J.N.,57
. JOSEPHINE,57;N.C.,112
. 117;REUBEN F.,207
. ROBERT,13,20-21,26,29
. 38,48,57,59;S.N.,57
. SYLVIA M.,49;W.R.,57
. WILLIAM,186,210-211
DANILL,RHODA JAY,456
. WILLIAM,456
DANISE,MILTON,387
DANNER,NENA,35
DANTZLER,JACOB,572;MARY
. ANN,603;MARY MAILON
. 572;R.F.,596;SARAH E.
. LOCKARD,596
DARBY,ARMINDA,310
. ARMINTA,310,321;ASA,7
. 25,57,68;CHARLES,297
. ELIZABETH KEITH,25
. ICY,300,317;JANE,300
. 351;JANE TAYLOR,553
. JOHN,57;JULIUS G.,553
. MARY F.,57;MINERVA,306
. 312;NANCY C.
. HAMBLETON,553;S.C.
. MAYES,7;SARAH C.,327
. SARAH G.,313;WILLIAM
. L.,553
DARDEN,JOHN,490
DARLY,JOHN,158;JULIAN
. WIDANELL,158
DARNAL,SARAH,162
DARNALL,M.A. COBT,422
. W.H.,422
DARNELL,A.J.,422;C.L.
. BLALOCK,422;CATHERINE
. 488;CATHERINE DOVER
. 479;DAVID,427;FANNIE
. 31;FLORENCE JOHNSON
. 479;HARRIET,491;J.W.
. 479;J.W.R.,479;JAMES
. P.,479;JAMES S.,479
. JOHN,475-476,478-481
. 485,487-489,491-492
. JOHN A.,482;JOSIE
. FITZSIMMONS,479;L.A.
. 31;LARENIA VINCENT,479
. LEVI J.,479;LOUISA,489
. M.J.,425;MANSON W.,479
. MARTHA,484;MARTHA E.
. 487;MARY DAWSON,427
. MARY E. BARTON,479
. MARY JANE PADGET,479
. MARY M,433;NANCY M.
. 492;NORA REAVES,479
. P.C.,427;ROXANNA,492
. S.A.,31;SARAH FLOYD
. 427;SUSIE HOTCHKISS,31
. W.J.,479;W.L.,479
. WILLIAM J.,479
DARNOL,GERLAD,547
DARTER,FRANCIS,464
DAUGHETY,
. CATHARINE FEW,553
. MASON,553
DAUVERGNE,ALDOLPHUS,231
DAVENPORT,ARTHUR E.,516
. E.N.,57;ELIJAH N.,40
. ELIZA J.,317,332
. HELEN,420;JOHN,302,315
. MAHALA MCGRAW,553
. MARCUS L.,57;MARY F.
. 425;MARY LOU CHECK,516
. RICHARD,553;S.A.
. PRICHARD,40;S.L.,57
. SANFORD H.,57;SARAH
. BOWMAN,330;SUSAN
. HENDRIX,302,315;T.J.
. 57;THOMAS,2,57,60,66
. W.L.,29,34,40,44

. WILLIAM F.,330
DAVID,AVERSON Y.,8
. EDWARD,276;FANNY E.
. 330;FRANCES E. HARRIS
. 315;FRANCIS E. HARRIS
. 329;FRANCIS L.,330
. IVERSON Y.,8;LAURA
. ANN,552;LODICY M.
. BURROUGHS,577;NANCY
. 331;NANCY ANN L.
. SEWEL,8;SIMEAN B.,329
. SIMON B.,315;THOMAS
. C.,577
DAVIDSON,A.F. SMITH,352
. AMANAHA ELLIOTT,352
. ASWELL,315;ASWELL W.
. 329;ELIZ. M. ROBERTS
. 156;HENRY H.,352;J.M.
. 425;JOHN B.,352;M.J.
. FOSTER,573;MARTHA A.
. MASHBURN,352;MARY
. TERRY,315,329,352
. W.C.,573;WILLIAM F.
. 156;WILLIAM H.,352
DAVIES,FRANCIS B.,570
. L.J.,570;MARY E.
. SIMMONS,570
DAVILL,ALEY,453
DAVIS,440;A.B.,32,36
. ADELAIDE VARNELL,568
. ALFORD B.,553;ALICE
. ROSSER,553;ALSEY,370
. AMELIA J. MARTIN,588
. ANCEL B.,479;ANCIL B.
. 479;ANNA,600
. ARCHIBALD,415;ARVINA
. 396;ASA S.,389
. BENJAMIN,352,442
. BENJAMIN W.M.,315,330
. BRITON,438;BRITTON,443
. C.C.,36,41,55;CALVIN
. W.,307,315;CAROLINE
. CROFT,580;CATHERINE
. E.,415;CHARLES C.,568
. CLARISSA,453;CORNELIA
. PEARCE,353;CULEN,297
. CULLEN,280,291,293,438
. CULLIN,449;DANIEL,150
. 184,216,229;DANIEL G.
. 353;E.,520,525,544
. E.A.,434;E.H.,422
. E.K.,244;E.R.,5,57
. EBY FUNDY,479
. EFFIE T. CAMP,434
. ELEANOR P. STRICKLAND
. 49;ELI H.,330;ELIJAH
. 231;ELISA,323;ELIZA,4
. 307;ELIZABETH,350,453
. 559;ELIZABETH J.
. ROBBINS,575;ELIZABETH
. JOHNSON,458;ELIZABETH
. PETTY,46;ELLEN,534
. ELLINDER HEADRICK,453
. EMILY GREEN,433;EMMA
. WILLMOTH,8;EPHRAIM,536
. F.M.,514,525;FANNIE
. WADE,430;FANNY E.
. DAVID,330;FRANCES
. HAMMONS,449;FRANCES
. L.,315;FRANCES POOR
. 301,315;FRANCES R.,304
. 319;FRANCIS,337
. FRANCIS I.,588
. FRANKLIN,353;G.E.
. MERRETT,330;G.F.D.,57
. G.W.,479,560;GARRY,2
. GARY,450;GEORGE W.,474
. GEORGIA,24;GEORGIANNA
. STROP,27;GRAY,57
. GREEN,547;GREENVILLE
. 470-471,473;H.C.,352
. H.O.,575;HARMON,441
. HARRIET J. JACKSON,586
. HARRISON,471,474

. HENRY,470-471;HENRY
. M.,32;HEZAKIAH B.,315
. IDA,57;ISRAEL P.,495
. J.B.,564;J.C.,579
. J.M.,162;JACKSON,563
. JAMES,298,300,315,452
. 461,479,511,530,553
. JAMES B.,57;JAMES L.,2
. 8;JAMES M.,309,315,405
. JAMES W.,72;JANE,19,45
. 320,336,592;JANE S.
. TATE,162;JEMIMA
. BARNETT,459;JESSE,3,88
. 110;JIMMIE,536;JIMMY
. 506;JOHN,465,553;JOHN
. D.,592;JOHN E.,496
. JOHN F.,7;JOHN P.,434
. JOHN S.,2;JOHNSON,465
. JONATHAN R.,2;JOSEPH
. 278,479;JOSEPH G.,449
. JOSHUA,149,300,315
. JULIA A.,26;JULIA A.
. MCMAHAN,583;JULIA ANN
. MATHEWS,553;JULIA ANN
. MATHINS,553;JULIA E.
. 588;K.A.,559;L.F.,525
. L.J. JACKSON,422;L.W.
. 606;LANREY ANN,552
. LAURA HIPPS,539
. LAVINA BAGWELL,315,330
. LEROY W.,595
. LITTLETON H.,471
. LOUISA CHADWICK,479
. LUCINDA MCDONALD,309
. 315;M.E.,539;MALINDA
. TARVER,598;MALISSA A.
. BRID,592;MANDY,367
. MARGARET GANNEY,353
. MARGARET L.,13;MARIAH
. 335;MARSHALL,46
. MARTHA,35,160,336,559
. MARTHA ANDERSON,315
. MARTHA C. COX,479
. MARTHA DAVIS,160
. MARTHA E.,333
. MARTHA J. HOLCOMB,573
. MARTHA K. BOOKER,592
. MARTHA L.,488;MARTHA
. SOMES,479;MARTHA
. TULLY,7;MARTIN,459
. MARY,310,316,320,336
. 365,563;MARY BAXLEY
. 449;MARY C. GOZEMAN
. 479;MARY E.,37,58
. MARY E. EDWARDS,595
. 606;MARY ELIZ.,336
. MARY L.,73;MARY S.
. BLACKSTOCK,352;MARY
. WARD,568;MASON,437
. MATTHEW,398;MATTIE L.
. 44;MATTIE LAY,434
. MOLLIE TIDWELL,520
. NANCY,307,316,557,572
. NANCY A. RAY,583
. NANCY BLACKSTOCK,352
. NANCY FLOYD,452
. OBEDIENCE BAKER,305
. 315;ORELIA,57;P.L.,57
. PARRY,430;PETE,498,515
. POLLEY MALCOM,553;R.
. 536;R.A.,583;R.W.,540
. RACHEL SAMPLES,300,315
. RICHARD D.,586
. RICHARD M.,573;ROBERT
. F.,305,315;ROBERT S.
. 475;RUTH,359;SALLY,450
. SALLY HUGGINS,301,315
. SALLY MITCHELL,31
. SAMUEL,27;SARAH,300
. 593;SARAH A.,303,305
. 379,568;SARAH ANN,318
. SARAH ANN SMITH,560
. SARAH BOWING,563
. SARAH C. WEST,32

. SARAH E.,573;SARAH E.
. ARNOLD,564;SARAH
. FLOYD,450;SARAH J.,314
. SARAH JANE,329;SARAH
. LEDBETTER,307,315
. SOPHIA,485;SURRAY,471
. SUSAN,581;SUSAN MCKAY
. 300,315;SUSAN W.,543
. T.J.,470;TEMPERANCE
. S.,23,57;TEMPY S.
. ROBERTS,5;THOMAS,463
. 474;THOMAS C.,577-578
. 583;URIAH,453;VAN,437
. VAN W.,330;W.A.,433
. W.H.,31;W.M.,391,580
. WALTON,471;WALTON H.
. 474;WARREN R.,592
. WILEY,105;WILLIAM,142
. 160,301,315,434,438
. 441-442,458,547,568
. WILLIAM B.,301,315
. WILLIAM J.,49;WILLIAM
. M.,1;WILLIS,598;Z.C.
. 579;Z.N.,568
. ZACHARIAH,153,222-223
DAVISON,HUGH,398
DAVITTE,JOHN C.,496
DAWES,MARY E.,39
. SUSANNAH,456
DAWN,EMMA C.,598
. JOSEPHINE,599
DAWNING,JANE,171
DAWNKOSS,362
DAWSON,ABEL,547;BERY,547
. E.A. WALRAVEN,45
. ENOCH,547;J.W.,422
. JANE MCCLESKY,8;JOHN
. 150,165,167;JONAS,547
. L.M.,45;LAWRENCE M.
. 135;LUSSAPHINE HILL
. 422;MARGARET,450;MARY
. 421,427;WILLIAM,57
. WILLIAM A.,404,547
. WILLIAM P.,8,57
DAY,330,498;ALLEN Y.,353
. AMY,323,340;ANDY,353
. ANDY L.,305,315
. BRELLEY WEST,479
. CHARLES,230;ELIZABETH
. PUGH,353;FRANCES,557
. JAMES,402;JESSE,150
. 170,230;JOSHUA DENNY
. 479;LOT,462;MAGGIE,485
. POLLY,370;REBECCA KEY
. 353;REBECCA W. KEY,305
. 315;SAMUEL,463
. ZACHARIAH,298
DEADMAN,BEDE POOL,453
. CINNAKE,453;LUCINDA
. 155
DEAL,
. CYNTHIA C. THOMAS,308
. 315;CYNTHIA C.
. THOMPSON,308;DANIEL
. 231;GEORGE,308,315
. I.P.,422;JACOB,58
. MARY,58;MESHACK,280
. 282,292
DEALE,P.,368
DEAN,507;ADA,534;ALLY
. 502;ARCHIBALD,439
. CHARLES,156;CORDELIA
. 526;DANIEL,502;E.B.
. 502;E.S.,577,579
. ELBERT J.,597
. ELIZABETH CHAMBLEE,380
. ELIZABETH CHEROKEE,353
. HARRIET CHADWICK,479
. J.B.,502;JEREMIAH,151
. JOHH M.,479;JOHN,433
. JOHN H.,479;JOSIAH M.
. 380;L.E.,502;LUCINDA
. WILSON,156;M.E.
. WALLACE,353;MARY,502

. MARY CARVER,479;NANCY
. 157;NAOMI GLADEN,597
. REBECCA,160;SALLIE
. GREASON,433;SARAH,454
. TRESSA CORBIN,491
. W.H.,14,45,479;W.J.
. 353;WILLIAM,152
. WILLIAM B.,256
. WILLIAM H.,14;ZARIAH
. M.,353
DEAR,JOHN POOR,261
DEARING,ELIZABETH,489
. JEREMIAH,479;LUCINDA
. EVANS,479;MARTHA JANE
. FULTON,479;MARY D.,481
. R.B.,479;ROBERT,479
. SARAHAN R. AKINS,479
DEARON,MICHAEL,230
DEASON,MICAJAH,495
DEATEN,WILLIAM,463
DEATON,HARRIET,372
DEAVENPORT,CHARLES,441
DEAVORS,A.J.,7
DEBORD,DANIEL,230
DECK,ALICE ANDERSON,602
. J.T.,369;JACOB,602
DECKER,
. MELISSA BALLARD,420
. SINGLETON,420
DEDMAN,WILLIAM,547
DEED,JOHN,387
DEEL,EPHRAIM G.,40
. VINY E. BINGHAM,40
DEEN,W.H.,16
DEES,ELIZABETH MOORE,559
. GREEN,149;MARION,559
DEFIER,JOHN,170
DEFOOR,JOHN,440-441
DEFOOT,S.L.,420
DEFREESE,WILLIAM,244-245
. 247-249
DEFRESE,CHARLIE,544
. MOLLIE PALMER,544
DEFUR,ROBERT,438
DEJOURNETT,JOHN,191
DEJOURNETTE,JOHN C.,241
DEJOUTNETTE,JOHN,183
DELANEY,JOHN B.,592
. JOHN L.,330;MARY M.
. HARRIS,330
. NARCISSA B. MOFFETT
. 592
DELANY,MARY,331
. ROSANNAH M.,156
DELAPERRIERE,ANGE,454
. MARY A. THURMAN,454
DELAY,HIRAM R.,14;JESSE
. W.,160;MARY PATON,160
. MATILDA S. JONES,14
DELENPORT,SARAH S.,335
DELK,112;DAVID,2,580
. ELIZABETH,58;FLETCHER
. L.,16;ISABELLA C.
. YORK,307,315;J.D.,58
. JACKSON,58,93,95,98-99
. 108,138,307,315
. JULIAH D.,5;MARY,302
. 321;MARY E. PARNELL,16
. MARY FRANCIS,13;MARY
. WALKER,5;OLYMPIA COX
. 580;R.D.,58;TEMPEY,320
. TEMPY,300;W.,111;W.P.
. 58;WILLIAM,74,111
. WILLIAM J.,58,94-95,98
. 102-103
DELLAFIELD,NANCY,456
DELONG,ELLEN BARBER,38
. R.,38
DEMBY,JAMES W.,445
. MATILDA W. CAMERON,445
DEMOND,A.Y.,387
DEMPSEY,A.F.,58;A.G.,11
. 13-14,16-17,20-21,23
. 30,36,47-48;ALVIN G.

. 137;BARNETT J.,440
. E.P.,433;ELIZABETH,418
. ELLIS,423;FANNIE,34
. FANNY LAND,433;HENSON
. 170;JOHN,439;L.,58
. L.E.,424;LEVI,436
. M.C.,418;M.D.P.,160
. MARY MCINTON,423;N.A.
. 58;N.E.,426;NEWTON A.
. 24;QUEEN CAPHORT,599
. ROBERT,77;S.A. DOBSON
. 601;SARAH J. MEEK,24
. SUSAN BAKER,160;T.,601
. WILLIAM,599
DENE,ELIJAH,156;ELIZA
. FOWLER,156
DENHAM,DIDIMAY TROUT,454
. P.G.,102,104,109
. PATRICK G.,104,110,454
. ROBERT,109
DENMAN,
. CAROLINE SPEARS,576
. CHAPLEY,576;ELIZABETH
. CARLTON,449;FELIX,392
. J.G.,392;JOHN,449
. NANCY,599;WILLIAM M.
. 392
DENMEAD,TOLBOTT,58
DENNING,CATHERINE,369
DENNIS,
. COMFORT PARKER,553
. HENRY,553;JACOB,440
. NARCISSA WILLIAMS,455
. RICHARD,172,465
. WILLIAM B.,455
DENNY,AZRIAH,463;ELHEED
. 463;ROBERT,170
DENSEMORE,DAVID,153
DENSMORE,DAVID,149,273
. MARY ANN,491
DENSON,BROOKS,521
. EMELINE CONGO,35
. JAMES,35,539;LAURA,519
DENT,JANE M.,155
DENTON,B.W.,574
. BENJAMIN,156;BENNY,504
. E.J. CAMPBELL,574
. ELIJAH,547;ELLA C.
. MCCRARY,598;EMA,577
. GEORGE,531;GEORGE R.
. 542;J.F.,598;J.G.,7
. 533;JAMES,504;JANE
. PITTMAN,156;JONAS,547
. JULIA PARKER,542;MARY
. 156,604;PERMELIA
. GARRETT,330;REUBEN,157
. 330;SAMUEL,92,105
. SUSAN PITMAN,157
DEPREIST,
. DEBORAH JONES,553
. GREEN,553
DERBY,
. CALDONIA D. WOLLEY,479
. EMILY,494;EMILY D.,494
. HENRY,479;JAMES,494
. JAMES S.,479;MARGARET
. SAMS,479;NANCY,490
DERIFIELD,NICHOLAS,450
. SALLY GORMAN,450
DERRICK,JOHN,547
DESHAYES,CAROLINE,596
DETREVILIE,ELIZA,58
. ROBERT,58;RUTH,58
DEVENPORT,115;F.L.,86
. JOSEPH,116
DEVERAUS,ABRAHAM,257
DEVETON,JOHN,96
DEW,J.C.,422;J.P. DODD
. 422
DEWBERRY,MARY E.,41
. WILLIAM,534
DEWELS,W.H.,140
DEWER,JOHN W.,110
DEWES,W.H.,140

DEWS,HENRY W.,29;LILA
. TRENHOHM,29;LILA
. TRENHOLM,29
DIAL,CHRISTY,558;JANE
. 551;JOHN,180,230,260
. JOSEPH S.,152,197,204
. 253;MARY J.,8;NANCY
. 555;PUNMELIA,552
DICKENKEY,JANE,322
DICKENS,ALFRED,204
. CAROLINE,556;TRESAM
. 447
DICKERD,SARAH,427
DICKERKEY,JANE,301
DICKERSON,547;ALLEN,58
. CAROLINE,37;E. PUTNAM
. 419;ECARILLA,456
. ELIZA J.,15;ELLEN,58
. EMILY,160;JAMES F.,419
. JOHN,456;LUCINDA,44
. MARY GARRISON,456
. MATILDA E.,33
. NANCY ANN MALCOM,553
. NANCY J. WHEELER,161
. NEHEMIAH S.,161
. NELSON,179,206,224,253
. 257,260,262-263,469
. R.J.,58;SELENIA KNOX
. 163;THOMAS E.,163
. THOMPSON,443;WELBORN
. T.,553
DICKINSON,
. CHARLOTTE JOHNSON,589
. JOHN J.,391;JOHN P.
. 285;NELSON,259;PERRY
. 589
DICKSON,114;D.W.,58,83
. E. FAULKS,600;E.A.,58
. 83;EDLEY P.,302,315
. JOHN,122,297;M.,421
. MAGGIE,593;MARY E.
. DAVIS,58;MILLY HOLDEN
. 302,315;SAMUEL,495
. W.C.,58;W.D.,58;W.M.
. 600;WILLIAM C.,58
DIDMAN,WILLIAM,465
DIEL,JOSEPH S.,152
DIFFEY,NANCY,450
DIGGS,NANCY,557
DIKES,JOHN,353;JOHN F.
. 353;SARAH DANIEL,353
. SARAH E. MCKINEY,353
DILBECK,MARVIS,475
DILDA,DENNIS,440;POLLY
. 547
DILDY,ELIAS,547
DILINGHAM,HIRAM,547
DILL,J.M.,523;J.N.,525
MARGARET,576
DILLAR,M.M.,428
DILLARD,C.C.,425;E.J.
. 427;EDMUND,445;ELIJAH
. 397;JAMES,547;JOHN,547
. LILLIE WILSON,434
. M.M.,428;MARGARET
. HICKS,572;MARGARET
. THURMOND,445;MARY
. ADCOX,427;MARY F.,433
. R.W.,434;SARAH,410
. THOMAS P.,572
DILLBECK,MALINDA,488
DILLINGHAM,JEHUE M.,479
. MARTHA E. LEMONS,479
DIMMOCK,T.W.,522
DIMSDALE,DAVID J.,161
. HIRAM,153,193-194,196
. 202 203,205,263,257
. 259-260,262-263
. MARTHA HENDRICKS,161
. SARAH L. HOLCOMB,479
. W.D.,479
DIMSDALL,HIRAM,191
DIMSEL,
. MARY E. WILSON,479

. SMITH,479
DINEMORE,DAVID,180
DINSMORE,
. CAROLINE REAVIS,162
. SYLVESTER,162
DISHAROON,
. ABBY BROOKS,480;B.B.
. 488;BETHEL Q.,476
. ERVIN C.,479-480;JOHN
. H.,480;MARGARET A.,482
. MARTHA M.,488;MARTHA
. PENDLEY,480;MARYAN,484
. SIS CHUMLEY,479
DISHEROON,ERWIN C.,159
DISKERT,MARY,330
DISMUKE,JESSE H.,553
. NANCY BROWN,553
. NANCY E. WAY,18
. WALTER B.,18
DIXON,MARTHA K.,307
. MARTHA R.,322
DLEY,HIRAM H.R.,553
. LOUISA VANDIFORD,553
DOAN,SEFIE,452
DOBBENS,JOHN A.,101
DOBBINS,C.C.,425;DRURIE
. 58;GEORGE,511;J.
. SIDNEY,47;JOHN A.,99
. 100,103-105,128;M.E.
. 424;MARY PACE,47
. NANNIE,32;SARAH F.,58
. THOMAS,511;WILLIAM,2
DOBBS,ADDIE M.,58
. ALBERT,58;ALICE,58
. ALICE C.,58;AMANDA C.
. 58;ANN,58;ASA,107
. BURWELL,253,257,263
. CAROLINE WILKS,157
. CYRUS,437,441-442
. D.W.,58;DAVID,58,86,93
. 94-95,161;DAVID J.,58
. 86,132;DINNIA,156
. E.A.,23-24,27,45,47-50
. 132-133;ELIAS B.,38
. ELIZA,32;ELIZABETH,452
. ELLERSON A.,133
. ELLISON A.,49;FRANCES
. 11;GEORGE H.,58;J.L.
. 58;J.P.,146;JAMES,87
. JAMES E.,58;JAMES P.
. 58,86,132;JANE,86
. JANE E.,58;JERRY,86
. JESSE,92;JOSEPH,156
. JULYAN,157;LEWIS,150
. 463;M.C.,58;MAMIE,58
. MARTHA,561;MARTHA 5.
. GRIFFIN,161;MARTIN,2
. 458;MARY M.,4;MATTIE
. J.,58;MELISSA TIPPIN
. 156;MOURMAN,441-442
. NANCY BARNWELL,452
. NANCY E. HARDMAN,38
. NANCY S. FOUNTAIN,161
. O.S.,58;PERRY,158
. PLEASANT C.,157
. ROSALINDA,58
. ROSALINDA HULSEY,458
. S.,112;SALLY,35;SILAS
. 161,452;SULSER,121
. TULSER,112;VESTY M.
. 158;VESTY M. DOBBS,158
. W.B.,58;W.J.,58;W.M.
. 86,129;W.O.,58;W.P.,58
. WILLIAM,58,86,100
. WILLIAM M.,58-59
. WILLIE,58
DOBS,BURWELL,262
DOBSON,A.P.,483;ANN,155
. HARRIT E. MANNING,583
. HENRY,181,211;HENRY
. H.,399;JAMES,211
. JOANNAH,455;JOSEPHINE
. 597;LAURA S.,582
. MARGARET EVANS,311,315

DRUMMOND,JANE,445
. LYDIA M. FINCHER,446
. MATHEW,446;NANCY,555
. W.H.,281;WILLIAM,442
. WILLIAM H.,276
DRYER,EDMOND H.,465
DRYSDALE,ISABEL J.,26
DUBERRY,WILLIAM,534
DUCK,
. MANERVA A. -
. WESTBROOK,480;MARY,482
. WILLIAM,480
DUCKET,ANNIE WHITE,604
. ARMINDA J.,582;E.N.
. 410;ESTER N.,564;J.W.
. 604;JESSE R.,564;M.E.
. MCCLAIN,573;MARTHA
. BENNET,586;NANCY
. MOORELAND,564;NATHAN
. A.,573;THOMAS,586
DUCKETT,
. CAROLINE DUNSON,599
. E.A.,599;E.J.,594
. ELIZABETH,571;JANE,579
. JANE DUNN,480;JOHN W.
. 480;LULA,492;MARGARET
. A.,580;MARY A.
. HARKINS,419;MARY J.
. DYCUS,594;SARAH,583
. WILLIAM A.,419
DUDLEY,ANDERSON,496
. DANIEL,2;DAVID,153,191
. 228,544;GENNETT,544
. JOHN W.,301;LINDA,424
. MALINDA PRUITT,301
. MARION,535
DUDLY,JOHN W.,315
. MALINDA PRUET,315
DUFFEN,M.E.,427;M.E.
. GAINES,426;WILLIAM C.
. 426-427
DUFFEY,JOHN M.,528
DUFFY,LUCINDA D.,8
DUGAN,D.R.,596;FRANCES
. FERINGTON,592;JOHN C.
. 592;M.J.,595;MARY ANN
. ROSE,596
DUGGAN,
. MINERVA A. JOHNSON,563
. W.H.H.,573;WILLIAM J.
. 563
DUGGER,SARAH ANN,432
DUKE,395;ALFRED G.,18
. CELIA COX,300,315
. CHARLES E.,553;G.R.
. 278;JAMES,553;JESSE
. 598;LUCY VAUGHN,598
. MARTHA COTTON,553
. MARTHA E. HILL,18
. MARTIN,397,401-402
. MARY ANN WHITE,553
. MINERVA HIGHTOWER,553
. SARAH ANN MURRAY,458
. THOMAS,553;TIMOTHY,300
. 315;W.L.,458
DUKES,MARTHA A.,12
. MOSES,2;SAMUEL,436
DUMAS,WINCHESTER,169
DUMMER,ELIZABETH,309,318
DUN,
. ANNY E.C. CAMERON,315
. EZEKIEL,315;JOHN,547
DUNAGAN,A.F.,518
. ELIZABETH,518;ISAIAH
. 456;JOSEPH,285;JOSHUA
. 463;LOUISA J.,577
. MARTHA,518;SUSANNAH
. EBERHART,456;T.C.,518
. T.G.,518
DUNAHOO,AMANDA,329
. JAMES M.,301;LUCY
. MONDAY,301
DUNAWAY,NANCY E.,335
. TABITHA,454

DUNBAR,JAMES P.,564
. MINERVA ANN ENNIS,564
DUNCAN,A.C.,478
. ALEXANDRIA,464;ANN N.
. GRISHAM,13;ANSELL,159
. ARMETTA SMITH,301
. BOBBIE,58;CATHERINE
. COOK,159;CHARLES,166
. 187,201,230,251
. CHOICE,159;DRURY,458
. EDMUND,201,251;ELIZA
. DODD,458;ELIZABETH C.
. 567;ELIZABETH TATE,159
. F.M.,520;FRANCES,23
. J.B.,86,520;JAMES,135
. JOHN,180,184,196,218
. JOHN B.,480;JOHN N.
. 330;LARAH E. PARTIN
. 480;LENA,58;MARTHA B.
. 58;MARY,493;MARY E.,19
. MARY M. TIDWELL,330
. MATILDA,456;MILLIA A.
. 564;NANCY,562;P.M.,500
. POLLY,577;POLLY
. BARNWELL,453;R.B.,265
. ROBERT,285;ROBERT S.
. 301;WILLIAM,453
. WILLIAM P.,13,62
. WILLIAM W.,1
DUNCIN,ISAAC RIGHT,330
. LUISA F. ANDERSON,330
DUNER,ISAAC E.,590;JANE
. BRANNER,590
DUNKIN,CALDONIA A.,483
. CLARA,455
DUNKING,
. ARMETTA SMITH,315
. ROBERT S.,315
DUNLAP,435,437;JONATHAN
. 547;JOSEPH C.,496
. MARY C. PHARIS,580
. MARY MOSS,480;MATHEW
. 548;R.H.,580;SARAH J.
. 329;THOMAS C.,495
. W.C.,417;WILLIAM,480
DUNMEAD,EDWARD,60,62
DUNN,
. ANN E.C. CAMERON,302
. D.D.,58;ELIZABETH
. HILL,449;ELIZABETH
. KELL,449;EZEKIEL,302
. FRANCIS,49;HASTEN,141
. 145;HASTON,24
. HENERITTA,24;HENRY,2
. 439;I.J.,59;J.H.,59
. J.M.,59;J.W.,573;JANE
. 36,480;JOHN,51,443,449
. 547;JULIA,42;LOU L.
. LOVE,573;M.E.,59;M.J.
. WILLIAMS,423;MARGARET
. 561;MARY,59;MAY,503
. MOSES,469;NANCY,58
. REBECCA TUCKER,24
. V.A.,575;W.G.,59;W.S.
. 59;W.W.,423;WILLIAM,2
. 59,106;WILLIAM N.,59
DUNNAGAN,ANN,452
DUNNAN,MOSES H.,96
DUNNEGAN,ELIZABETH,487
. JULIA A.E.,563
DUNNINGAN,B.S.,562
. MARY E. EDWARDS,562
DUNSON,CAROLINE,599
DUNTON,FRANCES P.,59
. JOHN C.,59;MARY,59
. NANCY,59
DUNWOODY,C.A.,146
. CHARLES A.,59;D.M.,69
. ELLEN C.,59;HATTIE W.
. MORRIS,48;HENRY A.,48
. JAMES B.,9;W.E.,81
DUPRE,C.W.,59
DUPREE,A.N.,59;C.C.,573
. D.D.,59;E.F.,59;E.M.

. 59;EMILY J.,593;J.A.
. 59;JANE GREEN,573
. MARY JANE,513;SAMUEL
. A.,59;W.A.,59;WILLIAM
. 543;WILLIAM A.,513
DUREN,CECILDA,554;POLLY
. VANN,553;SAMUEL,553
DURHAM,A.N.,59;ADOLPHUS
. 35;BETSY YOUNG,454
. C.A.,418;C.D.,563
. DAVID,454;E.O.,70
. FANNY,30;G.B.,167
. GEORGE,30,467;GREEN
. B.,149,165,170
. HARRIET,72;HARRIET M.
. 71;J.,111;J.P.,59
. JACOB O.,528;JAMES
. M.C.,330;JAMES S.,41
. JOHN,135;JOSEPHINE
. DOOLY,330;L.E.,515
. LACY W.,59;LAURA
. WHITFIELD,30;LUCY
. WOODLIFF,451;M.
. MONCRIEF,425;M.P.
. HARGROVES,35;MAMIE,59
. MATTIE J.,59;N.,111
. O.D.,563;ROWELL,451
. TALLULAH,44;UNICY
. JOHNSON,563;WILLIAM
. G.,425;WINNY CATH.,158
DUTREE,SAMUEL,133
DUTTON,D.S.,59;JOHN C.
. 524;MALISSA C. MOON
. 524;R.,59
DUVAL,EUGENE,500
DUVALL,J.B.,109
DUYCK,CELIA COX,300,315
. TIMOTHY,300,315
DYCUS,ANNIS COMPTON,589
. DAVID,563;EDWARD H.
. 571;JAMES G.,563;MARY
. J.,594;NANCY MCDUNE
. 571;NANCY MOORE,563
. NRACISSUS,576
. SARAH A. HAYLE,563
. STEPHEN B.,589
DYE,NANCY,419
DYENS,BIDDY WOOD,583
. T.L.,583
DYER,ALLEN,188;DAVID,231
. E.,177;EDWIN,445
. ELISHA,151,191-192,207
. 228,236,243,256
. HANNAH D.,578;HULDA
. A.,579;JAMES,578
. JOSEPH S.,149
. MARTHA E. ALEXANDER
. 582;MARY,426,565;N.
. 426;PAULINE,581
. SAMUEL,582;SIMPSON C.
. 191,222,256;SUSAN E.
. PHILLIPS,578;SYMPSON
. C.,152
DYERS,MARTHA,163
DYRE,JOHN,594;SUSAN A.
. SMITH,594
DYSON,J.C.,59;JAMES R.
. 59;MARION M.,59
E.ROLINS,MISSOURI,355
EACHEN,D.N.,8
EADS,W.C.,420;WILLIAM 236
EAKES,
. ALMYRA D. JOHNSTON,330
. M.H.,330;MARY A.,348
EAKS,R.A.,430
EARL,SAMUEL,64
EARLE,A.L.,59;ASPASIA
. 403;E.W.,59;R.H.,77
. RICHARD,66,78;SAM,61
. SAMUEL,59
EARLEY,ENOCH,166
EARLY,NEVEL S.,172
. RICHARD S.,553
. SARAH E. GUTHRY,553

. ZELPHER,373
EARNEST,JOHN,581;L.W.
. 582;M.L. MITCHELL,598
. M.M.,598;MAHALA CLICK
. 579;Q.T.,579;SALLIE
. SMITH,581
EARWOOD,ALLEN,520-521
. ANNIE,524;G.W.,524
. HENRY,502;JOHN,500,502
. SERRLING,502
EASLEY,JULIA,59
EASON,EARRALIE C.,6
. EMILY,59,84-85;J.L.,84
. J.S.,59,85;JOHN,589
. JOHN L.,59;JOHN S.,17
. JUDAH RUSSEL,589
. MANINSTER M.,59
. MARTHA JANE LEE,17
. NATHAN,59;O.R.,59,84
. OBED R.,59;R.,84;R.E.
. 112;RASBERRY,59,84
. REBECCA M.,9,59
. WILLIAM,99-100,102,105
EAST,ANNY,455;EMILY,533
. 534;NANCY,575;W.M.,561
. WILLIAM,560,562-563
. 566,568,573
EASTER,HARRIET,300
EASTERLING,
. CORDELIA A. GREENE,553
. GEORGIA MERIDITH,576
. J.M.,576;JOEL C.,553
. MARY J.,593;OBEDIENCE
. 495;SARAH,551;WILLIAM
. 111,495
EASTERS,HARRIET,321
EASTLAND,SALLIE,602
EATON,ALEXANDER,132;ANN
. 458;C.F.,40;CHARLOTTE
. 449;ELIZABETH TOLBERT
. 480;HANNAH,158;JAMES
. 232,244,246;JESSE W.
. 480;JOHN,440,464
. JOSEPH,149,167
. LUCINDA,304,314
. MALINDA,456;MARGARET
. 301;MARGRET,315;MARY
. ALDRIDGE,310,315
. MATTIE J.,38;OPILIALIA
. 479;PEGGY,453;REUBEN
. 150,310,315;ROANCY L.
. 20;RUTHA,162;SAMUEL
. 464;SIRRAH,452;SURRAY
. 181;SURRY,177-178
. SUSANNAH BECK,452
. T.I.,480;WILLIAM,464
. ZILPHIA DOBSON,480
EAVES,
. H.E. WOOLBRIGHT,418
. J.F.,428;JANE ROBERTS
. 428;LEDFORD B.,495
. LEWIS,495;M.L. FORD
. 540;M.V.,418;MARY,420
. NANCY L.,427;SHADY
. BROWN,526;T.M.,540
. W.T.,526
EBERHART,ELIZABETH,454
. 459;SUSANNAH,456
EBORD,DEWRY,548
ECHISON,FRANCES,552
ECHOLD,T.R.,144
ECHOLLS,ELIAS L.,304
. ELIZABETH STRICKLAND
. 304;MILLEY,316
ECHOLS,A.B.,395,400
. ALICE,516;BENJAMIN,308
. 315;CAROLINE FIELDS
. 308,315;CATHERINE,517
. CHARLES L.,510;E.M.
. 354;EBER,354,382;EBER
. B.,311,315;ELIAS L.
. 315;ELIJAH P.,330
. ELIZABETH,500
. ELIZABETH J. BROWN,315

. 330;ELIZABETH
. STRICKLAND,315
. EMALINE GANT,311,315
. FRANCIS E. GANT,382
. FRANCIS GANT,354
. HARRIET E. TERRY,354
. HENRY,599;HENRY L.,21
. J.R.,59;JAMES M.,307
. 315,330;JAMES T.,65
. JOSHUA,330;MANERVIA
. D.,382;MARGARET,307
. 325;MARY J.,20;MARY
. THOMAS,307,315
. MARY V. GILBERT,36
. MASON P.,306,315
. MILLY,331;MISSISSIPPI
. CAPE,330;NANCY M.,309
. 322;NANCY YANCY,306
. 315;R.W.,513;RHODA
. WALRAVEN,21;ROBERT M.
. 36;SARAH E. IVEY,599
. SARAH PURCELL,330
. T.G.,65;T.J.,516;T.R.
. 146,517;W.S.,504,513
. WILLIAM,59
EDDELMAN,JOSEPH,315
. MARY M. BRAMBLETT,315
EDDINGTON,LEAH,157
EDDLEMAN,GEORGE W.,586
. NANCY E.,9;NANCY
. WILLIAMS,586;RUTHA M.
. 313,327;SARAH F.,337
EDGAR,JOHN,553;POLLY
. HOLLOWAY,553
EDGE,JOHN M.,106;MARY
. ANN,581;NEWTON N.,162
. VIRGINIA A.S. HOLLAND
. 162
EDGERTON,WILLIAM,230
EDGEWORTH,E.G.,25
EDINGTON,WILLIAM,463
EDISON,R.L.,141
EDLEMAN,DAVID,97
EDMANSON,JAMES,297
. PHEOBE D.,328;SAMUEL
. 297
EDMANSONS,JAMES,297
EDMISON,JAMES,455
. SUSANNAH CARR,455
EDMONDS,BURWELL,553
. NANCY BEARDIN,553
EDMONDSON,A.L.,136,146
. A.S.,138,141;A.V.,395
. ANDREW J.,305,315
. BILL,510-511;CANSADA
. G.,338;FRANCES L.
. 411;JAMES,176,469,472
. JOHN,330;JOSEPH,472
. MARTHA KARR,453;MARY
. JEFFREYS,305,315
. NANCY E. SAMPLES,330
. PARTHY,321;PATSY,305
. SAMUEL,442,453;THOMAS
. 315
EDMONSON,ANDREW J.,354
. FRANCES E.,339;JAMES
. 176,441;JAMES O.,353
. LEROY,330;LUTITIE
. PHILLIPS,353;MARTHA
. R.,328;MARY,372;MARY
. BARKER,353;MARY C.
. JEFFERS,354;MARY L.
. 354;NANCY J. STEPHENS
. 330;NOAH,330;PINKNEY
. 353;SAMUEL,176,438,441
. SARAH J. WINDOWS,330
EDMUNDSON,
. FRANCIS L. DAVID,330
. JAMES,470;THOMAS,330
EDWARD,RACHAEL,50
. REBECCA E.,364
EDWARDS,A.,96;A.B.,91
. A.C.,51,59,70;A.D.,142

A.M.,59;A.N.,59
. A.T.A.,482;ABEL,474
. ALFRED,3;ALFRED B.,89
. ANNIE W.,59;BENJAMIN
. F.,315;CAROLINE,11
. CAROLINE C. JOHNSTON
. 315;CATHERINE,491
. CHARISTIANNA,383
. CHRISTINA,325,342
. DALEYANN TAYLOR,330
. DELITHA A.,9;E.H.,559
. 561-562,564-566,568
. EDWARD,149,171,215,217
. 221,235,242,257
. EDWARD HARPER,567
. ELEJAH,463;FRANCES C.
. CAPE,12;FRANCES E.,558
. FRANCES M.,160;FRED
. 518;G.R.,407;GUSSIE,59
. HENRY,466;J.W.,330
. JACK,510;JAMES,469
. JANE,333,376,379,488
. JANE OWENS,159;JOHN
. 151,192,203-204,213
. 214,228,236,242,330
. JOSEPH,159;JOSIE A.F.
. 342;JUDITH,450
. JULIA A.E. DUNNEGAN
. 563;L.B.,330;LEANDER
. 28;LITTLETON C.,223
. M.E. PHILLIPS,330
. M.H.,433-434;MALINDA
. 339,343;MARGARET E.
. 332;MARTHA E. MCGINTY
. 18;MARTHA G.,558;MARY
. 459;MARY A. BROADWELL
. 330;MARY E.,562,595
. 606;MARY FLETCHER,553
. MILES,102,105;NANCY
. 314,552;NANCY ALLIN
. 553;NANCY F.,339;O.G.
. 127;ROBERT L.,507
. ROSALEE CHAMBLEE,330
. RUTHA,158;S.B.,386
. SALLY,456;SARAH,305
. 325,353;SIMEON,59
. SOPHIA OFFUTT,307,315
. STEPHEN,467;SUSAN,302
. 321;T.S.,434;THOMAS
. 307,315,553;THOMAS P.
. 553;W.A.,330;W.N.,515
. WADE,465;WILLIAM,12
. WILLIAM T.,18,563
EEDES,S.M. TERRELL,421
. W.H.,321
EEDS,SIDNEY,428;WILLIAM
. 228,243-244
EIDS,WILLIAM,152
EIDSON,C.E. STEELE,48
. DAVID C.,496;R.S.,48
. 143
EIVENS,GEORGE,480
. HARRIET MCARTHUR,480
EIZEL,C. ABERNATHY,425
. SAMUEL,425
EKES,NANCY SIMS,330
. ROBERT A.,330
ELARD,AMOS,298
ELDER,MARY DISKERT,330
. WHITMAN,330
ELDERS,A.A.,529
ELDRIDGE,J.W.,59;M.J.,59
. MARTHA,22;WILLIE,59
ELINGTON,DAVID,168
ELIOT,ALPHA,495;SARAH
. R.,46
ELIS,AUGUSTA,7
ELISON,DUDLEY,315;MILLY
. 312;POLLY STONE,315
ELIT,JOHN W.,451;SARAH
. SCAGGS,451
ELLARD,AMOS,247,472,548
. JAMES,204,469,471,548
. JOSEPH,548;SARAH,339

. WILLIAM,471
ELLEGTON,WILLIAM,387
ELLER,ELEGOH,387
. MALINDA A. BRAMLETT
. 480;WILLIAM H.,480
ELLERD,JAMES,153
ELLIE,WILLIAM,256
ELLIETT,JAMES S.,151
ELLINGBERG,MARTHA C.,478
ELLINGTON,ANNIE,377;C.
. 59;DAVID B.,2,149,170
. FRANCES,457;LIZZA ANN
. LEDBETTER,480;PETER
. 377;RACHEL P.,417;S.
. ROBERT,480;SALINA H.
. COLEMAN,408;W.B.,417
. WATSON R.,408;WILLIAM
. 408
ELLIOT,
. ELIZABETH -
. ROBERTSON,582;EPHRAIM
. 548;RICHARD J.,582
ELLIOTT,143,165;AMANAHA
. 352;BURGETT MCCARTY
. 553;CICERO COLUMBUS
. 353;CORNELIUS,553
. D.N.,86;DAVID M.,35
. ELIZABETH,26
. ELIZABETH J.,334
. ELMIRA A.,59;F.A.,60
. G.L.,59;J.H.,138,140
. 142-143;JAMES H.,46
. JAMES JACKSON,353
. JAMES S.,191-192,207
. 225,253,257,259-260
. 262-263;JOHN,172,186
. L.V.,59;LULA,543;M.M.
. 60;MATILDA FREEMAN,353
. MINDA,524;RACHAEL R.
. MOON,46;SALLY DOBBS,35
. SARAH DOOLY,353;W...,60
ELLIS,A.L. HUGHES,365
. ALMYRA,163;ANDREW R.
. 480;BALIS,367
. BENJAMIN,365;C.F.
. FLOYD,422;ELIJAH,548
. ELIZABETH M.,565
. FANNIE A. HOGAN,430
. HARVEY,430;HESTER ANN
. 9;IDA,486;J.H.,422
. JAMES,474;JESSE,155
. JOHN,553;JOHN A.,581
. JOHN R.,508;JOHN W.
. 330;JOSHUA,301,315,553
. JOYCE BRUTON,330;L.C.
. 414;LIZZIE WATERS,430
. LUCINDA,359,385
. M.E.M.,560;MAHALIA,563
. MARGARET MARTIN,367
. MARY A.,328;MARY ANN
. 367;MARY B.,365;MILLY
. 423;NANCY,303,317
. NANCY LAY,155;R.D.,494
. SALLIE E. HUGHES,330
. SAMUEL J.,330
. SARAH ANN HUGHES,553
. SARAH J. MILFORD,330
. SARAH KELLY,301,315
. SARAH M. WHISENANT,480
. SILAS,1;SYTHA
. LASSETOER,553;THOMAS
. J.,330;W.A.,422;W.F.
. 430;W.S.,429;WILL,543
. WILLIAM,548
ELLISON,436-437;CHARITY
. 332;D.A.,516;DELILA
. 555;DUDLEY,300;E.
. JOLLY,603;E.C.,580
. EASTER,336;ELIZA E.
. LEACH,330;ELIZABETH
. STONE,553;EZRA T.,60
. FRANCIS,436-437;HENRY
. G.,152,222;JONATHAN
. G.,160;LUMPKIN J.,60

. M.A. AKERS,427;MAHALA
. E.,5;MILLY,301;MOSES
. 220-221,437;POLLY
. STONE,300;R.,603
. RACHEL,557;RALPH,474
. ROBERT,220-221;ROBERT
. E.,330;S.C.,579;S.M.
. 427;SAMUEL,244,436
. SERENA WHITLOCK,160
. WATSON,553;WILLIAM,232
ELLISTON,MALETHA,234
ELLMORE,500
ELLROD,
. ELIZABETH BRYANT,480
. JOHN T.,480;LEVIE,480
. MANDY C. DORSEY,480
. NARCISSA BRYANT,480
. THOMAS,480
ELLSBERRY,507;A.B.,502
. MARY,503
ELMER,J.B.,60
ELMOR,D.,465
ELMORE,DAVID,161;ELIZA
. 60;F.T.,60;HARRIET E.
. 12;LUCY MCCORMACK,161
. M.J.,425
ELROD,ALFRED,480
. CAROLINE,489
. ELIZABETH,31
. ELIZABETH SHOCKLEY,453
. GEORGE,453;JACOB,284
. 452,462;JOHN,189,461
. LINNEY BOYD,452
. LOUISA J. COGSWELL,163
. LUCINDA,352;M.A.
. BLALOCK,425;MARIAH,160
. MARTHA GODFREY,480
. T.H.,425;WILLIAM G.
. 163
ELSAS,JOSEPH,141
ELSBERRY,ANN,543;BETTIE
. 545;DELILAH HUBBARD
. 506;FLETCHER,540;G.R.
. 540;IKE,543;J.W.,506
. JAMES,531,538;JOHN,443
. LINCEY,436;LINSEY,2
. 544;W.T.,543
ELSBERY,Z.B.,539
ELUTT,MARY MULLINS,553
. WILLIAM,553
ELY,CHARLES A.,465
ELYARD,RACHEL E.,42
EMANIEL,ELIZABETH,28
EMANUEL,DAVID,60
. ELIZABETH,60;MARY,22
EMBER,JANE CALDWELL,571
. WILLIAM A.,571
EMBRY,ADDIE,536
. BENNETH J. SIMMS,23
. C.C.,499;J.M.,530
. WILLIAM P.,23
EMERSON,C.J.,409,561
. E.R. AUSTIN,566;M.C.
. AUSTIN,561;MARY J.,344
. MATILDA C. AUSTIN,409
. R.C.,566
EMERY,REUBEN,462
EMMERSON,
. ELIZA BETTIS,330
. MINERVA,155;WILLIAM
. 330
EMMONS,
. ELIZA H. FLETCHER,10
. LAURENCE E.,10
EMONS,NANNIE A.,33
EMORY,CHARLES W.,480
. ROXANAH L. DORSEY,480
ENGLAND,525;ELLEN
. TAMMERS,581;R.P.,581
ENGLASS,LOUESON,599
ENGLEHARDT,JOHN B.,577
. MARY C. BENDER,577
ENGLISH,DOCK,589;JAMES
. 516;LULA MCDONALD,516

632

. MARGARET J. LASSAMAN
. 29;S.E.,491;WILLIAM
. P.,29
FORSYTH,DORA,523;E.R.
. 534;ELIJAH,505;ELLA
. 537;J.J.,530;JAMES,495
. L.L.,545;MARTIN,496
. MIRIAH,589
FORSYTHE,LIZZIE,540
FORT,TOMLINSON,224,247
FORTER,
. MARTHA BONNETT,581
. ROBERT,581
FORTNER,DAVID F.,570
. LUTICIA M. ROMINES,570
FORTUNE,CAROLINE,567
. WILLIAM,443
FOSETT,MARTHA,481
FOSSETT,ALBERT,481
. CHAPPEL,481;ELIZABETH
. 459;FRANCES,433
. GEORGE W.,481;GEORGIA
. A.,432;LUCY ALLEN,481
. MARTHA,491;ROSETTA
. WARD,481;SARAH A.
. EVANS,481
FOSTER,530,539,543;A.J.
. 5;ABI A. HAYNES,306
. 316;ABSALOM,293
. AMANDA SAMPLES,331
. BENCY,314;BENJAMIN F.
. 331;BEREMIN,297
. BLUFORD,456;C.J.
. MARTIN,331;CARRIE,498
. 518;CLEMINTIN KERR,355
. COLLIER,209;ELIJAH,440
. 441;ELIZABETH,352
. EVELINE M. MCAFEE,331
. FLORENCE JORDAN,525
. GEORGE,548;GEORGIE
. GRIFFIN,532;GREEN B.
. 316,331;HANNAH,361
. IRA,288;IRA A.,283
. IRA R.,284,286,289-293
. 331;IRA ROW,305,316
. J.G.,60;J.Z.,52,60,66
. 77;JACOB,423;JAMES M.
. 131;JANE,602;JANE H.
. 301,316,366;JEMIMA C.
. 306;JEMINA C.,323
. JENSIE M.,60;JOHN,352
. 361,412,441,572;JOHN
. L.,60;JOSEPH D.,283
. 284,286,288-290,331
. JOSEPHINE WILLIAMS,331
. K.L.,42;KINDNESS E.
. JONES,357;KINDNESS
. JAMES,316,330;LAURA
. TREADWAY,432;LEE,432
. LELA,514;LEONNA,10
. LILA ALEXANDER,42
. LOUISA,304,316;LOUISA
. OLIVER,9;M.E.,428
. MALISSA,305,317
. MARGARET,324;MARGARET
. J.,308;MARTHA A,357
. MARTHA A.,562
. MARTHA F. HAYS,316,331
. MARTHA FOLDS,429
. MARTHA M. KEMP,355
. MARTHA MILNER,454
. MARY,357;MARY A.,301
. 325,329,340,342,359
. MARY A.R.,337;MARY
. ANN,310,325,375
. MARY J. MALONY,36
. MARY JANE SPROUCE,5
. MILLY A. C. HAYNES,305
. MILLY A.C. HAYNES,010
. MISSOURI,512;NANCY,302
. NANCY DELLAFIELD,456
. NANCY G. PAGE,352
. NANCY PAGE,361;PHIL
. 244;RANSOM,454;RANSOM

. E.,316,330,357;ROBERT
. T.,9;SALLIE,606;SARAH
. 324;T.A.,423;T.J.,498
. 511-512,514-515,525
. 530,545;THOMAS,285,548
. THOMAS A.,418-419,421
. 423-425;THOMAS E.,355
. TOLE,429;W.A.,532,536
. WALTER,179,183-184,198
. 214,219,252;WILLIAM
. 256;WILLIAM A.,355
. WILLIAM G.,462
. WILLIAM L.,18;WILLIAM
. P.,36,303,316;WILLIAM
. S.,28;WILLIAM T.,306
. 316;WILLIAM W.,391
. ZELFA PIRKLE,303,316
FOUNTAIN,
. AMANDA A. CAYLOR,481
. ARTAMINSA WILLIAMSON
. 161;JAMES F.,481
. JAMES M.,161;JESSE P.
. 161;MALISSA ODLE,161
. NANCY S.,161
FOURY,
. CHARLOTTE A. NORTHUP,8
. JOSEPH T.,8
FOUTS,
. EMMA A. MORRISON,481
. W.S.,481
FOWES,ELIZABETH,455
FOWLER,A.J.,331;AARON
. 297;ADALINE LANDSDOWN
. 307,316;AMANDA M.,21
. ANDELINE,159;C.A.,592
. CAROLINE WALLS,316,331
. CLARISSA CASTLEBERRY
. 156;COLUMBIA C.
. JULIAN,354
. CORNELIA A. GOOLSBY
. 331;D.H.,358;DAVID,548
. DELILAH VAUGHAN,310
. 316;DOTIA,163
. DRUCILLA L. SMITH,358
. E.F.,427;E.J.,16,19-20
. 49;ELENDER,337;ELIZA
. 156;ELIZA KING,354
. ELIZABETH,355,370,548
. ELIZABETH CARMICHAEL
. 163;ELIZABETH MILIGAN
. 354;ELPINA,111;EMILY
. A.,304,313;EMILY J.
. DOWDY,586;EMMA L.
. PADEN,43;FANNA
. COCKBURN,159;FANNIE
. HUGGINS,331;FANNY,453
. FRANCES,60;GEORGE T.
. 60,129,135,159;GEORGE
. W.,331;HARRIET L.,155
. JAMES A.,156,354
. JAMES M.,354;JAMES W.
. 331;JEREMIAH,548;JOEL
. M.,354;JOHN,156,163
. 298,309,316,331,457
. 548;JOHN C.,43;JOHN
. M.,310,316;JOSEPH,355
. 586;JOSHUA,331;L.W.,53
. LAVINIA,593;LETTIE M.
. ODUM,355;LOU V.
. HARRIS,354;LUCINDA,459
. LUCINDA E.F.,335;LUCY
. NIX,355;M.J.,350
. MARGARET CHADWICK,331
. MARTHA,18,354
. MARTHA J. GRAVITT,331
. MARTHA J. POOL,331
. MARY C.,319,335;MARY
. DAVIS,310,316;MARY
. DELANY,331;MARY JANE
. 331;MATTHEW C.,331
. MOSES,548;N.A.,62
. NANCY J. LEDBETTER,316
. 331;NANCY MOODY,156
. NATHAN,442;NEATA,301

. 313;NELSON,331;NICY
. HOUSE,455;OLIFFAN,320
. PHILLIP K.,316,331;R.
. BALEY,350;R.T.,167,177
. RACHAEL BALOTE,305,316
. RACHELL BETOTE,368
. REBECCA,455;ROBERT,165
. ROBERT T.,149,151,228
. S.W.,310,316;SAMANTHA
. J.,358;SAMUEL,465
. SARAH ALEXANDER,457
. SARAH E.,368;SARAH S.
. 324;SARAH WILEY,309
. 316;SUE M.,45;W.B.,350
. W.P.,60;WILEY,242,455
. WILLIAM,305,307,316
. 355;WILLIAM A.,354
. WILLIAM B.,368
FOX,AMANDA,432;EMILY
. ABBOTT,434;GEORGE A.
. 75;J.D.,434;J.H.,424
. JAMES,101;JOHN H.,401
. L.E. DEMPSEY,424;MARY
. 571;R.H.,582;S.C.
. LAYMANCE,582
FOXTER,J.Z.,78
FRAKER,CALEB S.,584
. MARGARET,589;MARY O.
. 594;S.J.,603;SARAH J.
. TYE,584
FRANCIS,
. GEORGIA A. TINSLEY,316
. MARY,340;SUSAN L.,333
. THOMAS H.,316
FRANK,AMANDA BROWN,578
JACKSON,578
FRANKLIN,ANN BODWELL,589
. B.P.,425;BENJAMIN,589
. ELIZABETH,563;JAMES
. 461;L.E.,564;LAURA
. ADAMS,425;MATTIE A.
. 426-427;NARCISSIA
. GAMBLE,564;SAMUEL,391
. SUSANNAH,453
FRASER,122;ANNA,60
. ELIZA J. DICKERSON,15
. JAMES A.,31;JAMES H.
. 15;JAMES O.,147
. MARY E. WARREN,31
. SIMON,122,147;WILLIAM
. 122
FRASIER,112;ELSIE,60
FRAY,BELLA,542
FRAZIER,EDWARD,60;ELLEN
. 41;EMMA H. KISER,47
. EMMA J. KISER,37
. HENRY,498;J.D.,37,47
. REBECCA L.,60;WILLIAM
. 60
FRAZURE,JOHN,461
FREADEL,JONATHAN,470
FREE,ELIZABETH,426;JOHN
. 418;M.A. LEWIS,418
. W.C.,82
FREEHAND,ISAAC,298
FREELAND,
. ELIZABETH KEY,316,331
. FRANCES E. KILGORE,11
. ISAAC,316,331
. JEREMIAH,11;SARAH REY
. 331;WILLIAM J.,331
FREEMAN,541;ADDIE MAY
. 500;AMANDA S.,581;ANN
. E.,407;BENJAMIN F.,161
. 162;ELIZA E.,162
. ELIZA E. FREEMAN,162
. ELIZABETH,162
. ELIZABETH HINTON,553
. ELIZABETH M. EVANS,162
. FANNIE M.,431
. FANNIE S. WARE,413
. G.W.L.,574,579;GEORGE
. 170,432;GREEN H.,582
. H.W.,501;HARRIET A.

. 590;HARTWELL D.,162
. HAY,501;JAMES,401,407
. 415;JAMES D.,413
. JAMES L.,514;JANE M.
. SUTTLES,574;JESSE P.
. 559;JESSE T.,568;JOE
. 500-501;JOHN,316;JOHN
. A.,604;JOHN R.,406
. LOTTY FRY,161;M.A.
. AULT,604;M.E.,419
. MARTHA,554;MARTHA A.
. SMITH,582;MARTHA E.
. 361;MARY,162;MARY
. A.A.,555;MARY C.,428
. MARY T. HAMILTON,406
. MATILDA,353;MELINDA
. CRAUS,316;METURIS
. MCMICKENS,514;REBECCA
. A.,557;REUBEN,112,118
. ROBERT,467;SARAH,427
. SARAH ELIZ. HUGHES,553
. TATIE GENTRY,432
. THOMAS,553;WILLIAM
. HENRY,553
FREENY,J.,125;L.A.E.,125
. L.J.A.,111;W.J.,125
FREEZE,A.L.,337
FRELTZ,J.C.,9;MARY A.
. LANE,9
FRESHAWERS,ELISHA,461
FREY,B.T.,60;E.W.,53-54
. 56,59,65,68,72,76-77
. 79;EDWARD W.,63
. MARTIN,60;MARTIN W.,60
FRICKS,A.J.,428;BERRY
. 424;JANE WISE,424;M.
. 394;MANDY,485;MARY,425
. MICHAEL,390,548
. RACHEL E.,422
FRIDELL,C.A.,47,60;J.L.
. 60;JOHN L.,60;LUCINDA
. 60;MALVINIA,39;N.E.
. SMITH,47;SARAH,35
FRIEDLEY,
. BRIDGET A. MCCANNA,316
. GEORGE,316
FRIEDMAN,
. ADELE SCHWARZ,586
. BENHARDT,586
FRIELAND,HOWEL,462
. JERRY,462
FRIERSON,
. ANNIE E. GEDARD,434
. THOMAS A.,434
FRISBY,F.M.,422;M.
. JOHNSON,422
FRITH,SARAH,29-30
FRIX,ADALINE,427;G.E.
. NUCKOLLS,331;G.W.,331
FROHAWK,JOHN,461
FROLEY,PATRICK,232
FROST,EFFIAH S.,557
. ELIS,442;HELAY WAIDE
. 459;JOHN M.,562;MARY
. 449;NANCY BURNET,562
. WILLIAM,459
FRY,JULIA L.,579;LOTTY
. 161;MARTHA JANE COUCH
. 606;MARY E.,333;PETER
. 470;W.D.,606
FRYLOCK,E.W.,606;M.E.
. COX,606
FUERSTENICK,
. CLARA GREMPLER,583
. EVON ENTRISS,583
FULCHER,SARAH,305,314
FULFORD,DANIEL,394
FULKS,JANE HICKS,571
. JOSEPH,571,591
. PARMELIA,572;SUSAN
. FARMER,591
FULLER,ABRAM,537
. AMANDA C. TALLEY,481
. ANN,545;B.F.,433

633

634

. 424;SALINA,486;SARAH
. A.,419;W.J.,410
. WILLIAM J.,393
. WILLIAM R.,410
GARTRELLE,HENRY A.,390
GARUM,CATHERINE,329
GARWOOD,F.P.,61;ROBERT
. B.,61
GASAWAY,ALMANNE,603
. JAMES,604;JOHN,600
. NANCY HAMBRIGHT,604
. SALLIE TALLEY,600
. WINNIE TOLLER,603
GASKEY,FANY SMITH,580
. J.W.,580
GASKILL,V.A.,48
GASP,MARTHA,564
GASSAWAY,OBEDIENCH,548
GASSETT,
. ANGELINE COLEMAN,5
. WILLIAM,5
GASTIN,ELIZABETH,423
. J.T.,428;M. ADAMS,428
GASTON,EULA FLEMING,525
. JAMES,280,292-293,301
. 316,525;JANE H.
. FOSTER,301,316
. WILLIAM,404
GASWICK,MATHIAS,465
GATES,ELIZABETH,308,312
. MARY MOBLEY,304,316
. SARAH E.,309;SARAH W
. 321;WILLIAM,304,316
GATHER,ELIZABETH,555
GATHRIGHT,WITTON H.,168
GATLING,ROBERT,149
GATON,URAIH,465
GATTY,JAMES M.,76
GAULT,EDWARD,61;EDWARD
. N.,61;ELIZABETH,61
. EMMA,61;FRANCES
. LUMMUS,316;JAMES L.,27
. JEFFERSON,316;JOSEPH
. 35,136;MARTHA,329
. MARY,337;MARY C.,12
. MARY E.,61;MILLY
. HADDER,370;MIRA
. HARDIMAN,27;PRESLY,370
. SARAH,370;WILLIAM,61
. WILLIAM L.,61
GAUNT,MARGARET A.,334
GAUSLIN,CAPTAIN,12
. MARTHA JOHNSON,12
GAVIN,MARY J.,564;R.,604
. SARAH MILLER,604
GAY,ALBERT,159;ELIZA,61
. JOHN,61;NANCY WARD,159
GAZAWAY,435-437;A.L.A.
. LEDBETTER,425;BERRY
. 582;DAVID,572
. ELIZABETH,19;G.,425
. JOHN G.,356;M.A.M.,601
. MALINDA C.,302,316
. MARGARET BENNETT,572
. MARTHA M. BLALOCK,582
. MARY M. PILCHER,356
. MARY O,587;RITHA A.
. ATTISON,356;W.R.,356
GEDARD,ANNIE E.,434
GEER,LOUISA K.,310
. LOUISE K.,309,315
GEIGER,C.A.,61;CAROLINE
. 61;CHARLES A.,61
GELLOGG,GEORGE,298
GEMER,JOHN A.,32
GENNING,C.M.,221
GENTRY,470;ALBELTINE
. RUTHERFORD,45;C.T.,575
. ELISHA,161;ELIZABETH
. CONN,161;ELSEY
. GREAVITT,459;FRANCES
. A.,594;G.W.,516,530
. GEORGE,536;GIFFEN,45
. HENRY H.,28;JERRY,470

. JOHN F.,332;M.L.
. ROACH,332;M.M.,332
. MELINDA HOOD,316,331
. NANCY KING,28;NANCY
. MATTOCKS,451;RACHEL
. 453;RACHEL GENTRY,453
. RODY ANN PUGH,332
. ROLLY,459;ROWLAND,451
. S.A. POTTER,575
. SIRENIA,455;TATIE,432
. THOMAS,453;WILLIAM,316
. 331
GEORGE,ALEY M. BURNS,567
. ALLEN,473;ARTHUR,548
. CAROLINE,568;EMMA,509
. H.M,425;ISAAC,153,181
. 204,548;J.L.,545;JACK
. 498,515;JAMES,437,548
. JANE THACKER,161
. JEREMIAH,437;JESSE,231
. 548;JOHN,95;MARMER D.
. 161;MATTIE A.,39
. WILLIAM,221;WILLIAM
. K.,567
GERER,JOSIAH,387
GERRY,WILLIAM,472
GERTHRA,J.,560
GHOLSTON,BENJAMIN,444
GIBBERT,MILAND,596
GIBBS,A.J.,525
. ELIZA ANN SMITHWICK
. 155;F.M.,393;HARRIET
. E.,159;JEREMIAH,171
. JERRY,467;JOHN,155,425
. L.A. FINDLEY,425;MARY
. 558;W.W.,100;WILLIAM
. W.,99
GIBSON,A.T.,61;ANNIE,61
. BAYLESS,517;D.C.,464
. E.,420;FANNIE SINSON
. 38;FRANK T.,61;I.R.,61
. J.F.,61;J.H.,481;J.L.
. 407;JOHN A.,148;JOHN
. S.,61;LOUISA,450
. NANCY,61;NANCY A.,61
. NATHANILL,38;S.C.
. CLARK,481;SARAH A.,163
. SUSIE BRON,517
GIDEON,A.A.,423
. BATHAELMA,421;GALSON
. B.,560;LARANA LACEY
. 560;S.,425
GIGNILIATT,C.T.,61
. JANETTE,61;JOSEPH,61
. WILLIAM R.,61
GIGNILLANT,
CHARLOTTE T.,61
GIGNILLIAL,N.G.,86
GIGNILLIAT,G.N.,67;L.N. 31
GIGRILLIANT,MADGE,44
GILBERT,
. ABBITHA E. PUGH,459
. E.G.,61;EDWARD,149,165
. 176,297,437,441,459
. ELIZABETH,159;G.R.,81
. 128-129;GEORGE,389
. GEORGE R.,127,129
. HARRIET,445;HULDA A.
. DYER,579;ISAAC,210
. ISHAM H.,331;J.J.,573
. 577;J.W.,587;JACOB,441
. JAMES,260;JOHN,441
. JOHN I.,565;JOHN J.
. 563-565,568,570,572
. 576,579;JULIE E.,345
. MARGARET BARNETT,587
. MARIAH,590;MARY A.,348
. MARY V.,36;MATILDA,328
. MILAND,596;NANCY C.
. BRASWELL,331;NARCISSA
. C.,348;NARCISSA C.
. GILBERT,348;PENELOPE
. SHIPP,565;S.A.L.,591
. S.P.,345;SARAH C.

. RIDEN,345;SARAH F.,328
. SIDNEY H.,348;W.E.,61
. 71,145;WILLIAM,292,441
GILBREATH,JOSEPH,434
. T.H.,395;TINY CURTISS
. 434
GILES,CLARE ANN,555
. EDWIN,433;ELIZABETH
. 578;JAMES,553;JAMES
. C.,67;MARTHA
. CHRISTOPHER,553;NANCY
. LONG,569;SALLIE ORR
. 433;WILLIAM C.,569
GILHAM,E.W.,25;EMMA,526
. S.M.E. MCKEY,25
GILLEHAN,JOHN,469;MOSES
. 470
GILLELAND,ALLEN,256,548
. ELIZABETH,548;MARY,157
GILLELEAN,HIRAM,471
GILLESPIE,ANNE,413
GILLEY,MARY,496;WILLIS 186
GILLHAM,E.W.,25;S.M.E.
. MCKEY,25;WILLIAM,131
GILLIAM,DAVID M.,454
. MARGARET S. GRADY,454
GILLIAN,FRANKLIN,565
. MARGARET TORBET,565
GILLMIRE,MARY,573
GILLY,JOURDAN,463
. WILLIS,230
GILMER,AUGUSTUS W.,331
. B.F.,332;GEORGE R.,210
. LYDDA A.,159;MARY J.
. BAGBY,332;MARY JANES
. 331;WILLIAM,464
GILMORE,DAN,453
. ELIZABETH,449;FRANCIS
. 450;LOUISA C.,155
. MATILDA RED,453;NANCY
. 449;NANCY BUFFINGTON
. 450
GILREATH,J.H.,402
. MARTHA E. HARDIN,161
. N.,402;NELSON,161
GILSTRAP,LARRA,487
GINGS,CALVIN,168
GINN,MARY,28;RUFFIN,548
GIP,533
GIPSON,JOHN Q.,156;JUDY
. 156;SARY ANN
. BROADWELL,156
GIRDY,REBECCA A.,568
GIRE,JAMES D.,591
. S.A.L. GILBERT,591
GIRLEY,MARY HARRISON,531
. ROBERT,531
GITCHEL,MARY,599;SARAH
. 580,601
GITCHELL,CLARINDA,586
. SARAH,587
GITON,JOHN W.,316,331
. REBECCA TERRY,316,331
GITTERY,LOUISA,6
GIVEN,G.W.,6,11-13
GEORGE W.,13
GIVENS,G.W.,6;LUCY,590
. W. ARNOLD,55
GLADDEN,A.S.,540;JAMES
. 584;M.A.,597;MARY
. ROBERTS,584
GLADEN,BIRTEE,61;NAOMI
. 597
GLADNEY,JO BAILEY,414
GLANTON,JAMES H.,424
. M.F. WINTER,424
GLASCO,MARY A.,4
GLASFOW,OBEDIAH,440
GLASGO,MILES,61
GLASGOW,JESSE,107;MILES
. 107
GLASS,
. ELIZABETH J. MINIS,571
. JAMES A.,316,331

. JAMES A.M.,227,243
. JOSEPH,554;MAHALA
. PORTER,457;MARY,338
. MARY ANN E. HELAD,554
. MARY E.,351;MARY J.
. HOWARD,316,331
. MELISSA,555;NANCY
. MCKENY,351;W.R.,571
. WILLIAM,457,466
. WILLIAM F.,351
GLASSCOCK,THOMAS,519
GLASSON,MARY,554
GLAZE,CAROLINE H.,574
. DANIEL,436;DAVID,181
. 183;JACOB,463;JOSEPH
. 463;PHOEBE,597
GLEN,JOHN,2;THOMAS S. 438
GLENN,ANNIE,602;G.R.,177
. GEORGE R.,149,166,168
. 170,173,181;HANNAH
. L.T.,554;JOHN W.,277
. JOSEPH,594;JULIA A.
. SHAW,429;MARTHA P.
. THOMSON,594;T.
. MILLISON,489;WILLIAM
. S.,429
GLORE,A.E.,61;ABRAM,61
. ELLIOT,543;EMILY
. BOSTWICK,554;GEORGE
. 554;GEORGE W.,61;J.B.
. 61;J.R.,61;JAMES R.,37
. JOHN G.,82;JOHN H.,61
. JOHN T.,61,66;MARY F.
. 61;MARY F. GANN,37
. NANIE C.,18;RHODA E.
. 61;TOBITHA,61
GLOSS,EMILY E.,336
GLOVER,AGNES BAGLEY,355
. ANNIE,61;ANNIS H.
. CHASTAIN,588;AZZIE
. BAGLEY,356;CAROLINE
. CANTRELL,596;EDWARD,61
. ELIZABETH NASH,311,316
. ELZA V.,62;GEORGIA A.
. FAGAN,355;H.P.,596
. HENRY P.,588;J.B.,58
. 62;JAMES B.,76,145
. JANE S.,61;JARRETT W.
. 311,316;JOHN E.,62
. JOHN H.,58,61;JOHN J.
. 600;JOHN O.,462
. JOSEPH,61;MARIA,61
. MARY CANTREL,562;MILZ
. E.,355;MINNIE,28
. NARCISSA,560;NED,522
. P.J. MOORE,600
. RICHARD,2;SAMUEL,355
. SUSANAH BAGLEY,356
. THOMAS W.,61;WILEY,93
. WILLIAM M.,356,562
. WILY,356
GLOWER,ALECK,515;NANCY
. 515
GNEN,MASS,387
GOBBE,ADDIE MULLIS,356
. ELIZABETH HORTON,356
. GEORGE W.,356
. LAWRENCE,356
GOBER,165;AMANDA P.,327
. ARILLIA H.,343;C.L.
. 424;G.W.,1;GEORGE F.
. 62;HENRY E.,316;J.A.
. 101;JAMES A.,253;JOHN
. T.,426-427;L.C.
. MANESS,332;L.F.,332
. M.W.,423;MARY,40;MARY
. E.,303,319;MARY E.
. DORSFY,424;MARY J.
. ROBINSON,316;N.M.,146
. N.N.,142;NANCY M.A.
. 378;NEWTON N.,50;S.E.
. 34;SARAH DOWNS,426-427
. SARAH HOLBROOK,332
. SARAH T. FARRINGTON,50

635

636

637

. TINSLEY,600
GROOVER,ANDREW R.,17
. E.C. LITTLE,423
. ELIZABETH,18;FANNIE
. MAE,62;HARRIET E.,493
. J.A.,63;J.C.,62,75
. J.N.,62;J.P.,62;JAMES
. P.,477;JAMES R.,482
. JOHN G.,65;L.C.,62
. L.H.,62;L.P.,62;LAURA
. 62;M.,45;M.C.,62
. MARIE,66;NANCY J.
. RICHARDSON,17;NANCY
. SIMMONS,482;P.F.,423
. P.L.,62;PETER,7,17
. REBECCA LEDBETTER,482
. SARAH J.,476;SUSANNAH
. FAULKNER,482;THOMAS
. P.,482;W.D.,418;W.F.
. 79;WILLIAM,482
. WILLIAM F.,62
GROSS,CAROLINE,273
GROVER,DANIEL,89;HOP
. GOOD,221;J.C.,59
. JAMES P.,492
GROVES,108;FANNY,589
. GRACE M.,62;JAMES M.
. 102;JAMES W.,105;JOHN
. W.,95,98-99;ROBERT,93
. WILLIAM,81,115
. WILLIAM F.,105-107,128
. 129,132,141
GROVIS,JOHN W.,92
GROWLER,REBECCA,354
GRUBB,FRANCES,598
GRUBBS,
. JANE SOPHIA WILSON,554
. LUISA W.,555;REBECCAH
. 558;THOMAS,554
GRUM,JESSE,152;ROGER,151
GUDGER,MARTHA A.,406
. WILLIAM,406
GUESS,ELIZABETH,32
. GERUSHA,87;H.N.,63
. HENRY,62,87;J.N.,63
. JERUSHA,62-63;JOSEPH
. N.,37;LOU P. MOORE,37
. LOUISA MCCURDY,44
. MARTHA,18;MOSES H.,90
. NATHANIEL,2;R.L.,63
. WILLIAM,2,90;WILLIE
. L.,63;WILLIS L.,44
GUICE,
. ELIZA ANN MCDONAL,567
. WILLIAM,567
GUILD,E.,508
GUINN,
. MARGARET M. -
. BRUSTER,554;MARY,572
. RICHARD R.,554;SALLY
. H.,552;SARAH,603
GUISE,TERENCE M.A.,389
GUISS,JOSEPH,96;WILLIAM 96
GULLAT,ALEXANDER A.,17
. MARY J. HEARN,17
GULLIVER,MARTHA,64
. MMARTHA,52
GUNBY,ROBERT M.,393
GUNN,GEORGE W.,554
. JESSE,554;MARTHA
. WHITE,157;MARY ANN
. WILLIS,554;TABITHA C.
. HILL,554;WILLIAM,157
GUNNELL,C.A.,62;G.A.,62
. W.B.,62
GUNNELLS,MARY ANN,324
GUNNELY,
. CATHERINE L. -
. COULTER,163;GEORGE,163
GUNNETT,WILLIAM B.,82
GUNTER,DAVID,62;JOEL,134
. JOEL A.,136
. MARGARET E. EDWARDS
. 332;S.C.,332;WILLIAM

. 149
GUNTHROP,MARGARET,418
GURIE,
. ELIZA ANN MCDONAL,567
. WILLIAM,567
GURING,
. MARY JANE COLLINS,482
. WILLIAM,482
GURLEY,ELIZABETH,2
GURTRIE,NANCY,422
GUSTINN,W.I.,561
GUTHER,ROBERT,173
GUTHERY,A.A.M. FORD,583
. ANDREW N.,309,316
. ELISA,320;FRANCES
. WADKINS,303,317
. FRANCES WATKINS,303
. MARY HARDIN,554;POLLY
. GRAVITT,309,316
. ROBERT,166;ROBERT M.
. 303,317,554;WILLIAM
. R.,583
GUTHREY,ELISA,310
. ELIZABETH C. ABNEY,23
. GEORGE W.,23;POLLY,457
. ROBERT,449;SARAH
. WILLIAMS,449
GUTHRIE,360;ANDREW W.
. 294;ASA,294
. CAROLINE M. SOUTHARD
. 317;CAROLINE SOUGHARD
. 331;ELISA,294
. ELIZABETH CAPE,455
. FRANCES CAPE,455;J.
. 561-562,564;JAMES,294
. 300,317;JEMIMAH,456
. JOHN F.,294,317,331
. LUCINDA,294,328,346
. LULA J.,604;MARY ANN
. 294;MORGAN,455;NANCY
. 294,458;RHODY,457
. ROBERT,151;ROBERT M.
. 294;SALLIE M.
. ALEXANDER,574;SARAH
. BIDDLE,300,317;THOMAS
. 455;W.R.,574
GUTHRY,DAVID,170
. ROBERTE,168;SARAH E.
. 553
GUTTERY,ANN,451;LETTY
. 452;MILLY,450;MOLLY
. 452
GUTURY,DAVID,149
GUY,WILLIAM,543
GUYTON,AMANDA BELL,482
. JOSEPH,456,482;ZEMILY
. MCCLUSKY,456
GWIN,G.W.,11-13;GEORGE
. W.,7;JOHN,29;MARY E.
. AYCOCK,29
GWINN,G.W.,6;RICHARD,220
GWINNETT,BUTTON,445
. EDWIN S.,415
HACKER,LARKEN,361
. MARCUS L.,361
. MARTHA E. FREEMAN,361
. MARTHA SATTERFIELD,361
HACKET,OLIVER,1
HACKETT,MARY,458;MARY
. C.,306,323;OLIVER,459
HACKNEY,JOHN,495;MARCUS
. L.,584;S.E. WRINKLE
. 584
HADARD,J.F.,6;LOUISA
. GITTERY,6
HADAWAY,JANE L.,6
. MATILDA,554;RICHARD
. P.,4;SUSAN HAYNES,4
HADDEN,MARTHA,313;MILLY
. S.,331
HADDER,CATHARINE,310
. CATHERINE,325;ELISA
. WILLIAMS,302,317
. FRANCES M.,308,324

. JOHN,302,317;MARTHA
. 307;MATILDA SCOTT,302
. 317;MILLY,370;SARAH
. J.C.,318,332;SOLOMON
. 302,317
HADDOCK,DAVID C.,583
. ELIZA C. RUSSELL,583
. ELIZABETH,597;I.,604
HAGAN,532;B.F.,530
. GEORGE T.,503;J.H.,539
. MANDY,520;MARGARET
. FARR,502;NED,502;NEWT
. 501
HAGANS,JAMES,442;NEWTON
. 442;REUBIN,443
. SANFORD,442;SILAS,442
HAGEN,CLARA,156
HAGER,
. ELIZABETH JENKINS,581
. J.R.,581
HAGERMAN,ASA F.,554
. MARGARET L. STEEL,554
HAGGARD,JAMES,562
. MARY H. MCDONALD,562
HAGGIE,A.C.,64
HAGGOOD,ATTICUS G.,8
HAGIN,B.F.,506;BERTHA
. 506;ELLA,537;ELLEN
. DAVIS,534;FANNIE,533
. FANNY,534;FLOYD,510
. G.F.,509;G.W.,510
. GEORGE,528;H.N.,528
. JENNIE,510;LUDELIA,506
. WILLIAM,533;WILLIAM
. F.,534
HAGOOD,AMANDA,335
. BENJAMIN,237,245
. CORDELIA ANDERSON,482
. ELIZABETH ROPER,333
. HANNAH E.,319;JAMES
. A.,333;JAMES L.,333
. M.A. RED,334;M.T.,482
. NANCY E. RED,333
. SUSAN L. FRANCIS,333
. TILMON D.,333;W.H.,334
HAGWOOD,SUSAN,454
HAIGLER,MARGARET,411
. WILLIAM VASTINE,411
HAILS,ALLEN J.,554
. NANCY WRIGHT,554
HAINBY,SAMUEL,466
HAINES,CHARLES,298
. JAMES,256;THOMAS,178
HAINSTON,L.P.,98
HAIR,EMILY L. CADY,592
. GEORGE W.,592;JANE
. WHITENER,598;M.A.,601
. NATHAN C.,598
HAIRSON,LITTLETON P.,99
HAIRSTON,ADOLPHUS B.,21
. JAMES B.,438;JOHN T.
. 22;JULIA,63;JULIA ANN
. WATSON,17;JULIA C.
. WALLACE,26;L.P.,98
. LITTLE B.,17;LITTLE
. P.,63;LITTLETON P.,100
. NANCY E. IRELAND,22
. P.M.,26;ROBERT,437
. SARAH L. BELL,21
. THOMAS,60,63;THOMAS
. J.,63
HAISE,SARY,453
HAISTEN,L.E.,536
HAIZ,FRANCIS,387
HAKER,HENRIETTE,568
HALCOMB,AMBROSE,580
. ELIZA BRIDGES,580
. MAHULDA MCCRAW,161
. WILLIAM,161
HALE,E.P.,464;JAMES,446
. 447;JANE,312
. LUCY JANE STROUD,554
. T.,105;WILLIAM,554
HALES,A.C.,42;AMANDA P.

. 63;DRAYTON C.,482
. ELIZABETH,63;ISAAC,482
. J.M.,489;JAMES,115-116
. JOHN,63;MARTHA,487
. MARY,476;RHODA P.,488
. SARAH A.E. REESE,482
. SARAH J. CASON,482
. T.J.,63
HALEY,ELLA,491;J.T.,86
. 132,140-141;LINEY,370
. MARY E.,161;SARAH L.
. 592
HALK,JULIA,489;THOMPSON
. 90
HALL,510;ALBERT H.W.,268
. ARAMINTA E.,565
. CALVIN,482;DARCUS
. SINGLETON,317,332
. DAVID,465;DAVID L.,268
. DAVID S.,596;E.P.,464
. ELIZA NEWMAN,161
. ELVIRA,330;EMILY,567
. EMILY HALL,567
. EZEKIEL,125;EZINK D.
. 109;FARRAR,100;FARRER
. 96;FARRIER,97
. FRANCIS E. BENNETT,570
. GEORGE,466;GEORGE A.
. 397;GEORGE W.,574
. HIRAM,149;ISOM R.,464
. J. THOMAS,570;J.C.
. NEEL,428;JOHN,464
. JOHN D.,49;JURISSA,567
. KATHERINE MARTIN,163
. LUCINDA SMITH,49
. M.E.B.,268;M.J.,596
. M.O.,63;MALINDA S.J.
. 268;MARGARET,347
. MARTHA A.E.B. WILKINS
. 309;MARTHA E.,268
. MARY A. HAYES,482
. MARY ANN,8;MARY E.
. DAVIS,37;MILLY,328
. MILY,382;NANNIE
. ROBERTS,530;NATHANIEL
. D.,268,309;PERRY M.
. 161;ROSWELL,462;SARAH
. 572;SARAH ANN E.,268
. SARAH E. SEAY,574
. SARAH S. GROGANS,596
. SUANNAH CLARK,560
. THOMAS,473;THOMAS J.
. 560;TISHA,494;W.J.,524
. W.T.,428;WILLIAM,317
. 332,439,465,567
. WILLIAM P.,438
. WILLIAM R.,37;WILLIAM
. T.,163
HALLEY,J.I.,394
HALLIDAY,
. DICKERSON T.,554
. MARY ANN HILL,554
HALLMAN,RODY,315,330
HALLMON,ELIZABETH,342
HALLOWAY,DARKY BECK,451
. JOHN,451
HALT,LURKEEN,387
HAM,
. ELIZABETH RUTHERFORD,7
. EZEKIEL,548;JAMES,7
. M.M.,179;MILTON M.,193
. 216
HAMBLETON,DENNIS,591
. JAMES A.,574;JOHN,298
. JOSEPH,298;M.C.
. FULTON,574;MARTHA
. KING,591;NANCY C.,553
HAMBRICK,AMILLER,483
HAMBRIGHT,B.F.,591
. MARTHA J. HOSKINS,591
. NANCY,604
HAMBRY,P.T.,40
. THERESA E. GOBER,40
HAMBY,A.S.,8;B.J.,63

638

. CHARLOTTE,368;D.C.,63
. E.T.,29;ELY MAYES,8
. FANNY B.,526;JEREMIAH
. 473-474;LEONARD,526
. M.E. MASTERS,569;MARY
. 477;MARY ANN,63;NANCY
. 333;NANCY A.,338;P.T.
. 63;REBECCA,455;SAMUEL
. 466;T.J.,569;T.K.,63
. WILLIAM,548
HAMES,FANNIE GRAHAM,27
. G.C.,27;GAZAWAY,7
. H.C.,143;J.S.,143
. JAMES W.,11;LASELL,143
. MARIETTA,7;MARIETTA
. HAMES,7;NANCY A.
. MCCRARY,317;PRESLEY
. 317;REBECCA,456
. W.J.M.,143
HAMILL,E.J.,582
HAMILTON,ALEXANDER,437
. ALEXANDER C.,440
. AMANDA,455,606
. ARCHABALD,435
. ARCHIBALD,441;C.A.,497
. 499;CHARLES H.,498
. D.B.,23;ELIZABETH A.
. SHIN,317;ELIZABETH A.
. SKIN,332;ELLEN MOYERS
. 590;EVERARD,245-246
. IDA,499;J.S.,424;JOHN
. 191-192;JOSEPHINE,63
. MARTHA,568;MARTHA A.
. WRIGHT,16;MARTHA J.
. 484;MARY T.,406
. MATHEW T.,437;MATTHEW
. T.,435;PAIRZADE WATE
. 413;RACHEL,576;RHODA
. ANN,412;ROBERT A.,16
. S.L.,571;SAMUEL L.,576
. SAVANNAH TOWNSEND,482
. THOMAS,392,406;W.B.,97
. WARREN,590;WILEY T.
. 413;WILLIAM,440
. WILLIAM B.,96,101,105
. 107;WILLIAM G.,317,332
. WILLIAM J.,484;WILLIE
. 482
HAMLING,J.W.,527
HAMMACK,HENRY,193,198
. R.B.,562;SARAH
. WILLIAMS,562
HAMMELLEN,WILLIAM H.,96
HAMMELTON,WILLIAM B.,97
HAMMEN,MALISSA,336
HAMMER,JACOB,515,518
HAMMET,H.M.,24
HAMMETT,
. A.J. WESTBROOK,482
. D.B.,56,482;H.M.,41-47
. 50,53-55,58,61,66-68
. 71,73-75,77-78,80-83
. 85,127-130,132-133,136
. 138,142-148;HAMILTON
. M.,128,141;J.H.,41
. JANE,46;MARY,453
. SARAH A.,42;SARAH L.
. 43;W.M.,76
HAMMITH,THOMAS,98
HAMMOCK,ASA,554
. BENJAMIN F.,554
. FRANCES M. SHEPHERD
. 554;LOUISA,586;R.,111
. 112;SARAH E. FLYNT,554
. W.,111;WILLIAM,112
HAMMON,ELIZABETH,385
. EMILY THOMAS,311,317
. HIRAM,311,317;J.M.,334
. LEROY,285;MARY A.
. MARTIN,334;SIRENIA
. GENTRY,455;WILLIAM,455
HAMMOND,ADELINE
. KEMP,333
. ALFRED H.,416;ANN E.

. 323,340,409;DANIEL,176
. 317,332;DANIEL J.,317
. DANNIEL,167;DRUSCILLA
. BENSON,317;ELIZ. ANN
. 304;ELIZABETH,306,312
. 319;ELIZABETH BENSON
. 317;ELIZABETH M.
. BENSON,332;EMILY
. THOMAS,311;FRANCES
. MILWOOD,333;HIRAM,311
. JANE,337;JOHN,176,298
. 391;JOSEPH,290,297
. LEROY,165,167,176,231
. 298;LUCY,416;LUCY E.
. 575;MAHALA,331;MAHALA
. PEARSON,317;MARGARET
. C.,163;MARTHA M.,339
. MARY,356;MARY ANN
. SARGENT,155;MARY
. ROLLIN,317,332;MILY
. 298;W.,409;WILLIAM,176
. 297-298,317,416,571
. WILLIAM N.,317,332-333
. WILLIAM O.,333
. WILLIAM P.,155
HAMMONDS,GEORGE,298
. JOSEPH,291;SARAH C.
. 342;WILLIAM,263
HAMMONS,
. CANZALA JEFFERS,163
. DANIEL,149,349;ENOCH
. 163;FRANCES,449;LEROY
. 149,170;LINDSEY,450
. MARY ROLIN,349;MATTIE
. 349;MILLY,452;WILLIAM
. 149
HAMMONTREE,
. DLEILAH TABEREAUX,482
. EMMA J. MURPHY,606
. GEORGE W.,482;L.T.,606
. NICY E. HOWELL,482
. SARAH L.,494;SUSAN
. SWAFFORD,482
. SYLVESTER,482;WILLIAM
. N.,482
HAMMRICK,S.,493
HAMONTREE,
MILLIE BROWN,597
HAMPHILL,JAMES,166
HAMPTON,CALLIE SMITH,482
. G.C.,482;MARTHA A.,34
. MORGAN,469,473;OLIVE
. 399;SARAH E.,340
. THOMAS W.,399
HAMRICK,CATHERINE,491
. JANE SMITH,431;R.A.
. 528;S.,476,478-480,488
. 494;SILVANUS,476,483
. 484,487,489-491
. SLYVANUS,485;SYLVANUS
. 431,482;T.B.,101,111
HAMSLEY,GEORGE,7
HANCE,THOMAS,181
HANCOCK,ELIZABETH,576
. H.H.,405;JOHN C.,404
. MARTHA,590;MARY ANN
. 570;THOMAS,473
. WILLIAM,469,473
HAND,258;EDMUND,554
. NANCY S. CROW,554
HANDRIX,WELER,387
HANES,E.T.,420;ELI T.
. 420;SUSAN,475
HANEY,415;A.J.,63
. ABIGAIL,304;DANIEL J.
. 63;DORA,502;E. GIBSON
. 420;ELIZABETH J.,63
. FRANCES BRAND,12;G.W.
. 63;GEORGIA A. RED,37
. HEZEKIAH,63;JAMES,420
. JANE,420;LARKIN V.,37
. MARTHA,63;MARTHA E.,25
. MARY E. CAMP,30
. SAMANTHA A.,37;SARAH

. A.,46,63;WILLIAM,63
. WILLIAM R.,12,30
. ZILLA,447
HANIE,F.A.,531;JULIA,531
HANKS,C.,428;CALVIN J.
. 266;J.A.R.,61,266,577
. 583;MOLLIE E.,600
. N.J. WRINKLE,579;S.M.
. 579
HANNA,HEPSY HANNAH,572
. ISAAC S.,572;WILLIAM
. 264
HANNAH,FRANCES,421
. HEPSY,572;MELISSA,420
HANNAN,SAM B.,63
HANNET,WILEY,177
HANNON,MARTHA E.,15
. SAMUEL C.,495
HANS,MARTHA C.S.,16
HANSARD,C.H. ROBERTS,334
. ELIZA J. DAVENPORT,317
. 332;GEORGE,317,332
. IRA W.,334;JAMES,334
. JAMES C.,317;L.E.
. SAMPLES,334
. LUCINDA A. BENSEN,334
. MARY E.,331;MINNIE B.
. 321;NARCUSSUS,332
. REBECCA SPRUCE,317
. SAMUEL L.,334;T.E.
. BARKER,334;WILLIAM E.
. 334
HANSEL,ANDREW J.,53
HANSELL,237;A.J.,63,113
. ANDREW J.,63,258;C.C.
. 63;CAROLINE,63;JULIA
. S.,15;MARY,43;W.A.,63
. WILLIAM,63
HANSFORD,JANE,158;POLLY
. 445
HANSHARD,MALINDA,160
HANSON,ELIZABETH A.,551
. GREEN,530;JOHN,513
. KATHERINE C.,457
HANSUCKER,JAMES,473
HANY,HEZEKIAH,6
. HISAKIAH,127;LAVINIA
. GANT,6
HAPGOOD,LEWIS,98
HAPPUCK,KARON,413
HAPPWEST,A.M.,579
. OCTAVIA HOPKINS,579
HARALSON,M.C.,566
HARAS,ELIZA A.,579
HARBEN,MATILDA,595
. NATHANIEL,466
. NATHANIEL B.,463
. SAMUEL,270;SUSAN,456
HARBIN,
. A.T.A. EDWARDS,482
. ABRAHAM,191;B.T.,63
. CATHERINE M. STRAIN
. 163;EARRALIE C. EASON
. 6;J.R.,84;JAMES R.,6
. 63;JESSE,465;JESSE W.
. 163;JOEL,63;JOHN
. DANIEL,155;M.,63
. MARTHA COLLEY,156
. MARY BOON,155;NANCY,18
. NATHANIEL,228,284
. RICHARD G.,63;SAMUEL
. C.,161;SAMUEL M.,482
. SANFORD V.,156;SARAH
. HARPER,161;SUSANNAH
. 453
HARBON,ABRAM,152
HARBOR,M.E.,421;SARAH
A.,422
HARBOUR,LITTLEBERRY,438
HARBUCK,JAMES,554
. MARTHA,552;SALLY
. THURMON,554
HARDAGE,EMALINE,44
. GEORGE W.,459

. GUSTAVUS A.,18;JAMES
. D.,458;JANE ROBESON
. 456;JOHN Y.,456
. MALINDA HOWARD,309-310
. 317;MARTHA GUESS,18
. MARY ANN COOK,459
. MARY B. CLEMENTS,458
. T.F.,60;T.J.,134
. WILLIAM C.,309-310,317
HARDBARGER,
. MARTHA M. TIPPINS,157
. RUFUS M.,157
HARDCASTLE,J.G.L.,567
. LOUISA,591;LOUISA
. CASH,567;M.E.,574
. MARY A. SCOGGINS,559
. WILLIAM,559
HARDCAUTT,JULIA A.,598
HARDEMAN,ADA,63;ANDREW
. J.,333;IDA LEE,63
. LEONORA A. HUTCHINS
. 333;NAAMAN,63;PARKS,63
. 75;S.O.,523
HARDEN,A.B.,459
. ELIZABETH,558;FANNY
. 555;FRANCES L.,431
. HARRIET WALLACE,333
. HARRIET WALLIS,379
. HATTIE L.,72;ISAAC,333
. 379;J.D.,532;J.H.,98
. JANE,458;LOUISA,307
. 317;MARTHA,63;MARY,400
. MARY A.,379;MARY
. BARNWELL,459;PERRY,400
. R.R.,63;ROBERT,298
. SOPHRONA,322;SUSAN,421
HARDIAN,JAMES W.,360
. MARY CLINKSCALES,360
. MARY F. BACON,360
HARDIE,J.J.,538;LILLIE
. 538;MARY,162
HARDIMAN,MIRA,27
HARDIN,86;ASA C.,94-95
. CALEB,482;D.A.,482
. H.A. ROPER,482;J.H.,95
. 98;JANE GARRETT,333
. JOANNAH HULSEY,317
. JOHN,285;JOSHUA H.,300
. 317;JOURDAN,317
. JULIA ANN F.,556
. LAFAYETTE,333;LILLIE
. PENN,510;MARTHA E.,161
. MARY,554;MARY A.B.,410
. MARY J.,603;MARY J.
. MARTIN,333;N.,410
. NANCY,445,447;NANCY
. GARRETT,300,317
. NATHANIEL,191;R.D.,510
. ROBERT,317,332
. SARAH E. SINGLETON,317
. 332;SARAH HUTCHENS,482
. SARAH M. CARVER,482
. SOPHRONA,338;WILLIAM
. 410;WILLIAM L.,333
HARDMAN,B.S.,149
. BENNETT M.,158;C.A.
. MEGARITY,19;HARRIET
. M.,63;JAMES,63;JAMES
. A.,11;JAMES N.,19
. JOHN J.,63;LUCINDA
. MCASKY,158;MARTHA M.,7
. MATILDA J.,14;MATILDA
. S.,63;NANCY E.,38
. PARKS,63,91,101,103
. 105;SYLVANIA A.
. JACKSON,11;THOMAS N.
. 63;WILLIAM,242,253,257
. 259,262-263
HARDMON,PARKS,103
HARDON,ELIZABETH,348
HARDRIDGE,JESSE D.,454
. JOHN,449;MAHALA COOK
. 454;MARGARET KERR,449
HARDWICK,CECILIA,517

. THOMAS,517
HARDY,111-112;ELIZABETH
. SWORDS,554;H.,63;I.H.
. 569;J. CALVIN,25
. JAMES,25;JANE ,63;JOHN
. 554;JULIA A.,43;JULIA
. RAKESTRAW,25;K.
. LUXICANAH,63;M.A.
. NICHOLS,428;M.C.,482
. MARGARET SLAY,569
. MARY,535;NORA,433
. ROZIE HARRIS,482
. SARAH BENSON,554
. SUSAN LEE,25;T.M.,63
. THOMAS,554;W.A.,428
HARDYMAN,ELIZA A.,158
HARGETT,JOHNSON,463
HARGROVE,A.N.,390
. ASHBURY,63;F.A.,63
. Z.B.,168,212,224-225
. 247,264
HARGROVES,FRANCES L.,28
. M.P.,35
HARIAN,CHARLOTTE,412
. JULIA ANN,412;SAMUEL
. 412
HARISTON,L.P.,93
HARKEY,JOSEPH,104
HARKINS,
. AMELIA BOISLCAIR,431
. EUGENIA M.,423;J.M.
. 429;J.S.,429,432-434
. JAMES,567;JAMES S.,422
. 423,425,427;JOHN,410
. JULIAN HOLDER,567
. M.M.,423;MAHALA J.,433
. MARY A.,419
. PERMELIA R. PERSONS
. 410;SARAH PULLEY,429
. SULTANA,429;T.F.,431
HARKLESS,
. EVALINA BACON,305,317
. ROBERT W.,305,317
HARKNESS,ELIZ. A.,311,314
HARLAN,CAROLINE,603
. E.A.,418;ELMINA,592
. J.M.,422-424;JAMES M.
. 396;JOSHUA,564,568
. M.J.,570;MAGGIE M.
. BORCH,434;S.J.,425
. T.H.,68;VINCENT V.,434
HARLAND,MISSOURI,589
HARLIN,
. CARTWHITE WALKER,589
. RILEY,589
HARLING,JANE,599
HARLOW,CINTHIA,63
. CLERICY,450;T.B.,63
HARMAN,SAMUEL,2
HARMINY,ALEXANDER,378
. LAURA A.M.,378;LOUISA
. BROWN,378
HARMON,FRANCIS,584
. HARRIET VENABLE,300
. 317;POLLIE,363
. WILLIAM,298,300,317
HARNAGE,A.,205;AMBROSE
. 149,165,169-172,183
. 186,199,215,229
. ANDREW,189
HARP,ANDREW J.,566
. EDMUND,449;FRANCES E.
. 158;PATTEY COMBS,449
. SARAH J.,568;SARAH J.
. CRUCE,566;SARAH J.
. CRUSE,566
HARPER,441;ALBERT,431
. ALEX T.,186;ALEXANDER
. T.,171;ALICE LAKE,431
. ASA,554;BROOKS,471,474
. CAROLINA ODOM,554
. CARRIE,432;CARRIE P.
. 63;GEORGE,1,89-90
. GEORGE W.,91,93-94

. MARY,522;ROBERT,90,96
. 508;ROD,544;SARAH,161
. THORNTON,509
HARRALSON,JOHN,474
HARREL,EDWARD,170;RILEY 1
HARRELL,ANN
. HOLBROOK,333
. EDWARD,166,297;JAMES
. 333;LAVINA,308,316
. MARY E. HARRIS,333
. NEWTON,333;SARAH,555
. WILSON,111
HARRES,BENJAMIN,435
. EDWARD,435
HARRIMAN,H.H.,434
. SAMANTHA RAY,434
HARRINGTON,JACKSON,63
HARRIS,A.C.,333;A.D.
. COWAN,423;ABRAHAM,281
. 306,317;ABRAM,298
. ADALINE,590;ALBRED,317
. ALEXANDER,307;ALFRED
. 307,465;ALICE RAGSDAL
. 539;ALSEY,184,216
. AMANDA,162,602;AMY,459
. ANNA LANGLEY,451
. ARCHIBALD,1,167,451
. AUGUSTIN,583;BENJAMIN
. 304,317;BENJAMIN J.
. 384;BESSIE S. CASON,64
. BETTIE S. NESBITT,434
. BETTIE STEWART,434
. BIRD,298;C.D.,423
. C.G.,576;C.N.P.,597
. C.R.A.,423;CAROLINE
. MESSINCER,595;CARON
. 301,314;CHARLES,1,91
. 150,170,275-276,285
. 286,291-292,298,301
. 317,504;CHARLEY,276
. 281;CLARINDA COWAN,421
. CLARINDA ROUCH,583
. CLARISSA J. GROGAN,600
. CLARK M.,446;COLDONA
. 476;CYNTHIA ADAMS,554
. D.D.,564;DAVID,333
. DEMARY F.,9;DRUCILLA
. 328;DRUCILLA A.,370
. E.C.,72;E.A.W.,604
. ELI,539;ELI S.,356
. 586;ELIZA A.
. BOATRIGHT,576;ELIZA
. C.,597;ELIZA COLLINS
. 275;ELIZABETH,384
. ELIZABETH BROWN,317
. ELIZABETH E. BROWN,302
. ELIZABETH EVANS,451
. ELIZABETH F.,39
. ELIZABETH FRANKLIN,563
. ELIZABETH JONES,334
. ELIZABETH LITTLE,317
. 332;ELIZABETH MCCALL
. 306,317;ELLEN COLE,334
. EPHRAIM,462;ESTER,1
. EUGENIA M. HARKINS,423
. EZEKIEL,285,287,292
. 298;EZEKIEL C.,42
. EZIKIAL,63;F.D.,477
. FRANCES E.,315
. FRANCES REDMON,309,317
. FRANCIS E.,325,329
. FRANCIS H.,583
. GEORGIA,580;H.M.,333
. H.P.,328;HANDY,67
. HANEY,85;HANNAH L.T.
. GLENN,554;HANNAH
. WALDROP,482;HARVEY,132
. HATTIE CARPENTER,27
. HENRY A.,309,317;HIGH
. 64;HIRAM,464;HUGH,64
. J.B.,479,490,492,537
. J.D.,432,493;J.F.,482
. J.H.,524;J.J.,411,491

. J.O.,475;J.P.,595
. J.T.,27,140;JAMES,1
. 287;JAMES C.,317,332
. 334;JAMES G.,354
. JAMES L.,270;JAMES W.
. 414;JANE,504;JANE
. COLLINS,301,317;JANE
. WEST,604;JANE
. WHITSITT,305,317
. JESSE,1;JOHN,443;JOHN
. L.,548;JOHN T.,139
. JOSA MANN,482;JOSEPH
. 243-244,248,252,254
. JOSHUA F.,158;JOSIAH
. F.,600;JULIA F.
. CHANDLER,414;KEZIA
. MALDEN,307,317;L.D.
. 287,297;L.P.,99
. LEMUEL C.,64;LETY,327
. LEWIS,554;LOU V.,354
. LOUISA HARDEN,307,317
. LUCINDA DEADMAN,155
. LUCINDA MICHAEL,554
. LUCY G.,48;M.D.,333
. M.T.,334;MARGARET,320
. MARGARET E.,568
. MARGARET L.,63
. MARGARET L. TUCKER,42
. MARGARET M.,307
. MARIAH ROBERTSON,158
. MARINA,555;MARTHA,311
. 325,385;MARTHA A.
. JULIAN,317,333,356
. MARTHA FOWLER,354
. MARTHA SHARP,304,317
. 384;MARY,342;MARY A.
. 488;MARY ANN,308,325
. MARY ANN TIPTON,564
. MARY C.A.,63,84;MARY
. E.,333,588;MARY E.
. BENNETT,317,332;MARY
. M.,330;MARY W. QUEEN
. 44;MATTIE,64;MILLEY
. G.,557;MILLIE J.,378
. MOLLIE,64;NAERRUCE,606
. NANCY C.,333;NANCY C.
. HARRIS,333;NANCY
. GARNER,446;NANCY
. STRONG,554;NARCISSA
. 323,340;NATHANIEL,437
. 443;NELLY,456;O.G.,430
. OVERTON,317,332
. PARKER,317,332
. PARMILIA,313;PERMELIA
. 327;R.A. CROW,333
. R.B.,281,285-286,291
. 292;R.J.K. WILLIAMS
. 333;RACHEL C. GARNER
. 317;RANCE B.,275-276
. REBECCA C. EVANS,597
. REBECCA JAY,301,317
. RICHARD,563;RODY,560
. ROSANNAH,437;ROSANNAH
. C.,304;ROXANA
. MITCHELL,411;ROZIE,482
. S.,339;S.J.,84;S.Y.,63
. SALLY,40;SALLY
. COLLINS,275;SARAH,281
. 314;SARAH JANE,322,338
. SARAH P. BRUTON,356
. SARAH TRAMMEL,333
. SINGLETON C.,482
. SMITH C.,317;SUSAN,281
. SUSAN COLLINS,275
. SUSIE,602;T.D.,476
. THOMAS,64,155;THOMAS
. H.,107;THOMAS P.,301
. 317;TYRIE S.,554
. VIRGINIA,603;W.M.,421
. W.W.,317,333;WILLIAM,1
. 89,93-95,256,275,281
. 285-286,291-292,298
. 305,317,399,451,554
. WILLIAM B.,333

. WILLIAM G.,466
. WILLIAM T.,44,146
. WILLIAM WESLY,356
. WILLIS,554;WILLIS
. WHITSETT,434;YENOBIA
. 30;ZACHARIAH B.,317
. ZACHARIAH N.,307
HARRIS.R.B.,281
HARRISON,337,536;A.H.,64
. A.J.,68-69,529;ALFRED
. G.,334;ANNA A.,568
. ATHALINDA MERRITT,333
. C.F.,529;D.A.,64
. FLORA A. HOPE,334
. GEORGE W.,394;J.P.,64
. JACOB C.,306;JASON,94
. JASON C.,317;JEREMIAH
. 408;JOHN F.,333;JOHN
. T.,392;JOSEPH B.,334
. JOSEPHUS,439;LEROY,334
. MALISSA,309,318
. MARGARET MILLER,453
. MARTIN,360;MARY,531
. MARY M.M. REED,360
. NANCY JENKINS,360
. REUBEN,204,453;REWBEN
. 152;ROBERT O.,360
. SARAH A. MCGINNIS,306
. 317;SARAH A.P. STUART
. 334;SARAH C.,552
. SARAH J. HENSON,334
. W.P.,24,425
HARRISS,HENSON,439
HARRSS,JOHN,387
HARRY,J.B.,39,484
HART,DOLL,541;FREDERICK
. 441;LANCELER,159;NAIL
. 604
HARTMAN,W.H.,252
HARTMANN,B.,585
. ELIZABETH WIGGIN,585
HARTSFIELD,JAMES M.,11
. 64;LOUISA M.A.,64
. MARTHA H. JACKSON,11
. MOSES A.,64;SAMUEL R.
. 230
HARVEL,RILEY,1
HARVELL,RILEY,116
. WILLIAM,112;WILSON,116
HARVEY,
. CHARLOTTE FLYNT,554
. ELINDER MARTIN,317
. EZEKIEL P.,317;GEORGE
. M.,305,317;ISAAC,245
. 246;LYDIA C.,322
. MURSYLEA MARTIN,305
. 317;PINKETHMAN,554
. REBECCA,552;STEPHEN
. 177
HARVILL,121;JOHN M.,49
. POLLY STEPHENS,49
HARVILLE,SARAH SELL,446
. THOMAS H.,446
HARVIN,
. ELVIRA E. STRAIN,155
. J.T.D.,155
HARVY,LYDIA C.,339
HARWELL,FREDERICK,357
. G. ANN,336;HOWARD,525
. JANE HODGES,357;L.L.
. 357;MARGARET SECRET
. 357;MINNIE BASS,525
. R.,111;R.J.,27;RILEY
. 104;WILSON,112
HASELFING,MANERVY,481
HASKINS,MARGARET,590
HASKY,MARTIN,92
HASLETT,
. SUSN AMANDA BROOKS,333
. WILSON F.,333
HASSLER,WILLIAM,473
HASTEY,MARY,494
HASTINGS,SARAH,28
HATAWAY,MARY,558

640

641

. T.,170,395;F.A.,418
. FRANCIS,347;G.W.,64
. GEORGIA,13,576
. GEORGIA WADE,541
. GREEN,298;HANNAH,567
. HARRIET TAYLOR,357
. HATTIE C. LOWERY,592
. ISAAC N.,334;ISABELL
. 450;J.A.,419;J.H.,581
. J.R.,334;J.T.,521
. J.W.,141,504;JAMES,1
. 545;JAMES R.,357;JANE
. 44;JANE R. BROWN,10
. JEMIMAH WILLIAMS,451
. JENNIE,602;JESSE B.
. 577;JOHN,156,545;JOHN
. M.,35;JOHN W.,64,482
. 601;JULIA A. MILLER
. 334;JULIA ANN
. STEPHENS,13;L.M. MOON
. 333;LETTIE BLACK,357
. M.,425;M.A.,333;M.S.
. 573;MADISON,451
. MAHAFFEY,3;MARGARET
. 570;MARGARET BRADLEY
. 300,317;MARIETTE,431
. MARTHA C. LIGHT,334
. MARTHA J. PHILLIPS,333
. MARY,340-341;MARY E.
. HOPE,334;MARY L.,604
. MARYAN GRICE,156
. MILLY,306,319;N.G.,333
. NANCY STRICKLAND,334
. NATHANIEL G.,300,317
. ORK.E.,172;ORKNEY,186
. PARKS,513;PELINA A.
. NICHOLSON,577
. PENELOPE J.,492
. PLEASANT,149,170
. RICHARD D.B.,334
. ROBERT,149,166,245,535
. ROXY A.,310,320;RUTH
. 453;S.B.,64;S.S.,64
. SALLY,453;SUSAN SNOW
. 581;SYRUS,458;TEMPY
. MCKENZIE,458;THOMAS,13
. THOMAS J.,592;WILL,64
. WILLIAM,51,64,145,170
. 541;WILLIAM E.,357
HENDRICK,JOHN,228
. MARGARET,450;MATILDA
. S.,432;MATTIE,432
. WILLIAM,150,333;ZEEDA
. COMPTON,333
HENDRICKS,ACA,510
. AMANDA GRAMLING,7
. CYNTHIA HUBBARD,449
. ELIZABETH FREEMAN,162
. EMILY PERSON,554;F.C.
. 421;GEORGE,7;JAMES,150
. JAMES M.,554;JOHN,149
. 222;LUKE,449;M.L.
. TATE,420;MARTHA,161
. RUSSELL,310,317
. THOMAS,207,222,237
. WILLIAM,162;WILLIS,150
. 420;ZERUAH A. HOWARD
. 310,317
HENDRIX,ANDREW J.,483
. CELIA GALAWAY,360
. CHIRA,81;CYNTHIA,305
. DAVID,81;ELIZABETH
. GRAVITT,334;ELIZABETH
. WOOD,334;EMANUEL,297
. G.D.,536;GEORGE W.,360
. INDER,302;IRANA,333
. ISAAC L.,334;JAMES W.
. 304,317,360;JANE A.
. COMPTON,304,317;JESSE
. 298;JOHN,153;JUDA,316
. LUCINDA CROW,458;LUKE
. 334,466;MALISSA A.,343
. MARTHA,158;MARY A.
. LEDBETTER,360;MARY M.

. 487;MARY PENDLEY,483
. MEBBY L.,324;MINNIE
. BADGETT,536;NANCY
. CLEMENTS,451;SUSAN,302
. 315;SYNTHA E.,334
. SYNTHIA,318;THOMAS,153
. 224;VIRGINIA,318
. VIRGINIA E.,306;WEBBY
. L.,308;WILLIAM,451,458
HENDRUS,LOIZA BATES,561
. WILLIAM H.,561
HENINGER,JOHN H.,602
. MARY L. FLINN,602
HENKEL,FREDERICK,569
. MARY K. KREISCHER,569
HENLEY,JOHN W.,111,120
. L.,120;LOTT,111
. NEWTIE,542
HENLY,J.W.,112
HENRON,W.N.,548
HENRY,509;ANDREW J.,65
. ANN COLEMAN,589
. DANIEL N.,470,473
. DAVID N.,470
. ELIZABETH MITCHELL,591
. EMELINE MINOR,446
. EPHRAIM L.,567;GEORGE
. 1;GEORGE W.,446;IDA
. 511;J.A.,596;J.B.,419
. K.A.D. HOPKINS,596
. K.A.D. KOPKINS,596
. MADISON,589;MARION,591
. MARTHA BROCK,419
. MARY ANN BLANTON,567
. MATTHEW,446;RUTHY J.
. 598
HENSELL,ALBERTA,30
HENSEN,MARY,495
HENSIN,AELLIN,352
HENSLEY,M.J. COWART,483
. W.J.,483
HENSON,ANDREW B.,548
. ANNA KILPATRICK,446
. ELIZA A. HARDYMAN,158
. ELIZABETH AASCEN,359
. ELIZABETH MANNING,359
. HIRAM L.,317;ISAAC,1
. 449,548;J.M.,425
. JAMES,393,512;JAMES
. B.,548;JAMES W.,300
. 317;JESSE,512;JOHN,333
. JOHN W.,359;M.J.
. ELMORE,425;MARY A.,327
. MARY ANN MASTERS,570
. MARY KIMBLE,449;MIREY
. 328;NANCY A. GRAVITT
. 317;NANCY A.L.,329
. PERMELIA,446;REBECCA
. 301,316;REBECCA A.,340
. REBECCA BRUCE,333
. REBECCA WHITE,300,317
. SARAH,359;SARAH A.,308
. SARAH ANN,313;SARAH
. J.,334;SUSAN,160
. THOMPSON M.,548
. VIRGIL,570;WILLIAM,247
. 249-250,259,446
. WILLIAM N.,495
. WILLIAN,158
HENTON,JOHN L.,567;MARY
. E.,568;PIETY E.,606
HERD,JAMES E.,465
HERINGTON,CALEB,466;J. 466
HERLICK,ALVERDA,486
HERNDEN,
. MARY E. NEISLER,334
. THOMAS J.,334
HERNDON,ARMINDA,340
. BENJAMIN,229;DAVID,18
. FRANCIS M.,554;JAMES
. M.,333;MARTHA FOWLER
. 18;MARY ANN MAYO,554
. MARY E. FRY,333
. MARY E. NEISLER,334

. NANCY,450;SARAH M.,552
. THOMAS J.,334
HEROLD,HENRY B.,158
. JANE PONDER,158
HERREN,
. ANGELINE D. -
. MCARTHUR,483;AUGUSTUS
. 483;LOVEY,452;MARTIN
. 483;MARY NELSON,483
. MILBERY T.,452
. NANCY E. BROWN,483
. SQUIRE,167,176-177,182
. 192,222;TALITHA C.,554
. WILLIAM,483
HERREON,SARAH,478
HERRIN,DANIEL,453;JANE
. 554;MARY PRISNELL,453
HERRING,ALEXANDER,317
. 332;LOUISA E.R. BROWN
. 317,332;SQUIRE,151,168
HERRINGTON,
. C.C. DOBBINS,425;H.B.
. 425;ILSA,65
HERRON,
. LUCINDA FOWLER,459
. SQUIRE,459
HERRS,246
HERSMAN,JOHN,582;JULIA
. COUCH,582
HERST,IBY,298
HERVEY,STEPHEN,177,182
HESLEP,D.D.,495
HESS,JOSEPH,559;MARY
. MCABEE,559
HESTALIR,JAMES,2
HESTER,
. ARMENIA ADCOCK,554
. BENJAMIN,461;JOHN,554
HETHCOCK,JOHN N.,483
. MARY L. SPENCE,483
HETTEN,JACOB,461;JAMES
. 461;JAMES C.,461
. SALLY,461
HEUGHS,
. ELINOR C. JARRETT,575
. HENRY P.,575
HEWETT,CASEY,427;NANCY
. GURTRIE,422;P.,422
. S.C.,423
HEWITT,JOHN M.,27
. SARAH ANN N. SMITH,27
HEWK,E.S.,47
HEYWARD,MARY D.,54
HI,JOHN,2
HIBBERTS,ISABELLA O.,571
. JOHN M.L.,568;MARTHA
. HAMILTON,568
HICE,FLORENCE,64
HICKEY,W.A.,425;W.H.,433
HICKMAN,REBECCA,599
HICKS,A.R.,106-107,139
. 140;ALVIRAH BOWAN,574
. ANDERSON,191,194,196
. 197,202,205;ANDREW,152
. 196;B.K.,595;BUCK,535
. DAVID,528;ELIZA
. RENFRO,587;ELIZABETH
. 28;EMMA E. WRIGHT,9
. EUNICE,528;GIP,540
. GUVICY J.,33;HENRY,548
. HENRY L.,3,64,102-104
. 106-107;JAMES J.,569
. JANE,571;JOEL D.,507
. JOHN B.,574;JOHN H.,26
. JOHN M.,509;JOHN W.,9
. LOUISA A.,600
. MARGARET,572;MARTHA
. J.,22;MARY,496
. MARY F. GANN,26
. MOLLIE BIRD,595
. NAPOLIEN,587;POLLY,64
. ROBERT S.,64;S.A.,64
. 107;S.A.E. REDWINE,569
. S.H.,140;SAIDIE,536

. STARLING A.,100,102
. 103;STERLIN A.,104
. TOLAVER L.,464
. TOLIVER,103,186
. WILLIAM,496
HIDE,ANCEL,358;ANCEL W.
. 358;AUSTIN,441
. ELIZABETH HOLLAND,358
. EMILY,368;ISAIAH,548
. MARY,561;REBECCA
. GARRETT,358;REUBEN,548
HIESS,PUTER,496
HIFF,W.T.,65
HIGDEN,ROBERT,405
HIGDON,L.,575;SARAH
. JORDAN,575
HIGG,
. ELIZABETH LOWERY,300
. 317;JOHN,300,317
. MARCUS A.,409;MARY E.
. BUTLER,409
HIGGIE,J.N.,106,108
HIGGIES,J.N.,106
HIGGINBOTHAM,
. DESSIE COPELAND,424
. ELIZABETH BROACH,554
. FRANCES,419;FRANCIS
. G.,548;HENRY O.,424
. JOHN,390,420;JOSEPH
. 554;MARY DONALDSON,420
HIGGINBOTHOM,WILLIAM,443
HIGGINS,ANN DACUS,317
. 332;BURREL,437
. CAROLINE L. TRIBBLE
. 357;CATHERINE,64
. DELILAH,350;ELIZABETH
. TRIBBLE,317;ENOCH,469
. HARRIETT,338;JAMES,303
. 317,437;JAMES D.,317
. 357;JOHN,317,332-333
. JOHN D.,582;JOSEPH,437
. JULIA GREEN,333
. LUCINDA BRAMLETT,446
. MARY E. WORDON,582
. NATHAN S.,357;POLLY
. BRAMBLETT,303,317
. R.T.,64;REUBEN,436
. SAMUEL G.,333;SANFORD
. 446;SARAH A.E.,333
. SARAH A.E. HIGGINS,333
. SYNTHA C.,336
. VICTORIA B. WINGO,357
HIGGS,L.P.,410;SARAH
. DILLARD,410;THOMAS,149
. 165
HIGH,MARY A.,568
HIGHFIELD,
. ELIZABETH J. -
. MURPHY,573;MARION L.
. 573
HIGHSMITH,THOMAS H.,93
. 94-95
HIGHT,JAMES L.,539
. LAVONIA,10
HIGHTOWER,COLUMBUS,483
. ELIZA E. HENDERSON,317
. GEORGE,483;GEORGE W.
. 483;J.N.,483;JOHN W.
. 523;KIZERE ARMSTEAD
. 554;LINEY,480
. MARTHA J. WILLIAMS,483
. MARY,555;MARY EVINS
. 483;MINERVA,553
. REBECCA YOUNG,483
. SAMANTHA PALMER,483
. T.J.,64;THOMAS,554
. THOMAS G.,317
HILBURN,ALLEN,495;BUD
. 520;ELIZABETH J.,64
. L.J.,64
HILDERBRAND,AARON A.,36
. CELIA,64;HARRIET A.
. BALDWIN,36;LUCY A.,42
. MARTHA,29

644

646

. THOMAS B.,39
ISAAC,111
ISHAM,W.M.,420,426
ISLEY,GEORGE,440-441
. MARY A.,447
ISRAEL,LOUISA,600
IVAY,LITTLETON,208
IVEY,ANDREW B.,9
. BENJAMIN,276
. CHARLOTTE,15
. DELITHA A. EDWARDS,9
. ELIZA ADCOCK,554
. ELIZABETH ANN,551
. FRANCIS,557;JANE
. HERRIN,554;L.C.,475
. L.S.,491-493;LEMUEL
. S.,480,484;MARTHA L.
. 491;NARCISA E.,475
. SARAH E.,599;SEABORN
. 554;WILKINS,554
IVIE,ABLE,295;DISA
. EVANS,484;FRANCES,295
. HUGH,295;JOHN,295
. MARIAH,477;NANCY,295
. RODA,295;STEPHEN,295
. SUSANNA,295;THOMAS,295
. W.H.,484;WINNEFORD,295
IVINS,GEORGE,66
IVY,CENITH,558;ELBIRT
. 555;EMILY UPSHAW,555
. JAMES,555;JOHN W.,361
. MARY A. MAYFIELD,361
. SAMUEL J.,361;SARAH
. A.,325;SARAH ANN
. UPSHAW,555;SARAH
. BUTLER,361;SYNTHA,557
JACK,
. ELIZ. ANN MEREDITH,555
. JOHN,149,165,167,176
. SAMUEL,465;SAMUEL S.
. 555;WILLIAM,465
JACKSON,206,242;ABEL,474
. ADALINE,601;ADALINE
. NAILOR,307;ADALINE
. NALER,307,318;ALFRED
. M.,318,334;AMANDA E.
. 163;ANN,66;ANNICE
. HOWARD,432;ARMINDA K.
. HUGHES,318;ARMINDA K.
. HUGHS,334;C.W.,334
. CAREY W.,473-474
. CAROLINE HUTCHESON,159
. CASEY W.,469
. CATHERINE,419
. CHARLOTTE,342
. CHARLOTTE R. TERRY,446
. CLERICY HARLOW,450
. D.C.,419;DANIEL M.,437
. DAVID,450,463;E.,266
. E.E.,329;EDWARD,470
. ELIJAH,155;ELIZ. JANE
. 162;ELIZA,592
. ELIZA J. BOND,318,334
. ELIZABETH,445,523
. ELIZABETH WRIGHT,155
. EMILY MILICAN,413
. FANNIE KIKER,428
. FRANCES,319;FRANCIS
. 335;GAMUEL,152;GEORGE
. 509;GIDEON,474;GOLA,66
. GRAL. A.,484
. GREENBERRY,159;H.C.,66
. 109,111;HARRIET J.,586
. HENRY,432;ISAAC L.,335
. ISABEL KELLEY,484;J.
. 132,146;J.C.,66;J.H.
. 426;JAMES,302,318,458
. JAMES B.,523;JAMES C.
. 109;JAMES M.,594;IANE
. STANLEY,25;JASPER N.
. 318,334;JOE,523;JOHN
. 446,590;JOHN E.W.,566
. JOHN M.,555;JOSHUA,71
. 81;JOSHUAH,130;JOSIAH

. 88;JUDY MCDENMAN,433
. KATY,590;KATY JACKSON
. 590;L.D.,25;L.J.,422
. LAURA F. ANDERSON,594
. LEVISA M.,557
. LITTLEBERRY,469,473
. LIZZIE,430;LOUEMMA
. WHITAKER,566;LYANT E.
. 194;M.C.,335;M.H.,428
. M.S. WESTRY,335
. MANERVA ADAMS,555
. MARGARET E.,563
. MARTHA,66,301,311,324
. 331,351,354,517
. MARTHA H.,11;MARTHA
. J.,66;MARY,454,551
. MARY E.,335
. MATILDA H. CHASTAIN
. 458;MILES,509-510
. MILTON C.,413;MINERVA
. LILES,432;NANCY E.
. BOND,318,334;NANCY H.
. 336;NANCY H. MCCLOUD
. 484;POLLY E. MCAFEE
. 334;POLLY E. MCAFRE
. 334;PYANT E.,180
. PYENT E.,180,208,210
. 212,215,218,232,245
. R.L.,56;REBECCA,341
. REBECCA TERRY,302,318
. ROBERT,433;S.L. HOPE
. 335;SAMUEL,152,191-192
. 307,318;SARAH,161,307
. 324;SEMMIA,454
. SHADRACH,66;SOPHRONIA
. M.,445;SUSAN,23
. SUSANNAH DAWES,456
. SYLVANIA A.,11
. TALLULAH DURHAM,44
. TIRE,466;TIREY,456
. TOM,510-511;VIOLET,454
. W.D.,432;W.F.,484
. W.H.,44;W.P.,66
. WESLEY H.,146;WILLIAM
. 66,462,466,548
. WILLIAM C.,318,334
JACOBS,ELISHA,555
. HANERETHA,560;JIM,543
. JOHN,230;MARY MEADOR
. 555
JAIM,JOHN,170
JAISON,MARTHA E.,157
JAMES,ALFRED I.,54
. AMANDA,10;AMANDA
. JAMES,10;ARMINDA J.
. DUCKET,582;CALENDER
. 345;CALINDER,301,312
. CLARINDA MAHEE,334
. CLARINDA MAHU,318
. CLARINDA MAY,361
. ELIZA,307,320
. ELIZABETH A. SIMS,318
. ELIZABETH OSBORN,318
. EMILY,301;EMMALY,321
. ERWIN M.,484;EZRAH,146
. F.,123;FELIX,102,109
. GEORGE,285,298,438
. GEORGE W.,318;HANNAH
. 321,336;HUIDA C.
. SHARYER,484;J.H.,484
. J.W.,361;JEMIMA COOK
. 446;JOASHLEY,496
. JOASHLY,88-89,110
. JOHN,1,66,88,110,139
. 143,146,170,318,437
. 529;JOHN A.,318,334
. JOHN T.,170;JOHN W.
. 335,361;JOSEPH,446,496
. JOSEPH N.,221
. KINDNESS,316,330;L.B.
. 298;L.V.,491;LANE,562
. LARKIN,10;LINDA
. EUBANKS,484;LIZZIE,484
. LUCINDA BUTLER,311,318

. 383;MAHLIN H.,383
. MAHLON HENRY,311,318
. MARGARET J. PHILLIPS
. 361;MARGARET PHILLIPS
. 335;MARTHA,597;MARY
. ANN,310,323;MARY E.
. 361;MARY I. MOORE,318
. MARY J.,570;MARY JANE
. 383;MOLLIE HOLBROOK
. 361;NANCY A.,591
. PULASKA D.,582;ROBERT
. 361;S.T.,66;SARAH,66
. SARAH ANN KEITH,562
. SARAH LINDSEY,302,318
. SHEROD,318;SHERROD,302
. THENA,551;THOMAS,109
. 318;WILLIAM M.,486
JANES,MARY,331
JANIS,SARAH,552
JANKINS,GRAFTON,555
. REBECCA SMITH,555
JARMON,AVERY,100
JARRELL,A.J.,28-29
JARRETT,
. ARSENA LEDFORD,576
. DEVERAUX,230;DREWERY
. R.,578;ELINOR C.,575
. FANNY,562;FRANK H.,524
. JANE A.,161;JOHN,576
. JOSEPH,548;LOUISIANNA
. 432;LYDIA,161;MARY,425
. MARY C. STEAVERSON,578
. NANCY,570;NANNIE L.
. 524;NANNIE L. JARRETT
. 524;SALLY,564;TILMEN
. 461
JARVIS,JOHN,565;MARY
. HODGE,565;SARAH,555
JAURDAN,
. MALINDAND LANE,560
. ROBERT,560
JAY,201;ANN YARBROUGH
. 452;ANNY,457
. ELIZABETH,454;JESSE
. 299,452,455;MARY,302
. 323;RACHEL CHARLES,455
. REBECCA,301,317,458
. RHODA,456;SARAH,457
. TEMPY BROCK,457
. WILLIAM,181,183,222
. 224,260,457
JEAN,DANIEL B.,555;MARY
. CARMICHAEL,555
JEFFERS,CANZALA,163
. JOHN,88,110;MARY C.
. 354
JEFFERSON,BASSELL,335
. BASWELL,335;CAROLINE
. 483;CAROLINE MILLS,431
. CINTHA E. CROW,335
. CUNIA ANN,488;E.D.,488
. ELSEY MCHAN,484
. FRANCES STAGGS,335
. GEORGE W.,155;HANAH
. MCHAN,484;JANE M.
. DENT,155;JONAS,484
. LARRA BLACKWELL,484
. LORI M.,371;MARTHA,342
. MARY,476;MARY E.,333
. MELINDA E.,486;SAMUEL
. 484;SARAH A.,161,333
. THOMAS,431
JEFFREY,ELIZABETH,322
JEFFREYS,MARY,305,315
JEFFRIES,ELIZABETH,308
JEFRIES,JOHN A.,318
JEMION,M.E.,47
JENINGS,HENRY,461;JOHN
. 603;S.J. WALSTON,603
JENKINS,ALBERT F.,66
. BARTLETT M.,306;C.S.
. 510;CARITY G.,308,324
. CHARLES J.,128;ELIZA
. J.,320;ELIZABETH,581

. ELIZABETH BLACK,161
. ELIZABETH J.,311;JOHN
. 301,318;JOHN R.,437
. KAREN BRADFORD,318
. MALINDA A. REED,309
. 318;MARY,157;MARY
. BARNETT,306;NANCY,360
. REUBEN M.,309,318
. ROBERT F.,161;ROSEA
. BRADFORD,301;SARAH,306
. 320;V.E.,66
JENKS,CATHERINE,310,320
. MARY,308,320
JENNINGS,ANN B.,551
. HENRIETTA,578;JOHN C.
. 497;MARTHA M.,497
JENSEN,ABREHAM,464
JENSON,SHADRICK,462
JENTRY,
. HARRIET A. FREEMAN,590
. JOHN,495;SAMUEL,495
. WILLIAM,590
JERRETT,
. MARGARET MANUS,569
. MARGARET MCMANIS,569
. THOMAS,569
JERVEY,MYRA MCCREA,66
JESCHKE,EMILIE,559
JESSUP,GEORGE R.,238
JESTER,ANDREW,437
JESTICE,MARY C.,578
JESTURE,ABDEN,298
JESTUS,MATILDA,602
JETT,FERDINAND,2-3
. JAMES M.,335;LEWSENDA
. GREEN,335
JEWELL,ADISON T.,563
. MARTHA PAGE,563
JILES,D.G.,66;ELLA,66
JINKENS,L.,372
JINKINS,BARTLETT M.,318
. MARY BARNETT,318
JINKS,JAMES M.,318,334
. LINNA F.,559
. MARGARET A. GAUNT,334
. MARGARET GANT,318
. MARTHA ANN,333
. WILLIAM,436;WILLIS,436
JOHN,D.W.,140;DOCK,66
. N.N.,86
JOHNS,ANGUS,93;ANNIE,517
. ARMINITHA FANNIN,32
. AUGUSTA ELIS,7;CLIAS
. E.,36;D.W.,135,139,142
. 143-145;DANIEL W.,33
. DAVID,7;ELIZABETH,423
. J.C.,66;J.E.,28;JOHN
. C.,149;JOHN D.,66
. JOSIE MOON,512
. MARKY S. SKINNER,33
. MARTHA,161;MARY,570
. MARY HIGHTOWER,555
. MARY M. WARD,28
. MATTIE CHATMAN,36
. PIERCE,528;RICHMOND
. C.,66;WILLIAM,555
. WILLIAM L.,32
JOHNSON,194,199,202-203
. 216,400;A.F.,128;A.G.
. 559-560;A.H.,130;A.J.
. 40,133,430;A.M.,486
. A.M. FRANCES,304,312
. A.O.,421;A.W.,490
. ALBERT,484;ALDOLPHUS
. R.,420;ALEXANDER,440
. ALFRED A.,570;ALONZO
. W.,429;AMERICA F.,128
. ANDREW,149,172,186
. ANGUS,108-109;ANN E.
. 413;ARTAMISSA KEMP,163
. B.F.,286-287;B.J.,417
. 421,424-425;B.S.,109
. 119;BEN,66;BENJAMIN
. F.,182,184-185,187,190

649

652

. 328;MARTHA MCAFEE,308
. 319;MARY L. MCAFEE,305
. 319;STARLING,308,319
. TABITHA,409
LERGMORANCE,
. A.D. AUSTIN,566;E.M.
. 566
LEROY,CARRIE,37;ELIZA,598
LERVY,BRIZZEL,566
LESETER,JACOB,99
LESEUR,C.L.,512
LESITER,SARAH ANN,334
LESLEY,ALVIN,319,335
. MARTHA A. HAWKINS,319
. 335;MARY A.
. WARREN D.,335
LESLIE,FRANK,538;JOHN
. 457;MARGARET EVANS,457
LESSLEY,
. MARY A. -
. BLANKINSHIP,335
. WARREN D.,319
LESTER,A.T.,535;ADAM J.
. 17;FANNIE C. SMITH,573
. HARRISON,303,319
. HENRY,533;JERMAN M.
. 301;JULIA A.,300
. JULIAN,315;LEON,533
. MARGARET J.,69;R.H.
. 282,297;RICHARD H.,280
. 288;SARAH A. PARKS,303
. 319;SARAH BORN,301,319
. SUSAN,69;TERMAN H.,319
. WILLIAM C.,573
LETHRAL,RICHARD,153
LEVELL,A.J.,69,533
. CHARLES F.,69;EDWARD
. F.,69;ELIZABETH,451
LEVERETT,JOHN E.,447
. NANCY,29;WILLIAM,436
LEVERTON,CALEDONIA,13
LEVINGSTON,E.,465
LEWALLEN,
. ELIZABETH BURT,450
. LUCINDA,558;MARY,555
. WORTHY,450
LEWELL,OPHELIA W.,29
LEWIS,502;A.F.,430
. AGNES,69;ANNY M.
. MOORE,561;C.K.,147
. C.L.,424;CRAWFORD K.
. 34;DEANNY PEARSON,310
. 319;ELEANOR J. GORDON
. 308,319;ELLEN
. MCGINLEY,363;ELSEY W.
. 319,364;ELSY W.,363
. EMMA,69;EVALINA J.
. LENOIR,305,319;FELIX
. 231;FRANK,542
. FRANKLIN P.,364
. FREDRICK T.,501
. GEORGE,530;GEORGE M.
. 517;HARRIET M.,310,317
. HATTIE,494;HENRY,465
. J.,411;J.A.,542;J.B.
. 363;J.H.,69;JAMES E.
. 424;JAMES W.,411;JOAB
. 389,430,432,434;JOHN
. 69,305,319;JOHN D.,530
. JOHN H.L.,485;JOSEPH
. B.,363;L.W.,363;LAURA
. KIRK,501;LULA B.
. JONES,308,319;M.A.,418
. 428;M.J.,419;MAJOR
. JOHN,305,319;MARGARET
. A.,566;MARTHA A.
. HAWKINS,363
. MARTHA ANN HAWKINS,319
. MARTHA HAWKINS,363-364
. MATTIE NEISE,364
. MAY E. ARNOLD,34
. MILES W.,561;MINERVA

. A.,486;MINNIE HAWKINS
. 363;MORIAH,551;NANCY
. 553;NANCY E.,317,332
. 363;NANCY JANE JONES
. 485;REBECCA,411;S.A.
. GOODWIN,424;S.N.,390
. TARELTON,392
. THEOPHILUS,411;THOMAS
. 308,319;WILEY H.,310
. 319;WILLIAM A.,308,319
LEWSUNDAY,211
LIGHT,341;ALLETHIA E.
. PHILLIPS,305
. AMANDA S.L. BOWMAN,335
. AMERICUS,375;ANNIE
. JONES,302,319
. CALIFORNIA,338
. CHRISTIAN MORGAN,364
. DANIEL F.,335
. ELIZ. A. PHILLIPS,319
. FLORA E. MOONEY,335
. GILFORD,302,319
. GUILFORD B.,375;HENRY
. B.,335;J.R.,297;JOHN
. RUSSELL,364;JOSEPH C.
. 364;KINDNESS B.,459
. LEAH S. ROLIN,364
. MARGARET BIB,302
. MARGARET BIBB,319,375
. MARGARET CROSS,319,335
. MARTHA C.,334
. MARTHA E. KING,335
. NANCY J.,348;NANCY
. JANE,333;NEWTON F.,319
. 335;PERNELA A.,304
. PERNELA ANN,325
. PLEASANT G.,302,319
. 335;R.A.,328;SUSAN
. MUNDAY,310,319;WILEY
. 305,319;YOUNG K.,310
. 319
LIGON,ROBERT,465
LILE,ELVINA MULLINS,162
. WILLIAM,162
LILES,H.M. BIRD,427
. JAMES,457;JOSEPHINE
. KAY,427;MINERVA,432
. RHODY GUTHRIE,457
. ROBERT,427;W.L.,427
LILLOMFIELD,W.,31
LILLY,JOSHUA,495;LEWIS,548
LIMLICK,J.N.,135
LIMMING,JOHN,473
LINALY,E.H.,137
LINCH,JOSEPH,169,219
LINDELY,ELISHA,101
LINDER,ELIZABETH,594
. JANE,570
LINDHEIMER,HETTIE,522
LINDLEY,ASEENATH,542
. E.A.,68;E.H.,4-5,14,19
. 21,60,65,69,81-82,86
. 103,131-133;ELISHA,98
. ELIZABETH E.,5
. GEORGIA,264
. GEORGIA A. TURNER,46
. H.,103;HATTIE,542
. HUTSON,35;J.F.,49,59
. 140,146;J.M.,137
. JAMES,18,39,47,101,103
. 105,130,133,135,139
. 143,145;JAMES F.P.,69
. JAMES M.,20;JOHN,177
. JOHN B.,68,130,132
. JOHN T.,69;JONATHAN,68
. 98;JONATHAN P.,542
. JULIA A.,28;K.K.,67
. KEREN H. KIRKPATRICK
. 49;M.,86;MAGGIE,69
. MARETTA SCOTT,35
. MARGARET JOHNSON,20
. T.P.,145;THOMAS,69,86
. 96,101;THOMAS A.P.,46
. WILLIAM,99

LINDLY,E.H.,8
LINDSAY,MARY,322
. RACHELL,49
LINDSEY,ANDERSON,302,319
. APPY REDD,305
. ARCHIBALD,149,298
. AZZY REDD,305
. ELIZABETH,207,457
. ELIZABETH HIX,311,319
. G.W.,465;GEORGIA A.O.
. BLAKE,336;HENDERSON
. 305;ISAAC,336;JAMES
. H.,319;LANTY
. SMALLWOOD,300,319
. LAWSON C.,311,319
. MARY ANN CRUSE,302,319
. MARY WALLACE,336
. NANCY J. HUGGINS,319
. RANSOM,300,319
. SANFORD,336;SARAH,302
. 318;SARAH C.,338
. WILLIAM,462-463
LINK,MOSES,461
LINKENFELT,JAMES,485
. MANDY FRICKS,485
LINLEY,JOHN,177
LINSEY,JOHN,2;MARIA,31
. MARION,510
LINSLEY,SARAH,515
LINTON,MARION,467
LINZAY,
. CATHERINE SANDERS,319
. P.H.,319
LION,NEPOLEON,461
. WILLIAM H.,462
LIONS,JAMES B.,443
LIPFORD,H.F.M.M.,439
LIPPER,JOHN,188
LIPSCOMB,
. MARY A. SAMS,363
. NANCY POOL,363;SMITH
. 363;THOMAS,363
LISLE,HIRAM,453;MARTHA
. BLALOCK,453
LISTER,SUE,430
LITCHFIELD,E.L.,59,69,71
. 77,142;L.A.,69;L.E.,78
. LEMUEL,69;LUTHER,69
. MARY K.,69
LITERAL,RICHARD,191,194
. 197,199,205,244-245
. 248;WILLIAM,199,245
. 248
LITTERAL,WILLIAM,244
LITTLE,ALONZO,430;CYRUS
. N.,335;E.C.,423
. ELIZABETH,317,332,551
. G.M.,542;GEORGIA
. MONTGOMERY,430;JACOB
. 541;JAKE,540;JAMES V.
. 593;JOSEPH,278,541
. JULIAN WHITFIELD,485
. MARTHA C.,328;MARTIN
. E.,485;MARY J.
. EASTERLING,593;MARY
. PACE,540;NANCY M.
. ROGERS,335;PENELOPE
. 513;SARAH,163
LITTLEFIELD,A.,423;D.H.
. 423;FANNIE BEAL,422
. G.W.,422;MARY STANTON
. 423;S. BOSMON,423
LITTLETON,MARK,464
LIVELY,ANDREW,504
. BARTHOLEMEW,372
. ELIZABETH COLLIER,418
. MARGARET M,372;MARY
. RAY,372;WILLIAM,418
LIVINGSTON,A.,230
. ALFRED,174
LOCHRIDGE,MALINDA,453
LOCK,JAMES J.,404
LOCKABEY,JAMES,440
LOCKABY,JOHN,438

LOCKAMY,
. AMANDA CHRISTIAN,336
. WILLIAM J.,336
LOCKARD,SARAH E.,596
LOCKE,JOHN,436
LOCKHART,B.J.,363;LEROY
. P.,363;RUTHA A.
. MCAFEE,363;SARAH M.
. MCEATCHEN,363
LOCKIBEE,JAMES,436
LOCKLER,BILL,534;LOU
. GORE,534
LOCKRIDGE,A.,578;A.J.
. 593;REBECCA,447
LOFTON,ELI,453;SUSAN
. WOODLIFF,453
LOGAN,A.J.,273;ANDREW
. J.,269-270,319;B.L.
. 270;BENJAMIN L.,270
. CANZADY ALLEN,485
. D.H.,269-270;DAVID H.
. 270;ELIZABETH CHAPMAN
. 335;F.,224,262;JACOB
. 485;JAMES,464;JAMES
. M.,270;JEFFERSON,462
. LEWIS G.,335;MARTHA
. JANE,317,332;MARY,305
. 325;MARY L.,337
. PLEASANT,151,222-223
. 253,257,456;SARAH A.
. THOMPSON,319;SARAH
. CASH,456;WILLIAM H.
. 270
LOGGAN,JICNY,459
LOGGIN,E.C.,364;J.O.
. HOPE,364;JAMES,364
. REBECCA E. EDWARD,364
LOGGINS,
. FRANCES M. HUBBARD,578
. WILLIAM A.,578
LOGINTHEWATER,220
LOGINWATER,216
LOKEY,E.J. JOHNSON,427
. HENRY,427
LOLLER,JAMES,436
LOLLIS,CYNTHA,372;JAMES
. 463;JOHN,463
LONEY,
. DAFFNY THOMPSON,589
. JAMES,589
LONG,ALICE,599;ANN JANE
. UNDERWOOD,565;ANN
. PETTY,595;ARIEY
. WIGDON,485;BENJAMIN
. 463;CHARLES,1;CHARLES
. R.,583;CHARLIE,485
. CLARISA M. GRIFFIN,485
. ELIZABETH HUGGINS,485
. ELIZABETH UNDERWOOD
. 583;EMER,477;FRANCES
. 335;HIRAM,305,485
. HYRAM,319;JOHN M.,485
. JOHN N.,485;JULIA A.
. 565;L.S.,423;LEWIS,298
. MAGGIE DAY,485
. MAHALY C. PEPPER,573
. MARGARET S.,492
. MARTHA JOHNSON,161
. MARY A. PROCTOR,305
. MARY ANN PROCTER,319
. NANCY,569;ROBERT,573
. SALLIE,337;SARAH J.
. KETCHEM,583;SARAH
. WOOD,428;THOMAS,161
. W.R.,583;WILEY,595
. WILLIAM R.,565
. WILLIAM S.,428;Y.J.
. MOON,423
LONGCRIER,
. CHRISTOPHER,438
LONGINO,HUGH A.,155
. MARGARET BREWSTER,155
LONGLEY,E.C. COLEY,427
. MARY OTYSON,594;W.A.

. 427;W.J.,594
LONGLY,E.C.,573;J.E.,573
. J.L.,573;M.E. BELL,573
. SALLIE,601
LONGSTREET,JAMES C.,408
. MARY ANN LAMAR,408
LONT,FRANCES HUNTER,428
. J.F.,428
LOOMIS,299
LOONEY,D.M.,533;MATTIE,543
LOOPER,J.H.,560;MARY
. STAAM,560
LOOTS,GEORGE,548;JOSEPH
. 548
LORD,ARMINDA,324,341
. ELEY,452
LOTHLIN,JOSEPH,463
LOTHRIDGE,J.C.,466
LOTT,
. ELIZABETH RANDALL,303
. 319;ENOCH,303,319
. MARIAH A.,336;MOSES
. 283;SAVANNAH C.,337
LOUDON,EMALINE,598
LOUER,MOLLIE,596
LOUGHRIDGE,WILLIAM,577
LOURY,J.M.,
LOVALADY,ANDREW,158
. SARAH MONROE,158
LOVE,502;ANDREW J.,421
. B.,465;D.K.,69;DANIEL
. 150;DAVID,65;EVA,598
. HARRY,132;JAMES,574
. JOHN M.,588;JOHN P.
. 566,598;LOU L.,573
. M.S.H.,69;MARY DAWSON
. 421;MARY E.,586
. MARY E. CLARK,574
. MARY E. HARRIS,588
. OSBORN,474;R.O.
. ROBERTS,601;R.R.,601
. S.E.,69;SALLIE,527
. SARAH,361,582;SEABORN
. B.,527;WILLIAM H.,168
. WILLIAM K.,150
LOVEJOY,MARY BRYSON,423
. WILLIAM,423
LOVELACE,MILTON,524
LOVELADY,DAVIS,548;MARY
. J.,494;SOLOMON,549
. THOMAS,549
LOVELESS,120;BARTON,485
. BENJAMIN F.,163
. CALLIE,482;ELLEN
. PRESLEY,485;EVAN J.,5
. H.H.,69;J.M.,485
. JAMES,69;LOUISA S.
. RUNYAN,5;MATTIE,21
. MICKY,159;S.J.,69
. SARA,69;SARAH ADAMS
. 163;SUSAN M. FERGUSON
. 485;WILLIAM,149,195
LOVELL,ISAAC,549
. JENNETTE N.,36
LOVEN,JONATHAN,452
. SUSANNAH BRIDGEMAN,452
LOW,ADDISON C.,319,335
. CHESTER,325;ELIZABETH
. 350,360;FRANCES
. JACKSON,319;FRANCIS
. JACKSON,335;HENRY,336
. HORAIN,336;JOHN C.,1
. MARGARET,458;MARIAH
. 602;MARY E. BOTTOMS
. 336;SYNTHA C. HIGGINS
. 336
LOWE,CHARLES A.,364
. CHARLEY,404;CYNTHIA
. ROGERS,307,319;DAVID
. G.,402;E.C.,580;ISAAC
. 390;JESSE,401;JOHN,307
. 319;JOHN L.,44;JOSEPH
. 364;MINTORIA E.
. PETYJOHN,364

. PERIBY L. MOBLE,44
. VIRGINIA JONES,364
LOWERY,ANDERSON D.,163
. AUGUSTUS,423;B.A.,425
. BAZZEL,24,403,405
. CHARLES,440;ELISHA,418
. 424;ELIZABETH,300,317
. F.,46;FANNIE E.,606
. GEORGE P.,69;HATTIE
. C.,592;ISAAC P.,305
. JAMES,69;JOHN W.,239
. JOHNSON B.,276
. MARIETTA,477;MARY
. CHAPMAN,163;MARY JANE
. MOTE,46;MARY JOINER
. 423;NANCY J. VESTAL
. 305;P.E.,606
. SHANERACH,474;SOLOMON
. R.,276;WILLIAM,474
LOWLIS,BURTTIN,466
LOWMAN,
. ELLENDER THOMAS,485
. GEORGE,467;MARTIN B.
. 485
LOWREY,BAZZEL,389;ISAAC
. P.,319;JOHN,463;JOHN
. W.,1;NANCY J. VESTAL
. 319;THOMAS F.,472
LOWRY,ALFRED B.,7
. AMANDA,366;ANN E.
. RICHARDSON,606;E.,534
. E.M.,418-419,422
. ELISHA,419-423
. ELIZABETH FAIN,7
. ELLENDOR,449;JAMES,534
. 537;JOHN A.,606;JOHN
. W.,161;M.A.V.,422
. MARTHA A.,14
. MARTHA M. HARDMAN,7
. MARY J.,421;NANCY,452
. SARAH M. FISHER,161
. WALTON R.,7
LOYD,BENJAMIN,567;JAMES
. R.,32;JOHN,437,439
. MARY,69;P. FINCHER,32
. SARAH J. JURELL,567
LUALLEN,JONATHAN,443
LUCAS,MARY D.,580
LUCY,WILLIAM,447
LULBRITE,LEONARD,495
LULUS,J.A.M.,93
LUMBUS,FANNY,421
LUMKIN,ELIZABETH,387
. F.M.,177;SARAH,387
LUMMUS,ANDREW J.,363
. CHARITY BAKER,363
. ELL.,335-336;FRANCES
. 316;FRANCIS M.
. TIDWELL,335-336;JAMES
. F.,363;JAMES M.,307
. 320;LENORA BARRETT,363
. LEVICY E.,336
. MARGARET HARRIS,320
. MARGARET M. HARRIS,307
. MARTHA A.,341;MARY A.
. BENTLEY,301,320;MARY
. E.,332;WILLIAM,320
. WILLLIAM,301
LUMPKIM,GEORGE W.,180
LUMPKIN,
. ESTHER HUDGINS,459
. GEORGE,393,399;H.P.
. 524;KERY,452
. WASHINGTON,169
. WILLIAM D.,459;WILSON
. 165,187,196,203,208
. 239,245
LUNCEFORD,GEORGE,549
. WILLIALM,549
LUPER,L.L.,427
LUSUNDAY,231
LUTE,M.E. WOOD,425;W.M.,
. 425
LUTES,ELIZABETH,406

. GEORGE,406;LEAH,406
LUTHER,373;ANNA,357
. JOSIAH,1
LYERS,GEORGIA,48
LYLE,522;ANNIE,543;HUGH
. G.,69;JAMES P.,69
. JOHN,443,496;JOHN P.
. 496;NANCY L.,69
. PLEASANT R.,439
LYMAN,CAROLINE,86
LYNCH,CAROLINE,575
. HENRY C.,598;JANE
. BAGLEY,156;JOHN,196
. JOSEPH,169,171,178-179
. 183-184,196,198,252
. JOSEPH M.,184;L.A.E.
. MARTIN,572;MARY A.,566
. 589;WILLIAM I.,156
. WILLIAM R.,572
LYNES,JOSEPH,549
LYNN,OLIN,419
LYON,ALBERT REDDEN,485
. E.H.,7;J.E.B.,479
. KINCY FINLEY,485
. LUCINDA MAULDIN,459
. P.H.,78,138-139,141
. 142,146;WILLIAM H.,459
M.,MARGARET,430
MABERRY,NANCY,496
MABLE,ALEX,61;ALEXANDER
. 70;JOHN,543;JOSEPH,70
. ROBERT,70
MABLES,JOHN,524
MABREY,EAPHUS,167
MABRY,ANN CHAMPION,457
. EPHRAIM,149;LIZZIE,28
. MARY,455;RUSSELL,457
. SARAH,455
MACK,JAMES K.P.,595
. MARTHA A.,592;MARY E.
. TIFFINS,595
MACKEN,EDWARD,442
MICHAEL,442
MACKEY,BENJAMIN F.,14
. ELIZABETH,45;EMELINE
. RUTHERFORD,14;FRANCES
. KIRK,26;JESSE,26;JOHN
. 472
MADDEN,N.M.,73;ROBERT
. J.,304,320;SARAH M.
. SEGARS,320;SARAH N.
. SAGERS,304;SARAH N.
. SEGERS,304
MADDOX,529;BENJAMIN W.
. 444;CHARLOTTE RHODES
. 155;E.J.,176;ED,177
. EDWARD,151;EDWARD H.
. 182;EDWARD J.,177,223
. 224,228,237,260,287
. ELIZABETH WELCHEL,458
. ESTHER,164;HENRY,177
. 523;HENRY H.,458;J.M.
. 70;JAMES A.,207,223
. 261;JEPTHA,151;JOHN
. 152,435;JOHN G.,177
. 182,204;JOHN Y.,192
. SEABORN,177;SEBRON,435
. WALTER,155
MADDUX,
. ELIZABETH J. SCOTT,13
. THOMAS F.,13
MAFFAHAY,JOHN,76
MAFFETT,
. N.G. CARPENTER,568
. R.G.W.,568
MAGARITY,MARY,49
MAGBEE,LABON,70;M.J.,70
MILTON J.,79
MAGILL,ISAAC L.,14
. SARAH E. ORR,14
MAHAFEY,KELLY,555
. MARTHA A.M. PEETERS
. 555
MAHAFFEY,CELESTIA,320

. JOHN,138,496
MAHAFFLEY,DOLPHUS,502
MAHAFFY,ALSTON,377;C.A.
. MASHBURN,377;CELESTIA
. 336;JACOB S.,377;JOHN
. 4,136-137;JOHN W.,336
. MALINDA,558;MARY E.
. WILLIAMS,336;SARAH A.
. LANDMOND,4;SUSAN BOYD
. 377
MAHAFPHY,JAMES,465
MAHALL,JOHN E.,486
. MELINDA E. JEFFERSON
. 486
MAHAN,CAGE,485;EMILY
. BARNETT,555;HARRIET
. MCCLURE,485;J.C.,145
. JAMES,461;LOUISA,486
. SALLIE,485;WILLIAM A.
. 555
MAHEE,333;CLARINDA,334
MAHON,GEORGE,24;JAMES,91
. WILLIAM B.,110
MAHORN,JAMES,103
MAHU,CLARINDA,318
MAILON,MARY,572
MAIN,ELIZABETH,557
MAJOR,CAROLINE E.,328
. DANNAL P.,363;FRANCES
. S.,383;JAMES T.,383
. JOHN H.,367;LUCINDA
. 457;LUELLA M.,363
. MARCENA BRANNON,383
. MARTHA RAINWATER,363
. MARY H.,335;MATILDA
. PRUETT,367;MATILDA
. WATERS,320;MOURNING
. HEATH,454;RICHARD,320
. 367,454;SAMUEL W.,157
. SARAH A.,341;SARAH C.
. BARKER,367
MAJORS,330;PEGGY,453
MALCOM,
. CATHARINE PETERS,555
. DANIEL,555;ELIZABETH
. GATHER,555;JAMES,555
. LUCINDA,557;NANCY ANN
. 553;POLLEY,553
. SUSANNAH R.,556
MALDEN,GRACE G.,310,323
. HANNAH H.,325;HANNAH
. M.,304;KEZIA,307,317
MALER,JAMES,463
MALEY,J.T.,146
MALLET,ABRAHAM,231
MALOM,ROBERT,1
MALON,WILLIAM B.,559
MALONA,ELLEN,24
MALONE,CORNELIA,17;D.J.
. 527;GEORGE,96;J.D.,527
. JOHN,395,402;JOHN T.
. 404;L.,70;LIZZIE B.,70
. MARANDAY C.,555
. MARTHA E.,422;NANCY
. DRUMMOND,555;NELLIE
. 434;PARMELIA FULKS,572
. ROBERT,1;SALLIE LOVE
. 527;SAMUEL M.,105
. WILLIAM,496,507
. WILLIAM B.,1,149,170
. 171,473-474,559-560
. 565,572
MALONEY,ELVIRA,32;S.N.
. 101;SAMUEL N.,100
. WILLIAM P.,1,96
. WILLIAM W.,2
MALONG,JOHN,112
MALONY,E. CHASTAIN,109
. J.N.,90;JOHN,101,109
. 112;MARY J.,36;S.N.
. 107;SAMUEL,100;SAMUEL
. N.,108;WILLIAM,115-116
. WILLIAM P.,90,102
MALOY,WILLIAM C.,584

656

657

659

. DOWDY,603
MIDDLEBROOKS,A.B.,227
. AMAZIAH B.,224;JAMES
. D.,522;LAURA A.,522
MIDDLETON,177,181;JAMES
. 149,176,276,285;JOHN
. 149,277,279,282,297
. THOMAS,549;WILLIAM,297
MIDWELL,PLEAS,531
MIERS,KATHERINE,458
MILAN,CHARLES,526;NELIA
. JONES,526
MILBURN,J.S.,428
MILER,SALLY,549
MILES,J.B.,71;JOHN,71
. 173;MARY,48
MILFORD,
. ELENDER THORNTON,303
. 320;ELENOR THORNTON
. 365;JAMES,303,320
. JAMES I.,365;LUVENIA
. E.,337;NANCY OWENS,365
. NANCY STOVALL,365
. SARAH J.,330
MILHENE,WILLIAM,165
MILICAN,EMILY,413
MILIGAN,ELIZABETH,354
MILIRONS,SARAH E.,578
MILLEN,ANN C.,71
. HEZEKIAH,276
MILLER,394,414;ADALINE
. CRUSE,320,336;ALEX,287
. ALEXANDER,66,152,204
. 207,217,242,454;ALLY
. 457;ANDREW,549;ANN,301
. 314;ANN C.,70-71
. CESLEY A. JOHNSON,306
. 320;CHARLES,71;CROSBY
. 365;D.,426-427;DAVID
. 397,421,602;DAVID I.
. 403;DAVID T.,71
. DEMPSEY,244,246,450
. DENNIS,151,191,244,418
. E.C.597;ED F.,502
. ELIAS,436;ELIE,440-441
. ELIZA BETTON,427
. EMILY ARNOLD,365
. EVELINE,343;EZEKIEL
. S.,403;G.,422;GEORGE
. A.,71;GREEN,309,320
. H.,281;HARDIN,276
. HENRY,157;HEZEKIAH,155
. HOMER,390;J.E.,418
. J.M.,434;J.N.,392,396
. J.R.,574;JAMES,285,298
. 421-422,439,456;JANE
. HILL,422;JESSE,392,395
. JESSE N.,393,400,402
. JOB,543;JOHN,71,151
. 204,207,210,214,217
. 228,236-239,298,306
. 320,336;JOHN C.,4,185
. 549;JOHN H.,71,77-78
. 112,118;JOHN S.,464
. JONES,359;JOSEPH,300
. 320;JULIA A.,334;L.A.
. 531;LETTY GUTTERY,452
. LEVI,473;LEWIS,455
. LOUISA MCDANIEL,426
. 427;LUCINDA,422;M.A.
. 427;M.A. MILLER,427
. M.E. HARDCASTLE,574
. M.H.,395;MARGARET,453
. MARGARET A. PICKARD
. 418;MARTHA BUTLER,502
. MARTHA NEEL,421
. MARTHA S. BELL,157
. MARY,5;MARY DAVIS,563
. MARY L. VEAL,421
. MARY R. ANDO,365
. MILBERY T. HERREN,452
. MINERVA EMMERSON,155
. NANCY,563;NANCY
. JOHNSTON,455;NICY,421

. ODBIAH,397;PETER,427
. POLLY,461;POLLY
. HULSEY,454;R.A.,581
. RACHEL,422;REBECCA
. GRAY,602;RICHARD,452
. ROBERT,451;RUSELL,563
. S.E.,426;SALLY,549
. SAMUEL,469,471,473
. SAMUEL NEAL,365;SARAH
. 604;SARAH A.,422
. SARAH SAUNDERS,456
. SARAH WALRAVENS,450
. SUSAN,555;SUSAN
. PENDERGRASS,309,320
. SUSANNA BROADNAX,451
. T.W.,422;TEMPEY DELK
. 320;TEMPY DELK,300
. THENAY,313;THENERY,306
. THOMAS W.,389;W.B.,508
. W.R.,427;WILLIAM,443
. WILLIAM F.,389
. WILLIAM S.,452
. ZEALOUS,463
MILLFORD,NANCY KELLY,336
. WILLIAM P.,336
MILLIAM,JOHN,405
MILLIAN,KARENHAPP,555
MILLICAN,JAMES,209,228
. 229,239,446;JOHN,405
. THOMAS,208-209,228-229
. 239
MILLINER,WILLIS,463
MILLIONS,NANCY,606
MILLIRONS,HENRY,573
. MARGARET E. OWENS,573
MILLISONS,J.A.,602
. MARGRET POTS,602
MILLNER,JEANETTE,606
. R.W.,30
MILLS,ADELA E.,315,330
. CAROLINE,431;COURTNEY
. MEUSE,456;DEMARSA,155
. E.R.,88-91,110;ENOCH
. 456;ENOCH R.,1,3,110
. H.J.,487;JAMES,466
. JESSE,465;JOHN,387
. JOSEPH L.,487;L.K.,604
. MARGARET C.,311,325
. MARY HITT,487;MITTY
. 589;SALLY,451;SUSAN
. A.,490
MILLSAP,ROSA,379
MILLSAPS,
. COUTNEY WHITLEY,556
. JOHN M.,556
MILLWOOD,ABRAHAM J.,365
. ELLA CHRISTIAN,365
. ELLA MARTIN,365
. JACKSON,320,336;JANE
. DAVIS,320,336;JESSY
. 336;MARTHY E. MCGEE
. 336;MARY DAVIS,320,336
. 365;S.W.,543;SARAH,340
. WALTER,543;WILLIAM,320
. 336;WILLIAM B.,365
MILNER,MARTHA,454;R.M.
. 11;R.W.,10,14,18,32,50
. WILLIS J.,174
MILNOR,WILLIAM,152
MILTON,
. EMILY E. GLOSS,336
. MINERVA C.,321,339
. WILLIAM C.,336
MILWOOD,FRANCES,333
. JACKSON,320;MARY
. DAVIS,320
MIMMS,CALVIN,435
MIMS,395;EDWARD,192
. EDWIN,177-178,191-192
. 207;J.A.,404,429,432
. 434
MINAR,L.A.,581
MINC,
. ELIZABETH LINDER,594

. WILLIAM R.,594
MINCE,ELIZA MCJUNKEN,594
. THOMAS W.,594
MINCHEW,ELISHA,436
. MARTHA,436;THOMAS,436
MINCY,AARON,463;AREN,463
. ISAAC,463
MINES,ELIZABETH,549
MINEY,ELIZA,379
MINHINETTE,FRANCIS,71
MINHINNETT,
. MARTHA ELDRIDGE,22
. THOMAS J.,22
MINIARD,A.E.,421
MINIS,ELIZABETH J.,571
. MARGARET A. NORTON,562
. WILLIAM,562
MINKINETTE,FRANCIS R.,71
MINNING,THOMAS,513
MINNIS,LATITIA,569
MINOR,EMELINE,446
. ROBERT M.,2
MINTON,ANNA COOK,159
. JAMES,152,207;JOHN,71
. JOHN P.,159;M.W.,71
. ROSANNA,71
MIRES,ANN STEWART,449
. JACOB,449
MIRILL,BENJAMIN,436
MISANGER,MARY,582
MITCHEL,ANGELINA,25
. D.P.,30;DANVILLE,437
. EINEFORE BASS,14
. ELIZABETH BUFFINGTON
. 600;HARDY,71;JOHN,14
. 72;JORDAN H.,556
. JULIA ANN F. HARDIN
. 556;MAGGIE J. BEATZ,30
. MARY ANN,582;PENN,72
. T.M.,600;THOMAS L.,72
. WILLIAM,55;ZULA G.
. RAY,72
MITCHELL,140,543;A.B.,23
. 26,32,40,47-48
. ABASHABA,311,316
. ALICE HOLLAND,592;ANN
. 20,602;ANN MITCHELL
. 602;CHARLOTTE E.,602
. D.R.,193,197,208-209
. 219,225,238-239,287
. 407;DANIEL R.,149,151
. 168,189,218,389;DAVID
. W.,564;DESIRE PALMER
. 556;E.C.,88;ELENDOR
. TANKERSLEY,449
. ELIZABETH,591
. ELIZABETH HENDERSON,15
. ELLA,513;F.M.,63
. FRANCES,592;G.T.,336
. GEORGE L.,17;GEORGIA
. 407;GEORGIA E. HUNT,17
. HARRIET C.,8;HENRY,71
. 98;ISAAC,449;JAMES,246
. JAMES C.,583-584
. JAMES M.,11;JAMES S.
. 209;JAMES W.,524;JANE
. WATTERS,307;JEDIDA T.
. PERKINS,556;JENETTIE
. 595;JOHN,71;JOHN B.
. 418;JOHN F.,588
. JOSEPH,15;JULIA A.
. KIRK,11;M.L.,598;M.M.
. 580;MARGARET,9
. MARGARET RILEY,588
. MARIAH ROACH,336
. MARTHA,71;MARTHA F.
. 587;MARY ANN,558;MARY
. BRUMBELOW,564;MARY D.
. LUCAS,580;MATTIE,35
. N.C.,602;NANCY,524
. NANCY E.,88;PENN,75
. R.,245;REBECCA,42,161
. ROBERT,175,179;ROXANA
. 411;SALEMA,49;SALLIE

. 603;SALLY,31;SAMUEL
. P.,556;SARAH A.
. BUFFINGTON,584
. SARAH C. NIX,418
. SARAH SMITH,556
. TABITHA T.,11;THOMAS
. M.,584;W.H.,405;W.T.
. 556;WILEY P.,602
. WILLIAM F.,592
. WILLIAM F.M.,63
. WILLIAM T.,556;WM.
. BENNETT,307
MITCHELLS,R.M.,147
MITCHEM,CLARA,18
MITCHENER,H.E.,320
. MARY H.E. SHIELDS,320
MITCHINER,E.E.C.,336
. M.E.E.,332;MARY H.E.
. SHIELDS,336
MIX,LODOWICK,204
MIXON,NOEL,231
MIZE,DANIEL G.,336
. ELVIRA M. REAVICE,336
MIZELL,L.F.,49;LUKE T.
. 46,49-50;M.T.,46
MOBLE,PERIBY L.,44
MOBLEY,ALLEN,535
. BURWELL,253;DEATON,474
. JOHN,505;L.C.,560
. LUCINDAY THARN,560
. M.A.V. LOWRY,422;MARY
. 304,316;NANCY A.E.,563
. REBECCA,531;THOMAS B.
. 422
MOBLY,E.W.,92;SARAH
. ROPER,556;SARAH
. ROSSER,556;WILLIAM,556
MOFFETT,NARCISSA B.,592
MOHAN,ALEXANDER,88,99
. 105,110;JAMES,88,90
. 100,105,110;JESSE,88
. 110;JOHN,135
MOHON,ALEXANDER,100
. J.C.,145,147;JOHN C.
. 29;MARGARET R.
. LEAVELL,29
MOHORN,ALEXANDER,99-100
. GEORGE W.,72;JAMES,99
. 100-101;JOHN A.,72
MOHORNE,JAMES,91,104
MOLEN,NELY,298
MOLLOY,JOHN,586;MEDE
. WRAN,586
MOLOCK,SAMUEL J.,49
. SARAH J. MARTIN,49
MONCRIEF,A.L.,425;D.H.
. 424;D.W.,422;M.,425
MONDAY,
. ALMIRA FITZSIMMONS,159
. B.,362;E. SHADBURN,362
. ELIZABETH E. SHADBURN
. 336;JANE E.,341;JOHN
. B.,336;JOHN L.,159
. LOUISA N.,362;LUCY,301
. 315;MARIEAS,385
. MARTHA J. CRUMP,385
. SAMUEL D.,385
MONEY,
. ELIZA J. JENKINS,320
. ELIZABETH J. JENKINS
. 311;FRANCIS,311,320
MONK,GEORGIA NOLUND,506
. J.T.,506;JAMES G.,72
. JAMES M.,72;THOMAS,442
MONKS,DENNIS,509
MONLYDE,S.G.,111
MONROE,ADALINE M.,342
. AMELIA C.,419
. ARTIMISA HOLLAND,337
. D.P.,267,270;DANIEL
. P.,268-269,274;DUGAL
. 453;ELIZABETH KELLY
. 303,320;ELIZABETH T.
. WINGO,336;JESSE B.,336

662

663

664

. T.J.,6
OVERBY,ELIZA,316,331
. MARTHA L. BENCE,562
. WILLIAM B.,562
OVERLOCK,
. ELIZA NORMAN,418
. EMERSON,418
OWEN,ASA,338;BETSY ANN
. LEAGUE,305;ELZIA,360
. EMALINE JOHNSON,309
. EMILY M. HUTCHINS,338
. FANNIE,536;FANNIE
. MOORE,23;FRANCES,310
. 314;G.A.,518,531
. GEORGE,73;GEORGE F.,74
. GEORGE S.,43,73
. GRIFFIN,212;GRIFFIN
. L.,556;HIRAM,73
. ISABELLA TURKET,579
. J.C.,525;JACTION,349
. JANE WHEELER,321,338
. JENNIE,73;JOHN,502
. JOHN A.,502;L.E.,518
. LEE,533;LUCY A.
. RAYBURN,43;M. HUTCHEN
. 349;MALINDA BEAVER,339
. MARY ANN ALLEN,556
. MENTORIA R.,349
. MILESBERRY,525;NANCY
. E.,321,336-337;OLIVER
. P.,305;OSWELL,339
. POWELL,309;ROSETTA,340
. S.M.,135;SANFORD,321
. 338;SARAH,305,324
. TAMPY,596;THADIUS C.
. 579;URIAH,23;W.C.,268
. W.R.,528,535
OWENBY,JOHN,461;WILLIAM
. 549
OWENS,ALFRED,310,321
. AMANDA A. WOOD,339
. BETSY A. LEAGUE,321
. CASANDRA,320
. CASSANDRA,337
. CATHARINE ROAN,556
. CHARLOTTE ALLEN,556
. COLEMAN P.,556;E.B.
. 514;E.H.,73;ELIJAH,159
. ELIZABETH,302,321,334
. ELIZABETH A. BROWN,321
. ELIZABETH BROWN,309
. ELIZABETH GRIFFIN,354
. ELIZABETH J. STONE,310
. 321;ELIZABETH OWENS
. 302,321;EMALINE
. JOHNSON,321;EMILY,344
. EMILY JAMES,301
. EMMALY JAMES,321;F.M.
. 339;GABRIEL T.,304,321
. GEORGE S.,47,131
. GEORGE W.,439;HARRIET
. F.,342;HARRIET P.
. ARMSTRONG,339;HIRAM,4
. HOWELL COBB,339
. ISABELLA I. HEARD,159
. JAMES,253,285;JAMES
. H.,556;JAMES M.,339
. 345;JANE,159;JOHN,301
. 321,495;JOHN R.,339
. JULIAN,324;LEE,533
. LENA WOOD,535;LONIZA
. M.,331;MALINDA,331
. MARGARET E.,573
. MARGARET GARRETT,339
. MARTHA,420;MARTHA
. TATUM,339;MARY,419
. MARY ANN E. FULLER,33
. MARY E.,341;MARY M.
. HUTCHINS,339;MATT,535
. 538;NANCY,385;NANCY
. J.,354;NANCY T.
. STOVALL,304,321
. OLIVER P.,321;OWEN,302
. 321;PERMELIA REEVES,4

. POWELL,321;RILEY,33
. RUFUS,418;S.,425;S.
. WILSON,418;S.L.,354
. SALLIE KNIGHT,47
. SARAH BURNEY,447
. SARAH JANE,564
. SARAH M. WHITMIRE,339
. SUSAN EDWARDS,302,321
. TERIA BENNETT,345
. WILEY W.,309,321
. WILLIAM,339,447
. WILLIAM S.,339
. WILLIAM W.,302,321
OWNINGS,M.C.,394
OWSLEY,THOMAS J.,133
OXFORD,
. CATHERINE BENDER,595
. DAVID,461,570;DAVID
. J.,595;JOHN,461,467
. 568;JONATHAN,461
. JONATHAN L.,574
. MAHALIA AUSTIN,568
. MARY B. POOL,574;S.J.
. SWEATMAN,570
PACE,ABRAHAM,2;ADELINE
. 505;B.L.,544;BARNABAS
. 496;DICK,500
. ELIZABETH C. RUFF,18
. FRANK,533;H.J.,321
. HARDY,73,92;HENRY T.
. 73,ISAAC,515,531-533
. J.L.,76;JAMES L.,13,73
. 128;JOHN,1-2,86,90,97
. JOHN N.,338;JULIA,13
. L. STEVA,73;LUCY J.
. 515;LULA,523;MARTHA
. A.,6;MARTHA S. FULTS
. 13;MARY,47,540;MARY
. L.,73;MINNIE B.
. HANSARD,321;NANCY
. KILLINGSWORTH,338
. RUSSELL,73;SOLOMON K.
. 132;SOLOMON R.,73
. STEPHEN,73,128;STEVE
. 533;TADDY,515;W.N.,73
. WILLIAM N.,18
PACK,ALICE NORRELL,431
. ALTHA GRIFFETH,488
. B.M.,431;JAMES,488
. ROXEY,486;SARAH E.,475
PACT,CLEMENTINE,484
PADDIS,JAMES,162
. SYNTHIA FINDLEY,162
PADEN,ALEXANDER D.,103
. ELIZABETH,161
. ELIZABETH S.,73;EMMA
. L.,43;JOHN T.,45
. MOSES W.,156;R.S.,73
. ROSANNAH M. DELANY,156
PADGET,
. ALLISON ALONZO,487
. ANNISE,483;COLUMBUS
. 487;FRANCES EVANS,487
. HENRY,487;IRE,487
. J.C.,476;JACOB A.,487
. JESSE,253,257,482,487
. 494;L.T.,479,492
. LEMUEL J.,163;LEROY
. T.,480;MARTHA E.
. DARNELL,487;MARY,476
. MARY FITTS,488;MARY
. HITT,487;MARY JANE,479
. MARY M. HENDRIX,487
. MARY M. SCRUGGS,163
. MELISSA E. BLACKWELL
. 487;PETER A.D.,487
. RHODA SMITH,487
. SANFORD W.,488;VINA
. 491;W.,482;WILLIAM,482
. 488
PADGETT,ABRAHAM,466;ASA
. 466;CARY G.,362
. ELVIRA,484;G.L.
. MOONEY,432;J.J.,432

. JAMES,372;JESSE,477
. 480,484;L.T.,488
. LIDDA BETTIS,372
. MALINDA,362;MALINDA
. DILLBECK,488;MARY
. EDMONSON,372;MARY
. JONES,362;NELSON,454
. RUSUS E.,370;SARAH
. GAULT,370;SEENETH,454
. SEENETH PADGETT,454
. TERRELL,372;W.,484
. WILLIAM,484,488
PADON,JOHN,453;SARAH
. COX,453
PAERSLEY,T.K.,581
PAGE,350;CARY,549
. CRAWFORD B.,372;DAVID
. 549;E.,132,136
. EBENEZER,73,129
. ELISE E. WILSON,372
. ELIZA A.,73;ELIZABETH
. C.,446;EMANUEL,373
. HULDAH L.,592;JACOB
. 225;JAMES M.,372;JANE
. 560;JASPER N.,598
. JOHN BENJAMIN,374
. JOHN P.,430;JUVANILL
. 372;MAHALA BROOK,373
. MAHALA BROOKS,372
. MARGRETT SHADER,374
. MARIETTA PHILLIPS,374
. MARTHA,563;MARY M.
. SUMMER,372;NANCY,361
. NANCY G.,352;RUTHY J.
. HENRY,598;SARAH M.
. HOLLAND,373;SOPHA
. SAMPLE,372;SUE LISTER
. 430;THOMAS,374
. WILLIAM,430;WILLIAM
. B.,244;WILLIAM J.,372
. 373
PAGETT,
. ARTILLA COWARD,156
. ISAAC,156;MELINDA
. BENT,158;PERRY C.,158
PAIGE,JOSEPH,73;SARAH
. C.,73
PAIN,ELIAS,339;ELIZA
. ORR,339;ELIZABETH,455
. ELIZABETH BATES,157
. M.C.,40;MARTHA,320,336
. MARY C.,339;MARY C.
. PAIN,339;NATHANIEL D.
. 157;P.,339;THOMAS,298
. U.W.,297;WILLIAM,297
. 339
PAINE,FRANCES,158
. GEORGE W.,162;J.L.,433
. MARY NEIGHBORS,5
. SALLIE COSTAIN,433
. TEMPEY GREGORY,162
. THOMAS,5
PAIR,FRANCES,73;J.W.,73
. JAMES L.,73,86;JAMES
. M.,73;JOHN,86;JOHN A.
. 73;S.P.,73;SARAH,73
. T.J.,73;W.E.,73
PALLY,MARY M.,580
PALMER,278;ABNER,307
. ANNEY HOLBROOKS,321
. ARNILL HOLBROOKS,309
. AUGUSTUS,427;AUGUSTUS
. H.,556;DESIRE,556;E.
. PORTER,10,17;E.P.,4-6
. 12-13,19;E.T.,5;ED
. PORTER,13;EDMAN T.,321
. EDMOND T.,307,309
. EDWARD PORTER,8;ELLA
. 408;ELLEN L. LANE,47
. EPENOLA,73;GEORGE S.
. 391;HENRY,95;JOHN,438
. 556;JOHN W.,529,544
. L.D.,414;MARY A.,598
. MARY CAMP,556;MARY F.

. 74;MARY FISHER,307
. MITTY MILLS,589
. MOLLIE,544;PORTER,8
. ROBERT,589;SAMANTHA
. 483;SARAH DOLLAR,307
. SARAH I. POWELL,427
. SARAH JONES,556
. SEABORN,459;W.F.,498
. W.J.,47,73,144
. WILLIAM CARTER,498
. WILLIAM J.,73;ZACH.
. 173
PALMOR,STEPHEN,461
PALMORE,LEOLER,544;MARY
. ANN,162;NANCY,552
PALMOUR,JOHN,466
. MALINDA,490;SARAH C.
. 494;SILAS,466;SOLOMON
. 466
PANE,ELIZABETH FOWES,455
. WILLIAM,455
PANNELL,JOHN A.,256
. LOUISA,454;MARY DELK
. 302,321;THOMAS,302,321
PANNIEL,
. NANCY D. WHITE,593
. WILLIAM T.,593
PANTER,HEZEKIAH,454
. SUSAN HAGWOOD,454
PANTHER,YOUNG,241
PARDON,
. ELIZABETH COCHRAN,370
. POLLY DAY,370;RILY,370
. WILLIAM,370
PARDUE,WILL,522
PARE,HARPER,462
PARIS,AARON,454;CELIA
. TIDWELL,454;DILLARD
. 501;ELIZABETH BLAG,454
. HOMER,532;JESSE,454
. N.D.,501;NATHAN,101
. OLIVER,498
PARK,ANDREW H.,306,321
. DELITHA W. TRYSON,306
. DELITHA W. TYSON,321
. JAMES,82;JOHN G.,474
. JOHN T.D.,473
. MARTHA P. PAXTON,556
. MOSES,556;SARAH A.,599
. WALLIS,464
PARKER,346;A.M.,79;ABE
. 372;ANN BROWN,556
. BARNETT,467;C.W.,506
. COMFORT,553;DARKEY,462
. ELIZA,431;ELIZABETH
. 451,552;EPHRAIM,392
. F.A.,338;FRANCIS,488
. FRANK,511;G.A.,465
. G.T.,519,542;GEORGE
. T.,523,536;GLENN,501
. HARRIETT HUTCHINS,556
. ISAAC L.,173;ISAAC W.
. 168;J.G.,372;J.H.,428
. J.L.,149;J.N.,490
. JAMES,166;JANE,151
. JEREMIAH,306,321;JOHN
. 549;JONSEY,461
. JOSEPHINE NORTON,488
. JULIA,542;JULIA A.,433
. L.J. KIRKPATRICK,603
. L.M.,518;LOUISA J.
. ALDRIDGE,584;LUKE,556
. M.E. BARTON,424
. MARGARET M LIVELY,372
. MARTHA,425;MARTHA A.
. CROW,338;MARY,490,594
. MARY ANDERSON,523
. MARY CARDELL,488
. MILLIE,345;PAT,501
. R.A.,603;RACHEL,518
. REASE C.,556;SALLIE
. M.,588;SAMUEL,488,603
. SARAH BRUMBELOW,306
. 321;SARAH E. GATES,309

665

. SARAH GUINN,603
. SARAH W GATES,321
. SELICIA,455;SOONIE,536
. WESTON,309,321
. WILLIAM,345,496
. WILLIAM H.,584
. WILLIAM M.,424
PARKINSON,MARTHA,303,324
. MARY,303,324
PARKS,ADA,535;BENJAMIN
. 453,463;C.A. FOWLER
. 592;CLEMON,464;E.E.,73
. E.F.,572;E.M.,73;ELAN
. N.,73;ELIZA A.,559
. ELIZA M.,340
. ELIZABETH,565;FRANCIS
. 597;GREEN B.,338;J.A.
. 424;JAMES,73,556;JOHN
. 534;LORENA YOUNG,528
. LUCY FORMBY,556
. MARTHA A. STEPLE,338
. MARY A.,341;MARY J.,73
. MARY TURNER,424
. MILTON,411;NANCY M.
. 334;PARMELIA,42;R.B.
. 528;RACHEL,457;RUTHA
. C.,586;S.J.,592;SALLY
. HENDERSON,453;SARAH
. A.,303,319;TULITHA,588
. W.G.,406;WILLIAM A.,40
. WILLIS,463
PARLEY,WILLIAM,150
PARLIER,JACOB,496
PARMER,ABNER,307,321;E.
. 596;EDMOND T.,307,321
. GEORGE,321;MAHALA
. MORTEN,321;MALIGA,321
. MARY FISHER,307,321
. MATLIDA HUBBARD,321
. SARAH DOLLAR,307,321
. SUSAN,455
PARNELL,JOHN R.,66;MARY
. E.,16
PARR,JOHN A.,42;JOICY
. WADE,10;LUCINDA J.
. SHAW,12;M.E.,428
. MATTHEW,442;NANCY
. CONGO,42;SIDNEY P.,12
. THOMAS,10
PARRAMORE,M.E.,521
PARRET,ELIZA,559;SARAH
. E.,565
PARRETT,
. NARCISSA AUSTIN,456
. WESLEY,456
PARRIS,ADDIE AUSTIN,538
. CAL,538;CELIA,309,316
. DICKSON,93-94;DOVER
. 507;EDIA,539;GEORGE
. 300;HENRY W.,339
. ISAAC,514;J.S.,541
. JOSEPH S.,488;LOU,504
. LULA HELMS,514;MAHALA
. MARTIN,301;MALOREY,301
. MARTHA WEBB,339
. MATILDA HUBBARD,300
. N.D.,504,522;N.J.,524
. NATHAN,92,94-95
. OCTAVIA,522;PHOEBE,520
. SARAH E. KILLIAN,488
. WARNER,538;WILLIAM,101
. 508
PARRISH,
. MARY CAMPBELL,423
PARROTT,EMILY CLARK,584
. JOHN,420;JOSIAH,584
. JULIE,519;MARY C.,566
. MELISSA HANNAH,420
PARSON,MARGARET DILL,576
. RUBIN P.,576;T.J.,528
PARSONS,EVAN,496;KESIAH
. COMBS,456;WADE,456
PARTIN,513;ADALINE
. MELTON,556;ALLEN,556

. ARTEMESIE,488;ISA
. WELLS,544;LARAH E.,480
. MARGARET MELTON,556
. ROBERT,556;SAMUEL,544
PARTRICK,
. MATILDA SMITH,556
. PAUL,556
PASCHAL,175;ANGESS,465
. SAMUEL,441
PASLEN,WILLIAM,474
PASS,SAVANNAH,422
PATE,BUTLER,308,321
. CYNTHIA,449;ELIZAR
. BLACKWELL,308,321
. HENRY,36,86;JANE
. HANNON,36;JOHNSTON,450
. MARY M.,19;REBECCA
. HURT,450;SAMUEL B.,515
. SUSAN,427
PATERSON,F.W.,495
. JOSEPH,156;MARY
. DENTON,156
PATMAN,DAVID,452
. NANCY M. CONNEL,452
PATON,MARY,160
PATRICK,
. MATILDA SMITH,556
. MATTHEW,393;PAUL,556
. PETER,573;POLLY,557
. RHODA HOLLAND,573
. ROBERT,473
PATTEN,
. CUNIA ANN -
. JEFFERSON,488;SAMUEL
. ANTHONY,488
PATTERSON,135;A.W.,476
. 483;AGNES WILSON,457
. AMANDA,568;AMOS,457
. BIDDY WOOD,451;DARCUS
. COCKBURN,308,321;DRED
. 207;ELIZABETH
. CANTRELL,459
. ELIZABETH WILSON,457
. ESTER N. DUCKET,564
. F.M.,426;FRANCES,328
. GEORGE,549;GEORGE W.
. 303,321;HARRIET,348
. HIRAM,345,459,463
. J.W.,410,564;JAMES,465
. JAMES C.,447;JANE
. CHAPMAN,456;JOHN,230
. 416,456,462,466,549
. JOSEPH,457,549;JOSHUA
. 308,321;JOSIAH B.,348
. 371;JULIA A.,345
. LOUISA SINGLETON,345
. MARGRET E. MCAFEE,371
. MARY,351,364;MARY B.
. MCNEAL,348,371;MARY
. E.,341;MARY P.
. STANSELL,49;MERRELL
. 451;NANCY,230,421
. ROBERT A.,49;ROLEY,549
. ROLLY,461;SAMUEL B.
. 371;SARAH BROWN,338
. SINTHER MORRIS,303,321
. SUSAN,492;WILLIAM,338
. 463
PATTILLO,ELIZABETH,553
. FANNIE,6;JAMES,106
. URBAN,104-105,107-108
. WESLEY H.,105
PATTON,B.F.,227
. CAROLINA,557;CHARLES
. 157;ELIZABETH Q.
. SUMMY,22;EMANUEL,50
. J.M.,392
. SARAH MATILDA GRESHAM
. 50;WILLIAM B.,22
PATTY,SUSANNAH,601
PATY,J.,408
PAUCL,
. ELIZABETH GAZAWAY,19
. WILLIAM B.,19

PAUL,SARY,158
PAW,BEAR,251
PAXSON,BENJAMIN F.,556
. SARAH CARTER,556
. STEPHEN,471
PAXTON,JOHN T.,597
. MARTHA P.,556;MARTIN
. R.,3;N.E. BRINKLEY,597
. RAY,181;RHEA,177
PAYNE,AMANDA WALKER,373
. ARCHIBALD,158;B.F.,502
. 516;BEULAH WILLIAMS
. 519;C.W.,488
. CHRISTIANA,159;DAVID
. H.,308,321;ELIAS,307
. 321;ELIZA,506
. ELIZABETH LAMPKIN,454
. ELIZABETH ORR,307,321
. ESTHER SIMMS,158
. FRANCIS E. JORDAN,373
. GEORGE W.,421;H.W.,501
. J.J.,537;J.L.,427
. JAMES,462;JAMES T.,454
. JEREMIAH,464;JULIA F.
. 73;JULIANN F. JONES
. 308,321;MARGARET,376
. MARTHA,320,352;MARTHA
. JOHNS,161;NANCY J.
. COOK,488;NANCY MAE,490
. OLIVER,161;PERMELIA
. POTTS,421;POLLY,456
. PRESLEY,373;RUTHE,453
. S.J. MELER,427;SARAH
. E.,9;SUSAN,308,314
. THOMAS,373,472,474
. WARREN,519;WILLIAM B.
. 222-223
PAYNOLDS,MARY ANN,159
PAYTHRESS,MARY,504
PEACOCK,171,174;E.C.,73
. L.S.,394;LOUIS,73
. PAYTON A.,73
PEADON,JAMES D.,440
. SAMUEL D.,443;WILLIAM
. 443
PEAK,L.,177;LINDSEY,191
. 228,236,244,246;NANCY
. 157;POLLY,387;SOLOMON
. 181
PEARCE,ANN DOBSON,155
. AUSTIN R.,155,556
. AXOM,435;CALEB C.,353
. CORNELIA,353;CRASY,453
. CYNTHA BELL,338
. DANIEL C.,447;EDMON
. 435;EDMOND,443;ELIZA
. CURTIS,488;ELIZA L.
. CAYLER,488;ELIZABETH,3
. ELIZABETH CLARK,577
. FLOYD A.,488;FRANCES
. C.,368;GADWELL,440
. JAMES J.,368;JOHN,454
. MAHALY,582;MARGARET
. 588;MARGARET WOODS,447
. MARTHA WILLIAMS,353
. MASTIN,3;MATILDA HUNT
. 556;MISSOURI V.,337
. P. DEALE,368;R.M.,578
. SARAH DEAN,454
. SARAH J. HOWARD,578
. W.L.,338;WILLIAM,1,88
. 577;WILLIAM A.,440
. WILLIAM T.,488
PEARDON,SAMUEL D.,444
PEARN,SALLY MILLS,451
. WILEY,451
PEARSON,AMANDA,340
. ARMINDA DARBY,310
. DEANNY,310,319
. EPHRIAM,488;EVAN C.
. 392;JOEL,310;JOHN,538
. LAFAYETTE,488;LAURA
. ANN,477;MAHALA,317
. MARTHA,342;MARTHA

. CHRISTENBERRY,321,339
. MARY J.,343;MARY
. REVIS,488;MELISSA,331
. P.M.,404;REBECCA
. REAVIS,488;S.A.,422
. SPARTIN,501;WILLIAM
. 321,339
PEASTER,BONY P.,73
PECK,J.,46;JAMES,45
. LINSEY,151;NANCY A.
. 560;SOLOMON,151
PEDEN,SAMUEL,276
PEEK,ANNIE,499;ESTHER
. MADDOX,164;JAMES,11,15
. JAMES M.,73;JULIUS A.
. 524;LINDSAY,164
. MARY ANN TINKER,157
. MARYAN TUCKER,158
. MATTIE,524;RACHEL,164
. SOLOMON W.,157-158,164
PEEPLES,
. MIRA M. ERWIN,407
. W.M.,390,392-394,396
. 397-398,402-403,407
. WILILAM M.,402
. WILLIAM,390;WILLIAM
. M.,389,401;WILLIAM N.
. 394
PEERS,MARY C.,337
PEETERS,MARTHA A.M.,555
. MARTHA J.,556;SARAH
. 551
PEGG,
. ELIZA JANE CARROLL,582
. JOHN,582
PELL,WILLIAM,549
PELLOM,EDWARD,297
PEMOY,JOHN,549
PENCE,JOHN,181,253,257
. MARTHA A.,486;WILLIAM
. 244
PENDEN,JOHN WESLEY,432
SALLIE GARDNER,432
PENDER,MATTHEW,288-289
. WILLIAM,288-289
PENDERGRASS,JOHN T.,321
. 339;MARTHE E.,557
. MARY GREEN,321,339
. SUSAN,309,320
PENDERGRAST,MARTHA,581
. MICHAEL,184
PENDLEY,435;ALFRED W.
. 488;BARBARA M.,478
. BARNABUS,488;BENJAMIN
. 438;CARTER,488
. CATHERINE DARNELL,488
. ELIAS W.,488
. ELIZABETH M.,479
. EMILY MARTIN,338
. ESTHER H. CATHLIN,488
. FRANCIS,43;FRANCIS
. DAVIS,337;GEORGE ANN
. LEDFORD,488;HARRIET
. EASTER,300;HARRIET
. EASTERS,321;HENRY I.
. 488;ISAAC,298,441
. J.M.,488;JAMES,298
. JAMES J.,337;JAMES T.
. 300,321;JANE EDWARDS
. 488;JESSE,305,321
. JOHN,95,338,441-442
. JOHN L.,488;JONATHAN
. 298,438,442;LEVI,297
. MAHALA HOWELL,304,321
. MALINDA,491;MARTHA,478
. 480,487;MARTHA E.
. BRUCE,488;MARTHA M.
. DISHAROON,488;MARTHA
. SHIRELY,447;MARY,483
. MARY SEAY,488;MARY
. STEGALL,488
. MISSOURI A. CHUMBLEY
. 488;N.H.,297;NANCY E.
. MOSS,488;NIMROD,285

. PHOEBE BOOKER,9
. SARAH A. BELL,35
. TEASSELY BROWN,381
. THOMAS,9;WILLIAM,373
POWEL,ABRAM,462;D.S.,489
. J.S.P.,410;LETTY ANN
. 342;LEWIS R.,1;MARY
. C.,410;RHODA ANN MOSS
. 489
POWELL,A.T.,425;ALLEN
. 304,310,322;AMANDA E.
. 430;CAROLINE ROBBINS
. 454;CHARLES,447;CLARA
. GREEN,447;DORA
. FORSYTH,523;EASTER
. BENNETT,310,322;ELIZA
. MCCRARY,310,322;F.T.
. 434;G.W.,110;GABRIEL
. 89;GEORGE W.,18,338
. HENRY F.,429;JACOB,418
. JAMES,54,523;JAMES B.
. 549;JAMES C.,339
. JAMES H.,390,398
. JAMES R.,489;JANE,463
. JEFFERSON,549;JOHN C.
. 14;L.R.,88;LARKIN D.
. 495;LAURA S. CLEMENT
. 338;LEWIS,88;LEWIS R.
. 88-90;LUCY ROACH,429
. MILDRED TODD,418
. NANCY,430;NANIE C.
. GLORE,18;NELLY
. CASSELBERRY,449
. OLIVER C.,310,322
. PLEASANT,463,549
. PRESLEY,495;PRESSLEY
. 449;R.A. GODFREY,489
. REBECCA A. POST,14;S.
. HARRIS,339;SARAH,324
. SARAH I.,427;SIDNEY
. F.,143;SLATERLI
. GARRETT,304;SLATNAH
. GARRETT,322;THOMAS,454
. 530;TILMAN,549
. VIRGINIA ANN,390
. WILLIAM H.,105
POWER,D.P.,527;EMILY T.
. 30;GEORGE H.,15;JAMES
. 3,106;JOHN,527
. MARTHA C. BISHOP,15
. MARY E.,18;SAMUEL A.,3
. SARAH M.,11;T.
. CHARLOTTE,5;T.D.,53,59
. 66,68-69,72,75-76
. W.R.,53,59,79;WILLIAM
. 18,25
POWERS,ALEXANDER G.,402
. GEORGE A.,127;P.A.,127
. REBECCA,457;S.H.,507
. W.P.,61;WILLIAM R.,61
PRANCE,ELLA FORSYTH,537
. GEORGE,537
PRATER,
. AMANDA A. BARRETT,489
. JAMES,465,471;JOHN
. DANIEL,489;LOYD,306
. 322;MARTHA BARRETT,489
. NANCY ASHWORTH,306,322
. SUSANAH,465;THOMAS,489
PRATHER,J.M.,523;JAMES
. Y.,74;MOLLIE TRUETT
. 523;P.H.,74
PRATT,ELVIRA MALONEY,32
. EMINA,576;GEORGE N.
. 556;MARTHA J. PEETERS
. 556;N.A.,22,38,43,45
. 74;NATHANIEL A.,28
. W.H.,32;W.N.,74
PREASE,JOHN,235
PREAST,JOHN,222-223,232
. 239;M. BRADLEY,457
. MARTIN,457;THOMAS,191
. WILLIAM,188,191,258
PREIST,MARANDA C.,328

PRESLEY,
. ABBALINE LANGLY,155
. ANDREW,457;B.C.,391
. CICERO,489;ELIZABETH
. HOPKINS,489;ELLEN,485
. EMALINE,552;EMILY C.
. MCCRARY,489;JORDON,493
. M. LARD,420;MAHALY
. RAY,162;MARY HOPKINS
. 489;MARY STRICKLAND
. 457;R.J. COOK,489
. R.M.,420;RHODA ANN,477
. ROBERT T.,489;W.T.,489
. WILLIAM,155,162
. ZACHARIAH,489
PRESSLEY,
. NANCY J. SHERMAN,22
. ROBERT C.,22
PRESSLY,ABSALOM,158
. DEMARIS LANGLY,158
PREST,JOHN,235
PRESTON,MARY ELIZ.,555
PREWETT,ANDERSON,535
. E.A.,383;ELIZA WRIGHT
. 21;ITTAI,21;J.R.,540
. JOHN L.,98;JOHN P.,383
. LUCINDA CHANDLER,447
. MARTHA,541;MARY C.
. NUNIE,383;WILLIAM,447
PREWITT,G.W.,514
PRICE,BENJAMIN,443
. CALVIN J.,489;CALVIN
. NEWTON,34;CATHERINE
. BROWN,489;CHARLES,489
. DANIEL,436,465
. ELIZABETH,558;ERVIN
. 549;ERWIN P.,432
. FRANCES E. BROOKS,34
. G.W.,519;GEORGIA
. JOHNSON,489;GREEN P.
. 519;I.J.,524;JAMES B.
. 549;JAMES J.,22;JOHN
. B.,549;JOSEPH,278
. LILLIE,524;LOUISA E.
. 33;MARY E. KIRK,22
. NANCY A.M. WATERS,37
. NANCY J.,34;ROSA C.
. RIVERS,519;THOMAS B.
. 37;WILLIAM,1,464
. WILLIAM C.,391
. WILLIAM P.,183;ZALONA
. A.,483
PRICHARD,GEORGE W.,84-85
. 109;ISAAC,451;JAMES
. 109;JORDAN,85;JOSHUA
. 84;S.A.,40;TEMPERANCE
. WYLEY,451
PRICHETT,MARTHA,583
PRICKETT,JAMES P.,21-22
. LUCY,538
PRIDES,LEWIS,297
PRIDGES,LEWIS,307
. OLIVIAT CHRISTOPHER
. 307
PRIEST,A.,330;ELIZABETH
. 457;JOHN,151,160,276
. LYDIA,160;MARY,159
. NANCY E.,337;P.C.,145
. 148;RACHEL NUMEN,160
. REBECCA,163;THOMAS,152
. 256;WILLIAM,152,177
. 181,183,213,234
PRINCE,A.W.,489;CYNTHIA
. KEITH,403;DELILAH
. PIEDMAN,453;EMILINE
. TATUM,489;JOSEPH,556
. K.,403;LUISA ROGERS
. 556;MALISSA,581
. MARGARET,588;NANCY B.
. 553;WILEY,453;WILLIS
. 462
PRINCEON,BURGESS,462
PRINTESS,MARY,579
PRINTUP,LAURA MANN,432

SIMON,432;WILLIAM,389
PRIOR,ASA,496;JACKSON,495
PRISNELL,MARY,453
PRITCHARD,ANDERSON,566
. ELLEN HOWARD,566
. GEORGE,74;GEORGE N.,74
. HETTIE,74;JAMES,74
. JOHN,2,474;JOHN R.,74
. JOSEPH H.,389;JOSHUA
. 74;MANIE,74;MARY,35
. NANCY,74,431;ROSETTA
. 432;RUTH,74;WILLIAM
. T.,94
PRITCHET,ANDERSON,593
. ANNA E. TATE,593
. ELIZA C. RICE,26;JOHN
. E.,26;SUSAN,595
PRITCHETT,
. FLORA S. MULLINS,374
. HESTER A.C. RED,374
. JAMES K.,374;JOSEPH
. 374;LUCINDA MILLER,422
. M.L.,523;MARGARET
. DAWSON,450;MARY,590
. R.S.,422,432;ROBERT
. 450;S.S. KINGSBURY,523
PRITCHITT,ROBERT,439
PRIVET,HIRAM,462
PROCTER,MARY ANN,319
PROCTOR,HIRAM,167,467
. MARY A.,305;POLLY,239
. 251;WILLIAM,467
PROPES,RICHARD W.,339
. SARAH J. CARROLL,339
PROVINCE,MINERVA,579
PRR,JOHN,122
PRSCKTOR,NICK,219
PRUET,MALINDA,315;REACE
. 438
PRUETT,ADALIZA ESTES,338
. BENJAMIN F.,339
. CHARLES,157;ELIAS,376
. ELIZABETH BENNET,157
. ENOCH E.,348,373
. INDIANA C.,12;ITAI,74
. JEREMIAH J.,18;JOHN
. 441;JOHN W.,339
. KESIAH,376;LETTY,303
. 320;M.C. ALBRIDGE,348
. MARGARET PAYNE,376
. MARTHA WILCOX,308,322
. MARY H. READMAND,339
. MATILDA,367;MICHAEL
. 441;MILLY M.,48;NANCY
. HARBIN,18;P. PAIN,339
. R.J. MOORHEAD,373
. R.J. SMITH,373
. RICHARD H.,338;ROSIE
. V.,348;S.D.,111
. WASHINGTON H.,373
. WILLIAM C.,111
. WILLIAM H.,308,322
. ZELPHER EARLY,373
PRUIT,ETIC,456;POLLY
. PAYNE,456;SARAH,158
. WILLIAM,2
PRUITT,BENJAMIN,276
. C.A. ESTES,339
. FRANCES E. EDMONSON
. 339;HANNAH M. ROGERS
. 322,339;HARVY M.,338
. J.T.,322,339;JOHN W.
. 322,339;LETTY,303
. MALINDA,301;MARGARET
. 330;MARGARET LOW,458
. MARY,343;MARY A.,106
. MARY BRADFORD,447
. NANCY C. REDMAN,339
. NANCY REDMAN,322;S.A.
. 339;SARAH M. PERY,338
. STEPHEN,458;WILLIAM
. C.,447;WILLIAM T.,339
. ZILPHA A.,327
PRUTT,NATHA,31

PRYOR,P.E. WHITE,420
. T.J.,420
PUCKET,ADALINE,333
. ALEXANDER,2;ELIJAH,455
. NANCY GRISSOME,455
PUCKETT,A.M.,141;AARON
. 406;BUD,509;ELIZA B.
. 333;ELIZABETH NEESE
. 374;ELIZABETH WOOD,455
. J.A.,374;J.R.,500
. JOHN,455;LAVADA,477
. M.,27,38-39;MALANY S.
. VANDVERE,593;MARGARET
. 341;MARY JANE,483;MAY
. 374;NANCY,360,455
. SISCO,374;WILLIAM,521
. 593
PUETT,E.J.,338;MARY A.
. JOHNSTON,338
PUGGETH,ASA,456;POLLY
. VILYARD,456
PUGH,ABBITHA E.,459
. ABNER,322,339
. ALEXANDER,297
. ANGELINE KARR,339
. ANNA WINTER,451
. BENJAMIN C.,161
. BENSON F.,338;DAVID
. 353;DRUCILLA,331
. ELENDER FOWLER,337
. ELIZABETH,306,318,332
. 353;ELIZER E.,161
. ELIZER E. PUGH,161
. FRANCES,371;FRANCES
. WHITWORTH,455;GADSEY
. CHAMBLEE,371;ISAAC,451
. JAMES,337,455;JOHN,152
. 204,339,454;JOHN M.
. 371;JOHN P.,322,339
. JOSEPHINE HAWKINS,322
. 339;L. BROWN,353
. LETTY,345;LORI M.
. JEFFERSON,371;MARY,303
. 323;MARY A.,338
. MARY A. PUGH,338
. 339;MARY HEATH,300,322
. MARY SAMPLES,322,339
. MARYAN,158;MILLY C.
. 335;NANCY,339;NANCY
. C.,160;NANCY PUGH,339
. NANCY WHEELER,454
. PHILIP,339;PHILLIP,322
. RODY ANN,332;SAMPSON
. 300,322;WILLIAM,339
PUGNE,WILLIAM B.,248
PULASKI,
. ISAAC JUSTICE,393
PULLEN,ELIZABETH,162
. WILLIAM,582,598
PULLEY,SARAH,429
PULLIAM,A.J.,425;A.P.
. 426;BETTY BALLEW,426
. 427;JANE,447;JULIA A.
. 429;LUCY,423;S. OWENS
. 425;SAMUEL,424-427,430
. 432-433;SARAH BAXTER
. 426
PULLIN,MARY A.,16
PULLIUM,ELIZA BLOON,590
. WILLIAM,590
PURCE,JAMES,297
PURCELL,HARRIET M.,330
. MARY E.,340;SARAH,330
PURON,SADIE J.,74
PURSEL,JAMES,461;JOHN,461
PURSLEY,C. MOREHEAD,426
. J.G.,588;MARY MATILDA
. 15;ROBERT,426;W.S.
. KIRKPATRICK,588
PURYEAR,ALEXANDER S.,419
. E. HURSTEN,428;NANCY
. DYE,419;S.S.,428
PUTMAN,DAVID,458

. ELIZABETH,451
. HARRIET M. HAWKINS,339
. LUCY CASTLEBERRY,458
. MALISSA GOSS,453
. REBECCA,453;SARAH,451
. WILLIAM,339;WILSON,453
PUTNAM,ANDERSON,474
. B.E.,423;DAVID,284-285
. 291;E.,419;ELIAS,151
. 166,168,173,177,192
. 222-223,234,243,401
. H.M.,74,142;JOHN B.,14
. 62;MALESSA,284
. MARY ANN BROOKE,161
. MARY GRISHAM,14
. PICKNEY,161;S.,423;S.
. PUTNAM,423;THOMAS,284
. WILSON,284-285,291
PUTNEY,
. JULIA A. BOWDOIN,421
. LOUIS,421
PYE,LOUISA GRANT,433
. THADDEUS B.,433
PYROM,C.W.,26;E.P.
. SPRAGIN,26
PYRON,CHARLES W.,56
. JAMES,74
QUALLS,DAVID,152,196,223
. 229,235;ELIZABETH
. BLALOCK,449;ELIZABETH
. LEDBETTER,489;JESSE
. 322,338;MARY MARTIN
. 322,338;MOSES,338
. PENNELL,449;ROBERT,246
. 489;SARAH HOLLINSHEAD
. 338
QUALS,DAVID,219
QUARLES,DAVIS,549
. ELIZABETH,162;GABRIEL
. W.,33;HUBBARD,549
. JESSIE,517;ROBERS,549
. SARAH E. STEPHENS,33
. TUENEAL,496
QUEEN,CYNTHIA C. POPE,19
. CYNTHIA S. STONE,578
. ELIZA RUSSELL,307,322
. FARENCY,15;FRANCES
. BEDINGFIELD,561
. FRANCIS,74;JAMES M.
. 578;JOEL P.,12;JOSEPH
. L.,561;LORENZA D.,129
. MARGARET,50;MARHEW,298
. MARY W.,44;NANCY,16
. SAMUEL M.,19
. SOPHRONIA HOOKER,12
. TIMOTHY,307,322
QUILLIAM,J.B.C.,6
QUILLIAN,ADALINE,590
. ANNA,407-408;B.B.,406
. 407,417;CLEM,474
. CLEMMONS,407;CLEMONDS
. 408;J.B.C.,5,9,28-29
. 507,515;M.P.,258
. MAGGIE R.,600
. MILLIGAN P.,254,264
. 266;POLLY ANN,407
. PRISCILLA,407;REBECCA
. L.,588;S.C.,407,567
. 568;SARAH J. TYE,592
. WILLIAM C.,592
QUILLIN,M.P.,261
QUILLION,509;B.B.,491
. CLEMAND,387;H.R.,387
QUIN,VIRGINIA HARRIS,603
. WILLIAM R.,603
QUINN,A.V.,426;FRANCES
. 598;J.C.,423;JAMES,600
. JOHN,591;LAURA
. MURDOCK,600;MARTHA A.
. 28;MARTHA BLACK,423
. MARTHA E. WHALEY,591
. MARY CARTER,426
QUINTON,BILL,475;J.,489
. JAMES,469;JOSEPH,2

. MARY,161;MOLLIE RAY
. 489;SARAH,477;SHARO
. 493
QUITE,EDWARD C.,396
RABUN,SARA F.,74
RABY,PETER,457;SARAH
. HUBBARD,457
RACK,MALINA,374
RACKLEY,ESTHER RED,339
. MALIRA,339;MINERVA C.
. 339;WARREN B.,339
RADAWAY,JAMES,573
. MELISSA BROUGHTON,573
RAFER,ECCA,463
RAGAN,ELIZAB ANN,558
. ELIZABETH A.,555
. FRANK,522;JANE,556
. WILLIAM,462
RAGEN,L.,281;T.,281
RAGIN,ROBERT,100
RAGINS,HARRIET,46
RAGLAND,278;L.A.,146
. LEMUEL A.,9;MARTHA A.
. BENNETT,9;R.A.,144
RAGSDAL,ALICE,539
RAGSDALE,249;ADDIE,535
. BENJAMIN,201,243,248
. 459;BERRY,535;BOB,536
. C.F.,503;CALTON,256
. CARLTON,205;DELILAH
. W.,9;ELEANOR,220,248
. 265-266;ELIJAH,95
. ELIZA,13;ELIZABETH,199
. 234;FANNIE BIGGERS,506
. FRANCIS,74;G.W.,111
. 531,536;GEORGE W.,95
. J.,105,536;J.F.,503
. JOHN,167-169,179,181
. 186,188,205,265;JOHN
. F.,500,506;JOHNATHAN
. H.,50;JOSEPH,508;JUDY
. GIPSON,156;LARKIN A.
. 156,177,253,257;LAURA
. DENSON,519;LUCINDA
. CARTER,536;MARY ALICE
. 539;MARY L. MCEVER,50
. MASON,100;MASON M.,100
. NELLY,201,251;PARSHA
. ANN,531;REBECCA M.
. EASON,9;REBECCA
. TERRELL,459;RICHARD
. 152,222;SANDER,508
. SANDERS,533;SANDERS
. B.,9;SANDERS W.,105
. SARAH A. GIBSON,163
. SARAH J.,50;SAUK,498
. SAUNDERS,95;SPENCER
. 163;T.J.,516;W.G.,519
. WILLIAM,95,105
. WILLIAM F.,503
RAIL,JESSE,465;WILLIAM,464
RAIMEY,SANFORD,436
RAINES,DALIAH,339;G.B.
. 489;J.M. HALES,489
RAINEY,B.,147-148
. BIRDING,64;D.,74;L.A.
. 65;O.H.,74;PITMAN,530
. WILLIAM P.,389
RAINS,DELILAH,454;SARAH
. 449
RAINWATER,JAMES,498
. JOHN,510,523,541
. MARTHA,363;MARTHA
. MCSIMMS,306;SIDNEY,306
RAINWATERS,J.M.,522
. JAMES E.,160;MARTHA
. MCGINNIS,322;SIDNEY
. 322;SUSAN HENSON,160
RAKESTRAW,544;C.,27,501
. C.R.,42;DALIAH RAINES
. 339;E.H.,75,83
. FRANCES,28;GROVER T.
. 535;HARRIETT FORESTER
. 42;IVEY,515;J.M.,535

. JAMES,339;JANE,18
. JANE RAKESTRAW,18
. JULIA,25;M.,446;P.,347
. W.B.,136;WESTLEY,42
. WILLIAM,18,75,83,445
. 446-447
RALSTON,LEWIS,170,178
. 179,183-184,196,214
. 218-219;SAMUEL A.,477
RALY,PETER,297
RAMBO,KINCHEN,445,447
RAMEY,CHRISTOPHER,470
. DIVINITY CONNER,322
. DIVINTIY CONNER,338
. ELENOR,549;GEORGE H.
. 474;ISAAC,549;JAMES
. 549;THOMAS,549
. WILLIAM,322,338,549
RAMSAUER,JAMES,523,525
RAMSAUR,
. CORDELIA S. ERWIN,417
. DAVID H.,417;J.W.,419
RAMSEY,AMELIA,405
. CASWELL,471;HENRY,541
. J.W.,560-562;JAMES,157
. 256;JAMES D.,339
. JAMES W.,563,568,571
. LULA GANN,540;MARY
. CASTLEBERRY,339
. NANCY M. ECHOLS,309
. 322;RICHARD,309,322
. S.J.,123,127;SALLY
. MARTIN,157;T.J.,112
RAMY,GEORGE,472;LOUISA
. M.,559;THOMAS,472
RAN,LOCK,603;MARY ANN
. DANTZLER,603
RANDAL,CHARLES,441;JOHN
. 441
RANDALL,ELIZABETH,303
. 319;JACKSON H.,91
. MARTHA A.,303,321
. P.H.,92;SAMANTHA,23
RANDOL,CHARLES,435
RANDOLPH,BEAUFORT,401
. GILBERT,561;J.,278
. JOHN,75,595;JULIA
. WILLIAMS,595
RANEON,G.W.,405
RANEY,
. AMERICA MOREHEAD,593
. EDWARD,593;WILLIAM,439
RANKFORD,LOUISA J.,45
RANKLEY,NANCY,378
RANSOM,G.W.,394,398,402
. 405,424,427-428;JAMES
. 392;JOHN,472
RANSOME,G.W.,396,399,401
. MARY E. HUFF,600
. WILLIAM,600
RANSON,G.W.,400,403
RANVER,MARY R.,409
RAPER,J.W.,489;JOSEPH,2
. 451,496;MAHALY BOX,451
. ROSETY MCLEON,489
RASBERRY,JOHN C.,496
. MARY B.,78
RASTON,RANDALL W.,394
RATAREE,ALEXANDER,536
. 544;E.L.,544;MARY,544
. WILL,542
RATCHFORD,EZEKIEL,278
. JAMES,395
RATCLIFF,ANDREW,588
. BETTIE PHILIPS,588
RATFORD,GILES,309,322
. NANCY PETTYJOHN,309
. 322
RATTAREE,JOHN,506
RATTY,WILLIAM,466
RAUCHENBERG,EMIL,565
. PAULINE WIRTH,565
RAUCHENBURG,
. FREDERICK,559

. LOUISA M. RAMY,559
RAULSTON,JOHN F.,465
. LEWIS,252
RAUNDSEVILL,J.H.,149
RAUNDSVILLE,DAVID,149
RAUSHENBERG,F.A.,591
RAVAN,JOHN,461
RAVEL,A.P.,75
RAVEN,JOHN,443
RAVENS,BARBAREY,329
RAVINS,BARBARY A.,314
RAWLEY,MA.,366
RAWLIN,PATSY GRAVITT,311
. TILMAN,311
RAWLINGS,ELIZABETH,301
. JONATHAN,442;PETER,439
RAWLINS,ELIZABETH,312
. NANCY J.,308,321
RAWLS,B.H.,502;BOB,515
. 541;EMANA COOPER,525
. ISAAC,278;J. IRA,502
. N.B.,520;R.L.,529
. ROBERT,520,535;ROBERT
. I.,502;ROBERT L.,525
. WILLIAM C.,398
RAY,AMANDA MANN,489
. AUGUSTUS,489;BETTY,480
. CICERO J.,429;DINGHAM
. 463;E.,420;ELIZABETH
. BARBER,36;ELVIRA WOOD
. 586;EMANUEL,75;EUGENE
. W.,75;F.A.,422
. FLORENA,75;FRANCES,15
. GEORGE,75;GEORGIA
. WARD,489;J.,520;J.W.
. 489;JAMES,10,557
. JAMES T.,586;JANE,561
. JANE ALLEN,311,322
. JENNIE,75;JOHN,75,463
. JOHN E.,36;JOHN F.,489
. JOSEPHINE,598;LEONNA
. FOSTER,10;LIZZIE,432
. LUCINDA CARVER,489;M.
. BENNETT,422;M.E.,423
. MAHALY,162;MARGARET
. COX,429;MARTHA ANN,75
. MARTHA B. ALLGOOD,557
. MARTHA JANE,483;MARY
. 372;MARY M.,480
. MOLLIE,489;NANCY A.
. 583;NANCY T. WHITSITT
. 300,322;ROBERT,463;S.
. ISABELLA,20;SALLIE,431
. SAMANTHA,434;THOMAS
. 476,482,484;WILLIAM,75
. 311,322;WILLIAM H.,149
. 165,167,170,172,300
. 322;ZULA G.,72
RAYBURN,LUCY A.,43
RAYS,E.A.,48;L.K.
. HUMPHRIES,48
REACE,RACHAEL,462
READ,ABIA A.,344;JOHN
. 146,375;JOSEPH,375
. LUCINDA E. PERRY,375
. MATILDA ROPER,375
. NANCY,329
READMAND,MARY H.,339
REAGAN,AGNES E. REED,409
. JACOB,473;WILLIAM A.
. 409
REAGEN,JESSIE P.,75
REAGIN,HENRY B.,75;R.L.
. 75;WILLIE B.,75
REAVES,ASA,464;DANIEL
. 464;ELIZABETH
. WILLIAMS,157;JAMES J.
. 157;JOHN D.,397;JOHN
. P.,304,322;MALACHI,91
. NORA,479;ROSANNAH C.
. HARRIS,304;ROSANNAH
. HARRIS,322;THOMAS,463
REAVICE,ELVIRA M.,336

. ELIZABETH TALLOW,159
. EVAN G.,396;F.C.,490
. HARTWELL,159;HENRY,496
. J.R.,395;JOHN,3,107
. 450;JOSEPHUS,322
. JOSEPHUS,300;M.C.,493
. MARY,425;MARY J.
. BARBERS,490;MOLLIE O.
. 603;NANCY HERNDON,450
. OCTAVIA ALLEN,490
. SALLIE,594;SAMANTHA
. CORNELLSON,490
. STEPHEN C.,490;THOMAS
. 437,441;W.J.,141,145
. W.N.,428;WILL,523
. WILLIAM,549;WILLIAM
. A.,490
RICHARDSON,ABEL,598
. AMOS,178,183-184,219
. 252;ANN E.,606
. BENJAMIN L.,578
. CAROLINE,578;COLUMBUS
. W.,587;DECIA NORTON
. 535;DELIA EVANS,578
. EFFIAH S. FROST,557
. EMILY MOORE,322,338
. FRANCES,571;J.M.,409
. 410-411,413-414,416
. 417,561,564,575,577
. J.R.,587;JOHN,528
. JOHN A.,12;JOHN C.,322
. 338;JOHN M.,557,570
. JOSEPH,472;JOSEPH B.
. 16;L.M.,565;M.J.,366
. MALISSA,584;MARTHA A.
. DUKES,12;MARTHA E.,577
. MARTHA SIMPSON,16
. MARY,447;MARY ANN,552
. MARY L. CHRISTOPHER
. 557;MARY STEELE,49
. MARY WORTHY,595
. MEVALINE WHITENER,587
. NANCY J.,17;R.F.,535
. ROBERT,595;SARAH A.
. KOWN,598;SARAH A.
. WHITENER,587;SUSANNAH
. 554;W.C.,566,569-570
. 572;W.H.,49,75
. WILLIAM,474,576
. WILLIAM H.,557
RICHARSON,ED,75;G.C.,75
. NANCY,75;T.B.,75
RICKER,SIMEON R.,191
RICKERSON,
. DECIA NORTON,535;R.F.
. 535
RIDDLE,A.F. NEWMAN,579
. M.S.,579;MARY A.,564
RIDEN,ELIZABETH,580
. HIRAM PARKS,347
. LUCINDA A. HAYNILL,347
. LUNIE A.,347;SARAH C.
. 345
RIDER,CHRISTOPHER,462
. 465;EVAN B.,490;JOHN
. 461-462;JONATHAN,461
. LOURANA CROW,490
. MARTHA A.,341;MARY
. LINDSAY,322;WILLIAM
. 462;WILLIAM A.,322
RIDINGS,CHARLES,490
. DICY CRENSHAW,490
. DICY GRENSHAW,490
. GEORGE,17;HOSEA,490
. JEPTHA,490;MARGARET
. STEPHENS,490;MARIA
. GADDEN,17;SARAH JANE
. HEARDEN,490;VIOLET,29
RIDLEY,MARY L.,593
RIED,ARCHOBOLD H.,374
. DANIEL,167;ELIZABETH
. HOLBROOK,374;HAMPTON
. 376;HUSTON,600;JETER
. J.,374;LAURA VENABLE

. 374;LOUISA ISRAEL,600
. MARTHA C. PERRY,376
. MARTHA HOLBROOK,376
. WILLIAM W.,376
RIEVES,BURWELL E.,339
. ELIZABETH TAYLOR,339
RIGGINS,NANCY,161,163
. 164;RODA WALKER,451
. TOLIVER,451
RIGGS,JAMES,435
RIGHT,ALEXANDER,442
. AMANDA J.,340;DELILA
. 458;HENRY,204;JOSEPH
. 463
RIGSBY,A.J.,109
RIKER,MARY M. SLOAN,576
. WILLIAM R.,576
RILEY,ADELINE L.,570
. ALICE WRENCH,600
. AMERICUS LIGHT,375
. CATHERINE THOMAS,162
. HARRIET BELL,375
. HARRISON,166;HARRISON
. W.,464;ISAAC,375
. JAMES,600;JAMES A.,375
. MARGARET,588;MARTHA
. T.,433;MARY ANN
. CLEVELAND,568;MATTIE
. F.,65;SPENCER,197
. THOMAS,568;WILLIAM H.
. 162,396,464
RIMINGTON,JAMES,465
. MARY HARDIE,162
RINEHARDT,ADAM H.,162
. JANE HARDEN,458;LEWIS
. W.,458
RINEHART,CHRISTOPHER,153
RIPLEY,MARTHA A.E.,312
. S.,312
RIPPLEY,MARTHA A.E.,327
RIPPY,
. LOUISA JANE -
. CRENSHAW,490;THOMAS
. E.,490
RISE,JAMES,450;SARAH
. WEAVER,450
RISENER,J.M.,579;S.C.
. ELLISON,579
RISK,DAVID,257
RITCH,ELIZABETH,449
. H.C.,498,529;LIZZIE
. 498,513
RIVERS,ROSA C.,519
RIVES,JOHN E.,273
ROACH,ADALINE PINDER,591
. AMANDA S. MCDANIEL,376
. ELIZ. ANN MCGULLION
. 300;ELIZA COLWELL,571
. ELIZABETH J.,569
. ELIZABETH MCGULLIAN
. 322;EMILY A.,579
. FRANCIS C.,569;HENRY
. 571;JAMES,549;JAMES
. B.,322,338,376
. JOHANNA,384;JOHN,150
. JOHN H.,601;JOSEPH
. BROWN,376;LEWIS,340
. LUCY,429;M.L.,332
. M.M. MARTIN,340
. MARIAH,336;MARTHA F.
. 359;MARTHA JANE,564
. MARY,601;MARY A.,334
. MARY A. PERRY,376
. MARY ANN PERRY,322,338
. MARY E.,366;MARY
. RHODES,581;MARY ROACH
. 601;MICHAEL,435;NANCY
. 385;NANCY COOK,359,366
. NARISSA,157;SAMUEL,581
. ULET,300,322;WILLIAM
. 359,366,591
ROAN,BERRY,306
. CATHARINE,556;MILLY
. HENDERSON,306

ROARK,JANE,455
ROBB,MARGARET R.,4
. WILDS,85
ROBBERTS,ELIZABETH,157
ROBBINETT,JOHN,256
ROBBINETTE,DANIEL,256
ROBBINS,A.,425;AUGUSTA
. A.,584;CAROLINE,454
. ELIZABETH J.,575
. GEORGE A.,389;JACOB
. J.,157;JANE DICKENKEY
. 322;JANE DICKERKEY,301
. LEVI,301,322;MARY A.
. OSBORN,587;REBECCA
. ALLRED,157;SAMUEL H.
. 587;WILLIAM A.,474
ROBBS,GEORGE W.,375
. NARCISSA E. GABLE,375
. PARTHENA JORDAN,322
. PARTHENA JORDON,309
. WILLIAM,309,322
ROBENSON,RICHARD,75
ROBERDS,SARAH,463
. SIDNEY,475;WILEY A.
. 153
ROBERS,JOHN,204;PATRICK
. W.,583;SARAH DUCKETT
. 583
ROBERSON,ELVINA,76
. EMELINE ADRAIN,453
. F.M.,339;JAMES B.,453
. JOSEPH,466;L.B.,402
. LEMUEL,466
. LITTLEBERRY B.,402
. MARTHA M. HAMMOND,339
. MARY E.,38;W.T.,76
ROBERT,B.F.,121;ELIJAH
. 196;FRANCIS W.,121
. L.K.,111;M.B.,340
. M.E. HUGHES,340
ROBERTS,A.B.,157;A.C.
. 266;A.J.,587;A.M.F.
. 571;A.P.,559;ABE,298
. ABEL,176;ALICE,431
. AUSTIN C.,256,266
. B.G.,76,139-140
. BENJAMIN F.,339
. BENSON,92-95;C.H.,334
. CAROLINE M.,407
. CATHARINE,310,313
. CLAUDE,519;CYNTHA
. MOORE,557;DAN,521
. DAVID J.,584;DAVID P.
. 158;DEBBY GOOLSBY,339
. E.J.,76;E.M.,340
. ELIJAH,104,150,186,230
. 395;ELIZ. M.,156
. ELIZA G.,75;ELIZA J.
. 560;ELIZABETH,309,317
. 565,581;ELIZABETH
. BECK,157;ELIZABETH C.
. 156,407;ELLEN,31
. ELMINA,455;ELVIRA,341
. EMMA,602;FRANKY,455
. FURMAN,86;G.,112;G.L.
. 419;G.P.,525,528
. GEORGE,107,109-112,124
. 157;GEORGE C.,75
. GEORGE W.,447;GRAY,436
. HUGH,221;J.H.,127
. JAMES,277,279,281-282
. 298,428;JAMES T.,557
. JANE,428;JANE JONES
. 420;JESSE C.,338
. JESSE J.,420;JESSEY
. C.,322;JOHN,75,232,549
. 566-567;JOHN B.E.,458
. JOHN T.,598;JOSEPH,435
. JOSEPHINE T. BERRY,559
. JOSHUA,156,278,524
. JOSIAH,339;LAFAYETT
. L.,575;LARKIN H.,339
. LAURA A.F. BELL,339
. LEWIS,261;LOUISA A.

. WOOD,584;LOUISA C.,575
. MALINDA EDWARDS,339
. MALINDA J.,583
. MARGARET,303,313
. MARIAN,499;MARION E.
. MARTHA,159;MARTHA E.
. 595;MARTIN,458;MARY,86
. 574,584;MARY A.,458
. MARY A. PALMER,598
. MARY A. ROBERTS,458
. MARY A. WILKINS,566
. 567;MARY ANN ANDERSON
. 322,338;MARY E.,75,307
. 325;MARY E. JONES,419
. MARY E. MCAFEE,340
. MARY E. SAMPLES,338
. MARY FANN,458;MARY M.
. GRAY,24;MARY
. MCCONNELL,156;MARY O
. GAZAWAY,587;MATTIE A.
. FRANKLIN,426-427
. MATTIE GREEN,428
. MITCHELL S.,496;N.W.
. 527,530;NANCY BLACK
. 158;NANCY DEAN,157
. NANCY EAST,575;NANCY
. HARDIN,447;NANNIE,530
. PINCKNEY W.,338;POLLY
. HYDE,447;R.O.,601
. ROADY,306,313;S.H.,75
. SARAH,277,327;SARAH
. J.,312;SARAH M.,159
. SUSAN,509;T.H.,101
. TEMPY S.,5;THOMAS,108
. W.,423,426;W.A.,426
. 427,496;W.G.,526;W.M.
. 24;WILEY,397;WILEY A.
. 153,222;WILL,108
. WILLIAM M.,227;WILLIE
. 400;WILLIS,112,124,502
. WYLIE,447
ROBERTSON,521;A.J.,581
. ALEXANDER,454
. ALICE M. BLALOCK,429
. B.A.,420;BENJAMIN E.
. 557;CATHERINE KELTON
. 454;CLABE,532;EASTER
. 10;EDITH A. HELTON,429
. ELISHA,149;ELIZA JANE
. 9;ELIZABETH,582
. ELIZABETH ELROD,31
. ELLA GREEN,521;ELLEN
. 29;FANNIE,499,527
. GERTRUDE,542;HOWARD
. 437;J.L.,432;J.T.,4,7
. 42,48,132;J.W.,34
. JACOB,458;JAMES,67
. JAMES M.,594;JAMES W.
. 147;JANE MOSELY,543
. JEP,111;JOHN,376;JOHN
. J.,31;JOHN L.,9;JOHN
. T.,9,16,80,85,133,135
. 136;JOHN W.,389;JOHN
. W.H.,376;JOSEPH,338
. LUCIA D. CHILDERS,17
. M.A.,426;M.A. WINN,34
. M.E. WARREN,424;M.R.
. 428;MARIAH,158;MARIAH
. NORRIS,458;MARTHA
. BYRD,376;MARTHA F.
. BOTTOMS,376;MARTHA
. FURGUSON,557;MARY E.
. SMITH,420;MATILDA,420
. MATTHEW,400;MOLLIE
. WORTHY,581;NANCY E.
. 568;NATHANIEL,431
. NATTIE,499;O.C.,528
. OLIVER H.,532;R.G.,429
. REBECCA ROPER,594
. REDDIN,438;RICHARD,132
. ROBERT,76;ROSA NOBLE
. 431;S.,500,536,542
. S.W.,101;SAM,76
. SARAH C. LINDSEY,338

. SIDNEY,543;SNOWDEN,499
. SUSAN A.C.,552
. TABITHA,39;THOMAS C.
. 400;W.B.,429;W.T.,76
. WILLIAM C.,76;WILLIAM
. G.,17;WILLIAM L.,107
. WILLIAM M.,424
ROBESON,CELIA HOLT,458
. ELIZA C.,459;J.A.
. MCBURK,561;JANE,456
. JOHN M.,561;ZEDECK H.
. 458
ROBINET,JOEL,253
ROBINETT,ARCHIBALD,160
. CAROLINE,457;REBECCA
. DEAN,160
ROBINNETT,JOEL,257
ROBINS,ALICE,539
. AUGUSTA A. ADAMS,578
. ELIZABETH SLOAN,597
. GEORGE,516;HENRY A.
. 578;J.S.N.,582;JAMES
. M.,516;JOHN,539;MARY
. L.,595;POLLY BATES,457
. THOMAS,457;THOMAS J.
. 474;WILLIAM E.,597
ROBINSON,A.,198,214
. ANDREW J.,270;ANNA,76
. BEDFORD,557;CAROLINE
. 340;CAROLINE SIMPSON
. 10;FANNIE,518;GEORGE
. M.,76;H.A.,10;JEP,111
. JEPTHA,111;JOANNA,76
. JOHN,10,76,396,398
. JOHN B.,270;JOHN C.
. 518;LOUISA J.
. RANKFORD,45;MALINDA
. 390;MARY J.,316
. MATTIE CAYLOR,518
. MOSES W.,439;REBECCA
. 270;REDDIN,442
. RICHARD,104;SARAH E.
. 270;SUSAN REYNOLDS,557
. THERESA,76;WILLIAM,76
. 270;WILLIAM F.,45
. WILLIAM H.,464
. WILLIAM T.,270
ROBISON,
. HULDA STANSELL,35
. RICHARD,137;SARAH,603
. WILLIAM,35
ROBNETT,EMILY,428
ROBSAN,RICHARD,110
ROBSON,MARK B.,463
RICHARD,130
ROCHESTER,MARY,531
ROCK,JOHN H.,604;JULIA
. BARNES,604;NAIL HART
. 604;S.J.,604
ROCKWELL,O.B.,4;S.,213
. 215;SAMUEL,214
RODD,BLANCHE L.,76
RODDY,JAMES,76;S.E.,76
RODGERS,CAROLINE,157
. DEMARSA MILLS,155
. JOHN,228;JOSEPH,155
. 583;MARY E.,565
. SALLIE,588
ROE,A.E. MOSS,425;A.T.
. 424;ANCIL,490;ARMINDA
. 486;BATHAELMA GIDEON
. 421;C. WARREN,427
. C.B.,420;CYNTHIA C.
. 421;DAVID J.,270-271
. EVELINE CANTRELL,490
. FRANCES ROGERS,420
. HIRAM C.,394;HORATIO
. V.,490;I.A.,421;JOHN
. 95;M.A.,421;MALINDA
. MCDONALD,160;MARGARET
. 478;MARY J. BOZEMAN
. 490;MARY T.,475;NANCY
. 433;R.D. BORDERS,424
. RANSOM,160;RICHARD,259

. 265;RUTHY,486;S.D.,425
. S.V.,427;SAMUEL,197
. SOLOMON,399;SUSAN,554
ROEBUCK,SARAH,419
ROGAN,SARAH,156
ROGER,PETER C.,151,191
. 236,243;R.P.,12
ROGERS,527;A.J.,32,76
. ADIE LEE,521;ALBINA
. M.,309;ALEXANDER,472
. ALF,516;ALMINA HAYNES
. 566;AMANDA M. WOOTEN
. 557;ANDREW,76;ANN C.
. 303,319;ANNA W.,76
. ANNIE E.,76;ARMINTA
. BOYD,451;CATHERINE,597
. CHARLES,76;CHARLES P.
. 76;CYNTHIA,307,319
. DAVID,557;DAVID M.,338
. DICEY SYDES,557;E.,381
. ELBINA M.,312;ELIZA
. ANN,335;ELIZA JANE,340
. ELIZA JANE ROGERS,340
. ELIZABETH HATCHER,566
. ELLA E.,599;EMELINE
. 348;EMMA,76;EMMA
. TAYLOR,32;ENOCH,151
. 182,190,192,222,256
. 286-287,292;EVA
. MCBRAYER,511;F.P.,76
. FLORIDA,45;FRANCES,420
. FRANCES WITZEL,596;H.
. 564-565;HANNAH,456
. HANNAH M.,322,339
. HARRIET,519;HENRY C.
. 311,322;HUGH,596;J.C.
. 513-514;J.E.,426;J.L.
. 40-41;JACK,516
. JACKSON,306,322;JAMES
. 285,400,405,557;JAMES
. A.,399;JAMES C.,474
. JAMES R.,76;JANE
. HENDERSON,44;JOHN,151
. 276,281,285,290,297
. 298,306,322,338,438
. 472,511,513;JOHN N.
. 322;JOHN P.,338;JOHN
. W.,44;JOHNSON,168,279
. JONATHAN M.,557
. JOSEPH,287,292,338,465
. 557,583;JOSEPH A.,585
. JUDY ANN CAWLEY,338
. LAURA,593;LEVI,539
. LOAMY,451;LOTTY
. BUCKNER,306,322;LOU
. ANNIE,600;LOUISA J.
. BLACKBURN,311
. LOUISA J. THOMPSON,311
. 322;LOVELY,276
. LUCINDA MALCOM,557
. LUISA,556;M.H.,599
. MALINDA MAYO,557
. MARTHA,343;MARTHA E.
. 565;MARTHA J.,321,336
. MARTHA SHANDS,338
. MARY,352,602;MARY A.
. 333;MARY J.
. STRICKLAND,338
. MENERVA,337;MINERVA,76
. NANCY,312,327;NANCY
. EZZARD,322;NANCY J.
. CAPE,339;NANCY J.
. COPE,339;NANCY M.,335
. PATSY WILSON,592
. PATTIE M. CRAWFORD,338
. PETER B.,339;R.P.,340
. ROBERT,276,290;ROBERT
. N.,340;S.,210;S.C.,596
. SAMUEL,592;SAMUEL L.
. 566;SAMUEL M.,566
. SARAH,426-427,556
. SARAH A.,321,336
. SARAH A. SPRINGFIELD
. 585;SARAH ARMSTRONG

. 426;SARAH BLACKBURN
. 322;SARAH E. JONES,340
. SARAH G. BLACKBURN,306
. SARAH L.,336;SIBBIE
. DANIEL,539;SOPHRONA
. HARDEN,322;SOPHRONA
. HARDIN,338;SUSAN,558
. SUSAN CHATHAM,339
. SUSAN E. HOWARD,596
. THOMAS,149,165,298
. THOMAS B.,338;THYRZA
. 518;VIANNA CAWLEY,340
. VIRGINIA,342;W.,281
. W.H.H.,340;WILLIAM,276
. 290,464,526;WILLIAM
. A.,39;WILLIAM B.,245
. WILLIAM J.,339
. WILLIAM S.,451
ROGGERS,JAMES,549
ROLCHE,GEORGE A.,252,255
ROLEN,MARY PARKER,490
ROBERT,298;THOMAS,490
ROLIN,LEAH S.,364
. MAHALA BENNETT,364
. MARY,349;MARY CRAME
. 338;THOMAS,338;TILMAN
. 364
ROLING,JANE JOHNSON,490
ROBERT,490
ROLINS,CAROLINE,378
. CATHERINE BRANNON,355
. 378;JAMES A.,355
. JAMES H.,378;JONATHAN
. 297;P.B.,74
ROLLIN,MARY,317,332
ROLLING,MATILDA,493
ROLLINGS,SAMUEL,437
ROLLINS,507;A.M.
. MCGAUGHY,589;ADDISON
. 590;CALVIN,472,474
. CATHERINE P. BRANON
. 338;GEORGE,469,471,473
. JAMES A.,338;JOHN,472
. JOHN F.,589;JOHN R.
. 473;JONATHAN,176
. MARIA E.,577;MARTHA
. 498;MARY M.,575;PHEBE
. MORRIS,590;W.I.,529
. W.L.,498,525,530,537
. WILLIAM,495
. WILLIAMSON,496
ROLLS,F.M.,427;MARY
. CORSSLEY,420;NANCY L.
. EAVES,427;W.F.,420
ROLON,SARAH ANN,344
ROMINES,LUTICIA M.,570
RONEY,ARDISHA,47
RONMAN,E.,532
ROOD,ASEL P.,76;B.E.,75
ROOKER,J.A.,424;JOHN B.
. 390;LOWERY,230;SUSAN
. REYNOLDS,424
ROONEY,S.A.,76;T.A.,76
ROOST,PIDGEON,263
ROOT,509;ALADA C.,523
. ALODA C.,76;CALEDONIA
. LEVERTON,13;EMMA,76
. JAMES L.,13,76;MARY
. E.,76;MARY H.,47
. WILLIAM,76,131,519
ROPER,A.H.,490;AARON,466
. AMY ELIZ. REID,338
. ANNIE RED,374
. BENJAMIN F.,490
. CHARLES F.,340
. CLAIBORN T.,340
. CRISSY,349;DORCAS
. TALANT,322;ELIJAH,478
. 493;ELIZA,305,314
. ELIZABETH,333
. ELIZABETH ELLIOTT,26
. ELIZABETH HOCKENHULL
. 338;ENOCH,180;EVALINE
. HOLBROOK,384;EVALINE

. HOLBROOKS,308,322
. GEORGE C.,338;H.A.,482
. HAMILTON,322,338
. HENRY F.,308,322,384
. HESTER,487;HULDA C.
. 310,318;J.W.,490
. JAMES P.T.,7;JASON,322
. JOHN,338,374;JOHN F.
. 374;JONES H.,380
. JOSEPH,2,496;M.C.,375
. MARTHA A. OGLESBY,7
. MARTHA F. MITCHELL,587
. MARTHA J.,380;MARTHA
. MARTIN,490;MARTHA
. TALLANT,340;MARY E.
. PURCELL,340;MARY E.
. TINSLEY,374;MATILDA
. 375;MISSEY ANN CAPE
. 322;NANNIE SMITH,490
. NELSON,587;NEPSEY ANN
. COPE,338;NEPSIAN CAPE
. 380;NEPSIAN COPE,380
. R.A.,591;R.P.,340
. RACHEL E.,325;REBECCA
. 594;REBECCA A. HENSON
. 340;ROSEYTY MCLEOD,490
. S.L.,26;SAMUEL,491
. SARAH,556;SARAH A.,315
. SARAH L. WIER,591
. SARAH T.,384;SARAH
. TALENT,338;SARAH
. TALLANT,322;SUSAN,466
. T.L.,138,140;THOMAS
. 549;WILLIAM A.,322,338
ROSE,
. CELESTIA M. COOMBS,14
. D.M.,399;ELIZABETH I.
. STEWART,569;JAMES,469
. JOHN,462,569;MALISSA
. 597;MARY,529;MARY ANN
. 596;SAMUEL P.,14
. SARAH,560
ROSS,A.E.,407;AMANDA A.
. 341;JAMES H.,37;M.L.
. TUGGLE,407;MARY,579
. MARY L. COLLIS,490
. PEGGY,456;SUSIE SMITH
. 37;W.A.,275,279-280
. 282-287;WILEY,278
. WILLIAM N.,490
ROSSEN,
. MARTHA M. KINNEY,433
. MIDDLETON M.,433
ROSSER,ALICE,553;SARAH
. 556
ROSWELL,JOHN C.,391
ROUCH,CLARINDA,583
ROUCHE,WILLIAM,519
ROUSE,ANN,308,313
. JOSEPH,564,577
. MARGARET
. MOORELAND,564
. MARY J. DANIEL,577
ROUSSEAU,ANDREW,176
ROUTH,ALFRED,395
. NANNIE V. BURSOW,596
. ROBERT F.,594
. S. EMILY GAMBRELL,588
. SAMUEL H.,596;TEBITHA
. BUNSON,594;WILLIAM F.
. 588
ROVIE,WILLIAM,76
ROWAN,B.C.,524;J.F.,36
. 44,47;JOHN F.,34,50
ROWDEN,HUBBARD A.,436
. LOT,445
ROWE,J.,89;JOHN,2,89-90
. 98;JOSEPH,91;SOLOMON
. 466;SUSAN,554
ROWEL,JAMES,2;WILLIAM,495
ROWLAN,
. MALINDA PALMOUR,490
. ROBERT,490
ROWLAND,A.W.,413;AMANDA

. J.,22;BAZELLE,196
. ELIZABETH HEATH,309
. 311,322;MATILDA,311
. 312;PATSY GRAVITT,311
. ROBERT,309,311,322,442
. SARAH,310,312;TILMAN
. 311
ROWLIN,MARY CRANE,322
. PATSY GRAVITT,311,322
. THOMAS,322;TILMAN,311
. 322
ROWNS,JOHN F.,20
ROZER,ALEXANDER,392
. DEXTER,392;ELIZABETH
. 392;FANNY,392;ROBERT
. 392;ROBERT A.,392
. SUSAN,392;THEOPHILUS
. 392;WILLIAM A.,392
RRUDALL,P.H.,93
RSSES,WILLIAM M.,28
RUCE,STEPHEN C.,405
RUCHER,SIMEON,187
RUCKEN,MARTHA BANKS,598
. SANDY,598
RUCKER,S.B.,207,285
. SIMEON,178,180;SIMEON
. B.,152,192,199,228
. SIMEON R.,253
RUCKS,JAMES F.,439-441
. WILLIAM,441
RUDASILL,MARY,162
RUDISILL,SARAH,162
RUEDIE,A.D.,133
RUFF,ELIZABETH C.,18
. H.C.,146;HENRY C.,21
. M.L.,76,146;MARTIN L.
. 76;MARY A.,48
. MINERVA A. DOWDA,21
. NANCY A.,20
RUGGLES,112
RUMPH,J.G.S.,121;JOHN
. B.,108
RUMSEY,
. ELVIRA BURCHFIELD,593
. FIELDS,76;JOSEPH,593
. RUBIN,76
RUNALS,CHARLES,462
RUNELLS,
. CAROLINE GEORGE,568
. JOHN W.,568
RUNION,HIRAM,470
RUNNELLS,JOHN,322
. LOUISA J. STAGG,322
RUNNELS,GALLANT,1;JOHN
. 338;LOUIZA J. STAGGS
. 338
RUNYAN,A.V. KIRK,5;E.C.
. 76;EMMA C. GARMON,33
. I.P.,62;ISRAEL P.,5
. LOUISA S.,5;R.H.,76
. ROBERT H.,33;T.,129
RUNYON,MARTHA A.,40
RUSE,THOMAS,465
RUSEL,JAMES R.,467
RUSH,JAMES,1;JOHN,557
. MARY JOHNSTON,557
RUSHTON,ANNIE,562;C.E.
. SIMS,417,586;ROBERT
. S.,417,586
RUSK,DAVID,152,186,191
. 192,198-199,207,228
. 253,259-260,262-263
. DAVIS,212;FANNIE,515
. H.L.,212;HUGH,196,198
. 223;HUGH G.,223,229
. 232,256;JANE
. KILLINGSWORTH,340
. THOMAS J.,230,340
RUSKE,THOMAS J.,174
RUSKIN,JOHN W.,76
. SAPHRONIA,76
RUSS,M.L.,99
RUSSEL,
. ADDIE BRINKLEY,599

. FANNIE WRIGHT,594
. HENSON,590;JUDAH,589
. LODICE RUSSELL,590
. WILLIAM,594,599
RUSSELL,A.B.,579
. CATHARINE,314
. CATHERINE,310;D.M.,519
. DAVID,425;ELISA,303
. 312;ELISHA,549;ELIZA
. 307,322;ELIZA C.,382
. 583;ELIZABETH RIDEN
. 580;F.J. BATES,424
. GEORGE,549;HARRIET,602
. HARRY A.,587;HENRY,339
. J.P.,580;JAMES F.,339
. JAMES R.,195;JANE,432
. JEREMIAH,441,447;JOHN
. 298,491;JOHN S.,155
. LODICE,590;M. GORDON
. 425;M.A.Q. ADAMS,579
. M.J. WOOD,587
. MARGARET HUTCHINS,339
. MARTHA,449;MARTHA
. BAKER,155;MARY,450
. MARY ANN VAUGHAN,322
. MATTIE V.,76;METTIE
. LOU,519;MINERVA C.
. RACKLEY,339;N.M.,424
. POLLY RED,447
. REBECCA A. YOUNG,587
. RHUHAMA,451;ROBERT,395
. SARAH,459;VICTORY,422
. W.H.,574;W.N.,587
. WILLIAM,322
RUSSEN,JOHN H.,286
RUSSOM,R.W.,518,541
RUSSON,R.W.,537
RUSTIN,MARY,153
RUSTK,FANNIE,515
RUTHE,MARY,571
RUTHERFORD,ALBELTINE,45
. ANALINE,37;CAROLINE
. WILSON,45;DULPHAS,463
. ELIZABETH,7,76
. EMELINE,14;ISAAC,17
. 420,444;J.,111;L.,76
. S.A.G.,112;SAMUEL,464
. THOMAS R.,45;WILLIAM
. 76,298
RUTLEDGE,A.B.,137,139
. 143;ALBERT B.,139
. ALDRED B.,27;DIANNA
. 446;ELIAS G.,436
. ELIZA A. KENNON,27
. JOHN,437;JOSEPH,305
. 322,463;MELISSA A.
. MCCOY,305,322;RUSSEL
. 436
RYALS,J.G.,23;JAMES G.
. 22,24,28,34,45,48
. JANUS G.,16;WALTER,524
RYBURN,P.M.,34-35
RYER,T.L.,142
RYMER,JO,508
RYSON,S.C. SITTON,579
. S.G.,579
SADDERFEE,KERTUS,152
SAFFOLD,196
SAG,WILLIAM,286-287
SAGERS,SARAH N.,304
SAILERS,GEORGE W.,586
. NANCY REESE,586
SAINDERS,NANCY,37
SALMON,WILLIAM,224
SALOMON,ABRAHAM,242
SALTER,ELIZA,445;JOHN
. B.,340;NANCY NELSON
. 340;PETER,435
SAMES,LEWIS,297
SAMMONS,HENRIETTA W.,448
SAMON,GEORGE,549
SAMPLE,CHARLES,298
. FRANCES MERITT,158
. JAMES,149,471,473

. JESSE,297;JOHN,298
. ROBERT J.,158;SOPHA
. 372;Z.M.,297
SAMPLER,112;E.,122;J.C.
. 429;MARIETTA AUSTIN
. 429
SAMPLES,357;A.G.,346
. ADALINE KARR,341
. AMANDA,331;AMANDA A.
. POSS,341;AMANDA A.
. ROSS,341;AMANDA J.,335
. ANDREW A.,376;ANDREW
. G.,379;CHARLES,371,557
. COLUMBIA S.,356
. DANIEL A.,379;E.
. DOOLEY,346;ELIZ. JANE
. PHILLIPS,340
. ELIZABETH JEFFREY,322
. ELIZABETH JEFFRIES,308
. ELIZABETH PHILLIPS,323
. EMA O. HAWKINS,381
. FRANCES,319,332
. FRANCES GREEN,341
. FRANCIS A.,346
. FRANCIS M.,335
. HENRIETTA,375;ISAAC
. N.,341;JAMES,341
. JAMES G.,376;JANE
. GRIMES,340;JESSE,308
. 322,340;JOHN,340,375
. JOHN C.,341;KESIAH
. PRUETT,376;L.E.,334
. LOUIE E.,381;MALINDA
. HANSHARD,160;MARTHA
. A.,327;MARY,322,339
. MARY A. FOSTER,340
. MARY ANN,384;MARY ANN
. FOSTER,375;MARY E.,338
. 379;MARY E. SAMPLES
. 379;MATTHEW,160
. MONROE M.,323,340
. NANCY A.,343;NANCY E.
. 330;OPHELIA H.,371
. PHEBE A.,573;POLLY A.
. 305;POLLY ANN,325
. POLLY PATRICK,557
. RACHEL,300,315
. REBECCA SCOTT,371
. SARAH,338;SARAH A.,331
. 355,381;SARAH A.
. DAVIS,379;SARAH A.
. DOLLAR,376;SARAH A.
. SAMPLES,381;SARAH
. DAVIS,300;SARAH E.
. DOLLAR,379;SARAH J.
. BLAKE,340;SARAH J.
. GREEN,323,340,356
. SARAH JANE BLAKE,323
. THOMAS C.,300,356,379
. THOMAS CALVIN,381
. THOMAS O.,323,340
. WILLIAM O.,340
. WILLIAM V.,323
SAMPSON,
. DIDEMA BURGESS,577
. JOHN,577
SAMS,AMERICA,584;ASA A.
. 584;CANDIS E.
. ANDERSON,159;CANSADY
. 342;CHRISTOPHER,490
. CICERO M.,378;CINTHA
. 314;D.F.,76;ELLA,604
. EMALINE J. WALLACE,323
. EMALINE WALLACE,340
. EMILY BAKER,323,363
. 378;FELAND,481;G.W.
. 159;GEORGIA,592;H.S.
. 76;JAMES,394;JAMES C.
. 490;JOHN F.,472;LENIE
. RED,378;LEWIS,458
. LEWIS A.,340;MARGARET
. 479;MARGARET BIDDY,458
. MARTHA M.E. HOGAN,490
. MARY,308,318;MARY A.

. 363;MARY CONNON,340
. MARY CONNOR,340;NANCY
. DERBY,490;NANCY E.,483
. REUBEN,149,165,168,340
. REUBIN,276,282-284,286
. 288-290,298;REUBIN J.
. 323;SAMUEL T.,490
. SUSAN A. MILLS,490
. SYNTHA,300;SYNTHIA,378
. WARREN,470-471
. WILLIAM N.,323,363,378
SAMUEL,ZACHARIAH,464
SAMUELS,THEODORE J.,490
. ZILPHIA E. REESE,490
SANDERS,A.C.,517;A.C.
. HUTCHINS,341;ALMENDY
. 76;ANNA,313;ARTILLA
. 302,319;ARTITIA,302
. BENJAMIN,91;CALEB,191
. 197,256;CALESS,152
. CATHERINE,319;CHARLEY
. A.N.,334;DIANNAH E.
. JONES,377;EDNA,48
. ELIZABETH,328;EMMA,47
. EVLIN LEDBETTER,377
. ISAAC,298,549;JACOB
. F.,341;JANE,308,323
. JOHN,229;JOHN CLARK
. 108;JOHN D.,140
. JOHNSON,300;JONSON,323
. JULIA,76;M.H.,424,426
. 427-428;MAHALA,303,319
. MALINDA,324,341
. MARTHA C.,308,319
. MARY A.,324,342;MARY
. HAWKINS,300,323;MOSES
. 377;NANCY,76
. PRISSELLA,332;ROBERT
. 183-184;S.A. SCOTT,424
. SINDEY,349;STEPHEN,495
. T.M.,521;TOM,511;W.J.
. 76;WILLIAM H.,377
SANDERSON,JOHN,92
SANDFORD,LUCY,538
SANDRES,B.B.S,2
SANDSDOWN,DAVID A.,285
SANFORD,210;CLARISA A.
. 338;DANIEL,445-447
. RAYMOND,273;WILLIAM
. 538
SANGER,J.R.,42;JOHN R.,12,14
SANGERS,JOHN R.,323
. MARTHA MORTEN,323
SANGES,GENEVA,42;J.R.,18
. 22,33,40,44,46-47
. JOHN,43;JOHN R.,31,45
. 76;KATE L.,21;M.T.,76
. SALLIE M.,13
SANLOON,EZRA,464
SANSDOWN,D.A.,285
SANSOM,J.C.,601;SARAH
. BEARDEN,601;WILLIAM,1
. 89
SANSON,JAMES L.,562
. JOSEPHINE JOHNSON,562
SANSOND,GEORGE,600
. LINDA BOYD,600
SANTETAKE,171
SARELLS,CHARLES J.,557
. POLLY PATRICK,557
SARGEANT,WILLIAM,112
SARGENT,MARY ANN,155
. W.C.,111
SARJEANT,JOHN,191-192
SARNES,GREENBERRY,456
. PEGGY ROSS,456
SARTAIN,
. SARAH A. HAWKINS,563
. WILLIAM,563
SARTER,
. ELMINA ROBERTS,455
. JOHNSTON,455
SARTIN,JOHN,307,323
. MARY SMITH,307,323

676

. C.H.B.,426;CAROLINE,10
. D.E.C. MCADAMS,426
. DICEY,1;DOXAY,9;E.J.,9
. 137;ELISHA H.,33
. ELIZA JANE ROBERTSON,9
. ELIZABETH J. BLAKE,341
. ELIZABETH MCKINNEY,156
. EMELINE,16;EMMA C.
. BLANKENSHIP,33
. FRANCIS M.,48
. GRACIE M. MCENTYRE,48
. J.H.,137;JACKSON,323
. JANE,155;JANE MAYHAN
. 557;JASPER,130-131
. JOHN,156,298;JOHN H.
. 77;JOHN L.,96,99-101
. 111;L.,101;L.A.,109
. L.M.,143-144;LARKIN
. 443;LEONARD,3;LEONARD
. A.,77;MALINDA,158
. MARTHA,16;MARTHA A.
. 323;MARTHA A. SIMPSON
. 323;MARY,157;MARY ANN
. 18;MARY M. CAMPBELL,19
. N.A.,421;RAYMOND B.,39
. REBECCA,77;ROBERT M.
. 341;SILAS M.,19
. TABITHA ROBERTSON,39
. W.W.,81,137;WILLIAM
. LAWRENCE,502;WILLIAM
. R.,557
SIMS,178;A.D. HUTCHINS
. 341;ANN M.,596;ARCHIE
. 77;BARNETT,462;BELLE
. 522;BENJAMIN,440,443
. C.E.,417,586;DAVID,170
. ELIZA ANN WILSON,155
. ELIZABETH,463
. ELIZABETH A.,318
. EMILY CLEMENTS,458
. F.A.,77;GEORGE,520-521
. H.L.,242,248,255,262
. HENRY L.,240-241,250
. 252,254,458,585;HENRY
. LIGHTFOOT,180
. ISABELLA CAMPBELL,323
. ISABELLA D. CAMPBELL
. 300;JOHN,3,443;JOHN
. A.,341;JOSEPH B.,155
. KELLEY,443;LEWIS,280
. 282,439;LIZZIE
. SELVIDGE,585;M.,299
. MICHAEL,256;NANCY,330
. REBECCA BLACKWELL,490
. RHODA HOUSE,451;SARAH
. 586;SARAH J.,584
. TOLBERT,439;VILETT
. THOMPSON,557;VIRGINIA
. M.,564;WALTAN,557
. WILLIAM,178,451
. WILLIAM B.,300,323,490
SIMSON,A.N.,47,50;M.W.,597
SINAS,SARAH J.,584
SINGLETARY,DILLA,582
. MARY P.,587
SINGLETCH,E.J.,538
SINGLETON,A.S.,570
. DARCUS,317,332;E.J.
. 538;HARRIET,330;HENRY
. 549;JAMES,549;LOUISA
. 345;MARY E. PATTERSON
. 341;POLLY A.,337
. PYRENUS,341;SARAH E.
. 317,332;THOMAS,447
. TRESAM DICKENS,447
. WILLIAM,549
SINSON,FANNIE,38
SINYARD,ADA PARKS,535
. ALECK,517;BUD,535
. DICY HULSEY,451
. ELIZABETH,532;HENRY
. 451;LUD,540;MARY
. STANCETT,600;THOMAS
. 600

SISK,533;J.W.,434;LULA
. DODD,434
SISNER,J.,187
SISSAN,SOPHIA,321
SISSEN,SARDA,462
SISSON,GEORGE W.,323,340
. NARCISSA HARRIS,323
. 340;NOAH B.,101
. SIPHIA,300
SITTEN,JAMES T.,152
SITTON,ANDREW J.,572
. ELIZABETH C. ROBERTS
. 156;JAMES T.,228;JOHN
. 156,461;MARY A.H.
. BREWER,572;S.C.,579
SIXKILLER,187
SIZEMORE,ABBY,362;ELIZ.,362
SKELTON,HULDAY,363
. JAMES,49;JAMES E.,108
. 109-110;JOHN M.,90
. M.V. CHALKER,49
. MARTIN,104;SABRINA,48
. W.T.,77
SKENE,KIZZA,453
SKILLREN,JOHN,420
. REBECCA CARLTON,420
SKIN,ELIZABETH A.,332
SKINNER,J.M.,142-143
. JAMES,99;JAMES M.,99
. 102;JAMES R.,447;JANE
. PULLIAM,447;MARKY E.
. 33
SKIT,JIM,224,232,235
SLAGLE,B.,409;D.E.,415
. DANIEL E.,407;DAVID
. M.,409;ELLA HALEY,491
. HELLENA EMOGENE,415
. J.,409;PRISCILLA,415
. PRISCILLA QUILLIAN,407
. W.F.,491
SLATE,SAMUEL,442
SLATEN,JOHN,422-424
. SARA,597
SLATER,JOHN B.,340
. NANCY NELSON,340
SLATIN,LUCINDA E.,308,324
SLATON,AARON,454;E.R.,38
. M.E. CAMPBELL,418
. REBECCA,451;SUSAN
. COLBERT,454;W.F.,418
. WILLIAM A.,464
SLATTON,MARY,463
SLAUGHTER,115;BILL,497
. CINDERELLA,453;J.W.,77
. SARAH,77
SLAY,MARGARET,569
SLEEDEL,MARGARET,160
SLEGAR,JOHN,471
SLEIG,DANIEL,606
. JEANETTE MILLNER,606
SLIGH,J.N.,507
SLOAN,A.M.,396;A.S.,399
. AMANDA,428;ARCHIBALD
. 469,472,562;ELIZABETH
. 597;FELIX A.,574;J.B.
. 425-426;J.C.
. KILLINGER,589;JAMES
. A.,399,576;JOHN,471
. LENORA,603;M.M.
. GREESON,418;MARY J.
. HOSKINS,574;MARY M.
. 576;MINERVA A.,588
. PARTHENA,302,320
. PERMELIA A. CARPENTER
. 562;R.P.,596;ROBERT
. 472;SAMUEL,303,323,589
. SARAH F. MARTIN,576
. SUSAN L. HELTON,434
. SUSANNAH TIDWELL,303
. 323;TAMPY OWEN,596
. W.A.,418;WILLIAM D.
. 434
SLOCUM,ANGELINA,31
SLOCUMB,JOSEPH,557

. NANCY DIGGS,557
SLOTTERBECK,A.J.,77
SLUDER,NANCY PINYAN,267
. WILLIAM,267
SMALL,HARVEY,180;LOU J.
. 591;LYDIA,590
SMALLWOOD,
. ANNIE ELLINGTON,377
. ELIZA J.,561;EVALINE
. 293;JOHN,379;LANTY,300
. 319;MARCUS A.,377
. MARKE,377;MCKINSEY,297
. MONROE,379;RENIE,300
. 313;SARAH TIPPINS,379
SMART,HESTER A.,566
. MARCUS,573;SARAH
. TALLEY,573
SMEARD,HENRY,496
SMEDLEY,J.R.,469;JOHN
. 557;NANCY BEARDIN,557
SMEN,JAMES,387
SMETHY,JOHN,457;MALINDA
. KITTLE,457
SMITELL,SARAH,464
SMITH,121,206,299,333
. 521,531;A.,409;A.C.
. 500;A.E.,424;A.F.,352
. A.L.,46;A.P.
. MCELWNATH,46;A.R.,183
. 195,225,233,240,276
. A.S.,78;A.W.,481
. AARON S.,106;ABASLOM
. 474;ABNER,162,298
. ABRAM,95,299,463
. ABSALOM,1;ACIL,464
. ADALINE BROCK,161
. ADENSAN,297;ALBERT G.
. 304,323;ALEXANDER,340
. ALEXANDRIA,466;ALFORD
. K.,379;ALFRED,491,561
. ALFRED A.,567;ALLEN
. 447;ALPHA,307,323,352
. AMANDA,6;AMANDA A.,567
. AMANDA HARRIS,162;AMY
. DAY,323,340;ANDREW J.
. 512;ANN,428,449;ANN
. E.,307,323;ANN M.,78
. ANNA MARIA,78;ANTHONY
. 474,582,584;ARCH,78
. ARCHIBALD,78
. ARCHIBALL,78;ARLENDAR
. 447;ARMETTA,301,315
. ARMINDA,362;ARMINDA
. HERNDON,340;ARTER C.
. 563;ASENITH,454;B.,100
. B.H.,98-100,103,105
. 106-107,508,521;B.J.
. 531;BARBERY KETTER,452
. BARTHY J.,379;BARTON
. 436;BENAJER,557
. BENJAMIN,98,508
. BENJAMIN F.,78;BENNY
. 511;BIDDY,557;BIDDY
. SMITH,557;BLARE,98
. BLARE BENJAMIN,98
. BRADLEY,3;167;C.H.,87
. C.V.,378;CABBIN,230
. CALLIE,482;CAROLINA
. PATTON,557;CAROLINE
. ADCOCK,421;CAROLINE
. BUTLER,430;CAROLINE
. ROBINSON,340
. CATHARINE,535;CATY M.
. WOODS,454;CELIA A.,78
. CHARLES,23,74,149,170
. CHARLEY,491;CHEROKEE
. ALEXANDER,432;CYRUS
. 474;D.C.,484;D.F.,428
. 562,564-566;D.W.,491
. DARAH,576;DAVID,33,425
. 464;DAVID L.,161
. DAVID N.,286;DEBBY
. ANN,572;DISEY,348
. DREWRY R.,562

. DRUCILLA L.,358;E.F.
. PARKS,572;E.F.
. SPENCER,422;E.J.,137
. 378,568,572;EDITH
. BROWN,557;EDITH
. MATTOCKS,447;EDMUND
. 469;EDNA SANDERS,48
. EDWARD,340;ELENORA
. BAILEY,569;ELIGAH W.
. 594;ELIJAH,340;ELIJAH
. B.,464;ELIJAH BUNION
. 505;ELIZ. ANN HAWKINS
. 340;ELIZA,599;ELIZA
. BROWN,155;ELIZA BURIN
. 561;ELIZA F. MORRIS
. 304,323;ELIZA MINEY
. 379;ELIZA PARRET,559
. ELIZA SHARPTIOR,491
. ELIZA THOMPSON,557
. ELIZABETH,40,379,529
. 556,563,566
. ELIZABETH A. POTTS,491
. ELIZABETH BARRETT,20
. ELIZABETH HUTCHENS,428
. ELIZABETH KING,447
. ELIZABETH MCPHERSIAN
. 447;ELIZABETH MULLINS
. 557;ELIZABETH RITCH
. 449;ELIZABETH WAMMOCK
. 557;ELLEN,424;ELVIRA
. 78;EMELINA D. FULLER
. 491;EMILY REDD,306,323
. EMILY REED,306;EMMA
. 520;EVALINE,575
. EVELIN CATES,378
. EVELINE ALLEN,491
. EVELINE YANCY,491
. EZEKIEL,245-246;F.M.
. 418,503,511,525
. FANNIE,24;FANNIE C.
. 573;FANY,580;FILLMOND
. 561;FLETCHER,508
. FRANCES DAY,557
. FRANCIS,525;FRANCIS
. IVEY,557;FRANCIS L.G.
. CASTLEBERRY,377;G.A.
. 500;G.B.,419;G.E.,410
. G.R.,422;GEORGE,423
. 491,549;GEORGE M.,8
. 192,204,222-223,226
. 229,234,244;GIDEON,2
. 466;GIDIEN,387
. GILFORD,496;GILMAN,135
. GUY W.,507;H.E.,505
. HALEY,557;HAMPTON,549
. HANNAH M.,78,314,329
. HARRIET C. MITCHELL,8
. HARVY,379;HELEN Z.,78
. HENRY,517,606;HOWARD
. 264;HULDAY SKELTON,363
. IBBIE,11;ISAAC,77
. ISHAM,557;J.A.,429
. J.B.,408;J.F.,498
. J.H.,536,601;J.J.,573
. J.N.,559;J.T.,41
. JACKSON,525;JAMES,377
. 404,437-438,465,549
. 557,561;JAMES A.,20
. JAMES B.,377;JAMES H.
. 26,89;JAMES L.C.,97
. 100-101;JAMES M.,48,78
. 86,173,306,323,363,592
. JAMES O.,78,107,130
. 135;JAMES S.C.,98
. JAMES W.,421;JANE,78
. 360,431;JANE ANDERSON
. 606;JANE HAMMETT,46
. JANE RAY,561;JEFFREY
. 167;JENNIE,78,517
. JENNIE A. CONLEY,592
. JESSE,149;JESSIE
. BEALL,536;JOB,105,107
. JOEL K.,491;JOHN,98
. 150,166,168,173-174

678

. GARY H.,522;J.M.,519
. 530,532,534;J.S.,509
. J.T.,545;JOHN T.M.,39
. JOHN W.,545;LUCIUS,524
. MALVINA,600;NANCY
. BOSWELL,11;S.P.,507
. SAMANTHA E. THOMAS,39
. SARAH A.,21;WILL,511
SPIVA,JOSEPHINE A.,575
SPIVY,MARTHA,558
. WILLIAM,550
SPOOR,MOLLY,31
SPRAGGINS,FRANCES,78
. ISABELLA,446;S.,78
. THOMAS E.,78
SPRAGIN,E.P.,26
SPRAGINS,
. ELIMIRA CHASTAIN,15
. M.J.,60;THOMAS D.,15
SPRIGGS,533
SPRINGER,498;JOHN E.,497
. JOSEPH,437;MARY,78
. MINNIE BENEDICT,497
. OLLIE,78;TOBITHA,78
SPRINGFIELD,BENNET,473
. FLORA FLEOFFRE,587
. GEORGIA ODELL,604
. H.G.,587;HUGH,472
. JAMES M.,562;JOSIAH
. 604;LANGSTON S.,472
. LINNA F. JINKS,559
. SARAH A.,585;SARAH
. BELL,562;W.A.,599
. WILLIAM F.,559
SPRINGS,ELIJAH,157
. ELIZABETH RICE,157
SPROUCE,MARY JANE,5
SPROUSE,JOHN H.,25
. JULIA,78;LOUELLA,78
. NANCY E. KEMP,25
SPROWL,CANDUS,593
SPRUCE,CALVIN,323
. CALVIN H.,340;CYNTHIA
. MASHBURN,323;JOHN C.
. 340;NANCY,313;REBECCA
. 305,317;SARAH BAILEY
. 340;SARAH E. HAMPTON
. 340;SARAH J.,595
. SUSAN M.,347
SPRUELL,NANCY A.,25
SPRUILL,NANCY,384
SPRUSE,NANCY,327
SPURLIN,LUCY KING,158
. THOMAS S.M.,158
SPURLING,HICKS,438
SPURLINGS,JAMES,439
SQUIRE,C.,210
STAAM,MARY,560
STABLEY,EZEKILL,144
STAFORD,HENRY M.,576
. NRACISSUS DYCUS,576
STAGG,FLORENCE C.,432
. LOUISA J.,322
STAGGS,FRANCES,335
. HESTER A.,307,320
. LOUIZA J.,338;ROSY J.
. 312,327
STALLINGS,S.W.,418
STANBACK,J.V.,148
STANCEL,DAVID,152,183
. 202,251;ELIJAH,3
. JESSE,461;JOHN,153,469
. KADER,264;LIZZIE,539
. M.E.,422;MALANA S.
. KEELE,418;THOMAS N.
. 418;W.H.,574
STANCELL,WILLIAM,112,121
STANCETT,MARY,600
STANCIL,DAVID,188,191
. 193,201,228;E.C.,107
. JESSE,177;JOHN,191,228
. 472;MARY WHITFIELD,491
. MINNIE,431;T.G.,491
. T.J.,483;THOMAS I.,477

. THOMAS J.,478-479,483
. 490-491,493;U.L.,491
. WILLIAM,170
STANCILL,CADER,257
STANCIPER,
. LOUISAH MESSEMORE,576
. P.J.,576
STAND,196,203
STANDFIELD,OLIVE,492
. TINIE,492
STANDFORD,JOHN R.,205
STANED,SARAH,577
STANELY,DORA,28
. FANNIE J. WADE,12
. WILLIAM P.,12
STANFIELD,ARMINDA M.,476
. BARBARA TABRIUAX,491
. E.L.,491
STANFORD,H.S.,378;J.E.
. JONES,378;JOHN R.,179
. 189;MILLEY S. HARRIS
. 557;MILLIE J. HARRIS
. 378;STEPHEN,378,557
. T.L.,402
STANIELL,ELIZABETH,451
STANLEY,B.M.,24;ELIZA
. M.,9;EULA,526;GEORGIA
. WILLIAMS,48;JAMES,48
. JANE,25;JANE WILLIAMS
. 24;JOHN,537;MARY H.,14
. WILLIAM,526
STANLY,
. MARTHA A. LUMMUS,341
. THOMAS J.,341
STANSBERRY,ALBERT G.,571
. J.M.,580;SUSAN
. CARLISLE,571
STANSEL,DAVID,181
. ELIJAH,167
STANSELL,BARON D.,83
. CALVIN L.,83;E.C.,56
. 78,83;EVA KIMBERLY,19
. GERTRUDE J. BRYSON,49
. HULDA,35;JAMESB.,83
. JOEL C.,19;JOHN,473
. KADER,219;MARY P.,49
. NANCY J.,83;W.D.,147
. 148;W.H.,570-573;W.S.
. 49;WILLIAM,109
STANSIL,WILLIAM,149
STANSILL,DAVID,78;JAMES
. N.,78
STANTON,ABIGAIL,429
. C.E.,423;JOHN,423,473
. LILLA G. FITE,431
. MARY,423;MISSOURI,431
. W.A.,431
STAPLER,AMOS,341
. MALINDA A.,380;SARAH
. STONE,341
STAPP,AARON,447
. BETSY A. WHITWORTH,447
. SARAH,163
STARK,JAMES P.,41
. JOANNA WOOD,41
STARNES,517;JOHN,459
. PERRY,513;REBECCA
. CARTER,459;RUTHY,160
STARNS,ARCHIBALD,340
. KASSY HYDE,340
STARNTON,JOHN,472
STARR,J.H.,412;JOHN H.
. 404;JOSEPH T.,427
. LIZZIE H.,412;M.R.,424
. NANCY,454;R.,412
. SARAH FREEMAN,427
STARRELL,TABITHA,161
STARRET,JOHN G.,411
STATAM,SUSAN,551
STATEN,ZEBEDEE,550
STATON,FALBY,578
STATTON,WILLEY,454
STATUM,SUSAN,551
STAUNTON,JOHN,469

STAVER,HANNAH,317
STEADHAM,ANDREW J.,36
. ELIZ. A. BLANKENSHIP
. 36
STEADMAN,NANCY,161
STEAGAL,
. ELIZABETH KELLY,311
. 323;PETER,311,323
STEAGALL,
. MARY ANN JAMES,310
. RICHARD,310
STEAL,
. ELIZA J. ROBERTS,560
. JAMES B.,560
STEAN,MARY,38
STEARNES,AUGUSTUS,430
. CLAUDIA A. HOPPER,430
STEARNS,A.H.,491;L.G.
. 491;L.V. JAMES,491
. R.E. STEPHENS,491
STEAVERSON,MARY C.,578
STEDHAM,ZACHARIAH,442
STEDMON,HENRY,341;MARY
. COLLINS,341
STEED,WILEY,30
STEEL,
. ELIZABETH ROBERTS,565
. ELVIRA A. E. EVANS,14
. GEORGE,565;H.J.,367
. HARIETT L. GODFREY,491
. HENRY J.,377;ISAAC,78
. J. MONROE,23;J.F.,464
. JAMES M.,491;JAMIMA,48
. M.J.M. JOHNSON,367
. MARGARET L.,554
. MARTHA M. BLACKSTON
. 377;MARY HOLLAND,377
. N.C.,367;RICHARD,550
. T.A. ADAMS,23;THOMAS
. N.,377;WILLIAM,78
. WILLIAM A.,14
STEELE,C.E.,48;JOHN V.
. 53;MARTHA A. W.
. EVERETT,4;MARY,49
. MILTON W.,4
STEELMAN,246;W.H.,247
. 265;WILLIAM H.,237,258
STEEN,
. ELIZABETH DOOLY,580
. GEORGE,440;NANCY A.
. EVERETT,36;NEWTON J.
. 36;SAMUEL G.,580
STEGAL,
. AMANDA SWAFFORD,491
. ANDREW H.,491;MALINDA
. PENDLEY,491;NANCY,293
. RUTHY ISBEL,293
. SHERMAN,491
STEGALL,ELIZABETH,155
. FARROW,465;LEWIS,509
. MARY,488;MARY ANN
. JAMES,323;RICHARD,323
STEGGALL,WILLIAM,509
STEIN,SAMUEL,132
STELL,HENRY,447;THOMAS
. J.,444;ZARILDA
. WILLIAMSON,447
STENCEL,NANCY,606
STENSON,L.H. CROW,566
. SAMUEL,566
STEONECYPER,JAMES,550
STEP,LUCINDA,569
. WILLIAM,463
STEPH,JOHN,387
STEPHENS,ALLEN,150
. AMANDA,350;ANNIE
. GARDNER,433;BENJAMIN
. 557;BENJAMIN C.,457
. CAROLINE PHILLIPS,379
. CORNELIA ANTOINETTE
. 411;DANIEL,341;DANIEL
. W.,379;DOROTHY,60,79
. E.H.,424;EDWARD D.,19
. ELIZA M. PARKS,340

. ELIZABETH,79
. ELIZABETH COLLEY,457
. ELIZABETH ESTES,308
. 323;ELIZABETH LOW,350
. 360;EMMA SANDERS,47
. EPHAME,379;EPHRAIM,308
. 323;H.P.,47;HANNAH A.
. 411;J.E.,60;J.H.,340
. JAMES,463;JAMES M.,157
. 491;JEPTHA K.,557
. JOEL,461;JOHN,350,360
. JULIA ANN,13;LENA E.
. 79;LEVISA M. JACKSON
. 557;LUCINDA SMITH,157
. MARGARET,458,490
. MARTHA A. RIDER,341
. MARTHA PHILLIPS,379
. MARY,360,556;MARY A.
. 337;MARY E. DUNCAN,19
. MARY J.,409;N.D.,140
. NANCY COLLEY,25;NANCY
. DAVIS,557;NANCY J.,330
. P. MORROW,424;POLLY,49
. R.E.,491;SARAH A.
. MOORE,49;SARAH E.,33
. SARAH FLORENCE,411
. SIMON,433;T.,69
. TELITHA MCLEOD,491
. TIMOTHY,25,69,79,136
. 141;URIAH,411;W.P.,76
. 79,131,135;WILLIAM J.
. 49;WILLIAM P.,133,136
. 141,145;WILLIS P.,79
. ZACHARIA,79
STEPHENSON,
. ELIZA CAGLE,603;FANNY
. JARRETT,562;JAMES S.
. 562;JOHN,496;MARTHA
. M.,567;MARY J. HOYLE
. 562;NATHAN,603
. WILLIAM,562
STEPLE,MARTHA A.,338
STERLING,ELISHA,241
. MARY CULVER,447
. PLEASANT A.,447
STETTON,ZEBODER,464
STEVENS,
. CAROLINE ESTES,376
. EPHRAM,376;J.A.
. BROWNLOW,427;JOSHUA
. P.,7;LIZZIE BAKER,429
. MARY C. BARNISTER,7
. NANCY E. PHILLIPS,376
. TIMOTHY,138;W.N.,427
. WILLIAM,392,429
. WILLIAM P.,376
. WILLIAM Y.H.,100
STEVENSON,AMANDA,579
. BENJAMIN F.,584;DAVID
. 564;ELIZABETH M.
. BATES,584;HARRIET
. VANDIKE,564;I.
. HADDOCK,604;J.H.,604
. NANCY A. WILLMUT,571
. W.B.,571
STEWARD,C.B.,526
. CORDELIA DEAN,526
. DAVID,297
STEWART,A.,399;A.J.,37.
. A.P.,380;AMANDA
. HAMILTON,606;ANDREW
. H.,380;ANDREW M.,302
. ANN,449;BARNEY,474
. BARNY,471;BETTIE,434
. CAROLINE,302,313
. CHARLES D.,78;CINTHY
. 451;CI ARK,274
. CORNELIUS,465;DICY
. MEREDITH,557;E.P.,78
. EDWARD A.,575
. ELIZABETH,327,418
. ELIZABETH I.,569;F.M.
. PATTERSON,426;FANNIE
. 427;FANNIE PATTILLO,6

684

UPSON,J.D.,505,509
UPTON,ELI,506;GEORGE,469
. JOHN A.,469;JOHN A.J.
. 472
USRA,JOHN,436
UTLEY,DAVID,201,207,251
. 458;OMA,201,251;OMA
. MARTIN,458
UTRY,DAVID,149
UTT,ANDREW,259
UWANA,JOHN,263;TINNY,263
VAN,NED,226,264;RACHEL
. MOORE,452;WYETT,452
VANABLE,JAMES,176
. NATHANIEL,176;W.R.,83
VANCE,MARY BROWN,590
. RICHARD,590
VANDERVIER,ENOCH,152
VANDEVER,W.H.,559
VANDEVERE,EMERLINE,565
VANDIFER,M.W.,561
VANDIFORD,LOUISA,553
VANDIKE,ATALINE,328
. HARRIET,564
VANDIVER,A.E.,400,568
. ENOCH,223;JULYAN
. DOBBS,157;M.A. ROE,421
. M.W.,560,569;SANFORD
. 157;T.A.,421
VANDIVERS,
. M.S. HENDERSON,573
. S.W.,573
VANDVERE,MALANY S.,593
VANDYKE,ROSANTE,575
VANHORN,LUCINDA E.,475
VANN,ASBERRY J.,11
. BURRELL T.,6;CHARLES
. M.,10;DAVID,172
. DYALPHIA BAKER,10
. ELIZA,448;ELIZABETH
. FANNIN,594;FRANCES
. DOBBS,11;JAMES,456
. JAMES B.,594;LUCINDA
. ATTAWAY,6;POLLY,553
. SALLY EDWARDS,456
VANTWERP,239
VANWICH,B.,57
VARDIVERE,HANNAH,569
VARICE,REBECCA,420
VARNELL,A.,575-576
. ADELAIDE,568;F.M.,572
. HARRIET CRESWELL,595
. MARTHA WHITTLE,572
. NAERRUCE HARRIS,606
. NANCY J.,578;SARAH,597
. WILLIAM,399;WILLIAM
. E.,606;WILLIAM M.,595
VARNER,CORNELIA
. MOORE,11
. JOHN,558;REBECCAH
. GRUBBS,558;WILLIAM S.,11
VARNUM,WILLIAM M.,238
VASSER,LUCY TAYLOR,37
. ROBERT,37
VAUGHAN,
. CHARLOTTE JACKSON,342
. CLABOURN,311,324
. CLAIBORNE,439;CLAYTON
. 112;CYNTHIA,304
. DELILAH,310,316
. ELIZABETH CARLISLE,301
. 324;FRANCES A. BOMAN
. 324;FRANCES A. BOWMAN
. 311;HAMILTON,342
. JAMES E.,324,342
. JERAMIAH,309;JEREMIAH
. 324;JOHN,324;LELAND
. F.,342;MARGARET,321
. MARGARET A.,306
. MARTHA E. CHAMBLEE,342
. MARY ANN,322;MARY E.
. 330;MELINDA NAYLOR,324
. 342;NANCY J.,310,321
. PATCHEY WIGGINS,324

. POLLY A. COGGINS,309
. POLLY ANN COGGINS,324
. SARAH POWELL,324
. SUSAN TIDWELL,309,324
. SYNTHA,318;W.W.,287
. WILLIAM B.,309,324
. WILLIAM W.,288-289,293
. 324;WILLIS,301,324
VAUGHN,520;ALBERT B.,40
. 42,44;AMANDA J.,369
. ANDY G.,383;C.,112
. CARY,481;FRANCES S.
. MAJOR,383;HARRIT
. ESTES,386;J.D.,32
. J.S.,530;J.T.,519,522
. JAMES E.,383;JAMES M.
. 386;LUCY,598;M.E.
. WALLACE,386;M.J.S,505
. MARTHA A. CHOPEALE,383
. MARTHA GRAVLEY,494
. NANCY E.,478;R.,530
. RANDALL,521;RANDOLPH
. 505;VIRGIL P.,494
. W.W.,297
VAVENDER,
. CRASY PEARCE,453
. WILLIAM,453
VEACH,J.S.,509
VEAL,ALEXANDER,497;MARY
. L.,4
VEAZEY,JOHN H.,496
VELVEN,JOHN,188
VELVIN,POLLY,557
VENABLE,
. ADALINE BAGLEY,311,324
. ELIZA BACON,374
. FRANCES,449;HARRIET
. 300,317;JAMES,285
. JUDITH,300,325;LAURA
. 374;MARTHA,301,312
. PATSEY STILL,449
. ROBERT,287,442;ROBERT
. R.,374;SANFORD,311,324
. THOMAS,449;W.R.,56
VENIBLE,JAMES,298
. ROBERT,298
VERHINE,J.E.,141;JAMES
. E.,148;JOISEY L.
. COLLINS,22;RICHARD T.
. 22
VERNER,JAMES M.,521
. S.S.,521
VERNON,ELIZA H. REED,324
. JOSIAH C.,324;L.L.,65
. 520
VESTAL,NANCY J.,305,319
VICERY,MARTHA,348
VICKERS,CHARLES D.,558
. MARTHA G. EDWARDS,558
VICKERY,CHARLES,279,301
. 324;CHARLOTTE,279
. ELIZA ANN ALLEN,558
. HARRY,174,279;HETTY
. 174;JOHN,279;JOHN W.
. 558;LUCY,279;MALINDA
. CLEMENTS,301;MALINDA
. CLEMMENS,324;MARTHA
. 328,372;MARY,279,300
. 312;MARY A. SANDERS
. 324;SAMPSON,461;SARAH
. 279;SUSAN,279
. SUSANNAH,310,314;T.N.
. 324
VICKORY,
. MARY A. SANDERS,342
. T.N.,342
VICKUS,SILAS,442
VILES,ALSFY HEAD,452
. SAMUEL,452
VILYARD,
. JANE WILLIAMS,458
. JOHN,458;POLLY,456
VINCENT,LARENIA,479
. LUCINDA H.,417

VINES,CHARLES,527
. FRANKY ROBERTS,455
. JOHN,455
VINSON,AMANDA LEA,10
. JONATHAN J.,10;LIZZIE
. 21
VINYARD,JOHN,437
VISAGE,WILLIAM,550
VISTELL,DAVID,299
VOLANTINE,BOB,528
VOSS,JOHN,163;OLIVE
. GANN,527;PHILLIP J.
. 527;SARAH A.,21;SUSAN
. FLETCHER,163
VOWEL,DAVIS,438
VOWELL,DAVID,442
VOYLES,J.E.,494;MANERVY
. CREIGE,494
WACAFER,MICHAEL,469
WACASA,GEORGE W.,471
WACASER,GEORGE W.,470
. MICHAEL,472;THOMAS,472
WACASON,
. ELIZA REYNOLDS,458
. GEORGE W.,458
WADDAIL,B.C.,574
. MARY E. MCCRARY,574
WADDALL,B.C.,413
. MARY E. MCCRARY,413
WADDEL,B.C.,574;MARY E.
. MCCRARY,574
WADDELL,EMILY,162;G.B.
. 53;JESSE,396;NICHOLAS
. 163;SARAH STAPP,163
WADE,543;AMANDA COX,42
. CAIN,459;CATHERINE
. MOOR,450;CLEMENTINE,12
. EDWARD,435;ELIJAH,456
. ELIZA E.,20;ELIZA
. SMITH,599;ELIZABETH
. 446;ELIZABETH COX,451
. FANNIE,430;FANNIE J.
. 12;GEORGIA,541
. GEORGIA DAVIS,24
. HARRIS,42,507
. HARRISON,497;HOMER,507
. JAMES,599;JESSE,559
. 572-573,575,577-578
. JOHN,24,437,581;JOICY
. 10;MARY,450;MARY
. EDWARDS,459;MATILDA
. WALSTON,581;PATEN,470
. 472;PATON,451;PHILIP
. 465;PHILLIP,450
. RASALIA M.,594
. REBECCA HAMES,456
. RICHARD,173,467
. SIDNEY A. CLARK,583
. TYLER,173;W.S.,583
. WILLIAM,343
WADKINS,A.J.,431
. ABRAHAM,589;ANN
. TATHAM,589;BRYANT,14
. DAVID,2;ELIZABETH
. BARNWELL,453;FRANCES
. 303,317;JESSA,91
. JESSE,2,91;JOHN,453
. MARTHA,303,315;MARY
. GRACE,14;MARY V.
. ALVERSON,431;NATHAN
. 342;NATHAN C.,306,324
. SARAH,303,319
. SARAH A. GRIFFIN,324
. 342;SARAH C. BUCHANAN
. 306,324
WADSWORTH,HOGAN,405
. TEMPY MARTIN,300,324
. WILLIAM,292 296,300
. 324
WADTS,JOSEPH,550
WAFFORD,JEREMIAH,152
. NATHANIEL,469
WAGGENOR,JOEL,474
WAGGONER,JAMES,191;JOHN

. 152,192,199,201,220
. 228,251,256
WAGNER,JOEL,471
WAGNON,JOHN,236,242,245
WAGONER,JOHN,191,207
WAIDE,HELAY,459
WAIN,D.C.,350
WAITER,JOHN,224
WAITES,JOHN,177,191-192
. 232,243-244,254,257
. JPHN,256;WILLIAM M.
. 240
WAITRS,JOHN,152
WAITS,ABSALOM,470;ANN
. EATON,458;JOHN,192,207
. 470;JULIA,21;MARTHY
. 452;MARY J.,43;SAMUEL
. 458
WAKEFIELD,JENNY,453
WALANETAH,261
WALAS,LUTHER,387
WALBRIT,WYATT,151
WALDRIP,ELI,297,343;IRA
. 297;MALISSA A.
. HENDRIX,343;REBECCA
. 448
WALDROP,HANNAH,482
. HAROY,127;HARVEY,127
. J.R.,530-531;MILTON
. 506;PARTILLA,303,324
. POLLY MORROW,303,324
. SARAH OWEN,324;W.C.
. 506;WILLIAM C.,324
WALDROUP,JULIA ANN,492
. SARAH J.,489
WALDRUP,ELIAS,343
. H.J.M. CROW,343;JANE
. 311,320;SARAH,304,314
. SARAH OWEN,305
. WILLIAM C.,305
WALES,FRANCIS A.,161
. MARY ANN EPPERSON,161
WALKER,A.P.,420;ABRAHAM
. 161;AMANDA,373;ANTUZA
. M.,156;C.L.,426
. CARTWHITE,589;CHARLES
. 571;DAN F.H.,561
. DAVID,309,325;DAWSON
. A.,399;DAWSON H.,575
. EDWIN A.,558;ELMINA
. HARLAN,592;FRANK,542
. GEORGE A.,265;GEORGE
. W.,401;HANNAH
. HENDERSON,567
. HARDRIDGE,256
. HARRIET C. WHITE,566
. HENRY,449;HENRY A.T.
. 569;HENRY M.,418
. HILLARD,592;ISAAC R.
. 231;J.H. JACKSON,426
. J.O.,540,542;JAMES,332
. 342,438,442,496;JAMES
. H.,567;JAMES S.,558
. JAMES W.,343;JERRY,528
. 550;JOHN M.,134
. JOSEPH,152,191,228,236
. 242;JOSEPH M.,593
. JOSEPH W.,139;L.A.F.
. BROWN,343;L.J.
. JOHNSON,601;LETTY ANN
. POOL,332;LETTY ANN
. POWEL,342;LEWIS G.,405
. LITTIE P.,540;M.E.,360
. M.W. MORROW,420
. MALINDA,363;MARIAH
. KIRK,161;MARTHA WINN
. 558;MARY,5,MARY E.,551
. MARY E. JONES,569
. MARY L.,587;MARY
. NICKS,450;MEMMARY,467
. MICAJAH,450;MOLLY J.
. HUTSON,418;NANCY C.
. 423;NANCY E. BRIDGES

. 593;NEWT,516;O.A.,424
. PATSEY HEAD,449
. REBECA PITTMAN,561
. RODA,451;SALLIE,592
. SALLIE J.E. BURRELL
. 343;SARAH,454;SARAH
. ADAMS,558;SARAH ANN
. 558;SARAH E. STROUP
. 571;SARAH J. BURRELL
. 343;SYLVANUS,175;T.
. 111,115;THEODOCIA C.
. WELLBORN,325
. THEODOCIA WELBORN,309
. THOMAS,471,473;THOMAS
. C.,343;THOMAS J.,601
. WEST,167;WILLIAM,472
. 474;WILLIAM D.,566
. WISLEY,467
WALKINS,
. AMANDA F. HINTON,558
. WILLIAM M.,558
WALL,ETHELD,550;FRANCES
. 411;FREWRY,550;ISAAC
. D.,181;JESSE,550;W.W.
. 390,393,395,411
. WILLIAM,550
WALLACE,ATHIE BISHOP,41
. CALVIN W.,41
. ELIZABETH,3,554
. ELIZABETH A. BARRETT
. 34;EMALINE,340
. EMALINE J.,323;EMMA,26
. EVELINE COPE,342
. FREDERIC,502;GEORGIA
. A.,17;GREEN B.,342
. H.B.,147;HARRIET,333
. J.B.,386;J.P.,147
. JAMES,16;JAMES A.,574
. 576-579;JANE T.,32
. JESSE B.,305,325,353
. JOE,543;JOHN,438,454
. JOSEPH P.,34;JULIA C.
. 26;LOTTIE WHITMORE,502
. LULA M.,37;M.E.,353
. 386;MARTHA JEFFERSON
. 342;MARTIN L.,342
. MARY,336;MARY A.,306
. 320;MITCHELL C.,558
. MOLLY COVINGTON,31
. NANCY,22;NANCY QUEEN
. 16;OSBORN,194;PETER
. 442;RACHEL GRESHAM,558
. S.B. EDWARDS,386
. SARAH,162,456;SARAH
. EDWARDS,305,325,353
. SEMMIA JACKSON,454
. SUSANNAH WATSON,456
. T.W.,147;TOLIVER,147
. TOLIVER W.,146
. URSULLAR,27;WADE H.,31
. WILLIAM,435,456
. WILLIAM T.,130;ZACH
. 394;ZACHARIAH,394
WALLER,J.B.,88-89;JAMES
. 88;JAMES B.,1,88,91
. 171;LAVINIA FOWLER,593
. SALLIE J.E,337
. WILLIAM,593
WALLES,GEORGE,462;W.B.
. 141
WALLICE,PETER,1
WALLIS,CLAIBON A.,385
. DAVID,342,384;DAVID
. J.,325;E.S.,338;ELIZA
. WHITMIRE,346,352
. ELIZA WOFFORD,385
. ELIZABETH,450;EVA,384
. GEORGE,462;GEORGE L.
. 385;H.B.,128,132,142
. 144,146;HARRIET,379
. HARRY O.,6;HARVY C.
. 343;JACOB,469;JAMES
. P.,342;JANE,310,319
. JANE T. WALLACE,32

. JESSE,153,204,207,228
. 236,244,248,252,254
. 352;JESSE B.,305
. JESSEE,346;JESSR T.
. 343;JOHANNA ROACH,384
. JOHN,299,343,385,466
. JOHN J.,343;JOHN M.
. 325;JOSEPH N.,47
. KEZIAH K. BRUCE,343
. LAURA B. HUGHES,385
. LAURA V.,29;LUTHER,284
. M.E. JEMION,47
. MANERVIA MARTIN,343
. MARIEAS MONDAY,385
. MARION T.W.,343
. MARTHA A.,336
. MARTHA A. RED,343
. MARTHA E.,352;MARTHA
. HARRIS,311,325,385
. MARY,329;MARY A.
. BLANTON,343;MARY
. GREEN,342;MARY J.,21
. 329;MATTIE,8;N.B.,144
. NALLY,381;NANCY,337
. S.E.,322;SARAH A.
. BARNWELL,325;SARAH C.
. NEWTON,325,342;SARAH
. CARRIE,346;SARAH
. COLLETT,343;SARAH
. MARTIN,385;T.W.,144
. W.B.,142;WILLIAM,299
. 385,462;WILLIAM A.,32
. WILLIAM B.,385
. WILLIAM W.,311,325,385
WALLRAVEN,JOHN,91
WALLS,CAROLINE,316,331
. M.C.,340;MARY JANE
. NIX,343;NANCY ROACH
. 385;NATH,385;SUSAN A.
. COX,385;W.J.,577-579
. WILLIAM L.,385
. WILLIAM T.,343
WALRAVEN,D.D.,425;DAVID
. 155;E.A.,45;E.F.
. SCOTT,425;ELIJAH,18
. ELIZABETH,111,116
. ELIZABETH WHITE,155
. EMILY TAYLOR,424
. ENOCH,14;F.C.,430
. F.E.,428;ISAAC,311,325
. 440;JOHN,100,116,424
. 462;L.J. CHAMBLEE,419
. LOUISA E. PHILIPS,14
. MARY C. CHANNELL,18
. MARY FISHER,420;MARY
. SOLOMON,311,325;MILLY
. A.,23;PERRY,419
. REBECCA,155;RHODA,21
. S.,181;SIMEON,179
. WILLIAM,298,420,435
. 440
WALRAVENS,SARAH,450
WALSH,JOSEPH,503
WALSTON,ALLEN,155
. ELIZABETH DANIEL,155
. MATILDA,581;S.J.,603
WALTERS,CHARLES F.,404
. JOHN S.,463
WALTHALL,L.M.,507
. TURMAN,495
WAMACH,ELIZABETH,557
WAMICK,MARY R.,594
WAMMACK,BIRD,443
WAMMOCK,ELIZABETH,557
WANIC,GEORGIA,475
WARD,531;ANDERSON,158
. ANN E.,593;C.A. MAYES
. 45;C.J.,45;CASINDA,156
. CATHERINE GREER,27
. DAVID,399;ELIZABETH
. 552;EMILINE TATUM,492
. G.A.,425;G.A. WARD,425
. GEORGIA,489;HANNAH

. VARDIVERE,569;J.R.,86
. 132,136;JAMES P.J.,161
. JERRY,529;JOHN,580
. JOHN R.,27,87,141,146
. JULIA,33;L.M.,423
. LABELIA,570;M.E.,425
. MARTHA OBRIANT,158
. MARY,434,568;MARY ANN
. REEVES,580;MARY L.,424
. MARY M.,28;NANCY,159
. NANCY A.,422;NANCY
. RIGGINS,161;NATHAN,436
. 469,473;RACHAEL,466
. ROSETTA,481;S.J.,504
. 582,584;STEPHEN D.,569
. T.M.,393,418-419,421
. 422-425,427;WESLEY,492
. WILLIAM,151,191,194
. 197,205,211,214-215
. 228,236,239-240,253
. 257-258;WILLIS,158
. WINNY CATH. DURHAM,158
WARDEN,JAMES,306,325
MARY BLAYLOCK,306,325
WARDLAW,LAURA,42
WARE,435-436;ALFRED,564
. EDWARD,409;ELIZABETH
. 178;FANNIE S.,413
. G.W.,421;HENRY H.,462
. JOHN,443;JOHN H.,464
. JOSEPH,431;M.A.,427
. MARIETTE HENDERSON,431
. MARTHA JANE ROACH,564
. NICHOLAS M.,178
. ROBERT,562-563,566-568
. S.A.C. CAPEHART,421
. SARAH D.,409;SUSANNAH
. 551
WARLICK,B.F.,475-476,482
. 485,489,491-492;E.A.
. MCMILLAN,493;T.J.,475
. W.H.,493
WARMACK,
. FANNIE ANN JONES,584
. JOHN W.,584;LUCY,591
. MARY E.,587
WARNER,80;R.,516
WARNICK,M.A.,427
WARNOCK,ELIZABETH,550
WARREN,ANN,450;ARTHUR
. 458;C.,427;EZEKIEL,441
. JESSE,438;JOHN T.,418
. LOT,462;M.E.,424;MARY
. 449;MARY E.,31;MONROE
. T.,493;NANCY
. NICHOLSON,493;REUBEN
. 438,467;REUBIN,442
. SARAH A. TURNER,418
. SARAH BABER,458
. WILLIAM,170
WARRENS,ELIZABETH,451
WASHINGTON,
. ELIZA MURPHEY,493
. EMMA,513;J.D.,527
. J.H.,525;JAMES H.,493
. JEFFERSON,448;L.M.,544
. SARAH WILLIAMS,448
WATE,PAIRZADE,413
WATER,ANNA HUMPHRIES
. 420;Z.L.,420
WATERS,
. ADDIE W. GRIMMETT,385
. ADDIE W. KELLOGG,385
. CHARLES A.,38;CYNTHIA
. 323;CYNTHIA A.M.,311
. DOUGLAS,405;ELIZABETH
. ACOCK,385;G.W.,406
. HANNAH M. MASON,6
. HELLEN,602;J. MATTIE
. ANDERSON,38;JOHN,259
. 464,526;JOHN C.,21,174
. JOSEPH,171,385,401
. JOSEPH C.,385;LIZZIE
. 430;MARTHA F.,314,329

. MARTHA L. WINN,406
. MARY J. WALLIS,21
. MATILDA,320;MOSES,284
. NANCY A.M.,37;R.L.,60
. R.M.,404;ROBERT,171
. SARAH A.,318;SARAH
. A.E.,332;T.A.,422
. WILLIAM O.,6
WATES,
. ELIZABETH BAILES,458
. LEVI,458;RICHARD J.
. 444
WATFORD,ANNIE TATE,50
. C.C.,50
WATKINS,ABNER,467;DICK
. 516;EASTER,481
. ELIZABETH,481;ELLEN
. KING,493;FANNIE
. CARTER,516;FRANCES,303
. G.H.,493;H.B.,444
. HENRY,467;HEZEKIAH,433
. JESSE,150;MARTHA,303
. MARY,484;MARY M
. DARNELL,433
. NANCY E.V. LEDFORE,493
. NATHAN C.,306;R.A.,465
. SARAH,303;SARAH C.
. BUCHANAN,306;THOMAS
. 550;UEL,467;WILLIAM
. A.,493
WATLEY,W.V.B.,496
WILSON,495
WATSON,278,542;ANSEL,325
. D.E. BENNETT,385
. DAVID M.,422;E.J.,475
. E.P.,480-481,483,485
. 493;ELIZABETH R.J.
. TYSON,162;EVIN,343;F.
. 86;FRANCIS M.,4
. GEORGE,30;GEORGIA
. HOOPER,541;H.F.,385
. HAMPTON F.,304,325
. HANNAH H. MALDEN,325
. HANNAH M. MALDEN,304
. HARRIET E. GROOVER,493
. HULDA CHATMAN,385
. J.F.,385;J.M.,498
. JAMES,558;JAMES B.,541
. JOHN,454;JOHN B.,60
. JOHN M.,160;JOSHUA N.
. 558;JULIA ANN,17;L.D.
. 162;LUCINDA BREWER,558
. MAHULDA CHAMPMAN,325
. MALINDA MAHAFFY,558
. MARTHA,302,315;MARTHA
. ALLEN,30;MARY A.
. GLASCO,4;MARY ANN,551
. MARY E. WIGGINS,343
. MARY H. STANLEY,14
. MARY HATAWAY,558;MARY
. J.,577;MARY J. TAYLOR
. 32;MARY OBARE,454
. NANCY BREWER,558
. NANCY C. PUGH,160
. NATHANIEL,459;PARIS
. 558;PHEBY,451;ROBERT,2
. ROBERT A.,14;S.H.,111
. SARAH A. HARBOR,422
. SARAH A. IVY,325
. SARAH BATES,459;SARAH
. E.,44;SUSANNAH,456
. WARREN L.,32;WILLIAM
. 436,558;WILSON,472
WATT,ANDERSON,471,473
. ELIZABETH HARRIS,384
. JAMES H.,384;JAMES M.
. 384;JOSEPH,152,222,224
. 228,237,239,241,260
. THERSA MCCRARY,384
WATTERS,ANDREW J.,399
. ANN,464;DAVID,464
. GEORGE,399;JAMES,466
. JANE,307;JOSEPH,397
. 399,403;LOUESA,318

687

. EMILY SHAW,28;GEORGE
. 403;GEORGE W.,403
. JAMES,403;MARTHA,308
. 322;NANCY ANN
. HUTCHINS,309;THOMAS
. 403;WILLIAM H.,28
WILDEN,MARY,562
WILDER,
. AMANDA BUCHANAN,308
. AMANDA BUCKANAN,325
. ETHELDRED,435,440
. ETHELDRID,437;FANNY
. JORDAN,325;FANNY
. JORDEN,307;JONATHAN
. 307,325;JULIA A.
. WILSON,493;MARY,328
. 347;SILAS,308,325
. WILLIAM,493
WILDES,A.D.,465
WILEY,193-194,217,229
. ALSEY BAXTER,431;D.G.
. 400;DAVID S.,64;DELIA
. 432;ELIZABETH PRIEST,457
. GILBERT,425;HANNAH
. MOORE,425;JAMES L.,160
. JOHN,457;JOHN P.,151
. 204,232,235;LUCINDA
. 558;N.H.,162;NANCY,458
. REBECCA JOHNSON,160
. SARAH,309,316;SARAH
. RUDISILL,162
WILFIELD,
. FRANCES COOPER,581
. OBEDIAH,581
WILKA,MILLA,590
WILKERSON,C.C.,495;JOHN
. 449;NANCY MATTOCKS,449
. ROBERT T.,433;SARAH
. 496;TARAH,496
WILKEY,A.H.,347;DAVID
. 149;ELIZA,428;L.A.
. ARMSTRONG,347;S.F.,426
WILKIE,ANDREW H.,309,342
. ANNA CROFFORD,155
. E.M.,427;ELIZABETH
. MCCLURE,342;FRANCIS
. 601;GEORGE,155;M.A.
. WARNICK,427;MARY
. TAILOR,309
WILKINS,510;A.W.,271,342
. ADALINE L. BRADWELL
. 325;ADALINE L.
. BROADWELL,342
. ANONYMUS W.,271
. BELARIAH,268;BISHOP
. 436;BREWSTER,536
. CHARLES S.,325,342
. HESEKIRE,384;HILL,268
. J.G.,325,342;J.W.,325
. JOHN W.,343;LOUISA A.
. PHILIPS,342;LOUISA A.
. PHILLIPS,325;LUCY C.
. COOK,343;M.E. BARRETT
. 325,342;MALINDA
. WHITMIRE,384;MARGARET
. 320;MARGARET H.,308
. MARTHA A.E.B.,309
. MARY,384;MARY A.,566
. 567;MARY A.D.,329
. W.W.,500;ZACHARIAH,268
WILKS,CAROLINE,157;JOHN
. A.,392
WILKY,WILLIAM,465
WILLBANK,ELIZA,156
WILLBANKS,HOSEA,448
. REBECCA WALDRIP,448
WILLBORN,ELIJAH,176
. W.E.,409
WILLCOX,GEORGE H.,163
. REBECCA PRIEST,163
WILLEY,JOHN P.,239
WILLIAMS,86,178;A.C.,568
. A.H.,343;A.V. KEMP,44

. ALEXANDER,157,472
. ALLICE COOPER,582
. AMANDA S. FREEMAN,581
. AMOS,550;AMY,309
. ANDREW J.,22;ANN,300
. 313;ANN ARMSTRONG,343
. ANN GUTTERY,451;ANNIE
. 309,312,349;ANSEN,435
. B.W.,504;BARBARY
. MYERS,457;BENJAMIN F.
. 266;BERRIEN,558
. BESSIE W.,31;BETTIE
. 503;BEULAH,519;BRIANT
. 2;BRITAIN,567;BRITIAN
. 562,564;BRITION,474
. BRITTAIN,578;CALIWAY
. 550;CAROLINE CLANTON
. 22;CHARITY W.,10
. CHARLES,289,305,325
. 384;CLARRISA T.,445
. CORA CHEEK,535
. CORNELIA MALONE,17
. DAVID,599;DELILA
. PETERS,558;DOW,285
. E.A. DAVIS,434;E.M.
. MARTIN,424;EDLEY,161
. EDNA CARLTON,545
. EDWARD,550;EFFA M.,575
. EGBERT C.,562;ELIJAH,2
. ELISA,302,317;ELISA
. BAGLEY,300;ELIZA E.
. 337;ELIZABETH,157,368
. ELIZABETH HOOD,561
. ELIZABETH STOVALL,379
. ELLIN CHEATHAM,50
. ELOISA BAGLEY,325
. EMILY CHASTAIN,596
. EMMA J.,434;ENVES,561
. ETHELD,550;EVA,522
. F.M.,343,476,486,490
. FANNIE J. BOYD,343
. FORIS,507;FRANCES A.
. GRAVITT,343;FRANCES
. B.,379;FRANCES
. TINSLEY,384;FRANCIS
. BOND,27;G.E.,530
. GEORGE,528;GEORGE K.
. 529;GEORGE W.,580
. GEORGIA,48;GREEF,297
. GRIEF,176;GROVER,545
. H.B.,140,148;H.P.,581
. H.S.,522;HAMPTON,558
. HANS,504;HANSILL J.
. 558;HENRY,522;HENRY
. S.,533;HUBBARD,438
. HULDA I. BENSON,384
. IBBY WIMMS,305,325
. ISAAC,27;ISAAC D.,17
. ISABELLE WILSON,368
. ISAIAH,101,285,300,325
. J.,465;J.A.,50;J.E.
. 545;J.F.C.,39;J.J.,535
. J.J. WINN,528;J.L.,596
. J.M.,503,530;JACOB,520
. JAMES,297,448,457
. JAMES C.,582;JAMES H.
. 285;JAMES I.,565
. JAMES R.,35;JANE,24
. 458;JANE A. JARRETT
. 161;JEMIMAH,451;JESSE
. 343,436;JESSE M.,384
. JOEL J.,593;JOEL W.
. 559;JOHN,149,167,186
. 297,342,368,436,438
. 439,451,472,601;JOHN
. B.,287;JOHN L.,343
. JOHN M.,384;JOHN T.
. 564;JOHNSON,69,513
. JOHNSTON,2;JONATHAN
. 161,451,550;JOSEPH,298
. 300,325,550;JOSEPHINE
. 331;JOSEPHINE DAWN,599
. JUDITH VENABLE,300,325
. JULIA,595;JULIA ANN

. 159;LEE,599;LEVI J.
. 494;LEWIS,276,305,325
. 444;LINER,156;LUCINDA
. BROADWELL,384;LULA,507
. M.J.,423;M.S.,485
. MADISON,343;MAGEE ANN
. HEAD,568;MALINDA
. JONES,358;MARGARET
. CROFT,342;MARGARET E.
. DRENNAN,565;MARGARET
. L.,8;MARGARET MARKS
. 451;MARGARET MOREHEAD
. 576;MARGARET R. MAYES
. 13;MARIAH,574;MARK,496
. MARTHA,19,162,353,544
. 545;MARTHA A.,339
. MARTHA ASHWORTH,343
. MARTHA HENDRIX,158
. MARTHA J.,483;MARTIN
. 550;MARY,556;MARY A.
. FULLER,494;MARY ANN
. 334;MARY ANN SAMPLES
. 384;MARY ANN TALLENT
. 456;MARY E.,336
. MARY E. COMPTON,343
. MARY E. NELSON,593
. MARY J.,340;MARY J.
. LOVELADY,494;MARY M.
. 329;MARY M. BELL,562
. MARY PRITCHARD,35
. MATILDA,453;MATTHEW
. J.,275;MATTHEW K.,325
. MATTIE A. GEORGE,39
. MELISSA,314;NANCY,350
. 575,586;NANCY A.
. PILGRIM,580;NANCY C.
. 11,38;NANCY D.
. MCMURRAY,559;NANCY M.
. 314,377;NANCY MOORE
. 558;NANCY PEAK,157
. NANCY WILLIAMS,575
. NARCISSA,455;NEAL E.
. 13;NOAH,158;PARALE,413
. 572;POLLY A. SAMPLES
. 305;POLLY ANN SAMPLES
. 325;QUNARTHY,581
. R.J.K.,333;RACHEL,455
. RACHEL E. ROPER,325
. RANDOL,440;REBECCA,458
. REBECCA BYRAM,307,325
. RICHARD,575;RICHARD
. A.,384;ROBERT,176,211
. 277,279-282,286-288
. 292,297;ROSANNAH,492
. ROWLAND,176;RUSSEL,173
. S. CHRISMAN,423;S.E.
. 347;S.M.,593;S.R.,591
. SAMUEL,231;SARAH,448
. 449,553,556,562
. SARAH E. STOVALL,325
. 342;SARAH ELIZ.,358
. SARAH F. BENNETT,311
. 325;SARAH WEBB,564
. SAVANNAH,516;SOLOMON
. 242;SUSAN A. PETERS
. 558;SUSAN BUICE,343
. SUSAN MOORE,591
. SUSANNAH PATTY,601
. TABITHA STARRELL,161
. THOMAS,463;THOMAS C.
. 325,342,358,379
. THOMAS W.,307,325,456
. URIAH,520;W.H.,423
. W.L.,424;W.N.,495
. W.R.,343,520;W.S.,60
. W.W.,504,507;WILLIAM,2
. 311,325,514,550,576
. WILLIAM G.,44;WILLIAM
. H.,243,434;WILLIE,545
. WYATT,545;ZACHARIAH
. I.,494
WILLIAMSON,ALLEN,112,122
. 123;ANDREW J.,389
. ARTAMINSA,161

. CAROLINE MCWHORTER,155
. ELISA JONES,325;ELIZA
. JONES,301;ETHELBERT
. 495;GEORGE B.,403
. J.A.,594;J.G.,123
. JAMES,442;JAMES G.,122
. JOHN,152,223,257,389
. JOHN R.,253;LAURA J.
. FORD,594;LOWRY,149
. MALINDA E.,159;MARTHA
. 572;SAMANTHA,487;SARY
. ANN,155;THOMAS,439
. WILLIAM,149,170,301
. 325,442;WILLIAM T.,149
. 150,179;WILLIAM W.,155
. ZARILDA,447
WILLIE,ELIZABETH,450
WILLIFORD,JOHN,89;JOHN
. M.,3,88,90,110;LENA
. D.,508;STEPHEN,442
. W.J.,508;WILLIAM E.
. 438
WILLINGHAM,A.G.,422
. BETSY,352;E.A. HARLAN
. 418;ELIZ. MONTGOMERY
. 325;ELIZABETH
. MONTGOMERY,302;GEORGE
. 292-296;JACKSON,302
. 325;JOSEPH H.,418
. LUCINDA WILEY,558
. LUCRETIA,370,557
. MAMIE,434;MARY A.,328
. MARY A. MASHBURN,343
. MARY L.,552;OBEDIENCE
. 300;OBEDIENT,315
. RILEY,558;S.E.
. CANTRELL,422;SARAH,337
. SUSAN J.,556;WILLIAM
. 510,537;WILLIAM E.,343
WILLIS,ANNA,553
. BREWSTER,513;DANIEL
. 175,493;ELIZABETH
. HARDEN,558;FRANCIS
. BOWMAN,532;H.M.,298
. J.M.,532;JOHN,455
. KISIAH CAYLOR,493
. LIZZIE SMITH,493;MARY
. 476;MARY ANN,554;MARY
. DOUGHERTY,451;NANY J.
. 4;PARTHENY,325,343
. PAUL T.,558;PICKINS
. E.,272;REBECCA,484
. SUSAN PARMER,455;T.J.
. 493;THOMAS B.,276
. WASHINGTON,149
. WILLIAM,149,170,451
WILLMOTH,
. ELIZABETH N. -
. BEAVERS,14;EMMA,8
. L.H.,14
WILLMUT,NANCY A.,571
WILLS,AUSTON A.,46
. FRANK,500,526;JOHN,544
. JOHN E.,343;KINNS L.
. WILSON,46;LOU
. MATTHEWS,526;MARTHA
. J.,342;MARY A.,347
. MASTIVE,347;SARAH J.
. THOMPSON,343;SUSAN M.
. SPRUCE,347
WILLSON,ALLEN,443
. EPHRAIM,298;JAMES,166
. 177,182,188,208,211
. 213,222-223,234;JOHN
. 209;LEE ROY,383;M.E.
. SCROGGINS,22;MARY,599
. MARY A.V.,476
. MARY JANE JAMES,383
. MOURNING COLILE,383
. NANCY,161;NANCY
. WILLSON,161;PHILIP,161
. RELING,167;RILEY,297
. THOMAS,170;W.N.,22
. WILLIAM,298;WILLIAMN.

. 383
WILLY,JOHN,550
WILS,J.,128
WILSEN,RICHARD,462
WILSON,A.,603;A.B.,426
. 428;A.W.,428;ABRAHAM
. 253;AGNES,457
. ANDERSON,307,325
. ANDREW S.,459;ANN
. CLOPSTON,589;BENJAMIN
. 310,325;BIRD,419-421
. 423-424,427,600;BOB
. 533;CAROLINE,45
. CHARLIE,542
. CIVELLA S. WELLBORN
. 307,325;CLERINDA V.
. 327;DANIEL N.,570
. DAVID M.,343;ELISE E.
. 372;ELIZ. ANN W.,459
. ELIZ. ANN W. WILSON
. 459;ELIZ.
. KILLINGSWORTH,325
. ELIZ. R. -
. KILLINGSWORTH,306
. ELIZA ANN,155
. ELIZABETH,457
. ELIZABETH BATES,453
. ELLENDER STONE,310,325
. EMILY,551;EMMA,542
. FRANCIS,395;FRANCIS
. A.,337;G.W.,545
. GEORGE,469;H.,533
. HANNAH,576;HARRIET L.
. FOWLER,155;HASELTINE
. 12;HATTIE LEWIS,494
. HENRY,153,222,256
. HUGH,495;ISABELLE,368
. J.,94;J.B.,343;J.C.,23
. J.M.,134;J.R.,494
. J.W.,325,342;JACK,432
. JAMES,86,149,192,208
. 217,256,266,304,325
. 439,455;JAMES H.,494
. JANE,155,449,490;JANE
. COLLINS,494;JANE
. MCCOY,456;JANE
. RUSSELL,432;JANE
. SOPHIA,554;JASON H.
. 174;JEFFERSON,589
. JENNIE,47;JOHN,151,453
. 495,535,571;JOHN A.
. 343;JOHN L.,439;JOHN
. S.,447;JOSEPH C.,35
. JULIA A.,493;KAY ANN
. JOHNSON,421;KINNS L.
. 46;L. JINKENS,372
. L.M.,36;LABEN,325
. LAVEN,306;LILLIE,434
. LIZZIE BROCKS,535
. LIZZIE BROOKS,535
. LOUIZA,570;LUCINDA,156
. LUGUESY,489;M.J.,418
. M.J. BENNETT,343;M.R.
. KING,419;MAGGIE,334
. MAGGIE R. QUILLIAN,600
. MALINDA E. WILLIAMSON
. 159;MANERVA TEDDER,343
. MARGARET,156,365,477
. MARGARET DOWDY,603
. MARTHA A.,582;MARTHA
. ANDERSON,575;MARTHA
. M.,485;MARTHA POOL,458
. MARY,38;MARY ANN
. HYFIELD,571;MARY E.
. 479;MARY E. MOOR,325
. 342;MARY G. KING,448
. MARY JANE REID,600
. MARY JOHNS,570
. MARY M. WHITTON,578
. MARY MAGARITY,49;MARY
. PRUITT,343;MARY R.
. CONGER,21;MARY
. SAUNDERS,455;MARY
. SCROGGINS,36;MATHEW

. W.,448;NANCY ANN,337
. 490;NANCY C.,163
. NANCY L. STOCKTON,570
. OLIVER,458,465;P.,419
. P.J.,49;PATSY,592
. PERNELA A. LIGHT,304
. PERNELA ANN LIGHT,325
. R.L.,535;R.V.,269
. R.W.,513;RANSEN,463
. REBECCA FOWLER,455
. RICHARD,442;RIDLEY
. SAUNDERS,458;RILEY,86
. 149,168,455,471
. ROBERT,550;ROBERT T.
. 372;S.,418;SAMANTHA
. RANDALL,23;SAMUEL,565
. SAMUEL H.,456;SAMUEL
. M.,438;SARAH,449
. SARAH A.R. BURTON,343
. SARAH FRIDELL,35
. SARAH JANE CONSTINE
. 565;SARAH L.
. HAMMONTREE,494
. SOPHRONIA,545;SUSAN
. 455;SUSAN E. CLINE,494
. T.H.,583;THOMAS,149
. 494;THOMAS P.,578
. THOMAS W.,343;URIAH
. 176;V.M.,574;V.W.,569
. W.A.,52;W.J.,476,478
. 479,481,483;WILLIAM,2
. 155,458,464,550,575
. WILLIAM L.,494
. WILLIAM R.,21;WILLIAM
. W.,159;WILLIS,570
. WILLIS H.,600;Z.F.,420
. 421,428-430,433-434
. Z.T.,432
WIMBERLY,ZACHARIAH,438
WIMBORN,DAVID,442
WIMMS,IBBY,305,325
WIMPEY,
. CATHERINE SHORT,603
. D.H.,603
WIMPLE,JULIA,590
WIMPY,B.R.,521;DANIEL
. 550;SUSAN,345;W.S.,414
WINDBACH,JONAS,518
WINDERS,ARABELLA A.,337
WINDOWS,SARAH J.,330
WINFRA,JESSE,2
WING,E.A.,86;EDWARD,441
. 465;JOHN,465;MARY,448
WINGAY,ELIZABETH,452
WINGINGTON,ING,481
. JOSEPH,493;SHARO
. QUINTON,493
WINGO,378;ELIZABETH,48
. ELIZABETH BALDWIN,325
. 342;ELIZABETH RED,343
. ELIZABETH T.,336;H.
. 375;HARRIET W.,338
. JANE H. FOSTER,366
. JESSE,343;MARTHA J.
. 359;MARY A. FOSTER,325
. 342,359;MARY FOSTER
. 357;PATIENCE A.,366
. SALLIE J.,39;THOMAS
. W.,325,342;VICTORIA
. B.,357;WILLIAM P.,325
. 342,357,359;ZACHARIAH,366
WININGHAM,ABELA,465
WINKLE,BENJAMIN,494
. JOSEPHINE HAWKINS,591
. LOUISANAN C.,407;MARY
. J.,591;ROSANA,578
. TISHA HALL,494
. WILLIAM,591
WINKLER,BENJAMIN,461
WINN,85,129;A.A.,135
. A.H.,524;ALBERT A.,177
. 199;ALEN,298;BISEY
. WIGLEY,519;DEWITT C.
. 50;ELISHA,276,281,444

. ELIZA,528;FANNIE E.
. LATIMER,15;G.,406
. GENNUBETH,150
. GENWLETH,166;GINNBETH
. 170;GLENNUBUTH,149
. HUGH L.,15;J.J.,528
. J.P.,174;JENNETT M.
. 558;JOHN,524;JOHN F.
. 217;JOHN P.,125,149
. 152,166,168,173,177
. 187,191-192,197-198
. 218,224,227-228,239
. 250,256,258;LEWIS,176
. LULA,37;M.A.,34
. MARGARET V.,412
. MARTHA,558;MARTHA L.
. 406;MARY A.,41
. MARY C. JOHNSON,50
. MATT,519;O.I.,528
. PRISCILLA BURNS,20
. ROBERT A.,228
. SARAH ANN WALKER,558
. THOMAS J.,20;WILL J.
. 533;WILLIAM A.,558
. WILLIAM T.,71
WINNE,A.H.,522
WINTER,ANNA,451;CHARLES
. L.,494;GEORGE W.,3
. JAMES,32;LALISIA
. GRIGGS,32;M.F.,424
. MARY HATEY,494
WINTERBOTTOM,MARY,475
WINTERS,
. ELIZABETH TOWNSEND,494
. G.W.,264;GEORGE W.,242
. 246;J.R.,521;JOHN R.
. 521;JOSEPH M.,494
. NOAH J.,494
. SARAH JANE BOLING,494
. WASHINGTON W.,167
WIRCHER,HENRY,170
WIRT,SARAH,452
WIRTE,EZEKIEL,172;JOHN,172
WIRTH,PAULINE,565
WISDOM,JESSE,149
WISE,JANE,424;NANCY E.,5
WISEMAN,JEREMIAH,100
WISENANT,JOHN N.,466
WISENER,537
WISENHUNT,HENRY,461
WISNER,DELILAH,452
. POLLEY,452
WISNOR,JEREMIAH,454
. NELLY WIGLEY,454
WITCER,LUCY,507
WITCHER,HENRY,149,166
. JOHN,149-150,166,173
. LACY,149,496
. MARTHA S. WRIGHT,420
. TALIAFARIO,398;W.A.
. 420;WILLIAM I.,398
WITEHER,JAMES,496
WITHCER,JOHN,168
WITHERSPOON,
. CHARLES W.,310,325
. G.G.,297,568,571,577
. MARY ANN FOSTER,310
. 325
WITTS,JOHN,525;MARY
. WOODALL,525
WITZEL,FRANCES,596
WIX,ADDISON,521;BEN,537
. CARRAH,545;DOVEY,537
. SARAH J.,499;ZACH,544
. ZODY,537
WIZ,ZACK,540
WOFFORD,A.F.,430
. BENJAMIN,342;CANDES
. 419;CAROLINE E.
. COWART,494;CICERO,494
. E.,477;E.E.,528;E.W.
. 490;ELIJAH,325;ELIZA
. 385;ELIZA JACKSON,592
. ELLA E. ROGERS,599

. HATTIE ELIZ. CAGLE,494
. HIRAM,101,105;ISAAC
. 390,393-394,396,400
. 404;JACOB,343;JANE
. HAYS,343;JANIE E.,528
. JEREMIAH,192,222-224
. 226;JOSEPH,101,195,243
. 244,264;MARTHA T.
. HURT,342;MARY M.
. TAYLOR,430;NATHAN,599
. NATHANIEL,149,170,230
. PACIFIC BURFORD,325
. RICHARD,592;SARAH E.
. 336;SOLOMON,278
. SOPHRONIA COWART,494
. THOMAS G.,494;W.,479
WOFL,CLYDE,544
WOLF,200-201;CLYDE,544
. MARY,1;POLLY,88
WOLLEY,CALDONIA D.,479
. FRANCES,454
WOMACK,BIRD,3,438;G.W.
. 545;MATHEY,535;THOMAS
. 3
WOMMACK,J.M.,522
WOOD,168;ABRAHAM,150,457
. AMANDA A.,339;AMANDA
. CALHOUN,564;AMANDA
. MULLINS,164;ANDREW,149
. 170,176,451,466
. ANGELINE BLANKENSHIP
. 343;BETTY HUBBARD,457
. BIDDY,451,583;C.L.,347
. CARY,558;CATHERINE
. JANE,164;CHARITY
. LANGLEY,451
. CONSTANTINE,570;DAN
. 531;DAVID BEAUREGARD
. 164;ELIZA PARKER,431
. ELIZABETH,334,455
. ELIZABETH HOLLINSHEAD
. 325;ELIZABETH
. HOLLINSHED,342
. ELIZABETH MREWOOD,156
. ELIZABETH WHITLEY,558
. ELLENDER F. COX,164
. ELVIRA,586;EMILY,301
. 312;EUGENE R.,164
. FLANADA,7;FRANCES D.
. 329;FRANCIS E. HARRIS
. 325;FRANK,531;GEORGE
. NEWTON,164;GRAVE G.
. 329;ISAAC,464;ISHAM
. 564;J.,121;J.J.,419
. J.T.,541;JAMES,162,180
. 210,215,218;JAMES E.
. 163;JAMES EDWARD,163
. JAMES J.P.,163-164
. JAMES R.,85;JANE
. BRIDGES,601;JASPER L.
. 163;JASPER LEWIS,164
. JERRY,529;JOANNA,41
. JOEL T.,93;JOHN,150
. 176,297,420,507,533
. 577;JOHN G.,533;JOHN
. H.,156,586;JOHN J.,325
. JOHN L.,161;JOHN R.
. 431;JOSEPH,156,533
. JOSEPHINE ZUBER,423
. LAURA A.,85;LAURA D.
. 163;LAURA VICTORIA,164
. LAZARUS,450;LENA,535
. LIDIA SMITH,430
. LORENZO D.,456;LOUISA
. A.,584;LOUISE
. MCCLUSKY,456;LUKE,298
. LYDIA C.,163;LYDIA
. CAROLINE,164;M.E.,425
. M.J.,85,587;MAGGIE E.
. 85;MALISSA,306,312
. MALISSA CARE,156
. MARGARET H.,418
. MARGARET L.,164
. MARGARET LULA,164

690

691